Contents

PARROQUIA DE SAN MIGUEL
ARCÁNGEL P665

ON THE ROAD

TRADITIONAL WOVEN
SOMBRERO HATS
JOHN & LISA MERRILL / GETTY IMAGES ©

lonely planet

Mexico

C800639918

PLAN YOUR TRIP

ON THE ROAD

Contents

Welcome to Mexico

Palm-fringed beaches, chili-spiced cuisine, steamy jungles, teeming cities, fiesta fireworks, Frida's creativity: Mexico conjures up diverse, vivid dreams. And the reality lives up to them.

An Outdoor Life

With steaming jungles, snowcapped volcanoes, cactus-strewn deserts and 10,000km of coast strung with sandy beaches and wildlife-rich lagoons, Mexico is an endless adventure for the senses and a place where life is lived largely in the open air. Harness the pounding waves of the Pacific on a surfboard, strap on a snorkel to explore the beauty beneath the surface of the Caribbean Sea and ride the whitewater of Mexico's rivers. Or stay on dry land and hike Oaxaca's mountain cloud forests, scale the peaks of dormant volcanoes or marvel at millions of migrating Monarch butterflies.

Art & Soul of a Nation

Mexico's pre-Hispanic civilizations built some of the world's great archaeological monuments, including Teotihuacán's towering pyramids and the exquisite Maya temples of Palenque. The Spanish colonial era left beautiful towns full of tree-shaded plazas and richly sculpted stone churches and mansions, while modern Mexico has seen a surge of great art from the likes of Diego Rivera and Frida Kahlo. Top-class museums and galleries document the country's fascinating history and its endless creative verve. Popular culture is just as vibrant, from the underground dance clubs and street art of Mexico City to the wonderful handicrafts of the indigenous population.

A Varied Palate

Mexico's gastronomic repertoire is as diverse as the country's people and topography. Dining out is an endless adventure, whether you're sampling regional dishes, such as Yucatán's *cochinita pibil* (slow-cooked pork) or a vast array of *moles* (complex sauces, their recipes jealously guarded) in Oaxaca and Puebla, or trying the artsy concoctions of world-class chefs in Mexico City. Some of Mexico's best eating is had at simple seafront *palapa* (thatched-roof shack) restaurants, serving achingly fresh fish and seafood, and the humble *taquerías*, ubiquitous all over Mexico, where tortillas are stuffed with a variety of fillings and slathered with homemade salsas.

Los Mexicanos

At the heart of your Mexican experience will be the Mexican people. A super-diverse crew, from Mexico City hipsters to the shy indigenous villagers of Chiapas, they're renowned for their love of color and frequent fiestas, but they're also philosophical folk, to whom timetables are less important than *simpatía* (empathy). You'll rarely find Mexicans less than courteous. They're more often positively charming, and know how to please guests. They might despair of ever being well governed, but they're fiercely proud of Mexico, their one-of-a-kind homeland with all its variety, tight-knit family networks, beautiful-ugly cities, deep-rooted traditions and agave-based liquors.

Why I Love Mexico

By Anna Kaminski, Writer

I first set foot in Mexico as a teenager, was beguiled by its ancient civilizations at university, and have now spent half of my life traversing the country on numerous trips. Having explored Mexico's cities, coasts, ruins and mountains, having surfed the couches of a motley crew of locals and expats – from a gangster in Tijuana to a Vietnam veteran painter in San Miguel de Allende – and having tasted Mexico's incredible food, from eyeball tacos and *mondongo* (tripe stew) to Michelin-starred set menus, I am still firmly in love with Mexico's remarkable diversity and its people.

For more about our writers, see p896

Above: Cenote X'Kekén y Samulá (p333)

Mexico

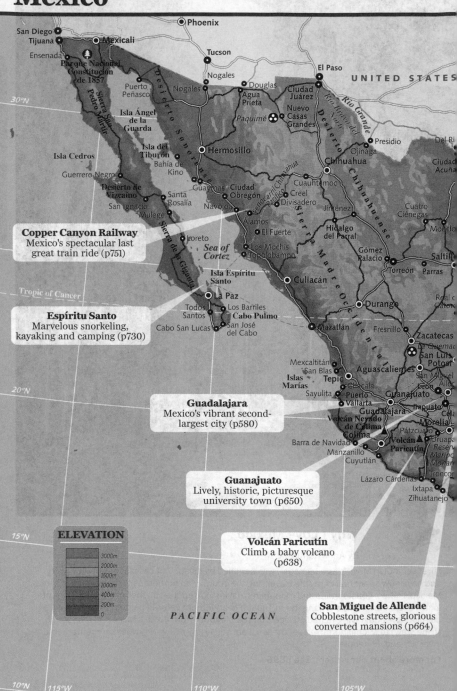

Copper Canyon Railway
Mexico's spectacular last
great train ride (p751)

Espíritu Santo
Marvelous snorkeling,
kayaking and camping (p730)

Guadalajara
Mexico's vibrant second-
largest city (p580)

Guanajuato
Lively, historic, picturesque
university town (p650)

Volcán Paricutín
Climb a baby volcano
(p638)

San Miguel de Allende
Cobblestone streets, glorious
converted mansions (p664)

ELEVATION

3000m
2000m
1500m
1000m
400m
200m
0

PACIFIC OCEAN

Teotihuacán
The awesome Pyramids of the Sun and Moon (p147)

Chichén Itzá
Simply spectacular ancient Maya ruins (p326)

Mexico City
Mammoth, fascinating, cultured metropolis (p62)

Mérida
Beautiful, cultured colonial city (p304)

San Cristóbal de las Casas
Colonial charm and Maya culture (p364)

Palenque
Exquisite Maya architecture in jungle setting (p383)

Reserva Mariposa Monarca
Monarch butterflies in their millions (p624)

Oaxaca
Gorgeous handicrafts, uniquely savory cuisine (p424)

Oaxaca Coast
Blissed-out beach-lovers' nirvana (p457)

Mexico's
Top 24

1

Peerless Palenque

1 Gather all your senses and dive head-first into the ancient Maya world at the exquisite Palenque (p383), where spectacular pyramids rise above emerald jungle treetops and furtive monkeys shriek and catapult themselves through dense canopies. Take your time to marvel at the abundance of reliefs, seek out the tomb of the mysterious Red Queen and her sarcophagus, wander the maze-like palace, gazing up at its iconic tower. Then, pay your respects to Pakal (Palenque's mightiest ruler) at the Temple of the Inscriptions, perhaps the most celebrated burial monument in the Americas.

Cabo Pulmo

2 Rediscover the magic of old Baja by visiting the largely undeveloped east coast, discovering world-class diving off Cabo Pulmo (p736), the only coral reef on the west coast of North America and, at 71 sq km, one of the largest and most successful marine protected regions in the world. In this beautiful place you can expect to see black coral bushes, schools of trigger fish, and yellowfin tuna and snapper. Depending on the seasons and currents, you may also spy hammerhead sharks, huge manta rays and whale sharks.

GERT OLSSON / SHUTTERSTOCK ©

LEONARDO GONZALEZ / SHUTTERSTOCK ©

ABERUGO / GETTY IMAGES ©

Mexico City, Cultural Capital

3 The nation's long-standing political capital (p62) clearly stands at the forefront of Mexico's cultural scene as well. Remember that this is where many of the country's top muralists left behind their most important works, such as Diego Rivera's cinematic murals in the Palacio Nacional (pictured; p71) and the social-realism work of José Clemente Orozco in the Palacio de Bellas Artes. Art, music, dance and theater are everywhere in Mexico City – even a gondola ride along the ancient canals of Xochimilco wouldn't be complete without taking in a fervent mariachi ballad.

Mexico's Last Train Journey

4 The Ferrocarril Chihuahua Pacífico (Copper Canyon Railway; p751) remains one of Latin America's best rail trips. Trains climb from sea level at Los Mochis to Chihuahua's high desert plains via the sensational rocky landscapes of the Copper Canyon. Vistas from your window include alpine forests, subtropical valleys, Tarahumara villages and glimpses of some of the world's deepest canyons. Alight at a photogenic stop for 15 minutes along the canyon's edge, or stay for days of exploring, hiking, biking and even zip-lining in one of Mexico's most breathtaking destinations.

The Pyramids of Teotihuacán

5 Once among Mesoamerica's greatest cities, Teotihuacán (p147) lies just an hour out of Mexico City. The immense Pirámide del Sol (Pyramid of the Sun) and Pirámide de la Luna (Pyramid of the Moon; pictured) dominate the remains of the ancient metropolis, which even centuries after its collapse in the 8th century AD remained a pilgrimage site for Aztec royalty. Today it is a magnet for those who come to soak up the mystical energies that are believed to converge here.

Oaxaca City

6 This highly individual city (p424) basks in bright upland light and captivates everyone with its deliciously inventive version of Mexican cuisine, gorgeous handicrafts, colorful fiestas, colonial architecture, booming arts scene and fine mezcals distilled in nearby villages. Within easy reach of the city are the superb ancient Zapotec capital, Monte Albán, dozens of indigenous craft-making villages with weekly markets, and the cool, forested hills of the Sierra Norte, perfect for hikers, mountain bikers and horseback riders. Celebrating Día de Nuestra Señora de Guadalupe (p105)

Marvelous Mérida

7 The cultural capital (p304) of the Yucatán Peninsula, this large but manageable city has a beautifully maintained colonial heart. It's veined with narrow cobbled streets and dotted with sunny plazas, with a wealth of museums and galleries and some of the best food in the region. Just out of town are wildlife reserves, graceful haciendas (estates) and jungle-shrouded cenotes (sinkholes) to swim in. A little further afield, the little-visited Maya sites along the Ruta Puuc allow you to step back in time without the tour groups.

JESS KRAFT / SHUTTERSTOCK ©

Shopping for Artisan Crafts

8 Mexico's bright, infinitely varied *artesanías* (handicrafts; p834) are today's successors to the costumes and ceramics of the pre-Hispanic nobility, and to the everyday handcrafted clothes, baskets and pots of their humbler subjects. Everywhere you go – whether wandering through markets, or visiting artisans in their village workshops to buy textiles, jewelry, ironwood carvings, bead-inlaid masks and more – the skill and creativity of potters, weavers, metalsmiths, carvers and leather workers delights the eye and tempts the pocket.

Magical San Cristóbal de las Casa

9 Saunter the cobblestone streets of hill-ringed San Cristóbal de las Casas (p364), the high-altitude colonial city in the heart of indigenous Chiapas. A heady mix of modern and Maya, with cosmopolitan cafes and traditional culture, it's also a jumping-off point for Chiapas' natural attractions and fascinating Tzotzil and Tzeltal villages. Spend sunny days exploring its churches and bustling markets, or riding a horse through fragrant pine forest, and chilly evenings warmed by the fireplace of a cozy watering hole.

Chichén Itzá

10 There's a reason why this Maya site (p326) is the most popular of Mexico's ancient sights – it is simply spectacular. From the imposing, monolithic El Castillo pyramid (where the shadow of the plumed serpent god Kukulcán creeps down the staircase during the spring and autumn equinoxes) to the Sacred Cenote and curiously designed El Caracol, the legacy of Mayan astronomers will blow your mind. Admire the Wall of Skulls and the stone carvings at the Temple of Warriors, or come back at night for the sound-and-light show.

Relaxing on the Oaxaca Coast

11 After a few days on this 550km sequence of sandy Pacific beaches (p457) you'll be so relaxed you may not be able to leave. Head for the surf mecca and fishing port of Puerto Escondido, the low-key resort of Bahías de Huatulco, or the ultra-laid-back hangouts of Zipolite, San Agustinillo or Mazunte. Soak up the sun, eat good food and imbibe in easygoing beach bars. When the mood takes you, have a swim, surf or snorkel, or board a boat to sight turtles, dolphins, whales, crocs or birdlife. Playa Carrizalillo (p459), Puerto Escondido

Savoring the Flavors

12 Mexican cuisine is like no other, and every part of the country has its own regional specialties, based on seasonal local ingredients and what's fresh on the day. For the tastiest travels, try local dishes from restaurants and busy market and street stalls – you'll lose count of the delicious culinary experiences (p836) you encounter. When it's time for fine dining, seek out some of the legion of creative contemporary chefs who concoct amazing flavor combinations from traditional and innovative ingredients. Quesadillas

La Huasteca Potosina, San Luis Potosí

13 Gorgeously green Huasteca Potosina (p690), a subregion of San Luis Potosí, offers ruins, cave visits and wild and wet experiences. You can plunge into, boat to or ogle at a number of stunning waterfalls and rivers. As for color? The turquoises, aquas and greens are as vibrant as any manipulated image. Huastec culture is strong here: don't miss trying a local *zacahuil,* a massive *tamal.* The region is home to surrealist garden, Las Pozas, where gigantic Dalí-esque structures strut their quirky stuff. Cascada de Tamul (p692)

JAKUB ZAJIC / SHUTTERSTOCK ©

FITOPARDO.COM/GETTYIMAGES ©

MAHAUX PHOTOGRAPHY / GETTYIMAGES ©

Volcán Paricutín

14 As volcanoes go, Paricutín (p638) is still in its adolescence. Blasting out of a Michoacán maize field in 1943, it's one of the youngest volcanoes on Earth, and one of only a few whose life cycle has been fully studied by scientists. And the dormant, 410m-high cone is relatively easy to climb. Some rock hop across barren lava fields to bag the peak, others ride horses through hot black sand before dismounting for the final summit scramble over volcanic scree. The goal's the same: a chance to stand atop a veritable geological marvel.

Pico de Orizaba

15 Touch the sky high above Mexico on the gruelling climb to the 5611m summit of Pico de Orizaba (p237), the snowcapped highest mountain in the country. The trek is no walk in the park. You'll need the help of an experienced local trekking operator, clothing for extreme cold and a sense of adventure as big as the mountain itself. If this all sounds a bit extreme for you, you can enjoy any number of less-demanding trails on the peak's lower slopes.

NORADOA / SHUTTERSTOCK ©

UROSR / GETTY IMAGES ©

San Miguel de Allende

16 This colonial beauty has it all: a spring-like climate, extraordinary light, architecture, handicraft shopping and some of the best culinary experiences in the country. Its frequent festivities mean that music, parades and fireworks are never hard to find, and its nearby hot springs are a joy to unwind in. Famously a place for retired gringos to spend the winter, San Miguel (p664) has so much more to offer than expat hangouts; spending time here is often a highlight of Mexico for many visitors. Dancers performing at Guanajuato International Film Festival (p670)

Monarchs in their Millions

17 Canopies of butterflies cover the forests and hillsides in the Reserva de la Biósfera Santuario Mariposa Monarca (Monarch Butterfly Biosphere Reserve; p624), an astonishing yearly natural phenomenon. It's the kind of annual event to plan your trip around – between late October and March the migrant monarchs cover every surface, weighing down fir tree branches and changing the landscape into a permanent sunset as the butterflies winter far from the freezing Great Lakes. It is one of the planet's most spectacular migrations and not to be missed.

Costa Maya

18 Do yourself a favor and get to this region while the going's still good. Unlike the over-developed Cancún and Riviera Maya, you can still find quiet fishing villages on the Costa Maya that put a premium on sustainable development, such as Mahahual (p296) and Xcalak, both of which boast some of the best dive sites on the Caribbean coast. Then head inland for Laguna Bacalar, a laid-back lakeside town known for its mesmerizing scenery, a 90m-deep cenote and an old Spanish fortress. Laguna Bacalar (p298)

Pacific Coastline

19 Running from the desert islands of Baja California to verdant coves backed by lush mountains, and from untrammeled expanses of sand to lagoons teeming with birdlife, Mexico's Pacific coastline (p492) is stunning in its natural beauty. Punctuating this primordial grandeur is a series of resort towns – Mazatlán, Puerto Vallarta, Manzanillo, Ixtapa, Zihuatanejo and Acapulco – interspersed with world-class surf spots such as Barra de Nexpa, Boca de Pascuales, Troncones and Puerto Escondido, where clear barrels of awesome power batter the shores.

Gregarious Guadalajara

20 Mexico's second-largest city (p580) manages to dazzle despite being more a collection of pueblos than a great metropolis. This charmer gets under your skin with colonial buildings, lofty churches, labyrinthine markets, awesome public spaces and craft shopping in the arty suburbs of Tlaquepaque and Tonalá. The young and middle class party all weekend in hip bars and dance clubs, and there's nowhere better in western Mexico to eat out, whether you're after local specialties such as spicy goat stew, or chic New Mexican and fusion cuisine. Catedral de Guadalajara (p581)

Espíritu Santo

21 Part of a Unesco-protected Biosphere Reserve, Espíritu Santo (p730) island is spectacular in every way. Pink sandstone has been eroded by wind and waves into finger-like protrusions, each harboring a beautiful cove. And if this otherworldly beauty isn't enough then you can descend into the endless blue with whale sharks, dive the many colorful reefs, camp under a canopy of stunning stars, watch frolicking sea lions at their island colony and paddle your way along myriad azure bays. Californian sea lion

JAVIER GARCIA / SHUTTERSTOCK ©

Tulum

22 Take a world-famous Maya ruin, plonk it down beside the achingly beautiful white sands and turquoise-blue waters of the Caribbean and you've got the rightly popular Tulum (p287). Add in accommodations for all budgets, from beach-side shacks to top-end resorts, some fantastic restaurants and bars, and numerous attractions in the surrounding area from cenotes (limestone sink-holes) to other Maya ruins, and it's no wonder many people come for a few days and find themselves staying for far longer.

Puerto Vallarta

23 Visitors adore colorful Vallarta's profusion of charms and it's undoubtedly a more genuine, vibrant place than most of Mexico's large beach-resort towns. Set on a long bay dotted with lovely beaches, it offers big-city nightlife, small-town friendliness, get-away-from-it-all excursions and a legendary LGBT scene. Beyond its lovely seafront boardwalk, one of the real delights of Puerto Vallarta (p520) is the abundance of top-quality street food, counterbalanced by a refined selection of fusion restaurants.

Traditional Mexican architecture, Puerto Vallarta

Guanajuato

24 The glorious World Heritage –listed city of Guanajuato (p650) packs a huge amount into its narrow valley. The former mining town turned colorful university city is a feast of plazas, fun museums, opulent colonial mansions and pastel-hued houses. Snake your way along pedestrian alleyways, people-watch in the squares, mingle with marvelous mariachi groups (pictured), or party hard at *estudiantinas* (traditional street parties) and in the many student bars. The underground tunnels – the town's major transport routes – make for a particularly quirky way to get around.

Need to Know

For more information, see Survival Guide (p849)

Currency
Peso (M$)

Language
Spanish, 68 indigenous languages

Visas
All tourists must have a tourist permit, available on arrival. Some nationalities also need visas.

Money
Mexico is largely a cash economy. ATMs and exchange offices are widely available. Credit cards are accepted in many midrange and top end hotels, restaurants and stores.

Cell Phones
Many US and Canadian cellular carriers offer Mexico roaming deals. Mexican SIM cards can be used in unlocked phones.

Time
Most of Mexico is on Hora del Centro (GMT/UTC minus six hours). Six northern and western states are on GMT/UTC minus seven or eight hours, while one eastern state is on GMT/UTC minus five hours.

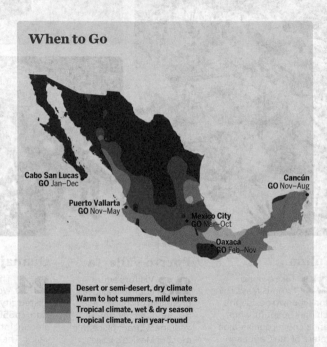

When to Go

Cabo San Lucas
GO Jan–Dec

Cancún
GO Nov–Aug

Puerto Vallarta
GO Nov–May

Mexico City
GO Mar–Oct

Oaxaca
GO Feb–Nov

- Desert or semi-desert, dry climate
- Warm to hot summers, mild winters
- Tropical climate, wet & dry season
- Tropical climate, rain year-round

High Season
(Dec–Apr)

➡ The driest months across most of Mexico, bringing winter escapees from colder countries.

➡ Christmas and Easter are Mexican holiday times, with transportation and coastal accommodations very busy.

Shoulder Season
(Jul & Aug)

➡ Vacation time for many Mexicans and foreigners. Hot almost everywhere and very wet on the Pacific coast. Accommodations prices go up in some popular areas.

Low Season
(May & Jun, Sep–Nov)

➡ May and June see peak temperatures in many areas.

➡ September is the heart of the hurricane season, which doesn't always bring hurricanes but does bring heavy rains on the Gulf and Pacific coasts.

Useful Websites

Lonely Planet (www.lonelyplanet.com/mexico) Destination information, hotel bookings, traveler forum, videos and more.

Mexico Cooks! (www.mexicocooks.typepad.com) Excellent blog on Mexican life.

México (www.visitmexico.com) Official tourism site with plenty of helpful ideas.

Planeta.com (www.planeta.com) Articles, listings, links, photos and more.

Geo-Mexico (www.geo-mexico.com) All sorts of informative and surprising stuff about Mexico.

Mexico Travel (www.tripsavvy.com) Mexico travel news and info.

Important Numbers

Country code	✆52
Emergency	✆911
International access code	✆00
National tourist assistance (including emergencies)	✆088

Exchange Rates

Australia	A$1	M$14.49
Belize	BZ$1	M$9.57
Canada	C$1	M$14.99
Euro zone	€1	M$23.02
Guatemala	Q1	M$2.63
Japan	¥100	M$17.66
New Zealand	NZ$1	M$13.52
UK	UK£1	M$26.12
USA	US$1	M$19.30

For current exchange rates, see www.xe.com.

Daily Costs

Budget: Less than M$800

➡ Hostel dorm bed: M$200; double room in budget hotel: M$370–620

➡ *Comida corrida* (fixed-price lunch) in low-budget restaurant: M$60–90

➡ 250km bus trip: M$230

Midrange: M$800–M$2300

➡ Double room in midrange hotel: M$630–1500

➡ Good dinner with drinks: M$250–350

➡ Museum entry: M$10–70

➡ City taxi ride: M$35–65

➡ Hiking/rafting/mountain-biking day trip M$900–2000

Top End: More than M$2300

➡ Double room in top-end hotel: M$1600–5000

➡ Fine dinner with drinks: M$360–500

➡ Personalized day tour: M$1500–2000

➡ Two-hour horseback ride: M$1000

Opening Hours

Where there are significant seasonal variations in opening hours, we provide hours for high season. Some hours may be shorter in shoulder and low seasons. Hours vary widely but the following are fairly typical.

Banks 9am-4pm Monday to Friday, 9am-1pm Saturday

Restaurants 9am-11pm

Cafes 8am-10pm

Bars and clubs 1pm-midnight

Shops 9am-8pm Monday to Saturday (supermarkets and department stores 9am-10pm daily)

Arriving in Mexico

Mexico City Airport Authorized taxis, with ticket offices inside the airport, cost M$250 to central areas. Metrobús buses (M$30 plus M$10 for a smart card sold by machines inside the airport) serve some central areas. The metro (subway; M$5) operates from 5am (6am Saturday, 7am Sunday) to midnight; its Terminal Aérea station is 200m from the airport's Terminal 1.

Cancún Airport Airport shuttles to downtown or the hotel zone cost around M$160 per person; taxis cost up to M$500. ADO buses run to downtown Cancún (M$72, frequent), Playa del Carmen (M$178, 1¼ hours, frequent) and Mérida (M$368, four hours, four daily).

Getting Around

Bus Mexico's efficient, comfortable and reasonably priced bus network is generally the best option for moving around the country. Services are frequent on main routes.

Air Over 60 cities are served by domestic flights, which are well worth considering for longer intercity trips. Fares vary widely depending on the airline and how far in advance you pay.

Car A convenient option giving maximum independence. Roads are serviceable, with speeds generally slower than north of the border or in Europe. Rental rates start around M$650 per day, including basic insurance.

Train Train travel is limited to one spectacularly scenic train route in northern Mexico.

For much more on **getting around**, see p863

First Time Mexico

For more information, see Survival Guide (p849)

Checklist

➡ Check that your passport is valid for at least six months beyond your stay

➡ Get necessary immunizations well in advance

➡ Check your government's Mexico travel information

➡ If flying, buy a return ticket

➡ Organize travel insurance

➡ Make bookings (for accommodations, travel, restaurants)

➡ Inform your credit-/debit-card company

➡ Check if you can use your cell phone in Mexico

What to Pack

➡ International electrical adaptor (for non-North Americans)

➡ Swimming and beach gear

➡ Flashlight (torch)

➡ Driver's license (if driving)

➡ Sun hat and sunglasses

➡ Sunscreen

➡ Waterproof jacket

➡ Sturdy footwear

➡ Warm clothing

➡ Charcoal tablets to treat Montezuma's Revenge

➡ Mexican Spanish phrasebook

Top Tips for Your Trip

➡ Try not to worry too much. Mexico's much-reported drug-gang violence happens mostly in a small number of places, chiefly in border towns, and tourists are rarely targeted. The country's most visited areas are little touched by the violence.

➡ Expect the unfamiliar. If the strangeness of a foreign land starts to get to you, stay somewhere where you feel comfortable. International cuisine is available in almost any town.

➡ Get out of the cities and coastal resorts into the countryside and smaller towns and villages, where you'll see a side of Mexican life that many tourists miss.

➡ Don't spread yourself too thin; pick a part of Mexico that you particularly want to explore.

What to Wear

In beach towns, shorts and short skirts are common; sleeveless tops are fine. Take some sleeved tops and long pants/skirts to protect against sun and mosquitoes, and for evenings. Dress conservatively when visiting churches. Pack a sweater or a warm jacket for cooler inland areas. A sun hat is essential; good, cheap options are sold throughout Mexico.

Sleeping

Mexico offers a full spectrum of accommodations. In popular destinations, book a couple of months ahead for peak times such as Christmas, Easter, and July/August.

Hostels Found largely in backpacker-heavy destinations, hostels are inexpensive, and are often run by savvy travelers.

Hotels Hotels range from nondescript to renovated historic residences.

Guesthouses Typically good value and family-run, guesthouses offer a great taste of local life.

Cabañas Cabins and huts, mostly found at beach destinations, range from basic to luxurious.

Camping and hammocks In more budget-oriented beach spots, you can often sleep in a hammock or pitch a tent cheaply.

Money

Plan on making cash purchases with pesos. Few businesses accept US dollars. It's easy to get pesos from ATMs using a major credit or debit card. You can pay with major credit and debit cards at many midrange and top-end restaurants, shops and hotels.

For more information, see p855.

Bargaining

It's worth asking if a discount is available on room rates, especially if it's low season or you're staying more than two nights. In markets some haggling is expected. Unmetered taxis will often shave some pesos off the initial asking price.

Tipping

Many service workers depend on tips to supplement miserable wages.

➡ **Restaurants** Tip 10% to 15% unless service is included in the check.

➡ **Hotels** It's nice (though optional) to leave 5% to 10% of your room costs for those who keep it clean and tidy.

➡ **Taxis** Drivers don't expect tips unless they provide some extra service.

➡ **Porters** Airport and hotel porters usually get M$50 to M$100.

➡ **Attendants** Car-parking and gas-station attendants expect M$5 to M$10.

Language

Mexico's main language is Spanish. Many Mexicans in the world of tourism also speak some English, often good English. In any accommodations catering to international travelers, you can get by with English. Still, it's useful and polite to know at least a few words of Spanish – Mexicans appreciate being greeted with *'Buenos días'* and appreciate you making the effort, even if they break into fluent English.

 Where can I buy handicrafts?
¿Dónde se puede comprar artesanías?
don·de se pwe·de kom·prar ar·te·sa·nee·as

Star buys in Mexico are the regional handicrafts produced all over the country, mainly by the indigenous people.

 Which *antojitos* do you have?
¿Qué antojitos tiene? ke an·to·khee·tos tye·ne

'Little whimsies' (snacks) can encompass anything – have an entire meal of them, eat a few as appetisers, or get one on the street for a quick bite.

3 **Not too spicy, please.**
No muy picoso, por favor. no mooy pee·ko·so por fa·vor

Not all food in Mexico is spicy, but beware – many dishes can be fierce indeed, so it may be a good idea to play it safe.

4 **Where can I find a *cantina* nearby?**
¿Dónde hay una cantina cerca de aquí?
don·de ai oo·na kan·tee·na ser·ka de a·kee

Ask locals about the classical Mexican venue for endless snacks, and often dancing as well.

5 **How do you say ... in your language?**
¿Cómo se dice ... en su lengua?
ko·mo se dee·se ... en su len·gwa

Numerous indigenous languages are spoken around Mexico, primarily Mayan languages and Náhuatl. People will appreciate it if you try to use their local language.

Etiquette

Mexicans are not huge sticklers for etiquette. Their natural warmth takes precedence.

➡ **Greetings** *'Mucho gusto'* (roughly 'A great pleasure') is a polite thing to say when you're introduced to someone, accompanied by a handshake. If it's a woman and a man, the woman offers her hand first.

➡ **Pleasing people** Mexicans love to hear that you're enjoying their country. They are slow to criticize or argue, expressing disagreement more by nuance than by blunt contradiction.

➡ **Visiting homes** An invitation to a Mexican home is an honor for an outsider; you will be treated very hospitably. Take a small gift, such as flowers or something for the children. Be at least 30 minutes late; being on time is considered rude.

What's New

Templo Mayor

A new entrance hall in this Mexico City temple displays artifacts unearthed over four years – funerary objects, a petrified tree and pre-Hispanic structures. A tower of more than 650 human skulls is planned to go on display. (p71)

Vegan Food

Meat-free, vegetarian, and especially vegan dishes are becoming more common in Mexico City. Seeing *comida vegana* is shorthand for hipness at any modern *bazar* (market), food hall, restaurant or even bar.

Baja Craft Beer

The craft beer scene of northern Baja is continually evolving, with plenty to sample in Ensenada, Mexicali and the creative center of it all, Tijuana.

Old Mazatlán

The streets and public spaces of Mazatlán's historic center have never looked better following an ambitious makeover. (p494)

Cenotes

Two newly discovered cenotes (sinkholes), X-Batún and Dzonbakal, are now accessible to swimmers and scuba divers. (p321)

High-speed Crossing

On Lago de Pátzcuaro, a 1200m-long zipline now links little Isla Janitzio with even tinier Isla Tecuéna. It costs M$250 one-way; a boat will return you to Janitzio. (p632)

Museo Francisco Villa

Housed in a colonial mansion with breathtaking murals, this new and well-conceived museum pays homage to Mexican revolutionary hero – and Durango native son – Pancho Villa. (p789)

Hotel Casa La Ola

The quiet beach village of San Agustinillo took a step upmarket with the opening of this slick boutique hotel perched on a rise over the beach, with an affiliated restaurant below. (p475)

Parque Nacional Revillagigedo

Mexico created this vast new marine reserve around the Revillagigedo archipelago in 2017. Known as the 'Galapagos of North America', it's home to hundreds of marine species. (p847)

Tren Turístico Puebla-Cholula

Cholula's pyramid and archaeological zone is now a pleasant 40-minute tram ride away from central Puebla. (p161)

For more recommendations and reviews, see lonelyplanet.com/mexico

If You Like...

Beach Resorts

Puerto Vallarta Pacific resort and LGBT capital with dazzling beaches, stylish restaurants and hot nightlife. (p520)

Playa del Carmen The chicest resort on the Caribbean coast. (p278)

Zihuatanejo Combines a livable feel and characterfully intimate center with pleasant beaches and great nearby coastline. (p551)

Cancún North of the megaresorts you'll be pleasantly surprised to find Cancún's quiet side: Isla Blanca. (p258)

Cabo San Lucas Three main family-friendly beaches, excellent facilities, numerous bars and restaurants, and water sports. (p740)

Mazatlán Attractively renovated colonial center, an old-time 1950s promenade and fun-in-the-sun beach-resort strip. (p494)

San Carlos The best stretches of sand in the north also come with mountain vistas. (p773)

Getaway Beaches

Playa Zicatela This 3km strip of golden sand and crashing waves in Puerto Escondido is heaven on Earth for surfers. (p459)

Xcalak Timeless Caribbean coast with a wonderful barrier reef. (p297)

Playa Maruata Tranquil, low-budget Michoacán fishing village beloved by beach bums and sea turtles. (p546)

Barra de Potosí Palm-fringed white sands, calm waters and a lagoon full of birds and crocs. (p560)

Isla Holbox Escape the Riviera Maya and wander the sandy roads of this palm-fringed Gulf coast getaway. (p273)

Espíritu Santo Shallow waters, pristine sandy beaches and boat trips. (p730)

Reserva de la Biosfera Los Tuxtlas The reserve's mountain-backed beaches are the Gulf of Mexico's ultimate chill-out spot. (p251)

Playa Escondida Battle your way along a rough road to reach this pristine sand crescent in southern Veracruz. (p253)

Luxury Spas & Hotels

Casa Oaxaca Boutique Oaxaca hotel dedicated to art, with gorgeous contemporary rooms and a colonial patio. (p436)

Banyan Tree Cabo Marqués Asian-influenced seclusion at this exclusive coastal retreat near Acapulco. (p569)

Posada La Poza Pacific-side retreat located at Todos Santos with lush gardens, a saltwater swimming pool and Jacuzzi, and a superb onsite restaurant. (p744)

Rosewood San Miguel de Allende Join well-heeled weekenders beside the fabulous pool at this historic palatial hotel. (p671)

Pueblo Lindo A rooftop pool overlooks the white houses of Taxco scattered across the hills. (p194)

Siete Lunas Stroll through jungle from fashionable Sayulita to reach this romantic cliff-top retreat. (p518)

Hotel Museo Palacio de San Agustín So fabulous it's also a museum, this impressive, elaborately decorated hotel is home to a fine collection of antiques. (p685)

Hacienda de los Santos A 300-year-old hacienda turned into a stunning boutique hotel situated in the colonial town of Álamos. (p777)

Amuleto Perched high over Zihuatanejo, this boutique retreat offers the ultimate in de-stress. (p556)

Le Blanc Ultramodern, ultrachic, adult-only spa just steps away from the Caribbean. (p262)

Pyramids & Temples

Palenque Exquisite Maya temples backed by jungle-covered hills. (p384)

Chichén Itzá A vast Maya temple complex, its step-pyramid design testimony to the Maya's exceptional astronomy skills. (p326)

Uxmal Set in hilly Puuc, this large Maya site is a riot of fascinating carved-stone ornamentation. (p52)

Yaxchilán Impressive temples in a Chiapas jungle setting, reached only by river. (p398)

Monte Albán The ancient Zapotec capital sits spectacularly on a flattened hilltop site just outside Oaxaca. (p445)

Tulum These late Maya temples and pyramids sit right on a rugged stretch of Caribbean coast. (p288)

Calakmul High pyramids in a huge, remote Maya city, still largely hidden in protected rainforest. (p349)

Teotihuacán Massive Pyramids of the Sun and Moon, and mural-decked palaces, in Mexico's biggest ancient city. (p147)

Tzintzuntzan Atmospheric Tarascan ruins with fantastic views of Lake Pátzcuaro, few crowds and unusual semicircular temples. (p634)

Edzná Marvel at the fine carvings at the Templo de Mascarones (Temple of Masks). (p345)

Historic Colonial Towns

Guanajuato The opulent mansions and winding streets of this university town squeeze into a picturesque valley. (p650)

Top: Relaxing at a tropical resort in LGBT-friendly Puerto Vallarta (p520)

Bottom: El Castillo (aka Pyramid of Kukulcán; p327), Chichén Itzá

San Miguel de Allende Artsy town of cobblestone streets and lovely stone architecture, with many foreign (mostly US) residents. (p664)

Oaxaca Gorgeous southern city with an indigenous flavor and stunning art and artisanry. (p424)

Zacatecas The magnificent cathedral in this former silver-mining city is the ultimate expression of colonial baroque. (p694)

Mérida Even if you're not big on architecture, the stately mansions here never cease to impress. (p304)

Álamos Wander the cobbled streets of northern Mexico's colonial jewel, nestled in the verdant Sierra Madre foothills. (p775)

Todos Santos This former cane-milling town has streets lined with handsome 19th-century brick-and-adobe haciendas. (p743)

Puebla Dense with restored colonial churches and mansions, sparkling with azulejos (painted ceramic tiles). (p153)

Morelia Unesco-listed since 1991, Morelia is anchored by what is arguably Mexico's most spectacular cathedral. (p614)

San Cristóbal de las Casas An indigenous highland town with winding cobblestone streets and old churches aplenty. (p364)

Shopping

Mexico City Everything from craft stores to boutiques to fashion, flea and food markets. (p129)

San Miguel de Allende A mind-boggling array of folk art from all over Mexico. (p674)

Guadalajara The artisans' suburbs of Tlaquepaque and Tonalá are replete with classy ceramics, furniture and glassware. (p599)

Tepotzotlán Colourful beaded jaguar heads and animal forms made by the Huichol people. (p144)

Taxco One of the best places in Mexico for silverwork, especially jewelry. (p191)

Oaxaca Its black clay pottery is highly prized. (p442)

Puebla Famous for colorful Talavera ceramics. (p160)

San Cristóbal de las Casas Head here for woollen crafts and colorful textiles. (p377)

León Buy your shoes, belts and bags at this leatherworks capital. (p661)

Mérida The one-stop shop for hammocks, guayaberas (men's shirts), huipiles (long, sleeveless tunics) and handicrafts. (p304)

Mexican Cuisine

Mexico City Unrivaled countrywide fare, from fusion restaurants serving nueva oocina mexicana to the world's best tacos. (p111)

Seafood Baja California's fish tacos, Veracruz' huachinango a la veracruzana and ceviche in Barra de Navidad. (p539)

Oaxaca Famed for its seven moles (chili-based sauces) and some of Mexico's best contemporary restaurants. (p438)

Puebla Home to mole poblano, chiles en nogada, tacos al pastor, escamoles (ant larvae) and festivals celebrating them. (p153)

Antojitos These ubiquitous 'little whims' made with masa (corn dough) include tacos, quesadillas, enchiladas and tamales. (p836)

Guadalajara Mexico's second city pitches forward-thinking fusion food against old staples such as birria (spicy-hot goat or lamb stew). (p593)

Baja Med Feast on Mexican-Mediterranean mélange cuisine in Tijuana (p705) and elsewhere in Baja California (p703).)

San Miguel de Allende One of Mexico's best dining scenes, combining quality Mexican cuisine with world-class fusion. (p664)

Yucatán Peninsula Flavorful dishes that are rooted in rich Maya culture, such as cochinita pibil (slow-roasted pork). (p255)

Coatepec Wake up and smell the coffee at the highland home of Mexico's brew. (p225)

Museums & Galleries

Museo Nacional de Antropología Mexico City's National Anthropology Museum is chock-full of stupendous relics from pre-Hispanic Mexico. (p85)

Museo Frida Kahlo The poignant Mexico City home of the haunted artist. (p96)

Museo Nacional de la Muerte All things related to death in this Aguascalientes museum, but far from macabre. (p677)

Museo de Antropología A superbly designed Xalapa space with Mexico's second-best archaeological collection after Mexico City. (p219)

Museo de las Culturas de Oaxaca Excellent Oaxaca museum situated in a beautiful ex-monastery demonstrates continuities between pre-Hispanic and contemporary culture. (p424)

Exploring Cenote Azul (p299), Laguna Bacalar,

Museo Jumex One of Latin America's leading contemporary-art collections at this Mexico City museum. (p89)

Horno3 Outstanding steel-making museum in the gigantic shell of a former blast furnace in Monterrey's newest urban park. (p800)

Gran Museo del Mundo Maya World-class museum in Mérida showcasing more than 1100 well-preserved Maya artifacts. (p304)

Museo de la Ballena Excellent La Paz museum featuring the California gray whale and related conservation efforts. (p730)

Palacio de Gobierno Wonderful multimedia museum on Jalisco and Guadalajara history with two impressive Orozco murals thrown in. (p581)

Diving & Snorkeling

Yucatán Peninsula With the world's second-largest barrier reef, it's world famous for its abundant coral and tropical fish. (p255)

Banco Chinchorro Wreck-studded coral atoll off the southern end of the Caribbean coast. (p296)

Isla Cozumel Diving and snorkeling for all abilities at the island's 65 reefs. (p283)

Bahías de Huatulco A string of beautiful Pacific bays with several coral plates and more than 100 dive sites. (p483)

Xel-Há This eco-park on the Riviera Maya offers snorkeling in a beautiful natural aquarium. (p277)

Laguna de la Media Luna Has an underwater cave ideal for advanced diving. (p691)

Cabo Pulmo A magnificent coral reef and spectacular diving and snorkeling experiences. (p736)

Espíritu Santo Swim and snorkel with whale sharks, the world's biggest fish. (p730)

Veracruz Excellent wreck diving, plus beautiful reefs around the Isla de Sacrificios. (p206)

Surfing

Puerto Escondido The Mexican Pipeline beach break is world famous, but Escondido has mellower waves, too. (p461)

Troncones A long, strong, world-class left point break and some excellent beach breaks. (p548)

Sayulita Dependable, medium-sized waves, good for practicing or learning, with a mellow party vibe. (p516)

Ensenada There's a perfect point break at San Miguel. (p715)

Barra de Nexpa One of several spots with healthy waves along the little-touched Michoacán coast. (p546)

San Blas For intermediates and beginners, with many beach and point breaks, and one of the world's longest waves. (p509)

Todos Santos The beaches surrounding this town offer some of the best swells in Baja. (p744)

Zipolite Clothing-optional beach on Oaxaca's unsullied coast that's also known for its big waves. (p471)

Hiking, Mountain Biking & Horseback Riding

Copper Canyon Bike down incredible trails, hike through extraordinary landscapes, or let the horse take the strain. (p750)

Pueblos Mancomunados These Oaxacan mountain villages are linked by a scenic trail network. (p455)

Rancho El Charro Horse treks into jungle-covered mountains behind Puerto Vallarta. (p523)

Bici-Burro Great mountain-bike outings from San Miguel de Allende. (p669)

Real de Catorce Explore the desert hills on foot, bike or horse from this magical old silver town. (p687)

Parque Marino Nacional Bahía de Loreto This beautiful national park is a world-class destination for a wide range of activities. (p727)

Pico de Orizaba Hikes in Mexico don't get more breathless or challenging than scaling the country's highest mountain. (p237)

Cañón del Sumidero Skip the bus and pedal 86km from San Cristóbal to this Chiapas landmark. (p362)

Wildlife

Whales Watch whales in Baja California's lagoons off Mazatlán, Puerto Vallarta or Puerto Escondido (December to March). (p30)

Sea turtles Cuyutlán, Playa Colola, Playa Escobilla, Tecolutla and Xcacel-Xcacelito beaches are all major turtle breeding grounds. (p844)

Birds Mexico's forests and coastal lagoons thrill bird-watchers. For flamingos head to Río Lagartos (p337) or Celestún (p320).)

Whale sharks Snorkel with gentle giants near La Paz, Baja, or Isla Contoy in Quintana Roo. (p32)

Parque Nacional Sierra San Pedro Mártir Look for California condors circling above, and bobcats, deer and bighorn sheep at ground level. (p713)

Reserva de la Biosfera Los Tuxtlas Explore the Americas' northernmost tropical rainforests in this impressively diverse reserve. (p251)

Reserva de la Biosfera Santuario Mariposa Monarca The fir trees in this reserve turn orange in winter with millions of monarch butterflies. (p624)

Reserva de la Biosfera El Pinacate y Gran Desierto de Altar Look for pumas and pronghorn antelope amid petrified lava flows and sand dunes. (p771)

Kayaking & Rafting

Baja California The islands and estuaries off the east coast are the stuff of kayakers' dreams. (p703)

Puerto Vallarta Kayak along the lagoons or islands off the Pacific coast. (p520)

Veracruz Ride the white-water rapids plunging down from the Sierra Madre Oriental from Jalcomulco or Tlapacoyan. (p204)

Oaxaca Rivers near Bahías de Huatulco have waters suitable for everyone from beginners to experienced rafters. (p421)

Mulegé Enjoy the mangrove- and palm-lined Río Mulegé via a kayak or raft. (p725)

Lagos de Montebello Paddle around these turquoise Chiapas lagoons in a traditional wooden *cayuco* (canoe). (p405)

Tequila & Mezcal

Oaxaca The world's mezcal capital boasts atmospheric mezcal bars ranging from hip hangouts to connoisseurs' cantinas. (p440)

Bósforo Duck into this Mexico City hideaway for the finest mezcals in town. (p123)

Tequila Visit the distilleries of the Jalisco town that the drink is named after. (p603)

Expo Tequila A prime Tijuana place to taste and rate tequila from all over Mexico. (p706)

La Fundación Mezcalería This Mérida bar pours organic mezcals, and has nightly live music. (p312)

Month by Month

January

It's warm in coastal and lowland areas, cool in the highlands and dry everywhere, attracting flocks of foreign tourists. The first week is Mexican holiday season, with transportation booked up and coastal resorts very busy.

🎊 Día de los Santos Reyes

January 6 (Three Kings' Day or Epiphany), rather than Christmas, is the day when Mexican children traditionally receive presents, commemorating the Three Kings' gifts for the baby Jesus. Mexicans eat *rosca de reyes,* a large oval sweetbread decorated with candied fruit.

🎊 Mérida Fest

Between January 5 and 28, Mérida celebrates its diverse culture with daily dance, music, theater, art, acrobatic shows and other cultural events. (p309)

🎊 Festival Alfonso Ortíz Tirado

In late January tens of thousands descend upon tiny Álamos for this multi-day festival featuring some of the world's top musicians playing classical and chamber music, blues, bossa nova and *trova* (troubadour-type music). (p776)

🏃 Migratory Bird Season

January is the peak season for migratory birds along Mexico's Pacific coast. Lagoons and rivers at places such as Laguna Manialtepec and Lagunas de Chacahua are packed with fowl, and San Blas even holds an International Migratory Bird Festival. (p509)

February

Temperatures are marginally higher than in January, but it remains dry, making this a great month to be in much of Mexico, though it can still be cold in the north and at high altitudes.

🎊 Día de la Candelaría

Candlemas (February 2), commemorating the infant Jesus' presentation in the temple, is widely celebrated. In Tlacotalpan several days of festivities feature bull-running in the streets, and a flotilla of boats following an image of the Virgin down the Río Papaloapan. (p245)

🎊 Carnaval

A big bash preceding the 47-day penance of Lent, Carnaval happens during the week leading up to Ash Wednesday (March 6, 2019; February 26, 2020). It's wildest in Veracruz, La Paz and Mazatlán, with parades and plenty of music, drinking, dancing, fireworks and fun.

🏃 Whale-Watching Season

Magnificent gray whales calve in bays and lagoons around Baja California from mid-December to mid-April. Whales can also be spotted along the whole Pacific coast during this period. Best months for Baja whale-watching are February and March.

March

It's getting steadily warmer all over Mexico, but it's still dry and the winter season for foreign tourism continues.

✵ Chacala Music & Arts Festival

The small Pacific coast fishing town of Chacala celebrates everything from music and dance to regional cuisine and local art at beachside venues. (p514)

✵ Festival Internacional del Cine

Mexico's biggest film event of the year draws top international actors and directors to Guadalajara for a week each March, with more than 250 films screened before more than 100,000 viewers. (p589)

✵ Festival de México

Mexico City's historic center hosts music, theater, dance and literary events featuring talent from Mexico and abroad – the capital's biggest cultural bash of the year. (p105)

☆ Spring Break

US students get a week's break in late February or March (dates vary between colleges) and many head to Mexican resorts such as Cancún, Puerto Vallarta or Cabo San Lucas for days of over-the-top partying.

✵ Vernal Equinox

Visitors mob Chichén Itzá for the spring (March 20 to 21) and autumnal (September 21 to 22) equinoxes, when shadows resemble a serpent ascending or descending El Castillo pyramid. Almost the same effect happens for a week preceding and following each equinox. (p326)

🏃 Ultra Caballo Blanco

Started by American runner Micah True, this 82km ultramarathon near Urique follows tough but gorgeous canyon trails, at altitude. The race pays homage to the native Tarahumara, who have a centuries-old tradition of long-distance running and whose very name means 'the running people'. (p756)

April

Temperatures continue to increase, but it stays dry. Semana Santa (Easter Week), which can be in March or April, is Mexico's major holiday week of the year, with tourist accommodations and transportation packed.

✵ Semana Santa

Semana Santa is the week from Palm Sunday to Easter Sunday (April 21, 2019; April 12, 2020). Good Friday sees solemn processions in many places, and enormous crowds attend a re-enactment of the Crucifixion in Iztapalapa, Mexico City. (p105)

🔒 Tianguis Artesanal de Uruapan

Semana Santa kicks off with a major crafts competition and Uruapan's main square is then filled with exhibitions and sales of Michoacán handicrafts for the following two weeks. (p636)

May

Temperatures reach annual peaks in cities such as Mérida (average daily high 35°C), Guadalajara (31°C), Oaxaca (30°C) and Mexico City (26°C). It's low season for tourism, meaning cheaper accommodations prices.

✵ Cinco de Mayo

Celebrating the battle (May 5) in 1862 when Mexican forces defeated French troops, the streets of Puebla, where the fighting happened, close for a huge parade of floats with the military, performers and dancers entertaining more than 20,000 people. The following two weeks feature other events. (p156)

✵ Expo Artesanal

Taking place at the Centro Cultural Tijuana, this superb arts-and-crafts festival (May 20 to 24) features handicrafts for sale from all over Mexico. (p706)

✵ Feria de Corpus Christi

Papantla's big bash features spectacular *voladores* performances (where men suspended by their ankles, whirl around a tall pole) and indigenous dances, plus *charreadas* (Mexican rodeos) and parades. (p240)

✵ Feria de Morelia

This three-week fair sees regional dance performances, bullfights, agricultural and handicraft exhibitions, plenty of partying and (at the end) fireworks in Michoacán's capital. (p619)

June

The rainy season begins, bringing heavy downpours in the southeast, in some places along the Pacific coast and in the central highlands. Tourist numbers and hotel prices remain low.

✤ Festival del Mole Poblano

Puebla celebrates its most famous contribution to Mexican cuisine, the chocolatey *mole poblano* sauce, in early June. (p156)

✤ Surf's Up

Countless spots along the Pacific coast, including Puerto Escondido with its legendary Mexican Pipeline, enjoy superb swells from April/May to October/November. June to August generally sees the biggest waves. Beginners can learn to surf almost year-round.

July

It's rainy in the southeast, central highlands and along the Pacific coast, but this is a summer vacation month for both foreigners and Mexicans, bringing busy times and higher prices at many tourist destinations.

✤ Guelaguetza

Oaxaca is thronged for this fantastically colorful feast of regional dance on the first two Mondays after July 16, with plenty of other celebratory events accompanying it. (p432)

✤ La Feria de las Flores

This week-long, major flower festival in Mexico City includes the display of myriad varieties of plants, family activities, performances, and botany-related paintings and sculpture. The festival has pre-Hispanic origins, when followers of Xiuhtecuhtli, Lord of Flowers, would make floral offerings in return for abundant crops. (p105)

✤ Swimming with Whale Sharks

Massive whale sharks congregate to feed on plankton off Isla Contoy, north of Cancún, between mid-May and mid-September. The best time to swim with these gentle giants is mid-June to July.

✤ Fiesta de Santa Magdalena

Xico, Veracruz, is abuzz with processions involving elaborate costumes and dance for much of July in celebration of the town's patron saint. A running of the bulls takes place through the streets on July 22 and at the most important processions between July 19 and 25. (p228)

August

The summer holiday season continues, as do the rains, although they're less intense in most areas. June to August is brutally hot in the north.

✤ Feria de Huamantla

Huamantla, east of Mexico City, lets rip over a few days and nights during its mid-August fair. On August 14 the streets are carpeted with flowers and colored sawdust. A few days later there's a Pamplona-esque running of the bulls. (p172)

☆ La Morisma

Zacatecas stages a spectacular mock battle with 10,000 participants, commemorating the triumph of the Christians over the Moors in old Spain, usually on the last weekend of August. (p699)

✤ Feria de la Uva

The Coahuila city of Parras celebrates wine every August. Think parades, live music performances, sporting events, religious ceremonies, and thousands and thousands of glasses of wine. The climax? A dance party at Casa Madero, the oldest winery in the Americas. (p796)

September

It's the height of the hurricane season on the Yucatán Peninsula and Mexico's coasts. It's also rainy in most places, with poor visibility for Caribbean divers.

✤ Día de la Independencia

On Independence Day (September 16) patriotic celebrations mark the anniversary of Miguel Hidalgo's 1810 call to rebellion against Spain, the Grito de Dolores. On the 15th, the Grito is repeated from every Mexican town hall, followed by fireworks. The biggest celebrations are in Mexico City. (p105)

October

Low season for tourism, with the possibility of hurricanes, but the rains ease off everywhere in the country except the Yucatán Peninsula.

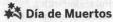 Copper Canyon Season

October, along with November and March, is one of the best months to visit northwest Mexico's spectacular canyon country, with temperatures not too hot at the bottom of the canyons, nor too cold at the top.

Festival Internacional Cervantino

Guanajuato's two- to three-week arts festival, dedicated to Spanish writer Miguel de Cervantes, is one of the biggest cultural happenings in Latin America, with performances by worldwide music, dance and theater groups. (p656)

November

The weather is mostly dry and hot temperatures are subsiding. Snow tops the high peaks of the central volcanic belt.

Día de Muertos

On the Día de Muertos (November 2) cemeteries come alive as families decorate graves and commune with their dead, some holding all-night vigils. Special altars appear in homes and public buildings. Associated events start days before, notably around Pátzcuaro, Uruapan, Mexico City and Oaxaca.

Festival Internacional de Música

This classical-music festival takes place in Morelia and is befitting of a city that is home to the oldest music conservatory in the Americas. Performances are held throughout the city in various plazas, churches and theaters. (p619)

Festival de las Ánimas

A new tradition in Mérida, this seven-day festival preceding Día de Muertos culminates in the Paseo de Ánimas (the Path of Souls) – a procession of participants who are dressed in traditional Yucatecan clothes, with skulls painted on faces, from the graveyard to Parque San Juan. (p309)

Festival Gourmet International

Guest chefs from around Mexico and the world descend on the Pacific resort of Puerto Vallarta for this 10-day feast of the culinary arts. (p524)

December

A dry month almost everywhere, and as cool as it gets. International winter tourism gets going and the Christmas–New Year period is Mexican holiday time, with accommodations busy and prices high.

Christmas

Christmas is traditionally celebrated with a feast in the early hours of December 25, after midnight mass. Pre- or post-Christmas events in some towns include *pastorelas* (nativity plays), as in Tepotzotlán and Pátzcuaro, and *posadas* (candlelit processions), as in Taxco.

Día de Nuestra Señora de Guadalupe

Several days of festivities throughout Mexico lead up to the feast day of the Virgin, the country's religious patron – the Day of Our Lady of Guadalupe (December 12). Millions converge on Mexico City's Basílica de Guadalupe. (p105)

Monarch Butterfly Season

From late October to March the forests of the Reserva de la Biosfera Santuario Mariposa Monarca (Monarch Butterfly Biosphere Reserve) turn orange as millions of large monarch butterflies winter here. The best time to watch them is on a warm, sunny afternoon. (p624)

Plan Your Trip
Itineraries

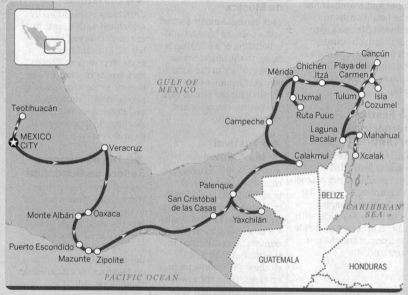

Beaches, Cities and Temples of Mexico's South
1 MONTH

This classic journey leads south from Mexico's central heartland to its glorious Caribbean beaches, and gives a superb sampling of the ruins, jungle, cities and beaches that make the country so fascinating.

Start by exploring the exciting megalopolis of **Mexico City**, key to any understanding of the country. Take a side trip to the awesome pyramids at **Teotihuacán**, capital of ancient Mexico's biggest empire. Then head east to the lively port city of **Veracruz**, before crossing the mountains south-

ward to **Oaxaca**. This cultured colonial city, with Mexico's finest handicrafts, sits at the heart of a beautiful region with a large indigenous population. Give yourself a day to explore the ancient Zapotec capital, **Monte Albán**, nearby.

Head to one of the relaxed beach spots on the Oaxaca coast, such as **Puerto Escondido**, **Mazunte** or **Zipolite**, for a few days' sun, surf and sand, before continuing east to **San Cristóbal de las Casas**, a beautiful highland town surrounded by intriguing indigenous villages. Move on to **Palenque**, perhaps the most stunning of

Pirámide del Sol (Pyramid of the Sun; p149), Teotihuacán

all ancient Maya cities, with its backdrop of emerald-green jungle, and **Yaxchilán**, another marvelous Maya city, accessible only by river.

Head northeast to **Campeche**, an attractive mix of colonial city and bustling modern town, detouring to the remote and ancient Maya city of **Calakmul** en route. Calakmul will take three days of your time – a day to get there, a day to explore and a day to get back, but it's worth every kilometer, we promise. Move on to colonial **Mérida**, the Yucatán Peninsula's lively cultural capital and the base for visiting the superb ruins of **Uxmal** and the **Ruta Puuc**. Next stop: **Chichén Itzá**, the most celebrated of all the Yucatán's Maya sites. From here it's on to **Tulum** on the Caribbean coast, another spectacular Maya site set beside a glorious beach. If it's too busy for you, opt for the quiet, laid-back vibe of **Laguna Bacalar**, or if you want to go diving, head to the coast and stay in **Mahahual** or remote **Xcalak**. Finally, make your way northward along the Riviera Maya to the resort town of **Playa del Carmen**, with a side trip to **Isla Cozumel** for excellent snorkeling and diving. End at Mexico's most popular and unabashed coastal resort, **Cancún**.

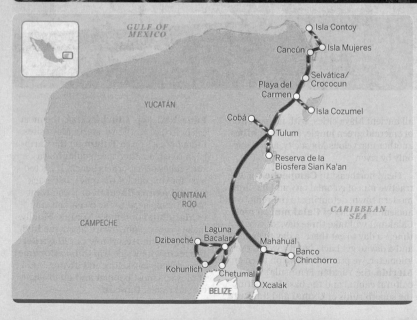

LEONARDO GONZALEZ / SHUTTERSTOCK ©

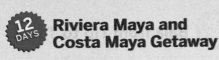

12 DAYS Riviera Maya and Costa Maya Getaway

This journey showcases the best of Mexico's Caribbean coast, from the bustling beaches and frenetic nightlife of the Riviera Maya to the soporific charm of seaside villages along the Costa Maya. Some wonderfully scenic Maya ruins and terrific diving and snorkeling add some action to a beach vacation.

Fly into Cancún and head straight for relaxed **Isla Mujeres** for beaches and snorkeling, taking a side trip to **Isla Contoy**, a national park with superlative bird-watching and, from June to September, the chance to swim with whale sharks that congregate nearby.

Alternatively, opt for hip **Playa del Carmen** with its own fine beaches, underwater activities and lively nightlife. 'Playa' is also the jumping-off point for the dive sites of **Isla Cozumel**. If you have kids, spend a day at the turtle farm on Isla Mujeres, one of the nearby 'eco-parks' such as **Selvática** with its 12 jungle zip-lines, or **Crococun** in Puerto Morelos, an interactive zoo with crocodiles and monkeys. Next stop: **Tulum**, with one of Mexico's most perfect beaches and its most spectacularly located Maya site. Nearby are the pyramids and temples of **Cobá**, as well as the wildlife-rich Reserva de la Biosfera Sian Ka'an. South of Tulum the Costa Maya is less developed and less touristed than the Riviera Maya. Head to **Mahahual**, a laid-back village with snorkeling and diving at the coral atoll **Banco Chinchorro**, or the tiny fishing town of **Xcalak**, another excellent water-sports base.

After three nights chilling in these towns, backtrack to the northern end of Chetumal Bay before heading south to the laid-back **Laguna Bacalar**, where you can bask in the sun and bathe in the cenote-clear water that is painted unreal shades of blue, turquoise and green. For a diversion, head into the jungle and find yourself exploring the ruins of **Kohunlich** and **Dzibanché**, where you're likely to have the places to yourself.

Finish your trip in the relaxed, low-key city of **Chetumal**, where you can either travel onwards to Belize or turn around and, if you're worried that you missed out on **Cancún's** nightlife, spend your last night there and paint the town red.

EMMA SHAW / LONELY PLANET ©

Top: Diver off Isla Cozumel (p282)
Bottom: Sea turtle

18 DAYS Baja from Tip to Toe

The world's second-longest peninsula seems tailor-made for road tripping, with 1200km of road snaking through picturesque villages, along dramatic coastline and past otherworldly rock canyons. Baja's charms are further enhanced by its appealing colonial towns, world-class diving and some of the best fish tacos you'll ever taste.

Enjoy a full-on day of Mexican life-on-the-streets in **Tijuana** before heading south via the **Valle de Guadalupe** winery route, stopping for a day or two to tour the vineyards and taste the terrific tipples. Then make a stop in **Ensenada** for great fish tacos and a stroll through the shopping streets before heading south via the Carretera Transpeninsular's spectacular desert scenery. If it's migration season (December to April), book a whale-watching tour at **Guerrero Negro**. Alternatively, continue south and detour to **Sierra de San Francisco** to view ancient petroglyphs in the local caves.

Further south, pass through San Ignacio to have a look at the most beautiful colonial church in Baja (pictured), and stop in **Mulegé** for a tranquil paddle in the cerulean **Sea of Cortez**. The highway then hugs the coast en route to **Loreto**, where you can spend a day or two discovering the artisan shops, great restaurants, historic architecture and 17th-century mission. Heading south again, the road passes several stunning beaches before ducking inland. Detour to **Puerto San Carlos** for a glimpse of sea-dwelling leviathans during whale-watching season, then make for the unspoiled charms of **La Paz**. Spend a day kayaking and snorkeling off the island of **Espíritu Santo**, or go swimming with whale sharks (October to March).

Next, stop at **Todos Santos**, a gorgeous little town with galleries, sea-turtle nesting grounds and beautiful historical buildings, before you hit wild **Cabo San Lucas**. Indulge in banana-boating, parasailing and other beach activities before hitting the bars, and don't forget to take a boat to **Land's End** for a glimpse of the magical stone arch. If you need a respite, head for **San José del Cabo**, Cabo's tamer twin, with its appealing colonial church, art galleries and a clutch of good restaurants. Or, go underwater for a closer glimpse of the reef at **Cabo Pulmo** – the only living reef in the Sea of Cortez.

Top: El Arco (the Arch) at Land's End (p740)
Bottom: Misión San Ignacio de Kadakaamán (p722), San Ignacio

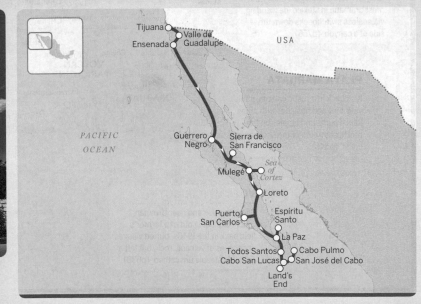

Off the Beaten Track: Mexico

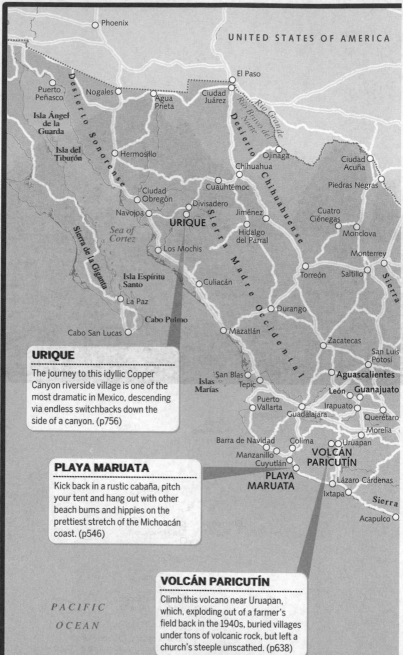

URIQUE

The journey to this idyllic Copper Canyon riverside village is one of the most dramatic in Mexico, descending via endless switchbacks down the side of a canyon. (p756)

PLAYA MARUATA

Kick back in a rustic cabaña, pitch your tent and hang out with other beach bums and hippies on the prettiest stretch of the Michoacán coast. (p546)

VOLCÁN PARICUTÍN

Climb this volcano near Uruapan, which, exploding out of a farmer's field back in the 1940s, buried villages under tons of volcanic rock, but left a church's steeple unscathed. (p638)

0 — 500 km
0 — 250 miles

SIERRA GORDA

This remote Querétaro biosphere reserve encompasses high-altitude cloud forests, semideserts, lowland tropical forests, historic Jesuit missions, isolated villages, waterfalls, caves and exotic wildlife. Explore with local guides from community-run ecolodges. (p651)

MINERAL DEL CHICO

You'll hold your breath round many a steep curve on the road up, but this charming old mining village, with moody mountain views, tumbling mists and good hiking, is well worth the trip. (p151)

RUTA PUUC

While the tour groups are shuffling from one site to another further north, check out these fascinating Maya ruins south of Mérida: there's a good chance you'll have them all to yourself. (p319)

Montgomery

Tallahassee

Nuevo Laredo

Reynosa   Matamoros

Ciudad Victoria

Gulf of Mexico

Tampico

SIERRA GORDA

Tuxpan

MINERAL DEL CHICO

MEXICO CITY   Xalapa

Veracruz

Puebla   Córdoba   Santiago Tuxtla

Ciudad del Carmen

Campeche   RUTA PUUC

Progreso
Mérida

Río Lagartos   Isla Mujeres
Tizimín   Cancún

Isla Cozumel

Felipe Carrillo Puerto

Escárcega   Chetumal

Chilpancingo

LACHATAO

Oaxaca

Madre del Sur

Villahermosa

Tuxtla Gutiérrez   LAGUNA MIRAMAR

Belize City

BELIZE

Puerto Escondido   Juchitán
Tehuantepec
Cocoleoco Surf Camp
Puerto Ángel   Tapachula

GUATEMALA   HONDURAS

LACHATAO

This tiny, remote mountain village has a certain intangible magic – which is perhaps why the ancient Zapotecs created a mysterious ceremonial site here. There's an excellent village ecotourism program with good cabañas and meals. (p455)

LAGUNA MIRAMAR

Via pockmarked dirt road or river boat, a day-long journey through the Lacandón Jungle takes you to this perfect clear blue lake with ancient petroglyphs and the haunting roars of howler monkeys. (p400)

Chiles en nogada

Plan Your Trip

Eat & Drink Like a Local

Mexican cuisine is far more tasty, fresh, varied, carefully prepared and creative than you could ever imagine before you start trying it. Venture into the flavors of Mexico, anywhere from simple street taco stands to refined contemporary fusion restaurants, and eating will be a highlight of your trip.

LINDSAY LAUGHNER GUNDLOCK / LONELY PLANET ©

Must-Try Dishes

Traditional dishes that will leave you with the taste of Mexico:

Chiles en nogada

Chiles en nogada comprises green, white and red ingredients, the colors of the Mexican flag: poblano chili, stuffed with minced meat and flavored with spices, topped with a cream sauce and sprinkled with pomegranate seeds.

Tacos al pastor

One of the country's favorites, *tacos al pastor* ('in the style of the shepherd') is a corn tortilla filled with thinly sliced pork that's been cooked on a spit, and served with onion and cilantro (coriander).

Mole negro

A Oaxacan specialty, the recipe of this dark, sultry sauce is jealously guarded, and the sauce itself is time-consuming and difficult to make. It tastes of chocolate, spices and... you'll see!

Food Experiences

Meals of a Lifetime

Quintonil, Mexico City (p118) This contemporary gem showcases Mexican ingredients, paraded in multiple courses.

Pujol, Mexico City (p118) A multiple-course tasting extravaganza of contemporary Mexican cuisine: reserve weeks ahead.

Alcalde, Guadalajara (p595) Acclaimed chef Francisco Ruano's latest venture is an unmissable contribution to the growing local gourmet scene.

Taco Fish La Paz, La Paz (p731) Cheap, basic, no view and – hands down – the best fish tacos in Baja.

Nohoch Kay, Mahahual (p297) Beautiful beach-front setting and scrumptious seafood.

Casa Oaxaca, Oaxaca (p439) Magically combines Oaxacan and other flavors in delectably original ways.

Áperi, San Miguel de Allende (p673) A cutting-edge, anything-goes experience enjoyed at the kitchen table.

El Presidio, Mazatlan (p502) Stellar food and meat dishes served in a beautifully restored 19th-century courtyard.

Ku'uk, Mérida (p311) A modern take on Yucatecan cuisine, with gorgeous presentation on slate, leaves and shells.

Cheap Treats

Mexico has one of the world's great street-food cultures. All over the country, street stands, markets and small eateries dole out endless supplies of filling and nutritious snacks and light meals, morning, noon and night. The busiest stands usually have the tastiest offerings and freshest ingredients.

Foremost are the many varieties of *anto-jito* ('little whim'), light dishes using *masa* (corn dough). The quintessential *antojito* is the taco – meat, fish or vegetables wrapped in a tortilla (Mexico's ubiquitous corn- or wheat-flour flatbread). Delicious varieties include *tacos al pastor* (with spit-cooked pork), *tacos de carne asada* (with grilled beef) and *tacos de pescado* (fish tacos, a favorite on the Pacific coast). There are many more types of *antojito* and an infinite variety of ingredients that can go into them. The most popular types include:

Quesadillas A tortilla folded in half with a filling of cheese and/or other ingredients.

Enchiladas Lightly fried tortillas with fillings, and covered in a chili sauce.

Tamales A wodge of *masa* mixed with lard, with stewed meat, fish or veggies in the middle, and steamed in corn husks or banana leaf.

Other common street foods:

Tortas Sandwiches (hot or cold) using a white bread roll.

Elotes Freshly steamed or grilled corn on the c̶ usually coated in mayonnaise and often sp̶ with chili powder.

PLAN YOUR TRIP EAT & DRINK LIKE A LOCAL

Dare to Try

Grasshoppers (*chapulines*) Fried with chili powder and garlic; they make a surprisingly munchable snack, especially accompanying a glass of mezcal. Plentiful in Oaxaca.

Corn fungus (*huitlacoche*) The black mold that grows on some cobs of corn (maize) has a truffle-like texture and has been considered a delicacy since pre-Hispanic times. Available during the mid-year rainy season at Mexico City's Mercado San Juan (p130) and as a sauce or stuffing ingredient at **Axitla** (Map p177; ☎739-395-05-19; Av Tepozteco; breakfast M$65-110, mains M$85-195; ☺10am-7pm Wed-Sun; ☑), Tepoztlán.

Cow's-eye tacos (*tacos de ojos*) Yes, that's right. Cows' eyes chopped up, steamed and put into tacos. Soft enough but not especially flavorsome and can be a bit greasy. Found at taco stands around the country and at Los Cocuyos (p112) restaurant in Mexico City.

Grubs and worms Ant larvae (*escamoles*) and maguey worms (*gusanos de maguey*) are seasonal fare from about March to June in the Puebla-Tlaxcala area. Elsewhere, at Onix (p621) in Morelia, you can wrap your tongue around scorpions.

Chilies for sale at a *mercado* (market)

Local Specialties

Central Mexico

Guadalajara is famed for its *birria* (chili-spiced goat or lamb stew eaten with tortillas, pickled onions, cilantro and salsa) and *tortas ahogadas* (drowned *tortas*) – sandwiches of chopped fried pork soaked in a spicy sauce. In Tequila, the town that gave Mexico its most famous drink, you can visit distilleries, or even take one of several express excursion trains from Guadalajara. The city of Puebla has a proudly distinctive cuisine including perhaps Mexico's single most famous dish – *mole poblano,* a thick sauce of chilies, fruits, nuts, spices and chocolate, usually served over chicken.

COOKING CLASSES

Estela Silva's Mexican Home Cooking School (p171) Long-established school near Tlaxcala, focusing on local cuisine.

La Casa de los Sabores (p432) Classes in cooking meals of Oaxacan and other Mexican origin at one of the best schools in Oaxaca.

La Villa Bonita (p178) Courses of several days including accommodations, run by celebrated chef Ana García.

Little Mexican Cooking School (p276) Classes on the Riviera Maya, preparing menus from seven different Mexican regions.

Patio Mexica Cooking School (p553) Highly recommended classes in local and national favorites.

Los Dos (p308) Renowned cooking school in Mérida, specializing in Yucatecan dishes.

Street stall vendor

Mexico City

The great melting pot of Mexican people and Mexican food, the capital has a vibrant street-food culture, with *antojitos* everywhere – at street stands, markets and thousands of taco stands. At the other end of the culinary scale, top chefs create fantastic fusion dishes in ultra-contemporary restaurants melding haute-cuisine techniques with traditional Mexican ingredients, especially in the neighborhoods of Condesa, Roma and Polanco.

Oaxaca

This southern state is famed for its unique dishes. Greatest renown belongs to its many *moles* – rich, thick sauces made with chilies, spices, nuts and often tomatoes, that go over meats. Oaxaca is also the world capital of mezcal, a potent sipping liquor made from agave plants which is enjoying an upsurge in popularity. *Tlayudas* (crunchy grilled tortillas topped with cheese, lettuce and refried beans) are also known as 'Mexican pizzas'. A more unconventional local specialty is *chapulines* (grasshoppers) which are far tastier than they sound.

Yucatán Peninsula

Caribbean flavors and indigenous Maya recipes influence the cuisine of Mexico's southeast corner. The most famous dish is *cochinita pibil* – slow-cooked pork marinated in citrus juices and *achiote* (a spice made from red seeds) and traditionally roasted in a pit in the ground. A staple is the fiery *chile habanero* – habanero sauce goes well on *papadzules* (tacos stuffed with hard-boiled eggs and pumpkin-seed sauce). Don't miss *sopa de lima*, a soup made from turkey, lime and tortilla pieces.

Veracruz

Two main factors strongly influence Veracruz cooking: its proximity to the ocean (and abundance of seafood), and centuries of Spanish and Afro-Caribbean influence. Standout dishes include *huachinango a la veracruzana* (red snapper in a spicy tomato sauce), *arroz a la tumbada* (a kind of paella-like soup), *camarones enchipotlados* (shrimp in a chipotle sauce) and *pollo encacahuatado* (chicken in a peanut sauce).

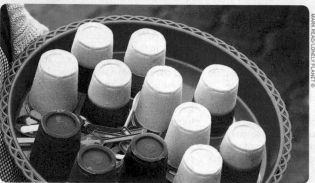

Top: *Tacos al pastor* (with spit-cooked pork)

Bottom: Oaxacan desserts

How to Eat & Drink

When to Eat

Desayuno (breakfast) Usually served from 8:30am to 11am, it tends to be on the hearty side. Egg dishes are popular and some Mexicans down serious meaty platefuls.

Comida (lunch) The main meal of the day, usually served between 2pm and 4:30pm and comprising a soup or other starter, main course (typically meat, fish or seafood) and a small dessert. *Comida corrida,* also known as *menú del día,* is an inexpensive fixed-price lunch menu.

Cena (dinner) For Mexicans, dinner is a lighter meal than lunch and often not eaten till 9pm. Nearly all restaurants serving dinner open from as early as 7pm though, offering full menus for those who want them.

Snacks At almost any time of day you can grab an *antojito* or *torta* at a cafe or street market stall. You can also get sandwiches (toasted) in some cafes.

Where to Eat

In general, *restaurantes* have full, multicourse menus and a range of drinks to accompany meals, while *cafés* and *cafeterías* offer shorter menus of lighter dishes and their drinks may focus on coffee, tea and soft drinks. Other types of eatery:

Comedor 'Eating room'; usually refers to low-budget restaurants serving simple, straightforward meals.

Fonda Small, frequently family-run eatery, often serving *comidas corridas.*

Mercado (market) Many Mexican markets have *comedor* sections where you sit on benches eating economical, home-style food cooked up on the spot.

Taquería Stall or small eatery specializing in tacos.

Menu Decoder

Our Food Glossary explans dishes you'll find on Mexican menus and the names of basic foods.

a la parrilla grilled on a barbecue grill

a la plancha grilled on a metal plate

al carbón cooked over open coals

aves poultry

bebidas drinks

LINDSAY LAUCKNER GUNDLOCK / LONELY PLANET ©

A typical Mexican *mercado* (market)

carnes meats

empanizado fried in breadcrumbs

ensalada salad

entradas starters

filete fillet

frito fried

huevos eggs

jugo juice

legumbres pulses

mariscos seafood (not fish)

menú de degustación tasting menu

mole rich, thick sauce, made with chilies, spices, nuts, often tomatoes and sometimes chocolate, poured over meats

pescado fish

plato fuerte main dish

postre dessert

salsa sauce

sopa soup

verduras vegetables

El Castillo (aka Pyramid of Kukulcán; p327), Chichén It

Plan Your Trip

Exploring Mexico's Ancient Ruins

Mexico's ancient civilizations were the most sophisticated and formidable in North and Central America. These often highly organized societies didn't just build towering pyramids and sculpt beautiful temples; they could also read the heavens, do complicated mathematics and invent writing systems. Exploring their sites is an unmissable Mexico travel experience.

Top 10 Sites & Best Times To Visit

Most of Mexico's major pre-Hispanic sites are scattered around the center, south and southeast of the country. Here's our top 10, along with the best time of year to visit them. Most sites open daily 9am to 5pm (some close Monday). Arriving early means fewer visitors and lower temperatures.

Teotihuacán, central Mexico
Year-round

Chichén Itzá, Yucatán Peninsula
September to November

Uxmal, Yucatán Peninsula
September to November

Palenque, Chiapas
October to May

Monte Albán, Oaxaca
October to May

Yaxchilán, Chiapas
October to May

Calakmul, Yucatán Peninsula
November to May

Tulum, Yucatán Peninsula
November to June

El Tajín, Veracruz
October to May

Templo Mayor, Mexico City
Year-round

Mexico's Ancient Civilizations

Archaeologists have been uncovering Mexico's ancient ruins since the 19th century. Many impressive sites have been restored and made accessible to visitors, others have been explored in part, and thousands more remain untouched, buried beneath the earth or hidden in forests. The major civilizations were these:

Olmec Mexico's 'mother culture' was centered on the Gulf coast, from about 1200 BC to 400 BC. It's famed for the giant stone sculptures known as Olmec heads.

Teotihuacán Based in the city of the same name with its huge pyramids, 50km from Mexico City, the Teotihuacán civilization flourished in the first seven centuries AD, and ruled the largest of all ancient Mexican empires.

Maya The Maya, in southeast Mexico and neighboring Guatemala and Belize, flowered most brilliantly in numerous city-states between AD 250 and AD 900. They're famed for their exquisitely beautiful temples and stone sculptures. Maya culture lives on today among the indigenous populations of these regions.

Toltec A name for the culture of a number of central Mexican city-states, from around AD 750 to AD 1150. The warrior sculptures of Tula are the most celebrated monuments.

Aztec With their capital at Tenochtitlán (now Mexico City) from AD 1325 to AD 1521, the Aztecs came to rule most of central Mexico from the Gulf coast to the Pacific. The best known Aztec site is the Templo Mayor in Mexico City.

Site Practicalities

➡ The most famous sites are often thronged with large numbers of visitors (arrive early). Others are hidden away on remote hilltops or shrouded in thick jungle, and can be the most exciting and rewarding to visit for those with an adventurous spirit.

➡ Admission to archaeological sites costs from nothing up to around M$250, depending on the site (only a handful of places, all in Yucatán state, cost more than M$90).

➡ Go protected against the sun and, at jungle sites, mosquitoes.

➡ Popular sites have facilities such as cafes or restaurants, bookstores, souvenir stores, audio guides in various languages and authorized (but not fixed-price) human guides.

➡ Little-visited sites may have no food or water available and may have poor road access.

➡ Guided tours to many sites are available from nearby towns, but public transportation is usually available, too.

➡ Major sites are usually wheelchair accessible.

➡ Explanatory signs may be in Spanish only, or in Spanish and English, or in Spanish, English and a local indigenous language.

Museo Nacional de Antropología (p85)

Resources

Colecciones Especiales Street View (www.inah. gob.mx/es/inah/322-colecciones-especiales-street-view) Take virtual tours of 27 sites in Google Street View.

Instituto Nacional de Antropología e Historia (www.inah.gob.mx) Mexico's National Institute of Anthropology and History administers 187 archaeological sites and 120 museums.

Mesoweb (www.mesoweb.com) A great, diverse resource on ancient Mexico, especially the Maya.

An Archaeological Guide to Central and Southern Mexico Joyce Kelly's book was published in 2001 and is still the best of its kind, covering 70 sites.

Top Museums

Some archaeological sites have their own museums, but there are also important city and regional museums that hold many of the most valuable and impressive pre-Hispanic artifacts and provide fascinating background on ancient Mexico.

Museo Nacional de Antropología (p85) The superb National Museum of Anthropology in Mexico City has sections devoted to all the important ancient civilizations, and includes such treasures as the famous Aztec sun stone and a replica of King Pakal's treasure-laden tomb from Palenque.

Museo de Antropología (p219) Mainly devoted to Gulf coast cultures, this excellent museum in Xalapa contains seven Olmec heads and other masterly sculptures among its 25,000-piece collection.

Parque-Museo La Venta (p416) This outdoor museum-cum-zoo in Villahermosa holds several Olmec heads and other fine sculptures from the site of La Venta, moved here in the 1950s when La Venta was under threat from petroleum exploration.

Museo Maya de Cancún (p258) One of Mexico's most important collections of Maya artifacts, assembled from sites around the Yucatán Peninsula.

PRE-HISPANIC NUMBERS

Ancient Mexicans loved numbers. We've assembled some of our own:

8km of tunnels dug by archaeologists beneath Cholula's Tepanapa Pyramid

70m – the height of Teotihuacán's Pyramid of the Sun

100km – the length of the *sacbé* (stone-paved avenue) from Cobá to Yaxuna

120 mural-covered walls in Teotihuacán's Tetitla Palace

300 masks of Chaac, the rain god, at Kabah's Palace of Masks

15,000 ritual ball-game courts found in Mexico (so far)

20,000 human hearts ripped out for the re-dedication of Tenochtitlán's Templo Mayor in 1487

25 million – estimated population of Mexico at the time of the Spanish conquest

Mexico's Ruins

SAN LUIS POTOSÍ

Paquimé (1500km)

GUANAJUATO

Celaya

MORELIA

Ciudad Valles

Tampico

Tuxpan

Poza Rica

Tula

PACHUCA

Teotihuacán

MEXICO CITY

Templo Mayor & Tlatelolco

Cholula

PUEBLA

CUERNAVACA

Xochicalco

El Tajín

El Cuajilote & Vega de la Peña

XALAPA

Cantona

Quiahuiztlán

Zempoala

Veracruz

Córdoba

Orizaba

Tehuacán

Presa Miguel Alemán

San Andrés Tuxtla

Coatzacoalcos

Minatitlán

CHILPANCINGO

Acapulco

Sierra Madre del Sur

Río Balsas

Puerto Escondido

Puerto Ángel

Bahías de Huatulco

Puerto Ángel

OAXACA

Monte Albán

Mitla

Yagul

Istmo de Tehuantepec

Juchitán

Tehuantepec

TUXTLA GUTIÉRREZ

San Cristóbal de las Casas

Presa La Angostura

Tapachula

GUATEMALA CITY

GUATEMALA

Bonampak

Yaxchilán

Toniná

Palenque

VILLAHERMOSA

Río Usumacinta

Ciudad del Carmen

CAMPECHE

Edzná

Calakmul

Becán

Xpuhil

Kohunlich

Dzibanché

CHETUMAL

BELMOPAN

BELIZE

Belize City

CARIBBEAN SEA

TEGUCIGALPA

HONDURAS

Cancún

Playa del Carmen

Ek' Balam

Tizimín

Tulum

Cobá

Chichén Itzá

Valladolid

Ruta Puuc

Kabah

Uxmal

MÉRIDA

Progreso

GULF OF MEXICO

PACIFIC OCEAN

200 km

100 miles

MAIN PRE-HISPANIC SITES

	SITE	PERIOD	DESCRIPTION
CENTRAL MEXICO	Teotihuacán (p52)	AD 0-700	Mexico's biggest ancient city, capital of the Teotihuacán empire
	Templo Mayor (p52)	AD 1375-1521	Center of Aztec capital, Tenochtitlán
	Cholula (p52)	AD 0-1521	City & religious center
	Tula (p52)	AD 900-1150	Major Toltec city
	Cantona (p52)	AD 600-1000	Huge, well-preserved city
	Tlatelolco (p52)	12th century–1521	Site of main Aztec market & defeat of last Aztec emperor Cuauhtémoc
	Xochicalco (p188)	AD 600-1200	Large, hilltop religious & commercial center
CHIAPAS	Palenque (p52)	100 BC-AD 740	Beautiful major Maya city
	Yaxchilán (p52)	7th-9th centuries AD	Maya city
	Toniná (p52)	c AD 600-900	Maya temple complex
	Bonampak (p52)	8th century AD	Maya site
NORTHERN MEXICO	Paquimé (p52)	AD 900-1340	Trading center linking central Mexico with northern desert cultures
OAXACA	Monte Albán	500 BC-AD 900	Hilltop center of Zapotec civilization
	Mitla (p52)	c AD 1300-1520	Zapotec religious center
	Yagul (p52)	AD 900-1400	Zapotec & Mixtec ceremonial center
VERACRUZ	El Tajín (p52)	AD 600-1200	Town & ceremonial center of Classic Veracruz civilization
	Quiahuiztlán (p52)	AD 600-1300	Totonac town & necropolis
	El Cuajilote (p52) & Vega de la Peña (p52)	AD 600-1400	Towns of unidentified civilization
YUCATÁN PENINSULA	Chichén Itzá (p52)	2nd-14th centuries AD	Large, well-restored Maya/Toltec city
	Uxmal (p315)	AD 600-900	Maya city
	Tulum (p52)	c AD 1200-1600	Late Maya town & ceremonial center
	Calakmul (p349)	Approx 1st-9th centuries AD	Huge, once very powerful Maya city, little restored
	Cobá (p52)	AD 600-1100	Maya city
	Kabah (p52)	AD 750-950	Maya city
	Ruta Puuc (p319)	AD 750-950	Three Puuc Maya sites (Sayil, Xlapak, Labná)
	Edzná (p52)	600 BC-AD 1500	Maya city
	Becán (p52)	550 BC-AD 1000	Large Maya site
	Xpuhil (p52)	Flourished 8th century AD	Maya settlement
	Ek' Balam (p52)	Approx AD 600-800	Maya city
	Dzibanché (p52)	Approx 200 BC-AD 1200	Maya city
	Kohunlich (p52)	AD 100-600	Maya city

HIGHLIGHTS	LOCATION/TRANSPORTATION
Pyramids of Sun and Moon, Calzada de los Muertos, palace murals	50km northeast of Mexico City; frequent buses
Ceremonial pyramid	Downtown Mexico City
World's widest pyramid	8km west of Puebla; frequent buses
Stone pillars carved as warriors	80km north of Mexico City; 1km walk/taxi from Tula station
24 ball courts, unique street system	90km northeast of Puebla; taxi or *colectivo* from Oriental
Aztec temple-pyramid	Northern Mexico City; trolleybus or metro
Pyramid of Quetzalcóatl	35km southwest of Cuernavaca; bus
Exquisite temples with jungle backdrop	7km west of Palenque town; frequent combis
Temples & other buildings in riverside jungle setting	Beside Río Usumacinta, 15km northwest of Frontera Corozal; boat from Frontera Corozal
Temples & pyramids on hillside	14km east of Ocosingo; combis from Ocosingo
Superb, if weathered, frescoes	150km southeast of Palenque; van or bus to San Javier (140km), then taxi and van
Adobe walls & buildings, clay macaw cages, rare geometric pottery	Casas Grandes village; bus or taxi from Nuevo Casas Grandes, 7km north
Pyramids, observatory, panoramas	6km west of Oaxaca; bus
Unique stone mosaics	46km southeast of Oaxaca; bus or *colectivo*
Large ball court, rock 'fortress'	35km southeast of Oaxaca; bus/*colectivo* and 1.5km walk
Rare niched pyramids, 17 ball courts, *voladores* ('fliers') performances	6km west of Papantla; bus or taxi
Unique temple-like tombs, lofty viewpoint	3km walk up from Hwy 180, opposite Villa Rica village
Remote jungle setting	17km south of Tlapacoyan; take *colectivo* or taxi then walk
El Castillo 'calendar temple', Mexico's biggest ball court, El Caracol observatory, Platform of Skulls	117km east of Mérida, 2km east of Pisté village; buses from Mérida, Pisté & Valladolid
Pyramids, palaces, riotous sculpture featuring masks of rain god Chaac	80km south of Mérida; buses from Mérida
Temples & towers on superb Caribbean-side site	130km south of Cancún; taxi, walk or cycle from Tulum
High pyramids with views over rainforest	60km south of Escárcega-Chetumal Rd; car, tour from Xpujil, Chicanná or Campeche/taxi from Xpujil or Escárcega
Towering pyramids in jungle setting	50km northwest of Tulum; bus or *colectivo* from Tulum, or bus from Valladolid
Palace of Masks, with 300 Chaac masks	104km south of Mérida; car, or bus or tour from Mérida
Palaces with elaborate columns & sculptures, including Chaac masks	Around 120km south of Mérida; car, or bus or tour from Mérida
Five-story pyramid-palace, Temple of Masks	53km southeast of Campeche; minibuses & shuttle service from Campeche
Towered temples	8km west of Xpujil; taxi, tour or car
Three-towered ancient 'skyscraper'	Xpujil town, 123km west of Chetumal; buses from Campeche & Escárcega, buses & *colectivos* from Chetumal
Acrópolis & high pyramid with unusual carving	23km north of Valladolid by taxi or *colectivo*
Semi-wild site with palaces & pyramids	68km west of Chetumal; car, taxi or tour from Chetumal or Xpujil
Temple of the Masks	56km west of Chetumal; car, taxi, or bus & 9km walk

Plan Your Trip
Travel with Children

The sights, sounds and colors of Mexico excite kids, and Mexicans love children, who are part and parcel of most aspects of life here. There are many child-friendly attractions and activities for kids of all ages, and with very few exceptions, children are welcomed at all accommodations and at almost any cafe or restaurant.

Best Regions for Kids

Yucatán Peninsula

Cancún, the Riviera Maya and nearby islands are geared to giving vacationers fun. The area is full of great beaches offering every imaginable aquatic activity, hotels designed to make life easy and attractions from jungle zip-lines to swimming in cenotes (sinkholes). Other parts of the peninsula are great if your kids will enjoy exploring Maya ruins.

Central Pacific Coast

The Pacific coast offers all conceivable types of fun in, on and under the ocean and lagoons. There's a vast range of places to base yourself, from sophisticated Puerto Vallarta to easygoing Zihuatanejo and countless smaller spots.

Mexico City

The capital keeps kids happy with a world-class aquarium, a hands-on children's museum, a first-rate zoo, dedicated kids entertainment and activities, and parks and plazas full of space and fun.

Mexico for Kids

Eating

Children may be less keen to experiment with exciting Mexican flavors than their parents are, but Mexico has plenty of places serving up familiar international fare. Italian restaurants are plentiful; foods such as eggs, steaks, bread, rice and cheese are available everywhere, and fresh fruit is abundant. Simpler Mexican snacks such as quesadillas, burritos and tacos, or steaming corn cobs straight from a street cart, are good options for introducing kids to local flavors. Restaurant staff are accustomed to children and can usually provide high chairs or an extra plate for dish-sharing, or prepare something that's not on the menu, if requested.

Sleeping

Mexico has some excitingly different places to stay that will please most kids – anything beachside is a good start, and rustic *cabañas* (cabins) provide a sense of adventure (but choose one with good mosquito nets!). Many hotels have a rambling layout and open-air space – courtyards, pool areas, gardens. Beach hotels countrywide are geared to families.

Family rooms and accommodations with kitchens are widely available, and most hotels will put an extra bed or two in a room at little extra charge. Baby cots may not be available in budget accommodations. Most accommodations have wi-fi access, and in the midrange and top end there will often be child-friendly channels on the TV.

Getting Around

Try to do your traveling in smallish chunks of a few hours, maximum. Many Mexican buses show nonstop movies (in Spanish), most of which are family-friendly and can help distract kids from a dull trip. If you're traveling with a baby or toddler, consider investing in deluxe buses for the extra space and comfort.

Car rental and, on some routes, flying are alternatives to buses. If you want a car with a child safety seat, the major international rental firms are the most reliable providers.

In northern Mexico most kids love riding the 'Chepe' railway (Ferrocarril Chihuahua Pacífico or Copper Canyon Railway).

Children's Highlights

On & In the Water

Learn to surf Kids as young as five can take classes at many spots with gentler waves along the Pacific coast, including Mazatlán, Sayulita, Ixtapa, Puerto Escondido and San Agustinillo.

Spot turtles, dolphins and whales Boat trips head out from many places along the Pacific coast and in Baja.

Snorkel tropical seas Many beaches on the Caribbean coast and islands, and some on the Pacific, provide calm waters and colorful marine life for beginners.

Ride a gondola Cruise ancient Aztec canals at Xochimilco, Mexico City (p93).

Uyo Ochel Maya (p290) Float down centuries-old, Maya-built canals through mangrove swamps filled with flowers and tropical fish.

Multi-Adventure

Parque de Aventura Barrancas del Cobre (p761) Kids adore the Copper Canyon Adventure Park with its spine-tingling seven zip-lines carrying you halfway to the canyon floor from its lip at 2400m. There's rappelling, climbing and a cable car, too.

Selvática (p277) Award-winning zip-line circuit through the jungle near Puerto Morelos, with its own cenote for swimming.

Boca del Puma (☑998-577-42-83; www.bocadelpuma.com; Ruta de los Cenotes Km 16; adult/child 5-14yr US$12/7; ☉9am-5pm; ◉) Zip-lining, horseback riding and a cenote to dip into, near Puerto Morelos.

Cobá (p294) This jungle-surrounded ancient Maya site near Tulum has pyramids, a zip-line and bicycles for pedaling around the network of trails.

Cuajimoloyas (p455) Horseback riding, mountain biking, hiking and a spectacular 1km zip-line in the mountains near Oaxaca.

Huana Coa Canopy (Map p496; ☑669-990-11-00; www.facebook.com/huanacoacanopy; Av del Mar 1111; per person US$75; ☉9am-1pm & 3:30-6pm Mon-Fri, 9am-1pm Sat; ◻Sábalo-Centro) Popular series of zip-lines in the forested hills near Mazatlán.

Teleférico de Orizaba (p234) Ride Mexico's second-highest cable car to a mountain-top playground.

Animals

Acuario Inbursa (p92) This world-class mega-aquarium in Mexico City wows kids with manta rays, piranhas and crocodiles, while the Soumaya and Jumex museums just across the road will entertain the parents.

Baja whale-watching (p723) See massive gray whales and their calves off the coasts of Baja California – usually requires several hours in a boat, so best for older kids.

Zoomat (p357) The zoo at Tuxtla Gutiérrez has 180 species, all from the state of Chiapas, including several types of big cat.

Playa Escobilla (p465) See thousands of turtles crawl out of the ocean in a single night to lay eggs on this Oaxaca beach.

Crococun (p276) Interactive zoo in Puerto Morelos with crocodiles and wild monkeys.

HEALTH & SAFETY

Children are more easily affected than adults by heat, disrupted sleep patterns, changes in altitude and foreign food. Take care that they don't drink tap water, be careful to avoid sunburn, cover them up against insect bites and ensure you replace fluids if a child gets diarrhea.

Don't hesitate to go to a doctor if you think it may be necessary. In general, privately run hospitals and clinics in Mexico offer better facilities and care than public ones. Adequate travel insurance will cover the cost of private medical care.

Museums

Museo Nacional de Antropología (p85) The carvings, statues and skulls inside Mexico's best museum are a huge hit with kids.

Papalote Museo del Niño There are two of these fun, hands-on, children's museums – one in Mexico City (p89), one in Cuernavaca (p185). Good for kids up to about 11.

Museo Interactivo de Xalapa (p220) Themed rooms on science, ecology and art, and an IMAX cinema.

La Esquina: Museo del Juguete Popular Mexicano (p665) Stunning museum in San Miguel de Allende where kids can see what toys were like before the digital revolution!

Museo de Historia Natural (Map p616; ☎443-312-00-44; Ventura Puente 23; ◷9am-4pm Mon-Fri, 11am-6pm Sat & Sun) FREE Small museum in Morelia directed at children has everything from fossils (including a mammoth's tusk) and dissected animals to a cactus garden.

Spectacles

Voladores This indigenous Totonac rite involves men (fliers) climbing up a 30m-high pole then casting themselves off backward, attached only by ropes. Performed regularly at El Tajín (p243) and at Mexico City's Museo Nacional de Antropología (p85).

Pirate Show (p340) Campeche recalls its pirate-battered past with Disney-esque spectaculars in an old city gate.

Folk dance Highly colorful, entertaining shows are given regularly by the Ballet Folklórico de México (p126) in Mexico City and Guelaguetza groups in Oaxaca, and at Mérida's Plaza Grande (p305).

Planning

➡ Bear in mind that few kids like traveling all the time. They're usually happier if they can settle into a place for a while, make friends and do some of the things they like doing back home.

➡ See a doctor about vaccinations at least one month – preferably two – before your trip.

➡ It's a good idea to book accommodations for at least the first couple of nights.

➡ Diapers (nappies) and sunscreen are widely available, but you may not easily find wet wipes, other creams, baby foods or familiar medicines outside larger cities and tourist towns.

➡ For all-round information and advice, check out Lonely Planet's *Travel with Children*.

Documents for Under-18 Travelers

Carrying notarized written permission from a parent or guardian is required by Mexican law for Mexican minors (under-18s, including those with dual nationality) or foreign minors residing in Mexico, if departing from Mexico without a parent or legal guardian. There have been cases of other minors being asked to show consent forms, especially when leaving Mexico by land borders, even though the law does not require them to do so. The US embassy in Mexico therefore advises all minors traveling without both parents to carry notarized consent letters. Check with a Mexican consulate well in advance of travel on what needs to be done.

Regions at a Glance

Mexico City

Museums
Fiestas
Food

Museums Galore

You name it, Mexico City probably has a museum for it: from avant-garde art to pre-Hispanic artifacts and antique toys. Don't miss the world-class Museo Nacional de Antropología and Frida Kahlo's famed blue house.

Enter the Night

Mexico City is the country's party capital, where old-world cantinas moonlight as hip bars or queer cabaret spaces. Learn salsa in a plaza by day, sip top mezcal on an exclusive rooftop bar at sundown, then let loose on the dance floor of a megaclub until the wee hours.

Culinary Melting Pot

The capital has fabulous eateries of many kinds and regional Mexican cuisine gets top billing. Everyone here seems to have an opinion on where you can find, say, the best Guerrero-style *pozole* (a hearty hominy, meat and veg soup) or the tastiest Yucatecan *cochinita pibil* (slow-roasted marinated pork).

p62

Around Mexico City

Archaeological Sites
Small-Town Escapes
Food

Ancient Architecture

Some of Mexico's most awe-inspiring ruins stand within a few hours' drive of the capital. Teotihuacán, with its stunning Pyramids of the Sun and Moon, is the most famous, but fascinating sites such as Cacaxtla, Xochitécatl, Xochicalco and Cantona can be explored in virtual solitude.

Pueblos Mágicos

With their leafy plazas, traditional crafts and gorgeous colonial edifices, remarkably well-preserved 'magical towns' such as Cuetzalan, Real del Monte, Malinalco and Valle de Bravo provide a perfect escape from the thick air and crowds of the capital.

Regional Specialties

An incredible variety of indigenous ingredients and imported culinary influences combine in complex regional cuisines. Many towns have their own specialty, such as the pasties from the mining villages above Pachuca, or Puebla's famed *mole poblano*.

p141

Veracruz

Archaeological Sites
Food
Outdoor Adventure

Ancient Cultures

Several distinct pre-Hispanic cultures graced Mexico's Gulf coast, and all have left a weighty legacy. Examine the Classic Veracruz ruins of El Tajín with its curious niched pyramid and the magnificence of Totonac Zempoala, and see the genius of ancient sculptors in Xalapa's Museo de Antropología.

Fish, Glorious Fish

Thanks to the state's 690km-long coastline, fish (and seafood) headlines most menus, in particular the spicy mélange known as *huachinango a la veracruzana*. Lining up behind it are the distinctive *moles* of Xico and the gourmet coffee of Coatepec.

River Deep, Mountain High

Mexico's highest mountain, Volcán Orizaba, towers over central Veracruz and presents the country's toughest trekking challenge. Down in the valleys, Río Antigua and Río Filobobos attract whitewater daredevils.

p204

Yucatán Peninsula

Beaches
Diving & Snorkeling
Maya Ruins

A Day at the Beach

Finding the right beach for you is simply a matter of hopping on a bus (or boat). From the debauchery of Cancún to lonely Costa Maya beaches such as Xcalak, the bleach-white sands and beautiful warm waters mustn't be missed.

Into the Blue

With hundreds of kilometers of Caribbean coastline and the world's second-largest barrier reef, the region is a diver's and snorkeler's dream. Banco Chinchorro and Isla Cozumel are the superstars and Cancún's underwater sculpture garden provides another unique experience.

Oldies but Goodies

From world-famous Chichén Itzá to virtually unheard-of sites such as Ek' Balam, the Yucatán is dotted with spectacular pyramids and temples. Many have a resonating atmosphere that even the loudest tour groups can't diminish.

p255

Chiapas & Tabasco

Nature
Outdoor Adventure
Indigenous Culture

Birds & Beasts

Nesting turtles, roaring monkeys and flashes of rainbow plumage are standard fare in the jungles and on the misty mountains and sandy beaches of this biodiverse region that's full of rare and endangered wildlife.

In Motion

Whether you're rappelling into a jungle sinkhole, bouncing over a stretch of white water in a rubber raft, or climbing a 4000m volcano, Chiapas has multiple ways to raise your adrenaline levels.

Temples & Tradition

The world of the Maya lives on everywhere you turn here, from the preserved stone temples of Classic Maya civilization to the persistence of dramatic pre-Hispanic religious rituals and the intricate hand-woven textiles and clothing still worn by many.

p353

Oaxaca

Beaches
Outdoor Activities
Culture

Coast of Dreams

With 550km of sandy Pacific strands and wildlife-rich lagoons, Oaxaca's coastline has it all – the pumping surf of Puerto Escondido, the blissed-out traveler scene of Zipolite and Mazunte, and the resort attractions of low-key Bahías de Huatulco.

The Great Outdoors

Hike through the Sierra Norte's mountain forests, surf the Pacific swells, raft rivers from the hills to the sea, snorkel or dive the beautiful Huatulco bays, and spot whales, dolphins and turtles off the Pacific coast.

Traditional & Cutting Edge

Oaxaca state is a cultural hub in so many senses, from Oaxaca City's vibrant arts scene to the distinctive Oaxacan cuisine and endlessly inventive handicrafts of the state's indigenous peoples. It all wraps up in a unique and proud Oaxacan regional identity.

p421

Central Pacific Coast

Outdoor Activities
Food
Beaches

Natural Highs

Kayak across a lagoon at dawn, ride horses into the Sierra Madre, swim among flitting butterflies in a boulder-strewn river, watch pelicans and whales parade through the waves, or scan the nighttime sands for nesting mama turtles.

Seafood Heaven

Sidle up to a beachside table at sunset, grab a cold beer and a fresh-cut lime and settle into a plateful of *pescado zarandeado* (grilled fish), *tiritas* (citrus-and-chili-marinated raw-fish slivers) or shrimp and red snapper cooked a dozen different ways.

Surf & Sand

Conjure up the beach of your dreams and you'll find it here, whether wiggling your toes in the sand with margarita in hand, or chasing perfect waves along an endless ultramarine horizon.

p492

Western Central Highlands

Culture
Food
Scenery

Art & Crafts

The highlands heave with indigenous culture, most notably that of the thriving Purépecha people, whose arts and crafts are sold around Pátzcuaro and Uruapan. You'll find superb art galleries and shopping in Guadalajara and its suburbs of Tlaquepaque and Tonalá.

Culinary Feast

When Unesco listed Mexican cuisine as Intangible Cultural Heritage in 2010, it made special mention of Michoacán, whose edibles are often termed the 'soul food' of Mexico. Throw in *birria* (a spicy goat or lamb stew) from Jalisco washed down with local tequila, and you've got a veritable feast.

Volcanic Drama

Tiny Colima state packs a scenic punch with its dramatic twin volcanoes. For equally glorious scenery don't miss the modern marvel of Volcán Paricutín in Michoacán.

p577

Northern Central Highlands

Museums
Outdoor Adventures
Colonial Cities

Historic & Contemporary

Home to fascinating indigenous cultures and most of the silver that brought opulence to Mexico's colonial grandees, this region was also the birthplace of Mexican independence. Excellent museums highlight everything from historical heroes to contemporary art.

Natural Playground

An emerging adventure playground, this region offers the chance to rappel into giant sinkholes and snorkel inland lakes in the Huasteca Potosina, ride into deserts around Real de Catorce and search for macaws in Sierra Gorda caves.

Pedestrian Paradise

Cobblestone streets lined by gorgeous colonial stone mansions and churches make for fascinating exploration on foot. Towns and cities here are made for getting lost in – up narrow *callejones* (alleys) or down steep steps. You'll eventually end up on a pretty, laurel-tree-filled plaza.

p640

Baja California

Scenery
Wine
Water Sports

Majestic Mountains, Tropical Paradise

Few places in the world have deserts just steps away from turquoise lagoons and high, pine-forested mountains just a couple of hours' drive inland. At every corner there are vistas that seem pulled from the pages of a vacation calendar.

Ruta del Vino

The Valle de Guadalupe is producing the best wines in Mexico and this 'Napa Sur' is garnering international acclaim. Its Wine Route makes for a great day (or two) out.

Surfing & Diving

Baja is a paradise for surfers of all levels, with beach, point and reef breaks up and down the Pacific coastline. Divers can do a two-tank dive in the Pacific and be in the natural aquarium of the Sea of Cortez in time for a night dive.

p703

Copper Canyon & Northern Mexico

Colonial Towns
Museums
Outdoor Adventures

Charming Continuity

The gorgeous old towns of Álamos, with its wonderful hotels and restaurants, Durango, with its expansive plazas and museum offerings, and Parras with its long-standing viticulture, seduce visitors with the pull of bygone centuries.

From Sarapes to Steel

Monterrey's spectacular Parque Fundidora is replete with cultural interest, particularly the Horno3 museum devoted to steelmaking. In Saltillo you'll find museums focusing on the desert environment, *sarape* textiles and birdlife, while Durango's and Chihuahua's impressive offerings include museums dedicated to Pancho Villa.

Great Outdoors

The north is all about topographical overload. An idyllic coastline, vast deserts, dramatic canyons and climates from alpine to subtropical all contribute to a wealth of wildlife and tantalizing hiking and biking.

p747

On the
Road

Baja
California
p703

Copper Canyon &
Northern Mexico
p747

Northern
Central
Highlands
p640

Central
Pacific
Coast
p492

Western
Central
Highlands
p577

Around Mexico
City p141

Mexico
City p62

Veracruz
p204

Oaxaca
p421

Yucatán
Peninsula
p255

Chiapas &
Tabasco
p353

Mexico City

📞 55 / POP 8.85 MILLION / ELEV 2240M

Best Places to Eat

➡ Pujol (p118)

➡ Contramar (p117)

➡ El Hidalguense (p117)

➡ Quintonil (p118)

➡ El Lugar Sin Nombre (p114)

➡ Hostería de Santo Domingo (p112)

Best Places to Stay

➡ Red Tree House (p109)

➡ Casa San Ildefonso (p106)

➡ Villa Condesa (p109)

➡ Casa Comtesse (p110)

➡ Gran Hotel Ciudad de México (p106)

➡ Chalet del Carmen (p111)

Why Go?

Mexico City is, and has always been, the sun in the Mexican solar system. Though much-maligned in the past, these days the city is cleaning up its act. Revamped public spaces are springing back to life, the culinary scene is exploding and a cultural renaissance is flourishing. On top of all that, by largely managing to distance itself from the drug war, the nation's capital remains a safe haven of sorts. Far from shaking off visitors, the earthquakes of 2017 revealed a young society who attracted admiration through their solidarity.

A stroll through the buzzing downtown area reveals the capital's storied history, from pre-Hispanic and colonial-era splendor to its contemporary edge. This high-octane megalopolis contains plenty of escape valves in the way of old-school cantinas, intriguing museums, inspired dining and boating excursions along ancient canals. With so much going on, you might consider scrapping those beach plans.

When to Go
Mexico City

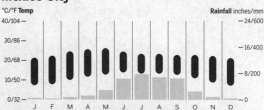

Mar & Apr Vacationing *chilangos* clear out for Easter, leaving the city remarkably calm.

May Catch the last of the warm, dry weather before the rainy season begins.

Nov Rainy season ends and the month begins with colorful Día de Muertos festivities.

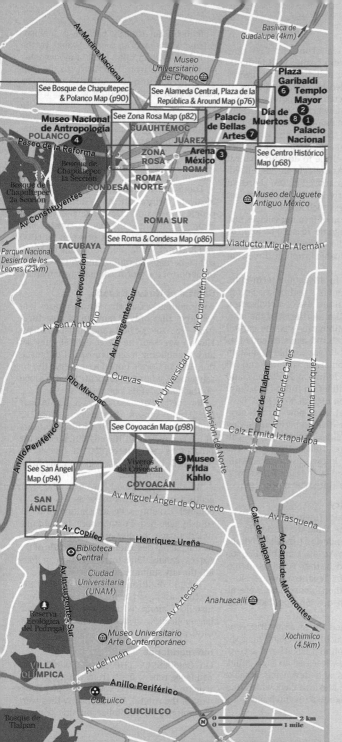

Mexico City Highlights

1 **Palacio Nacional** (p71) Studying Diego Rivera's tableau of Mexican history.

2 **Templo Mayor** (p71) Marveling at Aztec ruins in the heart of downtown.

3 **Arena México** (p129) Cheering on the masked heroes at the *lucha libre* (Mexican wrestling) bouts.

4 **Museo Nacional de Antropología** (p85) Gazing upon the Aztec sun stone and other superb pre-Hispanic relics.

5 **Museo Frida Kahlo** (p96) Sharing Frida's pain at her birthplace, Casa Azul in Coyoacán, now home to a museum.

6 **Plaza Garibaldi** (p73) Singing along to mariachi ballads in this soulful plaza.

7 **Palacio de Bellas Artes** (p76) Feasting your eyes on colorful murals and folkloric dance performances in an art deco theater.

8 **Día de Muertos** (p105) Celebrating the dearly departed while watching giant skeletons dance toward the Zócalo.

History

Driving over the sea of asphalt that now overlays this highland basin, you'd be hard-pressed to imagine that, a mere five centuries ago, it was filled by a chain of lakes. It would further stretch your powers to imagine that today's downtown was on an islet criss-crossed by canals, or that the communities who inhabited the island and the banks of Lago de Texcoco spoke a patchwork of languages that had as little to do with Spanish as Malay or Urdu. As their chronicles related, the Spaniards who arrived at the shores of that lake in the early 16th century were just as amazed to witness such a scene.

A loose federation of farming villages had evolved around Lago de Texcoco by approximately 200 BC. The biggest, Cuicuilco, was destroyed by a volcanic eruption three centuries later.

Breakthroughs in irrigation techniques and the development of a maize-based economy contributed to the rise of a civilization at Teotihuacán, 40km northeast of the lake. For centuries Teotihuacán was the capital of an empire whose influence extended as far as Guatemala. It was unable to sustain its burgeoning population, however, and fell in the 8th century to internal divisions, and was abandoned and left in ruins. Details are scarce as no written records were kept. Over the following centuries, power in central Mexico came to be divided between varying locally important cities, including Xochicalco to the south and Tula to the north. The latter's culture is known as Toltec (Artificers), a name coined by the later Aztecs, who looked back to the Toltec rulers with awe.

Aztec Mexico City

The Aztecs, or Mexica (meh-*shee*-kah), probably arrived in the Valle de México in the 13th century. A wandering tribe that claimed to have come from Aztlán, a mythical region in northwest Mexico, they acted as mercenary fighters for the Tepanecas, who resided on the lake's southern shore, and were allowed to settle on the inhospitable terrain of Chapultepec.

The tribe roamed the swampy fringes of the lake, finally reaching an island near the western shore around 1325. There, according to legend, they witnessed an eagle standing atop a cactus and devouring a snake (today seen on the Mexican flag), which they interpreted as a sign to stop and build a city, Tenochtitlán.

Tenochtitlán rapidly became a sophisticated city-state whose empire would, by the early 16th century, span most of modern-day central Mexico from the Pacific to the Gulf of Mexico and into far southern Mexico. The Aztecs built their city on a grid plan, with canals as thoroughfares and causeways to the lakeshore. In the marshier parts, they created raised gardens by piling up vegetation and mud and planting willows. These *chinampas* (versions of which still exist at Xochimilco in southern Mexico City) gave three or four harvests yearly.

The Spanish arrived in 1519, fracturing Mexican civilization and turning native people into second-class citizens in just two years. When these invaders arrived, Tenochtitlán's population was between 200,000 and 300,000, while the entire Valle de México had perhaps 1.5 million inhabitants, making it one of the world's densest urban areas.

Capital of Nueva España

So assiduously did the Spanish raze Tenochtitlán that only a handful of structures from the Aztec period remain visible today. Having wrecked the Aztec capital, they set about rebuilding it as their own. Conquistador Hernán Cortés hoped to preserve the arrangement whereby Tenochtitlán siphoned off the bounty of its vassal states.

Ravaged by disease, the Valle de México's population shrank drastically – from 1.5 million to under 100,000 within a century of the conquest. But the city emerged as the prosperous, elegant capital of Nueva España, with broad streets laid over the Aztec causeways and canals.

Building continued through the 17th century, but problems arose as the weighty colonial structures began sinking into the squishy lake bed. Furthermore, lacking natural drainage, the city suffered floods caused by the partial destruction in the 1520s of the Aztecs' canals. One torrential rain in 1629 left the city submerged for five years.

Urban conditions improved in the 18th century as new plazas and avenues were installed, along with sewerage and garbage-collection systems. This was Mexico City's gilded age.

Independence

On October 30, 1810, some 80,000 independence rebels, fresh from victory at Guanajuato, overpowered Spanish loyalist forces west of the capital. Unfortunately they were ill equipped to capitalize on this triumph and their leader, Miguel Hidalgo, chose not to advance on the city – a decision that cost Mexico 11 more years of fighting before independence was achieved.

Following the reform laws established by President Benito Juárez in 1859, monasteries and churches were appropriated by the government, then sold off, subdivided and put to other uses. During his brief reign (1864–67), Emperor Maximilian laid out the Calzada del Emperador (today's Paseo de la Reforma) to connect Bosque de Chapultepec with the center.

Mexico City entered the modern age under the despotic Porfirio Díaz, who ruled Mexico for most of the years between 1876 and 1911. Díaz ushered in a construction boom, building Parisian-style mansions and theaters, while the city's wealthier residents escaped the center for newly minted neighborhoods to the west.

Modern Megalopolis

After Díaz fell in 1911, the Mexican Revolution brought war, hunger and disease to the streets of Mexico City. Following the Great Depression, a drive to industrialize attracted more money and people.

Mexico City continued to mushroom in the 1970s, as the rural poor sought economic refuge in its thriving industries, and the metropolitan-area population surged from 8.7 to 14.5 million. Unable to contain the new arrivals, Mexico City spread beyond the bounds of the Distrito Federal (DF; Federal District) and into the adjacent state of México. The result of such unbridled growth was some of the world's worst traffic and pollution. At last count, the Greater Mexico City area had more than 22 million inhabitants.

For seven decades, the federal government ruled the DF directly, with presidents appointing 'regents' to head notoriously corrupt administrations. Finally, in 1997, the DF gained political autonomy. In 2000 Andrés Manuel López Obrador, of the left-leaning PRD (Party of the Democratic Revolution), was elected mayor. *Capitalinos* (capital-city residents) approved of 'AMLO.' His initiatives included an ambitious makeover of the *centro histórico* and the construction of an overpass for the city's ring road.

While López Obrador was narrowly defeated in the presidential election of 2006 (an outcome he fiercely contested based on fraud allegations), his former police chief, Marcelo Ebrard, won a sweeping victory in Mexico City, consolidating the PRD's grip on the city government. The PRD has passed a flood of progressive initiatives, including same-sex marriage and the legalization of abortion and euthanasia. In 2012 Ebrard passed the reins to his former attorney general, Miguel Ángel Mancera,

MEXICO CITY IN...

Two Days

Day one dawns and you find yourself standing in the **Zócalo** (p67), once the center of the Aztec universe. Explore the pre-Hispanic ruins at **Templo Mayor** (p71) then admire Diego Rivera's cinematic murals at **Palacio Nacional** (p71). On day two delve into Mexico's past at **Museo Nacional de Antropología** (p85) and **Castillo de Chapultepec** (p85). Come nightfall, do tequila shots over mariachi music at **Plaza Garibaldi** (p73).

Four Days

Greet the new day with a stroll around the fountains and leafy paths of **Alameda Central** (p77), making time to acquaint yourself with the art deco splendor and Diego Rivera mural of **Palacio de Bellas Artes** (p76). Next head for some *artesanías* (handicrafts) shopping at **La Ciudadela** (p129). If it's Saturday, spend the rest of the afternoon learning to dance at the adjacent **Plaza de Danzón** (p104).

One Week

Get to know the southern districts: visit **Museo Frida Kahlo** (p96) in Coyoacán and do dinner and mezcal sampling on the delightful **Jardín Centenario** (p97), or shop for quality crafts at San Ángel's **Bazar Sábado** (p132) market. Devote a day further south in Xochimilco and spend the afternoon gliding along ancient **canals** (p93) on a *trajinera* (gondola). Reserve Wednesday or Sunday evening for the **Ballet Folklórico de México** (p126).

who won the Mexico City mayoral race with more than 60% of the vote. In 2015 Mancera's government announced a major revamp of Avenida Chapultepec with new pedestrian (and, controversially, commercial) spaces, a sign of continual reinvention in CDMX (the city's new official name since 2016, ditching 'DF'). In late 2017 Mancera announced millions of pesos in funding for the reconstruction of areas of the city damaged by the 19 September 2017 earthquake. For many it felt like it was too little too late and highlighted the fact that despite being a megalopolis, real change in the city came from the people, neighborhoods and a new sense of community.

 Sights

You could spend months exploring all the museums, monuments, plazas, colonial-era buildings, monasteries, murals, galleries, archaeological finds, shrines and religious relics that this encyclopedia of a city has to offer – Mexico City shares billing with London for having the most museums of any city in the world.

Plan ahead as many museums close on Monday, while most waive their admission fees to residents on Sunday, thus attracting crowds.

CDMX comprises 16 *delegaciones* (boroughs), which are in turn subdivided into around 1800 *colonias* (neighborhoods).

MEXICO CITY FOR CHILDREN

As with elsewhere in Mexico, kids take center stage in the capital. Museums frequently organize hands-on activities for kids. The **Museo de la Secretaría de Hacienda y Crédito Público** (p73) often stages puppet shows on Sunday. For something that both adults and kids can love, the colorful Museo de Arte Popular (p78) tends to win over most children. Another great option is the Museo del Juguete Antiguo México (p81), a fascinating toy museum with more than 60,000 collectibles on display.

Mexico City's numerous parks and plazas are usually buzzing with kids' voices. Bosque de Chapultepec (p84) is the obvious destination, as it contains the Papalote Museo del Niño (p89), La Feria (p89) and several lakes such as the large Lago de Chapultepec with rowboat rentals. In neighboring Polanco is the world-class aquarium Acuario Inbursa (p92). Also consider Condesa's Parque México, where kids can rent bikes and where Sunday is family-activity day. Plaza Hidalgo (p97) in Coyoacán is another fun-filled spot with balloons, street mimes and cotton candy.

Many theaters, including the **Centro Cultural del Bosque** (Map p90; ☎ 55-5283-4600, ext 4408; www.ccb.bellasartes.gob.mx; Campo Marte, cnr Paseo de la Reforma; ⊗ box office noon-3pm & 5-7pm Mon-Fri & prior to events; ♿; Ⓜ Auditorio), **Centro Cultural Helénico** (Map p94; ☎ 55-4155-0919; www.helenico.gob.mx; Av Revolución 1500, Colonia Guadalupe Inn; ⊗ box office 10am-8:30pm; ♿; ☒ Altavista) and the Foro Shakespeare (p126), stage children's plays and puppet shows on weekends and during school holidays. Animated movies are a staple at cinemas around town, though keep in mind that children's films are usually dubbed in Spanish.

In Xochimilco (p92) kids will find riding the gondolas through the canals as magical as any theme park. Also in this part of town is the Museo Dolores Olmedo (p93), where peacocks and pre-Hispanic dogs occupy the gardens. Children's shows are performed in the patio on Saturday and Sunday at 1pm, and the museum offers workshops for children.

In late October look out for the parade and display of giant *alebrijes* (painted wooden carvings), and the Día de Muertos (p105) parade, both along Reforma.

For more on activities for children, see the 'Infantiles' section at the Conaculta (www.mexicoescultura.com) website; or the 'Family' events on the CDMX Travel (www.cdmxtravel.com) site in English.

Most metro stations and trains are too cramped and hot for prams and lack elevators. Baby-change facilities are available at most museums, but only in the larger restaurants. Even without children, walking through crowds in the *centro histórico* can be a tiring experience, while the leafy, compact centers at the heart of the neighborhoods of Roma, Condesa and Coyoacán allow for a little more freedom of movement without having to constantly hand hold.

Though the vast urban expanse appears daunting, the main areas of interest to visitors are fairly well defined and easy to traverse, contained mainly within the *colonias* of La Roma, La Condesa, Polanco, El Centro, Coyoacán and San Ángel.

Note that some major streets, such as Avenida Insurgentes, keep the same name for many kilometers, but the names (and numbering) of many lesser streets may switch every 10 blocks or so.

Often the easiest way to find an address is by asking for the nearest metro station.

Besides their regular names, many major streets are termed Eje (axis). The Eje system establishes a grid of priority roads across the city.

⊙ Centro Histórico

Packed with magnificent buildings and absorbing museums, the 668-block area defined as the *centro histórico* is the obvious place to start your explorations. More than 1500 of its buildings are classified as historic or artistic monuments and it is on the Unesco World Heritage list. It also vibrates with modern-day street life and nightlife, and is a convenient area to stay.

Since 2000, money has been poured into upgrading the image and infrastructure of the *centro*. Streets have been repaved, buildings refurbished, lighting and traffic flow improved and security bolstered. New museums, restaurants and clubs have moved into the renovated structures, and festivals and cultural events are staged in the plazas, spurring a continued downtown revival.

At the center of it all lies the massive Zócalo, downtown's main square, where pre-Hispanic ruins, imposing colonial-era buildings and large-scale murals convey Mexico City's storied past.

In true forward-looking, *chilango* (Mexico city inhabitants) style, the Zócalo, Plaza Tolsá and Gran Hotel opened themselves to international audiences when heavily featured in the James Bond *Spectre* film.

Metro station Zócalo is conveniently in the heart of the *centro,* but the area can also be approached from the west from metro Allende, or even metro Bellas Artes if you wish to experience the crowds of Calle Madero. In the far southern edge of the centro, metro Isabel La Católica allows you to cross the hip bars on and around Calle Regina.

Zócalo PLAZA

(Map p68; Plaza de la Constitución, Colonia Centro; Ⓜ Zócalo) The heart of Mexico City is the Plaza de la Constitución. Residents began calling it the Zócalo, meaning 'base,' in the 19th century, when plans for a major monument to independence went unrealized, leaving only the pedestal. Measuring 220m from north to south, and 240m from east to west, it's one of the world's largest city squares.

The ceremonial center of Aztec Tenochtitlán, known as the Teocalli, lay immediately northeast of the Zócalo. In the 1520s Cortés paved the plaza with stones from the ruins of the complex. In the 18th century the Zócalo was given over to a maze of market stalls until it was dismantled by General Santa Anna, who placed the unfinished monument in its center.

Today the Zócalo is home to the powers that be. On its east side is the Palacio Nacional (the presidential palace), on the north is the Catedral Metropolitana, and on the south are the city government offices. Jewelry shops and extravagant hotels line the arcade known as the Portal de Mercaderes on the plaza's west side.

As you emerge from metro Zócalo onto the vast central plaza, you may hear the booming of drums from the direction of the cathedral – the Aztec dancers are doing their thing. Wearing snakeskin loincloths, elaborately feathered headdresses and shell ankle bracelets, they move in a circle and chant in Náhuatl. At the center, engulfed in a cloud of fragrant copal smoke, drummers bang on the conga-like *huehuetl* (indigenous drum) and the barrel-shaped, slitted *teponaztli*.

Variously known as Danzantes Aztecas, Danza Chichimeca or Concheros, the dancers perform their ritual daily in the plaza. It is meant to evoke the Aztec *mitote,* a frenzied ceremony performed by preconquest Mexicans at harvest times, although scant evidence exists that the dancers' moves bear any resemblance to those of their forebears.

The square has variously served as a forum for mass protests, free concerts, a human chessboard, a gallery of spooky Día de Muertos (Day of the Dead) altars and an ice-skating rink. It's even been a canvas for photo artist Spencer Tunick, who filled the square with 18,000 nude Mexicans in May 2007.

The huge Mexican flag flying in the middle of the Zócalo is ceremonially raised at 8am by soldiers of the Mexican army, then lowered at 6pm.

Centro Histórico

0 km | 0.2 miles / 400 m

N

Paseo de la Reforma

Lerdo

Garibaldi (M)

Garibaldi

Salón Los Ángeles (660m)

Centro Cultural Universitario Tlatelolco (800m); Plaza de las Tres Culturas (890m)

Tianguis Dominical de la Lagunilla (270m)

Santa Muerte Altar (900m)

Lagunilla (M)

Héroe de Granaditas

Mercado Tepito

República de Costa Rica

Florida

Libertad

Rayón

República de Ecuador

Aztecas

República de Brasil

República de Paraguay

República de Nicaragua

República de Colombia

República de Bolivia

Metrobús República de Argentina

República de Argentina

República de Venezuela

Calle del Carmen

San Ildefonso

Justo Sierra

Rodríguez Puebla

Plaza de Loreto

Santísima

Secretaría de Educación Pública

4

91

87

81

66

20

3 Plaza Garibaldi

Plaza Garibaldi

Plaza Montero

Plaza de la Concepción

Eje Central Lázaro Cárdenas

70

75

74

77

Altuna

Comonfort

Incas

República de Honduras

República de Perú

Belisario Domínguez

Metrobús República de Chile

República de Chile

61

79

82

55

República de Cuba

Donceles

Allende (M)

13

28

Plaza Santo Domingo

31

53

La Palma

48

Tacuba

24

32

64

29

21

17

Condesa

Plaza Tolsá

Bellas Artes

Bellas Artes (M)

Santa Veracruz

Dos de Abril

25

30

Palacio de Bellas Artes

1

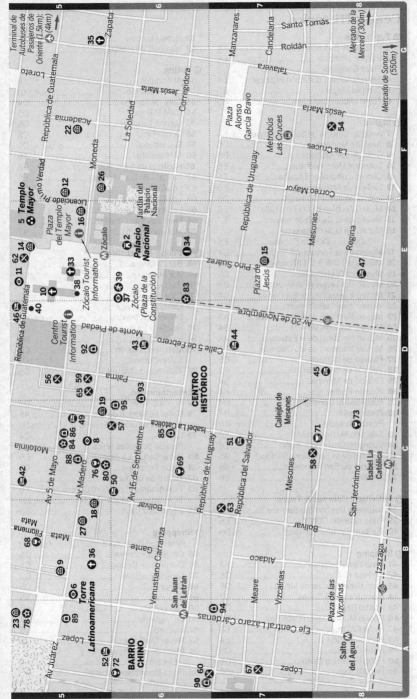

Centro Histórico

★**Templo Mayor** ARCHAEOLOGICAL SITE
(Map p68; ☑ 55-4040-5600; www.templomayor.
inah.gob.mx; Seminario 8; M$70; ⊘ 9am-5pm Tue-
Sun; M Zócalo) Before the Spaniards demolished it, the Teocalli of Tenochtitlán covered
the site where the cathedral now stands, as
well as the blocks to its north and east. It
wasn't until 1978, after electricity workers
happened on an eight-tonne stone-disc carving of the Aztec goddess Coyolxauhqui, that
the decision was taken to demolish colonial
buildings and excavate the Templo Mayor.

The temple is thought to be on the exact
spot where the Aztecs saw their symbolic eagle perching on a cactus with a snake in its
beak – the symbol of Mexico today. In Aztec
belief this was the center of the universe.

Like other sacred buildings in Tenochtitlán, the temple was enlarged several times,
with each rebuilding accompanied by the
sacrifice of captured warriors. What we see
today are sections of the temple's seven different phases. At the center is a platform
dating from about 1400. On its southern
half, a sacrificial stone stands in front of a
shrine to Huizilopochtli, the Aztec war god.
On the northern half is a chac-mool (a Maya
reclining figure) before a shrine to the water
god, Tláloc. By the time the Spanish arrived,
a 40m-high double pyramid towered above
this spot, with steep twin stairways climbing
to shrines of the two gods.

The entrance to the temple site and museum is east of the cathedral, across the hectic
Plaza del Templo Mayor. Authorized tour
guides (with Sectur ID) offer their services
by the entrance.

The on-site **Museo del Templo Mayor** (included in the site's admission price) houses a
model of Tenochtitlán and artifacts from the
site, and gives a good overview of Aztec, aka
Mexica, civilization. Pride of place is given to
the great wheel-like stone of Coyolxauhqui
(She of Bells on her Cheek), best viewed from
the top-floor vantage point. She is shown
decapitated, the result of her murder by Huizilopochtli, her brother, who also killed his
400 brothers en route to becoming top god.

Excavation continues to turn up major
pieces. Just west of the temple, a monolithic
stone carved with the image of Tlaltecuhtli,
the goddess of earth fertility, was unearthed
in October 2006 and is now prominently displayed on the museum's 1st floor.

Another key find was made in 2011 when
a ceremonial platform dating from 1469 was
uncovered. Based on historical documents,
archaeologists believe the 15m structure was
used to cremate Aztec rulers. A recent dig
also turned up what archaeologists believe
is the trunk of a sacred tree found at a newly
discovered burial site at the foot of the temple. Then in 2017 a tower of over 650 human
skulls 6m in diameter was found nearby,
believed to be Huey Tzompantli, mentioned
by Spanish conquistadors but undiscovered
until now. Most surprisingly, the remains of
the sacrificed included women and children.

A new entrance hall open to the public displays objects discovered over four years of the
hall's excavation – funerary objects, bones,
Colonial-era fine china and pre-Hispanic
structures of Cuauhxicalco ('the place of the
eagle vessel') – keeping Templo Mayor continually intriguing even for return visitors.

★**Palacio Nacional** PALACE
(National Palace; Map p68; ☑ 55-3688-1255;
www.historia.palacionacional.info; Plaza de la Constitución; ⊘ 9am-5pm Tue-Sun; M Zócalo) FREE
Inside this grandiose colonial palace you'll
see Diego Rivera murals (painted between
1929 and 1951) that depict Mexican civilization from the arrival of Quetzalcóatl (the
Aztec plumed serpent god) to the post-
revolutionary period. The nine murals covering the north and east walls of the first
level above the patio chronicle indigenous
life before the Spanish conquest.

The Palacio Nacional is also home to the
offices of the president of Mexico and the
Federal Treasury.

The first palace on this spot was built by
Aztec emperor Moctezuma II in the early
16th century. Cortés destroyed the palace
in 1521, rebuilding it as a fortress with three
interior courtyards. In 1562 the crown purchased the building from Cortés' family to
house the viceroys of Nueva España, a function it served until Mexican independence.

As you face the palace, high above the
center door hangs the **Campana de Dolores**, the bell rung in the town of Dolores
Hidalgo by Padre Miguel Hidalgo in 1810 at
the start of the War of Independence. From
the balcony underneath it, the president delivers the *grito* (shout) – ¡Viva México! – on
the evening of September 16 to commemorate independence.

Catedral Metropolitana CATHEDRAL
(Metropolitan Cathedral; Map p68; ☑ 55-5510-0440;
http://catedralmetropolitanacdmx.org; Plaza de la
Constitución; bell tower M$20; ⊘ cathedral 8am-
8pm, bell tower 10:40am-6pm; M Zócalo) One of

Mexico City's most iconic structures, this cathedral is a monumental edifice: 109m long, 59m wide and 65m high. Started in 1573, it remained a work in progress during the entire colonial period, thus displaying a catalog of architectural styles, with successive generations of builders striving to incorporate the innovations of the day. The conquistadors ordered the cathedral built atop the Templo Mayor and, as a further show of domination at a key historical moment, used most of these Aztec stones in its construction.

Original architect Claudio Arciniega modeled the building after Seville's seven-nave cathedral, but after running into difficulties with the spongy subsoil he scaled it down to a five-nave design of vaults on semicircular arches. The baroque portals facing the Zócalo, built in the 17th century, have two levels of columns and marble panels with bas-reliefs. The central panel shows the Assumption of the Virgin Mary, to whom the cathedral is dedicated. The upper levels of the towers, with bell-shaped tops, were added in the late 18th century. The exterior was completed in 1813, when architect Manuel Tolsá added the clock tower – topped by statues of Faith, Hope and Charity – and a great central dome.

The first thing you notice upon entering is the elaborately carved and gilded **Altar de Perdón** (Altar of Forgiveness). There's invariably a line of worshippers at the foot of the **Señor del Veneno** (Lord of the Poison), the dusky Christ figure on the right. Legend has it that the figure attained its color when it miraculously absorbed a dose of poison through its feet from the lips of a clergyman to whom an enemy had administered the lethal substance.

The cathedral's chief artistic treasure is the gilded 18th-century **Altar de los Reyes** (Altar of the Kings), behind the main altar. Fourteen richly decorated chapels line the two sides of the building, while intricately carved late-17th-century wooden choir stalls by Juan de Rojas occupy the central nave. Enormous painted panels by colonial masters Juan Correa and Cristóbal de Villalpando cover the walls of the sacristy, the first component of the cathedral to be built.

Visitors may wander freely, though you're asked not to do so during Mass. A donation is requested to enter the sacristy or choir, where guides provide commentary, and you can climb the **bell tower**. Mexico City's archbishop conducts Mass at noon on Sunday.

Adjoining the east side of the cathedral is the 18th-century Sagrario Metropolitano. Originally built to house the archives and vestments of the archbishop, it is now the city's main parish church. Its front entrance and mirror-image eastern portal are superb examples of the ultra-decorative Churrigueresque style.

Sagrario Metropolitano   CHURCH
(Map p68; Plaza de la Constitución s/n; ⊙8am-6:30pm; Ⓜ Zócalo) Adjoining the east side of the Catedral Metropolitana is the 18th-century Sagrario Metropolitano. Originally built to house the archives and vestments of the archbishop, it is now the city's main parish church. Its front entrance and mirror-image eastern portal are superb examples of the ultradecorative Churrigueresque style.

Centro Cultural de España   CULTURAL CENTER
(Spanish Cultural Center; Map p68; ☑55-6592-9926; www.ccemx.org; República de Guatemala 18; ⊙11am-9pm Tue-Fri, 10am-6pm Sat, 10am-4pm Sun; Ⓜ Zócalo) **FREE** The Centro Cultural de España always has a variety of cutting-edge art exhibitions going on. In the basement you'll find the **Museo de Sitio**, an interesting museum with the remains of 'El Calmécac,' a school where children of Aztec nobility received religious and military training during the reigns of Emperors Ahuízotl and Moctezuma II. It was built between 1486 and 1502.

Also in the museum are various artifacts unearthed as the cultural center was being expanded between 2006 and 2008, including several 2.4m-tall pre-Hispanic *almenas* (spiral-shaped decorative pieces), colonial-era ceramic objects and a weathered 20th-century handgun.

The cultural center's splendidly restored colonial-era building, which conquistador Hernán Cortés once awarded to his butler, has a cool terrace bar (p127) that stages live music and DJ sets.

Museo Archivo de la Fotografía   MUSEUM
(Photographic Archive Museum; Map p68; ☑55-2616-7057; www.cultura.cdmx.gob.mx/recintos/maf; República de Guatemala 34; ⊙10am-6pm Tue-Sun; Ⓜ Zócalo) **FREE** Occupying a 16th-century colonial-era building, the city's photo museum hosts changing exhibits focusing on all things Mexico City. Additionally, the museum has amassed a vast archive comprising a century's worth of urban images.

Plaza Tolsá
PLAZA

(Map p68; Ⓜ Bellas Artes) Several blocks west of the Zócalo is this handsome square, named after Manuel Tolsá, the illustrious late-18th-century sculptor and architect who completed the Catedral Metropolitana. He also created the bronze equestrian statue of the Spanish king Carlos IV (r 1788–1808), which is the plaza's centerpiece in front of the Museo Nacional de Arte; it originally stood in the Zócalo.

Museo Nacional de Arte
MUSEUM

(National Art Museum; Map p68; ☑55-5130-3400; www.munal.gob.mx; Tacuba 8; M$60, free Sun, camera use M$5; ⊙10am-5:30pm Tue-Sun; Ⓜ Bellas Artes) Built around 1900 in the style of an Italian Renaissance palace, this museum holds collections representing every school of Mexican art until the early 20th century. A highlight is the work of José María Velasco, depicting the Valle de México in the late 19th century.

Antiguo Colegio de San Ildefonso
MUSEUM

(Map p68; ☑55-5702-2834; www.sanildefonso.org.mx; Justo Sierra 16; adult/child under 12yr M$50/free, Tue free; ⊙10am-8pm Tue, to 6pm Wed-Sun; Ⓜ Zócalo) Diego Rivera, José Clemente Orozco and David Siqueiros painted murals here in the 1920s. Most of the work on the main patio is by Orozco; look for the portrait of Hernán Cortés and his lover La Malinche underneath the staircase. The amphitheater, off the lobby, holds Rivera's first mural, *La Creación*, undertaken on his return from Europe in 1923. Built in the 16th century, the former Jesuit college today hosts outstanding temporary art exhibitions.

Palacio de Minería
HISTORIC BUILDING

(Palace of Mining; Map p68; ☑55-5623-2982; www.palaciomineria.unam.mx; Tacuba 5; tours M$30; ⊙tours 11am & 1pm Sat & Sun; Ⓜ Bellas Artes) The Palacio de Minería was where mining engineers trained in the 19th century. A neoclassical masterpiece, the palace was designed by Tolsá and built between 1797 and 1813. Today it houses a branch of the national university's engineering department. Visits are by guided tour only.

Since 1893 the palace has displayed four restored meteorites that struck northern Mexico 50,000 years ago, one weighing more than 14 tons. There's also a small museum on Tolsá's life and work.

Palacio Postal
HISTORIC BUILDING

(Correo Mayor; Map p68; ☑55-5510-2999; www.palaciopostal.gob.mx; Tacuba 1; ⊙9am-6pm Mon-Fri, to 3:30pm Sat & Sun; 🚻; Ⓜ Bellas Artes) FREE More than just Mexico City's central post office, this early-20th-century palace is an Italianate confection designed by the Palacio de Bellas Artes' original architect, Adamo Boari. The beige stone facade features baroque columns and carved filigree around the windows. The bronze railings on the monumental staircase inside were cast in Florence.

The small **Postal Museum** (Map p68; ⊙9am-6pm Tue-Fri, to 3pm Sat & Sun) FREE, on the 1st floor, is where philatelists can ogle a design of the first stamp ever issued in Mexico.

Museo Interactivo de Economía
MUSEUM

(MIDE, Interactive Museum of Economics; Map p68; ☑55-5130-4600; www.mide.org.mx; Tacuba 17; adult/student M$95/75; ⊙9am-6pm Tue-Sun; Ⓜ Allende) The former hospital of the Bethlehemites religious order has been the home of this museum since 2006. A slew of hands-on exhibits is aimed at breaking down economic concepts. For coin connoisseurs, the highlight is the Banco de México's numismatic collection.

Museo de la Secretaría de Hacienda y Crédito Público
MUSEUM

(Finance Secretariat Museum; Map p68; ☑55-3668-1657; Moneda 4; ⊙10am-5pm Tue-Sun; Ⓜ Zócalo) FREE Sure, the name is a tough sell (yay, let's go to the Finance Secretariat Museum!), but it's actually a very interesting place. The museum shows off works from its collection of more than 30,000 pieces of Mexican art, much of it contributed by painters and sculptors in lieu of paying taxes. Built in the 16th century, the former colonial archbishop's palace also hosts a full program of cultural events (many free), from puppet shows to chamber music recitals.

The building sits atop the Templo de Tezcatlipoca, a temple dedicated to an Aztec god often associated with night, death and change through conflict. You'll see the temple's stairs just off the renovated main patio.

★ Plaza Garibaldi
PLAZA

(Map p68; Eje Central Lázaro Cárdenas, cnr República de Honduras; mariachi song M$130-150; Ⓟ; Ⓜ Garibaldi) Every night the city's mariachi bands belt out heartfelt ballads in this festive square. Wearing silver-studded outfits, they toot their trumpets and tune their guitars until approached by someone who'll pay for a song. Also roaming Garibaldi are white-clad *son jarocho* groups, hailing from Veracruz, and *norteño* combos, who bang out northern-style folk tunes. The notoriously seedy Garibaldi continues to undergo a makeover that includes heightened security, but it's still rough around the edges.

The latest addition to the plaza is the **Museo del Tequila y el Mezcal** (Map p68; www. mutemgaribaldi.mx; admission M$70; ⊙11am-10pm Sun-Wed, to midnight Thu-Sat), which has exhibits explaining the origins and production processes of Mexico's two most popular distilled agave drinks.

Avenida Madero   STREET
(Map p68) This stately avenue west of the Zócalo boasts a veritable catalog of architectural styles. Expect slow-moving throngs of families, teens, tourists, the occasional pickpocket, and street vendors on weekends.

Housed in a gorgeous neoclassical building two blocks from the square, **Museo del Estanquillo** (Map p68; ☑55-5521-3052; www. museodelestanquillo.com; Isabel La Católica 26; ⊙10am-6pm Wed-Mon; ⓂAllende) **FREE** contains the vast pop-culture collection amassed over the decades by DF essayist and pack rat Carlos Monsiváis. The museum illustrates various phases in the capital's development by means of the numerous photos, paintings and movie posters from the collection.

Palacio de Iturbide (Palacio de Cultura Banamex; Map p68; ☑55-1226-0091; www.fomento culturalbanamex.org; Av Madero 17; ⊙10am-7pm; ⓂAllende) **FREE**, with its late-18th-century baroque facade, is a few blocks west. Built for colonial nobility, in 1821 it became the residence of General Agustín Iturbide, a Mexican independence hero who became emperor here in 1822. (He abdicated less than a year later, after General Santa Anna announced the birth of a republic.) It hosts exhibits from the bank's extensive art collection.

Half a block past the pedestrian corridor Gante stands the amazing **Casa de los Azulejos** (House of Tiles; Map p68; ☑55-5512-1331; Av Madero 4; ⊙7am-1am; ⓂAllende). Dating from 1596, it was built for the Condes (Counts) del Valle de Orizaba. Most of the tiles that adorn the outside walls were produced in China and shipped to Mexico on the Manila naos (Spanish galleons used until the early 19th century). The building now houses a Sanborns restaurant in a covered courtyard around a Moorish fountain. The staircase has a 1925 mural by Orozco.

Across the way, the **Templo de San Francisco** (Map p68; Av Madero 7; ⊙8am-8pm; ⓂAllende) is a remnant of the vast Franciscan monastery erected in the early 16th century over the site of Moctezuma's private zoo. In its heyday it extended two blocks south and east. The monastic complex was divvied up under the post-independence reform laws, and in 1949 it was returned to the Franciscan order in a deplorable state and subsequently restored. The elaborately carved doorway is a shining example of 18th-century baroque. Open-air art exhibitions are held in the adjoining atrium.

Rising alongside the monastery, the **Torre Latinoamericana** (Latin American Tower; Map p68; ☑55-5518-7423; www.miradorlatino.com; Eje Central Lázaro Cárdenas 2; adult/child M$100/70; ⊙9am-10pm; ⓂBellas Artes) was Latin America's tallest building when constructed in 1956. Thanks to the deep-seated pylons that anchor the building, it has withstood several major earthquakes. If you want to learn more about the construction of the tower and downtown's centuries-long development, a museum on the 38th floor houses a permanent photo exhibition. Up above, views from the 41st-floor lounge bar and the 44th-floor observation deck are spectacular, smog permitting. Admission is free if you're just visiting the bar.

Ex Teresa Arte Actual   MUSEUM
(Map p68; ☑55-222-721; www.exteresa.bellas artes.gob.mx; Licenciado Primo Verdad 8, Colonia Centro; ⊙10am-6pm; ⓂZócalo) **FREE** Mexico City was built atop a sloshy lake bed and it's sinking fast, as evidenced by this teetering former convent. The 17th-century building now serves as a museum for performance art, contemporary exhibits, concerts and the occasional movie screening. Be sure to gaze up at the dual dome.

Museo Nacional de las Culturas   MUSEUM
(National Museum of Cultures; Map p68; ☑55-5512-7452; www.museodelasculturas.mx; Moneda 13; ⊙10am-5pm Tue-Sun; ⓂZócalo) **FREE** Constructed in 1567 as the colonial mint, this renovated museum exhibits the art, dress and handicrafts of the world's cultures. Explanatory text is in Spanish only.

Templo de la Santísima Trinidad   CHURCH
(Map p68; cnr Santísima & Zapata; ⓂZócalo) The profusion of ornamental sculpture on the facade, including ghostly busts of the 12 apostles and a representation of Christ with his head in God's lap, is the main reason to

visit the Church of the Holy Sacrament, five blocks east of the Zócalo as you walk along Calle Moneda. Most of the carving was done by Lorenzo Rodríguez between 1755 and 1783.

Suprema Corte de Justicia
PUBLIC ART

(Supreme Court; Map p68; ☑ 55-4113-1000; Pino Suárez 2; ◷ 9am-5pm Mon-Fri; Ⓜ Zócalo) FREE In 1940 muralist José Clemente Orozco painted four panels around the second level of the Supreme Court's central stairway, two dealing with the theme of justice. A more contemporary take on the same subject, *La historia de la justicia en México* (The History of Justice in Mexico), by Rafael Cauduro, unfolds over three levels of the building's southwest stairwell.

Executed in his hyper-realist style, Cauduro's series (*The Seven Worst Crimes*) catalogs the horrors of state-sponsored crimes against the populace, including the ever-relevant torture-induced confession. On the southeast corner of the building's interior, Ismael Ramos Huitrón's *La busqueda de la justicia* (The Search for Justice) reflects on the Mexican people's constant struggle to obtain justice, as does the social realism work *La justicia* (Justice), by Japanese-Mexican artist Luis Nishizawa, on the northwest stairwell. On the first level of the main stairway, American artist George Biddle painted *La guerra y la paz* (War and Peace) shortly after WWII ended. Photo ID required for admission.

Museo de la Ciudad de México
MUSEUM

(Museum of Mexico City; Map p68; ☑ 55-5522-9936; www.cultura.cdmx.gob.mx/recintos/mcm; Pino Suárez 30; adult/student M$29/15, Sun free; ◷ 10am-6pm Tue-Sun; Ⓜ Pino Suárez) FREE Formerly a palace of the Counts of Santiago de Calimaya, this 18th-century baroque edifice now houses a museum with exhibits focusing on city history and culture. Upstairs is the former studio of Joaquín Clausell, considered Mexico's foremost impressionist. The artist used the walls as a sketchbook during the three decades he worked here until his death in 1935.

Plaza Santo Domingo
PLAZA

(Map p68; cnr República de Venezuela & República de Brasil; ▣ República de Argentina) Smaller and less hectic than nearby Zócalo, this plaza has long served as a base for scribes and printers. Descendants of those who did the paperwork for merchants using the customs building (now the Education Ministry) across the square, the scribes work on the west side beneath the **Portales de Santo Domingo**, aka Portales de Evangelistas, as similar scribes have since the 18th century.

Nowadays Plaza Santo Domingo is also known for modern printers – peddlers of fake IDs, who often scam those who seek false papers. Since 2016 it has become the site for the annual UNAM Day of the Dead Megaofrenda.

To the north of the plaza stands the maroon stone **Iglesia de Santo Domingo** (Map p68; Belizario Dominguez; Ⓜ Allende), a beautiful baroque church dating from 1736. East of the church is the 18th-century **Palacio de la Inquisición** (Former Spanish Inquisition Headquarters; Map p68), headquarters of the Holy Inquisition in Mexico until Spain decreed its closure in 1812.

★ Secretaría de Educación Pública
PUBLIC ART

(Secretariat of Education; Map p68; ☑ 55-3601-1000; República de Brasil 31; ◷ 9am-3pm Mon-Fri; ▣ República de Argentina) FREE The two front courtyards here are lined with 120 fresco panels painted by Diego Rivera in the 1920s. Together they form a tableau of 'the very life of the people,' in the artist's words.

Each courtyard is thematically distinct: the one on the east end deals with labor, industry and agriculture, while the interior one depicts traditions and festivals. On the latter's top level is a series on proletarian and agrarian revolution, underneath a continuous red banner emblazoned with a Mexican *corrido* (folk song). A likeness of Frida Kahlo appears in the first panel as an arsenal worker. Bring photo ID to enter.

Museo José Luis Cuevas
MUSEUM

(Map p68; ☑ 55-5522-0156; www.museojoseluis cuevas.com.mx; Academia 13; M$20, Sun free; ◷ 10am-6pm Tue-Sun; Ⓜ Zócalo) This museum showcases the works of artist Cuevas, a leader of the 1950s Ruptura movement, which broke with the politicized art of the post-revolutionary regime. Cuevas' *La Giganta,* an 8m-tall bronze female figure with some male features, dominates the central patio.

◉ Alameda Central & Around

Emblematic of the downtown renaissance, the rectangular park immediately northwest of the *centro histórico* holds a vital place in Mexico City's cultural life. Surrounded by historically significant buildings, the Alameda Central has been the focus of ambitious redevelopment over the past decade. In particular, the high-rise towers on the Plaza Juárez and

Alameda Central, Plaza de la República & Around

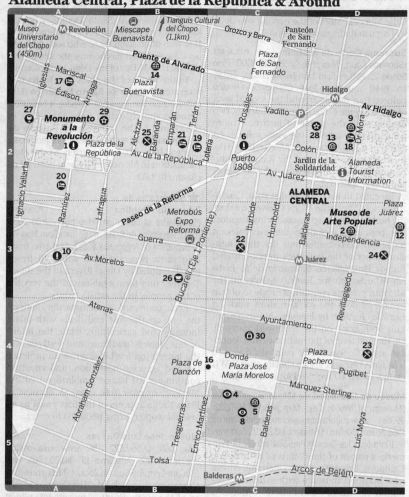

adjacent new restaurants have transformed the zone south of the park, much of which was destroyed in the 1985 earthquake. Metro stations Bellas Artes and Hidalgo are located on the Alameda's east and west sides, respectively. The north–south Eje Central Lázaro Cárdenas passes just east of the park.

★ **Palacio de Bellas Artes**   ARTS CENTER
(Palace of Fine Arts; Map p68; ☑ 55-4040-5300; www.palacio.bellasartes.gob.mx; cnr Av Juárez & Eje Central Lázaro Cárdenas; museum M\$60, Sun free; ⏰ 10am-6pm Tue-Sun; Ⓟ; Ⓜ Bellas Artes) Immense murals by world-famous Mexican

artists dominate the top floors of this white-marble palace – a concert hall and arts center commissioned by President Porfirio Díaz. Construction began in 1905 under Italian architect Adamo Boari, who favored neoclassical and art nouveau styles.

Complications arose as the heavy marble shell sank into the spongy subsoil, and then the Mexican Revolution intervened. Architect Federico Mariscal eventually finished the interior in the 1930s, utilizing the more modern art deco style.

On the 2nd floor are two early 1950s works by Rufino Tamayo: *México de hoy*

val de la vida mexicana (Carnival of Mexican Life). To the east is José Clemente Orozco's *La katharsis* (Catharsis), depicting the conflict between humankind's 'social' and 'natural' aspects.

The 4th-floor **Museo Nacional de Arquitectura** (MUNARQ; Map p68; ☎55-8647-5360; www.museonacionaldearquitectura.bellas artes.gob.mx; Av Juárez s/n; M$45, Sun free; ⊙10am-6pm Tue-Sun; M Bellas Artes) features changing exhibits on contemporary architecture. In addition, the palace stages outstanding temporary art exhibitions.

The renovated Bellas Artes theater (p126) is itself a masterpiece (though only viewable during performances), with a stained-glass curtain depicting the Valle de México. Based on a design by Mexican painter Gerardo Murillo (aka Dr Atl), it was assembled by New York jeweler Tiffany & Co from almost a million pieces of colored glass. The theater is the stage for seasonal opera and symphony performances and the Ballet Folklórico de México (p126). There are lofty views of the Palacio from the cafe terrace of the Sears building across the road.

Alameda Central   PARK
(Map p76; Av Juárez; ⚡; M Bellas Artes) Created in the late 1500s by mandate of then-viceroy Luis de Velasco, the Alameda took its name from the *álamos* (poplars) planted over its rectangular expanse. By the late 19th century the park was graced with European-style statuary and lit by gas lamps. It became the place to be seen for the city's elite. Today the Alameda is a popular refuge, particularly on Sunday when families stroll its pathways and lovers snuggle on benches.

The park is fitted out with dancing fountains, free wi-fi and well-manicured gardens rife with fragrant lavender plants; it's relatively safe and pleasant even on weekend nights. Don't expect to find any street food here – it's banned.

Museo Mural Diego Rivera   MUSEUM
(Diego Rivera Mural Museum; Map p76; ☎55-5512-0754; www.museomuraldiegorivera.bellasartes.gob. mx; cnr Balderas & Colón; adult/student M$30/15, Sun free, camera use M$5; ⊙10am-6pm Tue-Sun; M Hidalgo) This museum is home to one of Diego Rivera's most famous works, *Sueño de una tarde dominical en la Alameda Central* (Dream of a Sunday Afternoon in the Alameda Central), a 15m-long mural painted in 1947. Rivera imagined many of the figures who walked in the city from colonial times

(Mexico Today) and *Nacimiento de la nacionalidad* (Birth of Nationality), a symbolic depiction of the creation of the *mestizo* (mixed ancestry) identity.

At the west end of the 3rd floor is Diego Rivera's famous *El hombre en el cruce de caminos* (Man at the Crossroads), originally commissioned for New York's Rockefeller Center. The Rockefellers had the original destroyed because of its anti-capitalist themes, but Rivera re-created it here in 1934.

On the north side are David Alfaro Siqueiros' three-part *La nueva democracia* (New Democracy) and Rivera's four-part *Carna-*

Alameda Central, Plaza de la República & Around

onward, among them Hernán Cortés, Benito Juárez, Porfirio Díaz and Francisco Madero.

All are grouped around a *Catrina* (skeleton in pre-revolutionary women's garb). Rivera himself, as a pug-faced child, and Frida Kahlo stand beside the skeleton. Charts identify all the characters. The museum was built in 1986 to house the mural, after its original location, the Hotel del Prado, was wrecked by the 1985 earthquake.

Laboratorio de Arte Alameda   MUSEUM
(Alameda Art Laboratory; Map p76; ☑55-5510-2793; www.artealameda.bellasartes.gob.mx; Dr Mora 7; M$30, Sun free; ⊙9am-5pm Tue-Sun; Ⓜ Hidalgo) As is often the case with museums in the *centro*, the 17th-century former convent building that contains the Laboratorio de Arte Alameda is at least as interesting as its contents. Here you can catch installations by leading experimental artists from Mexico and abroad, with an emphasis on electronic and interactive media.

★ **Museo de Arte Popular**   MUSEUM
(Museum of Popular Art; Map p76; ☑55-5510-2201; www.map.df.gob.mx; Revillagigedo 11, cnr Independencia; adult/child/student M$60/free/free, Sun free; ⊙10am-6pm Tue & Thu-Sun, to 9pm Wed; Ⓜ;

Ⓜ Juárez) A major showcase for folk art, this is a colorful museum that even kids love. Contemporary crafts are thematically displayed from all over Mexico, including carnival masks from Chiapas, *alebrijes* (fanciful animal figures) from Oaxaca and trees of life from Puebla. The museum occupies the former fire department headquarters, itself an outstanding example of 1920s art deco by architect Vicente Mendiola. The ground-level shop sells quality handicrafts.

Plaza Juárez   PLAZA
(Map p76; Ⓜ Bellas Artes) Representing the new face of the Alameda zone, the row of chain restaurants, bars, stores and an upmarket hotel facing the park resembles an outdoor shopping plaza. One point of difference is the slick **Museo Memoria y Tolerancia** (Memory & Tolerance Museum; Map p76; ☑55-5130-5555; www.myt.org.mx; Plaza Juárez 12; admission M$75, temporary exhibitions M$30; ⊙9am-6pm Tue-Fri, 10am-7pm Sat & Sun), a maze-like museum dedicated to preserving the memory of genocide victims. Weekend evenings are very noisy, with bars and clubs aimed at students. On other nights it can feel a little deserted and rough.

Behind the fully restored **Templo de Corpus Christi**, which now holds the DF's archives, the plaza's centerpiece is a pair of Tetris-block towers by leading Mexican architect Ricardo Legorreta – the 24-story **Foreign Relations Secretariat** and the 23-story **Tribunales** building front a set of 1034 reddish pyramids in a broad pool, a collaboration between Legorreta and Spanish artist Vicente Rojo.

Museo Franz Mayer MUSEUM
(Map p76; ☑55-5518-2266; www.franzmayer.org.mx; Av Hidalgo 45; M$50, Tue free; ◉10am-5pm Tue-Fri, to 7pm Sat & Sun; ⓂBellas Artes) This museum is the fruit of the efforts of German-born Franz Mayer. Prospering as a financier in his adopted Mexico, Mayer amassed the collection of Mexican silver, ceramics, textiles and furniture now on display. The exhibit halls open onto a sumptuous colonial-era patio where you can grab a bite at the excellent Cloister Café.

Look out for the annual World Press Photo (www.worldpressphoto.org) exhibition held here between late July and late September.

Iglesia de la Santa Veracruz CHURCH
(Map p76; Plaza de Santa Veracruz, Av Hidalgo; ⓂBellas Artes) Originally constructed in 1586, this church was rebuilt in the 18th century and now houses the Museo Franz Mayer. It features two doors in Mexican baroque style.

Museo Nacional de la Estampa MUSEUM
(MUNAE; Map p68; ☑55-5521-2244; www.museonacionaldelaestampa.bellasartes.gob.mx; Av Hidalgo 39; M$45; ◉10am-6pm Tue-Sun; ⓂBellas Artes) Devoted to the graphic arts, this museum has thematic exhibits from its collection of more than 12,000 prints. The museum also does interesting temporary expositions that showcase works from Mexico and abroad.

La Ciudadela CULTURAL CENTER
(Map p76; Balderas, Colonia Centro; ⓂBalderas) The formidable compound now known as 'The Citadel' started off as a tobacco factory in the late 18th century, though it's best known as the scene of the Decena Trágica (Tragic Ten Days), the coup that brought down the Madero government in 1913. Today it's home to the **Biblioteca de México** (National Library; Map p76; ☑55-4155-0836; www.bibliotecademexico.gob.mx; Plaza de la Ciudadela 4; ◉8:30am-7:30pm) FREE.

Centro de la Imagen (Map p76; ☑55-4155-0850; http://centrodelaimagen.cultura.gob.mx; Plaza de la Ciudadela 2, Colonia Centro; ◉10-7pm Wed-Sun) FREE, the city's photography museum, is at the Calle Balderas entrance. Across the plaza, inside the Centro de Artesanías La Ciudadela (p129), vendors offer a wide array of crafts from around Mexico.

◉ Plaza de la República & Around

★**Monumento a la Revolución** MONUMENT
(Map p76; www.mrm.mx; Plaza de la República; all access adult/child M$80/60, 360 observation deck only M$50; ◉noon-8pm Mon-Thu, to 10pm Fri & Sat, 10am-8pm Sun; ⧆; ⓆPlaza de la República) Originally meant to be a legislative chamber, construction of the Monumento a la Revolución was interrupted by the Revolution, and there was talk of demolishing the building, but instead it was modified and given a new role. Unveiled in 1938, it contains the tombs of the revolutionary and post-revolutionary heroes Pancho Villa, Francisco Madero, Venustiano Carranza, Plutarco Elías Calles and Lázaro Cárdenas.

Both the monument and Plaza de la República on which it stands got a major makeover in 2010 to commemorate Mexico's centennial anniversary of the Revolution. Kids love frolicking in the plaza's geyser-like fountains, while at night the monument's renovated architectural features are highlighted by colorful lights.

The star attraction of the monument is the 65m-high summit **paseo linternilla** (Map p76; all access adult/child M$80/60) accessed by a glass elevator. The vertigo-inducing elevator opens to a spiraling staircase that ascends to a round terrace with a panoramic view of the city. Just below it is the equally impressive, though not as tall, **360 observation deck** (Map p76; ☑55-5592-2038; www.mrm.mx; adult/child M$50; ◉noon-8pm Mon-Thu, to 10pm Fri & Sat, 10am-8pm Sun), which is as high as you can go without the all-access pass.

You can also access the skeleton of the structure in the **1910 Structure Galleries**, and there is an interesting basement art gallery, the **Paseo Cimentación** (Map p76; ☑55-5592-2038; all access adult/child M$80/60; ◉noon-8pm Mon-Thu, to 10pm Fri & Sat, 10am-8pm Sun), where you can check out temporary art exhibitions amid a labyrinth of gigantic steel beams that serve as the structure's foundation.

Underlying the plaza and monument, the **Museo Nacional de la Revolución** (National Museum of the Revolution; Map p76; ☑ 55-5546-2115; www.cultura.cdmx.gob.mx/recintos/mnr; M$30, Sun free; ◷ 9am-5pm Tue-Fri, to 6:30pm Sat & Sun) covers a 63-year period, from the implementation of the constitution guaranteeing human rights in 1857 to the installation of the post-revolutionary government in 1920. Explanatory text is in Spanish only.

Museo Universitario del Chopo　MUSEUM
(☑ 55-5546-5484; www.chopo.unam.mx; Enrique González Martínez 10; M$30, Wed free; ◷ 11am-7pm Tue-Sun; Ⓜ San Cosme) You can't miss the prominent spires of this university-run museum. Parts of the old building, made of forged iron from Düsseldorf, were brought over in pieces and assembled in Mexico City around the turn of the 20th century. Chopo boasts wide, open spaces in which ramps serve as showroom floors and high ceilings permit larger-than-life exhibits for contemporary art works. The museum also hosts modern dance performances and screens international and Mexican indie movies.

Museo Nacional de San Carlos　MUSEUM
(Map p76; ☑ 55-5566-8342; www.mnsancarlos.com; Puente de Alvarado 50; adult/child under 3yr M$45/free, Sun free; ◷ 10am-6pm Tue-Sun; Ⓜ Revolución) The Museo Nacional de San Carlos exhibits a formidable collection of European art from the 14th century to early 20th century, including works by Rubens and Goya. The unusual rotunda structure was designed by Manuel Tolsá in the late 18th century.

◉ Paseo de la Reforma

Mexico City's grandest thoroughfare, known simply as 'Reforma,' traces a bold southwestern path from Tlatelolco to Bosque de Chapultepec, skirting the Alameda Central and Zona Rosa. Emperor Maximilian of Hapsburg laid out the boulevard to connect his castle on Chapultepec Hill with the old city center. After his execution, it was given its current name to commemorate the reform laws instituted by President Benito Juárez. Under the López Obrador administration, the avenue was smartly refurbished and its broad, statue-studded medians became a stage for book fairs and art exhibits. It is currently undergoing aggressive development, with office towers and new hotels springing up along its length.

Paseo de la Reforma links a series of monumental *glorietas* (traffic circles). A couple of blocks west of the Alameda Central is **El Caballito** (Map p76; Ⓜ Hidalgo), a representation of a horse's head by the sculptor Sebastián. It commemorates another equestrian sculpture (p73) that stood here for 127 years and today fronts the Museo Nacional de Arte. A few blocks southwest is the **Monumento a Cristóbal Colón** (Map p76), an 1877 statue of Columbus gesturing toward the horizon.

Reforma's intersection with Avenida Insurgentes is marked by the **Monumento a Cuauhtémoc** (Map p82; ☑ Reforma), memorializing the last Aztec emperor. Two blocks northwest is the Jardín del Arte (p132), site of a Sunday art market.

The **Centro Bursátil** (Map p82; Ⓜ Insurgentes), an angular tower and mirror-ball ensemble housing the nation's Bolsa (stock exchange), marks the southern edge of the Colonia Cuauhtémoc. Continuing west past the US embassy, you reach the symbol of Mexico City, the **Monumento a la Independencia** (El Ángel; Map p82; Ⓜ Insurgentes) 𝐅𝐑𝐄𝐄. Known as 'El Ángel,' this gilded Winged Victory on a 45m-high pillar was sculpted for the independence centennial of 1910. Inside the monument are the remains of Miguel Hidalgo, José María Morelos, Ignacio Allende and nine other notables. Thousands of people descend on the monument for occasional free concerts and victory celebrations following important Mexican *fútbol* matches.

At Reforma's intersection with Sevilla is the monument known as **La Diana Cazadora** (Diana the Huntress; Map p82; cnr Paseo de la Reforma & Sevilla), a 1942 bronze sculpture actually meant to represent the Archer of the North Star. The League of Decency under the Ávila Camacho administration had the sculptor add a loincloth to the buxom figure, and it wasn't removed until 1966.

A 2003 addition to the Mexico City skyline, the **Torre Mayor** (Map p82; ☑ 55-5283-8000; www.torremayor.com.mx; Paseo de la Reforma 505; Ⓜ Chapultepec) stands like a sentinel before the gate to Bosque de Chapultepec. The earthquake-resistant structure, which soars 225m above the capital, is anchored below by 98 seismic-shock absorbers. Unfortunately the building's observation deck is permanently closed.

Across from the Torre Mayor is the **Torre BBVA Bancomer** (Bancomer Tower; Map p82; Paseo de la Reforma s/n; Ⓜ Chapultepec),

DON'T MISS

MEXICO CITY'S QUIRKY SIGHTS

Mucho Mundo Chocolate Museum (Map p82; www.mucho.org.mx; Milán 45, Colonia Juárez; adult/child M$70/45; ⊗11am-5pm; 🚇Reforma) A beautifully restored 1909 building houses Mucho Mundo, a museum and store celebrating all things chocolate. The permanent exhibit includes an enclosed room of 2981 chocolate discs covering four walls, and you'll also find various sculptures made of, you guessed it, chocolate. 'Xico,' a local artist's take on a Mexican hairless dog, watches over the museum courtyard.

Museo del Calzado El Borceguí (El Borceguí Shoe Museum; Map p68; 🖉55-5510-0627; www.elborcegui.com.mx/museo.htm; Bolívar 27; ⊗10am-2pm & 3-6pm; Ⓜ Zócalo) At this shoe museum – and the oldest shoemaker in Mexico, operating since 1865 – there are more than 2000 pieces of footwear on show, many from famous feet such as Mexican authors Carlos Fuentes and Elena Poniatowska, Louis XIV of France and Queen Elizabeth II, plus Magic Johnson's size 14½ basketball shoes and Neil Armstrong's lunar boots. Fashionistas and fetishists will delight at the styles organized by decades. Who doesn't want to see Japanese sandals made of rice hay?

Museo del Juguete Antiguo México (Antique Toy Museum; 🖉55-5588-2100; www.museodeljuguete.mx; Dr Olvera 15, cnr Eje Central Lázaro Cárdenas; M$75; ⊗9am-6pm Mon-Fri, to 4pm Sat, 10am-4pm Sun; ⓅⓌ; Ⓜ Obrera) Mexican-born Japanese collector Roberto Shimizu has amassed more than a million toys in his lifetime, and this museum showcases about 60,000 pieces, ranging from life-size robots to tiny action figures. Shimizu himself designed many of the unique display cases from recycled objects.

Santa Muerte Altar (Alfarería, north of Mineros; ⊗rosary service 5pm, 1st day of the month; Ⓜ Tepito) Often garbed in a sequined white gown, wearing a dark wig and clutching a scythe in her bony hand, the Saint Death figure bears an eerie resemblance to Mrs Bates from the film *Psycho*. The Santa Muerte is the object of a fast-growing cult in Mexico, particularly in Tepito, where many of her followers have lost faith in Catholicism. Enter the notoriously dangerous Tepito 'hood at your own risk; the once-safe rosary service is no longer held following a shooting in 2016. It's three blocks north of metro Tepito.

Museo de la Tortura (Museum of Torture; Map p68; 🖉55-5521-4651; Tacuba 15; adult/student M$60/45; ⊗10am-6pm Mon-Fri, to 7pm Sat & Sun; Ⓜ Allende) Displaying European torture instruments from the 14th to 19th centuries, including a metal-spiked interrogation chair and the skull splitter, this museum has surefire appeal for the morbidly curious.

---

a bank's 50-story skyscraper that became Mexico's tallest building upon its completion in 2015, with sky gardens every nine floors. It was outdone in 2016 by wedge-shaped **Torre Reforma** (Map p82; Reforma 483; Ⓜ Chapultepec) across the road, now the city's tallest edifice. Nearby, the 104m-high **Estela de Luz** (Pillar of Light; Map p82; Paseo de la Reforma s/n; Ⓜ Chapultepec) was built to commemorate Mexico's bicentennial anniversary in 2010, though due to delays in construction and rampant overspending, the quartz-paneled light tower wasn't inaugurated until 2012. After eight former government officials were arrested in 2013 for misuse of public funds, it became known as the 'tower of corruption.' In the tower's basement you'll find the **Centro de Cultura Digital** (Map p82; 🖉55-1000-2637; www.centro culturadigital.mx; Estela de Luz, Paseo de Reforma s/n; ⊗11am-7pm Tue-Sun; Ⓜ Chapultepec) **FREE**, a hit-and-miss cultural center with expositions focusing on digital technology.

Metro Hidalgo accesses Paseo de la Reforma at the Alameda end, while the Insurgentes and Sevilla stations provide the best approach from the Zona Rosa. On the Insurgentes metrobús route, the 'Reforma' and 'Hamburgo' stops lie north and south of the avenue respectively. Along Reforma itself, any westbound 'Auditorio' bus goes through the Bosque de Chapultepec, while 'Chapultepec' buses terminate at the east end of the park at the **Chapultepec Bus Terminal** (Map p82). In the opposite direction, 'I Verdes' and 'La Villa' buses head up Reforma to the Alameda Central and beyond.

Zona Rosa

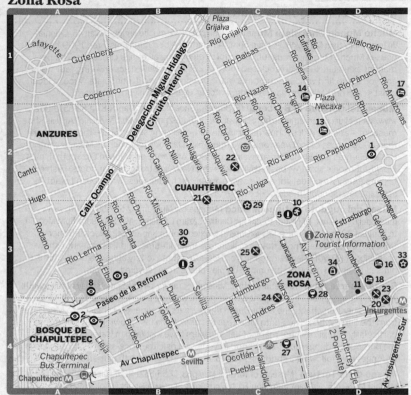

👁 Zona Rosa

Wedged between Paseo de la Reforma and Avenida Chapultepec, the 'Pink Zone' was developed as an international playground and shopping district during the 1950s, when it enjoyed a cosmopolitan panache. Since then, however, the Zona Rosa has been in gradual decline and has lost ground to more fashionable neighborhoods such as Condesa and Roma. It's now a hodgepodge of touristy boutiques, high-end hotels, clubs and fast-food franchises, though major 2017 refurbishments have provided wider, cleaner, more pedestrian-friendly streets, with the busy *glorieta* area around metro and metrobús Insurgentes seeing lit-up fountains and large CDMX signs for photo ops to create a sense of civic pride.

People-watching from its sidewalk cafes reveals a higher degree of diversity than elsewhere: it's one of the city's premier gay and lesbian districts and an expat magnet, with a significant Korean population (and associated Korean, Japanese and Chinese restaurants that outshine Chinatown). The pedestrianized Calle Génova corridor was earthquake damaged on the Reforma end, keeping the surrounding area closed until the planned demolition of a building for 2018. The southern end continues to get more polished with new bowl-food joints, and beauty product and gadget stores in an attempt to keep the zone in the pink.

Museo del Objeto del Objeto MUSEUM
(Museum of Objects; Map p86; www.elmodo. mx; Colima 145; adult/student/child under 12yr M$50/25/free; ⊙10am-6pm Tue-Sun; 🚊Durango) Packing a collection of nearly 100,000 pieces, some as old as the Mexican War of Independence (1810), this two-story design museum tells unique versions of Mexican history by compiling objects for thematic exhibits such as *fútbol* in Mexico. The

◉ Condesa

Colonia Condesa's striking architecture, palm-lined esplanades and joyful parks echo its origins as a haven for a newly emerging elite in the early 20th century. Mention 'La Condesa' today and most people think of it as a trendy area of informal restaurants, hip boutiques and hot nightspots. Fortunately much of the neighborhood's old flavor remains, especially for those willing to wander outside the valet-parking zones. Stroll the pedestrian medians along Ámsterdam, Avenida Tamaulipas or Avenida Mazatlán to admire art deco and California colonial-style buildings. The focus is the peaceful **Parque México**, the oval shape of which reflects its earlier use as a horse-racing track. Two blocks northwest is **Parque España**, which has a children's play area.

◉ Roma

Northeast of Condesa, Roma is a bohemian enclave in the rapid process of gentrification. Once inhabited by artists and writers, it's now also the home of designer labels and international dining, while still retaining its slower pace in the backstreets. This is where Beat writers William S Burroughs and Jack Kerouac naturally gravitated during their 1950s sojourn in Mexico City. Built at the turn of the 20th century, the neighborhood is a showcase for Parisian-influenced architecture, which was favored by the Porfirio Díaz regime. Some of the most outstanding examples stand along Colima and Tabasco. When in Roma linger in the cafes and check out the art galleries and specialty shops along Colima. A stroll down Orizaba passes two lovely plazas – Río de Janeiro, with a statue replica of Michelangelo's *David*, and Luis Cabrera, which has beautiful fountains (Beat writers once posed for a photo here). On weekends inspect the **Bazar de Cuauhtémoc** (Tianguis de Antigüedades; Map p86; Jardín Dr Chávez, Colonia Doctores; ☉10am-5pm Sat & Sun; ☐ Jardín Pushkin), an antique market in a small park – walk to the eastern end of Álvaro Obregón, the Roma's main thoroughfare, then one block north along Avenida Cuauhtémoc.

Small, independent art galleries and museums are scattered around Roma. Select 'Roma' from the website CDMX Travel (http://cdmxtravel.com) to view gallery listings.

permanent collection groups together items such as matchboxes, printing stamps and plenty of tins – for tobacco, shoe polish and gramophone needles. Many of the items are viewable on the website.

Centro de Cultura Casa Lamm ARTS CENTER
(Map p86; ☑55-5525-1332; www.galeriacasa lamm.com.mx; Álvaro Obregón 99, Colonia Roma; ☉10am-7pm Mon-Sat, to 5pm Sun; ☐Álvaro Obregón) **FREE** This cultural complex contains a gallery for contemporary Mexican painting and photography as well as an excellent art library.

MUCA Roma MUSEUM
(Map p86; ☑55-5511-0925; www.mucaroma.unam. mx; Tonalá 51; ☉10am-7pm Tue-Sun; ☐Durango) **FREE** Sponsored by the Universidad Nacional Autónoma de México (UNAM), this small university museum exhibits Mexican and international contemporary art with ties to science or new technology.

Zona Rosa

◉ Bosque de Chapultepec

Chapultepec (Náhuatl for 'Hill of Grasshoppers') served as a refuge for the wandering Aztecs before becoming a summer residence for their noble class. It was the nearest freshwater supply for Tenochtitlán. In the 15th century Nezahualcóyotl, ruler of nearby Texcoco, oversaw the construction of an aqueduct to channel its waters over Lago de Texcoco to the pre-Hispanic capital.

Today Mexico City's largest park, the Bosque de Chapultepec, covers more than 4 sq km, with lakes and several excellent museums. It also remains an abode of Mexico's high and mighty, containing the current presidential residence, **Los Pinos** (Map p90; ☑ 55-5093-53-00; Parque Lira s/n; ☺ 8am-10pm Mon-Fri; Ⓜ Constituyentes), and a former imperial palace, the Castillo de Chapultepec.

Sunday is the park's big day, as vendors line the main paths and throngs of families come to picnic, navigate the lake on rowboats and crowd into the museums. Most of the major attractions are in or near the eastern **1a Sección** (1st Section; Map p90; www.chapultepec.org.mx; Bosque de Chapultepec; ☺ 5am-6pm Tue-Sun; Ⓜ Chapultepec), while a large amusement park and children's museum dominate the 2da Sección.

A pair of bronze lions overlooks the main gate at Paseo de la Reforma and Lieja. Other access points are opposite the Museo Tamayo, Museo Nacional de Antropología and by metro Chapultepec. The fence along Paseo de la Reforma serves as the **Galería Abierta de las Rejas de Chapultepec** (Map p90; Paseo de la Reforma; ☺ 24hr) FREE, an outdoor photo gallery.

Chapultepec metro station is at the east end of the Bosque de Chapultepec, near the Monumento a los Niños Héroes and Castillo de Chapultepec. Auditorio metro station is on the north side of the park, 500m west of the Museo Nacional de Antropología. 'Auditorio' buses travel along the length of Paseo de la Reforma.

The 2da Sección of the Bosque de Chapultepec lies west of the Periférico. To get to the 2da Sección and La Feria amusement park from metro Chapultepec, find the 'Paradero' exit and catch a 'Feria' bus at the top of the stairs. These depart continuously and travel nonstop to the 2da Sección, dropping off riders at the Papalote Museo del Niño and La Feria. In addition to family attractions, there's a pair of upscale lake-view restaurants on Lago Mayor and Lago Menor.

★Museo Nacional de Antropología
MUSEUM

(National Museum of Anthropology; Map p90; ☑ 55-4040- 5300; www.mna.inah.gob.mx; cnr Paseo de la Reforma & Calz Gandhi; adult/child under 13yr M$70/free; ⏱ 9am-7pm Tue-Sun; P; M Auditorio) This world-class museum stands in an extension of the Bosque de Chapultepec. Its long, rectangular courtyard is surrounded on three sides by two-level display halls. The 12 ground-floor *salas* (halls) are dedicated to pre-Hispanic Mexico, while upper-level *salas* show how Mexico's indigenous descendants live today, with the contemporary cultures located directly above their ancestral civilizations. The vast museum offers more than most people can absorb in a single visit.

Everything is superbly displayed, with much explanatory text translated into English. At the entrance, you will find the starting point for free one-hour guided tours (four daily except Sunday, 10:30am to 5pm; reservation recommended) in English, which are worthwhile to make sense of Mexico's complicated history.

The best place to start is the Introducción a la Antropología and work counterclockwise from there. The first few halls are introductions to anthropology in general, and demonstrate how the hemisphere's earliest settlers got here and developed from nomadic hunting life to a more settled farming existence in Mexico's central highlands.

Many short-on-time visitors jump straight into the Teotihuacán hall displaying models and objects from the Americas' first great and powerful state. This then moves into the Los Toltecas, which displays one of the four basalt warrior columns from Tula's Temple of Tlahuizcalpantecuhtli.

The next hall is devoted to the Mexica, aka Aztecs. Come here to see the famous sun stone, unearthed beneath the Zócalo in 1790, and other magnificent sculptures from the pantheon of Aztec deities.

The halls that follow display the fine legacy of civilizations from Oaxaca and the Gulf of Mexico, including two stone Olmec head carvings weighing in at almost 20 tonnes.

If you rush through the Maya exhibits from Mexico, Guatemala, Belize and Honduras, be sure not to miss the breathtaking full-scale replica of the tomb of King Pakal, discovered deep in the Templo de las Inscripciones at Palenque.

The giant column fountain in the courtyard is known as *el paraguas* (the umbrella) and acts as a reminder of the connection to nature. Each side depicts a different sculpture – east showing the integration of Mexico; west, outward-looking Mexico; and north and south, the fight for liberty in Mexico's villages.

In a clearing about 100m in front of the museum's entrance, indigenous Totonac people perform their spectacular *voladores* rite – 'flying' from a 20m-high pole – every 30 minutes.

Castillo de Chapultepec
CASTLE

(Chapultepec Castle; Map p90; www.castillode chapultepec.inah.gob.mx; Bosque de Chapultepec; M$51, Sun free; ⏱ 9am-5pm Tue-Sun; M Chapultepec) A visible reminder of Mexico's bygone aristocracy, the 'castle' that stands atop Chapultepec Hill was begun in 1785 but not completed until after independence, when it became the national military academy. When Emperor Maximilian and Empress Carlota arrived in 1864, they refurbished it as their residence. The east end of the castle preserves their palace, with sumptuously furnished salons opening onto an exterior deck that affords sweeping city views.

The castle sheltered Mexico's presidents until 1939 when President Lázaro Cárdenas converted it into the **Museo Nacional de Historia** (National History Museum; Map p90; ☑ 55-4040-5215; www.mnh.inah.gob.mx; Parque de Chapultepec; adult/child under 13yr M$70/free; ⏱ 9am-5pm Tue-Sun).

On the upper floor, the opulent rooms are the work of Porfirio Díaz, who in the late 19th-century was the first president to use the castle as residences. In the center is a patio where a tower marks the top of Chapultepec Hill, 45m above street level.

To reach the castle, follow the road that curves up the hill behind the Monumento a los Niños Héroes. Alternatively, a trainlike vehicle (M$15 round trip) runs up every 15 minutes when the castle is open. Audio guides in English are available for M$65.

Kurimanzutto Gallery
GALLERY

(Map p90; www.kurimanzutto.com; Gobernador Rafael Rebollar 94, Colonia San Miguel Chapultepec; ⏱ 11am-6pm Tue-Thu, to 4pm Fri & Sat; M Constituyentes) FREE One of the city's most cutting-edge contemporary art galleries, temporary exhibits here showcase the works of up-and-coming talent from Mexico and abroad. Acclaimed Mexican artist Gabriel Orozco, one of more than 30 people represented by the gallery, helped to conceive the concept of Kurimanzutto with co-founders Jose Kuri

Roma & Condesa

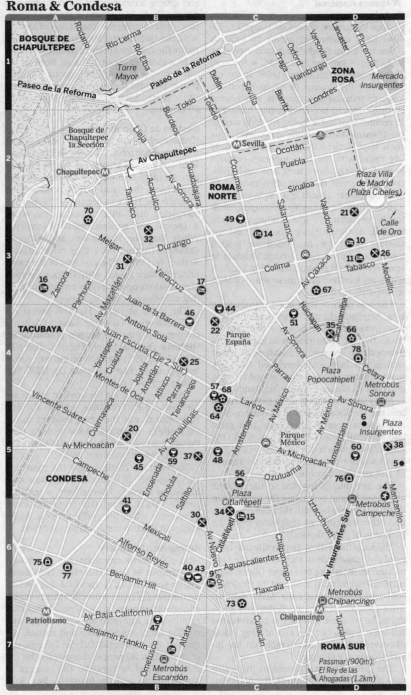

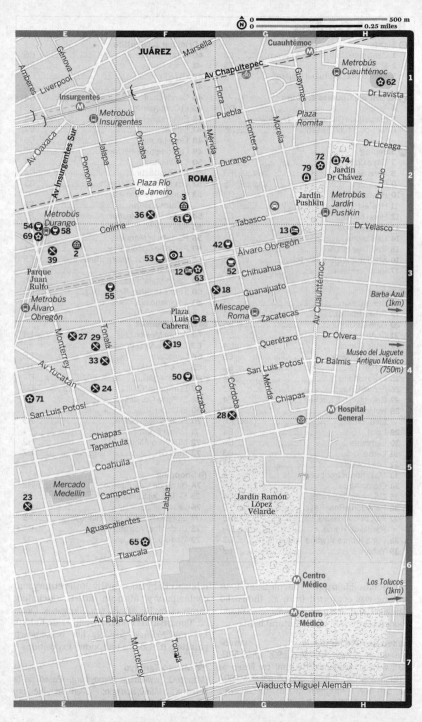

MEXICO CITY

0 — 500 m
0 — 0.25 miles

Roma & Condesa

and Monica Manzutto. The pleasant 1949 building was converted from an industrial patisserie and features expansive exposed wooden beams and lots of natural light.

Museo de Arte Moderno　MUSEUM
(Museum of Modern Art; Map p90; ☏55-5211-8331; www.museoartemoderno.com; cnr Paseo de la Reforma & Calz Gandhi; adult/student M$60/free, Sun free; ⊙10:15am-5:30pm Tue-Sun; Ⓟ; ⓂChapultepec) The small collection here ex-

hibits work by noteworthy 20th-century and contemporary Mexican artists, including canvases by Dr Atl, Rivera, Siqueiros, Orozco, Tamayo and O'Gorman, and Frida Kahlo's *Las dos Fridas,* possibly her best-known painting. It also has temporary expositions.

★**Museo Tamayo**　MUSEUM
(Map p90; www.museotamayo.org; Paseo de la Reforma 51; M$60, Sun free; ⊙10am-6pm Tue-Sun; Ⓟ; ⓂAuditorio) A multilevel structure built

to house international modern art, donated by Oaxaca-born painter Rufino Tamayo to the people of Mexico. The museum exhibits cutting-edge works from around the globe, which are thematically arranged with shows from the Tamayo collection. The renovated Tamayo has a new rustic-chic restaurant overlooking the park, an ideal breakfast stop before exploring Chapultepec's sights.

Jardín Botánico
GARDENS

(Botanical Garden; Map p90; ☑ 55-5553-8114; Paseo de la Reforma; ☺ 10am-5:30pm Mon-Fri, to 4pm Sat & Sun; Ⓜ Chapultepec) FREE Highlighting Mexico's plant diversity, this 4-hectare complex in Chapultepec is divided into sections that reflect the country's varied climatic zones. There are plenty of cacti and agave, and children might enjoy the straw creepy-crawly statues. The garden also features a greenhouse full of rare orchids.

Monumento a Los Niños Héroes
MONUMENT

(Map p90; Bosque de Chapultepec; ☺ Tue-Sun; Ⓜ Chapultepec) The six marble columns marking Chapultepec park's eastern entrance commemorate the 'boy heroes,' six young cadets who perished in battle. On September 13, 1847, 8000 US troops stormed Castillo de Chapultepec, which then housed the national military academy. Mexican General Santa Anna retreated before the onslaught, but the youths, aged 13 to 20, chose to defend the castle. Legend has it one of them, Juan Escutia, wrapped himself in a Mexican flag and leaped to his death rather than surrender.

Papalote Museo del Niño
MUSEUM

(Map p90; ☑ 55-5237-1773; www.papalote.org. mx; Bosque de Chapultepec; museum/planetarium M$199/99, family of 4 package M$849; ☺ 9am-6pm Mon-Wed & Fri, to 11pm Thu, 10am-7pm Sat & Sun; P ♿; Ⓜ Constituyentes) Your children won't want to leave this innovative, hands-on museum. Here kids can put together a radio program, channel their inner mad scientist, join an archaeological dig and try out all kinds of technological gadgets and games. Little ones also get a kick out of the planetarium and IMAX theater. Parking is M$20 per hour.

La Feria
AMUSEMENT PARK

(Map p90; ☑ 55-5230-2121; www.laferia.com.mx; Bosque de Chapultepec; M$200; ☺ 11am-6pm Tue-Fri, 10am-8pm Sat & Sun; P ♿; Ⓜ Constituyentes) An old-fashioned amusement park with some hair-raising rides. The Platino pass is good for everything, including La Feria's best roller coasters. Check the website

for current opening times as they change throughout the month.

Museo Jardín del Agua
PUBLIC ART

(Water Garden Museum; Map p90; ☑ 55-5281-5382; Bosque de Chapultepec; M$24; ☺ 9am-6pm Tue-Sun; Ⓜ Constituyentes) Diego Rivera painted a series of murals for the inauguration of Cárcamo de Dolores, Chapultepec's waterworks facility built in the 1940s. Experimenting with waterproof paints, Rivera covered the collection tank, sluice gates and part of the pipeline with images of amphibious beings and workers involved in the project.

Outside the building, you can't miss another of Rivera's extraordinary works, **Fuente de Tláloc**, an oval pool inhabited by a huge mosaic-skinned sculpture of the Aztec god of water, rain and fertility. About 150m north is the beautiful Fuente de Xochipilli, dedicated to the Aztec 'flower prince,' with terraced fountains around a pyramid in the *talud-tablero* style typical of Teotihuacán. Hold on to your ticket as it includes entry to the nearby Museo de Historia Natural (Natural History Museum; p56).

Fuente de Xochipilli
FOUNTAIN

(Map p90) This complex of cascade fountains opened in 1964, featuring architecture inspired by Tenochca (of Tenochtitlan) style with eagle-warrior heads and sloping walls. It was recently renovated.

◉ Polanco

The affluent neighborhood of Polanco, north of Bosque de Chapultepec, arose in the 1940s as a residential alternative for a burgeoning middle class anxious to escape the overcrowded *centro*. Metro Polanco is in the center of the neighborhood, while metro Auditorio lies at its southern edge.

Polanco is known as a Jewish enclave and also for its exclusive hotels, fine restaurants and designer stores along Avenida Presidente Masaryk. Some of the city's most prestigious museums and art galleries are here or in nearby Bosque de Chapultepec (p84).

Museo Jumex
MUSEUM

(Map p90; www.fundacionjumex.org; Blvd Miguel de Cervantes Saavedra 303, Colonia Ampliación Granada; adult/student & child M$50/free, Sun free; ☺ 11am-8pm Tue-Sun; P) Museo Jumex was built to house one of Latin America's leading contemporary art collections. Temporary exhibits draw on a collection of around 2600 pieces from renowned Mexican and

Bosque de Chapultepec & Polanco

4
17
16
33

Instituto
Nacional de
Migración

Av Ejército Nacional

LOS
MORALES

Horacio

Homero

Av Ferrocarril de Cuernavaca

Solón

Plinio

Sófocles

Cicerón

Séneca

Shaw

Av Molière

Ibsen

Goldsmith

Edgar Allan Poe

Calderón de la Barca

Lafontaine

France

Dumas

Tennyson

Eugenio Sue

Aristóteles

Galileo

Parque
América

Horacio

24

8

29

Anatole

Musset

Paseo de las Palmas

Molière

Ibsen

Av Castelar

27

Dickens

Av Presidente Masaryk

23

Oscar
Wilde

34

Verne

POLANCO

Newton

Campos Elíseos

Monte Elbruz

Parque Lincoln

Urbina

Montes Urales

Anatole
France

Dumas

Campos Elíseos

20

22

Andrés Bello

Paseo de la Reforma

Paseo de la Reforma

Av Prado Sur

Pedregal

30

31

LOMAS DE
CHAPULTEPEC

Alicama

Aguila y Seixas

Blvd López Mateos

Calz Molino del Rey

Calz Chivatito

Bosque de
Chapultepec
2a Sección

Lago
Mayor

11

6

Paseo de los Compositores

Margen
Oriente

15

Panteón
Civil de
Dolores

18

Lago
Menor

Terminal de Autobuses
del Poniente (3km)

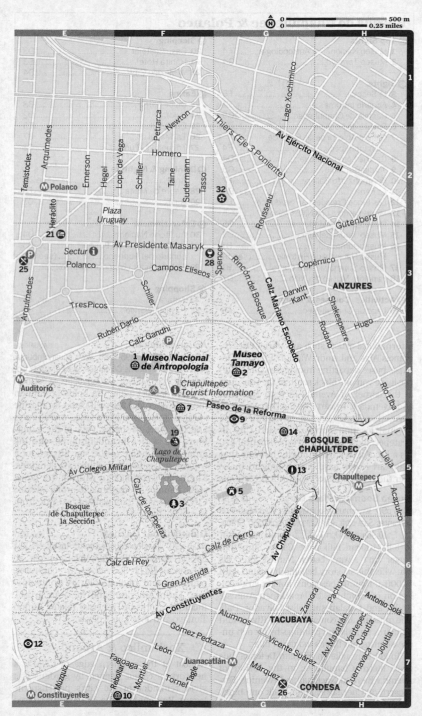

0 — 500 m
0 — 0.25 miles

E **F** **G** **H**

Lago Xochimilco

Av Ejército Nacional

Thiers (Eje 3 Poniente)

Newton

Petrarca

Homero

Arquímedes

Temístocles

Emerson

Hegel

Lope de Vega

Schiller

Taine

Sudermann

Tasso

Rousseau

32

Gutenberg

Heráclito

M Polanco

Plaza
Uruguay

21

Copérnico

ANZURES

Av Presidente Masaryk

Sectur **i**
Polanco

28

Spencer

Rincón del Bosque

Calz Mariano Escobedo

Darwin

Kant

Shakespeare

Rodano

Hugo

25

Campos Elíseos

Schiller

Tres Picos

Arquímedes

Rubén Darío

Calz Gandhi

P

1 **Museo Nacional
de Antropología**

**Museo
Tamayo**
2

Río Elba

M
Auditorio

Chapultepec
Tourist Information **i**

7

Paseo de la Reforma

9

14

**BOSQUE DE
CHAPULTEPEC**

19

Lago de
Chapultepec

Liela

Chapultepec
M

Acapulco

Av Colegio Militar

Calz de los Poetas

13

3

5

Av Chapultepec

Melgar

**Bosque
de Chapultepec
la Sección**

Calz de Cerro

Calz del Rey

Gran Avenida

Zamora

Pachuca

Antonio Solá

12

Av Constituyentes

Alumnos

TACUBAYA

Av Mazatlán

Yautepec

Cuautla

Jojutla

Gómez Pedraza

León

Vicente Suárez

Fagoaga

Montiel

Juanacatlán **M**

Márquez

Cuernavaca

Tagle

Tornel

26

CONDESA

M Constituyentes

10

Bosque de Chapultepec & Polanco

international artists such as Gabriel Orozco, Francis Alys and Andy Warhol. 'Ejército Defensa' buses departing from metro Chapultepec leave you one block south of the museum at the corner of Avenida Ejército Nacional and Avenida Ferrocarril de Cuernavaca.

Another Jumex branch, in the museum's original location north of Mexico City in Ecatepec, focuses on more experimental art. It's a bit of a trek from the city, but one that many art lovers have been willing to make over the years. See the website for directions.

Museo Soumaya Plaza Carso MUSEUM
(Map p90; www.museosoumaya.org; Blvd Miguel de Cervantes Saavedra 303, Colonia Ampliación Granada; ⊙10:30am-6:30pm) FREE Someone ought to tell Mexican billionaire Carlos Slim that bigger isn't always better. Named after his late wife, this six-story behemoth (plated with 16,000 aluminum hexagons) holds a large collection of sculptures by Frenchman Auguste Rodin and Catalan surrealist Salvador Dalí. The museum also contains worthy Rivera and Siqueiros murals and paintings by French impressionists, but there's too much filler.

To get here take an 'Ejército Defensa' bus from metro Chapultepec to the corner of Avenida Ejército Nacional and Avenida Ferrocarril de Cuernavaca, then walk one block north.

Acuario Inbursa AQUARIUM
(Map p90; ☑55-5395-4586; www.acuarioinbursa.com.mx; Av Miguel de Cervantes Saavedra 386, Colonia Polanco; M$195; ⊙10am-6pm; ⓜPolanco) Mexico's largest aquarium holds 1.6 million liters of water and 280 well-cared-for marine species, including barracuda, manta rays and five types of sharks. Four of the aquarium's five stories lie underground, with the ground level home to the star attraction: a colony of Gentoo and chinstrap penguins. The tanks were built to withstand a large-scale temblor in earthquake-prone Mexico City. It's about a 2km walk or taxi ride from metro Polanco.

Galeria López Quiroga GALLERY
(Map p90; www.lopezquiroga.com; Aristóteles 169, Colonia Polanco; ⊙10am-7pm Mon-Fri, to 2pm Sat; ⓜPolanco) FREE Specializes in sculptures, paintings and photography by contemporary Latin American and Mexican artists, including works by Francisco Toledo, Rufino Tamayo and José Luis Cuevas.

⊙ Xochimilco & Around

Almost at the southern edge of CDMX, a network of canals flanked by gardens is a vivid reminder of the city's pre-Hispanic legacy. Remnants of the *chinampas* (raised fertile land where indigenous inhabitants grew their food), these 'floating gardens' are still in use today. Gliding along the canals in a fancifully decorated *trajinera* (gondola) is an alternately tranquil and festive experience. On weekends a fiesta atmosphere takes over as the waterways become jammed with boats carrying groups of families and friends. Local vendors and musicians hover alongside the partygoers, serving food and drink. Midweek, the mood is much calmer.

Xochimilco (Náhuatl for 'Place where Flowers Grow') was an early target of Aztec hegemony, probably due to its inhabitants' farming skills. The Xochimilcas piled up vegetation and mud in the shallow waters of Lake Xochimilco, a southern offshoot of Lago de Texcoco, to make the fertile gardens known as *chinampas,* which later became an economic base of the Aztec empire. As the *chinampas* proliferated, much of the lake was transformed into a series of canals. Approximately 180km of these waterways remain today. The *chinampas* are still under cultivation, mainly for garden plants and flowers such as poinsettias and marigolds. Owing to its cultural and historical significance, Xochimilco was designated a Unesco World Heritage site in 1987.

Though the canals are definitely the main attraction, Xochimilco has plenty to see. East of **Jardín Juárez** (Xochimilco *centro's* main square) is the 16th-century **Parroquia de San Bernardino de Siena**, with elaborate gold-painted *retablos* (altarpieces) and a tree-studded atrium. South of the plaza, the bustling **Mercado de Xochimilco** covers two vast buildings: the one nearer the Jardín Juárez has fresh produce and an eating 'annex' for *tamales* (corn-based snacks with various fillings) and various prepared food; the other sells flowers, *chapulines* (grasshoppers), sweets and excellent *barbacoa* (savory barbecued mutton).

Xochimilco also boasts several visitor-friendly *pulquerías* (*pulque* bars), and about 3km west of Jardín Juárez is one of the city's best collection of Diego Rivera works, **Museo Dolores Olmedo** (🖉 55-5555-1221; www.museo doloresolmedo.org.mx; Av México 5843; M$100, Tue free; ⏲ 10am-6pm Tue-Sun; 🖭; 🚊 La Noria), which also has paintings by Frida Kahlo.

To reach Xochimilco, take metro line 2 to the Tasqueña station then follow the signs inside the station to the transfer point for the *tren ligero*, a light-rail system that extends to neighborhoods not reachable by metro. Xochimilco is the last stop. Upon exiting the station, turn left (north) and follow Avenida Morelos to the market, Jardín Juárez and the church. If you don't feel like walking, bicycle taxis will shuttle you to the *embarcaderos* (boat landings) for M$30.

Xochimilco Canals   HISTORIC SITE
(Xochimilco; boats per hour M$500, boat taxis one way per person M$30; 🅿 🖭; 🚊 Xochimilco) Hundreds of colorful *trajineras* (gondolas) await passengers at the village's 10 *embarcaderos* (jetties) to paddle you through the waterways dotted with birdlife and hedged by patchy trees. The tranquil city escape is only broken by the odd party boat or food and drink touts gliding up alongside – all part of the experience. Nearest to the center are Belem, Salitre and San Cristóbal, about 400m east of the plaza, and Fernando Celada, 400m west of the plaza on Avenida Guadalupe Ramírez.

On Saturday and Sunday, 60-person *lanchas colectivas* (boat taxis) run between the Salitre embarcadero and the Nativitas embarcadero (near the corner of Av Hermenegildo Galeana and Calle del Mercado) 1.4km southeast along the canal.

Boats seat from one to 20 people, making large group outings relatively cheap. Before boarding the *trajinera,* you can buy beer, soft drinks and food from vendors at the *embarcaderos* if you fancy an onboard picnic while cruising.

The official hourly price is fixed and per boat, not per person, so beware of markups.

◉ San Ángel

Settled by the Dominican order soon after the Spanish conquest, San Ángel, 12km southwest of the center, maintains its colonial splendor despite being engulfed by the metropolis. It's often associated with the big Saturday crafts market (p132) held alongside the Plaza San Jacinto. Though the main approach via Avenida Insurgentes is typically chaotic, wander westward to experience the old village's cobblestoned soul – it's a tranquil enclave of colonial-era mansions with massive wooden doors, potted geraniums behind window grills and bougainvillea spilling over stone walls.

La Bombilla station of the Avenida Insurgentes metrobús is about 500m east of the Plaza San Jacinto. Otherwise catch a bus from metro Miguel Ángel de Quevedo, 1km east, or from metro Barranca del Muerto, 1.5km north along Avenida Revolución.

San Ángel

San Ángel

⊚ **Top Sights**

1 Museo Casa Estudio Diego Rivera y
Frida Kahlo...A1

⊚ **Sights**

2 Jardín de la Bombilla..............................C2
3 Monumento a Álvaro Obregón..............C2
4 Museo Casa del Risco.............................B3
5 Museo de Arte Carrillo Gil....................B2
6 Museo de El Carmen................................B2
7 Parroquia de San Jacinto.......................B3
8 Plaza San Jacinto.....................................B3

⊗ **Eating**

9 Barbacoa de Santiago.............................B3
10 Cluny...B2
11 El Cardenal San Ángel............................C2

12 Montejo Sureste.......................................C2
13 San Ángel Inn...A2
14 Taberna del León.....................................A4

⊖ **Drinking & Nightlife**

15 La Camelia...B3

⊕ **Entertainment**

16 Centro Cultural Helénico.......................B1

⊖ **Shopping**

17 Bazar Sábado..B3
18 Gandhi..D2
19 Jardín del Arte El Carmen.....................B2
20 Jardín del Arte San Ángel......................B3
21 Plaza Loreto..B4

Plaza San Jacinto PLAZA
(Map p94; San Ángel Centro; 🚇 La Bombilla) Every
Saturday the Bazar Sábado (p132) brings
masses of color and crowds of people to this

San Ángel square, 500m west of Avenida
Insurgentes. **Museo Casa del Risco** (Map
p94; ☎55-5550-9286; www.museocasadelrisco.
org.mx; Plaza San Jacinto 15; ⊙10am-5pm Tue-

Sun) FREE is midway along the plaza's north side. The elaborate fountain in the courtyard is a mad mosaic of Talavera tile and Chinese porcelain. Upstairs is a treasure trove of Mexican baroque and medieval European paintings. About 50m west of the plaza is the 16th-century **Parroquia de San Jacinto** (Map p94; 55-5616-2059; Plaza San Jacinto 18-Bis, Colonia San Angel; ⊙8am-8pm) and its peaceful gardens.

★ **Museo Casa Estudio Diego Rivera y Frida Kahlo** MUSEUM
(Diego Rivera & Frida Kahlo Studio Museum; Map p94; 55-5550-1518; www.estudiodiegorivera.bellasartes.gob.mx; cnr Av Altavista & Diego Rivera; adult/student M$30/free, Sun free, camera use M$30; ⊙10am-5:30pm Tue-Sun; La Bombilla) If you saw the movie *Frida,* you'll recognize this museum, designed by Frida Kahlo and Diego Rivera's friend, architect and painter Juan O'Gorman. The artistic couple called this place home from 1934 to 1940. Frida, Diego and O'Gorman each had their own separate house: Rivera's abode preserves his upstairs studio, while Frida's (the blue one) and O'Gorman's have been cleared out for temporary exhibits.

Across the street is the San Ángel Inn (p119). Now housing a prestigious restaurant, the former *pulque* hacienda is historically significant as the place where Pancho Villa and Emiliano Zapata agreed to divide control of the country in 1914. It's a 2km walk or taxi ride from metrobús La Bombilla.

Museo de El Carmen MUSEUM
(Map p94; 55-5550-4896; http://elcarmen.inah.gob.mx; Av Revolución 4; adult/child under 13yr M$55/free, Sun free; ⊙10am-5pm Tue-Sun; La Bombilla) A storehouse of magnificent sacred art in a former school run by the Carmelite order. The collection includes oils by Mexican master Cristóbal de Villalpando, though the big draw is the collection of mummies in the crypt. Thought to be the bodies of 17th-century benefactors of the order, they were uncovered during the revolution by Zapatistas looking for buried treasure.

Museo de Arte Carrillo Gil MUSEUM
(Map p94; 55-5550-6289; www.museodeartecarrillogil.com; Av Revolución 1608, cnr Pabellón Altavista; M$45, Sun free; ⊙10am-6pm Tue-Sun; P; Altavista) One of the city's first contemporary-art spaces, this San Ángel museum was founded by Yucatecan businessman Álvaro Carrillo Gil to store a large collection he had amassed over many years. Long ramps in the building lead up to cutting-edge temporary exhibits and some lesser-known works by Diego Rivera, José Clemente Orozco and David Alfaro Siqueiros.

Jardín de la Bombilla PARK
(Map p94; btwn Av de la Paz & Josefina Prior, Colonia San Ángel; La Bombilla) In this tropically abundant, pruned park spreading east of Avenida Insurgentes, paths encircle the **Monumento a Álvaro Obregón**, a monolithic shrine to the post-revolutionary Mexican president. The monument was built to house the revolutionary general's arm, lost in the 1915 Battle of Celaya, but the limb was cremated in 1989.

'La Bombilla' was the name of the restaurant where Obregón was assassinated in 1928. The killer, José de León Toral, was involved in the Cristero rebellion against the government's anti-church policies. In July the park explodes with color as the main venue for La Feria de las Flores (p105), a major flower festival.

⊙ Ciudad Universitaria

Two kilometers south of San Ángel, the **Ciudad Universitaria** (University City; www.unam.mx; Centro Cultural Universitario) is the main campus of the Universidad Nacional Autónoma de México (UNAM). With about 330,000 students and 38,000 teachers, it's Latin America's largest university. Five former Mexican presidents are among its alumni, as is Carlos Slim, ranked the world's second-richest person in 2015, and Alfonso Cuarón, the first Latin-American to win a director's Oscar (for *Gravity*).

Founded in 1551 as the Royal and Papal University of Mexico, UNAM is the second-oldest university in the Americas. It occupied various buildings in the center of town until the campus was transferred to its current location in the 1950s. Although it is a public university open to all, UNAM remains 'autonomous,' meaning the government may not interfere in its academic policies. It is Mexico's leading research institute and has long been a center of political dissent.

An architectural showpiece, UNAM was placed on Unesco's list of World Heritage sites in 2007. Most of the faculty buildings are scattered at the north end. As you enter from Avenida Insurgentes, it's easy to spot the **Biblioteca Central** (Central Library), 10 stories high and covered with mosaics by Juan O'Gorman. The south wall, with two prominent zodiac wheels, covers colonial times, while the north wall deals with Aztec culture. **La Rectoría**, the administration building at the west end of the vast central lawn, has a vivid, three-dimensional Siqueiros mosaic on its south wall, showing students urged on by the people.

Across Avenida Insurgentes stands the **Estadio Olímpico** (☑ 55-5325-9000; Av Insurgentes Sur 3000, Ciudad Universitaria; ⬛CU), built of volcanic stone for the 1968 Olympics. With seating for over 72,000, it's home to UNAM's Pumas *fútbol* club, which competes in the national league's Primera División. Over the main entrance is Diego Rivera's sculpted mural on the theme of sports in Mexican history.

East of the university's main esplanade, the **Facultad de Medicina** (Faculty of Medicine) features an intriguing mosaic mural by Francisco Eppens on the theme of Mexico's *mestizaje* (blending of indigenous and European races).

A second section of the campus, about 2km south, contains the **Centro Cultural Universitario** (☑ 55-5622-7003; www.cultura. unam.mx; Av Insurgentes Sur 3000; ⬛ Centro Cultural Universitario), a cultural center with five theaters, two cinemas, the delightful Azul y Oro restaurant and two excellent museums.

To get to University City, take metrobús line 1 to the Centro Cultural Universitario (CCU) station, or go to metro Universidad and hop on the 'Pumabús,' a free on-campus bus. The Pumabús has limited service on weekends and holidays.

Museo Universitario Arte Contemporáneo   MUSEUM
(MUAC, ☑ 55-5622-6972; www.muac.unam.mx; Av Insurgentes Sur 3000, Centro Cultural Universitario; adult/student M$40/20; ☉ 10am-6pm Wed, Fri & Sun, to 8pm Thu & Sat; ℗; ⬛ Centro Cultural Universitario) Designed by veteran architect Teodoro González de León, the contemporary art museum's sloping, minimalist-style glass facade stands in stark contrast to the surrounding 1970s buildings. Inside you'll find cutting-edge temporary exhibitions occupying nine spacious halls with impressive lighting and high ceilings. The modern works include paintings, audio installations, sculptures and multimedia art from Mexico and abroad.

Museo Universitario de Ciencias   MUSEUM
(Universum; ☑ 55-5424-0694; www.universum. unam.mx; Circuito Cultural de Ciudad Universitaria s/n; adult/child M$70/60; ☉ 9am-6pm Mon-Fri, from

10am Sat & Sun; 🏃; ⬛ Centro Cultural Universitario) A huge science museum offering fun-filled attractions for kids, such as a planetarium and permanent exhibits that explore biodiversity, the human brain and much more. Nearby is the university **sculpture garden**, with a trail leading through volcanic fields past a dozen-or-so innovative pieces. The most formidable work is an enormous ring of concrete blocks by sculptor Mathias Goeritz.

⊙ Coyoacán

Coyoacán ('Place of Coyotes' in the Náhuatl language), about 10km south of downtown, was Cortés' base after the fall of Tenochtitlán. Only in recent decades has urban sprawl overtaken the outlying village. Coyoacán retains its restful identity, with narrow colonial-era streets, cafes and a lively atmosphere. Once home to Leon Trotsky and Frida Kahlo (whose houses are now fascinating museums), it has a decidedly countercultural vibe, most evident on weekends, when assorted musicians, mimes and crafts markets draw large but relaxed crowds to Coyoacán's central plazas.

The nearest metro stations to Coyoacán, 1.5km to 2km away, are Viveros, Coyoacán and General Anaya. If you don't fancy a walk, get off at Viveros station, walk south to Avenida Progreso and catch an eastbound 'Metro Gral Anaya' pesero (Mexico City name for a *colectivo*) to the market. Returning, 'Metro Viveros' peseros go west on Malintzin. 'Metro Coyoacán' and 'Metro Gral Anaya' peseros depart from the west side of Plaza Hidalgo.

San Ángel–bound peseros and buses head west on Avenida Miguel Ángel de Quevedo, five blocks south of Plaza Hidalgo.

★ Museo Frida Kahlo   MUSEUM
(Map p98; ☑ 55-5554-5999; www.museofrida kahlo.org.mx; Londres 247; adult Mon-Fri M$200, Sat & Sun M$220, student M$40, video guide M$80, camera use M$30; ☉ 10am-5:45pm Tue & Thu-Sun, from 11am Wed; Ⓜ Coyoacán) Renowned Mexican artist Frida Kahlo was born in, and lived and died in, Casa Azul (Blue House), now a museum. Almost every visitor to Mexico City makes a pilgrimage here to gain a deeper understanding of the painter (and maybe to pick up a Frida handbag). Arrive early to avoid the crowds, especially on weekends.

Built by Frida's father Guillermo three years before her birth, the house is littered with mementos and personal belongings that evoke her long, often tempestuous relationship with husband Diego Rivera and the leftist intellectual circle they often entertained here. Kitchen implements, jewelry, outfits, photos and other objects from the artist's everyday life are interspersed with art, as well as a variety of pre-Hispanic pieces and Mexican crafts. The collection was greatly expanded in 2007 after the discovery of a cache of previously unseen items that had been stashed in the attic.

Kahlo's art expresses the anguish of her existence as well as her flirtation with socialist icons: portraits of Lenin and Mao hang around her bed and, in another painting, *Retrato de la familia* (Family Portrait), the artist's Hungarian-Oaxacan roots are entangled.

Plaza Hidalgo & Jardín Centenario   PLAZA
(Map p98) The focus of Coyoacán life is its central plaza – actually two adjacent plazas: the **Jardín Centenario**, with the village's iconic coyotes frolicking in its central fountain; and the larger, cobblestoned **Plaza Hidalgo**, with a statue of the independence hero. It's the scene of most of the weekend fun when people congregate on its benches and in surrounding bars and restaurants.

The **Casa de Cortés** (Antiguo Palacio del Ayuntamiento de Coyoacán; Map p98; ☎55-5484-4500; Jardín Hidalgo 1, Colonia Coyoacán; ⊙8am-9pm; Ⓜ Coyoacán), on the north side of Plaza Hidalgo, is where conquistador Cortés established Mexico's first municipal seat during the siege

MEXICO CITY SIGHTS

FRIDA & DIEGO

A century after Frida Kahlo's birth, and more than 50 years after Diego Rivera's death, the pair's fame and recognition are stronger than ever. In 2007 a retrospective of Kahlo's work at the Palacio de Bellas Artes attracted more than 440,000 visitors. Though attendance at the Rivera survey that followed was not so phenomenal, the show reminded visitors that the prolific muralist had been an international star in his own lifetime. The artists are inseparably linked in memory, and both artists were frequent subjects in each other's work.

Rivera first met Kahlo, 21 years his junior, while painting at the Escuela Nacional Preparatoria, where she was a student in the early 1920s. Rivera was already at the forefront of Mexican art, and his commission at the school was the first of many semi-propaganda murals on public buildings that he was to execute over three decades. He had already fathered children by two Russian women in Europe, and in 1922 he married 'Lupe' Marín in Mexico. She bore him two more children before their marriage broke up in 1928.

Kahlo was born in Coyoacán in 1907 to a Hungarian-Jewish father and Oaxacan mother. She contracted polio at age six, leaving her right leg permanently thinner than her left. In 1925 she was horribly injured in a trolley accident that broke her right leg, collarbone, pelvis and ribs. She made a miraculous recovery but suffered much pain thereafter. It was during convalescence that she began painting. Pain – physical and emotional – was to be a dominating theme of her art.

Kahlo and Rivera both moved in left-wing artistic circles, and they met again in 1928. They married the following year. Frida's mother thought Diego was too old, fat, communist and atheist for her daughter, describing the liaison as 'a union between an elephant and a dove.' Their relationship was definitely always a passionate love-hate affair. Rivera wrote: 'If I ever loved a woman, the more I loved her, the more I wanted to hurt her. Frida was only the most obvious victim of this disgusting trait.'

In 1934, after a spell in the USA, the pair moved into a new home in San Ángel, now the Museo Casa Estudio Diego Rivera y Frida Kahlo (p95), with separate houses linked by an aerial walkway. After Kahlo discovered that Rivera had had an affair with her sister, Cristina, she divorced him in 1939, but they remarried the following year. She moved back into her childhood home, the Casa Azul (Blue House) in Coyoacán, and he stayed at San Ángel – a state of affairs that endured for the rest of their lives. Their relationship endured, too.

Despite the worldwide wave of Fridamania that followed the hit biopic *Frida* in 2002, Kahlo had only one exhibition in Mexico in her lifetime, in 1953. She arrived at the opening on a stretcher. Rivera said of the exhibition: 'Anyone who attended it could not but marvel at her great talent.' She died at the Blue House the following year. Rivera called it 'the most tragic day of my life... Too late I realized that the most wonderful part of my life had been my love for Frida.'

Coyoacán

of Tenochtitlán. The south side is dominated by the **Parroquia de San Juan Bautista** (Map p98; Plaza Hidalgo; ⊗8am-7pm; Ⓜ Coyoacán) and its adjacent former monastery.

Museo Nacional de
Culturas Populares   MUSEUM

(Map p98; ☎55-4155-0920; http://museoculturas populares.gob.mx; Av Hidalgo 289; M$13, Sun free; ⊗10am-6pm Tue-Thu, to 8pm Fri-Sun; Ⓜ Coyoacán) The Museo Nacional de Culturas Populares stages innovative exhibitions on folk traditions, indigenous crafts and celebrations in its various courtyards and galleries.

★Museo Casa de León Trotsky   MUSEUM

(Map p98; ☎55-5658-8732; www.museocasa deleontrotsky.blogspot.mx; Av Río Churubusco 410; adult/student M$40/20; ⊗10am-5pm Tue-Sun; Ⓜ Coyoacán) The Trotsky home, now a museum, remains much as it was on the day when an agent of Stalin, a Catalan named Ramón Mercader, caught up with the revo-

lutionary and smashed an ice axe into his skull. Memorabilia and biographical notes are displayed in buildings off the patio, where a tomb engraved with a hammer and sickle contains Trotsky's ashes.

Having come second to Stalin in the power struggle in the Soviet Union, Trotsky was expelled in 1929 and condemned to death in absentia. In 1937 he found refuge in Mexico. At first Trotsky and his wife Natalia lived in Frida Kahlo's Blue House, but after falling out with Kahlo and Rivera they moved a few streets northeast.

Bullet holes remain in the bedroom, the markings of a failed assassination attempt. The entrance is at the rear of the old residence, facing Av Río Churubusco. Ask about free guided tours in English at the entrance.

Anahuacalli   MUSEUM

(Diego Rivera Anahuacalli Museum; ☎55-5617-4310; www.museoanahuacalli.org.mx; Calle Museo 150, Colonia Coyoacán; adult/child under 16yr

Coyoacán

M$90/15; ⊙11am-5:30pm Wed-Sun; 🅿; 🚇Xotepingo) Designed by Diego Rivera to house his collection of pre-Hispanic art, this museum is a templelike structure of volcanic stone. The 'House of Anáhuac' (the Aztec name for the Valle de México) also contains one of Rivera's studios and some of his work, including a study for *Man at the Crossroads,* the mural whose original version was commissioned and destroyed by the Rockefeller Center in 1934.

In November elaborate Day of the Dead offerings pay homage to the painter, and from April to early December the museum hosts free concerts at 1pm on Sunday, which range from classical to regional folk music.

Anahuacalli is 3.5km south of Coyoacán. Admission includes entry to the Museo Frida Kahlo (p96), and for M$130 also includes weekend round-trip transportation departing from the Casa Azul.

You can also take the *tren ligero* from metro Tasqueña to the Xotepingo station. Exit on the west side and walk 200m to División del Norte. Cross and continue 600m along Calle Museo.

Ex-Convento de Churubusco
HISTORIC BUILDING

(☑55-5604-0699; 20 de Agosto s/n, Colonia San Diego Churubusco; ⊙Mass 7:30am Mon-Fri, 8:30am-7pm Sun; 🚇General Anaya) On August 20, 1847, this former convent was the scene of a historic military defeat, when Mexican troops defended it against US forces advancing from Veracruz in a dispute over the US annexation of Texas. The US invasion was but one example in a long history of foreign intervention in Mexico, as compellingly demonstrated in Churubusco's **Museo Nacional de las Intervenciones** (National Interventions Museum; M$52, Sun free; ⊙9am-6pm Tue-Sun; 🚇General Anaya). Entry into the church itself is during Mass only. From metro General Anaya, it's a 500m walk west.

Plaza Santa Catarina
PLAZA

(Map p98; 🚇Viveros) About a block south of Coyoacán's nursery is Plaza Santa Catarina, with the modest, mustard-colored church that gives the square its name. Across the street, the **Centro Cultural Jesús Reyes Heroles** (Map p98; ☑55-5554-5324; Av Francisco Sosa 202, Colonia Coyoacán; ⊙8am-8pm; 🚇Viveros) is a colonial-era estate with a coffee shop and lovely grounds, where yuccas and jacarandas spring from carefully tended gardens.

Viveros de Coyoacán
PARK

(Map p98; ☑55-5484-3524; www.viveros coyoacan.gob.mx; Av Progreso 1; ⊙6am-6pm; 🚇Viveros) **FREE** A pleasant approach to Coyoacán's central plazas is through the Viveros de Coyoacán, the principal nurseries for Mexico City's parks and gardens. The 38.9-hectare swath of greenery, 1km west of central Coyoacán, is popular with joggers and great for a stroll, but watch out for belligerent squirrels!

From metro Viveros, walk south (right, as you face the fence) along Avenida Universidad and take the first left, Avenida Progreso.

👁 Cuicuilco

One of the oldest significant remnants of pre-Hispanic settlement within the CDMX, Cuicuilco echoes a civilization that stood on the shores of Lago de Xochimilco as far back as 800 BC. In its heyday in the 2nd century BC, the 'place of singing and dancing' counted as many as 40,000 inhabitants – at that time the Teotihuacán civilization was only just beginning to rise to importance. The site was abandoned a couple of centuries later, however, after an eruption of the nearby Xitle volcano covered most of the community in lava.

Today archaelogical works continue to reveal new sections. The area is overgrown with grass in large areas, creating a real sense of discovery. The highlight is a 23m-tall, circular, pyramid-like mound.

Zona Arqueológica
Cuicuilco   ARCHAEOLOGICAL SITE
(www.inah.gob.mx; Av Insurgentes Sur s/n; ☺9am-5pm; **P**; 🚇 Villa Olímpica) **FREE** The principal structure here is a huge circular platform of four levels, faced with volcanic stone blocks, which probably functioned as a ceremonial center. Set amid a park with sweeping views of the area and studded with cacti and shade trees, it makes a nice picnic spot. The site has a small museum containing skulls and artifacts discovered during excavations.

👁 Tlalpan

Tlalpan today is what Coyoacán used to be – an outlying village with a bohemian atmosphere coupled with some impressive colonial-era architecture. The municipal seat of Mexico City's largest *delegación*, Tlalpan sits at the foot of the southern Ajusco range and enjoys a cooler, moister climate. There are some fine restaurants along the arcades of the charismatic plaza. To get here take metrobús Línea 1 to Fuentes Brotantes and walk four blocks east to the main square.

Museo de Historia de Tlalpán   MUSEUM
(✐55-5485-9048; Plaza de la Constitución 10; ☺2-8pm Mon-Fri, from noon Sat; 🚇 Fuentes Brotantes) **FREE** This museum hosts compelling contemporary art and historical exhibits in naturally lit galleries off the courtyard.

Casa Frisaac   CULTURAL CENTER
(✐55-5485-3266; Plaza de la Constitución 1; ☺8am-8pm; 🚇 Fuentes Brotantes) **FREE** This 19th-century estate, once the property of President Adolfo López Mateos, houses an art gallery with temporary exhibits, and a small auditorium for concerts and dance performances.

Capilla de las Capuchinas
Sacramentarias   CHAPEL
(✐55-5573-2395; Av Hidalgo 43, Colonia Tlalpan; M$200; ☺visiting hours 10am-noon & 4-6pm Mon-Thu; 🚇 Fuentes Brotantes) There's a sublime simplicity about this chapel, located inside a convent for Capuchin nuns. Designed by modernist architect Luis Barragán in 1952, the austere altar, free of the usual iconography, consists only of a trio of gold panels. In the morning, light streams through a stained-glass window made by German-Mexican artist Mathias Goeritz. Visits by appointment only.

👁 Tlatelolco & Guadalupe

Plaza de las Tres Culturas   HISTORIC SITE
(Plaza of the Three Cultures; ✐55-5583-0295; www. tlatelolco.inah.gob.mx; Eje Central Lázaro Cárdenas, cnr Flores Magón; ☺8am-6pm; **P**; **M**Tlatelolco) So named because it symbolizes the fusion of pre-Hispanic and Spanish roots into the Mexican *mestizo* identity, this plaza displays the architectural legacy of three cultural facets: the Aztec pyramids of Tlatelolco, the 17th-century Spanish Templo de Santiago and the modern tower that houses the Centro Cultural Universitario.

Recent archaeological finds have altered long-held views about Tlatelolco's history. According to the conventional version, Tlatelolco was founded by an Aztec faction in the 14th century on a separate island in Lago de Texcoco and later conquered by the Aztecs of Tenochtitlán. But a pyramid excavated on the site in late 2007 actually predates the establishment of Tenochtitlán by as much as 200 years. All agree, however, that Tlatelolco was the scene of the largest public market in the Valle de México, connected by a causeway to Tenochtitlán's ceremonial center.

During the siege of the Aztec capital, Cortés defeated Tlatelolco's defenders, led by Cuauhtémoc. An inscription about the battle in the plaza translates as, 'This was neither victory nor defeat. It was the sad birth of the *mestizo* people that is Mexico today.'

You can view the remains of Tlatelolco's main pyramid-temple and other Aztec buildings from a walkway around them. Tlatelolco's main temple was constructed in stages, with each of seven temples superimposed atop its predecessors. The double pyramid on view, one of the earliest stages, has twin staircases that supposedly ascended to temples dedicated to Tláloc and Huitzilopochtli. Numerous calendar glyphs are carved into the outer walls.

Recognizing the significance of the site, the Spanish erected the **Templo de Santiago** here in 1609, using stones from the Aztec structures as building materials. Just inside the main doors of this church is the **baptismal font of Juan Diego**.

Tlatelolco is also a symbol of modern troubles. On October 2, 1968, hundreds of student protesters were massacred here by government troops on the eve of the Mexico City Olympic Games. The weeks before the Olympics had been marked by a wave of protests against political corruption and authoritarianism, and president Gustavo Díaz Ordaz, anxious to present an image of stability to the world, was employing heavy-handed tactics to stop the unrest.

On that October day, helicopters hovered over the Plaza de las Tres Culturas and a massive police contingent cordoned off the protest zone. Suddenly shots rang out, apparently from the balcony that served as a speakers' platform. Police then opened fire on the demonstrators and mayhem ensued. A government-authorized account reported 20 protesters killed, though researchers and media reports estimate the real number is closer to 300.

The generally accepted theory, though there are many, is that the government staged the massacre, planting snipers on the balcony. To this day the incident still generates a massive protest march from Tlatelolco to the Zócalo on October 2.

Along Eje Central Lázaro Cárdenas, northbound trolleybuses pass right by the Plaza de las Tres Culturas.

Centro Cultural Universitario Tlatelolco
MUSEUM

(✏ ext 49646, 55-5117-2818; www.tlatelolco.unam. mx; Flores Magón 1; adult/student M$30/15, Sun free; ⏰10am-6pm Tue-Sun; Ⓜ Tlatelolco) The events that occurred before, during and after the 1968 massacre on Plaza de las Tres Culturas are chronicled in *Memorial del 68*, a compelling multimedia exhibit in the Centro Cultural Universitario Tlatelolco. The cultural center has two other outstanding permanent exhibits in the Museo de Sitio.

The shiny **Museo de Sitio** houses more than 400 objects unearthed at the archaeological site, such as pre-Hispanic offerings and ceramic artifacts. The interactive museum continues on the 2nd floor in the tower building across the way, where you can learn about colonial-era Tlatelolco and the area's flora and fauna. The tower's 3rd floor is home to the Colección Stavenhagen, an extraordinary collection of more than 500 pre-Hispanic clay and stone sculptures, including amusing animal figures and phallic works.

Basílica de Guadalupe
SHRINE

(www.virgendeguadalupe.org.mx; Plaza de las Américas 1, Colonia Villa de Guadalupe; ⏰6am-9pm; Ⓜ La Villa-Basílica) FREE A cult developed around this site after a Christian convert named Juan Diego claimed in December 1531 that the Virgin Mary appeared before him on the Cerro del Tepeyac (Tepeyac Hill). After numerous sightings, so the story goes, the lady's image was miraculously emblazoned on Diego's cloak, causing a bishop to believe the story and build a shrine in her honor. To this day the *basílica* remains a place of pilgrimage and worship.

Over the centuries Nuestra Señora de Guadalupe came to receive credit for all manner of miracles, hugely aiding the acceptance of Catholicism by Mexicans. Despite the protests of some clergy, who saw the cult as a form of idolatry (with the Virgin as a Christianized version of the Aztec goddess Tonantzin), in 1737 the Virgin was officially declared the patron of Mexico. Two centuries later she was named celestial patron of Latin America and empress of the Americas, and in 2002 Juan Diego was canonized by Pope John Paul II.

Today the Virgin's shrines around the Cerro del Tepeyac (formerly an Aztec shrine site) are the most revered in Mexico, attracting thousands of pilgrims daily and hundreds of thousands on the days leading up to her feast day, December 12. Some pilgrims travel the last meters to the shrine on their knees.

Around 1700, to accommodate the faithful flock, the four-towered Basílica de Guadalupe was erected at the site of an earlier shrine. But by the 1970s, the old yellow-domed building (now called the Antigua Basílica) proved inadequate to the task, so the new Basílica de Nuestra Señora de Guadalupe was built next door. Designed by Pedro Ramírez Vázquez, it

MEXICO CITY SIGHTS

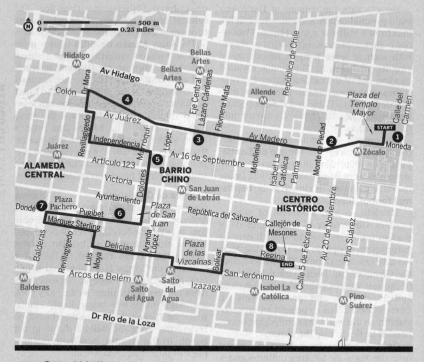

City Walk
Goin' Downtown

START EX TERESA ARTE ACTUAL
END REGINA CORRIDOR
LENGTH 5KM; THREE HOURS

Nothing beats wandering to fully appreciate the rich history of the *centro*.

Kick things off in the slanted 17th-century ❶ **Ex Teresa Arte Actual** (p74) building. If there's one place that can put the sinking-city phenomenon into perspective, it's here.

As you cross the ❷ **Zócalo** (p67), one of the world's largest squares, stop and contemplate that the surrounding buildings sit atop Aztec temples. Some of the imposing colonial-era structures were built with materials from the pre-Hispanic ruins.

Continue west along bustling Avenida Madero to reach the ❸ **Torre Latinoamericana** (p74) skyscraper. To get a feel for just how far Mexico City's concave valley spans, take in the view from the observation deck.

Next spend time strolling ❹ **Alameda Central** (p77), downtown's newly renovated

park with fun fountains and a famous Diego Rivera mural at the west end.

Cut across Avenida Juárez to Calle Dolores and drop by ❺ **El Tío Pepe** (p120), one of the city's oldest cantinas, for a beer or tequila.

Head south on Dolores to ❻ **Mercado San Juan** (p130), a 60-year-old market frequented by chefs and devout foodies. Look for Gastrónomico San Juan for wonderful deli treats and complimentary wine.

Exit the market on Pugibet and go west to Balderas to find ❼ **Centro de Artesanías la Ciudadela** (p129), a large crafts market with decent prices and great variety.

Return to the heart of downtown, walking east until you hit the ❽ **Regina corridor**, a happening pedestrian thoroughfare. Rest here at one of several sidewalk *mezcalerías*. If you prefer, cap off the walk at a nearby *pulque* joint on the corner of Mesones and Callejón de Mesones, a soulful spot that's been pouring the viscous fermented beverage for more than a century. ¡Salud!

is a vast, round, open-plan structure with a capacity of more than 40,000 people. The image of the Virgin, dressed in a green mantle trimmed with gold, hangs above and behind the main alter of the *basílica*, where moving walkways bring visitors as close as possible. Mass is performed hourly.

The rear of the Antigua Basílica is now the **Museo de la Basílica de Guadalupe** (☑55-5577-6022; Plaza Hidalgo, Colonia Villa de Guadalupe; adult/child under 12yr M$5/free; ⊙10am-5:30pm Tue-Sun; Ⓜ La Villa-Basílica), which houses a fine collection of colonial art interpreting the miraculous vision.

Stairs behind the Antigua Basílica climb 100m to the hilltop **Capilla del Cerrito** (Hill Chapel), where Juan Diego had his vision, then lead down the east side of the hill to the Parque de la Ofrenda, with gardens and waterfalls around a sculpted scene of the apparition. Continue on down to the baroque **Templo del Pocito**, a circular structure with a trio of tiled cupolas, built in 1787 to commemorate the miraculous appearance of a spring where the Virgen de Guadalupe had stood. From there the route leads back to the main plaza, re-entering it beside the 17th-century **Antigua Parroquia de Indios** (Parish of Indians).

To reach the Basílica de Guadalupe, take the metro to La Villa–Basílica station, then walk two blocks north along Calzada de Guadalupe, or you can take any 'Metro Hidalgo–La Villa' bus heading northeast on Paseo de la Reforma. To return downtown, walk to Calzada de los Misterios, a block west of Calzada de Guadalupe, and catch a southbound 'Auditorio' or 'Zócalo' bus.

 Activities

Boating

Isla de las Muñecas
BOATING

(Island of the Dolls; Embarcadero Cuemanco, Xochimilco; boat per hour M$500) For a truly surreal experience, head for Xochimilco and hire a gondola to the Island of the Dolls, where hundreds of creepy, decomposed dolls hang from trees. An island resident fished the playthings from the canals to mollify the spirit of a girl who had drowned nearby.

The best departure point for the four-hour round trip is Cuemanco *embarcadero*. To get here, go to metro General Anaya and exit the station on the east side of Calzada de Tlalpan, then walk 50m north to catch a 'Tláhuac Paradero' pesero. Get off at the Embarcadero Cuemanco entrance.

Cycling

On Sunday mornings Paseo de la Reforma is closed to auto traffic from Bosque de Chapultepec to the Alameda Central, and you can join the legions of *chilangos* who happily skate or cycle down the avenue.

Bicitekas
CYCLING

(Map p82; http://bicitekas.org; Monumento a la Independencia; ⊙9:30pm Wed) **FREE** For an ambitious trek, this urban cycling group organizes *Paseo Nocturno* rides departing from the Monumento a la Independencia Wednesday evenings. Groups of up to 200 cyclists ride to destinations such as Coyoacán and the northwestern suburb of Ciudad Satélite. Participants must be sufficiently robust to handle excursions of up to 40km. Helmets, reflective vests and rear lights are recommended.

Kayaking

Michmani
KAYAKING

(☑55-5676-6971; Embarcadero Cuemanco, Xochimilco, off Anillo Periférico Sur; per hour M$50) Take in some of the quieter parts of the Xochimilco canals while kayaking, and do some bird-watching while you're at it within this ecotourism park. You'll spot ducks, egrets and herons, among many other migratory and endemic species. You can also visit the many nurseries along the shores.

To get here, go to metro General Anaya and exit the station on the east side of Calzada de Tlalpan, then walk 50m north to catch a 'Tláhuac Paradero' pesero. Get off at the Embarcadero Cuemanco entrance and walk about 1km to Michmani, just beyond the *embarcadero*.

Lago de Chapultepec
KAYAKING

(Chapultepec Lake; Map p90; www.chapultepec.com.mx; 2-person kayaks/paddleboats/rowboats per hour M$60/50/60; ⊙9am-4:30pm Tue-Sun; Ⓜ Auditorio) Take a kayak, paddleboat or rowboat out for a spin with the ducks on Chapultepec Lake.

Ice-Skating

Pista de Hielo CDMX
ICE SKATING

(Map p68; www.cdmx.gob.mx/vive-cdmx/post/pista-de-hielo-cdmx) As part of a government program to bring fun recreational activities to the city's poorer inhabitants, a huge ice-skating rink is installed in the Zócalo during the Christmas holiday season. Ice-skates are loaned out free of charge, but the wait can be up to an hour.

Courses

Plaza de Danzón
DANCING

(Map p76; lessons M$20-50; ☺ 10am-2:30pm & 4:30-6pm Sat; Ⓜ Balderas) If you like to dance, learn a few great steps at the Plaza de Danzón, northwest of La Ciudadela, near metro Balderas. Couples crowd the plaza every Saturday afternoon to do the *danzón,* an elegant and complicated Cuban step that infiltrated Mexico in the 19th century. Lessons in *danzón* and other steps are given.

Escuela de Gastronomía Mexicana
COOKING

(Map p86; ☑ 55-5264-2484; www.esgamex.com; Coahuila 207; 3hr course incl ingredients M$950-1500; ☐ Campeche) Learn how to cook Mexican dishes from bilingual chefs. Popular classes include *pozole* (hominy soup), *mole poblano* (chicken in a chili and chocolate sauce) and *tamales.*

Centro de Enseñanza Para Extranjeros
LANGUAGE

(Foreigners' Teaching Center; ☑ 55-5622-2470; www.cepe.unam.mx; Av Universidad 3002, Ciudad Universitaria; 6-week course M$12,000; ☐ Ciudad Universitaria) The national university offers six-week intensive language classes, meeting for three hours daily from Monday through Friday. Students who already speak Spanish may take courses on Mexican art and culture.

Tours

Capital Bus
TOURS

(www.capitalbus.mx; Liverpool 155, Zona Rosa; day pass M$160-180, day trip M$650; ☺ ticket office 8:30am-6:30pm; Ⓜ Insurgentes) Take a day trip to the Teotihuacán pyramids and the Basílica de Guadalupe, or tour Mexico City with a hop-on, hop-off day pass (see website for ticket booth locations). Capital Bus also runs outings to nearby colonial towns, such as silver-making center Taxco and culinary capital Puebla.

Turibús Circuito Turístico
BUS

(Map p68; ☑ 55-5141-1360; www.turibus.com.mx; adult/child 4-12yr M$140/70, themed tours M$100-900; ☺ 9am-9pm; ⊕) Red double-decker buses run four *circuitos* (routes) across the city on the one ticket: Centro (downtown), Sur (south, including Frida Kahlo museum), Hipodromo (Polanco and Chapultepec) and Basílica (north). Buses pass every 15 to 60 minutes and you can hop off and on at any designated stop. All routes stop on the west side of the cathedral.

Buy ticket-wristbands on board or at major stops. Fares are slightly higher on Saturday and Sunday.

Turibús also offers themed tours, including cantinas, *lucha libre,* palaces, museums and food tasting. See the website for times.

Journeys Beyond the Surface
TOURS

(Map p68; ☑ cell 55-1745 2380; www.travelmexicocity.com.mx; group tours per person US$180-270) Eight-hour walking tours on aspects of the CDMX experience, with an off-the-beaten-track attitude. See murals, graffiti and street art, for example. Guides are well versed in history and anthropology if you choose to visit pre-Hispanic and colonial-era sites.

Mexico Soul & Essence
FOOD & DRINK

(Map p86; ☑ cell 55-29175408; www.ruthincondechi.com; tours US$100-175, cooking courses

US$300) Ruth Alegría, one of the city's foremost food experts, runs customized culinary and cultural excursions. She can arrange dining outings, market tours or specialized trips. She also offers an entertaining Mexican cooking course.

✨ Festivals & Events

★ Día de Muertos   CULTURAL
(Day of the Dead; ☺ Nov) In the lead-up to Day of the Dead (November 1 and 2), elaborate *ofrendas* (altars) show up everywhere. The huge annual street parade, Desfile de Día de Muertos, has been held since 2016 (initially in response to the faux parade in James Bond film *Spectre*) with over a thousand costumed dancers and performers joining giant *calavera* (skeleton) puppets along Reforma to the Zócalo.

Some of the best *ofrendas* can be seen at Anahuacalli (p98), Museo Dolores Olmedo (p93), the Zócalo (p67), Plaza Santo Domingo in el Centro (replacing Ciudad Universitaria since 2016), and in the neighborhood of San Andrés Mixquic in the extreme southeast of the Distrito Federal.

La Feria de las Flores   FERIA
(Jardín de la Bombilla; ☺ Jul; ♿) **FREE** This major flower festival explodes with color in the Jardín de la Bombilla. The weeklong cultural festivities include the display and sale of myriad varieties of plants, family activities, performances, and botany-related painting and sculpture. The festival has pre-Hispanic origins, when followers of Xiuhtecuhtli (Lord of Flowers) would make floral offerings in return for abundant crops.

Grito de la Independencia   FIREWORKS
(Palacio Nacional; ☺ Sep 15; M Zócalo) On September 15, the eve of Independence Day, thousands gather in the Zócalo to hear the Mexican president's version of the *Grito de Dolores* (Cry of Dolores), Hidalgo's famous call to rebellion against the Spanish in 1810, from the central balcony of the Palacio Nacional at 11pm. Afterward there's a fireworks display.

Festival del Centro
Histórico de CDMX   CULTURAL
(www.festival.org.mx; ☺ Mar/Apr) Across two weeks the *centro histórico* hosts music, theater, dance and culinary events featuring talent from Mexico and abroad – it's the city's biggest cultural bash of the year.

Día de Nuestra
Señora de Guadalupe   RELIGIOUS
(Day of Our Lady of Guadalupe; Basílica de Guadalupe; ☺ Dec; M La Villa-Basílica) At the Basílica de Guadalupe, the Day of Our Lady of Guadalupe caps 10 days of festivities that honor Mexico's religious patron. The number of pilgrims reaches millions by December 12, when groups of indigenous dancers perform nonstop on the basilica's broad plaza.

Foundation of Tenochtitlán   DANCE
(Plaza de las Tres Culturas; ☺ Aug 13; M Tlatelolco) Held on August 13 to celebrate the foundation of the Mexican capital, this is a major summit for Concheros (Aztec dancers) on Plaza de las Tres Culturas in Tlatelolco.

Semana Santa   RELIGIOUS
(☺ Mar/Apr) The most evocative events of Holy Week are in the Iztapalapa district, 9km southeast of the Zócalo, where a gruesomely realistic passion play is enacted on Good Friday.

🛏 Sleeping

Mexico City overflows with lodging options. The most reasonably priced places are in the centro histórico. Midrange lodgings abound in the Alameda and Plaza de la República areas, though often trade character for neutral modern comfort. In trendy Roma and Condesa offerings are mostly chic boutique hotels, with a few budget hostels. Cultural Coyoacán is a tranquil escape. Luxurious accommodations, including international chains, are concentrated in Polanco, the Zona Rosa and Reforma.

🛏 Centro Histórico

As a frequent destination for both Mexican and foreign visitors, the CDMX offers everything from no-frills guesthouses to topflight hotels. Some of the most reasonably priced places are in the *centro histórico*. Ongoing renovations of its infrastructure and preservation of its numerous historic edifices have boosted the zone's appeal, and it remains one of the more affordable areas.

More luxurious accommodations, including branches of some major international chains, are concentrated in Polanco and the Zona Rosa. In the trendy Roma and Condesa neighborhoods, the offerings are mostly chic boutique hotels, with a few budget hostels.

Midrange lodgings abound in the Alameda and Plaza de la República areas, though they tend to trade character for neutral modern comfort. (Note that places with the word 'garage' on the sign, or listing an hourly rate, generally cater to short-term guests.)

★ Casa San Ildefonso HOSTEL $

(Map p68; ☑ 55-5789-1999; www.casasanildefonso. com; San Ildefonso 38; dm/d M$300/800, s/tw without bathroom M$520/690, all incl breakfast; ☻@☞; MZócalo) A 19th-century building that most recently served as a storage facility for street vendors has been transformed into a cheerful hostel off a pedestrian thoroughfare. Unlike most downtown hostels, the high-ceiling dorms, private rooms and common areas here get wonderful sunlight. Guests have breakfast in a tranquil courtyard with a fountain, singing canaries and the gremlin-esque mascot Delfina. There's a tiny single room for M$330.

Hostal Regina HOSTEL $

(Map p68; ☑ 55-5434-5817; www.hostalcentro historicoregina.com; Calle 5 de Febrero 53; d/q without bathroom M$450/1050, ste M$1300, all incl breakfast; ☻@☞; MIsabel La Católica) Off the lively Regina corridor, this 18th-century historic building makes a great base to explore downtown. On offer are private rooms with wooden floors, high ceilings and shared bathrooms, and a two-story 'suite' that comfortably sleeps four. Guests socialize at the rooftop bar.

Mexico City Hostel HOSTEL $

(Map p68; ☑ 55-5512-3666; www.mexicocity hostel.com; República de Brasil 8; dm/tw incl breakfast M$190/600, tw without bathroom M$480; ☻@☞; MZócalo) Steps from the Zócalo, this colonial-era structure has been artfully restored, with original wood beams and stone walls as a backdrop for modern, energy-efficient facilities. Spacious dorms have four or six sturdy bunk beds on terracotta floors. Immaculate bathrooms trimmed with *azulejo* (painted ceramic tiles) amply serve around 100 occupants.

Hotel Castropol BUSINESS HOTEL $

(Map p68; ☑ 55-5522-1920; http://hotel castropol.com; Av Pino Suárez 58; s/tw/tr M$500/550/600; ☻☞; MPino Suárez) Minimalist, spacious rooms for peso watchers are hard to come by when the Zócalo is in sight at the end of the street. Here you not only get loads of cleanliness, marble and a flat-screen TV, but also a handy budget restaurant and the bar-filled Regina corridor kicking it nearby.

Hotel Isabel HOTEL $

(Map p68; ☑ 55-5518-1213; www.hotel-isabel. com.mx; Isabel La Católica 63; s/d/tr M$420/570/800, r without bathroom M$280-400; ☻@☞; ☐República del Salvador) A longtime budget-traveler's favorite, the Isabel offers large, well-scrubbed rooms with old but sturdy furniture, high ceilings and great (if noisy) balconies, plus a hostel-like social scene. Remodeled rooms cost a touch more. Single rooms with shared bathrooms are good value for the area.

Hostel Mundo Joven Catedral HOSTEL $

(Map p68; ☑ 55-5518-1726; http://mundojoven hostels.com; República de Guatemala 4; dm M$230, d with/without bathroom M$640/550, all incl breakfast; ☻@☞; MZócalo) Backpacker central, this HI affiliate is abuzz with a global rainbow of young travelers. Dorms are tidy and guests love the rooftop bar, but it's not the quietest of hostels. 'Quirky' bonuses include a free 10-minute massage.

Chillout Flat B&B $$

(Map p68; ☑ 55-5510-2665; www.chilloutflat. com.mx; Bolívar 8, Apt 102; s/d incl breakfast from M$950/1000; ☻@☞; MAllende) Chill with other travelers in one of two downtown apartments that have been converted into colorful guesthouses with hardwood floors. Street-facing rooms in this lovely 1940s historic building have double-pane windows for noise reduction. Reservations a must.

Hotel Catedral BUSINESS HOTEL $$

(Map p68; ☑ 55-5518-5232; www.hotelcatedral. com; Donceles 95; r incl breakfast M$1140-2000; P☻@☞; MZócalo) This comfortable lodging clearly benefits from its prime location in the heart of the *centro histórico*. Well-maintained rooms have flat-screens, desks, dark-wood furnishings and firm mattresses. For cityscape views, order a drink on the rooftop terrace.

Hotel Gillow HOTEL $$

(Map p68; ☑ 55-5518-1440; www.hotel gillow.com; Isabel La Católica 17; s/d/tw/ste M$840/900/1080/1140; ☻@☞; MAllende) In a historic building, Hotel Gillow has friendly, old-fashioned service and remodeled rooms done up with faux-wood floors and flat-screen TVs. If available, request a double room with a private terrace.

Gran Hotel Ciudad de México HOTEL $$$

(Map p68; ☑ 55-1083-7700; www.granhoteldela ciudaddemexico.com.mx; Av 16 de Sepiembre 82; r/ste incl breakfast from M$2275/3420; P☻

PARQUE NACIONAL DESIERTO DE LOS LEONES

Cool, fragrant pine and oak forests dominate this 20-sq-km **national park** (☑ 55-5814-1171; http://desiertodelosleones.mx; M$10.50; ☉9am-5pm Tue-Sun) in the hills surrounding the Valle de México. Around 23km southwest of Mexico City and 800m higher, it makes for a fine escape from the carbon monoxide and concrete.

The name derives from the **Ex-Convento Santo Desierto del Carmen** (Ex-Convento del Desierto de los Leones; ☑ 55-5814-1172; Camino al Desierto de los Leones; M$13; ☉10am-5pm Tue-Sun), the 17th-century former Carmelite monastery within the park. The Carmelites called their isolated monasteries 'deserts' to commemorate Elijah, who lived as a recluse in the desert near Mt Carmel. The 'Leones' in the name may stem from the presence of wild cats in the area, but more likely it refers to José and Manuel de León, who once administered the monastery's finances.

The restored monastery has exhibition halls and a restaurant. Tours in Spanish are run by guides (garbed in cassock and sandals) who lead you through expansive gardens around the buildings and the patios within, as well as some underground passageways.

The rest of the park has extensive walking trails (robberies have been reported, so stick to the main paths). Next to El León Dorado restaurant, stairs lead down to a gorgeous picnic area with several small waterfalls and a duck pond.

Most visitors arrive in a car, but green *camiones* head to the *ex-convento* hourly from metro Viveros (in front of the 7-Eleven), or from **Paradero las Palmas** (Map p94) in San Ángel, on Saturday and Sunday from 8am to 3:30pm. Monday to Friday departures are few (7:30am from Viveros; and 7:30am, noon and 3:30pm from Paradero las Palmas) and stop short in a mountain town called Santa Rosa from where you need to take a taxi.

✳@⌂; MZócalo) The Gran Hotel flaunts the French art nouveau style of the pre-revolution era. Crowned by a stained-glass canopy crafted by Tiffany in 1908, the atrium is a fin de siècle fantasy of curved balconies, wrought-iron elevators and chirping birds in giant cages. Rooms do not disappoint in comparison. Weekend brunch (M$250) is served on a terrace overlooking the Zócalo.

Breakfast deals and tour packages are available on the website. The hotel features in the James Bond film *Spectre*.

Hampton Inn & Suites   HOTEL $$$
(Map p68; ☑55-8000-5000; www.hampton mexicocity.com; Calle 5 de Febrero 24; r/ste incl breakfast from US$120/140; ⊖✳@⌂; ☐Isabel La Católica) This well-maintained historic gem underwent an elaborate makeover to preserve its facade and Talavera-tiled walls. Well-appointed rooms with contemporary furnishings surround a six-story atrium with a stained-glass ceiling. A good seafood restaurant shares the property.

Hotel Historico Central   HOTEL $$$
(Map p68; ☑55-5130-5138; www.central hoteles.com; Bolívar 28; d incl breakfast M$2916; P⊖✳⌂; MAllende) Occupying a restored 18th-century building in the historic center, this colonial-style hotel gives you plenty of

bang for your buck. All of the well-appointed rooms come with complimentary breakfast as well as free sandwiches and coffee at the 24-hour on-site cafe. Nearby sister property Zocalo Central offers more affordable digs but without the free grub.

🛏 Alameda Central & Around

Boutique offerings continue to spring up within strolling distance of the park and Bellas Artes to compete with a few international chain hotels along revitalized strips. By day the neighborhood bustles with shoppers, but after dark on weekdays it can feel a little too quiet in the backstreets.

Hotel Marlowe   HOTEL $$
(Map p68; ☑55-5521-9540; www.hotelmarlowe. com.mx; Independencia 17; s/d/tw/ste M$900/1050/1130/1400; P⊖@⌂; MSan Juan de Letrán) Marlowe stands across from China-town's pagoda gate. The lobby says modern, but the narrow, low-ceilinged rooms have brown-carpeted retro charm with marble bathrooms. Grab a suite for a larger, brighter room with small balcony. Fitness fans will appreciate the gym with a view.

Chaya   BOUTIQUE HOTEL $$$
(Map p76; ☑55-5512-9074; www.chayabnb.com; Dr Mora 9, 3rd fl; d/tw/ste US$130/155/225; ⊖⌂;

Ⓜ Hidalgo) Like a secret at the edge of Alameda Central, diminutive Chaya nestles on the top floor of an exquisite art deco building. Rooms exude utilitarian chicness, making slabs of gray, wood and cream look good. Plush beds and terrific Mexican breakfasts add to the feeling of escape within the city. Being so central brings occasional weekend noise from the park and bar below.

🛏 Plaza de la República & Around

Further away from the Zócalo, the area around the Monumento a la Revolución is awash with hotels, with a number of dives interspersed amid the business-class establishments. The semi-residential zone offers glimpses of neighborhood life.

Hostel Suites DF   HOSTEL $
(Map p76; ✆55-5535-8117; www.facebook.com/hostelsuitesdf; Terán 38; dm M$240, d M$620-720, all incl breakfast; ✉@🛜; 🚇Plaza de la República) Near the Monumento a la Revolución, this small HI-affiliated hostel offers pleasant common areas and a great central location that leaves you within walking distance of downtown. Dorm beds lack privacy curtains but have individual power points and bathrooms are spacious and clean.

Casa de los Amigos   GUESTHOUSE $
(Map p76; ✆55-7095-7413; www.casadelosamigos.org; Mariscal 132; dm/s/d without bathroom M$150/300/400; ✉@🛜; Ⓜ Revolución) 🍃 The Quaker-run Casa is a guesthouse popular with NGO workers, activists and researchers, but it welcomes walk-in travelers too. Breakfast (M$35) is available and on Tuesday and Thursday guests can take free yoga or Spanish classes. You're not allowed to smoke or drink alcohol in the house.

Plaza Revolución Hotel   HOTEL $$
(Map p76; ✆55-5234-1910; www.hotelplazarevolucion.com; Terán 35; d/ste M$920/1100; 🅿✉@🛜; 🚇Plaza de la República) On a quiet street four blocks east of Plaza de la República and Monumento a la Revolución, this glossy establishment is a stylish option in an area where cut-rate hotels are the norm. Modern rooms with wooden floors are done up in neutral colors and kept impeccably clean.

Palace Hotel   HOTEL $$
(Map p76; ✆55-5566-2400; www.palace-hotel.com.mx; Ramírez 7; s/d/tw M$600/670/730; 🅿✉@🛜; 🚇Plaza de la República) Run by gregarious Asturians, the Palace has large, neat rooms, some with broad balconies giving terrific views down palm-lined Ramírez to the domed Monumento a la Revolución. Request a street-facing room if you want brighter digs.

El Patio 77   B&B $$$
(✆55-5592-8452; www.elpatio77.com; Garcia Icazbalceta 77, Colonia San Rafael; ste incl breakfast from US$140; ✉@🛜; Ⓜ San Cosme) 🍃 Stay in a 19th-century mansion with eight tastefully appointed rooms, each decked out with crafts from a different Mexican state. Like that Huichol bead art or Oaxacan black ceramics in your room? Take them home with you – guests can purchase basically anything in the house that's not bolted down. A daily-changing breakfast is served in the eco-friendly B&B's pleasant patio.

🛏 Zona Rosa & Around

Foreign businesspeople and tourists check in at the upscale hotels in this international commerce and nightlife area. Less-expensive establishments dot the quieter streets of Colonia Cuauhtémoc, north of Reforma, and Juárez, east of Insurgentes.

★ Capsule Hostel   HOSTEL $
(Map p82; ✆55-5207-7903; www.capsulehostel.com.mx; Hamburgo 41; dm/d without bathroom M$225/545; ✉❄🛜; 🚇Hamburgo) This poshtel is less Japanese capsule hotel and more boutique hospital ward (with a similar level of cleanliness). Curtains wrap around the large dorm beds for privacy. Modern furnishings and surprisingly quiet rooms (request one away from the street) provide an excellent budget option (finally) near the embassies and action of Zona Rosa.

★ Casa González   GUESTHOUSE $$
(Map p82; ✆55-5514-3302; https://hotelcasagonzalez.com; Río Sena 69; d/tw/ste M$1095/1695/1395; 🅿✉❄@🛜; 🚇Reforma) A family-run operation for nearly a century, the Casa is a perennial hit with travelers seeking peace and quiet. Set around several flower-filled patios and semiprivate terraces, it's extraordinarily tranquil. Original portraits and landscapes decorate some rooms, apparently done by a guest in lieu of payment.

Hotel María Cristina   HOTEL $$
(Map p82; ✆55-5703-1212; www.hotelmariacristina.com.mx; Río Lerma 31; d/ste from M$995/1375; 🅿✉❄@🛜; 🚇Reforma) Dating from the 1930s, this facsimile of an Anda-

lucian estate makes an appealing retreat, particularly for the adjacent bar with patio seating. Though lacking the lobby's colonial-era splendor, rooms are generally bright and comfortable. It's in a quiet area near the Reforma 222 shopping plaza.

Hotel Bristol
BUSINESS HOTEL $$

(Map p82; ☑ 55-5533-6060; www.hotelbristol.com.mx; Plaza Necaxa 17; d/ste M$1260/1670; P ⊝ ✳ @ 🛜; 🚇 Reforma) A good-value option in the pleasant and central Cuauhtémoc neighborhood, the Bristol caters primarily to business travelers. Carpeted rooms are done in soothing colors and there's an above-average restaurant.

Hotel Geneve
HOTEL $$$

(Map p82; ☑ 55-5080-0800; www.hotelgeneve.com.mx; Londres 130; d/ste incl breakfast from M$3600/3980; P ⊝ ✳ @ 🛜; 🚇 Insurgentes) This Zona Rosa institution strives to maintain a belle epoque ambience despite the globalized mishmash around it. The lobby exudes class, with dark-wood paneling, oil canvases and high bookshelves. Rooms in the hotel's older rear section get a more pronounced colonial treatment, especially the 'vintage suites.'

Hotel Cityexpress EBC Reforma
BUSINESS HOTEL $$$

(Map p82; ☑ 55-1102-0280; www.cityexpress.com.mx; Havre 21; d/tw incl breakfast M$1800/1925; P ⊝ ✳ @ 🛜; 🚇 Hamburgo) The Cityexpress emphasizes functionality, providing a comfortable bed, desk, safe, blackout blinds and an on-site gym, but the decor and warm lighting here outshine the neutral-modern look favored by most hotels in this price category. It's conveniently next to a shopping plaza, Zona Rosa bars and Reforma's embassies.

Hotel Suites Amberes
APARTMENT $$$

(Map p82; ☑ 55-5533-1306; www.suitesamberes.com; Amberes 64; d/tr/q M$1800/2250/2610; P ⊝ 🛜; 🚇 Insurgentes) Sure to please families and small groups, the suites here are basically large one- and two-bedroom apartments with fully equipped kitchens, dining rooms and sofa beds. Street-facing rooms have the added plus of balconies. On the top floor you'll find a sun deck, gym and sauna room.

🛌 Condesa

Thanks to the recent appearance of several attractive lodgings, this neighborhood south of Bosque de Chapultepec makes an excellent leafy base with plenty of after-hours restaurants, bars and cafes.

★ Gael
HOSTEL $

(Map p86; ☑ 55-5919-1437; www.gaelcondesa.com; Nuevo León 179, Colonia Condesa; dm incl breakfast M$270-290; 🚇 Chilpancingo) In fancy Condesa, budget digs of this quality are hard to come by. Helpful English-speaking staff are quick to point out the co-working space for digital nomads and the rooftop terrace. The small neat dorms have individual privacy curtains and provide a tranquil rest. It's in a safe area near the metro and ample eating options.

Stayinn Barefoot Hostel
HOSTEL $

(Map p86; ☑ 55-6286-3000; www.facebook.com/stayinnbarefoot; Juan Escutia 125; dm/d incl breakfast from M$340/990; ⊝ 🛜; 🚇 Chapultepec) On the edge of Condesa, this artfully designed hostel is a breath of fresh air for a neighborhood lacking in budget accommodations. The cheerful lobby is done up in colorful mismatched tile floors and vintage furniture, while upstairs guests have use of a rooftop terrace. The Barefoot's welcoming mezcal bar seals the deal.

★ Red Tree House
B&B $$$

(Map p86; ☑ 55-5584-3829; www.theredtreehouse.com; Culiacán 6; s/d/ste incl breakfast from US$115/150/175; ⊝ 🛜; 🚇 Campeche) Condesa's first B&B has all the comforts of home, if your home happens to be decorated with exquisite taste. Each of the 17 bedrooms and suites is uniquely furnished, and the roomy penthouse has a private patio. Downstairs, guests have the run of a cozy living room and lovely rear garden, the domain of friendly pooch Abril.

The Red Tree also has five pleasant rooms in a house located a half-block away on Citlaltépetl.

★ Villa Condesa
BOUTIQUE HOTEL $$$

(Map p86; ☑ 55-5211-4892; www.villacondesa.com.mx; Colima 428; r incl breakfast from US$208; ⊝ 🛜; 🚇 Chapultepec) You can say *adiós* to hectic Mexico City from the moment you set foot in the Villa's leafy lobby. The 14 rooms in this striking historic building combine classic touches (each has a piece of antique furniture) with the modern trappings of a first-rate hotel. Reservations required; children under 12 not allowed. Guests have free use of bicycles.

★Casa Comtesse
B&B $$$

(Map p86; ☑55-5277-5418; www.casacomtesse. com; Benjamín Franklin 197; r incl breakfast from M$1245; P❄@❅; ☐Escandón) Run by an amiable French owner, this 1940s historic building houses eight rooms adorned with tasteful art and furnishings and a parquet-floored dining area where guests mingle over exceptionally good breakfasts that include quality pastries and fruit. Staff go out of their way to look after guests, helping plan an itinerary or affordable tours to the Teotihuacán ruins, or organizing mezcal tastings in the small bar.

The Casa also has a graphic-arts gallery with interesting works by Mexican artists.

🛏 Roma

Most of the places to stay in Roma are in the thick of things, with a slew of galleries, sidewalk cafes and bars within walking distance, and with more-upmarket Condesa conveniently nearby, you'll find more than enough late-night distractions.

★Hostel Home
HOSTEL $

(Map p86; ☑55-5511-1683; www.hostelhome. com.mx; Tabasco 303; dm incl breakfast M$250, r without bathroom M$600; ❄@❅; ☐Durango) Housed in a fine *porfiriato*-era building and managed by easygoing, English-speaking staff, this 20-bed hostel is on the narrow tree-lined Calle Tabasco, a gateway to the Roma neighborhood.

Hostel 333
HOSTEL $

(Map p86; ☑55-6840-6483; www.hostel333.com; Colima 333; dm incl breakfast M$220-250; @❅; ☐Durango) Guests revel in fiestas, barbecues and occasional gigs on a pleasant rooftop patio flanked by potted plants. Opt for neat dorm rooms or private digs with shared bathrooms at this renovated hostel with a clean shared kitchen. Sociable staff will point you toward the best local taco joints and bars, and may even join you.

Hotel Milán
HOTEL $$

(Map p86; ☑55-5584-0222; www.hotelmilan.com. mx; Álvaro Obregón 94; s/d M$685/715; P❄❆ @❅; ☐Álvaro Obregón) Sitting on the main corridor of bohemian Roma, the Milán goes for minimalist decor and contemporary art in its lobby. Well-maintained, small rooms come with quality bedding and feature bright bathrooms. One of the best-value modern options in the area.

Hotel Stanza
BUSINESS HOTEL $$$

(Map p86; ☑55-5208-0052; www.stanzahotel. com; Álvaro Obregón 13; r/ste from M$1690/2140; P❄❆@❅; ☐Jardín Pushkin) At the east end of Álvaro Obregón, the Stanza has its own restaurant and gym and makes a cushy base on the edge of Roma's hip restaurant and bar scene.

Casa de la Condesa
APARTMENT $$$

(Map p86; ☑55-5584-3089; www.casadelaconde sa.net; Plaza Luis Cabrera 16; ste incl breakfast from M$1400; ❄❆❅; ☐Álvaro Obregón) Right on delightful Plaza Luis Cabrera, the Casa makes a tranquil base for visitors on an extended stay, offering 'suites' that are more like studio apartments with kitchens. If the colorful furnishings and family-owned paintings feel too much like grandma's house, opt for the chic minimal penthouse. Call for weekly rates.

La Casona
BOUTIQUE HOTEL $$$

(Map p86; ☑55-5286-3001; www.hotellacasona. com.mx; Durango 280; r incl breakfast US$150; ❄❆❅; Ⓜ Sevilla) This stately mansion has been restored to its early-20th-century splendor to become one of the capital's most distinctive boutique hotels. Each of the 29 rooms is uniquely appointed with stylish wallpaper, ornate furniture and decorative musical instruments and artworks to bring out European charm.

🛏 Polanco

North of Bosque de Chapultepec, Polanco has excellent business and boutique hotel accommodations, but very little to offer if you're pinching pesos.

Casa Castelar
APARTMENT $$$

(Map p90; ☑55-5281-4990; www.casacastelar. com; Av Castelar 34; ste incl breakfast from US$184; ❄@❅; Ⓜ Auditorio) An affordable option by Polanco standards, the large comfy suites give you plenty of bang for your buck with minimalist designer furniture and quality plush bedding. The well-maintained Castelar has no common areas, but breakfast is served to your door. Chapultepec park's main sights are within walking distance.

Hábita Hotel
BOUTIQUE HOTEL $$$

(Map p90; ☑55-5282-3100; www.hotelhabita.com; Av Presidente Masaryk 201; d incl breakfast from US$280; P❄❆❅; Ⓜ Polanco) Architect Enrique Norten turned a functional apartment building into a smart boutique hotel. Decor in the 36 rooms is boldly minimalist and the most economical digs measure 20 sq meters (call them cozy or just plain small). The rooftop bar, Área (p124), is a hot nightspot.

W Mexico City
DESIGN HOTEL $$$

(Map p90; ☑55-9138-1800; www.wmexicocity. com; Campos Elíseos 252; r US$230-570; P☻ ✳@🖥; MAuditorio) One of the four sentinels opposite the Auditorio Nacional, this 25-floor designer business hotel is determined to break away from the stodginess of its neighbors. Cherry- and ebony-colored rooms feature silken hammocks hanging in the shower area. Rates drop considerably on Friday and Saturday.

🛏 Xochimilco

Michmani
CAMPGROUND $

(☑55-5489-7773, cell 55-5591 4775; www.facebook. com/parqueecoturisticomichmani; Embarcadero Cuemanco, off Anillo Periférico Sur; campsites per person incl tent M$150, cabin M$650; P) 🍽 In Xochimilco, the ecotourism center Michmani arranges stays at **La Llorona Cihuacoatl** campground, which sits on a peaceful off-grid *chinampa*. The center rents out tents, but you'll have to bring a sleeping bag, or you can stay in a tiny rustic cabin with two beds. Also available are barbecue grills and *temascals* (steam baths; M$250).

To get here, go to metro General Anaya and exit the station on the east side of Calzada de Tlalpan, then walk 50m north to catch a 'Tláhuac Paradero' pesero. Get off at the Embarcadero Cuemanco entrance and walk about 1km to Michmani, just beyond the *embarcadero*. From there a boat will take you to La Llorona.

🛏 Coyoacán & Ciudad Universitaria

The southern community has limited budget options but several appealing guesthouses. Check with the Coyoacán tourist office (p133) about short-term homestays.

Hostal Cuija Coyoacán
HOSTEL $

(Map p98; ☑55-5659-9310; www.hostalcuija coyoacan.com; Berlín 268; dm/d incl breakfast M$260/900; ☻@🖥; MCoyoacán) This lizard-themed (for the roaming critters in the garden) HI hostel offers a clean and affordable base to check out Coyoacán's nearby sights. The house has pleasant common areas, but don't expect the smallish dorms and private rooms to wow you.

El Cenote Azul
HOSTEL $

(☑55-5554-8730; Alfonso Pruneda 24, Colonia Copilco el Alto; dm M$250; ☻🖥; MCopilco) This laid-back hostel near the UNAM campus has six neatly kept four- or two-bed rooms sharing three Talavera-tiled bathrooms. The downstairs bar of the same name is a popular hangout for university students. It's tucked away off Privada Ezequiel Ordoñes. Monthly deals are available.

★ Chalet del Carmen
GUESTHOUSE $$

(Map p98; ☑55-5554-9572; www.chaletdelcarmen. com; Guerrero 94; s/d/ste from M$875/1175/1475; ☻🖥; MCoyoacán) 🍽 Run by a friendly Coyoacán native and his Swiss wife, this ecofriendly house strikes a warm blend of Mexican and European aesthetics. On offer are five rooms and two suites with antique furnishings and brilliant natural lighting. Guests have use of a kitchen and bicycles. Reservations a must.

Hostal Frida
GUESTHOUSE $$

(Map p98; ☑55-5659-7005; www.hostalfridabyb. com; Mina 54; d/tr M$650/870; ☻🖥; MCoyoacán) Don't let the 'hostal' tag fool you: this family-run place has well-appointed rooms more along the lines of a guesthouse. Each of the six wooden-floored doubles occupies its own level in adjacent structures, and three come with kitchens. Wi-fi is fast. Monthly rates available.

🛏 Airport

Hotel Aeropuerto
HOTEL $$

(☑55-5785-5318; www.hotelaeropuerto.com.mx; Blvd Puerto Aéreo 388; d/tw M$1000/1200; P☻✳🖥; MTerminal Aérea) Although there are several upscale hotels linked to the terminals, this affordable hotel across the street serves just fine for weary travelers. The only nonchain in the zone, it has helpful reception staff and neutral modern rooms, some overlooking the airport runway through soundproof windows.

Turn left outside the domestic terminal, and past the metro take a left onto Blvd Puerto Aéreo crossing the pedestrian bridge.

🍴 Eating

The capital offers eateries for all tastes and budgets, from soulful taco stalls to gourmet restaurants. Most of the hottest venues for contemporary cuisine show up in Roma, Condesa and Polanco.

Though places on the perimeter of the Alameda cater to tourists, head down Luis Moya or along Ayuntamiento, south of the Alameda, for pockets of the neighborhood's rustic heritage in the form of *torta* (sandwich) stands and chicken-soup vendors. Mexico City's modest Barrio Chino (Chinatown) covers a single paper-lantern-strung block of Calle Dolores, one block south of the park, but its mediocre restaurants are best avoided.

While the Zona Rosa is packed with places to eat and drink, with few exceptions the area is dominated by uninspiring 'international' fare and fast-food franchises, though increasingly there are excellent Korean and Japanese options here. North of Paseo de la Reforma, many new restaurants, good cafes and bars are cropping up in the Colonia Cuauhtémoc.

La Condesa has dozens upon dozens of informal bistros and cafes – many with sidewalk tables – competing for business along several key streets. The neighborhood's restaurant zone is at the convergence of Michoacán, Vicente Suárez and Tamaulipas; many good establishments ring Parque México.

✕ Centro Histórico

★Los Cocuyos   TACOS $

(Map p68; Bolívar 54; tacos M$12-18; ⊙10am-6am; Ⓜ San Juan de Letrán) *Suadero* (beef) tacos abound in the capital, but this place reigns supreme. Follow your nose to the bubbling vat of meats and go for the artery-choking *campechano* (mixed beef and sausage taco). For the more adventurous eater, there are *ojo* (eye) or *lengua* (tongue) tacos; for vegetarians, there are *nopales*.

Café El Popular   CAFE $

(Map p68; ☑55-5518-6081; Av 5 de Mayo 52; breakfast M$43-68; ⊙24hr; ✐; Ⓜ Allende) So popular was this tiny round-the-clock cafe that another more amply proportioned branch was opened next door. Fresh pastries, *café con leche* (coffee with milk) and good combination breakfasts are the main attractions.

Los Vegetarianos   VEGETARIAN $

(Map p68; ☑55-5521-6880; www.facebook.com/losvegetarianosdemadero; Av Madero 56; set lunch M$75-95; ⊙8am-8pm; ✐; Ⓜ Zócalo) Despite its austere entrance, this is a lively upstairs restaurant where a pianist plinks out old favorites. The meat-free menu includes a variations on Mexican standards, such as *chile en nogada* (stuffed green chilies) filled with soy meat, and there are vegan options as well.

Mercado San Camilito   MARKET $

(Map p68; Plaza Garibaldi; pozoles M$65-80; ⊙24hr; Ⓟ; Ⓜ Garibaldi) This block-long building contains more than 70 kitchens preparing, among other items, Jalisco-style *pozole* (a broth brimming with hominy kernels and pork) served with garnishes such as radish and oregano – specify *maciza* (meat) if pig noses and ears fail to excite you.

★Hostería de Santo Domingo   MEXICAN $$

(Map p68; ☑55-5526-5276; http://hosteria santodomingo.mx; Belisario Domínguez 72; chile en nogada M$220, mains M$90-230; ⊙9am-10:30pm Mon-Sat, to 9pm Sun; ☎; Ⓡ República de Chile) Whipping up classic Mexican fare since 1860, Mexico City's oldest restaurant has a festive atmosphere, enhanced by live piano music. The menu offers numerous dishes, but everyone comes here for the *chile en nogada* (an enormous *poblano* chili pepper stuffed with ground meat, dried fruit and bathed in a creamy walnut sauce). Beware: rumor has it the building is haunted.

Al Andalus   MIDDLE EASTERN $$

(Map p68; ☑55-5522-2528; m_andalus171@yahoo.com.mx; Mesones 171; mains M$80-220; ⊙9am-6pm; Ⓜ Pino Suárez) In a superb colonial-era mansion in the Merced textile district, Al Andalus caters to the capital's substantial Lebanese community with old standbys such as shawarma, falafel, baba ganoush, vine leaves, baklava and thick coffee.

Café de Tacuba   MEXICAN $$

(Map p68; ☑55-5521-2048; www.cafedetacuba.com.mx; Tacuba 28; mains M$100-280, 4-course lunch M$275; ⊙8am-11:30pm; ☎; Ⓜ Allende) Before the band there was the restaurant. Way before. A fantasy of colored tiles, brass lamps and oil paintings, this Mexican icon has served *antojitos* (snacks such as tacos and *sopes* – corn tortillas layered with beans, cheese and other ingredients) since 1912. Lively *estudiantinas* (student musical groups) entertain the dinner crowd Wednesday through Sunday.

Casino Español   SPANISH $$

(Map p68; ☑55-5521-8894; www.cassatt.mx; Isabel La Católica 29; 4-course lunch M$165, mains M$134-295; ⊙1-6pm Mon-Fri, restaurant also 8am-noon daily; ☎; Ⓜ Zócalo) This old Spanish social center, housed in a fabulous *porfiriato*-era building, has a popular *mesón* (cantina-style eatery) downstairs, where the courses keep coming, and an elegant restaurant upstairs, which features classic Spanish fare such as *paella valenciana* (paella Valencia-style).

★ **El Cardenal** MEXICAN $$$

(Map p68; ☑ 55-5521-8815; www.restauranteel
cardenal.com; Palma 23; breakfast M$75-95, lunch &
dinner M$130-250; ⊕8am-6:30pm Mon-Sat, from
8:30am Sun; P ?; M Zócalo) Possibly the finest
place in town for a traditional meal, El Carde-
nal occupies three floors of a Parisian-style
mansion and has a pianist playing sweetly in
the background. Breakfast is a must, served
with a tray of just-baked sweet rolls and a
pitcher of frothy, semi-sweet chocolate. For
lunch the house specialty is the *pecho de
ternera* (oven-roasted veal breast).

The latest branch, **El Cardenal San Án-
gel** (Map p94; ☑ 55-5550-0293; Av de la Paz 32;
breakfast M$75-95, lunch & dinner M$130-250;
⊕8am-8pm Mon-Sat, 8:30am-6:30pm Sun; P ?;
🚇 La Bombilla), is in the south.

Azul Histórico MEXICAN $$$

(Map p68; ☑ 55-5510-1316; www.azul.rest; Isabel
La Católica 30; mains M$160-330; ⊕9am-11:30pm;
P ?; M Zócalo) Chef Ricardo Muñoz reinvents
traditional Mexican recipes such as *pescado
tikin xic* (a grouper dish from the Yucatán
with plantain and tortilla strips). This branch
is in a beautiful complex of converted buildings and diners eat in an inner-courtyard
among trees and romantic lighting, enclosed
by stone archways.

Los Girasoles MEXICAN $$$

(Map p68; ☑ 55-5510-0630; www.restaurante
losgirasoles.com.mx; Tacuba 7, Plaza Tolsá; mains
M$175-239; ⊕8:30am-9pm Sun & Mon, to 10:30pm
Tue-Sat; P ?; M Allende) This fine restaurant
overlooking the grand Plaza Tolsá boasts an

AROUND MEXICO ON A PLATE

Pasillo de Humo (Map p86; www.facebook.com/pasillodehumo; Av Nuevo León 107, Colonia
Condesa; appetizers M$76-128, mains M$102-258; ⊕9am-7pm; ☑; 🚇 Campeche) If you can't
make it to culinary capital Oaxaca, here's your chance to delve into authentic traditional
cuisine from the region. You might try the *sopa oaxaqueña* (a delectable bean soup),
molotes istemeños (plantain balls in *mole* sauce) or *tlayudas* (large tortillas filled with
cheese, beans and aromatic herbs). The lovely dining area gets plenty of natural light. The
restaurant is on the 2nd floor of upscale food market Parián Condesa (p115).

Coox Hanal (Map p68; ☑ 55-5709-3613; Isabel La Católica 83, 2nd fl; mains M$65-135;
⊕10:30am-6:30pm; P ?; M Isabel La Católica) Started in 1953 by boxer Raúl Salazar, this
establishment prepares Yucatecan fare just as it's done in don Raúl's hometown of Méri-
da. The *sopa de lima* (lime soup with chicken), *papadzules* (tacos stuffed with chopped
hard-boiled egg and topped with pumpkin seed sauce) and *cochinita pibil* (pit-cooked
pork) are top-notch. Tables are set with the obligatory four-alarm *habanero* salsa.

Los Tolucos (☑ 55-5440-3318; Hernández y Dávalos 40, cnr Bolívar, Colonia Algarín; pozoles
M$65-80; ⊕10am-9pm; P; M Lázaro Cárdenas) A popular local favorite for some of the
best *pozole* (hominy and pork stew) in Mexico City. The Guerrero-style green *pozole*
here has been drawing people from far and wide for more than four decades. It's three
blocks east of metro Lázaro Cárdenas.

Yuban (Map p86; www.yuban.mx; Colima 268; appetizers M$80-120, mains M$180-270; ⊕1:30-
11pm Mon-Thu, to midnight Fri & Sat, to 6pm Sun; ?; 🚇 Durango) Savor Oaxaca-
inspired, elevated flavors such as exquisite *moles* and *tlayudas* (large tortillas folded
over chorizo and cheese), *chapulin* tacos and some darn-good mezcals. An adjoining
venue stages plays and screens Mexican indie flicks.

La Polar (☑ 55-5546-5066; www.lapolar.mx; Guillermo Prieto 129, Colonia San Rafael; birria
M$130; ⊕7am-2am; P; M Normal) Run by a family from Ocotlán, Jalisco, this boisterous
beer hall has essentially one item on the menu: *birria* (spiced goat stew). La Polar's ver-
sion of this Guadalajara favorite is considered the best in town. Spirits are raised further
by noisy mariachis and *norteña* combos who work the half-dozen salons here.

Tamales Chiapanecos María Geraldine (Map p98; ☑ 55-5608-8993; Plaza Hidalgo,
Coyoacán; tamales M$35; ⊕10am-10pm Sat & Sun; M Coyoacán) At the passageway next
to the arched wing of San Juan Bautista church, look for these incredible *tamales* by
Chiapas native doña María Geraldine. Wrapped in banana leaves, stuffed with ingredi-
ents such as olives, prunes and almonds, and laced with sublime salsas, they're a meal
in themselves.

encyclopedic range of Mexican fare, from pre-Hispanic ant larvae and grasshoppers to contemporary dishes such as red snapper encrusted with *huanzontle* flowers.

La Casa de las Sirenas
MEXICAN $$$

(Map p68; ☑ 55-5704-3345; www.lacasadelas sirenas.com.mx; República de Guatemala 32; mains M$240-310; ⏰ 11am-11pm Mon-Sat, to 7pm Sun; 🛜; Ⓜ Zócalo) Housed in a 17th-century relic, Sirenas has a top-floor terrace that looks toward the Zócalo via the Plaza del Templo Mayor. It's an ideal perch to enjoy regional dishes prepared with contemporary flair, such as chicken bathed in pumpkin seed *mole*.

✖ Alameda Central & Around

El Huequito
TACOS $

(Map p68; www.elhuequito.com.mx; Ayuntamiento 21; tacos al pastor M$17; ⏰ 8am-10pm; 🚇 Plaza San Juan) These old pros have been churning out delectable *tacos al pastor* (marinated pork roasted on a spit) since 1959, thus the higher than average asking price. Several downtown Huequito branches offer the sit-down experience, but for some reason the tacos are better here at the original hole-in-the-wall location.

El Cuadrilátero
SANDWICHES $

(Map p76; ☑ 55-5510-2856; Luis Moya 73; tortas M$72-95; ⏰ 7am-8pm Mon-Sat; 🚇 Plaza San Juan) Owned by wrestler Super Astro, this *torta* joint features a shrine to *lucha libre* (Mexican wrestling) masks. The mother of all *tortas*, the 1.3kg cholesterol-packed Torta Gladiador (egg, sausage, bacon, beef, chicken and hot dog) is free if you can gobble it in 15 minutes – only 99 people have managed it in over two decades. If the *torta* defeats you, it costs M$255.

Mi Fonda
SPANISH $

(Map p68; ☑ 55-5521-0002; López 101; paella M$75; ⏰ 11am-5pm Tue-Sun; 🚇 Plaza San Juan) Working-class *chilangos* line up for their share of *paella valenciana,* made fresh daily and patiently ladled out by women in white bonnets. Jesús from Cantabria oversees the proceedings.

★ El 123
ASIAN $$

(Map p76; ☑ 55-5512-1772; www.123comida tienda.com; Artículo 123; mains M$110-220; ⏰ 9am-11pm Mon-Sat, to 9pm Sun; 🛜🍴; Ⓜ Juárez) Good Japanese, Thai and Vietnamese food like this is rare in *el centro*. Equally so, this cafe-restaurant-gift shop's cool antique-store de-

sign, which reveals its relationship to the sister Mog Bistro restaurant in Roma. The same dependable sushi, green curry and green-tea *mochi* (glutinous rice cake) ice creams stand out here. Cash only.

★ El Lugar Sin Nombre
MEXICAN $$$

(Map p76; Luis Moya 31; mains M$175-200; ⏰ 7pm-midnight Tue-Sat) Too good to keep hidden, the 'restaurant with no name,' next to *mezcalaría* Bósfaro, prepares hand-crafted Mexican, slow-food dishes such as *conejo encacahuatado* (biodynamic rabbit in peanut salsa with sweet potato) and *pulpo en morita* (grilled squid with fruity smoked chilies) in earthenware cookware. Select ingredients are sourced from across Mexico and the industrial-chic atmosphere is just as charming. Spread the word. There is no phone number, website or reservations.

✖ Plaza de la República & Around

Gotan Restaurante
ARGENTINE $$

(Map p76; ☑ 55-5535-2136; www.gotan.com.mx; Baranda 17, Colonia Tabacalera; mains M$70-220; ⏰ 10am-8:30pm Mon-Fri; 🛜; 🚇 Plaza de la República) One of the best and most authentic Argentine restaurants in town, owned by a kind Buenos Aires native and her Mexican husband. It's all about the details here: bread is baked daily and the meats and other key ingredients are imported from Argentina. Don't leave without trying the *postre de la nonna,* a delightful caramel custard.

✖ Zona Rosa & Around

★ Café NiN
FRENCH $

(Map p82; ☑ 55-5207-7605; www.rosetta.com.mx; Havre 73, Colonia Zona Rosa; snacks/mains from M$10/130; ⏰ 7am-11pm Mon-Sat, 7:30am-5pm Sun; 🛜🍴; Ⓜ Insurgentes) This golden cafe-restaurant looks plucked from belle epoque Paris with glorious patisserie and bakery treats as part of the Rosetta Panadería empire by day. The bar is great for coffee, sandwiches or solo egg brunches. A newer food menu brings European fusion to pork belly with plantains and cilantro or green curry grouper fish. Save room for the grapefruit panna cotta.

Yug Vegetariano
VEGETARIAN $

(Map p82; ☑ 55-5333-3296; www.lovegetariano. com; Varsovia 3; buffet lunch M$105-120, mains M$67-80; ⏰ 7:30am-9pm Mon-Fri, 8:30am-8pm

Sat & Sun; 🛜 ⚡; Ⓜ Sevilla) The mostly Mexican menu is taste-bud heaven for vegetarians and vast enough for most carnivorous folk to find something they fancy. Choose from specialties such as squash-flower crepes, or gorge on the buffet lunch (1pm to 5pm) upstairs, with all-you-can-eat simple mains, salads, soup and sugarless drinks. Yug's old-world decor attracts an unpretentious local crowd.

Carnitas El Azul
MEXICAN $

(El Capote; Map p82; www.facebook.com/tacoselazul; Av Chapultepec 317, btwn Genova & Amberes, Colonia Juárez; tacos M$7-12, tortas M$18; ⊘ 9am-5pm Mon-Sat, to 4pm Sun; Ⓜ Insurgentes) Blink an eye and you'll walk right past this nondescript *carnitas* joint. El Azul (real name Rubén) has been slinging *tacos de carnitas* (pork simmered in lard) for more than 35 years and he has drawn praise from some of Mexico City's top chefs. Try the *costilla* (rib) tacos.

WanWan Sakaba
JAPANESE $$

(Map p82; ✆ 55-5514-4324; www.facebook.com/wanwansakaba; Londres 209; set lunch M$130-190, mains M$95-290; ⊘ 1-11pm Mon-Sat; ✳ ⚡; Ⓜ Insurgentes) The city's most authentic Japanese *izakaya* (pub-eatery) is casual enough to tuck into ramen at the bar (no tables here) with the mostly Japanese diners. Set lunches include perfectly simple grilled salmon, while the *gyoza* (pork dumplings) and the sake (rice wine) are Tokyo-good.

Rokai
JAPANESE $$$

(Map p82; ✆ 55-5207-7543; www.edokobayashi.com; Río Ebro 87, Colonia Cuauhtémoc; tasting menu M$1200-1800; ⊘ 1-4:30pm & 7-10:30pm Mon-Sat, 1pm-5:30pm Sun; 🛜; Ⓜ Insurgentes) Rokai takes Japanese food to a new level in Mexico City. Opt for the 'omakase,' a changing tasting menu consisting of meticulously prepared dishes, including fresh sushi and sashimi. Each course (there are up to nine) leaves you wanting more. The same owners run ramen restaurant Rokai Ramen-Ya next door if you're looking for something cheaper (ramen M$185). Reserve ahead.

Tezka
INTERNATIONAL $$$

(Map p82; ✆ 55-9149-3000; www.tezka.com.mx; Amberes 78; mains M$155-420, tasting menu M$560; ⊘ 1-5pm & 8-11pm Mon-Fri, 1-6pm Sat & Sun; Ⓟ 🛜; Ⓜ Insurgentes) Specializing in contemporary Basque cuisine, elegant but bistro-relaxed Tezka ranks among Mexico City's finest restaurants. The regularly changing menu fea-

tures elaborate dishes such as lamb glazed in coffee with potatoes in a vanilla sauce, and duck puff-pastry stuffed with raspberries. Or dabble in the four-course tasting menu (two appetizers, a main dish and dessert).

Don Asado
STEAK $$$

(Map p82; www.donasado.com.mx; Río Lerma 210; mains M$160-280; ⊘ 1-11pm Tue-Sat, to 7:30pm Sun; 🛜; Ⓜ Sevilla) One of the best and most reasonably priced steakhouses in town. Uruguayan-owned Don Asado rocks a large wood-burning grill to cook juicy cuts such as its popular *vacio con piel* (tender flank steak with a crispy outer layer of fat) or *bife de chorizo* (New York strip steak). Vegetarian options include handmade pasta and *empanadas* (turnovers).

🍴 Condesa

El Pescadito
SEAFOOD $

(Map p86; www.facebook.com/elpescadito condesadf; Atlixco 38, Colonia Condesa; tacos M$35; ⊘ 11am-6pm Mon-Fri, from 10am Sat & Sun; 🚇 Campeche) This bright-yellow taco joint is unmissable for the queue waiting for a (folding) seat. Nearly all nine fish/shrimp fillings are battered, Sonora style, for maximum crispy, juicy flavor. Pescadito's signature taco, *'que-sotote'* – a chili stuffed with shrimp and cheese – is worth holding out for.

Doña Blanca
MEXICAN $

(Map p86; ✆ 55-5553-2076; www.fondadonablanca.com; Av Veracruz 107; 8am-5pm Mon-Fri, to 4pm Sat, to 2pm Sun; ⊘ breakfasts M$55-65; Ⓜ Chapultepec) Blanca is *the fonda* for Condesa locals to eat breakfast in their pristine activewear. The encyclopedic menu includes figure-conscious egg-white omelettes with spinach, or *huevos Yucatán*, fried eggs floating atop tostadas and chunky *pico de gallo* salsa. It may be dressed up, but the excellent-value set breakfasts are definitely no nonsense.

Parián Condesa
INTERNATIONAL $

(Map p86; www.facebook.com/pariancondesa; Av Nuevo León 107, Colonia Condesa; mains M$95-220; ⊘ 9am-11pm Mon-Sat, to 7pm Sun; ⚡; 🚇 Campeche) If you're hankering for something special but can't decide what, peruse the food stalls at this sleek gourmet market. There's on-trend vegan or Japanese bowl food, Mexican classics, curry, pizza, grilled meat and seafood, and artisanal cheese, ice cream and drinks. Sit in the small courtyard for table service.

★**Lardo** FUSION $$
(Map p86; www.lardo.mx; Agustín Melgar 6, cnr Mazatlán; M$115-345; ⊙7am-10:45pm Mon-Sat, 8am-5pm Sun; ⊘) It always seems sunny in this convivial bistro, which takes Mexican flavors and matches them with European freshness. Part of the Rosetta patisserie family, Lardo's exquisite zucchini and spearmint pizzettas show baking prowess, and dishes such as red snapper with pepita sauce are expertly balanced.

Ojo de Agua HEALTH FOOD $$
(Map p86; ☑55-6395-8000; http://grupoojodeagua.com.mx; Calle Citlaltépetl 23; salads & sandwiches M$95-155; ⊙8am-10pm Mon-Thu, to 9pm Fri-Sun; ☎⊘; Ⓜ Chilpancingo) ✈ Missing those greens in Mexico City? Exciting salads with salmon steak or grilled apple and turkey keep this organic grocery-store-cafe full of those who want to keep healthy. The interesting juices and location next to a plaza and fountain are equally attractive.

Orígenes Orgánicos CAFE $$
(Map p86; ☑55-5208-6678; www.origenesorganicos.com; Plaza Popocatépetl 41A; mains M$115-180; ⊙8:30am-9:30pm Mon-Fri, 9am-6:30pm Sat & Sun; ☎⊘; Ⓡ Sonora) More than just a place to buy soy milk and certified-organic produce, this store-cafe emphasizes seasonal, organic ingredients in sandwiches, burgers, crepes, salads and tasty dishes such as salmon in a creamy walnut and cranberry sauce with brown rice. Vegetarians and vegans have a glut of options. It faces one of Condesa's loveliest plazas.

Taj Mahal INDIAN $$
(Map p90; www.tajmahaldf.com; Francisco Márquez 134, Colonia Condesa; mains M$120-190; ⊙1-10pm Sun-Wed, to 11pm Thu-Sat; ☎⊘; Ⓜ Juancatlán) A hard-working Bangladeshi man who once roamed Condesa selling clothes out of a suitcase now has his own restaurant specializing in Indian cuisine. Vegetarians will find many options here, including garlic naan, vegetable biryani and flavored yogurt drinks.

Café La Gloria FRENCH $$
(Map p86; ☑55-5211-4185; Vicente Suárez 41, Colonia Condesa; mains M$95-190; ⊙noon-midnight Mon-Thu, to 1am Fri-Sun; Ⓟ☎⊘; Ⓡ Campeche) A hip bistro in the heart of Condesa, La Gloria remains a popular meeting place thanks to the reliably good salads, zesty pastas and quirky art on display.

Lampuga SEAFOOD $$$
(Map p86; ☑55-5286-1525; www.lampuga.com.mx; Ometusco 1, cnr Av Nuevo León; mains M$162-297; ⊙1:30-11pm Mon-Wed, to 11:30pm Thu-Sat, to 6pm Sun; ☎⊘; Ⓜ Chilpancingo) Fresh seafood is the focus at this appealing bistro. Tuna *tostadas* make great starters, as does the smoked marlin carpaccio. For a main course, you'd do well to have the catch of the day grilled over coals.

La Capital MEXICAN $$$
(Map p86; ☑55-5256-5159; http://lacapitalrestaurante.com; Av Nuevo León 137; mains M$115-195; ⊙1:30pm-midnight Mon-Wed, to 1am Thu-Sat, to 6pm Sun; Ⓟ☎☎; Ⓜ Chilpancingo) The smart uniforms and sports on TV are the only traces of the 'cantina' at this large bistro. The Capital expertly accomplishes a casual but chic vibe while providing tasty traditional Mexican fare with a gourmet twist. Try the incredible *atún fresca* tostadas or duck enchiladas, with a well-balanced margarita Capital to accompany.

✕ Roma

El Parnita MEXICAN $
(Map p86; ☑55-5264-7551; www.elparnita.com; Av Yucatán 84; tacos M$25-38, tortas M$44-62; ⊙1:30-6pm Tue-Thu & Sun, to 7pm Fri & Sat; ☎; Ⓡ Sonora) What began as a small street stall has morphed into a see-and-be-seen restaurant in the Roma. This lunch-only establishment keeps it simple with a small menu of tried-and-true family recipes such as the *carmelita* (shrimp tacos with handmade tortillas) and the *viajero* (slow-cooked pork) taco. Reserve ahead for Saturday and Sunday.

Panadería Rosetta BAKERY $
(Map p86; ☑55-5207-2976; www.rosetta.com.mx/panaderia; Colima 179; bread M$20-50, baguettes M$52-115; ⊙7am-8pm Mon-Sat, to 6pm Sun; ☎; Ⓡ Durango) Sublime sweet bread, proper croissants and baguettes are made fresh daily at this tiny bakery, with a bench for coffee and sandwiches. It's owned by chef Elena Reygadas, sister of award-winning Mexican filmmaker Carlos Reygadas. It's a tight squeeze so if queues form, try the lovely Café NiN (p114) branch in Zona Rosa.

Por Siempre Vegana Taquería VEGAN $
(Map p86; ☑55-3923-7976; www.facebook.com/porsiemprevegana taqueria; cnr Manzanillo & Chiapas; tacos M$15; ⊙1pm-midnight Mon-Sat; ⊘; Ⓡ Sonora) Vegans can join in the street-food action with soy and gluten taco versions of *al*

pastor, loganiza and chorizo. The late-night experience is complete with self-serve tubs of toppings – potato, *nopales* (cactus paddles), beans and salsas. There are also dairy-free cakes and Oaxacan ice cream here.

Helado Obscuro
ICE CREAM $

(Map p86; ☑ 55-5564-8945; www.heladoobscuro. com; Córdoba 203; ice cream M$20-30; ☺ 11am-9pm Mon & Tue, to 10pm Wed-Sat, to 7pm Sun; ⃝⃔; ☐ Dr Márquez) Take a summery walk on the 'dark side' and try some alcohol-spiked ice cream. Concoctions with titillating names include the Mariachi en Bikini, with coconut milk, soursop and mezcal. Inventive flavors include tequila, wine, sake, whiskey cream and other tipples. Or go vanilla with dairy- and alcohol-free options. There's another branch inside Mercado Roma.

★ El Hidalguense
MEXICAN $$

(Map p86; ☑ 55-5564-0538; Campeche 155; mains M$90-240; ☺ 7am-6pm Fri-Sun; ⃝⃔; ☐ Campeche) Slow-cooked over aged oak wood in an underground pit, the Hidalgo-style *barbacoa* at this family-run eatery is off-the-charts delicious. Get things started with a rich consommé or *queso asado* (grilled cheese with herbs), then move on to the tacos. Top it off on a warm and fuzzy note, sampling the flavored *pulques*. Cash only.

★ Broka Bistrot
FUSION $$

(Map p86; www.brokabistrot.com; Zacatecas 126; set lunch M$165, mains M$155-255; ☺ 2pm-midnight Mon-Sat, 1:30-6pm Sun; ⃝; ☐ Álvaro Obregón) Set in a stylish hidden patio, Broka serves delectable Euro-Mexican fusion dishes such as a fish and *nopal* stack with blue-corn tortillas. The weekday lunch menu is hip and so photogenic that it's tweeted daily; check the website.

Bawa Bawa
BARBECUE $$

(Map p86; www.facebook.com/bawabawabbq; Córdoba 128; mains M$150-190; ☺ noon-10pm Mon-Wed, to 11pm Thu-Sat, 10am-7pm Sun; ⃝; ☐ Álvaro Obregón) Mexico City loves a barbecue and the Texas-style grub here ranks among the city's best. The pork belly and short rib reign supreme and can be ordered in combination with brisket, pork ribs and chicken, along with side dishes. The bottled Mexican microbrews go down nicely with the smoky meats.

Lalo!
BREAKFAST $$

(Map p86; www.eat-lalo.com; Zacatecas 173, Colonia Roma; breakfast M$100-210, lunch & dinner M$170-250; ☺ 8am-6pm Tue-Sun; ⃝⃔; ☐ Álvaro Obregón)

A popular breakfast spot in the trendy Roma neighborhood, Lalo refers to the nickname of owner and acclaimed chef Eduardo Garcia of Maximo Bistrot Local (p117). Menu faves here include *huevos con chorizo* (eggs with homemade Mexican sausage) and eggs Benedict. The colorful, feel-good drawings covering the wall are the work of Belgian graffiti artist Bue the Warrior.

★ Maximo Bistrot Local
EUROPEAN $$$

(Map p86; ☑ 55-5264-4291; www.maximobistrot. com.mx; Tonalá 133; mains M$350-900; ☺ 1-5pm & 7-11pm Tue-Sat, 1:30-4pm Sun; ☐ Álvaro Obregón) If there's one place that best represents Mexico City's exciting new culinary scene, it's Maximo Bistrot. The constantly changing menu, which draws on European and some Mexican recipes, features fresh, seasonal ingredients in dishes such as crab-stuffed courgette flowers, while simple ingredients like white string-beans dusted in Parmesan take on new life. Reservations a must.

Owner and chef Eduardo García honed his cooking skills at Pujol (p118) under the tutelage of famed chef Enrique Olvera.

★ Galanga Thai Kitchen
THAI $$$

(Map p86; ☑ 55-6550-4492; www.galangathai kitchen.com; Guanajuato 202, Colonia Roma; appetizers M$80-180, mains M$170-250; ☺ 1-10:30pm Tue-Sat, to 6pm Sun; ⃝⃔; ☐ Álvaro Obregón) Serving up classics like tom yum (hot and sour soup), gai satay (skewered chicken in peanut sauce) and pad thai (noodles in tamarind sauce), Galanga does the most authentic Thai cuisine in Mexico City. Tables fill up fast at this small restaurant so reserve ahead. All dishes are cooked to order by the owners, a Thai and Mexican couple.

★ Contramar
SEAFOOD $$$

(Map p86; ☑ 55-5514-9217; www.contramar.com. mx; Durango 200; appetizers M$85-229, mains M$179-327; ☺ 12:30-6:30pm Sun-Thu, to 8pm Fri & Sat; ⃟⃝; ☐ Durango) Seafood is the star attraction at this stylish dining hall with a seaside ambience. The specialty is tuna fillet Contramar-style – split, swabbed with red chili and parsley sauces and grilled to perfection. The creamy tuna *tostada* topped with avocado slices is another standout. Reservations recommended.

★ Los Loosers
VEGAN $$$

(Map p86; http://losloosers.com; Sinaloa 236, Colonia Roma; mains M$140-200; ☺ 1-9pm Tue-Fri, noon-9pm Sat, noon-6pm Sun; ⃝⃔;

Ⓜ Chapultepec) A rare find in the capital, and by that we mean vegan food done right. Reporter-turned-chef Mariana Blanco cooks up something a little different each day for a daily changing menu inspired by Mexican and Asian cuisine, such as ramen *chilaquiles* (ramen noodles in spicy chili sauce). Free delivery service available to your hotel room via Facebook. Cash only.

Fonda Fina
MEXICAN $$$

(Map p86; ☑ 55-5208-3925; www.fondafina.com. mx; Medellín 79, Colonia Roma; appetizers M$75-120, mains M$130-260; ⊘ 1-11pm Mon-Wed, to midnight Thu-Sat, to 7pm Sun; ☎ 🍴; 🚇 Álvaro Obregón) The 'fonda' concept of ordering a three-course meal off a set menu does not apply here; instead you select an entrée with your choice of sauce and side dish. Appetizer and main dish faves include *peneques rellenos de queso* (ricotta-filled tortillas in pumpkin seed *mole*) and *fideo seco con chilaquiles* (spicy tortilla wedges on a bed of pasta).

🍴 Bosque de Chapultepec & Polanco

Taquería El Turix
YUCATECAN $

(Map p90; Av Castelar 212; tacos M$15, tortas & panuchos M$26; ⊘ 11am-10pm; Ⓜ Polanco) This old-school *taquería* is a welcome sight in a neighborhood known for its pricey eats. With a recipe that's been in the family for 45 years, Turix does one thing and does it well: *cochinita pibil* (marinated pork). Top your taco or *torta* (sandwich) with pickled onion and a four-alarm habanero salsa, just like they do it in the Yucatán. It's 1.5km southwest of metro Polanco.

★ Pujol
MEXICAN $$$

(Map p90; ☑ 55-5545-4111; www.pujol.com. mx; Tennyson 133; menú degustación M$1840; ⊘ 1:30-10:30pm Mon-Thu, to 11pm Fri & Sat; Ⓟ; Ⓜ Polanco) Arguably Mexico's best gourmet restaurant, Pujol offers a contemporary take on classic Mexican dishes in a stylish and modern Mexican-designed setting. Famed chef Enrique Olvera regularly reinvents the menu, which is presented as a *menú degustación,* a multiple-course tasting extravaganza. Tasty morsels include a charred aubergine tamal, *infladita langosta* (a corn puff filled with lobster), and brown-sugar roasted pineapple with cilantro.

It might take up to several weeks to get a table here, so reserve well ahead.

★ Quintonil
MEXICAN $$$

(Map p90; ☑ 55-5280-1660; www.quintonil.com; Newton 55; mains M$390-650, menú degustación M$1950; ⊘ 1-4:30pm & 6:30-10pm Mon-Sat; ☎; Ⓜ Polanco) This contemporary innovator made the Top 50 Restaurants in the World list – in 2015, 2016 and 2017 – for creatively showcasing traditional Mexican dishes. Chef Jorge Vallejo gives local, organic ingredients starring roles, which dazzle when Wagyu beef meets an opulent *pulque* and *chile seco* reduction and elevate crab *tostadas* to a smoky revelation. It pays off, shining a spotlight on Mexico's culinary ascendancy. Book weeks ahead.

Dulce Patria
MEXICAN $$$

(Map p90; ☑ 55-3300-3999; www.dulcepatria mexico.com; Anatole France 100, Colonia Polanco; mains M$300-450; ⊘ 1:30-11:30pm Mon-Sat, to 5:30pm Sun; Ⓟ☎; Ⓜ Polanco) Cookbook author Martha Ortiz launched this restaurant several years ago, and it certainly lives up to her high standards, in spite of some unfortunate ruffled tablecloths and red velvet headrests. Reinvented traditional Mexican dishes such as *mole* enchiladas stuffed with plantain are deftly plated and delicious.

🍴 San Ángel

Barbacoa de Santiago
MEXICAN $

(Map p94; ☑ 55-5616-5983; Plaza San Jacinto 23, Colonia San Angel; tacos & flautas M$30; ⊘ 9am-6pm Mon-Fri, to 7pm Sat & Sun; 🚇 La Bombilla) A quick and affordable *taquería* off the plaza, this place is known for its *barbacoa* and *flautas ahogadas* (fried rolled tacos dipped in a *chile pasilla* and *pulque* sauce). You'll also find them at a mini-branch in Mercado Roma.

Cluny
FRENCH $$

(Map p94; ☑ 55-5550-7350; www.cluny.com. mx; Av de la Paz 57; mains M$143-297, prix fixe menu M$270; ⊘ 12:30pm-midnight Mon-Sat, to 11pm Sun; Ⓟ☎; 🚇 La Bombilla) For unpretentious French cuisine, this bistro located in an open-air shopping center hits the spot. Quiches, salads, crepes and decadently delicious desserts, all in generous portions, are the order of the day.

Taberna del León
MEXICAN $$$

(Map p94; ☑ 55-5616-2110; www.tabernadel leon.rest; Altamirano 46, Colonia San Ángel; mains M$240-495; ⊘ 1:30-11:30pm Mon-Wed, to midnight Thu-Sat, to 6pm Sun; Ⓟ☎; 🚇 Dr Gálvez) Chef Monica Patiño is one of the new breed of female stars stirring up traditional cuisine in innovative ways. Seafood is the specialty here, with the likes of *robalo a los tres chiles* (bass in three-pepper chili sauce) and corn blini with Norwegian salmon.

San Ángel Inn
MEXICAN $$$

(Map p94; ☑ 55-5616-1402; www.sanangelinn.com; Diego Rivera 50; breakfast M$90-160, lunch & dinner mains M$205-395; ☺ 7am-1am Mon-Fri, 8am-1am Sat, 8am-10pm Sun; P ☏ ♿; 🚍 Altavista) Classic Mexican meals are served in the garden and various elegant dining rooms of this historic estate next to the Museo Casa Estudio Diego Rivera y Frida Kahlo. On Saturday and Sunday mornings, the Inn provides activities for kids in the rear garden, meaning it's margarita time for mom and dad.

Montejo Sureste
YUCATECAN $$$

(Map p94; ☑ 55-5550-1366; Av de la Paz 16, Colonia San Angel; mains M$155-275; ☺ 1pm-midnight Mon-Sat, to 7pm Sun; P ☏; 🚍 La Bombilla) Along a cobbled street lined with restaurants, this inconspicuous Yucatecan establishment whips up regional favorites such as *sopa de lima* (lime soup), *cochinita pibil* (marinated pork) and *papadzules* (tortillas stuffed with diced hard-boiled eggs and bathed in pumpkin seed sauce).

Ciudad Universitaria

Azul y Oro
MEXICAN $$$

(☑ 55-5622-7135; www.azul.rest; Centro Cultural Universitario; mains M$160-330; ☺ 10am-6pm Mon & Tue, to 8pm Wed-Sat, 9am-7pm Sun; P ☏; 🚍 Centro Cultural Universitario) Chef Ricardo Muñoz searches Mexico high and low for traditional recipes and reinvents them to perfection. Fruits of his labor include *buñuelos rellenos de pato* (fried snacks filled with shredded duck and topped with *mole negro*) and *pescado tikin xic* (an elaborate grouper dish with plantain and tortilla strips). There's another branch downtown (p113).

Coyoacán

Super Tacos Chupacabras
TACOS $

(Map p98; cnr Avs Río Churubusco & México; tacos M$12; ☺ 24hr; Ⓜ Coyoacán) Named after Mexico's mythical 'goat sucker' (a vampire-like creature), this famous *taquería* under a freeway overpass slings wonderful beef and sausage tacos. The specialty is the *chupa,* a mixed-meat taco that contains 127 secret ingredients, or so they say. Avail yourself of the grilled onions, *nopales,* whole beans and other tasty toppings.

Churrería de Coyoacán
DESSERTS $

(Map p98; Allende 38; 4 churros from M$10; ☺ 9am-11pm Mon-Sat; Ⓜ Coyoacán) Here are Coyoacán's best deep-fried snacks. Get in line for a bag – chocolate-filled or straight up – then stroll over to the cafe (p124) next door for coffee. Figure about three hours in the gym to work off these bad boys.

La Casa del Pan Papalotl
VEGETARIAN $

(Map p98; ☑ 55-3095-1767; www.casadelpan.com; Av México 25; breakfast M$95, lunch & dinner M$60-95; ☺ 8am-10pm; ♿; Ⓜ Coyoacán) This hugely popular vegetarian restaurant draws a loyal breakfast crowd thanks to its organic egg dishes, *chilaquiles* (tortilla strips drenched in salsa) and fresh-made *pan* (bread). For lunch the lasagna with squash flower, mushrooms and *poblano* chili is a big hit.

Mercado de Antojitos
MARKET $

(Map p98; Higuera 6; pozoles M$70; ☺ 10am-11pm; Ⓜ Coyoacán) Near Coyoacán's main plaza, this busy spot has all kinds of snacks, including deep-fried quesadillas, *pozoles* and *esquites* (boiled corn kernels served with a dollop of mayo). Look for the 'Pozole Estilo Michoacán' stall.

El Kiosko de Coyoacán
ICE CREAM $

(Map p98; Plaza Hidalgo 6; per scoop M$25; ☺ 9am-midnight; Ⓜ Coyoacán) This obligatory weekend stop has homemade ice cream and popsicles in flavors ranging from mango with chili to *maracuya* (passion fruit).

Corazón de Maguey
MEXICAN $$$

(Map p98; ☑ 55-5659-3165; www.corazonde maguey.com; Jardín Centenario 9A; mains M$175-330; ☺ 12:30pm-1am Mon-Thu, to 2am Fri, 9am-2am Sat, 9am-midnight Sun; ☏; Ⓜ Coyoacán) Adorned with old glass jugs used for transporting booze, this attractive restaurant does traditional Mexican fare that's typically prepared in mezcal-producing regions, such as stuffed *chile ancho* peppers from Queretaro, Oaxacan *tlayudas* (large folded tortillas) and beef tongue in red *mole,* hailing from Puebla. It's also a prime spot to sample some of Mexico's finest mezcals.

Los Danzantes
MEXICAN $$$

(Map p98; ☑ 55-5554-1213; www.losdanzantes.com; Jardín Centenario 12; mains M$195-370; ☺ 12:30-11pm Mon-Thu, 9am-1am Fri & Sat, 9am-11pm Sun; ☏♿; Ⓜ Coyoacán) Los Danzantes puts a contemporary spin on traditional Mexican cuisine with dishes such as *huitlacoche* (trufflelike corn fungus) raviolis in *poblana* sauce, organic chicken in black *mole,* and *hoja santa* (Mexican pepperleaf) stuffed with cheese and *chipotle* chili. You'll also find mezcal from its own famous distillery. A different vegetarian option is featured each Monday.

✕ Tlalpan

La Voragine   ITALIAN $$
(☑ 55-2976-0313; Madero 107, Colonia Tlalpan; mains M$80-120, pizzas M$135-245; ☺ 1pm-2am Tue-Sat, to midnight Sun; ☎ ✐; ⬚ Fuentes Brotantes) Run by a fun-loving couple from New York and DF, this muraled pizzeria-bar prepares savory pizzas, exquisite manicotti and *fungi trifolati* (flambéed mushrooms in white-wine sauce). Or just drop in for a Mexican microbrew and enjoy the sunny patio upstairs. It's a half-block north of Tlalpan's main square.

✕ Colonia del Valle & Around

El Rey de las Ahogadas   MEXICAN $
(www.elreydelasahogadas.com; Av Coyoacán 360, Colonia del Valle; flautas M$17-19; ☺ 11am-midnight Mon-Thu, to 1am Fri & Sat, to 11pm Sun; ⓜ Poliforum) Deep-fried rolled tacos, aka *flautas,* are filled with your choice of refried beans, cheese, shredded beef, chicken, potato or marinated pork. They're topped with crumbled cheese, diced onion and served in a bowl of zesty *salsa verde. Flautas* are something of a fast-food staple throughout the city, but few can match the crunchy, spicy goodness of El Rey (The King).

Fonda Margarita   MEXICAN $
(☑ 55-5559-6358; www.fondamargarita.com; Adolfo Prieto 1354, Colonia Tlacoquemécatl del Valle; mains M$43-61; ☺ 5:30-noon Tue-Sun; ☎; ⬚ Parque Hundido) Possibly the capital's premier hangover-recovery spot, this humble eatery under a tin roof whips up batches of comfort food such as *longaniza en salsa verde* (sausage in green salsa) and *frijoles con huevo* (beans with egg). The *fonda* is beside Plaza Tlacoquemécatl, six blocks east of Avenida Insurgentes. There's usually a line to get in, but it moves fast.

▼ Drinking & Nightlife

Cafes, bars and cantinas are all key social venues on the capital's landscape. The traditional watering holes are, of course, cantinas – no-nonsense places with simple tables, long polished bars and old-school waiters.

▼ Centro Histórico

★ Hostería La Bota   BAR
(Map p68; ☑ 55-5709-9016; www.facebook.com/labotacultubar; San Jerónimo 40; ☺ 1:30pm-midnight Sun-Tue, to 2am Wed & Thu, noon-3am Fri & Sat; ☎; ⓜ Isabel La Católica) ✐ *Cerveza,* mezcal cocktails, tapas and deliciously oily pizza are served amid a profusion of warped bullfighting bric-a-brac and recycled objects. A portion of your bar tab sponsors local art projects.

Cantina Tío Pepe   BAR
(Map p68; Independencia 26; ☺ noon-11pm Mon-Sat; ⓜ San Juan de Letrán) A must-visit on the downtown cantina crawl circuit, Tio Pepe is one of the city's oldest and most traditional watering holes. Over a storied history that spans nearly 14 decades, the saloon has poured *cerveza* and tequila shots to influential Mexican politicians and famous artists. It's said that author William Burroughs wrote about this 'cheap cantina' in *Junky.*

Talismán de Motolinía   BAR
(Map p68; www.facebook.com/talismandemotolinia; Motolinía 31, Colonia Centro; ☺ 1pm-midnight Sun-Wed, to 2am Thu-Sat; ☎; ⓜ Allende) Potent mezcal is poured from a beautifully designed talisman-shaped bar at this downtown *mezcalería,* where you can catch nightly music acts (live bands, open mike or DJ sets). On Wednesday at 8pm there's usually mezcal tastings with a local expert, and affordable Oaxacan snacks are always available if you get the munchies.

Salón Corona   BEER HALL
(Map p68; ☑ 55-5512-5725; www.saloncorona.com.mx; Bolívar 24; ☺ 10:30am-2am; ⓜ Allende) Amiable staff serve up *tarros* (mugs) of light or dark *cerveza de barril* (draft beer) in this boisterous beer hall. It's a great place to get a taste of *fútbol*-mad Mexico when a match is on TV, which is almost always.

Bar La Ópera   BAR
(Map p68; ☑ 55-5512-8959; www.barlaopera.com; Av 5 de Mayo 10; ☺ 1pm-midnight Mon-Sat, to 6pm Sun; ⓜ Allende) With booths of dark walnut and an ornate copper-colored ceiling (said to have been punctured by Pancho Villa's bullet), this late-19th-century watering hole remains a bastion of tradition. The food is a little overpriced.

Bar Mancera   BAR
(Map p68; ☑ 55-5521-9755; Venustiano Carranza 49; ☺ 2-11pm Mon-Thu, to 2:30am Fri-Sun; ⬚ República

del Salvador) More than a century old, this atmospheric gentlemen's salon is now open to all but seems preserved in amber, with ornate carved paneling and well-used domino tables. Regulars come for the good stuff: mezcal and tequila as well as classics such as gin and tonic, and Campari and orange.

Downtown Mexico BAR
(Map p68; ☑ 55-5282-2199; www.downtownmexico. com; Isabel La Católica 30; ⊗ 10am-11pm Sun-Thu, to 2am Fri & Sat; ☎; M Zócalo) The rooftop lounge bar at boutique hotel Downtown Mexico has become a popular spot to chill over drinks. It's also been known to host the occasional pool party with open bar and DJ sets.

Café Jekemir CAFE
(Map p68; ☑ 55-5709-7086; www.cafejekemir.com; Isabel La Católica 88; ⊗ 8am-9pm Mon-Sat; ☎; M Isabel La Católica) Run by a family of coffee traders from Orizaba, this old distribution outlet, now transformed into a popular cafe, prepares good Veracruz coffee and Lebanese snacks.

☕ Zona Rosa

Jardín Chapultepec BEER GARDEN
(Map p82; www.facebook.com/jardinchapultepec mx; Av Chapultepec 398, Colonia Roma; ⊗ 1-10pm Tue-Thu, 1-11pm Fri, 11am-11pm Sat, 11am-10pm Sun; ☎☎; M Insurgentes) Mexico City's buzziest beer garden pours hoppy Mexican craft brew and grills a mighty fine burger. You may find yourself sharing a picnic bench in the perpetually packed garden, but that just makes for a more convivial experience when knocking 'em back. Note it's one of the exceedingly rare establishments nowadays that allows smoking.

Crisanta BAR
(Map p76; ☑ 55-5535-6372; www.crisantamx.com; Av Plaza de la República 51; ⊗ 1-10pm Mon-Wed, to 2am Thu & Fri, 10am-2am Sat, 11am-7pm Sun; ☎; ☐ Plaza de la República) A welcome sight in a nation where two breweries control about 98% of the market, Crisanta makes its own porter and sells Mexican and foreign craft beers. Jazz groups play twice a month on Friday and Saturday, and there's art on display in the back room. Antique furnishings and long wooden tables add character to the beer hall atmosphere.

Café La Habana CAFE
(Map p76; ☑ 55-5535-2620; Av Morelos 62; ⊗ 7am-11pm Sun-Thu, to 1am Fri & Sat; ☎;

☐ Expo Reforma) This coffeehouse is a traditional haunt for writers and journalists, who linger for hours over a *café americano*. Legend has it that Fidel and Che plotted strategy here prior to the Cuban revolution, and that Gabriel García Márquez wrote some of *Cien años de soledad* (One Hundred Years of Solitude) here.

☕ Condesa

Chiquitito CAFE
(Map p86; ☑ 55-5211-6123; www.chiquititocafe. com; Alfonso Reyes 232; ⊗ 7:30am-7:30pm Mon-Sat, 9am-5pm Sun; ☎; M Chilpancingo) 🍃 Small in size, huge on Veracruz flavor. Coffee shops are everywhere in the Condesa but few have the know-how to bring out the best in their beans. The baristas at this hole-in-the-wall have it all figured out.

Felina COCKTAIL BAR
(Map p86; ☑ 55-5277-1917; Ometusco 87; ⊗ 6pm-2am Tue-Sat; ☎; M Chilpancingo) Long-standing Felina has come of age. Quiet confidence is felt in its low-level music, and in cocktails that don't rely on sweetness but leverage real ingredients, such as fresh juniper berries in the gin. Psychedelic wallpaper and vintage chairs give a nod to a 'funky' past, but times have changed, and the lounging crowd is well-dressed but oh so casual.

Pastelería Maque CAFE
(Map p86; ☑ 55-2454-4662; Av Ozuluama 4; ⊗ 8am-10pm Mon-Sat, to 9pm Sun; ☐ Campeche) Condesa sophisticates gather for coffee in the mornings and Irish coffee in the evenings at this Parisian-style cafe-bakery near Parque México. Waiters bring around trays of freshly baked croissants and *conchas* (round pastries sprinkled with sugar).

Condesa df BAR
(Map p86; ☑ 55-5241-2600; www.condesadf.com; Veracruz 102; ⊗ 2-11pm Sun-Wed, to 1am Thu-Sat; ☎; M Chapultepec) The bar of the fashionable Condesa df hotel has become an essential stop on the Condesa circuit. Up on the roof, guests lounge on big-wheel wicker sofas and enjoy views of verdant Parque España across the way.

Enhorabuena Café CAFE
(Map p86; www.enhorabuenacafe.com; Atlixco 13; coffee M$30-58; ⊗ 8am-8pm Mon-Sat; ☎; ☐ Sonora) Mexico is a major coffee-producing nation and yet few baristas grasp the art of making a proper *café* like they do at

Enhorabuena. Sure, a cappuccino will cost a bit more, but you're paying for high-quality coffee from the Veracruz highlands. The cakes and sandwiches are excellent too.

Flora Lounge BAR

(Map p86; Michoacán 54, cnr Av Nuevo León; ⊙9am-midnight Mon-Wed, to 1am Thu & Sat, to 2am Fri; 🚇Campeche) Condesa is overflowing with bars, but Flora Lounge strikes the right balance between good, fairly priced cocktails and drinks, and a casual cute bistro atmosphere serving an excellent range of Mexican and international food.

Salón Malafama BAR

(Map p86; www.salonmalafama.com.mx; Av Michoacán 78; billiard table per hour M$100; ⊙1pm-midnight Sun & Mon, to 1am Tue & Wed, to 2am Thu-Sat; 🛜; 🚇Campeche) This sleek billiard hall doubles as a bar and gallery for photo exhibits. Board games, American diner food and happy hour specials on drinks and pool draw groups of friends. The well-maintained tables are frequented by both pool sharks as well as novices. Cash only.

El Centenario CANTINA

(Map p86; 🕿55-5553-5451; Vicente Suárez 42; ⊙noon-1am Mon-Wed, to 2am Thu-Sat; 🛜; 🚇Campeche) Laden with bullfighting memorabilia, this dark cantina with unrenovated tiles and brick arches is an enclave of tradition amid the modish restaurant and bar zone. Not a place to dress up for, but great to start the night with fair prices on beer, mezcal, tequila and rum.

Black Horse PUB

(Map p86; 🕿55-5211-8740; www.caballonegro.com; Mexicali 85; ⊙6pm-2:30am Tue-Sat; 🛜; Ⓜ Patriotismo) Besides its draw as a preferred spot to catch televised *fútbol* matches, this British pub boasts an international social scene and has excellent funk, jazz and indie-rock bands playing the back room. Check the website for events.

PataNegra Condesa BAR

(Map p86; 🕿55-5211-5563; www.patanegra. com.mx; Av Tamaulipas 30; ⊙1:30pm-2am; 🛜; 🚇Campeche) Nominally a tapas bar, this oblong salon draws a friendly mix of 20-something *chilangos* and expats. Live Veracruz-style *son jarocho* bands perform on Saturday, while the program during the week usually features jazz, salsa or funk music.

 Roma

★**Casa Franca** COCKTAIL BAR

(Map p86; 🕿55-5533-8754; www.facebook.com/ lacasamerida109; Mérida 109; ⊙5pm-1am Tue & Wed, to 2am Thu-Sat; 🛜; 🚇Jardín Pushkin) This upstairs bar is a labyrinth with more moods than a house party. The live jazz plays out in an intimate living room, while the corner balcony overlooking Álvaro Obregón captures that twinkle of Saturday night. The other (extremely) dark corners are made for lounging, sipping great cocktails and hand holding.

★**Traspatio** BEER GARDEN

(Map p86; www.facebook.com/traspatiomx; cnr Córdoba & Colima; ⊙1:30pm-midnight Tue & Wed, to 2am Thu-Sat, to 10pm Sun; 🛜; 🚇Durango) For the urban backyard barbecue experience, this open-air beer garden is a fine choice. It's a great little hideaway for chatting over a *cerveza* or mezcal and munching on a *choripán* (grilled sausage in a roll), tuna steak or portobello mushroom burger.

Quentin Café CAFE

(Map p86; 🕿55-7096-9968; www.facebook.com/ quentincafemx; Álvaro Obregón 64; ⊙8am-10pm Sun-Wed, to 11pm Thu-Sat; 🛜; 🚇Jardín Pushkin) Quentin's quietly cool baristas are serious about coffee whether it's dripped, poured-over or brewed. Beans are from Mexico and around the world. This contender for best coffee in CDMX is tiny but has enough table space for laptops.

Pan y Circo BAR

(Map p86; 🕿55-6086-4291; www.facebook.com/ panycircomxdf; Álavaro Obregón 160, Colonia Roma; ⊙1pm-2am Mon-Sat, to midnight Sun; 🛜; 🚇Álavaro Obregón) A buzzy nightspot in the trendy Roma district, this three-story bar makes a nice place to unwind over mezcal or cocktails, especially during the week when the crowd thins out. On the 2nd floor you can catch live music on Thursday nights in an interior patio, while upstairs you'll find a smoker-friendly *terraza* bar. See their Facebook page for weekly events.

La Chicha BAR

(Map p86; 🕿55-5574-6625; Orizaba 171; ⊙11am-midnight Mon-Wed, to 2am Thu-Sat; 🛜; 🚇Hospital General) Mix one part Mexican vintage decor, one shot of rock vibe and throw in mezcal, beer and snacks (including veg options) and you have a bar full to its low-lit brim, yet still chilled enough for

DON'T MISS

THE MEZCAL & PULQUE RENAISSANCE
....

In recent years the agave-based Mexican liquor mezcal, long thought of as just a poor rustic relative to tequila, has finally won the respect it deserves. Many bars around Mexico City now serve mezcal to the new breed of discerning aficionados.

A humbler kind of drinking establishment rooted in ancient Mexican tradition is the *pulquería*, which serves *pulque* (a pre-Hispanic, fermented alcoholic beverage). These places have also been experiencing a resurgence, with young *chilangos* rediscovering the joys of sharing a pitcher of the milky quaff.

Mezcalerías

Mano Santa Mezcal (Map p86; ☑55-6585-4354; Av Insurgentes Sur 219; ⊙6pm-2am Tue & Wed, from 4pm Thu-Sat, 6pm-midnight Sun; ⎚Durango) Often compared to having a drink at home because of the cheap, quality mezcal (or because you live in a designer-school laboratory), this small bar quickly overflows with droves of the young and hip on weekends.

Alipús (www.alipus.com; Guadalupe Victoria 15, Colonia Tlalpan; ⊙12:30-11pm Mon & Tue, to midnight Wed, to 1am Thu, 9am-1am Fri & Sat, 9am-11pm Sun; ⎚Fuentes Brotantes) From the makers of the popular Oaxaca-based mezcal brands Alipús and Los Danzantes, this quaint bar in Tlalpan stocks some of the finest mezcal in all of Mexico (ie Danzantes Pechuga Roja). The regional *antojitos* (snacks) are wonderful as well. There's also a chic Condesa (Map p86; ☑55-5211-6845; www.alipus.com/alipuscondesa; Aguascalientes 232; ⊙1-11:30pm Mon-Thu, to 1am Fri & Sat, 2-8pm Sun; Ⓜ Chilpancingo) branch.

La Clandestina (Map p86; Álvaro Obregón 298, Colonia Roma; ⊙6pm-midnight Mon-Sat; ⎚Álvaro Obregón) Fashioned after a rural mom-and-pop shop, the Clandestina provides a detailed menu describing the elaboration process of the mezcals dispensed from jugs on high shelves. In true clandestine fashion, the sign outside is tiny and for those in the know.

Bósforo (Map p76; Luis Moya 31, cnr Independencia; ⊙6pm-midnight Tue-Sat; Ⓜ Juárez) Blink and you might walk right past the friendliest neighborhood *mezcalería* in town. Behind the Bósforo's nondescript curtain await top-notch mezcals, an eclectic mix of music and surprisingly good bar grub in a dark and casual setting.

Pulquerías

Pulquería Los Insurgentes (Map p86; www.facebook.com/pulqueriaInsurgentes; Av Insurgentes Sur 226; ⊙2pm-1am Mon-Wed, 1pm-3am Thu-Sat; ⎚Durango) A testament to the city's *pulque* revival, this three-story *porfiriato*-era house may not please the purists, but unlike a traditional *pulquería*, here you get live music, DJ sets and other alcoholic drinks not called *pulque*.

Pulquería La Botijona (Av Morelos 109; ⊙10am-10pm; ⎚Xochimilco) Possibly the cleanest *pulque* dispenser in town, this institutional green hall near the Xochimilco train station is a friendly, family-run establishment with big plastic pails of the traditional quaff lining the shelves.

Pulquería El Templo de Diana (☑55-5653-4657; Madero 17, cnr Calle 5 de Mayo; ⊙10am-9pm; ⎚Xochimilco) This classic *pulquería*, a block east of the main market, Mercado de Xochimilco, has a cheerful sawdust-on-the-floor vibe, with a mixed-age crowd enjoying giant mugs of the *maguey*-based beverage. Even a few females may pop in. Delivered daily from Hidalgo state, the *pulque* is expertly blended with flavorings such as Nescafé, *pistache* (pistachio) and *piñon* (pine nut).

conversation. Part of a growing row of bars that are too cool for the swankiness of Álvaro Obregón – unfortunately staff seem more interested in posing than working.

Cantina Covadonga BAR
(Map p82; www.banquetescovadonga.com.mx; Puebla 121; ⊙1pm-3am Mon-Fri, from 2pm Sat; Ⓜ Insurgentes) Echoing with the sounds of

clacking dominoes, this old Asturian social hall is a traditionally male enclave, though hipsters of both sexes have increasingly moved in on this hallowed ground.

La Bodeguita del Medio
BAR

(Map p86; 55-5553-0246; www.labodeguita delmedio.com.mx; Cozumel 37; 1:30pm-2am Mon-Sat, to 12:30am Sun; Sevilla) The walls are tagged with verses and messages at this animated branch of the famous Havana joint. Have a mojito (a Cuban drink of rum, lime juice and mint leaves) and enjoy the excellent *son cubano* combos that perform here.

Maison Francaise de Thé Caravanserai
TEAHOUSE

(Map p86; 55-2803-1170; www.caravanserai. com.mx; Orizaba 101; 11am-9pm; ; Álvaro Obregón) This French- and 'Oriental'-style tearoom has more than 170 blends categorized by their intended use or effects. Visitors relax on comfortable sofas to enjoy their chosen brews, which are ceremoniously served on silver trays.

Los Bisquets Obregón
CAFE

(Map p86; 55-5584-2802; https://bisquets obregon.com; Álvaro Obregón 60; 7am-10:30pm Sun-Thu, to 11pm Fri & Sat; ; Álvaro Obregón) *Chilango* families flock to this quaint diner for the *pan dulce* (sweet bread) and *café con leche,* dispensed from two pitchers, Veracruz-style.

Polanco

Fiebre de Malta
BEER HALL

(Map p90; 55-5531-6826; www.fiebredemalta. com; Av Presidente Masaryk 48, Colonia Polanco; 10am-1am Sun-Tue & Thu, to 2am Wed, Fri & Sat; ; Polanco) At the forefront of Mexico City's craft beer boom, Fiebre de Malta has more 30 brews on tap, with suds ranging from hoppy IPAs to German-style Hefeweizens. The menu describes the characteristics of each beer, including their origin and flavor details. The large beer hall also does pub grub if you get the munchies.

Área
COCKTAIL BAR

(Map p90; 55-5282-3100; www.hotelhabita.com; Av Presidente Masaryk 201; 7pm-2am; ; Polanco) Atop the designer Hábita Hotel, this open-air roof lounge does a brisk trade in exotic martinis, with sweeping city views as a backdrop and videos projected on the wall of a nearby building.

San Ángel

La Camelia
BAR

(Map p94; 55-5615-5643; www.facebook.com/ lacamelia.cantabar; Madero 3; noon-8pm Sun-Thu, to 2am Fri & Sat; La Bombilla) This restaurant-cantina has been drawing Mexican celebrities since 1931, as evidenced by the stars' photos on the walls. On Friday and Saturday karaoke nights, it's your time to shine with a rendition of, say, a Michael Jackson or Madonna classic. Liquid courage comes in the form of tequila or *cerveza mexicana.*

Coyoacán

★ La Bipo
BAR

(Map p98; 55-5484-8230; Malintzin 155; noon-midnight Sun-Tue, to 2am Wed-Sat; ; Coyoacán) This popular cantina plays up the kitschier elements of Mexican popular culture, with wall panels fashioned from plastic crates and sliced tin buckets as light shades. The menu of Mexican snacks is hit and miss. DJs spin assorted tunes upstairs from Wednesday to Saturday.

Cantina La Coyoacana
BAR

(Map p98; http://lacoyoacana.com; Higuera 14; 1pm-midnight Sun-Wed, to 1:45am Thu-Sat; ; Coyoacán) Enter through swinging saloon doors and head to the open-air patio, where wailing mariachis do their thing in this traditional drinking establishment.

El Hijo del Cuervo
BAR

(Map p98; 55-5658-7824; www.elhijodelcuervo. com.mx; Jardín Centenario 17; 3pm-midnight Mon, 1pm-12:30am Tue-Sat, noon-midnight Sun; Coyoacán) A Coyoacán institution, this stone-walled 'cultu-bar' on the Jardín Centenario is a longtime favorite on the local cultural scene. Jazz and rock groups perform on Tuesday, Wednesday and Thursday nights.

Café El Jarocho
CAFE

(Map p98; 55-5658-5029; www.cafeeljarocho. com.mx; Cuauhtémoc 134; 6:30am-1am Sun-Thu, to 2am Fri & Sat; Coyoacán) This immensely popular joint churns out coffee from Veracruz for long lines of bean lovers. As there's no seating inside, people have their drink standing in the street or sitting on curbside benches. A branch (Map p98; Av México 25C; 6am-11pm; Coyoacán) with seats is several blocks northwest of Jardín Centenario.

Tlalpan

La Jalisciense
BAR

(☑55-5573-5586; Plaza de la Constitución 7; ⊙noon-11:30pm Mon-Sat; ⌨Fuentes Brotantes) This building opened its doors in 1870, making La Jalisciense the oldest cantina in Mexico City – now that's a good reason to pop in and wet your whistle with one of their many tequilas. The small *tortas* are also worthy.

Colonia del Valle

Passmar
CAFE

(☑55-5669-1994; http://cafepassmar.com; Adolfo Prieto s/n, local 237, cnr Av Coyoacán; ⊙7am-7:30pm; ☎; ⌨Amores) You'll be hard-pressed to find a place that takes a cup o' Joe more seriously than Passmar, and the proof is in the artful presentation of the cappuccino. You'll find the award-winning coffee in Mercado Lázaro Cárdenas, a block and a half southwest of metrobús Amores.

☆ Entertainment

There's so much going on in Mexico City on any given evening, it's hard to keep track.

Cinema

Mexico City is a banquet for movie-goers, with everything from open-air screenings, film festivals and art-house cinema to blockbusters, many from the strong Mexican film-production industry. Ticket prices are around M$60 in commercial cinemas, with many places offering discounts on Wednesday. Most movies are available in original languages with Spanish subtitles, except for children's fare. *El Universal* and *La Jornada* have daily listings.

Cineteca Nacional
CINEMA

(Map p98; ☑55-4155-1200; www.cineteca nacional.net; Av México-Coyoacán 389, Colonia Xoco; ☎; ⓂCoyoacán) Mexican and foreign indie movies are shown on 10 screens at the architecturally interesting Cineteca. In November the complex hosts the Muestra Internacional de Cine, an international film festival. From October to March you can catch free open-air screenings at dusk in the grass-covered rear garden.

On-site La Galería de la Cineteca Nacional is dedicated to Mexican cinema with exhibitions related to international film.

Cine Tonalá
CINEMA

(Map p86; www.cinetonala.com; Tonalá 261; ☎; ⌨Campeche) A small, hip multipurpose

venue for independent cinema, plays, stand-up comedy and concerts.

Cinemex Casa de Arte
CINEMA

(Cinemex Reforma; Map p82; ☑55-5257-6969; www.cinemex.com; Río Guadalquivir 104; ⓂInsurgentes) Primarily art-house flicks.

Cinemex Real
CINEMA

(Map p76; ☑55-5257-6969; www.cinemex.com; Colón 17; ⓂHidalgo) This Cinemex branch screens mostly Hollywood movies and the occasional Mexican hit.

Cinépolis Diana
CINEMA

(Map p82; ☑55-5511-3236; www.cinepolis.com; Paseo de la Reforma 423; ⓂSevilla) Screens commercial releases and international film-festival titles, many in their original language with Spanish subtitles.

Filmoteca de la UNAM
CINEMA

(☑55-5704-6338; www.filmoteca.unam.mx; Av Insurgentes Sur 3000; ⌨Centro Cultural Universitario) Two cinemas at the Centro Cultural Universitario screen films from a collection of more than 43,000 titles.

Dance, Classical Music & Theater

Orchestral music, opera, ballet, contemporary dance and theater are all abundantly represented in the capital's numerous theaters. Museums, too, serve as performance venues (often for free), including the Museo de la Secretaría de Hacienda y Crédito Público (p73) and the Museo de la Ciudad de México (p75). The national arts council (www.mexicoescultura.com) provides a rundown of events on its website.

If your Spanish is up to it, you might like to sample Mexico City's lively theater scene. **Mejor Teatro** (www.mejorteatro.com) covers the major venues.

★Patrick Miller
DANCE

(Map p82; ☑55-5511-5406; www.facebook. com/PatrickMillerMX; Mérida 17; admission M$30; ⊙10pm-3am Fri; ⓂInsurgentes) People-watching doesn't get any better than at this throbbing disco, founded by Mexico City DJ Patrick Miller. With a clientele ranging from black-clad '80s throwbacks to cross-dressers, the Friday fun begins when dance circles open and regulars pull off moves that would make John Travolta proud.

Salón Los Ángeles
DANCING

(☑55-5597-5181; www.salonlosangeles.mx; Lerdo 206, Colonia Guerrero; ⊙6-11pm Tue & 5-11pm Sun; ⓂTlatelolco) Fans of dance-hall music

TICKETS

Ticketmaster sells tickets for all the major venues online, or visit one of its branches:

Liverpool Centro (Map p68; Venustiano Carranza 92; ⊙11am-7pm; Ⓜ Zócalo)

Liverpool Polanco (Map p90; Mariano Escobedo 425; ⊙11am-8pm; Ⓜ Polanco)

Mixup Centro (Map p68; Av Madero 51; ⊙10am-9pm Mon-Sat, 11am-8pm Sun; Ⓜ Zócalo)

Mixup Zona Rosa (Map p82; Génova 76; ⊙11am-8pm; Ⓜ Insurgentes)

shouldn't miss the outstanding orchestras or the graceful dancers who fill the vast floor of this atmospheric ballroom. The live music, consisting of salsa and *cumbia* (dance music originating in Colombia) on Sunday and swing and *danzón* on Tuesday, draws a mostly older crowd. It's located in the rough Colonia Guerrero, so take an authorized taxi.

Two-hour dance classes are offered on Monday at 6pm and Tuesday at 4pm.

Palacio de Bellas Artes   PERFORMING ARTS
(Map p68; www.inba.gob.mx; Av Hidalgo 1; ⊙box office 11am-7pm; Ⓜ Bellas Artes) The Orquesta Sinfónica Nacional and prestigious opera companies perform in Bellas Artes' ornate theater, while chamber groups appear in the recital halls. The venue is most famous, though, for the **Ballet Folklórico de México** (Map p68; www.balletfolkloricodemexico.com. mx; tickets from M$365; ⊙performances 8:30pm Wed, 9:30am & 8:30pm Sun), a two-hour festive blur of costumes, music and dance from all over Mexico. Tickets are usually available on the day of the show or from Ticketmaster.

Foro Shakespeare   THEATER
(Map p86; ☑55-5553-4642; www.foroshakespeare. com; Zamora 7; ⛹; Ⓜ Chapultepec) A small independent theater in La Condesa with an eclectic program including live flamenco, stand-up comedy and children's programs. Jazz ensembles perform in the theater's restaurant-bar.

Mama Rumba   SALSA
(Map p86; ☑55-5564-6920; www.mamarumba. com.mx; Querétaro 230; admission M$110; ⊙9pm-3am Wed-Sat; ⛖ Sonora) Managed by a Havana native, Mama Rumba features contemporary salsa, with music by the house big

band. If you'd like to take a class (free with entrance fee), dance instructors will get you started Wednesday and Thursday at 9pm. Mama Rumba has a larger branch in San Ángel at Plaza Loreto.

Centro Nacional de las Artes   PERFORMING ARTS
(CNA; ☑55-4155-0000; www.cenart.gob.mx; Av Río Churubusco 79, Colonia Country Club; ⛖; Ⓜ General Anaya) This sprawling cultural institute near Coyoacán has many free events across the artistic spectrum, including contemporary dance, theater, art shows and classical concerts. To get here, exit metro General Anaya (Línea 2) on the east side of Calzada de Tlalpan, then walk north to the corner and turn right.

Teatro de la Ciudad   CONCERT VENUE
(Map p68; ☑55-5130-5740, ext 2006; http://tea tros.cultura.df.gob.mx; Donceles 36; ⊙box office 10am-3pm & 4-7pm; Ⓜ Allende) Built in 1918 and modeled after Milan's La Scala opera house, this lavishly restored 1300-seat hall gets some of the more interesting touring acts in music, dance and theater.

Live Music

Mexico City's eclectic music offerings rock. On any given night, you can hear traditional Mexican, Cuban, jazz, electronica, garage punk and so on. Music sounds off everywhere: in concert halls, bars, museums – even on public transportation. Free gigs often take place at the Zócalo and Monumento a la Revolución, while the thriving mariachi music scene at Plaza Garibaldi gets going by about 8pm and stays busy until 3am. The *'conciertos'* sections of Tiempo Libre (www. tiempolibre.com.mx) and Ticketmaster (www.ticketmaster.com.mx) include show listings. The street market Tianguis Cultural del Chopo (p132) has a stage at its north end every Saturday afternoon for young and hungry metal and punk bands.

★ **Salón Tenampa**   MARIACHIS
(Map p68; ☑55-5526-6176; Plaza Garibaldi 12; ⊙1pm-1am Sun-Thu, to 2am Fri & Sat; ⛖; Ⓜ Garibaldi) Graced with murals of the giants of Mexican song and enlivened by its own songsters – and an extensive tequila and mezcal menu – the Tenampa is a festive cantina on the north side of Plaza Garibaldi. If serenading at other tables is not enough, request a song (50 to 100 pesos) from mariachi, who travel from across the country. A visit here is obligatory.

★**Centro Cultural de España** LIVE MUSIC
(Map p68; ☑55-5521-1925; www.ccemx.org; República de Guatemala 18; ⊙10pm-2am Wed-Sat; Ⓜ Zócalo) Cool young things pack the terrace of this place each weekend for its excellent DJ and live-music sessions. Located directly behind the cathedral, the rebuilt colonial-era structure is usually quaking by midnight.

Parker & Lenox LIVE MUSIC
(Map p82; ☑55-5546-6979; www.facebook.com/ parkerandlenox; Milán 14; ⊙1pm-1am Tue, to 2am Wed-Sat; ☎; 🚇Reforma) Named after legendary saxophonist Charlie Parker and famed Harlem jazz club Lenox Lounge, Parker & Lenox is part American-style diner (specializing in hamburgers, M$140 to M$180) and part backroom concert venue featuring live jazz, blues, funk and swing bands.

Pasagüero + La Bipo CONCERT VENUE
(Map p68; ☑55-5512-6624; www.facebook.com/ pasaguero; Motolinía 33; ⊙10pm-3:30am Thu-Sat; ☎; Ⓜ Allende) Some visionary developers took a historic building and transformed its stonewalled ground level into a restaurant-bar for various cultural happenings, especially rock and electronica gigs.

Cafebrería El Péndulo LIVE MUSIC
(Map p86; www.forodeltejedor.com; Álvaro Obregón 86; ☎; 🚇Álvaro Obregón) Leading Mexican artists of varying musical genres play at this cafe-bookstore's rooftop venue. The adjoining open-air bar provides a nice atmosphere for hanging out after the show.

El Under LIVE MUSIC
(Map p86; ☑55-5511-5475; www.theunder.org; Monterrey 80; admission from M$50; ⊙9pm-5am Fri & Sat; 🚇Durango) At this underground favorite, black-clad youths dance to the likes of Morrissey and Bauhaus on the old house's lower level, while upstairs local bands grind out everything from garage punk and rockabilly to death metal.

Auditorio Nacional CONCERT VENUE
(Map p90; ☑55-9138-1350; www.auditorio.com. mx; Paseo de la Reforma 50; ⊙box office 10am-7pm Mon-Sat, 11am-6pm Sun; Ⓜ Auditorio) Major Mexican and visiting rock and pop artists take the stage at the 10,000-seat Auditorio Nacional. The adjoining **Lunario del Auditorio** (Map p90; www.lunario.com.mx;) is a large club reserved mostly for jazz and folk acts.

Barba Azul LIVE MUSIC
(www.facebook.com/barba.azul.cabaret; Gutiérrez Nájera 231, Colonia Obrera; ⊙8pm-3am Tue-Sat; Ⓜ Obrera) Welcome to the inferno. Red lighting and colorful artwork of dancers engulfed in flames set the mood at this cabaret-style nightclub, where you still see some *ficheras* (women who dance with men) at work (M$20). Since the 1950s, Barba Azul has staged some of the city's best salsa, merengue and *son* (folk) acts. Call for a secure taxi when leaving.

Multiforo Alicia CONCERT VENUE
(Map p86; ☑55-5511-2100; Av Cuauhtémoc 91A; 🚇Jardín Pushkin) Behind the graffiti-scrawled facade is Mexico City's premier indie-rock club. A suitably dark, seatless space, the Alicia stages mostly up-and-coming punk, surf and ska bands, who play at the store downstairs. See the Facebook page for show times.

Zinco Jazz Club JAZZ
(Map p68; ☑55-5512-3369; www.zincojazz.com; Motolinía 20; ⊙9pm-2am Wed-Sat; ☎; Ⓜ Allende) A vital component in the rebirth of the *centro*, Zinco is a supper club featuring local jazz and funk outfits as well as touring artists. The intimate basement room fills up fast when big-name acts take the stage.

El Bataclán CABARET
(Map p86; ☑55-5511-7390; www.labodega.com.mx; Popocatépetl 25; ⊙9pm-midnight Tue & Wed, to 2am Thu-Sat; 🚇Álvaro Obregón) A theater within a club (La Bodega), this classic cabaret venue showcases some of Mexico's more offbeat performers. Afterwards, catch top-notch Cuban *son combos* over a rum-based mojito.

Caradura CONCERT VENUE
(Map p86; ☑55-5211-8035; www.caradura.mx; Av Nuevo León 73, 2nd fl; ⊙9pm-2:30am Tue-Sat; 🚇Campeche) One of the best spots in town to exorcise your demons while rockin' out to garage, rockabilly and postpunk sounds.

El Imperial Club CONCERT VENUE
(Map p86; ☑55-5525-1115; www.elimperial.tv; Álvaro Obregón 293; ⊙10pm-2:30am Tue & Wed, to 4am Thu-Sat; Ⓜ Sevilla) Mexican alternative-rock bands and the occasional imported act perform in this ornate two-story house in La Roma with antique furnishings and vintage touches throughout.

Ruta 61 BLUES
(Map p86; ☑55-5211-7602; www.facebook.com/ El61BluesClub; Av Baja California 281; ⊙7pm-1am

Thu-Sat; ⓂChilpancingo) This split-level venue stages electric blues artists in the Buddy Guy/Howlin' Wolf mold. About once a month there's a direct-from-Chicago act, though you're more likely to see a local cover band.

El Plaza Condesa
CONCERT VENUE

(Map p86; ☑55-5256-5381; www.elplaza.mx; Juan Escutia 4; ⓆCampeche) At the heart of the Condesa nightlife scene, this former movie theater now raises the curtain for pop and rock acts from Mexico and abroad.

El Breve Espacio Mezcalería
LIVE MUSIC

(☑55-5781-9356; www.elbreveespacio.mx; Arequipa 734, cnr Montevideo; admission M$100-150; ☉7pm-midnight Wed, to 2am Thu-Sat; ☎; ⓂDeportivo 18 de Marzo) Folk singers in the Silvio Rodríguez mold take the stage at this temple of *trova* (troubadour-type folk music) in Lindavista.

Cabaret

La Perla
CABARET

(Map p68; ☑55-3916-2699; www.facebook.com/cabaret.laperla; República de Cuba 44;

GAY & LESBIAN MEXICO CITY

Since Mexico City approved a same-sex marriage law (with the nation following suit), the capital has been seen as a bastion of tolerance in an otherwise conservative country. The city's mayor, Miguel Ángel Mancera, even declared to the world that 'Mexico City is an LGBTTTI friendly city.'

The longtime heart of gay life is the Zona Rosa – in particular Calle Amberes – yet many night owls prefer the downtown 'alternative' scene along República de Cuba. GayCities (http://mexicocity.gaycities.com) has useful information on gay-friendly hotels, bars and clubs. The Marcha del Orgullo Gay (Gay Pride) takes place one Saturday each June and sashays along Reforma from the Ángel to the Zócalo.

The **Cliníca Condesa** (☑55-5515-8311; www.condesadf.mx; Gral Benjamín Hill 24; ☉7am-7pm Mon-Fri; ⓆDe La Salle) is a flagship health center specializing in sexual health, especially (but not only) LGBT issues, with rapid HIV and STI tests, treatment and prevention, such as PEP medication, at no charge, even for foreigners.

La Purísima (Map p68; República de Cuba 17, Colonia Centro; ☉7pm-2:30am Thu-Sat; ⓂBellas Artes) La Purísima is essentially two bars in one: join the sweaty throng downstairs to dance music, or head upstairs for mezcal, *pulque* and ironically bad/hip music. Drinks are cheap, but hold on tight as it gets crowded.

Nicho Bears & Bar (Map p82; www.bearmex.com; Londres 182; ☉8pm-2:30am Thu-Sat; ⓂInsurgentes) Popular with 30-somethings, this Zona Rosa bear den has a slightly more sophisticated air than many of the bars lining the raucous gay strip on nearby Amberes.

Marrakech Salón (Map p68; República de Cuba 18; cover charge M$50; ☉6pm-2:30am Thu-Sat; ⓂAllende) Typical sights and sounds at this gay bar include bare-chested bartenders serving cheap drinks, bar-top drag shows and festive music ranging from '80s pop to hip-shaking *cumbias* (dance music from Colombia) and current diva hits in English. It gets crowded and steamy, but no one seems to mind.

Tom's Leather Bar (Map p86; ☑55-5564-0728; www.toms-mexico.com; Av Insurgentes Sur 357; ☉9pm-3am Tue-Sun; ☎; ⓆCampeche) For those who dare to get medieval, Tom's provides the props, with heraldic shields and candelabras highlighting a decidedly decadent decor and a notorious dark room that must be crossed to reach the bathroom. Bears, cubs and daddies wear the crown here, though less so on busy Tuesdays.

Guilt (Map p90; ☑55-3500-5634; www.facebook.com/guiltpolanco; Anatole France 120, Colonia Polanco; cover M$300; ☉10:30pm-4:30am Sat; ⓂPolanco) A gay and lesbian club with a discerning, beautiful-people crowd (and wannabes) to match its swanky Polanco location. The T-shirt and blazer look is popular here while swaying to dance pop and electro and sipping pricey drinks. In fact you won't get in if you're wearing shorts, no sleeves or a cap.

Bar Oasis (Map p68; ☑55-5521-9740; República de Cuba 2G, Colonia Centro; ☉5pm-1am; ⓂBellas Artes) This packed disco attracts an older crowd and cuts across class lines, with both cowboys and businessmen dancing against a Day-Glo cityscape. Stick around past midnight Friday to Sunday for shows featuring lip-synching, cross-dressing performers.

⊙showtimes 11pm & 1am Fri & Sat; 🖵 República de Chile) Once a red-light venue, this cabaret has been reborn in the age of irony as a cradle of kitsch, with hilarious drag shows featuring traditional Mexican songstresses. Tickets go fast; reservations are possible by direct online messenger.

Teatro Bar El Vicio
CABARET

(Map p98; 🖋 55-5659-1139; www.elvicio.com.mx; Madrid 13, Colonia del Carmen; ⊙9:30pm-2am Thu-Sun; Ⓜ Coyoacán) With liberal doses of politically and sexually irreverent comedy and a genre-bending musical program, this alternative cabaret is appropriately located in Frida Kahlo's old stomping ground.

Sports

The capital stages *fútbol* (soccer) matches in the national Primera División almost every weekend of the year. Mexico City has three teams: América, nicknamed Las Águilas (the Eagles); Las Pumas of UNAM; and Cruz Azul. There are two seasons: January to June and July to December, each ending in eight-team play-offs and a two-leg final to decide the champion. The biggest match of all is El Clásico, between América and Guadalajara, which fills the **Estadio Azteca** (🖋 55-5487-3309; www.estadioazteca.com.mx; Calz de Tlalpan 3665; 🚊 Estadio Azteca) with 100,000 flag-waving fans. Get tickets in advance for this one.

Tickets to *fútbol* matches (M$90 to M$650 for regular-season games) are usually available at the gate, or from Ticketmaster. There are several stadiums that host games, including **Estadio Azul** (🖋 55-5563-9040; http://cruzazulfc.com.mx; Indiana 255, Colonia Nápoles; 🖵 Ciudad de los Deportes) for Cruz Azul matches and Estadio Olímpico (p96) to see UNAM's Pumas play.

Mexico City has one *béisbol* (baseball) team in the Liga Mexicana de Béisbol, the Diablos Rojos. During the regular season (April to July) it plays every other week at **Foro Sol** (http://diablos.com.mx; cnr Avs Río Churubusco & Viaducto Río de la Piedad, Colonia Granjas México; Ⓜ Ciudad Deportiva). From the metro, it's a five-minute walk to the ballpark. See the Diablos (www.diablos.com.mx) website for game times.

Most of the daily newspapers have a sports section where you can find out who is playing with which ball where. True enthusiasts should look for La Afición (www.laaficion.com), a daily devoted to sports.

Frontón México
SPECTATOR SPORT

(Jai Alai; Map p76; www.frontonmexico.com.mx; De la República 17, Colonia Tabacalera; tickets M$160-270; ⊙ticket office 10am-6pm Mon-Wed, 10am-9pm Thu-Sun; Ⓜ Revolución) Closed for two decades, the lovely art deco building Frontón México has reopened it doors for professional jai alai matches, one of the world's fastest ball sports. If you've never seen jai alai played live, you're in for a real treat. The season normally runs from March through June, but check the website for schedules. Frontón México doubles as a casino.

Arena México
MEXICAN WRESTLING

(Map p86; 🖋 55-5588-0266; Dr Lavista 197, Colonia Doctores; tickets M$40-210; ⊙7:30pm Tue, 8:30pm Fri, 5pm Sun; 🖵 Cuauhtémoc) One of Mexico City's two wrestling venues, the 17,000-seat Arena México is taken over by a circus atmosphere each week, with flamboyant *luchadores* (wrestlers) such as Místico and Sam Adonis going at each other in tag teams or one-on-one. There are three or four bouts, building up to the headline match. Also check out the smaller **Arena Coliseo** (Map p68; 🖋 55-5526-1687; República de Perú 77; tickets M$40-210; ⊙7:30pm Sat; 🖵 República de Chile).

Tickets are nearly always available at the door. Book in advance if you must have the pricier seats for Friday.

🔒 Shopping

Shopping can be a real joy in Mexico City, with *artesanías* (handicrafts) vendors, quirky shops and street markets all competing for your disposable income.

🔒 Centro Histórico & Around

★Mercado de la Merced
MARKET

(cnr Anillo de Circunvalación & General Anaya; ⊙5am-7pm Mon-Sat, 6am-5pm Sun; Ⓜ Merced) This gigantic market, Mexico City's largest, occupies four whole blocks dedicated to the buying and selling of daily needs, with photogenic displays of spices, chilies and every fresh Mexican foodstuff imaginable, from ant larvae to candied fruit. There is an atmospheric eating area with all varieties of fresh tacos, moles and *tlacoyos*.

★Centro de Artesanías La Ciudadela
ARTS & CRAFTS

(Map p76; 🖋 55-5510-1828; http://laciudadela.com.mx; cnr Balderas & Dondé; ⊙10am-7pm Mon-Sat, to 6pm Sun; Ⓜ Balderas) A favorite destination for good, and also mass-produced, handicrafts from all over Mexico. Worth seeking out are Oaxaca *alebrijes* (whimsical painted animals), guitars from Paracho and Huichol beadwork. Prices are generally fair, even before you bargain.

Mumedi
GIFTS & SOUVENIRS

(Mexican Design Museum; Map p68; ☑55-5510-8609; www.mumedi.org; Av Madero 74; ☺gift shop 11:30am-9pm Mon, 8am-9pm Tue-Sun; ☎; Ⓜ Zócalo) This design-museum gift shop sells interesting pop-culture knickknacks, handbags and jewelry crafted mostly by local artisans. Take a shopping break at the cute cafe.

Galería Eugenio
ARTS & CRAFTS

(Map p68; ☑55-5529-2849; Allende 84; ☺11am-5:30pm Mon-Sat; Ⓜ Garibaldi) Galería Eugenio sells more than 4000 traditional, mostly wooden and clay masks from artisans across the country. It's in the Lagunilla market area.

La Europea
DRINKS

(Map p68; ☑55-5512-6005; www.laeuropea.com.mx; Ayuntamiento 21; ☺9am-8pm Mon-Sat; ☐Plaza San Juan) Get reasonably priced tequila, mezcal and wine at this well-stocked liquor store with a better range than most. There are stores all over city.

Dulcería de Celaya
FOOD

(Map p68; ☑55-5521-1787; www.dulceriadecelaya.com; Av 5 de Mayo 39; ☺10:30am-7:30pm; Ⓜ Allende) This candy store has been operating since 1874 and it's worth a look for the ornate building alone. Candied fruits and coconut-stuffed lemons are some of the sweets on sale.

Plaza Downtown Mexico
MALL

(Map p68; www.facebook.com/TheShopsDT; Isabel La Católica 30; ☺11am-8pm Mon-Sat, to 6pm Sun; Ⓜ Zócalo) Shops surrounding the central courtyard of a beautifully restored 18th-century colonial-era building sell upmarket crafts, ceramics, chocolate and clothes.

Mercado de Sonora
MARKET

(http://mercadosonora.com.mx; cnr Fray Servando & Rosales, Colonia Merced Balbuena; ☺9am-7pm Mon-Sat, to 5pm Sun; Ⓜ Merced) This place has all the ingredients for Mexican witchcraft. Aisles are crammed with stalls hawking potions, amulets, voodoo dolls and other esoterica. This is also the place for a *limpia* (spiritual cleansing), a ritual involving clouds of incense and a herbal brushing. Sadly some vendors at the market trade illegally in endangered animals. It's two blocks south of metro Merced.

Gandhi
BOOKS

(Map p68; ☑55-2625-0606; www.gandhi.com.mx; Av Madero 32; ☺10am-9pm Mon-Sat, 11am-8pm Sun; Ⓜ Zócalo) This citywide bookstore chain has a voluminous range of texts on Mexico and Mexico City. More branches can be found at Bellas Artes (Map p68; ☑55-2625-0606; www.gandhi.com.mx; Av Juárez 4; ☺10am-9pm Mon-Sat, 11am-9pm Sun; Ⓜ Bellas Artes) and San Ángel (Map p94; ☑55-2625-0606; www.gandhi.com.mx; Av Miguel Ángel de Quevedo 121; ☺9am-10pm Mon-Fri, from 10am Sat & Sun; Ⓜ Miguel Ángel de Quevedo). There are two outlets on the same block in San Ángel.

Mercado San Juan
MARKET

(Map p76; www.mercadosanjuan.galeon.com; Pugibet 21; ☺8am-5pm Mon-Sat, to 4pm Sun; ☐Plaza San Juan) Specializes in top-price gourmet food items such as *huitlacoche* (trufflelike corn fungus), insects, crocodile, ostrich, deer and rare fruit. Local chefs and foodies come here to score ingredients not available elsewhere in the city.

Plaza de la Computación y Electrónica
ELECTRONICS

(Map p68; www.plazadelatecnologia.com/mexico; Eje Central Lázaro Cárdenas 38; ☺10am-8pm; Ⓜ San Juan de Letrán) Hundreds of electronics stalls huddle in the Plaza de la Computación y Electrónica, south of Uruguay. Best prices and availability in the city for laptop, phone and gadget chargers, cases and repairs.

Tianguis Dominical de la Lagunilla
MARKET

(cnr González Bocanegra & Paseo de la Reforma; ☺10am-6pm Sun; Ⓜ Garibaldi) At this collector's oasis you can hunt for antiques, old souvenirs and bric-a-brac. Books and magazines are alongside the Lagunilla building.

Never Die Gang
FASHION & ACCESSORIES

(Map p68; ☑55-5512-2183; www.neverdie.mx; Av 16 de Sepiembre 70, 2nd fl; ☺noon-8pm; Ⓜ Zócalo) If you're looking to tap into Mexico City's rap and hip-hop culture, the 'Gang' sells its own line of streetwear, accessories and music, and the shop doubles as a ticket outlet for live rap shows. It's run by a group of local musicians.

American Bookstore
BOOKS

(Map p68; ☑55-5512-0306; Bolívar 23; ☺10am-7pm Mon-Fri, to 6pm Sat; Ⓜ Allende) Has novels and books on Mexico in English, plus Lonely Planet guides.

La Lagunilla
MARKET

(Map p68; cnr Rayón & Allende; 10am-6:30pm; MGaribaldi) This enormous complex comprises three buildings: building No 1 contains clothes and fabrics, No 2 has food and No 3 sells furniture. Beware of petty theft, or wandering into the infamously unsafe Tepito area in the northeast.

Casasola Fotografía
GIFTS & SOUVENIRS

(Map p68; www.casasolafoto.com; Isabel La Católica 45, Office 201, 2nd fl; 10:30am-7pm Mon-Fri, to 3pm Sat; República del Salvador) Odds are you've probably seen this studio's world-famous revolution-era sepia photos. Items on sale include framed pictures, calendars, T-shirts and postcards. Photo ID required to enter the building.

Zona Rosa & Around

★Fonart
ARTS & CRAFTS

(Map p82; 55-5546-7163; https://fonart.gob.mx; Paseo de la Reforma 116; 10am-7pm Mon-Fri, to 4pm Sat & Sun; Reforma) This government-run crafts store sells quality wares from around Mexico, such as Olinalá-produced lacquered boxes and black pottery from Oaxaca. Another branch is at Mixcoac (Patriotismo 691; 10am-6pm Mon-Fri, to 7pm Sat; MMixcoac). Prices are fixed.

Fusión
DESIGN

(Map p82; http://casafusion.com.mx; Londres 37; noon-8pm Tue-Sat, 11am-7pm Sun; Hamburgo) From a converted house, a dozen boutique stores produce giftware, clothing and furniture, most with a Mexican spin. Each Friday to Sunday there's an ever-changing courtyard market showcasing products and food from a particular region, such as Michoacán. A cafe serves gourmet snacks such as grasshopper (or simply aubergine) pizza.

Antigüedades Plaza del Ángel
ANTIQUES

(Map p82; www.antiguedadesplazadelangel.mx; Londres 161, btwn Amberes & Av Florencia; market 9am-4pm Sat & Sun, stores 10:30am-7pm daily; MInsurgentes) Flea market within a mall of high-end antique shops selling silver jewelry, paintings, ornaments and furniture.

Condesa & Roma

Vértigo
ARTS & CRAFTS

(Map p86; 55-5207-3590; www.vertigogaleria.com; Colima 23; 10am-6pm Mon & Tue, noon-8pm Wed-Fri, 10am-5pm Sat; Jardín Pushkin) The store at this playfully hip art gallery sells silk screens, graphic T-shirts and etchings made by popular Argentine illustrator Jorge Alderete. In addition to 'low brow' art shows, Vértigo stages acoustic music performances every so often.

Libreria Rosario Castellanos
BOOKS

(Map p86; 55-5276-7110; www.fondodecultura economica.com; Av Tamaulipas 202, cnr Benjamín Hill; 9am-11pm; ; MPatriotismo) Inside the impressive art deco Centro Cultural Bella Época is one of the largest bookstores in Latin America where it is easy, and permitted, to sit for hours perusing. Shelves of books as well as CDs and DVDs.

La Naval
DRINKS

(Map p86; 55-5584-3500; www.lanaval.com.mx; Av Insurgentes Sur 373; 9am-9pm Mon-Sat, 11am-7pm Sun; Campeche) Name your poison: this gourmet store stocks a tantalizing selection of mezcals and tequilas, as well as Cuban cigars and hard to find imported gourmet food.

Under the Volcano Books
BOOKS

(Map p86; www.underthevolcanobooks.com; Celaya 25; 11am-6pm Mon-Sat; Sonora) Buys and sells used English-language titles. An excellent selection and very good prices.

El Hijo del Santo
GIFTS & SOUVENIRS

(Map p86; 55-5512-2186; www.elhijodelsanto.com.mx; Av Tamaulipas 219; 10am-9pm Mon-Sat; MPatriotismo) Owned by wrestler El Hijo del Santo – Mexico's most famous, iconic *lucha libre* star who rose to fame in the 1980s – this small specialty store sells (you guessed it) all things Santo. Among the offerings are kitschy portraits, hip handbags and the ever-popular silver Santo mask.

Polanco

Antara
MALL

(Map p90; www.antara.com.mx; Av Ejército Nacional 843B; 11am-11pm; MPolanco) This cluster of upmarket and chain stores is half open-air and is a designer destination in itself in the fashionable Polanco area.

Pasaje Polanco
SHOPPING CENTER

(Map p90; 55-5280-7976; Av Presidente Masaryk 360, cnr Oscar Wilde, Colonia Polanco; 9am-10pm; MPolanco) A classy complex flanked by sophisticated boutiques, specialty stores and a large crafts shop selling handbags, wrestling masks and Day of the Dead folk art.

San Ángel

Bazar Sábado
ARTS & CRAFTS

(Map p94; ☑55-5616-0082; Plaza San Jacinto 11; ⊘10am-7pm Sat; ☐La Bombilla) The Saturday bazaar showcases some of Mexico's best handcrafted jewelry, woodwork, ceramics and textiles. Artists and artisans also display their work in Plaza San Jacinto itself and in adjacent Plaza Tenanitla.

Jardín del Arte San Ángel
ART

(Map p94; www.jardindelarte.mx; Plaza San Jacinto; ⊘10am-4pm Sat; ☐La Bombilla) Local artists set up on the west side of Plaza San Jacinto in San Ángel to sell their paintings while vendors hawk art supplies. There is another location northeast of here in El Carmen (Map p94; www.jardindelarte.mx; ⊘10am-4pm Sat; ☐La Bombilla) and another in Colonia San Rafael (Map p82; btwn Sullivan & Villalongín, Colonia San Rafael; ⊘10am-6pm Sun; ☐Reforma).

Plaza Loreto
MALL

(Map p94; www.centrocomercialloreto.com.mx; Altamirano 46, cnr Av Revolución; ⊘11am-8pm; ☎; ☐Dr Gálvez) An attractive shopping mall converted from an old paper factory. Several patios and courtyards are set between the brick buildings and it's a lot more than just a place to shop – you'll find a mini-amphitheater for free concerts and puppet shows, an art-house cinema, an art museum and one of the city's best restaurants, Taberna del León (p118).

Other Neighborhoods

★Tianguis Cultural del Chopo
MUSIC

(Calle Aldama s/n; ⊘11am-4pm Sat; ⓜBuenavista) A gathering place for the city's various youth subcultures – especially goth, metal and punk – with most of the outdoor vendor stalls selling clothes or DVDs, or offering tattooing, body piercing and hair coloring. At the far north end of the market is a concert stage for young-and-hungry bands. The main entrance is one block east of metro Buenavista.

Mercado de Jamaica
MARKET

(https://mercadodejamaica.com; cnr Guillermo Prieto & Congreso de la Unión, Colonia Jamaica; ⊘24hr; ⓜJamaica) Huge, colorful flower market, featuring both baroque floral arrangements and exotic blooms. It's one block south of metro Jamaica.

ℹ Information

DANGERS & ANNOYANCES

While crime rates remain significant in the capital, a few precautions greatly reduce any dangers and first-time visitors are often surprised at how safe it feels. Most of the narco-related violence that makes the news abroad happens in the northern and Pacific states, far from Mexico City.

Assault

Although not as prevalent as in the 1990s, taxi assaults still occur. Many victims have hailed a cab on the street and been robbed by armed accomplices of the driver. Taxis parked in front of nightclubs or restaurants should be avoided unless authorized by the management. Rather than hailing cabs, find a *sitio* (taxi stand) or request a radio taxi or Uber.

Earthquakes

The danger posed by an earthquake is low, but they do occur. On September 19, 2017, a major earthquake rocked Mexico City, destroying and damaging buildings and displacing hundreds of people. While there were hundreds of deaths, it was far less devastating than the 1985 earthquake. It reflects, in part, the great improvements that have been to the city's buildings and their ability to resist seismic activity.

The *alerta sísmica* (public earthquake siren) can gives seconds of warning for you to evacuate a building and is now also connected to the official government app 911 CDMX.

Although it is difficult to predict an earthquake, the latest travel advice can be found on websites such as Smart Traveller (www.smarttraveller.gov.au) and the US Department of State (http://travel.state.gov).

Theft

Robberies happen most often in areas frequented by foreigners, including Plaza Garibaldi, the Zona Rosa and La Condesa late on weekend nights. Be on your guard at the airport and bus stations. Crowded metro cars and buses are favorite haunts of pickpockets, so keep a close eye on your wallet and avoid carrying ATM cards or large amounts of cash. In case of robbery, don't resist – hand over your valuables rather than risk injury or death.

EMERGENCIES

Fire (☑911)

Police (☑911)

INTERNET ACCESS

Free wi-fi is available in nearly all accommodations and cafes, and in many public parks and plazas. Internet services are everywhere; rates range from M$10 to M$30 per hour.

MEDICAL SERVICES

For recommendations for a doctor, dentist or hospital, call your embassy or **Sectur**, the tourism ministry. A list of area hospitals and English-speaking physicians (with their credentials) is on the US Embassy (p852) website. A private doctor's consultation generally costs between M$500 and M$1200. Call Cruz Roja (Red Cross) on 911 for emergency medical attention.

The pharmacies in Sanborns department stores are among the most reliable.

Farmacia París (☑55-5709-5000; www.farmaciaparis.com; República del Salvador 97, Colonia Centro; ⊗8am-11pm Mon-Sat, 9am-9pm Sun; ☑Isabel La Católica)

Farmacia San Pablo (☑55-5354-9000; www.farmaciasanpablo.com.mx; cnr Av Insurgentes Sur & Chihuahua, Colonia Roma; ⊗24hr; ☑Álvaro Obregón) Delivery service around the clock.

Hospital Ángeles Clínica Londres (☑55-5229-8400, emergency 55-5229-8445; https://hospitalesangeles.com/clinicalondres; Durango 50, Colonia Roma; ☑Cuauhtémoc) Hospital and medical clinic.

Hospital Centro Médico ABC (American British Cowdray Hospital; ☑55-5230-8000, emergency 55-5230-8161; www.abchospital.com; Sur 136 No 116, Colonia Las Américas; ☑Observatorio) English-speaking staff provide quality care.

Médicor (☑55-5512-0431; www.medicor.com.mx; Independencia 66, Colonia Centro; ⊗9am-9pm Mon-Sat, to 7pm Sun; ☑Juárez) For homeopathic remedies.

MONEY

Most banks and *casas de cambio* (exchange offices) change cash and traveler's checks, but some handle only euros and US or Canadian dollars. Rates vary, so check a few places. Mexico City is one of the few cities in the world where the exchange offices at the airport actually offer competitive rates. Exchange offices in town include **CCSole** (www.ccsole.com.mx; Niza 11, Zona Rosa; ⊗9am-6pm Mon-Fri; ☑Hamburgo) and **Centro de Cambios y Divisas** (☑55-5705-5656; www.ccd.com.mx; Paseo de la Reforma 87F; ⊗8am-9pm Mon-Fri, to 6pm Sat, 10am-5pm Sun; ☑Reforma).

The greatest concentration of ATMs, banks and *casas de cambio* is on Paseo de la Reforma between the Monumento a Cristóbal Colón and the Monumento a la Independencia.

POST

The Mexican postal service (www.correosdemexico.com.mx) website lists branches throughout the city. For important items, it is recommended to use a more reliable, private courier service.

Palacio Postal (p73) The stamp windows, marked '*estampillas*,' at the city's main post office stay open beyond normal hours. Even if you don't need stamps, check out the sumptuous interior.

Post Office Cuauhtémoc Branch (Map p82; ☑55-5207-7666; Río Tiber 87; ⊗8am-7pm Mon-Fri, to 3pm Sat & Sun; ☑Insurgentes)

Post Office Roma Norte Branch (Map p86; Coahuila 5; ⊗8am-6:30pm Mon-Fri, 9am-2:30pm Sat; ☑Hospital General)

TOILETS

Use of the bathroom is free at some Sanborns department stores, but otherwise costs M$5. Most market buildings, and holes-in-the-wall near metro stations, have public toilets; just look for the 'WC' signs. Hygiene standards vary at these facilities. Toilet paper is dispensed by an attendant on request.

TOURIST INFORMATION

Sectur (Map p90; ☑55-5250-0151, US 800-482-9832; www.gob.mx/sectur; Av Presidente Masaryk 172, Bosques de Chapultepec; ⊗9am-5pm Mon-Fri; ☑Polanco), the national tourism ministry, hands out brochures on the entire country, though you're better off at the tourism kiosks for up-to-date information about the capital.

The **Mexico City Tourism Secretariat** (☑800-008-90-90; www.mexicocity.gob.mx) has tourist information kiosks in key areas, including the airport and bus stations. Staff can answer your queries and distribute a map and practical guide. Staff members usually speak English. Most kiosks are open from 9am to 6pm daily.

Alameda Tourist Information (Map p76; cnr Av Juárez & Dr Mora, Colonia Centro; ⊗9am-6pm; ☑Hidalgo)

Basílica Tourist Information (☑55-5748-2085; Plaza de las Américas 1, Basílica de Guadalupe; ⊗9am-3pm Mon & Tue, to 6pm Wed-Sun; ☑La Villa-Basilica) On the plaza's south side.

Centro Tourist Information (Map p68; ☑55-5518-1003; Monte de Piedad; ⊗9am-6pm; ☑Zócalo) Outside the Catedral Metropolitana.

Chapultepec Tourist Information (Map p90; Paseo de la Reforma; ⊗9am-6pm Wed-Sun; ☑Auditorio) Near the Museo Nacional de Antropología.

Coyoacán Tourist Information (Map p98; ☑55-5658-0221; Jardín Hidalgo 1, Coyoacán; ⊗10am-8pm; ☑Coyoacán) Inside the Casa de Cortés.

Nativitas Tourist Information (☑55-5653-5209; Xochimilco; ⊗9am-4pm Mon-Fri, to 5pm Sat & Sun; ☑Xochimilco) At the Nativitas boat landing.

Xochimilco Tourist Information (☑55-5676-0810; www.xochimilco.df.gob.mx/turismo; Pino 36; ⊗8am-7pm Mon-Fri, 9am-6pm Sat & Sun; ☑Xochimilco) Just off the Jardín Juárez.

Zócalo Tourist Information (Map p68; Templo Mayor; ⊘ 9am-6pm; Ⓜ Zócalo) East of the Catedral Metropolitana.

Zona Rosa Tourist Information (Map p82; ☑ 55-5208-1030; cnr Paseo de la Reforma & Av Florencia; ⊘ 9am-6pm Wed-Sun; Ⓜ Insurgentes) On the Zona Rosa side of Monumento a la Independencia.

TRAVEL AGENCIES

A number of hostels and hotels have on-site *agencia de viajes* or can recommend one nearby.

Mundo Joven Airport (☑ 55-2599-0155; www.mundojoven.com; Sala E1, international arrivals, Terminal 1; ⊘ 9am-8pm Mon-Fri, 10am-5pm Sat, to 2pm Sun; Ⓜ Terminal Aérea) Specializes in travel for students and teachers, with reasonable airfares from Mexico City. Issues ISIC, ITIC, IYTC and HI cards. Additional branches in **Polanco** (☑ 55-5250-7191; www.mundojoven.com; Eugenio Sue 342, cnr Homero; ⊘ 10am-7pm Mon-Fri, to 2pm Sat; Ⓜ Polanco) and **Zócalo** (☑ 55-5518-1755; www.mundojoven.com; República de Guatemala 4, Zócalo; ⊘ 10am-7pm Mon-Fri, to 2pm Sat; Ⓜ Zócalo).

Turismo Zócalo (☑ 55-8596-9649; www.turismozocalo.com; Palma 34, 2nd fl, Colonia Centro; ⊘ 10am-7pm Mon-Fri, to 1pm Sat; Ⓜ Zócalo) Inside the Gran Plaza Ciudad de México mall. Also functions as a Miescape outlet for bus bookings.

USEFUL WEBSITES

CDMX Travel (www.cdmxtravel.com/en) The city's official travel site in English has a rundown on neighborhoods, experiences, tours and events.

Lonely Planet (www.lonelyplanet.com/mexico-city) Destination information, hotel bookings, traveler forum and more.

Mexico es Cultura (www.mexicoescultura.com) A government-run promotion of what's on in the city (and the whole country).

Secretaría de Cultura del Distrito Federal (www.cartelera.cdmx.gob.mx) Lists festivals, museums and cultural events.

Sistema de Información Cultural (sic.gob.mx) Directory-like listings of festivals, museums and goings-on in the city.

VISAS

Instituto Nacional de Migración (National Migration Institute; Map p90; ☑ 55-2581-0100; www.inm.gob.mx; Av Ejército Nacional 862; ⊘ 9am-1pm Mon-Fri) You'll need to come here if you want to extend your tourist permit, replace a lost one, or deal with other nonstandard immigration procedures. Catch the 'Ejercito' bus from metro Sevilla; it leaves you two blocks east of the office.

ⓘ Getting There & Away

AIR

Aeropuerto Internacional Benito Juárez (☑ 55-2482-2424; www.aicm.com.mx; Capitán Carlos León s/n, Colonia Peñón de los Baños; 🖥 ; Ⓜ Terminal Aérea) is Mexico City's only passenger airport, and Latin America's largest, with an annual capacity of about 32 million passengers. The airport has two terminals: terminal 1 (the main terminal) and terminal 2 (located 3km from the main terminal). Carriers operating out of terminal 2 include Aeromar, Aeroméxico, Copa Airlines, Delta and Lan. All other airlines depart from terminal 1.

Red buses (M$12.50, paid on board) run between the two terminals, making stops at *puerta* (door) 7 in terminal 1 and *puerta* 3 in terminal 2. The terminals also are connected by an *aerotrén*, a free monorail service for ticketed passengers only, between *puerta* 6 in terminal 1 and *puerta* 4 in terminal 2.

Both terminals have *casas de cambio* and peso-dispensing ATMs. Car-rental agencies and luggage lockers are in *sala* (hall) A and *sala* E2 of terminal 1.

More than 20 airlines provide international service to Mexico City. You can fly direct from more than 30 cities in the US and Canada, half a dozen each in Europe, South America and Central America/Caribbean, and from Tokyo. Seven different airlines connect the capital to about 50 cities within Mexico.

BUS

Mexico City has four long-distance bus terminals serving the four compass points: Terminal Norte (north), Terminal Oriente (called TAPO; east), Terminal Poniente (Observatorio; west) and Terminal Sur (south). All terminals have baggage-check services or lockers, as well as tourist information kiosks, newsstands, card phones, internet, ATMs and snack bars. There are also buses to nearby cities from the airport. For trips of up to five hours, it usually suffices to go to the bus station, buy your ticket and go. For longer trips, many buses leave in the evening and tickets may sell out earlier, so buy beforehand.

You can purchase advance tickets at Oxxo convenience stores throughout the city and **Miescape** (☑ 55-5784-4652; www.miescape.mx), a booking agency for more than a dozen bus lines out of all four stations (a 10% surcharge is added to the cost of the ticket up to a maximum of M$50). Miescape also offers purchase by phone with Visa or MasterCard. Miescape branches are at **Buenavista** (Ticketbus; Map p76; ☑ 55-5566-1573; www.miescape.mx; Buenavista 9, cnr Orozco y Berra; ⊘ 9am-2:30pm & 3:30-7pm Mon-Fri, to 3pm Sat; Ⓜ Revolución) and **Roma Norte** (Ticketbus; Map p86; ☑ 55-5564-6783; www.miescape.mx; Mérida 156, cnr Zacatecas;

⊙ 9am-2:30pm & 3:30-6:45pm Mon-Fri, to 2:45pm Sat; Ⓜ Hospital General).

Lines

Check the individual bus websites for schedules.

ADO Group (☑ 55-5784-4652; www.ado.com.mx) One of the largest and most reliable companies with services all across the country. Includes ADO Platino (deluxe), ADO GL (executive), OCC (1st class), ADO (1st class) and AU (2nd class).

Autobuses Teotihuacán (☑ 55-5587-0501; www.autobusesteotihuacan.com.mx) Services to the Teotihuacán ruins every 30 minutes. Ensure that your bus is marked *ruinas* and not to the nearby town of San Juan Teotihuacán.

Autovías (☑ 800-622-22-22; www.autovias.com.mx) Specializes in first-class services to Mexico State and Michoacán.

Estrella Blanca Group (☑ 800-507-55-00, 55-5729-0807; www.estrellablanca.com.mx) One of the largest and most reliable network of bus companies with services all across the country. Operates Futura, Costa Line and Elite (1st class).

Estrella de Oro (☑ 55-5549-8520, 800-900-01-05; www.estrelladeoro.com.mx) Specializes in services to Cuernavaca and cities in Guerrero state, such as Taxco and Acapulco. Executive and 1st class.

Estrella Roja (☑ 800-712-22-84, 55-5130-1800; www.estrellaroja.com.mx) Specializes in direct 1st-class services between Puebla and Mexico City's airport.

ETN (☑ 800-800-03-86, 55-5089-9200; www.etn.com.mx) Arguably the most luxurious network of buses with services all over the country. Includes ETN (deluxe) and Turistar (executive and deluxe).

Ómnibus de México (☑ 800-765-66-36, 55-5141-4300; www.odm.com.mx) The most popular routes from Mexico City include Monterrey and San Luis Potosí, and even for the US to Houston and Dallas. First class.

Primera Plus (☑ 800-375-75-87; www.primeraplus.com.mx) An extensive network of destinations, particularly for Jalisco, Michoacán, Guanajuato and Querétaro. Deluxe and 1st class.

Pullman de Morelos (☑ 55-5445-0100, 800-022-80-00; www.pullman.mx) Services to Cuernavaca. Executive, deluxe and 1st class.

Terminals

Terminal de Autobuses del Norte (☑ 55-5587-1552; www.centraldelnorte.com.mx; Eje Central Lázaro Cárdenas 4907, Colonia Magdalena de las Salinas; Ⓜ Autobuses del Norte) The largest of the four bus terminals. Serves points north, including cities on the US border, plus some points west (Guadalajara, Puerto Vallarta), east (Puebla) and south (Acapulco, Oaxaca). Deluxe and 1st-class counters are mostly in the southern half of the terminal. Luggage-storage services are at the far south

end and in the central passageway. Buses to Teotihuacán depart from here. Connects with metro Autobuses del Norte on Línea 5 (yellow).

Terminal de Autobuses de Pasajeros de Oriente (TAPO; ☑ 55-5522-9381; Calz Zaragoza 200, Colonia Diez de Mayo; Ⓜ San Lázaro) For eastern and southeastern destinations, including Puebla, Veracruz, Yucatán, Oaxaca and Chiapas. Known commonly as TAPO. Bus-line counters are arranged around a rotunda with a food court, internet terminals and ATMs. There's a left-luggage service in 'Túnel 1.' Connects with metro San Lázaro on Línea 1 (pink) and Línea B (dark green).

Terminal de Autobuses del Poniente (Observatorio; ☑ 55-5271-0149; Av Sur 122, Colonia Real del Monte; Ⓜ Observatorio) The point for buses heading to Michoacán, Valle de Bravo, Toluca and shuttle services running to nearby Toluca. In addition, ETN offers service to Guadalajara. Commonly referred to by the adjacent metro name Observatorio, which is as the western end of Línea 1 (pink).

Terminal de Autobuses del Sur (Tasqueña; ☑ 55-5689-9745; Av Tasqueña 1320, Colonia Campestre Churubusco; Ⓜ Tasqueña) Serves Tepoztlán, Cuernavaca, Taxco, Acapulco and other southern destinations, as well as Oaxaca, Huatulco and Ixtapa-Zihuatanejo. Estrella de Oro (Acapulco, Taxco) and Pullman de Morelos (Cuernavaca) counters are on the right side of the terminal, while OCC, Estrella Roja (Tepoztlán), ETN and Futura are on the left. In *sala* 3 you'll find luggage-storage service and ATMs. Connects with nearby metro Tasqueña at the southern end of Línea 2 (blue).

Aeropuerto Internacional Benito Juárez (p134) Departures from Mexico City's airport include Cuernavaca, Pachuca, Puebla, Querétaro, Toluca, Córdoba, San Juan del Rio, Orizaba and Celaya. Buses depart from platforms adjacent to *sala* E in terminal 1 and from *sala* D in terminal 2. Ticket counters in terminal 1 are on the upper level, off the food court. A pedestrian bridge off *sala* B leads to an ADO bus terminal with service to Acapulco and Veracruz. Updated bus times, destinations and prices can be found on the airport website.

CAR & MOTORCYCLE

Rental

Rental-car companies have offices at the airport, bus stations and in the Zona Rosa area of the city. Rates generally start at about M$600 per day, but you can often do better by booking online. You can find a list of rental agencies online at the CDMX Tourism Secretariat (www.mexicocity.gob.mx) website.

Roadside Assistance

If you leave the city, the **Ángeles Verdes** (Green Angels; ☑ 078; http://av.sectur.gob.mx) can provide 24-hour highway assistance for tourists. Just phone 078 and tell them your location.

Routes In & Out of the City

Whichever way you come into the city, once you're past the last *caseta* (toll booth) you enter a no-man's-land of poorly marked lanes and chaotic traffic. These *casetas* are also the points from which Hoy No Circula (p139) rules take effect.

➜ To Puebla (east of CDMX) Take the Viaducto Alemán (Río de la Piedad) east. From Roma and Zona Rosa, this is most conveniently accessed

BUSES FROM MEXICO CITY

DESTINATION	TERMINAL IN MEXICO CITY	BUS LINES	FARE (M$)	DURATION (HR)	FREQUENCY (DAILY)
Acapulco	Sur	Costa Line, Estrella de Oro	535-705	5	16
	Norte	Futura, Costa Line	535	5½-6	9
Bahías de Huatulco	Sur	OCC, Turistar, AltaMar	800-1100	15-15½	3
	Norte	AltaMar	1100	16	4:45pm
Campeche	Oriente (TAPO)	ADO, ADO GL	905-1742	16-18	6
	Norte	ADO	905	17-18	2
Cancún	Oriente (TAPO)	ADO, ADO GL	1120-2160	24-27	5
Chetumal	Oriente (TAPO)	ADO	1093-1556	19½-20	2
Chihuahua	Norte	Estrella Blanca, Ómnibus de México	1560-1640	18-19	7
Cuernavaca	Sur	Estrella Blanca, Estrella de Oro, ETN, Pullman de Morelos	111-140	1¼	frequent
Guadalajara	Norte	Estrella Blanca, ETN, Ómnibus de México, Primera Plus	657-850	6-7	frequent
	Poniente	ETN	806	6¼-7¾	4
Guanajuato	Norte	ETN, Primera Plus	513-680	5-5½	14
Matamoros	Norte	ETN, Futura	1203-1350	12½-13½	3
Mazatlán	Norte	Elite, ETN, Pacífico	1055-1420	13-16	13
Mérida	Oriente (TAPO)	ADO, ADO GL	898-1882	19-20½	5
Monterrey	Norte	ETN, Ómnibus de México	1130-1205	11-13	18
Morelia	Poniente	Autovías, ETN, Pegasso	327-486	4-4¼	frequent
Nuevo Laredo	Norte	ETN, Futura, Turistar	1335-1510	15-15½	8
Oaxaca	Oriente (TAPO)	ADO, ADO GL, ADO Platino	470-945	6-6½	frequent
	Sur	ADO GL, OCC	650-700	6½	5
Palenque	Oriente (TAPO)	ADO	1096	12¾	6:10pm
Papantla	Norte	ADO	382	5-6	7
Pátzcuaro	Norte	Primera Plus	482	5	7
	Poniente	Autovías	480	5	11
Puebla	Airport	Estrella Roja	290	2	every 40min
	Oriente (TAPO)	ADO, ADO GL, AU, Pullman de Morelos	141-200	2-2¼	frequent
Puerto Escondido	Sur	ETN, OCC, Turistar,	1082-1180	12-17½	2

off Avenida Cuauhtémoc (Eje 1 Poniente). Immediately after crossing over the Viaducto – by the Liverpool department store – turn left for the access ramp. From the Zócalo take Viaducto Tlalpan to get onto Viaducto Alemán then follow signs to Calzada Zaragoza. This leads to the highway to Puebla, or for Puebla airport head north along Blvd Puerto Aéreo.

➜ **To Oaxaca or Veracruz** Also take the Viaducto Alemán to Calzada Zaragoza following the signs for Oaxaca until you hit the Puebla Hwy.

DESTINATION	TERMINAL IN MEXICO CITY	BUS LINES	FARE (M$)	DURATION (HR)	FREQUENCY (DAILY)
Puerto Vallarta	Norte	ETN, Futura Primera Plus	984-1365	12-13½	5
Querétaro	Norte	Estrella Blanca, ETN, Primera Plus	265-345	2¾-3	frequent
	Airport	Primera Plus	385	3	frequent
	Poniente	Primera Plus	311	3½-4	17
San Cristóbal de las Casas	Oriente (TAPO)	ADO GL, OCC	801-1522	13-14	7
	Norte	OCC	1256	14-14½	4
San Luis Potosí	Norte	ETN, Primera Plus, Turistar	491-655	4½-5½	frequent
San Miguel de Allende	Norte	ETN, Primera Plus	388-510	3¼-4	7
Tapachula	Oriente (TAPO)	ADO GL, ADO Platino, OCC	830-1834	16½-19½	11
Taxco	Sur	ADO, Costaline, Estrella de Oro, Pullman de Morelos	209-275	2½	4
Teotihuacán	Norte	Autobuses Teotihuacán	50	1	hourly 6am-9pm
Tepoztlán	Sur	OCC	126	1	frequent
Tijuana	Norte	Elite	1998	4	12
Toluca	Airport	TMT Caminante	190	1¾	hourly
	Poniente	ETN, Flecha Roja	65-90	1	frequent
Tuxtla Gutiérrez	Oriente (TAPO)	ADO, ADO GL, ADO Platino, OCC	893-1670	11¾-12½	14
Uruapan	Poniente	Autovías, ETN	562-670	5¼-6	17
Veracruz	Oriente (TAPO)	ADO, ADO GL, ADO Platino, AU	580-720	5½-7¼	frequent
	Sur	ADO, ADO GL	664-748	5½-6¼	6
Villahermosa	Oriente (TAPO)	ADO, ADO GL, ADO Platino, AU	1022-1272	10-12¼	24
Xalapa	Oriente (TAPO)	ADO, ADO GL, ADO Platino, AU	184-682	4½-5	frequent
Zacatecas	Norte	ETN, Ómnibus de México	865-1120	8-9	14
Zihuatanejo	Sur	ADO, Costa Line, Estrella de Oro, Futura	723-900	9	4
	Poniente	Autovías	650	9	3

→ **To Querétaro** (north of CDMX) Take Reforma from the Diana roundabout until you reach the Estela de Luz and turn right onto Calz Gral Mariano Escobedo. Keep right and look for the signs to take the ramp to Querétaro. Pass through the toll at Tepotzotlán. Continue along for 200km. Take the exit toward Centro from Carretera México-Querétaro.

→ **To Pachuca, Hidalgo and northern Veracruz** (north of CDMX) Take Avenida Insurgentes north (also the route to Teotihuacán), which feeds into the highway.

→ **To Cuernavaca** (south of CDMX) Turn right (south) at the Zócalo onto Pino Suárez, which becomes Calzada Tlalpan. About 20km south, signs indicate a left exit for the *cuota* (toll highway) to Cuernavaca.

→ **To Toluca** (west of CDMX) Heading out of the city, take Paseo de la Reforma, which feeds right into the *cuota,* passing the high-rises of Santa Fe, to Toluca.

ⓘ Getting Around

TO/FROM THE AIRPORT

The metro is a cheap option for getting to the airport, though hauling luggage amid rush-hour crowds can be a Herculean task. Authorized taxis provide a painless, relatively inexpensive alternative, as does the metrobús if going to El Centro.

Metro

The airport metro station is Terminal Aérea, on Línea 5 (yellow). It's 200m from terminal 1: leave by the exit at the end of *sala* A (domestic arrivals) and continue past the taxi stand to the station.

To the city center, follow signs for 'Dirección Politécnico.' At La Raza (seven stops away) change for Línea 3 (green) toward 'Dirección Universidad.' Metro Hidalgo, at the west end of the Alameda, is three stops south; it's also a transfer point for Línea 2 (blue) to the Zócalo.

To get to the Zona Rosa from the airport, take Línea 5 to 'Pantitlán,' the end of the line. Change for Línea 1 (pink) and get off at metro Insurgentes.

There is no convenient metro link to terminal 2, but there is metrobús Línea 4, which connects to the TAPO bus terminal next to metro San Lázaro. Also, red buses at the entrance of terminal 2 go to metro Hangares (Línea 5).

Metrobús

Línea 4 of the metrobús has luggage racks and onboard security cameras, making it a more comfortable option than the metro.

Stops are at *puerta* 7 in terminal 1 and *puerta* 3 in terminal 2. The ride costs M$30, plus you'll need to purchase a smart card (valid for all metrobús trips) for M$10 at machines inside the terminals. From terminal 1, it's about 45 minutes to reach the Zócalo.

The line runs five blocks north of the Zócalo, along República de Venezuela and Belisario Domínguez, then it heads west along Avenida Hidalgo past metro Hidalgo. To return to the airport, catch it along Ayuntamiento or República del Salvador. See www.metrobus.cdmx.gob.mx for more information.

Taxi

Safe and reliable *taxis autorizados* (authorized taxis) are controlled by a fixed-price ticket system. Purchase taxi tickets from booths located in *sala* E1 (international arrivals) as you exit customs, and by the *sala* A (domestic arrivals) exit.

Fares are determined by zones. A ride to the Zócalo, Roma, Condesa or Zona Rosa costs M$235. One ticket is valid for up to four passengers. 'Sitio 300' taxis are the best. If you have phone internet access, an Uber will cost about M$170 to the same destinations, and will allow you to select which *puerta* (door) to be picked up from.

Porters may offer to take your ticket and luggage the few steps to the taxi, but hold on to the ticket and hand it to the driver. Drivers won't expect a tip for the ride, but will always welcome one.

TO/FROM THE BUS TERMINALS

The metro is the fastest and cheapest way to or from any bus terminal, but it's tricky to maneuver through crowded stations and cars. Taxis are an easier option – all terminals have ticket booths for secure *taxis autorizados,* with fares set by zone. A M$20 surcharge is applied from 9pm to 6am. An agent at the exit will assign you a cab.

Terminal Norte Metro Línea 5 (yellow) stops at Autobuses del Norte, just outside the terminal. To the city center, follow signs for 'Dirección Pantitlán,' then change at La Raza for Línea 3 (green) toward 'Dirección Universidad.' (The La Raza connection is a six-minute hike through a 'Tunnel of Science.') The taxi kiosk is in the central passageway; a cab for up to four people to the Zócalo, Roma or Condesa costs about M$135.

Terminal Oriente (TAPO) This bus terminal is next door to metro San Lázaro. To the city center or Zona Rosa, take Línea 1 (pink) toward 'Dirección Observatorio.' The authorized taxi booth is at the top (metro) end of the main passageway from the rotunda. The fare to the Zócalo is M$85; to the Zona Rosa, Roma or Condesa it's M$110.

Terminal Poniente Metro Observatorio, the eastern terminus of Línea 1 (pink), is a couple of minutes' walk across a busy street. A taxi ticket to Roma costs M$110, Condesa M$85 and the Zócalo M$135.

Terminal Sur It's a two-minute walk from metro Tasqueña, the southern terminus of Línea 2, which stops at the Zócalo. For the Zona Rosa, transfer at Pino Suárez and take Línea 1 to Insurgentes ('Dirección Observatorio'). Going to the terminal, take the 'Autobuses del

Sur' exit, which leads upstairs to a footbridge. Descend the last staircase on the left then walk through a street market to reach the building. Authorized taxis from Terminal Sur cost M$150 to the *centro histórico* and M$165 to Condesa and Roma. Ticket booths are in *sala* 3.

BICYCLE

Bicycles can be a viable way to get around town and are often preferable to overcrowded, recklessly driven buses. Although careless drivers and potholes can make Mexico City cycling an extreme sport, if you stay alert and keep off the major thoroughfares, it's manageable. The city government has encouraged bicycle use, with more bicycle-only lanes, and it's definitely catching on.

Bikes are loaned free from a kiosk on the west side of the Catedral Metropolitana. You'll also find booths at Plaza Villa de Madrid in Roma, at the intersection of Mazatlán and Michoacán in Condesa, and several along Paseo de la Reforma, near the Monumento a la Independencia and Auditorio Nacional. Leave a passport or driver's license for three hours of riding time. The kiosks operate from 10:30am to 6pm Monday to Saturday, and 9:30am to 4:30pm on Sunday.

CAR & MOTORCYCLE

Touring Mexico City by car is strongly discouraged, unless you have a healthy reserve of patience. Even more than elsewhere in the country, traffic rules are seen as suggested behavior. Red lights may be run at will, no-turn signs are ignored and signals are seldom used. On occasion you may be hit with a questionable traffic fine.

Don't Drive Today Program

To help combat pollution, Mexico City operates its 'Hoy No Circula' (Don't Drive Today; www.hoy-no-circula.com.mx) program, banning many vehicles from being driven in the city between 5am and 10pm on one day each week. Additionally, vehicles nine years and older are prohibited from operating one Saturday a month. Exempted from restrictions are rental cars and vehicles with a *calcomanía de verificación* (emissions verification sticker), obtained under the city's vehicle-pollution assessment system.

For vehicles without the sticker (including foreign-registered ones), the last digit of the license-plate number determines the day when they cannot circulate. See the official website for more information.

DAY	PROHIBITED LAST DIGIT
Monday	5, 6
Tuesday	7, 8
Wednesday	3, 4
Thursday	1, 2
Friday	9, 0

Parking

Avoid parking on the street whenever possible; most midrange and top-end hotels have guest garages. If you do park on the street, keep in mind that some neighborhoods, such as Cuauhtémoc, Roma and Polanco, have *parquímetros* (green parking meters usually located at the middle of the block). Feed them or your vehicle will be booted.

METRO

The metro system (www.metro.cdmx.gob.mx) offers the quickest way to get around Mexico City. Used by around 4.4 million passengers on an average weekday, it has 195 stations and more than 226km of track on 12 lines. Trains arrive every two to three minutes during rush hours. At M$5 a ride, it's one of the world's cheapest subways.

All lines operate from 5am to midnight weekdays, 6am to midnight Saturday and 7am to midnight Sunday and holidays. Platforms and cars can become alarmingly packed during rush hours (roughly 7:30am to 10am and 3pm to 8pm). At these times the forward cars are reserved for women and children, and men may not proceed beyond the *'Sólo Mujeres y Niños'* gate. The metro is also chaotic during heavy rain. With such crowded conditions, it's not surprising that pickpocketing occurs, so watch your belongings.

The metro is easy to use. Lines are color-coded and each station is identified by a unique logo. Signs reading 'Dirección Pantitlán,' 'Dirección Universidad' and so on name the stations at the end of the lines. Check a map for the direction you want. Buy a rechargeable smart card for M$10 at any station and then add credit (the card also works for all metrobús lines). Additionally, the metro sells *boletos* (tickets) at the *taquilla* (ticket window). Feed the ticket into the turnstile and you're on your way. When changing trains, look for 'Correspondencia' (Transfer) signs.

PESERO, METROBÚS & TROLEBÚS

Mexico City's buses and peseros operate from around 5am till 10pm daily, depending on the route. Electric trolleybuses generally run until 11:30pm. Only a few routes run all night, notably those along Paseo de la Reforma. This means you'll get anywhere by bus and/or metro during the day, but will probably have to take a few taxis after hours.

Pesero

Peseros (also called microbúses or combis) are gray-and-green minibuses operated by private firms. They follow fixed routes, often starting or ending at metro stations, and will stop at virtually any street corner. Route information is randomly displayed on cards attached to the windshield. Fares are M$5 for trips of up to 5km, and M$5.50 for 5km to 12km. Add 20% to all fares between 11pm and 6am. Privately run green-and-yellow buses charge M$6 and M$7 for the same distances. A useful resource for route planning with the confusing number of peseros is the ViaDF (www.viadf.mx) website.

Useful routes include the following:

Metro Sevilla–Presidente Masaryk Between Colonia Roma and Polanco via Álvaro Obregón and Avenida Presidente Masaryk (stops at metro Niños Héroes, Avenida Insurgentes, metro Sevilla and Leibnitz).

Metro Tacubaya–Balderas–Escandón Between *centro histórico* and Condesa, westbound via Puebla, eastbound via Durango (stops at Plaza San Juan, metro Balderas, metro Insurgentes, Parque España and Avenida Michoacán).

Metrobús

The metrobús is a wheelchair-accessible Volvo vehicle that stops at metro-style stations in the middle of the street, spaced at three- to four-block intervals. Access is by prepaid smart card, issued by machines for M$10 at the entrance to the platforms, and rides cost M$6. The rechargeable cards, which can also be used for the metro, are placed on a sensor device for entry. During crowded peak hours, the metrobús is a favorite for pickpockets. Unless mostly empty, the front of the bus is a dedicated area only for women and children, marked out with pink seating. Most metrobús lines run from 5am to midnight.

Línea 1 Plies a dedicated lane along Avenida Insurgentes from metro Indios Verdes in northern CDMX down to the southern end of Tlalpan.

Línea 2 Runs west to east along Eje 4 Sur from metro Tacubaya to metro Tepalcates. Connects with Línea 1 at the Nuevo León station.

Línea 3 Operates on a north–south route from the Tenayuca station to Ethiopia, where you can transfer to Línea 2.

Línea 4 Runs from metro Buenavista and cuts through the *centro histórico* to metro San Lázaro. The line also has an *'aeropuerto'* bus that goes to and from the airport for M$30.

Trolebús

Municipally operated *trolebuses* (trolleybuses) and full-sized cream-and-orange buses (labeled 'RTP') only pick up at bus stops. Fares are M$2 (M$4 for the express) regardless of distance

traveled. Trolleybuses follow a number of the key *ejes* (priority roads) throughout the rest of the city. They generally run until 11:30pm. Route maps are on the trolleybus website (http://ste.cdmx.gob.mx). Useful routes include the following:

Autobuses del Sur & Autobuses del Norte Eje Central Lázaro Cárdenas between north and south bus terminals (stops at Plaza de las Tres Culturas, Plaza Garibaldi, Bellas Artes/Alameda and metro Hidalgo).

TAXI

Mexico City has several classes of taxi. Cheapest are the cruising pink-and-white (or, being phased out, red-and-gold) street cabs, though they're not recommended due to the risk of assaults by the driver or accomplices. If you must hail a cab off the street, check that it has actual taxi license plates: numbers are preceded with the letters A or B. Check that the number on them matches the number painted on the bodywork. Also look for the *carta de identificación* (called the *tarjetón*), a postcard-sized ID that should be displayed visibly inside the cab, and ensure that the driver matches the photo. If the cab you've hailed does not pass these tests, get another one.

In *libre* cabs, fares are computed by *taxímetro*, which should start at about M$9. The total cost of a 3km ride in moderate traffic – say, from the Zócalo to the Zona Rosa – should be M$30 to M$40. Between 11pm and 6am, add 20%.

Radio taxis, which come in many different colors, cost about two or three times as much as the others, but this extra cost adds an immeasurable degree of security. When you phone, the dispatcher will tell you the cab number and the type of car. If you have a smartphone or device, you can order a cab via the popular app Easy Taxi or Uber.

Reliable radio-taxi firms, available 24 hours, include the following:

Sitio de Taxis Parque México (Map p86; ☑ 55-5286-7164, 55-5286-7129; Michoacán s/n)

Taximex (Map p86; ☑ 55-9171-8888; www.taximex.com.mx)

Taxis Radio Unión (Map p86; ☑ 55-5514-8074, 55-5514-7861; www.taxisradiounion.com.mx; Frontera 100)

Around Mexico City

Best Places to Eat

➡ Las Ranas (p158)

➡ La Sibarita (p179)

➡ El Mural de los Poblanos (p158)

➡ La Hostería del Convento de Tepotzotlán (p145)

➡ El Ciruelo (p179)

Best Places to Stay

➡ Hotel Los Arcos (p194)

➡ Hotel San Sebastian (p201)

➡ Hotel Hacienda de Cortés (p187)

➡ Posada del Tepozteco (p178)

Why Go?

With its daunting size and seemingly endless sprawl, the megalopolis of Mexico City might seem like a challenge to escape from, but even if you're in Mexico's capital for only a week, the ancient ruins, *pueblos mágicos* (magical villages) and stunning mountain landscape of the surrounding area should not be missed. Mexico City – like many capitals – has little in common with even its closest neighbors.

While many visitors to the region take a day trip to the awe-inspiring archaeological complex at Teotihuacán, the area offers much more – from the captivating colonial cities of Taxco, Puebla and Cuernavaca to the eccentric small towns of Valle de Bravo and Tepoztlán. For those eager to taste some crisp, particulate-free mountain air, there are *pueblitos* (small towns) such as Cuetzalan and Real del Monte, the volcanic giants of Popocatépetl and Iztaccíhuatl, and the lesser-known ruins of Xochicalco and Cantona to visit.

When to Go
Puebla City

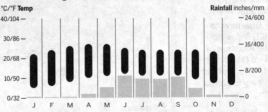

May–Oct Rainy season; afternoon showers wash the air clean and bring wild mushrooms to the forests.

Sep The weeks before Independence Day are the time to taste the seasonal specialty *chiles en nogada*.

Nov–Apr Drier months; nominally cooler, making for pleasant daytime city exploration and casual hikes.

Around Mexico City Highlights

1 Cuetzalan
(p174) Enjoying a sunset drink at the tiny *zócalo* amid the dramatic scenery of the Sierra Madre Oriental.

2 Teotihuacán
(p147) Being blown away by the spectacular pyramids.

3 Taxco (p191) Wandering the steep cobblestone streets linking the city's famed silver shops.

4 Tepotzotlán
(p144) Having a spiritual encounter in Tepotzotlán, home to a mountain-top pyramid dedicated to the Aztec god of *pulque*.

5 Mineral del Chico (p151) Feeling mountain mists sweep over you.

6 Puebla
(p153) Admiring the impressive Talavera-tiled historic churches.

7 La Malinche
(p162) Climbing slopes such as La Malinche, a dormant volcano with panoramic views.

8 Cuernavaca
(p182) Following in the footsteps of Mexico City's artists and high society while escaping to eternal spring.

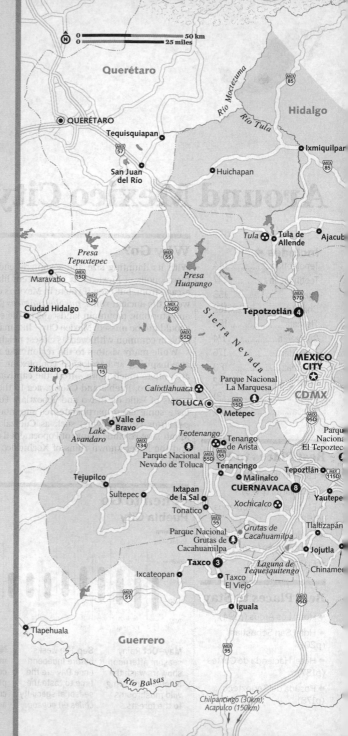

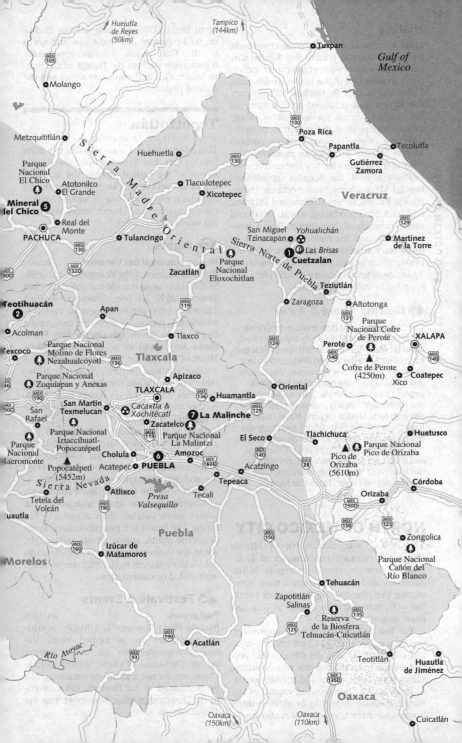

History

Long a cultural and economic crossroads, the region around present-day Mexico City has hosted a succession of important indigenous civilizations (notably the Teotihuacán, Toltec and Aztec). By the late 15th century, the Aztecs had managed to dominate all but one of central Mexico's states. Many archaeological sites and museums preserve remnants of pre-Hispanic history – Puebla's Museo Amparo provides an excellent overview of the region's history and cultures.

Post-conquest, the Spanish transformed central Mexico, establishing ceramic industries at Puebla, mines at Taxco and Pachuca, and haciendas producing wheat, sugar and cattle throughout the region. The Catholic Church used the region as a base for its missionary activities and left a series of imposing churches and fortified monasteries. Today, most towns retain a central plaza surrounded by colonial buildings.

ⓘ Getting There & Away

The cities, towns and (to a lesser extent) even the villages around Mexico City enjoy excellent, often 1st-class, bus links to both the capital and each other. Even the very smallest backwaters have comfortable daily services to Mexico City and to the closest transportation hub. While airports also serve Puebla, Toluca, Cuernavaca and Pachuca, it's nearly always cheaper and easier to fly to Mexico City and travel onward from there – these destinations even have direct bus routes from the airport. For all but the most obscure sights, traveling by bus is the easiest and most affordable option. Highway robbery is rarely an issue for major destinations, but aim to travel in daylight hours to smaller towns.

NORTH OF MEXICO CITY

The biggest attraction north of Mexico City is the extraordinary complex at Teotihuacán, once the largest metropolis in the Americas and one of Mexico's most spectacular pre-Hispanic sights. Further north, the well-preserved stone statues at Tula also draw visitors.

Far less visited, but equally impressive, are Parque Nacional El Chico and the mining village of Mineral del Chico – the perfect escape from the big city, with stunning views, wide-open spaces and friendly locals.

Pachuca, the fast-growing capital of dynamic Hidalgo state, has brightly painted houses, an attractive colonial center and a great line in Cornish pasties. From Pachuca, well-paved routes snake east and north to the Gulf coast, through spectacular countryside such as the fringes of the Sierra Madre Oriental mountain range and the coastal plain.

Tepotzotlán

⏱ 55 / POP 38,120 / ELEV 2300M

This *pueblo mágico* is an easy day trip from Mexico City, but feels far from the chaotic streets of the capital, despite the fact that urban sprawl creeps closer to Tepotzotlán's colonial center every year. A small, pleasant *zócalo,* market and church make Tepotzotlán worth a quick stop.

◉ Sights

Museo Nacional del Virreinato　　MUSEUM
(National Museum of the Viceregal Period; ⏱55-5876-0245; www.virreinato.inah.gob.mx; Plaza Virreinal; M$49, Sun free; ⊙9am-6pm Tue-Sun) There's a very simple reason to visit this wonderful, expansive museum comprising the restored Jesuit **Iglesia de San Francisco Javier** and an adjacent **monastery**. Much of the folk art and fine art on display – silver chalices, pictures created from inlaid wood, porcelain, furniture and religious paintings and statues – comes from Mexico City cathedral's large collection, and the standard is very high.

Once a Jesuit college of indigenous languages, the complex dates from 1606. Additions were made over the following 150 years, creating a showcase for the developing architectural styles of Nueva España.

Don't miss the **Capilla Doméstica**, with a Churrigueresque main altarpiece that boasts more mirrors than a carnival fun house. The facade is a phantasmagoric array of carved saints, angels, plants and people, while the interior walls and the Camarín del Virgen adjacent to the altar are swathed with gilded ornamentation.

✹ Festivals & Events

Pastorelas　　RELIGIOUS
(Nativity Plays) Tepotzotlán's highly regarded *pastorelas* are performed inside the former monastery in the weeks leading up to Christmas. Tickets, which include Christmas dinner and piñata smashing, can be purchased at La Hostería del Convento de Tepotzotlán after November 1 or via Ticketmaster.

🛌 Sleeping

Hotel Posada San José
HOTEL $

(☎ 55-5876-0835; Plaza Virreinal 13; r from M$450; 📶) Housed in a handsome colonial-era building on the south side of the *zócalo,* this centrally located budget hotel has 12 small rooms. Rooms overlooking the plaza and those near the hotel's water pump are noisy, though cheaper.

Hotel Posada del Virrey
HOTEL $

(☎ 55-5876-1864; Av Insurgentes 13; r with/without Jacuzzi M$600/400; 🅿📶) A short walk from the *zócalo,* this modern, motel-style posada (inn) is popular with weekenders. Rooms can be a bit dark, but they're clean, quiet and have TVs.

🍴 Eating & Drinking

It's best to avoid the many almost indistinguishable, tourist-centric restaurants on the *zócalo,* where the food is mediocre and prices are high. A better option is to join the locals at the market behind the Palacio Municipal, where food stalls serve rich *pozole* (a thin stew of hominy, pork or chicken), *gorditas* (round masa cakes) and freshly squeezed juices all day long.

Mesón Vegetariano Atzin
VEGETARIAN $

(☎ 55-5876-232; Plaza Tepotzotlán, Local A; comida corrida M$60; ⊙noon-6pm; 🍴) The yoga-instructor-owner-chef definitely sets the tranquil tone with her all-white outfits at this vegetarian restaurant in an inner courtyard. Set menus can include a simple salad, corn soup, sugar-free guava juice and natural yogurt with sunflower seeds. Tasty main dishes imitate meat favorites such as Veracruz-style 'fish' (from mushrooms) and gluten *milanesa* (Mexican schnitzel).

⭐ La Hostería del Convento de Tepotzotlán
MEXICAN $$

(☎ 55-5876-0243; www.hosteriadelconvento.mx; Plaza Virreinal 1; mains M$125-180; ⊙10am-5pm) Housed within the monastery's impressive bougainvillea-walled courtyard, La Hostería serves traditional brunch and lunch fare – *chiles tolucos* (Tepotzotlán specility of ancho chilies stuffed with chorizo and cheese) and *cecina adobada* (Oaxacan-style chili-marinated pork) – to a well-dressed clientele.

Los Molcajetes
PUB

(Los Molca; Pensador Mexicano s/n; ⊙6pm-late Tue-Sun) Los Molca (as locals call it) has homey yellow walls and a hodgepodge of paintings. Weekends get busy with students and older couples head-nodding (and sometimes spontaneously dancing) to pop hits and Mexican classics. Start the night with a *'cucaracha'* (cockroach), a potent shot of tequila and Kahlua. Hearty Mexican food is also served.

ℹ Getting There & Away

Tepotzotlán (not to be confused with Tepoztlán to the south of Mexico City) is on the Mexico City–Querétaro highway, about 40km from Mexico City.

From Mexico City's Terminal Poniente (Observatorio), Primera Plus buses (M$98, 1½ hours, hourly) run conveniently to the very center of Tepotzotlán. Return buses to Mexico City depart from the same terminal.

From Mexico City's Terminal Norte, 2nd-class Autotransportes Valle del Mezquital (AVM) buses (M$41, 40 minutes) stop at the Tepotzotlán bus terminal every 20 minutes en route to Tula. First-class *(directo)* buses stop every 40 minutes. Pegasso (www.pegasso.mx) buses (40 minutes, hourly) have a similar route. From the station, catch a combi (M$7.50) or secure taxi (M$35) to the *zócalo* (Plaza Virreinal).

Tula
☎ 773 / POP 29,560 / ELEV 2060M

A major city of the ancient, central Mexican culture widely known as Toltec, Tula is best known for its fearsome 4.5m-high stone warrior figures. Though less spectacular and far smaller than Teotihuacán, Tula is nonetheless fascinating and worth the effort of a day trip or overnight stay for those interested in ancient Mexican history.

The most attractive areas are the *zócalo* and Calle Quetzalcóatl, the pedestrianized street running north of the *zócalo* to a footbridge over the Tula river.

◉ Sights

⭐ Zona Arqueológica
ARCHAEOLOGICAL SITE

(☎ 773-100-36-54; www.centrohidalgo.inah.gob.mx; Carretera Tula–Iturbe Km 2; admission M$65, video camera use M$65; ⊙9am-5pm) Two kilometers north of Tula's center, ruins of the main ancient ceremonial site are perched on a hilltop. The highlight is standing atop a pyramid, virtually face-to-face with Toltec warrior statues, with views over rolling countryside (and the industrial sprawl nearby). Throughout the near-shadeless site, explanatory signs are in English, Spanish and Náhuatl. Near the main museum and the entrance to the site, you'll find souvenir markets on the weekends. Both of the on-site museums are free with site admission.

The main **site museum**, displaying ceramics, metalwork, jewelry and large sculptures, is near the entrance, at the north side of the *zona* from downtown on Calle Tollan. Outside the museum is a small, well-signed (in Spanish) cacti garden.

From the museum, the first large structure you'll reach is the **Juego de Pelota No 1** (Ball Court No 1). Archaeologists believe its walls were decorated with sculpted panels that were removed under Aztec rule.

Climb to the top of **Pirámide B**, also known as the Temple of Quetzalcóatl or Tlahuizcalpantecuhtli (the Morning Star), to see up close the impressive remains of three columnar roof supports – which once depicted feathered serpents with their heads on the ground and their tails in the air. The four basalt warrior telamones (male figures used as supporting columns; known as 'Los Atlantes') at the top, and the four pillars behind, supported the temple's roof. Wearing headdresses, breastplates shaped like butterflies and short skirts held in place by sun disks, the warriors hold spear throwers in their right hands and knives and incense bags in their left. The telamon on the left side is a replica of the original, now in Mexico City's Museo Nacional de Antropología. The columns behind the telamones depict crocodile heads (which symbolize the Earth), warriors, symbols of warrior orders, weapons and Quetzalcóatl's head.

On the pyramid's north wall are some of the carvings that once surrounded the structure. These show the symbols of the warrior orders: jaguars, coyotes, eagles eating hearts, and what may be a human head in Quetzalcóatl's mouth.

Now roofless, the **Gran Vestíbulo** (Great Vestibule) extends along the front of the pyramid, facing the plaza. The stone bench carved with warriors originally ran the length of the hall, possibly to seat priests and nobles observing ceremonies in the plaza.

Near the north side of Pirámide B is the **Coatepantli** (Serpent Wall), which is 40m long, 2.25m high and carved with geometric patterns and a row of snakes devouring human skeletons. Traces remain of the original bright colors with which most of Tula's structures were painted.

Immediately west of Pirámide B, the **Palacio Quemado** (Burned Palace) is a series of halls and courtyards with more low benches and relief carvings, one depicting a procession of nobles. It was probably used for ceremonies or reunion meetings.

On the far side of the plaza is a path leading to the **Sala de Orientación Guadalupe Mastache**, a small museum named after one of the archaeologists who pioneered excavations here. It includes large items taken from the site, including the huge feet of caryatids (female figures used as supporting columns) and a visual representation of how the site might have looked in its prime.

Catedral de San José   CATHEDRAL
(☏ 773-732-00-33; cnr Zaragoza & Calle 5 de Mayo) Tula's fortress-like cathedral, just off the *zócalo*, was part of the 16th-century monastery of San José. Inside, its vault ribs are decorated in gold.

🛏 Sleeping & Eating

Hotel Real Catedral   HOTEL $
(☏ 773-732-08-13; www.realhoteles.com/real_cat edral; Av Zaragoza 106; d M$700, incl breakfast M$800; P❋☎) A street back from the plaza, the Real Catedral has some luxurious perks (a small gym, in-room coffee makers, hair dryers and safes) for the price. Many of the inside rooms lack natural light, but the suites offer balconies and street views. There's a great selection of B&W photos of Tula in the lobby.

Hotel Casablanca   BUSINESS HOTEL $
(☏ 773-732-11-86; www.casablancatula.com; Pasaje Hidalgo 11; d/tr M$450/550; P☎) This comfortable, practical business hotel is right in the heart of Tula, located at the end of a narrow pedestrian street (look for the 'Milano' sign). Casablanca offers 36 rooms, all with cable TV, private bathroom and good wi-fi. Parking access is around back, via Avenida Zaragoza.

Hotel Cuellar   BUSINESS HOTEL $$
(☏ 773-732-29-20; www.hotelcuellar.com; Calle 5 de Mayo 23; s/d/tr incl breakfast M$715/1005/1300; P☎❄) You may be in Tula for the pyramids, but here you can add a dip in the pool to your city escape. The low ceilings, frilly bedding, clashing pastel decor, palm trees and ample parking might make you swear you're at an LA motel and not near the *zócalo*. Comfortable clean beds make up for it.

Best Western Tula
BUSINESS HOTEL **$$**

(☑ 773-732-45-75; www.bestwesterntula.com; Av Zaragoza s/n; r from M$970; P ❋ 🕾) Small and friendly enough not to feel like an anonymous chain hotel, this Best Western has 18 cozy rooms and gives other midrange hotels in Tula a run for their money.

Cocina Económica Las Cazuelas
MEXICAN **$**

(☑ 773-732-28-59; Pasaje Hidalgo 129; menú del día M$50; ⊗ 8am-6pm; 🕾) Come here for an excellent *menú del día* that includes your choice of soup, main dishes such as *chiles rellenos* (cheese-filled chilies) and *milanesa*, and *agua* (water flavored with fresh fruit). The upstairs balcony, away from the kitchen, is cooler than the steamy, main dining room.

Restaurant Casablanca
MEXICAN **$**

(☑ 773-732-22-74; www.casablancatula.com; Hidalgo 114; mains M$50-130; ⊗ 7am-9pm) While admittedly rather sterile – even Sanborns-esque – Casablanca has a full menu of Mexican standards, a good buffet (1pm to 6pm) and wi-fi. Just off the *zócalo*, it's one of the few sit-down options downtown, making it popular with business people and travelers alike.

Mana
VEGETARIAN **$**

(☑ 773-100-31-33; Pasaje Hidalgo 13; menú del día/ buffet M$50/70; ⊗ 8am-5pm Sun-Fri; 🖉) This simple vegetarian restaurant serves a generous *menú del día* that includes wholewheat bread, vegetable soup and a pitcher of oat milk. There's also a selection of veggie burgers, *taquitos,* quesadillas, soups and salads. Everything's fresh, hearty and homemade.

❶ Getting There & Away

Tula's **bus terminal** (Central De Autobuses Tula; Xicoténcatl 14) is three blocks downhill from the cathedral. First-class **Ovnibus** (☑ 800-839-21-30; http://ovnibus.com.mx) buses travel to/ from Mexico City's Terminal Norte (M$135, 1¾ hours, every 40 minutes) and direct to/from Pachuca (M$126, 1¼ hours, every 40 minutes). Primera Plus has services to Querétaro (M$234, 2¼ hours, eight daily).

❶ Getting Around

If you arrive in Tula by bus, the easiest way to get around is on foot. To reach the *zócalo* (known locally as 'El Jardín') from the station, turn right on Xicoténcatl then immediately left on Rojo del Río and walk two blocks to Hidalgo. Take a right on Hidalgo, which dead-ends at Plaza de la Constitución and Jardín de Tula, Tula's main square.

To reach the Zona Arqueológica, continue right for 200m along Calle Zaragoza until the bridge over the river and catch a *taxi colectivo* (M$8.50, 10 minutes) to the Oxxo store outside the *zona*. Return taxis also depart from here. The site's secondary, south entrance is locked and defunct.

Unfortunately, the town's bus station lacks an *empaque* (baggage check), which is problematic for day trippers traveling with luggage.

Teotihuacán

☑ 594 / ELEV 2300M

This complex of awesome pyramids, set amid what was once Mesoamerica's greatest city, is the region's most visited destination. The sprawling site compares to the ruins of the Yucatán and Chiapas for significance and anyone lucky enough to come here will be inspired by the astonishing technological might of the Teotihuacán (teh-oh-tee-wah-*kahn*) civilization.

Set 50km northeast of Mexico City, in a mountain-ringed offshoot of the Valle de México, **Teotihuacán** (☑ 594-956-02-76; www.teotihuacan.inah.gob.mx; admission/parking M$70/45; ⊗ 9am-5pm; P; 🚌 bound for Los Pirámides from Mexico City's Terminal Norte) is known for its two massive pyramids, the Pirámide del Sol (Pyramid of the Sun) and the Pirámide de la Luna (Pyramid of the Moon), which dominate the remains of the metropolis.

Though ancient Teotihuacán covered more than 20 sq km, most of what can be seen today lies along nearly 2km of the Calzada de los Muertos.

History

Teotihuacán was Mexico's biggest ancient city and the capital of what was probably Mexico's largest pre-Hispanic empire. It was a major hub of migration for people from the south, with multiethnic groups segregated into neighborhoods. Studies involving DNA tests in 2015 theorize that it was these cultural and class tensions that led to Teo's downfall.

The city's grid plan was plotted in the early part of the 1st century AD, and the Pirámide del Sol was completed – over an earlier cave shrine – by AD 150. The rest of the city was developed between about AD 250 and 600. Social, environmental and economic factors hastened its decline and eventual collapse in the 8th century.

Teotihuacán

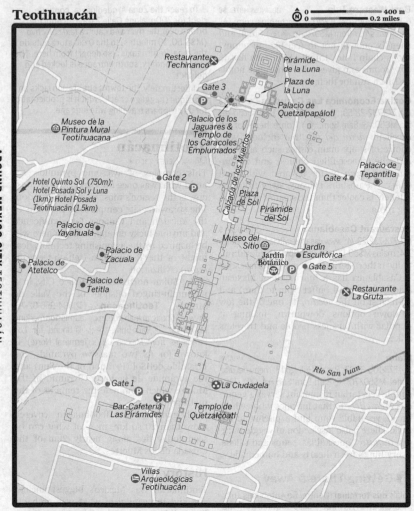

The city was divided into quarters by two great avenues that met near La Ciudadela (the Citadel). One of them, running roughly north–south, is the famous Calzada de los Muertos (Avenue of the Dead), so called because the later Aztecs believed the great buildings lining it were vast tombs, built by giants for Teotihuacán's first rulers. The major structures are typified by a *talud-tablero* style, in which the rising portions of stepped, pyramid-like buildings consist of both sloping *(talud)* and upright *(tablero)* sections. They were often covered in lime and colorfully painted. Most of the city was made up of residential compounds, some of which contained elegant frescoes.

Centuries after its fall, Teotihuacán remained a pilgrimage site for the Aztec royalty, who believed that all of the gods had sacrificed themselves here to start the sun moving at the beginning of the 'fifth world,' inhabited by the Aztecs. It remains an important pilgrimage site: thousands of New Age devotees flock here every year to celebrate the vernal equinox (between March 19 and March 21) and to soak up the mystical energies that are believed to converge here.

⊙ Sights

★ Pirámide del Sol ARCHAEOLOGICAL SITE

(Pyramid of the Sun) The world's third-largest pyramid – surpassed in size only by Egypt's Cheops (which is also a tomb, unlike the temples here) and the pyramid of Cholula – overshadows the east side of the Calzada de los Muertos. When Teotihuacán was at its height, the pyramid's plaster was painted bright red, which must have been a radiant sight at sunset. Clamber (carefully by rope) up the pyramid's 248 steps – yes, we counted – for an inspiring overview of the ancient city.

The Aztec belief that the structure was dedicated to the sun god was validated in 1971, when archaeologists uncovered a 100m-long underground tunnel leading from the pyramid's west flank to a cave directly beneath its center, where they found religious artifacts. It's thought that the sun was worshipped here before the pyramid was built and that the city's ancient inhabitants traced the origins of life to this grotto.

The pyramid's base is 222m long on each side, and it's now just over 70m high. The pyramid was cobbled together around AD 100, from three million tonnes of stone, without the use of metal tools, pack animals or the wheel.

No big backpacks are permitted up the Pirámide del Sol, and children must be accompanied by adults.

★ Pirámide de la Luna ARCHAEOLOGICAL SITE

(Pyramid of the Moon) The Pyramid of the Moon, at the north end of the Calzada de los Muertos, is smaller than the Pirámide del Sol, but more gracefully proportioned. Completed around AD 300, its summit is nearly the same height as Pirámide del Sol because it's built on higher ground, and is worth climbing for perspective on the dominance of the larger pyramid, not to mention the best photos of the whole Teotihuacán complex.

The **Plaza de la Luna**, just in front of the pyramid, is a handsome arrangement of 12 temple platforms. Some experts attribute astronomical symbolism to the total number of 13 (made up of the 12 platforms plus the pyramid), a key number in the day-counting system of the Mesoamerican ritual calendar. The altar in the plaza's center is thought to have been the site of religious dancing.

Calzada de los Muertos RUINS

(Avenue of the Dead) Centuries ago, the Calzada de los Muertos must have seemed absolutely incomparable to its inhabitants, who were able to see its buildings at their best. Today it is the main path that connects most of the sights at Teotihuacán. Gate 1 brings you to the avenue in front of La Ciudadela. For 2km heading north, the avenue is flanked by former palaces of Teotihuacán's elite and other major structures, such as the Pirámide del Sol. The Pirámide de la Luna looms large at the north end.

★ Templo de Quetzalcóatl RUINS

(Pyramid of the Feathered Serpent) Teotihuacán's third largest pyramid is the most ornate. The four surviving steps of the facade (there were originally seven) are adorned with striking carvings. In the *tablero* (right-angled) panels, the feathered serpent deity alternates with a two-fanged creature identified as the fire serpent, bearer of the sun on its daily journey across the sky. Imagine their eye sockets laid with glistening obsidian glass and the pyramid painted blue, as it once was. On the *talud* (sloping) panels are side views of the plumed serpent.

The fearsome plumed serpent is a precursor to the later Aztec god Quetzalcóatl. Some experts think the temple carvings depict war, while others interpret them as showing the creation of time.

La Ciudadela RUINS

(Citadel) This expansive, square complex is believed to have been the residence of the city's supreme ruler, and its rooms may have been the city's administrative center. Four wide walls topped by 15 pyramids enclose a huge open space, with a major pyramid, the Templo de Quetzalcóatl, built around AD 250, to the east. The pyramids represented mountains during rituals where the plaza, representing the world of the living, was deliberately flooded.

Skeletal remains of 137 human victims have been found under and around this temple. DNA tests reveal they were brought from diverse parts of Mesoamerica to be sacrificed.

In 2003, heavy rains sculpted a sinkhole beneath La Ciudadela to reveal a tunnel 17m underground, installed with an impressive miniature landscape representing the underworld. The tunnel was decorated with fool's gold to represent the starry night sky and pools of mercury to depict lakes. A vast collection of ritual treasures was also found, including eye-shaped crystals, jaguar sculptures and crocodile teeth-shaped diorite.

Museo del Sitio MUSEUM
(Museo de Teotihuacán; 594-958-20-81; 9am-4:30pm) Lying just south of the Pirámide del Sol, Teotihuacán's site museum makes a refreshing stop midway through a visit to the historic complex. The museum has excellent displays of artifacts, fresco panels and a confronting display of real skeletons buried in the ground, demonstrating ancient local beliefs on death and the afterlife. Information is provided in English and Spanish.

Nearby are the **Jardín Escultórica** (a lovely sculpture garden with Teotihuacán artifacts), a botanic garden, public toilets, snack bar, picnic tables and a bookstore with designer gifts.

Palacio de Tepantitla PALACE
This priest's residence, 500m northeast of the Pirámide del Sol, contains Teotihuacán's most famous fresco, the worn **Paradise of Tláloc**. The rain god Tláloc is shown attended by priests, with people, animals and fish nearby. Above is the sinister portrait of the **Great Goddess of Teotihuacán**, thought to be a goddess of the darkness and war because she's often shown with jaguars, owls and spiders – underworld animals. Look for her fanged nosepiece and her shields adorned with spiderwebs.

Museo de la Pintura Mural Teotihuacana MUSEUM
(594-958-20-81; admission incl with Teotihuacán Ruins ticket; 9am-4:30pm) This impressive museum showcases murals from Teotihuacán, as well as reconstructions of murals you'll see at the ruins.

Palacio de Quetzalpapálotl PALACE
Off the Plaza de la Luna's southwest corner is the Palace of the Quetzal Butterfly, thought to be the home of a high priest. The remains of bears, armadillos and other exotic animals were discovered here, showing that the area was used by the elite for cooking and rituals – not the kind of animals an average person would have eaten.

The **Palacio de los Jaguares** (Jaguar Palace) and **Templo de los Caracoles Emplumados** (Temple of the Plumed Conch Shells) are behind and below the Palacio de Quetzalpapálotl. The lower walls of several chambers off the patio of the Jaguar Palace display parts of murals showing the jaguar god blowing conch shells and praying to the rain god Tláloc. There are more complete murals in the Museo del Sitio.

The Templo de los Caracoles Emplumados, entered from the Palacio de los Jaguares' patio, is a now-subterranean structure of the 2nd or 3rd century. Carvings on what was its facade show large shells, possibly used as musical instruments.

Palacio de Tetitla & Palacio de Atetelco PALACE
A group of palaces lies west of Teotihuacán's main area, several hundred meters northwest of Gate 1. Many of the murals, discovered in the 1940s, are well preserved or restored and perfectly intelligible. Inside the sprawling **Palacio de Tetitla**, 120 walls are graced with murals of Tláloc, jaguars, serpents and eagles. Some 400m west is the **Palacio de Atetelco**, whose vivid jaguar or coyote murals – a mixture of originals and restorations – are in the Patio Blanco in the northwest corner.

About 100m further northeast are **Palacio de Zacuala** and **Palacio de Yayahuala**, a pair of enormous walled compounds that probably served as communal living quarters. Separated by the original alleyways, the two structures are made up of numerous rooms and patios but few entryways.

⭐ Festivals & Events

★ Experiencia Nocturna LIGHT SHOW
(Night Experience; www.ticketmaster.com.mx; Teotihuacán ruins; M$390; 6:30pm Mon, Fri & Sat Jan-Jun, Nov & Dec) A spectacular night event where colored lights and video are projected onto the Pyramids of the Sun and Moon at Teotihuacán to a soundtrack. The 45-minute show may be slightly cheesy but it does give an impressive glimpse at the pyramids in their original red splendor. The 'Night Experience' is staged erratically, so check the website regularly, months in advance, as tickets sell out quickly.

🛏 Sleeping & Eating

The town of San Juan Teotihuacán, 2km from the archaeological zone, has a few good overnight options, which make sense if you want to start early at the site before the crowds arrive.

Eating near the ruins is usually a pricey and disappointing experience. You're much better off bringing a picnic, though there are a couple of adequate restaurants worth seeking out.

Hotel Posada Sol y Luna
HOTEL $

(☑594-956-23-71, 594-956-23-68; www.posada solyluna.com; Cantú 13, San Juan Teotihuacán; d/tw/ste M$540/680/820; P 🛜) At the east end of town, en route to the pyramids, this well-run hotel has 16 fine but unexciting carpeted rooms, all with TV and bathroom. Junior suites have rather ancient Jacuzzis in them – not worth paying extra for.

Hotel Quinto Sol
HOTEL $$

(☑594-956-18-81; www.facebook.com/hotelquinto solteotihuacan; Av Hidalgo 26, San Juan Teotihuacán; s/d/tr M$955/1390/1570; P @ 🛜 ⚊) There's a reason most tourist groups stay at the Quinto Sol when visiting the ruins at Teotihuacán. With its fine facilities – including a decent-size pool, large, well-appointed rooms, good restaurant, in-room security boxes and room service – this is one of the best-equipped hotels in town.

Villas Arqueológicas Teotihuacán
HOTEL $$

(☑55-5836-9020; www.villasarqueologicas.com. mx; Periférico Sur s/n, Zona Arqueológica; d/ste Sun-Thu M$845/1461, Fri & Sat M$1095/1711; P ⚙ @ 🛜 ⚊) Just south of the Zona Arqueológica, this elegant hotel has a small gym, a heated outdoor pool, a lit tennis court, a playground and a spa with temascal (a traditional Mexican steam bath). There's also a refined Mexican restaurant. Wi-fi is only accessible in the lobby.

★ Restaurante Techinanco
MEXICAN $$

(☑594-958-23-06; Zona Arqueológica ring road; mains M$100-140; ⊙11am-5pm) A short walk from Gate 3, behind the Pirámide de la Luna, this homey restaurant serves excellent home cooking at comparatively reasonable prices. The small menu takes in local favorites from enchiladas to authentic homemade *moles* (chili-sauce dishes).

Ask about the curative massages or call in advance for a temascal.

❶ Information

Information Booth (☑594-956-02-76, reservations 594-958-20-81; www.teotihuacan. inah.gob.mx; ⊙7am-6pm) Near the southwest entrance (gate 1) of Teotihuacán.

❶ Getting There & Away

During daylight hours, Autobuses México–San Juan Teotihuacán runs buses from Mexico City's Terminal Norte to the ruins (M$50, one hour) every hour from 7am to 6pm. When entering Terminal Norte, turn left to Gate 8 for tickets, though ask which gate your bus departs from. Make sure your bus is headed for 'Los Pirámides,' not the nearby town of San Juan Teotihuacán (unless you are heading to accommodations in San Juan). Armed robberies occasionally occur on these buses; for current warnings, search the US State Department (www.travel. state.gov) website for 'Teotihuacán.'

At the ruins, buses arrive and depart from near gate 1, also making stops at gates 2 and 3 via the ring road around the site. Your ticket allows you to re-enter through any of the five entrances on the same day. The site museum is just inside the main east entrance (gate 5).

Return buses are more frequent after 1pm. The last bus back to Mexico City leaves at 6pm; some terminate at Indios Verdes metro station, but most continue to Terminal Norte.

Alternatively, tours to the ruins are plentiful and are better value for solo travelers than renting a guide alone and depart conveniently from Mexico City's Zócalo metro station or accommodations. **Capital Bus** (Map p82; https://capital bus.mx; Liverpool 155, Zona Rosa; one-day tour incl entrance fees M$650; ⊙departs Zona Rosa 8:30am, Zócalo 9am) runs daily minivan tours with a bilingual guide, including a visit to the Basílica de Guadalupe.

❶ Getting Around

To reach the pyramids from San Juan Teotihuacán, take a taxi (M$60) or any combi (M$14) labeled 'San Martín' departing from Avenida Hidalgo, beside the central plaza. Combis returning to San Juan stop on the main road outside gates 1, 2 and 3.

Mineral del Chico
☑771 / POP 481

The charming old mining village of Mineral del Chico is among the newest *pueblos mágicos* and outshines the much-larger Pachuca. You can take an easy and very lovely day trip or weekend retreat from Pachuca to this 'little' town or the nearly 3000-hectare **Parque Nacional El Chico** (www.parque elchico.gob.mx), which was established as a reserve in 1898.

The views are wonderful, the air is fresh and the mountains have some great hiking among spectacular rock formations and beautiful waterfalls. Most Mexicans who visit on the weekend hardly leave El Chico's cute main street (virtually the whole town) – not surprising when the locals are this friendly, proving their motto *'pueblo chico, gente grande'* (small town, great people).

DON'T MISS

REAL DEL MONTE

This gorgeous mountain town is a tangle of houses, restaurants and *pastie* shops scattered across a pine-tree-carpeted hillside. The air is thin here, so don't be surprised if you find yourself with a mild case of altitude sickness, but it's also clean, crisp and can get cold and windy suddenly (bring a sweater, if not a coat).

Two kilometers past the Hwy 105 turnoff for Parque Nacional El Chico, Real del Monte (officially known as Mineral del Monte) was the scene of a miners' strike in 1776, commemorated as the first strike in the Americas. Most of the town was settled in the 19th century, after a British company commandeered the mines. Cornish-style cottages line many of the steep, cobbled streets.

◉ Sights

Peña del Cuervo Mirador   VIEWPOINT

FREE There are lovely wide-angled views of the green mountains in El Chico National Park from the Peña del Cuervo lookout, located on a peak at 2770m. People have visited this natural viewing point since the 1920s. The large stone figures in the distance are called *Las Monjas* (The Monks) for their shape. Further away are more religiously named rocks, *Los Frailes* (The Friars).

From Mineral del Chico, *colectivos* marked 'Carboneras' (M$10) will drop you at the trailhead to the *mirador* (lookout). From there, it's about a 25-minute walk up a neglected cobbled staircase with a railing. Be careful after rain as there are plenty of loose stones.

🛏 Sleeping & Eating

Hotel El Paraíso   LODGE $$

(☏771-715-56-54; www.hotelesecoturisticos.com. mx; Carretera Pachuca s/n; r M$1100-1250; P 🛜) Nestled inside large, well-maintained grounds at the base of the mountain, with a fast-flowing stream running nearby, El Paraíso certainly has a location worthy of its name. The large, modern rooms lack individuality or charm, but they're very comfortable. A full-board option is available.

★ Restaurante y Cabañas San Diego   SEAFOOD $$

(☏771-209-33-63; Carretera Pachuca s/n; mains M$100-120; ⊙11am-4pm; P) Off the highway beside a rushing creek on the way into town (look for signs at the El Paraíso turnoff), San Diego is a true mountain escape. The owner's mother prepares excellent trout dishes. The fish *a la mexicana,* stuffed with Oaxacan cheese, tomatoes, chilies and thick chunks of garlic, is excellent. Breakfasts or dinners can be arranged by reservation.

There are also two comfortable but rustic cabins available for rent, one smaller (with a double bed, M$650 to M$750) than the other (sleeping up to 10 people, M$200 per person).

❶ Getting There & Away

From outside Iglesia de la Asunción, the pink church on Plaza de la Constitución in central Pachuca, blue-and-white *colectivos* climb the winding roads up to Mineral del Chico (M$15, 40 minutes) every 20 minutes from 8am to 6pm. The last service back to Pachuca is at 7pm.

There's no direct transit service from Real del Monte, but those wanting to avoid a trip back to Pachuca to transfer *colectivos* can hire a taxi for about M$150.

EAST OF MEXICO CITY

The views get seriously dramatic as you head east from the capital, with the landscape peppered with the snowcapped, volcanic peaks of Popocatépetl, Iztaccíhuatl, La Malinche and Pico Orizaba – the country's highest summit. The rugged Cordillera Neovolcánica offers anything from invigorating alpine strolls to demanding technical climbs. Unpredictable Popocatépetl, however, remains off-limits due to volcanic activity.

The gorgeous colonial city of Puebla – Mexico's fifth-largest city – is the dominant regional center, a local transportation hub and a big tourist draw with its churches dripping in tilework, plus rich culinary traditions, intriguing history and excellent museums. The surrounding state of Puebla is predominantly rural and home to approximately 500,000 indigenous people. Their rich handicraft culture ranges from pottery and carved onyx to embroidered textiles.

Attractive Cholula is now connected to Puebla by a convenient tourist train, making it easier than ever to drop by its youthful bars and chic restaurants.

Puebla

⌂ 222 / POP 1.5 MILLION / ELEV 2160M

Once a bastion of conservatism, Catholicism and tradition, Puebla has come out of its colonial-era shell. The city retains a fantastically well-preserved center, a stunning cathedral and a wealth of beautiful churches, while younger *poblanos* (people from Puebla) are embracing the city's increasingly thriving art and nightlife scenes.

The city is well worth a visit, with 70 churches in the historic center alone, more than 1000 colonial-era buildings adorned with the Talavera (painted ceramic tiles) for which the city is famous, and a long culinary history that can be explored at any restaurant or food stall. For a city of its size, Puebla is far more relaxed and less gridlocked than you might expect.

History

Founded by Spanish settlers in 1531 as Ciudad de los Ángeles, with the aim of surpassing the nearby pre-Hispanic religious center of Cholula, the city became known as Puebla de los Ángeles ('La Angelópolis') eight years later and quickly grew into an important Catholic center. Fine pottery had long been crafted from the local clay, and after the colonists introduced new materials and techniques, Puebla pottery evolved as both an art and an industry. By the late 18th century, the city had emerged as a major producer of glass and textiles. With 50,000 residents by 1811, Puebla remained Mexico's second-biggest city until Guadalajara overtook it in the late 19th century.

In 1862 General Ignacio de Zaragoza fortified the Cerro de Guadalupe against the French invaders and on May 5 that year his 2000 men defeated a frontal attack by 6000, many of whom were handicapped by diarrhea. This rare Mexican military success is the reason for annual (and increasingly corporate-sponsored and drunken) celebrations in the US, where the holiday is far more significant than in Mexico and hundreds of streets are named Cinco de Mayo. Few seem to remember that the following year the reinforced French took Puebla and occupied the city until 1867.

◉ Sights

★ Catedral de Puebla CATHEDRAL

(cnr Avs 3 Oriente & 16 de Septiembre; ⊙9am-1pm & 4-8pm) FREE Puebla's impressive cathedral, which appears on Mexico's M$500 bill, occupies the entire block south of the *zócalo*. Its architecture is a blend of severe Herreresque-Renaissance and early baroque styles. Construction began in 1550, but most of it took place under Bishop Juan de Palafox in the 1640s. At 69m, the towers are Mexico's tallest. The dazzling interior, the frescoes and the elaborately decorated side chapels are awe-inspiring; most have bilingual signs explaining their history and significance.

★ Museo Amparo MUSEUM

(⌂222-229-38-50; www.museoamparo.com; Calle 2 Sur 708; adult/student/child under 12yr M$35/25/free, Sun & Mon free; ⊙10am-6pm Wed-Mon, to 9pm Sat; 🚾) This superb private museum, housed in two linked 16th- and 17th-century colonial buildings, is loaded with pre-Hispanic artifacts, yet the interior design is contemporary and stylish. Displayed with explanatory information sheets in English and Spanish, the collection is staggering. Notice the thematic continuity in Mexican design – the same motifs appear again and again on dozens of pieces. An example: the collection of pre-Hispanic cult skeleton heads is eerily similar to the candy skulls sold during Día de Muertos.

The wonderful cafe terrace hosts free live music from 8pm to 9pm every Friday. There are often free art workshops for children on Saturday and Sunday.

Iglesia de la Compañía CHURCH

(cnr Av Palafox y Mendoza & Calle 4 Sur; ⊙Mass 7pm) This Jesuit church with a 1767 Churrigueresque facade is also called Espíritu Santo. Beneath the altar is a tomb said to be that of a 17th-century Asian princess who was sold into slavery in Mexico and later freed.

She was supposedly responsible for the colorful *china poblana* costume – a shawl, frilled blouse, embroidered skirt and gold and silver adornments. This costume became a kind of 'peasant chic' in the 19th century. But 'china' (chee-nah) also meant 'maidservant,' and the style may have evolved from Spanish peasant costumes.

Templo de Santo Domingo CHURCH

(cnr Avs 5 de Mayo & 4 Poniente) This fine Dominican church features a stunning

Puebla

Capilla del Rosario (Rosary Chapel), south of the main altar, which is the main reason to visit this church. Built between 1650 and 1690, it's heavy on gilded plaster and carved stone, with angels and cherubim seemingly materializing from behind every gold leaf. See if you can spot the heavenly orchestra.

Outside the entrance, in the Zona de Monumentos, you'll often find sculpture exhibitions.

Museo del Ferrocarril MUSEUM
(http://museoferrocarrilesmexicanos.gob.mx; Calle 11 Norte 1005; adult/child M$12/free, Sun free; ⊙9am-5pm Tue-Sun; ⊕) This excellent railway museum with activities for kids is housed in Puebla's former train station and the spacious grounds surrounding it. There are ancient steam-powered monsters through to relatively recent passenger carriages, many of which you can enter. One carriage contains an excellent collection of photos of

various derailments and other disasters that occurred during the 1920s and '30s.

Museo Casa del Alfeñique MUSEUM
(☑222-232-42-96; Av 4 Oriente 416; adult/student M$25/20, Sun free; ⊙10am-6pm Tue-Sun) This renovated colonial house is an outstanding example of the over-the-top 18th-century decorative style *alfeñique*, characterized by elaborate stucco ornamentation and named after a candy made from sugar and egg whites (evolving into modern-day Pueblan marzipan). The 1st floor details the Spanish conquest, including indigenous accounts in the form of drawings and murals. The 2nd floor houses a large collection of historic and religious paintings, local furniture and household paraphernalia. Labeling is in Spanish only.

Biblioteca Palafoxiana LIBRARY
(☑222-777-25-81; www.bpm.gob.mx; Av 5 Oriente 5; M$25, Sun free; ⊙10am-6pm Tue-Sun) Situated above the Casa de la Cultura and

N 0 — 400 m
0 — 0.2 miles

founded in 1646, Biblioteca Palafoxiana was the first public library in the Americas. For this, Palafoxiana has been listed on the Unesco Memory of the World register. The handsome library houses thousands of rare books on its gorgeous shelves – carved cedar and white pine – including one of the earliest New World dictionaries and the 1493 *Nuremberg Chronicle,* with more than 2000 engravings.

Casa de la Cultura
NOTABLE BUILDING

(☎222-232-12-27; Av 5 Oriente 5; ⊙8am-8pm Mon-Fri, 9am-1pm Sat) Occupying the entire block facing the south side of the cathedral, the former bishop's palace is a classic 17th-century brick-and-tile edifice that now houses government offices, the Casa de la Cultura and the State Tourist Office. Inside are art galleries, a bookstore and cinema, with a congenial cafe out back in the courtyard. Upstairs is the 1646 Biblioteca Palafoxiana, the first public library in the Americas.

Zócalo
PLAZA

Puebla's central plaza was originally a marketplace where bullfights, theater and hangings occurred, before assuming its current arboretum-like appearance in 1854. The surrounding arcades date from the 16th century. The plaza fills with an entertaining mix of clowns, balloon hawkers, food vendors and people using the free wi-fi on weekend evenings.

Museo San Pedro de Arte
MUSEUM

(☎222-246-58-58; Calle 4 Norte 203; adult/student M$25/20, Sun free; ⊙10am-6pm Tue-Sun) Opened in 1999 as Museo Poblano de Arte Virreinal, this top-notch museum is now named after the 16th-century Hospital de San Pedro in which it is housed. Galleries display excellent contemporary art and a fascinating permanent exhibit on the hospital's history.

Paseo Bravo
PLAZA

(btwn Reforma & 11 Poniente on Constitucion de 1917) This long, narrow park is an attractive counter to the *centro histórico's zocálo*. The park is festive and crowded in the afternoons, when kids in school uniforms, lunching office workers and rockers practicing guitar gather to eat, play and relax beneath trees from around the world – labeled with their species and origins. Capping off the Reforma end is the small but Talavera-heavy 17th-century church, **Sanitatario de Nuestra Señora de Guadalupe**.

Museo de la Revolución
MUSEUM

(Casa De Los Hermanos Serdan; ☎222-242-10-76; Av 6 Oriente 206; adult/student M$25/20, Sun free; ⊙10am-6pm Tue-Sun) This pockmarked 19th-century house was the site where the first battle of the 1910 Revolution was held. The renovated house retains its bullet holes and some revolutionary memorabilia, including a room dedicated to female insurgents.

Betrayed only two days before a planned uprising against the dictatorship of Porfirio Díaz, the Serdán family (Aquiles, Máximo, Carmen and Natalia) and 17 others fought 500 soldiers until only Aquiles, their leader, and Carmen were left alive. Aquiles, hidden under the floorboards, might have survived if the damp hadn't provoked a cough that gave him away. Both were subsequently killed.

Puebla

🚌 Tours

Turibus BUS

(☎ 222-231-52-17; www.turibus.com.mx; Puebla centro tour adult/child M$110/65, Cholula tour M$160/90; ⏰Cholula tour 1pm, centro tour every 40min 9am-7pm) Operated by ADO bus lines, this four-hour tour gives an overview of the nearby town of Cholula, including the pyramid (admission is a separate cost). There is also a red double-decker, hop-on, hop-off bus route around Puebla's *centro histórico* – better value than its slightly cheaper 1½-hour single tour. You can start either tour from the west side of the *zócalo* and buy tickets on board.

🎉 Festivals & Events

⭐**Día de Muertos** CULTURAL

(⏰Oct) Puebla has jumped on the bandwagon, with a two-week citywide cultural program starting in late October devoted to the Day of the Dead and including nighttime museum visits and viewings of *ofrendas* (altars).

Festival del Chile en Nogada FOOD & DRINK

(⏰Aug) Leaving no culinary stone unturned, the city's savvy restaurateurs promote the country's 'patriotic recipe,' *chiles en nogada* – green chilies stuffed with *picadillo* (a mix of ground meat and fruit) and topped with a luscious walnut cream sauce.

Festival del Mole Poblano FOOD & DRINK

(⏰Jun) In early June the city celebrates its most famous contribution to the culinary arts: *mole poblano,* a thick sauce of chilies, fruits, nuts, spices and chocolate.

Cinco de Mayo PARADE

(⏰May 5) The city's May 5 celebrations mark the day in 1862 when the Mexican army defeated the French. There is a huge parade and celebrations over the following fortnight. Cinco de Mayo celebrations are generally a much bigger deal in the US than in Mexico, except for in Puebla, which continue to grow in size.

Feria de Puebla MUSIC

(⏰Apr-May) Starting in late April and ending in late May, this fair honors the state's achievements with cultural and music events.

🛏 Sleeping

Puebla's hotel scene is competitive, with a huge range at all budgets and high standards in many boutique three- and four-star hotels. The Municipal Tourist Office (p161) on the *zócalo* provides flyers for budget hotels with prices. It's worth searching online for last-minute rates.

Many hotels can be spotted by illuminated 'H' signs over their entrance. Most colonial-era buildings have two types of room – interior (lacking windows) and exterior (exposed to a noisy street).

Hostal Casona Poblana   HOSTEL $

(☑ 222-246-03-83; http://casonapoblana.com; Calle 16 de Septiembre 905; dm/d/tr incl breakfast M$150/500/650; ☺☏) The rooms at this modern hostel have an openness to them, being built around a covered courtyard that is sociable without being party central. This setup means noise and cold travel easily, though wi-fi not so much. There is also a roof garden and small kitchen. Look for the large 'Hostal' banner out front.

Hotel Teresita   HOTEL $

(Hotel Teresa; ☑ 222-232-70-72; www.hotel teresita.com.mx; Av 3 Poniente 309; s/d/tr M$290/320/470; ☺☏) Among the multiple dreary posadas near the *zócalo,* Hotel Teresita sparkles with modern rooms boasting private bathrooms. The trade-off is a tiny space, ancient TVs and internal-facing windows (with footfall noise), but crisp white sheets, comfy beds and thorough cleanliness make Teresita a bargain.

Hostel Gente de Más   HOSTEL $

(☑ 222-232-31-36; www.gentedemashostel.com; Av 3 Poniente 713; dm/d/tw M$180/500/700; ☏) This fresh hostel has 'poshtel' aspirations with arty, rustic touches to the former house. Bathrooms are tiny and noise travels easily along the long halls, but rooms are clean and comfortable.

Gran Hotel San Agustín   HOTEL $

(☑ 222-232-50-89; Av 3 Poniente 531; r/tw/tr/q incl breakfast M$320/430/500/560; ℗☏) This straightforward budget option is near the *centro histórico* and has clean rooms, a plant-filled courtyard with a small fountain and includes very basic breakfast. It's not the kind of place where you'll want to spend the day (the rooms are dark and unexciting), but it's a perfectly fine base for exploring the city on a budget.

Hotel Colonial   HOTEL $$

(☑ 222-246-46-12, 800-013-00-00; www.colonial. com.mx; Calle 4 Sur 105; s/d/tr M$800/900/1000; ℗☏) Once part of a 17th-century Jesuit monastery and existing as a hotel in various forms since the mid-19th century, Colonial exudes heritage from its many gorgeously furnished rooms (half with colonial decor, half modern). There's a good restaurant and a fantastic 1890 gilt elevator. An unbeatable vibe and location despite occasional live-music and street noise.

Hotel Nube   HOTEL $$

(☑ 222-503-77-20; http://hotelnube.com.mx; Av 4 Oriente 407; d from $1140; ☺✳☏) Floating near the *zócalo* but without the noise, the almost-designer Hotel Nube offers fresh rooms with clean beds, modern bathrooms and a roof garden with a view. A mini-gym and helpful staff are pluses, but no English is spoken.

Hotel Mesón de San Sebastián   BOUTIQUE HOTEL $$

(☑ 222-242-65-23; www.mesonsansebastian. com; Av 9 Oriente 6; d/tw/ste incl breakfast M$990/1170/1345; ☏) This elegant boutique hotel has a colorful courtyard, accommodating staff who speak English, and a reputation for being family friendly. Each of the 17 rooms is individually decorated and named after a saint. All rooms have TV, phone, safe, minibar and antique furnishings. Discounts are offered during quiet periods.

★ La Purificadora   BOUTIQUE HOTEL $$$

(☑ 222-309-19-20; www.lapurificadora.com; Callejón de la 10 Norte 802; d/ste from US$130/200; ℗☏✲) From the trendy hotel company that runs Mexico City's chic Condesa df, Purificadora's stunning design has sharp, dramatic angles and a magnificent infinity pool on the roof. As its sister hotel did in the capital, La Purificadora has fast become the hip hangout of the *poblano* elite. Prices vary widely and rise Friday through Sunday, with frequent last-minute specials on the hotel website.

El Hotel Boutique Puebla de Antaño   BOUTIQUE HOTEL $$$

(☑ 222-246-24-03; www.hotelpuebladeantano. com; Av 3 Oriente 206; ste M$1765-2120; ℗✳☏✲) This boutique hotel has marble washbasins, crown molding, in-room fireplaces and Jacuzzis, and vintage photographs on the walls. The ground floor is home to one of Puebla's more refined French-influenced restaurants, Casa de los Espejos, while the rooftop Las Chismes de Puebla bar is almost painfully chic (think summertime in the Hamptons).

Mesón Sacristía de la Compañía
BOUTIQUE HOTEL $$$

(☑222-242-45-13; http://mesones-sacristia.com; Calle 6 Sur 304; ste incl breakfast M$1670-2050; P🛜) With eight rooms set around a bright, kitschy, pink courtyard, this small inn feels like the home of an eccentric grandmother. The junior suites are actually just standard rooms, while the two master suites are bigger and more worthy of the title. The downstairs restaurant, which serves aromatic US-style breakfasts and refined *poblano* cuisine, gets rave reviews from guests.

El Sueño Hotel & Spa
BOUTIQUE HOTEL $$$

(☑222-232-64-89, 222-232-64-23; www.elsueno -hotel.com; Av 9 Oriente 12; ste incl breakfast M$2205-4180; P❄🛜) An oasis of minimalist chic amid the colonial bustle of Puebla's old town, Sueño's 20 rooms are sleek, high-ceilinged and thematically decorated. Each is inspired by a different female Mexican artist. There's a hot tub and sauna, plasma TVs in the rooms and a martini bar in the lobby. Rooms are discounted on Sunday.

Casona de la China Poblana
LUXURY HOTEL $$$

(☑222-242-56-21; www.casonadelachinapoblana. com; cnr Calle 4 Norte & Av Palafox y Mendoza; d M$2530, ste M$2880-4025; P) This elegant boutique hotel is stunning and knows it. Shamelessly dubbing itself Puebla's 'most exclusive hotel,' China Poblana has massive, gorgeous suites decorated in a mixture of styles, a lovely courtyard and La Cocina de la China Poblana restaurant.

✗ Eating

Puebla's culinary heritage, of which *poblanos* are rightly proud, can be explored in a range of eateries throughout the city, from humble street-side food stalls to elegant colonial-style restaurants. However, given the city's renown as a culinary center, it's surprising how few truly excellent high-end restaurants there are.

★ La Zanahoria
VEGETARIAN $

(☑222-232-48-13; Av 5 Oriente 206; mains M$22-62, set meals M$76, daily buffet adult M$88-120, child M$53-72; ⊙7am-8:30pm; 🛜🍴♿) This godsend for vegetarians is an excellent place for lunch, just moments from the *zócalo*. The draw is the popular daily buffet from 1pm to 6pm in the spacious interior colonial courtyard. It features more than 20 dishes, salads and desserts, such as soy-meat lasagna, *chilaquiles* and Middle Eastern tabbouleh.

The extensive à la carte menu includes everything from veggie *hamburguesas* to *nopales rellenos* (stuffed cactus paddles). In the front of the restaurant is the express service area (including a juice bar and a health-food snack shop).

★ Las Ranas
TACOS $

(☑222-242-47-34; Av 2 Poniente 102; tacos & tortas M$8-27; ⊙noon-9:15pm Mon-Sat, 2pm-8:30pm Sun) This local institution is *the* place to try one of Puebla's great dishes: the *taco árabe*. Unbelievably moist *al pastor* (shepherd-style) pork is marinated and spit-grilled then rolled in fresh, slightly charred Middle Eastern–style flatbread. This restaurant and the annex across the street, **El Patio de las Ranas** (Av 2 Poniente 205), are perpetually full but worth the wait for the unforgettable tacos.

Antigua Churreria de Catedral
CAFE $

(☑222-232-13-24; cnr Calles 5 Oriente & 2 Sur; churros M$3-6; ⊙9am-midnight) There's always a hungry queue for the delicious, crispy *churros* (doughnut-like fritters) here. Half the fun is the spectacle of watching them being made behind the glass.

Mercado de Sabores Poblanos
MARKET $

(Av 4 Poniente, btwn Calles 11 & 13 Norte; ⊙7am-7pm) The 6570-sq-meter Mercado de Sabores Poblanos is a thrilling complement to Puebla's food scene. A sparkling food court serves local specialties such as *cemitas* (a style of sandwich/burger unique to Puebla), *pipián verde* (green pumpkin-seed sauce) and *tacos árabes* (Arabic taco) from 130-odd vendors.

★ El Mural de los Poblanos
MEXICAN $$

(☑222-242-05-03; www.elmuraldelospoblanos. com; Av 16 de Septiembre 506; mains M$170-295; ⊙8am-11pm Sun-Thu, to 11:30pm Fri & Sat; ❄🛜) Set back from the street in a gorgeous, plant-filled colonial courtyard, El Mural de los Poblanos serves excellent, traditional *poblano* dishes in an elegant setting. The house specialty is five kinds of *mole*. Other favorites include the smoky goat's-cheese-stuffed ancho *chile relleno* (dried *poblano* chili) and the trilogy of *cemitas* (a style of sandwich/burger unique to Puebla). Cocktails and other drinks are also excellent, and the service exceptional. Reservations are a good idea on busy Friday and Saturday nights and holidays.

PUEBLA'S SEASONAL TREATS

Justly famous for its incredible cuisine, Puebla also offers an array of seasonal, local delicacies that adventurous eaters should not miss.

Escamoles (March to June) Ant larvae; looks like rice and is usually sautéed in butter.

Gusanos de maguey (April to May) Worms that inhabit the maguey plant, typically fried in a drunken chili and *pulque* (a low-alcohol brew made from the maguey plant) sauce.

Huitlacoche (June to October) Inky-black corn fungus with an enchanting, earthy flavor. Sometimes spelt *cuitlacoche*.

Chiles en nogada (July to September) Green chilies stuffed with *picadillo* (a mix of ground meat and dried fruit), covered with a creamy walnut sauce and sprinkled with red pomegranate seeds.

Chapulines (October to November) Grasshoppers purged of digestive matter then dried, smoked or fried in lime and chili powder.

★ Augurio
MEXICAN $$

(222-290-23-78; www.augurio.mx; Av 9 Oriente 16; mains M$180-250; ⊙9am-11pm Mon-Sat, to 6pm Sun) Poblano chef Angel Vázquez has brought international flavours to Puebla in other ventures, but with Augurio he creates gourmet experiences in an intimate space out of local dishes such as starter of *camarones en costra de chicharrón* (shrimp crumbed in pork crackling) and 10 kinds of *mole* mains, including trout in a red pepita *mole* with buttery *escamoles* (ant larvae).

★ Restaurante Sacristía
MEXICAN $$

(222-242-45-13; Calle 6 Sur 304; mains M$120-195; ⊙1pm-11pm Mon-Sat, 9am-6pm Sun) Set in the delightful colonial patio of the Mesón Sacristía de la Compañía hotel, this is an elegant place for a meal of authentic *mole* and creative twists on rich *poblano* cuisine, or a cocktail or coffee in the intimate Confesionario bar. Live piano and violin soloists (and flower petals by request) lend a romantic ambience most nights from around 9pm.

If you like what you taste, inquire about the small-group cooking classes.

Amalfi Pizzeria
PIZZA $$

(222-403-77-97; Av 3 Oriente 207B; pizzas M$150-190; ⊙1-9:45pm Sun-Thu, to 11pm Fri & Sat) It's easy to see why this excellent wood-oven pizzeria – with dim lighting, terracotta walls and beamed ceilings – is a popular date spot. In addition to a wide selection of fine, thin-crust pizzas, there's decent wine and Italian classics such as caprese salads and pasta. Because the dining room is small, a reservation doesn't hurt.

La Purificadora
INTERNATIONAL $$$

(222-309-19-20; www.lapurificadora.com; Callejón de la 10 Norte 802, Paseo San Francisco, Barrio El Alto; mains M$160-350; ⊙7am-11pm Sun-Thu, to midnight Fri & Sat; ℗🛜) The restaurant at La Purificadora, one of Puebla's chicest boutique hotels, is set in a spare, loft-like space with unfinished walls and long, narrow wood-plank tables. The menu tends more toward the indulgent and elaborate, with dishes such as tequila-marinated sea bass or chicken *mole* with peanut polenta. There is also a good drinks list.

🍷 Drinking & Nightlife

During the day students pack the sidewalk tables along the pedestrian-only block of Avenida 3 Oriente, near the university. At night, mariachis lurk around Callejón de los Sapos – Calle 6 Sur between Avenidas 3 and 7 Oriente – but they're being crowded out by the bars on nearby Plazuela de los Sapos. These rowdy watering holes are packed on weekend nights, when many of them become live-music venues.

★ La Pasita
BAR

(222-232-44-22; Av 5 Oriente 602; shots from M$25; ⊙12:30-5:30pm Wed-Mon) This tiny bar among the antique stores of La Plazuela de Los Sapos has been serving liqueur shots for over century. Try sweet and strong *la pasita* (raisin), *rompope* (eggnog), *almendra* (almond) or the romantically named 'artist's blood' of quince and apricot. The eclectic kitsch decor and old world experience is worth the trip alone.

SHOPPING IN PUEBLA

The Zona Esmeralda, 2km west of the *zócalo*, is a stretch of Avenida Juárez with chichi boutiques, upscale restaurants and trendy nightclubs.

Antiques

For quirky antique stores, head to Callejón de los Sapos, around the corner of Avenida 5 Oriente and Calle 6 Sur. Most shops open from 10am to 7pm. On Saturday and Sunday, there is a lively outdoor antiques market here and at the Plazuela de los Sapos from 11am to 5pm.

Sweets

A number of shops along Avenida 6 Oriente, to the east of Avenida 5 de Mayo, sell traditional handmade Puebla sweets such as *camotes* (candied sweet-potato sticks) and *jamoncillos* (bars of pumpkin-seed paste).

Talavera

Puebla has plenty of shops selling the colorful, hand-painted ceramics known as Talavera. There are several good stores on Plazuela de los Sapos and the streets around it. Designs reveal Asian, Spanish-Arabic and Mexican indigenous influences. Bigger pieces are expensive, delicate and difficult to transport.

La Berenjena CRAFT BEER
(☎222-688-47-54; www.laberenjenapizza.com; Calle 3 Oriente 407; ☺2-11pm Mon-Sat, to 7pm Sun; ☞) Excellent artesanal pizzas are the specialty promoted at 'The Aubergine,' but the bar's long list of Mexican craft beers and mezcals are just as special. There is also wine, cocktails (mezcal mojito, anyone?) and fancy snacks to share such as honey roasted goat's cheese and *baba ganoush* (aubergine dip).

Café Milagros CAFE
(www.facebook.com/cafemilagros; Calle 6 Sur 4; frappé M$35, snacks M$30-70; ☺9am-10pm Sun-Wed, to midnight Thu-Sat) This is what a Mexican cafe would look like in a cartoon. Think shrines to Frida Kahlo, Day of the Dead trinkets, *lucha libre* (Mexican wrestling) paintings, devil masks and colorful wood tables. It's a popular backdrop for tacos with a friend or sipping a frappé solo with your electronic gadget.

Barra Beer SPORTS BAR
(☎222-298-05-54; Av 5 Poniente 705C; ☺noon-11:30pm Mon-Wed, to 1:30am Thu-Sat, 1pm-9pm Sun) With its impressive beer list, this shrine to *las cervezas del mundo* (beers of the world) serves beers from far and wide, including 21 varieties of German beer plus brews from China, Spain, Belgium and Ireland. Unless you're desperate for your native brew, try something from the good list of artisanal Mexican beers.

☆ Entertainment

★ Celia's Cafe LIVE MUSIC
(☎222-242-36-63; Av 5 Oriente 608; ☺9am-10pm Wed-Fri, to 11:30pm Sat, 10am-6pm Sun) Live music adds old-world romance to the *poblano* decor at this sprawling bar-restaurant. Dine to musicians playing *trova* (troubadour-type folk music; 8pm to 10pm Thursday), piano (8pm to 10pm Friday and breakfast and lunch Saturday and Sunday) or *bohemia* (love songs; 7pm to 9pm Saturday).

Every *mole poblano* (Mexico's most famous dish), coffee and tequila shot is served up in (purchasable) Talavera-ware that is crafted in Celia's own studio.

🔒 Shopping

★ Talavera Uriarte CERAMICS
(☎222-232-15-98; www.uriartetalavera.com.mx; Av 4 Poniente 911; ☺10am-7pm Mon-Fri, to 6pm Sat, to 5pm Sun) Unlike most of Puebla's Talavera shops, Uriarte still makes its pottery on-site. The showroom displays a gorgeous selection of high-quality, intricately painted pieces. Founded in 1824, the company is now owned by a Canadian expat. Factory tours are offered 10am to 1pm Monday through Friday.

ℹ Information

ATMs are plentiful throughout the city, but mostly on Avenida Reforma near the *zócalo*, where banks have exchange facilities. Expect long queues on Friday afternoons.

Nearly all accommodations and cafes have free wi-fi access. There is patchy access in the *zócalo*. There are also several places to get online along Calle 2 Sur. Most charge M$5 to M$10 per hour.

CAPU Tourist Kiosk (CAPU; ☉10am-6pm Thu-Mon) English-speaking staff with pamphlets and transportation information within the bus terminal.

Hospital UPAEP (☎222-229-81-34, ext 6035; www.christusmuguerza.com.mx; Av 5 Poniente 715) Well equipped for emergencies with short wait times, though only basic English is spoken.

Main Post Office (☎222-232-64-48; Av 16 de Septiembre s/n, cnr Av 5 Oriente; ☉8am-6pm Mon-Fri, 10am-3pm Sat)

Municipal Tourist Office (☎01-800-326-86-56; Portal Hidalgo 14; ☉9:30am-8pm) English- and French-speaking staff offer free maps, use of internet-connected PCs and excellent information about what's on. Through the archways on the north side of the *zócalo*.

State Tourist Office (Oficina de Turismo del Estado; ☎222-246-20-44; Av 5 Oriente 3; ☉8am-8pm Mon-Sat, 9am-2pm Sun) Information for destinations outside of Puebla. It's located in the Casa de Cultura building, facing the cathedral yard.

ℹ Getting There & Away

AIR
Aeropuerto Hermanos Serdán (☎222-232-00-32; www.aeropuerto-puebla.es.tl), 22km northwest of Puebla off Hwy 190, has Aeroméxico, Volaris and MexicanaLink flights to/from Guadalajara, Tijuana, Monterrey, Cancún and Hermosillo most days. There is one daily international flight to/from Houston with Continental; and one to/from Dallas with American Eagle.

Service can be patchy and the airport closes whenever there is volcanic ash in the air. The Toluca airport (p199) is likely a better option.

BUS
Puebla's **Central de Autobuses de Puebla** (CAPU; ☎222-249-72-11; www.capu.com.mx; Blvd Norte 4222) is 4km north of the *zócalo* and 1.5km off the autopista. It's more commonly referred to as CAPU.

From Mexico City and towns to the west, most buses to/from Puebla use the capital's TAPO station, though some travel to Terminal Norte or Terminal Sur in Tasqueña. The trip takes about two hours.

Both ADO (www.ado.com.mx) and Estrella Roja (www.estrellaroja.com.mx) travel frequently between the two cities, operating both 1st-class and wi-fi-enabled deluxe buses. They run a service to/from Mexico City's La Condesa neighborhood (five daily Monday to Friday, twice daily Saturday and Sunday), which is convenient for those staying in the area.

From CAPU, there are buses at least once a day to almost everywhere to the south and east. The bus station website has a useful list of most of the destinations and bus companies.

Frequent 'Cholula' *colectivos* (M$7.50, 40 minutes) leave from Avenida 6 Poniente, near the corner with Calle 13 Norte.

CAR & MOTORCYCLE
Puebla is 123km east of Mexico City by Hwy 150D. Traveling east of Puebla, 150D continues to Orizaba (negotiating a cloudy, winding 22km descent from the 2385m-high Cumbres de Maltrata en route), Córdoba and Veracruz.

TRAIN
The comfortable **Puebla–Cholula Tourist Train** (Tren Turístico Puebla–Cholula; https://tren turisticopuebla.com; Calle 11 Norte, cnr Av 18 Poniente; one way adult/child under 5yr M$60/free; ☉departs Puebla 7am, 8:30am, 4:50pm Mon-Fri, plus 3:20pm Sat & Sun) connects central Puebla with the pyramid in Cholula on a 17.4km, 40-minute route. The Puebla station is northwest of the *zócalo*.

ℹ Getting Around

Most hotels and places of interest are within walking distance of Puebla's *zócalo*.

Within the CAPU bus station, buy a ticket at a kiosk for an authorized taxi to the city center (about M$74). Alternatively, follow signs for 'Autobuses Urbanos' and catch combi 51 (M$6) to the corner of Avenida 4 and Blvd 5 de Mayo, three blocks east of the *zócalo*. The ride takes 15 to 20 minutes.

From the city center to the bus station, catch any northbound 'CAPU' *colectivo* from the same corner or anywhere along Blvd 5 de Mayo, or

BUSES FROM PUEBLA

DESTINATION	FARE (M$)	DURATION (HR)	FREQUENCY (DAILY)
Cuetzalan	210	3½	14
Mexico City (TAPO or Tasqueña)	150-200	2-2½	75
Oaxaca	347-780	4-4½	14
Veracruz	242-580	3½	29

WORTH A TRIP

LA MALINCHE VOLCANO

The long, sweeping slopes of this dormant 4460m volcano, named after Cortés' now much-maligned indigenous interpreter and lover, dominate the skyline northeast of Puebla, and are visible on a clear day. La Malinche, Mexico's fifth-tallest peak, is snow-capped only a few weeks each year, typically in May. Hiking here is most popular with families on weekends.

Centro Vacacional IMSS Malintzi (☑ 55-5238-2701; http://centrosvacacionales.imss. gob.mx; campsites M$60, cabins up to 6 people M$865-1278, up to 9 people M$1360; **P**), operated by the Mexican Social Security Institute, has 50 cabins, including rustic and 'luxury' options, at a frosty 3333m, and is the starting point of most hikes. The family-oriented resort has woodsy grounds and fine views of the peak. The remodeled cabins are basic, but include TV, fireplace, hot water and kitchen with refrigerator. It gets crowded from Friday to Sunday, but is quiet midweek. Prices are about M$100 higher on weekends and holidays. Those not staying can park here for M$40.

Beyond the vacation center, the road becomes impassable by car. It's about 1km by footpath to a ridge, from where it's an arduous five-hour round-trip hike to the top. Hikers should take precautions against altitude sickness.

The main route to the volcano is Hwy 136; turn southwest at the 'Centro Vacacional Malintzi' sign. Before you reach the center, you must register at the entrance of the Parque Nacional La Malintzi. Some *colectivos* to the entrance leave at 8:20am from the town of Apizaco (M$20, 40 minutes) from the corner of Av Hidalgo and Av Serdan, returning at 1pm, 3pm (Friday to Sunday) and 5pm.

along Calle 9 Sur. The most direct buses to CAPU are an off-white color and are branded with 'Boulevard CU' on the side. All city buses and *colectivos* cost M$6.

Call **Radio Taxi** (☑ 222-243-70-59), or use Uber, for a secure taxi service within the city – a good idea if you're traveling alone or going out at night.

Cholula

☑ 222 / POP 120,000 / ELEV 2170M

Cholula's transformation from a colorful satellite town of Puebla into a proper boutique city-break stepped up a notch with the introduction of a tourist train. Though Cholula is still (for now) far different from Puebla in its history and relaxed daytime ambience. Owing to its large student population, the town has a surprisingly vibrant nightlife and an increasing range of chic restaurants and accommodations options within a short walk of the huge *zócalo*.

Cholula is also home to the widest pyramid ever built (yes, wider than any in Egypt) – the Pirámide Tepanapa. Despite this claim to fame, the town's ruins are largely ignored because, unlike those of Teotihuacán or Tula, the shrubbery-covered pyramid has been so badly neglected over the centuries that it's virtually unrecognizable as a human-made structure.

History

Between around AD 1 and 600, Cholula grew into an important religious center, while powerful Teotihuacán flourished 100km to the northwest. Around AD 600, Cholula fell to the Olmeca-Xicallanca, who built nearby Cacaxtla. Some time between AD 900 and 1300 the Toltecs and/or Chichimecs took over and it later fell under Aztec dominance. There was also artistic influence from the Mixtecs to the south.

By 1519 Cholula's population had reached 100,000 and the Pirámide Tepanapa was already overgrown. Cortés, having befriended the neighboring Tlaxcalans, traveled here at the request of the Aztec ruler Moctezuma, but it was a trap and Aztec warriors had set an ambush. The Tlaxcalans tipped off Cortés about the plot and the Spanish struck first. Within a day they killed 6000 Cholulans before the city was looted by the Tlaxcalans. Cortés vowed to build a church here for every day of the year, or one on top of every pagan temple, depending on which legend you prefer. Today there are 39 churches – far from 365 but still plenty for a small city.

The Spanish developed nearby Puebla to overshadow the old pagan center and Cholula never regained its importance, especially after a severe plague in the 1540s decimated its indigenous population.

⊙ Sights

★**Zona Arqueológica**   ARCHAEOLOGICAL SITE
(☑222-247-90-81; Calzada San Andres; M$70; ⊘9am-6pm) Two blocks to the southeast of Cholula's central plaza, the **Pirámide Tepanapa** (☑222-247-90-81; Calzada San Andres; admission $70, Spanish/English guide $90/120; ⊘9am-6pm) looks more like a hill than a pyramid and has a domed church on top so it's tough to miss. The town's big drawcard is no letdown, with kilometers of tunnels veining the inside of the structure. The Zona Arqueológica comprises the excavated areas around the pyramid and the tunnels underneath.

The church grounds on the peak are worth the trip alone for panoramic views across Cholula to the volcanoes and Puebla.

Enter via the tunnel on the north side, which takes you on a spooky route through the center of the pyramid. Several pyramids were built on top of each other during various reconstructions, and more than 8km of tunnels have been dug beneath the pyramid by archaeologists to penetrate each stage, with 800m accessible to visitors. You can see earlier layers of the building from the access tunnel, which is a few hundred meters long.

The access tunnel emerges on the east side of the pyramid, from where you can follow a path around to the **Patio de los Altares** on the south side. Ringed by platforms and unique diagonal stairways, this plaza was the main approach to the pyramid. Three large stone slabs on its east, north and west sides are carved in the Veracruz interlocking scroll design. At its south end is an Aztec-style altar in a pit, dating from shortly before the Spanish conquest. On the mound's west side is a reconstructed section of the latest pyramid, with two earlier exposed layers.

Rather than following the path south, you can head straight up the stairs to the brightly decorated **Santuario de Nuestra Señora de los Remedios** (⊘8am-7pm) FREE that tops Pirámide Tepanapa and looks down upon the Patio de los Altares. It's a classic symbol of conquest, though possibly an inadvertent one as the church may have been built before the Spanish realized the mound contained a pagan temple. You can climb to the church for free on a path starting near the northwest corner of the pyramid.

The small **Museo de Sitio de Cholula** (Calz San Andrés; admission incl with Zona Arqueológica ticket; ⊘9am-5pm), across the road from the **ticket office** and down some steps, provides the best introduction to the site, with a cutaway model of the pyramid mound showing the various superimposed structures.

★**Capilla Real de Naturales**   CHURCH
(Zócalo; ⊘9:30am-1pm & 4-6pm Mon & Wed-Sat, 9am-3pm & 5-7pm Sun, closed Tue) The Arabic-style Capilla Real has 49 domes and dates from 1540. The mosque-inspired design makes the church unique to Mexico and creates a beautiful interior pattern of dome arches. It forms part of the Ex-Convento de San Gabriel. The church opens for extended hours (9am to 8pm) on the 25th of each month.

Parroquia de San Pedro   CHURCH
(Av 5 de Mayo 401; ⊘7am-7pm) This distinctively yellow baroque church has the tallest tower in Cholula and has become an often-photographed icon of the city, at least at ground level. It was built in 1640 and the dome was reconstructed in 1782.

Ex-Convento de San Gabriel   CHRISTIAN SITE
(Plaza de la Concordia; Zócalo; ⊘9am-7pm) The Ex-Convento de San Gabriel (also known as Plaza de la Concordia), facing the east side of Cholula's huge *zócalo*, includes a tiny but interesting Franciscan library and three fine churches – **Capilla de la Tercera Orden** (⊘9am-1pm & 4:30-6pm), Capilla Real and **Templo de San Gabriel** (⊘9am-7pm) – all of which will appeal to travelers interested in antique books and early religious and Franciscan history.

Museo de la Ciudad de Cholula   MUSEUM
(Casa del Caballero Águila; cnr Av 5 de Mayo & Calle 4 Oriente; M$20, Sun free; ⊘9am-3pm Thu-Tue) This excellent museum is housed in a fantastically restored colonial building on the *zócalo*. The small collection includes ceramics and jewelry from the Pirámide Tepanapa, as well as later colonial paintings and sculptures. Most interestingly, you can watch through a glass wall as museum employees painstakingly restore smashed ceramics and repair jewelry.

Zócalo   PLAZA
(Plaza de la Concordia) Cholula's *zócalo* (in San Pedro Cholula, which is not to be confused with Zócalo de San Andrés to the east) is so

Cholula

Cholula

⊙ Top Sights

⊙ Sights

⊙ Sleeping

⊗ Eating

⊕ Drinking & Nightlife

huge and exposed that most people prefer to congregate under the arches in the cafes and restaurants, or in the greener east side near to the 19th-century Capilla de la Tercera Orden (p163). Facing this leafier patch is the Ex-Convento de San Gabriel and the Arabic-style Capilla Real. In the center is the Templo de San Gabriel (p163), founded in 1530 on the site of a pyramid.

✨ Festivals & Events

Festival de la Virgen de los Remedios
DANCE

(☺ Sep) Perhaps the most important Cholulan holiday of the year, this festival is celebrated the week of September 1. There are traditional dances daily atop the Pirámide Tepanapa. It forms part of Cholula's regional *feria* held in the first few weeks of September.

Carnaval de Huejotzingo
HISTORICAL

(☺ Feb) On Shrove Tuesday, masked Carnaval dancers re-enact a battle between French and Mexican forces in Huejotzingo, 14km northwest of Cholula, off Hwy 190.

Quetzalcóatl Ritual
CULTURAL

On both the spring (late March) and autumn (late September) equinoxes, this pre-Hispanic ritual is re-enacted with poetry, dances, firework displays and music performed on traditional instruments at the pyramid in Cholula.

🛏 Sleeping

With an increasing range of good-value hotels, a few boutique favorites and even a hostel, Cholula makes an attractive alternative to staying in Puebla for those who prefer a laid-back pace. Stay near the pyramid, in the area known as San Pedro Cholula, for the churches, museums and *zócalo*.

Hostal de San Pedro
HOSTEL $

(☎ 222-178-04-95; www.hostaldesanpedro.com; Calle 6 Norte 1203; dm/d/tw/tr incl breakfast M$200/500/600/700; P☺@☎) The only true hostel in Cholula is a quick stroll from the *zócalo* and has clean, comfy beds in a quiet location. Upstairs rooms are built around a sunny terrace where you could easily pass an afternoon. If you end up staying even longer, there are long-term deals with laundry use. No alcohol is allowed in the hostel.

Hotel Real de Naturales
BUSINESS HOTEL $

(☎ 222-247-60-70; www.hotelrealdenaturales.com; Calle 6 Oriente 7; d/tw/tr/ste M$650/750/850/1050; P☎😎) This 45-room hotel was built in the colonial style to blend into the surrounding architectural landscape and it succeeds with its shady courtyards, tiled baths, tasteful B&W photography and elegant archways. Its central location and many considered details make it an excellent bargain.

Casa Calli
BOUTIQUE HOTEL $

(☎ 222-261-56-07; www.hotelcasacalli.com; Portal Guerrero 11; d/tw/tr M$650/850/1000; P☎😎) Right on the *zócalo*, this hotel contains 40 stylishly minimalist rooms, an attractive pool and an Italian restaurant-bar in the lobby. Rooms are discounted slightly in quiet periods (Sunday to Thursday) and there are weekend spa packages available.

★ Estrella de Belem
LUXURY HOTEL $$$

(☎ 222-261-19-25; www.estrelladebelem.com.mx; Calle 2 Oriente 410; r incl breakfast M$2005-2540; P❄☎😎) This beautiful hotel has just six rooms, each with gorgeous, thoughtful touches such as radiant-heat floors, noise-blocking windows, bathtubs and LCD TVs. The master suites are especially luxurious, with fireplaces and Jacuzzis. Common areas include a lovely, grassy courtyard and a small, rooftop swimming pool that has views over the town. No children under 12.

Hotel La Quinta Luna
LUXURY HOTEL $$$

(☎ 222-247-89-15; www.laquintaluna.com; Av 3 Sur 702; r incl breakfast M$1820, ste M$2230-3705; P☎) This rarefied hotel is popular with a wealthy weekender crowd. The seven stylish rooms occupy a thick-walled 17th-century mansion set around a charming garden and boast a gorgeous mix of colonial antiques, plush bedding, flat-screen TVs and contemporary art. Meetings with the featured *poblano* artists are happily arranged.

There's a great library and the excellent restaurant is open to nonguests who reserve.

🍴 Eating & Drinking

La Casa de Frida
MEXICAN $$

(☎ 222-178-23-03; www.facebook.com/lacasadefrida; Miguel Hidalgo 109; mains M$90-295, weekend buffet M$115; ☺ 9:30am-6pm Mon-Thu, to 10pm Fri & Sat, to 7pm Sun; ☎🍴🎵) This cavernous gem gives a nod to Frida Kahlo's home in Mexico City. Mexican handicrafts (plus the artist-owner's murals) are splashed throughout the courtyard, where Mexican musicians croon on one side and excellent flame-grilled steaks sizzle on the other. Service is excellent, there is a kids' playroom and the *pipián verde* (chicken in a spiced pepita sauce) is exceptionally complex.

A weekend buffet (9am to 1pm) is a popular way to have a taste of all of the classic Mexican dishes on offer.

Güero's
MEXICAN $$

(☎ 222 247-21-888; Av Hidalgo 101; mains M$55-130; ☺ 7:30am-11pm Mon-Sat, to 10pm Sun; 🎵) Decorated with antique photos of Cholula, this lively, family-friendly hangout has been a Cholula institution since 1955. Besides pizza, pasta and burgers, hearty Mexican choices include *pozole, cemitas* and quesadillas, all served with a delicious *salsa roja* (red sauce).

Container City
BAR

(www.containercity.com.mx; cnr Calle 12 Oriente & Av 2 Sur; ⊙11am-2am Tue-Sat) This collection of trendy bars, restaurants, clubs and shops buzzes at night. Set in revamped and stacked former shipping containers in eastern Cholula, it's the hangout of choice for the city's on-trend students and few fashionistas.

Bar Reforma
CANTINA

(☑222-247-01-49; cnr Avs 4 Sur & Norte; ⊙6pm-12:30am Mon-Sat, noon-6pm Sun) Attached to Hotel Reforma, Cholula's oldest drinking spot is a classic corner abode with swinging doors and plastic flowers, and specializes in iceless margaritas and freshly prepared sangrias. After 9pm it's popular with the university pre-clubbing crowd.

La Lunita
CANTINA

(☑222-247-00-11; cnr Avs Morelos & 6 Norte 419; ⊙8am-11pm) In the pyramid's shadow, this raucous, family-run bar has been in business since 1939. Painted in bright colors and decorated with an assortment of old advertising posters and knickknacks, La Lunita looks a lot like the movie version of a Mexican cantina. It's popular with locals who come for its broad-ranging menu (mains M$80 to M$180), live music, football on TV and plentiful drinks.

❶ Getting There & Away

The much-needed, comfortable **Puebla–Cholula Tourist Train** (Tren Turístico Puebla–Cholula; Av Morelos, cnr 6 Norte; one way adult/child under 5yr M$60/free; ⊙departs Cholula 7:45am, 12:20pm & 5:40pm Mon-Fri, 7:50am, 9:30am, 4:10pm & 5:50pm Sat & Sun) began operation in 2017. It connects central Puebla with the pyramid in Cholula on a 17.4km, 40-minute route. A taxi is similarly priced for two people at about M$150 and may be an appealing option instead of the early-morning train.

To travel to Puebla with locals on much windier routes, take a frequent **colectivo** (M$7.50, every 20 minutes) from the corner of Calle 5 Poniente and Av 3 Sur, or a larger **directo** (M$8, every 30 minutes) from the corner of Calles 2 Norte and 12 Oriente. Buses and *colectivos* stop two or three blocks north of the *zócalo*. The trip takes 20 to 40 minutes, depending on how direct they go.

From Mexico City's TAPO bus station, Estrella Roja runs four direct buses a day to Cholula for around M$130. Return buses to Mexico depart from the same stop.

Cacaxtla & Xochitécatl

The sister sites of Cacaxtla and Xochitécatl, about 20km southwest of Tlaxcala and 32km northwest of Puebla, are among Mexico's most intriguing.

Cacaxtla (ca-*casht*-la) is one of Mexico's most impressive ancient ruins with its many high-quality, vividly painted depictions of daily life. Rather than being relegated to a museum collection, these works – including frescoes of a nearly life-size jaguar and eagle warriors engaged in battle – are on display within the site itself. Discovered in 1975, the ruins are located atop a scrubby hill with wide views of the surrounding countryside.

The much older ruins at Xochitécatl (so-chi-*teh*-catl), 2km away and accessible from Cacaxtla on foot, include an exceptionally wide pyramid as well as a circular one. A German archaeologist led the first systematic exploration of the site in 1969, but it wasn't until 1994 that it was opened to the public.

◉ Sights

Cacaxtla
ARCHAEOLOGICAL SITE

(☑246-416-00-00; Circuito Perimetral s/n, San Miguel del Milagro; incl Xochitécatl & museums M$65; ⊙9am-5:30pm; ℗) The large murals at Cacxtla are intriguingly on display among the ruins rather than in a museum. They evoke a real sense of history where it happened and are worth seeing before they, unfortunately, continue to fade into history. The main attraction is a natural platform, 200m long and 25m high, called the **Gran Basamento** (Great Base), now sheltered under an expansive metal roof. Here stood Cacaxtla's main civic and religious buildings and the residences of its ruling priestly classes.

Starting at the parking lot opposite the site entrance, it's a 200m walk to the ticket office, museum and restaurant. From the ticket office it's another 600m downhill to the top of the entry stairs to the Gran Basamento in the **Plaza Norte**.

From here the path winds clockwise around the ruins until you reach the murals, many of which clearly show Maya influence among the symbols from the Mexican highlands. This combination of styles in a mural is unique to Cacaxtla.

Before reaching the first mural you'll come to a small patio, of which the main feature is an **altar** fronted by a small square pit, in which numerous human remains were discovered. Just beyond the altar you'll find the **Templo de Venus**, which contains two anthropomorphic sculptures – a man and a woman – in blue, wearing jaguar-skin skirts. The temple's name is attributed to the appearance of numerous half-stars around the female figure that are associated with Earth's sister planet, Venus.

On the opposite side of the path, away from the Plaza Norte, the **Templo Rojo** contains four murals, only one of which is visible. Its vivid imagery is dominated by a row of corn and cacao crops whose husks contain human heads.

Facing the north side of Plaza Norte is the long **Mural de la Batalla** (Battle Mural), dating from before AD 700. It shows two warrior groups, one wearing jaguar skins and the other bird feathers, engaged in ferocious battle. The Olmeca-Xicallanca (the jaguar warriors with round shields) are clearly repelling invading Huastecs (the bird warriors with jade ornaments and deformed skulls).

Beyond the Mural de la Batalla, turn left and climb the steps to see the second major **mural group**, behind a fence to your right. The two main murals (c AD 750) show a figure in a jaguar costume and a black-painted figure in a bird costume (believed to be the Olmeca-Xicallanca priest-governor) standing atop a plumed serpent.

Xochitécatl   ARCHAEOLOGICAL SITE
(☑246-416-00-00; Circuito Perimetral s/n, San Miguel del Milagro; incl Cacaxtla & museums M$65; ☺9am-5:30pm; P) About 2km from Cacaxtla, the much older ruins at Xochitécatl (so-chi-*teh*-catl) include a wide pyramid dedicated to a fertility god, and a circular pyramid. Because of its outline and the materials used, archaeologists believe the circular **Pirámide de la Espiral** was built between 1000 and 800 BC. Its form and hilltop location suggest it may have been used as an astronomical observation post, or as a temple to Ehécatl, the wind god. From here the path passes three other pyramids.

The **Basamento de los Volcanes**, which is all that remains of the first pyramid, is the base of the Pirámide de los Volcanes and it's made of materials from two periods. Cut square stones were placed over the original stones, visible in some areas, and then stuccoed over. In an interesting twist, the colored stones used to build Tlaxcala's municipal palace appear to have come from this site.

The **Pirámide de la Serpiente** gets its name from a large piece of carved stone with a snake head at one end. Its most impressive feature is the huge pot found at its center, carved from a single boulder, which was hauled from another region. Researchers surmise it was used to hold water.

Experts speculate that rituals honoring the fertility god were held at the **Pirámide de las Flores**, due to the discovery of several sculptures and the remains of 30 sacrificed infants. Near the pyramid's base – Latin America's fourth-widest – is a pool carved from a massive rock, where the infants were believed to have been washed before being killed.

ℹ **Getting There & Away**

Considering how close the archaeological zone is to Mexico City, Tlaxcala and Puebla – it's roughly smack in the middle of the three cities – getting to and from Cacaxtla and Xochitécatl on public transit is inconvenient and time-consuming.

Cacaxtla is 1.5km uphill from a back road between San Martín Texmelucan (near Hwy 150D) and Hwy 119, the secondary road between Tlaxcala and Puebla. To reach the site from Tlaxcala, catch a 'San Miguel del Milagro' *colectivo* (M$9, 40 minutes) from the corner of Escalona and Sánchez Piedras, which will drop you off about 500m from Cacaxtla.

From Puebla, Flecha Azul buses go direct from the CAPU terminal to the town of Nativitas, about 3km east of Cacaxtla. From there, catch a 'Zona Arqueológica' *colectivo* to the site.

Between Cacaxtla and Xochitécatl, taxis (M$60) are available on weekends, or walk the 2km (about 25 minutes).

Popocatépetl & Iztaccíhuatl

Mexico's second- and third-highest peaks, volcanoes Popocatépetl (po-po-ka-*teh*-pet-l; 5452m) and Iztaccíhuatl (iss-ta-*see*-wat-l; 5220m), form the eastern rim of the Valle de México, about 40km west of Puebla and 70km southeast of Mexico City. While the craterless Iztaccíhuatl is dormant, Popocatépetl (Náhuatl for 'Smoking Mountain' and also called Don Goyo and Popo) is very active and its summit has been off-limits since 1996.

The good news is that the fetching Iztaccíhuatl (White Woman), 20km north of Popo from summit to summit, remains open to climbers. From this vantage point there are panoramic views of the plateau, glaciers and across to Popo.

🏃 Activities

Hiking & Climbing

Izta's highest peak is **El Pecho** (5220m). All routes require a night on the mountain and there's a hut between the staging point at La Joya, the main southern trailhead, and Las Rodillas, one of the lesser peaks, that can be used during an ascent of El Pecho. It takes at least five hours to reach the hut from La Joya, then another six hours from the hut to El Pecho, and six hours back to the base.

Before making the ascent, climbers must register and pay the park entrance fee at the **Parque Nacional Iztaccíhuatl-Popocatépetl** (📞597-978-38-29; http://izta popo.conanp.gob.mx; Plaza de la Constitución 9B, Amecameca; per person per day M$30.50; ⊙7am-9pm) office, located on the southeast side of Amecameca's *zócalo*. The park website offers excellent maps and a handy downloadable English-language climbing guide.

About 24km up from Amecameca, there are lower-altitude trails through pine forests and grassy meadows near Paso de Cortés, the trailhead that leads to breathtaking glimpses of nearby peaks. La Joya is another 4km from Paso de Cortés.

Basic shelter with electricity is available at the Refugio de Altzomoni, roughly halfway between Paso de Cortés and La Joya. You must reserve in advance at the park office.

Climate & Conditions

It can be windy and well below freezing any time of year on Izta's upper slopes, and it's nearly always below freezing near the summit at night. Ice and snow are fixtures here; the average snow line is 4200m. The ideal months for ascents are November to February, when there is hard snowpack for crampons. The rainy season (April to October) brings with it the threat of whiteouts, thunderstorms and avalanches.

Guides

Iztaccíhuatl should be attempted *only* by experienced climbers. Because of hidden crevices on the ice-covered upper slopes, a guide is advisable. In addition to the guides following, the park office may have recommendations.

Livingston Monteverde (www.tierradentro. com; per person from US$290, with a minimum of 2 people) is a founding member of the Mexican Mountain Guide Association, with 25 years of climbing experience. He speaks fluent English, basic French and some Hebrew and Italian. Based in Tlaxcala.

Mario Andrade (📞cell 55-18262146; mountainup@hotmail.com) is an authorized, English-speaking guide, who has led many Izta climbs. His fee is US$350 for one person, and less per person for groups. The cost includes round-trip transportation from Mexico City, lodging, mountain meals and rope usage. Based in Mexico City.

🛏 Sleeping

Refugio de Altzomoni
LODGE **$**

(Altzomoni Lodge; dm per person M$30.50) Basic shelter is available at the Altzomoni Lodge, located by a microwave station roughly halfway between Paso de Cortés and La Joya. There are excellent views of Popo. Each of the three rooms has electricity and four bunk beds. Request the keys at Paso de Cortés before hiking up, and bring bedding, warm clothes and drinking water.

The bed cost is in addition to the national park fee for the same amount. Book in advance, especially for November to March, from the Parque Nacional Iztaccíhuatl-Popocatépetl office in Amecameca.

ℹ Getting There & Away

A guide is the most recommended option for climbing Iztaccíhuatl, with transportation included from Mexico City or Puebla. Otherwise, *colectivos* departing from Amecameca's *zócalo* for Paso de Cortés cost M$80. From the **national park office**, taxis will take groups to La Joya (40 minutes) for a negotiable M$300.

Tlaxcala

📞 246 / POP 90,000 / ELEV 2250M

The capital of Mexico's smallest state is unhurried and unself-conscious, with a compact colonial downtown defined by grand government buildings, imposing churches and a handsome central plaza. Despite its small stature, Tlaxcala is neither timid nor parochial. With a large student population, good restaurants and bars and a handful of excellent museums, the city has a surprisingly vibrant cultural life. Because there's no single attraction that puts Tlaxcala on tourist itineraries, it remains largely undiscovered, despite its location less than two hours' drive from Mexico City.

Two large plazas converge at the corner of Avenidas Independencia and Muñoz. The northern one, with colonial buildings, is the *zócalo* called Plaza de la Constitución. The southern square is Plaza Xicohténcatl.

History

In the last centuries before the Spanish conquest, numerous small warrior kingdoms (*señoríos*) arose in and around Tlaxcala. Some of them formed a loose federation that remained independent of the Aztec empire as it spread from the Valle de México in the 15th century. The most important kingdom seems to have been Tizatlán, now in ruins on the northeast edge of Tlaxcala.

When the Spanish arrived in 1519, the Tlaxcalans fought fiercely at first but ultimately became Cortés' staunchest allies against the Aztecs (with the exception of one chief, Xicoténcatl the Younger, who tried to rouse his people against the Spanish and is now a Mexican hero). In 1527 Tlaxcala became the seat of the first bishopric in Nueva España, but a plague in the 1540s devastated the population and the town has played only a supporting role ever since.

◉ Sights

★ Museo de Arte de Tlaxcala MUSEUM
(☑246-462-15-10; Plaza de la Constitución 21; adult/student/under 12yr M$30/15/free, Sun free; ☺9am-6pm Tue-Sun) This fantastic small contemporary-art museum houses an excellent cache of early Frida Kahlo paintings that were returned to the museum after several years on loan to other museums around the world. Both the museum's main building on the *zócalo* and the smaller **branch** (Avenida Guerrero 15; adult/student/under 12yr M$30/15/ free, Sun free; ☺9am-6pm Tue-Sun) hold interesting temporary exhibits and a good permanent collection of modern Mexican art.

★ Palacio de Gobierno PALACE
(Plaza de la Constitución; ☺10am-6pm Sat-Thu, 4-9pm Fri) FREE Inside the Palacio de Gobierno there are color-rich murals of Tlaxcala's history by Desiderio Hernández Xochitiotzin. His style is vividly realistic and detailed and reminiscent of modern graphic novels. The 500 sq meters of painting in this governmental palace was the last of the large-scale murals of the muralist movement in the country and a delight to fans of an illustration-style. English and Spanish speaking guides are available for M$200.

★ Santuario de la
Virgen de Ocotlán CHURCH
(Hidalgo 1, Ocotlán; ☺8am-7pm) FREE One of Mexico's most spectacular churches is an important pilgrimage site for those who believe the Virgin appeared here in 1541 – her image stands on the main altar in memory of the apparition. The classic Churrigueresque facade features white stucco 'wedding cake' decorations contrasting with plain red tiles. During the 18th century, indigenous artist Francisco Miguel spent 25 years decorating the altarpieces and the chapel beside the main altar.

The effigy is the central figure in Tlaxcala's most famous festival, the Bajada de la Virgen de Ocotlán. Visible from most of the town, the hilltop church is 1km northeast of the *zócalo*. Walk north from the *zócalo* on Avenida Juárez/Avenida Independencia for three blocks then turn right onto Zitlalpopocatl. Alternatively, 'Ocotlán' *colectivos* travel along this same route.

Zócalo PLAZA
(Plaza de la Constitución) It's easy to pass an afternoon reading or just people-watching in Tlaxcala's shady, spacious *zócalo*. The 16th-century **Palacio Municipal** (☺10am-6pm Sat-Thu, 4-9pm Fri), a former grain storehouse, and the Palacio de Gobierno occupy most of its north side. Off the *zócalo's* northwest corner is the orange-stucco and blue-tile **Parroquia de San José**. As elsewhere in the *centro histórico*, bilingual signs explain the significance of the church and its many fountains. The 16th-century building on the northwest side is the **Palacio de Justicia**.

Ex-Convento Franciscano
de la Asunción HISTORIC BUILDING
(Paseo San Francisco; ☺7am-3pm & 4-8pm) FREE Built between 1537 and 1540, this was one of Mexico's earliest monasteries and its church (the city's cathedral) has a Moorish-style wooden ceiling. It's up a path from the southeast corner of Plaza Xicohténcatl.

Just below the monastery, beside the 19th-century Plaza de Toros (bullring), is a **capilla abierta** (☺24hr) with three unique Moorish-style arches. One of the entrances is locked, but you can access the *capilla* from other entry points.

Museo Regional de Tlaxcala (☑246-462-0262; ☺10am-6pm) FREE, housed within the monastery, displays religious paintings and sculptures and some pre-Hispanic artifacts from nearby archaeological sites.

Museo Vivo de Artes y
Tradiciones Populares MUSEUM
(☑246-462-23-37; Blvd Sánchez 1; M$15; ☺10am-6pm Tue-Sun) This small popular arts museum has displays on Tlaxcalan village life, agave, weaving and *pulque*-making, sometimes with

Tlaxcala

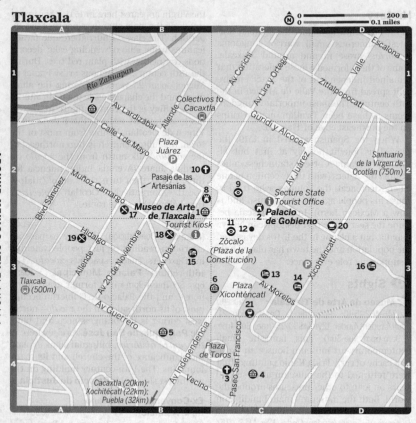

Tlaxcala

demonstrations. Artisans serve as guides to the more than 3000 artifacts on display. The cafe and handicrafts next door at the affiliated

Casa de Artesanías (☑246-462-23-37; http://artesanias.tlaxcala.gob.mx; Blvd Sánchez 1B; M$20, Tue free; ⊙9am-6pm) are also worth a look.

Museo de la Memoria
MUSEUM

(📞246-466-07-92; Av Independencia 3; adult/student M$20/10, Sun free; ⏰10am-5pm) This modern history museum looks at folklore through a multimedia lens and has well-presented exhibits on indigenous government, agriculture and contemporary festivals. Explanations are in Spanish only.

🍴 Courses

Estela Silva's Mexican Home Cooking School
COOKING

(📞246-468-09-78; www.mexicanhomecooking.com) Learn to cook *poblano* cuisine with Señora Estela Silva and her sous-chef husband, Jon Jarvis, in the couple's Talavera-tiled kitchen in Tlacochcalco, 10km south of Tlaxcala. The English-Spanish bilingual course includes all meals plus lodging in private rooms with fireplaces (transportation to/from the school can be arranged). An all-inclusive, six-night/five-day course is US$1798, but shorter stays can be arranged.

🧭 Tours

Tranvía El Tlaxcalteca
BUS

(📞246-458-53-24; Plaza de la Constitución, Portal Hidalgo 6; adult/child Mon-Fri M$100/90, Sat & Sun M$75/65; ⏰departs hourly noon-6pm) This motorized streetcar visits 33 downtown sights with a Spanish-speaking guide on board in a 45-minute tour on Saturday and Sunday. During the week the tour extends to two hours to include visiting and walking around the Basílica de Ocotlán. No reservations necessary. Departs from the east side on the *zócalo*.

🎊 Festivals & Events

Bajada de la Virgen de Ocotlán
RELIGIOUS

(⏰May) On the third Monday in May, the figure of the Virgen de Ocotlán is carried from its hilltop perch at Santuario de La Virgen de Ocotlán to churches, attracting equal numbers of onlookers and believers. Throughout the month, processions along flower-decorated streets commemorating the miracle attract pilgrims from around the country.

Gran Feria de Tlaxcala
CULTURAL

(⏰Oct-Nov) Also known as Tlaxcala's Fiesta de Todos los Santos, people come from around the state for three weeks between late October and mid-November, when *charrería* (horsemanship) and other rodeo-inspired pageantry take center stage. The festival includes Día de Muertos activities.

🛏️ Sleeping

Hostería de Xicohténcatl
GUESTHOUSE $

(📞246-466-33-22; Portal Hidalgo 10; s/d/tr M$460/510/600, ste M$720-1300; 🅿🛜) Half of the 16 rooms at this straightforward budget *hostería* are large, multiroom suites with kitchens, making it a bargain for families, groups or those in town for an extended stay. The *hostería* is clean, if a bit sterile, and the location – on Plaza Xicohténcatl – is excellent.

⭐Posada La Casona de Cortés
BOUTIQUE HOTEL $$

(📞246-462-20-42; http://lacasonadecortes.com.mx; Av Lardizábal 6; d/tw/tr from M$795/850/1385; 🅿🛜) Set around a lush courtyard with fruit trees and a fountain, this affordable boutique hotel seems almost too good to be true. The rooms, which have firm beds, tiled floors and high-pressure showers, are decorated with Mexican *artesanías* (handicrafts). The bar has a working 1950s jukebox and a roof deck with views of church steeples and volcanic peaks.

Hotel Minatzín
BOUTIQUE HOTEL $$

(📞246-462-04-40; Xicohténcatl 6; s/d/ste from M$650/750/950; 🅿❄🛜) This converted colonial house has stone tiling, is light, bright and airy and makes a fine match with Tlaxcala's nearby *zócalo*. All five spacious rooms have 3D TVs and feel more indulgent, and the beds much plusher, than the price suggests. The suite sleeps four.

⭐Hotel Posada San Francisco
LUXURY HOTEL $$$

(📞246-144-55-55; www.posadasanfranciscotlaxcala.mx; Plaza de la Constitución 17; d/ste incl breakfast M$1250/2460; 🅿❄🛜🅿) The bullfighter-themed bar at this hotel is the kind of place in which you'd expect to find a famous author swilling fine tequila – check out the stained-glass ceiling in the lobby, the pool and the airy patio restaurant.

🍴 Eating & Drinking

For a small city, Tlaxcala has an impressive number – and diversity – of good restaurants. The east side of the *zócalo* is overrun by underwhelming sidewalk cafes, but there are better options on the south side and on nearby Plaza Xicohténcatl. Tlaxcala's Mercado Emilio Sánchez Piedras is one of the most pleasant markets around. To get there from Parroquia de San José, walk along Avenida Lira y Ortega until the corner with Escalona.

La Granada
SPANISH

(☑ 246-462-77-72; Ignacio Allende 41; mains M$80-140; ⊙ 8am-8pm; ❋ 🐾) Seafood paella, potato tortilla and tapas are some of the favorites at this tidy little bistro-style restaurant. Drinks have a Mexican twist alongside sangria.

Jaque's
MEXICAN **$**

(☑ 246-466-09-53; Muñoz Camargo 2; menú del día M$80, mains M$45-85; ⊙ 8am-6:30pm; 🐾) Jaque's is just a few steps from the *zócalo*, but the Mexican fare is much better here than elsewhere in the area. Plus you still have the white tablecloths and bay windows peering down on the street. The *pechuga a la diabla* (chicken schnitzel stuffed with panela cheese in a spicy tomato sauce) is as devilishly good as the name suggests.

Desayunos Lupita
MEXICAN **$**

(☑ 246-462-64-53; Muñoz Camargo 14; set breakfasts M$50; ⊙ 8:30am-4pm Mon-Fri, to 1:30pm Sat & Sun) This ultra-popular breakfast and lunch spot serves quintessential *tlaxcalteco* food, like *huaraches* (an oblong, fried corn base with a variety of toppings), *tamales, atoles* (sweet, corn-based hot drinks) and quesadillas filled with everything from *huitlacoche* (corn mushrooms) to squash flower. It's glorified street food, perfect for those with a taste for central Mexican specialties who squeamish about eating from carts and stalls. Set breakfasts include your choice of main dish, fresh-squeezed juice, fruit salad and *café de olla*.

11:11 Cafe Boutique
CAFE

(☑ 246-144-01-81; www.facebook.com/11.11cafe; Xicohténcatl 19; ⊙ 10:30am-10pm Mon-Sat; 🐾) You would hardly know that this stylish cafe is down this quiet street, which makes it a popular spot for young couples and the local cool kids to hide away, sipping on frappés and good coffee.

Pulquería Tía Yola
PULQUERÍA

(☑ 246-462-73-09; Plaza Xicohténcatl 7; ⊙ 11am-9pm) Sip one of a dozen-or-so flavors of house-made *pulque* in a stone courtyard decorated with Día de Muertos figurines and mosaics of Aztec gods. The sidewalk tables along the plaza are a prime location for weekend people-watching. There is good Mexican food too.

ℹ Information

Several banks on Avenida Juárez, near the tourist office, exchange dollars and have ATMs. There is also an ATM inside the bus terminal.

Farmacia Cristo Rey (Av Lardizábal 15; ⊙ 24hr) Around-the-clock pharmacy.

Hospital General (☑ 246-462-35-55; Corregidora s/n; ⊙ 24hr) Emergency services.

Secture State Tourist Office (☑ 246-465-09-60; cnr Avs Juárez & Lardizábal; ⊙ 8am-5pm Mon-Fri) The English-speaking staff are eager to sing Tlaxcala's praises and equip travelers with colorful bird's-eye-view maps and a handful of brochures. These are also found at the handy **tourist kiosk** (Plaza de la Constitución; ⊙ 10am-5pm) on the west side of the *zócalo*.

ℹ Getting There & Away

Tlaxcala's **bus terminal** (cnr Castelar & Calle 1 Bis) sits on a hill 1km west of the central plaza. ATAH (☑ 246-466-00-87) runs (barely) 1st-class buses to Mexico City's TAPO terminal (M$150, two hours, every 30 minutes). Frequent 2nd-class Verde buses go to Puebla (M$29).

For Cacaxtla, take a colectivo (M$9, 40 minutes) marked 'San Miguel del Milagro' from the corner of Escalona and Sánchez Piedras.

ℹ Getting Around

Most *colectivos* (M$6.50) passing the bus terminal head into town, although it takes just 10 minutes to walk. Exit the terminal, turn right down the hill until you hit Avenida Guerrero then turn right past the towering steps of Escalinata de Héroes. To reach the terminal from the center, catch a blue-and-white *colectivo* on the east side of Blvd Sánchez. Taxis between the station and downtown cost M$35.

Huamantla

☑ 247 / POP 52,000 / ELEV 2500M

Colorful Huamantla has invested greatly in its downtown area, gussying up its colonial city center and adding pizazz to its charming *zócalo* with giant letters (an international trend) spelling 'Huamantla.' The most alluring recent addition is the monthly *Sábados Mágicos* (Magic Saturdays), where a small street is carpeted in colored sawdust and bright blooms. It's a taster of the flower parades held during Huamantla's larger annual *feria* in August.

With La Malinche looming over town, this is a pleasant base camp for exploring the surrounding countryside, once you get past its sprawling suburbs. Most escapees from Puebla will just stay in town and enjoy the eye-popping paint job atop Huamantla's church, Parroquia de San Luis Obispo.

CANTONA

Given its isolation from any town of significance, the vast and incredibly well-preserved Mesoamerican city of **Cantona** (M$46; ⊗9am-6pm) is virtually unknown to travelers. With 24 ball courts discovered, this is now believed to have been the biggest single urban center in Mesoamerica, stretching over 12 sq km in an ethereal lava-bed landscape dotted with cacti and yucca and enjoying incredible views of Pico de Orizaba to the south.

The site was inhabited from AD 600 to 1000 and is of interest for two main reasons. Unlike most other Mesoamerican cities, no mortar was used to build it, meaning all the stones are simply held in place by their weight. It's also unique in its design sophistication – all parts of the city are linked by an extensive network of raised roads connecting some 3000 residences. There are several small pyramids and an elaborate acropolis at the city's center. With good information panels in English and an access road, Cantona is now being promoted as a tourist attraction. The **Museo de Sitio de Cantona** (☑276-596-53-07; adult/student M$55/free; ⊗9am-6pm Wed-Sun) is worth a visit, especially if you can read Spanish.

From Oriental, which is the nearest decent-sized town, Grupo Salazar covered pick-up-truck *colectivos* leave every 20 minutes from the corner of Carretera Federal Puebla-Teziutlan and 8 Poniente for Cantona (M$35, 45 minutes). The trucks have 'Tepeyahual-co' on their windshield. Tell the driver your destination when you board.

Otherwise, taxis to the site are M$150 or more for a round trip. If you have your own transportation, visiting Cantona makes for a good side trip en route to Cuetzalan.

⊙ Sights

★ Museo Nacional del Títere   MUSEUM
(☑247-472-10-33; Parque Juárez 15; adult/student & senior/child M$20/10/5, Sun free; ⊗10am-5pm Tue-Sat, to 3pm Sun; ⊕) The national puppet museum displays dolls and marionettes from all around the world in a fantastic renovated building on the *zócalo*. It's a fun stop for the young and young at heart.

⚝ Festivals & Events

★ Feria Huamantla   FERIA
(⊗Aug) For two weeks in August, this festival features parades of cyclists, candlelight, and locals blanketing the town's streets with carpets of flowers and colored sawdust, plus a night known as La Noche Que Nadie Duerme ('The Night That Nobody Sleeps'). There's a running of the bulls, similar to that in Pamplona – but more dangerous since the uncastrated males charge from two directions.

★ Sábados Mágicos   ART
(www.facebook.com/turismoenhuamantla; Pasaje Margarita Maza de Juárez; ⊗11am-4pm 3rd Sat of the month) If you can't make it to the annual Feria Huamantla, you can get a taster every 'Magic Saturday' on the third Saturday of every month when an alleyway next to the Presidencia Municipio gets blanketed in colored *aserrín* (sawdust) and flowers. Later in the afternoon, dancers perform and firecrackers are let off.

Weather permitting, the colorful *tapete* (carpet) is left in place for viewing the following day. Times can vary so check ahead to make sure the *tapete* will go ahead.

🛌 Sleeping & Eating

Hotel Centenario   HOTEL $
(☑247-472-05-87; Juárez Norte 209; r M$380-550, ste M$700; ℙ@🛜) Just a short walk from the *zócalo*, Hotel Centenario has 33 salmon-pink, clean and spacious rooms with renovated bathrooms and wi-fi access. The staff are helpful and there's a good coffee shop in the lobby.

★ Hacienda Soltepec   HISTORIC HOTEL $$$
(☑247-472-14-66; www.haciendasoltepec.com; Carretera Huamantla-Puebla Km 3; d/tw/ste from M$1605/1780/2850; ℙ🛜🏊) A 4.5km drive south of town, this gorgeous renovated hacienda is a former movie set (María Félix stayed here for months while filming one of her classics) with views of Malinche, horse stables, tennis courts and a fantastic in-house restaurant. Bright rooms have high ceilings and polished floorboards. Its own *pulque* brewery is open for visits on Saturday and Sunday.

La Casa de los Magueyes   MEXICAN $$
(☑247-472-28-63; Reforma Sur 202; mains M$90-170; ⊗9am-10pm Mon-Sat, to 6pm Sun) This wonderful home-style restaurant just southeast of the *zócalo* serves regional dishes

made with seasonal ingredients such as *maguey* buds, wild mushrooms or even *escamoles* (agave ant eggs).

① Getting There & Away

Surianos (www.autobusesoro.com.mx) has services to/from Puebla CAPU (M$39, two hours) every 15 to 30 minutes. ATAH runs buses from Tlaxcala's main station (M$38) every seven minutes. The bus doesn't always stop at a station, so be sure to tell the driver you're going to Huamantla *centro* to avoid missing the town entirely. There are no direct services from Cuetzalan; you must first head to Puebla.

Supra operates a direct service between Mexico City's TAPO station (M$175, three hours, hourly) and Huamantla.

Cuetzalan

♪ 233 / POP 6000 / ELEV 980M

The gorgeous drive to Cuetzalan is one of the most exhilarating trips in the region and an adventure in itself. Beyond the Zaragoza turnoff, the road becomes dramatic, snaking up hills and around hairpin bends and offering breathtaking views. At the end of it all is the remote, humid town of Cuetzalan (Place of the Quetzals). A striking village built on a precipitous slope, the town is famed for its vibrant festivals, weekend *voladores* perfomances, and Sunday *tianguis* (street market) that attracts scores of indigenous people in traditional dress. On the clearest days you can see all the way from the hilltops to the Gulf coast, 70km away, as the quetzal flies.

◎ Sights

Three structures rise above Cuetzalan's skyline: the plaza's freestanding clock tower, the Gothic spire of the Parroquia de San Francisco and, to the west, the tower of the French Gothic Santuario de Guadalupe, with its highly unusual decorative rows of *los jarritos* (clay vases).

Casa de la Cultura
Museum MUSEUM

(Alvarado 18; ⊙ 9am-4pm) FREE This small museum alongside the tourist office exhibits traditional daily dress of the region, arts and crafts, and some archaeological pieces from nearby Yohualichán. Fans of the *voladores* will find a rundown of the history of this and other dances and ceremonial performances.

Cascada Las Brisas
& Cascada del Salto WATERFALL

About 5km southeast of town, there's a pair of lovely waterfalls. The natural swimming pools beneath the falls are enticing – bring your bathing kit. Rickshaw mototaxis will deposit you at the trailhead and await your return. From here it's an easy 15-minute walk to the waterfalls.

✪ Festivals & Events

Feria del Café y del Huipil CULTURAL

(Plaza Celestino Gasca s/n; ⊙ Oct) For several lively days around October 4, Cuetzalan celebrates both its patron saint, St Francis of Assisi, and the start of the coffee harvest with the Festival of Coffee and Huipiles. It features hearty drinking, traditional quetzal dancing and airborne *voladores* (literally 'fliers'), the Totonac ritual in which men, suspended by their ankles, whirl around a tall pole.

☰ Sleeping

Posada Jaqueline GUESTHOUSE $

(♪ 233-331-03-54; Calle 2 de Abril 2; s/d M$200/250; ☎) Jaqueline's 20 basic but clean-enough rooms, overlooking the uphill side of the *zócalo*, are one of Cuetzalan's best-value options with cable TV and 24-hour hot water. Some upstairs rooms share a balcony and have views over the town.

Posada Quinto Palermo HOTEL $$

(♪ 233-331-04-52; Calle 2 de Abril 2; r M$750; ☎) This basic hotel has the best location in town and a roof deck overlooking the palm trees and steeples of Cuetzalan's gorgeous *zócalo*. The 15 rooms have almost comically bad color schemes and tacky art. Ask for a room facing the front of the hotel, which has windows onto the plaza. Rates are greatly reduced in low season. Parking (M$30) at a nearby lot can be arranged at check-in.

Tosepan Kali LODGE $$

(♪ 233-331-09-25; www.tosepankali.com; Km 1.5 de la Carretera Cuetzalan, San Miguel Tzinacapan; dm/r/cabins per person incl breakfast M$250/350/450; P☎❀) ✿ High on a hill between Cuetzalan and the nearby town of San Miguel Tzinacapan to the north, Tosepan Kali resembles a tree house nestled in dense foliage. With clean rooms constructed largely of bamboo and stone and a large pool with valley views, this beautiful, if rundown, ecohotel – its name means 'our house' in Náhuatl – is the work of a local indigenous cooperative who collect rainwater.

Hotel Posada Cuetzalan HOTEL $$
(☑ 233-331-01-54; www.posadacuetzalan.com;
Zaragoza 12; s/d/tr/q M$655/913/1085/1220;
[P][⛱][❄]) This handsome hotel, 100m uphill
from the *zócalo* and a short walk from the
bus station, has three large courtyards full of
chirping birds, a swimming pool, a good res-
taurant featuring local fruit liqueurs and 36
simple rooms with tropical colors, tiled floors,
lots of lightly stained wood and cable TV.
There's wi-fi in the front rooms near the office.

Hotel La Casa de la Piedra BOUTIQUE HOTEL $$
(☑ 233-331-00-30; www.lacasadepiedra.com; Car-
los García 11; d/tw/ste from M$960/1580/1680;
[P][⛱][❄]) All 16 rooms in this renovated-yet-
rustic former coffee-processing warehouse
have picture windows and refinished wooden
floors. Upstairs, the two-level suites accommodate up to four people and offer views of
the valley. Downstairs rooms have tiled bathrooms, stone walls and one or two beds.

✗ Eating

Regional specialties, sold at many roadside
stands, include fruit wines and smoked
meats. Look for *xoco atol* (fermented rice
drink), *yolixpan* (coffee liquer) and *dulce de
tejocote* (yellow hawthorn fruit in anise syrup). Try the regional *café de la sierra* while
you can as climate change has decimated
crops in recent decades.

Sazón Jarocho SEAFOOD $
(☑ 233-119-18-83; Zaragoza 13; comida corrida
M$50, mains M$50-120; ⊙ 9am-10pm Tue-Sun)
There's something about Cuetzalan's steamy,
tropical ambience that demands *mariscos*.
Thankfully, this straightforward seafood
restaurant serves delicious seafood dishes,
ranging from Veracruz-style fish to *caracoles* (sea snail), crab, octopus and shrimp,
prepared however you like it. The house specialty, a coconut or pineapple stuffed with
seafood, is excellent.

Restaurante Yoloxóchitl MEXICAN $
(☑ 233-331-03-35; Calle 2 de Abril No 1; mains
M$50-75; ⛱) Beautifully decorated with
plants, antiques and ancient jukeboxes,
Yoloxóchitl has views over the cathedral
and a selection of salads, *antojitos* (tortilla-based snacks) and meat dishes, as well as
wild mushrooms pickled in chipotle chili.

La Terraza SEAFOOD $$
(☑ 233-331-04-16; Hidalgo 33; breakfasts M$58,
mains M$58-162; ⊙ 8:30am-9pm) This family-
run restaurant west of the *zócalo*, decorated

YOHUALICHÁN RUINS

This ceremonial pre-Hispanic **site**
(M$40; ⊙ 9am-5pm) inhabited by Los
Totonacas has niche 'pyramids' similar
to El Tajín's (Veracruz) that are in varying
states of ruin. The site is impressive and
well worth a visit, not least for the great
views from this side of the valley. It lies
about 8km northeast of Cuetzalan, the
last 2km along a steep cobblestone
road. To get here, ask at the tourist office
(p176) for a *camión* (truck) passing by
the pyramids. The entrance is adjacent
to Yohualichán's church and town plaza.

with photos of the town's annual festivities,
is extremely popular with locals for its large
selection (and servings) of breakfasts, *maris-
cos* (seafood), quesadillas, *platillos de la
región* and crawfish (in season).

☆ Entertainment

★ Los Voladores PERFORMING ARTS
(Parroquía de San Francisco de Asís, Plaza Celestino
Gasca s/n; by donation; ⊙ from 4pm Sat, from noon
Sun) In the *danza de los voladores* (dance of
the 'flyers'), airborne performers whirl around
a 30m pole, suspended by their ankles while
playing flutes. On weekends *voladores* twirl
outside the church at the *zócalo*, several times
a day for tourists (and tips). It's a remarkable,
not-to-be-missed performance. This Mesoa-
merican ritual was recognized as an Intangi-
ble Cultural Heritage by Unesco in 2009.

Four dancers represent the cardinal points
and a fifth represents the sun. They spin 13
times, a number derived from 52 (the number
of years in a pre-Hispanic century) divided by
four ropes, to represent the dawn of a new
sun. The ritual is estimated to have originat-
ed some time in the preclassic period (1000
BC to AD 250) in Veracruz. Performances are
canceled during heavy rain or wind.

🔒 Shopping

Mercado de Artesanías
Matachiuj ARTS & CRAFTS
(Hidalgo 917; ⊙ 9am-7pm Wed-Mon) This fair-
trade market a few blocks west of the *zócalo*
has a range of quality weavings and other
crafts that come with the benefit of meeting
the producer, as many wares are made on-
site by local artisans. Food stalls and tourist
guides can also be found here.

ℹ Information

The **tourist office** (Casa de la Cultura de Cuetzalan; ☎ 233-331-05-27; Av Miguel Alvarado 18; ⊙ 9am-5pm Mon-Fri, to 9pm Sat & Sun) inside the Casa de la Cultura, two blocks west of the *zócalo*, has much-needed town maps and accommodations information, but no English is spoken. Next door there's a Santander ATM.

ℹ Getting There & Away

Vía buses run between Puebla and Cuetzalan (M$210, 3½ hours, hourly) from Puebla 6:45am to 8pm, returning 5am to 6pm. It pays to check road conditions and buy your return bus tickets in advance during the rainy season. AU runs at least six buses a day, from 9am to 10pm, from Mexico City's TAPO bus station (M$360, six hours), returning from Cuetzalan between 4:30am and 2:30pm. Additional services are offered by ADO Friday to Sunday.

ℹ Getting Around

On the town's steep streets, three-wheeled mototaxis (from M$25 or about M$100 an hour) offer rides with a thrill. Covered pickup trucks provide transportation to nearby *pueblitos* (M$8).

SOUTH OF MEXICO CITY

A host of great destinations sits south of the Mexican capital, including mystical Tepoztlán, breathtaking silver-mining tourist mecca Taxco and the superb complex of caves at Grutas de Cacahuamilpa. Cuernavaca, 'the city of eternal spring,' is a longtime popular escape from Mexico City and a home-away-from-home for many North Americans and *chilangos* (Mexico City inhabitants) who own second houses here.

The state of Morelos, which encompasses Cuernavaca and Tepoztlán, is one of Mexico's smallest and most densely populated. Unfortunately, it suffered major damage in the earthquake of 19 September 2017 and many sights were forced to close (at least temporarily) for restoration work. Valleys at different elevations have a variety of microclimates, and many fruits, grains and vegetables have been cultivated here since pre-Hispanic times. You can visit palaces and haciendas in the region, along with 16th-century churches and monasteries. Those interested in the peasant revolutionary leader Emiliano Zapata should head to Cuautla, the first city that the Morelos hero conquered, and 6km further south to Anenecuilco, where he was born.

Tepoztlán

⏹ 739 / POP 14,000 / ELEV 1700M

A weekend trip from the capital to Tepoztlán rarely disappoints. This beautifully situated small town with a well-preserved historic center surrounded by soaring cliffs is just 80km south of Mexico City. As the birthplace of Quetzalcóatl, the omnipotent serpent god of the Aztecs over 1200 years ago (according to Mesoamerican legend), Tepoztlán is a major Náhuatl center and a mecca for New Agers who believe the area has a creative energy.

This *pueblo mágico* boasts a great crafts market and a host of charming restaurants and hotels. It also retains indigenous traditions, with some elders still speaking Náhuatl and younger generations learning it in school, making it a rarity among the towns ringing the Mexican capital.

◉ Sights

Everything in Tepoztlán is easily accessible on foot, except the impressive cliff-top Pirámide de Tepozteco, a 2.5km strenuous hike away.

★ Pirámide de Tepozteco
ARCHAEOLOGICAL SITE

(M$47, Sun free; ⊙ 9am-5pm) Tepoztlán's main sight is this 10m-high pyramid perched atop a sheer cliff at the end of a very steep paved path that begins at the end of Avenida Tepozteco. Built in honor of Tepoztécatl, the Aztec god of harvest, fertility and *pulque,* the pyramid is more impressive for its location than actual size. At the top, depending on haze levels, the serenity and the panorama of the valley make the hike worthwhile.

Spotting the plentiful coati (raccoon-like animal) here is also a bonus.

Tepotzteco is some 400m above the town. Be warned that the path is tough, so head off early to beat the heat and wear decent shoes. The 2.5km walk is not recommended to anyone not physically fit. A store at the peak sells refreshments, but you should bring water with you anyway. Video-camera use is M$47. The hike itself is free, but to get close to the pyramid (and the view) you must pay the admission fee.

Ex-Convento Domínico de la Natividad
CHRISTIAN SITE

This monastery, situated east of the *zócalo,* and the attached church were built by Dominican priests between 1560 and 1588. The plateresque church facade has Dominican

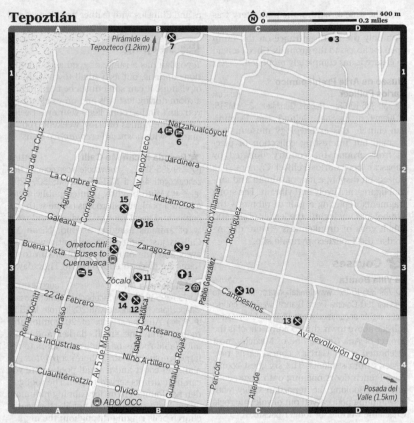

Tepoztlán

Tepoztlán

⊙ Sights
1 Ex-Convento Domínico de la
  Natividad B3
2 Museo de Arte Prehispánico Carlos
  Pellicer.......................................B3

❸ Activities, Courses & Tours
3 La Villa Bonita............................. D1

⊜ Sleeping
4 Hotel Posada Ali.........................B2
5 Posada del Tepozteco.................A3
6 Posada Nican Mo Calli.................B2

❽ Eating
7 Axitla..B1
8 El Brujo...B3
9 El Ciruelo......................................B3
10 El Mango Biergarten-Restaurante C3
11 El Tlecuil......................................B3
12 La Luna Mextli..............................B3
  La Sibarita.............................(see 5)
13 La Sombra del Sabino..................C4
14 Los Buenos Tiempos....................B3
15 Los Colorines...............................B2

❷ Drinking & Nightlife
16 La Terraza Yecapixtla..................B3

seals interspersed with indigenous symbols, floral designs and various figures, including the sun, moon and stars, animals, angels and the Virgin Mary. Upstairs, various cells house a bookstore, galleries and a regional history museum.

The monastery's arched entryway is adorned with an elaborate seed mural of pre-Hispanic history and symbolism. Every year during the first week of September, local artists sow a new mural from 60 varieties of seeds.

At the time of writing the monastery was closed for earthquake-damage assessment with only the south entrance on the ramp open for access to the grounds. Check ahead to ensure it has completely reopened.

Museo de Arte Prehispánico
Carlos Pellicer   MUSEUM
(☑739-395-10-98; Pablo González 2; M$15; ☺10am-6pm Tue-Sun) Behind the Dominican church, this archaeology museum has a small but interesting collection of pieces from around the country, donated by Tabascan poet Carlos Pellicer Cámara. The objects on display, a mix of human and animal figures, are lively and vibrant. The stone fragments depicting a pair of rabbits – the symbol for Ometochtli, the leader of the 400 rabbit gods of drunkenness – were discovered at the Tepozteco pyramid site.

🕏 Courses

La Villa Bonita   COOKING
(☑739-395-15-15; www.lavillabonita.com; Aniceto Villamar 150, Colonia Tierra Blanca; weekend course incl 2 nights accommodations US$450-925) On a hillside above town, this cooking school is the project of Ana García, one of Mexico's most celebrated chefs. García's course earns rave reviews from students. The six guest rooms have French doors opening onto a gorgeous patio overlooking the Tepoztlán valley, with a swimming pool carved out of volcanic rock. Check the website for longer packages.

🎊 Festivals & Events

Tepoztlán is a festive place, with many Christian feasts superimposed on pagan celebrations. With eight *barrios* (neighborhoods) and an equal number of patron saints, there always seems to be some excuse for fireworks.

Fiesta del Templo   RELIGIOUS
(☺Sep 7) On September 7 an all-night celebration goes off on Tepozteco hill near the pyramid, with copious consumption of *pulque* in honor of Tepoztécatl. The following day is the Fiesta del Templo, a Catholic celebration featuring theater performances in Náhuatl.

The holiday was first intended to coincide with – and perhaps supplant – the pagan festival, but the *pulque* drinkers get a jump on it by starting the night before.

Carnaval   DANCE
During the five days preceding Ash Wednesday (46 days before Easter Sunday), Carnaval features the colorful dances of the Huehuenches and Chinelos with feather headdresses and beautifully embroidered costumes.

🛏 Sleeping

Tepoztlán has a range of good accommodations options, but as a small town with lots of visitors, it can sometimes be hard to find a room during festivals and on weekends. If you can't find a room, keep your eyes peeled for private homes offering weekend rooms, marked with *hospedaje económico* signs.

★ Posada Nican Mo Calli   HOTEL $$
(☑739-395-31-52; www.hotelnican.com; Netzahualcóyotl 4A; d M$1400, ste M$1500-2200; ⓅⓈⓍ) With brightly painted public areas, a heated pool, stylish rooms (some with balconies and great mountain views) and plenty of animals hanging around, Nican Mo Calli is just right for a romantic weekend away and one of the best options in town. Rates are discounted Sunday to Thursday.

Hotel Posada Ali   GUESTHOUSE $$
(☑739-395-19-71; www.facebook.com/hotelposadalitepoztlan; Netzahualcóyotl 2C; d from M$1150; ⓅⓈⓍ) Ali has a mix of 20 comfortable rooms, from the small, darker and more affordable rooms on the lower floors to the larger rooms upstairs. There's a *frontón* (jai alai) ball court and a small pool where you can have drinks served to you. The roof garden has lounge chairs for calming mountain views. Light sleepers may not like the nearby church bells ringing throughout the night.

Posada del Valle   RESORT $$
(☑739-395-05-21; www.posadadelvalle.com.mx; Camino a Mextitla 5; r from M$1650, spa packages M$4220-5220; ⓅⓍ) East of town, this hotel-spa has quiet, romantic rooms and a good Argentine restaurant. Spa packages include accommodations for one or two nights, breakfast, massages and a visit to the temascal (steam bath). It's 2km down Ave Revolución 1910 – just follow the signs for the final 100m to the hotel. Children under 16 not allowed.

★ Posada del Tepozteco   LUXURY HOTEL $$$
(☑739-395-00-10; www.posadadeltepozteco.com; Paraíso 3; ste M$3295-3660; ⓅⓐⓈⓍ) This refined hotel was built as a hillside mansion in the 1930s. The 20 rooms are airy and individually decorated, with most boasting magnificent views over town, and share a wonderful garden and pool. The guest book contains famous names, including Angelina Jolie, who stayed in Room 5 when she dropped by. Rates are discounted up to 40% during the week.

Eating

This small town is hopping on weekends, when cafes and bars fill up with enthusiastic visitors. Unfortunately for those visiting midweek, many of the best spots are only open Friday to Sunday.

El Tlecuil
VEGAN $

(www.facebook.com/eltlecuiltepoztlan; Mercado Municipal de Tepotzlán s/n; snacks M$40; ⊙9am-6pm; ✔) The chaotic market hides a stall with vegan pre-Hispanic food. Mainly this means croquette taste bombs wrapped up as tacos or with rice and *mole* sauce. Flavor highlights include *siete semillas* (mixed sunflower, pepita and other seeds) and an inventive apple hash.

El Brujo
BAKERY $

(Av 5 de Mayo; breakfasts M$60-95; ⊙9am-9pm; ✔) This wonderful bakery-restaurant on the town's main drag is the best bet for a full breakfast, with excellent omelettes and Mexican standards such as *chilaquiles* (strips of fried corn tortillas bathed in sauce). It also has great coffee and fantastic desserts. Just looking at the cake display is likely to start you salivating.

Los Buenos Tiempos
BAKERY $

(✆739-395-05-19; Av Revolución 1910 No 14B; pastries M$8-35; ⊙8:30am-10:30pm; 🕾✔) Head here for the best pastries around – the smell drifting over the *zócalo* alone will probably bring you in on autopilot. There's also good coffee and a lively social scene, and it's a great place to buy a pastry breakfast to take up to the pyramid with you.

Los Colorines
MEXICAN $$

(✆739-395-08-90; www.facebook.com/loscolorines oficial; Av Tepozteco 13; mains M$75-165; ⊙9am-9pm; ✔🖶) Inside the pink exterior of this buzzing restaurant, the hearty traditional Mexican fare bubbles away in *cazuelas* (clay pots) – try the regional *chiles rellenos* or *huauzontle* (broccoli-like flower buds). More than the food, eating here is a joy for the piñatas, terrace views, spaciousness and the sense of being at a fiesta at grandma's colorful ranch. Cash only.

El Mango Biergarten-Restaurante
GERMAN $$

(✆739-395-22-53; www.elmangotepoztlan.com; Campesinos 7; mains M$70-165; ⊙2-11pm Fri & Sat, noon-8pm Sun; 🕾) Craving goulash, spaetzle, bratwurst and hearty, freshly baked bread? This German-run beer garden, just down the hill from the *zócalo*, serves genuine German food on weekends. To wash it down, Mango's beer list includes both imported European beers and domestic artisanal *cerveza*. There's live jazz and blues; see the event calendar on the website.

La Sombra del Sabino
CAFE $$

(✆739-395-03-69; www.lasombradelsabino. mx; Av Revolución 1910 No 45; mains M$150-165; ⊙10am-7pm Wed-Sun; 🕾) This 'literary cafe' and bookstore serves coffee, tea, wine or beer and simple fare – pastries, sandwiches and salads – in a contemplative garden setting. La Sombra del Sabino also hosts readings and events and sells a small selection of English-language books.

La Luna Mextli
INTERNATIONAL $$

(✆739-395-11-14; www.facebook.com/lalunamextli; Av Revolución 1910 No 16; mains M$85-220; ⊙noon-9pm Mon-Fri, 9am-10pm Sat & Sun) La Luna Mextli has its own in-house gallery stuffed with local art. The food is also excellent, from the Mexican standards to an entire list of Argentine steaks and *parrillada* (mixed grill).

★ La Sibarita
MEXICAN $$$

(✆777-101-16-00; www.posadadeltepozteco. com.mx; Posada del Tepozteco, Paraíso 3; mains M$200-300; ⊙8:30am-10pm Sun-Thu, to 11pm Fri & Sat; 🅿🕾) High on a hill above town, the restaurant at Posada del Tepozteco has gorgeous views of the valley below. With surreal cliffs and a pyramid overhead, the restaurant's setting is striking. The menu features dishes such as chicken breast stuffed with goat's cheese, *róbalo* (snook) carpaccio in vinaigrette and rose-petal *nieve* (sorbet), all paired with imported wines.

★ El Ciruelo
MEXICAN $$$

(✆777-219-37-20; www.elciruelo.com.mx; Zaragoza 17; mains M$193-369; ⊙1-6:30pm Sun-Thu, to 10:30pm Fri & Sat; 🖶) Set in a courtyard with impressive views of the cliffs and pyramid, this long-standing favorite serves an upscale menu of dishes from *pechuga con plátano macho* (chicken with plantain in *mole*) and *salmón chileno a la mantequilla* (Chilean salmon in butter sauce) to good salads and Mexican soups, though prices are inflated for the scenery. On Saturday and Sunday there are play areas for kids.

🍸 Drinking & Nightlife

La Terraza Yecapixtla
ROOFTOP BAR

(✆735-172-85-85; Av Tepozteco; ⊙9am-11pm; 🕾) It looks unassuming from the street, but climb the stairs and this open-air bar has good views of the cliff face and greenery. There are grills and Mexican snacks to go with the beer, cocktails and spirits. The music leans toward *ranchero* at low volume.

Shopping

Tepoz has a fantastic daily **market** that convenes on the *zócalo*. It's at its fullest on Wednesday and Sunday. As well as the daily fruit, vegetable, clothing and crafts on sale, on Saturday and Sunday stalls around the *zócalo* sell a wide selection of handicrafts.

ℹ Getting There & Away

Don't confuse Tepoztlán (in Morelos) with Tepotzotlán to the north of Mexico City.

ADO/OCC (www.ado.com.mx; Av 5 de Mayo 35) runs 1st-class buses mainly to/from Mexico City's Terminal Sur (M$126, one hour, every 20 to 30 minutes, 5am to 8pm), but also to Terminal Norte (M$130, 2¼ hours, two daily), direct to/from Mexico City's airport (M$184, 1½ hours, four daily), and to Cuautla (M$24, 45 minutes, every 30 minutes). ADO/OCC buses in Tepotzlán arrive at the ADO terminal 'Terminal Tepoztlán-Gasolinera' beside a gas station, from where a white *micro* (M$8, five minutes, frequent) can take you the 1.5km to the *zócalo*.

Ometochtli runs direct buses to Cuernavaca (M$24, 40 minutes, every 20 minutes 6am to 9pm). They leave from opposite the Auditorio (with its mosaic mural of *chinelos*); buy tickets from sellers at the blue-and-white umbrella before boarding. Do not take the indirect route, only the safer buses that say '*directo*' on their front. Buses drop you off in Cuernavaca at *La Fuente*, a church at Calle Chamilpa 1B, from where it is a pleasant walk south to the *zócalo*. A secure taxi to Cuernavaca is about M$230.

Cuautla

735 / POP 154,360 / ELEV 1300M

Cuautla (*kwout*-la) has none of Tepoztlán's scenic beauty, or the architectural merit of Cuernavaca, but it does have sulfur springs that have attracted people for centuries, as well as serious revolutionary credentials.

Cuautla was a base for one of Mexico's first leaders in the independence struggle, José María Morelos y Pavón, until he was forced to leave when the royalist army besieged the town in 1812. A century later it became a center of support for Emiliano Zapata's revolutionary army. However, if Mexican history and *balnearios* (bathing places) aren't your thing, there's not much for you here – modern Cuautla is a perfectly pleasant town, but there's little to see and do aside from the above.

◎ Sights

The two main plazas are Plaza Fuerte de Galeana, better known as the Alameda (a favorite haunt of mariachis-for-hire at weekends), and the *zócalo*.

Ex-Convento de San Diego HISTORIC BUILDING (Batalla 19 de Febrero s/n) In 1911 presidential candidate Francisco Madero embraced Emiliano Zapata at Cuautla's old train station in the Ex-Convento de San Diego. Steam enthusiasts will want to come on Saturday, when Mexico's only steam-powered train fires up for short rides from 4pm to 9pm. The Ex-Convento is now home to Cuautla's **tourist office** (735-352-52-21; 9am-8pm).

DON'T MISS

CUAUTLA'S BALNEARIOS

Cuautla's best-known *balneario* (thermal bath) is the riverside **Agua Hedionda** (Stinky Water; 735-352-00-44; http://balnearioaguahedionda.com; end of Av Progreso, cnr Emiliano Zapata; adult/child Mon-Fri M$50/30, Sat & Sun M$75/40, before 9am Mon-Fri M$25; 6:30am-5:30pm Mon-Fri, to 6pm Sat & Sun;). Waterfalls replenish two lake-sized pools with sulfur-scented tepid water. Take an 'Agua Hedionda' bus (M$7) from Plazuela Revolución del Sur. There's a two-for-one deal on Thursday. Check the website for any warnings about closures before making the trip as Agua Hedionda was closed because of earthquake damage at the time of writing.

Other *balnearios* worth visiting include **El Almeal** (Hernández; adult/child M$80/50; 9am-6pm) and **Los Limones** (Gabriel Teppa 14; adult M$65-75, child M$50; 8:30am-6pm). Both are served by the same spring (no sulfur) and have extensive shaded picnic grounds. Prices are reduced Monday to Friday. Children under three go free. Check Balnearios Morelos (www.balneariosenmorelos.com.mx) for a full list of thermal baths in the area.

¡QUE VIVA ZAPATA!

A peasant leader from Morelos state, Emiliano Zapata (1879–1919) was among the most radical of Mexico's revolutionaries, fighting for the return of hacienda land to the peasants with the cry '*¡Tierra y libertad!*' (Land and freedom!). The Zapatista movement was at odds with both the conservative supporters of the old regime and their liberal opponents. In November 1911 Zapata disseminated his *Plan de Ayala*, calling for restoration of all land to the peasants. After winning numerous battles against government troops in central Mexico (some in association with Pancho Villa), he was ambushed and killed in 1919.

Ruta de Zapata

In Anenecuilco, 6km south of Cuautla, what's left of the adobe cottage where Zapata was born (on August 8, 1879) is now the **Museo de la Lucha para la Tierra** (Museo y Casa de Emiliano Zapata; ☑735-308-89-01; Ayuntamiento 33, cnr Av Zapata; M$35; ☺10am-5pm), with a rousing mural of Zapata's life story.

About 20km south is the **Ex-Hacienda de San Juan Chinameca** (☑735-170-00-83; Cárdenas s/n; M$30, Sun free; ☺9am-5pm Tue-Sun), in the town of the same name, where in 1919 Zapata was lured into a fatal trap by Colonel Jesús Guajardo, following the orders of President Carranza, who was eager to dispose of the rebel leader and consolidate the post-revolutionary government. Pretending to defect to the revolutionary forces, Guajardo set up a meeting with Zapata, who arrived at Chinameca accompanied by a guerrilla escort. Guajardo's men shot the general before he crossed the abandoned hacienda's threshold.

The hacienda has a small and, unfortunately, horribly maintained museum with a meager collection of photos and newspaper reproductions. But there's a statue of Zapata astride a rearing horse at the entrance, where you can still see the bullet holes where the revolutionary died and where old men gather to celebrate their fallen hero.

From Chinameca head 20km northwest to Tlaltizapán, the site of the excellent **Cuartel General de Zapata** (Museo de la Revolución del Sur; ☑734-341-51-26; Guerrero 2; ☺10am-5pm Tue-Sun) `FREE`, the main barracks of the revolutionary forces. Here you can see Zapata's rifle (the trigger retains his fingerprints), the bed where he slept and the outfit he was wearing at the time of his death (riddled with bullet holes and stained with blood).

Though it's possible to do this route via *colectivo* (yellow 'Chinameca' combis traveling to Anenecuilco and Chinameca leave from the corner of Garduño and Matamoros in Cuautla every 10 minutes), it can be an all-day ordeal. The Morelos state tourist office (p190) in Cuernavaca arranges tours of the route.

Museo Histórico del Oriente MUSEUM
(☑735-352-83-31; Callejón del Castigo 3; M$39, Sun free; ☺10am-5pm Tue-Sun) The former residence of José María Morelos houses the Museo Histórico del Oriente. Each room here covers a different historical period with displays of pre-Hispanic pottery, good maps and early photos of Cuautla and Zapata. The Mexican War of Independence rebel leader's remains lie beneath the imposing Zapata monument in the middle of Plazuela Revolución del Sur.

🛏 Sleeping & Eating

Hotel Defensa del Agua HOTEL $
(☑735-352-16-79; Defensa del Agua 34; d M$340-440, tr M$410-515, q M$475-590; P🛜❄) This modern, clean hotel is set out in a motel style with a small pool and spacious rooms with TV, phone and fan. There's a very handy Italian Coffee Company branch in the building for breakfast. Avoid rooms with windows facing the noisy street.

Hotel & Spa Villasor RESORT $$
(☑735-303-55-03; www.hotelvillasor.com.mx; Av Progreso; s/d/ste M$540/700/1150; P❄🛜❄) Out of town and opposite the Agua Hedionda baths, this modern place has a large pool and comfortable rooms equipped with cable TV. With its own spa treatments, Villasor is the best option for relaxation, but it's not convenient for those without transportation.

Así Es Mi Tierra MEXICAN $
(☑735-398-47-54; Reforma 113; mains M$90-240; ☺1-9pm Mon-Fri, 8am-midnight Sat, 8am-10pm Sun; 🛝) Housed in a bright, airy kiosk resembling an ample circus tent, Tierra makes a grand show of steaks, grills and Mexican dishes such as *chiles en nogada* (green chilies stuffed with picadillo, covered with a

creamy walnut sauce and sprinkled with red pomegranate seeds) and chunky chicken tacos with all the trimmings of salad, rice and guacamole. The Saturday and Sunday brunch buffets are popular with groups and families.

Las Golondrinas MEXICAN $$
(☑735-354-13-50; www.restaurantelasgolondrinas. com; Catalán 19A; mains M$85-190; ⊙8am-10pm) Set in a 17th-century building filled with plants and koi ponds, Golondrinas offers an attractive atmosphere and excellent service. House specialties include a range of *molcajetes* (spicy stews cooked in a large stone mortar). Breakfasts include egg-white omelettes.

❶ Getting There & Away

OCC (☑800-702-80-00; www.ado.com.mx; Calle 2 de Mayo 97) has 1st-class buses to Mexico City's Terminal Sur (M$140, two hours, every 15 to 30 minutes) and Tepoztlán (M$24, 50 minutes, every 15 to 40 minutes).

Cuernavaca

☑777 / POP 339,000 / ELEV 1480M

There's always been a formidable glamour surrounding Cuernavaca (kwehr-nah-*vah*-kah), the capital of Morelos state. With its vast, gated haciendas and sprawling estates, it has traditionally attracted high-society visitors year-round for its warmth, clean air and attractive architecture. Today this tradition continues, even though urban sprawl has put a decisive end to the clean air and you're more likely to see vacationing North Americans and college students studying Spanish on monthlong courses than meet international royalty or great artists in the street.

Cuernavaca is an easygoing weekend escape from Mexico City for its strollable town center, touches of fine dining, artworks by Diego Rivera and Frida Kahlo, and as a launchpad for the well-maintained ruins of nearby Xochicalco.

History

The first settlers to the valleys of modern Morelos are believed to have arrived in 1500 BC. In the centuries between AD 200 and 900 they organized a highly productive agricultural society and developed Xochicalco and other large constructions throughout the region. Later, the dominant Mexica (Aztecs) called them Tlahuica, which means 'people who work the land.' In 1379 a Mexica warlord conquered Cuauhnáhuac, subdued the

Tlahuica and exacted an annual tribute that included 16,000 pieces of *amate* (bark paper) and 20,000 bushels of corn. The tributes payable by the subject states were set out in a register the Spanish later called the Códice Mendocino, in which Cuauhnáhuac was represented by a three-branch tree. This symbol now graces Cuernavaca's coat of arms.

The Mexica lord's successor married the daughter of the Cuauhnáhuac leader, and from this marriage was born Moctezuma I Ilhuicamina, the 15th-century Aztec king, who was a predecessor to Moctezuma II Xocoyotzin, encountered by Cortés. Under the Aztecs, the Tlahuica traded and prospered. Their city was a learning and religious center, and archaeological remains suggest they had a considerable knowledge of astronomy.

When the Spanish arrived the Tlahuica were fiercely loyal to the Aztecs. In April 1521 they were finally overcome and Cortés torched the city. Soon the city became known as Cuernavaca, a more Spanish-friendly version of its original appellation.

In 1529 Cortés received his belated reward from the Spanish crown when he was named Marqués del Valle de Oaxaca, with an estate that covered 22 towns, including Cuernavaca, and 23,000 indigenous Mexicans. After he introduced sugarcane and new farming methods, Cuernavaca became a Spanish agricultural center, as it had been for the Aztecs. Cortés' descendants dominated the area for nearly 300 years.

With its salubrious climate, rural surroundings and colonial elite, Cuernavaca became a refuge for the rich and powerful in the 1700s and 1800s, including José de la Borda, the 18th-century Taxco silver magnate. Borda's lavish home was later a retreat for Emperor Maximilian and Empress Carlota. Cuernavaca has also attracted many artists and achieved literary fame as the setting for Malcolm Lowry's 1947 novel *Under the Volcano*.

◉ Sights

★**Museo Robert Brady** MUSEUM

(☑777-318-85-54; Netzahualcóyotl 4; M$45; ⊙10am-6pm Tue-Sun) Let's face it, who wouldn't want to be independently wealthy and spend their life traveling around the world collecting art for their lavish Mexican mansion? If that option isn't open to you, visit this museum – easily one of Cuernavaca's best – and live vicariously. The onetime home of American artist and collector

Robert Brady (1928–86), the museum, which is housed in the Casa de la Torre, is a wonderful place to spend time appreciating the exquisite taste of one person.

Originally part of the monastery within the Recinto de la Catedral, the house is a stunning testament to a man who knew what he liked. Brady lived in Cuernavaca for 24 years after a spell in Venice, and never married or had children. His collections range from Papua New Guinea and India to Haiti and South America.

Every room, including the two gorgeous bathrooms and kitchen, is bedecked in paintings, carvings, textiles, antiques and folk arts from all corners of the Earth. Among the treasures are works by well-known Mexican artists, including Rivera, Tamayo, Kahlo and Covarrubias, as well as Brady's own paintings (check out his spot-on portrait of his friend Peggy Guggenheim). There is a bedroom dedicated to his friend Josephine Baker, the French-American actor and black civil-rights activist. The gardens are lovely too, with a very tempting (but off-limits) swimming pool in one of them and a little cafe in the other.

Classic and contemporary films are shown in the museum's courtyard every Wednesday at 4pm and 6pm for a M$30 donation. Movies are in their original language with Spanish subtitles.

Guided tours (10am to 6pm Tuesday to Saturday) are available by appointment for groups up to 20 people for M$300.

MMAPO
MUSEUM

(Museo Morelense de Arte Popular; ☎777-318-62-00; Hidalgo 239; ⊙10am-5pm Tue-Sun) FREE An excellent addition to Cuernavaca, this bright and inviting museum showcases handicrafts from Morelos, including life-size *chinelos* (costumed dancers with upturned chins from Morelos). Most of the pieces are displayed out in the open, not behind glass, so you can get close and admire the handiwork. The attached store sells quality pieces that you won't see in your average craft market.

Catedral de Cuernavaca
CHURCH

(www.catedraldecuernavaca.org; Hidalgo 17; ⊙7:30am-8pm) FREE Cuernavaca's cathedral stands in a large high-walled *recinto* (compound). It was built in a grand, fortress-like style in an effort to impress, intimidate and defend against the natives. Franciscans started work on what was one of Mexico's earliest Christian missions in 1526, using indigenous labor and stones from the rubble of Cuauhnáhuac. The first structure was the **Capilla Abierta de San José**, an open chapel on the cathedral's west side. The compound entrance is on Hidalgo.

The cathedral itself, the **Templo de la Asunción de María**, is plain and solid, with an unembellished facade. The side door, which faces north to the compound entrance, shows a mixture of indigenous and European features – the skull and crossbones above it is a symbol of the Franciscan order. Inside are frescoes rediscovered early in the 20th century. Cuernavaca was a center for Franciscan missionary activities in Asia and the frescoes – said to show the persecution of Christian missionaries in Japan – were supposedly painted in the 17th century by a Japanese convert to Christianity.

The cathedral compound also holds two smaller churches. On the right as you enter is the **Templo de la Tercera Orden de San Francisco**. Its exterior was carved in 18th-century baroque style by indigenous artisans and its interior has ornate, gilded decorations. On the left as you enter is the 19th-century **Capilla del Carmen**, where believers seek cures for illness.

The cathedral was damaged by the earthquake of September 19, 2017. At the time of writing it was scheduled to remain closed for some time. Check ahead of your visit to ensure that is has reopened.

Palacio de Cortés
HISTORIC BUILDING

(☎777-312-81-71; M$55, Sun free; ⊙8am-6pm Tue-Sun) Cortés' imposing medieval-style fortress stands opposite the southeast end of the Plaza de Armas. This two-story stone palace was built in 1535 on the base of the city pyramid that Cortés destroyed after taking Cuauhnáhuac. The base is still visible from various points on the ground floor. The palace houses the excellent **Museo Regional Cuauhnáhuac** (Leyva 100; M$55, Sun free; ⊙9am-6pm Tue-Sun, last entry 5:30pm), which has two floors of exhibits highlighting Mexican cultures and history. On the upstairs balcony is a fascinating mural by Diego Rivera, *Historia del Estado de Morelos*.

The mural was commissioned in the mid-1920s by Dwight Morrow, the US ambassador to Mexico. Flowing from right to left, scenes from the conquest through to the 1910 Revolution emphasize the cruelty, oppression and violence that have characterized Mexican history.

Cuernavaca

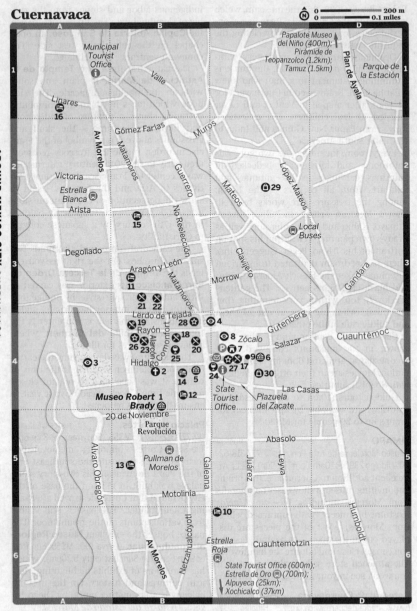

While upstairs covers events from the Spanish conquest to the present, the ground floor focuses on pre-Hispanic cultures, including the Tlahuica and their relationship with the Aztec empire. Most labeling is in Spanish only, with a few well-translated exceptions.

Cortés resided here until he turned tail for Spain in 1541. The palace remained with Cortés' family for most of the next century, but by the 18th century it was being used as a prison. During the Porfirio Díaz era it became government offices.

Cuernavaca

AROUND MEXICO CITY CUERNAVACA

On September 19, 2017, a powerful earthquake rocked the region and damaged the building's clock, which has since been removed. At the time of writing the Palacio was to remain closed to the public for at least a year, for damage assessment and reparations. Check ahead to ensure that it is open again, or simply enjoy the building's facade.

Jardín Juárez GARDENS
(Guerrero) [FREE] Adjoining the northwest corner of the Plaza de Armas is the Jardín Juárez, where the central gazebo (designed by tower specialist Gustave Eiffel) houses juice and sandwich stands. Live-band concerts on Thursday and Sunday evenings start at 6pm. Roving vendors sell balloons, ice cream and corn on the cob under the trees, which fill up with legions of cacophonous grackles at dusk.

Even more entertaining are the guitar trios who warm up their voices and instruments before heading to the cafes across the street to serenade willing patrons. You can request a ballad or two for around M$80.

Papalote Museo del Niño MUSEUM
(www.papalotecuernavaca.org.mx; Av Vicente Guerrero 205; adult/child under 15yr M$50/60, group of 4 M$185; ⊙9am-6pm Mon-Fri, from 10am Sat & Sun; P ⊕) Built as part of a land deal with the city, this excellent children's museum has an odd location in a shopping center beside a Costco, about 4km north of downtown, but for travelers with children it's well worth seeking out. Geared toward education, technology and play, the museum includes a large Lego exhibit, musical elements and lots of bright colors. There's an IMAX theater in the same complex and discounts for families and groups.

It's 500m south of the Pullman de Morelos bus terminal 'Casino de la Selva.'

Pirámide de Teopanzolco RUINS
(☑777-314-12-84; cnr Río Balsas & Ixcateopan; M$50, Sun free; ⊙9:30am-5:30pm) This very small archaeological site, 1km northeast of the center, actually has two pyramids, one inside the other. You can climb on the outer base and see the older pyramid within, with a double staircase leading up to the remains of a pair of temples. Tlahuicas built the older pyramid over 800 years ago; the outside one was being constructed by the Aztecs when Cortés arrived, and was never completed. The name Teopanzolco means 'Place of the Old Temple.'

There are a few explanatory signs in English. The site was damaged by the earthquake of September 19, 2017. At the time of writing it was closed for restoration work. Check before your visit to ensure that is has completely opened again.

Jardín Borda
GARDENS

(📞777-318-82-50; Av Morelos 271; adult/child M$30/15, Sun free; ⊙10am-5:30pm Tue-Sun) Beside the 1784 Parroquia de Guadalupe, this extravagant property, inspired by Versailles, features gardens formally laid out in a series of terraces with paths, steps and fountains. Duck into the house to get an idea of how Mexico's 19th-century aristocracy lived. In typical colonial style, the buildings are arranged around courtyards. In one wing, the **Museo de Sitio** has exhibits on daily life during the empire period and original documents with the signatures of Morelos, Juárez and Maximilian.

The property was designed in 1783 for Manuel de la Borda as an addition to the stately residence built by his father, José de la Borda. From 1866 Emperor Maximilian and Empress Carlota entertained their courtiers here and used the house as a summer residence.

Several romantic paintings in the **Sala Manuel M Ponce**, a recital hall near the entrance of the house, show scenes of the garden in Maximilian's time. One of the most famous paintings depicts Maximilian in the garden with La India Bonita, the 'pretty Indian' who later became his lover. Originally there was a botanical collection to show off, with hundreds of varieties of ornamental plants and fruit trees. Because of a water shortage, the baroque-style fountains now operate only on weekends.

Plaza de Armas
PLAZA

(Zócalo; Gutenberg) Cuernavaca's *zócalo*, Plaza de Armas, is flanked on the east by the Palacio de Cortés, on the west by the **Palacio de Gobierno** and on the northeast and south by restaurants and roving bands of mariachis. It's the only main plaza in Mexico without a church, chapel, convent or cathedral overlooking it.

🎓 Courses

Cuernavaca is a well-established center for studying Spanish at all levels and has dozens of language schools. As such, standards are high, teaching is usually very thorough and prices competitive (generally US$240 to US$310 per week, plus registration- and study-material fees and housing). The best schools offer small-group or individual instruction at all levels with four to five hours per day of intensive instruction, plus a couple of hours' conversation practice. Classes begin each Monday and most schools recommend a minimum enrollment of four weeks.

With so many teaching styles and options, prospective students should research carefully. Contact the **tourist office** (📞777-329-44-04; www.cuernavaca.gob.mx/turismo; Av Morelos 278; ⊙9am-6pm) for an extensive list of schools.

🎉 Festivals & Events

Feria de la Primavera
CULTURAL

(⊙Mar-Apr) From late March to early April, the city's Spring Fair includes cultural and artistic events, plus concerts and a beautiful exhibit of the city's spring flowers.

Carnaval
STREET CARNIVAL

(⊙Feb/Mar) Over the five days leading up to Ash Wednesday, Cuernavaca's colorful Carnaval celebrations feature parades, art exhibits and street performances by Tepoztlán's Chinelo dancers.

🛏 Sleeping

Some of the best boutique hotels in the country are here, aimed at weekend escapees from the capital. Budget hotels tend to be simple, while midrange hotels are few. The town fills up with visitors at weekends and holidays, when rates rise significantly. Light sleepers should avoid anywhere within earshot of Plazuela del Zacate on rowdy weekends.

Hotel Colonial
HOTEL $

(📞777-318-64-14; Aragón y León 19; s/d/tw/tr incl breakfast M$350/455/500/590; 🛜) While this relaxed budget hotel may be basic, it's also excellent value. There's a garden at its center, cable TV, a free water cooler and decorative floors. The upstairs rooms with balconies and tall ceilings are best.

Hotel Las Hortensias
HOTEL $

(📞777-318-52-65; www.hotelhortensias.com; Hidalgo 13; s/d/tw/tr M$390/440/510/660; 🛜) Cheap and central, Las Hortensias has small, sparse rooms, a lush garden and staff who seem to constantly be cleaning. Streetside rooms are noisy, so bring earplugs or ask for one of the dark interior rooms.

Hotel Juárez
HOTEL $

(📞777-314-02-19; Netzahualcóyotl 19; r M$300-400, without bathroom M$250-350; 🅿🛜🐕) The rooms at this well-located hotel are large and airy but have tired beds. To compensate, a breezy terrace overlooks a large grassy backyard, an attractive swimming pool and Cuernavaca's clay-tiled rooftops. It's not pretty, but it's a good budget option, especially for a dip in the water.

Hotel Laam
BUSINESS HOTEL $$

(✆777-314-44-11; www.laamhotel.com.mx; Av Morelos 239; d/tw M$960/1520; ▣🅿🛜🌊) With a motel feel and comfortable, if sterile, rooms (some with huge terraces), this slick hotel is good value. Set back from the road, giving it distance from street noise, Hotel Laam comes with a heated swimming pool and well-tended grounds.

Hotel Antigua Posada
HOTEL $$

(✆777-310-21-79; Galeana 69; r M$850-1000, ste M$1150-1300, all incl breakfast; 🅿🛜🌊) This exclusive little hideaway is a short walk from the center of town and boasts just 11 rooms behind its unpromising exterior. But once inside you'll find a lovely courtyard and great service. Rooms are gorgeous, complete with wooden beams and rustic touches.

★Hotel Hacienda de Cortés
HISTORIC HOTEL $$$

(✆777-315-88-44, 800-220-76-97; www.hotelhaciendadecortes.com.mx; Plaza Kennedy 90; d/ste from M$2135/2990; 🅿🛜🌊) Built in the 16th century by Martín Cortés (successor to Hernán Cortés as Marqués del Valle de Oaxaca), this former sugar mill was renovated in 1980 and boasts 23 rooms of various levels of luxury, each with its own private garden and terrace. There's also a swimming pool built around old stone columns, a gym and an excellent restaurant.

It's approximately 5km southeast of the center of town. Good online promotions available via the website.

Las Mañanitas
LUXURY HOTEL $$$

(✆777-362-00-00; www.lasmananitas.com.mx; Linares 107; ste incl breakfast M$2950-5885; 🅿❄🛜🌊) If you're really out to impress someone, book a room at this stunning place. It's a destination hotel – you may not want to leave the whole weekend – so the fact that it's not in the center of town isn't too important. The large rooms are beautifully understated, many with terraces overlooking the gardens, which are full of peacocks and boast a heated pool. Rates are cheaper midweek.

La Casa Azul
BOUTIQUE HOTEL $$$

(✆777-314-21-41, 777-314-36-34; www.hotelcasaazul.com.mx; Arista 17; r M$2915-3330; 🅿🛜🌊) This 24-room boutique hotel is a short walk from the town center and has lots of charm. Originally part of the Guadalupe Convent, the hotel has soothing fountains, two pools, a gym, and a great selection of local arts and crafts throughout.

✗ Eating

Cuernavaca is a great food town with a few excellent high-end restaurants and plenty of good cafes. There are, however, surprisingly few enticing midrange options.

Emiliano's
MEXICAN $

(Rayon 5; menú del día M$43-70, mains M$30-85; ⏰8am-7pm) Quiz any local on their favorite place to eat and you'll be directed to the thatched roof of homey Emiliano's. Complex *mole* and other Mexican sure things, such as stuffed chilies, are only enhanced by tortillas you can watch being handmade. Add breakfast and you'll be here all day.

Iguana Green's
MEXICAN $

(Rayón 190; menú del día M$45, mains M$40-90; ⏰8am-6:30pm) With food this good and this cheap it would easy for Iguana to be just another anonymous *fonda* (family restaurant) and still draw crowds, but the friendly family in charge take obvious pride in creating a festive space – with brightly colored chairs and tables and messages of appreciation for the authentic Mexican dishes scrawled on the walls.

La Cueva
CAFE $

(Galeana; mains M$40-90; ⏰8am-10pm) This sloped bar, which opens onto the bustling crowds of Calle Galeana, serves up superb *pozole* (shredded meat and hominy in a pork-based broth) and other delicious snacks and dishes such as stewed *conejo* (rabbit). This is a great place to eat with the locals at local prices. Excellent breakfasts start at just M$35.

★La India Bonita
MEXICAN $$

(✆777-312-50-21; www.laindiabonita.com; Morrow 115; mains M$150-240; ⏰8am-10pm Sun-Thu, to 11pm Fri & Sat) Set in a lush courtyard, Cuernavaca's oldest restaurant also has some of its best traditional Mexican food – from *brocheta al mezcal* (skewered meats marinated in mezcal) to *chile en nogada* (*poblano* pepper in walnut sauce) – with the occasional enticing twist. India Bonita operates a tasty bakery-cafe next door.

★La Maga Café
MEXICAN $$

(www.lamagacafe.com; Morrow 9; buffet M$103; ⏰1-5pm Mon-Sat; 🛜🍴) The colorful buffet at La Maga features multitudes of glazed pots filled with salads, pastas, fruit, vegetables, and daily specials such as glistening *pollo en adobo* (chicken marinated in chili and herbs) and *tortas de elote* (cheesy corn croquettes).

WORTH A TRIP

XOCHICALCO

Atop a desolate plateau with views for miles around, **Xochicalco** (☎737-374-30-92; http://turismo.morelos.gob.mx/zona-arqueologica-de-xochicalco; admission M$70, video permit M$35; ☉9am-6pm, last entry 5pm) is an impressive and relatively easy day trip from Cuernavaca that shouldn't be missed. It's large enough to make the journey worthwhile, but not so well known as to be overrun by tourists.

A Unesco World Heritage site and one of central Mexico's most important archaeological sites, Xochicalco (so-chee-cal-co) is Náhuatl for 'place of the house of flowers.' The collection of white stone ruins, many still to be excavated, covers approximately 10 sq km. They represent the various cultures – Tlahuica, Toltec, Olmec, Zapotec, Mixtec and Aztec – for which Xochicalco was a commercial, cultural and religious center. When Teotihuacán began to weaken around AD 650 to 700, Xochicalco began to rise in importance, achieving its peak between AD 650 and 900, with far-reaching cultural and commercial relations. Around AD 650, Zapotec, Maya and Gulf Coast spiritual leaders convened here to correlate their respective calendars. Xochicalco remained an important center until around 1200, when its excessive growth precipitated a demise similar to that of Teotihuacán.

The site's most famous monument is the **Pirámide de Quetzalcóatl**. Archaeologists have surmised from its well-preserved bas-reliefs that astronomer-priests met here at the beginning and end of each 52-year cycle of the pre-Hispanic calendar. Signage here is in English and Spanish, but information at the excellent, ecologically sensitive **museum**, situated 200m from the ruins, is in Spanish only.

From October through May, the site offers an occasional **light show** (☎reservations 737-374-30-90; xochicalco.mor@inah.gob.mx; M$7; ☉Oct-May) on Friday and Saturday nights. It's quite a spectacle, but call ahead because the shows aren't regular.

From Cuernavaca's market, *colectivos* with 'Xochi' on their windshield (M$15) depart every 30 minutes for the site entrance. Larger buses from the Pullman de Morelos terminal make the same trip, directly, but only on Saturday and Sunday. On arrival, you'll need to walk to the museum to buy tickets. The last return *colectivo* leaves around 6pm. Alternatively, take a taxi (M$30) from the site to the nearby town of Alpuyeca, where there are frequent *colectivos* back to Cuernavaca.

There are great vegetarian options and a community vibe, sometimes with live music. Arrive early to nab a window seat.

★**L'arrosoir d'Arthur** FRENCH $$
(☎777-243-70-86; Calle Juan Ruiz de Alarcón 13; menú del día M$110, mains M$140-180; ☉1pm-midnight Mon & Wed, from 10am Tue & Thu-Sun; 🖎) As much a hangout and nightspot as a restaurant, this French-owned place in a loft space downtown has excellent, affordable French dishes (crepes, cassolette, chicken in mustard sauce), plus good cocktails and wines. On weekends, the chilled, European vibe gets more energetic with live music, theater, dance and poetry events.

★**Restaurante Hacienda de Cortés** INTERNATIONAL $$$
(☎800-220-76-97, 777-315-88-44; www.hotel haciendadecortes.com.mx; Plaza Kennedy 90; mains M$105-385; ☉7am-11pm; 🅿❄🖎🍴) Situated within Hotel Hacienda de Cortés, a 15-minute drive south east of central Cuernavaca, this elegant but unpretentious hotel restaurant serves an excellent selection of salads and delicious international dishes, including a fantastic vegetarian lasagna, tuna in almond sauce with risotto, and well-prepared Angus steaks. The dining room is spectacular, with massive vines climbing the walls and wrought-iron chandeliers overhead.

Restaurant Las Mañanitas FRENCH $$$
(☎777-362-00-00; www.lasmananitas.com.mx; Linares 107; breakfasts M$110-285, mains M$265-490; ☉8am-10:30pm) The restaurant and bar of Cuernavaca's most famous hotel, Las Mañanitas, is a luxurious splurge that's open to all. The expansive menu has a heavy French accent, with dishes such as entrecôte Bourguignon and sumptuous desserts. Traditional dishes include *maguey* grubs. Reserve a table inside the mansion or on the terrace, where you can watch wildlife wander among modern garden sculptures.

Tamuz INTERNATIONAL $$$
(www.tamuz.mx; Reforma 501; mains M$160-270; ☉8am-6pm Tue-Wed, to 10pm Thu, to 11pm Fri &

Sat, to 6pm Sun) The Israeli chef here dishes up an eclectic menu that includes dishes like chicken marsala Tel Aviv–style, pita with smoked salmon dip, and polenta. The restaurant, in one of the Cuernavaca's more posh neighborhoods, has a LA-esque design (modern, spare and characterless) with a lovely backyard.

Casa Hidalgo   MEXICAN $$$
(🖉777-312-27-49; www.casahidalgo.com; Jardín de los Héroes 6; menú del día M$230, mains M$155-295; ⏾8am-11pm Sun-Thu, to midnight Fri & Sat) Directly opposite the Palacio de Cortés, with a great terrace and upstairs balcony, this popular restaurant attracts a well-heeled crowd of local socialites. The menu is eclectic – try cold mango-agave soup with jicama, or *tlaxcalteca* chicken breast stuffed with cheese and roasted *poblano* pepper with three salsas: squash blossom, spinach and chipotle. Breakfast and lunch set menus available.

🍷 Drinking & Nightlife

Cuernavaca's nightlife is kept buzzing by a student population, especially at rowdy bars and clubs at Plazuela del Zacate and the adjacent alley Las Casas (home of pumping house and techno clubs with that tell-tale accordion of Mexican *norteño*). All stay open until the last patron leaves, which is usually sunrise on weekends. For something more sophisticated the best options are L'arrosoir d'Arthur, the cafes opposite the cathedral or Mercado Comonfort.

★**Mercado Comonfort**   BEER GARDEN
(www.facebook.com/mercadocomonfort; Comonfort 4; ⏾noon-11pm or later) A great addition to the city's drinking scene away from roudy La Plazuela, this 'market' is a secluded courtyard with pubs and small terraced bars from where cool locals can be seen drinking cocktails or lattes. Beer and wine snacks include pizza, tapas, vegetarian meals, and Yucatecan and Oaxacan dishes. Some bars stay open well after midnight on weekends.

★**House Cafe + Lounge**   LOUNGE
(🖉777-318-37-82; www.lascasasbb.com; Las Casas 110; ⏾8am-11pm Sun-Wed, to 12:30am Thu-Sat; 🛜) Housed inside a boutique hotel, the food and cocktails at House are excellent, but the real reason that the beautiful people are drawn here is to be seen lounging around the pool by night in a more tranquil environment than the clubs on the same street.

☆ Entertainment

Hanging around the central plazas is a popular activity, especially on Sunday evenings, when open-air concerts are often staged. There are often recitals at Jardín Borda (p186) on Thursday nights, too.

If your *español* is up to it, sample Cuernavaca's theater scene.

Los Arcos   DANCE
(🖉777-312-15-10; Jardín de los Héroes 4; minimum spend M$60; ⏾salsa 9:30-11:30pm Thu, Fri & Sun) Come here to dance salsa, not on a stage but around the tables of families having dinner on the terrace, with crowds of appreciative onlookers. The live band's carnival beats can be heard from the other side of the plaza and have a magnetic effect on your swiveling hips.

Cine Teatro Morelos   CINEMA
(🖉777-318-10-50; www.cinemorelos.com; Av Morelos 188; tickets from M$30; 🖐) Morelos' state theater hosts quality film festivals, plays and dance performances. There's a full schedule posted out front and a bookstore and cafe inside.

Teatro Ocampo   THEATER
(🖉777-318-63-85; http://cartelera.morelos.gob.mx/tags/teatro-ocampo; Jardín Juárez 2) This theater near Jardín Juárez stages contemporary plays. A calendar of cultural events is posted at its entrance.

🛍 Shopping

There are some good quality *guayaberas* (men's appliqued shirts), *huipiles* (long, sleeveless tunics) and upmarket souvenirs in the plaza opposite the cathedral and along the same street.

**Mercado de Artesanías
y Plata**   ARTS & CRAFTS
(Handicrafts & Silver Market; Juárez, cnr Hidalgo; ⏾8am-9pm) This relaxed market has handicrafts such as coconut lamps and hand-painted ceramics, found all over Mexico, as well as a plethora of handmade *chinelo* dolls with upturned beards, a specialty of Morelos. It's a shady place to browse and prices are reasonable. To find the market, look for the huge statue of Morelos, the revolutionary himself, at the entrance.

Mercado Adolfo López Mateos   MARKET
(🖉777-417-68-59; Adolfo López Mateos; ⏾6am-8pm) A sprawling, semi-covered market selling fresh produce and other wares, Mercado Adolfo López Mateos bursts with the smells of fruit, meat, flowers and smoked chilies.

❶ Information

There's internet access at the Futura and Estrella Blanca bus station and internet cafes all over town.

There's an information booth in the cathedral, at the north end of the zócalo (9am to 6pm daily) and other kiosks around town, including at most bus stations. Ask for maps.

Cruz Roja (Red Cross; ☎777-315-35-15; Rio Pánuco, cnr Leñeros; ⊙24hr) The Red Cross has professional medical consultations for under M$100. It's a 20-minute drive east of central Cuernavaca.

Main Post Office (Plaza de Armas; ⊙8am-5pm Mon-Fri, 10am-2pm Sat)

Municipal Tourist Office (p186) Also has a tourist police office.

State Tourist Office (☎777-314-38-81, 800-987-82-24; www.morelosturistico.com; Av Morelos Sur 187; ⊙9am-6pm) This excellent tourist office has a wealth of brochures, maps and information. Also has a **city center** (☎777-314-39-20; www.morelosturistico.com; Hidalgo 5; ⊙9am-6pm) branch.

Tourist Police (☎800-903-92-00)

❶ Getting There & Away

Hwy 95D (the Mexico City–Acapulco toll road) skirts the city's east side. If you're driving from the north, take the Cuernavaca exit and cross to Hwy 95 (where you'll see a statue of Zapata on horseback). Hwy 95 becomes Blvd Zapata then Avenida Morelos as you descend south into town. From Avenida Matamoros (still traveling south) the Avenida Morelos is one way, northbound only. To reach the center, veer left down Matamoros.

BUS

Cuernavaca's main-line bus companies operate separate long-distance terminals.

Estrella de Oro (EDO; ☎777-312-30-55; www.estrelladeoro.com.mx; Av Morelos Sur 812) Departures to Taxco (M$91, 1¼ hours, once or twice daily) and Mexico City's Terminal Sur (M$132, 1½ hours, seven daily). Pluss also departs from here.

Estrella Roja (ER; ☎777-318-59-34; www.estrellaroja.com.mx; cnr Galeana & Cuauhte-

motzin) Tiny terminal with services to Tepoztlán and Cuautla.

Estrella Blanca (☎777-312-26-26; www.estrellablanca.com.mx; Av Morelos 503, btwn Arista & Victoria) Futura, Costa Line and executive ETN services to Toluca (M$235, three hours, twice daily) with Turistar leave from here. Departures to Puebla (M$270, three hours, three to four daily), Taxco, Tepoztlán, Tepotzotlán and Mexico City's Terminals Norte (two hours) and Sur.

Pullman de Morelos (PDM; ☎777-318-09-07; www.pullman.mx; cnr Calles Abasolo & Netzahualcóyotl) The most conveniently located station. Comfortable buses to Mexico City's airport and Terminal Sur.

CAR & MOTORCYCLE

Cuernavaca is 89km south of Mexico City, a 1½-hour drive on Hwy 95 or a one-hour trip on Hwy 95D. Both roads continue south to Acapulco – Hwy 95 detours through Taxco; Hwy 95D is more direct and much faster.

❶ Getting Around

You can walk to most places of interest in central Cuernavaca. Local buses (M$6.50) advertise their destinations on their windshields. Many local buses, and those to nearby towns, leave from the **southern corner** of the city's labyrinthine market, Mercado Adolfo López Mateos. There have been reports of robberies on local buses in Cuernavaca, so exercise caution if you must use them. Taxis to most places in town cost the base fare of M$35.

The bus depots are in walking distance of the zócalo, except the Estrella de Oro bus terminal, 1km south (downhill) of the center, which is reachable on Ruta 17 or 20 down Galeana. In the other direction, catch any bus heading up Avenida Morelos. Ruta 17 and 20 buses head up Avenida Morelos and stop within one block of the Pullman de Morelos terminal at Casino de la Selva.

The **Cuernabús** (Hidalgo, cnr Juárez; per person M$100; ⊙ departs zócalo 11am, 1pm & 3pm Sat & Sun) is a double-decker tourist bus taking in 22km of sights, starting at the zócalo and including parks and sights such as Jardín Borda, the Catedral de Cuernavaca and, most usefully, the Pirámide de Teopanzolco. It has only a Spanish-speaking guide.

BUS FROM CUERNAVACA

DESTINATION	FARE (M$)	DURATION (HR)	FREQUENCY (DAILY)
Cuautla	64	1½	28
Mexico City	100-140	1½	40
Mexico City Airport	250	2	24
Taxco	90	1¾	13
Tepoztlán	24	¾	28

Taxco

📍 762 / POP 53,000 / ELEV 1800M

The first sight of Taxco's (*tahss*-ko) white buildings scattered across the steep valley as you approach it is enough to take your breath away. Surrounded by dramatic mountains and cliffs, its perfectly preserved colonial architecture and the twin belfries of its baroque masterpiece, Templo de Santa Prisca, make for one of the most beguiling views anywhere in the central highlands.

Taxco, 160km southwest of Mexico City, has ridden waves of boom and bust associated with wealthy silver deposits discovered here in the 16th century and then repeatedly until the early 20th century. With its silver now almost depleted, Taxco thrives on tourism. As such, it's a rare example of preservation-centric development in Mexico. Unlike many colonial-era towns, Taxco has not been engulfed by industrial suburbs, and new buildings must conform to the old in scale, style and materials. This preserves Taxco as a striking small city and one of the best weekend trips from the capital.

History

Taxco was called Tlachco (Ball-Playing Place) by the Aztecs, who dominated the region from 1440 until the Spanish arrived. The colonial city was founded by Rodrigo de Castañeda in 1529, with a mandate from Hernán Cortés. Among the town's first Spanish residents were three miners, Juan de Cabra, Juan Salcedo and Diego de Nava, and the carpenter Pedro Muriel. In 1531 they established the first Spanish mine in North America.

The Spaniards came searching for tin, which they found in small quantities, but by 1534 they had discovered tremendous lodes of silver. That year the Hacienda El Chorrillo was built, complete with water wheel, smelter and aqueduct – the remains of the latter form the old arches (Los Arcos) over Hwy 95 at the north end of town.

The prospectors quickly depleted the first silver veins and fled Taxco. Further quantities of ore were not discovered until 1743. Don José de la Borda, who had arrived in 1716 from France at the age of 16 to work with his miner brother, accidentally unearthed one of the region's richest veins. According to the legend, Borda was riding near where the Templo de Santa Prisca now stands when his horse stumbled, dislodged a stone and exposed the precious metal.

Borda went on to introduce new techniques of draining and repairing mines, and he reportedly treated his indigenous workers better than most colonial mine owners. The Templo de Santa Prisca was the devout Borda's gift to Taxco. His success attracted more prospectors, and new silver veins were found and played out. With most of the silver gone, Taxco became a quiet town with a dwindling population and economy.

In 1929 a US architect and professor named William (Guillermo) Spratling arrived and, at the suggestion of the then US ambassador Dwight Morrow, set up a silver workshop as a way to rejuvenate the town. (Another version has it that Spratling was writing a book and resorted to the silver business because his publisher went bust. A third has it that Spratling had a notion to create jewelry that synthesized pre-Hispanic motifs with art deco modernism.) The workshop evolved into a factory, and Spratling's apprentices began establishing their own shops. Today Taxco is home to hundreds of silver shops, many producing for export.

◉ Sights

★ Templo de Santa Prisca   CHURCH

(Plaza Borda 1) The icon of Taxco, Santa Prisca is one of Mexico's most beautiful and striking pieces of baroque architecture. Its standout feature (best viewed side-on) is the contrast between its belfries, with their elaborate Churrigueresque facade, and the far more simple, constrained and elegant nave. The rose-colored stone used on the facade is extraordinarily beautiful in sunlight – look for the oval bas-relief depiction of Christ's baptism above the doorway. Inside, the intricately sculpted, gold-covered altarpieces are equally fine Churrigueresque specimens.

Santa Prisca was a labor of love for town hero José de la Borda. The local Catholic hierarchy allowed the silver magnate to donate this church to Taxco on the condition that he mortgage his mansion and other assets to guarantee its completion. The project nearly bankrupted him, but the risk produced an extraordinary legacy. It was designed by Spanish architects Juan Caballero and Diego Durán, and was constructed between 1751 and 1758.

Museo Guillermo Spratling   MUSEUM

(📞 762-622-16-60; Delgado 1; M$40; ⊙9am-5pm Mon-Sat, to 3pm Sun) This very well laid-out three-story history and archaeology

Taxco

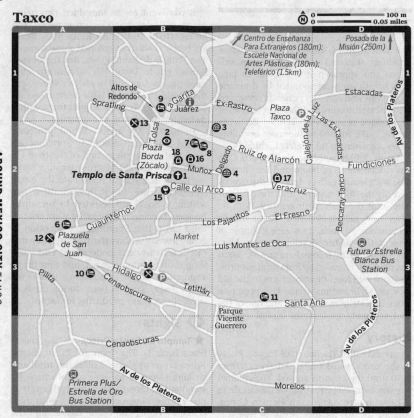

Taxco

◎ Top Sights
1 Templo de Santa Prisca B2

◎ Sights
2 Casa Borda B2
3 Museo de Arte Virreinal C2
4 Museo Guillermo Spratling C2

🛏 Sleeping
5 Hostel Casa Taxco C2
6 Hotel Casa Grande A3
7 Hotel Emilia B2
8 Hotel Los Arcos B2
9 Hotel Mi Casita B1
10 Hotel Santa Prisca A3
11 Pueblo Lindo C3

✖ Eating
12 Hostería Bar El Adobe A3
13 La Hacienda de Taxco B2
   La Susheria .... (see 7)
14 Restaurante Santa Fe B3

🍷 Drinking & Nightlife
15 Bar Berta B2

🛍 Shopping
16 EBA Elena Ballesteros B2
17 Nuestro México Artesanías C2
18 Patio de las Artesanías B2

museum is off an alley behind Templo de Santa Prisca. It contains a small but excellent collection of pre-Hispanic jewelry, art, pottery and sculpture from US silversmith William Spratling's private collection. The phallic cult pieces are a particular eye-opener. On the basement floor there are examples of Spratling's designs using pre-Hispanic motifs. The top floor hosts occasional temporary exhibits.

Museo de Arte Virreinal
MUSEUM

(📞762-622-55-01; Ruiz de Alarcón 12; M$50; ⏱10am-6pm Tue-Sun) This charming, rather ragtag religious-art museum is housed in a wonderful old house. It hosts a small but well-displayed collection of art, labeled in English and Spanish. The most interesting exhibit describes restoration work on Santa Prisca, during which some fabulous material (including tapestries, woodwork altarpieces and rich decorative fabrics) was discovered in the basement of the house. There is also an interesting display on the Manila Galleons, which pioneered trade between the Americas and the Far East.

The Museo de Arte Virreinal is often referred to as Casa Humboldt, even though the famous German explorer and naturalist Friedrich Heinrich Alexander von Humboldt slept here for only one night in 1803.

Casa Borda
NOTABLE BUILDING

(📞762-622-66-34; Centro Cultural Taxco, Plaza Borda; ⏱10am-6pm Tue-Sun) **FREE** Built by José de la Borda in 1759, the Casa Borda serves as a cultural center hosting experimental theater and exhibiting contemporary sculpture, painting and photography by Guerrero artists. The building, however, is the main attraction. Due to the unevenness of the terrain, the rear window looks out on a precipitous four-story drop, even though the entrance is on the ground floor.

🏃 Activities

Teleférico
CABLE CAR

(www.montetaxco.mx; one way/round trip adult M$65/95, child M$45/65; ⏱7:45am-7pm Sun-Thu, to 10pm Fri & Sat) From the north end of Taxco, a Swiss-made gondola ascends 173m to the Hotel Monte Taxco resort, affording fantastic views of Taxco and the surrounding mountains from the hotel pool – ask at reception for directions.

Combis marked 'Arcos/Zócalo' (M$6.50) stop downhill from the cable car entrance. Walk uphill from the south side of Los Arcos and turn right through the Escuela Nacional de Artes Plásticas gate.

The Hotel Monte bar-restaurant, El Taxqueño, has great views and is surprisingly more economical than the balcony restaurants around Taxco's zócalo.

🍴 Courses

Taxco's cozy mountain atmosphere and relative safety makes it a popular place for foreigners, especially Americans, to study Spanish and silverwork.

Centro de Enseñanza Para Extranjeros
LANGUAGE

(CEPE; 📞762-622-34-10; www.cepe.unam.mx; Ex-Hacienda El Chorrillo s/n; 6-week intensive course M$12,000) This branch of Mexico City's Universidad Nacional Autónoma de México offers intensive Spanish-language courses in the atmospheric Ex-Hacienda El Chorrillo.

Escuela Nacional de Artes Plásticas
ART

(📞762-622-36-90; www.fad.taxco.unam.mx; Del Chorrillo; courses from US$1200) This school offers arts workshops in painting, sculpture and jewelry.

🎉 Festivals & Events

Be sure to reserve your hotel in advance if your visit coincides with one of Taxco's annual festivals. Check exact dates of movable feasts with the tourist office (p195).

Feria de la Plata
FERIA

(⏱Nov/Dec) The weeklong national silver fair convenes in late November or early December. Craft competitions are held and some of Mexico's best silverwork is on display. Other festivities include rodeos, concerts, dances and burro (donkey) races.

Las Posadas
CULTURAL

(⏱Dec) From December 16 to 24, nightly candlelit processions fill Taxco's streets with door-to-door singing. Children are dressed up to resemble biblical characters. At the end of the night, they attack piñatas.

Día del Jumil
FOOD & DRINK

(⏱Nov) The Monday after the Día de Muertos (Day of the Dead; November 2), locals celebrate the jumil – the edible beetle said to represent the giving of life and energy to Taxco residents for another year. Many families camp on the Cerro de Huixteco (above town) over the preceding weekend, and townsfolk climb the hill to collect jumiles and share food and camaraderie.

Fiestas de Santa Prisca & San Sebastián
RELIGIOUS

(⏱Jan) Taxco's patron saints are honored on January 18 (Santa Prisca) and January 20 (San Sebastián), when locals parade by the Templo de Santa Prisca for an annual blessing, with their pets and farm animals in tow.

🛏 Sleeping

Taxco has a wealth of hotels, from large four- and five-star resorts to charming family-run posadas. During holiday weekends, when the hordes arrive from Mexico City, it's a good idea to reserve ahead.

Earplugs are also a good idea. Owing to the innumerable Volkswagen taxis that serve as transportation in this, the steepest of hill towns, street noise is a problem nearly everywhere.

Hostel Casa Taxco   HOSTEL $
(☑ 762-622-70-37; www.hostelcasataxco.com; Veracruz 5; dm/d M$250/550, tw/q with shared bathroom M$500/800; 🛜) You know Taxco is getting with the times when you lay eyes on this beautiful converted house with its artisanal tiles and furnishings – it's almost a poshtel. The dorms only have two or four beds, and there's the calm vibe of a colonial home. There's also an open-plan kitchen and a roof terrace with cathedral views.

Hotel Casa Grande   HOTEL $
(☑ 762-622-09-69; www.hotelcasagrandetaxco. com.mx; Plazuela de San Juan 7; with/without bathroom s M$330/220, tw M$515/330, tr M$600/420; 🛜) Its excellent location and hypnotic terrace views over the *plazuela* make Casa Grande an attractive budget option, but bring your earplugs as the music from the restaurant-bar La Concha Nostra goes late into the night on weekends. Rooms are small but have fresh cotton sheets.

★ Hotel Los Arcos   HISTORIC HOTEL $$
(☑ 762-622-18-36; www.hotellosarcosdetaxco. com; Juan Ruiz de Alarcón 4; d M$1080; 🛜) With plenty of plant-filled terraces, courtyards, rooftop space and chic cushioned areas to lounge about it, this beautiful old hotel could be a destination in itself. Rooms are large and rustic with comfortable beds and touches of Mexican decoration, and the location near the *zócalo* is convenient, though street-facing rooms have some traffic noise.

★ Hotel Mi Casita   INN $$
(☑ 762-627-17-77; www.hotelmicasita.com; Altos de Redondo 1; r incl breakfast from M$1020; 😊@🛜) This elegant colonial home run by a family of jewelry designers boasts 12 beautifully and individually decorated rooms just moments from the *zócalo,* with wraparound balconies giving views over the cathedral. The comfortable rooms feature original hand-painted bathroom tiles, three with Ta-

lavera bathtubs, some with private terraces and all with fans.

Hotel Emilia   HOTEL $$
(☑ 762-622-13-90; www.hotelemilia.com.mx; Ruiz de Alarcón 7; d/tr M$850/950; 🛜❄) All 14 rooms are spotlessly clean and have beautiful tiled bathrooms. Owned by a family of famous silver workers, this intimate hotel has colonial charm and includes free use of the pools at nearby Hotel Agua Escondida. Sadly, it's in an especially noisy location – ask for a room at the back, but don't miss the views from the rooftop terrace.

Hotel Santa Prisca   HOTEL $$
(☑ 762-622-00-80; www.facebook.com/santa prisca.hotel; Cenaobscuras 1; r M$585-770, ste/f M$860/1100; 🅿🛜) The 31-room Santa Prisca has traditional Mexican decor and a welcoming courtyard garden. It has a great location too, right in the thick of things. Rooms are smallish, but most have breezy private balconies. All have two beds, and newer, sunnier rooms cost a bit more. The parking lot is reached through a tunnel at the hotel's uphill end.

Pueblo Lindo   HOTEL $$$
(☑ 762-622-34-81; www.pueblolindo.com.mx; Hidalgo 30; r & ste incl breakfast M$1290-2990; 🅿@🛜❄) This luxurious hotel manages to balance style and substance, embracing a modern Mexican-inspired aesthetic with bright colors and wooden furnishings. There's a bar-lounge and excellent service. The rooftop pool has fantastic views over Taxco, as do many of the rooms.

Posada de la Misión   LUXURY HOTEL $$$
(☑ 800-008-29-20, 762-622-00-63; http://posada mision.com; Cerro de la Misión 32; r incl breakfast M$2145-5355; 🅿🛜❄) On a steep hill overlooking town, the rambling grounds of La Misión are a luxurious escape from Taxco's bustle. Rooms are large, bright and airy, and many have balconies with breathtaking views. There's also a gorgeous pool and Jacuzzi under a mosaic of Cuauhtémoc, and an excellent restaurant.

🍴 Eating

The *jumil* (similar to a stink beetle) is a delicacy in Taxco, notably during the Día del Jumil (p193) festivity – look for them in a *cucurucho* (paper cone) in the market. They are traditionally eaten live in a tortilla, but are more commonly seen crushed into a sauce.

For street food, try the excellent barbecued pork tacos in Plazuela de San Juan at night.

La Sushería
JAPANESE $

(www.facebook.com/lasusheriataxco; Ruiz de Alarcón 7; sushi M$70-105; ⊙1-11pm; 🕾🍽) This sushi restaurant in the lobby of Hotel Emilia reflects modern Taxco with its designer furniture but casual vibe. The sushi is fresh and finished nicely with the green-tea ice cream – heaven in a cocktail glass. If you're here on a date or a business lunch, the slick booths are the perfect place to impress.

Restaurante Santa Fe
MEXICAN $

(🖉762-622-11-70; Hidalgo 2; mains M$70-115; ⊙8am-8pm) In business for over 50 years, Santa Fe is a favorite among locals for its fairly priced traditional fare such as *conejo en chile ajo* (rabbit in garlic and chili). The walls are plastered with patron photos and some excellent B&W shots of ye olde Taxco. A three-course *menú de hoy* is available at lunch, and sometimes later, for M$87.

★ El Sotavento
MEXICAN $$

(🖉762-627-12-17; Alarcón 4; mains M$90-185; ⊙9am-11pm Thu-Tue) It's easy to be wooed by the cobblestone arches in the warm lighting of Sotavento's tranquil courtyard. Classic Mexican dishes such as enchiladas and chicken *mole* are some of the best in town and there are cocktails and some surprisingly good European options too. The Sunday breakfast buffet (M$130) is a wonderful indulgence.

La Hacienda de Taxco
MEXICAN $$

(🖉762-622-11-66; Plaza Borda 4; mains M$80-175; ⊙7:30am-10:30pm; 🍽♿) Offering an extensive menu of traditional Mexican dishes (including house-made jam in the morning and a 20-ingredient, house-made *mole* in the afternoon), La Hacienda also has considerate touches, like the option of egg-white-only breakfasts, vegetarian dishes and smaller portions for kids.

Hostería Bar El Adobe
MEXICAN $$

(🖉762-622-14-16; Plazuela de San Juan 13; mains M$65-225; ⊙8am-11pm) This place doesn't have the *zócalo* views, but the interior is charmingly decorated with B&W photos of everyone from Pancho Villa to Elvis, and the cute balcony tables are more private. Good, simple dishes include pan-fried chicken or fish in salsa with rice and veg. There's *pozole* (M$65) on Thursday, live *trova* music on Saturday night and a buffet (M$125) on Sunday.

🍸 Drinking & Nightlife

Bar Berta
CANTINA

(🖉762-107-55-90; www.facebook.com/barbertataxco; Cuauhtémoc; ⊙noon-10pm Wed-Mon) By rights Berta should be flooded with lost-looking tourists, but instead there's a clientele of local roughs knocking back stiff drinks and watching *fútbol*. There's a tiny upstairs terrace for people-watching over the *zócalo*. Try a Berta (tequila, honey, lime and mineral water), the house specialty.

🛍 Shopping

Nuestro México Artesanías
ARTS & CRAFTS

(🖉762-622-09-76; Veracruz 8; ⊙10am-6pm) Treasure hunters will love fossicking in this storehouse of handicrafts from across Mexico. Most of the favorite souvenirs are here – coconut masks, papier-mâché devils, flying cherubs, fish wind chimes and, yes, silver. The prices are marked and close to what you pay on the street outside.

Patio de las Artesanías
JEWELRY

(Plaza Borda; ⊙9am-6pm Tue-Sun) If you are looking for silver, there are several shops to wander through in the Patio de las Artesanías building.

EBA Elena Ballesteros
JEWELRY

(🖉762-622-37-67; www.ebaplata.com; Muñoz 4; ⊙9:30am-7pm Mon-Sat, 10am-6pm Sun) EBA Elena Ballesteros produces creative, well-crafted silver designs in Taxco.

ℹ Information

Several banks around the main plazas and bus stations have ATMs.

Hospital General (🖉762-622-93-00; Los Jales 120)

Tourist Office (cnr Juárez & Plazuela del Exconvento; ⊙9am-8pm) Next to the post office, it offers maps and good information. Note that the tourism kiosk in the main plaza mostly exists to hand out brochures and push tours.

ℹ Getting There & Away

The shared **Futura/Estrella Blanca terminal** on Avenida de los Plateros offers luggage storage. The **Primera Plus/Estrella de Oro (EDO) terminal** is at the south end of town. The Futura bus to Mexico City runs mostly on the hour.

For more frequent bus services to the coast, take a shared taxi (M$30) from in front of the bus station to the nearby town of Iguala, about 30 minutes away.

Buses serve Acapulco (M$300, four to five hours, seven daily) from the EDO and Futura

WORTH A TRIP

CACAHUAMILPA CAVERNS

One of central Mexico's most stunning natural sights, the **Cacahuamilpa Caverns** (Grutas de Cacahuamilpa; ☎721-104-01-55; http://cacahuamilpa.conanp.gob.mx; adult/child incl guide M$80/70; ⊙10am-5pm; P) are a must-see for anyone visiting Taxco or Cuernavaca. The scale of the caves is hard to imagine, with vast chambers up to 82m high leading 1.2km beneath the mountainside, inside of which are mind-blowing stalactites and stalagmites.

Unfortunately, individual access to the (perfectly safe) pathway through the caves is not allowed. Instead, visitors are allocated free guides who lead large group tours (departures each hour on the hour), with constant stops to point out shapes (Santa Claus, a kneeling child, a gorilla) in the rock. At the end of the hour-long tour, you can wander back to the entrance – with the lights now off – at your own pace. Most guides do not speak English.

From the cave exit it's possible to follow a steep path for 15 minutes to the fast-flowing Río Dos Bocas. There are spectacular views year-round and tranquil pools for swimming during the dry season. Bring bug spray.

Weekends are often very crowded, with long lines and large group tours – making midweek a more pleasant time for a visit. There are restaurants, snacks and souvenir stores near the entrance. Between the entrance and the caves, it's possible to take a short zipline (M$70) across the treetops, or you can just walk the 150m around.

To reach the caves, take an Estrella Roja 'Grutas' bus from the Futura bus terminal in Taxco (M$40, 40 minutes, every 40 minutes) or taxi (M$180). Buses deposit you at the crossroad where the road splits off to Cuernavaca. From there, walk 350m downhill to the park's visitor center. Return buses leave from the same crossroad (every 40 minutes, last bus 6:30pm). Pullman de Morelos have direct services from Cuernavaca Centro (M$70, two hours, every two hours until 7:43pm) to the caves; the last return bus is at 6pm.

terminals; Cuernavaca from EDO (M$100, two hours, five daily) and Futura (M$90, 1½ hours, 12 daily); and Mexico City's Terminal Sur (M$209, 2½ hours) from EDO (four to six daily) and Futura (eight daily).

ℹ Getting Around

While one of the joys of Taxco is getting lost while aimlessly wandering the pretty streets, it's actually a very easy place to find your way around. The twin belfries of Santa Prisca make the best landmark, situated as they are on the zócalo, Plaza Borda.

Nearly all of the town's streets are one way, with the main road, Avenida de los Plateros, being the only major two-way street. This is where both bus stations are located and is the road for entering and leaving the town. The basic colectivo route is a counterclockwise loop going north on Avenida de los Plateros and south through the center of town.

Apart from walking, combis and taxis are the best way to navigate Taxco's steep and narrow cobbled streets.

Combis (white Volkswagen minibuses; M$6.50) are frequent and operate from 7am to 8pm. 'Zócalo' combis depart from Plaza Borda, travel down Cuauhtémoc to Plazuela de San Juan then head down the hill on Hidalgo. They turn right at Morelos, left at Avenida de

los Plateros and go north, passing the Futura bus station, until La Garita, where they turn left and return to the zócalo. 'Arcos/Zócalo' combis follow the same route except that they continue past La Garita to Los Arcos, where they do a U-turn and head back to La Garita. Combis marked 'PM' (for Pedro Martín) go to the south end of town from Plaza Borda, past the Estrella de Oro bus station. Taxis cost M$25 to M$35 for trips around town.

WEST OF MEXICO CITY

The area to the west of Mexico City is dominated by the large industrial, transportation-hub city of Toluca, the capital of the state of Mexico. While pleasant, Toluca has little to recommend it to travelers and most bypass it en route to the area's two wonderful small-town, colonial gems. Malinalco is a sleepy and remote village with some fascinating pre-Hispanic ruins perched above it, and Valle de Bravo, a cosmopolitan getaway, is located on the shores of a large, artificial reservoir, a dramatic two-hour drive west of Toluca. The countryside surrounding Toluca itself is scenic, with pine forests, rivers and a huge extinct volcano, Nevado de Toluca.

Toluca

☑722 / POP 490,000 / ELEV 2660M

Like many colonial Mexican cities, Toluca's development has created a ring of urban sprawl around what remains a very picturesque old town. The traffic problems alone can be enough to dampen the city's appeal, but those who make time to visit will find Toluca a pleasant, if bustling, small city. It's an enjoyable place to spend a day exploring attractive plazas, lively shopping arcades, art galleries and museums.

The vast Plaza de los Mártires, with the cathedral and Palacio de Gobierno, marks the town center. Most of the action, however, is concentrated a block south in the pedestrian precinct ringed by *arcos* (archways). Shady Parque Alameda is three blocks west along Hidalgo.

◉ Sights

The 19th-century **Portal Madero**, running 250m along Avenida Hidalgo, is lively, as is the commercial arcade along the pedestrian street to the east, which attracts mariachis after 9pm. A block north, the large, open expanse of **Plaza de los Mártires** is surrounded by fine old government buildings; the 19th-century **cathedral** and the 18th-century **Templo de la Santa Veracruz** are on its south side. On Plaza Garibay's north side is the 18th-century **Templo del Carmen**.

★ **Cosmovitral Jardín Botánico**   GARDENS
(Cosmic Stained-Glass Window Botanical Garden; ☑722-214-67-85; Juárez s/n, cnr Lerdo de Tejada; adult/child M$10/5; ⊙9am-6pm Tue-Sun) At the northeast end of Plaza Juárez the stunning and unique Cosmovitral Jardín Botánico was built in 1909 as a market. The building now houses 3500 sq meters of lovely gardens, lit through 48 stained-glass panels designed by the Tolucan artist Leopoldo Flores with the help of 60 artisans. The 500,000 pieces of glass come in 28 different colors from seven countries, including Japan, Belgium and Italy.

★ **Museo de Culturas Populares**   MUSEUM
(Museum of Popular Culture; ☑722-274-54-58; Blvd Reyes Heroles 302; adult/child M$10/5; ⊙10am-6pm Mon-Sat) This museum has a wonderfully varied collection of Mexico's traditional arts and crafts, with some astounding 'trees of life' from Metepec, whimsical Day of the Dead figures and a fine display of *charro* (cowboy) gear. There are also mosaics, traditional rugs, a loft and a gift shop.

Museo de Arte Moderno   MUSEUM
(Museum of Modern Art; ☑722-274-12-66; Blvd Reyes Heroles 302; M$10, Sun free; ⊙9am-6pm Mon-Sat, to 3pm Sun) The Museo de Arte Moderno traces the development of Mexican art from the late-19th-century Academia de San Carlos to the Nueva Plástica and includes paintings by Tamayo, Orozco and many others. There's an impressive spherical mural of people fighting against slavery, which makes up part of the building itself, as well as exhibits of challenging pieces of contemporary art.

Museo de Antropología e História   MUSEUM
(Museum of Anthropology & History; ☑722-274-12-00; Blvd Reyes Heroles 302; M$10, Sun free; ⊙9am-6pm Mon-Sat, to 3pm Sun) This standout museum presents exhibits on the state's history from prehistoric times to the 20th century, with a good collection of pre-Hispanic artifacts. It also traces pre-Hispanic cultural influences up to the modern day in tools, clothing, textiles and religion. Most labeling is in Spanish only.

Museo Luis Nishizawa   MUSEUM
(☑722-215-74-65; Bravo Norte 305; adult/child M$10/5; ⊙10am-6pm Tue-Sat, to 3pm Sun) This musuem exhibits the work of modern Mexican-Japanese muralist and landscape artist Luis Nishizawa (1918–2014). Nishizawa was born in the state of Mexico and trained in both Mexican and Japanese artistic styles, which is reflected in murals constructed from ceramics. He is known for his mixed-media sculptures and intensely colorful ink paintings of nature and people. His works are held in collections across the world, including MOMAK in Kyoto.

Centro Cultural Mexiquense   MUSEUM
(State of Mexico Cultural Center; ☑722-274-12-22; Blvd Reyes Heroles 302; ⊙10am-6pm Mon-Sat, to 3pm Sun) FREE This cultural center, 4.5km west of the city center, houses three good museums (which all keep the same hours). It's no must-see, but still a worthwhile free diversion for visitors interested in local arts and crafts, local archaeology and modern art.

From downtown you can take a cab (M$40), though it's easy to take one of the plentiful *colectivos* from outside Mercado Juárez – just look for 'Centro Cultural' on its destination board. The circuitous ride takes 20 minutes. Get off by the large grass roundabout near the Monterrey University Toluca campus, cross to the opposite side and the museum complex is through the gate and down the road.

Museo de Bellas Artes de Toluca MUSEUM
(Museum of Fine Art; ☑722-215-53-29; Degollado
102; adult/child M$10/5; ⊙10am-6pm Tue-Sun)
The ex-convent buildings adjacent to the
Templo del Carmen, on the north side of
Plaza Garibay, house Toluca's Museo de Bel-
las Artes, which exhibits paintings from the
colonial period to the early 20th century.

☞ Tours

Tranvía TRAM
(☑722-330-50-52; www.turismotolucalabella.com;
Independencia, cnr Bravo; adult/child M$60/40;
⊙departs hourly 11am-5pm Fri-Sun) This motorized trolley visits two dozen sites in the
city in an hour with a Spanish-only guide.
Most of the year, there are also *leyendas*
night tours (adult/child M$90/70, 6:30pm
to 11pm Friday to Sunday, 1½ hours, every
1½ hours), visiting 12 sites accompanied by
a guide recounting 'legends' associated with
each building.

🛏 Sleeping

★ Hotel Colonial INN $
(☑722-215-97-00; Hidalgo Oriente 103; s/d/tr
M$400/500/650; P🅿🛜) The rooms overlook-
ing the busy main road are the best, but also
the loudest, at this well-run and excellent-val-
ue hotel. The impressive lobby and friendly
staff are other good reasons to stay here.
Rates include free parking nearby in a lot on
Juárez. Popular with groups, so call ahead.

Hotel Maya HOTEL $
(☑722-214-48-00; Hidalgo 413; r with/without
bathroom M$400/300; 🛜) The extremely cen-
tral location of this one-grandma-run posada makes a handy, if very no-frills, base for
a quick visit of Toluca's sights. If street noise
bothers you, choose a darker interior room.

Hotel Don Simón BUSINESS HOTEL $$
(☑722-213-26-96; www.hoteldonsimon.com; Matamoros 202; d/tr M$1200/1400; P@🛜) The
rooms at Don Simón are immaculately clean
and bright, if a little heavy on the brown
furnishings of yesteryear, which continue
into the attached restaurant. It's a balanced
all-rounder in central Toluca – the staff are
friendly, the street is quiet and it's just a
short walk to Cosmovitral.

Fiesta Inn Toluca Centro BUSINESS HOTEL $$$
(☑722-167-89-00; www.fiestainn.com; Allende Sur
124; r/ste M$1685/2570; P@🛜) This modern,
sleek, 85-room Fiesta Inn has airy, comfortable rooms, a small gym and a cafe-bar-

restaurant in the lobby. There's a second
Fiesta Inn near the airport.

🍴 Eating

Toluqueños take snacking and sweets very
seriously and you can join them in the arcades around Plaza Fray Andrés de Castro.
Other stalls sell candied fruit and *jamoncillos* (bars of pumpkin-seed paste), and *mo-
stachones* (sweets made of burned milk).
Most eateries in the center are open from
around 8am to 9pm.

★ La Gloria Chocolatería
y Pan 1876 CAFE $
(Quintana Roo; snacks M$10-35; ⊙9am-11:30pm)
You'll probably be the only foreigner at
this wonderful, friendly, family-run cafe.
It serves a tempting menu of local cuisine,
from *tacos al pastor* (spicy pork tacos) to
delicious *sermones* (sandwiches) stuffed
with oven-baked pork or shredded chicken
bathed in *mole poblano*.

La Vaquita Negra
del Portal SANDWICHES $
(☑722-167-13-77; Portal Reforma 124B; sandwiches
M$24-34; ⊙8:30am-8pm) On the northwest
corner of the arcades, smoked hams and
huge green-and-red sausages hanging over
the deli counter signal first-rate *tortas*. Try
a messy *toluqueña* (red pork chorizo sausage, white cheese, cream, tomato and *salsa verde*), and don't forget to garnish your
heaped sandwich with spicy pickled peppers
and onions.

Hostería Las Ramblas MEXICAN $$
(☑722-215-54-88; Calle 20 de Noviembre 107D;
mains M$110-180; ⊙9am-8pm Mon-Sat, to 7pm
Sun; 🥗) On a pedestrian mall, this atmospheric restaurant feels like a throwback to
the 1950s, with white tablecloths and retro
decor. Attentive waiters serve full breakfasts,
including excellent vegetarian options such
as the *omelette campesino* – panela cheese,
rajas (*poblano* chili) and zucchini – and a
variety of lunch and dinner mains such as
mole verde and *conejo al ajillo* (liberally
garlicked rabbit).

🛍 Shopping

★ Casart ARTS & CRAFTS
(Casa de Artesanía; ☑722-217-52-63; Aldama 102;
⊙10:30am-7pm Mon-Sat, to 5pm Sun) This downtown location of Casart – the state organization promoting local crafts – is fantastic both
for its beautiful home, set around a court-

BUSES FROM TOLUCA

DESTINATION	FARE (M$)	DURATION (HR)	FREQUENCY (DAILY)
Cuernavaca	71-235	2	24
Mexico City (Poniente)	50-90	1	55
Morelia	258-332	2	16
Taxco	189	3	7
Valle de Bravo	77	2¼	10
Zihuatanejo	643	9	1

yard, and its wonderful selection of quality arts and crafts. Prices are fixed and therefore higher than you might be able to get haggling in markets for an inferior product (for the best prices, go directly to the source).

ⓘ Information

There are banks with ATMs near Portal Madero.

City Tourist Office (☑722-384-11-00, ext 104; www.toluca.gob.mx/turismo; Plaza Fray Andrés de Castro, Edificio B, Local 6, Planta Baja; ☉9am-6pm Mon-Fri, 10am-7pm Sat & Sun) English-speaking staff provide free city maps and can help book accommodations.

State Tourist Office (☑722-212-59-98; www.edomexico.gob.mx; Urawa 100, cnr Paseo Tollocan; ☉9am-6pm Mon-Fri) Inconveniently located 2km southeast of the center, but with English-speaking staff and good maps.

Tourist Information Kiosk (www.turismotolucalabella.com; Palacio Municipal; ☉9am-6pm Mon-Fri, 10am-7pm Sat & Sun) Helpful kiosk with free city map.

ⓘ Getting There & Away

AIR

The modern, efficient and low-stress **Aeropuerto Internacional de Toluca** (TOL; ☑722-279-28-00; Blvd Miguel Alemán Valdez) is an excellent alternative to Mexico City's massive and intimidating airport. Conveniently located off Hwy 15, about 10km from downtown, the airport is adjacent to the industrial zone and a group of business-friendly chain hotels.

Toluca is the hub for budget airline Interjet (www.interjet.com.mx), which offers flights to Las Vegas and all over Mexico.

Spirit Airlines (☑800-772-7117; www.spirit.com) and **Volaris** (☑800-122-80-00; www.volaris.com.mx) also offer international service, flying travelers between Toluca and several cities in the US, including Los Angeles, Chicago, Las Vegas, Houston, San Francisco, Seattle, Newark, Miami, New York and Atlanta.

Europcar, Dollar and Alamo all have rental-car offices at the airport.

BUS

There are frequent Caminante shuttle buses from Toluca's airport to Mexico City's Observatorio bus terminal (M$202) daily to about 7pm or 8pm; and to the capital's Aeropuerto Internacional (M$200, five daily). Both take an hour or two, depending on traffic. Interjet has shuttles to Cuernavaca (M$255). An authorized taxi from the airport to downtown Toluca costs about M$35 and takes 20 to 30 minutes.

Toluca's **bus station** (Terminal Toluca; www.terminaltoluca.com.mx; Berriozábal 101) is 2km southeast of the center. Ticket offices for many destinations are on the platforms or at the gate entrances, and it's fair to say it can be a confusing place. Look for monitors at gate entrances that reveal which gates sell which destination.

ⓘ Getting Around

The main road from Mexico City becomes Paseo Tollocan on Toluca's eastern edge, before bearing southwest and becoming a ring road around the city center's southern edge. Toluca's bus station and the huge Mercado Juárez are 2km southeast of the center, off Paseo Tollocan.

Large 'Centro' buses depart from outside Toluca's bus station to the town center (M$10, 20 minutes) along Lerdo de Tejada and by Plaza de los Mártires. From Juárez in the center, 'Terminal' buses go to the bus station. Taxis from the bus station to the city center cost around M$45.

Nevado de Toluca

Among the highest peaks in the region, the long-extinct volcano Nevado de Toluca (also known as Xinantécatl) is Mexico's fourth-tallest peak. Nevado has two summits on the crater rim, each worth hiking for magnificent views across two snow-fringed crater lakes – Sol and Luna. The lower summit, Pico del Aguila (4620m), is closer to the parking area and is the more common day hike. The main or highest summit is called Pico del Fraile (4704m) and requires an additional three to four hours of hike time.

In 2013 the Mexican government redesignated the national park a *zona protegida* (protected area), legalising and legitimising the unregulated mining activity that had been going on there. Most people still continue to call it a national park.

🏃 Activities

Mario Andrade CLIMBING
(📞55-1826-2146; mountainup@hotmail.com; transportation, one meal & park entrance US$200) English-speaking Mario Andrade leads one-day private climbs up Nevado de Toluca and also guides climbers on Izta ascents.

🛌 Sleeping

Posada Familiar HOSTEL $
(📞722-214-37-86; campsite/dm M$85/150) Just beyond the Parque de los Venados gate, Posada Familiar, the only accommodations in the park, offers basic lodging at a heavily used refuge with shared hot showers, a kitchen (without utensils) and a common area with a fireplace. Bring extra blankets. It is best to reserve two weeks ahead.

❶ Getting There & Away

The best way to get to Nevado de Toluca is with a private guide or tour.

From Toluca, taxis will take you to the trailhead for upwards of M$250, or there and back (including time for a look around) for a negotiable M$600. Be sure to hire a newer taxi (the road up is very rough and dusty) from an official taxi stand with the driver's photo displayed inside the vehicle. Most international car-rental companies also have offices in Toluca.

From the park entrance a road winds 3.5km up to the main gate (Carretera Temascaltpec Km 18, San Antonio Acahualco; admission per vehicle/camioneta M$20/40; ⏰10am-5pm, last entry 3pm). From there it's a 17km drive along an unsurfaced road up to the crater. Dress warmly – it gets chilly up top.

Valle de Bravo

📞726 / POP 28,000 / ELEV 1800M
With one of the loveliest colonial centers in central Mexico, the *pueblo mágico* of Valle de Bravo is an utter charmer and a wonderful spot for an escape from Mexico City. The setting here is reminiscent of the northern Italian lakes, with thickly wooded, mist-clad hills and red terracotta roofing used throughout the town. Valle, as it's known, is famous for being the weekend retreat of choice for the capital's well-connected upper classes.

There are stunning views at the shore of Lago Avándaro – an artificial lake, the result of the construction of a hydroelectric station – but the beguiling and largely intact colonial center is arguably the real draw here. Boating on the lake is very popular as well, as are hiking and camping in the hills around the town. Valle is set up well for visitors while still feeling authentic.

🏃 Activities

Boating on the pleasant lake is the main activity here and you will be approached by plenty of operators anywhere near the water. *Lanchas* (small boats) with a captain run about M$400/700 for 30 minutes/one hour. Many include visits to a waterfall. Make sure the boat includes *chalecos salva vidas* (life jackets) – child-sized, if required.

Hiking opportunities to haciendas, butterfly farms, waterfalls and even a Buddhist temple are possible through tour operators or self-guided (the most popular trail is 'La Pena' for lofty lake views); ask at the tourist information stand on the *zócalo*. Paragliding and parasailing are also popular.

✨ Festivals & Events

Festival de las Almas CULTURAL
(⏰Oct/Nov) In late October or early November, the weeklong Festival de las Almas, an international arts and culture extravaganza, brings in music and dance troupes from all over Europe and Latin America.

🛌 Sleeping

For a small town, this popular weekend escape from Mexico City has a good selection of budget posadas and midrange hotels. The most affordable, shabby options are within two blocks of the bus station. Camping and sleeping in huts is also possible; the tourist information stand on the *zócalo* has information.

★ Hotel San José HOTEL $
(📞726-262-09-72; Callejón San José 103; d/tw/tr M$600/700/1350; 🛜) This converted ranch-style hotel is just a block from the *zócalo,* but hidden down an alley away from the noise, with a small terrace garden where you can admire the view of the hills. Huge rooms have extremely comfortable beds, and light-filled bathrooms with luxury trimmings – heavy shower curtains and plush bath rugs. Most have kitchenettes. The biggest steal in Valle.

★**Hotel San Sebastian** BOUTIQUE HOTEL **$$**
(☑726-688-50-15; hotel_sansebastian@outlook.
es; San Sebastian 101, cnr Callejon Machinhue-
pa; d/tr/penthouse M$1000/1200/4000; ❋🛜)
Some of the best lake and terracotta-tile
views are from the balcony of the small
rooms at this fresh hotel. Bathrooms are
modern and spotless and beds are very
comfortable, making for a top romantic
getaway, even for solo travelers. There is
also room service from the adjacent res-
taurant. A penthouse sleeps six and has a
kitchen and terrace.

Hotel Casanueva BOUTIQUE HOTEL **$$**
(☑726-262-17-66; Villagrán 100; d/tw/ste
M$1000/1300/1700; 🛜) Set on the west side
of the *zócalo*, the Casanueva has individually designed rooms decorated with tasteful arts and crafts. One of the most stylish
options downtown, the hotel's suite, which
sleeps four, is especially lovely. Some rooms
have private balconies over the square.

El Santuario RESORT **$$$**
(☑726-262-91-00; www.elsantuario.com; Car-
retera Colorines, San Gaspar; r from M$5570;
🅿❋🛜♨) Twenty minutes northwest out-
side town, this gorgeous hillside hotel has
an infinity pool, fountains, an in-house spa
and rooms with magnificent lake views
and personal mini-pools. There's also a golf
course, horse stables and a marina with sail-
boat rentals.

✕ Eating & Drinking

There are scores of restaurants and cafes
along the wharf and around the *zócalo*,
many of which only open Friday through
Sunday. If there ever was a time to try *es-
quite* (lime and chili-flavored corn in a cup)
from street stalls, this is it. Villagrán, on the
west side of the *zócalo*, has very clean food
stands. The *trucha* (trout) on most menus
is farmed in the mountains, not from
the lake.

La Michoacana MEXICAN **$$**
(Calle de la Cruz 100; mains M$100-205; ⊘8am-
11pm; 🛜) A large restaurant with colorful
indoor spaces and a great terrace with excellent wide-angled views of the town and
lake. Mexican favorites include chicken
mole, *salmón en salsa de almendra* (al-
mond-sauce salmon) and lots of snacks and
drinks to take it slowly. Waiters are eager to
practice their English.

Soleado FUSION **$$**
(☑726-262-58-31; Pagaza 314; mains M$135-265;
⊘1-10pm Sat-Thu, to midnight Fri, closed Mon;
🛜🍴♿) Soleado calls itself *cocina del mun-
do* and indeed there is a dish and a dessert
from many a 'kitchen of the world' on offer.
Admittedly, most dishes, from Indian curry
to Italian veg lasagna, have a (tasty) Mexican
twist. The low-lit restaurant with lofty views
is a great place for groups, with dishes to
please all tastes.

There are breakfasts with organic eggs,
and a menu for kids.

Restaurante Paraíso SEAFOOD **$$**
(☑726-262-47-31; Fray Gregorio Jiménez de la
Cuenca s/n; mains M$75-160, set lunch M$140;
⊘8am-10pm) Restaurante Paraíso has fantastic lake views and a sprawling menu of
seafood specialties, plus excellent and im-
aginatively prepared local trout. Come early
and watch the sunset from the rooftop patio.
A set lunch with fish options is good value.

LocaL CAFE
(☑726-262-51-74; www.facebook.com/local.
valledebravo; Calle 5 de Mayo 107; ⊘9am-6:30pm;
🛜🍴) LocaL tries to be a bit of everything –
cafe, co-working space with free printing
deals, a library with design and architecture
books, roof terrace with nursery, and a small
bakery with vegan items – but its most solid
triumph is being the hippest place in Valle
de Bravo.

❶ Information

There's a tourist-info kiosk on the wharf and
essential services, including ATMs and internet cafes, are found around the main plaza, a
10-minute walk uphill from the waterfront.

Tourist Information Stand (Bocanegra, cnr Independencia; ⊘9am-5pm) At this stand on the
zócalo, staff speak a bit of English, give directions and have free maps and tour brochures.

❶ Getting There & Away

Considering the hordes of tourists who descend
on Valle each weekend, transportation options
are relatively few. Most visitors are affluent
Mexicans, who come by car.

Zina-bus (www.autobuseszinacantepec.com.
mx) runs 1st-class *directo* buses from early
morning to late afternoon between Mexico City's
Terminal Poniente and Valle de Bravo's small bus
terminal on Calle 16 de Septiembre (M$238, 2¼
hours, every one to two hours). For a scenic ride
ask for the southern, 'Los Saucos' route, which
travels along Hwy 134 and through a national
park. If driving, that's the route to take as well.

There is no direct bus between Malinalco and Valle de Bravo. You have to travel via Toluca (M$77, frequent) on a 2nd-class bus or via Mexico City.

Malinalco

☑714 / POP 7000 / ELEV 1740M

Set in a valley of dramatic cliffs and ancient ruins, this *pueblo mágico* continues its transformation into the next Tepoztlán. Weekends see crowds, but still far fewer than those that descend on more easily accessible weekend escapes. The drive to Malinalco is one of the most enjoyable to be had in the area, with dramatic scenery lining the road south of Toluca.

There are a clutch of 'hippie' stores, a handful of international restaurants and a surprising number of boutique hotels. The town is far from fully developed, though, and it's almost unnervingly quiet midweek, when it can still be a challenge to find a decent place to eat outside of the *zócalo*.

The village itself has a charming colonial core set around a well-preserved convent and two central plazas, which sit side by side.

◉ Sights

Aztec Temples ARCHAEOLOGICAL SITE
(Zona Arqueológica Cuauhtinchan; ☑722-215-85-69; Av Progreso s/n; M$55; ☺10am-5pm Tue-Sun, last entry 4pm) An invigorating 358-step hike up the mountainside above Malinalco takes you to one of the country's few reasonably well-preserved temples (even surviving recent earthquakes), from where there are stunning views of the valley and beyond. The fascinating site includes *El paraíso de los guerreros* (a mural that once covered an entire wall), depicting fallen warriors becoming deities and living in paradise. From the main square follow signs to the *zona arqueológica*, taking you up the hillside on a well-maintained, signed footpath.

The Aztecs conquered the region in 1476 and were busy building a ritual center here when they were conquered by the Spanish. **El Cuauhcalli** (Temple of the Eagle and Jaguar Knight, where sons of Aztec nobles were initiated into warrior orders) survived because it was hewn from the mountainside itself. The entrance is carved in the form of a fanged serpent.

Temple IV, located on the far side of the site, continues to baffle archaeologists.

As the room is positioned to allow the first rays of sunlight to hit it at dawn, there has been speculation that this place was part of a Mexican sun cult, a solar calendar or a meeting place for nobles – or some combination of these.

Situated near the site entrance, the **Museo Universitario Dr Luis Mario Schneider** explores the region's history and archaeology in a beautiful, modern museum space.

Augustinian Convent CHURCH
(Convento Agustino de Malinalco; Morelos s/n, cnr Hidalgo; ☺9am-6pm) A well-restored 16th-century convent, fronted by a tranquil tree-lined yard, faces the central plaza. Impressive frescoes fashioned from herb- and flower-based paint adorn its cloister.

☞ Tours

Tour Gastronómico Prehispánico FOOD & DRINK
(☑cell55-55091411; https://gastrotourprehispanico malinalco.weebly.com; tours per person M$1200) This pre-Hispanic food tour includes a visit to the market, a cooking class using traditional utensils and methods, and a three-course meal. Discounts for groups of over five people.

🛏 Sleeping & Eating

This small town has an inordinate number of hotel rooms, but reservations remain a good idea. Because Malinalco is geared toward weekend visitors, you'll have no trouble finding a room Sunday to Thursday night (often with a negotiable discount), though some of the nicer hotels aren't open for walk-ins (or at all) midweek.

Perhaps surprisingly for such a small town, Malinalco has a few very good restaurants. Unfortunately for those visiting midweek, though, most of the better options (on Avenida Hidalgo and around the *zócalo*) are only open Thursday through Sunday. There is a small but well-stocked supermarket on the north east corner of the *zócalo*.

El Asoleadero HOTEL $
(☑714-147-01-84; Aldama, cnr Comercio; s/d M$600/700, r with kitchen M$800; P🅟🛜❄) Just uphill from Malinalco's main drag, El Asoleadero offers spacious, modern and airy rooms with stunning views of the *pueblito* and surrounding cliffs. You can enjoy the million-peso vista from the courtyard's small pool with a cold beer from the lobby. Discounts of M$100 Sunday to Thursday.

★ **Casa Navacoyan** BOUTIQUE HOTEL $$$
(☎714-147-04-11; www.casanavacoyan.mx; Prolangación Calle Pirul 62; s/d/ste incl breakfast from M$2500/2700/3200; ⓟ🛜❄) This beautiful hotel on the outskirts of town has just six rooms, each decorated in a sort of upscale, home-style aesthetic, like staying at your wealthy aunt's house in the country. The immaculately groomed yard is the real attraction, with palm trees, a gorgeous heated pool and views of Malinalco's famed hills and cliffs.

Casa Limón BOUTIQUE HOTEL $$$
(☎714-147-02-56; www.casalimon.com; Río Lerma 103; r/ste incl breakfast from M$2700/3100; ⓟ🛜❄) Surrounded by a stark high-desert landscape, this ultra-trendy hotel with bright fan-cooled rooms, a slate pool and intriguing artworks has a seductive indoor-outdoor bar and an elegant tree house–like restaurant (mains M$300). Pricey mains are classic international, from coq au vin to almond trout, and the wine list is superb. Limón can be fiendishly difficult to find in the poorly signposted backstreets.

★ **Los Placeres** INTERNATIONAL $$
(☎714-147-08-55; https://losplaceresmalinalco.com; Plaza Principal s/n; mains M$85-190; ⊙2-7pm Thu, to 10pm Fri, 10am-10pm Sat & Sun; 🛜🅿) This artsy garden restaurant on Malinalco's zócalo serves international fare (Nicoise salad or chicken curry) alongside creative takes on traditional Mexican dishes, such as omelettes with poblano sauce, trout with ancho chilies or fondue al tequila. There are elaborate murals, tile-mosaic tabletops and the likes of Robert Johnson on the sound system.

Mari Mali MEXICAN $$
(☎714-147-14-86; Av Juárez 4; menú del día M$80, mains M$90-165; ⊙10am-6pm Sun-Thu, to 9pm Fri & Sat; 🛜) The only casual, classy and clean place serving set-menu breakfasts and lunches midweek. Mexican classics such as enchiladas and pozole make it on the menu, as does mains of trucha (trout) complete with salad and rice. The fruit sellers outside are a colorful bonus.

El Puente de Má-Li INTERNATIONAL $$
(☎714-147-01-29; Hidalgo 22; mains M$140-250; ⊙1-6pm Sun-Tue & Thu, to 11pm Fri & Sat) After the tiny bridge as you leave the zócalo for the ruins, this atmospheric restaurant is set around a colonial dining room and a great back garden where you can try a selection of antojitos, pastas, soups and steaks.

ℹ Information

Tourist Information Kiosk (☎714-147-21-08; www.malinalco.net; ⊙9am-4pm Mon-Fri, to 5pm Sat & Sun) Tour brochures, a free map and help with accommodations. It's at the north end of the zócalo.

ℹ Getting There & Away

Águila (☎800-224-84-52; www.autobuses aguila.com) runs two direct buses each afternoon (4:20pm and 6:20pm), with an additional service Saturday and Sunday (8:30am) from Mexico City's Terminal Poniente (M$110, 2½ hours). If you can't wait, Águila also runs every 20 minutes between Terminal Poniente and Chalma (M$115, 2½ hours), from where you can take a taxi (M$15, 15 minutes) to nearby Malinalco.

The direct Águila bus from Malinalco to Terminal Poniente only runs at 3:50am and 5:15am Monday to Friday and only at 5pm Saturday and Sunday, from outside the Santander bank on Hidalgo. To avoid the red-eye hours, take a taxi (M$15, 15 minutes) back to Chalma for Águila buses to Mexico City's Terminal Poniente (M$115, 2½ hours, every 20 minutes). Águila buses do not have toilets on board.

From gate 6 of Toluca's bus station, take a Flecha Roja bus to Tenango (M$44, 1½ hours, every 10 minutes), and from outside the Elektra store take a colectivo to Malinalco (M$22, 50 minutes).

Though the distances are short, traveling from Malinalco to Cuernavaca can take hours. It is, however, possible to hire a taxi (M$175, about one hour) and travel between the two towns via the incredibly scenic trip through Puente Caporal–Palpan–Miacatlán to the town of Alpuyeca, near the Xochicalco ruins. From there it's easy to flag one of the frequent buses traveling along Hwy 95, and continue either north (to Cuernavaca and Mexico City) or south (to Taxco and the coast).

Veracruz

Includes ➡

Best Places to Eat

➡ El Brou (p223)

➡ Villa Rica Mocambo (p213)

➡ Marrón Cocina Galería (p236)

➡ El Cebichero (p236)

➡ La Barra (p254)

➡ Taquería Los Nuevos 4 Vientos (p238)

Best Places to Stay

➡ Mesón del Alférez Xalapa (p222)

➡ Casa Real del Café (p226)

➡ Hotel Tres79 (p235)

➡ Rodaventa Natural (p229)

➡ Posada Bugambilea (p250)

➡ Las Magdalenas (p228)

Why Go?

Taking up much of Mexico's Gulf coastline, the long and diverse state of Veracruz is where the Spanish conquest of the Aztecs began. It was also the cradle of the aptly named Veracruz Mesoamerican culture at El Tajín and is home to Mexico's highest peak – soaring, snowcapped Orizaba.

As a destination, it's routinely overlooked by travelers, and while it's true that the beaches are better in the Yucatán and the colonial towns can be more impressive in Mexico's central and western highlands, Veracruz has both, without the hassle. It also lays claim to the World Heritage site of colonial Tlacotalpan, the inspiring Biosphere Reserve of Los Tuxtlas and some gorgeous *pueblos mágicos* (magical villages), including hilly Papantla, coffee-growing Coscomatepec and smaller, equally appealing Xico.

Its biggest attraction, however, is its quietness. Wherever you go here, you'll find yourself well off the beaten path, with discoveries just waiting to be made.

When to Go
Veracruz City

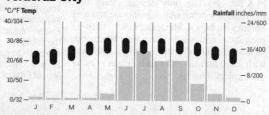

July Nonstop processions and masked dances in Xico in honor of the town's patron saint.

Feb & Mar The Veracruz Carnaval kicks off the biggest party on Mexico's eastern coast.

Nov–Feb Peak tourist season for non-Mexicans with less rain and balmy temperatures.

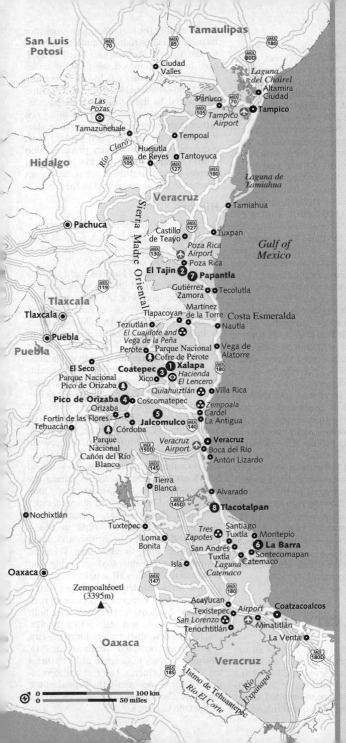

Veracruz Highlights

❶ Museo de Antropología (p219) Deciphering a triumvirate of Mesoamerican cultures in Xalapa's architecturally magnificent museum.

❷ El Tajín (p242) Imagining past glories at these extensive ruins.

❸ Coatepec (p225) Sipping gourmet coffee in this cloud forest–encased highland town.

❹ Pico de Orizaba (p237) Standing breathless atop the summit of Mexico's highest mountain.

❺ Jalcomulco (p229) Riding the white water of one of Mexico's best rivers for rafting and then relaxing in a *temazcal* (traditional herbal steamroom).

❻ La Barra (p254) Taking a boat across Laguna de Sontecomapan for some superbly fresh fish right on the beach.

❼ Papantla (p240) Watching grown men fly at a one-of-a-kind *voladores* (fliers) ceremony.

❽ Tlacotalpan (p245) Marveling at the many colors of this sleepy colonial town, perhaps Mexico's least known World Heritage site.

History

The Olmecs, Mesoamerica's earliest known civilization, built their first great center around 1200 BC at San Lorenzo in southern Veracruz state. In 900 BC the city was violently destroyed, but Olmec culture lingered for several centuries at Tres Zapotes. During the Classic period (AD 250–900), the Gulf coast developed another distinctive culture, known as the Classic Veracruz civilization. Its most important center was El Tajín, which was at its peak between AD 600 and 900. In the post-Classic period the Totonacs established themselves in the region south of Tuxpan. North of Tuxpan, the Huastec civilization flourished from AD 800 to 1200. During this time, the warlike Toltecs also moved into the Gulf coast area. In the mid-15th century, the Aztecs took over most of the Totonac and Huastec areas, exacting tributes of goods and sacrificial victims, and subduing revolts.

When Hernán Cortés arrived in April 1519, he made Zempoala's Totonacs his first allies against the Aztecs by vowing to protect them against reprisals. Cortés set up his first settlement, Villa Rica de la Vera Cruz (Rich Town of the True Cross), and by 1523 all the Gulf coast was in Spanish hands. Forced slavery, newly introduced diseases and the ravages of war severely reduced indigenous populations.

Veracruz harbor became a trade and communications link with Spain and was vital for anyone trying to rule Mexico, but the climate, tropical diseases and pirate threats inhibited the growth of Spanish settlements.

Under dictator Porfirio Díaz, Mexico's first railway linked Veracruz to Mexico City in 1872, stimulating industrial development. In 1901, oil was discovered in the Tampico area, and by the 1920s the region was producing a quarter of the world's oil. In the 1980s, the Gulf coast still held well over half of Mexico's reserves and refining capacity. Today, the region is not as large a player as it used to be, but is still a significant contributor to Mexico's oil economy.

VERACRUZ CITY

🖉 229 / POP 892,000

Veracruz, like all great port cities, is an unholy mélange of grime, romance and melted-down cultures. Conceived in 1519 and due to celebrate its 500th birthday in 2019, this is Mexico's oldest European-founded settlement. But usurped by subsequent inland cities, it's neither the nation's most historic nor its most visually striking. Countless sackings by the French, Spanish and North Americans have siphoned off the prettiest buildings, leaving a motley patchwork of working docks and questionable hybrid architecture, punctuated by the odd stray colonial masterpiece. But Veracruz' beauty is in its grit rather than its grandiosity. A carefree spirit reigns in the *zócalo* (main square) most evenings, where the primary preoccupation is who to cajole into a *danzón* (traditional couples dance), and there are some decent beaches in the southern part of the city.

History

Hernán Cortés arrived at the site of present-day Veracruz on Good Friday, April 21, 1519, and began his siege of Mexico. By 1521 he had crushed the Aztec empire.

Veracruz provided Mexico's main gateway to the outside world for 400 years. Invaders and pirates, incoming and outgoing rulers, settlers, silver and slaves – all came and went, making Veracruz a linchpin in Mexico's history. In 1569, English sailor Francis Drake survived a massive Spanish sea attack here. In 1683, vicious Frenchman Laurent de Gaff and his 600 men held Veracruz' 5000 inhabitants captive, killing escapees, looting, drinking and raping. Soon after, they left much richer.

Under bombardment from a French fleet in the Pastry War, General Antonio López de Santa Anna was forced to flee Veracruz in 1838, wearing nothing but his underwear. But the general managed to respond heroically, expelling the invaders. When Winfield Scott's army attacked Veracruz during the Mexican-American War, more than 1000 Mexicans died before the city surrendered.

In 1861, Benito Juárez announced that Mexico couldn't pay its debts to Spain, France and Britain. The British and Spanish planned only to take over Veracruz' customhouse, but retreated on seeing that Frenchman Napoleon III sought to conquer Mexico. After Napoleon III's five-year intervention ended, Veracruz experienced revitalization. Mexico's first railway was built between Veracruz and Mexico City in 1872, and foreign investment poured into the city.

US troops occupied Veracruz in 1914, halting a delivery of German arms to dictator Victoriano Huerta. Later in the Revolution, Veracruz was briefly the capital of the reformist Constitutionalist faction led by Venustiano Carranza.

THE FOUNDING OF VERACRUZ – MARKS I, II AND III

There is an intriguing murkiness about the first Spanish settlement on mainland America north of Panama.

Popular myth suggests that Hernán Cortés was the first European to arrive in the Veracruz area, but, in truth, fellow Spaniard Juan de Grijalva beat him to it by about six months. Grijalva docked on the Isla de Sacrificios (a short way offshore of Veracruz) in late 1518, where he found evidence of human sacrifice and spent 10 days trading with Mesoamerican natives.

Cortés' more famous flotilla arrived via the Yucatán coast in 1519, and quickly set up a temporary camp on a beach opposite the island of San Juan de Ulúa, on the site of present-day Veracruz. However, a real city wasn't established here for another 80 years. Instead, Cortés and his men quickly abandoned their malaria-ridden camp and trekked 40km north to the Totonac settlement of Zempoala, where they were courted by the corpulent chief, Xicomecoatl, with whom they made a cynical alliance against the Aztecs. Xicomecoatl sent Cortés' entourage 30km further north to the city of Quiahuiztlán with 400 Zempoala-hired porters, where they were met by a population of 15,000 curious citizens. With their ships already docked on the adjacent coast, Cortés was determined to cut legal ties with Diego Velázquez, his overseer in Cuba, and decided to found a town near Quiahuiztlán, declaring himself the legal *adelantado* (governor). Christened Villa Rica de la Vera Cruz (Veracruz Mk I), it consisted of little more than a fort, a chapel and some barracks, but small as it was, it was the first recorded European-founded settlement in North America. Around 1524, due to its limitations as a port, the town was moved south to La Antigua (Veracruz Mk II) and sited several kilometers inland on the banks of the Río Antigua, where small ships could be docked. But as the Spanish empire grew, Antigua's river location made it less practical for larger ships, meaning supplies had to be hauled overland to San Juan de Ulúa, where they often fell prey to smugglers. As a result, around 1599, Veracruz was moved for a third time back to the site of the original encampment on the coast opposite San Juan de Ulúa.

Today, Veracruz is an important deep-water port, handling exports, manufacturing and petrochemical industries. Tourism, particularly from the domestic sector, is another large income earner.

◉ Sights

★ Zócalo   PLAZA

Any exploration of Veracruz has to begin with its *zócalo* (also called the Plaza de Armas and Plaza Lerdo), the city's unofficial outdoor 'stage' where inspired organized events overlap with the day-to-day improvisation of Mexican life. The handsome public space is framed on three sides by *portales* (arcades), the 17th-century **Palacio Municipal** (Zamora s/n) and an 18th-century **cathedral** (⊗8am-7pm). The level of activity accelerates throughout the day until the evening, when the *zócalo* becomes thick with music, entertainers, merrymakers and bystanders.

★ Museo Histórico Naval   MUSEUM

(☑229-931-40-78; Arista 418; adult/student/child under 6yr M$45/30/free; ⊗10am-5pm Tue-Sun) Occupying a former naval academy, this high-tech museum offers a titanic lesson in Mexico's maritime heritage, with plenty of interactive displays and a beautifully planned layout. Displays run the gamut from pre-Colombian navigation and Columbus' discovery of the New World, to trade with Asia, the growth of Veracruz and the role of the present-day navy. There are also exhibits focusing on the US attacks on Veracruz in 1847 and 1914, a ship simulator and plenty of armaments through the ages.

The in-house cafe offers a place for a quiet rest. The big drawback for non-Spanish speakers is that most of the displays are in Spanish only.

Centro Cultural La Atarazana   CULTURAL CENTRE

(☑229-932-89-21; Montero s/n; ⊗10am-7pm Tue-Fri, to 2pm & 3-7pm Sat & Sun) FREE This colonial-era warehouse has been beautifully converted into an exhibition space. Worthwhile temporary exhibitions, such as ceramic art and installations by contemporary artists, are held regularly.

Veracruz

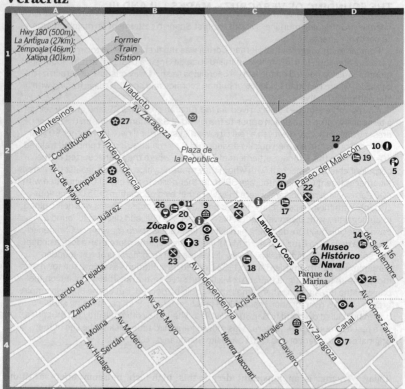

Instituto Veracruzano de Cultura
CULTURAL CENTRE

(☎229-932-89-21; www.ivec.gob.mx; cnr Av Zaragoza & Canal; ⊙10am-8pm Tue-Sun) FREE A converted church and cloister house some excellent temporary exhibitions, such as art by Diego Rivera, as well as works by local contemporary artists.

San Juan de Ulúa
FORTRESS

(☎229-938-51-51; adult/student & child M$60/free; ⊙9am-4:30pm Tue-Sun) The city's colonial fortress has been almost swallowed up by the modern port – it's almost hidden amid the container ships and cranes across the harbor. The central part of the fortress was a prison, and a notoriously inhumane one, during the Porfirio Díaz regime. Today, San Juan de Ulúa is an empty ruin of passageways, battlements, bridges and stairways undergoing lengthy renovations. To get here, take a taxi (M$55) or a *lancha* (boat taxi; M$40) from the *malecón*.

The fort was originally built on an island that's since been connected to the mainland by a causeway. The earliest fortifications date from 1565, and a young Francis Drake got his comeuppance here in a violent battle in 1569. During the colonial period, the fort and island became the main entry point for Spanish newcomers to Mexico.

Guided tours are available in Spanish and, quite often, in English. Entry is free on Sundays.

Acuario de Veracruz
AQUARIUM

(☎229-931-10-20; www.acuariodeveracruz.com; Blvd Camacho s/n; adult/child M$130/75, shark feeding M$440/240; ⊙10am-7pm Mon-Thu, to 7:30pm Fri-Sun) One of Veracruz' biggest attractions and allegedly the best of its kind in Latin America, this aquarium does a good job of showcasing the denizens of the Gulf of Mexico, as well as fishy oddities such as arapaima and albino shark catfish. Situated 2km south of the center, on the waterfront,

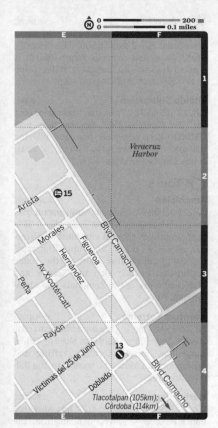

VERACRUZ VERACRUZ CITY

its centerpiece is a large doughnut-shaped tank filled with tiger, reef and nurse sharks, barracuda, and eagle rays that glide around visitors. Visitor participation in shark feedings is possible.

The aquarium also features a dolphin show and a tank full of sad manatees. Aquarium authorities claim they are aiding dolphin and manatee conservation and research, but animal-welfare groups around the world claim that such exhibits are cruel.

Museo Agustín Lara   MUSEUM
(☏229-937-02-09; Ruíz Cortines s/n, Boca del Río; adult/student M$30/15; ◷10am-2:30pm & 4-6pm Tue-Fri, 10am-4pm Sat & Sun) A monument to one of Veracruz' most famous musical icons, this museum displays a range of Agustín Lara's personal belongings, furniture and memorabilia in the musician's old city residence. It is situated just off Blvd Camacho, 4km south of the city center.

Museo de la Ciudad de Veracruz   MUSEUM
(Veracruz City Museum; ☏229-931-63-55; Av Zaragoza 397; ◷10am-5pm Tue-Sun) FREE Housed in a charming colonial-era building, this museum recounts the city's history from the pre-Hispanic era, and also gives a feel for the essence of this proud and lively city through explanations of its music, diverse ethnic roots and politics. Standout exhibits include some Totonaca and Huastec figures.

There is some labeling in English, and plenty about Veracruz at different stages in its history.

The attractive courtyard often hosts cultural experiences such as dance shows, Día de Muertos events and more.

Faro Carranza
LIGHTHOUSE

(Paseo del Malecón) Facing the waterfront on the *malecón,* Faro Carranza holds a lighthouse and navy offices guarded by a large **statue of Venustiano Carranza**. It was here that the 1917 Mexican Constitution was drafted. Every Monday morning the Mexican navy goes through an elaborate parade in front of the building.

Fototeca
ARTS CENTER

(☑229-932-87-67; Callejón El Portal de Miranda 9; ⊘10am-1pm & 2-5pm Mon-Fri) `FREE` On the southeast side of the *zócalo,* this small arts center has rotating photographic and video exhibitions. It's spread over three floors of a restored colonial building, though sometimes only the ground floor is open.

✖ Activities

Diving & Snorkeling

You wouldn't expect high-visibility diving right near such an oil-rigged city, but Veracruz has some pretty good options (including at least one accessible wreck) on the reefs near the offshore islands. Visibility is best in May.

★ Scubaver
DIVING

(☑229-932-39-94; www.scubaver.net; Hernández y Hernández 563; 2 dives M$900) This friendly, professional and centrally located outfit is used to dealing with foreigners. PADI courses and all manner of dives on offer.

Mundo Submarino
DIVING

(☑229-980-63-74; www.mundosubmarino.com.mx; Blvd Camacho 3549; beginner dives from M$1000) Recommended operator offering day and night dives, plus a range of PADI courses and excursions.

☞ Tours

Amphibian
ADVENTURE

(☑229-931-09-97; www.amphibianveracruz.com; Lerdo 117, Hotel Colonial lobby; ⊘9am-5pm) This outfit conducts themed city tours of Veracruz, as well as rafting and rappelling expeditions to Jalcomulco, tours of the coffee region that include Xico and Xalapa, and historical tours of the Zempoala and Quiahuiztlán ruins.

Aventura Extrema
ADVENTURE

(☑229-150-83-16; www.aventuraextrema.com; Sánchez Tagle 973; ⊘11am-6pm Mon-Fri) Offers rappelling, horseback riding, rafting and hiking around Veracruz, mostly in the Jalcomulco area.

Harbor Tours
BOATING

(☑229-935-94-17; www.asdic.com.mx; adult/child from M$100/55; ⊘9am-6pm) Boats from the

---

VERACRUZ BEACHES & LAGOONS

Inseparable from the *jarocho* (Veracruz) identity is the beach. You'll find pleasant stretches of beach all the way down through Boca del Río. As a rule of thumb, the further from the oil rigs the better, but locals can be seen enjoying them all.

Alternatively, you can find *lanchas* (M$110 Monday to Thursday and M$150 Friday to Sunday) by the aquarium that will take you to **Cancuncito**, a sandbar off the coast touted as the best beach in Veracruz, with light sand and clear water. Another part of the *lancha* beat is the **Isla de Sacrificios**, an island once used for Totonac human sacrifice and later as a leper colony. It's now part of a protected nature and marine reserve called **Parque Marino Nacional Sistema Arrecifal Veracruzano**. Sometimes, when tourism is low, *lanchas* aren't to be found, but harbor-tour boats stop there on some tours.

Some 11km from the center, the gritty, off-shoot town of **Boca del Río** has a smattering of brightly colored seafood restaurants overlooking the mouth of the river on Blvd Camacho. *Lanchas* offering boat tours to mangrove forests leave from here. Over the bridge, the coastal road continues about 8km further down the coast from Boca del Río to **Mandinga**, known for its seafood (especially *langostinos bicolores* – two-colored prawns), where you can hire a boat (from the *zona de restaurantes*) to take you around mangrove lagoons rich with wildlife.

malecón offer 45-minute tours of the harbor, plus a variety of other excursions.

✳ Festivals & Events

★ Carnaval
CARNIVAL

Veracruz erupts into a nine-day party before Ash Wednesday in February or March. Flamboyant parades wind through the city daily, beginning with one devoted to the 'burning of bad humor' and ending with the 'funeral of Juan Carnaval.' Throw in fireworks, dances, salsa and samba music, handicrafts, folklore shows and children's parades, and it adds up to be one of Mexico's greatest fiestas. See the tourist office (p215) for a program of events.

🛏 Sleeping

At busy times (mid-July to mid-September, Carnaval, Semana Santa, Christmas and New Year) prices may increase by 10% to 40%. There are historic hotels around the *zócalo* and some inexpensive places are dotted around the city center, while the hostels are found further south, closer to the aquarium. Boca de Río and around is full of business and resort hotels.

★ Oyster Hostel
HOSTEL $

(☑ 229-931-06-76; www.facebook.com/oysterhostel veracruz; Xicotencatl 1076, Flores Magon; incl breakfast dm/d/q M$129/302/431; ✳🛜) Smart, bright, clean and well run, with an often fun-loving crowd in residence and clued-up management, the Oyster Hostel is currently the best backpackers in town. The breakfast spread is unusually good for this price bracket, and it's close to the waterfront and within walking distance of many of the town's sights. Dorms have a maximum of six beds.

Hotel Amparo
HOTEL $

(☑ 229-932-27-38; www.hotelamparo.com.mx; Serdan 482; s/d/tr M$250/450/550; P✳🛜) A few blocks from the *zócalo*, this mosaic-fronted, family-run hotel represents the best value for your peso in the historic center, if not the city. Yes, the rooms are snug bordering on cozy and are fan-cooled rather than air-conditioned, but they're clean, have en suites, and are steps away from most of Veracruz's attractions.

El Faro
HOTEL $

(☑ 229-931-65-38; www.facebook.com/HotelElFaro Veracruz; Av 16 de Sepiembre 223; r/q M$399/699; P✳🛜) This no-frills place is a central budget option, just a short wander from the seafront. Room prices depend on the size and number of beds, and the cheaper ones can be very dark, with no natural daylight. That said, it's clean, safe and in the heart of the city. The receptionist speaks excellent English.

Nû Hotel
HOTEL $

(☑ 229-937-09-17; www.nuhotel.com.mx; Av Lafragua 1066; s/d M$600/650; P🛜✳🛜) The Nû has pitched itself amid the scruffy next-to-bus-station hovels and declared war. It's no contest really, especially at these prices. Savor the clean, minimalist-chic rooms; young, casual staff; and cool downstairs cafe. The only real drawback is the location, 3km south of the *zócalo*, which isn't really handy for anything – except the buses, of course.

★ Mesón del Mar
BOUTIQUE HOTEL $$

(☑ 229-932-50-43; www.mesondelmar.com. mx; Morales 543; r/ste from M$950/1293; ✳🛜) This colonial charmer boasts friendly staff and well-cared-for rooms with tall ceilings (many have mezzanines with extra sleeping spaces). Balconies, beautifully tiled bathrooms, ceiling fans and wooden furniture all add to the mix, and while rooms facing Avenida Zaragoza can be noisy if you open the windows, this is one of Veracruz' most atmospheric midrange options.

Balajú Hotel & Suites
HOTEL $$

(☑ 229-201-08-08; www.bajalu.com; Blvd Camacho 1371; r from M$870; P✳🛜🏊) The room design follows the tried and tested tiled floor/neutral color scheme formula, but on the upside, this smart, pleasant hotel overlooks the sea (pick a corner room for best views), the staff are efficient and friendly, and it's close both to the aquarium and the city center.

Hotel Imperial
HISTORIC HOTEL $$

(☑ 229-816-15-30; www.hotelimperialveracruz. com; Lerdo 153; r/ste from M$1200/2000; 🛜✳🛜🏊) Claiming to be the oldest hotel in the Americas, the Imperial has been open nonstop since 1794. Its suites and public areas are suitably ornate (check out the 1904 stained-glass elevator!) and will certainly please colonial history buffs, and you can't beat the location. The standard rooms, however, are as bland as unseasoned porridge.

Hawaii Hotel
HOTEL $$

(☑ 229-989-88-88; www.hawaiihotel.com.mx; Paseo del Malecón 458; s/d/tr M$700/800/1000; P✳🛜🏊) Who knows why it's called the

Hawaii Hotel? The 30-room hotel looks more like the prow of a boat, with marble and white decor inside. However, it's the best value on the *malecón,* and some of the spacious, sunlight-filled rooms have marvelous views. Extras such as hairdryers and fridges make for a comfortable stay.

★ Hotel Emporio   LUXURY HOTEL $$$

(✆229-989-33-00; www.hotelesemporio.com/hoteles/emporio-veracruz; Paseo del Malecón 244; r from M$2567; ⏏🔁❄🛜🏊) Hands down the best hotel in Veracruz. The whole place is shot through with arty touches, and the rooms are spacious, with beautifully appointed bathrooms. Each comes with a large balcony, and it's worth splurging on a sea view. It also has three pools, a gym, a cocktail bar and a dynamite location on the most picturesque stretch of the *malecón.*

Out-of-season deals can see prices drop 40% on the listed rack rates.

Fiesta Inn   BUSINESS HOTEL $$$

(✆229-923-15-00; www.fiestainn.com; Figueroa 68; r from M$1591; ⏏🔁❄🛜🏊) A block away from the *malecón* and overlooking the sea, this solid business-style hotel is all spacious rooms and blond-wood furniture, like the other brethren in the chain. A good on-site restaurant, pool, gym, helpful bilingual staff and proximity to the city's attractions, plus a quiet location, add to its charm.

Gran Hotel Diligencias   LUXURY HOTEL $$$

(✆229-923-02-80, 800-505-55-95; www.granhoteldiligencias.com; Av Independencia 1115; r/ste from M$3000/3800; ⏏🔁❄🛜🏊) The fanciest option on the *zócalo* has a smart lobby full of fresh flowers and buzzes with livery-clad bellhops. Upstairs the huge rooms deliver solid old-fashioned elegance and perks such as cable TV and coffee makers. Outdoor pool, spa, and gym are among other boons. You'll find more atmosphere downstairs in the adjoining **Bar El Estribo** (✆229-923-02-80; ⏱9am-late; 🛜) and Villa Rica seafood restaurant.

✖ Eating

Excellent seafood features heavily on the menus of most restaurants, from the condensed strip of *palapas* (thatched-roof shelters) on the *malecón* just south of the aquarium to seafood restaurants in Boca del Río. Fusion and international places are scattered throughout the city, and some of

the best cheap eats, including street food, are found in the historical center.

★ Tacos David   STREET FOOD $

(cnr Morales & Farías; tacos M$10; ⏱10am-4pm Mon-Sat) Late morning and lunchtime, locals congregate at simple tables around this locally beloved taco stand that specializes in one thing: *cochinita pibil* (slow-cooked pork) tacos served in a fragrant, mildly spicy broth. Four tacos is a good-sized portion and there are extra chilies if you want to spice it up.

Antojitos Emily   MEXICAN $

(✆229-955-09-36; Zapata 436; mains from M$10; ⏱9am-2:30pm) Red plastic tables, fans rotating lazily overhead and a generally low-key appearance belie the fact that this little neighbourhood eatery does some of the best *gordas* (filled pastry), *pellizcadas con chicharrón* (cornflour 'nests' topped with pork crackling), *antojitos con chorizo* (fried tortillas with tomato salsa, chorizo and cheese) and other snacks. Lunchtimes get pretty crowded.

Mercado Hidalgo   STREET FOOD, MARKET $

(Av Hidalgo; mains M$30-70; ⏱8am-3pm Mon-Fri) Join *jarochos* in the mazes of the Hidalgo Market, where you can find nooks that serve cheap, delectable local favorites. Tampico Mariscos is a good bet for the monster seafood cocktail *vuelvealavida* ('come back to life' – a hangover remedy), while Los Michoacanos serves all manner of meaty tacos, as does Taquería Rosita.

Nieves del Malecón   ICE CREAM $

(✆229-931-70-99; www.nievesdelmalecon.com; Av Zaragoza 286; scoops from M$25; ⏱8am-midnight) *Jarochos* prefer sorbets *(nieves)* over ice cream and this is one of the town's sorbet favorites, sandwiched between the *malecón* and the *zócalo*. Loquacious 'callers' stand outside drumming up business, competing with a rival place (with its own 'callers') directly across the street. Try the delicious *mamey* (apple) flavor, or opt for the Veracruz staple, vanilla.

★ Gran Café de la Parroquia   CAFE $$

(✆229-932-25-84; www.laparroquia.com; Gómez Farías 34; mains M$70-200; ⏱6am-midnight) To say that Veracruz' greatest 'sight' is a cafe might seem like a slur on this grizzled port city's reputation, but walk into the Gran Café de la Parroquia – over two centuries old – and the penny will drop. The de rigueur drink is *lechero,* a milky coffee brought to your table as an espresso measure in the bottom of a glass.

Tap your spoon on the glass rim and – hey presto – a bow-tied, white-jacketed waiter quickly appears, extends his jug high in the air, and tops your coffee up with hot milk to create the perfect *lechero.*

The Parroquia has inspired some spinoffs in recent years (including one right next door that some people confuse with the original), but none comes close to matching the atmosphere and spirit of the original on Veracruz' Paseo del Malecón. It's a solid breakfast joint, too, with eggs prepared at least a dozen different ways.

Bistro Marti   FRENCH $$
(✆229-213-95-73; www.facebook.com/bistromarti veracruz; Calle Magallanes 213; mains M$120-230; ⊙1-11:30pm Tue-Fri, 5pm-midnight Sat, 1-7pm Sun; 🕾) This highly regarded French restaurant, with just a hint of Italian to it, serves a seasonally changing menu that can be loaded with treats, such as delicately presented scallops or classic mussels in white wine sauce, as well as more unusual items such as cheese soup. The setting manages to be romantic, modern and cozy all at once.

Los Canarios   SPANISH, MEXICAN $$
(✆229-989-33-00; http://loscanarios.com.mx/emporio-veracruz; Paseo del Malecón 224; mains M$140-290; ⊙1-11pm; 🕾) With large windows overlooking the *malecón,* it's hard to resist this fancy place in the super-smart Hotel Emporio. Slink inside and reacquaint yourself with à la mode Spanish cooking, mixed, of course, with a few Mexican inflections. Catalan-style *arróz negro* (rice with squid ink and calamari) is excellent, the red wine arrives chilled, and the service doesn't miss a beat.

The hungry should watch out for the seafood buffet (M$280) served all day Friday to Sunday.

Gran Café del Portal   INTERNATIONAL $$
(✆229-931-27-59; Av Independencia 1187; mains M$70-200; ⊙7am-midnight; 🕾) This smart and impressively decorated place just off the *zócalo* is actually quite relaxed despite its surface formality. Indeed, service can be positively laid-back, though the deft aim of the coffee/milk-pouring waiters is as precise as any you'll find in Veracruz. Full meals are available, as well as the mainstays of milky coffee and pastries.

★**Villa Rica Mocambo**   SEAFOOD $$$
(✆229-922-21-13; www.villaricamocambo.com.mx; Calz Mocambo 527, Boca del Río; mains M$120-325; ⊙11am-10pm Sun-Wed, to midnight Thu-Sat; 🕾🚹) Food – and this restaurant in particular – is reason enough to make the pilgrimage to Boca del Río. Fish is the all-encompassing ingredient, from *camarones enchipotlados* (smoky chipotle shrimp) to stuffed sea bass, and the beachside service is attentive. More than a few people say it serves the best seafood in Veracruz, and we concur.

There's a second branch at Gran Hotel Diligencias on the *zócalo.*

Mardel   ARGENTINE $$$
(✆229-937-56-42; www.mardel.com.mx; Blvd Camacho 2632; mains M$160-380; ⊙7am-11pm Mon-Sat, 8am-11pm Sun; 🕾) Owned by a retired Argentine football player, this upscale restaurant has a great seafront position and specializes in rib-eye steaks. There are also Mexican and Spanish influences on the extensive menu, but regulars advise sticking to the staple: a perfectly cooked slab of cow. The TVs showing sports can be a distraction or a delight, depending on your point of view.

🍷 Drinking & Nightlife

The *portales* cafes on the *zócalo* are drinking strongholds. But head south some distance on the *malecón* and you'll find the majority of the city's fast-paced and ever-changing nightlife along Blvd Camacho.

Bar Prendes   BAR
(✆229-922-21-13; Lerdo; ⊙9am-late) For a front-row seat for whatever's happening in the *zócalo* on any given night, look no further than Prendes; its trendy modern furniture occupies a prize slice of real estate under the *portales.* Beers come in long tubes with taps at the bottom for groups.

Velitas   BAR
(cnr Blvd Camacho & Militar; ⊙5pm-close) With its romantic, tiki-torch ambience, this popular little seaside *palapa* is a laid-back place to grab a cocktail while checking out the ocean and the people strolling past on the boulevard. On weekends there's live music.

☆ Entertainment

Of course, there are always marimbas and mariachis on the *zócalo.* And the coastline boulevard is known as *la barra más grande del mundo* (the biggest bar in the world),

DANZÓN DAYS

It's hard to wander far in Veracruz without stumbling into a plaza full of romantic *jarochos* (inhabitants of Veracruz) indulging in the city's favorite pastime, the *danzón*. An elegant tropical dance, it melds aspects of the French contradance with the rhythms of African slaves.

As with most Latin American dances, the *danzón* has its roots in Cuba. It was purportedly 'invented' in 1879 by popular band leader Miguel Failde, who showcased his catchy dance composition *Las Alturas de Simpson* in the port city of Matanzas. Elegant and purely instrumental in its early days, the *danzón* required dancers to circulate in couples rather than groups, a move that scandalized white polite society of the era. By the time the dance arrived in Mexico, brought by Cuban immigrants in the 1890s, it had become more complex, expanding on its peculiar syncopated rhythm, and adding other instruments such as the conga to form an *orquesta típica*.

Though the *danzón* faded in popularity in Cuba in the 1940s and '50s with the arrival of the *mambo* and the *chachachá*, in Mexico it continued to flourish. Indeed, since the 1990s the *danzón* has undergone a huge revival in Veracruz, particularly among mature citizens. The bastion of the dance is the *zócalo* on Friday and Saturday evenings, and if you hang out on the square for long enough it's quite probable that someone will whisk you off your feet and make you join in (which can be something of a mixed blessing).

barra referring both to the sandbar and the drinks bar. There is also a bona fide theater and some live-music venues.

Las Barricas
LIVE MUSIC

(Constitución 72; cover Sat & for live music M$50; ⊙2pm-4am Mon-Sat) This *jarocho*-recommended live-music venue and club plays a variety of music: reggaeton, salsa, pop, rock etc. It's on the small side, so expect to be packed in with the raucous, jovial crowd, especially on weekends.

Teatro Principal Francisco Javier Clavijero
THEATER

(☑229-200-22-47; Emparán 166; ⊙hours vary) This theater has a long history and has had many incarnations. It moved here in 1819 and adopted its current architectural style (French neoclassical with some tremendous mosaics) in 1902, though it's looking somewhat dilapidated now. Plays, musicals and classical concerts are performed here.

La Casona de la Condesa
LIVE MUSIC

(www.facebook.com/casona.condesa; Blvd Camacho 1520; cover Fri & Sat M$50-80; ⊙10pm-5am Tue-Sun) La Casona attracts an older (ie not teenage) crowd and offers solid live music at night, and at other times even hosts occasional art exhibitions. It is situated close to the seafront, 5km south of the city center on Blvd Camacho.

Shopping

Avenida Independencia is the city's main shopping thoroughfare. Souvenirs, including bottles of vanilla and good-quality coffee, can be procured at the **Mercado de Artesanías** (Paseo del Malecón; ⊙9am-7pm). Jewelry – especially silver – is also economical and sometimes engraved with interesting Aztec/Maya motifs.

Libros y Arte Fototeca
BOOKS

(☑229-934-22-33; Callejón El Portal de Miranda 9; ⊙10am-1pm & 2-5pm Mon-Fri) Inside the Fototeca building on the corner of the *zócalo*, this place has good regional and international selections.

ⓘ Information

Most banks change US dollars, and some change euros as well. ATMs are generally widely available throughout the city. There's a cluster of banks with ATMs a block north of the *zócalo*, including the following:

Banco Santander (Av Independencia & Juárez; ⊙24hr)

HSBC (Av Independencia & Juárez; ⊙24hr)

Hospital Beneficencia Española de Veracruz (☑229-931-40-00; www.heveracruz.mx; Av 16 de Sepiembre 955; ⊙24hr) Best hospital in the city, with general medical services.

Hospital Regional (☑229-932-11-71; Av 20 de Noviembre 1074; ⊙24hr) General hospital.

Post Office (Plaza de la República 213; ⊙9am-4pm Mon-Fri, to 1pm Sat) A five-minute walk north of the *zócalo*.

Tourist Office (☑229-922-95-33; http://veracruz.mx; Palacio Municipal; ⊙8am-3pm) Has helpful staff and plenty of maps and brochures.

Tourist Office Booth (cnr Paseo del Malecón & Landero y Cos; ⊙9am-9pm) At the far western end of Mercado de Artesanías.

ⓘ Getting There & Away

AIR

Veracruz International Airport (VER; www.asur.com.mx) is 18km southwest of the center, near Hwy 140. There are flights to Cancún, Guadalajara and Monterrey with VivaAerobus (www.vivaaerobus.com), to Cuidad del Carmen, Támpico and Mérida with TAR Aerolíneas (https://tarmexico.com), Villahermosa with Aeromar (www.aeromar.com.mx) and MAYAir (www.mayair.com.mx), and frequent flights to Mexico City with Aeroméxico (www.aeromexico.com), Aeromar, Interjet (www.interjet.com.mx) and a number of international airlines. Volaris (www.volaris.com) and Interjet also fly to Guadalajara. Direct flights to/from Houston are offered by United (www.united.com).

BUS

Veracruz is a major hub, with good services up and down the coast and inland along the Córdoba–Puebla–Mexico City corridor. Buses to and from Mexico City can be heavily booked at holiday times.

The **bus station** (☑229-937-04-58; Av Díaz Mirón btwn Tuero Molina & Orizaba) is located 3km south of the *zócalo* and has ATMs. The 1st-class/deluxe area is in the part of the station closest to Calle Orizaba. For more frequent, slightly cheaper and slower 2nd-class services, enter on the other side from Avenida Lafragua. There's a 24-hour luggage room here.

CAR & MOTORCYCLE

Local and international car-rental agencies, such as Hertz (www.hertz.com) and Dollar (www.dollar.com) have desks at Veracruz airport. There are also some other agencies scattered around town. Rates start at M$400 per day.

ⓘ Getting Around

Veracruz International Airport is small, modern and well organized, with a cafe and several shops. There's no bus service to or from town; official taxis cost M$280 to the *zócalo*. You must buy a ticket upfront from a booth in the arrivals hall, which helps to avoid being ripped off. Going the other way, just M$160 is the going rate, but agree on a price before you get in.

To get downtown from the 1st-class bus station, take a bus marked 'Díaz Mirón y Madero' (M$10). It will head to Parque Zamora then up Avenida Madero. For the *zócalo*, get off on the corner of Avenida Madero and Lerdo and turn

BUSES FROM VERACRUZ

Daily 1st-class ADO departures from Veracruz include the following:

DESTINATION	FARE (M$)	DURATION (HR)	FREQUENCY (DAILY)
Campeche	1170	11½	10pm
Cancún	1102	20-22¾	4
Catemaco	91-132	3¾	10
Chetumal	814	17¼	4:45pm
Córdoba	146-164	1¾-2¼	frequent
Mérida	896-1071	15¼-18¼	4
Mexico City	228-686	5½-7¼	frequent
Oaxaca	235-371	6¾-8½	5
Orizaba	79-186	2½	frequent
Papantla	306	3½-4¼	7
Puebla	176-384	3¾-5¼	frequent
San Andrés Tuxtla	196	3¼	12
San Cristóbal de las Casas	521-1160	8¾-10	3
Santiago Tuxtla	192	2¾	10
Tuxpan	394-446	5½-6	frequent
Villahermosa	610	6½-8¾	frequent
Xalapa	134-384	1½-2¼	frequent

right. Returning to the bus stations, pick up the same bus service going south on Avenida 5 de Mayo. Booths in the 1st- and 2nd-class stations sell taxi tickets to the center (zócalo area; M$45 to M$50). In some hotels, such as the Gran Hotel Diligencias (p212), you can get a summary sheet of official taxi-ride costs, which is helpful for guarding against tourist price inflation.

Buses marked 'Mocambo-Boca del Río' (M$10 to Boca del Río) leave regularly from the corner of Avenida Zaragoza and Arista, near the zócalo; they go via Parque Zamora and Blvd Camacho to Playa Mocambo (20 minutes) and on to Boca del Río (30 minutes). AU buses also go there from the 2nd-class station.

CENTRAL VERACRUZ

From Veracruz, curvy Hwy 180 follows the coast past dark-sand beaches to the busy transportation hub of Cardel, where Hwy 140 branches west to Xalapa, the state capital, surrounded by coffee-growing highland villages and home to one of Mexico's best museums. Two of Mexico's white-water-rafting hubs, Tlapacoyan and Jalcomulco, lie north and south of Xalapa, respectively. Just south of Veracruz, Hwy 150D heads southwest to Córdoba, Fortín de las Flores and Orizaba, on the edge of the Sierra Madre. Orizaba is a particularly appealing town, with Mexico's highest mountain looming beyond it.

Between Nautla and Veracruz, the coast is remarkably wild and unexplored, despite its weighty historical significance. The sleepy village of Antigua makes a delightful stopover, while the town of Zempoala hides a significant archaeological site of the same name. If rarely visited archaeological sites thrill you, you'll be in raptures at Quiahuiztlán, further along the coast.

La Antigua

♪ 296 / POP 988

The village of Veracruz's second incarnation (1525–99) and the second-oldest Spanish settlement in Mexico, La Antigua reveals little of its past identity with its languid grid of sleepy, cobbled streets and moss-covered ruins. It's a pleasant, soporific backwater these days, well worth a detour for its historical significance and good seafood.

A Spanish settlement was established here in 1525, and it's rumored that this is where conquistador Cortés moored his

boats to a **ceiba tree**. The tree – gnarly and gigantic – is still standing, with a boat lying beside it. The eye-catching ruined building, half-strangled by tree roots and vines, is a 16th-century customs house, sometimes erroneously called the 'Casa de Cortés.' The **Ermita del Rosario** (⊙8am-6pm) church, probably dating from 1523, is considered to be the oldest in the Americas.

Lanchas will motor you along the pleasant Río Antigua for around M$100 per person, depending on how many people want to go.

✗ Eating

★**Las Delicias Marinas**   SEAFOOD $$

(☏296-971-60-38; www.lasdeliciasmarinas.com; Río Huitzilapan waterfront; mains M$130-255; ⊙10am-7pm) On the waterfront, closest to a pedestrian-only suspension bridge, the celebrated Las Delicias Marinas serves exquisite fresh and saltwater fish and seafood that could emulate anything in Veracruz. The charcoal-grilled seafood mix and the *camarones enchipotlados* (shrimp in chipotle sauce) have to be tasted to be believed. You'll encounter music and dance entertainment here on weekends.

❶ Getting There & Away

Colectivo taxis charge M$10 or so from the village to the highway 1km away, where buses to Veracruz and Cardel pass every 15 minutes or so. Flag down the driver just north of the toll booth or just walk for 20 minutes from the highway.

Villa Rica

♪ 296

Standing in this tiny, dusty fishing village situated 69km north of modern-day Veracruz, it's hard to believe you're gazing at the site of the first European-founded settlement north of Panama in mainland America. These days the historic settlement hardly merits a label on most maps, though there is a smattering of houses here, along with several lodgings, a couple of rustic restaurants and the weed-covered foundations of some buildings constructed by Cortés and his men soon after their arrival.

Never properly consolidated, the 'Veracruz that once was,' founded as Villa Rica de la Vera Cruz in 1519, lasted only until 1524 when it was moved to present-day La Antigua. There's a small and attractive curved

ZEMPOALA

As Hernán Cortés approached the Totonac settlement of Zempoala in 1520, one of his scouts reported that the buildings were made of silver – but it was only white paint shining in the sun. Zempoala's chief – a corpulent fellow nicknamed el cacique *gordo* (the fat chief) by the Spanish – struck an alliance with Cortés for protection against the Aztecs. But his hospitality didn't stop the Spanish from smashing statues of his gods and lecturing his people on the virtues of Christianity. It was at Zempoala in 1520 that Cortés defeated the expedition sent by Cuba's Spanish governor to arrest him. A smallpox epidemic in 1575–77 decimated Zempoala and most of the survivors moved to Xalapa.

The **archaeological remains** (Morelos Oriente s/n; M$50; ⊙9am-6pm) of this Totonac town of around 30,000 people date back to around AD 1200 and sit on the outskirts of modern-day Zempoala, reachable by frequent bus services from Cardel (M$20). The temples and buildings at this quiet, grassy site have undergone extensive renovation works, and most are studded with smooth, rounded riverbed stones, though many were originally plastered and painted. Zempoala once had defensive walls, underground water and drainage pipes, and human sacrifices were held in its temples.

As there is no labeling at the site itself, have a look inside the adjoining **museum** first. Apart from interesting clay figurines, polychrome plates, obsidian flints and pottery used in ceremonies, there are photos and descriptions (in Spanish) of every major building on the site. Also, check out the clay figure of Xipe Totec – a deity in whose honor slaves and prisoner were sacrificed and skinned, the skin then placed on ill people to cure them of their ailments.

It may be possible to have a guide show you around for a tip. Roberto del Moral Moreno is the only one who knows some English. He charges approximately M$120 per tour. If he's not on site, ask the caretaker to call him.

By the entrance, the **Templo del Muerte** (Temple of the Dead) once featured a tomb containing Mixtecachihuatl, the goddess of dead women. The **Templo Mayor** (Main Temple), uncovered in 1972, is an 11m-high pyramid with a wide staircase ascending to the remains of a shrine. When they first encountered Zempoala, Cortés and his men lodged in the **Templo de Las Chimeneas**, whose battlement-like teeth *(almenas)* were thought to be chimneys – hence the name. The circle of stones in the middle of the site is the **Círculo de los Guerreros**, where lone captured soldiers were made to fight against groups of local warriors. Few won.

There are two main structures on the west side. One is known as the **Templo del Sol** and has two stairways climbing its front in typical Toltec-Aztec style. The sun god was called Tonatiun and sacrifices were offered to him here on the **Piedra de Sacrificios**. The 'fat chief,' officially known as Xicomacatl, sat facing the macabre spectacle on the appropriately large altar. To its north, the second structure is the **Templo de la Luna**, with a structure similar to Aztec temples to the wind god, Ehecatl. East of Las Chimeneas is **Las Caritas** (Little Heads), named for niches that once held several small pottery skulls, now displayed at the museum.

Another large temple to the wind god, known as the **Templo Dios del Aire**, is in the town itself – go back south on the site entrance road, cross the main road in town and then go around the corner to the right. The ancient temple, with its characteristic circular shape, is beside an intersection.

beach, and you can trace it around past some dunes and across an isthmus to the Cerro de la Cantera, a rocky outcrop famed for its plunging *quebraditas* (ravines). Weekends are lively with visiting Veracruz residents.

◉ Sights

★**Quiahuiztlán**   ARCHAEOLOGICAL SITE
(off Hwy 180; M$40; ⊙9am-4:30pm) Perched like a mini–Machu Picchu on a plateau beneath a horn-shaped mountain, Quiahuiztlán is a pre-Hispanic Totonac town and

necropolis. Counting 15,000 inhabitants at the time of Cortés' arrival in 1519, its history before that is sketchy, although there was certainly a settlement here by AD 800. Enjoying a commanding view of the Gulf coast, the now-deserted site has two pyramids, more than 70 tombs and some carved monuments.

The inhabitants of Quiahuiztlán (place of the rains) were the only pre-Columbian civilization to bury their dead in tombs resembling miniature temples. A short trail leads up from the main plateau that overlooks the ocean to a higher site with four tombs. Yet another trail, partially overgrown and requiring some serious, almost vertical scrambling up rocks (around 20 minutes each way), continues on from there almost to the top of the mountain (the Cerro de Metates), rewarding your exertions with a bird's-eye view of the ruins and unparalleled views of the coast and the greenery-clad valley, with buzzards circling overhead.

Buses plying Hwy 180 drop you at the Quiahuiztlán turnoff.

Quiahuiztlán is reachable via a pleasant 3km walk up a winding paved road from Hwy 180. In spite of its lofty location, the settlement was subjugated first by the Toltecs between AD 800 and 900, and then by the Aztecs around AD 1200. You can contemplate this amid nature and in solitude, as you're likely to have the place entirely to yourself.

🏃 Activities

★ EcoGuías La Mancha OUTDOORS

(📞296-100-11-63; www.ecoturismolamancha.com; La Mancha-Actopan, Carretera Federal Cardel-Nautla Km 31; campsites with own/borrowed tent M$60/100, cabañas per person/entire M$150/1200) 🍃 All hail this progressive local association for developing a grassroots environment education center. The facilities, 1km from the beach, offer interpretive walks, bird-watching excursions, horseback riding and kayak tours where you can see mangroves and wildlife, all for M$150 per person. Follow the 'El Mangal' signs from the La Mancha eastbound turnoff on Hwy 180 for 1km. Bring repellent.

Accommodations are rustic (eight-person cabins with thatched roofs or rent-a-tents), but it's a great off-the-beaten-path choice that supports the local community.

🛏 Sleeping & Eating

Villas Arcon HOTEL $$

(📞296-964-91-72; www.villasarcon.com; Villa Rica; s/d M$900/1150; 🅿️❄️🛜🏊) At the northern entrance to Villa Rica, this bright orange, low-rise resort hotel sits amid immaculate grounds in the shade of trees and bamboo thickets. Spartan, reasonably clean but characterless rooms surround two pools, and it's a short walk through the village to the beach. The on-site restaurant serves fish and seafood dishes, including excellent *camarones encipotlados* (chipotle shrimp).

Restaurant Miriam SEAFOOD $

(Villa Rica; mains M$60-130; ⊙10am-7pm) Friendly Miriam and her extended family serve up delicious seafood dishes to order, in what is essentially an extension of their living room. Be warned, when she offers you her *picantísimo* (spiciest) dish, she's not kidding!

❶ Getting There & Away

Villa Rica is about 1km east of the main Hwy 180. Ask any bus driver on the Cardel–Nautla run to stop at the entrance road to the Quiahuiztlán ruins. From here it's an easy walk to the village.

Xalapa

📞228 / POP 719,591 / ELEV 1417M

Familiar to the world primarily due to the super-hot green chili that was named after it, Xalapa (also spelled Jalapa, but always pronounced ha-*la*-pa) is actually about as different to the fiery jalapeño pepper as can be – unlike sweaty coastal Veracruz city, Xalapa's highland location makes it temperate and often quite cloudy. Thanks to its alternative vibe and large student population, the city is lively at night and has a thriving cultural scene (it has its own branch of the Hay Festival of Literature & the Arts, for example).

Traffic-choked Xalapa has an alluring center, full of well-kept parks, bustling pedestrian streets and colonial architecture. The superb anthropological museum is the main draw for visitors here, but the gargantuan pre-Hispanic relics are supplemented by hip bars, weighty bookstores and a superb array of quality coffee joints, making this one of Mexico's most enjoyable state capitals.

History

Founded by Totonacs in the early 1200s, Xalapa was part of the Aztec empire when Hernán Cortés and his men passed through in 1519. Because of its appealing climate and location, Spain strategically placed a monastery here to proselytize the indigenous population. By the 17th century it had evolved into a commercial axis and meeting hub. Today Xalapa is still a commercial center for coffee, tobacco and flowers.

⊙ Sights

★ Museo de Antropología   MUSEUM
(☑ 228-815-09-20; www.uv.mx/max; Av Xalapa s/n; adult/student M$55/30, audio guide M$50; ☺ 9am-5pm Tue-Sun) Set in spacious gardens off Avenida Xalapa, 4km northwest of the center, this remarkable museum (containing Mexico's second-finest archaeological collection) is a work of art in its own right. The focus is on the main pre-Hispanic civilizations from the Gulf coast, principally the Olmecs, the Totonacs, the Huastecs and Classic Veracruz, and the beautifully displayed artifacts are presented in chronological order in a series of interconnecting galleries that descend the side of a lush hill.

The exhibits' scale and breadth rival the museum's intricate layout. Standout exhibits include the world's largest collection of giant Olmec heads, a reconstruction of the Las Higueras temple, jade masks, and the museum's most celebrated piece: the jade Olmec sculpture, *El señor de las Limas*, from southern Veracruz. There are also dramatic stone representations of the main pre-Columbian deities, namely Quetzalcoal (aka the Feathered Serpent), god of creation and knowledge; Tlaloc, the bespectacled god of rain and fertility; Tlazolteotl (aka the Eater of Filth), the patron deity of adulterers and goddess of carnal desire; and Xipe Totec, deity of life-death-rebirth, celebrated with the sacrifice of a slave and the priest wearing the flayed skin of the corpse. There is also an array of fine work associated with the pre-Hispanic ball game.

It has a small cafe on the upper floor and a truly excellent bookstore, while the walk back up the hill through the beautifully kept garden is a delight.

It's well worth paying extra for the excellent audio guide (bring ID to leave as collateral), or else download the museum's app.

If taking public transportation, hop on a 'Camacho-Tesorería' **bus** (Av Camacho; M$10)

from Enríquez near Parque Juárez. To return, take a bus marked 'Centro.' A taxi here costs M$30.

Parque Juárez   PLAZA
Xalapa's central main square feels like a terrace, with its south side overlooking the valley below and the snowcapped cone of Pico de Orizaba beckoning in the distance. Greener and better kept than most other plazas in Mexico, you'll find monkey puzzle trees and manicured hedges among the shoe-shiners, balloon sellers and wandering minstrels.

On the plaza's north side is the 1855 neoclassical **Palacio Municipal** (Av Enríquez) and on the east side is the **Palacio de Gobierno** (Parque Juárez), the seat of Veracruz' state government. The Palacio de Gobierno has a fine mural by Mario Orozco Rivera depicting the history of justice above the stairway near the eastern entrance on Enríquez.

Catedral Metropolitana   CATHEDRAL
(cnr Enríquez & Revolución; ☺ 8am-6pm) An unfinished masterpiece, Xalapa's cathedral lacks a second tower but still impresses with its scale and grandiosity. Moreover, rather than compensating for its steep hillside position, the architecture makes full use of it to inspire awe as you enter, forcing you to raise your head to see the altar and giant crucifix centerpiece. A mélange of neo-Gothic and baroque, the church contains the remains of St Rafael Guízar y Valencia, beatified by Pope John Paul II in 1995.

Parque Paseo de los Lagos   PARK
(Zona Universitaria) 🌿 Xalapans escape the monstrous traffic just south of Parque Juárez in this serendipitous park, which has 3km of delightful lakeside paths, most commonly used for jogging (and making out). At its northern end is the **Centro Cultural Los Lagos** (☑ 228-812-12-99; Paseo de los Lagos s/n; ☺ 8am-5pm), a lovely cultural center; check out the bulletin board to find out about cultural events and drop-in dance or yoga classes.

Pinacoteca Diego Rivera   GALLERY
(☑ 228-818-18-19; www.facebook.com/Pinacoteca DiegoRivera.IVEC; Herrera 5; ☺ 10am-7pm Tue-Sat) **FREE** Tucked beneath the west side of the plaza, this small gallery houses a modest collection of Rivera's works, and sometimes exhibits paintings by other Mexican artists, such as Jose García Ocejo.

Xalapa

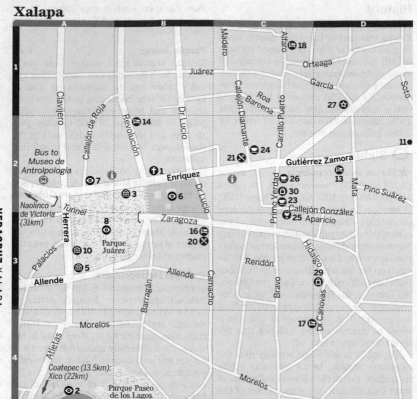

Parque Ecológico Macuiltépetl PARK
(off García Barna; ⊙5am-7pm) Atop a hill north of the city, this 40-hectare park is actually the heavily wooded cap of an extinct volcano. Spiraling to the top, the park's paths are a treasure for the city's robust fraternity of joggers, and provide expansive views of Xalapa and the surrounding area.

Museo Casa de Xalapa MUSEUM
(☑228-841-98-02; Herrera 7; ⊙10am-7pm Tue-Sun) FREE For a quick exposé of Xalapan history, head to this museum in an old colonial house close to Parque Juárez. Exhibits (in Spanish) run the gamut from prehistory to the growth and urbanization of Xalapa, the city's culture and commerce, and a replica Xalapeño kitchen.

Galería de Arte Contemporáneo GALLERY
(☑228-817-03-86; Xalapeños Ilustres 135; ⊙9am-6pm Tue-Sun) FREE The town's contemporary art gallery is in a renovated colonial building

1km east of the center. Showing an interesting range of temporary exhibitions, such as abstract ceramics by Gloria Carasco, it also has a small movie theater that screens arthouse films, mostly for free.

Parroquia de San José CHURCH
(cnr Xalapeños Ilustres & Arieta; ⊙8am-6pm) In the learned San José quarter, this church dates from 1770 and confirms Xalapa's penchant for asymmetrical one-towered religious edifices. Architecturally, it displays an unusual blend of baroque and Mudejar styles, including some horseshoe arches. Directly behind is the **Mercado Alcalde y García**, a covered market spiced up by some cool cafe-restaurants in the lower levels.

Museo Interactivo de Xalapa MUSEUM
(www.mix.org.mx; Av Murillo Vidal 1735; M$50; ⊙9am-5pm Mon-Fri, 10am-7pm Sat & Sun; ⊛) In one of the city's less intriguing suburbs, this new jack-of-all-trades museum works

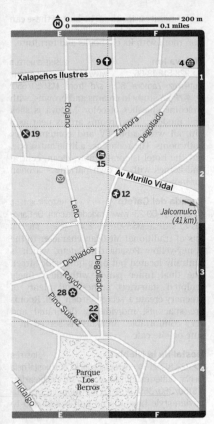

VERACRUZ XALAPA

wonders on rainy days with hyperactive kids. There are six themed rooms (science, ecology, art etc), a planetarium and an IMAX cinema. The latter two cost extra.

El Ágora de la Ciudad　　　　GALLERY
(📞228-818-57-30; www.agora.xalapa.net; Parque Juárez; ⏰10am-10pm Tue-Sun, 9am-6pm Mon) [FREE] A busy and sleekly modern art gallery with a cinema, theater, gallery, bookstore and cafe. Temporary exhibitions have included the psychedelic, sensual paintings of contemporary artist Lázaro Gracia.

🏃 Activities

Local tour operators offer cultural trips to the outlying *pueblos mágicos* (magical cities) of Xico, Coatepec and Naolinco, as well as archaeological sites, and also provide easygoing sports-oriented outdoor excursions, such as hiking, rafting and rappelling.

Robert Straub　　　　BIRDWATCHING
(📞228-818-18-94; http://wildsidenaturetours.com/leaders/robert-straub) Local bird-watching guide Robert Straub, a member of COAX (a conservation-minded bird-watching club), offers tours in the area, or can hook up birders with experienced local guides if he is busy. Straub authored a bird-watching guide to Veracruz, *Guía de Sitios* – proceeds go to Pronatura, a conservation nonprofit.

Veraventuras　　　　ADVENTURE SPORTS
(📞228-818-97-79; www.veraventuras.com; Degollado 81; ⏰9am-5pm Mon-Sat) Offers rafting

excursions, camping trips and many other activities, including trips to nearby hot springs.

Courses

Escuela para Estudiantes Extranjeros
LANGUAGE

(School for Foreign Students; ☎228-817-86-87; www.uv.mx/eee; Gutiérrez Zamora 25; 6-week courses from US$390, plus registration fee US$100) The Universidad Veracruzana's Escuela para Estudiantes Extranjeros offers short-term, accredited programs on the Spanish and Náhuatl languages and on Mexican culture and history. Most students chose to stay in one of the homestay programs organized by the univeristy.

☞ Tours

Aventura en Veracruz
CULTURAL

(☎228-979-26-16; www.facebook.com/aventuraver) Experienced guide Armando Lobato can arrange tours of Xalapa's surroundings, from cultural jaunts to Naolinco de Victoria to coffee tours of Coatepec's *fincas* (coffee farms) and rafting excursions to Jalcomulco.

Sleeping

Xalapa is blessed with some charming places to stay, such as several centrally located hotels inside centuries-old colonial mansions. There's also a bona fide hostel. Prices are reasonable.

★ Mesón del Alférez Xalapa
HISTORIC HOTEL $

(☎228-818-01-13; www.pradodelrio.com; Sebastián Camacho 2; r M$669, ste from M$839, all incl breakfast; ❋☎) This gorgeous place right in the center of town manages to get it all just right. A quiet, classy, 19th-century colonial mansion, it's a retreat from the roaring traffic outside, with beautiful split-level rooms (beds upstairs, living room below), heavy wooden beams, flower-filled greenery and the best breakfast in town in its refined La Candela restaurant. A bargain.

★ Posada La Mariquinta
GUESTHOUSE $

(☎228-818-11-58; www.lamariquinta.xalapa.net; Alfaro 12; s/d/ste M$580/720/1150; ☺☎) Set in an 18th-century colonial residence, this guesthouse is built like a fortress. Inside, tranquility reigns. The airy, individually decorated rooms are arranged around a quiet, bougainvillea-filled garden, and the place is quiet, friendly and stuffed with art, antiques

and general curiosities. The best of these can be found in the fabulous library-cum-reception room with its old books and furniture.

Majova Inn
BUSINESS HOTEL $

(☎228-818-18-66; www.hotelmajovainn.com; Gutiérrez Zamora 80; s/d from M$550/650; P❋☎) A study in creams and browns, with welcome splashes of color, Majova is slick and modern. Tiled rooms are as neat as a pin, all with cable TV and contemporary bathrooms. The rooms are a little antiseptic, but the hotel is comfortable, clean, central and comes with its own parking – a boon for motorists.

Posada del Cafeto
HISTORIC HOTEL $

(☎228-817-00-23; www.pradodelrio.com; Dr Canovas 8; s/d/ste M$590/690/890; ❋☎) There's lots of traditional Mexican character to the honey-yellow Posada del Cafeto, which is centrally located but on a quiet side street. The dual inner patios with their finely sculpted stairways, arches and plenty of greenery create a 'secret garden' feel. Rooms are spacious, individually decorated and very comfortable. Breakfast is served in a cute on-site cafe.

Hostal de la Niebla
HOSTEL $

(☎228-817-21-74; www.facebook.com/hostal.dela niebla; Gutiérrez Zamora 24; dm/s/d incl breakfast M$150/360/360; P☎) This modern Scandinavian-style hostel is no half-baked nod to the backpacker market. Rather, it's a spotless, well-organized, community-oriented place featuring airy rooms with decks and terraces. There's access to lockers and a kitchen. Accommodations are in either six-bed dorms or large private rooms.

Hotel Limón
HOTEL $

(☎228-817-22-04; Revolución 8; s/d M$200/230; P☎) The term 'musty jewel' could have been invented with this hotel in mind. The 'musty' part refers to the rooms on the ground floor, with high ceilings and fans but no windows and inadequate ventilation. The 'jewel' is the blue-tiled courtyard, seemingly inherited from richer past owners. An economical option for the unfussy, it's also very central.

Colombe Hotel Boutique
BOUTIQUE HOTEL $$

(☎228-818-89-89; www.colombehotel.com; Calle Vista Hermosa 16; s/d from M$997/1077, ste M$2380; P❋☎) A short way out of the city center, this small hotel has 13 rooms that all differ from one another and range from the Río, which is a bit like sleeping inside a technicolor rainbow, to the mellow tones of the Aqua room and the local-flavored Suite México. A cozy hookah bar, a restaurant and helpful staff are among the perks.

✖ Eating

Stylish cafes and restaurants abound in Xalapa, many offering interesting regional menus and vegetarian choices. Some are centrally located, but a number of dining options require a taxi ride. Callejón González Aparicio, between Primo Verdad and Mata, is an alley loaded with hip international eateries. One local specialty worth trying is *chiles rellenos* (stuffed peppers).

Verde Raiz
VEGAN $

(☑228-200-16-31; www.facebook.com/verderaiz xalapa; Leño 28; mains M$50-65; ☺8:30am-7pm Mon-Sat; 🛜) 🍴 Raw food and tofu tacos have arrived in Xalapa and have become hugely popular with the resident student population. Get here early to grab one of the three tiny tables and tuck into a bowl of muesli, some *chilaquiles* (fried tortilla strips with salsa and fresh cheese) or one of its celebrated smoothies or juices.

Postodoro
ITALIAN $

(☑228-841-20-00; www.postodoro.com; Primo Verdad 11; mains M$39-98; ☺9am-midnight; 🛜) With its cheery yellow walls, beautiful courtyard dining space lit with fairy lights and comfy leather booths, this place has won itself many local fans. It confuses malfatti with tagliatelle, but that aside, the pasta dishes are nicely executed, portions are ample, and inexpensive sangria and wine flow generously.

La Fonda
MEXICAN $

(☑228-818-72-82; Callejón Diamante 1; dishes M$50-100; ☺8am-5:30pm) A microcosm of the Xalapa eating experience, La Fonda invites you to squeeze past the tortilla-making señorita at the door and climb upstairs, where the mural-festooned interior gives onto a narrow plant-adorned balcony overlooking the main street. The menu juxtaposes formidable *mole* with *chileatole de pollo* (chicken soup with little floating cobs of corn), but standards have slipped a bit.

Mercado de la Rotonda
MARKET $

(Revolución s/n; ☺7am-6pm) Located at the north end of Revolución, this untouristed market has several basic eateries offering regional food on the cheap.

★El Brou
MEDITERRANEAN $$

(☑228-165-49-94; Soto 13; mains M$98-248; ☺9am-5pm; 🛜🍴) Housed in a delightful high-ceilinged colonial lounge, El Brou gets it right on all counts. The varied menu offers a delicious and arty take on Mediterranean, Middle Eastern and Mexican cuisine, and the modern touches to its traditional decor give it a chic look and feel. Settle in for a memorable meal of tuna tartare, tabbouleh and Greek-style moussaka.

★La Candela
BREAKFAST $$

(☑228-818-01-13; www.pradodelrio.com; Sebastián Camacho 2; mains M$75-160; ☺8am-3:30pm; 🛜) Hidden downstairs in the Mesón del Alférez Xalapa, this brightly decorated place attracts a crowd of loyal regulars who come for the inventive Mexican cuisine and great steaks at lunchtime, but it's the breakfasts, which are accepted by nearly all Xalapeños as being the best in town, that really please hungry tummies.

★Vinissimo Xalapa
INTERNATIONAL $$$

(☑228-812-91-13; www.vinissimo.com.mx; Av Araucarias 501; mains M$130-280; ☺2pm-midnight Mon-Sat; 🛜) Elegant, but certainly not pretentious, the Vinissimo Xalapa offers outstanding *'alta cocina'* dishes created with imagination and fresh market produce. The often-changing menu takes its risottos and pastas from Italy, and seafood flavors from the wild coastline of Spanish Galicia. It has a comprehensive wine and cocktail list and service is attentive. It's a 10-minute cab ride east of the center.

🍷 Drinking & Nightlife

Xalapa has numerous cafes serving highland coffee grown in nearby Coatepec. Being a university town, Xalapa has a vivacious nightlife. The loudest buzz can be found in jam-packed Callejón González Aparicio, the covered alley off Primo Verdad filled with trendy bars.

★Café Cali
CAFE

(☑228-818-13-39; www.cafecali.com.mx; Callejón Diamante 23A; breakfasts M$170; ☺9am-10pm Mon-Sat, 10am-7pm Sun) The enticing smell of roasting coffee beans wafts down the alleyway and seems to envelop the entire block surrounding the wonderful Café Cali. The interior of the cafe is classic bohemia, and the range of coffees is pure caffeine-drenched bliss.

VERACRUZ XALAPA

Espresso 58
COFFEE

(Primo Verdad 7; ⊙7am-10:30pm Mon-Sat; 🔊) A branch of a sleek mini-chain that attracts loquacious student debaters and those who just want to be glued to their smartphones. The in-house Café Mahal coffee (locally grown, of course) is *muy rico* and the baristas are charming.

Cubanías
BAR

(www.facebook.com/BarCubanias; Callejón González Aparicio; ⊙5pm-1:30am; 🔊) Veracruz' Cuban influences rise to the surface in this boisterous bar, with mojitos, beer and – should you be peckish – large Cuban sandwiches on offer. It guards the entrance to Callejón González Aparicio and live music rocks up later on.

Angelo Casa de Té
CAFE

(☑228-841-08-39; Primo Verdad 21A; tea from M$15; ⊙8am-9pm) The shelves at this cute little place are lined with tins of different kinds of tea, the walls are adorned with pictures of tea-pickers and fields the world over, and it has good chocolate and homemade cookies to tuck into.

☆ Entertainment

Xalapa has a lively cultural life, with entertainment running the gamut from poetry slams to theater.

Centro Recreativo Xalapeño
ARTS CENTER

(☑228-195-82-24; Xalapeños Ilustres 31; ⊙9am-8pm) On bookish Xalapeños Ilustres, this cultural center is the font of pretty much everything that passes for 'art' in Xalapa. Jam sessions, tango classes, art expos, sculpture competitions and Cine Francés all kick off here; keep your eye on the poster board or check out the Facebook page for upcoming events.

The building is an attractive 19th-century colonial gem with a courtyard and small cafe (Luna Negra).

Tierra Luna
PERFORMING ARTS

(☑228-812-13-01; http://tierraluna.com.mx; Rayón 18; ⊙9am-10pm Mon-Thu, to 2am Fri & Sat; 🔊) A sanctuary for arty types, the historic high-ceilinged Tierra Luna provides a changing roster of poetry readings, theater performances and music gigs. It also serves tasty cafe fare, including a breakfast menu and a range of alcoholic drinks. It has a small bookstore and a craft store too.

Teatro del Estado Ignacio de la Llave
THEATER

(☑228-818-43-52; cnr Llave & Av Ávila Camacho; ⊙from 8pm) The impressive state theater hosts both the Orquesta Sinfónica de Xalapa and the Ballet Folklórico of the Universidad Veracruzana. It is situated 1.5km northwest of Parque Juárez, up Avenida Ávila Camacho.

Shopping

An epicenter of Xalapa's alternative culture is Callejón Diamante, an alley lined with boutiques and street vendors selling cheap jewelry, incense and paraphernalia. Bookstores line Xalapeños Ilustres.

360 by Negro Distaster
FASHION & ACCESSORIES

(☑228-284-35-28; Hidalgo 48; ⊙11am-9pm Mon-Sat, to 3pm Sun) Head for this outlet of the edgy Mexico City fashion label and stock up on designer T-shirts and tops with grungy skull motifs and more.

Café Colón
COFFEE

(☑228-817-60-97; Primo Verdad 15; ⊙9am-8pm Mon-Sat, 10am-1pm Sun) 🍴 Old-school coffee roasters will grind Coatepec's best in front of your eyes in this aromatic store. It sells for around M$180 per kilogram.

ⓘ Information

There are banks with 24-hour ATMs along Enríquez and Gutiérrez Zamora.

Centro de Especialidades Médicas (☑228-814-45-00; www.cemev.gob.mx; Ruíz Cortines 2903) Medical care; open 24/7.

Information Booth (www.xalapa.gob.mx; Enríquez s/n, inside Palacio Municipal; ⊙10am-3pm Mon-Fri) Located in the Palacio Municipal, this place has helpful info and maps.

Information Booth (Enríquez; ⊙9am-8pm) Next to Banco Santander.

Post Office (cnr Gutiérrez Zamora & Diego Leño; ⊙9am-5pm Mon-Fri, to 2pm Sat)

Xalapa Mio (www.xalapamio.com) Official tourist-office site.

Xalapa Tourist Network (www.xalapa.net) General tourist information site about things to see and do in and around the city.

ⓘ Getting There & Away

Xalapa is a transportation hub with excellent connections throughout the state and beyond.

BUS

Xalapa's modern and well-organized bus station, the **Central de Autobuses de Xalapa** (CAXA; ☑228-842-25-00; Av 20 de Noviembre), is 2km

BUSES FROM XALAPA

The daily ADO services listed in the table leave from CAXA. Destinations also served by ADO include Acayucan, Campeche, Cancún, Catemaco and Mérida.

DESTINATION	COST (M$)	DURATION (HR)	FREQUENCY (DAILY)
Cardel	98	1	18
Córdoba	120-181	3	11
Mexico City (TAPO)	334	5	12
Orizaba	129-260	3¾	11
Papantla	314	4¼	8
Puebla	239-341	2½-3	frequent
Veracruz	79-384	2	frequent
Villahermosa	547-802	8½	8

east of the center and has an ATM, cafes and telephones. Second-class buses for Xico and Coatepec regularly leave from Mercado Los Sauces, about 1km west of the center on Circuito Presidentes. First-class services are offered by ADO and good 2nd-class services by AU.

Buses to Jalcomulco leave from the **Azteca bus station** (☑228-818-74-56; Niños Héroes 85), 2km north of the center.

CAR & MOTORCYCLE

Xalapa is famous for its traffic-choked streets, and driving here can be a challenging prospect; just negotiating the sprawling suburbs to find the center can be difficult as signage is poor.

Hwy 140 to Puebla is narrow and winding until Perote; the Xalapa–Veracruz highway is very fast and smooth. Going to the northern Gulf coast, it's quickest to go to Cardel, then north on Hwy 180. There are numerous parking lots in the center (M$15 to M$17 per hour).

❶ Getting Around

For buses from CAXA to the center, follow signs to the taxi stand, then continue downhill to the main Avenida 20 de Noviembre. The bus stop is to the right. Any bus marked 'Centro' will pass within a block or two of Parque Juárez (M$10). For a taxi to the center, you have to buy a ticket in the bus station (M$35 to M$45). To return to the bus station, take the 'Camacho-CAXA-SEC' bus from Avenida Ávila Camacho or Hidalgo. Taxi rides across Xalapa cost M$20 to M$40, depending on the distance.

Coatepec

☑ 228 / POP 52,621 / ELEV 1200M

Waking up and smelling the coffee has rarely been this epiphanic. Cradled in the Sierra Madre foothills, Coatepec's coffee production has long been its raison d'être, a fact that will become instantly clear as soon as you step

off the bus and inhale. The settlement dates from 1701 and coffee has been grown in the surrounding cloud forests for almost as long. The crop has brought wealth to the town; Coatepec – which lies a mere 15km south of Xalapa – is adorned with rich, gaudily painted colonial buildings. In 2006 it was nominated as a *pueblo mágico* (magical village) by the Mexican government. It makes a laid-back alternative to nearby Xalapa.

In late September, Coatepec vivaciously celebrates its patron saint, San Jerónimo, making it an excellent time to visit.

◉ Sights

★ **Museo El Cafétal Apan**   MUSEUM
(☑228-816-61-85; www.elcafe-tal.com; Carretera Coatepec-Las Trancas Km 4; M$40; ⊙9am-5pm) 🖉 If you want to learn a bit more about the history of coffee in the region, visit this excellent museum, which displays antique coffee-making tools alongside modern machinery. There are hands-on demonstrations showing how coffee is grown, washed, sorted and roasted, and also coffee tastings. Purchase your coffee beans, coffee and chipotle salsa and other caffeinated goodies here. It's a bit out of town; a taxi will cost around M$45.

Cascada Bola de Oro   WATERFALL
(Camino a Chopantla s/n) FREE The nearest waterfall to town is in the environs of a well-known Coatepec coffee *finca* (estate), which also has various trails and a natural swimming pool. To get there, follow Calle 5 de Mayo north to a bridge, continue north on Calle Prieto and then turn left into Calle Altamirano. After passing the last shop, hang a right, cross a bridge and turn left onto a path. The tourist office dispenses useful maps.

VERACRUZ COATEPEC

WORTH A TRIP

MUSEO EX-HACIENDA EL LENCERO

Almost as old as New Spain itself, this former **posada** (☑228-820-02-70; off Carretera Xalapa-Veracruz Km 10; adult/child M$40/30; ⊙10am-5pm Tue-Sun) was initiated in 1525 by Juan Lencero, a soldier loyal to Hernán Cortés, and served as a resting place for tired travelers toiling between a newly Europeanized Mexico City and the coast. Today the house-museum incorporates a superbly restored house furnished with antiques, along with some delightful gardens with a lake and a 500-year-old fig tree. Catch one of the regular 'Miradores' buses (M$12) from Xalapa's Plaza Cristal shopping center.

If driving to the estate, travel 12km southeast of Xalapa on the Veracruz highway, and then turn down a signposted road branching off to the right for 1km or so.

Museo de la Orquídea   GARDENS

(☑228-231-05-58; www.facebook.com/Museode laOrquidea; Aldama 20; M$30; ⊙10am-5pm Tue-Sun) FREE A 40-year labor of love by local botanist Dr Contreras Juárez, this orchid garden features more than 5000 species of orchids from around the world, including all of Mexico's 1200 indigenous species, some of which are so minuscule that they can only be properly appreciated with a magnifying glass. A quick guided tour shows off some of the beauties.

Cerro de las Culebras   VIEWPOINT

(off Independencia; ⊙24hr) Cerro de las Culebras (Snake Hill; Coatepec in the Náhuatl language) is easily accessible from the town center. The walk takes you up cobbled steps to a lookout tower with a white statue of Christ on top. From here there are magnificent city and mountain views (it's best to go in the morning). To get there, walk three blocks west from the main plaza on Lerdo, then north all the way up Independencia.

Parque Miguel Hidalgo   PLAZA

Coatepec's main square is green and avoids the worst of the town's traffic. In its center stands a exceptional *glorieta* (bandstand), which doubles as a cafe. Set back from the road on the eastern side is the unashamedly baroque Parroquia de San Jerónimo, named after the city's patron saint.

🛏 Sleeping & Eating

★Casa Real del Café   HISTORIC HOTEL $$

(☑228-816-63-17; www.casarealdelcafe.com; Gutiérrez Zamora 58; r incl breakfast M$1100-1500; P❂🔊) This colonial-style hotel is owned by local coffee farmers whose aromatic products fortuitously find their way into the onsite Antiguo Beneficio cafe. Split-level rooms offer historic luxury with dark wood, close-up photos of coffee being grown, coffee-

bean-adorned mirrors and gorgeously tiled bathrooms with rain showers, while the communal courtyard sports reclining chairs, a spa and a reading room.

Hotel Boutique Casabella   BOUTIQUE HOTEL $$

(☑228-979-07-18; www.hotelcasabellacoatepec. com.mx; Calle 16 de Sepiembre 33; r M$980; P🔊) Its split-level rooms clustered around two greenery-filled courtyards, this historic hotel has plenty of charming features: a bona fide well in the central courtyard, heavy wooden beams and antique coffee presses scattered about. This blends seamlessly with contemporary creature comforts: good beds, cable TV and rain showers.

Hotel Mesón del Alférez Coatepec   BOUTIQUE HOTEL $$

(☑228-816-67-44; www.pradodelrio.com; Jiménez del Campillo 47; d/ste incl breakfast M$853/1026; P❂✳🔊) Behind the mustard-yellow walls of this historical townhouse lies a secret courtyard with a fountain and a jungle of flowers. Surrounding it is a horseshoe of split-level rooms filled with heavy timber furnishings, polished floors, wood beam ceilings and colonial accents. It's a gorgeous place to stay and has helpful staff, but you have to rely on artificial ventilation. An excellent breakfast is included.

Posada de Coatepec   HISTORIC HOTEL $$$

(☑228-816-05-44; www.posadacoatepec.com. mx; Hidalgo 9; d/ste incl breakfast M$1700/2000; P❂🔊🏊) Coatepec's hallmark hotel is in a resplendent colonial-era building; the atmospheric central courtyard is overflowing with plants and features a gurgling fountain. It boasts a pool, exhibits from local artists, tranquil gardens and a full-sized antique coach. The rooms are spacious and individually decorated, but a little on the dark and musty side, as is typical with colonial mansions.

★ Café Santa Cruz
MEXICAN $$

(📞 228-200-40-59; Zamora 24; mains M$110-175; ⊙ 1-10pm) From the outside, this blushing terracotta building resembles a country farmhouse, but the tiny dining room (there's only a handful of tables) is all light, modern and very relaxed. The folk who work here serve memorable Mexican gourmet dishes, such as rabbit in carrot and macadamia sauce, and honey-glazed salmon with apples.

Finca Andrade
MEXICAN $$

(📞 228-816-48-87; www.fincaandrade.com; Lerdo 5; mains M$106-184; ⊙ 7:30am-9pm; 🐾) This large, colorful restaurant is renowned for its smoky, flavorful *chilpochole de camarón* (chili-laden shrimp soup), as well as chicken served with the restaurant's secret *mole* recipe and a variety of tasty *antojitos* (small bites).

🍸 Drinking & Nightlife

★ El Café de Avelino
CAFE

(www.facebook.com/elcafedeavelino; Rebolledo 21; ⊙ 1-8pm Fri-Wed) Some of the best coffee in Coatepec comes from a cafe with two tables and four chairs (five if you count the owner's). Owner Avelino Hernández – known locally as the *Poeta del Café* (coffee poet) – brews minor miracles from his Coatepec, Cosailton, Xico and Teocelo brands.

You can buy the beans for M$200 per kilogram.

El Cafésitio
COFFEE

(📞 228-202-27-31; www.facebook.com/cafesitio coatepec; Rebolledo; ⊙ 10:30am-8:30pm; 🐾) This thimble-sized cafe is primarily a place to purchase locally grown, gourmet coffee beans (M$160 to M$325 per kilogram), but there are three stools at the counter on which you can perch to try the wares in the form of a *cortado,* cappuccino, macchiato, espresso, *lágrima* (for those who like some coffee in their milk) or a *coatepecano* (like *americano,* only local).

Casú
CAFE

(La Casa del Café; 📞 228-816-57-11; www.facebook. com/cafecasucoatepec; Calle 5 de Mayo; ⊙ 9am-9pm; 🐾) A charming cafe run by a friendly team of coffee roasters, who serve up their delicious wares (think fantastic coffee and mouthwatering cakes) in a lovely back garden space a short distance from the main square.

🛍 Shopping

Enriqueta
COFFEE

(📞 228-816-86-59; www.facebook.com/enriqueta mx; Rebolledo 11; ⊙ 9am-8pm) At one of the better coffee shops in town, the heady brew can be purchased as beans or ground – fine, extra fine and coarse. For 500g you'll pay around M$90.

ℹ Information

Tourist Office (📞 228-816-04-34; http://somoscoatepec.com; cnr Rebolledo & Arteaga, Palacio Municipal s/n; ⊙ 9am-2pm & 4-7pm Mon-Fri, 9:30am-6:30pm Sat & Sun) A helpful office in the Palacio Municipal on Parque Hidalgo.

ℹ Getting There & Away

Regular buses (M$15) arrive from Xalapa's CAXA and Los Sauces terminals, or a taxi is around M$100. Buses for Xico (M$15) leave from Constitución between Aldama and Juárez. The ADO **bus station** (📞 228-816-96-19; Río Sordo s/n) serves Puebla and Mexico City

---

Xico

📞 228 / POP 18,652 / ELEV 1297M

Quiet and hilly Xico is a small, beguiling town; in 2011 it joined the ranks of Mexico's government-sanctioned *pueblos mágicos.* Just 8km from Coatepec, Xico attracts devotees of *mole* and handicrafts rather than coffee, while its cobbled streets and varied colonial architecture make it an increasingly popular weekend retreat. Exuberant masked and costumed dances are a vital part of Xico's many fiestas, and within Mexico the town is best known for its annual Fiesta de Santa Magdalena, held each July and famous for a running of the bulls à la Pamplona in Spain.

◎ Sights

The tourist office might be able to organize a coffee-farm tour.

★ Cascada de Texolo
WATERFALL

(off Camino a la Cascada; ⊙ 24hr) **FREE** From Xico, it's a pleasant, signposted 3km walk (or short drive along a potholed road) past an ex-hacienda to the spectacular, plunging, 80m Cascada de Texolo. From the viewpoint, cross the bridge. A five-minute walk leads to the **Cascada de la Monja**, featured in the film *Romancing the Stone* (1984); the said 'stone' was hidden behind it. The main trail continues up to a viewpoint restaurant; take the steep Sendero de Ocelot (M$10) down for an up-close look at Cascada de Texolo.

Though some locals swim in the Cascada de la Monja, à la Kathleen Turner and Michael Douglas, the current is strong, so you take your safety into your own hands.

Museo del Danzante Xiqueño MUSEUM

(☑228-129-66-97; Av Hidalgo 76, Casa de Cultura; ⏰10am-6pm Tue-Fri) **FREE** Inside the Casa de Cultura, this excellent, colorful museum takes you through the centuries-old history of Xico's costumed dances that take pride of place during the town's celebrations dedicated to its patron saint. The mask-carving tradition is also explained, as is the role of each masked character – the bull, the clown, the *negro separado* – in each dance.

Café Gourmet Pepe PLANTATION

(☑228-855-09-70; Carretera Xico-Coatepec Km 1; tour M$60; ⏰10am-5pm) 🌿 This plantation produces almost-organic, shade-grown coffee. It also offers tours (call ahead) and sells delicious coffee and liquors. Get off at the first bus stop in Xico and walk back 150m to where you'll see signs on the right.

Casa Museo Totomoxtle MUSEUM

(cnr Aldama & Juárez; ⏰4-7pm) **FREE** A small museum highlighting the town's peculiar artisanal pastime of making intricate and detailed figures from *hojas de maiz* (maize leaves). Only in Xico! Opening hours can be flexible.

🎊 Festivals & Events

★ Fiesta de Santa Magdalena RELIGIOUS

(⏰Jul 15-24) The mother of all festivals, involving exuberant costumed dances, processions and more. The Magdalena statue in the Parroquia de Santa María Magdalena (located at the end of Avenida Hidalgo) is clothed in a different elaborate dress each day for 30 days around the fiesta. A running of the bulls takes place through the streets on July 22.

Gigantic floral arches are raised, and streets are artistically decorated with carpets of colored sawdust in preparation for the saint's procession.

🛏 Sleeping & Eating

Hotel Paraje Coyopolan HOTEL $

(☑228-813-12-66; www.coyopolan.com; Venustiano Carranza Sur s/n; s/d incl breakfast from M$550/685; P🐕🛜) It's all about bright colors and lively Mexican design at this OK place right on the river just outside the town. The hotel arranges hiking, canyoning and rappelling in the surrounding mountains and canyons, making it a great base for outdoor activities. Some rooms are windowless but open out onto balconies.

Posada los Naranjos HOTEL $

(☑228-153-54-54; Av Hidalgo 193; r from M$400; P🛜) With just nine rooms and right in the center of town, this no-frills place is a willdo-for-a-night budget option. Rooms have high ceilings and, though clean, are windowless and musty. It's a short amble down Xico's main street from the church. The dawn chorus of the church bells is either a boon or a bane, depending on your outlook.

★ Las Magdalenas BOUTIQUE HOTEL $$$

(☑228-813-03-14; www.lasmagdalenas.com.mx; Hidalgo 123; r incl breakfast from M$1590; P🛜) This gorgeous colonial house has been impressively transformed into an outstanding boutique hotel. It boasts a fabulous garden full of flowers, common areas with gilded mirrors, and split-level rooms that are surprisingly light and modern for such an old-world setting. The on-site restaurant is atmospheric, but the food is only so-so.

Los Portales Texolo MEXICAN $

(☑228-129-81-43; Av Hidalgo 109; mains M$60-120; ⏰9am-8pm Tue-Sun) Some way down Avenida Hidalgo from the church, you'll arrive at a small square that is popular with ecstatic birds at sunset. Here you'll find this friendly local place, where delicious *xiqueño* specialties such as *chiles en nogada* and *mole* are served outside, amid Xico's colonial splendor.

★ Restaurante Mesón Xiqueño MEXICAN $$

(☑228-813-07-81; Av Hidalgo 148; mains M$55-350; ⏰9am-9pm) Near the corner with Calle Carranza is Xico's best known restaurant. Dine inside the lovely courtyard and sample the famous local *mole* (a complex mix of chocolate, almonds sucrose and numerous secret ingredients), served in a number of different ways, as well as stuffed xalapeños, soup with the fragrant *xonequi* herb and more.

🛍 Shopping

Casa Doria ARTS & CRAFTS

(☑228-044-22-81; Av Hidalgo 193; ⏰11am-7pm) A good place for local handicrafts, including the distinctive, painted wooden masks worn by dancers during the town's many festivals.

La Casa de Lilu
FOOD

(Av Hidalgo 150; ⊙9am-7pm) Xico's trademark *mole* can be procured at this friendly shop. Also sells organic coffee.

ℹ Information

Tourist office (☑228-813-16-18; Av Hidalgo 76; ⊙9am-6pm) Inside the Casa de la Cultura; a good source of local info.

ℹ Getting There & Away

From the **bus terminal** (☑228-813-03-91; Nava s/n), frequent buses run to Xalapa's Los Sauces terminal (M$18) and to Coatepec (M$12).

Jalcomulco

☑279 / POP 4690 / ELEV 350M

Sitting in a lush valley just 30km southeast of Xalapa, tiny Jalcomulco hugs the Río Antigua (this stretch known as the Río Pescados) and is surrounded by jungle-covered hills. The area is rich with caves and luscious swimming spots, but it's most famous for its rapids – some of Mexico's best white water – which accommodate white-water enthusiasts from the beginner through to the more advanced.

Numerous operators offer multiday rafting packages and typically include other adventure activities, such as rappeling, horseback riding, mountain biking, canyoning and trekking.

While on weekends the place comes to life with numerous adventurers descending on it, the rest of the time Jalcomulco remains a soporific village amid mango plantations and sugarcane fields.

⚡ Activities

★ Jalco Expediciones
RAFTING

(☑279-832-36-87; www.jalcoexpediciones.com. mx; Calle 20 de Noviembre 17; day package M$780; ⊙9am-6pm) Very professional rafting company with excellent equipment. It offers rafting/rappelling/zip-lining packages, with the bonus of wood-fired pizza waiting for customers upon return. Day packages and multiday adventures available.

★ Expediciones México Verde
TOUR

(☑800-362-88-00; www.mexicoverde.com; Carretera Tuzamapan-Jalcomulco Km 6; 5hr rafting trip M$790, kayaking M$890; ⊙9am-5pm) The list of white-knuckle, wet and wild adrenaline activities offered by this professional establishment will get the heart of even the most reckless racing. This is one of the longest-standing operators in Jalcomulco, with luxurious accommodations in the form of spacious safari tents scattered in jungly grounds, its own restaurant, spa and *temascal* (herbal steam room). Located around 6km north of town.

Armonía Rafting
TOUR

(☑279-832-35-80; www.armoniarafting.com; Zaragoza 56; rafting day trip M$850; ⊙9am-6pm Mon-Fri, to 3pm Sat, to 1pm Sun) One of the top rafting operators in Jalcomulco, with three-day, two-night packages that include accommodations (camping/hostel/hotel M$2390/2590/2790 per person), two rafting outings, rappelling, zip-lining, meals, transportation, guide and a steaming session in a *temascal* (traditional herbal steam room). Day activities also available.

🛏 Sleeping & Eating

Posada del Río
HOTEL $

(☑279-832-35-27; cnr Zaragoza & Madero; r M$680; ❄🖎🏊) Centrally located, this small, ochre-colored hotel has just 14 compact rooms, clustered around a courtyard filled with greenery and a pool. There's a rustic mansion vibe to the place, the on-site restaurant prepares delicious local dishes, and the service is helpful and friendly.

Aldea Ecoturismo
TENTED CAMP $$

(☑279-832-37-51; www.aldeajalcomulco.com.mx; Carretera Tuzamapan-Jalcomulco Km 3; tent per person M$555, s/d bungalow from M$647/1200; 🏊) Around 3km out of town, this leafy property allows you to live out your jungle fantasies by camping amid the tangled vines or sleeping in tree-house bungalows (there are terrestrial ones as well). Rafting, rappeling and other adrenaline-packed activities are on the menu, and you can steam your aching muscles afterward in a traditional *temascal*.

★ Rodaventa Natural
RESORT $$$

(☑279-822-35-97; www.rodaventonatural. com; Constitución s/n; 3-/4-person bungalow M$1638/1810, safari tent M$2155; ❄🖎🏊) Just south of the river, adorable, snug thatch-roofed bamboo bungalows (with extra loft beds) and luxurious, spacious safari tents surround a pool and a *palapa*-style restaurant that sit amid lush grounds. The decor inside the lodgings is vibrant, with bold splashes of color, and there also a luxury spa and traditional *temascal* to chill out in.

The resort specializes in multiday packages that include rafting, rappelling, whitewater kayaking, canyoning, zip-lining and more.

★ **Restaurante Nachita**　　SEAFOOD **$$**
(☑ 228-832-35-19; Madero 4; mains M$95-320; ⊗ 8am-9pm; 🐾) Sit on the deck overlooking the river and order one of the restaurant's specialties: *manuelitos* (locally caught crawfish) in salsa verde or chipotle sauce, a hearty *torta be mariscos* (seafood pie) or seafood *cazuela* (casserole), served with amazing homemade salsas and washed down with cups of *agua de jamaica* (hibiscus iced tea) the size of goldfish bowls. Popular with groups.

🛈 Getting There & Away

Buses to Xalapa's Azteca terminal (M$40, 1½ hours, six daily) and to Coatepec (M$30, 45 minutes, hourly) leave from the main square. Adventure tour operators from Veracruz City and elsewhere offer transfers to Jalcomulco as part of their rafting packages.

Tlapacoyan

☑ 225 / POP 35,338

At the mouth of the Río Filobobos (known as Río Bobos and famous for its rapids), head 60km inland from Nautla on Hwy 129 and you'll hit Tlapacoyan, where a handful of rafting companies are based, and where the waterfall Cascada de Encanto provides a gorgeous swimming spot. Tlapacoyan itself is fairly unexciting agricultural town, surrounded by banana plantations and citrus fruit groves, but it's worth an overnight stopover, if only to visit the two exciting and recently discovered archaeological sites nearby, Caujilote and Vega de la Peña, collectively referred to as Filobobos.

👁 Sights

★ **El Cuajilote**　　ARCHAEOLOGICAL SITE
(M$55; ⊗ 9am-5pm) This beautiful site consists of temples, platforms and shrines, partially reclaimed from the jungle, around a long, rectangular plaza, and dates back to AD 600–900 and was once home to peoples unknown. It's worth visiting for the beauty of the surroundings alone; you are likely to have the serene place to yourself.

Follow the 'Filobobos' signs south from Tlapacoyan along a paved road; the last 1km is unpaved and very bumpy. Rancho Grande-bound taxis can drop you at the 1km turnoff.

As you enter the site, the first two buildings on your right are a ball court. Directly opposite is the excavated **Templo Mayor**, an impressive multi-tiered pyramid. Along the two sides of the plaza you can make out the shapes of other platforms and temples beneath the lush vegetation. A brook separates the Templo Mayor from the remains of shrines in the middle of the plaza. The archaeological project is ongoing and the origins of El Cuajilote's residents are yet to be determined. Over 1500 phallic fertility figures were found at **Shrine A4**, suggesting the influence of a Huastec fertility cult, whereas the earliest buildings at the site (possibly dating back to BC 1000) seem to be Olmec in appearance and stone sculptures found here appear to be similar to Totonac in style. Archaeologists believe that it is also possible that the two sites that make up Filobobos were, in fact, settled by a hitherto unknown Mesoamerican civilization.

Vega de la Peña　　ARCHAEOLOGICAL SITE
(M$55; ⊗ 9am-5pm) Reachable only on foot and covering 8 sq km, Vega de la Peña is a seldom-visited, recently discovered site of a pre-Hispanic settlement that's been only partially excavated. It shows Olmec, Huastec, Totonac and Toltec influences and its history spans more than 1500 years, from BC 100 to AD 1500, though its heyday seems to have been between AD 1200 and 1500. It's 2.5km away from the El Cuajilote site, where you can get directions.

It's not as visually impressive as its sister Filolobos site, El Cuajilote; there's a small ball court and some residential buildings, but the underlying idea is mindblowing. It is possible that the yet to be excavated ruins are considerably more extensive than currently believed, and that the complex civilization that flourished here played a considerably more prominent role in terms of Mesoamerican trade and influence than previously believed.

🏃 Activities

★ **Aventurec**　　RAFTING
(☑ 225-315-43-00; www.aventurec.com; off Hwy 129, El Encanto; day rafting packages from M$800) Highly regarded operator who runs three types of rafting trips on Río Filobobos,

including one that combines wet and wild river adventure with stopping by the two archaeological sites on the way. Multiday packages that include kayaking, zip-lining and other adrenaline-packed activities come highly recommended. Choose between camping or staying in dorms or cabins.

🛏 Sleeping & Eating

Hotel Posada Oliver   HISTORIC HOTEL $
(☑225-315-42-12; Av Cuauhtemoc 400; r M$500; ❄🛜) The pick of Tlapacoyan's hotels (not that it's much of a horse race), Posada Oliver is just off the main square, with stone arches and greenery-filled courtyard adding much-needed character. Rooms are simple but comfortable, with cable TV and air-con.

Las Acamallas   MEXICAN $
(☑225-315-02-91; Heroes de Tlapacoyan s/n; mains M$60-130; ⊗8am-10pm) Just off the main square, two-tiered Las Acamallas is a sure bet for some enchiladas, chicken cooked a dozen ways and cups of *horchata* (rice milk drink) as big as your head.

❶ Getting There & Away

From the **bus terminal** (Zaragoza s/n) there are ADO services to Mexico City (M$395, 5½ hours, nine daily), Puebla (M$250, 3½ hours, seven daily) and Xalapa (M$134, 2½ hours, 10 daily). For connecting services to Veracruz or Papantla, you need to take a 2nd-class bus to Martínez de la Torre, 22km east, and change there.

Córdoba

☑271 / POP 142,500 / ELEV 817M

Not to be confused with its famous namesakes in Spain and Argentina, Córdoba has an illustrious history and a justifiable sense of civic pride; the contract that sealed Mexico's independence was signed here in 1821. The city itself was originally founded in 1618 as a staging post between Mexico City and the coast, with the purpose of protecting the Spanish crown's interests from the local slave rebellion, led by Gaspar Yanga, which was strong in the area.

As an overnight stop, Córdoba is less lovely than nearby Orizaba but more lively, on the sheer strength of its main plaza. It's a 24-hour live 'show,' where theater-goers in high heels dodge hungry pigeons and grandpas moonlight as marimba players. Watching over it all is an impressive baroque cathedral, easily the most resplendent in the state.

⊙ Sights

Most of Córdoba's sights ring its main plaza, Parque de 21 de Mayo, which is a sight in itself.

**Catedral de la
Inmaculada Concepción**   CATHEDRAL
(Parque de 21 de Mayo; ⊗hours vary) Dating from 1688, this blue baroque cathedral has an elaborate facade flanked by twin bell towers. The interior is surprisingly ornate for Mexico, with gold-leaf detailing and marble floors. The chapel features candlelit statues with altars, such as a gruesome Jesus on the cross and an eerily despairing Virgen de la Soledad. The mixture of glitz and gore is a visual metaphor for a disturbing historical dichotomy: the richness of the conquistadors and the misery that the indigenous people endured.

Ex-Hotel Zevallos   HISTORIC BUILDING
(Parque de 21 de Mayo) Built in 1687, this is the former home of the *condes* (counts) of Zevallos. It's on the northeast side of Parque de 21 de Mayo, behind the *portales*. Plaques in the courtyard record that Juan O'Donojú and Agustín de Iturbide met here on August 24, 1821, and agreed on the terms for Mexico's independence. They also concurred that a Mexican, not a European, should be head of state. The building is now full of restaurants and cafes.

Parque de 21 de Mayo   PLAZA
You don't come to Córdoba's main plaza to tick off a list of 'sights.' You come here to live life. The square vies with Veracruz city's as the region's most jazzy and vibrant. It's far larger than the port city's plaza, though a seemingly unending line of musicians makes up for any lack of intimacy. Opposite the cathedral on the square's west side is the splendiferous **Palacio Municipal**, replete with a memorable Diego Rivera interior mural.

Parque Ecológico Paso Coyol   PARK
(cnr Calle 6 & Av 19, Bella Vista; M$10; ⊗7am-6pm) 🌿 Formerly a 4-hectare abandoned lot overrun by 'delinquents,' this eco-conscious park is now patronized by *cordobeses,* who run and walk trails that snake around gardens punctuated with exercise stations. Your meager entrance fee pays for both *campesinos* (country people) and biologists alike to maintain the place. Follow Calle 3 south from the plaza for 1.5km. The street changes

name, weaves through a suburb and bottoms out at the park.

Museo de la Ciudad
MUSEUM

(☑ 271-712-09-67; Calle 3 btwn Avs 3 & 5; ⊙ 9am-5pm Mon-Fri) FREE This museum, which is a part of the city university, has a modest but interesting collection of artifacts including a fine Aztec ball-court marker and some Olmec figurines. There's also a replica of the magnificent statue of *El señor de las Limas* that resides in Xalapa's Museo de Antropología (p219). You'll find it just off the main square, opposite the Centro Cultural Municipal.

☞ Tours

Cecila Rábago
CULTURAL

(☑ 271-120-20-30; cecirabago@hotmail.com; Fortín de las Flores; 1-4 people per day from M$1400) A well-established, bilingual tour guide in the area, Cecila is an expert on history and sites in the Fortín–Córdoba–Orizaba area. A firecracker of a woman, she can offer tours of the city and organic coffee plantations, take you on all-day hiking excursions off the tourist track, and many other things in between. Contact her in advance.

✵✍ Festivals & Events

Good Friday
RELIGIOUS

On the evening of Good Friday, Córdoba marks Jesus' crucifixion with a procession of silence, in which thousands of residents walk through the streets behind an altar of the Virgin. Everyone holds a lit candle, no one utters a word and the church bells are strangely quiet.

🛏 Sleeping

Hotel Los Reyes
HOTEL $

(☑ 271-712-25-38; www.losreyeshotel.com; cnr Calle 3 & Av 2; s/d M$250/299; ❄🖥) Just half a block from the main square, this excellent cheapie distinguishes itself with friendly service and its attention to detail, with good beds and quality bed linens (embroidered with the hotel name) in the fan-cooled rooms. Half the rooms face indoors; of the outdoor-facing ones, rooms 203 to 206 are the best, as they face the quieter Calle 3.

Hotel Bello
HOTEL $

(☑ 271-712-81-22; www.hotelbello.com/cordoba; cnr Av 2 & Calle 5; s/d/tr M$635/696/720; P🖥@🖥) Brightly painted in yellow and thus hard to miss, this modern hotel is spotless and well located just moments from the main square. The rooms are fresh, with balconies, and some have great views toward Pico de Orizaba. The staff are affable. Go for the top-floor balcony rooms. It's on a busy street, so gets noisy.

Hotel Layfer
HOTEL $$

(☑ 271-714-05-05; www.hoteleslayfer.com; Av 5 No 908; s/d M$810/1000; P🖥🖥🏊) Definitely Córdoba's fanciest hotel (if not necessarily its best value), the Layfer has modern, but not wildly exciting, rooms arranged around a central swimming pool. Mileage is added with a wide array of extras, including complimentary body-care products, a bar, gym, restaurant and games room.

Hotel Mansur
HOTEL $$$

(☑ 271-712-60-00; www.hotelmansur.com.mx; Av 1 No 301; r M$1642-2552; P🖥🖥) Claiming five stories of prime viewing space above Córdoba's main plaza, the venerable Mansur, with its vast balconies equipped with thick wooden chairs, makes you feel as if you're part of the 'show' going on below. The hotel has undergone a complete face-lift, exchanging old-world glamour for contemporary art. The rooms are suitably luxurious, and some have private terraces.

There's no price hike for rooms at the front, so request one of these if you relish a view, and one at the back if all you desire is peace and relative quiet.

🍴 Eating

Córdoba has a lively eating scene with plenty of choice. Numerous restaurants are found on, or within a couple of blocks of, the main square, and there's a cluster of upmarket eateries where Avenida 9 intersects with Calles 22 and 20.

El Patio de la Abuela
MEXICAN $

(☑ 271-712-06-06; Calle 1 No 208; mains M$35-120; ⊙ 8am-midnight; 🖥) This friendly, informal eatery serves a variety of tacos, *picaditas* (thick tortillas with different toppings) and *tamales*, as well as hearty *pozole* (spiced hominy and pork stew), *mondongo* (cow tripe soup – a hangover cure!) and gut-busting helpings of grilled meats. Just like *abuela* used to make.

Calufe Café
CAFE $

(Calle 3 No 212; coffee from M$25; ⊙ 8am-9pm Sun-Wed, to midnight Thu-Sat; 🖥) If only all cafes could be like this. Calufe occupies the interior of an agreeably peeling colonial mansion with eclectic nooks arranged

BUSES FROM CÓRDOBA

Deluxe and 1st-class buses from Córdoba include the following:

DESTINATION	FARE (M$)	DURATION (HR)	FREQUENCY (DAILY)
Fortín	20	½	frequent
Mexico City (TAPO)	434	5½	frequent
Oaxaca	278-400	5¼-7	4
Orizaba	40	¾-1	frequent
Puebla	169	3¼	frequent
Veracruz	70-164	1¾-2¼	frequent
Xalapa	108-242	3	11

around a dimly lit plant-filled courtyard. Guitar and vocal duos provide a melancholy musical backdrop in the evenings. Calufe sells its own blend of coffee, along with melt-in-the-mouth coffee cake and other diet-busting snacks.

Roof Garden Restaurant FUSION $$
(☑ 271-716-41-42; Av 9 Bis btwn Calles 26 & 28; mains M$75-240; ☺9:30am-11pm) Offering creatively crafted and presented contemporary Mexican cooking with flashes of inspiration from a sun-soaked Mediterranean, this plant-filled and cheery little restaurant out in the western reaches of the city is one of the best places to eat in Córdoba. Alongside modern takes on Mexican classics there's a range of carpaccios, pastas, multi-layer burgers, and good coffee and homemade lemonade.

El Balcón del Zevallos MEXICAN $$$
(☑ 271-714-66-99; Av 1 No 101; mains M$130-420; ☺5pm-1am Mon-Thu, from 2pm Fri-Sun; ☎) The upper floor of the beautiful former Hotel Zevallos claims the prize for Córdoba's most famous restaurant. It has a wonderful setting – a balcony overlooking the plaza – an extensive wine list (including some decent Mexican reds) and good (though overpriced) meat and seafood dishes cooked *a la parrilla* (on the barbecue) at your table. Service is not overly officious.

Drinking & Nightlife

★**Hêrmann Thômas**
Coffee Masters COFFEE
(☑ 271-712-50-71; http://hermann-thomas.com; Calle 2 104, btwn Avs 1 & 3; ☺7:45am-10pm; ☎) Its sleek interior decked out with books on art, design and history, the region's loveliest coffee shop carefully sources its beans from select *fincas* (farms) in Mexico's coffee regions. Have your coffee in a variety of ways,

including iced Vietnamese style, and get a bag of gourmet beans to go. Teas and fruit juice mixes also available.

ℹ️ Information

Banks around the Plaza de Armas have 24-hour ATMs.

Hospital Covadonga (☑ 271-714-55-20; www. corporativodehospitales.com.mx; Av 7 No 1610; ☺24hr) Urgent medical care at all hours.

Tourist Office (☑ 271-712-43-44; Centro Cultural Municipal, cnr Av 3 & Calle 3; ☺8:30am-4pm & 6-7:30pm Mon-Fri, 10am-2pm Sat & Sun) Helpful staff offer maps and information. Volunteers sometimes give tours of the city.

ℹ️ Getting There & Away

BUS

Córdoba's **bus station** (Blvd Augin Millan), which has deluxe, 1st-class and 2nd-class services, is 2.5km southeast of the plaza. To get to the town center from the station, take a local bus marked 'Centro' or buy a taxi ticket (M$40). To Orizaba, it's more convenient to take a local bus from the corner of Avenida 11 and Calle 3 than to go out to the Córdoba bus station.

CAR & MOTORCYCLE

Córdoba, Fortín de las Flores and Orizaba are linked by toll Hwy 150D, the route that most buses take, and by the much slower Hwy 150. A scenic back road goes through the hills from Fortín, via Huatusco, to Xalapa.

Orizaba

☑ 272 / POP 124,000 / ELEV 1219M

Orizaba manages to surprise you. At first sight it's a workaday medium-sized Mexican town, but it quickly turns out to be one of the more appealing towns in Veracruz and is home to a number of idiosyncratic sights, a pleasant old colonial center, some lovely parks and a gorgeous riverside walk. It's also within

VERACRUZ ORIZABA

easy reach of Mexico's highest mountain, the magnificent Pico de Orizaba (5611m), and a vertigo-inducing cable car has made viewing this dormant volcano easier than ever before. The most striking sight in the town itself is Gustave Eiffel's unique art nouveau Palacio de Hierro (Iron Palace), while the most revealing is the excellent art museum, home to the second-largest Diego Rivera collection in Mexico. Add to that a varied dining scene and the smell of roasted beans wafting from numerous coffee shops, and you may find yourself lingering longer than expected.

⊙ Sights

★ Teleférico de Orizaba   CABLE CAR
(☑ 278-114-72-82; Sur 4 btwn Calles Poniente 3 & Poniente 5; M$50; ⊘ 9am-7pm Mon-Fri, to 7pm Sat, Sun & holidays) This cable car rattles and sways visitors from its riverside site across from the Palacio Municipal right up to the top of the Cerro del Borrego hill (1240m) for incredible views over the city and easy access to hiking routes. It takes just five minutes to travel nearly 1km and climb some 320m. Vertigo sufferers will probably just have to ask people to describe the view to them!

It's a fab excursion, and once you reach the top of the Cerro del Borrego, you'll find signed walking trails and an 'eco-park,' which has picnic areas, a small military museum, playgrounds and, between 1pm and 6pm on weekends, a re-creation of a military battle that took place here in the late 19th century.

★ Palacio de Hierro   MUSEUM
(☑ 272-728-91-36; Parque Castillo; ⊘ 9am-7pm) **FREE** The 'Iron Palace' is Orizaba's fanciful art nouveau landmark. The palace's interior has been converted into half a dozen small museums. Most notable are the Museo de la Cerveza, tracking Orizaba's beer industry; the Museo de Fútbol (soccer); the Museo de Presidentes y Banderas, with info on *every* Mexican president as well as a whole load of flags; and the Museo Interactivo, with a small planetarium and some science exhibits, including a bed of nails you can lie on.

Also on site are the Museo de Geográfico de Orizaba (geography of the Orizaba area) and Museo de las Raíces de Orizaba (archaeological artifacts).

Alexandre Gustave Eiffel, a master of metallurgy who gave his name to the Eiffel Tower and engineered the Statue of Liberty's framework, designed this pavilion, which was built in Paris. Orizaba's mayor, eager to acquire an impressive European-style Palacio Municipal, bought it in 1892. Piece by piece it was shipped, then reassembled in Orizaba.

Museo de Arte del Estado   MUSEUM
(State Art Museum; ☑ 272-724-32-00; cnr Av Oriente 4 & Sur 25; M$20; ⊘ 10am-7pm Tue-Sun) Orizaba's wonderful Museo de Arte del Estado is housed in a gorgeously restored colonial building dating from 1776 and attached to the side of a church. The museum is divided into rooms that include Mexico's second-most-important permanent Diego Rivera collection, with 33 of his original works. There are also contemporary works by regional artists. Guides give complimentary tours in Spanish. The museum is 2km east of Parque Castillo.

Parque Alameda   PARK
(Av Poniente 2 & Sur 10; ⊘ 24hr; ⊕) About 1km west of the center, Parque Alameda is either a very large plaza or a very small park, depending on your expectations. What it doesn't lack is activity. Aside from the obligatory statues of dead heroes, you'll find an outdoor gym, a bandstand, food carts, shoe-shiners and a playground for kids, including a huge jungle of bouncy castles and air-filled slides. Practically the whole city rolls in at weekends after Sunday Mass.

Parque Castillo   PLAZA
(Av Colón Oriente; ⊘ 24hr) Smaller than your average Mexican city plaza, Parque Castillo is bereft of the normally standard Palacio Municipal (town hall), which sits several blocks away on Avenida Colón Poniente. Instead, it is watched over by the eclectic Palacio de Hierro and a 17th-century parish church, the Catedral de San Miguel Arcángel. On the south side is the neoclassical and still-functioning Teatro Ignacio de la Llave (1875), which hosts opera, ballet and classical-music concerts.

🏃 Activities

Paseo del Río   WALKING
This excellent 3km-long riverside walk, bordering Orizaba's clean eponymous river, has murals and abstract sculpture toward its southern end, beyond the cable car. There are 13 bridges along the way, including a suspension bridge and the arched Puente La Borda, dating from 1776. A good starting point is Avenida Poniente 8, about 600m northwest of the Palacio de Hierro.

From Avenida Poniente 8 you can head north to the Puente Tlachichilco or toward the southern end of the walk that culminates in a miniature Eiffel Tower, just beyond the railway bridge. If, as you walk you hear a deep growl that sounds suspiciously like a tiger, don't run away. There's a collection of animal enclosures along the walkway containing monkeys, parrots, crocodiles, lamas and, yes, even a tiger. All of the animals were born in captivity and cannot be released into the wild.

☞ Tours

Alberto Gochicoa
OUTDOORS
(☑cell 272-1037344) A recommended guide who can help organize various outdoor activities in nearby hills, mountains and canyons, including climbs partway up Pico de Orizaba. Highlights of the area include the gorgeous Cañón de la Carbonera near Nogales and the Cascada de Popócatl near Tequila.

Erick Carrera
OUTDOORS
(☑cell 272-1345571) A recommended guide to the Orizaba environs.

🛏 Sleeping

Orizaba has something to suit all budgets, from higher-end options on the Avenida Oriente 6 traffic strip and near Parque Alameda to lower-end choices in or near the center.

Hotel del Río
HOTEL $
(☑272-726-66-25; http://hoteldelrio.tripod.com; Av Poniente 8 No 315; s/d from M$360/380; P❋🕸) A pleasant place for an exceptional price make this a surefire winner. It has an attractive location right by the Río Orizaba, simple modern rooms with tacky 'art' in an old building, and a congenial, bilingual owner. It might not be as flowery and fancy as some hotels in Veracruz state, but it's certainly among the best value.

Hotel Plaza Palacio
HOTEL $
(☑272-725-99-23; Av Poniente 2 2-Bis; s/d/tr M$305/390/450; 🕸) You can't get more central than this place; the windows look directly onto the Palacio de Hierro. It's nothing special architecturally, and the rooms are clean but not particularly characterful. But you do get cable TV and a fan, as well as the town right on your doorstep.

Orizaba Inn
HOTEL $$
(☑272-725-06-26; www.hotelorizabainn.com. mx; Av Oriente 2 No 117; r/ste from M$690/890; ❂❋🕸) A fresh and funky hotel with turquoise accents in the bright, whitewashed rooms, thoroughly modern bathrooms and

mod cons. Some rooms come with balconies; have a look at a few if you can. Friendly staff and a decent breakfast up this hotel's game.

Hotel Mision Orizaba
BOUTIQUE HOTEL $$
(☑272-106-92-94; www.hotelesmision.com.mx; Av Oriente 6 No 64; s/d from M$1008/1313; P❋🕸🛗) Officially the smartest place in town, this revamped place has comfortable if surprisingly plain rooms set around a courtyard and a tiny swimming pool. There are some thoughtful touches to the rooms such as fresh flowers, writing desks and coffee machines. Plus the staff are very helpful.

★Hotel Tres79
BOUTIQUE HOTEL $$$
(☑272-725-23-79; http://tres79hotelboutique. com; r from M$1918; P❂❋🕸) This immaculate hotel punches way above Veracruz's weight. Each of its 14 rooms is individually styled to represent a Mexican writer, musician or artist (we particularly like the Agustín Lara room), with bold furnishings and great attention to creature comforts (hypoallergenic bedding, rain showers). The courtyard incorporates a vertical garden and tiled fountain, and the international restaurant is excellent.

🍴 Eating

In sedate Orizaba many restaurants close early, though the dining scene is excellent and incorporates fusion, steak and seafood restaurants, as well as atmospheric cafes. Head to the plaza for noteworthy Orizaban snacks including *garnachas* (open tortillas with chicken, onion and tomato salsa) or scour Avenida Oriente 4 in search of the best tacos.

Taco T
STREET FOOD $
(☑272-106-10-49; Av Oriente 4 1247; tacos from M$10; ⊙1pm-midnight) Join the locals in the bustling dining hall of the most popular *taquería* of the many strung along Avenida Oriente 4, and watch the cooks expertly slice off sizzling hunks of meat from the rotating skewers. Or get your tacos to go and enjoy them in the tranquility of the leafy plaza across the street.

Metlapilli
MEXICAN $
(☑272-705-24-82; Madero 350; dishes from M$10; ⊙8am-2pm Tue-Sun; 🍴) Run by a friendly mother-daughter team, this tiny eatery comprises exactly four tables that fill up come breakfast or lunch with customers clamoring for tacos filled with *flor de calabaza* (squash blossom) or mushrooms, and *picaditas* with assorted toppings. Most dishes

are vegetarian. Wash them down with a fresh juice or *licuado* (milkshake).

★ El Cebichero
SEAFOOD $$

(📞272-106-33-22; Av Oriente 4 No 855; mains M$65-250; ⏰11am-10pm Mon-Sat; 🤚) Spot this tiny *cevichería* by the puffer fish dangling outside and the fishing nets strung along the ceiling. Young chef Toni Serrano (who studied English in Bournemouth, UK) prepares such delights as scallop ceviche with tabaquero and habanero chili. He also grills steaks, since the place is a *parrilla* as well. Write a message on an M$20 note before you leave.

★ Marrón Cocina Galería
FUSION $$

(📞272-724-01-39; www.facebook.com/marron cocinagaleria; Av Oriente 4 No 1265; mains M$80-169; ⏰2-11pm Tue-Thu & Sun, to midnight Fri & Sat; 🤚) With buckets for lampshades, sunflowers on the tables and mildly distressed furniture, this cool and very good fusion restaurant has an easy, informal and convivial atmosphere. Some of the best items on the menu are Italian-Mexican fusion, such as wonderful, spicy *lasagna de mi suegra* (my mother-in-law's lasagna). The crunchy, thin pizzas are another treat.

🍷 Drinking & Nightlife

★ Gran Café de Orizaba
CAFE

(📞272-724-44-75; www.grancafedeorizaba.com; cnr Av Poniente 2 & Madero, Palacio de Hierro; snacks M$40-80; ⏰8am-10:30pm; 🤚) How often in Mexico can you sit back and enjoy a coffee and cake on the balcony of a regal cafe, inside an iron palace designed by Gustave Eiffel? Exactly – but this is your chance. The delightful decor, smart staff and selection of sandwiches, crepes and cake make

this an obvious place to break up your exploration of Orizaba.

Cafino
COFFEE

(📞272-100-57-36; www.facebook.com/cafino. orizaba; Oriente 4 No 327; ⏰10am-9pm Mon-Sat) A thimble-sized cafe that accommodates around 2½ people comfortably. Worth popping in for a brew, since it uses only high-quality, high-altitude arabica from Mexico's coffee region.

El Interior
COFFEE

(📞272-726-45-31; cnr Av Oriente 4 & Sur 9; ⏰9am-8:30pm; 🤚) Books, coffee and art. This small literary cafe connected to a book and craft store is just what we wish all bookstores were like! El Interior is handily located between Parque Castillo and the Museo Arte del Estado.

ℹ Information

Banks with ATMs are on Avenida Oriente 2, a block south of the plaza.

Hospital Covadonga (📞272-725-50-19; www. corporativodehospitales.com.mx; Sur 5 No 398)

Orizaba Pueblo Mágico It's well worth downloading this app, a comprehensive guide to the town's attractions.

Tourist Office (📞272-728-91-36; www.orizaba. travel; Palacio de Hierro; ⏰9am-7pm) Has enthusiastic staff and plenty of brochures.

ℹ Getting There & Away

BUS

Local buses from Fortín and Córdoba (cnr Av Oriente 9 & Norte 14) stop four blocks north and six blocks east of the town center, while the **AU 2nd-class bus station** (Poniente 8 No 425) is northwest of the center.

BUSES FROM ORIZABA

Daily 1st-class buses include the following:

DESTINATION	FARE (M$)	DURATION (HR)	FREQUENCY (DAILY)
Córdoba	40	¾	frequent
Fortín de las Flores	34	½	frequent
Mexico City (TAPO)	364	4½	frequent
Mexico City (Terminal Norte)	366-414	4½-5½	4
Oaxaca	374	5¼-6	6
Puebla	212-250	2¼	frequent
Veracruz	176	2-3¼	frequent
Xalapa	260	3¼-4	12

The modern 1st-class **bus station** (☎222-107-22-55; cnr Av Oriente 6 & Sur 13) handles all ADO, ADO GL and deluxe UNO services.

CAR & MOTORCYCLE

Toll Hwy 150D, which bypasses central Orizaba, goes east to Córdoba and west, via a spectacular ascent, to Puebla (160km). Toll-free Hwy 150 runs east to Córdoba and Veracruz (150km) and southwest to Tehuacán, 65km away over the hair-raising Cumbres de Acultzingo.

Pico de Orizaba

Rising high above the region, the snow-capped tip of this mighty volcano throws down a gauntlet to those who cannot resist the siren call of a peak not conquered.

🏃 Activities

★ Pico de Orizaba   TREKKING

At a cloud-scraping and breathless 5611m, the snowcapped Pico de Orizaba is Mexico's tallest mountain (and the third tallest in North America after USA's Mt Denali and Canada's Mt Logan) and it dominates the horizons for miles around. Climbing it is a serious, six-day undertaking, suitable only for experienced high-altitude trekkers prepared for extreme cold and possible altitude sickness.

Called Citlaltépetl (Star Mountain) in the Náhuatl language, the views from the summit of this massive dormant volcano take in the mountains of Popocatépetl, Iztaccíhuatl and La Malinche to the west and the Gulf of Mexico to the east. You might imagine then that thoughts of scaling this monster would tempt tourists from far and wide, but it gets relatively few takers, because you need a couple of weeks to spare and must be prepared to take a short technical course on traversing ice fields, as the last section of the ascent is particularly demanding.

Anyone climbing the mountain should be well equipped, and all but the most experienced will need a guide. There are a number of recommended guide companies from the US, but the only local one is Servimont, a climber-owned outfit passed down through the Reyes family. Do not attempt to rush up this mountain because altitude sickness, which at these heights can be deadly, is a very real concern. If you experience any kind of symptoms, descend immediately.

The best climbing period is October to March, with the most popular time being December and January.

★ Servimont   TREKKING

(☎245-451-50-19, cell 222-6275406; www.servimont.com.mx; Ortega 1A, Tlachichuca) Servimont is a climber-owned outfit passed down through the Reyes family since the 1930s. As the longest-running operation in the area, it also acts as a Red Cross rescue facility. It's based in the small town of Tlachichuca (2600m), which is a common starting point for expeditions. It is the only Mexican operator to offer Pico de Orizaba ascents.

Book your expedition with Servimont two to four months in advance and allow four to seven days to acclimatize, summit and return. Shorter and less demanding ascents on offer are those of Iztaccíhuatl, Malinche and Nevado de Toluca volcanoes.

❶ Getting There & Away

Autobuses Valles (Av Hidalgo 13A) runs 2nd-class buses to Ciudad Serdán (M$20, one hour), where you can change to another bus to Orizaba (M$60, two hours).

NORTHERN VERACRUZ

The northern half of Veracruz state, between the coast and southern fringes of the Sierra Madre Oriental, mainly consists of lush rolling pastureland. Laguna de Tamiahua is the region's largest wetland, while the Gulf's Costa Esmeralda has some fine isolated (though sometimes polluted) beaches, which are popular with local holidaymakers. The major attraction is El Tajín archaeological site; it's reachable from the historic town of Papantla and is refreshingly untouristed compared to some of Mexico's more renowned archaeological sites. Just north of Papantla is busy, unattractive Poza Rica, which can be a useful pit stop. Tecolutla is a quintessential Mexican beach resort with black sand and some very good seafood, while Tuxpan is a worthwhile stopover if you're heading north to Tampico and beyond.

Tuxpan

📞 783 / POP 89,800

Tuxpan (sometimes spelled Túxpam), 300km north of Veracruz and 190km south of Tampico, is a steamy fishing town and minor oil port. If you pass through, you can enjoy excellent seafood, take a trip across the broad Río Tuxpan to visit a little museum devoted to Cuban-Mexican friendship, or join vacationing Mexicans on Playa Norte, the beach 12km to the east. The town itself is no great beauty, but is well set up for overnighting travelers passing through en route to Tampico.

◉ Sights

Museo de la Amistad
México-Cuba   MUSEUM
(Mexican-Cuban Friendship Museum; Obregón s/n; ☺9am-5pm) FREE Commemorating the colonial histories of Mexico and Cuba and their significance to Fidel Castro's ill-fated uprising of 1956, this museum is filled with pictures of Che Guevara and Castro, a model of the revolutionary yacht, *Granma*, and more. To get here, take a boat (M$5) across the river from the quay near the ADO bus station, walk several blocks south to Obregón, then turn right. The museum is at the western end of Obregón, on the river.

On November 25, 1956, the errant lawyer-turned-revolutionary, Fidel Castro, set sail from the Río Tuxpan with 82 poorly equipped soldiers to start an uprising in Cuba. The sailing was made possible thanks to an encounter in Mexico City between Castro and Antonio del Conde Pontones (aka 'El Cuate'). On meeting Castro for the first time, Pontones, a legal arms dealer, was immediately taken by the Cuban's strong personality and agreed to help him obtain guns and a boat. To smooth the process, he bought a house on the south side of the Río Tuxpan, where he moored the boat and allowed Fidel to meet in secret. Today that house is the Museo de la Amistad México-Cuba.

☞ Tours

Paseos Turísticos
Negretti   BOAT TOUR, DIVING
(☑783-835-45-64; Recreo s/n) A local tour operator that organizes diving (M$2500 per eight-person group, not including equipment), fishing (M$450 per boat per hour), boat trips to the nearby mangroves (M$600 for two hours), kayaking (M$120 per person) and water-skiing (M$320 for 30 minutes). It has an office located on the south side of the Río Tuxpan where the cross-river ferry docks.

🛏 Sleeping & Eating

Hotel Reforma   HOTEL $$
(☑783-834-11-46; http://hotel-reforma.com.mx; Av Juárez 25; s/d/ste M$835/950/1200; P ❄ ☎) The grand exterior of the Reforma leads into a smart atrium lobby with a small waterfall and some 98 comfortable if rather functional rooms. They include flat-screen TVs and relentless brown carpeting. There's a smart restaurant downstairs.

★ Taquería Los
Nuevos 4 Vientos   STREET FOOD $
(☑783-134-48-76; Morelos s/n; tacos M$10; ☺9:30am-midnight) One of four *taquerías* (taco stands) in a row, this one wins our praise and loyalty with its extensive collection of fresh salsas, which complement the six types of meat (*asado*, tripe, *pastór* etc) that are deftly fried and scooped into tacos. Perpetually packed with locals at mealtimes, it clearly gets their vote, too.

Restaurante Mora   SEAFOOD $$
(☑783-837-09-93; Ribera del Pescador s/n; mains M$100-160; ☺noon-9pm) The first of a long row of simple seafood restaurants along the Laguna de Tampamachoco, Mora serves up stuffed crabs, *camarones enchipotlados*

BUSES FROM TUXPAN

First-class departures from the ADO station include the following.

DESTINATION	FARE (M$)	DURATION (HR)	FREQUENCY (DAILY)
Mexico City (Terminal Norte)	396	4¼	13
Papantla	92	2	12
Tampico	294	3¼	frequent
Veracruz	394	6	11
Villahermosa	771	13	4
Xalapa	398	6½	9

(chipotle shrimp), oysters on the half shell, and the fresh catch of the day, which is grilled, fried, stuffed with shrimp or *a la diabla* (hot!).

ℹ️ Information

Tourist Booth (📞783-110-28-11; http://tuxpan. com.mx; Juárez 25, Palacio Municipal; ⊙9am-7pm Mon-Fri, 10am-2pm Sat) Staff at this booth have vast reserves of enthusiasm: you'll go away overloaded with maps and brochures.

ℹ️ Getting There & Away

Most 1st-class buses leaving Tuxpan are *de paso* (passing through). Booking a seat in advance might be a good idea. There are several bus terminals, but the 1st-class ADO **bus station** (📞783-834-01-02; cnr Rodríguez & Av Juárez) is the most convenient from the center.

There is a M$5 ferry service across the river at various points between Guerrero and Parque Reforma.

Papantla

📞784 / POP 53,546 / ELEV 180M

Spread across a succession of wooded hills, the solidly indigenous city of Papantla has a history, look and feel that stares firmly back in time to a pre-Hispanic or, more precisely, Totonac period of grandeur. Predating the Spanish conquest, the city was founded around AD 1230. Traditionally a launching pad for people visiting the nearby ruins of El Tajín, Papantla has carved its own niche in recent years, stressing its indigenous heritage and promoting its central position in the world's best vanilla-growing region. You'll see Totonacs wearing traditional clothing here – the men in loose white shirts and trousers, and the women in embroidered blouses and *quechquémitls* (traditional capes). Meanwhile *voladores* 'fly' and local artisans peddle handicrafts in the attractive main square.

◉ Sights

Iglesia de Nuestra Señora de la Asunción   CHURCH
(Zócalo; ⊙8am-7pm) Overlooking the *zócalo* from its high platform, this church is notable for its large cedar doors and quartet of indoor canvases by a Jalisco artist. Begun in 1570 by the Franciscans, it was added to in stages over the subsequent centuries; the bell tower wasn't completed until 1875.

Outside stands a 30m-high *voladores* pole. Ritualistic performances normally take place every two hours between 11am and 7pm Monday to Saturday. During low season (October to April), performances can be seen at 9am, noon, 4pm and 7pm Friday to Sunday.

Zócalo   PLAZA
Officially called Parque Téllez, Papantla's *zócalo* is terraced into the hillside below the Iglesia de la Asunción. Wedged beneath the cathedral and facing the square is a symbolic 50m-long bas relief mural. Depicting Totonac and Veracruz history, it was designed by Papantla artist Teodoro Cano in 1979. A serpent stretches along the mural, bizarrely linking a pre-Hispanic stone carver, El Tajín's Pirámide de los Nichos, and an oil rig.

Museo de la Ciudad Teodoro Cano   MUSEUM
(📞784-842-47-51; Curti 101; M$50; ⊙10am-6pm Tue-Sun) 🎨 Legendary Paplanta artist Teodoro Cano (b 1932) was once a student of Mexican art giant Diego Rivera. This small museum displays a handful of Cano's fine paintings, an alluring combination of both dark and ebullient scenes that are drawn almost exclusively from Totonac culture. The Totonac theme extends to the museum's other artifacts, including photos and traditional clothing displays. It's small, but immensely satisfying. A modern on-site auditorium hosts regular cultural events.

Volador Monument   MONUMENT
(Callejón Centenario s/n) At the top of the hill towers Papantla's *volador* monument, a 1988 statue by Teodoro Cano portraying a musician playing his pipe and preparing for the four fliers to launch. To reach the monument, take Calle Centenario heading uphill from the southwest corner of the cathedral yard, before turning left into steep Callejón Centenario. Good city views from the top.

👣 Tours

Gaudencio Simbrón   WALKING
(📞783-842-01-21, 784-121-96-54; per day M$450) Guide Gaudencio Simbrón is more commonly known as *el de la ropa típica* (the guy who wears traditional clothes) because he sports Totonac costume. He works through Hotel Tajín (p240) and can guide you through El Tajín, Papantla and its environs.

✨ Festivals & Events

Feria de Corpus Christi
CULTURAL

(☺late May-early Jun) The fantastic Feria de Corpus Christi is the big annual event in Papantla. As well as the bullfights, parades and *charreadas* (Mexican rodeos) that are usual in Mexico, Papantla celebrates its Totonac cultural heritage with spectacular indigenous dances. The main procession is on the first Sunday when *voladores* fly in elaborate ceremonies several times a day.

Festival de Vainilla
FOOD & DRINK

(☺Jun 18) A major celebration in Papantla, the Vanilla Festival features indigenous dancers, gastronomic delights sold in street stalls, and all manner of vanilla products.

🛏 Sleeping

Papantla has a decidedly small and uninspiring selection of budget and midrange places to stay. However, prices are low and rooms are more or less clean.

Hotel Tajín
HOTEL $

(☏784-842-01-21; http://hoteltajin.mx; Núñez y Domínguez 104; s/d/tr M$690/770/940, ste from M$1200; P❋🤖🐾) So what if the interior is a little dated and worn? The Tajín is an intrinsic part of the Papantla experience with a prime edge-of-*zócalo* location and a stone-arch-fringed pool and on-site restau-rant. It's not a fancy hotel by any means, but the whole place oozes character, even if its 62 rooms range from the cozy to the ho-hum. It's just off the *zócalo*; if you're facing the chuch, follow the road beneath it to the left.

Hotel Hostal del Moncayo
GUESTHOUSE $$

(☏784-842-04-98; http://hotelpapantla.webcind ario.com; Zaragoza 108; s/d from M$595/797; P❋🤖) This quiet, family-run place has pleasant, airy rooms upstairs, though no amount of cheery tilework on walls can make up for the smell of mildew in the downstairs room. There's limited parking on site.

🍴 Eating

Papantla's *zócalo* is home to a good selection of local restaurants and cafes. Mercado Juárez, at the southwest corner of the plaza opposite the cathedral, has stalls that sell cheap, fresh regional food and there are two excellent restaurants worth seeking out away from the town center.

Café Catedral
BAKERY, CAFE $

(☏784-842-53-17; cnr Núñez y Domínguez & Curato; cakes from M$30; ☺8am-8pm) The town's best coffeehouse (ask any local) doubles as a bakery. Grab a cake, muffin or *pan dulce* (sweet bread) from one of the display cases, sit at a cheap cafe table and wait for the chief

---

DON'T MISS

PAPANTLA'S VOLADORES: BUNGEE-JUMPING PIONEERS

The idea of launching yourself head first from a great height with only a rope tied around your ankles for support is popularly thought to have been conceived by bungee jumping New Zealanders in the 1980s. But in truth, Papantla's Totonac *voladores* (fliers) have been flinging themselves off 30m-high wooden poles (with zero safety equipment) for centuries. Indeed, so old is this rather bizarre yet mystic tradition, no one is quite sure how or when it started.

The rite begins with five men in elaborate ceremonial clothing climbing to the top of the pole. Four of them sit on the edges of a small frame at the top and rotate the frame to twist the ropes around the pole. The fifth man dances on the platform above them while playing a *chirimía,* a small drum with a flute attached. When he stops playing, the others fall backward. Arms outstretched, they revolve gracefully around the pole and descend to the ground, upside down, as their ropes unwind.

One interpretation of the ceremony is that it's a fertility rite and the fliers make invocations to the four corners of the universe. It's also noted that each flier circles the pole 13 times, giving a total of 52 revolutions. The number 52 is not only the number of weeks in the modern year but also was an important number in pre-Hispanic Mexico, which had two calendars: one corresponding to the 365-day solar year, the other to a ritual year of 260 days. The calendars coincided every 52 solar years.

Voladores ceremonies are best observed at El Tajín, outside Papantla's cathedral, and occasionally at Zempoala.

BUSES FROM PAPANTLA

First-class ADO services include the following:

DESTINATION	FARE (M$)	DURATION (HR)	FREQUENCY (DAILY)
Mexico City (Terminal Norte)	200-296	4-5	7
Tuxpan	92	2	8
Veracruz	224	4¼	4
Xalapa	314	4¼	7

señora to come round with an old-fashioned tin jug to fill up your cup. Everyone seems to know everyone else here, and local gossip bounces off the walls.

Naku Restaurante Papanteco　MEXICAN $$
(☑784-842-31-12; www.kinkachikin.com; Colegio Militar s/n; mains M$70-200; ⊙8am-8pm; ☜) This restaurant, a couple of kilometers northeast of town, has traditionally dressed waitstaff serving supposedly authentic Totonac cuisine (though we suspect/hope they've removed some of the less savory items that people probably ate back then...). The garden setting is nice, the food very tasty and the bread is baked in a big mud-clay oven.

Plaza Pardo　MEXICAN $$
(☑784-842-00-59; www.facebook.com/RestaurantePlazaPardo; Enríquez 105, 1st fl; mains M$85-170; ⊙7:30am-11:30pm; ☜) There's no place better to absorb the atmosphere of Papantla than the Plaza Pardo's delightful balcony overlooking the *zócalo*. While the interior is perfectly pleasant, it's a big step down in romance and views. The menu offers a large range of *antojitos,* fish and meats, all cooked in pleasant but unmemorable ways.

Restaurante la Parroquia　INTERNATIONAL $$
(☑784-842-01-21; http://hoteltajin.mx/restaurantes; Núñez y Domínguez 104, Hotel Tajín; mains M$75-140; ⊙8am-10pm; ☀☜) With its exposed stone arches, this hotel bar-restaurant has plenty of atmosphere (particularly on the poolside terrace) and an extensive international menu that runs the gamut from *antojitos* and enchiladas to burgers. It also serves cocktails made with locally produced vanilla extract.

★Ágora Alta Cocina　FUSION $$$
(☑784-842-75-64; www.facebook.com/agora papantla; Libertad 301, 3rd fl; mains M$295-1250; ☀☜) An unexpected surprise in a quiet residential part of town, Ágora Alta Cocina is indeed high – both in terms of location and the sky-high aspirations. The food? Nicely executed fusion, from smoked salmon with pear, goat's cheese and asparagus to delicate, herb-filled Asian-style shrimp and noodle soup and seared steak. Attentive young service and good desserts, too.

🛍 Shopping

Here in Mexico's leading vanilla-growing center, you'll find quality vanilla extract, vanilla pods and *figuras* (pods woven into the shapes of flowers, insects or crucifixes). There's a good artisan store on the southwest corner of the *zócalo*. You'll also encounter traditional Totonac clothing and handmade baskets.

ℹ Information

Tourist office (Reforma 100; ⊙8am-5pm Mon-Fri) A kiosk inside the Ayuntamiento building, off the *zócalo*. It offers helpful maps of the town center and the surrounding region.

ℹ Getting There & Away

A few long-distance buses leave from Papantla's **Terminal ADO** (☑784-101-35-01; cnr Juárez & Venustiano Carranza), a short, steep walk from the center. Taxis from the ADO to the center are M$25. You can make bus reservations online (www.ado.com.mx) or at the **ticket counter** (Juan Enríquez s/n; ⊙9am-5pm) just east of the plaza. At the **Terminal Transportes Papantla** (cnr Av 20 de Noviembre & Olivo), just off the plaza by the Pemex station, Transportes Papantla (TP) serves the coastal towns to the south and has slightly less expensive buses to Poza Rica and Tuxpan.

El Tajín

This evocative and under-visited ancient city was 'rediscovered' accidentally by an officious Spaniard looking for illegal tobacco plantations in 1785. Today, one of the best-preserved and important pre-Hispanic cities in Mesoamerica, El Tajín's pyramids and temples burst off a plain surrounded

El Tajín

▲ 0 ⎯⎯⎯⎯ 200 m
Ⓝ 0 ⎯⎯⎯⎯ 0.1 miles

Plaza de las Columnas
Edificio B
Edificio A
Gran Greca
Edificio D
Plaza El Tajín Chico
Edificio C
Edificio I
Juego de Pelota Norte
Estructura 3
Pirámide de los Nichos
Plaza De Dios Tajín
Juego de Pelota de las Pinturas
Templo de las Alamenas
Juego de Pelota de Venus
Juego de Pelota Sur
Juego de Pelota de las Serientes
Plaza del Arroyo
Visitor Center, Parking Lot (150m)

by low, verdant hills 7km west of Papantla. These extensive ruins are the most impressive reminder of Classic Veracruz civilization. Try to come and visit as late in the day as possible in order to catch the reddening sky, bubbling clouds and reflective calm of the site shortly before closing.

Among El Tajín's special features are rows of square niches on the sides of buildings, numerous ball courts, and sculptures depicting human sacrifice connected with the ball game. Archaeologist José García Payón believed that El Tajín's niches and stone mosaics symbolized day and night, light and dark, and life and death in a universe composed of dualities.

History

It was originally thought that El Tajín (the name is Totonac for 'thunder,' 'lightning' or 'hurricane') was settled in three phases between BC 100 and AD 1200, but the most recent research suggests that it reached its zenith as a city and ceremonial center between AD 800 and 900. Around 1200 the site was abandoned, possibly after a fire and attacks by Chichimecs. Quickly engulfed by the jungle, it lay unknown to the Spanish until 1785.

◉ Sights

The **El Tajín site** (off Hwy 127; M$70; ☺9am-5pm) stretches across 10 sq km. To see everything, you'll walk a few kilometers over a couple of hours. There's little shade and it can get blazingly hot, so come early or late. Most buildings and carvings have some sort of labeling in English and Spanish, but a guide would greatly aid your understanding of the ruins.

★ Pirámide de los Nichos
ARCHAEOLOGICAL SITE

El Tajín's most emblematic structure, the beautifully proportioned Pyramid of the Niches, is just off the Plaza Menor. The six lower levels, each surrounded by rows of small square niches, climb to 18m. Archaeologists believe that there were originally 365 niches, suggesting that the building may have been used as a kind of calendar. In its heyday, it was painted red with black niches.

Museo El Tajín
MUSEUM

(☺9am-5pm) Do drop in to the on-site museum at entrance to the El Tajín site (included in your ticket price) to see an excellent model of the site. It also displays a collection of statuary, pottery, delicate bas reliefs and part of a burial site from the ruins.

Juego de Pelota de Las Pinturas
ARCHAEOLOGICAL SITE

The Juego de Pelota de las Pinturas (Ball Court of the Paintings), to one side of the Pirámide de los Nichos, is so called as it has two very impressively preserved red and blue geometric friezes on its north-facing side.

El Tajín Chico
ARCHAEOLOGICAL SITE

El Tajín Chico was the government area of the ancient city and would have been home to the ruling classes. Many of the buildings at El Tajín Chico have geometric stone mosaic patterns known as 'Greco' (Greek).

The path north toward Plaza El Tajín Chico passes the **Juego de Pelota Norte** (Northern Ball Court), which is smaller and older than the southern court and has fainter carvings on its sides.

The raised boardwalk gives an excellent view of the lower site.

Edificio I, probably once a palace, has some terrific carvings and beautifully preserved, blue, yellow and red paintwork. **Edificio C**, on the east side, with three levels and a staircase facing the plaza, was initially painted blue and sports some unusual whorled decorations. **Edificio A**, on the plaza's north side, has an arch construction known as a corbeled arch, with two sides jutting closer to each other until they are joined at the top by a single slab, which is typical of Maya architecture. Its presence here is yet another oddity in the jigsaw puzzle of pre-Hispanic cultures.

Northwest of Plaza El Tajín Chico is the unreconstructed **Plaza de las Columnas** (Plaza of the Columns), one of the site's most important structures. It originally housed a large open patio and adjoining buildings stretching over the hillside. Some wonderful reassembled carved columns are displayed in the museum.

Juego de Pelota Sur ARCHAEOLOGICAL SITE
(Southern Ball Court) Some 17 ball courts have been found at El Tajín. The Juego de Pelota Sur dates from about 1150 and is the most famous of the courts, owing to the six relief carvings on its walls that depict various aspects of the ball-game ritual.

The panel on the northeast corner is the easiest to make out: in the center, three ball-players perform a ritual post-game sacrifice with one player ready to plunge a knife into the chest of another, whose arms are held by the third player. Death gods and a presiding figure look on. The other panels depict various scenes of ceremonial drinking of *pulque* (a milky, low-alcohol brew made from the *maguey* plant).

Plaza Menor PLAZA
Beyond the Plaza del Arroyo in the south of the site, flanked by pyramids on four sides, is the Plaza Menor (Lesser Plaza), part of El Tajín's main ceremonial center and possible marketplace, with a low platform in the middle. All of the structures around this plaza were probably topped by small temples, with some decorated with red or blue paint, traces of which remain.

✨ Festivals & Events

★ Voladores Performances CULTURAL
A 30m-high *voladores* pole stands outside the entrance to the ruins. Totonacs perform the *voladores* rite (which was traditionally carried out only once a year) three times per day beside the visitor center. Before they start, a performer in Totonac regalia requests donations (around M$20 per person should suffice) from the audience.

ℹ Information

The **visitor center** (off Hwy 127; ⊙ 9am-5pm) has a left-luggage room and information desk. Those seeking more information should look for the book *Tajín: Mystery and Beauty*, by Leonardo Zaleta, sometimes available in several languages in the souvenir shops.

A multilingual guide service is available for M$300 per hour for one to six people.

ℹ Getting There & Away

Frequent buses come from Poza Rica. From Papantla, buses (M$20) marked 'Pirámides Tajín' leave every 20 minutes or so from Calle 16 de Septiembre, directly behind Hotel Tajín. The site is 300m from the highway – buses drop you off near the market, before the entrance to Tajín. Taxis to/from Papantla cost M$80. There are usually one or two waiting outside the ruins.

Tecolutla

📞 766 / POP 4591
This lazy seaside town, with a reasonable strip of sand and a slew of seafood restaurants and cheap hotels nearby, passes for one of Veracruz' more pleasant beachfronts. Cancún this most definitely isn't. Instead, the place is as dead as a doornail midweek, though on weekends, in high summer and during Semana Santa it's a different story. There are banks and ATMs on the plaza.

⊙ Sights & Activities

Playa Tecolutla BEACH
Stretching for miles, this black-sand beach is extremely popular with Mexican holidaymakers. On weekends and holidays it's packed with families picnicking on plastic chairs by the water, buying snacks from wandering vendors, riding giant inflatable bananas and splashing in the waves. On weekdays, expect to have the place largely to yourself.

★ Grupo Ecologista
Vida Milenaria VOLUNTEERING
(📞 766-846-04-67; www.vidamilenaria.org.mx; Niños Héroes 1; donation required; ⊙ 7am-9pm May-Nov) 🐾 This small turtle conservation place (at the beach end of Niños Héroes) is run by Fernando Manzano Cervantes, known locally as 'Papá Tortuga'. In addition to educating the public, he has been effectively protecting and releasing green and Kemp's ridley turtles here for over 35 years. Visitors gather in droves to watch baby-turtle releases most mornings in season.

If you stop by, think about buying a souvenir because this is a privately funded show. Volunteers are especially needed here in April and May, when patrolling the beaches (35km worth) and collecting the turtle eggs is imperative (when possible the eggs are left in their original nest site but at others time they're reburied in a safer area). Most of the patrolling is done at night between 10pm and 6am. Camping and the use of kitchen and bathroom facilities is free to volunteers.

The highest number of turtles are released in June, but in late October you can join hundreds of locals in celebrating the release of the baby turtles in the Festival de Las Tortugas.

☞ Tours

Boat Trips   BOATING
(off Ribera del Río; per group M$400-500) Walk toward the Río Tecolutla on Emilio Carranza and you'll hit the *embarcadero* (pier), where boats will take you fishing or through dense mangrove forests rich with wildlife, including pelicans.

🛏 Sleeping & Eating

Budget and midrange hotels abound in this tourist-reliant town. Smarter options are outside the town itself, but there are plenty of cheap hotels near the plaza, and nicer ones toward the ocean.

Aqua Inn Hotel   HOTEL $
(☎766-846-03-58; www.tecolutla.com.mx/ aquainn; cnr Aldama & Av Obregón; r from M$700; P❋🛜🏊) This modern place in the middle of town and a short walk from the water has clean, functional rooms, all with cable TV. It has a small rooftop pool and a cool cafe and restaurant. Prices drop steeply outside high season, making it a bargain during off-peak times.

★ Hotel Azúcar   DESIGN HOTEL $$$
(☎232-321-06-78; www.hotelazucar.com; Carretera Federal Nautla-Poza Rica Km 83.5; r incl breakfast from US$283; P❋🛜🏊) Some 45km south of Tecolutla, this impressive beachside design hotel goes for the minimalist Zen look. The rooms are scorching white with rustic-chic decor, gorgeous whitewashed public areas topped in thatch, a sumptuous pool, an impressive spa and a sublimely laid-back restaurant.

★ El Camarón Desvelado   SEAFOOD $
(☎766-846-02-35; Aldama s/n; mains M$50-120; ⊙8am-9pm) The Sleepless Shrimp is the busiest of the seafood restaurants in town, briskly serving platters of *arroz a la tumbada* (seafood rice with a tomato base), garlic shrimp, octopus in its own ink and fish stuffed with seafood, among other ocean goodies.

Taquería Los Jairos   STREET FOOD $
(cnr Obregón & Hidalgo; tacos M$60; ⊙9am-10pm) Perch at one of the plastic tables at this bustling taco joint, order a plate of tacos *pastór* (with shawarma-like pork), *cabeza* (with cow head meat) or *suadero* (cut of beef between the belly and the leg), slather some salsa on it and wash it down with a *michelada* (beer with lime juice, spices and salt on the rim). Perfect.

🍷 Drinking & Nightlife

Porteño Café   COFFEE
(cnr Aldama & Av Obregón; ⊙8am-10pm) This handy town center cafe serves a full range of *lecheros* (coffee with milk), espressos, lattes and cappucinos, as well as frappés and iced coffees for those hot days at the beach. Coffee's the draw here, but there's also a supporting cast of *bocadillos* (sandwiches).

ℹ Getting There & Away

Tecolutla is 41km east of Papantla. There are regular 2nd-class Transportes Papantla buses between Tecolutla and Papantla (M$50) that arrive and depart from outside the church on Avenida Obregón, one block west of the main plaza. There is also a small but swanky 1st-class ADO **bus station** (cnr Abasolo & Ahumada) a few blocks from the main plaza. Many buses to and from Tecolutla have to transfer through Gutiérrez Zamora. ADO offers services to some major cities including Mexico City's Terminal Norte (M$404, 5¼ hours, seven daily), as well as services to Papantla (M$68, one hour, eight daily).

SOUTHERN VERACRUZ

Southeast Veracruz is arguably the most beautiful part of the state, and yet tourism is still on a very modest scale. Here you'll find languorous wetlands, volcano-dappled rainforest, breathtaking lakes, some beautiful beaches along the little-visited Costa de Oro, and the superb Reserva de la Biosfera Los Tuxtlas, a well-run biosphere reserve that will appeal to anyone wanting to get off the beaten track. The wilder, volcanic portion of the reserve is accessed via San Andrés Tuxtla, whereas the Laguna Catemaco portion is renowned for bird-watching and is closer to the eponymous town. As part of the former heartland of ancient Olmec culture, the area is laden with archaeological sites, not to mention Tlacotalpan, a Unesco World Heritage site that will enchant anyone lucky enough to head this way. If you're heading south into Tabasco, the unpretty commercial center of Acayucan is a passable stopover.

Tlacotalpan

♪ 288 / POP 7600

Once an important river port, this Uneco World Heritage town has changed little since the 1820s. The color palette is extraordinary here; the lucid sunsets over the adjacent Río Papaloapan add subtle oranges and yellows to the rainbow of single-story colonial houses, bringing to mind a more soporific Havana.

In September 2010, Tlacotalpan was hit by devastating floods, which inundated 500 historic buildings and prompted the evacuation of 8500 people. The recovery has been remarkable, with only a high watermark drawn onto a wall on Calle Alegre to show how disastrous the flooding was.

Its smattering of ho-hum museums aside, this is the kind of town where the greatest pleasure is found in walking the streets and taking in the atmosphere. Tlacotalpan has two appealing plazas, Parque Hidalgo and Plaza Zaragoza, directly adjacent to each other. Be sure to take a stroll by the riverside and down Cházaro.

⊙ Sights

Capilla de la Candelaria CHURCH
(Parque Hidalgo; ⊘ 8am-6pm) Looking a little worn from the outside, the salmon-colored Capilla de la Candelaria dates from 1779 and is furnished with local coral stone.

Parroquía San Cristobal CHURCH
(Plaza Zaragoza; ⊘ 8am-6pm) This neoclassical church, begun in 1812, is gorgeously painted in blue and white and is the star of Plaza Zaragoza.

Villin Montalio GALLERY
(Av 5 de Mayo 53; ⊘ 9am-6pm Mon-Sat) Tlacotalpan is well known for its locally made cedar furniture, including rocking chairs. Drop by this office/workshop to see it being made,

and to see some of the finished products on display as well.

Casa Cultural de Agustín Lara MUSEUM
(cnr Carranza & Noel; M$10; ⊘ 10am-6pm Mon-Sat) This museum features old photos of Tlacotalpan, and those of *tlacotalpeño* Agustín Lara (1900–70) – a legendary musician, composer and Casanova – as well as a Frankenstein-lookalike mannequin of the man seated by a piano. Its appeal is perhaps greater to Mexicans than it is to foreign tourists.

Museo Salvador Ferrando MUSEUM
(Alegre 6; M$20; ⊘ 11am-6pm Tue-Sat, 12:30-7pm Sun) The Ferrando, named for a Tlacotalpan artist, is the best of Tlacotalpan's handful of mini-museums. It displays a motley bunch of old cannons, vintage Singer sewing machines, old muskets and paintings of local notables within a charming old colonial mansion.

Activities

Bici Cletando CYCLING
(♪ 288-100-46-86; Parque Hidalgo; per 30min/1hr/2hr M$25/40/70; ⊘ 9am-6pm) Wonderfully flat, Tlacotalpan is a perfect spot for bike riding. You can arrange bike hire through Bici Cletando, which rents out bikes from a stand outside the Capilla de La Candelaria on Plaza Zaragoza.

⏻ Tours

Boat Rides BOATING
(1hr M$350) If you walk the *malecón* near the restaurants, you're bound to run into a *lanchero* (boatman) offering to whisk you down the scenic river for an hour-long boat ride to see a nearby lagoon. It's not the Amazon, but it's a lovely way to spend a late afternoon.

✲ Festivals & Events

Día de la Candelaria RELIGIOUS
(⊘ Jan & Feb) In late January and early February, Tlacotalpan's huge Candelaria festival features bull-running in the streets. An image of the Virgin is also floated down the river, followed by a flotilla of small boats.

⌕ Sleeping

There's a smattering of mostly midrange guesthouses inside beautiful colonial buildings. Prices triple or quadruple during the Candelaria holiday, during which reservations, made weeks ahead of time, are essential.

★ **Hotel Doña Juana** GUESTHOUSE $
(☑288-884-34-80; http://hoteldonajuana.com; Juan Enríquez 32; r M$600-730; ❀🛜) This is a modern multi-layered building that has small, but very well-kept rooms. The ample use of terracotta colors and statement art make it stand out from many similarly priced places, as do the helpful, smiling staff. Avoid the single dark room with a partial view of the inner courtyard.

Hostal El Patio GUESTHOUSE $
(☑288-884-31-97; www.hostalelpatio.com.mx; Alvarado 52; r M$550-650; P@🛜) This guesthouse combines a warm color scheme with spacious, well-appointed rooms (with rain showers) and a leafy courtyard. The resident miniature schnauzer provides canine love.

Hotel Posada Doña Lala HISTORIC HOTEL $
(☑288-884-24-55; http://hoteldonalala.mx; Av Carranza 11; s/d/ste M$650/750/1000; P❀❀🛜❀) With its sun-bleached pink facade looking toward the river, Doña Lala is a gorgeous colonial-style hotel with spacious, elegant rooms with high ceilings. For great views try to get a room overlooking the square; half the rooms are dark and face the inner courtyard. It has an excellent restaurant downstairs and even a pool to enjoy.

Hotel Casa del Río HOTEL $$
(☑288-884-29-47; www.casadelrio.com.mx; Cházaro 39; r/ste M$850/1100; ❀❀🛜) Creating modern, stylish, minimalist rooms in a colonial mansion is definitely a challenge, but the Hotel Casa del Río does a good job of it with its nine spacious offerings. Its best feature is definitely the terrace overlooking the river. Oh, and the breakfast. We liked that a lot! Wi-fi in the lobby only.

✖ **Eating & Drinking**

The riverside is lined with fish restaurants that operate from lunchtime to sunset each day, serving up the catch of the day. See which one looks busiest and join the locals. There are several dining options on and around Plaza Zaragoza as well.

Restaurant Doña Lala MEXICAN $$
(Av Carranza 11; mains M$80-180; ⊙7am-10pm; 🛜) The smartest eating option in town, this place inside the hotel of the same name has a friendly staff and is patronized by a crowd of local eccentrics who vie for the best seats on its terrace. The wide-ranging selection of Mexican dishes won't disappoint and the locally caught seafood is very good.

Rokala MEXICAN $$
(☑288-884-22-92; Plaza Zaragoza; mains M$100-190; ⊙6pm-midnight; 🛜) With its unbeatable position under the colonial arches on the Plaza Zaragoza, this friendly place with alfresco dining buzzes year-round. Mains range from fresh fish and prawns plucked from the river to meat grills and typical *antojitos* (snacks). For atmosphere alone it's a clear winner, but the food itself is only average. Mosquito repellent is a boon in the evenings.

El K-Fecito CAFE
(www.facebook.com/elkfe; Plaza Zaragoza; ⊙5pm-2am) On the joining point of the two main plazas and serving great coffee, cakes and various simple snacks, El K-Fecito seems to have it all, and becomes packed in the late evening. Bring mosquito repellent.

☆ **Entertainment**

Teatro Netzahualcoyotl THEATER
(Av Carranza; ⊙hours vary) The gorgeous French-style Teatro Netzahualcoyotl, built in 1891, hosts highbrow events.

ℹ **Information**

Tourist Office (☑288-884-33-05; www.tlacotalpan-turismo.gob.mx/turismo.html; Plaza Zaragoza, Ayuntamiento; ⊙9am-3pm Mon-Fri) Right on Plaza Zaragoza, with helpful maps and info.

ℹ **Getting There & Away**

Hwy 175 runs from Tlacotalpan up the Papaloapan valley to Tuxtepec, then twists and turns over the mountains to Oaxaca (320km).

BUSES FROM TLACOTALPAN

DESTINATION	COST (M$)	DURATION (HR)	FREQUENCY (DAILY)
Mexico City (TAPO)	676	8½-11	2
Puebla	285	6½	10pm
San Andrés Tuxtla	108	2	4
Xalapa	292	3	6:20am

DON'T MISS

TRES ZAPOTES

One of Veracruz's most important archaeological sites, the late-Olmec settlement of Tres Zapotes, lies around 21km west of Santiago Tuxtla. The site was an Olmec settlement for over 2000 years, from around 1200 BC to AD 1000, and was probably first inhabited while the great Olmec center of La Venta (Tabasco) still flourished. After the destruction of La Venta (about 400 BC), the city carried on in what archaeologists call an 'epi-Olmec' phase – the period during which the Olmec culture dwindled, as other civilizations (notably Izapa and Maya) came to the fore.

Tres Zapotes is now just a series of mounds in cornfields, but the eponymous archaeological **museum** (📞294-947-01-96; www.inah.gob.mx/es/red-de-museos/226-museo-de-sitio-de-tres-zapotes; Estela Nuñez, Tres Zapotes; M$40; ⊙9am-5pm Tue-Sun) showcases important finds from the site. The biggest piece, Stela A, depicts three human figures in the mouth of a jaguar. Other pieces include a sculpture of what may have been a captive with hands tied behind his back, and the upturned face of a woman carved into a throne or altar. The Olmecs preceded Mexico's other major civilizations, and are notable for sculpting giant human heads, a 1.5m example of which, dating from 100 BC, takes pride of place in the museum. The museum attendant is happy to answer questions in Spanish or give a tour (tipping is appreciated).

From Santiago Tuxtla, take a 2nd-class bus (M$35) or taxi (M$40/140 *colectivo/ private*). If driving, the road to Tres Zapotes goes southwest from Santiago Tuxtla; a 'Zona Arqueológica' sign points the way from Hwy 180. Eight kilometers down this road, you fork right onto a paved stretch for the last 13km to Tres Zapotes. It comes out at a T-junction, from where you go left then left again to reach the museum.

The riverside ADO **station** (📞288-884-21-25; Cházaro 37) is situated outside the Mercado Municipal, three blocks east of the center.

Santiago Tuxtla

📞294 / POP 15,500 / ELEV 300M

Santiago Tuxtla centers on a lovely, verdant main plaza – one of the state's prettiest and all atweet with Mexican grackles – and is surrounded by the rolling green foothills of the volcanic Sierra de los Tuxtlas. It's far more laid-back and considerably more charming than its built-up neighbor San Andrés, with its plaza strewn with women arm-in-arm, couples lip-to-lip and shoes getting vigorously shined. Its museum and its giant Olmec head alone make it worth a visit.

◉ Sights

Olmec Head   MONUMENT

(Plaza Olmeca) Dominating the main plaza, this stone monolith is known as the 'Cobata Head,' after the estate where it was found. Thought to be a very late Olmec production, it's the biggest known Olmec head, weighing in at 40 tonnes, and is unique in that its eyes are closed.

Museo Tuxteco   MUSEUM

(📞294-947-10-76; Plaza Olmeca; M$50; ⊙9am-5pm Tue-Sun) This museum on Santiago Tuxtla's main plaza focuses on the pre-Columbian peoples that inhabited this region from 1600 BC to around AD 1200, with a particular emphasis on the Olmecs, Mexico's first known major civilization. Artifacts include a Totonac effigy of a woman who died in childbirth, ceramic plates used in human-sacrifice ceremonies on the Isla de Sacrificios, Olmec stone carvings (including a colossal head), a monkey-faced *hacha* (ax) with obsidian eyes, and a Tres Zapotes altar replica.

🛏 Sleeping & Eating

★**Mesón de Santiago**   HOTEL $

(📞294-947-16-70; Calle 5 de Mayo No 8; d M$760; 🅿❉🛜≋) With a well-preserved colonial exterior and enormous, creeper-covered trees in the peaceful courtyard, this fantastic place right on the main plaza is unexpected in such a quiet and little-visited place. Rooms are tastefully decorated, with deeply burnished wood furniture, beautifully tiled bathrooms and domed staircases. The small pool was looking a little neglected when we visited.

BUSES FROM SANTIAGO TUXTLA

First-class bus services include the following:

DESTINATION	FARE (M$)	DURATION	FREQUENCY (DAILY)
Córdoba	304	4hr	3
Mexico City	334-744	9½hr	6
Puebla	438-588	6¾-7½hr	4
San Andrés Tuxtla	52	20min	18
Tlacotalpan	90	1½hr	3
Veracruz	93-192	2¾hr	9
Villahermosa	322	5¾hr	8:50pm
Xalapa	234	4¾hr	3

La Joya
MEXICAN $

(☑294-947-01-77; cnr Juárez & Comonfort; mains M$50-80; ⊙7am-11pm) The plastic tablecloths, alfresco-only chairs and rustic open-to-view kitchen scream 'Moctezuma's revenge,' but fear not: La Joya delivers where it matters – good, tasty Mexican food. It's on a corner of the main plaza, to one side of the Olmec head.

ℹ Getting There & Away

Most buses arrive and depart from the **bus station** near the junction of Morelos and the highway. ADO buses stop on the highway, at the corner with Guerrero. To get to the center, continue down Morelos, then turn right into Ayuntamiento, which leads to the main plaza, a few blocks away.

All local and regional buses and *colectivos taxis* to San Andrés Tuxtla are frequent and stop at the junction of Morales and Hwy 180. A private taxi between the towns is M$80. Frequent 2nd-class buses also go to Catemaco, Veracruz, Acayucan and Tlacotalpan.

Taxis to Tres Zapotes (Zaragoza) leave from the Sitio Puente Real, on the far side of the pedestrian bridge at the foot of Zaragoza (the street going downhill beside the Santiago Tuxtla museum).

San Andrés Tuxtla

☑294 / POP 63,800 / ELEV 360M

Like a lot of modern towns, San Andrés puts function before beauty. The busy service center of the Las Tuxtlas region is best used for bus connections and link-ups to its more enticing peripheral sights, including a volcano and a giant waterfall. Cigar aficionados will definitely want to visit, as San Andrés is Mexico's cigar capital. The center of town is orderly, with a soaring orange and yellow tiled church on the main plaza.

◉ Sights

★ Salto de Eyipantla
WATERFALL

(Salto de Eyipantla; M$10; ⊙8am-6pm) Twelve kilometers southeast of San Andrés, in the eponymous village, a 250-step staircase leads down to the absolutely spectacular Salto de Eyipantla, a 50m-high, 40m-wide waterfall. To avoid the steps (and a soaking), you can also enjoy it from a *mirador* (lookout). Follow Hwy 180 east for 4km to Sihuapan, then turn right to Eyipantla. Frequent TLT buses (M$15) and shared taxis (M$30) run from San Andrés, leaving from the corner of Cabada and 5 de Mayo, near the market. Part of Mel Gibson's movie *Apocalypto* was filmed here.

⌣ Sleeping & Eating

Hotel Posada San Martín
HOTEL $

(☑294-942-10-36; Av Juárez 304; s/d/tr M$490/575/660; ⏏❋☎☒) Midway between the main road and the main plaza, this hacienda-style posada is a good deal and a very unexpected find. It has a pool set in a peaceful garden and antiques scattered about its public areas. The rooms are spacious and clean and all have charmingly tiled sinks.

★ Mr Taco Segovia
STREET FOOD $

(www.facebook.com/Mr.TacoSegovia; cnr Madero & Allende; tacos M$8; ⊙6pm-2am) Satisfying late-night munchies for over 20 years, this taco stand is a study in nose-to-tail eating, Mexico-style. Watch the guys fry up the tortillas and top them with *suadero* (cut of beef from between the belly and the leg), *tripita* (tripe), *seso* (brain) and more, and add some spice with homemade salsa.

BUSES FROM SAN ANDRÉS TUXTLA

The services listed run from ADO.

DESTINATION	FARE (M$)	DURATION (HR)	FREQUENCY (DAILY)
Córdoba	314	4½	3
Mexico City (TAPO)	642-744	9½-10½	5
Puebla	414-596	7½-8¼	4
Santiago Tuxtla	52	½	17
Tlacotalpan	108	2	3
Veracruz	196	3	15
Xalapa	317	5	6

ⓘ Information

Tourist Office (Madero 1; ⊙8:30am-3:30pm) The tiny office inside the Palacio Municipal has up-to-date info on the Reserva de la Biosfera Los Tuxtlas.

ⓘ Getting There & Away

San Andrés is the transportation center for Los Tuxtlas, with fairly good bus services in every direction. First-class buses with ADO and 2nd-class with AU depart from their respective **stations** (☑294-942-08-71; cnr Juárez & Blvd 5 de Febrero) on Juárez just off the Santiago Tuxtla–Catemaco highway, and about a 10-minute walk from the center.

Frequent **colectivo taxis** (5 de Mayo s/n) to Catemaco and Santiago leave from the market – they're the fastest way of getting to local destinations but cost a fraction more than the rickety 2nd-class TLT buses that also leave from a block north of the market and skirt down the north side of town on Blvd 5 de Febrero (Hwy 180).

Catemaco

☑ 294 / POP 29,000 / ELEV 340M

The sleepy town of Catemaco is an unlikely traveler hot spot, and yet it's the obvious base for exploring Reserva de la Biosfera Los Tuxtlas. Small and a little scruffy, it's reminiscent of a dusty backpacker destination from the 1980s, but without a significant number of backpackers. With a long tradition of witchcraft – including shamans who will exorcise your nasty spirits – a gorgeous lakeside setting, proximity to great bird-watching opportunities, swimming holes and pristine, isolated beaches, Catemaco makes a good base for exploring the area.

⊙ Sights

Basílica del Carmen　　　　CHURCH
(Zócalo; ⊙8am-6pm) Catemaco's main church was named a basilica (ie a church with

---

THE WITCHING HOUR

On the first Friday in March each year, hundreds of *brujos* (shamans), witches and healers from all over Mexico descend on Catemaco to perform a mass cleansing ceremony on Cerro Mono Blanco, a little way north of the town. The event is designed to rid them of the previous year's negative energies, though in recent years the whole occasion has become more commercial than supernatural. Floods of Mexicans also head into town at this time to grab a shamanic consultation or *limpia* (cleansing), and eat, drink and be merry in a bizarre mix of otherworldly fervor and hedonistic indulgence.

Witchcraft traditions in this part of Veracruz go back centuries, mixing ancient indigenous beliefs, Spanish medieval traditions and voodoo practices from West Africa. Many of these *brujos* multitask as medicine men or women (using both traditional herbs and modern pharmaceuticals) and shrinks, or black magicians who cast evil spells on enemies of their clients. Catemaco is known for its brotherhood of 13 prominent *brujos* (Los Hermanos), who are seen as the high priests of their profession. If you want to arrange a consultation, it's best to take advice from locals, to find out what services are provided during the rituals and how much you're likely to be paying, and also to avoid scammers.

Catemaco

Catemaco

◎ Sights
1 Basílica del Carmen	B2

🛏 Sleeping
2 Hotel Acuario	B2
3 Hotel Los Arcos	B2

✦ Eating
4 Il Fiorentino	C3
5 La Casa de Los Tesoros	B3
6 La Ola	B3

special ceremonial rights) in 1961, due primarily to its position as a pilgrimage site for the Virgen del Carmen. It's said she appeared to a fisherman in a cave by Laguna Catemaco in 1664, in conjunction with a volcanic eruption. A statue of the virgin resides in the church and is venerated on her feast day every July 16.

The intricate interior and haunting stained glass of the church belie its modernity; the current building only dates from 1953, though it looks at least a century older.

🛏 Sleeping & Eating

★ **Posada Bugambilea** GUESTHOUSE $
(☎294-110-01-80; 20 de Octobre 5; s/d M$300/450)
On the edge of town and drowning in bou-

gainvillea blossoms, with kittens playing on the patio, this yellow guesthouse is run by the loveliest proprietress in town, who'll shower you with advice and attention. Rooms are spacious and airy and benefit from the quiet you won't find in the town center. Hammocks on the upstairs terrace catch the breeze.

Hotel Los Arcos HOTEL $
(☎294-943-00-03; www.arcoshotel.com.mx; Madero 7; r/q from M$720/766; 🅿✳🛜🏊) This one of the better options in the town itself. Centrally located, it's a friendly, well-run place with small rooms and reasonably stable wi-fi. Each room has its own semi-private outdoor space and seating area. There's even a (very) small pool. Sound carries, though, so you may feel as if you're in bed with your neighbors.

Hotel Acuario HOTEL $
(☎294-943-04-18; cnr Boettinger & Carranza; r/tr from M$593/759; 🅿🛜) This friendly budget accommodations option has 25 clean rooms that are located just off the *zócalo*. It is well kept, though plain and fan-cooled. Some of the rooms have balconies and views – try to book one of these, as rooms situated at the back of the hotel lack natural light. Cable TV is a bonus.

BUSES FROM CATEMACO

ADO's 1st-class bus services include the following:

DESTINATION	FARE (M$)	DURATION (HR)	FREQUENCY (DAILY)
Mexico City	342-463	10-11	6
Puebla	330-468	8-8¾	4
San Andrés Tuxtla	38	½	16
Santiago Tuxtla	52	1	14
Veracruz	92-204	3½-4	11
Xalapa	198	5½	4

La Casa de Los Tesoros   CAFE $

(☏ 294-943-29-10; Aldama 4; mains M$50-120; ☺10am-10pm Mon-Thu, 9am-10pm Fri-Sun; 🛜) This very popular hippie-styled place is part cafe-restaurant, part used bookstore (spot some vintage LP guides here), part gallery and part arty gift shop, selling locally produced handicrafts. It's renowned among locals for its breakfasts (build-your-own omelettes) in particular, but there are also burgers, root-beer floats and more. There's also a good range of herbal teas.

La Ola   SEAFOOD $$

(Paseo del Malecón s/n; mains M$80-175; ☺11am-9pm; 🛜) A vast waterfront restaurant on the *malecón*, serving all the seafood you could want, including reasonable *pargo* (red snapper), barbecued shrimp and more.

Il Fiorentino   ITALIAN $$

(☏ 294-943-27-97; Paseo del Malecón 11; mains M$100-160; ☺6:30-11pm; 🛜) Smarter than your average Italian-abroad restaurant, Il Fiorentino serves handmade pasta, Piedmontese wine, cappuccinos and great cake. It's on the *malecón* and run by an Italian – of course.

❶ Getting There & Away

ADO and AU buses operate from a lakeside **bus terminal** (cnr Paseo del Malecón & Revolución). Local **2nd-class TLT buses** (Hwy 180) run from a bus station 700m west of the plaza by the highway junction and are a bit cheaper and more frequent than the 1st-class buses. *Colectivo* taxis arrive and depart from **El Cerrito** (Carranza s/n), a small hill about 400m to the west of the plaza on Carranza.

To arrive at communities surrounding the lake and toward the coast, take inexpensive *piratas* (*colectivo* pickups). They leave from a stop five blocks north of the bus station, on the corner of Lerdo de Tejada and Revolución.

Reserva de la Biosfera Los Tuxtlas

The various nature reserves around San Andrés Tuxtla and Catemaco were conglomerated in 2006 into this biosphere reserve under Unesco protection. This unique volcanic region, rising 1680m above the coastal plains of southern Veracruz, lies 160km east of the Cordillera Neovolcánica, making it something of an ecological anomaly. Its complex vegetation is considered the northernmost limit of rainforest in the Americas. The nature reserve spans the Laguna Catemaco and its surrounds, and its heart is the Volcán San Martín, at the bottom of which sits the village of Ruíz Cortines. Despite its many charms, the region receives few international visitors and has little tourism infrastructure. This all makes it a wonderful area to explore for those with a love of nature and the offbeat. Get the latest update on Ruíz Cortines at the San Andrés tourist office (p249), and take a local guide with you, as locals are wary of strangers.

❍ Sights

Laguna Encantada   LAKE

(off Valencia) The 'Enchanted Lagoon' occupies a small volcanic crater 3.5km northeast of San Andrés in jungle-like terrain. A dirt road goes there, but no buses do. Some locals advise not walking by the lake alone as muggings have occurred in the past; check with the guides at the nearby Yambigapan homestay for updates.

Cerro de Venado   NATURE RESERVE

(off Valencia; M$10; ☺8am-6pm) 🌿 This 23-hectare reserve, which was created in 2009 with the planting of thousands of trees, is 2.5km from Laguna Encantada on the road to Ruíz Cortines. There are 500 steps up to a

Los Tuxtlas

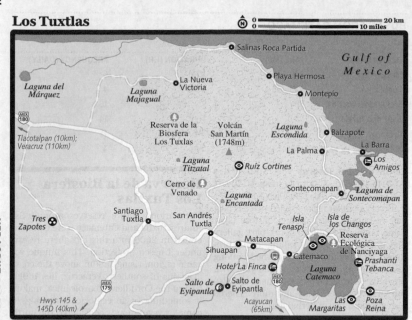

0   20 km
0   10 miles

Salinas Roca Partida

Gulf of Mexico

Playa Hermosa

La Nueva Victoria

Laguna del Márquez

Laguna Majagual

Montepío

MEX 180

Tlacotalpan (10km); Veracruz (110km);

Reserva de la Biosfera Los Tuxlas

Volcán San Martín (1748m)

Laguna Escondida

Balzapote

La Palma

La Barra

Los Amigos

Laguna Titzatal

Ruíz Cortines

Cerro de Venado

Laguna Encantada

Sontecomapan

Laguna de Sontecomapan

Tres Zapotes

Santiago Tuxtla

San Andrés Tuxtla

Isla Tenaspi

Isla de los Changos

Reserva Ecológica de Nanciyaga

Matacapan

Sihuapan

Catemaco

Prashanti Tebanca

Hotel La Finca

Laguna Catemaco

MEX 179

Salto de Eyipantla

Salto de Eyipantla

MEX 180

Hwys 145 & 145D (40km)

Acayucan (65km)

Las Margaritas

Poza Reina

650m hill with fabulous views of San Andrés Tuxtla, lake and mountains.

🏃 Activities

Ruíz Cortines
HIKING

(☑ cell 294-1005035; Ejido Ruíz Cortines; campsites/cabañas M$70/450) 🖉 Tucked at the base of a volcano, an hour north of San Andrés Tuxtla, this little village has installed very rustic *cabañas* and offers horseback riding, and hikes to caves. Its highlight is the breathtaking all-day hike up Volcán San Martín (1748m). A taxi from San Andrés Tuxtla costs M$120, while a *pirata* (pickup truck) costs M$30.

🛏 Sleeping & Eating

Yambigapan Estancia Rural
CAMPGROUND $

(☑ 294-115-76-34; www.facebook.com/Restaurant Yambigapan; Camino a Arroyo Seco Km 3.5; camping per person M$35, s/d M$350/450; 🅿) 🖉 Three kilometers or so from San Andrés Tuxtla, this family-run rural homestay has two very rustic *cabañas* with spectacular views. Not to be missed are the cooking classes from the *doña* of the house, Amelia, who will teach you traditional Mexican cooking and its history (in Spanish) in her homey kitchen for M$250. Taxi (around M$45) is the easiest way to arrive.

There's a great restaurant on the premises; swimming in the nearby river, Arroyo Seco; and guided hikes. An all-day summit of Volcán San Martín can also be arranged. If you're counting your pesos, ask a *pirata* (pickup truck) going to Ruíz Cortines to leave you at the turnoff and follow the signs for Yambigapan that eventually lead you up a long dirt driveway. It should cost about M$10.

Yambigapan
MEXICAN $

(☑ 294-115-76-34; www.facebook.com/Restaurant Yambigapan; Camino a Arroyo Seco Km 3.5; mains M$70-100; ⏱ 9am-5pm Sat & Sun; 🛜) This small cozy restaurant (open weekends only), serving exceptionally tasty and interesting local dishes whipped up by the talented *doña* Amelia, is found at the campground of the same name situated on the banks of the Laguna Encantada, located just 3km from San Andrés.

ℹ Getting There & Away

From San Andrés Tuxtla, there are *piratas* (pickup trucks) and *colectivo* taxis to Ruíz Cortines; these pass by Laguna Encantada. From Catemaco, *piratas* and *colectivo* taxis ply the lakeshore road along the Laguna Catemaco.

Costa de Oro

📞 294

From Catemaco, a mostly paved, 92km-long road runs toward the coast, passing through what's known as 'the Switzerland of Mexico' (presumably because of the green hills and cows) before it reaches the lagoon-side town of Sontecomapan, known for its boat trips through the mangroves. Further north along the coast, it passes by the idyllic fishing villages or La Barra and Montepío, renowned for their seafood, and several beautiful, pristine beaches, including those at the appropriately named villages of Playa Hermosa and Costo de Oro, before turning inland again and rejoining Hwy 180, some 22km north of Santiago Tuxtla. Take a day or two to slowly explore some of least-visited and most beautiful parts of the Veracruz coast.

⊙ Sights

Playa Escondida
BEACH

Traveling north, turn right off the main road onto a dirt road just before Balzapote village. Follow a gorgeous wreck of a road for 10 minutes to a moldering relic of a hotel.

From there, you'll find a path leading to a long set of crumbling stairs going to Playa Escondida (Hidden Beach), which earns its name: during the work week in the low season, you'll probably have the gorgeous blond sands and turquoise waters to yourself.

This used to be a nude beach in the '70s and '80s. For our money, this is probably the single best beach in the whole state.

La Barra
VILLAGE

The small fishing village of La Barra, with its pleasant beach overlooking the Laguna Sontecomapan, can be reached by a *lancha* from Sontecomapan (M$650 including a tour of the mangroves on the way), or via a bumpy side road going east from La Palma, 8km north of Sontecomapan. Do not miss a lunch of super-fresh catch of the day at one of the seafood-serving *palapas*.

🏃 Activities

Laguna de Sontecomapan
BOATING

In the town of Sontecomapan, 15km north of Catemaco, there are some lagoonside eateries where you can hire a boat (for up to six people) for an hour-long jaunt through

VERACRUZ COSTA DE ORO

LAGO DE CATEMACO

To explore Laguna Catemaco, there are *lancheros* along the *malecón* in Catemaco offering boat trips. Boats can be paid for *colectivo* (ie per place) or can be hired for up to six people. Expect to pay M$120 for a *colectivo* (in busy times only) or M$650 for a private *lancha* for an hour's boat trip. You can visit several islands on the lake; on the largest, **Isla Tenaspi**, Olmec sculptures have been discovered. **Isla de los Changos** (Monkey Island) shelters red-cheeked monkeys, originally from Thailand. They belong to the Universidad Veracruzana, which acquired them for research.

On the northeast shore of the lake, 8km or so from Catemaco, the **Reserva Ecológica de Nanciyaga** (📞294-943-01-99; www.nanciyaga.com; Carretera Catemaco-Coyame; ⊙cabin reservations 9am-2pm & 4-6pm Mon-Fri, 9am-2pm Sat; P) 🏊 is a kind of reserve within a reserve and pushes an indigenous theme in a small tract of rainforest. The grounds are replete with a *temascal* (traditional herbal steam room), a ye olde planetarium and Olmec-themed decor. Day visitors are welcome. One night's lodging (M$1780 for two people with meals) in solar-powered rustic cabins includes a mineral mud bath, a massage, a guided walk and kayak use. Only you can say whether a torchlit walk to the communal bathrooms at night thrills you or repels you, but it's a fantastic amid-unbridled-nature experience. From Catemaco, arrive by *pirata* (M$12), taxi (M$90) or boat (around M$60 per person).

Follow the lake's eastern shore along perhaps the most potholed road in the history of Mexico for another 8km and you can reach the rustic-chic (read: a bit rundown) **Prashanti Tebanca** (📞294-115-88-86; www.prashanti.com.mx; Camino Laguna Catemaco Km 17; r M$750-2000; P 🅿 🐕). It's a bit more plush than Nanciyaga (rooms have their own bathrooms, for example), but since it's in the middle of nowhere, all meals and activities, such as kayaking and boat rides, are best booked in advance.

the beautiful mangroves (M$450) or for a trip to La Barra (M$650 for the whole boat or M$100 per person). From Catemaco you can catch a taxi (M$70) or *pirata* (M$20) to Sontecomapan.

Pozo de los Enanos SWIMMING
(Sontecomapan) The idyllic Pozo de los Enanos (Well of the Dwarfs) swimming hole, where local youths launch, Tarzanlike, from ropes into the water, is a five-minute walk from the boat landing in Sontecomapan.

🛏️ Sleeping & Eating

⭐ Rancho Los Amigos ECOLODGE $
(📞294-107-46-99, 294-100-78-87; www.losamigos. com.mx; Sontecomapan; incl breakfast dm M$270, cabañas 2 people M$580-900, 6 people M$1200-1700; 🐾) 🏄 Los Amigos is a well-run, peaceful retreat close to where the Laguna Sontecomapan enters the ocean. The fantastic *cabañas* tucked into the verdant hillside have lovely hammocked balconies with spectacular views of the bay. There are nature trails to a beautiful lookout, and a restaurant serving fresh seafood. The boat ride there from Sontecomapan is about 20 minutes.

Kayaking in the mangroves, yoga and relaxing in a traditional herbal steam room *(temascal)* are among the get-away-from-it-all attractions.

⭐ La Barra SEAFOOD $
(mains M$70-120; ⊙10am-9pm) Wiggle your toes in the sand and dig into fish so fresh it may have just jumped onto your plate from the ocean in front of you. Whether grilled, or cooked *al mojo de ajo* (with garlic), and served with homemade salsa, fried plantain, rice and an ice-cold beer, it's as close as it gets to perfection.

The fare at the several *palapas* is comparable in quality, but we particularly like the palapa at the very end of the road because of the estuary views.

ℹ️ Getting There & Away

Piratas (pickup trucks) run reasonably frequently from Catemaco to Montepío (M$40) via Sontecomapan (M$15). For La Barra, if you don't have your own wheels, it's best to take a boat from Sontecomapan. *Piratas* beyond Montepío are infrequent, so to drive the whole Costa de Oro it's best to have your own car.

The road is mostly paved, but somewhat potholed, and with one really slow stretch of giant cobblestones near the turnoff for Playa Escondida and Balzapote.

Yucatán Peninsula

Why Go?

Few Mexican destinations can dazzle you with ancient Maya ruins, azure Caribbean and Gulf of Mexico waters and colonial cities all in one fell swoop. Actually, there's only one – the Yucatán Peninsula. The peninsula comprises parts of Belize and Guatemala, as well as three separate Mexican states: Yucatán, Quintana Roo and Campeche. Quintana Roo is probably the best known thanks to the tourism mega-destinations of Cancún, Tulum and Playa del Carmen, where millions flock annually to get their share of vitamin D on brochure-perfect beaches or resort infinity pools. But head just a couple of hours west and you hit Mérida, the capital of Yucatán state, whose colonial vestiges and contemporary restaurants are a satisfying change of pace, not to mention the many cenotes (freshwater springs) nearby. Neighboring Campeche state is home to mind-blowing Maya ruins galore. This entire compact peninsula holds wonderful, varied and accessible travel surprises.

Best Places to Eat

➡ Ku'uk (p311)

➡ Apoala (p311)

➡ Harry's (p263)

➡ Posada Margherita (p292)

➡ Hartwood (p292)

Best Places to Stay

➡ Luz en Yucatán (p309)

➡ Hacienda Hotel Santo Domingo (p325)

➡ Río Bec Dreams (p349)

➡ Hacienda Puerta Campeche (p342)

➡ Mezcal Hostel (p262)

When to Go
Playa del Carmen

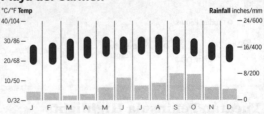

Dec–Apr Mérida Fest is held in January; the weather is much cooler.

Jul & Aug Hot and humid throughout the peninsula. Hurricane season begins. Hotel rates rise.

Sep–Nov Weather cools down from September to November. Great hotel deals. Crowds thin out at ruins.

Yucatán Peninsula Highlights

1 **Mérida** (p304) Wandering this magnificent colonial capital and feasting on local treats.

2 **Parque Dos Ojos** (p289) Diving in this extraordinary underground cave system.

3 **Isla Holbox** (p273) Snorkeling with 15-ton whale sharks or spotting rare birds in nearby islands.

4 **Calakmul** (p349) Exploring some of the Maya's

tallest pyramids, with awesome views of the surrounding jungle.

5 **Chichén Itzá** (p326) Staring in awe at the El Castillo pyramid and learning about Maya culture.

6 Laguna Bacalar (p298)
Plunging into the 90m-deep
Cenote Azul and delighting at
the lake of seven colors.

7 Cobá (p293) Marveling
as the jungle awakens with

birdcalls and morning light
filtering through the canopy.

8 Isla Cozumel (p282)
Diving amid coral reefs at one
of the world's best underwater
destinations.

9 Campeche (p338)
Meandering through colorful
streets and chilling in the
main plaza of this delightfully
relaxed capital.

QUINTANA ROO

Cancún

🖉 998 / POP 628,000

Cancún is a tale of two cities. There's a glitzy hotel zone with its famous white-sand beaches, unabashed party scene and sophisticated seafood restaurants. Then there's the actual city itself, with neighborhood taco joints and undeveloped beaches.

Had your fill of raucous discos in the hotel zone? Escape to a downtown salsa club. Tired of lounging around the pool in Ciudad Cancún? Simply hop on a bus and head for the sapphire waters of the hotel zone.

Or even better, venture out and explore more of Quintana Roo state. Just a day trip away from Cancún, the pristine national park of Isla Contoy beckons with a fascinating variety of bird and plant species. Cobá, with its Maya ruins, jungle, and croc-infested lagoon, seems like a different world. Even further south, Bacalar's lagoon seems almost CGI-created, with Photoshop gradients of blue, green and sand.

👁 Sights

⭐ **Museo Maya de Cancún** MUSEUM

(Maya Museum; Map p260; www.inah.gob.mx; Blvd Kukulcán Km 16.5; M$70; ⏱9am-6pm Tue-Sun; 🚌R-1) Holding one of the Yucatán's most important collections of Maya artifacts, this modern museum is a welcome sight in a city known more for its party scene than cultural attractions. On display are some 400 pieces found at key sites in and around the peninsula, ranging from sculptures to ceramics and jewelry. One of the three halls shows temporary Maya-themed exhibits.

Cancún's original anthropology museum shut down in 2006 due to structural damage from hurricanes. The new museum features hurricane-resistant reinforced glass. The price of admission includes access to the adjoining San Miguelito archaeological site.

All Ritmo AMUSEMENT PARK

(Map p260; 🖉998-881-79-00; www.allritmocancun.com/en/waterpark; Puerto Juárez-Punta Sam Hwy Km 1.5; adult M$320-350, child 5-12yr M$270-290; ⏱10am-5pm Wed-Mon) Little ones can splish and splash to their heart's content at this water park, which also has mini-golf and shuffleboard. The turnoff is 2km north of the Ultramar ferry terminal. 'Punta Sam'

colectivos on Avenida Tulum (opposite the bus terminal) will drop you at the turnoff, and it's a short walk from there.

Zona Arqueológica

El Rey ARCHAEOLOGICAL SITE

(Map p260; Blvd Kukulcán Km 18; M$50; ⏱8am-4:30pm; 🚌R-1, R-2) In the Zona Arqueológica El Rey, on the west side of Blvd Kukulcán, there's a small temple and several ceremonial platforms. The site gets its name from a sculpture excavated here of a noble, possibly a *rey* (king), wearing an elaborate headdress. El Rey, which flourished from AD 1200 to 1500, and nearby San Miguelito were communities dedicated to maritime trade and fishing.

Beaches

Starting from Ciudad Cancún in the northwest, all of Isla Cancún's beaches are on the left-hand side of the road. (The lagoon is on your right; don't swim in the lagoon because of crocodiles!) The first beaches are Playas Las Perlas, Juventud, Linda, Langosta, Tortugas and Caracol. With the exception of Playa Caracol, these are Cancún's most swimmable beaches.

When you round Punta Cancún the water gets rougher (though it's still swimmable) and the beaches become more scenic as white sands meet the turquoise-blue Caribbean, from Playa Gaviota Azul all the way down south to Punta Nizuc at Km 24.

Playa Las Perlas BEACH

(Map p260; Km 2.5) A small beach with a great kids' playground, bathrooms and free *palapa*-topped tables. Free parking. Access from north side of the Holiday Inn.

Playa Langosta BEACH

(Map p260; Km 5) In the middle of the north end of Zona Hotelera, Playa Langosta is a gem of a place for swimming. Facing Bahía de Mujeres, the beach is coated with Cancún's signature powdered coral sand and the waters are quite shallow, making it good for snorkeling. If you've had enough of the water there are lots of beach restaurants and bars.

Playa Caracol BEACH

(Map p260; Km 8.7) Next to the Isla Mujeres ferry dock, this tiny stretch of sand is probably the least inviting of Cancún's beaches, but you can head left when you hit the water to get to the lovely beach 'belonging' to the Hotel Riu. No parking.

PARQUE NACIONAL ISLA CONTOY

Spectacular **Isla Contoy** (☎998-234-99-05; contoy@conanp.gob.mx) is a bird-lover's delight: an uninhabited national park and sanctuary that is an easy day trip from Cancún and from Isla Mujeres. About 800m at its widest point and more than 8.5km long, it has dense foliage that provides ideal shelter for more than 170 bird species, including brown pelicans, olive cormorants, turkey birds, brown boobies and frigates, and is also being a good place to see red flamingos, snowy egrets and white herons.

Whale sharks are often sighted north of Contoy between June and September. In an effort to preserve the park's pristine natural areas, only 200 visitors are allowed access each day. Bring binoculars, mosquito repellent and sunblock.

Guided tours to Isla Contoy give you several hours of free time to explore the island's interpretive trails, climb a 27m-high observation tower and get in a little snorkeling.

For more information on the island, Amigos de Isla Contoy (p266) has a website with detailed information on the island's ecology.

Tour operators based out of Cancún and Isla Mujeres run trips to Contoy.

Playa Chac-Mool   BEACH
(Map p260; Km 9.5) With no parking, this is one of the quieter beaches in Cancún, with a lifeguard on duty. There's no food, but there are stores and restaurants near the access, opposite Señor Frogs.

Playa Marlin   BEACH
(Map p260; Km 12.5) A long, lovely stretch of sand with lifeguards on duty and deck chairs, umbrellas and tables for rent. There's no food, but there is an Oxxo out on Blvd Kukulcán, north of the Kukulcán Plaza where the beach access is.

Playa Delfines   BEACH
(Map p260; Km 17.5; P) Delfines 1s about the only beach with a public car park; unfortunately, its sand is coarser and darker than the exquisite fine sand of the more northerly beaches. On the upside, the beach has great views, there are some nearby Maya Ruins to check out and, as the last beach along the boulevard, it is rarely crowded. Heed the signs regarding swimming conditions as undertows are common here.

Activities
Diving & Snorkeling
★ Museo Subacuático
de Arte   DIVING, SNORKELING
(MUSA Underwater Museum; Map p260; ☎998-206-01-82; www.musacancun.com; snorkeling tour US$41.50, 1-tank dive US$64.50; ⊙9am-5pm) Built to divert divers away from deteriorating coral reefs, this one-of-a-kind aquatic museum features more than 500 life-size sculptures in the waters of Cancún and Isla Mujeres. The artificial reefs are submerged at depths of 4m and 8m, making them ideal for snorkelers

and first-time divers. Organize dives through diving outfits; Scuba Cancún is recommended. The underwater museum is a creation of British-born sculptor Jason deCaires Taylor.

Scuba Cancún   DIVING
(Map p260; ☎998-849-52-25; www.scubacancun.com.mx; Blvd Kukulcán Km 5.2; 1-/2-tank dives US$62/77, equipment rental extra) A family-owned and PADI-certified dive operation with many years of experience, Scuba Cancún was the city's first dive shop. It offers a variety of snorkeling, fishing and diving expeditions (including cenote and night dives). It also runs snorkeling and diving trips to the underwater sculpture museum, aka MUSA.

☞ Tours
Captain Hook   BOATING
(Map p260; ☎998-849-49-31; www.capitanhook.com; Blvd Kukulcán Km 5, Marina Capitán Hook; adult US$84-109, child under 13yr US$5; ⊙tour 7-10:30pm) There's nothing like a swashbuckling adventure with sword fights and cannon battles to get kids' imaginations running wild. This 3½-hour tour aboard a Spanish galleon replica includes dinner service, and it costs a pretty doubloon if you opt for the steak and lobster option (US$95).

Asterix   TOURS
(Map p260; ☎998-886-42-70; www.contoytours.com; Blvd Kukulcán Km 5.2; adult/child 5-12yr US$99/54; ⊙tours 9am-6pm Tue-Sun) Tours to Isla Contoy depart from **Marina Scuba Cancún** (Map p260). They include guide, breakfast, lunch at Isla Mujeres, open bar and snorkeling gear. Hotel pickup can be arranged for US$10 extra per person.

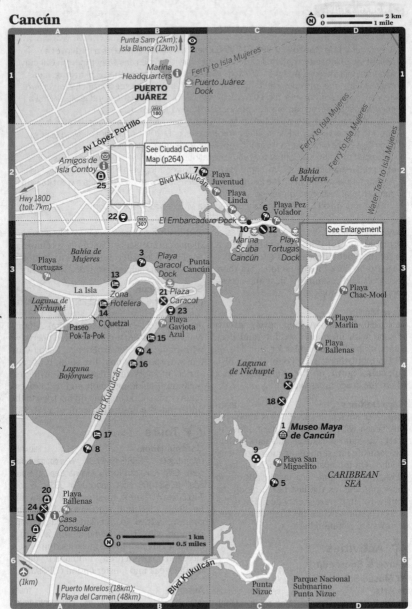

Cancún

Punta Sam (2km);
Isla Blanca (12km)

Marina
Headquarters

PUERTO
JUÁREZ

Puerto Juárez
Dock

Ferry to Isla Mujeres

MEX 180

Av López Portillo

Amigos de
Isla Contoy

See Ciudad Cancún
Map (p264)

Hwy 180D
(toll; 7km)

Blvd Kukulcán

Playa
Juventud

Playa
Linda

Bahía
de Mujeres

Ferry to Isla Mujeres

Ferry to Isla Mujeres

Ferry to Isla Mujeres

Water Taxi to Isla Mujeres

El Embarcadero Dock

Playa Pez
Volador

Marina
Scuba
Cancún

Playa
Tortugas
Dock

See Enlargement

MEX 307

Playa
Tortugas

Bahía de
Mujeres

La Isla

Zona
Hotelera

Laguna de
Nichupté

Paseo
Pok-Ta-Pok

C Quetzal

Playa
Caracol
Dock

Plaza
Caracol

Punta
Cancún

Playa
Chac-Mool

Playa
Gaviota
Azul

Playa
Marlin

Laguna
Bojórquez

Blvd Kukulcán

Laguna
de Nichupté

Playa
Ballenas

Museo Maya
de Cancún

Playa San
Miguelito

CARIBBEAN
SEA

Playa
Ballenas

Casa
Consular

0   1 km
0   0.5 miles

Puerto Morelos (18km);
Playa del Carmen (48km)

Blvd Kukulcán

Punta
Nizuc

Parque Nacional
Submarino
Punta Nizuc

See Ciudad Cancún Map (p264)

🛏 Sleeping

The city has a variety of accommodations ranging from budget all the way to mind- and budget-blowing. Almost all hotels offer discounts during 'low' season, but many have up to five different rate peri-ods: Christmas and New Year are always at a premium, with high rates from late February to early March (US spring break), at Easter, and in July and August (when lo-cals have their holidays). Many places have great online promotions.

Cancún

Hostel Mundo Joven
HOSTEL $

(Map p264; ☎ 998-898-21-03; www.facebook.com/mundojovenhostelcancun; Av Uxmal 25; dm/d incl breakfast from US$11/37; ❄ ❋ @ ☎; 🚍 R-1) One of downtown's budget deals, common-area offerings at this HI affiliate include a rooftop bar and a hot tub (that seems to be constantly undergoing repair). Dorm rooms are tidy and cost slightly more with air-conditioning. With other hostels offering far more nearby, the best reason to book here is its proximity to the bus station.

Grand Royal Lagoon
HOTEL $$

(Map p260; ☎ 998-883-27-49, 800-552-46-66; www.gr-lagoon.com; Quetzal 8A; r M$1100; P ❄ ❋ ☎ ☒; 🚍 R-1) A breezy place, and relatively affordable for the Zona Hotelera, the Grand Royal offers cable TV, safes and a small pool. Most rooms have two double beds, while some have kings, lagoon views and balconies. It's 100m off Blvd Kukulcán Km 7.5. Wi-fi is in the lobby only.

Hotel Antillano
HOTEL $$

(Map p264; ☎ 998-884-11-32; www.hotelantillano.com.mx/eng; Claveles 1; s/d incl breakfast M$1120/1270; P ❄ ❋ ☎ ☒; 🚍 R-1) Just off Avenida Tulum is this very pleasant and quiet place with a relaxing lobby, nice pool, good central air-con and cable TV. Rooms on the Avenida catch more street noise. Rates drop considerably during low season.

Hotel Plaza Caribe
HOTEL $$

(Map p264; ☎ 998-884-13-77; www.hotelplazacaribe.com; Pino s/n; r M$1295; P ❄ ❋ ☎ ☒; 🚍 R-1) Directly across from the bus terminal, this hotel offers comfortable rooms, a pool, restaurant and gardens with peacocks roaming about. The remodeled 'executive' rooms sport a more modern look than the 'standard' digs.

Hotel Colonial Cancún
HOTEL $$

(Map p264; ☎ 998-884-15-35; www.hotelcolonial-cancun.com; Tulipanes 22; d M$850; ❄ ❋ ☎ ☒; 🚍 R-1) Rooms are anything but colonial, but they're pleasant enough and they overlook a leafy central courtyard with a gurgling fountain. The hotel has a small pool area.

Hotel Bonampak
HOTEL $$

(Map p264; ☎ 998-884-02-80; www.hotelbonampak.com; Av Bonampak 225; r incl breakfast M$1220; P ❄ ❋ @ ☎ ☒; 🚍 R-1, R-2) Good value by Cancún standards, rooms at this business-style hotel have comfy mattresses, dark-wood furnishings and flat-screen TVs. Ask for one overlooking the sunny pool area.

🛏 Ciudad Cancún

'Budget' is a relative term; prices in Cancún are higher for what you get than most anywhere else in Mexico. There are many cheap lodging options within several blocks of the bus terminal, northwest on Avenida Uxmal. The area around Parque de las Palapas has numerous hostels and budget digs as well.

Midrange in Cancún is a two-tiered category; the Ciudad Cancún area is much cheaper than the Zona Hotelera and only a short bus ride away from the Zona's beaches.

Hostel Ka'beh
HOSTEL $

(Map p264; ☎988-892-79-02, 998-168-80-27; www.cancunhostel.hostel.com; Alcatraces 45; dm/r incl breakfast M$380/880; ❂❄@☎; ➤R-1) A friendly central option just off the buzzing Parque de las Palapas, this small hostel has a lived-in feel that goes hand in hand with the relaxed vibe. Expect many social activities at night, most organized around food and drink. Vans depart to the beach in the mornings and to the Zona Hotelera after dinner.

★Mezcal Hostel
HOSTEL $$

(Map p264; ☎998-125-95-02, 998-255-28-44; www.mezcalhostel.com; Mero 12; dm/r incl breakfast US$20/64; ❂❄☎; ➤R-1) If getting a made-to-order omelette in the morning doesn't grab you, perhaps the swimming pool, the bar, the numerous activities or the nightly excursions to the clubs will. Mezcal Hostel occupies a beautiful two-story house in a quiet residential area. Sunday barbecue parties are perfect for sipping smoky mezcal. Smoke can be thick in the common areas, but the dorms are smoke-free.

Cancún International Suites
HOTEL $$

(Map p264; ☎998-884-17-71; www.cancuninternationalsuites.com; Gladiolas 11, cnr Alcatraces; r/ste M$1100/2000; ❂❄☎; ➤R-1) Colonial-style rooms and suites in this remodeled hotel are comfortable and quiet and the location is great – right off Parque de las Palapas and conveniently close to downtown's restaurant and bar zone.

Soberanis Hotel
HOTEL $$

(Map p264; ☎998-884-45-64; www.hotelsoberanis.com; Av Cobá 5 s/n; d incl breakfast M$1300; ❂@☎; ➤R-1) Location, location, location. The Soberanis sits right on a corner where buses stop before continuing on to the Zona Hotelera, plus there's a supermarket right next door. The rooms have comfortable, clean beds and wood furnishings. No elevator means the lotsa-luggage crowd may want to look elsewhere.

Náder Hotel & Suites
HOTEL $$

(Map p264; ☎998-884-15-84; www.suitesnadercancun.com; Av Náder 5; d/ste incl breakfast US$54/75; ❂❄☎; ➤R-1) The Náder caters to business travelers, but it's also a hit with families thanks to its ample rooms and suites with large common areas and kitchens. Even the 'standard' setup here gets you digs with some serious elbow room.

★Hotel El Rey del Caribe
HOTEL $$$

(Map p264; ☎998-884-20-28; www.elreydelcaribe.com; Av Uxmal 24; r incl breakfast M$3400; ❂❄❄❄; ➤R-1) 🗲 El Rey is a true ecotel – it recycles, employs solar collectors and cisterns, uses gray water on the gardens, and has some rooms with composting toilets. This beautiful spot has a swimming pool and Jacuzzi in a jungly courtyard that's home to a small family of *tlacuaches* (opossums). All rooms have a fully equipped kitchenette, comfortable beds and fridges. Offers good online deals.

🛏 Zona Hotelera

With few exceptions, most hotels lining Blvd Kukulcán are of the top-end variety. Many offer all-inclusive packages, often at reasonable rates if you're willing to forgo eating elsewhere. Often the best room rates are available through hotel-and-airfare packages, so shop around.

Hostel Natura
HOSTEL $$

(Map p260; ☎998-883-08-87; www.facebook.com/HostelCancunNatura; Blvd Kukulcán Km 9.5; dm/r US$30/65; ❂❄☎; ➤R-1) Up above a health-food restaurant of the same name, this fun, vibrant Zona Hotelera hostel offers private rooms with lagoon views and somewhat cramped dorms, offset by the airy rooftop terrace, and a nice common kitchen area. The party zone is just a stumble away, and the staff are helpful and friendly.

★Le Blanc
RESORT $$$

(Map p260; ☎800-272-02-15, 998-881-47-48, US 877-883-3696; www.leblancsparesort.com; Blvd Kukulcán Km 10; d/ste all-inclusive US$766/806; 🅿❂❄❄☎; ➤R-1, R-2) You can't miss the glaring white exterior of the aptly named Le Blanc, arguably Cancún's most sophisticated resort. This adults-only retreat comes with all the amenities you'd expect in this category: gorgeous infinity pool, cold welcome drink on check-in, coconut-scented hand towels – the works. There's even butler service should life in Cancún become too complicated. Discounts for multiple-night stays.

★Beachscape Kin Ha Villas & Suites
HOTEL $$$

(Map p260; ☎998-891-54-00; http://beachscapekinhavillas.com; Blvd Kukulcán Km 8.5; r from

US$108; P ⊖ ✳ @ 🛜 ☲; 🚃R-1) A good family spot, Beachscape offers a babysitting service, a play area for kids and a swimmable beach with calm waters. You'll never need to leave the hotel's grounds (though we think you should), as there are bars, markets, travel agencies and more on the premises. All rooms feature a balcony and two double beds or one king-sized bed. The price listed is for the European plan, but you can arrange an all-inclusive stay.

Me by Melia
LUXURY HOTEL **$$$**

(Map p260; ☑ 998-881-25-00; www.mebymelia. com; Blvd Kukulcán Km 12; d all-inclusive from US$320; P ⊖ ✳ 🛜 ☲; 🚃R-1, R-2) Just reopened after extensive renovations, this is an uber-modern, expressionist-inspired hotel. A Times Square–sized TV dazzles behind the reception desk, and futuristic-rustic swing hammocks await you outside. It won't suit everyone, but if you prefer clean lines over standard Cancún baroque, it's the place for you. Only half the rooms have ocean views, so be sure to request one that does.

✕ Eating

Where you go to eat often is based on where you are staying: the Hotel Zone or the city centro. Either place has a range of options, though meals are (not surprisingly) pricier in the Hotel Zone.

Rooster Café Sunyaxchen
CAFE **$**

(Map p264; ☑ 998-310-46-92; Avenida Sunyaxchen, Supermanzana 24, At Plaza Sunyaxchen; mains M$60-120; ☺7am-11pm) A main go-to café for locals in search of a place to write, work or hang out, this trendy coffee shop has a central location in downtown Cancún, close to Market 28. Try items like Monte Cristo waffles and homemade breads from the breakfast menu, or stop by in the afternoon for desserts, salads, burgers and paninis.

Taco Factory
MEXICAN **$**

(Map p260; ☑ 998-883-48-64; www.facebook.com/ taco.factory.cancun; Blvd Kukulcán Km 9; tacos M$20-37; ☺11:30am-7am Mon & Wed-Sun, 1pm-4am Tue; 🚃R-1) This casual open-air eatery boasts the best authentic Mexican tacos in the Cancún Hotel Zone, and its convenient location in the central alley right by the nightclub strip makes it perfect for late-night cravings. For great flavor, try the tacos *al pastor*.

★ El Tigre y El Toro
ITALIAN **$$**

(Map p264; ☑ 998-898-00-41; Av Náder 64; mains M$140-170; ☺6pm-midnight; 🛜 ✒; 🚃R-1, R-2)

Gourmet thin-crust pizza and homemade pastas are served in a pebbly candlelit garden at El Tigre y El Toro ('tiger' and 'bull' are the owners' nicknames). Many locals rank this as Cancún's *numero uno* pizza joint.

La Parrilla
MEXICAN **$$**

(Map p264; ☑ 998-287-8118; www.laparrilla.com. mx; 51 Av Yaxchilán; mains M$130-550; ☺noon-2am) Colorful decoration, a large outdoor bull, and the sounds of a mariachi band invite you in to La Parrilla on Avenida Yaxchilán, a downtown street known for its dive bars and classic Mexican food. Open since 1975, La Parrilla fills up with locals and tourists alike thanks to its tasty tacos *al pastor* (M$184) and extensive menu of authentic Mexican cuisine.

La Fonda del Zancudo
INTERNATIONAL **$$**

(Map p264; ☑ 998-884-1741; www.facebook.com/ lafondadelzancudo; 23 Av Uxmal; mains M$95-225; ☺7pm-midnight Mon-Sat; 🚃R-1) Softly illuminated by strings of lights, lanterns and moonlight, this alluring little restaurant sits within an enchanting walled patio on downtown Cancún's central Avenida Uxmal. The main menu boasts artisanal creations made primarily with local organic ingredients, and the daily specials wall always has tempting culinary surprises and inventive cocktails to try.

Irori
JAPANESE **$$**

(Map p264; ☑ 998-892-30-72; www.iroricancun. com.mx; Av Tulum 226; mains M$85-220; ☺1-10:30pm Mon-Sat, to 9:30pm Sun; 🛜 ✒; 🚃R-27) Enjoy the show as the chef slices and dices the night away at this Japanese-run restaurant serving sushi and many other Japanese favorites in an intimate setting. There's even a kids' menu and playroom for those with little sushi-scoffers in tow. You'll find the entrance on Calle Viento. Note that it may close early on slow nights.

★ Harry's
STEAK **$$$**

(Map p260; ☑ 998-840-65-50; www.harrys.com. mx; Blvd Kukulcán Km 14.2; mains M$470-1500; ☺1pm-1am; 🚃R-1, R-2) Stunning, renowned Harry's serves house-aged steaks, plus super-fresh fish and a famous cotton candy treat. The architecture's impressive too, with indoor waterfalls, plenty of decking over the lagoon and two bars – one indoors and one out. Service is impeccable too. Try the jungle-theme lounge or new club upstairs, and don't miss peeking at their mezcal display. Yum!

Ciudad Cancún

N

0 — 400 m
0 — 0.2 miles

A **B** **C** **D**

Hwy 180 (1km);
Puerto Juárez (4km)

21

Flamboyan

Av Tulum

Av Náder

Naranja

Hwy 180
(850m)

Flamboyan

Cereza

Av Uxmal

Roble

Roble

Palmera

Palmera

Laurel

Chaca

Bus Stop to
Zona Hotelera

Colectivos to Puerto
Juárez & Punta Sam

Punta Allen

Av Yaxchilán

3

Laurel

8

Pino

Nicchehabi

Cancún Bus
Terminal

Playa Express
Buses

7

Av Uxmal

16

Rosas

Margaritas

Margaritas

14

Punta Conoco

Jazmines

12

Av Sunyaxchén

18

15

Azucenas

20

9

Jazmines

Ayuntamiento
Benito
Juárez

Mercado 28
(200m)

Gladiolas

Tulipanes

Av Yaxchilán

Parque Las
Palapas

6

Av Tulum

Gladiolas

Tulipanes

1

Av Náder

Orquídeas

Claveles

4

10

2

Claveles

Orquídeas

Alcatraces

Alcatraces

Crisantemos

Av Cobá

11

FONATUR
City Tourism
Office

17

Sierra

Av Cobá

19

Av Xcaret

Av Cobá

Brisa

Nube

Jaleb

Lluvia

Av Bonampak

Lluvia

Nube

Tejón

Av Tulum

Cielo

Pecari

Agua

Cielo

Pecari

Agua

Tierra

Viento

Av Bonampak

Viento

13

Tierra

5

Mar

Fuego
Park

Fuego

Av Sayil

Ciudad Cancún

⭐ **La Habichuela**   FUSION $$$

(Map p264; ☎998-884-31-58; www.lahabi
chuela.com; Margaritas 25; mains M$190-345;
⊙1pm-midnight; P🐶; 🚇R-1) This elegant res-
taurant has a lovely courtyard dining area,
just off Parque de las Palapas. The specialty
is the *cocobichuela* (shrimp and lobster in
curry sauce served inside a coconut with
tropical fruit, M$545), but almost anything
on the menu is delicious. The menu even has
a Maya-English dictionary! **La Habichuela
Sunset** (Map p260; ☎998-840-62-80; www.
lahabichuela.com; Blvd Kukulcán Km 12.6; mains
M$250-400; ⊙noon-midnight; 🐶; 🚇R-1, R-2),
the restaurant's slightly pricier Zona Hotel-
era branch, affords a gorgeous lagoon view.

Crab House   SEAFOOD $$$

(Map p260; ☎998-193-03-50; www.crabhousecan
cun.com; Blvd Kukulcán Km 14.7; dishes M$450-
1250; ⊙noon-11:30pm; P🐶; 🚇R-1) Offering a
lovely view of the lagoon that complements
the seafood, the long menu here includes
many shrimp and fish-fillet dishes. Stone
crab is the specialty, which (along with lobster) is priced by the pound. Both are served
from crystal-clear tanks. The establishment
prides itself in having no holidays: not even
for hurricanes.

Peter's Restaurante   INTERNATIONAL $$$

(Map p264; ☎998-251-93-10; http://petersestau
rante.restaurantwebexperts.com; Avenida Bonam-
pak, btwn Calles Sierra & Robalo; dinner M$400-
1200; ⊙6-10pm Tue-Sat) Set on one of down-
town Cancún's busiest avenues, Peter's Res-
taurante has a homey charm and some of
the best cooking in the city. Dutch Chef Peter
Houben has blended European, Mexican and
international cuisine, with beautifully pre-
pared dishes like the mushroom ravioli ap-
petizer and fresh salmon filet in lemon sauce
with a spicy hint of *chile de àrbol* (tree chili).

Drinking & Nightlife

Many clubs and restaurants are open for
drinks for much of the day. Cancún doesn't
offer much in the way of a gay and lesbian
scene, but downtown has a few nightspots.

⭐ **Mambocafé**   CLUB

(Map p264; ☎998-884-45-36; www.mambocafe.
com.mx; Plaza Hong Kong, cnr Avs Xcaret & Tankah;
cover M$200; ⊙10pm-5am Wed-Sat; 🚇R-2) The
large floor at this happening club is the per-
fect place to practice those Latin dance steps
you've been working on. Live groups play
Cuban salsa and other tropical styles.

Nomads Cocina & Barra   COCKTAIL BAR

(Map p264; ☎998-898-31-92; http://nomadscancun.
com; cnr Av Náder & Mero; ⊙3pm-2am, to 3am Fri
& Sat; 🚇R-1) Showing off with an artsy vibe
where geometric tiles meet concrete and
brick, Nomads draws in Cancún's young 'in
crowd' with classic Mexican street food, cre-
ative cocktails and innovative cuisine. The
indoor area allows friends to sit down to a
late dinner (mains M$110 to M$280), while
the back area under the stars is standing
-room-only for socializing by the bar.

The City   CLUB

(Map p260; ☎998-883-33-33; http://thecitycan
cun.com; Blvd Kukulcán Km 9; incl drinks from
US$65; ⊙10:30pm-5am Fri; 🚇R-1) The largest
nightclub in Latin America still manages to
fill up every Friday night. Frequently hosting
world-famous DJs and musicians, this mas-
sive place offers wild nightlife whether you're
dancing on top of the central stage or watch-
ing it all from the stadium-style side levels.
Due to the crowds and 'party hearty' atmos-
phere, be aware that it can be nuts at times.

Marakame Café   BAR

(Map p260; ☎998-887-10-10; www.marakamecafe.
com; Av Circuito Copán 19, near Av Nichupté; ⊙8am-
1am Mon-Fri, 9am-2am Sat, 9am-midnight Sun; 🐶)

An excellent open-air breakfast and lunch spot by day, and a popular bar with live music by night. The bartenders, or mixologists if you will, prepare interesting concoctions such as kiwi-flavored mojitos and margaritas blended with *chaya* (tree spinach), cucumber and lime. It's a short taxi ride from downtown.

Shopping

Shopaholics will enjoy the city's colorful markets. Locals head to either **Mercado 28** (Mercado Veintiocho; Map p260; cnr Avs Xel-Há & Sunyaxchén; ⊙6am-7pm) or **Mercado 23** (Map p264; Av Tulum s/n; ⊙6am-7pm; ⊠R-1) for clothes, shoes, inexpensive food stalls and so on. Of the two, Mercado 23 is the less frequented by tourists. If you're looking for a place without corny T-shirts, this is the place to go. There's definitely no shortage of modern malls in Cancún.

La Europea   DRINKS

(Map p260; ☑998-176-82-02; www.laeuropea.com.mx; Blvd Kukulcán Km 12.5; ⊙10am-9pm Mon-Sat, 11am-7pm Sun; ⊠R-1) A gourmet liquor store with reasonable prices, knowledgable staff and the best booze selection in town, including top-shelf tequilas and mezcals. Most airlines allow you to travel with up to 3L of alcohol, but check first. Salud!

Plaza Kukulcán   MALL

(Map p260; www.kukulcanplaza.mx; Blvd Kukulcán Km 13; ⊙10am-10pm; ☎; ⊠R-1) The largest of the indoor malls is Plaza Kukulcán. Of note here are the temporary art exhibits, the many stores selling silverwork, and La Ruta de las Indias, a shop featuring wooden models of Spanish galleons and replicas of conquistadors' weaponry and body armor.

Information

EMERGENCY

Cruz Roja (Red Cross)	☑911, ☑065
Fire	☑911, ☑998-884-12-02
Police	☑911, ☑066
Tourist Police	☑911, ☑066, ☑998-885-22-77

IMMIGRATION

Instituto Nacional de Migración (Immigration Office; ☑998-881-35-60; www.gob.mx/inm; cnr Avs Náder 1 & Uxmal; ⊙9am-1pm Mon-Fri) Go here to replace lost immigration forms.

MEDICAL SERVICES

Hospital Playa Med (☑998-140-52-58; www.hospitalplayamed.com; Av Náder 13, cnr Av Uxmal; ⊙24hr; ⊠R-1) Modern facility with 24-hour assistance.

MONEY

There are several banks with ATMs throughout the Zona Hotelera and downtown on Avenida Tulum. Cancún's airport also has ATMs and money exchange.

Scotiabank (La Isla Shopping Village, Zona Hotelera; ⊙24hr) One of the many options.

POST

There is no post office in the Zona Hotelera, but most hotels' reception desks sell stamps and will mail letters.

The **Main Post Office** (Map p260; cnr Avs Xel-Há & Sunyaxchén; ⊙8am-4pm Mon-Fri, 9am-12:30pm Sat) is downtown at the edge of Mercado 28. You can also post mail in the red postal boxes sprinkled around town.

TOURIST INFORMATION

Amigos de Isla Contoy (Map p260; ☑998-884-74-83; www.islacontoy.org; Plaza Bonita Mall; ⊙9:30am-5pm Mon-Fri) Has helpful info about Isla Contoy and works to conserve the island.

Cancún Visitors Bureau (www.cancun.travel) An informative website, but no tourist office.

Casa Consular (Map p260; ☑998-840-60-82; www.casaconsular.org; Kukulcán Km 13; ⊙10am-2pm Mon-Fri) While they don't provide consular assistance themselves, Casa Consular will find the exact information you need and tell you where you need to go. It is a service for all visitors, not just those with an embassy or consulate in the city. Located inside the police and fire department building.

FONATUR City Tourism Office (Map p264; ☑998-887-33-79, 555-090-42-00; www.fonatur.gob.mx; cnr Avs Cobá & Náder; ⊙9am-4pm Mon-Fri) City tourist office with ample supplies of printed material and knowledgable staff.

Marina Headquarters (Map p260; ☑998-880-13-63, 998-234-99-05; contoy@conanp.gob.mx; Capitanía Regional de Puerto Juárez)

Getting There & Away

AIR

Aeropuerto Internacional de Cancún (☑998-848-72-00; www.asur.com.mx; Hwy 307 Km 22) is the busiest airport in southeast Mexico. It has all the services you would expect from a major international airport: ATMs, money exchange and car-rental agencies. It's served by many direct international flights and by connecting flights from Mexico City. Low-cost

Mexican carriers VivaAerobus, Interjet and Volaris have service from Mexico City.

There are flights to Cancún from Guatemala City and Flores (Guatemala), Havana (Cuba), Panama City and São Paulo (Brazil). Some Havana–Cancún flights continue to Mérida.

For a full list of the carriers with flights to Cancún, see the airport website. Mexican carriers include the following:

Aeroméxico (☏998-193-18-68; www.aeromexico.com; Av Cobá 80; ⊙9am-6:30pm Mon-Fri, to 6pm Sat; ☐R-1) Direct flights from Mexico City and New York. Office just west of Avenida Bonampak.

Interjet (☏998-892-02-78; www.interjet.com; Av Xcaret 35, Plaza Hollywood) Flies direct to Miami and Havana.

Magnicharters (☏800-201-14-04, 998-884-06-00; www.magnicharters.com.mx; Av Náder 94, cnr Av Cobá; ☐R-1) To Mexico City.

VivaAerobus (☏81-8215-0150; www.vivaaerobus.com; Cancún airport, Hwy 307 Km 22) Non-stop to Houston.

Volaris (☏551-102-80-00; www.volaris.com; Cancún airport, Hwy 307 Km 22) Service to Mexico City and many other parts of Mexico.

BOAT

There are several points of embarkation to reach Isla Mujeres from Cancún by boat. **El Embarcadero** (Map p260), **Playa Caracol** (Map p260) and **Playa Tortugas** (Map p260) docks are among the options. From **Puerto Juárez** (Map p260) it costs M$160; leaving from the Zona Hotelera it is US$14. If you want to transport a vehicle you'll need to head to **Punta Sam**, 8km north of Ciudad Cancún (basic auto fares M$292 to M$511, including driver).

For Isla Contoy boats depart from the Marina Scuba Cancún (p259). For more on hours and departure points to Isla Mujeres, see www.ultramarferry.com/en.

BUS

Cancún's modern **bus terminal** (Map p264; www.ado.com.mx; cnr Avs Uxmal & Tulum) occupies the wedge formed where Avenidas Uxmal and Tulum meet. It's a relatively safe area, but be aware of your bags and cautious of people offering to do anything for free. If you do accept help, make sure to establish the price before you get in the vehicle.

Across Pino from the bus terminal, a few doors from Avenida Tulum, is the ticket office and mini-terminal of **Playa Express** (Map p264; Calle Pino), which runs air-conditioned buses down the coast to Playa del Carmen every 10 minutes until early evening, stopping at major towns and points of interest. **ADO** (☏800-009-90-90; www.ado.com.mx) covers the same ground and beyond with its 1st-class service.

ADO sets the 1st-class standard. Mayab provides good 'intermediate class' (tending to make more stops than 1st class) to many points.

BUSES FROM CANCÚN

DESTINATION	COST (M$)	DURATION (HR)	FREQUENCY (DAILY)
Bacalar	360-400	4-5	frequent
Chetumal	404-518	5½-6	frequent
Chichén Itzá	151-298	3-4	14
Chiquilá	128-230	3-3½	3 (Mayab)
Felipe Carrillo Puerto	168-210	3½-4	6
Mérida	412-498	4-4½	frequent
Mexico City	2074	27	1 to Terminal Norte; 6:30pm
Mexico City (TAPO)	2074	24½-28	2; 6:30am, 8pm
Palenque	1326	13-13½	1; 5:45pm
Playa del Carmen	38-106	1-1½	frequent ADO & Playa Express
Puerto Morelos	28	½-¾	frequent ADO & Playa Express
Ticul	288	8½	frequent
Tizimín	133	3	3
Tulum	116-206	2½	frequent
Valladolid	117-216	2-2¼	8
Villahermosa	1086-1286	12¾-14½	frequent

CAR & MOTORCYCLE

Cancún can get congested at times and driving inside the city may not be worth the stress, but you can certainly get around by car. Be careful to park in white curb areas only unless you've been specifically told parking in yellow is OK. Red, green and anything else than white is prohibited or reserved. Be aware that Hwy 180D, the *cuota* (toll road) running much of the way between Cancún and Mérida, costs M$450. An economy size rental car with liability insurance costs about M$600 per day.

Alamo (🖉 998-886-01-00; www.alamo.com.mx; Airport, Terminal 2)

Avis (🖉 800-288-88-88, 998-176-80-30; www.avis.com.mx; Blvd Kukulcán Km 12.5, Centro Comercial La Isla)

Hertz (🖉 800-709-50-00; www.hertz.com; Cancún airport)

National (🖉 998-881-87-60; www.nationalcar.com; Cancún airport)

❶ Getting Around

TO/FROM THE AIRPORT

Frequent ADO buses go to Ciudad Cancún (M$72) between 8:20am and 12:30am. They depart from outside the terminals. Once in town, the buses travel up Avenida Tulum to the bus terminal on the corner of Avenida Uxmal. Going to the airport from Ciudad Cancún, the same ADO airport buses (Aeropuerto Centro) leave regularly from the bus station. ADO also offers bus services out of the airport to Playa del Carmen and Mérida.

Airport shuttle vans Green Line and Super Shuttle run to and from Ciudad Cancún and the Zona Hotelera for about US$50 per person.

Yellow Transfers (🖉 998-193-17-42, 800-021-8087; www.yellowtransfers.com) is a pick-up and drop-off service from the airport to many area hotels.

Colectivos (Map p264) are an inexpensive way to get to the airport. Regular taxis run from the airport into town or to the Zona Hotelera and cost up to M$650 (up to four people). Expect to pay about M$370 for a city cab when returning to the airport.

BUS

To reach the Zona Hotelera from Ciudad Cancún, catch any **bus** (Map p264) with 'R-1' 'Hoteles' or 'Zona Hotelera' displayed on the windshield as it travels along Avenida Tulum toward Avenida Cobá then eastward on Avenida Cobá. South of Avenida Cobá, along Avenida Tulum, you can also catch the 'R-27' to the Zona Hotelera.

To reach Puerto Juárez and the Isla Mujeres ferries, you can either take a northbound 'Punta Sam' or 'Puerto Juárez' **colectivo** (Map p264) from a bus stop on Avenida Tulum (across from the ADO terminal), or you can wait on Avenida Tulum for an R-1 'Puerto Juárez' bus.

TAXI

Cancún's taxis do not have meters. Fares are set, but you should always agree on a price before getting in; otherwise you could end up paying for a 'misunderstanding.' From Ciudad Cancún to Punta Cancún it's usually M$100 to M$130, to Puerto Juárez M$50 to M$70. Trips within the Zona Hotelera or downtown zones cost around M$50. Hourly and daily rates should be about M$240 and M$2000, respectively.

Isla Mujeres

🖉 998 / POP 12,600

Some people plan their vacation around Cancún and pencil in Isla Mujeres as a side trip. But Isla Mujeres is a destination in its own right, and it's generally quieter and more affordable than the options you get across the bay.

Sure, there are quite a few ticky-tacky tourist shops, but folks still get around by golf cart and the crushed-coral beaches are undeniably lovely. As for the calm turquoise water of Isla Mujeres, well, you really just have to see it for yourself.

There's just enough here to keep you entertained: snorkel or scuba dive, visit a turtle farm or put on your sunglasses and settle in with that book you've been dying to finish. Come sunset, there are plenty of dining options, and the nightlife scene moves at a relaxed island pace.

◉ Sights

Isla Mujeres Turtle Farm   FARM

(Isla Mujeres Tortugranja; 🖉 998-888-07-05; Carretera Sac Bajo Km 5; M$30; ⊙9am-5pm; ⊕) 🖉
Although they're endangered, sea turtles are still killed throughout Latin America for their eggs and meat. In the 1980s, efforts by a local fisherman led to the founding of this *tortugranja* (turtle farm), 5km south of town, which safeguards breeding grounds and protects eggs.

It's a small spot, with a number of sizes of turtles and a few different species. The farm is easily reached from town by taxi (M$80) or golf cart.

Hatchlings are liberated immediately. The turtles that leave this secure beach return each year, which means their offspring receive the same protection. The sanctuary releases about 125,000 turtles each year, but only one of every 1000 will survive.

The farm provides refuge for loggerhead, hawksbill and green turtles ranging in weight from 150g to more than 300kg. It also has a small but interesting aquarium, displays on marine life and a pen that holds large nurse sharks. Tours are conducted in Spanish and English. The public is not always able to watch the releases (you can ask), but the farm usually does them around 7pm from July through November. It's quite a sight to see the tiny creatures scurrying into the great big sea.

Punta Sur   VIEWPOINT, GARDENS

(ruins M$30) At the island's southernmost point you'll find a lighthouse, a sculpture garden and the worn remains of a temple dedicated to Ixchel, Maya goddess of the moon and fertility. Various hurricanes have pummeled the ruins over time and there's now little to see other than the sculpture garden, the sea and Cancún in the distance. Taxis from town cost about M$150.

Beaches

★ Playa Garrafón   BEACH

Head to this beach for excellent snorkeling. It's 6.5km from the tourist center. A cab costs M$120.

Playa Norte   BEACH

Once you reach Playa Norte, the island's main beach, you won't want to leave. Its warm, shallow waters are the color of blue raspberry syrup and the beach is crushed coral. Unlike most of the island's east coast, Playa Norte is safe for swimming and the water is only chest deep even far from shore.

Playa Secreto   BEACH

(🏊) The lagoon separating a large hotel complex from the rest of the island has a shallow swimming spot that's ideal for kids. Despite the depth (or lack of it) a number of pretty fish circle around the swimmers looking for handouts.

🏃 Activities

Diving & Snorkeling

Within a short boat ride of the island there's a handful of lovely dives, such as **La Bandera**, **Arrecife Manchones** and **Ultrafreeze** (El Frío), where you'll see the intact hull of a 60m-long cargo ship, thought to have been deliberately sunk in 30m of water. Expect to see sea turtles, rays and barracuda, along with a wide array of hard and soft corals.

Isla Mujeres 1 km / 0.5 miles

There's good shore-snorkeling near **Playa Garrafón** and at **Yunque Reef**. As always, watch for boat traffic when you head out snorkeling.

Snorkeling with whale sharks is another popular activity. The peak season runs from mid-June through August. It can get downright crazy, with up to a dozen boats circling one whale shark, but they limit the number of swimmers in the water to three people (including one guide). Most dive shops offer whale-shark excursions.

Isla Mujeres Town

YUCATÁN PENINSULA ISLA MUJERES

Isla Mujeres Town

◉ Sights
1 Playa Norte	A2
2 Playa Secreto	B1

◆ Activities, Courses & Tours
3 Aqua Adventures Eco Divers	C4
4 Mundaca Divers	C3

◉ Sleeping
5 Apartments Trinchan	C2
6 Casa El Pío	D4
7 Hotel Francis Arlene	C3
8 Hotel Kinich	B3
9 Hotel Na Balam	B1
10 Hotel Rocamar	D3
11 Poc-Na Hostel	C2

✖ Eating
12 Aluxes Coffee Shop	B3
13 Café del Mar	A3
14 La Lomita	D4
15 Lola Valentina	B3
16 Olivia	B3
17 Rooster Café	B3

⊙ Drinking & Nightlife
18 Buho's	A2
19 El Patio	C3
20 Fenix Lounge	B1

ⓘ Transport
21 Ferries to Zona Hotelera & Cancún	C4
22 Ferry to Puerto Juárez	C4

★ **Hotel Garrafón de Castilla** SNORKELING
(☎ 998-877-01-07; Carretera Punta Sur Km 6; M$70, snorkel-gear rental M$80; ⊙10am-6pm) Avoid the overpriced Playa Garrafón Reef Park and instead visit Hotel Garrafón de Castilla's beach club for a day of snorkeling.

Aqua Adventures Eco Divers DIVING
(☎ 998-251-74-23, cell 998-3228109; www.diveisla mujeres.com; Juárez 1, cnr Morelos; 2-tank dives incl

equipment from US$75, whale-shark tour US$125; ☺ 9am-7pm Mon-Sat, 10am-6pm Sun) Great option for snorkeling with whale sharks and goes to 15 sites for reef dives.

Mundaca Divers DIVING
(☑ 998-877-06-07, cell 998-1212228; www.munda cadiversisla.com; Madero s/n; 2-tank dives US$90, snorkeling US$47, bay fishing US$450; ☺ 8am-8pm) Does everything from shark-cave dives and fishing expeditions to snorkeling trips to a one-of-a-kind underwater sculpture museum known as MUSA (p259).

🛏 Sleeping

★ Poc-Na Hostel HOSTEL $
(☑ 998-877-00-90; www.pocna.com; Matamoros 15; dm/d incl breakfast from M$300/600; ☻ ✳ 🛜) You can't beat this hostel's common areas. For starters, the hostel is right on a lovely palm-shaded beach, home to one of the town's most happening beach bars at night – and you can also pitch a tent if you bring your own. Guests can chill in a cool *palapa* lobby bar, where breakfast is served and local bands play nightly.

If at some point you get bored with all the lazing around, Poc-Na keeps things interesting by offering activities ranging from salsa and Spanish classes to snorkeling tours and bike rental (M$180 per day).

Apartments Trinchan APARTMENT $$
(☑ cell 998-1666967; atrinchan@prodigy.net.mx; Carlos Lazo 46; r with fan/air-con M$700/800; ✳ 🛜) Since it has no website, you'll have to take our word for it when we say this is one of the best budget deals in town – and the beach is right around the corner. If it's available, opt for one of the large apartments with full kitchen.

Hotel Francis Arlene HOTEL $$
(☑ 998-877-03-10; www.francisarlene.com; Guerrero 7; r with fan/air-con from M$1200/1500; ☻ ✳ 🛜) This place offers comfortable, good-sized rooms with fan (or air-con) and fridge. Most have a king-sized bed or two doubles, and many have balconies and partial sea views. The lounging frog sculptures are cute. Good low-season rates.

Hotel Na Balam BOUTIQUE HOTEL $$$
(☑ 998-881-47-70; www.nabalam.com; Zazil-Ha 118; r/ste incl breakfast from US$196/283; ☻ ✳ 🛜 ☵) Iguanas roam the beautiful hibiscus and palm gardens at this beachfront hotel on Playa Norte. All rooms are decorated with simple elegance and have safes, hammocks, private balconies or patios, and some come with TVs. The hotel offers yoga and meditation classes as well as massage services and a swimming pool.

Hotel Kinich BOUTIQUE HOTEL $$$
(☑ 998-888-09-09; www.islamujereskinich.com; Juárez 20; s/d/ste incl breakfast M$1500/1800/2500; ☻ ✳ 🛜) Boutique Hotel Kinich gives you plenty of bang for your buck in low season, when rates drop by about 40%, and even in high season the huge rooms with balconies are still a pretty good deal, especially the family-friendly suites. Wi-fi in the lobby only.

Casa El Pío BOUTIQUE HOTEL $$$
(www.casaelpio.com; Hidalgo 3; r US$95-113; ☻ ✳ 🛜) Book rooms well in advance if you want to stay at this small – and very popular – boutique hotel. One of the five rooms has an ocean view, as does the rooftop terrace, and all rooms have interesting design details. The pool is for splashing more than swimming, but with the beach right around the corner who cares? Online reservations only.

Hotel Rocamar HOTEL $$$
(☑ 998-877-01-01; www.rocamar-hotel.com; cnr Bravo & Guerrero; r M$2261-3094, casas M$6664; 🅿 ☻ ✳ 🛜) Modern rooms (the glass-walled bathrooms in some may not appeal if you're sharing with a casual acquaintance) feature private balconies with sea views. The view from the pool isn't too shabby either. Casas are available with a full kitchen. Prices drop considerably in low season.

Wi-fi extends through the lobby only.

🍴 Eating

Aluxes Coffee Shop CAFE $
(Matamoros 11; mains M$30-210; ☺ 8am-9pm Wed-Mon; 🛜) Aluxes serves bagels, baguettes and mighty fine banana bread (M$25), and it's one of the friendliest joints in town.

★ Mango Café BREAKFAST $$
(☑ 998-274-01-18; Payo Obispo 101, Colonia Meterológico; mains M$85-125; ☺ 7am-3pm & 4-9pm; 🛜) See the south side of town and drop by Mango Café for some self-serve coffee and a hearty Caribbean-inspired breakfast. The hot items here are coconut French toast (M$100) and eggs Benedict in a curry hollandaise sauce (M$125). It's a short bike or cab ride away, about 3km south of the ferry terminal.

★ Rooster Café
CAFE **$$**

(☑ 998-274-01-52; Hidalgo 26; breakfasts M$85-195; ◷ 7am-6pm; 🛜) The undeniable king of the breakfast providers on the island is this cute little cafe with a couple of tables out front and chilly air-con inside. The menu covers the classics and throws in a couple of inventive twists, all served up with excellent coffee and attentive service.

La Lomita
MEXICAN **$$**

(☑ 998-179-94-31; Juárez Sur 25; mains M$120-200; ◷ 9am-10pm) The 'Little Hill' serves good, cheap Mexican food in a small, colorful setting. Seafood and chicken dishes predominate. Try the fantastic bean and avocado soup, or the ceviche (seafood marinated in lemon or lime juice, garlic and seasonings). The walls are cutely painted and outdoors there's a little alfresco dining section with umbrellas.

★ Lola Valentina
FUSION **$$$**

(☑ 998-315-94-79; Av Hidalgo s/n; mains M$175-345; ◷ 8am-11pm; 🛜🍴) Overlooking the quieter north side of the restaurant strip, Lola does excellent Mexican fusion with dishes along the line of Thai-style shrimp tacos (M$175). Also on the menu are several vegan, gluten-free items, and the very popular and decidedly non-vegan, non-GF Latin Surf n' Turf (M$375). They've added swings at the bar (fun!) and redone their tasty cocktail menu (yum!).

★ Olivia
MEDITERRANEAN **$$$**

(☑ 998-877-17-65; www.olivia-isla-mujeres.com; Matamoros; mains M$170-250; ◷ 5-9:45pm Mon-Sat; 🛜) This delightful Israeli-run restaurant makes everything from scratch, from Moroccan-style fish served on a bed of couscous to chicken shawarmas wrapped in fresh-baked pita bread. Ask for a candlelit table out back in the garden, where Olivia (the cat) may stop by to say hi, and save room for the house-made cherry ice cream. Closes mid-September to mid-October. Reservations recommended.

Café del Mar
INTERNATIONAL **$$$**

(☑ 998-848-8470, ext 806; Av Rueda Medina; mains M$198-290; ◷ 8am-11pm) The loungiest and beach-clubbiest place on the island also has some of the best food, with a small but inventive fusion menu focusing on salads, seafood and pastas. The deck chairs and beach beds are a great place to finish off that daiquiri (and maybe order another). *Palapas* are an option for shade. Live music daily.

🍷 Drinking & Nightlife

Buho's
BAR

(☑ 998-877-03-01; Carlos Lazo 1, Playa Norte; ◷ 9am-11pm; 🛜) The quintessential swinger experience. Literally: they have swings at the bar. You can also take morning and afternoon yoga classes here. Any closer to the beach and you'll be in the water.

Fenix Lounge
BAR

(☑ 998-274-00-73; www.fenixisla.com; Zazil-Ha 118; ◷ 11am-10pm Mon-Sat, to 8pm Sun; 🛜) A waterfront *palapa* bar where you can go for a swim in calm waters, enjoy excellent cocktails, such as the spicy mango margarita (M$130), and groove to live music on weekends.

El Patio
BAR

(Av Hidalgo 17; ◷ 4pm-midnight; 🛜) The self-proclaimed 'house of music' has an open-air patio and rooftop terrace where on a good night you can catch blues or jazz acts and on a bad night mediocre '80s cover bands. Happy hour is from 5pm to 7pm, with food specials as well as discount drinks.

ℹ Information

Several banks are directly across from the ferry dock. Most exchange currency and all have ATMs.

HSBC (cnr Av Rueda Medina & Morelos; ◷ 9am-5pm Mon-Fri, to 3pm Sat)

Hospital Integral Isla Mujeres (☑ 998-877-17-92; Guerrero, btwn Madero & Morelos) Doctors available 24/7.

Hyperbaric Chamber (☑ 998-877-17-92; Morelos s/n) Next to Hospital Integral Isla Mujeres. It's often closed; inquire at the hospital.

Tourist Information Office (☑ 998-877-03-07; direcciondeturismo@hotmail.com; Av Rueda Medina 130, btwn Madero & Morelos; ◷ 9am-4pm Mon-Fri) Offers a number of brochures. Some staff members speak English.

ℹ Getting There & Away

There are several points of embarkation from Cancún to reach Isla Mujeres. Most people cross on Ultramar passenger ferries. The R-1 'Puerto Juárez' city bus in Cancún serves all Zona Hotelera departure points and Puerto Juárez, in Ciudad Cancún. If you arrive by car, daily parking fees in and around the terminals cost between M$130 and M$200, but it can be as low as M$50 if you go further from the terminal.

Fares for ferries departing from the Zona Hotelera are in US dollars. If you're on a tight budget, it's much cheaper to leave from Puerto Juárez. Ferries (www.granpuerto.com.mx) depart from the following docks:

El Embarcadero (Blvd Kukulcán Km 4) Six daily departures; one way US$14.

Playa Caracol (Blvd Kukulcán Km 9.5) Six daily departures; one way US$14.

Playa Tortugas (Blvd Kukulcán Km 6.5) Eight daily departures; one way US$14.

Puerto Juárez (4km north of Ciudad Cancún) Depart every 30 minutes; one way M$160.

Punta Sam, 8km north of Ciudad Cancún, is the only ferry that transports vehicles and bikes. From Punta Sam, drivers are included in prices for the following one-way fares: cars (M$292), motorcycles (M$99) and bicycles (M$93); additional passengers pay M$40. Get there an hour before if you're transporting a vehicle. See www.maritimaislamujeres.com for departure times. To reach Punta Sam, take a taxi or northbound 'Punta Sam' *colectivo* along Avenida Tulum. Ferries for **Punta Sam** and the **Zona Hotelera** leave from different docks, as does the ferry to **Puerto Juárez**.

ⓘ Getting Around

BICYCLE

Cycling is a great way to get around on the island's narrow streets and to explore outlying areas.

Rentadora Fiesta (Av Rueda Medina s/n, btwn Morelos & Bravo; per hour/day M$100/250; ⊘8am-5pm) Rents mountain bikes and beach cruisers.

MOTORCYCLE & GOLF CART

Inspect all scooters carefully before renting. Costs vary, and are sometimes jacked up in high season, but generally start at about M$380 per day (9am to 5pm).

Many people find golf carts a good way to get around the island, and caravans of them can be seen tooling down the roads. The average cost is M$700 per day (9am to 5pm).

Gomar (⌨998-877-16-86; Av Rueda Medina, cnr Bravo; per day M$700) Offers reasonable golf-cart rentals.

Mega Ciro's (⌨998-857-52-66; www.facebook.com/CirosGolfCartRentals; Av Guerrero 11; scooter/golf cart per day M$350/55; ⊘9am-5pm) Rents out scooters and golf carts.

TAXI

Taxi rates are set by the municipal government and posted at the taxi base just south of the passenger-ferry dock. Rates start at M$25. There's a **taxi stand** (Av Rueda Medina) near the ferries.

Isla Holbox

⌨984 / POP 1500

Isla Holbox (hol-bosh) has sandy streets, colorful Caribbean buildings, lazing, sun-drunk dogs, and sand so fine it's texture is nearly clay. The greenish waters are a unique color from the mixing of ocean currents, and on land there's a mixing too: of locals and tourists, the latter hoping to escape the hubbub of Cancún.

'Hoping' is the operative word, because while there are no throbbing nightclubs here, and while it's beautiful, it's not exactly peaceful (what with the throngs of people and constant buzzing of noisy gasoline-powered golf carts), unless you really do get away from it all: to the more remote beaches either by golf cart or boat.

It's a fantastic spot for wildlife. Lying within the Yum Balam reserve, Holbox is home to more than 150 bird species, including roseate spoonbills, pelicans, herons, ibis and flamingos. In summer, whale sharks congregate nearby.

⊙ Sights

For most people, the island is synonymous with powdery sand, but there are some lovely lagoons, low forest and lots of wildlife. Some of the best 'sights' are underwater: whale sharks and sea turtles.

★ Punta Mosquito   BEACH

On the eastern side of the island, Punta Mosquito is about 2.5km east of the downtown area. It has a large sandbar and is a good place to spot flamingos.

☞ Tours

★ VIP Holbox Experience   TOURS

(⌨984-875-21-07; www.vipholbox.com; whale shark tours per person US$125) VIP Holbox Experience goes the extra mile to ensure that guests understand they are part of a delicate ecosystem – for the whale shark tours, they offer biodegradable sunscreen and follow strict guidelines to make sure these incredible animals are properly protected. Tours include delicious ceviche (seafood marinated in lemon or lime juice, garlic and seasonings) and a stop for snorkeling. They also offer a variety of other island tours, from kayaking to 4WD trips through the jungle.

⌦ Sleeping

Not surprisingly, *cabañas* (cabins) and bungalows are everywhere along the beach. Some of the most upscale places can be found east of town, out along the island's northern shore in what locals call the Zona Hotelera. Budget and midrange hotels are clustered around the plaza.

SWIM WITH THE WHALE SHARKS

Between mid-May and late August, massive whale sharks congregate around Isla Holbox to feed on plankton. They are the largest fish in the world, weighing up to 15 tonnes and extending as long as 15m from gaping mouth to arching tail. Locals call them 'dominoes' because of their speckled skin.

The best time to track these gentle giants is in July and August, but that also happens to be shoulder season, when you can get up to two dozen boats rotating around a single whale shark. It's unpleasant for both shark and swimmer, so think twice about taking a tour during this season. The alternative is going in June, but you risk not spotting any whale sharks.

The World Wildlife Fund has been working with the local community since 2003 to develop responsible practices for visiting the whale sharks, trying to balance the economic boon of these tours with the environmental imperatives of protecting a threatened species.

When swimming with the whale shark only three swimmers (including your guide) are allowed in the water at a time. You are not allowed to touch the fish, and are required to wear either a life jacket or wetsuit to ensure you do not dive below the shark.

Hostel Tribu
HOSTEL **$**

(☑ 984-875-25-07; www.tribuhostel.com; Av Pedro Joaquín Coldwell; dm/r from M$280/800; ☻❄☎) With so many activities available here (from salsa lessons to yoga and kayaking), it doesn't take long to settle in with the tribe. Six-bed dorms and private rooms are clean, colorful and cheerful. Tribu also has a book exchange and a bar that stages weekly jam sessions. From the plaza, it's one block north and two blocks west.

★ Casa Takywara
HOTEL **$$$**

(☑ 984-875-22-55; www.casatakywara.com; Paseo Carey s/n; d/bungalows incl breakfast M$3230/3990; ☻❄☎) Out on the quiet western end of town, this beautiful waterfront hotel stands out for its striking architecture and stylishly decorated rooms with kitchenettes and sea-view balconies. It's built next to a patch of protected wetland where you'll hear the song of chirping cicadas. Rates drop considerably during the low season. It's 1km west of Avenida Tiburón Ballena.

Hotel Casa Barbara
HOTEL **$$$**

(☑ 984-875-23-02; www.hotelcasabarbara.mx; Av Tiburón Ballena s/n; r incl breakfast M$2600; ☻❄☎☒) A very comfortable hotel with a swimming pool surrounded by a verdant garden. Rooms are decked out with rustic furnishings and cushy beds, and most have porches overlooking the garden. It's halfway between the ferry dock and the beach.

Hotel La Palapa
HOTEL **$$$**

(☑ 984-875-21-21; www.hotellapalapa.com; Morelos; r US$250; ☻❄☎) La Palapa offers cozy beachfront rooms, some with balconies overlooking the sea, and a cloistered beach area complete with an outdoor bar that serves scrumptious international food. The ocean view from the rooftop terrace is simply awesome. It's 100m east of Avenida Tiburón Ballena along the beach.

✗ Eating

★ Le Jardin
FRENCH **$**

(☑ 984-115-81-97; www.facebook.com/LeJardin Panaderia; bread M$25-30, coffee M$40-65; ☺8:30am-12:30pm Wed-Sun; ☜) Very tasty French pastries and morning breakfast selections make this a welcome spot if you're craving something other than Mexican morning food. Coffee is delicious as well, and the plumeria and butterfly bordered, airy *palapa* makes for a comfortable spot to sit and chat with fellow diners. Kids will love the large toy selection to play with as adults dine.

★ Limoncito
BREAKFAST **$**

(☑ 984-875-23-40; Av Damero s/n; breakfast M$80-110; ☺8am-9:30pm Thu-Tue; ☎) This colorful little *palapa*-covered restaurant on the square slings excellent Mexican breakfasts all day long. The *motuleños* (eggs in tomato sauce served with fried plantain, ham and peas) is a local favorite, as are the enchiladas.

Las Panchas
MEXICAN **$$**

(☑ 984-875-2413; Morelos s/n, btwn Avs Damero & Pedro Joaquín Coldwell; antojitos M$25-36, mains M$95-170; ☺8am-11:30am & 1-6pm) Ask just about anyone in town where to go for good, cheap eats and they'll probably point to Las Panchas, where you can get delicious Yucatecan *antojitos* (snacks) such as *chaya* (tree spinach) *tamales, panuchos* and *salbutes* (fried tortillas with tasty toppings).

Edelyn Pizzería & Restaurant   PIZZA $$

(📞 984-875-20-24; Plaza Principal; pizzas from M$100; ⏲ noon-11:30pm) We would be remiss if we didn't mention the self-proclaimed creators of Holbox's famous lobster pizza (from M$300), but locals say you can find much better pies with the coveted lobster topping elsewhere in town (hint: one is right across the square).

★ El Chapulím   MEXICAN $$$

(📞 984-137-60-69; Tiburón Ballena s/n; mains from M$350; ⏲ from 6pm Mon-Sat) El Chapulím doesn't take reservations, has no menu, and the kitchen closes when the food runs out – usually by 10pm – so you come here aware of the quirks involved. Food is excellent, and chef Erik comes to your table personally, offering four meal options, usually including some type of fish or seafood creation. Vegetarians must book 24 hours in advance. Cash only.

Raíces   SEAFOOD $$$

(📞 984-136-00-17; Beachfront; mains M$200-420; ⏲ 11-8pm) Don't let the humble surrounds of this beachfront eatery put you off – this is some of the best seafood in town. The coconut lobster is definitely worth a look, and butter and garlic fish is mouthwatering. The seafood platter for two would easily feed a small army, and eating steps away from the lapping waves is priceless.

Note that they close the kitchen promptly and aren't usually willing to stay open for latecomers.

🍷 Drinking & Nightlife

Carioca's   BAR

(📞 984-234-23-32; ⏲ 8pm-2am) Located beachside just northeast of 'downtown,' this little *palapa* beach bar is a great chill-out spot. There's a disco here from midnight Friday to Sunday, which runs until the wee hours if anyone's there to enjoy it.

ℹ Information

Holbox has no banks. There's an ATM on the plaza above the police station, but it often runs out of money so bring lots of cash.

ℹ Getting There & Around

Ferries run to Holbox from the port town of Chiquilá, usually from 5:30am to 9:30pm (M$90). It takes about 25 minutes to reach the island. Smaller, faster and wetter *lanchas* (motorboats) make the crossing after dark for M$1250.

Buses from the terminal in Cancún (M$86, 3½ hours) leave for Chiquilá at 7:50am, 10:10am and 12:50pm. Alternatively, you have the option of taking a taxi from Cancún for about US$100.

Private air charters with **Flights Holbox** (📞 984-136-88-52; www.flights-holbox.com; Holbox Airport) are surprisingly economical if you have a small group. Per plane (up to five passengers), a Cancún flight costs US$470. They also run to Playa (US$560), Tulum (US$675), Cozumel (US$631) and Mérida (US$1290).

If you're driving, your vehicle will be safe in Chiquilá parking lots for M$50 per 24 hours. You won't be allowed to bring a tourist car to the island. While technically a freight and car ferry runs to Holbox, nobody will allow you to board.

The good news is that you really won't need a car there. Holbox's sand streets are narrow and deeply rutted, and golf carts have become ubiquitous, buzzing noisily up and down like giant bumblebees. You can rent them easy enough, but consider using your walking shoes instead. Golf-cart taxis cost M$30 in town and M$80 out to Punta Coco.

Rentadora El Brother (📞 984-875-20-18; Av Tiburón Ballena s/n; cart per hour/day M$200/1000; ⏲ 9am-5pm) rents out golf carts.

Puerto Morelos

📞 998 / POP 9200

Halfway between Cancún and Playa del Carmen, Puerto Morelos retains its quiet, small-town feel despite the building boom north and south of town. While it offers enough restaurants and bars to keep you entertained by night, it's really the shallow Caribbean waters that draw visitors here. Brilliantly contrasted stripes of bright green and dark blue separate the shore from the barrier reef – a tantalizing sight for divers and snorkelers – while inland a series of excellent cenotes beckon the adventurous. There's a nice market just south of the plaza with a good selection of crafts and handmade hammocks that are much higher quality than ones you'll find in Cancún or Playa.

⊙ Sights

Crococun Zoo ZOO

(☏ 998-850-37-19; www.crococunzoo.com; Hwy 307 Km 31; adult/child 6-12yr US$32/22; ⊙ 9am-5pm) About 23km south of the Cancún airport, this former crocodile farm now calls itself a conservationist zoo that protects some of the area's endangered species. The price of admission includes a guided tour in which visitors are allowed to interact with some of the animals, such as white-tailed deer, boa constrictors, macaws, crocs and spider monkeys.

Jardín Botánico
Dr Alfredo Barrera Marín GARDENS

(Jardín Botánico Yaax Che; ☏ 998-206-92-33; www.jardinbotanico.com; Hwy 307 Km 320; adult/child 3-10yr M$120/50; ⊙ 8am-4pm Mon-Sat;) One of the largest botanical gardens in Mexico, this 65-hectare reserve has about 2km of trails and sections dedicated to epiphytes (orchids and bromeliads), palms, ferns, succulents (cacti and their relatives) and plants used in traditional Maya medicine. The garden also holds a large animal population, including the only coastal troops of spider monkeys left in the region.

🏃 Activities

The barrier reef that runs along most of the coast of Quintana Roo is only 600m offshore here, providing both divers and snorkelers with views of sea turtles, sharks, stingrays, moray eels, lobsters and loads of colorful tropical fish. Several sunken ships make great wreck diving, and the dive centers have cenote trips as well.

Aquanauts DIVING

(☏ 998-206-93-65; www.aquanautsdiveadventures.com; Av Melgar s/n; 1-/2-tank reef dives US$70/90, snorkeling US$30-80; ⊙ 8am-4pm Mon-Sat) Runs many interesting tours, including drift diving, cenote and shipwreck dives, and lionfish hunting. The dive shop is one block south of the plaza, in Hotel Hacienda Morelos.

🎓 Courses

Little Mexican Cooking School COOKING

(☏ 998-251-80-60; www.thelittlemexicancookingschool.com; Av Rojo Gómez 768, cnr Lázaro Cárdenas; per class US$128; ⊙ 10am-3:30pm Tue & Thu) Ever wonder how to cook delicious regional Mexican cuisine? Here's your chance. During this six-hour course you'll learn all about ingredients used in Mexican cooking and how

to prepare at least seven dishes. See website to book a class; days sometimes vary.

🛏 Sleeping & Eating

Casitas Kinsol GUESTHOUSE $$

(☏ 998-206-91-52; www.casitas-kinsol.com; Av Zetina Gazca Lote 18; r US$49; ⊝ ⛱ 🐾) Great for people who want to see what life's like on the other side of town (yes, there are signs of life west of the highway!), Kinsol offers eight *palapa*-style huts with beautiful design details such as Talavera tile sinks and handcrafted furnishings. It's a peaceful spot where even the dogs and cats get along. It's 3km west of town.

A resident tortoise wanders around in the verdant garden.

Posada Amor HOTEL $$

(☏ 998-871-00-33; Av Rojo Gómez s/n; d M$800; ⊝ ⊛ ⛱) About 100m southwest of the plaza, Posada Amor has been in operation for many years. The simple white-walled rooms have some creative touches. There's a shady back area with tables and plenty of plants, the restaurant offers good meals, and there's a friendly expat bar.

★ Posada El Moro HOTEL $$$

(☏ 998-871-01-59; www.hotelelmoro.mx; Av Rojo Gómez s/n; r incl breakfast US$92, ste US$125; P ⊝ ⊛ ⛱ ⛲) A well-run property, with cheery geraniums in the halls and courtyard. Some rooms have kitchenettes, all have couches that fold out into futons, and there's a small pool in a tropical garden. Prices drop substantially in low season or on their webpage (not the booking megasites). It's northwest of the plaza.

Casa Caribe B&B $$$

(☏ 998-251-80-60; www.casacaribepuertomorelos.com; Av Rojo Gomez 768; r incl breakfast US$185; ⊝ ⊛ ⛱) Just follow your nose to Casa Caribe, an elegantly decorated B&B that shares its lovely grounds with the Little Mexican Cooking School. Rooms have sweeping beach views from private balconies, and though only one comes with aircon, all five get fantastic sea breezes. Breakfast is a creation of the culinary school, so you know it will be good. There's a three-night minimum stay.

El Nicho BREAKFAST $$

(www.elnicho.com.mx; cnr Avs Tulum & Rojo Gómez; breakfast M$65-125, lunch M$90-190; ⊙ 7am-2pm Fri-Wed; ⛱🍴) Puerto Morelos' best and most popular breakfast spot, El

Nicho serves organic egg dishes, eggs Benedict, *chilaquiles* (fried tortilla strips in salsa) with chicken, and organic coffee from Chiapas. Vegetarians will find many good options here.

★ **John Gray's Kitchen** INTERNATIONAL $$$
(998-871-06-65; www.facebook.com/johngrays kitchen; Av Niños Héroes 6; breakfast M$65-100, dinner M$270-450; 8am-10pm Tue-Sat, from 5pm Mon) One block west and two blocks north of the plaza, this 'kitchen' turns out some truly fabulous food. The chef's specialty, though not listed on the regularly changing menu, is the duck in chipotle, tequila and honey sauce. It opens for breakfast, too.

★ **Al Chimichurri** STEAK $$$
(998-241-82-20; http://alchimichurri.restaurant webx.com; Av Rojo Gómez s/n; mains M$155-340; 5pm-midnight Tue-Sun) You definitely can't go wrong with the fresh pasta and wood-fired pizza here, but this Uruguayan grill is best known for its steaks. The star cuts are a *Flintstones*-size rib eye, tender flank steak and filet mignon in homemade beef gravy. It's just south of the plaza.

🛍 Shopping

★ **Artisans Market** ARTS & CRAFTS
(Av Rojo Gómez s/n; 9am-8pm) The hammocks sold here differ from what you'll find elsewhere because they're created right here in Puerto Morelos by a local family that's been making them for decades. (Ask for Mauricio!) You can also buy dream catchers, *alebrijes* (colorful, hand-carved wooden animals from San Martín Tilcajete), handbags, masks, jewelry and more.

ℹ Getting There & Away

Playa Express and ADO buses that travel between Cancún and Playa del Carmen drop you on the highway. Buses and Playa Express vans from Cancún's ADO terminal cost M$28. If you're

---

RIVIERA THEME PARKS

Always a big hit with children, there are several theme parks between Cancún and Tulum, many of which have fantastic scenery – truly some of the most beautiful lagoons, cenotes and natural areas on the coast. Sure, some will find these places too cheesy, but the kids couldn't care less.

It's worth mentioning that some parks offer an optional swim with dolphins activity, and though it may seem like a lovely idea, animal welfare groups suggest interaction with dolphins and other sea mammals held in captivity creates stress for these creatures.

Here are some of the most popular parks.

Aktun Chen (800-099-07-58, 984-806-49-62; www.aktun-chen.com; Hwy 307 Km 107; full tour incl lunch adult/child US$128/102; 9:30am-5:30pm;) Forty kilometers south of Playa del Carmen, this small park features a 585m-long cave, a 12m-deep cenote, 10 zip-lines and a small zoo.

Xplor (984-803-44-03; www.xplor.travel; adult/child 5-11yr all-inclusive US$119/59.50; 9am-5pm;) This large park 6km south of Playa del Carmen features circuits that take you zip-lining, rafting, driving amphibious jeeps, swimming in an underground river and hiking through caverns.

Xel-Há (998-883-05-24, 984-803-44-03, USA/Canada 855-326-2696; www.xelha.com; Hwy Chetumal-Puerto Juárez Km 240; adult/child 5-11yr from US$89/44.50; 9am-6pm;) Billing itself as a natural outdoor aquarium, it's built around an inlet 13km north of Tulum. There are lots of water-based activities on offer, including a river tour and snorkeling.

Xcaret (984-206-00-38; www.xcaret.com; Hwy Chetumal-Puerto Juárez Km 282; adult/child 5-12yr from US$188/94; 8:30am-10:30pm;) One of the originals in the area, with loads of nature-based activities and stuff for grown-ups like a Mexican wine cellar and day spa. It's 6km south of Playa del Carmen.

Selvática (800-365-7446, 998-881-30-30; www.selvatica.com.mx; Ruta de los Cenotes Km 19; adult/child 8-11yr US$199/99; tour 9am, 10:30am, noon & 1:30pm;) Inland from Puerto Morelos, this adventure outfit only runs prearranged tours. Come for adrenaline-pumping zip-lining, swimming in a cenote and more. Check the website for age restrictions for each tour.

arriving at the Cancún airport, there are bus departures from there to Puerto Morelos for M$104. They run frequently from 7am to 10pm daily. Going to Cancún or Playa costs M$28.

Taxis are usually waiting at the turnoff to shuttle people into town; cabs parked at the plaza will take you back to the highway. Some drivers will tell you the fare is per person or overcharge in some other manner; strive for M$30 for the 2km ride, for as many people as you can stuff in.

Playa del Carmen

984 / POP 150,000

Playa del Carmen, now the third-largest city in Quintana Roo, ranks up there with Tulum as one of the Riviera's trendiest cities. Sitting coolly on the lee side of Cozumel, the town's beaches are jammed with super-fit Europeans. The waters aren't as clear as those of Cancún or Cozumel, and the beach sands aren't quite as champagne-powder-perfect as they are further north, but still Playa (as it's locally known) grows and grows.

The town is ideally located: close to Cancún's international airport, but far enough south to allow easy access to Cozumel, Tulum, Cobá and other worthy destinations. The reefs here are excellent, and offer diving and snorkeling close by. Look for rays, moray eels, sea turtles and a huge variety of corals. The lavender sea fans make for very picturesque vistas.

A cruise ship destination, Playa can feel pretty crowded, but that's usually only in the hotel zone.

◉ Sights & Activities

Playa del Carmen is primarily known for its beaches and outdoor party life, but there are a few spots worth checking out on rainy days.

Aquarium   AQUARIUM
(El Acuario de Playa del Carmen; 998-287-53-13, 984-873-38-59; www.elacuariodeplaya.com; Calle 14 Norte 148; M$233; ⊙11am-7pm) An impressive aquarium with lots of exhibits, information and activities. One of the few options in Playa for non-beach days.

Beaches
Avid beachgoers won't be disappointed here. Playa's lovely white-sand beaches are much more accessible than Cancún's: just head down to the ocean, stretch out and enjoy. Numerous restaurants front the beach in the tourist zone and many hotels in the area offer an array of water-sport activities.

If crowds aren't your thing, go north of Calle 38, where a few scrawny palms serve for shade. Here the beach extends for uncrowded kilometers, making for good camping, but you need to be extra careful with your belongings, as thefts are a possibility.

Some women go topless in Playa (though it's not a common practice in most of Mexico, and is generally frowned upon by locals – except the young, of course). **Mamita's Beach**, north of Calle 28, is considered the best place to let loose.

About 3km south of the ferry terminal, past a group of all-inclusives, you'll find a refreshingly quiet stretch of beach that sees relatively few visitors. Going even further north will get you to remoter areas too.

Diving & Snorkeling
In addition to great ocean diving, many outfits offer cenote dives. Prices are similar at most shops: two-tank dives (US$85), cenote dives (US$175), snorkeling (US$30), whaleshark tour (US$350) and open-water certification (US$450).

Phocea Mexico   DIVING
(984-873-12-10; www.phocea-mexico.com; Calle 10 s/n; 2-tank dive US$89; ⊙8am-6pm) French, English and Spanish are spoken at Phocea Mexico. The shop does dives with bull sharks (US$90) from November to March.

⤳ Courses & Tours

International House   LANGUAGE
(984-803-33-88; www.ihrivieramaya.com; Calle 14 No 141; per week US$230) Offers 20 hours of Spanish classes per week. You can stay in residence-hall rooms (US$36), even if you're not taking classes, but the best way to learn a language is to take advantage of the school's homestays (including breakfast, US$33 to US$39) with Mexican host families.

Río Secreto   ADVENTURE
(998-113-19-05; www.riosecreto.com; Carretera 307 Km 283.5; adult/child 6-11yr US$79/40; ⊙9am-6pm) Hike and swim through a 600m-long underground cavern 5km south of Playa del Carmen. Some aspects are hyped, but there is a lot that is just plain awesome.

🛏 Sleeping

Enjoy Playa Hostel   HOSTEL $
(984-147-77-76; www.enjoyplayahostel.com; Calle 4, btwn Av 15 & 20; dm M$250-300, d M$1200; ❄🕸😺) A welcoming and convenient hostel that's very close to the

beach, the bus station and the tourist zone. While the dorm rooms are a bit dark, they have outlets for charging phones and lockers for secure storage. A rooftop terrace area offers a place to meet people, though you might also find people in the lobby downstairs.

Hostel Playa HOSTEL $
(☎984-803-32-77; www.hostelplaya.com; Calle 8 s/n; dm/d/tr incl breakfast M$200/490/735; P☺🤙) Though temporarily closed at the time of research, this place was made for mingling with its central common area, a cool garden spot and a rooftop terrace. In a town where new hostels pop up overnight, this one has been around since 2002. Hopefully it will reopen soon.

★ Hotel Playa del Karma BOUTIQUE HOTEL $$
(☎984-803-02-72; www.hotelplayadelkarma.com; 15 Av, btwn Calles 12 & 14; d M$1050-1250; ☺❄🤙❄) The closest you're going to get to the jungle in this town; rooms here face a lush courtyard with a small – no, make that tiny – pool. All rooms have air-con and TV, and some come with kitchenette, sitting area and sweet little porches with hammocks. The hotel arranges tours to nearby ruins and diving sites.

Grand Velas RESORT $$$
(☎322-226-86-89, 800-831-11-65; www.rivieramaya.grandvelas.com;Hwy307Km62;dall-inclusive from US$894; P☺❄🤙❄) The mother of all beach resorts, the sprawling Grand Velas boasts one of the best spas on the coast; an azure, free-form infinity pool; marble-floored rooms that put other so-called luxury accommodations to shame; loads of activities for kids and grown-ups; and the list goes on. It's 6km north of Playa del Carmen.

Petit Lafitte RESORT $$$
(☎984-877-40-00; www.petitlafitte.com; Carretera Cancún-Chetumal Km 296; d/bungalow incl breakfast & dinner from US$294/357, child 3-11yr additional US$60; P☺❄🤙❄) Occupying quiet Playa Xcalacoco, 6km north of Playa del Carmen, Petit Lafitte is an excellent family vacation spot. Stay in a room or a 'bungalow' (essentially a wood cabin with tasteful rustic furnishings, some of which sleep up to five guests). Kids stay entertained with the large pool, small animal shelter/pen, games room and various water activities. See website for directions.

✖ Eating

For cheap eats, head away from the tourist center, or try the small **market** (Av 10 s/n, btwn Calles 6 & 8; mains M$30-80; ☺7:30am-11pm) for some homestyle regional cooking.

Kaxapa Factory SOUTH AMERICAN $
(☎984-803-50-23; www.kaxapafactory.com; Calle 10 s/n; mains M$65-125; ☺10am-10pm Tue-Sun; 🤙) The specialty at this Venezuelan restaurant on the park is *arepa,* a delicious corn flatbread stuffed with your choice of shredded beef, chicken or beans and plantains. There are many vegetarian and gluten-free options here and the refreshing fresh-made juices go nicely with just about everything on the menu.

Don Sirloin MEXICAN $
(☎984-148-04-24; www.donsirloin.com; 10 Av s/n; tacos M$14-65; ☺2pm-6am; 🤙) *Al pastor* (marinated pork) and sirloin beef are sliced right off the spit at this popular late-night taco joint, which now has three branches in Playa.

Chez Céline BREAKFAST $
(☎984-803-3480; cnr 5 Av & Calle 34; breakfast M$66-109; ☺7:30am-11pm; ❄) Good, healthy breakfasts and a range of yummy baked goods are what keeps this French-run bakery-cafe busy.

100% Natural VEGETARIAN $$
(Cien Por Ciento Natural; ☎984-873-22-42; www.100natural.com; Quinta Av s/n, cnr Calle 10; mains M$86-286; ☺7am-11pm; 🤙) The trademark offerings of this quickly establishing chain – vegetable- and fruit-juice blends, salads, various vegetable and chicken dishes and other healthy foods – are delicious and filling. The Zona Hotelera location is in a jungle- and tiki-hut-type setting.

La Famiglia ITALIAN $$$
(☎984-803-53-50; www.facebook.com/lafamiglia pdc; 10 Av s/n cnr Calle 10; mains M$130-390; ☺3-11pm Tue-Sat, from 5pm Sun; 🤙) Pay a visit to the family and enjoy superb wood-fired pizza and handmade pasta, ravioli and gnocchi. Playa is a magnet for Italian restaurants, but this definitely ranks among the best of them.

🍷 Drinking & Nightlife

You'll find everything from mellow, tranced-out lounge bars to thumping beachfront discos here. The party generally starts on Quinta Avenida then heads down toward the beach on Calle 12.

Playa del Carmen

YUCATÁN PENINSULA PLAYA DEL CARMEN

0 — 200 m
0 — 0.1 miles

Chez Céline (600m);
La Bodeguita del Medio (650m)

Calle 16 Bis

Calle 14 Bis

15 Av

Calle 14

● 2

Calle 12 Bis

20 Av

Quinta Av (5 Av)

1 Av

1 Av Bis

● 6

8 ✕

10 Av

1 ◉

Terminal
ADO

Calle 12

Calle 10 Bis

12

10
✕

9 ✕

15 Av

Calle 10

✕ 7

3

Parque 28
de Julio

Calle 8

Playa

5

Calle 6 Norte Bis

11
✕

Calle 6

14

10 Av

Calle 4

4

15 Av

13

20 Av

10 Av

Quinta Av (5 Av)

CARIBBEAN
SEA

Calle 2

Playa
Express

Parque
Turístico
Leona
Vicario

Terminal
del Centro

Av Juárez

Plaza
Mayor

Hwy 307 (450m);
Cozumel (10km)

20 Av

10 Av

Quinta Av (5 Av)

Calle 1 Sur

16

18 15

Calle 1 Sur

17

Cozumel
(19km)

Playa del Carmen

★ **Dirty Martini Lounge**　　　　BAR
(www.facebook.com/dirtymartinilounge; ◷noon-2am Sun-Thu, to 3am Fri & Sat) The Dirty Martini Lounge doesn't have a foam machine, there's no mechanical bull and there's minimal nudity – a refreshing change for crazy Playa. The decor is something you'd find in the American West, with comfy cowhide upholstery and brown wood panels, and it's a place where you can sip something tasty while actually hearing yourself think.

La Bodeguita del Medio　　　DANCING
(📞984-803-39-51; www.labodeguitadelmedio.com.mx; Quinta Av s/n; ◷12:30pm-2am; 🛜) The writing is literally on the walls (and on the lampshades, and pretty much everywhere) at this Cuban restaurant-bar. After a few mojitos you'll be dancing the night away to live *cubana* music. Get here at 7:30pm for free salsa lessons.

Playa 69　　　　　　　　　　GAY
(www.facebook.com/sesentaynueveplaya; off Quinta Av, btwn Calles 4 & 6; cover after 11pm M$60; ◷9pm-5am Wed-Sun) This popular gay dance club proudly features foreign strippers from such far-flung places as Australia and Brazil, and it stages weekend drag-queen shows. It may also open Tuesdays at key vacation times, such as the holidays. Find it at the end of the narrow alley.

☆ Entertainment

★ **Fusion**　　　　　　　　LIVE MUSIC
(📞984-803-54-77; Calle 6 s/n; ◷7am-1am) This beachside bar and grill stages live music, such as belly dancing or even fire-dancing shows. The schedule varies, but it's always later in the evening (around 11pm) and al-ways fun. Earlier, it's just a pretty spot to have a beer or cocktail and listen to the waves.

ℹ Information

Tourist Information Kiosk (Plaza Mayor; ◷9am-5pm) Get basic tourist info and maps here.

ℹ Getting There & Away

BOAT

Ferries depart frequently to Cozumel from Calle 1 Sur, where you'll find three companies with **ticket booths**. Barcos Caribe is the cheapest of the bunch. Prices are subject to change. Transcaribe, south of Playa, runs car ferries to Cozumel.

Barcos Caribe (📞987-869-20-79; www.barcoscaribe.com; one-way fare adult/child 5-12yr M$135/70; ◷6:45am-11pm)

Mexico Waterjets (📞984-879-31-12; www.mexicowaterjets.com; one-way fare adult/child 6-11yr M$162/96; ◷9am-9pm) Price promotions can bring fares down to M$69 for all travelers.

Transcaribe (📞987-872-76-71; www.transcaribe.net; Hwy 307 Km 282, Calica-Punta Venado; one-way fare M$1000) Runs daily ferries to Cozumel if you want to cross with your vehicle. One-way fare includes passengers. The terminal is 7km south of Playa del Carmen.

Ultramar (📞984-803-55-81, 998-293-90-92; www.ultramarferry.com/en; one-way fare adult/child 6-11yr M$163/97; ◷6:45am-11pm) The most spiffy of the ferries, and claims to be the least prone to seasickness due to extra stabilizers. Also offers a 1st-class option with a lounge, more room, priority boarding and leather seats.

BUSES FROM PLAYA DEL CARMEN

DESTINATION	FARE (M$)	DURATION (HR)	FREQUENCY (DAILY)
Cancún	38-68	1¼	frequent
Cancún international airport	178	1	frequent
Chetumal	250-346	4¼-5	frequent
Chichén Itzá	155-314	4	7:30am (2nd class), 8am (1st class), 2:30pm (2nd class)
Cobá	92-142	2	11 (1st & 2nd class)
Mérida	258-464	4¼-5¾	frequent
Palenque	634-934	11½-12	3
San Cristóbal de las Casas	836-1158	17-17½	3
Tulum	45-74	1	frequent
Valladolid	132-216	2¾	6

BUS

Playa has two bus terminals; each sells tickets and provides information for at least some of the other's departures. You can save money by buying a 2nd-class bus ticket, but remember that it's often stop-and-go along the way. A taxi from Terminal ADO to the Plaza Mayor costs about M$30.

Playa Express shuttle buses are a much quicker way to get around the Riviera Maya, or to Cancún.

The **Terminal ADO** (www.ado.com.mx; 20 Av s/n, cnr Calle 12) is where most 1st-class bus lines arrive and depart.

All 2nd-class bus lines (including Mayab) are serviced at the old bus station, **Terminal del Centro** (Quinta Av s/n, cnr Av Juárez).

Playa Express (Calle 2 Norte) offers quick, frequent service to Puerto Morelos for M$25 and downtown Cancún for M$38 .

COLECTIVO

Colectivos (Calle 2, cnr 20 Av; ⊙4am-midnight) are a great option for cheap travel southward to Tulum and north to Cancún. They depart as soon as they fill (about every 15 minutes) and will stop anywhere along the highway between Playa and Tulum, charging M$45. Luggage space is somewhat limited, but they're great for day trips. From the same spot, you can grab a *colectivo* to Cancún (M$38).

Isla Cozumel

☏987 / POP 100,000

Cozumel at first glance is just another cheesy cruise-ship destination – at least, if you just stay in the hotel zone. But leave the tourist area behind and you'll see an island of quiet cool and authenticity. Garages still have shrines to the Virgin, there's a spirited Caribbean energy and, of course, there are some holiday things to do, such as diving some of the best reefs in the world.

While diving and snorkeling are the main draws, the town square is a pleasant place to spend the afternoon, and it's highly gratifying to explore the less-visited parts of the island on a rented scooter or convertible bug. The coastal road leads to small Maya ruins, a marine park and captivating scenery along the unforgettable windswept shore. And while the nightlife here doesn't rival Playa's or Cancún's, there's plenty to do after the sun goes down.

⊙ Sights

Punta Molas
RUINS

(Map p284; ⊙24hr) FREE Head to the far northeast of the island and you'll find yourself at the deserted lighthouse of Punta Molas, but take a 4WD, as this point isn't the easiest to reach. You'll want to fill up that gas tank and be prepared – there isn't much traffic around here to flag down for help. Once in the vicinity, you'll find some fairly good beaches and some minor ruins. The best camping spot along the road is at the lovely Playa Bonita.

El Cedral
ARCHAEOLOGICAL SITE

(Map p284; M$35; ⊙24hr) This Maya ruin, a fertility temple, is the oldest on the island. It's the size of a small house and has no ornamentation. El Cedral is thought to have been an important ceremonial site; the small church standing next to the tiny ruin today is evidence that the site still has religious significance for locals.

The village of El Cedral is 3km west of Carretera Costera Sur. The turnoff is near Km 17, across from the Alberto's Restaurant sign. Look for the white-and-red arch.

Museo de la Isla de Cozumel   MUSEUM
(Map p286; ☑ 987-872-14-34; Av Melgar s/n; M$72; ⊘ 9am-4pm Mon-Sat) The Museo de la Isla de Cozumel presents a clear and detailed picture of the island's flora, fauna, geography, geology and ancient Maya history. Thoughtful and detailed signs in English and Spanish accompany the exhibits. It's a good place to learn about coral before hitting the water, and it's one not to miss before you leave the island.

Beaches

Access to many of Cozumel's best stretches of beach has become limited. Resorts and residential developments with gated roads create the most difficulties. Pay-for-use beach clubs occupy some other prime spots, but you can park and walk through or around them and enjoy adjacent parts of the beach without obligation. Sitting under their umbrellas or otherwise using the facilities requires you to fork out some money, either a straight fee or a *consumo mínimo* (minimum consumption of food and drink), which can add up in some places. It's not always strictly applied, especially when business is slow.

Playa Palancar   BEACH
(Map p284; Carretera Costera Sur Km 19) About 17km south of town, Palancar is a great beach to visit during the week when the crowds thin out. It has a beach club renting snorkel gear (M$130) and there's a restaurant. Near the beach, Arrecife Palancar (Palancar Reef) has some excellent diving (it's known as Palancar Gardens), as well as fine snorkeling (Palancar Shallows).

🏃 Activities

Cozumel and its surrounding reefs are among the world's most popular diving spots.

The sites have fantastic year-round visibility (commonly 30m or more) and a jaw-droppingly impressive variety of marine life that includes spotted eagle rays, moray eels, groupers, barracudas, turtles, sharks, brain coral and some huge sponges. The island can have strong currents (some-times around 3 knots), making drift dives the standard, especially along the many walls. Even when diving or snorkeling from the beach you should evaluate conditions and plan your route, selecting an exit point down-current beforehand, then staying alert for shifts in currents. Always keep an eye out (and your ears open) for boat traffic as well. It's best not to snorkel alone away from the beach area.

Prices are usually quoted in US dollars. In general expect to pay anywhere between US$80 and US$100 for a two-tank dive (equipment included) or an introductory 'resort' course. PADI open-water certification costs US$350 to US$420.

Multiple-dive packages and discounts for groups or those paying in cash can bring rates down significantly.

If you encounter a decompression emergency, head immediately to the hyperbaric chamber at **Cozumel International Clinic** (☑ 987-872-14-30; Calle 5 Sur, btwn Avs Melgar & 5 Sur; ⊘ 24hr).

There are scores of dive operators on Cozumel. All limit the size of their groups to six or eight divers, and the good ones take pains to match up divers of similar skill levels. Some offer snorkeling and deep-sea fishing trips as well as diving instruction.

Deep Blue   DIVING
(Map p286; ☑ 987-872-56-53; www.deepbluecozumel.com; Calle Salas 200; 2-tank dives incl equipment US$100, snorkeling incl gear US$60; ⊘ 7am-9pm) This PADI and National Association of Underwater Instructors (NAUI) operation has knowledgable staff, state-of-the-art gear and fast boats that give you a chance to get more dives out of a day. A snorkeling outing visits three sites.

🛏 Sleeping

Amigo's Hostel   HOSTEL $
(Map p286; ☑ 987-872-38-68, cell 987-1199664; www.cozumelhostel.com; Calle 7 Sur 571, btwn Avs 25 Sur & 30 Sur; dm/r US$12/45; ❀❋ 🛜 🌊) Unlike some cramped budget digs, here you get a large garden with labels on the trees and vines, an inviting pool and a good lounge area stocked with reading material. Some guests say it's too far removed from the tourist center; others like it that way. Snorkel-gear rentals available (M$100 per day). Air-con is May to October only and from 10pm to 8am.

Isla Cozumel

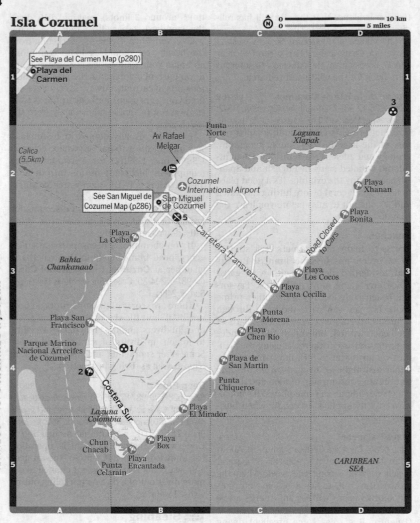

N
0 ——————— 10 km
0 ——————— 5 miles

See Playa del Carmen Map (p280)
○ Playa del Carmen

Calica
(5.5km)

Punta Norte

Av Rafael Melgar

Laguna Xlapak

4 ⌂

Cozumel International Airport

Playa Xhanan

See San Miguel de Cozumel Map (p286)
○ San Miguel de Cozumel

Playa Bonita

5 ✕

Playa La Ceiba

Carretera Transversal

Road Closed to Cars

Bahía Chankanaab

Playa Los Cocos

Playa Santa Cecilia

Punta Morena

Playa San Francisco

Playa Chen Río

Parque Marino Nacional Arrecifes de Cozumel

✕ 1

Playa de San Martín

2 ⊙

Punta Chiqueros

Costera Sur

Playa El Mirador

Laguna Colombia

Chun Chacab

Playa Box

CARIBBEAN SEA

Punta Celarain

Playa Encantada

YUCATÁN PENINSULA ISLA COZUMEL

Isla Cozumel

⊙ Sights
1 El Cedral B4
2 Playa Palancar A4
3 Punta Molas D1

⌂ Sleeping
4 Hotel B Cozumel B2

✕ Eating
5 Camarón Dorado B2

Sun Suites Cozumel HOTEL $$
(Map p286; ☎987-872-29-28; www.sunsuitesczm.com; Av 10 Norte 19; s/d M$800/900) Tiled floored rooms are spick and span, and there's a small swimming pool in the back. Interestingly enough, as well as the usual amenities of a hotel (fridge, air-con, TV) there are also several instruments that guests are welcome to use, such as a guitar and even a saxophone.

★ **Hotel B Cozumel** BOUTIQUE HOTEL $$$
(Map p284; ☎987-872-03-00; www.hotelbcozumel.com; Carretera Playa San Juan Km 2.5; r/ste from

US$85/185;) This hip hotel on the north shore may not have that sand beach you're after, but just wait till you get a look at the azure infinity pool and oceanfront hot tub. Rooms here are fashioned with recycled objects, and bikes are available to hit the town. Rates are for jungle-view rooms; ocean views cost extra. It's about 3km north of the ferry terminal.

Casa Mexicana HOTEL $$$
(Map p286; 987-872-9090; www.casamexicana cozumel.com; Av Melgar 457; d incl breakfast from US$159;) The breezy open-air lobby with swimming pool and ocean view is pretty awesome here. Rooms are standard issue for the most part, but all in all Casa Mexicana offers a good deal given its prime location and free breakfast buffet. Rooms with ocean views cost a little extra.

Hotel Flamingo BOUTIQUE HOTEL $$$
(Map p286; 987-872-12-64, USA 800-806-1601; www.hotelflamingo.com; Calle 6 Norte 81; r incl breakfast from US$101;) The colorful Hotel Flamingo is a nicely decorated place offering spacious rooms loaded with amenities. There's a large penthouse apartment here, too (US$298). Common areas include a leafy courtyard, a pool-table room, a popular bar and a rooftop sundeck with a hot tub. The hotel can arrange various activities for you, such as cycling, horseback riding, windsurfing and fishing.

✗ Eating

Taquería El Sitio TACOS $
(Map p286; Calle 2 Norte; tacos & tortas M$14-35; 7:30am-12:30pm) For something quick, cheap and tasty, head over to El Sitio for breaded shrimp and fish tacos or a *huevo con chaya torta* (egg and tree spinach sandwich). The folding chairs and concrete floor aren't fancy, but the food is good.

Camarón Dorado SEAFOOD $
(Map p284; 987-872-72-87, cell 987-1121281; camarondoradoczm@hotmail.com; cnr Av Juárez & Calle 105 Sur; tortas M$38, tacos M$17-28; 7am-1:30pm Tue-Sun;) If you're headed to the windward side of the island or just want to see a different aspect of Cozumel, drop by the Camarón Dorado for a bite, assuming you're early enough. Be warned: these items are highly addictive. It's 2.5km southeast of the ferry terminal.

Jeanie's MEXICAN $$
(Map p286; 987-878-46-47; www.jeaniescoz umel.com; Av Melgar 790; breakfasts M$79-125, mains M$110-230; 7am-10pm;) The views of the water are great from the outdoor patio here. Jeanie's serves waffles, plus hashbrown potatoes, eggs, sandwiches and other tidbits like vegetarian fajitas. Frozen coffees beat the midday heat. Between 5pm and 7pm they do a lovely happy hour, too!

★ **Guido's Restaurant** ITALIAN $$$
(Map p286; www.guidoscozumel.com; Av Melgar 23; mains M$205-305, pizzas M$180-225; 11am-11pm Mon-Sat, 3-11pm Sun;) Drawing on recipes from her father, Guido, chef Yvonne Villiger has created a menu ranging from wood-fired pizzas and homemade pastas to prosciutto-wrapped scallops. To accompany the meal, order sangria, the house specialty. The cocktail menu is equally impressive; they even offer house-made tonic syrup for your G&Ts.

★ **Kinta** MEXICAN $$$
(Map p286; 987-869-05-44; www.kintarestau rante.com; Av 5 Norte s/n; mains M$260-340; 5-11pm;) Putting a gourmet twist on Mexican classics, this chic bistro is one of the best restaurants on the island. The Midnight Pork Ribs (M$340) are a tried-and-true favorite, and they've added a wood-fired oven recently, with a delicious oven-baked fish (M$320). For dessert treat yourself to a *budín de la abuelita,* aka granny's pudding.

🍷 Drinking & Nightlife

La Cocay BAR
(Map p286; 987-872-55-33; www.lacocay.com; Calle 8 Norte 208; 5:30-11pm;) A great place for an after-dinner drink, La Cocay has a good wine list and serves Mexican craft beers. Unlike most places in Yucatán, here you can actually order a Negroni and they'll say: 'Coming right up!'

ℹ Information

Tourist Information Office (Map p286; 987-869-02-11; Av 5 Sur s/n, Plaza del Sol, 2nd fl; 8am-3pm Mon-Fri) Pick up maps and travel brochures here.

ℹ Getting There & Away

AIR

Cozumel's small **airport** (Map p284; 987-872-20-81; www.asur.com.mx; Blvd Aeropuerto Cozumel s/n) is about 3km northeast of the ferry terminal; follow the signs along Avenida Melgar. Some airlines fly direct from the US; European flights are usually routed via the US or Mexico City. Mexican carriers Interjet and MayAir serve Cozumel.

San Miguel de Cozumel

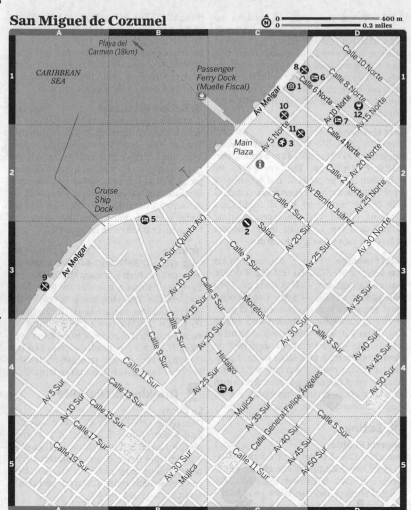

Interjet (☎ 800-011-23-45, USA 866-285-9525; www.interjet.com) Flies direct to Mexico City.

MayAir (☎ 987-872-36-09; www.mayair.com. mx) Service to Cancún with continuing flight to Mérida.

BOAT

Passenger ferries operated by México Waterjets (www.mexicowaterjets.com) and Ultramar (www.granpuerto.com.mx) run to Cozumel from Playa del Carmen hourly from 6am to 9pm (one way M$165), leaving from and arriving at the **Passenger Ferry Dock** (Map p286).

To transport a vehicle to Cozumel, go to the Calica car-ferry terminal (officially known as the Terminal Marítima Punta Venado), about 7km south of Playa del Carmen. There are four daily departures (two on Sundays). See www.tran-scaribe.net for the schedule. You'll need to line up at least one hour before departure, and two hours beforehand in high season. Fares start at M$1000 and go up depending on the size of the vehicle. Passengers are included in the price.

ℹ Getting Around

TO/FROM THE AIRPORT

Frequent, shared shuttle vans run from the airport into town (M$57), to hotels on the island's north end (M$96) and to the south side (M$97 to

San Miguel de Cozumel

M$140). To return to the airport in a taxi, expect to pay M$85 from town.

BICYCLE & SCOOTER

Solo touring of the island by scooter is a blast, provided you have experience with them and with driving in Mexico. Two people on a bike is asking for trouble, though, as the machines' suspension will be barely adequate for one. Riders are injured in crashes on a regular basis, so always wear a helmet and stay alert. Collision insurance is not usually available for scooters: you break, you pay. Be sure to carefully inspect the scooter for damage before driving off or you may get hit with a repair bill.

To rent, you must have a valid driver's license and leave a credit-card slip or put down a cash deposit. There is a helmet law, and it is enforced.

Rentadora Isis is a good rental place; **Shark Rider** (Map p286; ☎ 987-120-02-31; Av 5 Norte s/n, btwn Av Juárez & Calle 2 Norte; bikes/scooters per day US$10/20; ☉ 8am-7pm) rents out bikes as well.

CAR

A car is the best way to get to the island's further reaches, and you'll get plenty of offers to rent one. All rental contracts should automatically include liability insurance (*daños a terceros*). Check that taxes are included in the price you're quoted: they often are not. Collision insurance is usually about M$150 extra, with a M$5000 deductible for the cheapest vehicles.

Rates start at around M$500 all-inclusive, though you'll pay more during late December and January. There are plenty of agencies around the main plaza, but prices are about 50%

lower from the dock to the fringes of the tourist zone, where you can sometimes find a jalopy or clunker for US$30 or so.

When renting, check with your hotel to see if it has an agreement with any agencies, as you can often get discounts. Some agencies will deduct tire damage (repair or replacement) from your deposit, even if tires are old and worn. Be particularly careful about this if you're renting a 4WD for use on unpaved roads; straighten out the details before you sign. And always check your car's brakes before driving off.

If you rent, observe the law on vehicle occupancy. Usually only five people are allowed in a vehicle. If you carry more, the police will fine you. You'll need to return your vehicle with the amount of gas it had when you signed it out or pay a premium. There's a gas station on Avenida Juárez, five blocks east of the main square, and several **gas stations** near the town center.

Rentadora Isis (☎ 984-879-31-11, 987-872-33-67; www.rentadoraisis.com.mx; Av 5 Norte 181; per day from US$20; ☉ 8am-6:30pm) is a fairly no-nonsense place with cars ranging from great shape to total clunkers; this branch rents out convertible VW Beetles, Golfs and scooters, with little seasonal variation in prices.

TAXI

As in some other towns on the Yucatán Peninsula, the taxi syndicate on Cozumel wields a good bit of power. Fares are around M$35 (in town), M$100 (to the Zona Hotelera) and M$2000 for a day trip around the island. Fares are posted just outside the ferry terminal.

Tulum

🗐 984 / POP 18,200

Tulum's spectacular coastline – with all its confectioner-sugar sands, jade-green water and balmy breezes – makes it one of the top beaches in Mexico. Where else can you get all that *and* a dramatically situated Maya ruin? There's also excellent cave and cavern diving, fun cenotes and a variety of lodgings and restaurants to fit every budget.

Some may be put off by the fact that the town center, where the really cheap eats and sleeps are found, sits right on the highway, making the main drag feel more like a truck stop than a tropical paradise. But rest assured that if Tulum Pueblo isn't to your liking, you can always head to the coast and find that tranquil beachside bungalow.

Exploring Tulum's surrounding areas pays big rewards: there's the massive Reserva de la Biosfera Sian Ka'an, the secluded fishing village of Punta Allen and the ruins of Cobá.

DON'T MISS

PARQUE DOS OJOS

About 4km south of Xcacel-Xcacelito – and 1km south of amusement park Xel-Há – is the turnoff to the enormous Dos Ojos cave system. Operating as a sustainable tourism project by the local Maya community, Parque Dos Ojos offers guided **snorkeling and diving tours** (📞 984-160-09-06; www.parquedosojos.com; Hwy 307 Km 124; 1-/3-tank dive incl guide & equipment M$475/1900; ⊙9am-5pm) of some amazing underwater caverns, where you float past illuminated stalactites and stalagmites in an eerie wonderland.

With an extent of about 83km and some 30 cenotes, it's one of the largest underwater cave systems in the world. One of the most popular sites for experienced divers is the Pit, a 110m-deep cenote in which you can see ancient human and animal remains. If you are not a certified diver, you can pay the price of admission and go swimming or snorkeling.

History

Most archaeologists believe that Tulum was occupied during the late post-Classic period (AD 1200–1521) and that it was an important port town during its heyday. The Maya sailed up and down this coast, maintaining trading routes all the way down into Belize. When Juan de Grijalva sailed past in 1518, he was amazed by the sight of the walled city, its buildings painted a gleaming red, blue and yellow and a ceremonial fire flaming atop its seaside watchtower.

The ramparts that surround three sides of Tulum (the fourth side being the sea) leave little question as to its strategic function as a fortress. Several meters thick and 3m to 5m high, the walls protected the city during a period of considerable strife between Maya city-states. Not all of Tulum was situated within the walls. The vast majority of the city's residents lived outside them; the civic-ceremonial buildings and palaces likely housed Tulum's ruling class.

The city was abandoned about 75 years after the Spanish conquest. It was one of the last of the ancient cities to be abandoned; most others had been given back to nature long before the arrival of the Spanish. But

Maya pilgrims continued to visit over the years, and indigenous refugees from the War of the Castes took shelter here from time to time.

'Tulum' is Maya for 'wall,' though its residents called it Zama (Dawn). The name Tulum was apparently applied by explorers during the early 20th century.

Present-day Tulum is growing fast: since 2006 the population has more than doubled and there are no signs of it slowing down.

◉ Sights

★ **Tulum Ruins**   ARCHAEOLOGICAL SITE
(www.inah.gob.mx; Hwy 307 Km 230; M$70, parking M$100, tours from M$700; ⊙8am-5pm; P)
The ruins of Tulum preside over a rugged coastline, a strip of brilliant beach and green-and-turquoise waters that'll leave you floored. It's true the extents and structures are of a modest scale and the late-post-Classic design is inferior to those of earlier, more grandiose projects – but, wow, those Maya occupants must have felt pretty smug each sunrise.

Tulum is a prime destination for large tour groups. To best enjoy the ruins without feeling like part of the herd, you should visit them early in the morning. A train (M$20) takes you to the ticket booth from the entrance, or just hoof the 500m. You'll find cheaper parking just east of the main parking lot, along the old entrance road. There's a less-used southern foot entrance from the beach road.

Exploring the Ruins

Visitors are required to follow a prescribed route around the ruins. From the ticket booth, head north along nearly half the length of Tulum's enormous **wall**, which measures approximately 380m south to north and 170m along its sides. The **tower** at the corner, once thought to be a guard post, is now believed by some to have been a type of shrine. Rounding the corner, you enter the site through a breach in the north wall.

Once inside, head east toward the **Casa del Cenote**, named for the small pool at its southern base, where you can sometimes see the glitter of little silvery fish as they turn sideways in the murky water. A small tomb was found in the casa. Walk south toward the bluff holding the **Templo del Dios del Viento** (Temple of the Wind God), which provides the best views of El Castillo juxtaposed with the sea below.

Below the Wind God's hangout is a lovely little stretch of **beach** (roped off at last visit). Next, head west to **Estructura 25**, which has some interesting columns on its raised platform and, above the main doorway (on the south side), a beautiful stucco frieze of the Descending God. Also known as the Diving God, this upside-down, part-human figure appears elsewhere at Tulum, as well as at several other east-coast sites and Cobá. It may be related to the Maya's reverence for bees (and honey), perhaps being a stylized representation of a bee sipping nectar from a flower.

South of Estructura 25 is **El Palacio**, notable for its X-figure ornamentation. From here, head east back toward the water and skirt the outside edge of the central temple complex (keeping it to your right). Along the back are some good views of the sea. Heading inland again on the south side, you can enter the complex through a corbeled archway past the restored **Templo de la Estela** (Temple of the Stela), also known as the Temple of the Initial Series. Stela 1, now in the British Museum, was found here. It was inscribed with the Maya date corresponding to AD 564 (the 'initial series' of Maya hieroglyphs in an inscription gives its date). At first this confused archaeologists, who believed Tulum had been settled several hundred years later than this date. It's now thought that Stela 1 was brought to Tulum from Tankah, a settlement 4km to the north dating from the Classic period.

At the heart of the complex you can admire Tulum's tallest building, a watchtower appropriately named **El Castillo** (The Castle) by the Spaniards. Note the Descending God in the middle of its facade, and the Toltec-style 'Kukulcánes' (plumed serpents) at the corners, echoing those at Chichén Itzá. To the Castillo's north is the small, lopsided **Templo del Dios Descendente**, named for the relief figure above the door. South of the Castillo you'll find steps leading down to a (usually very crowded) beach, where you can go for a swim.

After some beach time, heading west toward the exit will take you to the two-story **Templo de las Pinturas**, constructed in several stages around AD 1400 to 1450. Its decoration was among the most elaborate at Tulum and included relief masks and colored murals on an inner wall. The murals have been partially restored, but are nearly impossible to make out. This monument might

have been the last built by the Maya before the Spanish conquest and, with its columns, carvings and two-story construction, it's probably the most interesting structure at the site.

On the way, you'll likely see iguanas, frigate birds soaring overhead and, if you're lucky, a shy *agouti* or two (a rabbit-sized rodent indigenous to the area).

🏃 Activities

Zacil-Ha
SWIMMING

(☎984-218-90-29; Hwy 109 s/n; M$80, snorkel gear M$30, zip-line M$10; ⏰10am-6pm) At this cenote you can combine swimming, snorkeling and zip-lining. It's 8km west of Avenida Tulum on the road to Cobá. There's even a bar, too!

Xibalba Dive Center
DIVING

(☎984-871-29-53; www.xibalbadivecenter.com; Andromeda 7, btwn Libra Sur & Geminis Sur; 1-/2-tank dive US$100/150) One of the best dive shops in Tulum, Xibalba is known for its safety-first approach to diving. The center specializes in cave and cavern diving, but it also does ocean dives. Xibalba doubles as a hotel (rooms from M$1500) and offers attractive packages combining lodging, diving and cave-diving classes.

Tulum Ruins ⓝ N   0 ▬▬▬ 50 m

Tower
Entrance
Gate
Casa del Cenote
Mini-temples
Templo del Dios del Viento
Estructura 25
Parking (700m); Toilets (700m); Hwy 307 (800m); Tulum (3km)
Estela 2
El Palacio
Templo del Dios Descendente
Estructura 20
Oratorio
El Castillo
Tickets
Exit
Templo de las Pinturas
Templo de la Estela
Plataforma de la Danza
Archway
(No Public Vehicle Access)
Punta Allen (60km)
Guard Tower
Muralla Fortificada
Gate
Gate
CARIBBEAN SEA

YUCATÁN PENINSULA TULUM

Tulum

👉 Tours

★ Uyo Ochel Maya
TOURS

(☎ 983-124-80-01; adult/child M$700/350, parking M$50; ⊙8am-4pm) Tour Chunyaxche and Muyil lagoons before donning a life jacket and floating down a centuries-old Maya canal. It's a lovely way to see the second-largest lagoon in Quintana Roo, and the mangroves harbor orchids, saprophytes and numerous birds.

🛌 Sleeping

The biggest decision, aside from budget, is whether to stay in the town center or out along the beach. Both have their advantages: most of the daytime action is at the beach or ruins, while at night people tend to hit the restaurants and bars in town.

You'll find better deals in town, where hostels and midrange options abound.

Weary Traveler
HOSTEL $

(☎ 984-106-71-92; www.wearytravelerhostel.com; Polar s/n, Tulum Pueblo, btwn Orión Norte & Beta Norte; dm/r M$250/800; ⊝❋🛜) Once the only hostel in a tiny, out-of-the-way spot called Tulum, the Weary Traveler is now one of many options for the budget traveler in the town center. The hostel offers a free breakfast, which can include custom-made omelettes, or guests can make their own meals at the communal kitchen. The common areas are a great way to meet people.

Hotel Latino
HOTEL $$

(☎ 984-871-26-74; www.hotellatinotulum.com; Andromeda Oriente 2013; r/ste from M$850/980; ⊝❋🛜📺) The tiny TVs and petite plunge pool must be part of the whole minimalist concept here. Request one of the rooms upstairs that come with balconies and hammocks.

Zazil-Kin
CABAÑAS $$

(☎ 984-124-00-82; www.hotelzazilkintulum.com; Carretera Tulum-Boca Paila Km 0.47; cabañas with/without bathroom M$1880/1372, r from M$3346; 📍⊝❋🐾🛜) About a 10-minute walk from the ruins, this popular place resembles a little Smurf village with its dozens of painted *cabañas* (cabins). Zazil-Kin also has more expensive air-conditioned, double-occupancy rooms. If you opt for the bare bones cabins, be aware electricity is available from 7am to 7pm. Bring insect repellent! There are swings and a jungle gym for kiddos.

Diamante K
CABAÑAS $$$

(☎ cell 984-8762115; www.diamantek.com; Carretera Tulum-Boca Paila Km 2.5; cabin/ste US$92/250; ⊝🛜) Diamante K is one of those spots that really can't be any closer to the beach. It's nine cabins have a shared bathroom and thus remain affordable; all rooms are lovely, with hammocks, incredible ocean views, palm trees, and almost Tolkeinesque accents and decor.

Tankah Inn
HOTEL $$$

(☎ USA 918-582-3743, cell 984-1000703; www.tankah.com; Tankah 3, Lote 16; d incl breakfast US$149; 📍❋🛜) Tankah Inn has five comfortable rooms with tiled floors, all with private terraces, good beds and nice cross-ventilation. A large upstairs kitchen, dining room and common area afford splendid views. A slew of activities is offered here, including diving, fishing and kayaking. It's less than 2km east of the highway.

Tulum

Cabañas Playa Condesa
CABIN $$$

(☏984-234-14-13; Carretera Tulum-Boca Paila Km 3, Zona Hotelera; d with/without bathroom M$2500/1500; ☜) About 1km north of the T-junction, this group of thatched *cabañas* (cabins) is one of the cheaper options in the hotel zone. Along with the basic rooms – which are actually rather clean – you also get mosquito nets (believe us, you'll need them). The coast is rocky here, but there's a sandy beach just 100m away.

Casa Cenote
HOTEL $$$

(☏USA 646-634-7206, cell 984-1156996; www.casacenote.com; r incl breakfast US$180; ᴘ⊛☜) Across the road from a cenote, the beachside bungalows are lovingly done up with Maya touches, each with a screened sliding glass door leading to its own little terrace. The Casa offers rustic cabins and an on-site restaurant as well. To get here, turn east at the 'Casa Cenote' sign and it's about 2km from the highway.

Teetotum
BOUTIQUE HOTEL $$$

(☏984-143-89-56; www.hotelteetotum.com; Av Cobá Sur 2; r incl breakfast US$161; ⊖⊛☜⊛) There are just four stylish rooms in this hip boutique hotel. Common areas include a sundeck upstairs, a dip pool just below and an excellent restaurant. It's a bit overpriced for not being on the beach, but a nice place to stay all the same. It's 200m south of Avenida Tulum. Rates can drop to around US$100 at times.

El Paraíso
HOTEL $$$

(☏USA 310-295-9491, cell 984-1137089; www.elparaisohoteltulum.com; Carretera Tulum-Boca Paila Km 1.5; r US$318; ᴘ⊖⊛☜) Has 11 rooms in a one-story hotel-style block, each with two good beds, private hot-water bathroom, fine cross-ventilation and 24-hour electricity. The restaurant is very presentable, and the level beach, with its palm trees, *palapa* parasols, swing-chaired bar and soft white sand, is among the nicest you'll find on the Riviera Maya. Bike rentals available.

⊨ Tulum Pueblo

El Jardín de Frida
HOSTEL $

(☏984-871-28-16; www.fridastulum.com; Av Tulum s/n, Tulum Pueblo, btwn Av Kukulcán & Chemuyil; dm/r/ste incl breakfast M$200/800/1100; ᴘ⊖☜) ✿ The main house, dorms and private rooms are painted in colorful Mexican pop-art style at this eco-hostel. Most rooms are fan-cooled with the exception of the suites, which come with optional air-con. The mixed dorms are clean and cheerful, and the staff are super friendly and helpful.

Hotel Kin-Ha
HOTEL $$

(☏984-871-23-21; www.hotelkinha.com; Orión Sur s/n, btwn Sol & Venus; d with fan/air-con US$75/95; ᴘ⊛☜) A small Italian-run hotel with pleasant rooms surrounding a small courtyard with hammocks. The location is ideal – the bus stop for *colectivos* going to the beach and ruins is right around the corner. Guests are allowed to use Kin-Ha's sister property facilities on the beach.

★L'Hotelito
HOTEL $$$

(☏984-160-02-29; www.hotelitotulum.com; Av Tulum s/n; d incl breakfast US$120; ⊖⊛@☜) Brick and wood boardwalks pass through a jungle-like side patio to generous, breezy rooms at this character-packed, Italian-run hotel. The attached restaurant does good breakfasts, too. Two rooms upstairs come with wide balconies, but they also catch more street noise from the main strip down below. Towels are twisted into the shape of rabbits or swans. Check online for discounts.

⊨ Zona Hotelera

Cenote Encantado
CAMPGROUND $

(☏cell 984-1425930; www.cenoteencantado.com; Carretera Tulum-Boca Paila Km 10.5; tents per person M$500; ⊖) A rare budget option near the beach, this new-agey spot gets its name from a pretty cenote right in the campground's backyard. Guests here stay in large furnished tents with beds, rugs and nightstands. It's not in front of the beach, but you

YUCATÁN PENINSULA TULUM

WORTH A TRIP

GRAN CENOTE

About 4km west of Tulum, **Gran Cenote** (Hwy 109 s/n; US$10, snorkeling gear M$80, diving M$200; ⊗8:10am-4:45pm) is a worthwhile stop on the highway out to the Cobá ruins, especially if it's a hot day. You can snorkel among small fish and see underwater formations in the caverns if you bring your own scuba gear. A cab from Tulum costs M$80 to M$100 one way (but check first to avoid surprises).

can walk or bike there. Kayaks are planned in the near future. There's also a yoga/meditation room.

You can swim or snorkel in the cenote, but watch out for the 'legendary' crocs! It's 6.5km south of the T-junction, near the Reserva de la Biosfera Sian Ka'an entrance.

★ Hotel La Posada Del Sol
BOUTIQUE HOTEL $$$

(☑ cell 984-1348874; www.laposadadelsol.com; Carretera Tulum-Boca Paila Km 3.5; r incl breakfast US$250-350; ➌🛜) 🖉 Employing recycled objects found on the property after a hurricane, Posada Del Sol stands out for its naturally beautiful architecture. The solar-and wind-powered hotel has no air-con, but rooms catch a nice ocean breeze and just wait till you see the many wonderful design details set around a 'jungle' garden. The beach here is pretty darn sweet, too.

Rooms do not have TVs. The hotel works with local turtle-nesting organizations, too. It's just before the much larger Marina del Sol hotel.

Posada Margherita
HOTEL $$$

(☑ Whatsapp 984-8018493; www.posadamargherita.com; Carretera Tulum-Boca Paila Km 7; d from US$380; ⊗noon-9:30pm; ➌🛜) 🖉 This is a beautiful spot right in the center of the Hotel Zone, with the beach just steps away. The restaurant below makes incredible food using fresh, local, organic ingredients. All rooms have good bug screening, 24-hour lights and a terrace or balcony, some with hammocks. Cash only.

Note that the phone number is for Whatsapp only. They are out of the cellular service area and cannot accept regular phone calls.

✗ Eating

Tulum has everything from cheap tourist food to high-end cuisine. Be aware that many of the restaurants in the Zona Hotelera cannot accept credit cards because they're off the grid. Most hotel restaurants welcome nonguests.

★ Azafran
BREAKFAST $$

(☑984-129-61-30; www.azafrantulum.com; Av Satélite s/n, cnr Calle 2; mains M$65-170; ⊗8am-3pm Wed-Mon; 🛜) A great little German-owned breakfast spot in a shady rear garden, the favorite dish is the 'hangover breakfast,' a hearty portion of homemade sausage, mashed potatoes, eggs, rye toast and bacon – you might even have a lettuce sighting. There are lighter items on the menu, too, such as freshly baked bagels topped with brined salmon.

La Gloria de Don Pepe
TAPAS $$

(☑984-152-44-71; Orion Sur; tapas M$60-160; ⊗1-10:30pm Tue-Sun) With its 'A meal without wine is called breakfast' sign, this spot tickles the taste buds with delicious tapas plates and small bites. And wine – did we mention there's wine? A perfect place to come to talk to a friend for a couple hours without being drowned out by noise. Alfresco seating is also possible.

★ El Asadero
STEAK $$$

(☑984-157-89-98; Satélite 23; mains M$195-480; ⊗4:30-11pm; 🛜) Pricey but worth it, this spot has grilled *arrachera* (flank steak) served with sides of potato, *nopal* (cactus paddle) and sausage, which pairs nicely with the Mexican craft beers on offer. Pescatarians won't be disappointed with the grilled tuna.

★ Hartwood
FUSION $$$

(www.hartwoodtulum.com; Carretera Tulum-Boca Paila Km 7.5; set menu M$500; ⊗6-10pm Wed-Sun) 🖉 Assuming you can get in (and you won't without a reservation), this sweet 'n' simple nouveau cuisine restaurant down on the beach road will definitely impress. Ingredients are fresh and local, flavors and techniques are international. The set menu changes daily, and the solar-powered open kitchen and wood-burning oven serve to accentuate the delicious dishes. It's about 4.5km south of the T-junction.

★ Posada Margherita
ITALIAN $$$

(☑Whatsapp 984-8018493; www.posadamargherita.com; Carretera Tulum-Boca Paila Km 7; mains M$295-520; ⊗7:30am-9:30pm) This hotel's beachside restaurant is candlelit at night, making it a beautiful, romantic place to dine. The fantastic food, including pasta, is made fresh daily and consists mostly of organic ingredients. The wines and house mezcal are excellent. It's 3km south of the T-junction. Cash only.

Drinking & Nightlife

★ Batey

BAR

(Centauro Sur s/n, btwn Av Tulum & Andrómeda; ⏱8am-2am Mon-Sat, 4pm-1am Sun) Mojitos sweetened with fresh-pressed cane sugar are the main attraction at this popular Cuban bar, with fun music acts in the rear garden. Most nights the crowd spills into the street, with cane-pressing contests and discussions around the iconic painted VW bug outside.

ⓘ Getting There & Away

The 24-hour bus terminal is simple but adequate, with a few chairs for waiting, but not much else. If you're headed for Valladolid, be sure your bus is traveling the short route through Chemax, not via Cancún. *Colectivos* leave from Avenida Tulum for **Playa del Carmen** (M$45, 45 minutes). **Colectivos for Felipe Carrillo Puerto** (Av Tulum s/n) (M$75, one hour) depart from a block south of the **ADO bus terminal** (www.ado.com.mx; Av Tulum s/n, btwn Calles Alfa & Júpiter; ⏱24hr). Others leave for Cobá.

ⓘ Getting Around

Colectivos to the beach (M$30) run about hourly from a stop on the corner of Venus and Orión from 6am to 7:30pm. You can also catch *colectivos* from there to the ruins. Returning, just flag them down.

Bicycles and scooters can be a good way to go back and forth between the town and beach. Many hotels have free bikes for guests. **I Bike Tulum** (🖰984-802-55-18; www.ibiketulum.com; Av Cobá Sur s/n, cnr Venus; bicycle per day M$140-190, scooter per day incl insurance M$650; ⏱8:30am-5:30pm Mon-Sat) has a good selection of bike and scooter rentals.

Taxi fares are fixed, from either of the two taxi stands in Tulum Pueblo: **one** (Av Tulum s/n) south of the **ADO bus terminal**, which has fares posted; the **other** (Av Tulum s/n), four blocks north. They charge M$100 to the ruins and M$100 to M$150 from town to the Zona Hotelera, depending on how far south you need to go.

Cobá

🖰984 / POP 1300

Cobá's ruins are a treat and there's little reason to come here if you're not planning to explore them: the state's tallest pyramid, a beautiful ball court and a variety of other structures make for a fun few hours exploring. The village is quiet and cute, with a croc-filled lagoon, a couple other sights and attractions, and a few hotels and restaurants...but people come for the ruins. In droves. By the busload. In fact, that's its biggest problem: arrive after 11am and you'll be one of literally hundreds of other people coming in from Cancún, Playa and Tulum.

From a sustainable-tourism perspective, it's great to stay the night in small communities like Cobá, but don't plan on staying up late.

History

Cobá was settled earlier than Chichén Itzá or Tulum, and construction reached its peak

YUCATÁN PENINSULA COBÁ

BUSES FROM TULUM

DESTINATION	COST (M$)	DURATION (HR)	FREQUENCY (DAILY)
Cancún	152	2	frequent
Chetumal	308	3¼-4	frequent
Chichén Itzá	220	2½-2¾	9am & 2:45pm
Cobá	80	1	10:10am
Felipe Carrillo Puerto	64	1¼	frequent; consider taking a *colectivo*
Laguna Bacalar	210-224	3	frequent
Mahahual	278	2½	12:30am, 8:55am & 6:40pm
Mérida	338	4-5	frequent
Playa del Carmen	74	1	frequent
Valladolid	126	2	frequent

between AD 800 and 1000. Archaeologists believe that this city once covered 70 sq km and held some 40,000 Maya.

Cobá's architecture is a mystery; its towering pyramids and stelae resemble the architecture of Tikal, which is several hundred kilometers away, rather than the much nearer sites of Chichén Itzá and the northern Yucatán Peninsula.

Archaeologists say they now know that between AD 200 and 600, when Cobá had control over a vast territory of the peninsula, alliances with Tikal were made through military and marriage arrangements in order to facilitate trade between the Guatemalan and Yucatecan Maya. Stelae appear to depict female rulers from Tikal holding ceremonial bars and flaunting their power by standing on captives. These Tikal royal females, when married to Cobá's royalty, may have brought architects and artisans with them.

Archaeologists are still baffled by the extensive network of *sacbés* (ceremonial limestone avenues or paths between great Maya cities) in this region, with Cobá as the hub. The longest runs nearly 100km from the base of Cobá's great Nohoch Mul pyramid to the Maya settlement of Yaxuna. In all, some 40 *sacbés* passed through Cobá, parts of the huge astronomical 'time machine' that was evident in every Maya city.

The first excavation at Cobá was led by the Austrian archaeologist Teobert Maler in 1891. There was little subsequent investigation until 1926, when the Carnegie Institute financed the first of two expeditions led by Sir J Eric S Thompson and Harry Pollock. After their 1930 expedition, not much happened until 1973, when the Mexican government began to finance excavation. Archaeologists now estimate that Cobá contains more than 6500 structures, of which just a few have been excavated and restored, though work is ongoing.

◎ Sights

Cobá Ruins   ARCHAEOLOGICAL SITE
(www.inah.gob.mx; M$70, guides M$600-650; ☺8am-5pm; P) Cobá's ruins include the tallest pyramid in Quintana Roo (the second tallest in all of Yucatán) and the thick jungle setting makes you feel like you're in an Indiana Jones flick. Many of the ruins are yet to be excavated, mysterious piles of root-and vine-covered rubble. Walk along ancient *sacbés* (ceremonial limestone avenues or paths between great Maya cities), climb up

ancient mounds, and ascend to the top of Nohoch Mul for a spectacular view of the surrounding jungle.

Juego de Pelota   ARCHAEOLOGICAL SITE
(Cobá Ruins) An impressive ball court, one of several in the ruins. Don't miss the relief of a jaguar and the skull-like carving in the center of the court.

Templo 10   ARCHAEOLOGICAL SITE
(Cobá Ruins) Here you can see an exquisitely carved stela (AD 730) depicting a ruler standing imperiously over two captives.

Exploring the Ruins
Grupo Cobá   ARCHAEOLOGICAL SITE
(Cobá Ruins) The most prominent structure in the Grupo Cobá is **La Iglesia** (the Church). It's an enormous pyramid; if you were allowed to climb it, you could see the surrounding lakes (which look lovely on a clear day) and the Nohoch Mul pyramid. To reach it walk just under 100m along the main path from the entrance and turn right.

Take the time to explore Grupo Cobá; it has a couple of corbeled-vault passages you can walk through. Near its northern edge, on the way back to the main path and the bicycle concession, is a very well-restored juego de pelota (ball court).

Grupo Macanxoc   ARCHAEOLOGICAL SITE
(Cobá Ruins) Grupo Macanxoc is notable for its numerous restored stelae, some of which are believed to depict reliefs of royal women who are thought to have come from Tikal. Though many are worn down by the elements, a number of them are still in good condition and are worth a detour.

Grupo de las Pinturas   ARCHAEOLOGICAL SITE
(Cobá Ruins) The temple at Grupo de las Pinturas (Paintings Group) bears traces of glyphs and frescoes above its door and remnants of richly colored plaster inside. You approach the temple from the southeast. Leave by the trail at the northwest (opposite the temple steps) to see two stelae. The first of these is 20m along, beneath a *palapa*. Here, a regal figure stands over two others, one of them kneeling with his hands bound behind him.

Sacrificial captives lie beneath the feet of a ruler at the base. You'll need to use your imagination, as this and most of the other stelae here are quite worn. Continue along the path past another badly weathered stela and a small temple to rejoin a path leading to the next group of structures.

Grupo Nohoch Mul   ARCHAEOLOGICAL SITE
(Cobá Ruins) Nohoch Mul (Big Mound) is also known as the Great Pyramid (which sounds a lot better than Big Mound). It reaches a height of 42m, making it the second-tallest Maya structure on the Yucatán Peninsula (Calakmul's Estructura II, at 45m, is the tallest). Climbing the old steps can be scary for some. Two diving gods are carved over the doorway of the temple at the top (built in the post-Classic period, AD 1100–1450), similar to sculptures at Tulum. The view from up top is over many square kilometers of flat scrubby forest, with peeks of lake.

Xaibé   ARCHAEOLOGICAL SITE
(Cobá Ruins) This is a tidy, semicircular stepped building, almost fully restored. Its name means 'the Crossroads,' as it marks the juncture of four separate *sacbés* (ceremonial limestone avenues or paths between great Maya cities).

🏃 Activities

**Cenotes Choo-Ha, Tamcach-Ha
& Multún-Ha**   SWIMMING
(per cenote M$55; ⊗8am-6pm) About 6km south of the town of Cobá, on the road to Chan Chen, you'll find a series of three locally administered cenotes: Choo-Ha, Tamcach-Ha and Multún-Ha. These cavern-like cenotes are nice spots to cool off with a swim, or a snorkel if you bring your own gear. Children under 10 are free.

🛏 Sleeping & Eating

★Hacienda Cobá   HOTEL $$$
(☑cell 998-2270168; www.haciendacoba.com; Av 1 Principal Lote 114; d incl breakfast US$87; 🅿😊🛜) Lovely if simple hacienda-style rooms with rustic furniture sit in a pleasant jungle setting with lots of chirping birdies and the occasional spider-monkey sighting. It's about 200m south of the Hwy 109 turnoff to Cobá and 2.5km from the ruins, so you'll either need a car or be willing to walk or cab it into town.

Chile Picante   MEXICAN $$
(mains M$85-180; ⊗7am-11pm) Located at Hotel Sac-Be, Chile Picante does everything from vegetarian omelettes with *chaya* (Mexican tree spinach) and fresh fruit plates to *panuchos* (handmade fried tortillas with beans and toppings).

Restaurant La Pirámide   MEXICAN $$
(☑984-206-71-75, 984-206-70-18; mains M$80-150; ⊗8am-5pm; 🛜) At the end of the town's main drag, by the lake, this restaurant is pretty touristy but does decent Yucatecan fare like *cochinita* or *pollo pibil* (achiote-flavored pork or chicken). The open-air set-up allows for nice lagoon views.

ℹ Getting There & Away

Most buses serving Cobá swing down to the ruins to drop off passengers at a small bus stop; but you can also get off in town. Buses run five times daily between Tulum and Cobá (M$50 to M$80, 45 minutes), Playa del Carmen (M$91 to M$142, two hours). Buses also go seven times daily to Valladolid (M$52, one hour) and Chichén Itzá (M$75 to M$82, 1½ hours), then on to Merida (M$115, three hours).

Day-trippers from Tulum can reach Cobá by taking **colectivos** (M$110) that depart from Av Tulum and Calle Osiris.

The road from Cobá to Chemax is arrow-straight and in good shape. If you're driving to Valladolid or Chichén Itzá, this is the way to go.

Punta Allen
📞 984 / POP 470

The tiny town of Javier Rojo Gómez is more commonly called by the name of the point 2km south, Punta Allen. The village, which is truly the end of the road, exudes a laid-back ambience reminiscent of the Belizean cays. There's also a healthy reef 400m from shore that offers snorkelers and divers wonderful sights.To get here you have to enter the incredible Sian Ka'an Biosphere Reserve, a vast tract of mangrove swamp, lagoon, beaches and jungle that supports a variety of endemic species, including the elusive jaguar.

The village is known primarily for its catch-and-release bonefishing; tarpon and snook are very popular sportfish as well. Cooperatives in town offer fishing trips, dolphin-watching outings and snorkeling expeditions.

Hurricane Gilbert nearly destroyed the town in 1988, and there was some damage and a lot of wind-scrubbed palms after Hurricane Dean. But Punta Allen is still standing.

◉ Sights

**Reserva de la Biosfera
Sian Ka'an**   NATURE RESERVE
(Sian Ka'an Biosphere Reserve; M$37; ⊗sunrise-sunset) Sian Ka'an (Where the Sky Begins) is home to a small population of spider and howler monkeys, American crocodiles, Central American tapirs, four turtle species,

giant land crabs, more than 330 bird species (including roseate spoonbills and some flamingos), manatees and some 400 fish species, plus a wide array of plant life.

There's an entrance gate to the reserve about 10km south of Tulum. At the gate, there's a short nature trail taking you to a rather nondescript cenote (Ben Ha). The trail's short, so go ahead and take a second to have a look.

About 10km south of the reserve entrance is a modest visitors area, a pull-off where you'll find a watchtower that provides tremendous bird's-eye views of the lagoon.

The road can be a real muffler-buster between gradings, especially when holes are filled with water from recent rains, making it difficult to gauge their depth. The southern half, south of the bridge beyond Boca Paila, is the worst stretch – some spots require experienced off-road handling or you'll sink into the mud. It is doable even in a non-4WD vehicle, but bring along a shovel and boards just in case – you can always stuff palm fronds under the wheels to gain traction – and plan on returning that rental with a lot more play in the steering wheel.

There are no hiking trails through the heart of the reserve; it's best explored with a professional guide. If you'd like to see more of Sian Ka'an, Maya-run Community Tours Sian Ka'an runs various expeditions into the sprawling biosphere reserve.

For remote coastal camping, this is where intrepid adventuring really takes off. Bring a tent, a couple of hammocks, lots of water, mosquito nets and food supplies. Around 30km from the entrance gate is an excellent camping spot with the lagoon on one side and glorious blue ocean on the other.

🛏 Sleeping & Eating

Grand Slam Fishing Lodge HOTEL $$$

(☑998-800-10-47; www.grandslamfishinglodge.com; r US$375; P🌀❄🔝🏊) If you've got money to burn, this place at the town entrance is for you. The upscale lodge boasts 12 oceanfront rooms with Jacuzzi, large balconies and around-the-clock electricity (a true luxury in Punta Allen). Fly-fishing enthusiasts can request lodging and all-inclusive fishing packages.

Muelle Viejo SEAFOOD $$

(mains M$90-160; ⊙12:30-9pm Tue-Sun; P) Service here can be as slow as the frigates circling overhead, but it's hard not to use this as a chance to relax and enjoy. Overlooking a dock where fishermen bring in the daily catch, this colorful beach house serves fresh seafood cocktails, decent fried fish dishes and lobster when it's in season.

ℹ Getting There & Away

The best way to reach Punta Allen is by driving a rental car or scooter, but prepare to drive very slowly and expect more than a few transmission-grinding bumps. The ride can take three to four hours or as little as two, depending on the condition of the road. Keep a sharp eye out while driving for the numerous sunbathing iguanas, snakes and other wildlife.

Mahahual

☑983 / POP 920

Mahahual changed forever when the cruise ship dock was completed, and grows larger every year. Despite the (literally) boatloads of tourists, there's a lovely, relaxed, Caribbean vibe that you won't find further north, and it's the only spot in the Costa Maya that's large enough to support a diversity of sleeping and eating options, while still being right on the beach. Xcalak is tiny (and wants to stay that way); Bacalar is inland, next to a lagoon not the open sea. Many feel it's just right. At least for now.

Tourism has brought a few tacky shops and gringo bars to the north side of town. If that's not you, go south toward Xcalak and you'll have no problem finding your own private beach with sugar-white sand.

There's great diving and snorkeling here, and there's just enough nightlife along the beachfront *malecón* (waterfront promenade) to keep you entertained.

🏃 Activities

★ Banco Chinchorro DIVE SITE

Divers won't want to miss the reefs and underwater fantasy worlds of the Banco Chinchorro, the largest coral atoll in the northern hemisphere. Some 45km long and up to 14km wide, Chinchorro's western edge lies about 30km off the coast, and dozens of ships have fallen victim to its barely submerged ring of coral.

The atoll and its surrounding waters were made a biosphere reserve (Reserva de la Biosfera Banco Chinchorro) to protect them from depredation. But the reserve lacks the personnel and equipment needed to patrol such a large area, and many abuses go undetected.

Most dives here go to a maximum of 30m, as there are no decompression chambers for miles. And with a ban on wreck dives recently lifted, there are plenty of shipwreck sites worth exploring. Along the way you'll also spot coral walls and canyons, rays, turtles, giant sponges, grouper, tangs, eels and, in some spots, reef, tiger and hammerhead sharks.

There's good snorkeling as well, including *40 Cannons,* a wooden ship in 5m to 6m of water. Looters have taken all but about 25 of the cannons, and it can only be visited in ideal conditions.

Mahahual Dive Centre   DIVING
(✍ 983-102-09-92, cell 983-1367693; www.mahahualdivecentre.com; Malecón Km 1; 2-/3-tank dives US$80/110, snorkeling US$25; ☺ 9am-5pm) In a new location, right on the *malecón*, Mahahual Dive Center does trips to nearby sites and the fishing village of Punta Herrero.

Doctor Dive   DIVING
(✍ cell 983-1036013; www.doctordive.com; Av Mahahual s/n, cnr Coronado; 2-tank dive US$95, snorkeling incl equipment US$25; ☺ 8am-9pm) In addition to scuba and snorkeling excursions, the Doctor can offer training courses at many different levels.

🛏 Sleeping & Eating

Hostal Jardín Mahahual   HOTEL $
(✍ 983-834-57-22; www.facebook.com/hostal.jardin; Sardina s/n, cnr Rubia; dm/r M$220/650; ❂❋🖧) For the price, this is a surprisingly stylish little hostel with five private rooms and an eight-bed coed dorm. Rooms are spotless and the dorms are the best in town by far. It's set back two blocks from the beach, near Calle Rubia.

★ Posada Pachamama   HOTEL $$
(✍ 983-834-57-62; www.posadapachamama.net; Huachinango s/n; d/q M$1000/1500; 🅿❂❋🖧🐾) Rooms at the Pachamama (which means Mother Earth in Inca) range from small interior singles and doubles with ocean views to more ample digs that sleep four. The staff are very knowledgable about local activities.

Ko'ox Quinto Sole   BOUTIQUE HOTEL $$$
(✍ 983-834-59-42; www.kooxquintosoleboutiquehotel.com; Carretera Mahahual-Xcalak Km 0.35; r/ste M$3775/5775; 🅿❂❋🖧) One of the fanciest hotels in town, the spacious rooms here have heavenly beds and private balconies (some with Jacuzzi). It's on a quiet beach

north of the boardwalk and 350m south of the lighthouse at town's entrance. There's also a restaurant on premises. Rates are for jungle views; ocean views cost more.

★ Nohoch Kay   SEAFOOD $$
(Big Fish; ✍ 983-733-60-68; cnr Malecón & Cazón; mains M$190-235; ☺ 1-9:30pm Mon-Sat, to 8pm Sun; 🖧) Nohoch Kay, aka the Big Fish, definitely lives up to its name. Don't miss this beachfront Mexican-owned restaurant, where they prepare succulent whole fish in a garlic and white-wine sauce, or opt for the surf-and-turf platter for two (M$670), which includes lobster, steak, octopus and shrimp.

Luna de Plata   ITALIAN $$
(✍ 983-119-22-73; www.lunadeplata.info; Av Mahahual Km 2; mains M$100-360; ☺ 8am-10pm; 🖧) The 'ristorante' of this Italian-owned hotel prepares fresh bread and pasta, pizza and seafood dishes. Try the scrumptious lobster-filled ravioli in shrimp sauce.

🛈 Getting There & Away

Mahahual is 127km south of Felipe Carrillo Puerto, and approximately 100km northeast of Bacalar.

There's no official bus terminal in Mahahual. At last visit, liquor store **Solo Chelas** (at Calles Huachinango and Cherna) was selling tickets for a daily ADO northbound bus, which departs Mahahual at 5:30am for Tulum (M$278, three hours), Playa del Carmen (M$350, four hours) and Cancún (M$426, five hours). A Xcalak-bound Caribe bus (M$58, 40 minutes) passes through town along Calle Huachinango, usually at 6:30am. Southbound buses to Bacalar (M$78, two hours) and Chetumal (M$80, 2½ hours) leave about every two hours from 5:30am to 7:30pm.

Shuttle vans leave hourly from 5:20am to 8:20pm to Chetumal (M$80, 2½ hours), Laguna Bacalar (M$75, two hours) and Limones (M$50, one hour), where you can catch frequent northbound buses. The terminal is on the corner of Calles Sardina and Cherna, on the soccer field's north end.

There's a Pemex gas station in Mahahual if you need to fill your tank. The Xcalak turnoff is about 100m west of the gas station.

Xcalak
✍ 983 / POP 380

The rickety wooden houses, beached fishing launches and lazy gliding pelicans make this tiny town plopped in the middle of nowhere a perfect escape. And by virtue of its remoteness and the Chinchorro Atoll, Xcalak may yet escape the development boom.

Come here to walk along dusty streets and sip frozen drinks while frigate birds soar above translucent green lagoons. Explore a mangrove swamp by kayak, or just doze in a hammock and soak up some sun. Xcalak has a few nice restaurants and an easygoing mix of foreigners and locals.

The mangrove swamps stretching inland from the coastal road hide some large lagoons and form tunnels that invite kayakers to explore. They and the drier forest teem with wildlife; in addition to the usual herons, egrets and other waterfowl, you can see agoutis, jabirus (storks), iguanas, javelinas (peccaries), parakeets, kingfishers, alligators and more.

🏃 Activities

XTC Dive Center
DIVING

(www.xtcdivecenter.com; Coast Rd Km 0.3; 2-tank dives US$275, snorkeling trips US$50-75; ⊙9am-5pm) XTC is the one-stop shop for all your needs. It offers dive and snorkel trips to the wondrous barrier reef offshore, and to Banco Chinchorro. It also rents out diving equipment, provides PADI open-water certification (US$600), and operates fishing and bird-watching tours.

Additionally, XTC rents three nice, affordable rooms (US$50 to US$70) and has a good restaurant-bar. It's 300m north of town.

🛏 Sleeping & Eating

Accommodations here are simple, even the nicer ones. Most places don't accept credit cards without prior arrangements, and are best contacted through their websites or via email. Food in Xcalak tends to be tourist-grade seafood or Mexican, though some of it is quite good.

Casa Paraiso
HOTEL $$$

(☑USA 404-502-9845, Whatsapp 678-446-9817; http://casaparaisoxcalak.com; Coast Rd Km 2.5; r incl breakfast US$130; 🛜) Bright, cheery yellow Casa has four guest rooms with large, hammock-equipped balconies facing the sea. Each room has a king-sized bed and a kitchen with fridge, and the bathrooms try to outdo one another with their beautiful Talavera tilework. Includes free use of kayaks, snorkel gear and bicycles.

Hotel Tierra Maya
HOTEL $$$

(☑USA 330-735-3072; www.tierramaya.net; Coast Rd Km 2; r from US$107, ste US$179; P🖥🛜) This modern beachfront hotel has six lovely rooms (three quite large), each tastefully appointed with many architectural details. Each of the rooms has a balcony facing the sea; the bigger rooms even have small refrigerators. Look for the large Maya mural on the building's wall.

Costa de Cocos
INTERNATIONAL $$

(www.costadecocos.com; Coast Rd Km 1; breakfast US$5, lunch & dinner US$5-26; ⊙7am-8:30pm; P🅿🛜) This fishing lodge's restaurant-bar is one of the better options in town for eating and drinking. It serves both American- and Mexican-style breakfasts and does fish tacos for the lunch and dinner crowd. The bar produces its own craft whiskey and has pale ale on tap.

Toby's
SEAFOOD $$

(☑983-107-54-26; mains M$85-155; ⊙11am-8:30pm Mon-Sat) On the main drag in town, the friendly chitchat and well-prepared fish and seafood dishes make this a popular expat spot. Try the coconut shrimp or lionfish and you'll know why. Open Sundays...occasionally.

ℹ Getting There & Away

Buses to Chetumal (M$130) and Limones (a stop where you can grab northbound buses) leave at 5:30am and 2pm; they stop on the coast road behind the lighthouse. From Chetumal, buses leave at 6am and 4pm.

Cabs from Limones, on Hwy 307, cost about M$700 (including to the northern hotels). From Felipe Carillo Puerto a cab costs about M$1000.

Driving from Limones, turn right (south) after 55km and follow the signs to Xcalak (another 60km). Keep an eye out for the diverse wildlife that frequents the forest and mangrove; a lot of it runs out onto the road. Large land crabs, snakes and tortoises are common.

You can take a bumpy coastal road from Xcalak to Mahahual, but don't be surprised if it's closed during the rainy season, and there's a bridge that seems to wash out frequently, so ask first before heading out only to find that you'll have to swim part of the way.

Laguna Bacalar

☑983 / POP 11,000

Laguna Bacalar, the peninsula's largest lagoon, comes as a surprise in this region of scrubby jungle. More than 60km long with a bottom of sparkling white sand, this crystal-clear lake offers opportunities for camping, swimming, kayaking and simply lazing around, amid a color palette of blues, greens and shimmering whites that seems more out of Photoshop than anything real life could hold.

CORREDOR ARQUEOLÓGICO
....

The Corredor Arqueológico comprises the archaeological sites of Dzibanché and Kohunlich, two intriguing and seldom-visited Maya ruins that can be visited on a day trip from Chetumal.

Dzibanché (M$55; ⊙8am-5pm) Though it's a chore to get to, this site is definitely worth a visit for its secluded, semi-wild nature. Dzibanché (meaning 'writing on wood') was a major city extending more than 40 sq km and there are a number of excavated palaces and pyramids, though the site itself is not completely excavated. On the way there you'll pass beautiful countryside.

The turnoff for Dzibanché from Hwy 186 is about 44km west of Chetumal, on the right just after the Zona Arqueológico sign. From there it's another 24km north and east along a narrow road. About 2km after the tiny town of Morocoy you'll need to turn right again. It's easy to miss the sign unless you're looking for it.

Kohunlich (off Hwy 186; adult/child under 13yr M$65/free; ⊙8am-5pm) This archaeological site sits on a carpeted green. The ruins, dating from both the late pre-Classic (AD 100–200) and the early Classic (AD 300–600) periods, are famous for the great **Templo de los Mascarones** (Temple of the Masks), a pyramid-like structure with a central stairway flanked by huge, 3m-high stucco masks of the sun god.

Kohunlich's turnoff is 3km west along Hwy 186 from the Dzibanché turnoff, and the site lies at the end of a 9km road. It's a straight shot from the highway.

Some would say this area is the 'new' Tulum. Small and sleepy, yet with enough tourism to have things to do and places to eat, the lakeside town of Bacalar lies east of the highway, 125km south of Felipe Carrillo Puerto. It's noted mostly for its old Spanish fortress and popular *balnearios* (swimming grounds). There's not a lot else going on, but that's why people like it here. Around the town plaza, you'll find an ATM, a small grocery store, a taxi stand and tourist information office.

◉ Sights & Activities

Fortress FORTRESS
(☑983-834-28-86; cnr Av 3 & Calle 22; M$73; ⊙11am-7pm Tue-Sun) The fortress above the lagoon was built to protect citizens from raids by pirates and the local indigenous population. It also served as an important outpost for the Spanish in the War of the Castes. In 1859 it was seized by Maya rebels, who held the fort until Quintana Roo was finally conquered by Mexican troops in 1901.

Today, with formidable cannons still on its ramparts, the fortress remains an imposing sight. It houses a museum exhibiting colonial armaments and uniforms from the 17th and 18th centuries.

Balneario SWIMMING
(Av Costera s/n, cnr Calle 14; ⊙9am-5pm) FREE
This beautiful public swimming spot lies several blocks south of the fort, along Avenida Costera. Admission is free, but parking costs M$10.

Cenote Azul SWIMMING
(☑983-834-24-60; Hwy 307 Km 34; adult/child under 10yr M$25/free; ⊙10am-6pm) Just shy of the south end of the *costera* (coast highway) and about 3km south of Bacalar's city center is this cenote, a 90m-deep natural pool with an on-site bar and restaurant. It's 200m east of Hwy 307, so many buses will drop you nearby.

🛏 Sleeping & Eating

★**Yak Lake House Hostel** HOSTEL $
(☑983-834-31-75; www.facebook.com/theyaklakehouse; Av 1, btwn Calles 24 & 26; dm M$300-350, r M$1200; P❄✳🛜) If lounging around all day in your bikini is your idea of fun, then Yak House won't disappoint. It's steps away from Laguna Bacalar and there are ample chairs, docks and decks on which to soak up the sun. Free breakfast, friendly staff, clean rooms and good lockers make this a sweet spot to park yourself for a few days. At the time of research, there was no signpost of any kind. Look for the large brown and white facade with a heavy wood door.

Hotel Laguna Bacalar HOTEL $$
(☑983-834-22-05; www.hotellagunabacalar.com; Av Costera 479; d with fan/air-con M$1360/1500, bungalow from M$2100; P❄✳🛜🏊) This breezy place boasts a small swimming pool, a restaurant and excellent views of

YUCATÁN PENINSULA LAGUNA BACALAR

the lagoon, which you can explore by way of kayak or boat tours. It's 2km south of Bacalar town and only 150m east of Hwy 307, so if you're traveling by bus you can ask the driver to stop at the turnoff.

★ Rancho Encantado   CABIN $$$

(📞998-884-20-71; www.encantado.com; Hwy 307 Km 24; d/ste incl breakfast from $2480/4600; 🅿️➖❄️🛜🏊) Laguna Bacalar is absolutely beautiful in and of itself, so imagine what it's like to stay at one of the most striking locations along the shore. A typical day on the *rancho* goes something like this: wake up in comfy thatch-roof cabin, have breakfast with lagoon view, snorkel in crystalline waters (tours are not included in the price). The ranch is 3km north of Bacalar.

★ Mango y Chile   VEGAN $$

(📞983-688-20-00; www.facebook.com/mangoy chile; Av 3, btwn Calles 22 & 24; mains M$90-130; ⊙1pm-9pm Wed-Mon) Bacalar's first and only all-vegan dining option, Mango y Chile has a beautiful large deck overlooking the fort and the lagoon, and friendly service. Vegans will rejoice that there's a spot here to dine at worry-free. The burgers are tasty, though the food is on the salty side.

★ La Playita   SEAFOOD $$

(📞983-834-30-68; www.laplayitabacalar.com; Av Costera 765, cnr Calle 26; mains M$137-351; ⊙noon-11pm; 🛜) A sign outside reads, 'Eat, drink and swim' – and that pretty much sums it up. Fish and seafood dishes are tasty, albeit on the smallish side, but the Alipús mezcal and fine swimming certainly make up for that. An enormous rubber tree, which provides shade in the pebbly garden, was nearly uprooted in 2007 when Hurricane Dean pummeled the coast.

☆ Entertainment

Galeón Pirata Espacio Cultural   LIVE MUSIC

(📞983-157-75-58; www.facebook.com/Galeon PirataBacalar; Av Costera s/n, btwn Calles 30 & 32; ⊙4pm-11pm Tue-Thu, 7pm-3am Fri & Sat) This indie cultural center stages live music, art exhibits, movie screenings and plays. It doubles as a restaurant-bar. Hours can be erratic, but when it's happening, it's a fun time.

❶ Getting There & Away

Buses don't enter town, but taxis and most combis will drop you at the town square. Buses arrive at the Bacalar's ADO terminal on Hwy 307, near Calle 30. From there it's about a 10-block

walk southeast to the main square or you can grab a local taxi for M$18.

From the **ADO station** (📞983-833-31-63; Hwy 307), buses go to Chetumal (M$38 to M$62), Cancún (M$262 to M$400), Mahahual (M$78), Xcalak (M$94) and Tulum (M$166 to M$224), to name just some of the destinations.

If you're driving from the north and want to reach the town and fort, take the first Bacalar exit and continue several blocks before turning left (east) down the hill. From Chetumal, head west to catch Hwy 307 north; after 25km on the highway you'll reach the signed right turn for Cenote Azul and Avenida Costera, aka Avenida 1.

Chetumal

📞983 / POP 151,200

The capital of Quintana Roo, Chetumal is a relatively quiet city going about its daily paces. The bayside esplanade hosts carnivals and events, and the modern Maya museum is impressive (though a bit short on artifacts). Excellent Maya ruins, amazing jungle and the border to neighboring Belize are all close by. Though sightings are rare (there are no tours), manatees can sometimes be seen in the rather muddy bay or nearby mangrove shores. The lagoon should not be used for swimming, as there is a risk of crocodiles, despite the locals' joke that there's only one (named Harry) and he's tame. It may be their way of getting rid of pesky tourists, so swim in your hotel pool to be sure.

History

Before the Spanish conquest, Chetumal was a Maya port used for shipping gold, feathers, cacao and copper to the northern Yucatán Peninsula. After the conquest, the town was not actually settled until 1898, when it was founded by the Mexican government to put a stop to the arms and lumber trade carried on by descendants of the Maya who fought in the War of the Castes. Dubbed Payo Obispo, the town changed its name to Chetumal in 1936. In 1955, Hurricane Janet virtually obliterated it, and 2007's Hurricane Dean did a bit of damage to the town's infrastructure.

◉ Sights

Museo de la Cultura Maya   MUSEUM

(📞983-832-68-38; Av de los Héroes 68, cnr Av Gandhi; M$73; ⊙9am-7pm Tue-Sun) The Museo de la Cultura Maya is the city's claim to cultural fame – a bold showpiece that's beautifully

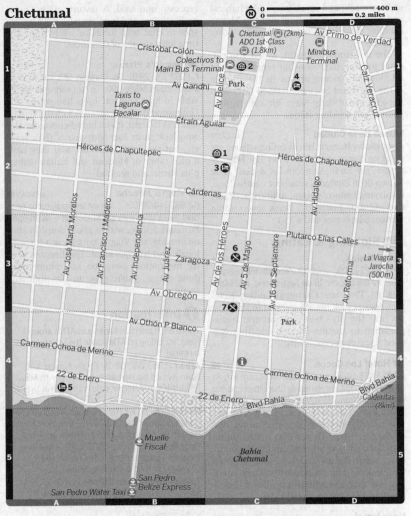

Chetumal

Chetumal

◎ Sights
1 Museo de la Ciudad C2
2 Museo de la Cultura Maya C1

🛏 Sleeping
3 Hotel Los Cocos C2
4 Hotel Xcalak C1
5 Noor Hotel A4

🍴 Eating
6 Café Los Milagros C3
7 Sergio's Pizzas C3

conceived and executed, though regrettably short on artifacts. It's organized into three levels, mirroring Maya cosmology. The main floor represents this world, the upper floor the heavens, and the lower floor Xibalbá the underworld. The various exhibits cover all of the Mayab (lands of the Maya).

Scale models show the great Maya buildings as they may have appeared, including a temple complex set below Plexiglas that you can walk over. Though original pieces are in short supply, there are replicas of stelae and a burial chamber from Honduras' Copán, reproductions of the murals found in Room 1 at Bonampak, and much more. Mechanical and computer displays illustrate the Maya's complex calendrical, numerical and writing systems.

The museum's courtyard, which you can enter for free, has salons for temporary exhibitions of modern artists. In the middle of the courtyard is a *na* (thatched hut) with implements of daily Maya life on display: gourds and grinding stones.

Museo de la Ciudad
MUSEUM

(Local History Museum; Héroes de Chapultepec, cnr Av de los Héroes; adult/child under 11yr M$27/8; ⊙9am-7pm Tue-Fri, 9am-5pm Sat & Sun) The Museo de la Ciudad is small but neatly done, displaying historic photos, military artifacts and old-time household items (even some vintage telephones and a TV).

🛏 Sleeping & Eating

Hotel Xcalak
HOTEL $

(☑983-129-17-08; http://xcalakhotelboutique.com; Av Gandhi, cnr 16 de Septiembre; r M$450; ⊜❄🐕) That rare Chetumal budget hotel that doesn't look like it's trapped in the '70s. It's near the city's best museum and transportation to Laguna Bacalar, and there's a good restaurant downstairs.

★ Hotel Los Cocos
HOTEL $$

(☑983-835-04-30; www.hotelloscocos.com.mx; Av de los Héroes 134, cnr Héroes de Chapultepec; d/ste with air-con from M$912/1824; 🅿⊜❄@🐕🏊) With a great location, Hotel Los Cocos has a mirrored lobby that gets your inner disco-dancer rising. There's also a swimming pool, Jacuzzi, gym and restaurant. All rooms have small fridges and balconies. It runs 'promotions' year-round, so it's likely you'll pay less than the official rates listed here – check the website for details.

Noor Hotel
HOTEL $$

(☑983-835-13-00; Blvd Bahía 3, cnr Av Morelos; r M$900-1020; 🅿⊜❄🐕🏊) Right on the bay, the Noor will appeal to those looking to get away from the bustling center. Bayview rooms are your best bet here, as the interior rooms tend to get poor ventilation. There's a decent pool and the restaurant prepares international cuisine. The boardwalk across the way is sweet for afternoon strolls.

Café Los Milagros
CAFE $

(☑983-832-44-33; Zaragoza s/n; breakfast M$84-130, lunch M$28-95; ⊙7am-4pm Mon-Fri; 🐕) Simple and laid-back spot that serves great espresso and food. A favorite with Chetumal's student and intellectual set, it's a good spot to chat with locals or while away the time with a game of dominoes.

★ Sergio's Pizzas
PIZZA $$

(☑983-832-29-91; Av Obregón 182, cnr Av 5 de Mayo; mains M$86-300; ⊙7am-midnight; ❄🐕) Walk in here and you'll feel like you're in a Hollywood mafia movie: not a chatty female waitress in sight. It's all barrel-chested males who look more like bodyguards than waiters, but the food's delicious, and they have a nice range of Mexican and Italian dishes, plus steaks and seafood.

La Viagra Jarocha
MEXICAN $$

(☑983-144-39-05; www.laviagrajarocha.com; Blvd Bahía 98A; mains M$135-200; ⊙8am-9pm) Fun and festive, with a goofy dolphin statue outside, the Viagra Jarocha is a hit with locals and tourists alike. The breezes keep the mosquitoes away, too, and when you're done eating, you're close to the nightclub scene.

ℹ Information

There are numerous banks and ATMs around town, including an ATM inside the 1st-class bus terminal.

Arba (☑983-832-09-15; Efraín Aguilar s/n, btwn Avs de los Héroes & Juárez; per hr M$13; ⊙7am-10pm) Internet cafe with several similar cafes nearby.

Banorte (Av de los Héroes, btwn Plutarco Elías Calles & Cárdenas; ⊙8:30am-4pm Mon-Fri, 9am to 2pm Sat) For ATM and bank services.

Cruz Roja (Red Cross; ☑065, 911; cnr Avs Independencia & Héroes de Chapultepec; ⊙24hr) For medical emergencies.

Tourist Information Office (☑983-833-24-65; Av 5 de Mayo 21, cnr Ochoa de Merino; ⊙8am-5pm Mon-Fri) Has brochures and well-meaning staff.

ℹ Getting There & Away

AIR

Chetumal's small airport is roughly 2km northwest of the city center along Avenida Obregón.

Interjet (☑800-011-23-45; www.interjet.com) offers direct flights from Mexico City.

BOAT

Belize-bound ferries depart from the **muelle fiscal dock** (Blvd Bahía) on Bahía Blvd. Remember that in addition to the ferry fee you'll pay an exit fee of M$500 on departure.

San Pedro Belize Express (☑ 983-832-16-48; www.belizewatertaxi.com; Av Blvd Bahía s/n, Muelle Fiscal; one way US$55; ⊙ 9am-3:30pm) Boat transportation to Belize City, Caye Caulker and San Pedro.

San Pedro Water Taxi (http://belizewatertaxi express.com; Blvd Bahía s/n, Muelle Fiscal; one way US$50; ⊙ 9am-3:30pm) Runs water taxis to San Pedro and Caye Caulker, in Belize.

BUS

Double-check bus details as the departure locations can be confusing and this information is subject to change. At the time of writing, the following departure information applied.

ADO 1st-Class Terminal (☑ 983-832-51-10; www.ado.com.mx; Salvador Novo 179, off Av Insurgentes) Located 2km north of the center, with services to Cancún, Campeche, Mérida, Valladolid, Xcalak and other destinations.

Old Chetumal Terminal (Salvador Novo s/n; ⊙ 6am-10pm) Now used only for buses to Corozal, Belize City and Orange Walk. Also Guatemala.

Minibus Terminal (cnr Avs Primo de Verdad & Hidalgo) Minibuses serve Laguna Bacalar (M$62) from 8am to 2pm.

TAXI & CAR

City cabs charge about M$25 for short trips, but always ask the price before getting in. **Taxis** on Avenida Independencia (between Efraín Aguilar and Avenida Gandhi) charge M$180 per person for Laguna Bacalar. Night trips have an additional surcharge.

Gibson's Tours & Transfers (☑ 501-6002605; Santa Elena-Corozal border; transport starts at US$100 for up to 4 people) can provide transportation between Mexico and Corozal, can arrange permits for border crossing with your rental car and also offers various tours in Belize.

ⓘ Getting Around

Most places in Chetumal's tourist zone are within walking distance. To reach the main bus terminal from the center, catch a **colectivo** from the corner of Avenidas Belice and Cristóbal Colón, in front of the 2nd-class bus station. Ask to be left at the *glorieta* at Avenida Insurgentes. Head left (west) to reach the terminal.

You'll also find Calderitas buses departing from the same corner.

BUSES FROM CHETUMAL

Unless noted otherwise, the following buses depart from **ADO 1st-class terminal**.

DESTINATION	FARE (M$)	DURATION (HR)	FREQUENCY (DAILY)
Bacalar	45-62	¾	frequent
Belize City, Belize	300	4-4½	frequent; from old Chetumal terminal
Campeche	498	6-7	3
Cancún	404-518	5½-6½	frequent
Corozal, Belize	50	1	frequent; from old Chetumal terminal
Escárcega	316	4	frequent
Felipe Carrillo Puerto	116	2½-3	5
Flores, Guatemala (for Tikal)	700	7½-8	7am; from old Chetumal terminal
Mahahual	85-110	2½-3½	3
Mérida	446	5½-6	4
Orange Walk, Belize	100	2¼	frequent; from old Chetumal terminal
Palenque	584-694	6½-7½	5
Tulum	308	3¼-4	11
Valladolid	228	5½	3
Veracruz	1206	17	1 at 6:30pm
Villahermosa	662-762	8¼-9	7
Xcalak	130	4-4½	2 at 5:40am and 4:10pm
Xpujil	164	2-3	5

YUCATÁN PENINSULA CHETUMAL

YUCATÁN STATE & THE MAYA HEARTLAND

Sitting regally on the northern tip of the peninsula, Yucatán state sees less mass tourism than its flashy neighbor, Quintana Roo. It is sophisticated and savvy, and the perfect spot for travelers more interested in cultural exploration than beach life. While there are a few nice beaches in Celestún and Progreso, most people come to this area to explore the ancient Maya sites peppered throughout the region, like the Ruta Puuc, which will take you to four or five ruins in just a day.

Visitors also come to experience the past and present in the cloistered corners of colonial cities, to experience *henequén* haciendas (vast estates that produced agave plant fibers, used to make rope) lost to time or restored by caring hands to old glory, and to discover the energy, spirit and subtle contrasts of this authentic corner of southeastern Mexico. For planning, a useful website is www.yucatan.travel.

Mérida

🎵 999 / POP 800,000

Since the Spanish conquest, Mérida has been the cultural capital of the entire Yucatán Peninsula. A delightful blend of provincial and *'muy cosmopolitano,'* it is a town steeped in colonial history. It's a great place to explore, with narrow streets, broad central plazas and the region's best museums. It's also a perfect place from which to kick off your adventure into the rest of Yucatán state. It has excellent cuisine and accommodations, thriving markets and events happening just about every night.

Long popular with European travelers looking to go beyond the hubbub of Quintana Roo's resort towns, Mérida is a tourist town, but a tourist town too big to feel like a tourist trap. And as the capital of Yucatán state, Mérida is also the cultural crossroads of the region. There's something just a smidge elitist about Mérida: locals have a beautiful town, and they know it.

History

Francisco de Montejo (the Younger) founded a Spanish colony at Campeche, about 160km to the southwest, in 1540. From this base he took advantage of political dissension among the Maya, conquering T'ho (now Mérida) in 1542. By decade's end Yucatán was mostly under Spanish colonial rule.

When Montejo's conquistadors entered T'ho, they found a major Maya settlement of lime-mortared stone that reminded them of the Roman architecture in Mérida, Spain. They promptly renamed the city and proceeded to build it into the regional capital, dismantling the Maya structures and using the materials to construct a cathedral and other stately buildings. Mérida took its colonial orders directly from Spain, not from Mexico City, and Yucatán has had a distinct cultural and political identity ever since.

During the Caste War, only Mérida and Campeche were able to hold out against the rebel forces. On the brink of surrender, the ruling class in Mérida was saved by reinforcements sent from central Mexico in exchange for Mérida's agreement to take orders from Mexico City.

Mérida today is the peninsula's center of commerce, a bustling city that has been growing rapidly ever since *maquiladoras* (low-paying, for-export factories) started cropping up in the 1980s and '90s, and as the tourism industry picked up during those decades as well. The growth has drawn migrant workers from all around Mexico and there's a large Lebanese community in town.

◉ Sights

★ Gran Museo del Mundo Maya   MUSEUM

(www.granmuseodelmundomaya.com.mx; Calle 60 Norte 299E; M$150; ⊙8am-5pm Wed-Mon; 🅿) A world-class museum celebrating Maya culture, the Gran Museo houses a permanent collection of more than 1100 remarkably well-preserved artifacts, including a reclining chac-mool sculpture from Chichén Itzá and a cool underworld figure unearthed at Ek' Balam (check out homeboy's punk-rock skull belt and reptile headdress). If you're planning on visiting the area's ruins, drop by here first for some context and an up-close look at some of the fascinating pieces found at the sites.

Inaugurated in 2012, the contemporary building was designed in the form of a ceiba, a sacred tree believed by the Maya to connect the living with the underworld and the heavens above. On a wall outside, the museum offers a free light-and-sound show at night.

You'll find it about 12km north of downtown on the road to Progreso. Public transportation running along Calle 60 will leave you at the museum's entrance.

★ Palacio Cantón   MUSEUM
(Regional Anthropology Museum; ☎ 999-923-05-57; www.palaciocanton.inah.gob.mx; Paseo de Montejo 485; adult/child under 13yr M$52/free; ⊙ 8am-5pm Tue-Sun) This massive mansion was built between 1909 and 1911, though its owner, General Francisco Cantón Rosado (1833–1917), lived here for only six years before his death. The Palacio's splendor and pretension make it a fitting symbol of the grand aspirations of Mérida's elite during the last years of the Porfiriato – the period from 1876 to 1911 when Porfirio Díaz held despotic sway over Mexico. It hosts temporary exhibitions and the entry fee may depend on what's on.

★ Casa de Montejo   MUSEUM
(Museo Casa Montejo; www.casasdeculturaban amex.com/museocasamontejo; Calle 63 No 506, Palacio de Montejo; ⊙ 10am-7pm Tue-Sat, to 2pm Sun) FREE Casa de Montejo is on the south side of Plaza Grande and dates from 1549. It originally housed soldiers, but was soon converted into a mansion that served members of the Montejo family until the 1800s. Today it houses a bank and museum with a permanent exhibition of renovated Victorian, neo-rococo and neo-renaissance furnishings of the historic building.

Outside, take a close look at the facade, where triumphant conquistadors with halberds stand on the heads of generic barbarians (though they're not Maya, the association is inescapable). Typical of the symbolism in colonial statuary, the vanquished are rendered much smaller than the victors; works on various churches throughout the region feature big priests towering over or in front of small indigenous people. Also gazing across the plaza from the facade are busts of Montejo the Elder, his wife and his daughter.

★ Parque Santa Lucía   PARK
(cnr Calles 60 & 55) The pretty little Parque Santa Lucía has arcades on the north and west sides; this was where travelers would get on or off the stagecoaches that linked towns and villages with the provincial capital. Today it's a popular restaurant area and venue for **Serenatas Yucatecas** (Yucatecan Serenades), a free weekly concert on Thursday at 9pm.

Museo Fernando García Ponce-Macay   MUSEUM
(Museo de Arte Contemporáneo; ☎ 999-928-32-36; www.macay.org; Pasaje de la Revolución s/n, btwn Calles 58 & 60; ⊙ 10am-5:15pm Wed-Mon) FREE Housed in the former archbishop's palace, the attractive museum holds permanent exhibitions of three of Yucatán's most famous painters of the Realist and Ruptura periods (Fernando Castro Pacheco, Fernando García Ponce and Gabriel Ramírez Aznar), as well as revolving exhibitions of contemporary art from Mexico and abroad.

Paseo de Montejo   ARCHITECTURE
Paseo de Montejo, which runs parallel to Calles 56 and 58, was an attempt by Mérida's 19th-century city planners to create a wide boulevard similar to the Paseo de la Reforma in Mexico City or the Champs-Élysées in Paris. Though more modest than its predecessors, the Paseo de Montejo is still a beautiful green swath of relatively open space in an urban conglomeration of stone and concrete. There are occasional sculpture exhibits along the paseo (promenade).

Plaza Grande   PLAZA
FREE One of the nicest plazas in Mexico, huge laurel trees shade the park's benches and wide sidewalks. It was the religious and social center of ancient T'ho; under the Spanish it was the Plaza de Armas, the parade ground, laid out by Francisco de Montejo (the Younger).

A ceremony is held daily marking the raising and lowering of the Mexican flag, there's a crafts market on Sunday, and dance or live music nearly every night.

Catedral de San Ildefonso   CATHEDRAL
(Calle 60 s/n; ⊙ 6am-midday & 4:30-8pm) On the site of a former Maya temple is Mérida's hulking, severe cathedral, begun in 1561 and completed in 1598. Some of the stone from the Maya temple was used in its construction. The massive crucifix behind the altar is **Cristo de la Unidad** (Christ of Unity), a symbol of reconciliation between those of Spanish and Maya heritage.

To the right over the south door is a painting of Tutul Xiu, *cacique* (indigenous chief) of the town of Maní paying his respects to his ally Francisco de Montejo at T'ho. (De Montejo and Xiu jointly defeated the Cocomes; Xiu converted to Christianity, and his descendants still live in Mérida.)

In the small chapel to the left of the altar is Mérida's most famous religious artifact,

Mérida

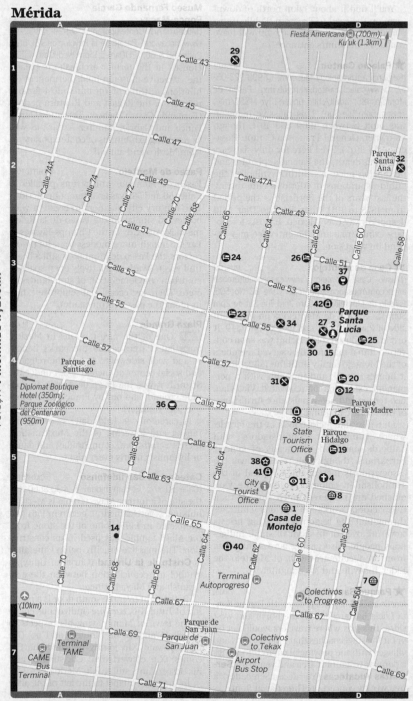

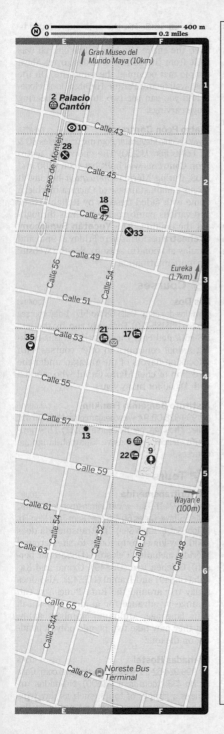

Mérida

YUCATÁN PENINSULA MÉRIDA

a statue called **Cristo de las Ampollas** (Christ of the Blisters). Local legend says the statue was carved from a tree that was hit by lightning and burned for an entire night without charring. It is also said to be the only object to have survived the fiery destruction of the church in the town of Ichmul (though it was blackened and blistered from the heat). The statue was moved to the Mérida cathedral in 1645.

Other than these items, the cathedral's interior is largely plain, its rich decoration having been stripped away by angry peasants at the height of anticlerical fervor during the Mexican Revolution.

Museo de Arte Popular de Yucatán   MUSEUM
(Yucatán Museum of Popular Art; Calle 50A No 487; ⊙10am-5pm Tue-Sat, to 3pm Sun) FREE In a building built in 1906, the Museo de Arte Popular de Yucatán has a small rotating exhibition downstairs that features popular art from around Mexico. The permanent exhibition upstairs gives you an idea of how locals embroider *huipiles* (long, woven, white sleeveless tunics with intricate, colorful embroidery) and it explains traditional techniques used to make ceramics. Watch out for jaguars drinking toilet water!

Museo de la Ciudad   MUSEUM
(City Museum; ☑999-924-42-64; Calle 56 No 529A, btwn Calles 65 & 65A; ⊙9am-6pm Tue-Fri, to 2pm Sat & Sun) FREE The Museo de la Ciudad is housed in the old post office and offers a great reprieve from the hustle, honks and exhaust of this market neighborhood. There are exhibits tracing the city's history back to pre-Conquest days up through the belle epoque period, when *henequén* (sisal) brought riches to the region, and into the 20th century.

Iglesia de Jesús   CHURCH
(Iglesia de la Tercera Orden; Calle 60 s/n) The 17th-century Iglesia de Jesús was built by

Jesuits in 1618. It's the sole surviving edifice from a complex of buildings that once filled the entire city block. The church was built from the stones of a destroyed Maya temple that occupied the same site. On the west wall facing Parque Hidalgo, look closely and you can see two stones still bearing Maya carvings.

Teatro Peón Contreras   THEATER
(www.sinfonicadeyucatan.com.mx; cnr Calles 60 & 57; tickets from M$150) The enormous Teatro Peón Contreras was built between 1900 and 1908, during Mérida's *henequén* heyday. It boasts a main staircase of Carrara marble, a dome with faded frescoes by Italian artists, and various paintings and murals throughout the building. The **Yucatán Symphony Orchestra** performs here Friday at 9pm and Sunday at noon (in season). See the website for more information.

🍃 Courses

Los Dos   COOKING
(www.los-dos.com; Calle 68 No 517; 1-day courses & tours US$185-210) Formerly run by the late US-educated chef David Sterling, this cooking school continues to offer courses with a focus on flavors of the Yucatán under the direction of chef Mario Canul who worked with David for many years.

Instituto Benjamín Franklin   LANGUAGE
(☑999-928-00-97; www.benjaminfranklin.com.mx; Calle 57 No 474A; per 1hr course US$12) This nonprofit teaches intensive Spanish-language courses.

👉 Tours

★Turitransmérida   TOURS
(☑999-924-11-99; www.turitransmerida.com.mx; Calle 55, btwn Calles 60 & 62; ⊙8am-7pm Mon-Fri, to 1pm Sat, to 10am Sun) Turitransmérida does good day-long group tours to sites around Mérida, including Celestún (US$56 per person), Chichén Itzá (US$49), Uxmal and Kabah (US$49) and Izamal (US$42). Also does a day trip around the Ruta Puuc. You can arrange in advance for guides who speak your language. Minimum numbers apply, but they may take two people only depending on the tour.

Nómadas Hostel   TOURS
(☑999-924-52-23; www.nomadastravel.com; Calle 62 No 433; tours from M$600) Nómadas arranges a variety of tours, such as day trips including transportation and guide to the

---

BIKE-FRIENDLY MÉRIDA

In an effort to make the city more bike-friendly, Mérida closes down stretches of Paseo de Montejo and Calle 60 to traffic on Sunday morning. For night tours, the bicycle activist group **Ciclo Turixes** (www.cicloturixes.org) gathers at Parque Santa Ana on Wednesday at around 8:30pm. See its blog for times.

ecological reserve of Celestún (M$850) and outings to the Maya ruins of Chichén Itzá (M$600) and Uxmal and Kabah (M$600). The hostel also provides informative DIY sheets with written instructions detailing costs and transportation tips for more than a dozen destinations in the region.

✸✸ Festivals & Events

Paseo de Ánimas   STREET CARNIVAL
(Festival of Souls; ☉ around Oct 31) Hundreds of locals flaunt their skeleton-style and parade through the altar-lined streets for Day of the Dead celebrations. Musical renditions, artist performances and local food carts add to the festivities.

Toh Bird Festival   FESTIVAL
(Festival de las Aves Toh; www.festivalavesyucatan.com; ☉ Feb-Nov) Holds various events throughout the year, culminating with a 'bird-a-thon' (bird-counting competition) in late November.

Otoño Cultural   CULTURAL
(www.culturayucatan.com; ☉ Sep & Oct) Typically held in September and October, this three-week autumn fest stages more than 100 music, dance, visual-art and theater events.

Mérida Fest   CULTURAL
(www.merida.gob.mx/festival; ☉ Jan) This cultural event held throughout most of January celebrates the founding of the city with art exhibits, concerts, theater and book presentations at various venues.

🛏 Sleeping

★ Nómadas Hostel   HOSTEL $
(☏ 999-924-52-23; www.nomadastravel.com; Calle 62 No 433; dm from M$200, d M$690, without bathroom M$450, incl breakfast; P❄@🛜🏊) One of Mérida's best hostels, it has mixed and women's dorms, as well as private rooms. Guests have use of a fully equipped kitchen with fridge, as well as showers and hand-laundry facilities. It even has free salsa, yoga, and cooking classes, and an amazing pool out back. See the hostel's website for various tours available to nearby ruins.

The owner, Señor Raul, was one of the first 'contemporary' hosteliers in Mexico, and he knows his stuff.

★ Luz en Yucatán   HOTEL $$
(☏ 999-924-00-35; www.luzenyucatan.com; Calle 55 No 499; r US$58-100; P❄❄🛜🏊) While many much blander hotels are loudly claiming to be 'boutique,' this one is quietly ticking all the boxes while creating its own guesthouse niche – individually decorated rooms, fabulous common areas and a wonderful pool-patio area out back. Knowledgeable and enthusiastic owners Tom and Donard and their helpful, English-speaking staff assist with every need and can arrange tours and more.

The front suites-cum-apartments with kitchenettes are fabulous. The house it offers for rent across the road, which sleeps seven people and has a hot tub, is just as good, if not better.

Hotel La Piazzetta   HOTEL $$
(☏ 999-923-39-09; www.hotellapiazzettamerida.com; Calle 50A No 493; btwn Calles 57 & 59; d incl breakfast M$750-1100; ❄❄🛜) Off a quiet side street overlooking **Parque de la Mejorada**, this friendly little guesthouse-cum-hotel has lovely views of the park or the pleasant patio area. Each of the well-appointed rooms is decked out with a contemporary feel: stressed wooden tables, hanging baskets with towels and the like. Free bike loans are available. An airy, pleasant on-site cafe forms the lobby.

Casa Ana B&B   B&B $$
(☏ 999-924-00-05; www.casaana.com; Calle 52 No 469; r incl breakfast US$50; ❄❄🛜🏊) Casa Ana is a casual but intimate escape and one of the best deals in town. It has a small natural-bottom pool and a cozy overgrown garden. The rooms are spotless and have Mexican hammocks and (phew) mosquito screens. The Cuban owner Ana is on site, which adds a personal, friendly touch.

Hotel Julamis   BOUTIQUE HOTEL $$
(☏ 999-924-18-18; cell 998-1885508; www.hoteljulamis.com; Calle 53 No 475B; r incl breakfast US$69-99; ❄🛜) The highlight of this B&B is its breakfast, prepared by the gourmet-chef owner, Alex. The rooms are very pleasant (each features unique design details, such as colorful murals and original tiled floors), if a tad tired. But the 6pm tequila tastings and service make for a pleasant stay. All rooms come with fridges stocked daily with free beverages.

Gran Hotel   HOTEL $$
(☏ 999-923-69-63; www.granhoteldemerida.com; Calle 60 No 496; d M$730-790, ste M$1400-1600; P❄❄🛜) This was indeed a grand hotel when built in 1901. Most rooms in this old-timer are pretty tired; some have

slightly more modern features, while several still have the same old-period furnishings and faded carpets. Despite the wear, the lobby retains many elegant and delightful decorative flourishes. And the central location is a plus.

62 St Guesthouse
GUESTHOUSE $$

(☑999-924-30-60; www.casaalvarezguesthouse. com; Calle 62 No 448, btwn Calles 51 & 53; d M$750; P➘✳❄🛜🏊) Impeccably clean and about as tranquil as you can get, this old-school guesthouse offers a friendly, one-of-the-family ambience, along with nice showers, spotless bathrooms and in-room fridges. The house is full of antiques, including a cylinder-style gramophone player. Guests have use of a kitchen and small pool out back. Charming caretaker hosts.

★Casa Lecanda
BOUTIQUE HOTEL $$$

(☑999-928-01-12; www.casalecanda.com; Calle 47 No 471, btwn 54 & 56; d incl breakfast from US$325; ✳🛜🏊) Behind its beautiful but unassuming facade, Casa Lecanda is a huge cut above Mérida's other boutique options thanks to attention to detail in both the design and the guest service. A 19th-century mansion restored to stunning effect, it only has seven rooms, each decorated with a nod to traditional styles but including mod-cons and luxurious bathrooms.

A small pool in the lush gardens is a welcome touch, as is the choose-your-own-room-scent at check-in. Hearty breakfasts are served in the colonial-style dining room and an array of tequilas and Mexican wines can be sampled at the bar.

Diplomat Boutique Hotel
B&B $$$

(☑999-117-29-72; www.thediplomatmerida.com; Calle 78 No 493A, btwn Calle 59 & 59A; r US$275; ✳🛜🏊) This beautiful, intimate oasis, just southwest of the historic center in a local neighborhood of Santiago, oozes style and charm. The four rooms err on minimalist, with touches of flair such as greenery and tasteful ornamentation. The hospitable Canadian hosts provide a gourmet breakfast spread served in the patio, treats by the pool, and fabulous ideas for cuisine and exploration.

After a day of hitting the streets (if you've managed to pull yourselves away), relax in a hammock or loll in the pool (sigh moment). While high-season rates may be pushing the budget, low-season rates provide better value.

Los Arcos Bed & Breakfast
B&B $$$

(☑999-928-02-14; www.losarcosmerida.com; Calle 66 No 448B; d incl breakfast US$85-95; P➘✳❄🛜🏊) Certainly not for minimalists – there's art on every wall and knicknacks filling every space – Los Arcos is a lovely, gay-friendly B&B with two guestrooms at the end of a drop-dead-gorgeous garden and pool area. Rooms have an eclectic assortment of art and antiques, excellent beds and bathrooms.

Hotel Casa del Balam
HOTEL $$$

(☑999-924-88-44; www.casadelbalam.com; Calle 60 No 488, btwn Calles 55 & 57; d/ste from M$1200/1800; P➘✳@🛜🏊) This place is centrally located, has an attractive pool and large, quiet colonial-style rooms with shiny tiles and extra-firm beds with wrought-iron bedheads. It often offers hefty discounts during quiet times, which make it solid value.

✖ Eating

Don't miss 'Mérida en Domingo,' an all-day food and crafts market on the main plaza every Sunday. It's a great place to try a wide variety of regional dishes, and it's cheap, too!

★Pola
ICE CREAM $

(www.polagelato.com; Calle 55 s/n, btwn Calles 62 & 64; from M$30) You'd head to this place even if you were you in the Arctic, it's that good. Get your tongue around full-cream, 100% natural (no additives) gelati with some of the quirkiest flavours in ice-cream land. Mondays is traditionally 'pork and beans' night in Yucatán, so you can try this flavor, too (Mondays only). Don't miss the conventional chocolate flavor, however. *Muy rico* (delicious).

★Wayan'e
TACOS $

(cnr Calles 59 & 46; tacos M$12-17, tortas M$20-32; ⏱7am-2:30pm Mon-Sat) Popular for its *castakan* (crispy pork belly), Wayan'e (meaning 'here it is' in Maya) is one of Mérida's premier breakfast spots. Vegetarians will find options here, such as the *huevo con xkatic* (egg with chili) taco and fresh juices. But if you eat meat, it's all about the greasy goodness of the *castakan torta* (sandwich).

Bistro Cultural
FRENCH $

(Calle 66 377c, btwn 41 & 43; breakfast mains M$45-60, lunch mains M$65-80; ⏱8:30am-5:30pm Mon-Fri, to 4:30pm Sat & Sun) It's worth the hike a few blocks from the tourist hubbub to enjoy this cute little French-run cafe. After viewing some local artworks in a little salon, you can enjoy a snack or meal in its lovely garden. While the cuisine is French, the influence is Yucatecan and locally grown, organic products are used where possible.

The small menu includes the likes of *croque chaya* (a play on a French *croque monsieur*) and there is a daily special on top of the fixed plates. It sells delectable French pastries too (M$12 to M$17). It plans to open Thursday through Saturday evenings between October and April.

Bar de Café Sukra
CAFE $

(www.facebook.com/sukracafe; Paseo de Montejo 496, btwn 43 & 45; mains M$60-90; ⊘9am-6pm Mon-Sat, to 2pm Sun) This easygoing spot, at the beginning of Paseo de Montejo, is framed by pretty plants and features an eclectic mix of tables and chairs, more reminiscent of a great aunt's house than an eatery overlooking the poshest street in town. The excellent salads and sandwiches are equally as down to earth. Dig in and watch the world go by.

La Socorrito
YUCATECAN $

(Calle 47, btwn Calles 58 & 60; tortas M$20; ⊘7am-4pm) One of many in this strip, these old pros were one of the first; they've been slow-cooking *cochito* in underground pits for more than six decades. You'll find this delightful hole-in-the-wall on the plaza side of the Mercado de Santa Ana.

★ Oliva Enoteca
ITALIAN $$

(☑999-923-30-81; www.olivamerida.com; Calle 47, cnr Calle 54; mains M$180-320; ⊘1-5pm & 7pm-midnight Mon-Sat) This contemporary restaurant with black-and-white tiled floors, Edison light bulbs, designer chairs and a viewable kitchen is a magnet for the local cool cats who descend on this smart place for excellent Italian cuisine.

Nectar
YUCATECAN $$

(☑999-938-08-38; http://nectarmerida.mx; Av A García Lavín 32; mains M$220-500; ⊘1:30-5pm & 7pm-12:30am Tue-Thu, to 1am Fri & Sat, 1:30-5pm Sun; ✲) Inventive but delicious takes on traditional Yucatecan cuisine, a setting that would win design awards, and superfriendly and helpful staff make for a winning combination at this north Mérida (take a taxi) destination restaurant. The *cebollas negras* (blackened onions; M$150) might look unappealing but the taste soon dispels any

doubts. And you can't go wrong with the meat and fish mains.

Its imaginative cocktails are a great start to a meal and the imaginative desserts a great way to finish.

Lo Que Hay
VEGAN $$

(www.hotelmediomundo.com; Calle 55 No 533; mains M$80-150, 3-course menu M$280; ⊘7-10pm Tue-Sat; ⬗⯌) Even nonvegans usually give an enthusiastic thumbs up to this dinner-only restaurant, where three-course vegan meals are served in a serene courtyard. The dishes range from Mexican and Lebanese cuisine to raw vegan. Lo Que Hay is in the **Hotel Medio Mundo** (☑999-924-54-72; d incl breakfast US$80-90; ⬗✲⬗⬗) and it welcomes nonguests.

La Chaya Maya
MEXICAN $$

(www.lachayamaya.com; Calle 55 No 510; mains M$65-200; ⊘1-10pm Mon-Sat, 8am-11pm Sun) Popular with locals and tourists alike, this restaurant opened a new location in a lovely downtown colonial building. Consider La Chaya your introduction to classic Yucatecan fare (and it's a good one): *relleno negro* (black turkey stew) or *cochinita pibil* (slow-cooked pork). The **original location** (www.lachayamaya.com; cnr Calles 62 & 57; mains M$65-200; ⊘7am-11pm) opens for breakfast.

★ Ku'uk
INTERNATIONAL $$$

(☑999-944-33-77; www.kuukrestaurant.com; Av Rómulo Rozo No 488, cnr Calle 27; mains M$220-500, tasting menu M$1350) The stunning historic home, at the end of Paseo Montejo, sets the scene for what's to come: a high-end, alto-gourmet meal that will end up setting a very high benchmark for Mexican cuisine. You can dine in a number of elegant, if slightly bare, rooms. The cuisine gives a nod to Yucatecan cuisine with contemporary preparation and flavor twists. Go the whole way on a tasting menu (M$1350, with wine pairing M$2200).

★ Apoala
MEXICAN $$$

(☑999-923-19-79; www.apoala.mx; Calle 60 No 471, Parque Santa Lucía; mains M$155-300; ✆) With influences of dishes from Oaxaca, which like the Yucatán is known for its extraordinary regional cuisine, Apoala reinvents popular dishes such as *enmoladas* (stuffed tortillas in a rich *mole* sauce) and *tlayudas* (a large tortilla with sliced beef, black beans and Oaxaca cheese). It's in a lovely spot on Parque Santa Lucía (p305) and rubs shoulders with some other great eateries.

YUCATÁN PENINSULA MÉRIDA

Eureka

ITALIAN $$$

(📞 999-926-26-94; www.facebook.com/eureka
cucinaitaliana; Av Rotary Internacional 117, cnr
Calle 52; mains M$130-260; ⏱1-11pm Tue-Sat, to
6pm Sat; 🅿🛜🅿) This is another of many
eateries that is on the list of Mérida's ex-
cellent *cucina Italiana*, and this one has
a touch of style. The signature dish of chef
Fabrizio Di Stazio is the *riccioli eureka*,
freshly made pasta in white ragu sauce
with mushrooms and an aromatic hint of
truffle. It's east of Paseo Montejo and an
easy taxi ride.

🍷 Drinking & Nightlife

★ Mercado 60

COCKTAIL BAR

(www.mercado60.com; Calle 60, btwn 51 & 53;
⏱6pm-late) For a fun night of booze and
cheap(ish) international eats, head to this
atmospheric, lively and diverse culinary
market, where the margaritas (or fine
wines) will have you dancing alongside
trendy locals to live salsa music. This mod-
ern concept is a cocktail bar meets beer hall,
with different businesses serving up differ-
ent concoctions.

The cuisine – ranging from Mexican
gourmet tacos to ramen noodles – is also
served from small kiosks. Dishes, while
tasty, could be better but they do the 'soak-
ing-up' trick...

★ Manifesto

COFFEE

(http://manifesto.mx; coffee from M$30; ⏱8am-
9pm Mon-Fri, to 6pm Sat) You won't find any
spiced-pumpkin-latte-with-a-twist non-
sense here. This place offers a tasty 'man-
ifesto' indeed: coffee for focused coffee
drinkers. Thanks to a trio from Calabria,
Italy, you can find your cappuccinos, es-
pressos and, yes, even flat whites, made by
well-trained baristas. And the fit-out just
happens to be great, too – minimalist and
funky.

They roast their beans here, too, and you
can buy packets with beans originating from
Veracruz, Chiapas and more. Disappointing-
ly, Manifesto is closed on Sundays.

La Fundación Mezcalería

BAR

(www.facebook.com/lafundacionmezcaleriameri
da; Calle 56 No 465, btwn 53 & 55; ⏱8pm-2:30am
Wed-Sun; 🛜) A popular cyclist hangout,
especially on Wednesday, this loud, ret-
ro-styled bar with nightly live music has
an excellent selection of organic mezcals

and an atmosphere conducive to knocking
'em back. Careful though: this stuff packs a
mean punch.

☆ Entertainment

Mérida organizes many folkloric and musi-
cal events in parks and historic buildings,
put on by local performers of considerable
skill. Admission is mostly free. The tourist
publication *Yucatán Today* has a good sum-
mary of weekly events.

Centro Cultural Olimpo

CONCERT VENUE

(📞 999-924-00-00, ext 80152; www.merida.gob.
mx/capitalcultural; cnr Calles 62 & 61) Always has
something going on: films, concerts, art in-
stallations, you name it.

🛍 Shopping

Guayaberas Jack

CLOTHING

(www.guayaberasjack.com.mx; Calle 59 No 507A;
⏱10am-8:30pm Mon-Sat, to 2:30pm Sun) The
guayabera (embroidered dress shirt) is the
classic Mérida shirt, but in buying the wrong
one you run the risk of looking like a waiter.
Drop into this famous shop to avoid getting
asked for the bill.

Hamacas Mérida

ARTS & CRAFTS

(📞 999-924-04-40; www.hamacasmerida.com.mx;
Calle 65 No 510, btwn Calles 62 & 64; ⏱9am-7pm
Mon-Fri, to 2pm Sat) Has a large catalog with
all kinds of sizes, shapes and colors of ham-
mocks (and chairs), plus it ships worldwide.

Tejón Rojo

GIFTS & SOUVENIRS

(www.tejonrojo.com; Calle 53 No 503; ⏱noon-
9pm Mon-Sat, 1-6pm Sun) Sells trendy graph-
ic T-shirts and an assortment of Mexican
pop-culture souvenirs, including coffee
mugs, jewelry, handbags and wrestling
masks.

Librería Dante

BOOKS

(www.libreriadante.com.mx; cnr Calles 61 & 62, Pla-
za Grande; ⏱8am-10:30pm) Shelves a selection
of archaeology and regional history books in
English and has good Yucatecan cookbooks,
too. The bookstore has other branches
throughout the city.

ℹ Information

INTERNET ACCESS

Free public wi-fi access is available on several of
the main plazas and in many cafes.

Chandler's Internet (Calle 61 s/n, btwn Calles 60 & 62; per hour M$15; ⊗9am-10pm) Just off Plaza Grande.

MEDICAL SERVICES

Yucatán Today (www.yucatantoday.com/en/topics/healthcare-merida-yucatan) has a good list of doctors and hospitals.

Clínica de Mérida (☑999-942-18-00; www.clinicademerida.com.mx; Av Itzáes 242, cnr Calle 25; ⊗24hr; ▣R-49) Good private clinic with laboratory and 24-hour emergency service.

Hospital O'Horán (☑999-930-33-20; Av de los Itzáes, cnr Av Jacinto Canek) A centrally located public hospital for emergencies. For less urgent matters, such as prescriptions and consultations, consider going to a private clinic.

MONEY

Banks and ATMs are scattered throughout the city. There is a cluster of both along Calle 65 between Calles 60 and 62, one block south of Plaza Grande. *Casas de cambio* (money-exchange offices) have faster service and longer opening hours than banks, but often have poorer rates.

POST

Post Office (☑999-928-54-04; Calle 53 No 469, btwn Calles 52 & 54; ⊗8am-7pm Mon-Fri, to 3pm Sat) Central post office.

TOURIST INFORMATION

You'll find tourist information booths at the airport. Two tourist offices downtown have basic brochures and information and maps.

City Tourist Office (☑999-942-00-00, ext 80119; www.merida.gob.mx/turismo; Calle 62, Plaza Grande; ⊗8am-8pm) Right on the main plaza, it is staffed with helpful English speakers. Here you can hook up free walking tours of the city, which depart daily at 9:30am.

State Tourist Office (☑999-930-31-01; www.yucatan.travel; Calle 61 s/n, Plaza Grande; ⊗8am-8pm) In the entrance to the Palacio de Gobierno. There's usually an English speaker on hand.

ⓘ Getting There & Away

AIR

Mérida's **Aeropuerto Internacional de Mérida** (Mérida International Airport; ☑999-940-60-90; www.asur.com.mx; Hwy 180 Km 4.5; ▣R-79) is a 10km, 20-minute ride southwest of Plaza Grande off Hwy 180 (Avenida de los Itzáes). It has car-rental desks, an ATM, currency-exchange service and a tourist information booth.

Most international flights to Mérida make connections through Mexico City. Nonstop international services are provided by Aeroméxico and United Airlines.

Low-cost airlines Interjet, VivaAerobus and Volaris serve Mexico City. Mayair operates prop planes to Cancún and Cozumel.

Aeroméxico (☑800-021-40-00; www.aeromexico.com) Flies direct from Miami.

Interjet (☑800-011-23-45, USA 866-285-9525; www.interjet.com) Serves Mexico City, where you can catch connecting flights to New York, Miami and Houston.

Mayair (☑800-962-92-47; www.mayair.com.mx) Runs prop planes to Cancún that continue on to Cozumel.

VivaAerobus (☑818-215-01-50, USA 888-935-98-48; www.vivaaerobus.com) Service to Mexico City and Monterrey.

Volaris (☑Mexico City 55-1102-8000, USA 866-988-3527; www.volaris.com) Direct to Mexico City and Monterrey.

BUS

Mérida is the bus transportation hub of the Yucatán Peninsula. Take care with your bags on night buses and those serving popular tourist destinations (especially 2nd-class buses); there have been reports of theft on some routes.

There are a number of bus terminals, and some lines operate from (and stop at) more than one terminal. Tickets for departure from one terminal can often be bought at another, and destinations overlap greatly among bus lines. Check out www.ado.com.mx for ticket info on some of the lines.

CAME Bus Terminal (Terminal de Primera Clase; ☑999-920-44-44; Calle 70 s/n, btwn Calles 69 & 71) Mérida's main bus terminal has (mostly 1st-class) buses – including ADO, OCC and ADO GL – to points around the Yucatán Peninsula and faraway places such as Mexico City.

Fiesta Americana Bus Terminal (☑999-924-83-91; cnr Calle 60 & Av Colón; ▣R-2) A small 1st-class terminal on the west side of the Fiesta Americana hotel complex servicing guests of the luxury hotels on Avenida Colón, north of the city center. ADO buses run between here and Cancún, Playa del Carmen, Villahermosa and Ciudad del Carmen.

Noreste Bus Terminal (Autobuses del Noreste y Autobuses Luz; ☑999-924-63-55; Calle 50, cnr Calle 67) Noreste and Luz bus lines uses this terminal. Destinations served from here include many small towns in the northeast part of the peninsula, including Tizimín and Río Lagartos; Cancún and points along the way; and small towns south and west of Mérida, such as Celestún, Ticul, Ruinas de Mayapán and Oxkutzcab. Some Oriente buses depart from Terminal de Segunda Clase and stop here,

Parque de San Juan (Calle 69, btwn Calles 62 & 64) From all around the square and church, combis (vans and minibuses) depart for Muna, Oxkutzcab, Tekax, Ticul and other points.

Terminal Autoprogreso (Progreso Bus Terminal; ☎ 999-928-39-65; www.autoprogreso.com; Calle 62 No 524) There's a separate terminal with buses leaving for the northern beach town of Progreso.

Terminal TAME (Terminal de Segunda Clase; ☎ 999-924-08-30; Calle 69, btwn Calles 68 & 70) This terminal is just around the corner from the CAME bus terminal. ADO, Mayab, Oriente,

Sur, TRT and ATS run mostly 2nd-class buses to points in the state and around the peninsula, including Felipe Carrillo Puerto and Ticul.

Colectivo to Tekax

Colectivo to Progreso (Calle 60)

CAR & MOTORCYCLE

The most flexible way to tour the many archaeological sites around Mérida is to travel with a rental car. Assume you will pay M$500 to M$550 per day (tax and insurance included) for short-term rental of an economy-size vehicle.

BUSES FROM MÉRIDA

DESTINATION	COST (M$)	DURATION (HR)	FREQUENCY (DAILY)
Campeche	226	2½-3	frequent
Cancún	210-412	4½-6½	frequent; CAME Bus Terminal & Terminal TAME
Celestún	56	2½	frequent; Noreste Bus Terminal
Chetumal	446	5½-6	3-4; Terminal TAME
Chichén Itzá	91-144	1½-2	frequent; CAME Bus Terminal; Noreste terminal
Escárcega	288	4-4½	4; Terminal TAME
Felipe Carrillo Puerto	218	6	frequent; Terminal TAME
Izamal	28	1½	frequent; Noreste terminal
Mayapán	25	1½	hourly; Noreste terminal
Mexico City	1792-1882	20	7; CAME Bus Terminal & Segunda Clase
Palenque	628-638	7½-10	4; CAME Bus Terminal & Segunda Clase
Playa del Carmen	464	4-6	frequent; CAME Bus Terminal & Segunda Clase
Progreso	20	1	frequent; Terminal Autoprogreso
Río Lagartos/San Felipe	160-225	3½	3; Noreste terminal
Ruta Puuc (round-trip; 30min at each site)	179	8-8½	8am Sundays only; Terminal TAME
Ticul	55	1¾	frequent; Terminal TAME
Tizimín	105-170	60	frequent; Noreste terminal
Tulum	190-338	4-4½	5; CAME Bus Terminal & Segunda Clase
Uxmal	63	1½	5; Terminal TAME
Valladolid	204	2½-3	frequent; CAME Bus Terminal & Terminal TAME

Getting around Mérida's sprawling tangle of one-way streets is better done on foot or bus.

Several agencies have branches at the airport and on Calle 60, between Calles 55 and 57. You'll get the best deal by booking online.

There is an expensive toll highway between Mérida and Cancún (M$450).

Easy Way (☑ 999-930-95-00; www.easyway rentacar-yucatan.com; Calle 60 No 484, btwn Calles 55 & 57; ◷7am-11pm)

National (☑ 999-923-24-93; www.nationalcar. com; Calle 60 No 486F, btwn Calles 55 & 57; ◷8am-1pm & 4-8pm)

❶ Getting Around

TO/FROM THE AIRPORT

The taxi companies **Transporte Terrestre** (☑ 999-946-15-29; www.transporteterrestre demerida.com; per car M$200-220) and **ADO** (☑ 999-946-03-68) provide speedy service between the airport and downtown, charging M$200 (same price for hotel pickup). A street taxi from the city center to the airport should cost about M$100 to M$120. If you want to get this same price *from* the airport, you'll need to walk out to the main street and flag down a city cab.

A city bus labeled 'Aviación 79' (M$8) travels between the main road of the airport entrance (the bus does not enter the airport) and the city center every 15 to 30 minutes until 9pm, with occasional service until 11pm. The best place to catch the same bus to the airport is at Parque San Juan, from the corner of Calles 62 and 69.

BUS

City buses are cheap at M$8, but routes can be confusing. Some start in suburban neighborhoods, skirt the city center and terminate in another distant suburban neighborhood. Transpublico.com (https://merida.transpublico.com) provides detailed maps of all the routes.

To travel between Plaza Grande and the upscale neighborhoods to the north along Paseo de Montejo, catch the R-2 'Hyatt' or 'Tecnológico' line along Calle 60. To return to the city center, catch any bus heading south on Paseo de Montejo displaying the same signs and/or 'Centro.'

TAXI

More and more taxis in town are using meters these days. If you get one with no meter, be sure to agree on a price before getting in. M$30 to M$50 is fair for getting around downtown and to the bus terminals. Taxi stands can be found at most of the barrio parks (dispatch fees may cost extra).

Radio Taxímetro del Volante (☑ 999-928-30-35) For 24-hour radio taxi service.

Uxmal

Uxmal, pronounced oosh-mahl, is an impressive set of ruins, easily ranking among the top (and unfortunately most crowded) Maya archaeological sites. It is a large site with some fascinating structures in good condition and bearing a riot of ornamentation. Adding to its appeal is Uxmal's setting near the hilly Puuc region, which lent its name to the architectural patterns in this area. *Puuc* means 'hills,' and these, rising up to about 100m, are the first relief from the flatness of the northern and western portions of the peninsula.

For an additional cost, Uxmal projects a nightly light-and-sound show.

For an entirely different experience, outside the ruins, the **Choco-Story** (www. choco-storymexico.com; Hwy 261 Km 78, near Hotel Hacienda Uxmal; adult/child 6-12yr M$120/90; ◷9am-7:30pm) museum takes a look at the history of chocolate.

◉ Sights

Exploring the Ruins

Casa del Adivino ARCHAEOLOGICAL SITE
(Pirámide del Adivino) As you approach Uxmal, the Casa del Adivino comes into view. This 35m-high temple (the name translates as 'Magician's House') was built in an unusual oval shape. What you see is a restored version of the temple's fifth incarnation, consisting of round stones held rudely together with lots of cement. Four earlier temples were completely covered in the final rebuilding by the Maya, except for the high doorway on the west side, which remains from the fourth temple.

Decorated in elaborate Chenes style (a style that originated further south), the doorway proper forms the mouth of a gigantic Chaac mask.

Cuadrángulo de las Monjas ARCHAEOLOGICAL SITE
The 74-room, sprawling Nuns' Quadrangle is directly west of the Casa del Adivino. Archaeologists guess variously that it was a military academy, royal school or palace complex. The long-nosed face of Chaac appears everywhere on the facades of the four separate temples that form the quadrangle. The northern temple, the grandest of the four, was built first, followed by the southern, then the eastern and finally the western.

South of Mérida

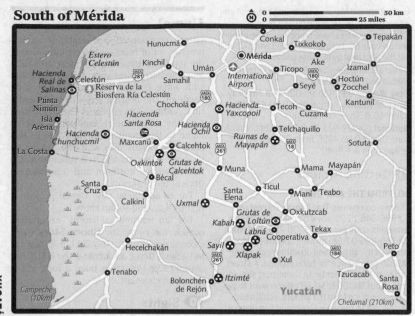

Several decorative elements on the exuberant facades show signs of Mexican, perhaps Totonac, influence. The feathered-serpent (Quetzalcóatl, or in Maya, Kukulcán) motif along the top of the west temple's facade is one of these. Note also the stylized depictions of the *na* (traditional Maya thatched hut) over some of the doorways in the northern and southern buildings.

Passing through the corbeled arch in the middle of the south building of the quadrangle and continuing down the slope takes you through the **Juego de Pelota** (Ball Court). From here you can turn left and head up the steep slope and stairs to the large terrace. If you have time, you could instead turn right to explore the western **Grupo del Cementerio** (which, though largely unrestored, holds some interesting square blocks carved with skulls in the center of its plaza), then head for the stairs and terrace.

Casa de las Tortugas   ARCHAEOLOGICAL SITE
The House of the Turtles, which you'll find south of the Juego de Pelota (Ball Court), takes its name from the turtles carved on the cornice. The Maya associated turtles with the rain god, Chaac. According to Maya myth, when the people suffered from drought, so did the turtles, and both prayed to Chaac to send rain.

The frieze of short columns, or 'rolled mats,' that runs around the temple below the turtles is characteristic of the Puuc style.

On the west side of the building a vault has collapsed, affording a good view of the corbeled arch that supported it.

Palacio del Gobernador   ARCHAEOLOGICAL SITE
The Governor's Palace, with its magnificent facade nearly 100m long, is arguably the most impressive structure at Uxmal. The buildings have walls filled with rubble, faced with cement and then covered in a thin veneer of limestone squares; the lower part of the facade is plain, the upper part festooned with stylized Chaac faces and geometric designs, often lattice-like or fretted.

Other elements of Puuc style are decorated cornices, rows of half-columns (as in the Casa de las Tortugas) and round columns in doorways (as in the palace at Sayil).

Researchers recently discovered some 150 species of medicinal plants growing on the east side of the palace. Due to the high concentration of plants growing there it's believed they were cultivated by the Maya to treat stomach infections, snake bites and many other ailments.

Gran Pirámide
ARCHAEOLOGICAL SITE

The 30m-high, nine-tiered pyramid has been restored only on its northern side. Archaeologists theorize that the quadrangle at its summit was largely destroyed in order to construct another pyramid above it. That work, for reasons unknown, was never completed. At the top are some stucco carvings of Chaac, birds and flowers.

El Palomar
ARCHAEOLOGICAL SITE

West of the Gran Pirámide sits a structure whose roofcomb is latticed with a pattern reminiscent of the Moorish pigeon houses built into walls in Spain and northern Africa – hence the building's name, which means the Dovecote or Pigeon House. Honeycombed triangular 'belfries' sit on top of a building that was once part of a quadrangle.

Casa de la Vieja
ARCHAEOLOGICAL SITE

(Old Woman's House) Off the southeast corner of the Palacio del Gobernador's platform is a small complex, now largely rubble, known as the Casa de la Vieja. In front of it is a small *palapa* (thatch-roof shelter) that covers several large phalluses carved from stone.

🛏 Sleeping

There is no town at Uxmal, only several hotels, and there are no budget options. A good range of midrange lodgings can be found in Santa Elena, 16km southeast, or in Ticul, 30km east.

Hotel Hacienda Uxmal
HISTORIC HOTEL $$$

(☎800-719-54-65, USA 877-240-58-64; www.mayaland.com; Hwy 261 Km 78; r from US$136; 🅿❋🛜🏊) This attractive Mayaland Resort is 500m from the ruins. It housed the archaeologists who explored and restored Uxmal. Wide, tiled floors, lots of wrought iron, high ceilings, great bathrooms and a beautiful swimming pool make for a pleasant stay. There are even rocking chairs to help you kick back after a hard day of exploring.

For those on a budget, the attached Casa del Mago may have cheaper rooms but was closed for unknown reasons at the time of research.

Lodge at Uxmal
LUXURY HOTEL $$$

(☎800-719-54-65, USA 877-240-58-64; www.mayaland.com; Hwy 261 Km 78; r from US$235; 🅿❋🛜🏊) Rooms could be nicer for the price, but you can't beat the easy access to the ruins and the pool certainly adds value. Some of the more expensive rooms have Jacuzzis. We don't suppose Stephens and Catherwood enjoyed such luxury when they passed through the area in the late 1830s.

❶ Getting There & Away

Uxmal is 80km from Mérida. Departures (around M$70, 1½ hours, four daily) on the Sur bus line leave from Mérida's Terminal TAME (p314). But going back to Mérida, passing buses may be full. If you get stuck, a taxi to nearby Santa Elena costs M$150 to M$200.

Tours offered by Nómadas Hostel (p308) in Mérida are always a good option, or rent a car and also visit other ruins in the area.

Santa Elena
📶 997 / POP 3500

Originally called Nohcacab, the town known as Santa Elena today was virtually razed in 1847 in the Caste War. '*Ele*-na' means burnt houses in Maya. The Mexican government changed the name to Santa Elena in a bold PR stunt.

If you're up for a little DIY adventure, head 4km outside town to the Mulchic pyramid; locals can tell you how to get there.

Santa Elena makes a great base to explore the nearby ruins of Uxmal, Kabah and those along the Ruta Puuc.

⊙ Sights

Santa Elena Museum
MUSEUM

(M$10; ⊙9am-6pm) The only reason you go to this tiny museum is for the view (it's perched on a hill) and to support the locals – both worth doing. As for the displays? While they are termed '18th-century child mummies,' in truth they are four sub-composed bodies that were found buried beneath the adjoining cathedral.

🛏 Sleeping

★Pickled Onion
B&B $$

(☎cell 997-1117922; www.thepickledonion yucatan.com; off Hwy 261; d/f incl breakfast from US$50/65; 🅿🌀🛜🏊) Offers the chance to stay in a modern adobe-walled hut with lovely tiled floors and bathrooms. The well-maintained rooms all come with coffee makers and mosquito netting and keep you cool with *palapa* roofs. We love the pool and surrounding lush and landscaped gardens, and the excellent **restaurant** (mains M$110-120; ⊙7:30am-8:30pm; 🅿🛜) does food to go for picnics in the nearby ruins. It's on the south end of town, off Hwy 261.

Uxmal

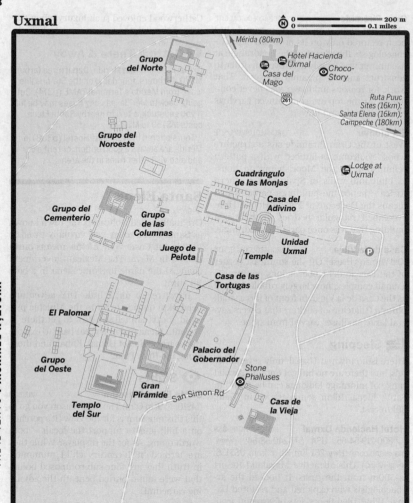

Nueva Altia B&B $$

(📱cell 998-2190176; Hwy 261 Km 159; d incl breakfast US$66; 🅿️☕🛜) 🍃 If you're looking for some peace and quiet, this is *the* place. Geometrically designed to get nice cross breezes, the spiral-shaped bungalows were inspired by ancient Maya architecture. And, as with many locales, unearthed Maya ruins are tucked away on the pretty, wooded grounds.

Flycatcher Inn B&B $$

(📱997-978-53-50; www.flycatcherinn.com; off Hwy 261; d incl breakfast from M$1200-1800; 🕐mid-Oct–Aug; 🅿️❄️🛜) Flycatcher Inn features seven squeaky-clean rooms, all with great porches, hammocks, excellent screenage and spiffy bathrooms. It is surrounded by a pleasant garden and a number of bird and animal species can be seen here, including the flycatchers that gave their name to the place.

The inn's driveway is less than 100m north of Santa Elena's southern entrance, near **Restaurant El Chac-Mool** (📱997-978-51-17; www.facebook.com/chacmooluxmal; Calle 18 No 211B; mains M$110-120; 🕐7am-10pm; 🅿️🛜).

ⓘ Getting There & Away

It's handy to have your own wheels here, especially if you're using it as a base to visit the ruins of Uxmal, plus to explore the Ruta Puuc. Second-class Sur Mayab buses run between Mérida and Campeche stopping in Uxmal and Santa Elena (plus Oxcutzcab, five daily, around M$70).

Kabah

Kabah   ARCHAEOLOGICAL SITE
(Hwy 261; M$50, guides M$500; ⊙8am-5pm) On entering, head right to climb the stairs of **El Palacio de los Mascarones** (Palace of the Masks). Standing in front of it is the Altar de los Glifos, whose immediate area is littered with many stones carved with glyphs. The palace's facade is an amazing sight, covered in nearly 300 masks of Chaac, the rain god or sky serpent. Most of their huge noses are broken off; the best intact beaks are at the building's south end.

These curled-up noses may have given the palace its modern Maya name, Codz Poop (Rolled Mat; it's pronounced more like 'Codes Pope' than some Elizabethan curse). This section was recently restored.

When you've had your fill of noses, head north and around to the back of the Poop to check out the two restored **atlantes** (an *atlas* – plural *'atlantes'* – is a male figure used as a supporting column). These are especially interesting, as they're some of the very few 3D human figures you'll see at the main Maya sites. One is headless and the other wears a jaguar mask atop his head.

Descend the steps near the *atlantes* and turn left, passing the small **Pirámide de los Mascarones**, to reach the plaza containing **El Palacio**. The palace's broad facade has several doorways, two of which have a column in the center. These columned doorways and the groups of decorative *columnillas* (little columns) on the upper part of the facade are characteristic of the Puuc architectural style.

Steps on the north side of El Palacio's plaza put you on a path leading about 200m through the jungle to the **Templo de las Columnas**, which has more rows of decorative columns on the upper part of its facade. At last visit, access to the temple was closed for restoration.

West of El Palacio, across the highway, a path leads up the slope and passes to the south of a high mound of stones that was once the **Gran Pirámide** (Great Pyramid).

The path curves to the right and comes to a large restored **monumental arch**. It's said that the *sacbé*, or cobbled and elevated ceremonial road, leading from here goes through the jungle all the way to Uxmal, terminating at a smaller arch; in the other direction it goes to Labná. Once, all of the Yucatán Peninsula was connected by these marvelous 'white roads' of rough limestone.

At present nothing of the *sacbé* is visible, and the rest of the area west of the highway is a maze of unmarked, overgrown paths leading off into the jungle.

The souvenir ticket office sells snacks and cold drinks. For good lodging, stay in Santa Elena (p317), about 8km north of Kabah.

Kabah is 104km from Mérida. It's easiest to reach the site by car, or from Mérida you can take a Sur bus (five daily).

Turitransmérida (p308) does Ruta Puuc tours on a more regular basis and Nómadas Hostel (p309) also runs tours to Kabah.

Ruta Puuc

The Ruta Puuc (Puuc Route) meanders through rolling hills dotted with seldom-visited Maya ruins sitting in dense forests. A road branches off to the east (5km south of Kabah) and winds past the ruins of Sayil, Xlapak and Labná, eventually leading to the Grutas de Loltún. The sites offer some marvelous architectural detail and a deeper acquaintance with the Puuc Maya civilization.

◉ Sights

Labná   ARCHAEOLOGICAL SITE
(Ruta Puuc; M$50; ⊙8am-5pm; **P**) This is *the* Ruta Puuc site not to miss. Archaeologists believe that, at one point in the 9th century, some 3000 Maya lived at Labná. To support such numbers in these arid hills, water was collected in *chultunes* (cisterns); there were some 60 *chultunes* in and around the city; several are still visible. **El Palacio**, the first building you encounter, is one of the longest in the Puuc region, and much of its decorative carving is in good shape.

On the west corner of the main structure's facade, straight in from the big tree near the center of the complex, is a serpent's head with a human face peering out from between its jaws, the symbol of the planet Venus. Toward the hill from this is an impressive Chaac mask, and nearby is the lower half of a human figure (possibly a ballplayer) in loincloth and leggings.

The lower level has several more well-preserved Chaac masks, and the upper level contains a large *chultun* that still holds water. The view of the site and the hills beyond from there is impressive.

Labná is best known for **El Arco**, a magnificent arch once part of a building that separated two quadrangular courtyards. It now appears to be a gate joining two small plazas. The corbeled structure, 3m wide and 6m high, is well preserved, and the reliefs decorating its upper facade are exuberantly Puuc in style.

Flanking the west side of the arch are carved *na* with multi-tiered roofs. Also on these walls, the remains of the building that adjoined the arch, are lattice patterns atop a serpentine design. Archaeologists believe a high roofcomb once sat over the fine arch and its flanking rooms.

Standing on the opposite side of the arch and separated from it by the *sacbé* is a pyramid known as **El Mirador**, topped by a temple. The pyramid itself is largely stone rubble. The temple, with its 5m-high roofcomb, is well positioned to be a lookout, hence its name. Labná is 14km east of the Ruta Puuc junction with Hwy 261.

Sayil
ARCHAEOLOGICAL SITE

(Ruta Puuc; M$50; ⊙8am-5pm) Sayil is best known for **El Palacio**, the huge three-tiered building that has an 85m-long facade and is reminiscent of the Minoan palace on Crete. The distinctive columns of Puuc architecture are used here often, either as supports for the lintels, as decoration between doorways or as a frieze above them, alternating with stylized Chaac masks and 'descending gods.'

Xlapak
ARCHAEOLOGICAL SITE

(Ruta Puuc; ⊙8am-5pm) FREE The ornate *palacio* at Xlapak (shla-pak), also spelled Xlapac, is quite a bit smaller than those at nearby Kabah and Sayil, measuring only about 20m in length. It's decorated with the inevitable Chaac masks, columns and colonnettes and fretted geometric latticework of the Puuc style. The building is interesting and on a bit of a lean.

❶ Getting There & Away

Turitransmérida (p308) offers Ruta Puuc tours as do some of the hostels and accommodations.

On Sundays only, an ATS bus leaves Terminal de Segunda Clase at 8am and costs M$176. It returns at between 3pm and 4pm so it's a whirlwind trip to three ruins, plus Kabah and Uxmal.

Ruinas de Mayapán

Ruinas de Mayapán
ARCHAEOLOGICAL SITE

(M$50; ⊙8am-5pm) Though far less impressive than many Maya sites, Mayapán is historically significant – it was one of the last major dynasties in the region and established itself as the center of Maya civilization from 1200 to 1440. The site's main attractions are clustered in a compact core, and visitors usually have the place to themselves. It is one of few sites where you can ascend to the top of the pyramid.

The city of Mayapán was large, with a population estimated to be around 12,000; it covered 4 sq km, all surrounded by a great defensive wall. More than 3500 buildings, 20 cenotes and traces of the city wall were mapped by archaeologists working in the 1950s and in 1962. The late-post-Classic workmanship is inferior to that of the great age of Maya art.

Among the structures that have been restored is the **Castillo de Kukulcán**, a climbable pyramid with fresco fragments around its base and, at its rear side, friezes depicting decapitated warriors. The reddish color is still faintly visible. The **Templo Redondo** (Round Temple) is vaguely reminiscent of El Caracol at Chichén Itzá.

Don't confuse the ruins of Mayapán with the Maya village of the same name, which is about 40km southeast of the ruins, past the town of Teabo.

The Ruinas de Mayapán are just off Hwy 184, a few kilometers southwest of the town of Telchaquillo and some 50km southeast of Mérida. Although some 2nd-class buses run to Telchaquillo (M$50, 1½ hours, hourly), consider renting a car to get here.

Celestún

☑988 / POP 6800

West of Mérida, Celestún is a sleepy sunscorched fishing village that moves at a turtle's pace – and that's the way locals like it. There's a pretty-enough little square in the town center and some nice beaches, but the real draw is Reserva de la Biosfera Ría Celestún, a wildlife sanctuary abounding in waterfowl, with flamingos the star attraction.

It makes a good beach-and-bird day trip from Mérida, and it's somewhere you can kick back and do nothing for a day or two, especially if you've become road weary.

BACK ROADS SOUTH OF MÉRIDA

Hacienda Yaxcopoil (📱cell 999-9001193; www.yaxcopoil.com; Hwy 261 Km 186; adult/child under 12yr M$100/free; ⊘8am-6pm Mon-Sat, 9am-3pm Sun; [P][🚻]) If you visit one hacienda, this is the one. This vast estate grew and processed *henequén;* many of its numerous French Renaissance–style buildings have undergone picturesque restorations. The interior of the main building is superb. You can enter the sheds with the giant rasping machines that turned the leaves into fiber. The caretaker used to work cutting *henequén* (sisal) and has stories to share (should you speak Spanish; tip suggested).

Hacienda San Pedro Ochil (📱999-924-74-65; www.haciendaochil.com; Hwy 261 Mérida-Muna Km 175; M$30; ⊘10am-6pm; [P][🚻]) There's no lodging (nor old house) here, but it provides an interesting look at how *henequén* was grown and processed. From the parking lot, follow the tracks once used by small wheeled carts to haul materials to and from the processing plant. You'll pass hemp and filigree workshops, and a small museum with changing exhibitions. The *casa de maquinas* (machine house) and smokestack still stand.

Grutas de Calcehtok (Grutas de X'Pukil; 📱cell 999-2627292; off Hwy 184; tour 1-/2hr M$100/130; ⊘8am-5pm; [P][🚻]) The Calcehtok caves are said to comprise the longest dry-cave system on the Yucatán Peninsula. More than 4km have been explored so far, and two of the caves' 25 vaults exceed 100m in diameter (one has a 30m-high 'cupola'). The caves hold abundant and impressive natural formations; however, if you're claustrophobic, have a fear of dark spaces or don't like getting dirty, this definitely isn't for you.

Oxkintok (www.inah.gob.mx; M$50, guides around M$600; ⊘8am-5pm; [P]) Archaeologists have been excited about the ruins of Oxkintok for several years. Inscriptions found at the site contain some of the oldest-known dates in the Yucatán, and indicate the city was inhabited from the pre-Classic to the post-Classic period (300 BC to AD 1500), reaching its greatest importance between AD 475 and 860.

Cenote X-Batún & Dzonbakal (📱cell 999-2565508; San Antonio Mulix; M$50; ⊘9:30am-6:15pm) Some will say we've given a 'best kept secret' away. But the word is out: a cooperative from the tiny village San Antonio Mulix runs this gorgeous spot, consisting of two cenotes, 800m apart. Pay at the Centro Comunitario, then drive 2km along a dirt road. At the end of the road turn right to X-Batún or left to Dzonbakal.

X-Batún, although small, is one of the prettiest sinkholes around, its aquamarine waters open to the sky.

At the entrance to the 2km stretch is a community-run restaurant (mains M$40 to M$95) and you can stay in some simple Maya *cabañas,* complete with fans and mosquito nets (M$600 for four people).

Fishing boats dot the appealing white-sand beach that stretches north for kilometers, and afternoon breezes cool the town on most days. Celestún is sheltered by the peninsula's southward curve, resulting in an abundance of marine life and less violent seas during the season of *nortes* (winds and rains arriving from the north).

⊙ Sights

Hacienda Real de Salinas HISTORIC BUILDING
This abandoned hacienda, a few kilometers southeast of town, once produced dyewood and salt, and served as a summer home for a Campeche family. It's 5km in from the mouth of the estuary. Out in the *ría* (estuary) you can see a cairn marking an *ojo de agua dulce* (freshwater spring) that once supplied the hacienda.

The buildings are decaying in a most scenic way; you can still see shells in the wall mixed into the building material, as well as pieces of French roof tiles that served as ballast in ships on the journey from Europe. Many intact tiles with the brickworks' name and location (Marseille) are still visible in what's left of the roofs.

The hacienda makes a good bicycle excursion from town. Coming south on Calle 4, go left at the Y junction (a dirt road that flanks Puerto Abrigo), then turn right to reach El Lastre (the Ballast), a peninsula between the estuary and its western arm. Flamingos, white pelicans and other birds

GRUTAS DE LOLTÚN

One of the largest **dry-cave systems** (adult/child under 13yr M$127/free, parking M$22; ⊙ tours 9:30am, 11am, 12:30pm, 2pm, 3pm & 4pm; ⬆) on the Yucatán Peninsula, Loltún ('stone flower' in Maya) provided a treasure trove of data for archaeologists studying the Maya. Carbon dating of artifacts found here reveals that the caves were used by humans 2200 years ago. Chest-high murals of hands, faces, animals and geometric motifs were apparent as recently as 25 years ago, but so many people have touched them that scarcely a trace remains, though some handprints have been restored.

A few pots are displayed in a niche, and an impressive bas-relief, **El Guerrero**, guards the entrance. Other than that, you'll mostly see illuminated limestone formations.

To explore the labyrinth, you must take a scheduled guided tour, usually in Spanish but sometimes in English if the group warrants it. The services of the guides are included in the admission price, though they expect a tip afterward (at least M$50 per person is fair). Tours last about one hour and 20 minutes, with lots of lengthy stops. Some guides' presentations are long on legends (and jokes about disappearing mothers-in-law) and short on geological and historical information. The sign says the route is 2km, but in reality it's around 1.1km. Colored lights illuminate the route.

Colectivos (shared vans) to Oxkutzcab (osh-kootz-kahb, M$60, 1½ hours, frequent) depart from Calle 67A in Mérida, beside Parque San Juan. Loltún is 7km southwest of Oxkutzcab, where you can catch *colectivos* (M$17) to the caves from Calle 51 (in front of the market). A taxi costs about M$120.

Renting a car is the best option for reaching the Grutas, though; once you're out of Mérida it's easy going on pretty good roads.

are sometimes seen here. If the water is high enough, it's possible to ask your flamingo-tour captain to try stopping here on the way back from the birds. You'll find bike rentals on the town square.

Reserva de la Biosfera Ría Celestún
WILDLIFE RESERVE

The 591-sq-km Reserva de la Biosfera Ría Celestún is home to a huge variety of animals and birdlife, including a large flamingo colony. You can see flamingos (via boat tours) year-round in Celestún, but they're usually out in full force from November to mid-March.

Tours

Flamingo tours in the Reserva de la Biosfera Ría Celestún are Celestún's main draw. Normally the best months for viewing the flamingos are from around end November to mid-March.

Trips from the beach last 2½ hours and begin with a ride along the coast for several kilometers, during which you can expect to see egrets, herons, cormorants, sandpipers and many other bird species. The boat then turns into the mouth of the *ría* (estuary).

Continuing up the *ría* takes you under the highway bridge where other boat tours begin and beyond which lie the flamingos.

Depending on the tide, hour, season and climate conditions, you may see hundreds or thousands of the colorful birds. Don't encourage your captain to approach them too closely; a startled flock taking wing can result in injuries and deaths (for the birds). In addition to taking you to the flamingos, the captain will wend through a 200m mangrove tunnel and visit freshwater springs welling into the saltwater of the estuary, where you can take a refreshing dip. Tours from the bridge run 1½ hours.

Hiring a boat on the beach can be frustrating at times. Operators tend to try to collect as many people as possible, which sometimes means a lot of waiting around. Prices are often quoted based on six passengers, but if fewer people show up, the quoted price rises. You can avoid this problem by coming up with a group of six on your own. Expect to pay around M$250 per passenger (for a boat of six people) plus the M$15 entry to the biosphere reserve.

With either the bridge or beach option, your captain may or may not speak English.

⭐ Manglares de Dzinitún
ECOTOUR

(☎ cell 999-6454310; dzinitun@gmail.com; 90min tour per canoe & 2-person kayak from M$800) ✎ About 1km inland past the bridge (follow the signs to 'Paseos: canoas y kayak') you'll find an ecotour operator offering ecofriendly tours in a double kayak (where you do the work) or canoe (the guide paddles). These run through a rehabilitated mangrove tunnel and good birding spots, made better by the lack of engine noise and knowledgable guides; a couple have basic English.

To get here from the beach, turn right on the street after the second transmission tower. It's about 300m ahead.

🛏 Sleeping & Eating

Most of Celestún's hotels are on Calle 12, within a short walk of one another. Book ahead for a sea view.

Hotel Flamingo Playa   HOTEL $
(☑ 988-916-21-33; drivan2011@hotmail.com; Calle 12 No 67C; r M$700; 🅿 ❄ 🐾 🛜 ⛱) A family-run hotel on the beach with a pool overlooking the coast. Weathered sinks and showers could use some maintenance, and the rooms are humid, but the place is clean nonetheless. It's 800m north of Calle 11.

Hotel Manglares   HOTEL $$
(☑ 988-916-21-04; hotelmanglares@hotmail.com; Calle 12 No 63; d/cabañas M$1100/1600; 🅿 ❄ 🛜 ⛱) Although the modern architecture doesn't blend perfectly with the laid-back town, this is a nice midrange choice. The 24 rooms all have sea views and private balconies. The well-appointed *cabañas* face the beach and come with mini-kitchens, Jacuzzis and a small common area.

★ Casa de Celeste Vida   GUESTHOUSE $$$
(☑ 988-916-25-36; www.hotelcelestevida.com; Calle 12 No 49E; r/apt US$95/130; 🅿 ❄ 🛜 🐾) This friendly Canadian-owned place offers comfortably decked-out rooms with kitchenette (with toaster and coffee maker) and an apartment that sleeps four – all with water views and the beach at your doorstep. Kayak and bike use are free for guests. The hosts are happy to arrange flamingo tours and a nighttime crocodile excursion. It's 1.5km north of Calle 11.

A large communal kitchen means you can cook your own meals. Breakfast baskets cost US$10 for two people. It's open all year.

Dolphin   BREAKFAST $$
(Calle 12 No 104, cnr Calle 13; mains M$55-110; ⊙ 8:30am-1pm Wed-Sun; 🅿 🛜) It's as casual as it comes with plastic chairs and a 'picnic' feel (sandy floor), but it's an excellent breakfast spot at Hotel Gutiérrez. Full breakfasts include coffee, juice, freshly made bread, marmalade and some mighty fine egg dishes.

La Playita   SEAFOOD $$
(Calle 12 No 99; mains M$70-150; ⊙ 10am-6pm) Of all the sandy-floored, plastic table-and-chairs beachfront joints here, this one gets the thumbs-up from the locals. Fresh seafood and ceviche are its main draws.

La Palapa   SEAFOOD $$
(☑ 998-916-20-63; restaurant-lapalapa@hotmail. com; Calle 12 No 105; mains M$120-215; ⊙ 11am-7pm) A cut above the other seaside joints, La Palapa has an expansive dining area looking down to the sea, plus savory seafood dishes. The go-to dish is the coconut-coated shrimp served in a coconut shell.

❶ Information

There are no banks in town. You'll find an ATM inside Super Willy's, also located on the plaza. The best bet is to bring cash in case the ATMs run out of money (which occurs frequently).

❶ Getting There & Away

Calle 11 is the road into town (it comes due west from Mérida), ending at Calle 12, the road paralleling the beach.

Frequent buses head for Celestún (M$60, 2½ hours) from Mérida's Noreste bus terminal. The route terminates at Celestún's plaza, a block inland from Calle 12.

There are also *colectivos* on the plaza that will take you to downtown Mérida for around M$60.

By car from Mérida, the best route to Celestún is via the new road out of Umán.

Progreso
☑ 969 / POP 39,000

If Mérida's heat has you dying for a quick beach fix, or if you want to see the longest pier (6.5km) in Mexico, head to Progreso (aka Puerto Progreso). The front strip *(malecón)* can get packed with diners, drinkers and oversunned tourists, as can the beach (even though it's loooong). Nevertheless, Progreso maintains a relaxed beach-town vibe. As with other Gulf beaches, the water is murky, even on calm days. Winds can hit full force in the afternoon and evenings, especially from December to March when *los nortes* (northern winds) kick up.

Méridanos come in droves on weekends, especially during July and August when it can be difficult to find a room with a view and, sadly, you'll see more litter on the beach. Once or twice a week the streets flood with cruise-ship tourists, but the place can feel empty on off nights, which makes a refreshing change.

🏃 Activities

El Corchito
SWIMMING

(📞999-158-51-55; Hwy 27 s/n, cnr Calle 46; M$35; ⊙9am-4pm) Take a refreshing dip in one of three fresh-water swimming holes surrounded by mangroves at nature reserve El Corchito. Motorboats take visitors across a canal to the reserve. El Corchito is home to iguanas, boa constrictors, small crocs, raccoons and a band of coatis. The coons and coatis are skilled food thieves, something to consider if you bring lunch.

El Corchito sees a lot of visitors, especially on weekends, so get there early for a more peaceful swim.

'Tecnológico' buses departing from a bus station at Calles 82 and 29 will leave you a block and a half from El Corchito. If you're driving, take Calle 46 south to Hwy 27.

🛏 Sleeping & Eating

Hotel Yaxactún
HOTEL $$

(📞969-103-93-26; yaxactun@outlook.com; Calle 66 No 129, btwn Calles 25 & 27; r from M$650-750; ❄❋🅿🛜🏊) The Yaxactún has earned bragging rights as one of the most modern (plus very brown and cream) hotels in town. Street-facing rooms get good natural light and have balconies. The hotel also has a small on-site restaurant specializing in Yucatecan food, and there's a swimming pool with a kiddie corral. It's three blocks from the beach. There's little greenery and lots of concrete.

El Naranjo
YUCATECAN $

(Calle 27 s/n, btwn Calles 78 & 80; tacos/tortas M$10/18; ⊙6am-noon) One of the best options in the market for cochito (slow-cooked pork) – and it's squeaky clean.

Milk Bar
CAFE $$

(Malecón s/n, btwn 72 & 74; mains M$69-180; ⊙8am-midnight) The huge 'cow in a rowboat' indicates you've arrived at this laid-back Texan-run spot. Despite the name, it doesn't specialize in milk-based drinks, but is definitely the place to go for hefty sandwiches, burgers and salads. It's a popular hangout for expats who enjoy the eclectic decor and large servings. Decent breakfasts will cure the dog of hangovers.

Crabster
SEAFOOD $$$

(📞969-103-65-22; www.crabster.mx; M$135-320; ⊙8-11am & noon-8pm) At the current posh spot on the strip, with its blond-wood chairs, pink velvet trim and designer lighting, you could be in an international hotel, not smack on the beachfront. But this fancy spot pulls in the moneyed visitor for, you guessed it, seafood dishes (not to mention to be spotted). Another hook? Service is extremely professional.

ℹ Getting There & Away

Progreso is 33km north of Mérida along a fast four-lane highway that's basically a continuation of the Paseo de Montejo.

To get to Progreso from Mérida, go to the Progreso bus terminal (p314) or catch a colectivo one block east of the terminal on Calle 60.

Traveling to Mérida, frequent buses (M$20) depart from Progreso's bus terminal (Calle 29 No 151, btwn Calles 80 & 82).

Izamal

📞988 / POP 16,000

In ancient times Izamal was a center for the worship of the supreme Maya god, Itzamná, and the sun god, Kinich-Kakmó. A dozen temple pyramids were devoted to these or other gods. No doubt these bold expressions of Maya religiosity are why the Spanish colonists chose Izamal as the site for an enormous and impressive Franciscan monastery, which still stands at the heart of this town, about 70km east of Mérida.

The Izamal of today is a quiet provincial town, nicknamed La Ciudad Amarilla (the Yellow City) for the traditional golden-yellow buildings that spiral out from the center like a budding daisy. It's easily explored on foot, and horse-drawn carriages add to the city's charm.

⊙ Sights

★ Centro Cultural y Artesanal
MUSEUM

(www.centroculturalizamal.org.mx; Calle 31 No 201; M$25; ⊙10am-late) 🅿 Just across the square from the monastery, this cultural center and museum showcases popular art from around Mexico. Explanatory cards in English give an excellent summary. Its excellent shop sells fair-trade-certified crafts made by artisans from 12 indigenous communities. Any purchase you make is a direct source of income for rural indigenous families.

DZIBILCHALTÚN

Lying about 17km due north of central Mérida, **Dzibilchaltún** (Place of Inscribed Flat Stones; adult M$132, parking M$20; ⊘ site 8am-5pm, museum 9am-4pm Tue-Sun; P) was the longest continuously used Maya administrative and ceremonial city, serving the Maya from around 1500 BC until the European conquest in the 1540s. At the height of its greatness, Dzibilchaltún covered 15 sq km. Some 8400 structures were mapped by archaeologists in the 1960s; few of these have been excavated. Aside from the ruins, the site offers a lovely, swimmable cenote and a Maya museum.

In some ways it's unimpressive if you've already seen larger places, such as Chichén Itzá or Uxmal, but twice a year humble Dzibilchaltún shines. At sunrise on the equinoxes (approximately March 20 and September 22), the sun aligns directly with the main door of the **Templo de las Siete Muñecas** (Temple of the Seven Dolls), which got its name from seven grotesque dolls discovered here during excavations. As the sun rises, the temple doors glow, then 'light up' as the sun passes behind. It also casts a cool square beam on the crumbled wall behind. Many who have seen both feel the sunrise here is more spectacular than Chichén Itzá's famous snake, and is well worth getting up at the crack of dawn to witness.

Enter the site along a nature trail that terminates at the modern, air-conditioned **Museo del Pueblo Maya**, featuring artifacts from throughout the Maya regions of Mexico, including some superb colonial-era religious carvings and other pieces. Exhibits explaining both ancient and modern Maya daily life are labeled in Spanish and English. Beyond the museum, a path leads to the central plaza, where you'll find an open chapel that dates from early Spanish times (1590–1600).

Within the site, the **Cenote Xlacah** is more than 40m deep and a fine spot for a swim after exploring the ruins. In 1958 a National Geographic Society diving expedition recovered more than 30,000 Maya artifacts, many of ritual significance, from the cenote. The most interesting of these are now on display in the site's museum. South of the cenote is **Estructura 44** – at 130m it's one of the longest Maya structures in existence.

Chablekal-bound *colectivos* depart frequently from Calle 58 (between Calles 57 and 59) in Mérida. They'll drop you about 300m from the site's entrance.

Kinich-Kakmó   ARCHAEOLOGICAL SITE
(Calle 27 s/n, btwn Calles 26B & 28; ⊘ 8am-5pm) FREE Three of the town's original 12 Maya pyramids have been partially restored. The largest (and the third largest in Yucatán) is the 34m-high Kinich-Kakmó, three blocks north of the monastery. Legend has it that a deity in the form of a blazing macaw would swoop down from the heavens to collect offerings left here.

**Convento de San
Antonio de Padua**   MONASTERY
(Calle 31 s/n; museum M$5; ⊘ 6am-8pm, sound & light show 8pm Thu-Sat, museum 7am-8pm) When the Spaniards conquered Izamal, they destroyed the major Maya temple, the Ppapp-Hol-Chac pyramid, and in 1533 began to build from its stones one of the first monasteries in the western hemisphere. Work on Convento de San Antonio de Padua was finished in 1561. Under the monastery's arcades, look for building stones with an unmistakable maze-like design; these were clearly taken from the earlier Maya temple. There's a **sound-and-light show** here three nights a week.

🍴 Sleeping & Eating

Several *loncherías* occupy spaces in the market on the monastery's southwest side.

Hotel Casa Colonial   HOTEL $
(☏ 988-954-02-72; hotelcasacolonializamal@ hotmail.com; Calle 31 No 331, cnr Calle 36; s/d M$500/600; P ✳ ⬡ ✺) A clean and spacious option compared to some of the other more rundown and cramped budget hotels in town. All rooms are even decked out with dining tables, microwaves and minifridges.

**★ Hacienda Hotel
Santo Domingo**   HOTEL $$
(☏ cell 988-9676136; www.izamalhotel.com; Calle 18, btwn Calles 33 & 35; r M$900-1590, ste from M$1690; P ⬡ ⬡ ✺) Set on a 13-hectare property with lush gardens, walking trails, a pool

BUSES FROM IZAMAL

DESTINATION	FARE (M$)	DURATION (HR)	FREQUENCY (DAILY)
Cancún	182	5	frequent
Mérida	40	1½	frequent; Terminal de Autobuses Centro
Tizimín	85	2½	3; Oriente
Valladolid	66	2	frequent; Terminal de Autobuses Centro

and *palapa* restaurant, this serene, upscale and extremely well-run spot (the owner is always on site) will win over nature lovers and those who enjoy a touch of style. All rooms are very attractive, some with natural stone sinks and indoor-outdoor showers. The pool and small bar are wonderful.

On top of this, meals can be preordered and breakfast – enjoyed around the pool – is à la carte. Those missing their pet pooches will be sated: it has a few dogs. It's five blocks from the monastery.

★ **Kinich** MEXICAN **$$**
(www.restaurantekinich.com; Calle 27 No 299, btwn Calles 28 & 30; mains M$75-230; ☺10am-8pm; ☏) Sure, it's touristy, but this is fresh, handmade Yucatecan cuisine at its finest. The *papadzules kinich* – rolled tortillas stuffed with diced egg and topped with pumpkin-seed sauce and smoky sausage – is a delightful house specialty. Kinich is also famous for its *dzic de venado*, a shredded venison dish (M$230).

The setting is a massive *palapa* and the servers are dressed in traditional *huipiles* (long, sleeveless tunics).

ℹ Getting There & Around

Frequent buses run out of Izamal's **Oriente bus terminal** (☏ cell 988-9540107; Calle 32 s/n, cnr Calle 31A) and the nearby **Terminal de Autobuses Centro** (☏ 988-967-66-15; www.autobusescentro.com; Calle 33 No 302, cnr Calle 30).

Taxis around town charge M$25; a base is at Calles 32 and 31A.

Horse-carriage rides cost M$250 per hour.

Chichén Itzá

☏ 985 / POP 5500 (PISTÉ)

The most famous and best restored of the Yucatán Maya sites, **Chichén Itzá** (Mouth of the Well of the Itzáes; http://chichenitza.inah.gob.mx; off Hwy 180, Pisté; adult/child under 13yr M$242/70, guided tours Spanish/English

M$800/900; ☺8am-4pm; P), while tremendously overcrowded – every gawker and his or her grandmother is trying to check off the new seven wonders of the world – will still impress even the most jaded visitor. Yes, it's goose-bump material. Many mysteries of the Maya astronomical calendar are made clear when one understands the design of the 'time temples' here. Other than a few minor passageways, climbing on the structures is not allowed.

The heat, humidity and crowds in Chichén Itzá can be fierce, as can competition between the craft sellers who line the paths (not to mention the irritating habit of hordes clapping to illustrate the pyramid acoustics). To avoid this, try to explore the site either early in the morning or late in the afternoon.

A nightly sound and light show gets some people fired up; others less so.

History

Most archaeologists agree that the first major settlement at Chichén Itzá, during the late Classic period, was pure Maya. In about the 9th century, the city was largely abandoned for reasons unknown.

It was resettled around the late 10th century, and shortly thereafter it is believed to have been invaded by the Toltecs, who had migrated from their central highlands capital of Tula, north of Mexico City. The bellicose Toltec culture was fused with that of the Maya, incorporating the cult of Quetzalcóatl (Kukulcán, in Maya). You will see images of both Chac-Mool, the Maya rain god, and Quetzalcóatl, the plumed serpent, throughout the city.

The substantial fusion of highland central Mexican and Puuc architectural styles makes Chichén unique among the Yucatán Peninsula's ruins. The fabulous El Castillo and the Plataforma de Venus are outstanding architectural works built during the height of Toltec cultural input.

The sanguinary Toltecs contributed more than their architectural skills to the Maya: they elevated human sacrifice to a near obsession, and there are numerous carvings of the bloody ritual in Chichén demonstrating this.

After a Maya leader moved his political capital to Mayapán while keeping Chichén as his religious capital, Chichén Itzá fell into decline. Why it was subsequently abandoned in the 14th century is a mystery, but the once-great city remained the site of Maya pilgrimages for many years.

⊙ Sights

El Castillo ARCHAEOLOGICAL SITE
Upon entering Chichén Itzá, El Castillo (aka the Pyramid of Kukulcán) rises before you in all its grandeur. The first temple here was pre-Toltec, built around AD 800, but the present 25m-high structure, built over the old one, has the plumed serpent sculpted along the stairways and Toltec warriors represented in the doorway carvings at the top of the temple. You won't see the carvings, however, as ascending the pyramid was prohibited after a woman fell to her death in 2006.

The structure is actually a massive Maya calendar formed in stone. Each of El Castillo's nine levels is divided in two by a staircase, making 18 separate terraces that commemorate the 18 20-day months of the Maya Vague Year. The four stairways have 91 steps each; add the top platform and the total is 365, the number of days in the year. On each facade of the pyramid are 52 flat panels, which are reminders of the 52 years in the Maya calendar round.

To top it off, during the spring and autumn equinoxes, light and shadow form a series of triangles on the side of the north staircase that mimic the creep of a serpent (note the carved serpent's heads flanking the bottom of the staircase).

The older pyramid inside El Castillo has a red jaguar throne with inlaid eyes and spots of jade; also lying behind the screen is a chac-mool (Maya sacrificial stone sculpture). The entrance to **El Túnel**, the passage up to the throne, is at the base of El Castillo's north side. You can't go in, though.

Researchers in 2015 learned that the pyramid most likely sits atop a 20m-deep cenote, which puts the structure at greater risk of collapsing.

Gran Juego de Pelota ARCHAEOLOGICAL SITE
The great ball court, the largest and most impressive in Mexico, is only one of the city's eight courts, indicative of the importance the games held here. The court, to the left of the visitor center, is flanked by temples at either end and is bounded by towering parallel walls with stone rings cemented up high. Along the walls of the ball court are stone reliefs, including scenes of decapitations of players.

There is evidence that the ball game may have changed over the years. Some carvings show players with padding on their elbows and knees, and it is thought that they played a soccer-like game with a hard rubber ball, with the use of hands forbidden. Other carvings show players wielding bats; it appears that if a player hit the ball through one of the stone hoops, his team was declared the winner. It may be that during the Toltec period, the losing captain, and perhaps his teammates as well, was sacrificed.

The court exhibits some interesting acoustics: a conversation at one end can be heard 135m away at the other, and a clap produces multiple loud echoes.

Templo del Barbado ARCHAEOLOGICAL SITE
The structure at the ball court's north end, called the Temple of the Bearded Man after a carving inside of it, has finely sculpted pillars and reliefs of flowers, birds and trees.

Plataforma de los Cráneos ARCHAEOLOGICAL SITE
The Platform of Skulls (Tzompantli in Náhuatl, a Maya dialect) is between the **Templo de los Jaguares y Escudos** and El Castillo. You can't mistake it, because the T-shaped platform is festooned with carved skulls and eagles tearing open the chests of men to eat their hearts. In ancient days this platform was used to display the heads of sacrificial victims.

Plataforma de las Águilas y los Jaguares ARCHAEOLOGICAL SITE
Adjacent to the Platform of Skulls, the carvings on the Platform of the Eagles and Jaguars depict those animals gruesomely grabbing human hearts in their claws. It is thought that this platform was part of a temple dedicated to the military legions responsible for capturing sacrificial victims.

Chichén Itzá

A DAY TOUR

It doesn't take long to realize why the Maya site of Chichén Itzá is one of Mexico's most popular tourist draws. Approaching the grounds from the main entrance, the striking castle pyramid **1 El Castillo** jumps right out at you – and the wow factor never lets up.

It's easy to tackle Chichén Itzá in one day. Within a stone's throw of the castle, you'll find the Maya world's largest **2 ball court** alongside eerie carvings of skulls and heart-devouring eagles at the Temple of Jaguars and the Platform of Skulls. On the other (eastern) side are the highly adorned **3 Group of a Thousand Columns** and the **4 Temple of Warriors**. A short walk north of the castle leads to the gaping **5 Sacred Cenote**, an important pilgrimage site. On the other side of El Castillo, you'll find giant stone serpents watching over the High Priest's Grave, aka El Osario. Further south, marvel at the spiral-domed **6 Observatory**, the imposing Nunnery and Akab-Dzib, one of the oldest ruins.

Roaming the 47-hectare site, it's fun to consider that at its height Chichén Itzá was home to an estimated 90,000 inhabitants and spanned approximately 30 sq km. So essentially you're looking at just a small part of a once-great city.

El Caracol
Observatory
Today they'd probably just use a website, but back in the day priests would announce the latest rituals and celebrations from the dome of the circular observatory.

Edificio de las Monjas (Nunnery)

6

Akab-Dzib

Entrance

Grupo de las Mil Columnas
Group of a Thousand Columns
Not unlike a hall of fame exhibit, the pillars surrounding the temple reveal carvings of gods, dignitaries and celebrated warriors.

TOP TIPS

➤ Arrive at 8am and you'll have a good three hours or so before the tour-bus madness begins. Early birds escape the merchants, too.

➤ Remember that Chichén Itzá is the name of the site; the actual town where it's located is called Pisté.

El Castillo
The Castle
Even this mighty pyramid can't bear the stress of a million visitors ascending its stairs each year. No climbing allowed, but the ground-level view doesn't disappoint.

Gran Juego de Pelota
Great Ball Court
How is it possible to hear someone talk from one end of this long, open-air court to the other? To this day, the acoustics remain a mystery.

Entrance

Parking Lot

Visitors Center

Tumba del Gran Sacerdote (High Priest's Grave)

Templo de los Jaguares (Temple of Jaguars)

Plataforma de los Cráneos (Platform of Skulls)

① ② ③ ④ ⑤

Cenote Sagrado
Sacred Cenote
Diving expeditions have turned up hundreds of valuable artifacts dredged from the cenote (limestone sinkhole), not to mention human bones of sacrificial victims who were forced to jump into the eternal underworld.

Templo de los Guerreros
Temple of Warriors
The Maya associated warriors with eagles and jaguars, as depicted in the temple's friezes. The revered jaguar, in particular, was a symbol of strength and agility.

Chichén Itzá

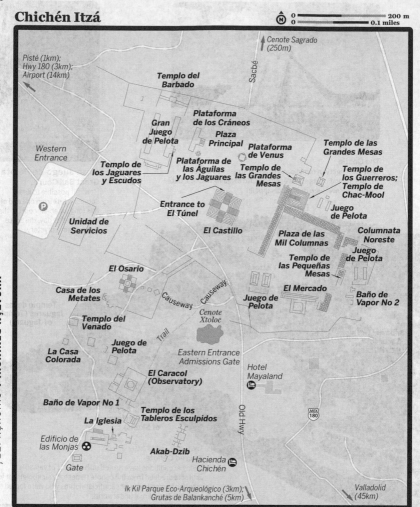

Cenote Sagrado
ARCHAEOLOGICAL SITE

From the Platform of Skulls (p327), a 400m rough stone *sacbé* (path) runs north (a five-minute walk) to the huge sunken well that gave this city its name. The Sacred Cenote is an awesome natural well, some 60m in diameter and 35m deep. The walls between the summit and the water's surface are ensnared in tangled vines and other vegetation. There are ruins of a small steam bath next to the cenote.

Grupo de las Mil Columnas
ARCHAEOLOGICAL SITE

This group east of El Castillo (p327) pyramid takes its name – which means 'Group of the Thousand Columns' – from the forest of pillars stretching south and east. The star attraction here is the **Templo de los Guerreros** (Temple of the Warriors), adorned with stucco and stone-carved animal deities. At the top of its steps is a classic reclining chac-mool figure, but ascending to it is no longer allowed.

Many of the columns in front of the temple are carved with figures of warriors. Archaeologists working in 1926 discovered a Temple of Chac-Mool lying beneath the Temple of the Warriors.

You can walk through the columns on its south side to reach the **Columnata Noreste**, notable for the 'big-nosed god' masks on its facade. Some have been reassembled on the ground around the statue. Just to the south are the remains of the **Baño de Vapor** (Steam Bath or Sweat House) with an underground oven and drains for the water. The sweat houses (there are two on site) were regularly used for ritual purification.

El Osario
ARCHAEOLOGICAL SITE

The Ossuary, otherwise known as the Bonehouse or the Tumba del Gran Sacerdote (High Priest's Grave), is a ruined pyramid to the southwest of El Castillo. As with most of the buildings in this southern section, the architecture is more Puuc than Toltec. It's notable for the beautiful serpent heads at the base of its staircases.

A square shaft at the top of the structure leads into a cave below that was used as a burial chamber; seven tombs with human remains were discovered inside.

El Caracol
ARCHAEOLOGICAL SITE

Called El Caracol (the Snail) by the Spaniards for its interior spiral staircase, this observatory, to the south of the Ossuary, is one of the most fascinating and important of all Chichén Itzá's buildings (but, alas, you can't enter it). Its circular design resembles some central highlands structures, although, surprisingly, not those of Toltec Tula.

In a fusion of architectural styles and religious imagery, there are Maya Chaac rain-god masks over four external doors facing the cardinal points. The windows in the observatory's dome are aligned with the appearance of certain stars at specific dates. From the dome the priests decreed the times for rituals, celebrations, corn-planting and harvests.

Edificio de las Monjas
ARCHAEOLOGICAL SITE

Thought by archaeologists to have been a palace for Maya royalty, the so-called Edificio de las Monjas (Nunnery), with its myriad rooms, resembled a European convent to the conquistadors, hence their name for the building. The building's dimensions are imposing: its base is 60m long, 30m wide and 20m high.

The construction is Maya rather than Toltec, although a Toltec sacrificial stone stands in front. A smaller adjoining building to the east, known as **La Iglesia** (the Church), is covered almost entirely with carvings.

Akab-Dzib
ARCHAEOLOGICAL SITE

East of the Nunnery, the Puuc-style Akab-Dzib is thought by some archaeologists to be the most ancient structure excavated here. The central chambers date from the 2nd century. The name means 'Obscure Writing' in Maya and refers to the south-side annex door, whose lintel depicts a priest with a vase etched with hieroglyphics that have yet to be successfully translated.

🛏 Sleeping & Eating

Most of Chichén Itzá's lodgings, restaurants and services are arranged along 1km of highway in the town of Pisté to the western (Mérida) side of the ruins. It's about 1.5km from the ruins' main (west) entrance to the nearest hotel in Pisté, and 2.5km from the ruins to Pisté's town plaza. Don't hesitate to haggle for a bed in low season (May through June and August to early December).

The highway (Calle 15) through Pisté is lined with dozens of eateries, large and small. The cheapest are clustered in a roadside market, known as Los Portales, on the west end of town.

Pirámide Inn
HOTEL $

(☎985-851-01-15; www.piramideinn.com; Calle 15 No 30; campsite M$100, r without/with air-con M$500/600; 🅿 ❂ ❄ 🛜 🏊 ❂) Campers can pitch a tent, enjoy the inn's pool and use tepid showers in this dated spot. The spacious rooms have decent bathrooms and two spring-me-to-the-moon double beds.

Located on the main drag in Pisté, this place has the closest budget rooms to Chichén Itzá (p326), though it's still a hike of about 1.5km. Animals are welcome.

Hotel Chichén Itzá
HOTEL $$

(☎985-851-00-22, USA 800-235-4079; www.mayaland.com; Calle 15 No 45; r/ste M$1310/1750; 🅿 ❂ ❄ 🛜 ❂) On the west side of Pisté, this hotel has 42 pleasant rooms with tiled floors and old-style brick-tiled ceilings. Rooms in the upper range face the pool and the landscaped grounds, and all have firm beds and minibars. Parents may bring two kids under 12 years old for free. The resort is one of the Mayaland chain, which is prominent in the district.

★ Hacienda Chichén
RESORT $$$

(☎ 999-920-84-07, USA 877-631-00-45; www.haciendachichen.com; Zona Hotelera Km 120; d from US$224; P☯❋☎☂) About 300m from the Chichén Itzá (p326) entrance, this resort sits on the well-manicured grounds of a 16th-century hacienda with an elegant main house and towering ceiba trees. The archaeologists who excavated Chichén during the 1920s lived here in bungalows, which have been refurbished and augmented with new ones. Monthly activities on offer include Maya cooking classes and bird-watching.

One small downer is that the restaurant's prices are exorbitant.

Hotel Mayaland
HOTEL $$$

(☎ 998-887-24-95, USA 877-240-5864; www.mayaland.com; Zona Hotelera Km 120; d/ste from M$2100/3500; P☯❋☎☂) Every world dignitary has stayed at the resort-style Mayaland, it seems. This smart spot in a lovely garden setting is less than 100m from Chichén Itzá and has a 'private' entrance. The rooms, garden bungalows and pools are very (very) nice, but when you're on site at the observatory, El Caracol, you'll see the hotel cuts a swath through the jungle.

As well as restaurants and all the services, it also offers cultural programs, including a popular 'Be Maya' activity where you cook Maya cuisine plus visit the resort's own replica 'observatory,' while learning about the roles of Maya people. The Mayaland Lodge is the second option nearby, and features smart bungalows in a far more private setting.

Cocina Económica Fabiola
MEXICAN $

(Calle 15 s/n; mains M$45-70; ☺7am-10pm) For a good, honest, cheap meal hit this humble little place at the end of the strip of eateries opposite the church. For 25 years it's been churning out *sopa de lima* (lime soup) and *pollo yucateco* (Yucatecan chicken).

Las Mestizas
MEXICAN $$

(☎ 985-851-0069; Calle 15 s/n; mains M$70-110; ☺9am-10pm; ❋☎) *The* place to go in town if you're craving decent Yucatecan fare (photos of each dish help you decide). There's indoor and outdoor seating – depending on the time of day, an outdoor table may mean you'll be getting tour-bus fumes (and lines of people) to go along with that *poc chuk* (pork marinated in orange juice and garlic and grilled).

ⓘ Getting There & Away

Oriente has ticket offices near the east and west sides of Pisté, and 2nd-class buses passing through town stop almost anywhere along the way.

Many 1st-class buses arrive and depart from the ruins only. These also head to Mérida and Valladolid, as well as to coastal locations in Quintana Roo: Playa del Carmen, Tulum and Cancún. If you plan to see the ruins and then head directly to another city by 1st-class bus, buy your bus ticket at the visitor center before hitting the ruins, to secure your seat.

Colectivos (shared vans) to Valladolid (M$35, 40 minutes) enter the car park.

ⓘ Getting Around

Buses to Pisté generally stop at the plaza; you can make the hot walk to and from the ruins in 20 to 30 minutes. First-class buses stop at the ruins; for others, check with the driver. The 2nd-class buses will also leave you near Cenote Ik Kil and the Grutas de Balankanché.

There is a taxi stand near the west end of town; the prices are around M$40 to M$50 to the ruins, M$80 to Cenote Ik Kil and M$150 to Grutas de Balankanché.

BUSES FROM CHICHÉN ITZÁ

DESTINATION	COST (M$)	DURATION (HR)	FREQUENCY (DAILY)
Cancún	151-298	3-4½	9
Cobá	69	2	7:30am
Mérida	91-168	1¾-2½	frequent
Playa del Carmen	155-314	3½-4	3
Tulum	104-220	2½-3	3
Valladolid	31-100	1	frequent

Valladolid

📞 985 / POP 52,000

Also known as the Sultaness of the East, Yucatán's third-largest city is known for its quiet streets and sun-splashed pastel walls. It's worth staying here for a few days or longer, as the provincial town makes a great hub for visits to Río Lagartos, Chichén Itzá, Ek' Balam and a number of nearby cenotes. The city resides at that magic point where there's plenty to do, yet it still feels small, manageable and affordable.

History

Valladolid has seen its fair share of turmoil and revolt. The city was first founded in 1543 near the Chouac-Ha lagoon some 50km from the coast, but it was too hot and there were way too many mosquitoes for Francisco de Montejo, nephew of Montejo the Elder, and his merry band of conquerors. So they upped and moved the city to the Maya ceremonial center of Zací (sah-*see*), where they faced heavy resistance from the local Maya. Eventually the Elder's son – Montejo the Younger – took the town. The Spanish conquerors, in typical fashion, ripped down the town and laid out a new city following the classic colonial plan.

During much of the colonial era, Valladolid's physical isolation from Mérida kept it relatively autonomous from royal rule, and the Maya of the area suffered brutal exploitation, which continued after Mexican independence. Barred from entering many areas of the city, the Maya made Valladolid one of their first points of attack following the 1847 outbreak of the Caste War in Tepich. After a two-month siege, the city's occupiers were finally overcome. Many fled to the safety of Mérida; the rest were slaughtered.

Today Valladolid is a prosperous seat of agricultural commerce, augmented by some light industry and a growing tourist trade.

💿 Sights

★**Casa de los Venados**   MUSEUM
(📞985-856-22-89; www.casadelosvenados.com; Calle 40 No 204, btwn Calles 41 & 43; admission by donation; ⊙ tours 10am or by appointment) Featuring over 3000 pieces of museum-quality Mexican folk art, this private collection is interesting in that objects are presented in a house, in the context that they were originally designed for, instead of being roped off in glass cases. The tour (in English or Spanish) brushes on the origins of some of the more important pieces and the story of the award-winning restored colonial mansion that houses them.

Catedral de San Servasio   CATHEDRAL
(San Gervasio) The original edifice was built from the main pyramid in 1545, then it was demolished and rebuilt in the early 1700s. This is the only church with a north-facing entrance in the Yucatán (all the others are east-facing), a way of castigating recalcitrant locals.

🏃 Activities

★**Hacienda San Lorenzo Oxman**   SWIMMING
(off Calle 54; cenote M$70, cenote & pool M$100; ⊙9am-6pm) Once a *henequén* plantation and a refuge for War of the Castes insurgents in the mid-19th century, today the hacienda's main draw is a gorgeous cenote that's far less crowded than other sinkholes in and around Valladolid, especially if you visit Monday through Thursday. If you buy the entry to both you have a M$60 debit to use at the cafe.

To get there by bike or car, take Calle 41A (Calzada de los Frailes) past the Templo de San Bernardino along Calle 54A, turn right on Avenida de los Frailes, then hang a left on Calle 54 and head about 3km southwest. A taxi to the hacienda costs M$80 to M$100.

Cenote X'Kekén y Samulá   SWIMMING
(Cenote Dzitnup & Samulá; 1/2 cenotes M$60/90; ⊙8:30am-5:20pm) One of two cenotes at Dzitnup (also known as X'Kekén Jungle Park), X'Kekén is popular with tour groups. A massive limestone formation with stalactites hangs from its ceiling. The pool is artificially lit and very swimmable. Here you can also take a dip in cenote Samulá, a lovely cavern pool with *álamo* roots stretching down many meters.

Pedaling a rented bicycle to the cenotes takes about 20 minutes. By bike from Pisté's center take Calle 41A (Calzada de los Frailes), a street lined with colonial architecture. Go one block past the **Templo de San Bernardino** (Convento de Sisal; cnr Calles 49 & 51; Mon-Sat M$30, Sun free; ⊙9am-7pm) along Calle 54A, then make a right on Calle 49, which becomes Avenida de los Frailes and hits the old highway. Follow the *ciclopista* (bike path) paralleling the road to Mérida for about 3km, then turn left at

Valladolid

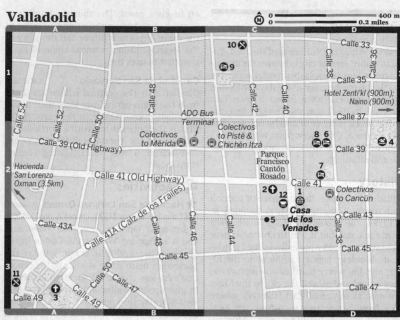

N
0 — 400 m
0 — 0.2 miles

Valladolid

◎ Top Sights
1 Casa de los Venados C2

◎ Sights
2 Catedral de San Servasio C2
3 Templo de San Bernardino A3

✦ Activities, Courses & Tours
4 Cenote Zací D2
5 MexiGo Tours C3

🛏 Sleeping
6 Casa Marlene D2
7 Casa San Roque D2
8 Casa Tía Micha D2
9 Hostel La Candelaria C1

✖ Eating
10 La Palapita de los Tamales C1
11 Yerba Buena del Sisal A3

◎ Drinking & Nightlife
12 Coffee Bike Station C2

the sign for Dzitnup and continue for just under 2km. Shared *colectivos* also depart for Dzitnup.

Cenote Zací   SWIMMING
(☑ 985-856-0818; Calle 36 s/n, btwn Calles 37 & 39; adult M$30, child 3-11yr M$15; ◎ cenote 8:30am-5:30pm, restaurant 9am-6pm) One of few cenotes in a downtown location, Cenote Zací, an open-air swimming hole, is a handy place to cool off. While it's pleasant enough, don't expect crystalline waters. You might see catfish or, overhead, a colony of bats. The park also holds small souvenir stands plus a pleasant restaurant under a large *palapa* (mains M$85 to M$140).

👉 Tours

★ Yucatán Jay
Expeditions & Tours   BIRDWATCHING, CULTURAL
(☑ cell 985-1118000, cell 985-1034918; www.yucatanjay.com; ◎ 8am-8pm) This cooperative, run by five informative and enthusiastic individuals from the Xocén community, 14km south of Valladolid, offers a fabulous array of tours, from bird-watching to tours based on Maya culture and gastronomy. They can take you to cenotes and other locations, providing excellent insights into their culture.

Birders are usually delighted at the spotting successes (plus the guides have access to areas of flora and wildlife where you'd normally not be able to enter). They can arrange breakfasts in the community as well.

🛏 Sleeping & Eating

⭐ Hostel La Candelaria   HOSTEL $

(☑985-856-22-67; www.hostelvalladolidyucatan.com; Calle 35 No 201F; dm/r incl breakfast from M$230/500; ❄@🛜) A friendly place right on a quiet little square, this hostel can get a little cramped and hot (but some dorms have air-con). The kitchen, a gorgeous elongated garden complete with hammocks, a gals-only dorm and plenty of hangout space, make it one of the best hostels in town. The hostel also rents out bikes for M$20 per hour.

One of the most organized hostels around, its has folders with lists of activities and ideas to keep you there for days, not to mention bike rental, laundry services, dinner options and more. Lovely owner Tania is a woman 'in the know'!

Casa San Roque   B&B $$

(☑985-856-26-42; www.casasanroquevalladolid.com; Calle 41 No 193B; r M$1582; 🅿❄✻🛜🌬) With just six colonial rooms on offer you'll get more privacy and personalized attention here than at some of the larger hotels on the main plaza. The full breakfast and a pool with dual fountains in the rear garden are the clinchers.

Hotel Zenti'k   BOUTIQUE HOTEL $$$

(☑985-104-9171; www.zentikhotel.com; Calle 30 No 192C, btwn 27 & 29; cabañas M$2400; 🅿✻🛜🌬) It bills itself as a boutique hotel and indeed the multilingual staff and excellent service back this up. It is, in fact, more like a miniresort, with a series of spacious cabañas (if set ever-so-too slightly together) within intimate surrounds. A gorgeous pool, spa, underground swimming cave and fabulous restaurant make this a clincher.

You'll need your own transportation to get here as it's just beyond walkable from the center for some, especially at night. Prices are significantly lower outside high season and that's when you get real value for money. Several walls are covered in impressive murals by contemporary artists.

Casa Tía Micha   BOUTIQUE HOTEL $$$

(☑985-856-04-99; www.casatiamicha.com; Calle 39 No 197; r incl breakfast M$1700-2100; 🅿❄✻🛜🌬) The corridor and rear garden are beautifully lit at night in this family-run boutique hotel just off the plaza. Some of the tastefully adorned colonial-style rooms have king-sized beds, and the upstairs suite comes with a Jacuzzi. If the Tía is booked, on the same block you'll find sister property **Casa Marlene** (r incl breakfast M$1700-2100; 🅿❄🛜🌬).

⭐ Yerba Buena del Sisal   MEXICAN $

(☑985-856-14-06; www.yerbabuenadelsisal.com.mx; Calle 54A No 217; mains M$80-120; ⏱8am-10pm Tue-Sun; 🛜🍴) Wonderfully healthy and delicious dishes are served in a peaceful garden. Tortilla chips and three delectable salsas come to the table while you look over the menu, which offers many great vegetarian and mostly organic dishes, such as the delightful *tacos maculum* (with handmade corn tortillas, beans, cheese and aromatic Mexican pepper leaf).

At the time of research, they were about to move three houses away but were hoping to re-create the same atmosphere – we believe they will be able to.

⭐ La Palapita de los Tamales   MEXICAN $

(Calle 42 s/n, cnr Calle 33; tamales M$40; ⏱8-10pm Mon-Sat; 🍴) You've probably never had *tamales* like these before. The menu changes daily here. At last visit, which may or may not have been a Friday, the *tamal* of the day had a pork, egg and bean filling and was lightly fried in *manteca* (lard) to give the exterior a hardened texture. Let's just say it was quite a snack. Great juices, breakfasts and vegan options too.

⭐ Naino   INTERNATIONAL $$

(☑985-104-90-71; www.facebook.com/zentikproject; Calle 30, btwn Calles 27 & 29; mains M$80-150; ⏱7am-noon & 3-10:30pm; 🅿🛜) Located on the outskirts of town, on the premises of the resort Zenti'k, this pleasant open-air restaurant is a wonderful place for breakfast, lunch or dinner. It serves good international food; well-to-do locals love coming here at any time of day.

🍷 Drinking & Nightlife

⭐ Coffee Bike Station   CAFE

(☑985-122-24-39; www.facebook.com/coffeebikestation2016; Calle 40 No 203, btwn Calles 41 & 43; snacks from M$40; ⏱8:30am-1:30pm & 6-10pm Mon-Fri) A welcome addition to Valladolid is this funky little coffee and bike-centric cafe. Yes, it really does boast a proper espresso machine and, yes, the owner (Enrique) really does know how to make great coffee. Beware unconventional opening hours, however. Get in while you can as

Enrique also takes bike tours. You can rent bikes from here (M$160 per day).

❶ Getting There & Away

BUS

Valladolid's main bus terminal is the convenient **ADO bus terminal** (www.ado.com.mx; cnr Calles 39 & 46). The main 1st-class services are by ADO, ADO GL and OCC; Oriente and Mayab run 2nd-class buses. Buses to Chichén Itzá/ Pisté stop near the ruins during opening hours (but double-check).

COLECTIVO

Colectivos depart as soon as their seats are filled (or you can elect to pay the full fare). Most operate from 7am or 8am to about 7pm.

Direct services run to **Mérida** (Calle 39; near the ADO bus terminal; M$180, two hours) and **Cancún** (Calle 41, cnr Calle 38; M$200, two hours); confirm they're nonstop. *Colectivos* for **Pisté and Chichén Itzá** (Calle 39; M$35, one hour) leave north of the ADO bus terminal. For **Ek' Balam** (Calle 44 btwn Calles 35 & 37; M$50) take a 'Santa Rita' *colectivo* from Calle 44 between Calles 35 and 37.

It's possible to get to many of the cenotes. *Colectivos* depart from different points around the center; ask the locals. Note that these tend to leave in the mornings only.

❶ Getting Around

The old highway passes through the town center, though most signs urge motorists toward the toll road north of town. To follow the old highway eastbound, take Calle 41; westbound, take Calle 39.

Bicycles are a great way to see the town and get out to the cenotes. You can rent them at Hostel La Candelaria (p335) or **MexiGo Tours** (☏985-856-07-77; www.mexigotours.com; Calle 43 No 204C, btwn Calles 40 & 42; ☺4-7pm) for around M$20 per hour.

Ek' Balam

The tiny village of Ek' Balam is worth a visit to see what a traditional Maya village looks like. There's not a lot here, except a handful of artisan stands along the main plaza, which also serves as the town's soccer field, and a decent accommodation option.

◉ Sights

Ek' Balam ARCHAEOLOGICAL SITE
(adult M$205, guide M$600; ☺8am-4pm) The fascinating ruined city of Ek' Balam reached its peak in the 8th century, before being suddenly abandoned. Vegetation still covers much of the archaeological site, but it's well organized and has a lovely, lush setting. Interesting features include a ziggurat-like structure near the entrance, as well as a fine arch and a ball court. Most impressive, though, is the gargantuan **Acrópolis**, whose well-restored base is 160m long and holds a 'gallery' – actually a series of separate chambers.

Built atop the base of the Acrópolis is Ek' Balam's massive **main pyramid**, reaching a height of 32m and sporting a gaping jaguar mouth. Below the mouth are stucco skulls, while above and to the right sits an amazingly expressive figure. On the right side stand unusual winged human figures (some call them Maya angels, although a much more likely explanation is that they are shaman or medicine men).

The turnoff for the archaeological site is 17km north of Valladolid, and the ruins are another 6km east from the turnoff.

From the Ek' Balam entrance you can visit the **X'Canché Cenote** (☏cell 985-1009915; www. ekbalam.com.mx/cenote-xcanche; M$50; ☺8am-5pm), believed to have been a ceremonial site.

BUSES FROM VALLADOLID

DESTINATION	FARE (M$)	DURATION (HR)	FREQUENCY (DAILY)
Cancún	117-261	2½-3½	frequent
Chichén Itzá/Pisté	31-28	¾	frequent
Chiquilá (for Isla Holbox)	115-170	4	1
Cobá	49	1	frequent
Izamal	66	2½	12:50pm
Mérida	117-204	2-3½	frequent
Playa del Carmen	132-216	2½-3	frequent
Tizimín	30	1	frequent
Tulum	92-126	1½-2	frequent

🛏 Sleeping

★ Genesis Eco-Oasis   GUESTHOUSE $$
(☑ cell 985-1010277; www.genesisretreat.com; Ek' Balam pueblo; d US$65-79; 🕿🕿) 🢆 This retreat offers B&B intimacy in a quiet, laid-back ecofriendly setting. Mostly it's environmentally friendly: gray water is used for landscaping, the rooms' architecture (pitched, thatched roofs) encourages passive cooling, and there's a dehydrating toilet or two. There's a chilling swimming pool and a temascal (pre-Hispanic steam bath) on site – and it offers delicious veggie meals made from scratch.

❶ Getting There & Away

Colectivos (M$50) to Ek' Balam depart Valladolid from Calle 44, between Calles 35 and 37.

Río Lagartos

☑ 986 / POP 3000

On the windy northern shore of the peninsula, sleepy Río Lagartos (Alligator River) is a fishing village that also boasts the densest concentration of flamingos in Mexico, supposedly two or three flamingos per Mexican, if one believes the provided math. Lying within the **Reserva de la Biosfera Ría Lagartos**, this mangrove-lined estuary shelters bird species, including snowy egrets, red egrets, tiger herons and snowy white ibis, as well as the crocodiles that gave the town its name. It's a beautiful area. At the right time of year you can see numerous species of birds without even getting out of your vehicle.

Most residents aren't sure of the town's street names, and signs are few. The road into town is the north–south Calle 10, which ends at the waterfront *malecón*.

There are no banks or ATMs in town and many places do not accept plastic, so bring plenty of cash.

ᗑ Tours

★ Río Lagartos Adventures   BOATING
(☑ cell 986-1008390; www.riolagartosadventures.com; Calle 19 No 134; per boat 2hr from US$110, fly-fishing per boat US$195) This outfit run by local expert Diego Núñez Martinez does various water and land expeditions, including flamingo- and crocodile-watching, snorkeling to Isla Cerritos, fly-fishing and excursions designed for photography. Diego is a licensed, fluent, English-speaking guide with formal training as a naturalist. He's well up to date on the area's fauna and flora, which includes some 400 bird species.

He organizes the tours out of **Ría Maya Restaurante** (www.riolagartosadventures.com; Calle 19 No 134, cnr Calle 14; mains M$150-300, lobster M$250-500; ☉9am-9pm) and trains local guides.

Flamingo Tours   BIRDWATCHING
The brilliant orange-red flamingos can turn the horizon fiery when they take wing. Depending on your luck, you'll see either hundreds or thousands of them. The best months for viewing them are June to August. The four primary haunts, in increasing distance from town, are Punta Garza, Yoluk, Necopal and Nahochín (all flamingo feeding spots are named for nearby mangrove patches).

🛏 Sleeping & Eating

Restaurant y Posada Macumba   GUESTHOUSE $
(☑ 986-862-00-92; www.restaurantmacumba.com; ☉d M$650-850, apt M$900-1200) One of the village's best choices to stay, the waterfront Macumba has six smallish and very comfortable rooms, decked out in funky Caribbean design, courtesy of the ultracreative owner. The panoramic view from the apartment makes it a great deal.

El Perico Marinero   HOTEL $$
(☑ 986-862-00-58; www.elpericomarinero.com; Calle 9, near Calle 19; d incl breakfast M$800-900; 🅿❄🕿🕿) Río Lagartos' smartest hotel offers 14 pleasant rooms, some with estuary vistas and handmade wood furnishings, and all with excellent beds.

Restaurant y Posada Macumba   SEAFOOD $$
(☑ 986-862-00-92; www.restaurantmacumba.com; Calle 16 No 102, cnr Calle 11; mains M$85-135; ☉8am-7pm; 🕿) You may feel like you've swum into a mermaid's cave here, such is the owner's creative flair. Beyond the shell-focused crafts that line the walls, and the fanciful light shades, it's a decent eatery with excellent seafood. The menu is massive so the photo board (à la Chinese restaurant) will help get you started.

❶ Getting There & Away

Several Noreste buses run daily between Río Lagartos and Tizimín (M$45, 1¼ hours), Mérida (M$210, three to four hours) and San Felipe (M$20, 20 minutes). Noreste serves Valladolid and Cancún, but you'll need to transfer in

Tizimín. If you are traveling to Valladolid, be sure to catch the 4pm bus from Río Lagartos; the 5pm doesn't make the connection in Tizimín.

The bus terminal is on Calle 19, between Calles 8 and 10.

CAMPECHE STATE

Tucked into the southwestern corner of the Yucatán Peninsula, Campeche state is home to low-key villages, vast stretches of tangled jungle, bird-dotted mangroves and lagoons, and some of the region's most imposing Maya ruins – many of which you might have all to yourself. On deserted beaches endangered turtles lay their eggs, while offshore playful dolphins frolic in the surf. The walled capital city of Campeche is the region's cultural epicenter, providing a great jumping-off point for your adventures into this offbeat hinterland.

Campeche is the least visited of the Yucatán's states, laced through with lonely back roads, friendly people, quiet coastlines and a provincial, lost-land charm. It makes a welcome break from the tourist hordes that descend on the peninsula's more popular destinations; here you'll find peace, surprising attractions and very genuine, local experiences.

Campeche

☑ 981 / POP 250,000

Campeche is a colonial fairyland, its walled city center a tight enclave of restored pastel buildings, narrow cobblestone streets, fortified ramparts and well-preserved mansions. Added to Unesco's list of World Heritage sites in 1999, the state capital lacks a little of a 'daily life' ambience as few people actually live in the historic center. But leave the inner walls and you'll find a genuine Mexican provincial capital complete with a frenetic market, peaceful *malecón* (boardwalk) and old fishing docks.

Besides the walls and numerous mansions built by wealthy Spanish families during Campeche's heyday in the 18th and 19th centuries, seven of the *baluartes* (bastions or bulwarks) have also survived. Two preserved colonial forts guard the city's outskirts, one of them housing the Museo de la Arquitectura Maya, an archaeological museum with many world-class pieces.

Campeche is the perfect base for day trips to Edzná, the Chenes sites and neighboring beaches.

History

Once a Maya trading village called Ah Kim Pech (Lord Sun Sheep-Tick), Campeche was first briefly approached by the Spaniards in 1517. Resistance by the Maya prevented the Spaniards from fully conquering the region for nearly a quarter-century. Colonial Campeche was founded in 1531, but later abandoned due to Maya hostility. By 1540, however, the conquistadors had gained sufficient control, under the leadership of Francisco de Montejo (the Younger), to found a permanent settlement. They named the settlement Villa de San Francisco de Campeche.

The settlement soon flourished as the major port of the Yucatán Peninsula, but this made it subject to pirate attacks. After a particularly appalling attack in 1663 (p348) left the city in ruins, the king of Spain ordered construction of Campeche's famous bastions, putting an end to the periodic carnage. Today the economy of the city is largely driven by tourism.

◉ Sights

★ **Museo Arqueológico de Campeche & Fuerte de San Miguel**   MUSEUM, FORT

(Campeche Archaeological Museum; Av Escénica s/n; M$55; ⊙ 8:30am-5pm Tue-Sun; ℗) Campeche's largest colonial fort, facing the Gulf of Mexico some 4km southwest of the city center, is now home to the most important of Maya museums, the excellent Museo Arqueológico de Campeche, and the city's one must-see museum. Here you can admire emblematic pieces from the sites of Calakmul and Edzná, and from Isla de Jaina, an island north of town once used as a burial site for Maya aristocracy.

Stunning jade jewelry and exquisite vases, masks and plates are thematically arranged in 10 exhibit halls. The star attractions are the jade burial masks from Calakmul. Also displayed are stelae, seashell necklaces and clay figurines.

Equipped with a dry moat and working drawbridge, the fort itself is a thing of beauty. The roof deck, ringed by 20 cannons, affords wonderful harbor views.

To get here take a bus or combi (minibus; marked 'Lerma') from the market. Ask the driver to let you off at the access road (just say 'Fuerte de San Miguel'), then hike 300m up the hill. Taxis cost around M$40 to M$50.

Plaza Principal PLAZA

Shaded by carob trees and ringed by tiled benches and broad footpaths radiating from a belle epoque kiosk, Campeche's appealingly modest central square started life in 1531 as a military camp. Over the years it became the focus of the town's civic, political and religious activities and remains the core of public life. *Campechanos* come here to chat, smooch, have their shoes shined or cool off with an ice cream after the heat of the day.

Malecón WATERFRONT

A popular path for joggers, cyclists, strolling friends and cooing sweethearts, the *malecón*, Campeche's 7km-long waterfront promenade, makes for a breezy sunrise ramble or sunset bike ride.

Mansión Carvajal HISTORIC BUILDING

(Calle 10, btwn Calles 51 & 53; ☉8am-2:45pm Mon-Fri) FREE Once the mansion of wealthy landowner Fernando Carvajal, this beautiful building now houses state offices. Visitors are welcome to take a peek inside, however. Black-and-white tiled floors, Doric columns, elaborate archways and a dramatic marble and ironwork staircase are highlights. Note the historical plaque.

Monument to the City Gates MONUMENT

Next to the Plaza Moch-Couoh is a monument of the city's four gates (land, sea, San Román and Guadalupe); these entrances were in the city walls that surrounded the city. The first two are still standing.

Museo del Archivo
General de Estado MUSEUM

(✆981-816-09-39; Calle 12 No 159; ☉8am-3pm Mon-Fri) FREE At this small museum, learn how Campeche came to be. It's free and air-conditioned, and you get to check out old documents and maps, and watch a video (in Spanish or English) that recounts the history of the state.

Catedral de Nuestra Señora
de la Purísima Concepción CATHEDRAL

(Calle 55; ☉6:30am-9pm) FREE Dominating Plaza Principal's east side is the two-towered cathedral. The limestone structure has stood on this spot for more than three centuries, and it still fills beyond capacity most Sundays. Statues of Sts Peter and Paul occupy niches in the baroque facade; the sober, single-nave interior is lined with colonial-era paintings. And at night, the gauzy lights on the illuminated church and other central landmarks creates a magical atmosphere.

Centro Cultural
Casa Número 6 CULTURAL CENTER

(Calle 57 No 6; M$20, audio guide M$15; ☉8am-9pm Mon-Fri, 9am-9pm Sat & Sun) During the prerevolutionary era, when this mansion was occupied by an upper-class *campechano* family, Número 6 was a prestigious plaza address. Wandering the premises, you'll get an idea of how the city's high society lived back then. The front sitting room is furnished with Cuban-style pieces of the period. Inside are exhibition spaces, a pleasant back patio and a gift shop.

Ex-Templo de San José
& Bazar Artesanal HISTORIC BUILDING

(former San José Church; cnr Calles 10 & 63; ☉10am-8pm) Faced with blue-and-yellow tiles, the Ex-Templo de San José is a wonder; note the lighthouse, complete with weather vane, atop the right spire. Built in the early 18th century by Jesuits who ran it as an institute of higher learning until they were booted out of Spanish domains in 1767, it now serves as the temporary location for the Bazar Artesanal. This is a one-stop shop for regional crafts, at least while the artisans' market near the Convention Center is being remodeled.

Museo de la Arquitectura Maya MUSEUM

(Calle 8; M$40; ☉8:30am-5:30pm Tue-Sun) The Baluarte de Nuestra Señora de la Soledad, designed to protect the Puerta del Mar, contains the fascinating Museo de la Arquitectura Maya. It provides an excellent overview of the sites around Campeche state and the key architectural styles associated with them. Five halls display stelae taken from various sites, accompanied by graphic representations of their carved inscriptions with brief commentaries in flawless English.

Baluartes

After a particularly blistering pirate assault in 1663, the remaining inhabitants of Campeche set about erecting protective walls around their city. Built largely by indigenous labor with limestone extracted from nearby caves, the barrier took more than 50 years to complete. Stretching more than 2.5km around the urban core and rising to a height of 8m, the hexagonal wall

Campeche

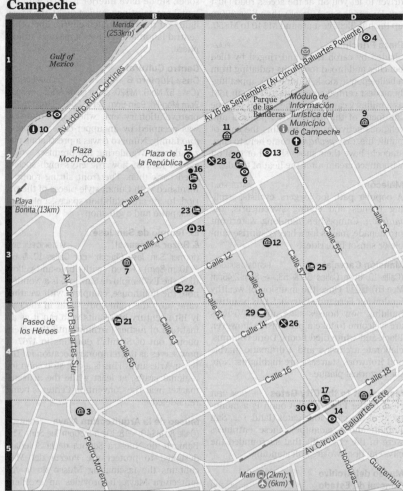

Merida
(253km)

Gulf of
Mexico

Av Adolfo Ruiz Cortines

Plaza
Moch-Couoh

Playa
Bonita (13km)

Av 16 de Septiembre (Av Circuito Baluartes Poniente)

Parque
de las
Banderas

Módulo de
Información
Turística del
Municipio
de Campeche

Plaza de
la República

Plaza de
la República

Av Circuito Baluartes Sur

Calle 8

Calle 10

Calle 12

Calle 14

Calle 16

Calle 18

Calle 53

Calle 55

Calle 57

Calle 59

Calle 61

Calle 63

Calle 65

Paseo de
los Héroes

Pedro Moreno

Av Circuito Baluartes Este

Honduras

Guatemala

Main (2km);
(6km)

YUCATÁN PENINSULA CAMPECHE

was linked by eight bulwarks. The seven that remain display a treasure trove of historical paraphernalia and artifacts of varying degrees of interest. You can climb atop the bulwarks and stroll sections of the wall for sweeping views of the port.

Two main entrances connected the walled compound with the outside world. The **Puerta del Mar** (Sea Gate; cnr Calles 8 & 59) **FREE** provided access from the sea, opening on to a wharf where small craft delivered goods from ships anchored further out. (The shallow waters were later reclaimed so the gate is now several blocks

from the waterfront.) The **Puerta de Tierra** (Land Gate; Calle 18; ⊙9am-6pm) **FREE**, on the opposite side, was opened in 1732 as the principal ingress from the suburbs. It is now the venue for a **sound-and-light show** (adult M$60, child 4-10 yr M$30; ⊙8pm Thu-Sun).

Baluarte de San Francisco & Baluarte de San Juan
HISTORIC BUILDING
(Calle 18; M$25; ⊙8am-9pm Mon-Wed, to 6pm Thu & Fri, 9am-6pm Sat & Sun) **FREE** Once the primary defensive bastion for the adjacent Puerta de la Tierra, the Baluarte de San

Baluarte de San Pedro HISTORIC BUILDING
(cnr Avs Circuito Baluartes Este & Circuito Baluartes Norte) **FREE** Directly behind Iglesia de San Juan de Dios, the Baluarte de San Pedro served a post-piracy defensive function when it repelled a punitive raid from Mérida in 1824. Carved in stone above the entry is the symbol of San Pedro: two keys to heaven and the papal tiara. It is currently closed to visitors.

Baluarte de Santiago & Jardín Botánico Xmuch Haltún GARDENS, HISTORIC BUILDING
(cnr Calles 8 & 49; M$15; ☉8am-9pm Mon-Fri, 9am-9pm Sat & Sun) Completed in 1704 – the last of the bulwarks to be built – the Baluarte de Santiago houses the **Jardín Botánico Xmuch Haltún**, a botanical garden with numerous endemic and some introduced plants. It's not a huge place, but provides a green and peaceful respite when the sun gets particularly brutal.

Tours

Kankabi' Ok TOUR
(☎981-811-27-92; Calle 59 No 3; ☉9am-1pm & 5-9pm Mon-Sat) A very reliable outfit that offers four-hour city tours (minimum two people; M$905), trips to archaeological sites such as Edzná (around M$930), Chenes (around M$1733) and the Ruta Puuc (around M$2272). Further afield they go to Cenote Miguel Colorado (M$1463) and Calakmul (M$2500). Also rents out bikes and does ecotourism and beach trips.

Sleeping

Hostal Viatger HOSTEL $
(☎981-811-4500; Calle 51 No 28, btwn 12 & 14; dm/d/tr incl breakfast M$250/790/830; P🕸) Of the plethora of hostels that have popped up here in the last few years, we like this one for its location in the historic center (but away from the crowds), plus its friendly ambience. Dorms are slightly squishy, but women can enjoy their own space and there's the option of private doubles and triples.

Hotel Campeche HOTEL $
(☎981-816-51-83; hotelcampeche@hotmail.com; Calle 57, btwn Calles 8 & 10; s/d with fan M$285/380, r with air-con M$448; ❄🕸) Not much in the way of frills here, but the plaza-side location and big rooms in this classically crumbling building make this about the best budget bet in town. A couple of rooms have little balconies looking out over the plaza.

Francisco houses a pirate exhibition in both English and Spanish. You also enter here, to walk along the Baluarte de San Juan, the smallest of the seven bulwarks. Here you can see the bell that was rung to alert the population in times of danger. (Different bells around the city had different sounds and meanings.)

Baluarte de Santa Rosa HISTORIC BUILDING
(cnr Calle 14 & Av Circuito Baluartes Sur; ☉8am-8pm) **FREE** The Baluarte de Santa Rosa has a gallery that houses temporary exhibitions.

Campeche

◎ Sights

1 Baluarte de San Francisco &
Baluarte de San Juan...................D4
2 Baluarte de San Pedro F4
3 Baluarte de Santa Rosa...................A5
4 Baluarte de Santiago & Jardín
Botánico Xmuch Haltún D1
5 Catedral de Nuestra Señora de la
Purísima Concepción...................C2
6 Centro Cultural Casa Número 6 ....C2
7 Ex-Templo de San José & Bazar
Artesanal....................................B3
8 Malecón A2
9 Mansión Carvajal............................D2
10 Monument to the City Gates A2
11 Museo de la Arquitectura Maya...........C2
12 Museo del Archivo General de
Estado.....................................C3
13 Plaza Principal.............................C2
14 Puerta de Tierra D5
15 Puerta del Mar B2

☉ Activities, Courses & Tours

16 Kankabi' Ok....................................B2

ⓛ Sleeping

17 Hacienda Puerta Campeche.................D4
18 Hostal Viatger E2
19 Hotel Boutique Casa Don Gustavo.......B2
20 Hotel Campeche...............................C2
21 Hotel Francis Drake.........................B4
22 Hotel López..................................B3
23 Hotel Misión Campeche.......................B3
24 Hotel Plaza Campeche........................E1
25 Hotel Socaire................................D3

⊗ Eating

26 Cafe Luan....................................C4
27 La Pigua......................................E1
28 Marganzo.....................................C2

⊖ Drinking & Nightlife

29 Chocol-Ha....................................C4
30 Salón Rincón Colonial D5

⊛ Entertainment

Puerta de Tierra..........................(see 14)

⊚ Shopping

31 Casa de Artesanías Tukulná.................B3

★ Hotel López   HOTEL $$

(☑981-816-33-44; www.hotellopezcampeche.com.
mx; Calle 12 No 189; s/d/ste M$950/1080/1250;
✳🖥📶) This business hotel is by far one of
Campeche's best midrange options. Small
but modern, comfortably appointed rooms
open on to curvy art deco-styled balconies
around oval courtyards and pleasant greenery. Bring your swimsuit for the lovely pool
out back. Prices are considerably lower outside high season.

Hotel Misión Campeche   HOTEL $$

(☑981-816-45-88; www.hotelmision.com.mx; Calle
10 No 252; r M$1162; 🅿✳@📶) A large central
hotel and part of a Mexican chain, this is a
good midrange choice. The highlight is the
pretty colonial courtyard with 42 large and
clean rooms and arcaded corridors. The
downside is that the rooms can vary widely
in size and the general 'feng shui' (read size
of windows, orientation and the like); check
some out first.

Hotel Socaire   BOUTIQUE HOTEL $$

(☑981-811-21-30; www.hotelsocaire.com; Calle 56
No 17; r from US$82; 📶🏊) A charming con-
verted colonial building (the reception area)
leads through to a variety of spacious rooms
in the rear. At the time of research, some
were showing slight signs of humidity. The
lovely pool area adds to a pleasant stay. The

website photos slightly (over)do it justice,
but it's in a great central location and it's
excellent value.

Hotel Francis Drake   HOTEL $$

(☑981-811-56-26; www.hotelfrancisdrake.com;
Calle 12 No 207; s/d M$890/990, ste from M$1120,
incl breakfast; ✳📶) A somewhat baroque
lobby leads to cool, fresh rooms with a
sprinkling of tasteful decoration. Bathrooms and balconies are tiny, but the
rooms are huge (other hotels would call
them suites) with king-sized beds and separate sitting areas.

★ Hacienda Puerta
Campeche   BOUTIQUE HOTEL $$$

(☑981-816-75-08; www.luxurycollection.com;
Calle 59 No 71; r from US$210; ✳@📶🏊) This
beautiful boutique hotel has 15 suites with
high ceilings and separate lounges. Perfectly
manicured gardens and grassy lawns offer
peace, while the partly covered pool has
nearby hammocks that are fit for a Maya
king. It also runs a restored luxury hacienda 26km outside the city, on the way to the
Edzná ruins.

Hotel Boutique Casa
Don Gustavo   BOUTIQUE HOTEL $$$

(☑981-816-80-90; www.casadongustavo.com; Calle
59 No 4; r/ste from M$4250/5000; 🅿✳📶🏊)

Just 10 rooms decorated with antique furniture (and huge modern bathrooms), though everything is so perfectly museum-like it's almost hard to relax. There's a small pool with hammocks nearby, or try the rooftop Jacuzzi. Colorful tiled hallways line an outdoor courtyard, and there's a restaurant too. Call or check the website for promotions.

✕ Eating

You can try some good local dishes in Campeche, especially seafood and the likes of *cochinita pibil* (roasted suckling pig). One of two high-end places steals the show for quality cuisine, but the rest offer fairly straightforward menus, especially eateries in the historic center. However, traditional atmosphere and old-fashioned service make up for bland offerings. Several restaurants offer musical entertainment.

Cafe Luan CAFE $
(Calle 14 No 132; ⊗8am-2pm; ☎) This friendly, well-lit spot serves excellent lighter breakfast and lunch snacks, from eggs (any way you want them) to hot cakes and freshly made sandwiches. Reasonable coffee and excellent smoothies make it a great place to grab a welcome break from the heat.

★ Marganzo MEXICAN $$
(☎981-811-38-98; www.marganzo.com; Calle 8 No 267; mains M$160-250; ⊗7am-11pm; ☎) Marganzo is popular with tourists and locals, for good reason – the food is great, the portions large and the complimentary appetizers numerous. An extensive menu offers everything from international fare to regional treats such as *cochinita pibil*. Wandering musicians provide entertainment. Thursday breakfasts come with a 50% discount for females.

★ La Pigua SEAFOOD $$$
(☎981-811-33-65; Miguel Alemán 179A; mains M$230-300; ⊗1-9pm) Some of Campeche's finest meals are served at this upscale restaurant just outside the walls and behind **Hotel Plaza** (☎981-811-99-00; www.hotelplaza campeche.com; cnr Calle 10 & Av Circuito Baluartes; r/ste M$1667/1851; P❀☎☎). Service is attentive and the specialties include seafood dishes – *camarones al coco* (coconut shrimp), whole fish in cilantro sauce and grilled squid with ground almonds and paprika.

☕ Drinking & Nightlife

★ Chocol-Ha CAFE
(☎981-811-78-93; Calle 59 No 30; drinks M$25-55, snacks M$55-80; ⊗8am-1pm & 5-11pm Mon-Sat) When that chocolate craving hits, head on over to this cute little cafe with a patio in front and grassy yard in back. Drinks include bittersweet hot chocolate with green tea or chili, and a chocolate frappé. Sweet treats such as cake, crepes and even *tamales* (yep, all chocolate!) will give you a sugary high.

★ Salón Rincón Colonial BAR
(Calle 59 No 60; ⊗10am-9pm) With ceiling fans high over an airy hall and a solid wood bar amply stocked with rum, this Cuban-style drinking establishment appropriately served as a location for *Original Sin*, a 2001 movie with Antonio Banderas and Angelina Jolie that was set in Havana. The *botanas* (appetizers) are exceptionally fine and go down well with a local beer.

🛍 Shopping

Casa de Artesanías Tukulná ARTS & CRAFTS
(☎981-816-21-88; Calle 10 No 33; ⊗9am-9pm) A central shop selling a lovely and high-quality range of textiles, clothing, hats, hammocks, wood chairs, sweets and so on – all made in Campeche state.

ℹ Information

Campeche has numerous banks with ATMs.
Call 911 in an emergency.

Central Post Office (cnr Av 16 de Sepiembre & Calle 53; ⊗8:30am-4pm Mon-Fri)

Hospital General De Especialidades (☎981-127-39-80; Las Flores)

Hospital Dr Manuel Campos (☎981-811-17-09; Av Circuito Baluartes Norte, btwn Calles 14 & 16)

HSBC Bank (Calle 10, btwn Calles 53 & 55; ⊗9am-5pm Mon-Fri, to 2pm Sat) Open Saturday.

Módulo de Información Turística del Municipio de Campeche (☎981-811-39-89; Plaza Central; ⊗8am-9pm Mon-Fri, 9am-9pm Sat & Sun) Basic information on Campeche city.

Secretaría de Turismo (☎981-127-33-00; www.campeche.travel) About the only thing this place has going for it is its website with information on the state.

ℹ Getting There & Away

AIR

Campeche's small but modern airport is 6km southeast of the center; it has car-rental offices and a tiny snack bar. **Aeroméxico** (☑ Mexico City 55-51-33-4000; www.aeromexico.com) provides services.

BUS

Campeche's **main bus terminal** (☑ 981-811-99-10; Av Patricio Trueba 237), usually called the ADO or 1st-class terminal, is about 2.5km south of Plaza Principal via Av Central. Buses provide 1st-class services to destinations around the country, along with 2nd-class services to Sabancuy (M$36, two hours), Hecelchakán (M$45, one hour) and Candelaria (M$199, four hours).

The **2nd-class terminal** (Terminal Sur; ☑ 981-816-34-45; Av Gobernadores 479), often referred to as the 'old ADO' station or Autobuses del Sur, is 600m east of the Mercado Principal. Second-class destinations include Hopelchén (M$68, 1½ hours), Xpujil (M$220, four hours) and Bécal (M$60, 1¾ hours).

Transportes Crígar (Calle 10 No 329) is a handy spot to buy ADO (1st-class) bus tickets. Or try or other travel agencies around town.

To get to the main bus terminal, catch any 'Las Flores,' 'Solidaridad' or 'Casa de Justicia' microbus by the post office. To the 2nd-class terminal, catch a 'Terminal Sur' bus from the same point.

A taxi costs around M$40.

CAR & MOTORCYCLE

If you're arriving in Campeche from the south, via the *cuota* (toll road), turn left at the roundabout signed for the *universidad* and follow that road straight to the coast, then go north.

If you're heading to either Edzná, the long route to Mérida or the fast toll road going south, take Calle 61 to Av Central and follow signs for the airport and either Edzná or the *cuota*. For the non-toll route south, just head down the *malecón*. For the short route to Mérida go north on the *malecón*.

In addition to some outlets at the airport, several car-rental agencies can be found downtown, including **Avis** (☑ 981-811-07-85; www.avis.mx; Calle 10, btwn 57 & 59; ⊙ 8am-2pm & 4-6pm). Rates start from M$700 per day depending on the season.

ℹ Getting Around

Taxis from the airport to the center cost M$160 (shared taxis M$70 per person); buy tickets at the taxi booth inside the terminal. Going to the airport, some street taxis (ie those not called from your hotel, which are more expensive) charge M$120 to M$150; penny-pinchers can try taking the hourly bus to Chiná (a village outside Campeche; around M$15) from the market, and getting off at the airport entrance, then walking 500m to the airport doors.

Within Campeche city, taxis charge M$30 to M$60; prices are 10% more after 10pm, and 20% more from midnight to 5am.

Most local buses (around M$7) have a stop at or near the Mercado Principal.

Consider pedaling along the *malecón;* get bike rentals at Kankabi' Ok (p341).

Drivers should note that even-numbered streets in the *centro histórico* take priority, but go slowly until you get the hang of the cross streets.

Northern Campeche

Northern Campeche offers a fascinating blend of experiences. An enticing mix of colonial and Maya elements, blended with

BUSES FROM CAMPECHE

DESTINATION	FARE (M$)	DURATION (HR)	FREQUENCY (DAILY)
Cancún	652	7	7
Chetumal	305-498	6½	1
Ciudad del Carmen	250	3	hourly
Mérida	226	2½	hourly
Mérida (via Uxmal)	157	4½	5 from 2nd-class terminal
Mexico City	1646	18	3
Palenque	440	5	5
San Cristóbal de las Casas	630	10	2
Villahermosa	283-524	6	frequent
Xpujil	220-362	5	2pm

centuries-old tradition and lush nature, it's worth spending time here. Hang out with the locals in a colonial plaza of small towns, wander through the alluring complex of Edzná (one of the region's finest set of ruins) or marvel over the unique features of architecture at the Chenes sites. Top off your experience by trying and buying one of the Yucatan's traditional panama hats. Another plus? Most of these places are doable as separate day trips from Campeche.

Chenes Sites

Northeastern Campeche state is dotted with more than 30 sites in the distinct Chenes style, recognizable by the monster motifs around doorways in the center of long, low buildings of three sections, and temples atop pyramidal bases. Most of the year you'll have these sites to yourself. The three small sites of El Tabasqueño, Hochob and Dzibilnocac make for an interesting day trip from Campeche if you have your own vehicle, or you can take a tour from Campeche with Kankabi' Ok Tours (p341) – at the time of research they went to Hochob, Tohcok and Dzibilnocac.

⊙ Sights

Dzibilnocac   ARCHAEOLOGICAL SITE
(M$40; ⊘8am-5pm) FREE Though it only has one significant structure, Dzibilnocac possesses an eerie grandeur that merits a visit. Unlike the many hilltop sites chosen for Chenes structures, Dzibilnocac ('big painted turtle' is one translation) is on a flat plain, like a large open park. As Stephens and Catherwood observed in 1842, the many scattered hillocks in the zone, still unexcavated today, attest to the presence of a large city.

The single, clearly discernible structure is A1, a palatial complex upon a 76m platform with a trio of raised temples atop rounded pyramidal bases. The best preserved of the three, on the east end, has fantastically elaborate monster-mask reliefs on each of its four sides and the typically piled-up Chac masks on three of the four corners.

Dzibilnocac is located beside the village of Iturbide (also called Vicente Guerrero), 20km northeast of Dzibalchén. From Campeche's 2nd-class bus terminal there are several buses daily to Iturbide via Hopelchén (M$108, three hours). There's no place to stay here so you'll need to make it back to Hopelchén by nightfall.

Hochob   ARCHAEOLOGICAL SITE
(M$40; ⊘8am-5pm) About 60km south of Hopelchén, Hochob, 'the place where corn is harvested,' is among the most beautiful and terrifying of the Chenes-style sites. The Palacio Principal (Estructura 2, though signposted as 'Estructura 1') is on the north side of the main plaza, faced with an elaborate doorway representing Itzamná, creator of the ancient Maya, as a rattlesnake with open jaws.

Facing it across the plaza, Estructura 5 has two raised temples on either end of a long series of rooms; the better preserved eastern temple retains part of its perforated roofcomb.

To reach Hochob, go 5km south from El Tabasqueño, then turn right just before the Pemex station at Dzilbalchén. Now go 7.5km to the Chencoh sign, turn left, then after 400m go left again. Drive another 3.5km to Hochob.

El Tabasqueño   ARCHAEOLOGICAL SITE
(⊘8am-5pm) FREE Supposedly named after a local landowner from Tabasco, El Tabasqueño boasts a temple-palace (Estructura 1) with a striking monster-mouth doorway, flanked by stacks of eight Chac masks with hooked snouts. Estructura 2 is a solid free-standing tower, an oddity in Maya architecture.

To reach El Tabasqueño, go 30km south from Hopelchén. Just beyond the village of Pakchén, there's an easy-to-miss sign at a turnoff on the right; follow this rock-and-gravel road 2km to the site.

⊙ Getting There & Away

If you don't have your own wheels, head off on a day trip from Campeche with Kankabi' Ok Tours (p341). There is no easy public transportation to these, or other Chenes, sites.

Edzná

If you only have the time or inclination to visit one archaeological site in northern Campeche, Edzná should be your top pick. It's located about 60km southeast of Campeche.

⊙ Sights

★**Edzná**   ARCHAEOLOGICAL SITE
(M$55; ⊘8am-5pm) Edzná's massive complexes, that once covered more than 17 sq km, were built by a highly stratified society that flourished from about 600 BC to the 15th

CHRISONTOUR84 / SHUTTERSTOCK ©

. Cenote, Valladolid (p333)
s possible to visit, and swim in, many of the
'unning cenotes (natural sinkholes) within easy
stance of this charming city.

. Becán (p350), Campeche
ne of the largest and most elaborate Maya sites,
urrounded by lush forest.

. Laguna Bacalar (p298)
trikingly beautiful Laguna Bacalar is a 60km-long
goon – the largest on the Yucatán Peninsula –
nd a great place to relax and unwind.

. Mérida (p304)
tunning Mérida – the cultural capital of the
ucatán Peninsula – is full of narrow cobbled
reets and plazas studded by beautifully
aintained ornate colonial-era buildings..

TATI NOVA PHOTO MEXICO / SHUTTERSTOCK ©

THE MARAUDING PIRATES OF CAMPECHE

Where there's wealth, there are pirates – this was truer in the 1500s than it is today. And Campeche, which was a thriving timber, chicle (gum) and logwood (a natural source of dye) port in the mid-16th century, was the wealthiest place around.

Pirates (or 'privateers,' as some preferred to be called) terrorized Campeche for two centuries. Time and time again the port was invaded, ships sacked, citizens robbed and buildings burned – typical pirate stuff. The buccaneers' hall of shame included the infamous John Hawkins, Francis Drake, Henry Morgan and the notorious 'Peg-Leg' himself. In their most gruesome assault, in early 1663, the various pirate hordes set aside rivalries to converge as a single flotilla upon the city, massacring Campeche's citizens.

This tragedy finally spurred the Spanish monarchy to take preventive action, but it was another five years before work on the 3.5m-thick ramparts began. By 1686 a 2.5km hexagon incorporating eight strategically placed bastions surrounded the city. A segment of the ramparts extended out to sea so that ships literally sailed into a fortress to gain access to the city. With Campeche nearly impregnable, pirates turned to other ports and ships at sea. In 1717 the brilliant naval strategist Felipe de Aranda began a campaign against the buccaneers, and eventually made this area of the Gulf safe from piracy. Of course, all that wealth from chicle and timber was created using indigenous slaves, leading one to question: who were the real bad guys, anyway?

For a taste of the pirate life, take a 50-minute cruise on a 'pirate ship' that heads out Tuesday through Sunday at noon and 5pm (or noon and 6pm in warmer seasons), conditions permitting. Get information at a kiosk near the *tranvía* kiosk, in the Plaza Principal. (The ship was under maintenance at time of research so check if it's afloat.)

century AD. During that period the people of Edzná built more than 20 complexes in a melange of architectural styles, installing an ingenious network of water-collection and irrigation systems. (Though it's a long way from such Puuc Hills sites as Uxmal and Kabah, some of the architecture here has elements of the Puuc style.)

Most of the visible carvings date from AD 550 to 810.

The causes leading to Edzná's decline and gradual abandonment remain a mystery; the site remained unknown until its rediscovery by *campesinos* in 1906.

Edzná means 'House of the Itzáes,' a reference to a predominant governing clan of Chontal Maya origin. Edzná's rulers recorded significant events on stone stelae. Around 30 stelae have been discovered adorning the site's principal temples; a handful are on display underneath a *palapa* just beyond the ticket office.

A path from the *palapa* leads about 400m through vegetation; follow the 'Gran Acropolis' sign. Soon, to your left, you'll come upon the **Plataforma de los Cuchillos** (Platform of the Knives), a residential complex highlighted by Puuc architectural features. The name is derived from an offering of silica knives that was found within.

Crossing a *sacbé* (stone-lined, grass walkway), you arrive at the main attraction, the **Plaza Principal**. Measuring 160m long and 100m wide, the Plaza Principal is surrounded by temples. On your right is the Nohochná (Big House), a massive, elongated structure topped by four long halls likely used for administrative tasks, such as the collection of tributes and the dispensation of justice.

Across the plaza is the **Gran Acrópolis**, a raised platform holding several structures, including Edzná's major temple, the 31m-high Edificio de los Cinco Pisos (Five-Story Building). The current structure is the last of four remodels and was done primarily in the Puuc style. It rises five levels from its base to the roofcomb and contains many vaulted rooms. Note the well-preserved glyphs along the base of the central staircase.

South of Plaza Principal is the **Templo de los Mascarones** (Temple of the Masks), with a pair of reddish stucco masks underneath a protective palapa. Personifying the gods of the rising and setting sun, these extraordinarily well-preserved faces display dental mutilation, crossed eyes and huge earrings, features associated with the Maya aristocracy.

ℹ Getting There & Away

Combis (around M$50, one hour) leave when full from Calle Chihuahua near Campeche's Mercado Principal. Most drop you 200m from the site entrance unless the driver is feeling generous. The last combi back is midafternoon (some say 2pm, others 3pm...you get the idea), so ask the driver to make sure!

Kankabi' Ok (p341) in Campeche provides guided tours of Edzná (including transportation) for around M$930 per person.

Southeastern Campeche

The southern peninsular region from Escárcega to Xpujil, which borders modern-day Guatemala, was the earliest established, longest inhabited and most densely populated region in the Maya world. Here you'll find the most elaborate Maya archaeological sites on the Yucatán Peninsula.

Among the region's archaeological sites, the Río Bec architectural style dominates. It is actually a hybrid of styles fusing elements from the Chenes region to the north and Petén to the south. Río Bec structures are characterized by long, low buildings divided into three sections, with a huge 'monster' mouth glaring from a central doorway. The facades are decorated with smaller masks and geometric designs. At each end are tall, smoothly rounded towers with banded tiers supporting small false temples flanked by extremely steep, nonfunctional steps.

The most significant is the spectacular Calakmul set amid the ecologically diverse, and very lush, **Reserva de la Biosfera Calakmul**.

Calakmul

The most remote of all the Maya ruins, Calakmul is also one worth making the effort to get to. Simply put, it's a magnificent experience, made even better by its history as a leading city from around AD 250. Many buildings survive, giving an evocative sense of a powerful place.

But visiting Calakmul is not just a historical experience, it's also an ecological one. Lying at the heart of the vast, untrammeled Reserva de la Biosfera Calakmul (which covers close to 15% of the state's total territory), the ruins are surrounded by rain forest and seemingly endless canopy of vegetation. You might glimpse ocellated turkeys, parrots, toucans and more – around 350 bird species reside or fly through here. You'll no doubt see or hear spider and howler monkeys, too, but you're much less likely to spot a jaguar – one of five kinds of wildcat in the area.

◉ Sights

★**Calakmul** ARCHAEOLOGICAL SITE
(M$184; ⊘8am-5pm) Possibly the largest city during Maya times, Calakmul was 'discovered' in 1931 by American botanist Cyrus Lundell. The site bears comparison in size and historical significance to Tikal in Guatemala, its chief rival for hegemony over the southern lowlands during the Classic Maya era. It boasts the largest and tallest known pyramid in Yucatán, and was once home to over 50,000 people.

A central chunk of the 72-sq-km expanse has been restored, but most of the city's approximately 6000 structures lie covered in jungle. In 2004, amazingly well-preserved painted murals were discovered at the Chiik Naab acropolis of Estructura 1. They depicted something never before seen in Maya murals – the typical daily activities of ordinary Maya (as opposed to the usual political, ceremonial or religious themes). A few years before that, a significant 20m-long, 4m-high stucco frieze was uncovered at Estructura II, whose features seemed to mark a transition between Olmec and Maya architecture.

Unfortunately, the murals and frieze are not open to the public, but their reproductions can be seen at Calakmul's modern **Museo de Naturaleza y Arqueología** (⊘7am-3pm) 𝗙𝗥𝗘𝗘, at Km 20 on the 60km side road to Calakmul. This worthwhile museum also has geological, archaeological and natural-history exhibits.

At the time of research, you pay three different fees: the community entrance (M$50), biosphere entrance (M$64) and the site entrance M$70. This combination seems subject to change.

⛺ Tours

From Campeche, Kankabi' Ok (p341) runs tours to Calakmul. Alternatively, from Xpujil, **Ka'an Expeditions** (☎983-871-60-00; www.kaanexpeditions.com; Av Calakmul s/n; per person US$75; ⊘noon-8pm Tue-Sun) also runs a fairly 'cookie-cutter' but convenient tour, or a good English-speaking outfit is **Calakmul Adventures** (☎cell 983-1841313; www.calakmuladventures.com; around M$1300). Just west of Xpujil, **Río Bec Dreams** (www.riobecdreams.com; Hwy 186 Km 142, Becán; 2-person cabaña

M$1050-1350, 3-person cabaña M$1400-1550, 4-person cabaña M$1750; (P😊) arranges tours with English-speaking guides, but these are only available to its guests.

If you want to arrange something on the hop, certified guides wait at the turnoff from Hwy 186 (at the entrance to the 20km of lands owned by the local community of Conhuas). They charge around M$600 for a multihour visit, but you need your own transportation. Most speak Spanish only.

If you want a real DIY experience, you can hire a taxi from Escárgeca or Xpujil (around M$1400 with a three-hour wait).

🛏 Sleeping

Campamento Yaax' Che   CAMPGROUND $
(Servidores Turísticos Calakmul; 📱cell 983-1348818; www.ecoturismocalakmul.com; own/fixed tent US$6/19) The closest campground to the Calakmul site, and the nearest thing to a camping experience in the jungle, this is located several kilometers after the turnoff from Hwy 186 on the road to Calakmul and another 700m in on a rough road. It's a relaxed, wilderness-style campground with sites for BYO tents. Or you can opt for ready-pitched tents.

It can be muddy when wet. There are environmentally friendly dry toilets and 'natural' showers plus a communal *palapa*. Meals can be arranged. Head honchos Fernando and Leticia offer tours, too (from around M$900 per person for the three-hour jungle tour; from M$1200 to archaeological sites; minimum numbers apply).

❶ Getting There & Away

Calakmul is 60km south of Hwy 186 at the end of a good paved road (the turnoff is 56km west of Xpujil).

Chicanná & Becán

Chicanna & Becan are two interesting sites that are easily accessible from Hwy 186, located 10km and 8km respectively west of Xpujil. They represent fascinating examples of Chenes and Río Bec styles.

◉ Sights

Chicanná   ARCHAEOLOGICAL SITE
(M$50; ⊙8am-5pm) Aptly named 'House of the Snake's Jaws,' this Maya site is best known for one remarkably well-preserved doorway with a hideous fanged visage. Located 11km west of Xpujil and 400m south of Hwy 186, Chicanná is a mixture of Chenes and Río Bec architectural styles buried in the jungle. The city attained its peak during the late Classic period, from AD 550 to 700, as a sort of elite suburb of Becán.

Beyond the admission pavilion, follow the rock paths through the jungle to **Estructura XX**, which boasts two monster-mouth doorways, one above the other. The top structure is impressively flanked by rounded stacks of crook-nosed Chac masks.

A five-minute walk along the jungle path brings you to **Estructura XI**, with what remains of some of the earliest buildings. Continue along the main path about 120m northeast to reach the **main plaza**. Standing on the east side is Chicanná's famous **Estructura II**, with its gigantic Chenes-style monster-mouth doorway, believed to depict the jaws of the god Itzamná – lord of the heavens and creator of all things. Note the painted glyphs to the right of the mask. A path leading from the right corner of Estructura II takes you to **Estructura VI**, which has a well-preserved roofcomb and some beautiful profile masks on its facade. Circle around the back, noting the faded red-painted blocks of the west wing, then turn right to hike back to the main entrance.

Becán   ARCHAEOLOGICAL SITE
(M$55; ⊙8am-5pm) The Maya word for 'canyon' or 'moat' is *becán,* and indeed a 2km moat snakes its way around this must-visit Maya site. Seven causeways provide access across the moat to the 12-hectare site, within which are the remains of three separate architectural complexes. A strategic crossroads between the Petenes civilization to the south and Chenes to the north, Becán displays architectural elements of both, with the resulting composite known as the Río Bec style.

The elaborate defenses surrounding the site allude to the militaristic nature of the city, which, from around AD 600 to 1000, was a regional capital encompassing Xpujil and Chicanná.

Enter the complex via the western causeway, skirting Plaza del Este on your left. Proceed through a 66m-long arched passageway and you will emerge on to the **Plaza Central**, ringed by three monumental structures. The formidable 32m **Estructura IX,** on the plaza's north side, is Becán's

HORMIGUERO

The buildings of **Hormiguero** (⊗8am-5pm) date as far back as AD 50; the city (whose name is Spanish for 'anthill') flourished during the late Classic period. Until recent times, the site was not easy to reach; the road, although overgrown, is largely sealed. Hormiguero has two impressive and unique buildings in a stunning, lush setting that are worth the trek. You are likely to have the site to yourself.

As you enter you'll see the 50m-long **Estructura II**. The facade's chief feature is a very menacing Chenes-style monster-mouth doorway, jaws open wide, set back between a pair of Classic Río Bec tiered towers. Around the back is intact Maya stonework and the remains of several columns. Follow the arrows 60m north to reach **Estructura V**, with a much smaller but equally ornate open-jawed temple atop a pyramidal base. Climb the right side for a closer look at the incredibly detailed stonework, especially along the corner columns that flank the doorway.

This site is reached by heading 14km south from Xpujil's stoplight, then turning right and going 8km west on a sealed road (the final 2km are on a rough, dirt road).

tallest building – though the sign says not to climb it, a rope is provided! **Estructura VIII** is the huge temple on your right, with a pair of towers flanking a colonnaded facade at the top. It's a great vantage point for the area; with binoculars, you can make out Xpujil's ruins to the east. Across the plaza from VIII is **Estructura X**, with fragments of an Earth Monster mask still visible around the central doorway. The other side of X opens on to the west plaza, with a ritual **ball court**. As you loop around Estructura X to the south, check out the encased stucco mask on display.

Follow around the right side of the mask to another massive edifice, **Estructura I**, which takes up one side of the eastern plaza. Its splendid south wall is flanked by a pair of amazing Río Bec towers rising 15m. Ascend the structure on the right side and follow the terrace alongside a series of vaulted rooms back to the other end, where a passage leads you into the **Plaza del Este**. The most significant structure here is **Estructura IV**, on the opposite side of the plaza; experts surmise it was a residence for Becán's aristocrats. A stairway leads to an upstairs courtyard ringed by seven rooms with cross motifs on either side of the doorways. Finally, go around Estructura IV to complete the circle. Becán is located 8km west of Xpujil, 500m north of the highway.

ⓘ Getting There & Away

Your own transportation is required to get to these sites. Alternatively, a taxi from Xpujil costs around M$500 with one-hour wait at each.

Xpujil

☑ 983 / POP 4000

Although unremarkable, the small town of Xpujil (shpu-*heel*) has expanded over the last few years, especially given its proximity to the area's many ruins. As such, it's a useful base. It has a few hotels, some unexceptional eateries, several ATMs (one at supermarket Willy's), an exchange house (Elektra Dinero on Calle Chicanna near Xnantun) and a bus terminal. Most services are along the seven-block main drag, Av Calakmul (aka Hwy 186) and one street heading inland. There are three gas stations in the area.

◉ Sights

Xpuhil   ARCHAEOLOGICAL SITE
(M$50; ⊗8am-5pm) The ruins of Xpuhil are a striking example of the Río Bec style. The three towers (rather than the usual two) of Estructura I rise above a dozen vaulted rooms. The 53m central tower is the best preserved. With its banded tiers and impractically steep stairways leading up to a temple that displays traces of a zoomorphic mask, it gives you a good idea of what the other two towers must have looked like in Xpuhil's 8th-century heyday. Go around back to see a fierce jaguar mask embedded in the wall below the temple.

The ruins are located on the western edge of Xpujil town; it's about a 1km walk from the entrance to the ruins, which are in a pretty setting.

🛏 Sleeping & Eating

Xpujil's sleeping options are all along the main highway, which can be noisy. Around the bus terminal at the east end of town you'll find cheap hotels; the nicer hotels are at the west end of town. Some of the best options are near Bécan, around 12km west of Xpujil.

Aside from the hotel restaurants, various greasy spoons are clustered around the bus station and roadside *taquerías* (taco stands) toward the Xpuhil ruins. There's a small supermarket next to the bus station. There is an excellent **restaurant** (https:// riobecdreams.com; Hwy 186 Km 142; mains M$120-220; ⊙ 7:30am-9pm; P) near Bécan, around 12km west of Xpujil.

Hotel Maya Balam   HOTEL $$
(Calle Xpujil s/n, btwn Av Calakmul & Silvituc; d M$490-690, tr M$590; P✳🅟) The best of a fairly basic lot in town, this place is small and modern with clean rooms. There's not much outlook (back rooms face on to the car park), but it's fine for a night or two if you're exploring the area.

Sazon Veracruzano   MEXICAN $$
(Av Calakmul 92; mains M$130-170; ⊙ 7am-11pm Mon-Sat) Even though it's a casual place with bright orange exterior and even more vibrant plastic tablecloths, it's as smart as you'll get in Xpujul. It offers a big menu of Mexican dishes (with a focus on Veracruz, where the owners are from). Think the likes of *fajita la arrachera* (beef strips; M$170) and fried fish fillet.

ℹ Getting There & Away

The **bus terminal** (✆ 983-871-65-11) is just east of the Xpujil stoplight next to the Victoria Hotel. Services head to/from Campeche (M$260 to M$370, one daily, 4½ hours; via Champotón), plus Chetumal.

There are also taxi *colectivos* to Chetumal (M$120 per person, 1½ hours). You'll find these near the traffic circle opposite the bus terminal.

Chiapas & Tabasco

Best Places to Eat

➡ Santo Nahual (p375)

➡ Restaurante LUM (p375)

➡ Restaurant Los Geranios (p404)

➡ Ta Bonitio (p404)

➡ Cocina Chontal (p420)

Best Places to Stay

➡ Hostal Tres Central (p357)

➡ La Joya Hotel (p373)

➡ Puerta Vieja Hostel (p372)

➡ Las Guacamayas (p401)

➡ Parador-Museo Santa María (p404)

Why Go?

Chilly pine-forest highlands, sultry rain-forest jungles and attractive colonial cities exist side by side within Mexico's southernmost state, a region awash with the legacy of Spanish rule and the remnants of ancient Maya civilization. Palenque and Yaxchilán are evocative vestiges of powerful Maya kingdoms, and the presence of modern Maya is a constant reminder of the region's rich and uninterrupted history. The colonial hubs of San Cristóbal de las Casas and Chiapa de Corzo give way to sandbar beaches and fertile plots of coffee and cacao in the Soconusco, and for outdoor adventurers, excursions to Laguna Miramar and the Cañón del Sumidero are unmissable.

To the north, the state of Tabasco has more water than land with lagoons, rivers and wetlands. Well off the tourist trail, the region harbors some Maya ruins and an expansive biosphere reserve.

When to Go
San Cristóbal de las Casas

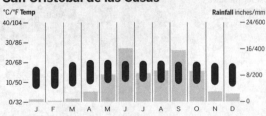

Jan Fiesta Grande de Enero in Chiapa de Corzo, and San Juan Chamula's change of cargo-holders.

Jun–Nov Nesting season for sea turtles along the Pacific coast. Heavy rains in Tabasco.

Nov–Apr The driest month, though evenings in San Cristóbal are chilly November to February.

Chiapas & Tabasco Highlights

1 **Palenque** (p383) Scaling the jungly hills and soaring Maya temples.

2 **San Cristóbal de las Casas** (p364) Strolling the high-altitude cobblestone streets.

3 **Cañón del Sumidero** (p362) Cruising through the waterway and sheer high rock-cliffs.

4 **Laguna Miramar** (p400) Spending a few splendid days hiking and relaxing at this pristine mountain-ringed lake.

5 **Madre Sal** (p411) Exploring the towering mangroves and watching for nesting turtles.

6 **Lagos de Montebello** (p405) Flitting between the sapphire and emerald lakes.

7 **Yaxchilán** (p398) Wandering amid the roar of howler monkeys at the riverside Maya ruins.

8 **Reforma Agraria** (p401) Scanning the forest for massive scarlet macaws.

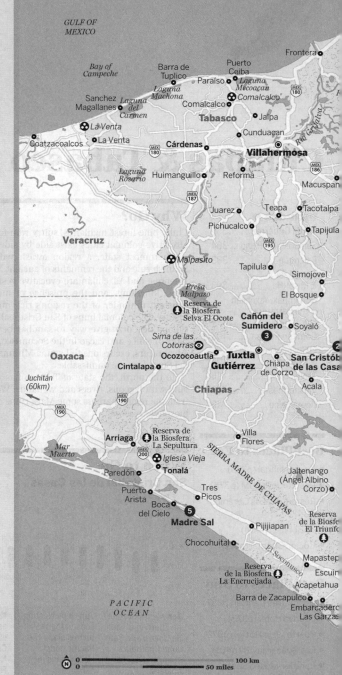

CHIAPAS

History

Low-lying, jungle-covered eastern Chiapas gave rise to some of the most splendid and powerful city-states of Maya civilization. During the Classic period (approximately AD 250–900), places such as Palenque, Yaxchilán and Toniná were the centers of power, though dozens of lesser Maya powers – including Bonampak, Comalcalco and Chinkultic – prospered in eastern Chiapas and Tabasco during this time, as Maya culture reached its peak of artistic and intellectual achievement. The ancestors of many of the distinctive indigenous groups of highland Chiapas today appear to have migrated to that region from the lowlands after the Classic Maya collapse around AD 900.

Central Chiapas was brought under Spanish control by the 1528 expedition of Diego de Mazariegos, and outlying areas were subdued in the 1530s and '40s, though Spain never gained full control of the Lacandón Jungle. New diseases arrived with the Spaniards, and an epidemic in 1544 killed about half of Chiapas' indigenous population. Chiapas was ineffectively administered from Guatemala for most of the colonial era, with little check on the colonists' excesses against its indigenous people, though some church figures, particularly Bartolomé de Las Casas (1474–1566), the first bishop of Chiapas, did fight for indigenous rights.

In 1822 a newly independent Mexico unsuccessfully attempted to annex Spain's former Central American provinces (including Chiapas), but in 1824 Chiapas opted (by a referendum) to join Mexico rather than the United Provinces of Central America. From then on, a succession of governors appointed by Mexico City, along with local landowners, maintained an almost feudal control over Chiapas.

Periodic uprisings bore witness to bad government, but the world took little notice until January 1, 1994, when Zapatista rebels suddenly and briefly occupied San Cristóbal de las Casas and nearby towns by military force. The rebel movement, with a firm and committed support base among disenchanted indigenous settlers in eastern Chiapas, quickly retreated to remote jungle bases to campaign for democratic change and indigenous rights. The Zapatistas have failed to win any significant concessions at the national level, although increased government funding steered toward Chiapas did result in noticeable improvements in the state's infrastructure, the development of tourist facilities and a growing urban middle class.

In September 2017 a magnitude 8.2 earthquake struck around 87km off the coast of Chiapas. Around 98 people were killed and over 40,000 homes were damaged. The damage could have been much worse, but the earthquake occurred far underground. By late October 2017 reconstruction work was well under way and most signs of earthquake damage had been repaired.

⊕ Getting There & Away

Bus links within the region and to other states are very good; for regional routes, minibuses, combis and *colectivo* taxis are speedier (though less spacious) alternatives.

There aren't lots of car-rental options in Chiapas. Tuxtla Gutiérrez has a number of agencies both at the airport and in town, but otherwise it's pretty thin. San Cristóbal has one rental company, and there are a few in Tapachula. The only other convenient place to rent is Villahermosa, Tabasco.

Tuxtla Gutiérrez Region

From the hot and heaving city of Tuxtla Gutiérrez to the cool splash of a waterfall or the screech of a parrot in the jungle, the Tuxtla Gutiérrez region has a lot going for it. Sadly though, most visitors hurry straight through the region in their haste to reach the nearby colonial town of San Cristóbal de las Casas.

Tuxtla Gutiérrez

☑ 961 / POP 550,000 / ELEV 530M

In Chiapas, Tuxtla Gutiérrez is as close to a big city as you're going to get. A busy modern metropolis and transportation hub, the state capital doesn't overwhelm with style, though it makes up for it with lots of amenities and nightlife. Most travelers pass through either the shiny modern airport or the bus station on the way to somewhere else, but it's a comfortable, worthwhile and welcoming place to spend a day or two.

A few blocks west of the Jardín de la Marimba, Avenida Central becomes Blvd Belisario Domínguez; many of the Tuxtla's best hotels and restaurants are strung along this road, as well as the city's big-box megastores.

⊙ Sights

★ Jardín de la Marimba PLAZA
To take your *paseo* (stroll) with the locals, stop by this leafy plaza in the evening. It's eight blocks west of Plaza Cívica, and the whole city seems to turn out here for the free nightly marimba concerts (6pm to 9pm), especially at weekends. Couples of all ages dance around the central bandstand, and the scores of sidewalk cafes – which stay open until at least 10pm or 11pm – serve some of the best coffee in town.

★ Zoológico Miguel Álvarez del Toro ZOO
(Zoomat; ☑ 961-639-28-56; www.zoomat.chiapas. gob.mx; Calz Cerro Hueco s/n; adult/child M$60/20, adult before 10am Wed-Sun M$30, Tue free; ⊙ 8:30am-4:30pm Tue-Sun) Chiapas, with its huge range of natural environments, has the highest concentration of animal species in North America, including several varieties of big cat, 1200 butterfly species and more than 600 birds. About 180 of these species, many of them in danger of extinction, are found in spacious, forested and generally natural-looking enclosures at Tuxtla's excellent zoo. Beasts you'll see here include ocelots, jaguars, pumas, tapirs, red macaws, toucans, snakes, spider monkeys and three species of crocodile.

Most interpretive materials are in both English and Spanish. To get to the zoo take a Ruta 60 'Zoológico' **colectivo** (M$8, 20 minutes) from the corner of 1a Calle Oriente Sur and 7a Avenida Sur Oriente. A taxi from the center costs around M$55.

Parque Madero PARK
The park's **Museo Regional de Chiapas** (☑ 961-225-08-81; Calz de los Hombres Ilustres; M$55; ⊙ 9am-6pm Tue-Sun), an imposing modern building, has a sampling of lesser archaeological pieces from Chiapas' many sites, and a slightly more interesting history section, running from the Spanish conquest to the revolution, all in Spanish only.

Parque Madero also contains the lush oasis of the **Jardín Botánico** (⊙ 9am-4pm) FREE and a low-key **children's theme park** (admission free, rides M$10-18; ⊙ 11am-8pm Tue-Sun). Take a Ruta 3 or 20 *colectivo* from 6a Av Norte Poniente.

Museo de la Marimba MUSEUM
(☑ 961-600-01-74; 9a Calle Poniente Norte; M$10, Sun free; ⊙ 10am-9pm) On the Jardín de la Marimba, this small museum showcases 100 years of this ubiquitous instrument, with both antique and modern models on display and a photo exhibition of the most revered marimba performers.

Museo del Café MUSEUM
(☑ 961-611-14-78; https://turismo.tuxtla.gob.mx/mcafe.php; 2a Calle Oriente Norte 236; M$25; ⊙ 9am-5pm Mon-Sat) Operated by the state government, this small museum, housed inside an attractive colonial building, contains exhibits on the cultivation and processing of everyone's favorite bean. Descriptions are in Spanish only, but English-speaking guides are available. The rooms are pleasantly air-conditioned and at the end of the tour visitors receive a cup of brew to savor in the building's pretty courtyard.

Plaza Cívica PLAZA
Bustling and broad, Tuxtla's main plaza occupies two blocks flanked by an untidy array of concrete government and commercial structures. At its southern end, across Avenida Central, you'll find nice hill views in front of the whitewashed modern **Catedral de San Marcos** (Av Central). The cathedral's clock tower tinkles out a tune on the hour to accompany a kitsch merry-go-round of apostles' images, which emerges from its upper levels.

☞ Tours

Transporte Panorámico Cañón del Sumidero TOURS
(☑ cell 961-1663740) Daily bus tours leave from Tuxtla's Jardín de la Marimba at 9:30am and 1pm if a minimum of five people show up. Three tours are available: viewing the canyon from above at five *miradores* (lookout points; M$150, 2½ hours), a *lancha* (motorboat) trip with return transportation (M$390, 4½ hours) and an all-day *miradores* and *lancha* trip (M$450, morning departure only). Call a day beforehand to confirm departures. Private regional tours also available.

🛏 Sleeping

Good budget hotels cluster in the city center, while most midrange and luxury hotels – primarily big international chains – are strung out along Avenida Central Poniente and Blvd Belisario Domínguez west of the center. The larger hotels offer sizable online and weekend discounts.

★ Hostal Tres Central HOSTEL $
(☑ 961-611-36-74; www.facebook.com/TresCentral; Central Norte 393; dm M$134, r with/without bathroom M$521/350; P ⊙ ✳ @ 🎘) Tuxtla's one

Tuxtla Gutiérrez

and only hostel is actually one of the best in Mexico. A stylish Ikea-esque affair with uber-comfortable beds in either four-person dorms or spacious private rooms (those with shared bathroom have a shower and sink in the room). The rooftop terrace views of the surrounding hills can't be beat. No kitchen facilities, though there is an on-site cafe-bar.

★ **Holiday Inn Express** BUSINESS HOTEL $
(☑800-907-458; www.ihg.com; Ave Central Pte 1254; r from M$686; P☺✱🕾) Even if you're not a fan of chain hotels this one is well worth a look. It has a prime position just two blocks from the Jardín de la Marimba, slick and friendly service, soothing color combinations, well-equipped rooms, lightning-fast internet and an impressive breakfast spread.

All up it will be hard for any other hotel in town to match the Holiday Inn Express for price and quality.

Hotel Casablanca HOTEL $
(☑961-611-03-05; 2a Av Norte Oriente 251; s with fan from M$219, s with air-con M$415, d with fan/air-con M$285/415; ☺✱🕾) Practice your jungle explorer moves as you wade through the foliage-filled courtyard of this super helpful and friendly little hotel absolutely square in the middle of town. The rooms might be dated, but they're kept polished and clean and there are little desks to work at and big mirrors to admire yourself in.

Hotel del Carmen HOTEL $
(☑961-612-30-84, 800-841-31-91; www.hoteldel carmen.net; 2a Av Sur Poniente 826; r from M$466; ✱🕾) An excellent option that offers real value for money. It's got a plumb spot between the old and new parts of town. Rooms are large and charmingly simple with starched white sheets and dark-wood furnishings. There's a good restaurant in the flower-filled covered central courtyard.

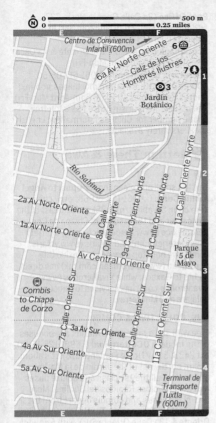

CHIAPAS & TABASCO TUXTLA GUTIÉRREZ REGION

✖ Eating

Lots of upscale and international chain options are west of the center, along Blvd Belisario Domínguez, and a number of enjoyable cafes cluster in the center around the Jardín de la Marimba.

★ Taquitos Casa Blanca TACOS $
(cnr 16 Poniente & 3a Norte 428; tacos/pozol M$10/13; ◷ 7:30am-3:30pm) One of a number of earthy eateries around this neighborhood, Taquitos Casa Blanca has made a name for itself for serving no-frills, filling, cheap and delicious tacos as well as rich cocoa *pozole* (these are something of an acquired taste!) and no trip to Tuxtla is really complete without eating here once. Busy with local workers at lunchtime.

Restaurante La Casona MEXICAN $
(☏ 961-612-75-34; 1a Av Sur Poniente 134; breakfast M$40-70, mains M$60-95; ◷ 7am-11pm; ℗) Beyond the stately carved wooden doors is a dramatic tablecloth dining room with high ceilings and interior arches in a century-old building. Dine on regional dishes such as *pollo juchi* (fried chicken with pickled vegetables and potatoes) or *tasajo*

Hotel Catedral HOTEL $
(☏ 961-613-08-24; www.hotel-catedral.net; 1a Av Norte Oriente 367; s/d M$350/400, with air-con M$450/500; ℗ ◐ ✳ ☈) A friendly, family-run place, this excellent budget option has neat, super-clean rooms with dark wood furniture and ceiling fans. It also has comfortable hall couches. Pass on the noisier downstairs rooms off the lobby. Free drinking water and morning coffee.

Hilton Garden Inn HOTEL $$
(☏ 961-617-18-00; www.tuxtlagutierrez.hgi.com; cnr Blvds Belisario Domínguez & Los Castillos; r/ste from M$1050/1350; ℗ ◐ ✳ @ ☈ ▨) The luxurious 167-room Hilton sits in a commercial area 2.5km west of the Jardín de la Marimba. Gadget-lovers will appreciate the MP3 player/alarm clock, adjustable pillow-top mattresses and internet-ready TVs, and style fans will groove on the rain-forest showerheads and Herman Miller chairs.

en salsa de chirmol (sliced beef in tomato sauce) and listen to marimba performances from 2pm to 6pm.

Florentina Pizza
PIZZA $$

(☑ 961-613-91-91; 12a Poniente Norte 174; pizzas from M$110; ⊙ 5pm-midnight Tue-Fri, 2:30pm-12:30am Sat, 2:30-10:30pm Sun; ☎) Thin-crust, wood-fired pizza, washed down with craft beer *in Tuxtla*? Yep – this is the most frequently recommended pizzeria in town, for good reason. The atmosphere's just right, the colors are bright, prices are reasonable and there's occasional live music.

★ La Mansión
MEXICAN $$$

(☑ 961-617-77-33; www.lamansion.com.mx; Sur Poniente 105; mains M$120-250; ⊙ 1pm-midnight Mon & Tue, to 1am Wed-Sat, to 9pm Sun; P ✳) Mixing classic white-tablecloth elegance with blue-and-red disco lighting, this upmarket restaurant, which is inside the Marriott Hotel, serves creative, sassy modern Mexican cuisine. Think tacos in a rainbow of colors, giant chocolate eggs and simply exquisite red meats served with lightly barbecued vegetables.

❶ Information

There's an ATM at the departure level of the airport.

Banorte (Av Central Oriente, btwn 2a Calle Oriente Sur & 3a Calle Oriente Sur; ⊙ 9am-5pm Mon-Fri, to 2pm Sat) Changes dollars.

Municipal Tourism Office (9a Calle Poniente Norte; ⊙ 9am-2pm & 4-8pm) Inside the Museo de la Marimba.

Post Office (2a Calle Oriente Norte 227; ⊙ 8am-5pm Mon-Fri, 10am-2pm Sat) In the Palacio Federal.

Scotiabank (cnr Ave Central Oriente & 4a Calle Oriente; ⊙ 8:30am-4pm Mon-Fri)

Secretaría de Turismo (☑ 961-617-05-50, 800-280-35-00; www.turismochiapas.gob.mx; Andrés Serra Rojas,1090; ⊙ 8am-4pm Mon-Fri) The main state tourism office has a toll-free phone number for Chiapas information; English speakers rarely available.

❶ Getting There & Away

AIR

Tuxtla's small and gleaming **Aeropuerto Ángel Albino Corzo** (☑ 961-153-60-68; www.chiapas aero.com; Sarabia s/n) is 35km southeast of the city center and 18km south of Chiapa de Corzo. Aeroméxico (www.aeromexico.com), Interjet (www.interjet.com) and Volaris (www.volaris.com) have nonstop services to Mexico City. Aerotucán (www.aerotucan.com.mx) has direct flights to Oaxaca, while VivaAerobus (www.vivaaerobus.com) has services to Cancún, Guadalajara and Monterrey.

BUS, COLECTIVO & COMBI

Free wi-fi and a huge supermarket are bonuses of the modern **OCC terminal** (☑ 961-125-15-80, ext 2433; 5a Av Norte Poniente 318). It's about 2.5km northwest of the Jardín de la Marimba and houses all the 1st-class and deluxe buses and the 2nd-class Rápidos del Sur line. More 2nd-class buses and combis depart from the **Terminal de Transporte Tuxtla** (cnr 9a Av Sur Oriente & 13a Calle Oriente Sur), with frequent departures for destinations including San Cristóbal, Ocosingo and Ozozocoautla.

BUSES FROM TUXTLA GUTIÉRREZ

DESTINATION	FARE (M$)	DURATION (HR)	FREQUENCY (DAILY)
Cancún	859-1055	17-20	5
Comitán	112-132	3	frequent
Mérida	1006-1342	13-14	5
Mexico City (TAPO & Norte)	898-1570	11½-12	11
Oaxaca	380-589	10	4
Palenque	268-364	6-6½	frequent
Puerto Escondido	541-666	11-12	2
San Cristóbal de las Casas	56-76	1¼	frequent
Tapachula	446-504	4½-6	frequent
Tonalá	168-202	2-2½	frequent
Villahermosa	384-412	4-5	12

For Chiapa de Corzo (M$14, 45 minutes), combis leave every few minutes between 5am and 10:30pm from 1a Avenida Sur Oriente.

To San Cristóbal

For San Cristóbal de las Casas (M$50, one hour), minibuses and combis are faster and more frequent (every 10 minutes) than the bus.

Corazón de María (☑ 961-600-12-12; 13a Calle Oriente Sur) Combis depart from a storefront near Av Central Oriente; services 4am to 9pm.

Ómnibus de Chiapas (☑ 961-611-26-56; cnr 7a Calle Oriente Sur & 1a Av Sur Poniente) Comfortable minibuses (called 'sprinters'); departures 5am to 10pm.

CAR & MOTORCYCLE

In addition to companies at the airport, in-town rental agencies include **Alamo** (☑ 961-153-61-23; www.alamo.com; 5a Av Norte Poniente 2260; ☺ 7am-10pm), near the OCC bus station, and **Europcar** (☑ 961-121-49-22; www.europcar. com; Blvd Belisario Domínguez 2075; ☺ 8am-11pm Mon-Fri, to 4pm Sat & Sun).

ⓘ Getting Around

TO/FROM THE AIRPORT

From the airport, prepay taxis (one to three passengers) meet all flights and go to central Tuxtla (M$350, 40 minutes), Chiapa de Corzo (M$300, 30 minutes) and San Cristóbal (M$1100 private or M$300 shared, one hour). OCC runs frequent buses directly from the terminal to San Cristóbal (M$240) roughly every one or two hours between 8am and 11pm, although there is a three-hour pause in the service between 10am and 1pm.

BUS

A biodiesel bus service called **ConejoBus** (☺ 5am-11pm) plies Blvd Belisario Domínguez–Avenida Central; you'll need a prepaid card (M$5.50 from the Palacio de Gobierno on the Parque Central) to ride. For other areas, consult www.tuxmapa.com.mx for local combi routes. Taxi rides within the city cost M$40 to M$50.

West of Tuxtla Gutiérrez

Sima de las Cotorras   CENOTE

(Abyss of the Parrots; www.simaecoturismo.com; adult/child over 9yr M$30/15) The Sima de las Cotorras is a dramatic 160m-wide sinkhole that punches 140m down into the earth into a crater thick with rain forest. At sunrise, a green cloud of screeching parrots spirals out for the day, trickling back before dusk. With binoculars you can see a series of red pre-Hispanic rock paintings that decorate one side of the cliff face, and you can also

hike or rappel (M$700) down into the hole. For serious bird-watchers this is an essential stop.

Lodging (☑ cell 968-1178081; www.simaeco turismo.com; campsites M$100, tent & sleeping bag rental M$250-300, d/q M$400/600, 6-person cabañas M$800; ℗ ☻) is available (the spacious six-person, two-room *cabañas* are well worth the extra cost), and there is a good **restaurant** (mains from M$85; ☺ 8am-6pm) serving scrumptious *tamales* and hand-made tortillas.

From the last stop in Ocozocoautla (Coita), located on Hwy 190 right at the signed turnoff for the Sima, take a taxi (around M$300, 50 minutes). Three daily Piedra Parada *colectivos* (M$14) also leave from this stop, but let you off 4km before the Sima. Driving from Tuxtla, it's reasonably well signed all the way. Go all the way through Ocozocoautla, turning right at the minibus terminal (there's a blue turnoff sign here, but it's not visible coming from this direction), go 3.5km north, then 12km on a good dirt road.

El Aguacero   WATERFALL

(www.cascadaelaguacero.com; M$32; ☺ 7am-5pm) Plunging into the sheer Río La Venta canyon, El Aguacero is a gorgeous series of frothy stairsteps that tumble and spray. In drier months (usually December through May), you can stroll along sandy riverbed beaches to the waterfall. When the water's high, it's a half-hour hike along a shady jungle trail.

From December through May, you can also explore an underground river running through the 200m-long **El Encanto cave.** An hour-long tour (M$200) includes all equipment (helmet, headlamp etc).

In the past access to the waterfalls was via 724 well-built steps, but at the time of research access to these was temporarily blocked and you could only see the falls from a couple of watchtowers.

Camping (campsites per person M$65, campsite & equipment for 4 M$300) and hammock space (with showers) is available, and a small *comedor* (food stall) usually serves quesadillas (M$20).

From Ocozocoautla (Coita), *colectivos* to El Gavilán/Las Cruces (M$12) can drop you off at the highway turnoff, and it's a 3km walk down to the entrance. Drivers should look for the turnoff sign about 15km west of Ocozocoautla.

Chiapa de Corzo

☑ 961 / POP 45,000 / ELEV 450M

Set 12km east of Tuxtla Gutiérrez on the way to San Cristóbal, Chiapa de Corzo is a small and attractive colonial town with an easygoing, provincial air. Set on the north bank of the broad Río Grijalva, it's the main starting point for trips into the Cañón del Sumidero.

Chiapa de Corzo has been occupied almost continuously since about 1200 BC. Before the Spaniards arrived, the warlike Chiapa tribe had their capital, Nandalumí, a couple of kilometers downstream, on the opposite bank of the Grijalva. When Diego de Mazariegos invaded the area in 1528, the Chiapa hurled themselves by the hundreds to their death in the canyon rather than surrender. Mazariegos founded a settlement called Chiapa de Los Indios here, but quickly shifted his base to San Cristóbal de las Casas, where he found the climate and indigenous inhabitants more manageable.

◉ Sights

The *embarcadero* (jetty) for Cañón del Sumidero boat trips is two blocks south of the plaza down Calle 5 de Febrero. Look for the road lined with vendors.

★ Cañón del Sumidero   CANYON

The Sumidero Canyon is a spectacular fissure in the earth, found north of Tuxtla Gutiérrez. In 1981 the Chicoasén hydroelectric dam was completed at its northern end, damming the Río Grijalva, which flows through the canyon, and creating a 25km-long reservoir. Traveling between Tuxtla and Chiapa de Corzo, the road crosses the Grijalva just south of the canyon mouth.

The most impressive way to see the canyon is from a **lancha** (return trip M$215; ◷ 8am-4pm) that speeds between the canyon's towering rock walls. It's about a two-hour return trip, starting at either Chiapa de Corzo or the Embarcadero Cahuaré, 5km north of Chiapa along the road to Tuxtla. You'll rarely have to wait more than half an hour for a boat to fill up. Bring a drink, something to shield you from the sun and, if there's any chance of bad weather, some warm clothing or a waterproof jacket.

It's about 35km from Chiapa de Corzo to the dam. Soon after you pass under Hwy 190, the canyon walls tower an amazing 800m above you. Along the way you'll see a variety of birds – herons, cormorants, vultures and kingfishers – plus probably a crocodile or two.

The boat operators will point out a few odd formations of rock and vegetation, including one cliff face covered in thick hanging moss, resembling a giant Christmas tree. *Lanchas* sometimes have to plow through a sheen of floating plastic garbage when wet-season rains wash in trash from Tuxtla Gutiérrez.

Plaza   PLAZA

Impressive arcades frame three sides of the plaza, and a beefy tree called **La Pochota** buckles the sidewalk with its centuries-old roots. Venerated by the indigenous people who founded the town, it's the oldest ceiba tree along the Río Grijalva. But the focal point of the plaza is **La Pila** (also called the Fuente Colonial), a handsome brick fountain completed in 1562 in Mudejar-Gothic style. It's said to resemble the Spanish crown.

Chiapa de Corzo   ARCHAEOLOGICAL SITE

(Av Hidalgo, Barrio Benito Juárez; ◷ 9am-5pm) **FREE** On a trade route between the Pacific and the Gulf, the sprawling Chiapa de Corzo settlement had close ties to neighboring Maya and Olmec cultures. At its peak, it counted about 200 structures, but was abandoned around AD 500. After years of excavation, three Zoque pyramid structures are now on view here, 1.5km east of the main plaza. These visible structures were built between 1600 and 1800 years ago, but sit on mounds dating back as far as 750 BC.

Though the guarded ruins receive few visitors, it's worth an hour to climb around the deserted temples and marvel at the big-sky countryside. Recent excavation of one nearby mound (not open to the public) unearthed the oldest known pyramid tomb in Mesoamerica and new evidence linking it to Olmec centers such as La Venta.

The site entrance is near the Nestlé plant and the old highway (on the road that goes to La Topada de la Flor), but the site isn't signed from the road. Taxis charge about M$150 round trip from the plaza with an hour of wait time, but you can walk there in 20 minutes.

Templo de Santo Domingo
de Guzmán   CHURCH

(Mexicanidad Chiapaneca 10; ◷ 8am-5pm) The large Templo de Santo Domingo de Guzmán, one block south of the main plaza, was built in the late 16th century by the Dominican order. Its adjoining convent is now the **Centro Cultural** (☑ 997-616-00-55; www.facebook.com/CentroculturalExconvento; ◷ 10am-5pm Tue-Sun) **FREE**, home to an exposition of the wood and lino prints of talented Chiapa-born Franco Lázaro Gómez (1922–49), as well as the **Museo de la Laca**, which is dedicated to the local craft specialty: lacquered gourds. The museum holds pieces dating back to 1606.

🎎 Festivals & Events

Fiesta Grande de Enero   CULTURAL
(🕙 Jan) Held for a week in mid-January, this is one of Mexico's liveliest and most extraordinary festivals, including nightly dances involving cross-dressing young men, known as Las Chuntá. Women don the highly colorful, beautifully embroidered *chiapaneca* dress, and blond-wigged, mask-toting *Parachicos* (impersonating conquistadors) parade on a number of days. A canoe battle and fireworks extravaganza follow on the final evening.

🛏 Sleeping & Eating

Restaurants on the *embarcadero* have near-identical, and equally overpriced, menus. The river views are nice, though battling marimba players tend to amp up the noise level. The market (southeast of the plaza) is your best bet for an inexpensive meal. *Tascalate* (a sweet concoction of ground cacao, pine nuts, toasted corn, cinnamon and annatto) can be found on most menus, and many shops sell the drink powder.

Posada Rocio   HOTEL $
(📞 961-616-02-04; Zaragoza 347; d/tr from M$300/310; 🐕) Just off the main plaza, this humble little faded orange guesthouse ticks all the budget-hotel boxes with its decent-sized, clean rooms, friendly management and a good location.

INDIGENOUS PEOPLES OF CHIAPAS

Of the 4.8 million people of Chiapas, approximately a quarter are indigenous, with language being the key ethnic identifier. Each of the eight principal groups has its own language, beliefs and customs, a cultural variety that makes Chiapas one of the most fascinating states in Mexico. Travelers to the area around San Cristóbal are most likely to encounter the Tzotziles and the Tzeltales. Their traditional religious life is nominally Catholic, but integrates pre-Hispanic elements. Most people live in the hills outside the villages, which are primarily market and ceremonial centers.

Tzotzil and Tzeltal clothing is among the most varied, colorful and elaborately worked in Mexico. It not only identifies wearers' villages but also continues ancient Maya traditions. Many of the seemingly abstract designs on these costumes are in fact stylized snakes, frogs, butterflies, birds, saints and other beings. Some motifs have religious-magical functions: scorpions, for example, can be a symbolic request for rain, since they are believed to attract lightning.

The Lacandones dwelled deep in the Lacandón Jungle and largely avoided contact with the outside world until the 1950s. They now number less than 1000 and mostly live in three main settlements in that same region (Lacanjá Chansayab, Metzabok and Nahá), with low-key tourism being one of their major means of support. Lacandones are readily recognizable in their white tunics and long black hair cut in a fringe. Most Lacandones have now abandoned their traditional animist religion in favor of Presbyterian or evangelical forms of Christianity.

Traditionally treated as second-class citizens, indigenous groups mostly live on the least productive land in the state, with the least amount of government services or infrastructure. Many indigenous communities rely on subsistence farming and have no running water or electricity, and it was frustration over lack of political power and their historical mistreatment that fueled the Zapatista rebellion, putting a spotlight on the region's distinct inequities.

Today, long-standing indigenous ways of life are challenged both by evangelical Christianity – opposed to many traditional animist-Catholic practices and the abuse of alcohol in religious rituals – and by the Zapatista movement, which rejects traditional leadership hierarchies and is raising the rights and profile of women. Many highland indigenous people have emigrated to the Lacandón Jungle to clear new land, or to Mexican and US cities in search of work. Despite all obstacles, indigenous identities and self-respect survive. Indigenous people may be suspicious of outsiders, and may resent interference in their religious observances or other aspects of their life, but if treated with due respect they are likely to respond in kind.

Hotel La Ceiba
HOTEL $$

(☑ 961-616-03-89; www.laceibahotel.com; Av Domingo Ruíz 300; r M$745; P❂✳❈❂✿) The most upscale place in town (though the rooms are quite simple), La Ceiba has a full-service spa and restaurant, an inviting pool, a lush garden and 87 well-kept air-conditioned rooms in an arched and domed colonial-flavored building. It's two blocks west of the main plaza.

Hotel Santiago
HOTEL $$

(☑ cell 961-1531049; www.hoteldesantiago.com; López s/n; r from M$434; ❂) Down by the port, this medium-sized hotel has plenty of colonial stylings from the outside but very few on the inside. Rooms are arranged around a central patio/lightwell and are big, comfortable and simple. It's a quiet spot (except in festival time of course) despite its central location. If you're here in low season definitely ask for a discount.

Los Sabores de San Jacinto
MEXICAN $

(☑ 961-218-46-88; Calle 5 de Febrero 144; mains M$80-120; ❂1pm-midnight Wed-Tue) This no-frills place, with a handful of tables inside the orange dining room and a couple more outside on the terrace overlooking the street, serves hearty, simple but very tasty south Mexican staples. The service is fast and it's one of the few places open in the evenings.

Restaurant Jardines de Chiapa
MEXICAN $$

(☑ 961-616-01-98; www.restaurantesjardines.com. mx; Madero 395; mains M$95-180; ❂9am-7pm) Not too far from the main plaza, this large place is set around a garden patio with atmospheric brick columns. The long menu includes the tasty house special *cochinito al horno* (oven-baked pork). Be warned that it can get a bit hectic at lunchtime with tour groups pouring in for the buffet lunch (M$279). Stick with à la carte!

D'Avellino
ITALIAN $$

(☑ 961-153-07-33; www.davellino.com.mx; Calz Grajales 1103; mains M$55-130, pizza M$99-155; ❂1pm-1am Mon-Sat, to midnight Sun) A cute Italian restaurant with a rustic old-world dining room and patio seating, D'Avellino serves fresh pastas and good pizza in a warm and convivial atmosphere. It's an easy five- to 10-minute stroll northwest of the plaza, along the main Tuxtla-bound road.

❶ Information

The **state tourism office** (☑ 961-616-10-13; Calle 5 de Febrero s/n; ❂8am-4pm Mon-Fri, 9am-1pm Sat) is in the Municipal building in front of the main plaza.

❶ Getting There & Away

Combis from Tuxtla Gutiérrez (M$14, 45 minutes) leave frequently from 1a Avenida Sur Oriente (between Calles 5a and 7a Oriente Sur) between 5am and 10:30pm. They arrive (and return to Tuxtla) from the north side of the main plaza.

There's no direct transportation between San Cristóbal and the center of Chiapa de Corzo. From San Cristóbal, catch a Tuxtla-bound combi and ask to be let off at the Chiapa de Corzo stop on the highway (M$35, 30 minutes). From there, cross the highway and flag down a combi (M$7) to the plaza. From Chiapa de Corzo to San Cristóbal, catch a combi from the plaza back to the highway and then flag down a combi heading to San Cristóbal. You'll rarely wait more than a few minutes for a connecting combi in either direction.

San Cristóbal Region

All tourist roads in Chiapas lead, sooner or later, to the pastel painted, cobbled streets of the gorgeous mountain city of San Cristóbal de las Casas. Although the city is rich in cultural attractions, for many visitors it's the bright highland light, humming street life and the chance to mingle with the local indigenous people – a people who are descended from the ancient Maya and maintain some unique customs, traditional dress and beliefs – that is the greatest draw.

Markets and festivals often give the most interesting insight into indigenous life, and beyond the valley bowl in which San Cristóbal nestles, lots of village markets take place. Full of life and the hues of a hundred different colors, the weekly markets at the villages are today nearly always held on Sunday. Proceedings start as early as dawn, and wind down by lunchtime.

San Cristóbal de las Casas

☑ 967 / POP 185,000 / ELEV 1940M

Set in a gorgeous highland valley surrounded by pine forest, the colonial city of San Cristóbal (cris-*toh*-bal) has been a popular travelers' destination for decades. It's a pleasure to explore San Cristóbal's cobbled streets and markets, soaking up the unique ambience and the wonderfully clear highland light. This medium-sized city also boasts a comfortable blend of city and countryside, with restored century-old houses giving way to grazing animals and fields of corn.

Surrounded by dozens of traditional Tzotzil and Tzeltal villages, San Cristóbal is at the heart of one of the most deeply rooted indigenous areas in Mexico. A great base for local and regional exploration, it's a place where ancient customs coexist with modern luxuries.

The city shook violently during the September 2017 Chiapas earthquake: though some buildings were damaged or collapsed, in general the town escaped serious damage.

History

Diego de Mazariegos founded San Cristóbal as the Spanish regional base in 1528. Its Spanish citizens made fortunes from wheat, while the indigenous people lost their lands and suffered diseases, taxes and forced labor. The church afforded some protection against colonist excesses. Dominican monks reached Chiapas in 1545, and made San Cristóbal their main base. The town is now named after one of them, Bartolomé de Las Casas, who was appointed bishop of Chiapas and became the most prominent Spanish defender of indigenous people in colonial times. In modern times Bishop Samuel Ruiz, who passed away in 2011, followed in Las Casas' footsteps, defending the oppressed indigenous people and earning the hostility of the Chiapas establishment.

San Cristóbal was the state capital of Chiapas from 1824 to 1892, but remained relatively isolated until the 1970s, when tourism began to influence its economy.

Recent decades have seen an influx of indigenous villagers into the 'Cinturón de Miseria' (Belt of Misery), a series of impoverished, violence-ridden, makeshift colonies around San Cristóbal's *periférico* (ring road). Many of these people are here because they have been expelled from Chamula and other communities as a result of internal politico-religious conflicts. Most of the craft sellers around Santo Domingo church and the underage hawkers around town come from the Cinturón de Miseria.

San Cristóbal was catapulted into the international limelight on January 1, 1994, when the Zapatista rebels selected it as one of four places from which to launch their revolution, seizing and sacking government offices in the town before being driven out

DON'T MISS

TWO VIEWPOINTS

Want to take in the best views in town? Well, you'll have to work for them, because at this altitude the stairs up these hills can be punishing. The **Cerro de San Cristóbal** (off Hermanos Dominguez) and **Cerro de Guadalupe** (off Real de Guadalupe) lord over the town from the west and east, respectively, and churches crown both lookouts. The Iglesia de Guadalupe becomes a hot spot for religious devotees around the **Día de la Virgen de Guadalupe**. These areas are not considered safe at night.

within a few days by the Mexican army. The city remains a hot spot for sympathizers (and some opponents) of the Zapatista rebels, and a central location for organizations working with Chiapas' indigenous people. Political and social tensions remain, but San Cristóbal continues to attract travelers, real-estate investment and a growing middle class.

◉ Sights

San Cristóbal is very walkable, with straight streets rambling up and down several gentle hills. Heading east from Plaza 31 de Marzo, Real de Guadalupe has a pedestrian-only section with a concentration of places to stay and eat. Another pedestrian mall, the Andador Turístico, runs up Hidalgo and Avenida 20 de Noviembre.

★**Na Bolom**   HISTORIC BUILDING
(☎967-678-14-18; www.na-bolom.org; Guerrero 33; M$40, with tour M$50; ☉9am-7pm) An atmospheric museum-research center, Na Bolom for many years was the home of Swiss anthropologist and photographer Gertrude Duby-Blom (Trudy Blom; 1901–93) and her Danish archaeologist husband Frans Blom (1893–1963). Na Bolom means 'Jaguar House' in the Tzotzil language (as well as being a play on its former owners' name). It's full of photographs, archaeological and anthropological relics and books.

The house tour provides a revealing insight into the lives of the Bloms and the Chiapas of half a century and more ago – though the picture presented of the Lacandones does dwell more on their past than their present. The Bloms bought the

San Cristóbal de las Casas

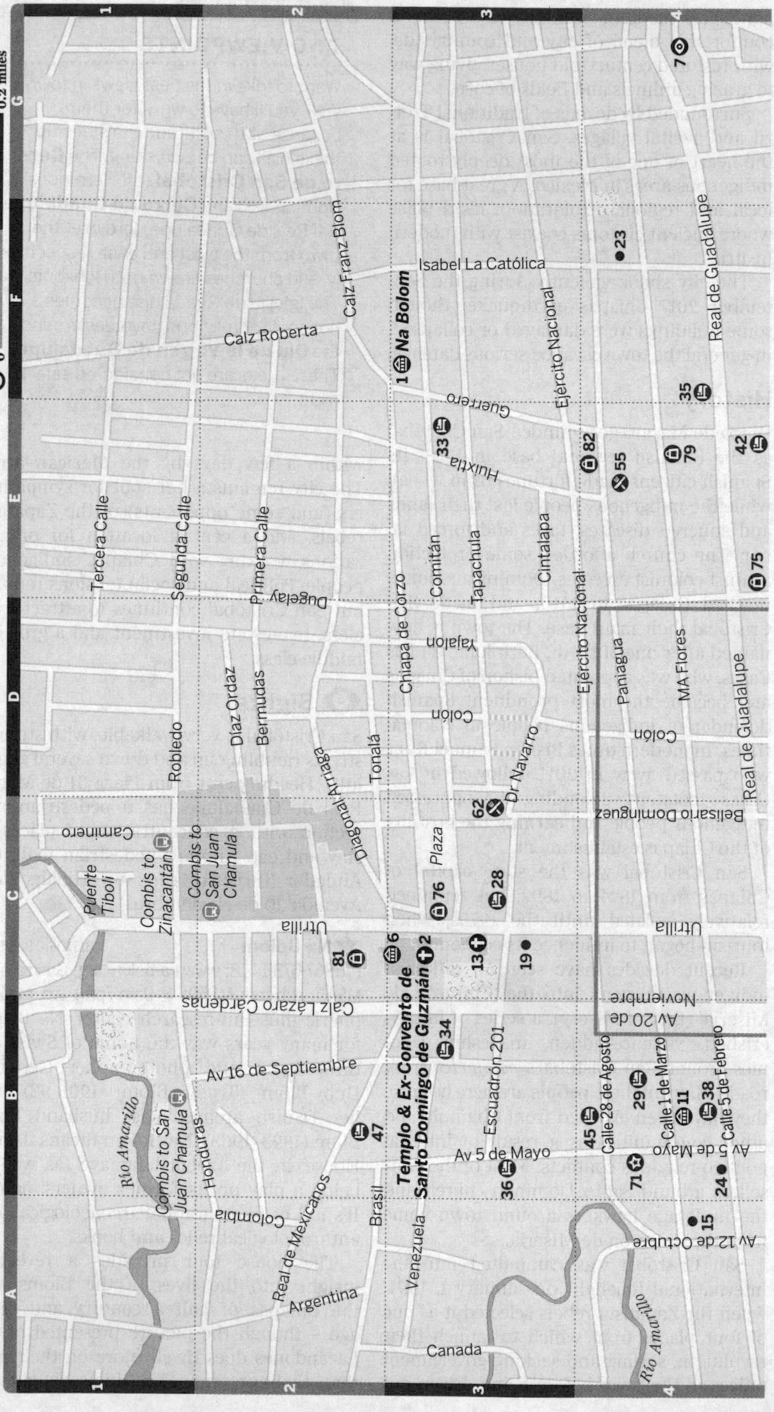

CHIAPAS & TABASCO

0 0
400 m
0.2 miles

Río Amarillo

Combis to San Juan Chamula

Colombia
Honduras
Real de Mexicanos
Brasil
Venezuela
Argentina
Canada
Río Amarillo

Av 12 de Octubre

Av 16 de Septiembre

Calz Lázaro Cárdenas

Puente Tiboli
Combis to Zinacantán
Caminero
Combis to San Juan Chamula

Tercera Calle
Segunda Calle
Primera Calle
Robledo
Díaz Ordaz
Bermudas
Diagonal Arriaga
Tonalá
Colón

Duguelay
Chiapa de Corzo
Yajalon
Dr. Navarro

Calz Roberta
Calz Franz Blom

Isabel La Católica

Real de Guadalupe

Ejército Nacional
Guerrero
Huixtla
Comitán
Tapachula
Cintalapa

Paniagua
MA Flores
Colón
Belisario Domínguez
Utrilla
Real de Guadalupe

Av 20 de Noviembre
Escuadrón 201
Av 5 de Mayo
Calle 28 de Agosto
Calle 1 de Marzo
Calle 5 de Febrero
Av 5 de Mayo

Utrilla

Plaza

Templo & Ex-Convento de Santo Domingo de Guzmán

1 Na Bolom

7
23
35
42
75
79
82
55
33
62
76
28
81
6
2
13
19
34
47
36
71
45
29
11
38
15
24

367

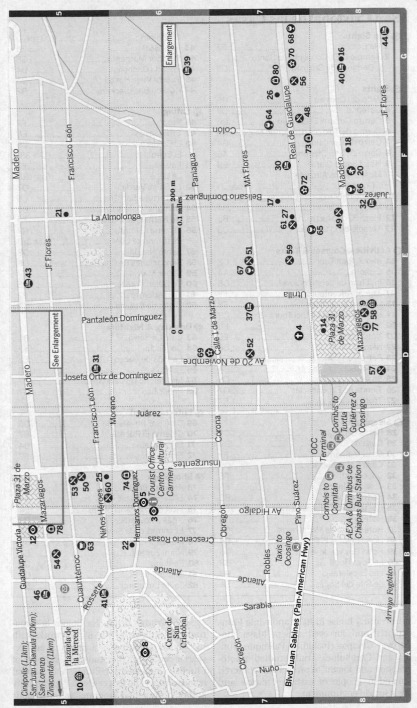

CHIAPAS & TABASCO

San Cristóbal de las Casas

19th-century house in 1950, and while Frans explored and surveyed ancient Maya sites all over Chiapas (including Palenque, Toniná and Chinkultic), Trudy studied, photographed and fought to protect the scattered Lacandón people of eastern Chiapas and their jungle environment.

Since Trudy's death, Na Bolom has continued the thrust of the Bloms' work, with the house operating as a museum and research center for the study and support of Chiapas' indigenous cultures and natural environment, and as a center for community and environmental programs in indigenous areas. The library of more than 9000 books and documents here is a major resource on the Maya.

Na Bolom also offers guest rooms (p373) and meals made with organic vegetables grown in its garden.

★ **Templo & Ex-Convento de Santo Domingo de Guzmán**   CHURCH
(Utrilla; ⊙ 6:30am-2pm & 4-8pm) FREE Located just north of the center of town, the imposing 16th-century Templo de Santo Domingo is San Cristóbal's most beautiful church, especially when its facade catches the late-afternoon sun. This baroque frontage, with outstanding filigree stucco work, was added in the 17th century and includes the double-headed Hapsburg eagle, then the symbol of the Spanish monarchy. The interior is lavishly gilded, especially the ornate pulpit.

On the western side, the attached former monastery contains a regional museum and the excellent **Centro de Textiles del Mundo Maya** (http://fomentoculturalbanamex.org/ctmm; Calz Lázaro Cárdenas; M$55; ⊙ 9am-5:45pm Tue-Sun). Around Santo Domingo and the neighboring **Templo de la Caridad**, built in 1712, Chamulan women and bohemian types from around Mexico conduct a colorful daily crafts market. The weavers' showroom of Sna Jolobil (p377) is now in a separate light-filled building on the northwest section of the grounds.

Plaza 31 de Marzo   PLAZA
The leafy main plaza is a fine place to take in San Cristóbal's unhurried highland atmosphere. Shoe-shiners, newspaper sellers and *ambulantes* (mobile street vendors) gather around the elaborate iron bandstand.

The **Hotel Santa Clara**, on the plaza's southeast corner, was built by Diego de Mazariegos, the Spanish conqueror of Chiapas. His coat of arms is engraved above the main portal. The building is a rare secular example of plateresque style in Mexico.

Catedral   CATHEDRAL
(Plaza 31 de Marzo) On the north side of the plaza, the candy-colored cathedral was begun in 1528 but wasn't completed until 1815 because of several natural disasters. Sure enough, new earthquakes struck in 1816 and also 1847, causing considerable damage, but it was restored again from 1920 to 1922. The gold-leaf interior has lots of incense smoke and candlelight as well as five gilded altarpieces featuring 18th-century paintings by Miguel Cabrera.

Museo de los Altos de Chiapas   MUSEUM
(✆ 967-678-16-09; Calz Lázaro Cárdenas s/n; M$55; ⊙ 9am-5:30pm Tue-Sun) One of two museums inside the Ex-Convento de Santo Domingo, which is located on the western side of the Templo de Santo Domingo, this museum has several impressive archaeological relics – including stelae from Chincultik – as well as exhibits on the Spanish conquest and evangelization of the region. Admission is bundled with Centro de Textiles del Mundo Maya.

Museo del Ámbar de Chiapas   MUSEUM
(✆ 967-674-58-99; www.museodelambar.com; Plazuela de la Merced; M$25; ⊙ 10am-2pm & 4-8pm Tue-Sun) Chiapas amber – fossilized pine resin that's around 30 million years old – is known for its clarity and diverse colors. Most is mined around Simojovel, north of San Cristóbal. This small museum explains all things amber (with information sheets in English, French, German, Japanese and Italian). There are some gorgeous pieces on display with magnifying glasses so you can make out all the detail, and various films are shown. Afterward you can shop for some exquisitely carved items and insect-embedded pieces.

Note that a number of nearby jewelry shops have appropriated the museum's name, but this is the only place around that's housed in an ex-convent – you can't miss it.

Arco del Carmen   GATE
The Arco del Carmen, at the southern end of the Andador Turístico on Hidalgo, dates from the late 17th century and was once the city's gateway.

Centro Cultural El Carmen   NOTABLE BUILDING
(Hermanos Domínguez s/n; ⊙ 9am-2pm & 4-8pm Mon-Fri) FREE This ex-convent, just east of the Arco del Carmen, is a wonderful colonial building, with a large, peaceful garden. It's now the Centro Cultural El Carmen, hosting art and photography exhibitions and the occasional musical event.

Museo del Cacao   MUSEUM
(✆ 967-631-79-95; www.kakaw.org; 1ro de Marzo 16; M$30; ⊙ 10am-7pm Mon-Sat, 11am-4pm Sun) This chocolate museum runs along an open upstairs balcony of a cafe. Learn about the history of chocolate and how it was used by the Maya. Also on display are modern chocolate drinking vessels and utensils, and the process to create the delicious substance. Includes a free sample.

❧ Courses

Several good language schools offer instruction in Spanish, with flexibility to meet most level and schedule requirements. Weekly rates normally include three hours' tuition five days a week, but many variations (classes only, hourly instruction, homestays etc) are available.

La Casa en el Árbol
LANGUAGE

(☎967-674-52-72; www.lacasaenelarbol.org; Madero 29; individual classes 1/10/20hr M$150/1350/2400, homestay & meals per week M$1700) The 'Tree House' is an enthusiastic, socially committed school that teaches Tseltal and Tsotzil. It offers lots of out-of-school activities and is also a base for volunteer programs. Mexican cooking classes are also available.

Instituto de Lenguas Jovel
LANGUAGE

(☎967-678-40-69; www.institutojovel.com; Madero 45; individual/group classes per week from US$215/140, homestay per week from US$140) Instituto Jovel is professional and friendly, and has a top-class reputation among students. Most tuition is one-to-one, and it has a beautiful location. Classes in indigenous cultures of Chiapas (US$110), Mexican cooking (US$26 to US$34), history (US$110) and salsa dancing (US$6) are offered too.

Shaktipat Yoga
HEALTH & WELLBEING

(☎cell 967-1025053; http://shaktipatyoga.com.mx; Niños Héroes 2; class M$65) A studio in the healing-arts complex of Casa Luz with multilingual vinyasa, ashtanga and hatha yoga classes. Multiclass discounts.

☞ Tours

Agencies in San Cristóbal (open approximately 8am to 9pm) offer a variety of tours, often with guides who speak English, French or Italian, though many offer transportation only. Typical day trips run to Chiapa de Corzo and Cañón del Sumidero (from M$400, six to seven hours), Lagos de Montebello and El Chiflón waterfalls (M$450, nine to 10 hours) and Palenque, Agua Azul and Misol-Ha (M$550, 14 hours). All prices are per person (usually with a minimum of four people).

Alex & Raúl Tours
CULTURAL

(☎967-678-91-41; www.alexyraultours.wordpress.com; per person M$250) Enjoyable and informative minibus tours in English, French or Spanish. Raúl and/or a colleague wait at the wooden cross in front of San Cristóbal's cathedral from 8:45am to 9:30am daily, going to San Juan Chamula and Zinacantán. Trips to Tenejapa, San Andrés Larraínzar or Amatenango del Valle can also be arranged for a minimum of four people.

Jaguar Adventours
CYCLING

(☎967-631-50-62; www.adventours.mx; Belisario Domínguez 8A; bicycle rental per hour/day M$50/250; ⊗9am-2:30pm & 3:30-8pm Mon-Sat, 9am-2:30pm Sun) Does bicycle tours to Chamula and Zincantán (M$650), plus longer expeditions. Prices start at M$450 per person. Also rents out quality mountain bikes with helmet and lock.

Marcosapata o En Bici Tours
CYCLING, HIKING

(☎967-141-72-16; http://marcosapata1.wordpress.com) Offers tailored hiking tours (M$250) and bike tours visiting San Lorenzo Zinacantán, San Juan Chamula, Rancho Nuevo or the Cañón del Sumidero. Tours cost between M$440 and M$700. English and French spoken. Ask for Marco Antonio Morales at the clothing store at Utrilla 18.

Petra Vertical
ADVENTURE

(☎967-631-51-73; www.petravertical.com; Isabel la Católica 9B) Regional climbing, rappeling and rafting excursions, with destinations including the Sima de las Cotorras, El Aguacero, the Cañón de la Venta, and the Chorreadero waterfall and cave system near Chiapa de Corzo. Also organizes walking trips from San Cristóbal to the Arcotete river cave and the Huitepec reserve.

Nichim Tours
ADVENTURE

(☎967-631-63-40; www.nichimtours.com.mx; Hermanos Domínguez 15) Full-service agency offering adventurous tours to the Selva El Ocote, as well as regional day trips to amber mines and workshops, and indigenous markets. Multilingual guides.

Natutours
OUTDOORS

(☎967-674-63-52; www.natutours.com.mx; Vicente Guerrero 20; ⊗9am-4pm Mon-Sat) 🍃 Specializes in ecotourism (including intriguing tree-climbing outings), jungle treks and cultural tourism, and also holds workshops to promote recycling and sustainable use in the region – although hopefully you're already doing that!

Tienda de Experiencias
TOUR, BUS TOUR

(☎800-841-66-09; www.facebook.com/pg/Tiendade Experiencias; Real de Guadalupe 40A) Offers small group tours to artisan cooperatives, scuba/snuba diving in cenotes and other eclectic 'experiences.' Its Jungle Connection hop-on/hop-off bus route circles the Lacandón.

THE ZAPATISTAS

On January 1, 1994, the day the North American Free Trade Agreement (Nafta) was implemented, a previously unknown leftist guerrilla army emerged from the forests to occupy San Cristóbal de las Casas and other towns in Chiapas. The Ejército Zapatista de Liberación Nacional (EZLN; Zapatista National Liberation Army) linked antiglobalization rhetoric with Mexican revolutionary slogans, declaring that they aimed to both overturn the oligarchy's centuries-old hold on land, resources and power, and improve the wretched living standards of Mexico's indigenous people.

The Mexican army evicted the Zapatistas within days, and the rebels retreated to the fringes of the Lacandón Jungle to wage a propaganda war, mainly fought via the internet. The Zapatistas' balaclava-clad, pipe-puffing Subcomandante Marcos (a former university professor named Rafael Guillén) rapidly became a cult figure. High-profile conventions against neoliberalism were held, international supporters flocked to Zapatista headquarters at La Realidad, and Zapatista-aligned peasants took over hundreds of farms and ranches in Chiapas.

A set of accords on indigenous rights and autonomy was negotiated between the Zapatistas and the Mexican government but never ratified, and tension and killings escalated in Chiapas through the 1990s. According to Amnesty International, the paramilitary groups responsible for a massacre in Acteal in 1997 were armed by the authorities. By 1999 an estimated 21,000 villagers had fled their homes after a campaign of intimidation.

After a high-profile Zapatista media campaign, La Otra Campaña (The Other Campaign), during Mexico's 2006 presidential election, the EZLN has mostly remained dormant, with only the occasional conference and mobilization, its political influence slight outside its own enclaves. The movement still maintains five regional 'Juntas de Buen Gobierno' (Committees of Good Government) and many autonomous communities, though some former supporters have grown disillusioned and many have left the movement.

In 2016, in a break with tradition, the Zapatista's elected to put forward a candidate for the 2018 presidential elections. This has ended 20 years of the Zapatista's rejection of Mexican politics.

Further background is available in *The Zapatista Reader,* an anthology of writers from Octavio Paz and Gabriel García Márquez to Marcos himself, and Bill Weinberg's *Homage to Chiapas: The New Indigenous Struggles in Mexico.*

SendaSur
ECOTOUR

(📱 967-678-39-09; www.sendasur.com.mx; Calle 5 de Febrero 29; ⊙ 9am-2pm & 4-7pm Mon-Fri, 9am-noon Sat) ✐ A partner-based ecotourism network based in San Cristóbal de las Casas, but operating throughout Chiapas, Senda-Sur can help with independent travel and reservations in the Lacandón and El Ocote jungle regions.

Explora
ADVENTURE

(📱 967-631-74-98; www.ecochiapas.com; Calle 1 de Marzo 30; ⊙ 9:30am-2pm & 4-8pm Mon-Fri, 9:30am-2pm Sat) Adventure trips to the Lacandón Jungle, including multiday river kayaking and rafting.

Trotamundos
TOURS

(📱 967-678-70-21; www.facebook.com/trotamundos agencia; Real de Guadalupe 26C) Regional transportation, Tuxtla airport transfers and trips to Laguna Miramar.

🎉 Festivals & Events

Semana Santa
RELIGIOUS

The Crucifixion is acted out on Good Friday in the Barrio de Mexicanos, northwest of town.

Feria de la Primavera y de la Paz
CULTURAL

(Spring & Peace Fair) Easter Sunday is the start of this weeklong town fair, with parades, musical events and bullfights.

Festival Cervantino Barroco
CULTURAL

(Cervantes Festival; ⊙ Oct/Nov) A fair with art, music, dance and theater.

Festival Internacional Cervantino Barroco
ART

(www.conecultachiapas.gob.mx; ⊙ late Oct) **FREE** This free weeklong cultural program keeps things hopping with world-class music, dance and theater.

🛏 Sleeping

San Cristóbal has a wealth of budget accommodations, but also a number of appealing and atmospheric midrange hotels, often set in colonial or 19th-century mansions, along with a smattering of top-end luxury. The high seasons here are during Semana Santa and the following week, and the months of July and August, plus the Día de Muertos and Christmas–New Year holidays. Most prices dip at least 20% outside high season.

🛏 Real de Guadalupe Area

Le Gite del Sol   HOTEL $
(☑967-631-60-12; www.legitedelsol.com; Madero 82; s/d M$250/320, d without bathroom M$220; @⊛) A bountiful breakfast complements simple rooms with floors of radiant sunflower yellow and bathrooms that look a bit like oversized shower stalls, or pleasant rooms with shared facilities in a newer location across the street. French and English spoken, and kitchen facilities available.

Hostal Rincón de los Camellos   HOSTEL $
(☑967-116-00-97; www.loscamellos.over-blog.com; Real de Guadalupe 110; dm M$100, s/d/q without bathroom M$200/280/400; ⊖⊛) A clean, tranquil little spot run by a welcoming French-Mexican duo. The brightly painted rooms are set around two patios, with a grassy little garden out back. A small kitchen has free drinking water and coffee.

Casa Margarita   HOTEL $$
(☑967-678-09-57; www.hotelcasamargarita.mx; Real de Guadalupe 34; d incl breakfast from M$920; P⊖⊛) This popular and well-run travelers' haunt offers impeccably clean, though rather dark, rooms with reading lights and a good city-center location.

🛏 West of Plaza 31 de Marzo

★Puerta Vieja Hostel   HOSTEL $
(☑967-631-43-35; www.puertaviejahostel.com; Mazariegos 23; dm incl breakfast M$140, r with/without bathroom M$390/320; ⊖⊛) A spacious, modern, traveler-savvy hostel in a high-ceilinged colonial building with a large garden strung with hammocks, kitchen, temascal (pre-Hispanic steam bath) and sheltered interior courtyard. Its dorms (one for women only) are a good size, and the rooftop ones have fab views. Private rooms have one queen and a bunk bed. There's occasional live music in the garden.

Hostal Akumal   HOSTEL $
(☑cell 967-1161120; Av 16 de Sepiembre 33; dm/d incl breakfast M$130/400; ⊛) Friendly, live-in owners and a big cooked breakfast that changes daily (a prominent sign quite rightly states 'Continental breakfast is not real breakfast') are some of the winning points at this centrally located hostel. There's a roaring fireplace in the lounge for chilly nights, a funky courtyard hangout area and the rooms and dorms are adequate, if nothing exciting.

Posada Ganesha   GUESTHOUSE $
(☑967-678-02-12; www.posadaganesha.com; Calle 28 de Agosto 23; dm M$177, d without bathroom incl breakfast M$350-530; ⊖⊛) This cute little incense-infused hostel, trimmed in Indian fabrics, wouldn't look out of place on the backstreets of Kathmandu. It's a friendly and vibrant place to rest your head, with a simple guest kitchen and a pleasant lounge area. Most of the time yoga sessions (additional payment) are held twice daily Monday to Friday.

Hotel Posada El Paraíso   HOTEL $$
(☑967-678-00-85; Calle 5 de Febrero 19; s/d M$755/900; ⊖⊛) Combining colonial style with a boutique-hotel feel, El Paraíso has a bright-blue wood-pillared patio, a jungly garden sitting area and loads of bohemian character. The high-ceilinged rooms are not huge, but all have natural light, and several are bi-level with an extra bed upstairs. The in-house restaurant, L'Eden, is excellent.

★Casa de Alma   BOUTIQUE HOTEL $$$
(☑967-674-77-84; Av 16 de Sepiembre 24; ste incl breakfast from M$3215; P⊖⊛) Wow! This outstanding, and very central, boutique hotel has it all. The rooms, which offer just the right mix of colonial charm and modern comforts, are notable for the floor-to-ceiling artworks and creative bed heads with a Maya touch. Beautiful bathrooms and views over terracotta tiled roofs from the private terraces and balconies.

The communal areas are just as impressive with a stylish reception area and a covered courtyard restaurant (great food) with a modern art ceiling and lots of leafy plants. Service is top-notch and there's a spa and secure underground parking – a huge plus in the city center.

Hotel b¨o   BOUTIQUE HOTEL $$$
(☑967-678-15-15; www.hotelbo.mx; Av 5 de Mayo 38; r from M$4390; P⊖@⊛) 🖉 San Cristóbal meets Miami Beach in a boutique hotel that

breaks the traditional colonial-architecture barrier with supermodern, trendy lines and unique, artsy touches. The large rooms and suites are very elegant and boast glass-tile bathrooms with ceiling showers, while the flowery gardens host fine water features. Compared to much of the competition, though, it comes across as a bit overpriced.

Las Escaleras BOUTIQUE HOTEL $$$
(📞967-678-81-81; www.lasescalerashotel.com; Isauro Rossette 4; r from M$3000; 🛜) With lip-stick-red walls and discreet arty touches, this is a sophisticated and charming hotel that oozes with cool character. The hilltop location might not be for the leg-weary (there are even more stairs than the name implies), but if you're looking for style, it's one of the best options in town.

South of Plaza 31 de Marzo

Parador Margarita HOTEL $
(📞967-116-01-64; www.hotelparadormargarita.mx; JF Flores 39; s/d/tr incl breakfast M$650/785/1230; 🅿🛜) A three-story hotel with moderately sized rooms sporting one king- or two queen-sized beds, and some include details like fireplaces, stained-glass windows and bathroom skylights. Other pluses include in-room heaters and a pleasant back patio overlooking a large lawn.

Docecuartos HOTEL $$
(📞967-678-10-53; www.docecuartos.com; Benito Juárez 1; r from M$912; 🛜) Set around a charming courtyard, there are indeed only 12 rooms here, which adds to the intimate feel but makes booking a necessity pretty much any time of year. The rooms themselves are gorgeously decked out, with just the right balance of colonial stateliness, indigenous color and modern amenity, and the super-central location gets a big thumbs up.

Nuik B&B B&B $$
(📞967-631-71-54; http://nuikbb.com; Madero 69; r incl breakfast from M$1000; ⊖🛜) Always smiling and always with time for a chat, it's the owner, Claudia, who really makes this place what it is. Mind you, even without her bubbly presence, this six-room B&B, which is strung with ethnic art and touches of the bohemian, would still attract those in search of a place to stay with genuine character.

★**La Joya Hotel** B&B $$$
(📞967-631-48-32; www.lajoyahotelsancristobal.com; Madero 43A; r incl breakfast US$170-220; 🅿⊖

@🛜) This extraordinary boutique hotel is a visual feast in which every corner contains something interesting and beautiful. The five rooms have been ripped from a design magazine and have exquisite cabinetry, enormous bathrooms and antiques curated from the owners' world travels. Fireplace sitting areas and heaters grace each room, and a rooftop terrace beckons with hill views.

Attentive service includes afternoon snacks, bedtime tea, and a specially prepared light dinner for late arrivals. Don't be surprised if you end up considering this one of the very best boutique hotels you've ever stayed in. Needless to say booking ahead is essential. Minimum two-night stay.

Casa Santa Lucía BOUTIQUE HOTEL $$$
(📞967-631-55-45; www.hotelcasasantalucia.mx; Av Josefa Ortíz de Domínguez 13; r M$1600-2000, ste M$2500-3000; 🅿⊖🛜) This discreet boutique hotel has been touched by the hand of an artist. Moroccan lamps hang from polished wood beams, geraniums add a touch of pink, leopards and Day of the Dead skulls grin from shady corners, and ethnic textiles and antique carved furnishings fill the bedrooms. Lucky guests rave about the warm welcome, free laundry service and delicious breakfasts. Other thoughtful touches are the complimentary cookies.

North of Plaza 31 de Marzo

Rossco Backpackers HOSTEL $
(📞967-674-05-25; www.backpackershostel.com.mx; Real de Mexicanos 16; dm from M$110, d with/without bathroom M$530/400; 🅿⊖@🛜) Rossco Backpackers is a friendly, sociable and well-run hostel with good dorm rooms (one for women only), a guest kitchen, a movie-watching loft and a grassy garden. Private upstairs rooms have nice skylights. A free night's stay if you arrive by bicycle or motorcycle!

Hotel Posada Jovel HOTEL $$
(📞967-678-17-34; www.hoteljovel.com; Paniagua 28; s/d from M$650/850; 🅿✳🛜) Recently renovated, the colonial-style Joval now offers one of the better deals in town. The rooms are filled with the light, color and character of Mexico and they surround a pretty garden with fountains and tropical flowers where you can have breakfast.

Na Bolom HOTEL $$
(📞967-678-14-18; www.nabolom.org; Guerrero 33; r incl breakfast from M$1110; 🅿⊖🛜) This famous museum/research institute (p365),

about 1km from Plaza 31 de Marzo, has 16 cutesy (though not necessarily luxurious) guest rooms, all loaded with character and all but two with log fires. Meals are served in the house's stately dining room. Room rates include a house tour.

Guayaba Inn
HOTEL $$$

(☑ 967-674-76-99; www.guayabainn.com; Comitán 55; r incl breakfast from M$2200; 🛜) With something of an old country farmhouse to it, this gorgeous, rustic and quirky place is one of the best-looking boutique hotels in town. The artist owners' attention to detail shines through in everything from the tranquil garden spaces to the light, spacious and divinely decorated rooms. All rooms have fireplaces, big separate tubs and mini-bars, and there's a sauna/massage suite.

Bela's B&B
B&B $$$

(☑ 967-678-92-92; www.belasbandb.com; Dr Navarro 2; s US$40-80, d US$60-95, all incl breakfast; 🅿 😺 🛜 🐕) A dreamy oasis in the center of town, this tranquil American-run B&B will seduce you with its lush garden, electric blankets, towel dryers and on-site massages. The five comfortable rooms are trimmed in traditional local fabrics and some have lovely mountain views. There's a virtual Noah's Ark of dogs, so if you're not a doggy fan look elsewhere. There's a three-night minimum stay.

Hotel Diego de Mazariegos
HOTEL $$$

(☑ 967-678-08-33; www.diegodemazariegos.com; Calle 5 de Febrero 1; r M$1600, ste M$1900-2500; 🅿 🛜) This long-established hotel occupies two 18th-century mansions built around beautiful, wide courtyards. The 76 rooms are large and decked out with traditional fabrics and fittings, but also have modern comforts including cable TV. Some have fireplaces, and the suites have spa tubs.

🍴 Eating

The foodie jackpot of Chiapas, San Cristóbal has more tantalizing food options than any other place in the state. If you can verbalize a culinary craving, the chances are some restaurant exists here to fulfill it. Vegetarians are spoiled for choice. ¡Provecho!

🍴 Real de Guadalupe Area

Self-caterers can stock up at the centrally located **Super Más** (Real de Guadalupe 22; ⊙8am-10pm) market, and there are a number of fruit and vegetable shops on Dugelay where the pedestrianized section of Real de Guadalupe ends.

TierrAdentro
MEXICAN $

(☑ 967-674-67-66; Real de Guadalupe 24; set menu M$55-130; ⊙8am-11pm; 🛜 🍴) A popular gathering center for political progressives and coffee-swigging, laptop-toting locals (not that they're mutually exclusive), this large indoor courtyard-restaurant, cafe and pizzeria is a comfortable place to while away the hours. It's run by Zapatista supporters, who hold frequent cultural events and conferences on local issues.

Arez
MIDDLE EASTERN $

(☑ 967-678-63-08; Real de Guadalupe 29; wraps M$25-45, mains M$60-100; ⊙noon-11pm) Stare at paintings of the Lebanese coastline as you tuck into hunks of lamb shawarma and other delicious Lebanese dishes at San Cristóbal's original Middle Eastern restaurant. Try the barbecue Arez, with grilled beef, chicken, onions and peppers.

La Lupe
MEXICAN $$

(☑ 967-678-12-22; Real de Guadalupe 23; mains M$70-120, breakfast M$83; ⊙7am-midnight) This very popular cafe has farmhouse decorations splayed across the walls and good, filling authentic Mexican country fare served in clay pots or on wooden boards. It's renowned for its filling breakfasts of *huevos mexicanos* and its tasty fruit juices.

Pizzería El Punto
PIZZA $$

(☑ 921-110-31-63; Real de Guadalupe 47; pizzas M$100-160; ⊙noon-11:30pm; 🍴) Forget the cardboard crap that passes for pizza in some parts, these crispy slices are the best in town, bar none. The central branch of this excellent pizzeria has a full bar, swanky black-and-red decor and a lovely balcony overlooking Real de Guadalupe.

Crustaceos
SEAFOOD $$

(☑ 967-116-05-24; Madero 22; mains M$100-150; ⊙noon-7pm; 🛜) Seriously good seafood, including the perennial favorites: ceviche and garlic-marinated shrimp. The atmosphere's very laid back and things can get a bit rowdy, especially when there are two-for-one beers on offer.

🍴 West of Plaza 31 de Marzo

Namandí Café & Crepas
CREPERIE, CAFE $

(☑ 967-678-80-54; Mazariegos 16C; crepes M$71-99; ⊙8am-11pm Mon-Sat, 8:30am-10:30pm Sun; 🛜 🍴) Nattily attired staff serve baguette

CHIAPAS & TABASCO SAN CRISTÓBAL REGION

sandwiches, pastas and good coffee at this large modern cafe and restaurant, but the fresh-off-the-griddle crepes are the main draw. Try a savory *crepa azteca* with chicken, corn and peppers drizzled with *salsa poblana*. Kids love the glassed-in modern play space, and frazzled parents can take advantage of free childcare while they're onsite (paid babysitting also available).

★Restaurante LUM
MEXICAN $$

(☑967-678-15-15; Hotel b˚o, Av 5 de Mayo 38; mains M$150-250; ⊙7am-11pm) This swanky indoor-outdoor restaurant in San Cristóbal's first designer hotel serves up exciting blends of Chiapas, Veracruz and Yucatán cuisine fused with tastes and ideas from around the culinary planet. Custom-made lamps, reflecting pools and walls of geometrically stacked firewood create a funky contemporary ambience. We're still in raptures of delight over the octopus and the beef with lentils.

El Eden
MEXICAN, INTERNATIONAL $$

(☑967-678-00-85; Hotel El Paraíso, Calle 5 de Febrero 19; mains M$85-180; ⊙7am-11pm; ☑) This luminously colorful restaurant has a tempting European and Mexican menu that includes an authentic *fondue suiza* (Swiss fondue), *sopa azteca* (tortilla, chili, onion and herb base topped with shredded chicken, fresh cheese, lime, avocado and coriander) and succulent meat dishes, all served around a cozy fireplace or out in the leafy courtyard. There's a good-sized wine list too.

✕ South of Plaza 31 de Marzo

Te Quiero Verde
VEGETARIAN $

(Niños Heroes 4; mains from M$60; ⊙noon-9pm Wed-Mon; ☎☑) If you've ever doubted that a vegan burger can be truly tasty, you need to get down here. The soups and salads are OK too, but the burgers and homemade fries steal the show.

La Tertulia San Cris
CAFE $

(☑967-116-11-45; Cuauhtémoc 2; mains M$40-80; ⊙8am-11pm Tue-Sun, to 5pm Mon) This small, theatrical, boho cafe does great breakfasts, yummy salads and a passable pizza, all served up in a paintbox of colors. A little onsite gift store selling local produce and souvenirs rounds out the picture.

El Caldero
MEXICAN $

(☑967-116-01-21; Av Insurgentes 5; soups from M$68; ⊙11am-10pm) Perfect for a cold day, simple, friendly little El Caldero special-

izes in delicious Mexican soups – *pozole* (shredded pork in broth), *mondongo* (tripe), *caldo* (broth). Although calling them mere 'soups' does them an injustice, these are more thick, hearty stews than watery soups and they come with a spread of avocados, tortillas and various salsas. One vegetarian option too.

★Santo Nahual
FUSION $$

(☑967-678-15-47; www.santonahual.com; Hidalgo 3; mains M$130-240; ⊙9am-midnight; ☎) Even before you've tasted the food this wonderful new venture impresses with its glass-roofed courtyard dining area filled with worn timbers, smooth pebbles, glossy-leafed banana plants and even a day-glo piano. And when the food, which is best described as modern fusion Mexican, does come you'll find it every bit as unexpected and imaginative as the decor.

Try the scallop with pesto and tomato or the Thai chicken and follow up with a pavlova of forest fruits.

Sensaciones de Chiapas
MEXICAN $$

(☑967-674-55-06; Plaza 31 de Marzo 10A; mains M$80-130; ⊙8am-midnight) Inside the Hotel Ciudad Real, this is a great place to try authentic Chiapas cuisine including *chipilín* soup, quesadilla de Cochinita, a great range of *mole* (chili sauce) dishes and the house specialty: chicken thighs stuffed with cheese, ham and other goodies. Occasional live marimba bands accompany your meal.

✕ North of Plaza 31 de Marzo

★No Name Quesadillas
MEXICAN $

(Paniagua 49B; quesadillas M$40; ⊙8-11pm Thu-Tue; ☑) A sweet couple sells gourmet quesadillas and flavored *atoles* (sweet, corn-based hot drinks) at this signless storefront with romantic courtyard seating. The menu changes daily: vegetarian Sunday through Tuesday, seafood Thursday, meat on Friday and a mixed bag on Saturday, but there are always around six different variations available.

Get a taste of ingredients like wild mushrooms, crunchy seasonal ants, squash flowers and spicy chorizo, and line up early before the food sells out.

Falafel
FELAFEL $

(MA Flores 4; mains M$45-90; ⊙1-9pm Mon-Sat; ☑) A small cheerful place with a brilliant mural of a mustachioed sun; its filling namesake meal, which is as good as any you'll find in the Middle East, comes wrapped in freshly baked pitas and with a plate of deliciously creamy hummus. Hebrew readers should browse the book exchange.

La Salsa Verde
TACOS $

(☑ 967-678-72-80; Av 20 de Noviembre 7; 5 tacos M$60-120; ☺ 8am-11:30pm; 🖳) Meat sizzles on the open-air grill and TVs blare at this taco institution (more than 30 years in business), with tables of families and club-goers packed into its two large, noisy dining rooms.

Trattoria Italiana
ITALIAN $$

(☑ 967-678-58-95; Dr Navarro 10; mains M$135-180; ☺ 1:30-10pm Wed-Mon) Set inside a pastel-colored colonial building and with some tables outside under the trees, this mother-and-daughter-run Italian restaurant really feels as if it's been transferred straight from Tuscany. The house special is ravioli, handmade fresh every day and you can expect fillings of sea bass with eggplant, cheeses with walnut and arugula, or rabbit with rosemary and olive. The sauces are divine – don't miss the mango, chipotle and gorgonzola if it's around.

🍷 Drinking & Nightlife

The aroma of roasted highland-grown coffee beans wafts through the streets of San Cristóbal, and a strong dose is never far away.

Cocoliche
COCKTAIL BAR

(☑ 967-631-46-21; Colón 3; mains M$75-120; ☺ 1pm-midnight; 🖳) By day Cocoliche is a bohemian restaurant with lots of Asian dishes, but in the evening its mismatched Chinese lanterns and wall of funky posters set the scene for drinking boozy *licuados* (milkshakes) with friends. Jostle for a sofa near the fireplace on chilly nights, and check out the nightly Latin jazz and salsa, and occasional theater events at 9pm.

Café La Selva
CAFE

(www.cafelaselva.com; Crescencio Rosas 9; coffee M$15-25; ☺ 8:30am-11pm; 🖳) One of the first coffee shops in San Cristóbal and still about the best. La Selva is housed in an attractive old building with eye-catching wall murals. There are around 10 different types of coffee on offer here and the beans for all of them are roasted on the spot, which lends a delicious aroma to the place.

Panóptico
BAR

(Real de Guadalupe 63A; ☺ Noon-midnight) A small bar with more of a local clientele than many city-center places, has good range of artisan beers and the barman knows how to mix a mean mojito. It also does a small range of tapas and has board games to play.

Mezcalería Gusana Grela
MEZCALERÍA

(MA Flores 2; ☺ 7pm-3am Mon-Sat) Wedge yourself in at one of a handful of tables and try some of the dozen or so artisanal mezcals (M$40 to M$60) from Oaxaca, many of which are fruit-infused.

La Viña de Bacco
WINE BAR

(☑ 967-119-19-85; Real de Guadalupe 7; ☺ 2pm-midnight Mon-Sat) At San Cristóbal's first wine bar, chatty patrons spill out onto the street, a pedestrian block off the main drag. It's a convivial place, pouring a large selection of Mexican options (among others), starting at a reasonable M$20 per glass. A free tapa comes with every glass of wine.

Latino's
CLUB

(☑ 967-678-99-27; Madero 23; Fri & Sat M$50; ☺ 8pm-3am Mon-Sat) A bright restaurant and dance spot where the city's *salseros* (salsa musicians) gather to groove. A salsa/merengue/cumbia/bachata band plays at 11pm Thursday through Saturday.

☆ Entertainment

Most live-music venues are free, and clubs generally enforce the no-smoking law.

San Cristóbal is a fine place to immerse yourself in Mexican and Latin American cinema, political documentaries and art-house movies. West of the center, the **Cinépolis** (www.cinepolis.com; tickets M$60) multiplex plays first-run flicks.

★ Cafe Bar Revolución
LIVE MUSIC

(☑ 967-678-66-64; www.facebook.com/cafebarrevolucion; Calle 1 de Marzo 11; ☺ 11am-3am) There's always something fun at Revolución, with two live bands nightly (at 9pm and 11pm) and an eclectic line up of salsa, rock, blues, jazz and reggae. Dance downstairs or order a mojito or caipirinha and chat in the quieter upstairs *tapanco* (attic).

El Paliacate
ARTS CENTER

(☑ 967-125-37-39; Av 5 de Mayo 20; ☺ 6-11pm Tue-Sat) An alternative cultural space with a small restaurant and a bar serving wine, beer and artisan mezcal, El Paliacate's main stage hosts music events including rock en Tzotzil, *son jarocho* (a type of folk music) and experimental bands, plus the occasional documentary film or theater presentation. There's bike parking inside and chill-out rooms upstairs.

Cinema El Puente
CINEMA

(☑967-678-37-23; Centro Cultural El Puente, Real de Guadalupe 55; tickets M$30; ⊗Mon-Sat) Screenings at 6pm and 8pm.

Kinoki
CINEMA

(☑967-678-50-46; http://forokinoki.blogspot.com; Belisario Domínguez 5A; tickets M$30; ⊗12:30pm-midnight; ⊕) With a beautiful upstairs space and terrace, this art gallery and tea salon screens two films nightly at 6:30pm and 8:30pm. Private cinema rooms available with over 3500 movies on hand.

🛍 Shopping

Real de Guadalupe and the Andador Turísti-co have some upscale craft shops, but the busy daily crafts market around the Santo Domingo and La Caridad churches is also a good place to check out. In addition to textiles, another Chiapas specialty is amber, sold in numerous jewelry shops. When buying amber, beware of plastic imitations: the real thing is never cold and never heavy, and when rubbed should produce static electricity and a resiny smell.

Posheria
DRINKS

(Real de Guadalupe 46A; ⊗10am-9pm) Pick up a bottle of artisanal *pox* (pronounced 'posh'; alcohol made from sugarcane) infused with honey, chocolate or fruits like *nanche* (a sweet, yellow fruit). Definitely not what the common folk are drinking, since bottles sell for M$50 to M$200 and the alcohol content averages only about 14%.

Sna Jolobil
ARTS & CRAFTS

(☑967-678-26-46; www.facebook.com/SnaJolobil; Calz Lázaro Cárdenas s/n; ⊗9am-2pm & 4-7pm Mon-Sat) Next to the Templo de Santo Domingo, Sna Jolobil – Tzotzil for 'The Weaver's House' – exhibits and sells some of the very best *huipiles* (long, sleeveless tunics), blouses, skirts, rugs and other woven items, with prices ranging from a few dollars for small items to thousands for the best *huipiles* (the fruit of many months' work).

A cooperative of 800 weavers from the Chiapas highlands, it was founded in the 1970s to foster the important indigenous art of backstrap-loom weaving, and has revived many half-forgotten techniques and designs.

Abuelita Books
BOOKS

(Colón 2; ⊗noon-8:30pm Thu-Mon; ⊕) A great place for a leisurely browse over homemade brownies, hot coffee or a steamy tea; come

---

AMATENANGO DEL VALLE

The women of this Tzeltal village by the Pan-American Hwy, 37km southeast of San Cristóbal, are renowned potters. Pottery here is still fired by a pre-Hispanic method, building a wood fire around the pieces rather than putting them in a kiln. Amatenango children find a ready tourist market with *animalitos* – little pottery animal figures that are inexpensive but fragile. If you visit the village, expect to be surrounded within minutes by young *animalito* sellers. From San Cristóbal, take a Comitán-bound bus or combi.

---

here to replenish your reading material from an excellent selection of new and used books in English (other languages also available). Free English movies on Thursday nights.

Fruit & Vegetable Shops
FOOD

(Santiago; ⊗8am-8pm) Stock up for a picnic at these fruit and veg shops.

Taller Leñateros
ARTS & CRAFTS

(☑967-678-51-74; www.tallerlenateros.com; Paniagua 54; ⊗9am-5pm Mon-Fri, to 2pm Sat) 🖉 A society of Maya artists, the 'Woodlanders' Workshop' crafts exquisite handmade books, posters and fine-art prints from recycled paper infused with local plants, using images inspired by traditional folk art. It's an open workshop, so you can watch the art in progress.

Lágrimas de la Selva
JEWELRY

(Plaza 31 de Marzo; ⊗10am-9pm Mon-Sat, noon-9pm Sun) A lovely jewelry store where you can watch jewelers work with amber.

El Camino de los Altos
ARTS & CRAFTS

(www.facebook.com/elcaminodelosaltosAC; Av Insurgentes 19; ⊗noon-10pm Wed-Mon) Creators of exquisite furnishings and textiles, El Camino de los Altos is a collaboration of French textile designers and 130 Maya weavers.

J'pas Joloviletik
CLOTHING

(Utrilla 43; ⊗9am-2pm & 4-7pm Mon-Fri) A 30-year-old cooperative, J'pas Joloviletik – the name means 'those that weave' in Tzotzil – is comprised of nearly 200 women from 12 communities, and they have a spacious shop on the east side of the Templo de Santo Domingo. Sometimes open Saturday and Sunday – opening hours are very flexible!

Meltzanel CLOTHING

(Diego de Mazariegos 8; ☺9am-2pm & 4-8pm Mon-Fri, 10am-8pm Sat) Modern designs fashioned from traditional Maya textiles.

Nemi Zapata ARTS & CRAFTS

(www.nemizapata.com; MA Flores 57; ☺9am-7pm Mon-Fri, 9:30am-3:30pm Sat) ✍ A fair-trade store that sells products made by Zapatista communities: weavings, embroidery, coffee and honey, as well as Ejército Zapatista de Libéracion Nacional (EZLN; Zapatista National Liberation Army) cards, posters and books.

❶ Information

Most banks require your passport if you want to change cash, though they only change money Monday through Friday. There are also handy ATMs at the OCC bus station and on the southern side of the Plaza 31 de Marzo.

There are two tourist offices in the city and staff are generally knowledgable in both of them.

Banamex (Av Insurgentes, btwn Niños Héroes & Cuauhtémoc; ☺9am-4pm Mon-Sat) Has an ATM; exchanges dollars.

Banco Azteca (Plaza 31 de Marzo; ☺9am-8pm) Hidden in the back of the Elektra furniture store; exchanges dollars and euros.

Dr Luis José Sevilla (☎967-678-16-26, cell 967-1061028; Calle del Sol 12; ☺6am-10pm) Speaks English and Italian; can make house calls. Located west of the center near the Periférico.

Hospital de la Mujer (☎967-678-38-34; Av Insurgentes 24; ☺24hr) General hospital with emergency facilities.

Lacantún Money Exchange (Real de Guadalupe 12A; ☺9am-9pm Mon-Sat, 9am-2pm & 4-7pm Sun) Open outside bank hours but rates are worse.

Main Post Office (Allende 3; ☺8am-4pm Mon-Fri, to 2pm Sat)

Tourist Office Centro Cultural Carmen (Av Hidalgo 15; ☺9am-8pm) Tourist information is available inside this cultural center.

Tourist Office Zebadua Theater (☎967-678-06-65; Calle 1 de Marzo 11; ☺9am-8pm) Staff are generally knowledgable about the San Cristóbal area; English spoken.

❶ Getting There & Away

A fast toll autopista (M$56 for cars) zips to San Cristóbal from Chiapa de Corzo. Follow the highways signs that say 'cuota' (toll).

At the time of research buses were not traveling to Palenque via Ocosingo because of security concerns. Most buses were instead taking the much more circular route via Villahermosa. If you do travel to Palenque via Ocosingo it's best to travel during daylight, as highway holdups – though by no means common – do occasionally occur. When taking a bus along this route, consider stowing valuables in the checked luggage compartment.

AIR

San Cristóbal's airport has no regular passenger flights; the main airport serving town is at Tuxtla Gutiérrez. Ten daily direct OCC minibuses

BUSES FROM SAN CRISTÓBAL DE LAS CASAS

DESTINATION	COST (M$)	DURATION (HR)	FREQUENCY (DAILY)
Campeche	630	10	2 OCC
Cancún	1362-1422	18-19	3 OCC, 1 AEXA
Ciudad Cuauhtémoc (Guatemalan border)	156	3¼	3
Comitán	78-90	1¾	frequent OCC & *colectivos*
Mérida	934	12¾	6:20pm
Mexico City (TAPO & Norte)	1390-1684	13-14	10
Oaxaca	428-672	11-12	4
Palenque	306	5	frequent
Pochutla	672	11-12	2
Puerto Escondido	740	12½-13	2
Tuxtla Gutiérrez	62	1-1¼	frequent OCC; 4 AEXA
Tuxtla Gutiérrez airport (Ángel Albino Corzo)	242	1½	10
Villahermosa	466	5½-7	5

WORTH A TRIP

GRUTAS DE SAN CRISTÓBAL

The entrance to this long **cavern** (M$20, parking M$10; ⏰8am-6pm) is situated in pine woods 9km southeast of San Cristóbal, a five-minute walk south of the Pan-American Hwy. The first 350m or so of the cave is lit and open for viewing, with a concrete walkway threading through a dazzling chasm of stalagmites and stalactites. Beyond that you have the option of continuing (extra M$30) in total darkness with just a flashlight (provided) for company for another few hundred meters. Horseback riding is available from the parking area, where you'll also find *comedores* (food stalls).

To get here, take a Teopisca-bound combi (M$20) from the Pan-American Hwy, about 150m southeast of the OCC bus station in San Cristóbal, and ask for 'Las Grutas.'

(M$242) run to the Tuxtla airport from San Cristóbal's main bus terminal; book airport-bound tickets in advance, and consult www.ado.com.mx for schedules to/from 'Ángel Albino Corzo Aeropuerto.'

A number of tour agencies run shuttles to the Tuxtla airport for around M$280 to M$300 per person. Taxis from the airport will cost at least M$600.

BUS & COLECTIVO

The Pan-American Hwy (Hwy 190, Blvd Juan Sabines, 'El Bulevar') runs through the southern part of town, and nearly all transportation terminals are on it or nearby. From the OCC bus terminal, it's six blocks north up Insurgentes to the central square, Plaza 31 de Marzo.

The main 1st-class **OCC terminal** (☑967-678-02-91; cnr Pan-American Hwy & Av Insurgentes) is also used by ADO and UNO 1st-class and deluxe buses, plus some 2nd-class buses. Tickets can also be purchased at **Ticketbus** (☑967-678-85-03; Real de Guadalupe 16; ⏰7:30am-10pm) in the center of town. AEXA buses and Ómnibus de Chiapas minibuses share a terminal across the street from the OCC terminal.

All *colectivo* vans (combis) and taxis have depots on the Pan-American Hwy a block or so from the OCC terminal. They generally run from 5am until 9pm and leave when full, including to Comitán, Tuxtla Gutiérrez & Ocosingo. Combis to Zinacantán and San Juan Chamula (Utrilla) leave from further north (Honduras). *Colectivo* taxis to Tuxtla, Comitán and Ocosingo are available 24 hours; if you don't want to wait for it to fill, you must pay for the empty seats.

For Tuxtla Gutiérrez, comfortable Ómnibus de Chiapas 'sprinter' minibuses (M$50) are the best bet; they leave every 10 minutes.

For Guatemala, most agencies offer a daily van service to Quetzaltenango (M$350, eight hours), Panajachel (M$350, 10 hours) and Antigua (M$450, 12 hours); Viajes Chincultik is slightly cheaper, and also has van service to Guatemala City and Chichicastenango. Otherwise, go to Ciudad Cuauhtémoc and pick up onward transportation from the Guatemala side.

CAR & MOTORCYCLE

San Cristóbal's only car-rental company, **Optima** (☑967-674-54-09; optimacar1@hotmail.com; Mazariegos 39; ⏰9am-7pm Sun-Fri, 9am-2pm & 4-7pm Sat) rents out manual transmission cars. Rates vary wildly depending on the season and demand. Sizable discounts are given for payment in cash. Drivers must be 25 or older and have a credit card.

ℹ Getting Around

Combis (M$8) go up Crescencio Rosas from the Pan-American Hwy to the town center. Taxis cost M$30 within town and M$34 at night.

To self-propel, Jaguar Adventours (p370) rents out good-quality mountain bikes.

Croozy Scooters (☑cell 967-6832223; Belisario Domínguez 7; scooters per 3hr/day M$300/450, motorcycles M$400/540; ⏰10am-7pm) rents well-maintained Italika CS 125cc scooters and 150cc motorcycles. The price includes a free tank of fuel, maps, locks and helmets; passport and M$500 deposit required.

San Juan Chamula

☑967 / POP 3300 / ELEV 2200M

The Chamulans are a fiercely independent Tzotzil group. Their main village, San Juan Chamula, 10km northwest of San Cristóbal, is the center for some unique religious practices and is an interesting place to visit, but do be aware of local sensibilities.

Chamulan men wear loose homespun tunics of white wool (sometimes, in cool weather, thicker black wool), but *cargo*-holders – those with important religious and ceremonial duties – wear a sleeveless black tunic and a white scarf on the head. Chamulan women wear fairly plain white or blue blouses and/or shawls and woolen skirts.

Sunday is the weekly market, when people from the hills stream into the village to shop, trade and visit the main church.

Around San Cristóbal de las Casas

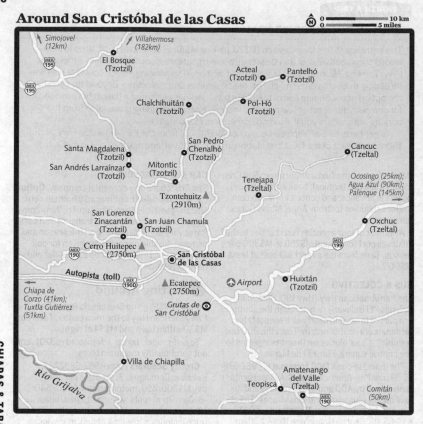

A corresponding number of tourist buses also stream in, so you might prefer to come another day (though due to local superstitions, there are fewer worshippers on Wednesdays).

👁 Sights

★ Templo de San Juan

CHURCH

(M$70) Standing beside the main plaza, Chamula's main church is a ghostly white, with a vividly painted arch of green and blue. Inside the darkened sanctuary, hundreds of flickering candles, clouds of copal incense, and worshippers kneeling with their faces to the pine-needle-carpeted floor make a powerful impression. Chamulans revere San Juan Bautista (St John the Baptist) above Christ, and his image occupies a more important place in the church.

Chanting *curanderos* (literally 'curers'; medicine men or women) may be rubbing patients' bodies with eggs or bones, and worshippers often drink soft drinks (burps are believed to expel evil spirits) or copious amounts of *pox* (alcohol made from sugarcane). Images of saints are surrounded with mirrors and dressed in holy garments.

You must obtain tickets (M$70) at the **tourist office** (⊙7am-6pm) beside the plaza before entering.

Nearby, around the shell of an older church, is the village **graveyard**. Though it's no longer practiced, traditionally black crosses were for people who died old, white for the young, and blue for others.

🎊 Festivals & Events

Carnaval

CARNIVAL

(⊙Feb/Mar) During Carnaval, groups of minstrels stroll the roads in tall, pointed hats with long, colored tassels, strumming guitars and chanting. Much *pox*, an alcoholic drink made from sugarcane, is drunk. Festivities also mark the five 'lost' days of the ancient Long Count calendar, which divided time into 20-day periods (18 of these make 360 days, leaving five to complete a year).

❶ Getting There & Away

From San Cristóbal combis to San Juan Chamula (M$18) leave from spots on Calle Honduras and Utrilla frequently. It's best to come with a guide.

San Lorenzo Zinacantán

📋 967 / POP 3900 / ELEV 2558M

The orderly village of San Lorenzo Zinacantán, about 11km northwest of San Cristóbal, is the main village of the Zinacantán municipality (population 36,000). Zinacantán people, like Chamulans, are Tzotzil. The men wear distinctive pink tunics embroidered with flower motifs and may sport flat, round, ribboned palm hats. Women wear pink or purple shawls over richly embroidered blouses.

The people of Zinacantán are great flower growers. They have a particular love for the geranium, which – along with pine branches – is offered in rituals for a wide range of benefits.

◉ Sights

Iglesia de San Lorenzo   CHURCH
(M$15) The huge central Iglesia de San Lorenzo was rebuilt following a fire in 1975. Today there are often masses of flowers on the altar. Photography is banned in the church and churchyard.

❶ Getting There & Away

For Zinacantán, combis (M$18) and *colectivo* taxis (M$20) go at least hourly, from a yard off Robledo in San Cristóbal de las Casas. Transportation runs from before daybreak to around dusk.

Ocosingo & Toniná

📋 919 / POP 42,000 / ELEV 900M

A respite from both the steamy lowland jungle and the chilly highlands, the bustling regional market town of Ocosingo sits in a gorgeous and broad temperate valley midway between San Cristóbal and Palenque. The impressive Maya ruins of Toniná are just a few kilometers away.

At the time of research the town of Ocosingo was perfectly safe to visit but there have been some serious security issues on roads in and out of the city. Check the latest before venturing here.

Ocosingo spreads east (downhill) from Hwy 199. Avenida Central runs down from the highway to the broad central plaza, overlooked from its east end by the Templo de San Jacinto. Some hotels, restaurants and services are along Calle Central Norte, running off the north side of the plaza.

◉ Sights

★**Toniná**   ARCHAEOLOGICAL SITE
(📋919-108-22-39; ⊘8am-5pm) **FREE** The towering ceremonial core of Toniná, overlooking a pastoral valley 14km east of Ocosingo, is one of the most spectacular archaeological sites in Chiapas. This was the city that brought mighty Palenque to its knees. However, despite the ruins being veritable poems in stone, and the sheer importance of the site, few people bother to visit – which is all the better for those who do.

The year AD 688 saw the inauguration of the Snake Skull–Jaguar Claw dynasty, with ambitious new rulers bent on controlling the region. Palenque was their rival state, and when Toniná captured the Palenque ruler K'an Joy Chitam II in 711, it's likely that he had his head lopped off here.

Toniná became known as the Place of the Celestial Captives, because its chambers held the captured rulers of Palenque and other Maya cities, who were destined to be ransomed for large sums or decapitated. A recurring image in Toniná sculpture is of captives before decapitation, thrown to the ground with their hands tied.

To enter the site, follow the road from the entrance and **site museum** (⊘Tue-Sun) **FREE**, which details Toniná's history (in Spanish) and contains most of the best artifacts. The road turns into a footpath, crosses a stream and climbs to the broad, flat **Gran Plaza**. At the south end of the Gran Plaza is the **Templo de la Guerra Cósmica** (Temple of Cosmic War), with five altars in front of it. Off one side of the plaza is a **ball court**, inaugurated around AD 780 under the rule of the female regent Smoking Mirror. A decapitation altar stands cheerfully beside it. In 2011 archaeologists discovered two life-size stone sculptures of captive warriors inscribed as being from Copán (in Honduras), confirming that Maya kingdom's wartime alliance with Palenque.

To the north rises the ceremonial core of Toniná, a hillside terraced into a number of platforms, rising 80m above the Gran Plaza. At the right-hand end of the steps, rising

ⓘ ROAD TRAVEL TO OCOSINGO

The valleys known as Las Cañadas de Ocosingo, between Ocosingo and the Reserva de la Biosfera Montes Azules to the southeast, form one of the strongest bastions of support for the Zapatistas, and Ocosingo saw the bloodiest fighting during the 1994 uprising, with about 50 rebels killed here by the Mexican army. Fighting continues to flare up to this day and at the time of research buses were not running to Ocosingo due to trouble on some of the roads surrounding the town. It is still possible to get to the town by *colectivo* but even these might travel by a much longer route. It's imperative that you check with authorities before traveling to and from Ocosingo.

from the first to the second platform, is the entry to a **ritual labyrinth of passages**.

Higher up on the right-hand side is the **Palacio de las Grecas y de la Guerra** (Palace of the Grecas and War). The *grecas* are a band of geometrical decoration forming a zigzag x-shape, possibly representing Quetzalcóatl. To its right is a rambling series of chambers, passages and stairways, believed to have been Toniná's **administrative headquarters**.

Higher again is Toniná's most remarkable sculpture, the **Mural de las Cuatro Eras** (Mural of the Four Eras). Created between AD 790 and 840, this stucco relief of four panels – the first, from the left end, has been lost – represents the four suns, or four eras of human history. The people of Toniná believed themselves to be living in the fourth sun – that of winter, the direction north, mirrors and the end of human life. At the center of each panel is the upside-down head of a decapitated prisoner. Blood spurting from the prisoner's neck forms a ring of feathers and, at the same time, a sun. In one panel, a dancing skeleton holds a decapitated head. To the left of the head is a lord of the underworld, resembling an enormous rodent.

Up the next set of steps is the seventh level, with remains of four temples. Behind the second temple from the left, more steps descend into the very narrow **Tumba de Treinta Metros** (Thirty-Meter Tomb), an

impossibly slim passageway that's definitely not for the claustrophobic!

Above here is the **acropolis**, the abode of Toniná's rulers and site of its eight most important temples – four on each of the two levels. The right-hand temple on the lower level, the **Templo del Monstruo de la Tierra** (Temple of the Earth Monster), has Toniná's best-preserved roof-comb, built around AD 713.

On the topmost level, the tallest temple, the **Templo del Espejo Humeante** (Temple of the Smoking Mirror), was built by Zots-Choj, who took the throne in AD 842. In that era of the fourth sun and the direction north, Zots-Choj had to raise this, Toniná's northernmost temple, highest of all, which necessitated a large, artificial northeast extension of the hill.

Combis to Toniná (M$16) leave from a roofed depot just behind Ocosingo's Tianguis Campesino every 30 minutes. The last one returns around 5:30pm. A taxi costs around M$130. There are currently no security issues surrounding a visit.

🛏 Sleeping & Eating

Hotel Central   HOTEL $
(☏919-673-00-24; Av Central 5; r M$500; 🅿️🕙 ❄🛜) Fronting the plaza and with great views from the 1st-floor terrace, the comfortable Hotel Central has smallish rooms with cable TV and fan. Ask for one of the upstairs rooms; corner room 12 is especially bright and breezy.

Restaurant Los Rosales   MEXICAN $
(☏919-673-12-15; Hotel Margarita, Calle Central Norte 19; breakfast M$60-80, mains M$80-130; ⏱7am-11pm; 🛜) With a wall of windows looking out over the rooftops to views of never-ending green mountains, this eatery, which is a part of a hotel, makes a pleasant place to plot your day.

🔒 Shopping

Fábrica de Quesos Santa Rosa   FOOD
(☏919-673-00-09; 1a Calle Oriente Norte 11; ⏱8am-2pm & 4-8pm Mon-Sat, 8am-2pm Sun) Ocosingo is known for its *queso amarillo* (yellow cheese). There are nine main types sold by this cheesemaker, including 'de bola,' which comes in 1kg balls with an edible wax coating and a crumbly, whole-fat center. Free factory tours available during business hours.

Tianguis Campesino MARKET
(Peasants' Market; cnr Av 2 Sur Oriente & Calle 5 Sur Oriente; ☺6am-5pm) The Tianguis Campesino is for the area's small-scale food producers to sell their goods direct; only women are allowed to trade here, and it's a colorful sight, with most of the traders in traditional dress.

❶ Information

The **Municipal Tourism Office** (☺8am-4pm Mon-Fri), in the plaza-front Palacio Municipal, has regional and city maps, though you're better off getting actual information from the hotels.

❶ Getting There & Away

Ocosingo's **OCC bus terminal** (☎919-673-04-31) is on Hwy 199, 600m west of the plaza; the 1st-class **AEXA bus terminal** (☎cell 919-1140679; www.autobusesaexa.com.mx) is across the road. The main *colectivo* terminal is across the street from AEXA. Due to serious security issues at the time of research no buses were actually traveling to and from Ocosingo. You could still get there by *colectivo* but these often take very roundabout kind of routes to avoid roadblocks or known trouble areas.

A walled lot behind the market is the terminus for trucks to Nahá (M$50, 2½ hours, 11am and noon) and Laguna Miramar.

Palenque

☎916 / POP 43,000 / ELEV 80M

Swathed in morning jungle mists and echoing to a dawn chorus of howler monkeys and parrots, the mighty Maya temples of Palenque are deservedly one of the top destinations of Chiapas and one of the best examples of Maya architecture in all of Mexico. By contrast, modern Palenque town, a few kilometers to the east, is a sweaty, humdrum place without much appeal except as a jumping-off point for the ruins and a place to find internet access. Many prefer to base themselves at one of the forest hideouts along the road between the town and the ruins, including the funky travelers' hangout of El Panchán.

History

The name Palenque (Palisade) is Spanish and has no relation to the city's ancient name, which may have been Lakamha (Big Water). Palenque was first occupied around 100 BC, and flourished from around AD 630 to around 740. The city rose to prominence under the ruler Pakal, who reigned from AD 615 to 683. Archaeologists have determined that Pakal is represented by hieroglyphics of sun and shield, and he is also referred to as Escudo Solar (Sun Shield). He lived to the then-incredible age of 80.

During Pakal's reign, many plazas and buildings, including the superlative Templo de las Inscripciones (Pakal's own mausoleum), were constructed in Palenque. The structures were characterized by mansard roofs and very fine stucco bas-reliefs.

Pakal's son Kan B'alam II (r 684–702), who is represented in hieroglyphics by the jaguar and the serpent (and is also called Jaguar Serpent II), continued Palenque's expansion and artistic development. He presided over the construction of the Grupo de las Cruces temples, placing sizable narrative stone stelae within each.

During Kan B'alam II's reign, Palenque extended its zone of control to the Río Usumacinta, but was challenged by the rival Maya city of Toniná, 65km south. Kan B'alam's brother and successor, K'an Joy Chitam II (Precious Peccary), was captured by forces from Toniná in 711, and probably executed there. Palenque enjoyed a resurgence between 722 and 736, however, under Ahkal Mo' Nahb' III (Turtle Macaw Lake), who added many substantial buildings.

After AD 900, Palenque was largely abandoned. In an area that receives the heaviest rainfall in Mexico, the ruins were soon overgrown, and the city remained unknown to the Western world until 1746, when Maya hunters revealed the existence of a jungle palace to a Spanish priest named Antonio de Solís. Later explorers claimed Palenque was capital of an Atlantis-like civilization. The eccentric Count de Waldeck, who in his 60s lived atop one of the pyramids for two years (1831–33), even published a book with fanciful neoclassical drawings that made the city resemble a great Mediterranean civilization.

It was not until 1837, when John L Stephens, an amateur archaeology enthusiast from New York, reached Palenque with artist Frederick Catherwood, that the site was insightfully investigated. Another century passed before Alberto Ruz Lhuillier, the tireless Mexican archaeologist, uncovered Pakal's hidden crypt in 1952. Today it continues to yield fascinating and beautiful secrets – most recently, a succession of sculptures and frescoes in the Acrópolis del Sur area, which have vastly expanded our knowledge of Palenque's history.

◉ Sights

Hwy 199 meets Palenque's main street, Avenida Juárez, at the **Glorieta de la Cabeza Maya** (Maya Head Statue; Map p388), a roundabout with a large statue of a Maya chieftain's head, at the west end of the town. The main ADO bus station is here, and Juárez heads 1km east from this intersection to the central square, **El Parque** (Map p388).

A few hundred meters south of the Maya head, the paved road to the Palenque ruins, 7.5km away, diverges west off Hwy 199. This road passes the site museum after about 6.5km, then winds on about 1km further uphill to the **main entrance to the ruins** (Map p385).

Museo de Sitio   MUSEUM

(Map p385; Carretera Palenque-Ruinas Km 7; with ruins ticket free; ⊙9am-4:30pm Tue-Sun) Palenque's site museum is worth a wander, displaying finds from the site and interpreting, in English and Spanish, Palenque's history. Highlights include a blissfully air-conditioned room displaying a copy of the lid of Pakal's sarcophagus (depicting his rebirth as the maize god, encircled by serpents, mythical monsters and glyphs recounting his reign) and finds from Templo XXI. Entry to the sarcophagus room permitted every half hour.

El Panchán   AREA

(Carretera Palenque-Ruinas Km 4.5) Just off the road to the ruins, El Panchán is a legendary travelers' hangout, set in a patch of dense rainforest. It's the epicenter of Palenque's alternative scene and home to a bohemian bunch of Mexican and foreign residents and wanderers.

Once ranchland, the area has been reforested by the remarkable Morales family, some of whom are among the leading archaeological experts on Palenque. Today, El Panchán has several (mostly rustic) places to stay, a couple of restaurants, a set of sinuous streams rippling their way through every part of the property, nightly entertainment (and daily drumming practice), a meditation temple, a temascal (pre-Hispanic steam bath) and a constant stream of interesting visitors from all over the world.

Exploring the Ruins

Ancient **Palenque** (Map p385; M$48 plus M$22 national park entry fee; ⊙8am-5pm, last entry 4:30pm) stands at the precise point where the first hills rise out of the Gulf coast plain, and the dense jungle covering these hills forms an evocative backdrop to Palenque's exquisite Maya architecture. Hundreds of ruined buildings are spread over 15 sq km, but only a fairly compact central area has been excavated. Everything you see here was built without metal tools, pack animals or the wheel.

As you explore the ruins, try to picture the gray stone edifices as they would have been at the peak of Palenque's power: painted blood red with elaborate blue and yellow stucco details. The forest around these temples is still home to howler monkeys, toucans and ocelots. The ruins and surrounding forests form a national park, the Parque Nacional Palenque, for which you must pay a separate admission fee at Km 4.5 on the road to the ruins.

Palenque sees more than 1000 visitors on an average day, and visitation spikes in the summer holiday season. Opening time is a good time to visit, when it's cooler and not too crowded, and morning mist may still be wrapping the temples in a picturesque haze. Refreshments, hats and souvenirs are available outside the main entrance. Vendors line many of the paths through the ruins.

Official site guides are available by the entrance and ticket office. Two Maya guide associations offer informative two-hour tours for up to seven people, which cost M$880 in Spanish or M$1050 in English, French, German or Italian. French, German and Italian speakers may have to wait a bit longer as there are fewer guides available.

Most visitors take a combi or taxi to the ruins' main (upper) entrance, see the major structures and then walk downhill to the museum, visiting minor ruins along the way.

Combis to the ruins (M$24 each way) run about every 10 minutes during daylight hours. In town, look for 'Ruinas' combis anywhere on Juárez west of Allende. They will also pick you up or drop you off anywhere along the town–ruins road.

Be aware that the mushrooms sold by locals along the road to the ruins from about May to November are the hallucinogenic variety.

Templo de las Inscripciones Group

As you walk in from the entrance the vegetation suddenly peels away to reveal many of Palenque's most magnificent buildings in one sublime vista. A line of temples rises in front of the jungle on your right, culminating in the Templo de las Inscripciones about 100m ahead; El Palacio, with its trademark

Palenque Ruins

0 | 200 m
0 | 0.1 miles

Mayabell (400m);
El Panchán (2km);
Palenque (7km)

Palenque Ruins

Top Sights

Sights

Activities, Courses & Tours

CHIAPAS & TABASCO PALENQUE

tower, stands to the left of the Templo de las Inscripciones; and the Grupo de las Cruces rises in the distance beneath a thick jungle backdrop.

The first temple on your right is Templo XII, called the **Templo de la Calavera** (Temple of the Skull) for the relief sculpture of a rabbit or deer skull at the foot of one of its pillars. The second temple, **Templo XI**, has little interest. Third is **Templo XIII**, containing a tomb of a female dignitary, whose remains were found colored red (as a result of treatment with cinnabar) when unearthed in 1994. You can look into the **Tumba de la Reina Roja** (Tomb of the Red Queen) and see her sarcophagus. With the skeleton were found a malachite mask and about 1000 pieces of jade. Based on DNA tests and resemblances to Pakal's tomb next door, the theory is that the 'queen' buried here was his wife Tz'ak-b'u Ajaw. The **tomb of Alberto Ruz Lhuillier**, who discovered Pakal's tomb in 1952, lies under the trees in front of Templo XIII.

The **Templo de las Inscripciones** (Temple of the Inscriptions), perhaps the most celebrated burial monument in the Americas, is the tallest and most stately of Palenque's buildings. Constructed on eight levels, the Templo de las Inscripciones has a central front staircase rising 25m to a series of small rooms. The tall roofcomb that once crowned it is long gone, but between the front doorways are stucco panels with reliefs of noble figures. On the interior rear wall are three panels with the long Maya inscription, recounting the history of Palenque and this building, for which Mexican archaeologist Alberto Ruz Lhuillier named the temple. From the top, interior stairs lead down into the **tomb of Pakal** (now closed to visitors indefinitely, to avoid further damage to its murals from the humidity inevitably exuded by visitors). Pakal's jewel-bedecked skeleton and jade mosaic death mask were removed from the tomb to Mexico City, and the tomb was re-created in the Museo Nacional de Antropología. The priceless death mask was stolen in an elaborate heist in 1985 (though recovered a few years afterward), but the carved stone sarcophagus lid remains in the closed tomb – you can see a replica in the site museum.

El Palacio

Diagonally opposite the Templo de las Inscripciones is **El Palacio** (The Palace; Map p385), a large structure divided into four main courtyards, with a maze of corridors and rooms. Built and modified piecemeal over 400 years from the 5th century on, it was probably the residence of Palenque's rulers.

Its **tower**, built in the 8th century by Ahkal Mo' Nahb' III and restored in 1955, has remnants of fine stucco reliefs on the walls,

but you're not allowed to climb up inside it. Archaeologists believe the tower was constructed so that Maya royalty and priests could observe the sun falling directly into the Templo de las Inscripciones during the winter solstice.

The northeastern courtyard, the **Patio de los Cautivos** (Patio of the Captives), contains a collection of relief sculptures that seem disproportionately large for their setting; the theory is that they represent conquered rulers and were brought from elsewhere.

In the southern part of the complex, the extensive subterranean bathrooms included six toilets and a couple of sweat baths.

Grupo de las Cruces

Pakal's son, Kan B'alam II, was a prolific builder, and soon after the death of his father started designing the temples of the Grupo de las Cruces (Group of the Crosses). All three main pyramid-shaped structures surround a plaza southeast of the Templo de las Inscripciones. They were all dedicated in AD 692 as a spiritual focal point for Palenque's triad of patron deities.

The **Templo del Sol** (Temple of the Sun), on the west side of the plaza, has the best-preserved roofcomb at Palenque. Carvings inside, commemorating Kan B'alam's birth in AD 635 and accession in 684, show him facing his father. Some view this beautiful building as sure proof that Palenque's ancient architects were inspired by the local hallucinogenic mushrooms. Make up your own mind!

Steep steps climb to the **Templo de la Cruz** (Temple of the Cross), the largest and most elegantly proportioned in this group. The stone tablet in the central sanctuary shows the lord of the underworld smoking tobacco on the right and Kan B'alam in full royal attire on the left. Behind is a reproduction of a panel depicting Kan B'alam's accession.

On the **Templo de la Cruz Foliada** (Temple of the Foliated Cross), the corbel arches are fully exposed, revealing how Palenque's architects designed these buildings. A well-preserved inscribed tablet shows a king (probably Pakal) with a sun shield emblazoned on his chest, corn growing from his shoulder blades, and the sacred quetzal bird on his head.

The 'cross' carvings in some buildings here symbolize the ceiba tree, which in Maya belief held up the universe.

Acrópolis Sur

In the jungle south of the Grupo de las Cruces is the Southern Acropolis, where archaeologists have made some terrific finds in recent excavations. You may find part of the area roped off. The **Acrópolis Sur** (Map p385) appears to have been constructed as an extension of the Grupo de las Cruces, with both groups set around what was probably a single long open space.

Templo XVII, between the Cruces group and the Acrópolis Sur, contains a reproduction carved panel depicting Kan B'alam, standing with a spear, with a bound captive kneeling before him (the original is in the site museum).

In 1999, in **Templo XIX**, archaeologists made the most important Palenque find for decades: an 8th-century limestone platform with stunning carvings of seated figures and lengthy hieroglyphic texts that detail Palenque's origins. A reproduction has been placed inside Templo XIX. The central figure on the long south side of the platform is the ruler Ahkal Mo' Nahb' III, who was responsible for several of the buildings of the Acrópolis Sur, just as the Grupo de las Cruces was created by Kan B'alam II. Also on view is a wonderful reproduction of a tall stucco relief of U Pakal, the son of Ahkal Mo' Nahb'.

Also discovered in 1999, **Templo XX** contains a red-frescoed tomb built in 540 that is currently Palenque's most active dig. Archaeologists began restoration work inside the tomb in 2012, and now believe that it might be the final resting place of K'uk B'alam I, an ancestor of Pakal.

In 2002 archaeologists found in **Templo XXI** a throne with very fine carvings depicting Ahkal Mo' Nahb', his ancestor the great Pakal, and his son U Pakal.

Grupo Norte

North of El Palacio is a **Juego de Pelota** (Ball Court; Map p385) and the handsome buildings of the Northern Group. Crazy Count de Waldeck lived in the so-called **Templo del Conde** (Temple of the Count), constructed in AD 647.

Palenque Northeastern Groups

East of the Grupo Norte, the main path crosses Arroyo Otolum. Some 70m beyond the stream, a right fork will take you to **Grupo C** (Map p385), a set of jungle-covered buildings and plazas thought to have been lived in from about AD 750 to 800.

If you stay on the main path, you'll descend some steep steps to a group of low, elongated buildings, probably occupied residentially from around AD 770 to 850. The path goes alongside the Arroyo Otolum, which here tumbles down a series of small falls forming natural bathing pools known as the **Baño de la Reina** (Queen's Bath). Unfortunately, you can't bathe here anymore.

The path then continues to another residential quarter, the **Grupo de los Murciélagos** (Bat Group), and then crosses the **Puente de los Murciélagos**, a footbridge across Arroyo Otolum.

Across the bridge and a bit further downstream, a path goes west to **Grupo I** and **Grupo II**, a short walk uphill. These ruins, only partly uncovered, are in a beautiful jungle setting. The main path continues downriver to the road, where the museum is a short distance along to the right.

☞ Tours

Transportador Turística Scherrer & Barb   TOURS

(☏ cell 916-1033649; fermerida_69@hotmail.com; Av Juárez 13) Offers the most eclectic tours in town, including the remote Lacandón communities of Metzabok and Nahá (day trip M$1400, two days M$2500), Guatemala's Piedras Negras archaeological site (M$2500), and cool day trips off the Carretera Fronteriza like the Cascada de las Golondrinas, Cascada Welib-já and various bird-watching and kayaking destinations. All with a minimum of four people; English and Italian spoken.

Palenque Guides   TOURS

(Map p385; 2hr tour for up to 7 people in English/Spanish M$1050/880) A good guide brings the ruins to life. A bad guide can put a damp cloud over your visit. On the trail up to the ruins you'll pass by dozens of people (including children) claiming to be guides. It's best to wait until you reach the entry gate and take an official guide. Note that prices are rather flexible!

🛏 Sleeping

The first choice to make is whether you want to stay in or out of Palenque town. While Palenque town hosts traffic and commerce, the surrounding area, especially between the town and the ruins, offers some magical spots where howler monkeys romp in the tree canopy and unseen animals chirp after dark. The compound of El Panchán (p384) is a traveler favorite, with low-key budget *cabañas* nestled in the stream-crossed jungle. Frequent

Palenque

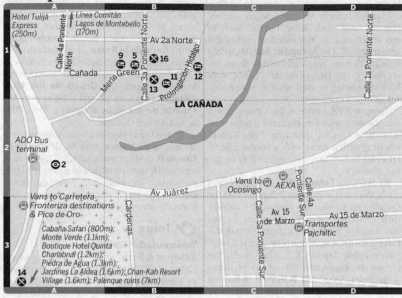

Palenque

daytime combis between town and the ruins will drop you off and pick you up anywhere along this road.

Except for the leafy La Cañada area in the west, Palenque town is not particularly attractive, but if you stay here you'll have plenty of restaurants and services nearby.

⌂ In Town

★ Yaxkin
HOSTEL $

(☏916-345-01-02; www.hostalyaxkin.com; Prolongación Hidalgo 1; dm M$180, d without bathroom M$472/330, d with air-con & bathroom M$727; P❄✳@⊙) Channeling laid-back El Panchán from pretty La Cañada, this former disco has been revamped into a modern hostel with a guest kitchen, a ping-pong table, multiple lounges and a swanky restaurant-bar and cafe. Rooms without air-con are monastic but funky. The fan-cooled dorms (one for women only) and private rooms with air-con feel more pleasant and comfortable.

There's a positive environmental outlook as well, with solar water heaters in use, lots of recycling, no plastic usage and other forward looking ideas.

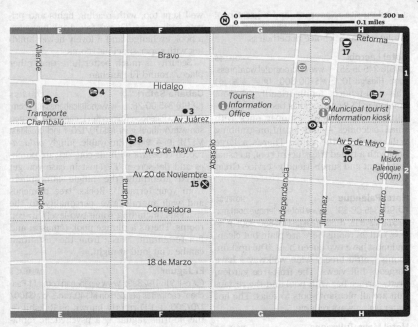

Hostal San Miguel

HOTEL $

(☎916-345-01-52; hostalmiguel1@hotmail.com; Hidalgo 43; dm M$150, s/d with fan M$250/400, with air-con M$400/550; ❄❄❄) Very much a no-frills option, but the rooms have good natural light and views from the upper floors and it's clean and quiet. Dark two- and four-bed dorms don't have hot water or air-con, and all air-con rooms have two queen beds.

Hotel Lacandonia

HOTEL $

(☎916-345-00-57; Allende 77; r M$500; P❄❄) A modern hotel with tasteful, airy rooms all have wrought-iron beds, reading lights and cable TV, and there's a good restaurant. The upstairs rooms facing the street have cute balconies and the best light.

Hotel Xibalba

HOTEL $$

(☎916-175-08-60; www.hotelxibalba.com; Merle Green 9, La Cañada; r from M$551; P❄@❄) Located in the tranquil neighborhood of La Cañada, this midrange hotel is one of the better deals in town. It offers 35 pleasant, clean rooms many of which have murals on the walls and birds on the bedspreads. The common areas have rock-accented architectural details and a replica of the lid from Pakal's sarcophagus on display. Restaurant on premises.

Hotel Chablis Palenque

HOTEL $$

(☎916-345-08-70; www.hotelchablis.com; Merle Green, 7; r M$1000-1280; ❄❄❄❄) With sunny colors, high-quality, thick mattresses, neatly tiled (if small) bathrooms, a decent restaurant and an attractive flora-filled courtyard with a pristine pool, this appealing little hotel is hard to beat. Although it's in the center of town, it's set a little way back from the road, which keeps things fairly quiet. Our only real quibble is that the prices are a little steep.

Hotel Maya Rue

HOTEL $$

(☎916-345-07-43; www.hotelmayaruepalenque.com; Aldama s/n; r M$600-900; ❄@❄) Tree-trunk beams, dramatic lighting and impressive black-and-white photographs hanging from the walls add a dose of style to this 12-room offering combining traditional materials and industrial chic. Some rooms have shaded private balconies, but all are spacious and come with cable TV. Cafe on premises.

Hotel Tulijá Express

HOTEL $$

(☎916-345-01-04; www.tulijahotelpalenque.com; Blvd Aeropuerto Km 0.5; r incl breakfast from M$880; ❄❄❄❄) Just on the edge of town (but within easy walking distance), this is an excellent-value midrange hotel. There's a good on-site restaurant, and a great pool area. It's not bursting with character, but is a solid midrange choice nonetheless.

Hotel Lacroix
HOTEL $$

(☎916-345-15-35; www.lacroixhotel.wordpress.com; Hidalgo 10; r M$700-800; P⊝❄🛜🌊) This well-tended, family-friendly 16-room hotel near El Parque sports tasteful sponge-painted peach rooms – upper ones with small balconies – and attention-grabbing wall murals of the ruins. There's a large pool with a tinted translucent roof, a casual restaurant and super-friendly service. Great value.

Hotel Palenque
HOTEL $$

(☎916-345-00-39; www.hotelpalenque.com.mx; Av 5 de Mayo 15; d incl breakfast M$850-950; P❄🛜🌊) All 28 rooms here are plain but clean, and most have two queen beds. The upstairs rooms – off a breezy wide walkway – have gorgeous hill views. The fruit-tree garden, pretty terrace bar with pool and the restaurant are all pleasant spots to relax. The hot water isn't always reliable.

Hotel Maya Tulipanes
HOTEL $$

(☎916-345-02-01; www.mayatulipanes.com.mx; Cañada 6, La Cañada; r M$935-1232; P⊝❄@🛜🌊) Entered through a muraled foyer, the slightly overpriced La Cañada hotel has plain, comfortable, air-conditioned rooms with wrought-iron double beds and minimalist decor. It's designed around a pretty garden with a small pool and a restaurant.

Misión Palenque
HOTEL $$

(☎916-345-02-41; www.hotelmisionpalenque.com; Periférico Oriente s/n; r from M$1035; P❄🛜🌊) Set on lush, sprawling grounds just to the east of the center, this 207-room behemoth has all the trimmings you'd expect: comfy rooms with lime-green splashes of color, fabulous gardens and pool area, a good on-site restaurant and ultra-attentive staff.

🛏 Outside Town

Margarita & Ed Cabañas
GUESTHOUSE $

(☎916-348-69-90; www.margaritaandedcabanas.blogspot.com; Carreterra Palenque-Ruinas Km 4.5, El Panchán; cabañas M$285, r with fan M$320-410, s/d with air-con M$480/570; P❄) With the most spotless digs in the jungle, Margarita has welcomed travelers to her exceptionally homey place for decades. Bright, clean and cheerful rooms have good mosquito netting, and the more rustic screened *cabañas* are

well kept too, with reading lights and private bathrooms. There's free drinking water, a book exchange, and a lovely newer building with super-spacious rooms.

Security is much better here than other places around El Panchán.

Cabaña Safari
CABAÑAS $

(☎916-345-00-26; www.hotelcabanasafari.com; Carretera Palenque-Ruinas Km 1; campsites per person with/without gear M$170/120, r incl breakfast M$711; P❄🛜🌊) Enjoyable, jungly *palapa*-roofed *cabañas* with air-con, private porches and flat-screen TV (just in case you get bored absorbing the jungle atmosphere from your terrace!). Rocks, tree branches and wall murals give personality to the spacious (including some two-level) air-con rooms. There's a plunge pool, temascal and full restaurant. Music from the restaurant can be a bit loud at night.

El Jaguar
CABAÑAS $

(☎cell 916-1192829; www.elpanchan.com; El Panchán; campsites per person M$40, dm/s/d M$100/170/300; P) Formerly known as Rakshita's, the no-frills Jaguar is a psychedelic fantasy of colorful murals and DIY construction. Dorm mosquito netting and ground-level room security are iffy; the two-story units are pretty groovy. All have hot water and fans.

Jardines La Aldea
HOTEL $$

(☎916-345-16-93; www.hotellaaldea.net; Carretera Palenque-Ruinas Km 2.8; r from M$1050; P❄🛜🌊) The four-star Aldea has 33 large, beautiful and bright *palapa*-roofed rooms set amidst lovely grounds. Each room has an outside terrace with hammock and easy chair. It's a simple, stylish place, with a peaceful hilltop restaurant and a wonderful pool area. There are no TVs, making it an ideal place to get away from it all.

Maya Bell
HOTEL $$

(☎916-341-69-77; www.mayabell.mx; Carretera Palenque-Ruinas Km 6; cabañas without bathroom M$350, r with fan/air-con M$820/1100; P❄🛜🌊) With a sprawling jungleside pool frequented by (very vocal!) howler monkeys, this spacious grassy spot has tons of clean and comfortable sleeping options, plus a very average restaurant. Rooms with air-con are very homey and comfortable; those with fan are more basic, as are the shared bathrooms.

It's the closest accommodation to the ruins (it's just 400m from Palenque's site museum), but being inside the national park means you have to pay the park entry fee if you arrive between 7am and 8pm.

Hotel Paraiso Inn
GUESTHOUSE $$

(☑916-348-08-28; Carretera Palenque-El Naranjo km 1; d/ste M$847/1250; ❄🖥) Modern, open-plan rooms with lots of space, tiled floors and forest views. It's out on its own a short walk away from the other hotel zones, which is great if you like peace and quiet but can be a bit of a hassle when it comes to getting to and from restaurants in the evening.

You'd better be on very personal terms with anyone you share a room with be-cause there are glass shower doors facing the beds here!

Chan-Kah Resort Village
RESORT $$

(☑916-345-11-34; www.chan-kah.com.mx; Car-retera Palenque-Ruinas Km 3; r/ste M$1580/4100; Ⓟ❄🖥@🖥🏊) This large, quality resort on the road to the ruins is an ideal choice for families. It has arty, well-spaced wood-and-stone cottages some of which have four beds and all come with generous bathrooms, ceil-ing fans, terrace and air-con. Kids and swim-mers will also love the Chan-Kah's stupen-dous multilayer 70m stone-lined swimming pool in lush jungle gardens.

★ Boutique Hotel Quinta Chanabnal
BOUTIQUE HOTEL $$$

(☑916-345-53-20; www.quintachanabnal.com; Carretera Palenque-Ruinas Km 2.2; r US$150-350; Ⓟ❄🖥🏊) The Maya-inspired architecture and impeccable service at this decadent boutique hotel will leave you swooning. En-ter through heavy wood doors (carved by lo-cal artisans) into spacious stone-floor suites that contain majestically draped four-poster beds, outlandish Mexican art and cavernous bathrooms. Water features on the premises include a creek, a small lagoon and a natural rock, multi-tiered swimming pool.

Massages, a temascal and a fine restau-rant are available. The Italian owner, a Maya expert, also speaks German, French, English and Spanish.

Piedra de Agua
BOUTIQUE HOTEL $$$

(☑916-345-08-42; www.palenque.piedradeagua. com; Carretera Palenque-Ruinas Km 2.5; r incl breakfast from M$1920; Ⓟ❄🖥🏊) Elegant and romantic off-white-and-wood minimalism marks this fab designer *cabaña* compound that pampers guests with oodles of natural bath products, plush robes, private terrace tubs with bubble bath and hammocks out-side every room. Massages are available,

though the lap pool and Jacuzzi are the most popular amenities. A perfect place to indulge after a sweaty day at the ruins.

✕ Eating

Palenque is definitely not the gastronomic capital of Mexico. There's a decent variety of restaurants, though some are laughably overpriced. A number of inexpensive stands and sit-down spots can be found near the AEXA bus terminal and on the east side of El Parque in front of the church.

★ Café Jade
MEXICAN, CHIAPANECO $

(☑916-345-48-15; Prolongación Hidalgo 1; break-fast M$50-100, mains M$60-120; ⏱7am-11pm; 🖥) This very cool bamboo construction has indoor and outdoor seating and is one of the most popular places in town. Its growing fame hasn't led to a reduction in taste qual-ity though, and it serves good breakfasts, some Chiapan specialties and international traveler classics such as burgers. A reasona-ble number of vegetarian options and really good fresh juices, too.

Don Mucho's
MEXICAN, INTERNATIONAL $

(☑916-112-83-38; Carretera Palenque-Ruinas Km 4.5, El Panchán; mains M$60-150; ⏱7am-11pm) The hot spot of El Panchán, popular Don Mucho's provides great-value meals in a jungly setting, with a candlelit ambience at night. Busy waiters bring pasta, fish, meat, plenty of *antojitos* (typical Mexican snacks), and pizzas (cooked in a purpose-built Italian-designed wood-fired oven) that are some of the finest this side of Naples.

★ El Huachinango Feliz
SEAFOOD $$

(☑916-345-46-42; Hidalgo s/n; mains M$90-160; ⏱9am-11pm) A popular, atmospheric restau-rant in the leafy La Cañada neighborhood. It has an attractive front patio with tables and umbrellas, and there's also an upstairs cov-ered terrace. Seafood is the specialty here: order seafood soup, seafood cocktails, grilled fish that's beautifully crunchy on the outside and soft on the inside or shrimp served 10 different ways. The service is slooow but the food is worth the wait.

Monte Verde
ITALIAN $$

(☑916-119-17-87; mains M$100-180; ⏱1-11pm) There's a real Mediterranean vibe to this Italian restaurant tucked away in the for-est (do a bit of bird and monkey watching while waiting for your lunch!) and though most people go for the delicious thin-crust pizzas, the meat and pasta dishes are worthy of your time. Try the seafood tagliatelle piled high with prawns and you'll leave happy. Frequent live music in the evenings.

Restaurant Las Tinajas MEXICAN $$
(cnr Av 20 de Noviembre & Abasolo; mains M$85-130; ⊙7am-11pm) It doesn't take long to figure out why this place is always busy. It slings enormous portions of excellent home-style food – enough to keep you fueled up for hours. *Pollo a la veracruzana* (chicken in a tomato, olive and onion sauce) and *camarones al guajillo* (shrimp with a not-too-hot type of chili) are both delicious, as is the house salsa.

La Selva MEXICAN $$
(☑916-345-03-63; Hwy 199; mains M$85-220; ⊙11:30am-10:30pm) An upscale and slightly formal (for Palenque anyway) restaurant serving up well-prepared steaks, seafood, salads and *antojitos* under an enormous *palapa* roof, with jungle-themed stained-glass panels brightening one wall. Try the *pigua* (freshwater lobster) when it's available in the fall.

Restaurant Maya Cañada MEXICAN $$
(☑916-345-02-16; Merle Green s/n; breakfast M$85-110, mains M$85-200; ⊙7am-11pm; 🛜) This relatively upmarket and professionally run restaurant in the shady La Cañada area serves fine steaks, regional specialties and terrific seafood kebabs, all of which is beautifully presented. It's open to the air and has a cool upstairs terrace.

★ Restaurante Bajlum MEXICAN $$$
(☑916-107-85-18; www.facebook.com/Restaurante -Bajlum-276562802519284; mains M$150-250; ⊙2-10pm) Creative and stunningly presented modern Maya fusion food fills the menu at this upmarket but very inviting restaurant. The house specials include the delicious rabbit with 'jungle herbs' and duck with orange. Much of the produce is locally produced and whatever you order the owner is sure to come over and explain the story behind each dish. Impressive cocktail list. It's a little tucked away down a side lane on the left shortly before the ruins.

🍸 Drinking & Nightlife

Palenque doesn't have much of a nightlife scene. In the evenings you'll often spot more travelers waiting for a night bus than out on the town. Along the ruins road you can listen to live music in a few places, and in town

there are one or two other options. Bars in the center tend toward the unsavory.

Italian Coffee Company CAFE
(www.italiancoffee.com; cnr Jiménez & Reforma; coffee M$20-40; ⊙8am-11pm; 🛜) Weary traveler, welcome to air-conditioned nirvana complete with a huge menu of coffees and board games to while away a wet afternoon.

ⓘ Information

Whichever direction you come from it's safer to travel to Palenque in daylight hours as armed hold ups along roads leading to Palenque are not unheard of. For the moment it's best not to travel directly from Ocosingo to Palenque, and at the time of research most transportation was taking alternative and much longer, but safer routes. There have also been recent reports of thefts on the night bus from Mérida. When taking buses along these routes, consider stowing valuables in the checked luggage compartment.

Both of the below banks change dollars and euros (bring a copy of your passport).

Banco Azteca (Av Juárez, btwn Allende & Aldama; ⊙9am-9pm)

Bancomer (Av Juárez 96; ⊙8:30am-4pm Mon-Fri) Also has an ATM.

Clínica Palenque (Velasco Suárez 33; ⊙8:30am-1:30pm & 5-9pm) English-speaking clinic.

Municipal tourist information kiosk (El Parque; ⊙9am-2pm & 6-9pm Mon-Fri)

Post Office (Independencia s/n; ⊙8am-8:30pm Mon-Fri, to noon Sat)

Tourist Information Office (cnr Av Juárez & Abasolo; ⊙9am-8pm Mon-Sat, to 1pm Sun) The state tourism office's help center has the most reliable town, regional and transportation information, as well as maps. However, more accurate information is normally available from hotel staff.

ⓘ Getting There & Away

AIR

In 2014 Palenque's long-deserted **airport** (☑916-345-16-92) finally opened to commercial flights. Interjet has twice-weekly service to Mexico City. Otherwise, the closest major airport is Villahermosa; ADO runs a direct airport service (M$330) in comfortable minibuses.

BUS

In a spacious location behind the Maya head statue, **ADO** (☑916-345-13-44) has the main bus terminal, with deluxe and 1st-class services, an ATM and left-luggage facilities; it's also used by OCC (1st class). It's a good idea to buy your outward bus ticket a day in advance. Note that due to security issues buses are not currently running direct to Ocosingo and most companies are routing buses through Villahermosa instead.

AEXA (☑ 916-345-26-30; www.autobuses aexa.com.mx; Av Juárez 159), with 1st-class buses, and Cardesa (2nd class) is about 300m east on Avenida Juárez.

Línea Comitán Lagos de Montebello (☑ 916-345-12-60; Velasco Suárez btwn Calles 6a & 7a Poniente Norte), west of Palenque market, runs hourly vans to Benemérito de las Américas (M$130) 10 times daily (3:30am to 2:45pm), with most continuing around the Carretera Fronteriza to the Lagos de Montebello (M$300, seven hours to Tziscao) and Comitán (M$350, eight hours).

COLECTIVOS

Vans to Ocosingo (M$76) wait on Calle 5a Poniente Sur and leave when full. The route is prone to security issues and vans do not always go on the most direct road. Be prepared for canceled services or very circuitous routing.

Many **combis** for destinations along the Carretera Fronteriza (including Lacanjá Chansayab, Bonampak, Yaxchilán and Benemérito de las Américas) and for Pico de Oro leave from an outdoor *colectivo* terminal just south of the ADO bus station.

Vans operated by **Transportes Pajchiltic** (Av 15 de Marzo), run to Metzabok (M$55, three hours) and Nahá (M$60, four hours) whenever they're full (morning is best). Transportation back again often leaves in the middle of the night.

🛈 Getting Around

Taxis charge M$55 (up to M$70 at night) to El Panchán or Maya Bell, and M$60 to the ruins. Combis run by **Transporte Chambalú** (☑ 916-345-28-49; Hidalgo; M$25) from the center ply

the ruins road until dark. **Radio Taxis Santo Domingo** (☑ 916-345-01-26) has on-call service. There's a **taxi stand** on El Parque.

Agua Azul & Misol-Ha

These spectacular water attractions – the thundering cascades of Agua Azul and the 35m jungle waterfall of Misol-Ha – are both short detours off the Ocosingo–Palenque road. During the rainy season they lose part of their beauty as the water gets murky, though the power of the waterfalls is magnified.

Both are most easily visited on an organized day tour from Palenque.

👁 Sights

Agua Azul   WATERFALL
(M$40) Agua Azul is a breathtaking sight, with its powerful and dazzling white waterfalls thundering into turquoise (outside rainy season) pools surrounded by verdant jungle. On holidays and weekends the place is packed; at other times you'll have few companions. The temptation to swim is great, but take extreme care, as people do drown here. The current is deceptively fast, the power of the falls obvious, and there are many submerged hazards like rocks and dead trees.

If you're in decent shape, keep walking upstream – the crowds thin out the further up you go.

The turnoff for Agua Azul is halfway between Ocosingo and Palenque, some 60km from each. A paved road leads 4.5km down to Agua Azul from Hwy 199. A well-made

CHIAPAS & TABASCO AGUA AZUL & MISOL-HA

BUSES FROM PALENQUE

DESTINATION	FARE (M$)	DURATION (HR)	FREQUENCY (DAILY)
Campeche	440	5-5½	4 ADO
Cancún	722-994	12-13½	4 ADO
Mérida	628	8	4 ADO
Mexico City (1 TAPO & 1 Norte)	1096	13½	2 ADO
Oaxaca	946	15	ADO at 5:30pm
San Cristóbal de las Casas	306-354	8-9	6 ADO, 4 AEXA
Tulum	576-645	10-11	4 ADO
Tuxtla Gutiérrez	268-364	6½	11 ADO, 5 AEXA
Villahermosa	140-204	2½	frequent ADO & AEXA
Villahermosa airport	330	2¼	5 ADO

stone and concrete path with steps runs 700m up beside the falls from the parking area, which is packed with food and souvenir stalls. Basic lodging is also available.

Unfortunately, theft isn't uncommon, so don't bring valuables, keep an eye on your belongings and stick to the main paved trail.

Misol-Ha

WATERFALL

(total M$30) Just 20km south of Palenque, spectacular Misol-Ha cascades approximately 35m into a wonderful wide pool surrounded by lush tropical vegetation. It's a sublime place for a dip when the fall is not excessively pumped up by wet-season rains. A path behind the main fall leads into a cave, which allows you to experience the power of the water close up. Misol-Ha is 1.5km off Hwy 199 and the turnoff is signposted, and two separate *ejidos* (communal landholdings) charge admission.

🛏 Sleeping

Centro Turístico Ejidal Cascada de Misol-Ha

CABIN $

(☏916-345-12-10; www.misol-ha.com; cabin M$290; ⊘restaurant 7am-7pm, to 10pm high season; ℗🖳🛜) Has atmospheric wooden cabins among the trees near the waterfall, with fans, hot-water bathrooms and mosquito netting, plus a good open-air restaurant (mains M$80 to M$160). Nighttime swims are dreamy.

ℹ Getting There & Away

Most Palenque travel agencies offer daily Misol-Ha and Agua Azul trips. Trips cost around M$350 including admission fees, and last six or seven hours, spending 30 to 60 minutes at Misol-Ha and two to three hours at Agua Azul. Trips can also be organized to deposit you in San Cristóbal afterward for an additional M$120. *Colectivos* (M$40) run from Palenque to the turn off for Misol-Ha from where it's a 20- to 30-minute walk to the falls.

Due to security issues, for the moment it's not safe to travel to/from Agua Azul and Ocosingo.

Bonampak, Yaxchilán & the Carretera Fronteriza

Close to the Guatemala border, the ancient Maya cities of Bonampak and Yaxchilán might not be the largest or even among the best known of Maya ruins, but one thing's for sure: they're certainly among the most

wildly romantic. Fringed by the Lacandón Jungle, the daylight hours are characterized by bright tropical birds flitting between crumbling monuments and monkeys hooting from the trees. Night is even more atmospheric with the sky awash with stars and the ground twinkling with fireflies. Bonampak, famous for its frescoes, is 152km by road from Palenque; the bigger and more important Yaxchilán, with a peerless jungle setting beside the broad and swift Río Usumacinta, is 173km by road, then about 22km by boat.

Access to Bonampak and Yaxchilán is via the Carretera Fronteriza, which also gives handy access to a number of excellent ecotourism projects, dreamy waterfalls, Lacandón villages and lesser-known archaeological ruins.

☞ Tours

Organized tours can be helpful in this region if you have limited time and aren't driving. Always check package inclusions and exclusions, so you can plan your meals and park fees. Following are the standard tours (including entry fees and some meals) per person offered by Palenque travel agencies:

Bonampak and Yaxchilán Day trips (M$1750 to M$2500) usually include two meals and transportation in an air-conditioned van – a good deal since independent transportation to both is time-consuming and tours include the Bonampak transportation fee; two-day trips (M$3000 to M$4000) include an overnight stay at Lacanjá Chansayab.

Transportation to Flores, Guatemala Transportation (around M$1300, 10 to 11 hours) is by van to Frontera Corozal, river launch up the Usumacinta to Bethel in Guatemala, and public bus on to Flores. It's just as easy to organise it all yourself and go entirely by public transportation.

Flores via Bonampak and Yaxchilán Two days (around M$3100) with an overnight in Lacanjá Chansayab.

In Palenque, Transportador Turística Scherrer & Barb (p387) organizes more off-the-beaten-path trips to the region, including the Lacandón villages of Nahá and Metzabok and waterfalls in the area; San Cristóbal–based SendaSur (p371) can help with reservations for independent travelers.

ℹ Information

DANGERS & ANNOYANCES

Drug and human trafficking are facts of life in this border region, and the Carretera Fronteriza more or less encircles the main area of Zapatista rebel activity and support, so expect numerous military checkpoints along the road and from this area to Palenque and Comitán. These checkpoints generally increase security for travelers, but don't tempt easy theft by leaving money or valuables unattended during stops. For your own security, it's best to be off the Carretera Fronteriza before dusk. No public transportation ever runs after dark. For similar reasons, all border crossings with Guatemala are places you should aim to get through early in the day.

In the rainy months of September and October, rivers are usually too swollen for safe swimming.

Don't forget insect repellent.

ℹ Getting There & Away

The Carretera Fronteriza (Hwy 307) is a good paved road running parallel to the Mexico–Guatemala border, all the way from Palenque to the Lagos de Montebello. From Palenque, Autotransporte Chamoán runs vans run to Frontera Corozal (M$145, 2½ to three hours, every 40 minutes from 4am to 5pm), leaving from the outdoor *colectivo* terminal near the Maya head statue and south of the bus station. Use them for visits to Bonampak and Lacanjá Chansayab, because upon request they'll stop at the junction closest to the ruins, known as Crucero Bonampak (M$95, two hours), instead of the San Javier stop on the highway.

Línea Comitán Lagos de Montebello (p393), west of Palenque market, runs hourly vans to Benemérito de las Américas (M$125) 10 times daily (3:30am to 2:45pm), with most continuing around the Carretera Fronteriza to the Lagos de Montebello (M$310, seven hours to Tziscao) and Comitán (M$368, eight hours).

Both companies stop at San Javier (M$85, two hours), the turnoff for Lacanjá Chansayab and Bonampak, 140km from Palenque, and at Crucero Corozal (M$100, 2½ hours), the intersection for Frontera Corozal. For Cascada Welib-Já and Nueva Palestina, take any Carretera Fronteriza–bound combi from Palenque.

Gas stations along the Carretera Fronteriza are limited. From Palenque to Comitán (via the Chajul cutoff road) you'll find them in Chancalá and Benemérito only, but plenty of entrepreneurial locals sell reasonably priced gasoline from large plastic containers. Look for homemade 'Se vende gasolina' signs. If you're driving yourself make sure you are safely off the roads before dark.

Palenque to Bonampak

Cascada de las Golondrinas   WATERFALL

(Nueva Palestina; M$25, campsite M$60; ⊙ restaurant 9am-4pm) A lovely water feature tucked 10km off the highway, where two rivers cascade dramatically from a high point of 35m and you can swim in clear blue water during the dry season. A wooden boardwalk crosses the outflow, and at dusk hundreds of swallows duck in to bed down in a cave beneath the falls, streaming out at dawn.

You can camp here in lovely shady spots with basic facilities. From Palenque take a combi to the turnoff for Nueva Palestina (M$55, two hours), where taxis charge M$130 one way to the falls. Arrange a return pickup. Drivers should go 9km toward Nueva Palestina to the signed turnoff; the falls are another 1km in.

Cascada Welib-Já   WATERFALL

(M$25; ⊙ 8am-7pm) Thirty kilometers from Palenque, these 25m-high curtains of water aren't the most dramatic water features in the area, but the turquoise river pools make excellent swimming spots and there are generally few other people around. Amenities include a cross-river zip-line (M$50) and a simple restaurant. From Palenque, take a combi to the well-signed highway entrance (M$40, 30 minutes); it's a 700m walk in.

Plan de Ayutla   ARCHAEOLOGICAL SITE

(near Nueva Palestina; M$50; ⊙ 8am-5pm) The remote Maya ruins of Plan de Ayutla sit on an evocatively overgrown site, with buildings in various states of excavation and abandonment. From the dirt lot under dense tree canopy, follow a winding path up the rise to the **North Acropolis**, one of three constructed on natural hills. Visitors can explore a maze of interconnected rooms over four levels of the former residential palace complex.

The most significant building in this acropolis is **Structure 13**, a dramatically vaulted structure with an exterior decorated with unique stepped apron moldings. It was here that archaeologists recently discovered an **astronomical observatory** with two upper rooms containing window channels aligned to view the winter solstice and the solar zenith.

Plan de Ayutla was inhabited between 150 BC and AD 1000 and is believed to have been a regional seat of power between 250 BC and AD 700. Based on its size and

Bonampak

Site Entrance
(500m)

Edificio 15

Edificio 16

Templo de
las Pinturas
(Edificio 1)

Stele 1   Gran Plaza

Stele 3   Edificio 17

Stele 2

Edificio 3

Edificio
2

Edificio 6

features (including its ball court – at 65m long the largest in the upper Río Usumacinta region), archaeologists have two theories about the site's history. One hypothesis is that it was the city of Sak T'zi' (White Dog), which battled Toniná, Yaxchilán and Piedras Negras – and whose bloody defeat by Bonampak may be depicted in that site's famed murals, or perhaps it is the ancient city of Ak'e' (Turtle), where the royalty of Bonampak originated.

By car, drive 11km into Nueva Palestina from the highway; when the paved road turns left next to a clutch of lodgings signs, continue straight onto a gravel road. After about 4.5km, follow the signed left at the junction (the right turn goes to the village of Plan de Ayutla, not the ruins) and then travel another 3km to the clearly visible site. *Ejido* (common landholding) representatives, if present, may charge a small fee. Arriving by combi at the Nueva Palestina highway turnoff, you can negotiate a taxi fare with waiting time.

Bonampak

One of the outstanding archaeological sites of Chiapas, the setting of Bonampak in dense jungle hid it from the outside world until 1946. The **site** (M$65; ⊙8am-5pm) is most renowned for its vivid frescoes, which really bring the Maya world to life. Getting here is a bit of a hassle but the reward is well worthwhile. The ruins are spread over 2.4 sq km, but all the main ruins stand around the rectangular Gran Plaza.

The Bonampak site abuts the Reserva de la Biosfera Montes Azules, and is rich in

wildlife. Keep your eyes peeled for monkeys and macaws.

◉ Sights

The most impressive surviving monuments at the ruins were built under Chan Muwan II, a nephew of Yaxchilán's Itzamnaaj B'alam II, who acceded to Bonampak's throne in AD 776. The 6m-high **Stele 1** in the **Gran Plaza** depicts Chan Muwan II holding a ceremonial staff at the height of his reign. He also features in **Stele 2** and **Stele 3** on the **Acrópolis**, which rises from the south end of the plaza.

However, it's the vivid **frescoes** inside the modest-looking **Templo de las Pinturas (Edificio 1)** that have given Bonampak its fame – and its name, which means 'Painted Walls' in Yucatecan Maya. Some archaeologists theorize that the murals depict a battle between Bonampak and the city of Sak T'zi', which is believed to be Plan de Ayutla.

Diagrams outside the temple help interpret the murals, which are the finest known from pre-Hispanic America, but which have weathered badly since their discovery. (Early visitors even chucked kerosene over the walls in an attempt to bring out the colors!)

Room 1, on the left as you face the temple, shows the consecration of Chan Muwan II's infant son, who is seen held in arms toward the top of the right end of the room's south wall (facing you as you enter). Witnessing the ceremony are 14 jade-toting noblemen. The central **Room 2** shows tumultuous battle scenes on its east and south walls and vault, while on the north wall Chan Muwan II, in jaguar-skin battle dress, presides over the torture (by fingernail removal) and sacrifice of prisoners. A severed head lies below him, beside the foot of a sprawling captive. Recently restored and now blazing with vivid color, **Room 3** shows a celebratory dance on the Acrópolis steps by lords wearing huge headdresses, and on its east wall three white-robed women puncture their tongues in a ritual bloodletting.

The sacrifices, the bloodletting and the dance may all have been part of the ceremonies surrounding the new heir. In reality, the infant prince probably never got to rule Bonampak; the place was abandoned before the murals were finished, as Classic Maya civilization evaporated. Don't forget to look up at the intricately carved lintels when entering **Edificios 1** and **6**.

ℹ Getting There & Away

Bonampak is 12km from San Javier, the turnoff town on the Carretera Fronteriza. If you get dropped off at San Javier instead of Crucero Bonampak (8km further in), taxis from San Javier charge M$30.

Get ready to open your wallet: the community charges M$30 per person to enter the town of Lacanjá, and private vehicles are prohibited beyond the Crucero Bonampak, where van drivers charge an exorbitant M$250 round trip per van to the ruins and back.

Lacanjá Chansayab

POP 380 / ELEV 320M

Lacanjá Chansayab, the largest Lacandón Maya village, is 6km from San Javier on the Carretera Fronteriza, and 12km from Bonampak. Its family compounds are scattered around a wide area, many of them with creeks or even the Río Lacanjá flowing past their grassy grounds. Tourism is now an important income earner, and many families run *campamentos* with rooms, camping and hammock space. As you approach the village, you'll cross the Río Lacanjá on a bridge, from which it's about 700m to a central intersection where tracks go left (south), right (north) and straight (west).

🏃 Activities

Sendero Ya Toch Kusam
HIKING

The Sendero Ya Toch Kusam is a 2.5km self-guided walking trail that starts 200m west from the central intersection.

🛏 Sleeping & Eating

Campamento Río Lacanjá
CABAÑAS $$

(www.ecochiapas.com/lacanja; r without bathroom M$645; P) This fabulous set-up might lack material luxury, but it's rich in jungle atmosphere. Comfortable, semi-open-air, wood-framed cabins with mosquito nets stand close to the tree-shrouded Río Lacanjá and are open to the sights and sounds of the forest and river. A separate group of larger rooms (triple/quad M$750/850) have two solid wooden double beds, tiled floors, fans and hot-water bathrooms.

As well as guided walks, rafting trips on the Río Lacanjá – which has waterfalls up to 2.5m high but no rapids – are offered for a minimum of four people. A half-day outing including Lacanjá ruins and Cascada Ya Toch Kusam (both reached on foot from the river) costs M$600 per group (up to 10 people), and overnight rafting and camping

trips also visiting the Bonampak ruins are around M$1400 per person. Set dinners cost M$100 and breakfast is M$85.

Campamento Topche
CABAÑAS $$

(www.sendasur.com.mx; r with/without bathroom M$1294/733; P🐾🛜) About 550m west of the central intersection, this recently refurbished *campamento* has a few options: comfortable rooms with terracotta-tiled floors and a vaulted and mosquito-proofed *palapa* roof; wood-cabin rooms with shared bathroom, mosquito nets and walls that don't reach the ceiling; and detached jungly *cabañas* next to the river. All have hot water.

Restaurant Chankin
MEXICAN $

(meals around M$90; ⏱7am-9pm) This calm and quiet garden restaurant has fragrant walls of flowers that attract swarms of hyperactive hummingbirds, while the food, which is hearty country fare, attracts travelers who are a lot less hyperactive.

ℹ Getting There & Away

Combis for Lacanjá Chansayab (M$140) and other destinations along the Carretera Fronteriza leave Palenque from an outdoor *colectivo* terminal just south of the ADO bus station. The community collects M$30 per person at the town entrance. If you're traveling from Yaxchilán, combis charge M$53 between Crucero Corozal and San Javier.

Frontera Corozal

POP 5200 / ELEV 200M

This riverside frontier town (formerly Frontera Echeverría) is the stepping-stone to the beautiful ruins of Yaxchilán, and is on the main route between Chiapas and Guatemala's Petén region. Inhabited mainly by Chol Maya, who settled here in the 1970s, Frontera Corozal is 16km by paved road from Crucero Corozal junction on the Carretera Fronteriza. The broad Río Usumacinta, flowing swiftly between jungle-covered banks, forms the Mexico–Guatemala border here.

Long, fast, outboard-powered *lanchas* (motorboats) come and go from the river *embarcadero* (jetty). Almost everything you'll need is on the paved street leading back from the river here, including the **immigration office** (⏱8am-6pm), 400m from the *embarcadero,* where you should hand in/obtain a tourist permit if you're leaving for/arriving from Guatemala.

⊙ Sights

Museo de la Cuenca del Usumacinta
MUSEUM

(Museum of the Usumacinta Basin; M$26; ⊙ 9am-5pm) The Museo de la Cuenca del Usumacinta, opposite the immigration office, has good examples of Chol Maya dress, and some information in Spanish on the area's postconquest history, but pride of place goes to two fine and intricately carved stelae retrieved from the nearby site of Dos Caobas. If it's not open, inquire at the Restaurante Imperio Maya next door.

⌁ Sleeping & Eating

Nueva Alianza
CABAÑAS $$

(☑ in Guatemala 502-463-824-47; www.hotelnueva alianza.org; r with/without bathroom M$600/300; P🐾) Friendly Nueva Alianza, among trees 150m along a side road from the museum, has small, plain but cheerful budget rooms with wooden walls that don't reach the ceiling, and newer stand-alone rooms with bathrooms. All have fans and wooden furniture. There's a good on-site restaurant (mains from M$80) and the only internet access in town.

Escudo Jaguar
CABAÑAS $$

(☑ in Guatemala 502-5353-56-37; www.escudo jaguar.com; campsites per person M$150, s/d M$580/680; P🐾) Often used by tour groups, Escudo Jaguar overlooks the river 300m from the embarcadero. Its solidly built thatched cabañas are all kept spotless, and come equipped with fan and mosquito netting. The best are very spacious and have hot showers and terraces strung with hammocks. The restaurant serves straightforward, but well-prepared Mexican dishes (mains from M$65, breakfasts M$40 to M$75).

Restaurante Imperio Maya
MEXICAN $

(mains M$75-110; ⊙ 7:30am-3pm) Attached to the museum, this spacious palapa-topped restaurant has a lengthy menu of Mexican standards and caters to Yaxchilán-bound tourists.

ⓘ Getting There & Away

If you can't get a bus or combi direct to Frontera Corozal, get one to Crucero Corozal, 16km southeast of San Javier on the Carretera Fronteriza, where taxis (M$40 per person colectivo) run to Frontera Corozal. The ejido (community) hits up visitors entering or leaving Frontera Corozal for a M$30 per person toll; keep your ticket for exiting unless you're continuing on to Guatemala.

Autotransporte Chamoán vans run hourly from Frontera Corozal embarcadero to Palenque (M$90, 2½ to three hours), with the last departure at 4pm or when full.

Lancha organizations have desks in a thatched building near the embarcadero, and all charge about the same prices for service to Bethel, Guatemala (boat for 1-3 people M$450, 4 people M$530, 5-7 people M$650, 8-10 people M$800), which is 40 minutes upstream. From Bethel, hourly buses depart to Flores (4½ hours) from 8am to 4pm. Make sure that the driver stops at the Bethel immigration office.

Yaxchilán

Jungle-shrouded Yaxchilán (M$70; ⊙ 8am-5pm, last entry 4pm) has a terrific setting above a horseshoe loop in the Río Usumacinta. The location gave it control over river commerce, and along with a series of successful alliances and conquests, Yaxchilán was one of the most important Classic Maya cities in the Usumacinta region. Archaeologically, Yaxchilán is famed for its ornamented facades and roofcombs, and its impressive stone lintels carved with conquest and ceremonial scenes. A flashlight is helpful for exploring parts of the site.

Howler monkeys (saraguates) inhabit the tall trees here, and are an evocative highlight. You'll almost certainly hear their visceral roars, and you stand a good chance of seeing some. Spider monkeys, and occasionally red macaws, can also be spotted here at times.

History

Yaxchilán peaked in power and splendor between AD 681 and 800 under the rulers Itzamnaaj B'alam II (Shield Jaguar II, 681–742), Pájaro Jaguar IV (Bird Jaguar IV, 752–68) and Itzamnaaj B'alam III (Shield Jaguar III, 769–800). The city was abandoned around AD 810. Inscriptions here tell more about its 'Jaguar' dynasty than is known of almost any other Maya ruling clan. The shield-and-jaguar symbol appears on many Yaxchilán buildings and stelae; Pájaro Jaguar IV's hieroglyph is a small jungle cat with feathers on its back and a bird superimposed on its head.

Most of the main monuments have information boards in three languages, including English.

Yaxchilán

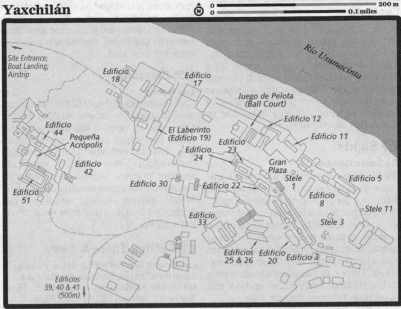

Rio Usumacinta

Site Entrance;
Boat Landing;
Airstrip

Edificio 18

Edificio 17

Juego de Pelota (Ball Court)

Edificio 12

Edificio 11

Edificio 44

Pequeña Acrópolis

El Laberinto (Edificio 19)

Edificio 23

Edificio 24

Gran Plaza

Edificio 42

Edificio 30

Edificio 22

Stele 1

Edificio 5

Edificio 8

Edificio 51

Stele 11

Edificio 33

Stele 3

Edificios 25 & 26

Edificio 20

Edificio 3

Edificios 39, 40 & 41 (500m)

Sights

As you walk toward the ruins, a signed path to the right leads up to the **Pequeña Acrópolis**, a group of ruins on a small hilltop – you can visit this later. Staying on the main path, you soon reach the mazelike passages of **El Laberinto (Edificio 19)**, built between AD 742 and 752, during the interregnum between Itzamnaaj B'alam II and Pájaro Jaguar IV. Dozens of bats shelter under the structure's roof today. From this complicated two-level building you emerge at the northwest end of the extensive **Gran Plaza**.

Though it's difficult to imagine anyone here ever wanting to be any hotter than they already were, **Edificio 17** was apparently a sweat house. About halfway along the plaza, Stele 1, flanked by weathered sculptures of a crocodile and a jaguar, shows Pájaro Jaguar IV in a ceremony that took place in AD 761. **Edificio 20**, from the time of Itzamnaaj B'alam III, was the last significant structure built at Yaxchilán; its lintels are now in Mexico City. **Stele 11**, at the northeast corner of the Gran Plaza, was originally found in front of Edificio 40. The bigger of the two figures visible on it is Pájaro Jaguar IV.

An imposing stairway climbs from Stele 1 to **Edificio 33**, the best-preserved temple at Yaxchilán, with about half of its roof-comb intact. The final step in front of the building is carved with ball-game scenes, and splendid relief carvings embellish the undersides of the lintels. Inside is a statue of Pájaro Jaguar IV, minus his head, which he lost to treasure-seeking 19th-century timber cutters.

From the clearing behind Edificio 33, a path leads into the trees. About 20m along this, fork left uphill; go left at another fork after about 80m, and after some 10 minutes, mostly going uphill, you'll reach three buildings on a hilltop: **Edificio 39, Edificio 40** and **Edificio 41**.

Getting There & Away

Lanchas (motorboats) take 40 minutes running downstream from Frontera Corozal, and one hour to return. The boat companies are in a thatched building near the Frontera Corozal *embarcadero* (jetty), all charging about the same price for trips. The return journey with 2½ hours at the ruins for one to three people costs M$800, four people M$1050, five to seven people M$1450 or eight to 10 people M$1800. *Lanchas* normally leave frequently until 1:30pm or so; try to hook up with other travelers or a tour group to share costs.

Las Nubes

At Las Nubes milky-blue river waters spill over smooth granite boulders and crash and tumble over a series of impressive waterfalls surrounded by tropical forest. It's a deliciously laid-back spot in which to while away a couple of days swimming, walking or, for the more active, throwing caution to the wind by going zip-lining, rappelling or trying other adrenaline sports.

◉ Sights

Río Santo Domingo   RIVER
The Río Santo Domingo is a beautiful, turquoise mess of cascades and rapids. Some of the river pools are great swimming spots; it's M$20 per person to swim here if you're not staying the night. A swinging bridge straddles a fierce section of water-carved canyon, making an excellent vantage point from which to swoon over the grandest waterfalls. There's also an adrenaline-pumping zip-line (M$150), and you can spelunk and rappel from February through June.

There are some enjoyable walking opportunities along the riverbank and into the forest. The most popular short walk is the 15-minute amble up to a *mirador* where you will be rewarded with blue-green jungle views. The bird watching all around here is great. Activities are paid for through Las Nubes.

🏃 Activities

Ecoturismo Xbulanjá   RAFTING
(☑in Guatemala 502-3137-56-91; www.xbulanja. com) From Embarcadero Jerusalén, just east of the Las Nubes highway turnoff, this Tseltal cooperative offers Class III rafting to Las Nubes for M$2200 (two to six passen-

gers, three hours), and its lodging (*cabañas* M$600 to M$800) and restaurant (mains M$60 to M$100) are a less-expensive alternative to Las Nubes. Rafting-trip prices include the drive back.

🛏 Sleeping

Las Nubes   LODGE $$
(☑in Guatemala 502-4972-02-04; www.causas verdeslasnubes.com; cabañas M$1500) Beautifully situated close to the main falls, this nicely landscaped and very peaceful complex has 15 well-built but frustratingly overpriced *cabañas* with hot water and pleasant porches, as well as a waterside restaurant that serves meals (mains around M$90), but no alcohol, though you can bring your own. Lodging rates drop 25% in low season.

❶ Getting There & Away

Las Nubes is 12km off the Carretera Fronteriza, 55km from Tziscao. From Comitán there are between four and six daily combis (M$95, 3½ to four hours) between 7:30am and 4:30pm.

Laguna Miramar

ELEV 400M

Ringed by rainforest, pristine Laguna Miramar, 140km southeast of Ocosingo in the Reserva de la Biosfera Montes Azules (Montes Azules Biosphere Reserve), is one of Mexico's most remote and exquisite lakes. Frequently echoing with the roars of howler monkeys, the 16-sq-km lake is bathtub-warm and virtually unpolluted. Rock ledges extending from three small islands make blissful wading spots, and petroglyphs and a turtle cave are reachable by canoe. The area is rich in wildlife. As you swim you might find yourself being ogled by spider monkeys, tapirs, macaws and toucans; butterflies are also prolific. Locals fish for *mojarra* (perch), and will assure you that the lake's few crocodiles are not dangerous. Well, not *that* dangerous anyway! Take note though: getting to the lake can be a real mission. Don't bother coming unless you have several days at your disposal.

◉ Sights

Emiliano Zapata   AREA
(☑community phone 200-124-88-80/81/82) The Laguna Miramar is accessible thanks to a successful ecotourism project in the small Maya community of Emiliano Zapata,

---

---

❶ LAS NUBES–LAGUNA MIRAMAR SHORTCUT

If you're visiting both Las Nubes and Laguna Miramar via public transit, you can avoid the east–west backtracks to the highway by walking between Las Nubes and Loma Bonita, a town about halfway in along the road to the *lanchas* for Laguna Miramar. It's approximately a 5km hike (40 minutes, with some hills) from the swinging bridge at Las Nubes to Loma Bonita, where you can catch onward combis.

REFORMA AGRARIA

Reforma Agraria is the home of an impressive community program to protect the endangered scarlet macaw (*guacamaya*). This huge and spectacular member of the parrot family, which is so colorful it looks like a flying rainbow, once ranged as far north as Veracruz, but sadly its only Mexican home today is far eastern Chiapas. Numbers at Reforma Agraria have increased to more than 110 pairs since 1991, when the 14.5-sq-km macaw reserve was founded. Guides here can take you in search of the birds, but remember that they can move in and out of the reserve in seasonal pursuit of food; the best months for observing them are December to June, when they are nesting. Ask to see the chick aviary onsite and about the possibility of accompanying staff when they monitor nests.

Las Guacamayas (📞 in Guatemala 502-5157-96-10; www.ecoturismoaramacao.com; Ejido Reforma Agraria; dm M$330, cabaña M$1635-1965, ste M$2070-2260; 🅿 ⊜ 🛜), a beautiful and welcoming ecolodge, is situated on the bank of the broad Río Lacantún, one of the Usumacinta's major tributaries, with the Reserva de la Biosfera Montes Azules on the opposite bank. Large, superbly comfortable thatch-roofed *cabañas* – with a jungle decor theme, mosquito screens, verandas and bathrooms with hot showers – are spread around the extensive grounds, linked by wooden walkways. Dorms are shared two-bed rooms with common bathrooms.

near its western shore. If you arrive independently, ask for the Comité de Turismo or El Presidente.

🛏 Sleeping

At the lakeshore, you can sling a hammock or camp (per person M$40) under a *palapa* shelter. But if you arrive after noon, you'll need to stay in Emiliano Zapata, as the guides want to make it home before dark. The village has a handful of simple *cabañas* (M$150 per person) with river views, all with one queen and one twin-bed room, a fan and shared bathrooms.

ℹ Getting There & Away

BOAT

Take a combi from Comitán to La Democracia (across the bridge from Amatitlán) or Plan de Río Azul and hire a *lancha* (M$1400 one way, maximum eight passengers, two hours) to Emiliano Zapata via the Río Jatate. Most boats depart from Plan de Río Azul, where *lanchas* (M$1400 to M$2600 per boat, depending on boat size and bargaining skills) leave on demand until about 3pm. La Democracia and Plan de Río Azul are a rough 16km and 20km respectively from the Carretera Fronteriza highway; the first half is paved.

BUS & COLECTIVO
From Comitán

Transportes Las Margaritas (6a Calle Sur Oriente 51, btwn 4a & 5a Av Oriente Sur) combis service Las Margaritas (M$20, 25 minutes) frequently from Comitán. From Las Margaritas there are very uncomfortable collectivos running a couple of times daily to

San Quintín (M$100, 4½ to six hours) from 5am to noon. There tends to be one departure every hour but it all depends on supply and demand. Combis return from San Quintín from 2am until noon.

From Ocosingo

Trucks leave for San Quintín (M$100 to M$120, five to six hours in the dry season) from a large walled lot at the back of the market. Departures are roughly every two hours from 8am until 2pm, but it all depends on how many passengers there are. Get there early and be prepared to wait around.

Metzabok & Nahá

Situated in the Lacandón Jungle between Ocosingo and the Carretera Fronteriza town of Chancalá, the small and isolated Lacandón villages of Metzabok and Nahá straddle a network of underground rivers in a protected biodiversity zone that's home to wildlife including jaguars, tapirs, howler monkeys and ocelots. Inhabitants here still follow many Lacandón traditions and customs.

🏃 Activities

In Metzabok, villagers offer *lancha* (motorboat) trips (up to M$800 per boat) along forest-ringed Laguna Tzibana, where you can see a moss-framed limestone wall painted with vivid red prehistoric pictograms, and hike to a lookout point above the tree canopy.

CHIAPAS & TABASCO BONAMPAK, YAXCHILÁN & CARRETERA FRONTERIZA

In Nahá you can hire a guide (one/two hours M$400/700) to travel on foot or by canoe to various lagoons and learn about the area's flora and fauna.

🛏 Sleeping

Centro Ecoturístico Nahá
CABAÑAS $$

(☑in Guatemala 555-150-59-53; www.nahaeco turismo.com; s/d M$750/850, without bathroom M$300/450) A friendly place with simple well-screened thatched huts with mosquito nets and bags of Tarzan character or startlingly luxurious *cabañas* with hot-water bathrooms.

ℹ Getting There & Away

From Palenque, Transportes Pajchiltic (p393) vans leave for Metzabok (M$55, three hours) and Nahá (M$60, four hours) whenever they're full (morning is best). Transportation back again often leaves in the middle of the night. Note that service to Metzabok is unreliable in both directions; it will stop at the junction (6km away) if the driver decides there aren't enough passengers to bother with the detour. From Ocosingo, trucks to Nahá (M$65, 2½ hours) leave from a walled lot behind the market whenever there are enough passengers.

Comitán Region

With a heady mixture of natural world wonders, towns laced in pretty colonial architecture and impressive ancient sites, the Comitán region has a lot going for it. So, it's a little odd then that the region isn't more heavily touristed. But, for those in the know, this is one of the most enticing parts of Chiapas to explore. The regional capital is Comitán, a likeable small town of attractive buildings and lots of local color.

Comitán

☑ 963 / POP 98,000 / ELEV 1560M

With a pretty plaza of modern sculpture pieces, an eye-catching church and mature, carefully manicured flat-topped trees where birds flock and chirp in the evening, the colonial-flavoured town of Comitán has a pleasant, artsy atmosphere. Set on a high plain 90km southeast of San Cristóbal, Comitán has a gentle climate, some memorable places to stay and eat, a few interesting museums and few visitors. To top it all off, there are several natural and archaeological attractions less than an hour away in the verdant countryside.

◉ Sights

★Museo Arqueológico de Comitán
MUSEUM

(☑963-632-57-60; 1a Calle Sur Oriente; ⊙9am-6pm Tue-Sun) FREE Although this museum is very small it's crammed with treasures from the area's many archaeological sites (Spanish signage only). Despite all the beautiful artistic items from across the ages, the highlights for most people are the misshapen pre-Hispanic skulls on display – deliberately 'beautified' by squeezing infants' heads between boards. Going to the dentist will never seem quite so bad again...

Iglesia de Santo Domingo
CHURCH

(⊙7am-2pm & 4-8pm) On the **plaza**, the pretty apricot-yellow Iglesia de Santo Domingo dates back to the 16th and 17th centuries, and sports unusual and handsome blind arcading on its tower. Its former monastic buildings next door are now the **Centro Cultural Rosario Castellanos** (☑963-632-06-24; www.facebook.com/CentroCulturalRosario Castellanos; 1a Av Oriente; ⊙9am-9pm) FREE, which has a pretty wood-pillared patio featuring a mural on local history.

Casa Museo Dr Belisario Domínguez
MUSEUM

(☑963-632-13-00; Av Central Sur 35; ⊙10am-6pm Tue-Sat, 9am-12:45pm Sun) FREE Just south of the main plaza, the recently renovated Casa Museo Dr Belisario Domínguez is the family home of Comitán's biggest hero and the site of his medical practice. It provides (in Spanish) fascinating insights into the state of medicine and the life of the professional classes in early-20th-century Chiapas (with a reconstruction of the on-site pharmacy and home), as well as the heroic tale of Domínguez' political career, ending in his assassination.

🛏 Sleeping

★Hotel Nak'am Secreto
HOTEL $$

(☑963-636-73-85; www.nakan.mx; 1a Av Oriente Norte 29; r incl breakfast from M$947; ❇🤖) With sharp, modern and spacious rooms, some charming common areas and fabulously detailed service, this is Comitán's best-value hotel. The super-central location, big leafy plants in terracotta pots and views from the rooftop garden seal the deal.

Hotel Lagos de Montebello
HOTEL $$

(☑963-632-10-92; www.hotelloslagosdemonte bello.com; Blvd Belisario Dominguez Norte 14;

Comitán

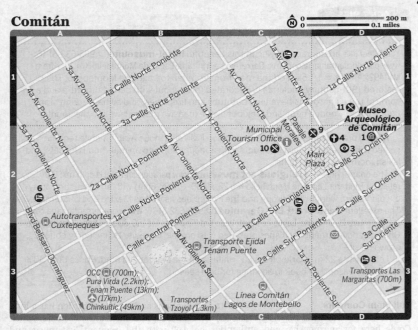

d M$832; 😋🛜❄) It's all about form and functionality at this large, well-run hotel on the edge of the city center. The rooms are of a good size and are well equipped with desks and flat-screen TVs, and it's pretty quiet at night. The covered courtyard swimming pool is a big bonus and there's a cafe next door.

La Casa Del Marques de Comillas
BOUTIQUE HOTEL **$$**

(☏ 612-175-08-60; www.lacasadelmarquesdecomillas.com; Av Central Sur 24; r from M$816; 😋❄🛜❄) We love the hidden garden courtyard with its sun-drenched swimming pool at this popular and good-value hotel. The slightly old-fashioned rooms are given a dose of life through the use of strong, contrasting colors and there are plenty of other arty touches throughout. Some of the staff speak English. A great deal.

★ Hotel Casa Delina
BOUTIQUE HOTEL **$$$**

(☏ 963-101-47-93; www.hotelcasadelina.com; 1a Calle Sur Poniente 6; r from M$1300; 🅿😋🛜) When a team of contemporary Mexican and international artists were let loose in this stunningly restored 250-year-old mansion they really created something truly memorable. Think outlandish light fittings hanging from original wood-pillared arches, walls festooned with pouting lips and leaping horses, and a gorgeous, leafy tropical garden surrounded by eight industrial-chic rooms. This is truly something special. An on-site cafe serves excellent organic Chiapan coffees.

🍴 Eating & Drinking

A handful of good, typical restaurants lines the west side of the plaza.

PARADOR-MUSEO SANTA MARÍA

You'll feel like aristocracy staying in this beautiful **hotel-museum** (☎963-632-51-16; www.paradorsantamaria.com.mx; Carretera La Trinitaria-Lagos de Montebello Km 22; r from M$1492; P ❄ 🛜 🏊), 1.5km off the road from Comitán to Lagos de Montebello. The restored 19th-century hacienda is decorated throughout with period furniture and art; some of the eight rooms have tiled bathtubs and fireplaces, and all have rough stone floors, grand wooden beds and look out over expansive grassy lawns to the countryside beyond.

An odd but opulent newer lodging addition is an enormous Arabian-style tent, furnished with Oriental rugs, a bathroom with a Jacuzzi tub and animal-mouth faucets, and lavish room-dividing curtains.

The chapel here is a **religious art museum** (www.paradorsantamaria.com.mx; Carretera La Trinitaria-Lagos de Montebello Km 22; M$30; ☉9am-6pm) with an interesting array of colonial-era work from Europe and the Philippines as well as Mexico and Guatemala. The excellent **Restaurant Los Geranios** (☎963-632-51-16; www.paradorsantamaria.com.mx; Carretera La Trinitaria-Lagos de Montebello Km 22; mains M$150-300; ☉8am-9pm) serves Chiapan and international dishes prepared with organic ingredients (including coffee) grown on site.

Look for the 22km marker from La Trinitaria on the Montebello road. Prices drop 30% in the low season, but book in advance for high season.

Yuli Moni Comedor
MEXICAN $

(Mercado; quesadillas M$20-30; ☉8am-5pm; 🍴) Come here for inexpensive and authentic street food. This mercado *comedor* has tasty and filling quesadillas; the *nopales* (cactus) and mushrooms are also good options for vegetarians.

★ Ta Bonito
MEXICAN $$

(☎963-565-95-06; www.facebook.com/tabonitio.mx; Ave Central Norte 5; mains M$80-120; ☉8am-11pm) Ever had an octopus tentacle burger? No, we didn't think so. Highly imaginative and quirky modern Chiapas dishes are served up at this easygoing place that as much as possible uses only local produce. As well as unexpected main courses and great mezcal, it's also well regarded for its large and varied breakfast spreads.

500 Noches
SPANISH $$

(☎963-101-38-11; Calle Central, Main Plaza; mains M$120-170; ☉11am-11pm; 🛜) Soaring ceilings and romantic nooks populate this cavernous restaurant-bar specializing in fondues, tapas and 80-plus wines, as well as craft beers. The big draw is the live *trova* folk music (starting at 7pm nightly), so it's worth coming by for drinks or dessert even if small plates aren't your thing. Plaza seating too.

Pura Vida
BEER GARDEN

(www.facebook.com/PuraVidaBeerStation; De Abasolo; beer M$25-60; ☉2-11pm Tue-Sun) A little way to the west of the city center this unpretentious and cool beer garden has a long list of local and international beers, which go well with the frequent live music and blazing bonfires.

ⓘ Information

BBVA Bancomer (cnr 1a Av Oriente Sur & 1a Calle Sur Oriente; ☉8:30am-4pm Mon-Fri) Changes euros and dollars Monday through Friday; has an ATM.

Municipal Tourism Office (http://visit comitan.com; Av Central Norte; ☉8am-8pm Mon-Wed, to 9pm Thu-Sun)

Post Office (Av Central Sur 45; ☉8:30am-4:30pm Mon-Fri, to noon Sat)

ⓘ Getting There & Away

The Pan-American Hwy (Hwy 190), named Blvd Belisario Domínguez here but usually just called 'El Bulevar,' passes through the west of town. **Mototaxis** (per person M$8) will get you quickly and easily around the town.

Comitán's **OCC bus terminal** (☎963-632-09-80; Blvd Belisario Domínguez Sur 43) is on the Pan-American Hwy. Among many others there are buses to Mexico City, Villahermosa, Playa del Carmen and Cancún. Across the road from the OCC terminal, 'centro' combis (M$8) run to the main plaza; a taxi is M$35.

Numerous *colectivos* have terminals on Hwy 190 between 1a and 2a Calles Sur Poniente, about 500m north of the OCC terminal; they depart when full. For San Cristóbal, vans (M$55) and *colectivo* taxis (M$60) are available until

9pm. Vans for Ciudad Cuauhtémoc (M$47, until 8pm), which usually say 'Comalapa,' and Tuxtla Gutiérrez (M$95, until 6pm) are also available.

Línea Comitán Lagos de Montebello (☑ 963-632-08-75; 2a Av Poniente Sur 23) runs vans to the Lagos de Montebello and along the Carretera Fronteriza, with departures to Laguna Bosque Azul (M$45, one hour) and Tziscao (M$50, 1¼ hours) every 20 minutes from 3am to 5pm; to Reforma Agraria (M$160, 4½ hours) 10 times from 3am until 2pm; and to Palenque (M$350, eight hours) eight times daily from 3:30am to 11am. Schedules don't use daylight saving time.

Transportes Tzoyol (☑ 963-632-77-39; cnr 4a Av Poniente Sur 1039 & 13a Calle Sur Poniente) runs vans to Reforma Agraria (M$145) eight times daily from 2:30am to 3pm, as well as to Plan de Río Azul (M$100, 3½ hours), the connection for boats to Laguna Miramar, four times a day between 4:30am and 2pm. It doesn't use daylight saving time.

Autotransportes Cuxtepeques (Blvd Belisario Domínguez Sur btwn 1a & 2a Calles Norte Poniente) runs hourly vans and buses to the El Chiflón waterfall turnoff on Hwy 226 (M$35, 45 minutes) from 4am to 8pm.

GETTING TO GUATEMALA

Very frequent *colectivos* (M$50) and intermittent buses (M$65) run between Ciudad Cuautémoc and Comitán (1½ hours). From Ciudad Cuautémoc, three daily OCC buses run to San Cristóbal de las Casas (M$156, 3½ hours) and beyond from 11am to 10pm, but it's usually quicker to get to Comitán and pick up onward transportation there. Other (infrequent) destinations include Palenque, Cancún and Tapachula.

The **Mexican immigration office** (Ciudad Cuautémoc; ☉ 8am-10pm) is across the street from the OCC terminal; *colectivos* generally assume that travelers need to be dropped off there. The Guatemalan border post is 4km south at La Mesilla, and 'Línea' combis (M$8) and taxis (M$15 *colectivo*, M$50 private) ferry people between the two sides.

There are banks and money changers on both sides of the border, which closes to car traffic from 9pm to 6am.

From La Mesilla, **mototaxis** (M$8/Q5) can drop you at the 2nd-class bus depot. Second-class buses leave very frequently from 6am to 6pm for Huehuetenango (two hours) and Quetzaltenango (four hours), where you can find onward connections to Guatemala City. About 1km inside the border (just past the curve in the highway), 1st-class Línea Dorada (www.lineadorada.info) has direct daily departures to Guatemala City (eight hours).

There's a **Guatemalan consulate** (☑ 963-110-68-16; www.minex.gob.gt; 1a Calle Sur Poniente 35, Int 3 4th fl, Comitán; ☉ 9am-1pm & 2-5pm Mon-Fri) in town that issues tourist visas.

Lagos de Montebello

The temperate pine and oak forest along the Guatemalan border east of Chinkultic is dotted with more than 50 small lakes of varied hues, known as the Lagos (or Lagunas) de Montebello. The area is very picturesque, peaceful and, after the steamy heat of the nearby jungles, beautifully cool and refreshing. Most people just come on a day trip from Comitán, but the lakes make an ideal place at which to spend a couple of peaceful days walking.

◉ Sights

◉ Lagunas de Colores

From the park ticket booth, the northward road leads to the Lagunas de Colores, five lakes with vivid hues that range from turquoise to deep green: **Laguna Agua Tinta**, **Laguna Esmeralda**, **Laguna Encantada**, **Laguna Ensueño** and, the biggest, **Laguna Bosque Azul**, on the left where the paved road ends.

CHIAPAS & TABASCO COMITÁN REGION

BUSES FROM COMITÁN

DESTINATION	FARE (M$)	DURATION (HR)	FREQUENCY (DAILY)
Ciudad Cuauhtémoc	120	1½	3
Palenque	368	10	1
San Cristóbal de las Casas	78	2	frequent
Tapachula via Motozintla	300	6	6
Tuxtla Gutiérrez	102-112	3	frequent

Lagos de Montebello

Lagos de Montebello

CHIAPAS & TABASCO EL SOCONUSCO & BEACHES

👁 Laguna Pojoj & Laguna Tziscao

Near to Tziscao, a track leads 1km north to cobalt-blue Laguna Pojoj, which has an island in the middle that you can visit on simple rafts. Laguna Tziscao, on the Guatemalan border, comes into view 1km past the Pojoj junction. The turnoff to the Chuj-speaking village of **Tziscao**, a pretty and spread-out place stretching down to the lakeside, is a little further on.

👣 Tours

In the Laguna Ensueño (and sometimes Bosque Azul) parking lot, *camiones* (trucks) do shared three- to five-hour lake tours for about M$600 per vehicle, though it can be harder to get a group together on weekdays. Local boys offer multilake horseback excursions that include **Dos Cenotes** (M$200, two to three hours), a pair of sinkholes in the forest, or to the **Laguna de Montebello** (about one hour away). From Laguna de Monebello, more boys offer horseback rides to Dos Cenotes.

🛏 Sleeping & Eating

La Esmeralda CABIN $
(📲 cell 963-1094329; cabin M$665; 🅿️😊) Like a cute little summer camp, these simple but well-built two-story wood chalets have hot water and a five-star location (though they are crammed in quite close to one and other). Each cabin can sleep up to five. There's a restaurant (mains M$60 to M$85) serving basic Mexican staples.

It's located 500m east off the road between Laguna Ensueño and Laguna Encantada.

Comedores MEXICAN $
(dishes from M$45; ⊙ 7am-3pm) Beside the Laguna Bosque Azul parking lot are several basic *comedores* that serve drinks and simple plates of *carneasada* (roasted meat) or quesadillas, and food options exist at most other lakes as well.

ℹ Getting There & Away

The paved road to Montebello turns east off Hwy 190 just north of La Trinitaria, 16km south of Comitán. It passes Chinkultic after 32km, and enters the Parque Nacional Lagunas de Montebello 5km beyond. A further 800m along is a ticket booth, where you must pay a M$25 park-admission fee. Here the road forks: north to the Lagunas de Colores (2km to 3km) and east to the village of Tziscao (9km), beyond which it becomes the Carretera Fronteriza, continuing east to Ixcán and ultimately circling back up to Palenque. Public transportation from Comitán is a snap, making it an easy day trip. Vans go to the end of the road at Laguna Bosque Azul and to Tziscao, and will drop you at the turnoffs for Museo Parador Santa María, Chinkultic and the other lakes. The last vehicles back to Comitán leave Tziscao and Laguna Bosque Azul in the early evening.

From San Cristóbal, a number of agencies offer tours that take in the lakes, throw in a visit to El Chiflón and get you back by dinnertime.

El Soconusco & Beaches

Chiapas' fertile coastal plain, 15km to 35km wide, is called the Soconusco, and is named for the Aztecs' most distant 15th-century province, called Xoconochco. It's hot and humid year-round, with serious rainfall from mid-May to mid-October. The lushly vegetated Sierra Madre de Chiapas, rising steeply from the plain, provides an excellent environment for coffee, bananas and other crops. Olive ridley and green sea turtles and the occasional leatherback nest along the coastline from June through November, and turtle preservation projects exist in Puerto Arista, Boca del Cielo, La Encrucijada and Chocohuital/Costa Azul.

The endless beach and ocean here is more wild and wooly than the tropical cliche and you should take care where you go in – the surf is often rough, and riptides (known as *canales*) can quickly sweep you out a long way. Bring bug repellent for overnights, as sandflies can be fierce from May through October.

Tonalá

📍 966 / POP 35,000

This sweaty, bustling town on Hwy 200 is the jumping-off point for the beaches in the northern part of El Soconusco. The town has no attractions as such and, assuming you don't arrive too late in the day, there's little reason to spend the night here.

There are good travel connections to larger inland towns and you'll need to get cash if you're heading for nearby beaches such as Puerto Arista (p409), as there are no ATMs there.

◉ Sights

Iglesia Vieja ARCHAEOLOGICAL SITE
(☉8am-5pm) FREE Believed to be the regional capital of the Zoque during the Classic period, these ruins were inhabited between AD 250 and AD 400. The site's most prominent characteristics are its use of megalithic granite architecture, and its most impressive structure, the namesake 'Old Church,' is a 95m by 65m pyramid utilizing stone blocks weighing over a ton each. Instead of steps, the apex is reached via a ramp – look for the petroglyph cross at the south side of its base.

The other distinctive feature here is the presence of many carved anthropomorphic

---

THE LACANDÓN JUNGLE

Chiapas contains swaths of wild green landscape that have nourished its inhabitants for centuries. But this rich trove of natural resources also makes it a contentious prize in the struggle for its water, lumber and oil and gas reserves.

The Selva Lacandona (Lacandón Jungle), in eastern Chiapas, occupies just 0.25% of Mexico. Yet it contains more than 4300 plant species (about 17% of the Mexican total), 450 butterfly species (42% of the national total), at least 340 bird species (32% of the total) and 163 mammal species (30% of the Mexican total). Among these are such emblematic creatures as the jaguar, red macaw, white turtle, tapir and harpy eagle.

This great fund of natural resources and genetic diversity is the southwest end of the Selva Maya, a 30,000-sq-km corridor of tropical rainforest stretching from Chiapas across northern Guatemala into Belize and the southern Yucatán. But the Lacandón Jungle is shrinking fast, under pressure from ranchers, loggers, oil prospectors, and farmers desperate for land. From around 15,000 sq km in the 1950s, an estimated 3000 to 4500 sq km of jungle remains today and it continues to shrink at a rate of about 5% per year. Waves of land-hungry settlers deforested the northern third of the Lacandón Jungle by about 1960. Also badly deforested are the far eastern Marqués de Comillas area (settled since the 1970s) and Las Cañadas, between Ocosingo and Montes Azules. Most of what's left is in the Reserva de la Biosfera Montes Azules and the neighboring Reserva de la Biosfera Lacan-tun.

The Mexican government deeded a large section of the land to a small number of Lacandón families in the 1970s, creating tensions with other indigenous communities whose claims were put aside. Land within the region remains incredibly contested. Lacandones and their advocates consider themselves to be an environmentally sensitive indigenous group, defending their property against invasive settlers. Other communities within the reserve, who provide some of the Zapatista rebels' strongest support, view it as an obfuscated land grab and pretext for eviction under the guise of environmental protection. Zapatista supporters also argue that the settlers are using the forests in unsustainable ways, and claim that the government seeks to exploit the forests for bio-prospecting (patenting) traditional plants.

SIGHTS AROUND COMITÁN

With a dearth of other tourists, **Chinkultic** (⊗8am-5pm) is one of those magical archaeological sites where the sense of wild atmosphere is as enthralling as the stories written into the stones. Chinkultic was a minor Maya power during the late Classic period and, like Tenam Puente, may have survived into post-Classic times. Of 200 mounds scattered over a wide area of dramatically situated ruins, only a few have been cleared, but it's easy to let your imagination color in the rest.

The ruins are in two groups. From the entrance, first take the path to the left, which curves around to the right below one of Chinkultic's biggest structures, **E23**, which is covered in vegetation. The path reaches a grassy plaza with several weathered **stelae**, some carved with human figures, and a ball court on the right.

Return to the entrance, from which another path heads to the **Plaza Hundida** (Sunken Plaza), crosses a stream, then climbs steeply up to the **Acrópolis**, a partly restored temple atop a rocky escarpment, with remarkable views over the surrounding lakes and forests and down into a cenote (sinkhole) 50m below – into which the Maya used to toss offerings of pottery, beads, bones and obsidian knives.

Guides – some of whom we're pretty sure should be in school – wait about outside the site to offer their services to the few visitors.

Chinkultic is about 48km from Comitán, on the road to the Lagos de Montebello. Combis for the lakes can drop you at the intersection (M$50 from Comitán); the site is 2km north via a paved access road.

Note that the site is closed periodically; it's best to check with the Comitán tourist office (p404) before heading out.

El Chiflón

These mighty waterfalls tumble 120m off the edge of an escarpment 20km southwest of Comitán. In a region with a surfeit of impressive waterfalls these ones really are something special. In the dry season, from roughly February through July, the falls form a foamy line and the blue river water is safe enough to swim in. But during the rainy season, rapid currents turn the river a muddy brown, the falls gush with abandon and swimming is a life-threatening proposition.

A 1km approach road heads up from Hwy 226 to the parking area, from which a well-made path leads 1.3km up alongside the forest-lined river (which has nice swimming spots) to a series of increasingly dramatic and picturesque waterfalls. Reaching the main Velo de Novia falls, prepare to be drenched by flying spray. You can also fly across the river on a zip-line (M$150).

A small **interpretive center** provides information (in Spanish) on the river and wildlife in the area.

From Comitán, Autotransportes Cuxtepeques (p405), runs hourly vans and buses to the El Chiflón turnoff on Hwy 226 (M$35, 45 minutes) from 4am to 8pm. Mototaxis wait there to ferry passengers up the road. Drivers should take the Tzimol turnoff from the Pan-American Hwy, 5km south of central Comitán.

Tenam Puente Maya Ruins

(M$50; ⊗8am-5pm) These sprawling Maya ruins feature three ball courts, a 20m tiered pyramid and other structures rising from a wooded hillside. Tenam Puente was one of a set of Classic Maya settlements in this region that seem to have survived in the post-Classic period, possibly to as late as AD 1200. Although the main structures have been fully restored, the lesser ones remain half buried in the undergrowth, which, combined with the lack of visitors, gives the site a reflective, dreamy atmosphere.

A 5km-long paved road leads west to the site from Hwy 190, 9km south of Comitán. **Transporte Ejidal Tenam Puente** (3a Av Poniente Sur 8) runs combis (M$25) every 45 minutes from 8am to 6pm. The last combi from the ruins returns at 4pm. A taxi costs about M$300 return (with an hour at the ruins).

and zoomorphic monuments scattered throughout the site. The most well-known are the **Sapodrilo** (it appears to be a cross between a toad and a crocodile) and the **Altar de las Cuatras Caras** (Altar of the Four Faces).

Few people make the really quite minimal effort required to visit, which gives the ruins a haunting, deserted quality. From the signed turnoff at Km 10 on the Tonalá–Arriaga hwy, it's about 9km (30 minutes) east off the main road; a high-clearance vehicle is required mid-May through November because the last 2km up can be washed out, but walking a section may still be required. There is no public transportation.

An exuberant authority on regional archaeological sites, the distinguished **Ricardo López Vassallo** (☏966-663-01-05, cell 966-1042394; rilova36@hotmail.com) lives in Tonalá and can organize transportation.

🛏 Sleeping & Eating

Hotel Galilea
HOTEL $

(☏966-663-02-39; Hidalgo 138; s/d M$425/465; P❄️🛜) The good-value, mellow yellow Hotel Galilea has a convenient restaurant and clean medium-sized rooms with dark wooden furniture that give it an old-world feel. It's virtually on the central plaza.

Restaurant Nora
MEXICAN $$

(☏966-663-02-43; www.facebook.com/norarestau rante; Independencia 10; mains M$85-165; ⊙8am-5pm Mon-Fri, to 2pm Sat) There's always a fun family atmosphere at the Restaurant Nora, one block east from the plaza (behind the Hotel Galilea). The prawns are something of a house specialty, but then they have had plenty of time to get them right because they've been in business since 1964.

ℹ Getting There & Away

From the central plaza, the **OCC bus terminal** (Hidalgo) is 600m west and the 2nd-class **Rápidos del Sur** (RS; Hidalgo btwn Belisario Domínguez & Iturbide) is 250m east. Both lines have frequent services to Tapachula (M$142 to M$318, three to four hours), Pijijiapan (M$82 to M$112, one hour) and Tuxtla Gutiérrez (M$114 to M$202, 2½ to three hours).

Colectivo taxis for Puerto Arista (M$25, 20 minutes), Boca del Cielo (M$38, 35 minutes) and Madre Sal (M$70) run from Matamoros between 20 de Marzo and Belisario Domínguez, four blocks east of the plaza and one block downhill. Puerto Arista combis (M$20) leave from Juárez between 20 de Marzo and 5 de Mayo, one block further downhill. Combis to Madre Sal (M$45) depart from near the market on 5 de Mayo between Juárez and Allende; a private taxi costs M$300. *Colectivo* taxis for Pijijiapan (M$50) can be found on Hidalgo between 5 de Mayo and 20 de Mayo. Taxis and combis run until about 7pm.

Puerto Arista
☏994 / POP 900

The state's most developed beach town is 18km southwest of Tonalá, though unless you visit during weekends, summer or holidays – when hotel prices rise and vacationing *chiapanecos* jam the place and its beachfront *palapa* seafood eateries – it's a small, ultra-sleepy fishing town. With flowers and trees lining the roads, and a shiny white three-story lighthouse in the center of town, it's an attractive little place and will suit those after an easy, 100% Mexican beach holiday experience.

◉ Sights

Centro de Protección & Conservación de la Tortuga Marina en Chiapas
ANIMAL SANCTUARY

(⊙10am-5pm) FREE During the nesting season, the state government collects thousands of newly laid olive ridley turtle eggs from 40km of beach, incubating them in protected beachside nests and releasing the hatchlings when they emerge seven weeks later. At this center located about 3km northwest along the single street from the lighthouse (taxis charge M$30), you can stop in to see the turtle nursery. To volunteer (M$3500 per eight days including basic food and board) with beach patrols and hatchling release, contact San Cristóbal-based **Natáté** (☏967-631-69-18; www.natate.org.mx; Madero 29). Entry is by donation.

🛏 Sleeping

Garden Beach Hotel
HOTEL $$

(☏994-600-90-42; www.gardenbeach.mx; Blvd Mariano Matamoros 800; r from M$1000; P❄️🛜🏊) Across the street from the beach and 800m southeast of the lighthouse, this hotel has pastel-shaded, air-conditioned rooms that are well past their best. All rooms have flat-screen TVs and up to three double beds. The upper floors have great ocean views.

It has a beachfront open-air restaurant (mains M$120 to M$170) and a big double pool overlooked by a bright green frog the size of a small car.

CHIAPAS & TABASCO EL SOCONUSCO & BEACHES

ℹ️ Getting There & Away

At weekends and in holidays there's a near-constant stream of *colectivo* taxis bustling between Puerto Arista and Tonalá (M$25, 20 minutes). During the working week you'll likely have to wait a little longer for transportation.

Reserva de la Biosfera La Encrucijada

This large biosphere reserve protects a 1448-sq-km strip of coastal lagoons, sandbars, wetlands, seasonally flooded tropical forest and the country's tallest mangroves (some above 30m). The ecosystem is a vital wintering and breeding ground for migratory birds, and harbors one of Mexico's biggest populations of jaguars, plus spider monkeys, turtles, crocodiles, caimans, boa constrictors, fishing eagles and lots of waterfowl. Despite the apparent quantity of wildlife, you'd have to be very dedicated and patient to see many of the flagship creatures. Bird-watching, however, is good at any time of year, but best during the November-to-March nesting season. The reserve can be visited via access points from Pijijiapan and Escuintla, and *lancha* rides take you through towering mangroves.

◉ Sights

◉ Ribera Costa Azul

A laid-back coastal jewel, the beautiful black sandbar of Ribera Costa Azul (also called Playa Azul) is a thin strip of palm-fringed land between ocean and lagoon accessed from the Chocohuital *embarcadero,* 20km southwest of Pijijiapan. Camping is generally free, though restaurants ask that you eat your meals (seafood M$130–150) there to do so. Outside of the busy high season many places are closed. *Lanchas* (M$15 one way) ferry passengers to the sandbar, and birding and mangrove trips (M$320 per boat per hour) can also be organized.

If you don't want to camp, head 300m north of the Chocohuital dock and pull up a pool chair at the **Refugio del Sol** (☏ cell 962-6252780; www.refugiodelsol.com.mx; Ribera Costa Azul; r from M$1770; ﾟ🄿✲🛜🅂) hotel.

◉ Embarcadero Las Garzas

Lost among the swamps and backwaters in the heart of the reserve at Embarcadero Las Garzas is the large thatched roof

Red de Ecoturismo La Encrucijada (Embarcadero Las Garzas; ⊘ 8am-5pm). This is a clearinghouse for information on tours and lodging run by local community ecotourism groups. Activities on offer include private *lancha* tours (M$1100 to M$1800, up to 10 passengers) to local beaches and to some superb bird-watching spots. *Lanchas* also serve a number of small communities where you can camp or overnight in simple *cabañas*. At the settlement of **Barra de Zacapulco** – which also has a sea-turtle breeding center – you can usually camp or sling a hammock for free if you eat your meals at one of its simple *comedores* (seafood plates around M$100). A community cooperative there offers six basic solar-powered **cabañas** (☏918-596-25-00; Embarcadero Las Garzas; r M$500) with fans, screened windows and cold-water bathrooms.

ℹ️ Getting There & Away

For Ribera Costa Azul, combis for Chocohuital (M$25, 40 minutes, 5am to 6pm) leave hourly from 1a Av Norte Poniente 27 in Pijijiapan between 2a and 3a Poniente Norte; the last one returns at 8pm.

To get to Embarcadero Las Garzas , take a bus along Hwy 200 to Escuintla, then a *colectivo* taxi to Acapetahua (M$9, 10 minutes). Beside the abandoned railway in Acapetahua, take a combi 18km to Embarcadero Las Garzas (M$25, 20 minutes, every 30 minutes until 5pm). From Embarcadero Las Garzas, *colectivo lanchas* go to communities including Barra de Zacapulco (M$55, 25 minutes). The last boat back from Barra de Zacapulco may be as early as 4pm, and the last combi from Embarcadero Las Garzas to Acapetahua goes at about 5pm.

Tapachula Region

Often treated as a mere stepping stone between northern Guatemala and better known attractions elsewhere in southern Mexico, it's nevertheless well worth devoting a few days to the Tapachula area. This area is known for producing some of the best coffee in Mexico and a few of the coffee farms offer tours and boutique accommodations. Highlights elsewhere in the region include the pretty village of Santo Domingo, reaching for the clouds by climbing one of the tallest volcanoes in Mexico and exploring little known pre-Hispanic ruins. The regional capital, Tapachula, is a workaday town but makes for a convenient overnight stop.

MADRE SAL

Drift to sleep pondering the waves crashing onto the black-sand beach at **Madre Sal** (☑ cell 966-6666147, cell 966-1007296; www.elmadresal.com; Manuel Ávila Camacho; campsites M$50-100, cabañas M$600-800; ℗), an ecotourism project 25km south of Puerto Arista. Named for a mangrove species, its restaurant (meals from M$100) and thatched two-bed en suite *cabañas* sit astride a skinny bar of pristine land between a lagoon and the Pacific that's reached via *lancha* (M$25) through mangroves.

Guests use candles after the 11pm power shutoff, and crabs skitter along the sand when stars fill the night sky. In season, sea turtles come ashore to lay eggs, and the night watchman can wake you if you want to watch or help collect the eggs for the Boca del Cielo hatchery.

Though the water can be rough, the beach is spotless, and there's excellent bird-watching in the mangroves, including 13 species of heron. Three-hour *lancha* trips are available (M$750 per boat, maximum 12 people), including one for bird- and crocodile-spotting.

From Tonalá, take a taxi (M$70 shared, M$300 private) or combi (M$45) to Manuel Ávila Camacho; combis charge an extra M$5 to the *embarcadero*, or you can walk five minutes or ride on the back of a motorbike (M$10).

Tapachula

☑ 962 / POP 320,000 / ELEV 100M

Mexico's bustling southernmost city, the 'Pearl of the Soconusco,' doesn't quite live up to its nickname, though it does have an interesting combination of urban sophistication and tropical tempo. The city is an important commercial center, not only for the Soconusco but also for cross-border trade with Guatemala.

A hot, humid and busy place year-round, most travelers simply pass through here on their way to or from Guatemala, but it makes a good base for a number of interesting nearby attractions.

Tapachula's heart is the large, lively **Parque Hidalgo**, with vistas of the towering 4100m cone of Volcán Tacaná to the north on clear days. The city's stately **cathedral** (⊙ 8am-6pm) overlooks the western edge of the plaza.

A few blocks away, **Parque Bicentenario** is a quiet, although not especially attractive, spot that has fountains lining the main walkways and some shady spots for watching the world go by

🛏 Sleeping

Hotel Diamante   HOTEL $

(☑ 962-628-50-32; www.hoteldiamante.com.mx; Calle 7a Poniente 43; r with fan/air-con M$350/$627; ℗✳🛜) A rather uninspired hotel but the average rooms are well-priced and clean. Rooms 12 through 16 have dynamite views of Volcán Tacaná.

⭐ Casa Maya Mexicana   BOUTIQUE HOTEL $$

(☑ 962-626-66-05; www.casonamaya.com; Av 8a Sur 19; r incl breakfast from M$908; ℗😊✳@🛜🏊) A vine-covered, exquisite boutique hotel paying homage to Mexican women in history. Guests can choose from sumptuous rooms named for heroines such as human rights lawyer Digna Ochoa or Zapatista commander Ramona. Antiques, lush plants and all kinds of interesting art create a soothing, creative feel. The 10 rooms on two floors surround a tropical garden-patio with a small pool.

In addition there's a small bar and a restaurant with excellent homemade meals and great service, all of which makes this a fabulous place to stay.

Hotel Mo Sak   HOTEL $$

(☑ 962-626-67-87; www.hotelmosak.com; Av 4a Norte 97; s/d from M$575/640; ℗✳🛜) A popular choice, this modern and fair-priced hotel has big windows, bold artwork and minimalist furniture. Helpful, attentive staff and free morning coffee help round out the deal. King-bed rooms have kitchenettes.

Suites Ejecutivas Los Arcos   HOTEL $$

(☑ 962-625-31-31; www.suitesejecutivasarcos.com; Av 1a Sur 15; s/d from M$696/814; ✳🛜) This is one of those delightfully arty hotels which Mexico so excels at. Paper butterflies and real plants enliven common areas and a tangle of art fills the walls. It has a great downtown location, rooms are generously sized and come equipped with

Tapachula

Tapachula

◎ Sights
1 Cathedral..B2
2 Parque Hidalgo..............................B3

🛏 Sleeping
3 Casa Maya Mexicana.....................A4
4 Hotel Diamante..............................C3
5 Hotel Mo Sak.................................D1
6 Suites Ejecutivas Los Arcos...........C5

✗ Eating
7 La Jefa...C4
8 La Parrilla Tap................................B3

kitchenette and balconies overlooking the lush gardens.

Hotel San Francisco HOTEL $$
(☎ 962-620-10-00; www.sucasaentapachula.com; Av Central Sur 94; s/d from M$627/796; ❄ 🛜 ⌦) If you're craving a good night's sleep and guaranteed comforts then this large, business-style hotel to the south of the center ticks all the boxes. The light-filled rooms are spacious and the hotel has a whole bunch of amenities, including an inviting garden-pool area.

✕ Eating

★ La Jefa
MEXICAN $$

(☑962-118-17-20; 1a Ave Norte Esquina; mains M$80-140; ☺noon-8pm) This classic Tapachula *parrillada* is a great night out with a group friends. Huge hunks of meat sizzle over the barbecue, cold beers are slapped down onto the tables, TVs blare out and a couple of oversized wooden chickens stand guard over diners. This is rustic Mexican eating at its finest.

Ostionería El Rinconcito
SEAFOOD $$

(☑962-626-49-13; Hormiguillo 4; mains M$50-150; ☺9am-8pm) Take a taxi to this popular, cheap and cheerful seafood spot and try to choose between the 17 different shrimp dishes, a freshly cooked *róbalo* (snook) and the in-season *langosta* (lobster). Weekend lunches are prime time, when an organ serenades diners with *ranchera, cumbia* and *romántica*. Kids will love the pufferfish dangling from the ceiling and the trampoline.

La Parrilla Tap
PARRILLA $$

(☑962-118-14-28; Av 8a Norte 14; tacos & tortas M$25-70, mains $70-120; ☺7am-midnight) Share an arty and hearty platter of *parrilla*, snack on a quick taco or try the lush house *pollo con mole* (chicken with *mole* sauce) at this buzzing grill right off the plaza. It's deservedly one of the most popular places in town.

El Mito-t
MEXICAN $$

(☑962-620-02-80; 4 Ave Sur, 133; mains M$80-120; ☺Mon-Sat 1pm-midnight, to 7pm Sun) You get to be the chef at this fun place – well, kind of anyway. Known far and wide for its salsas, they pile a dozen or more different kinds onto your table when you sit down and then leave it to you to order the tacos and fillers. The prawns and calamari are a hit with everyone.

★ Ristorante Marinni
ITALIAN $$$

(☑962-625-39-97; www.facebook.com/Marinni Ristorante; Av 11a Sur 1; mains M$100-200; ☺1-11pm Mon-Thu, to midnight Fri & Sat, to 7pm Sun) Held in high regard by locals, this Italian restaurant has a sophisticated and softly lit indoor dining room and an outdoor patio cloaked in dramatic greenery. Taste highlights include the *tallarines con camarones* (pasta with shrimp), wood-fired thin-crust pizza and the *medallón al balsámico* (beef medallions in red wine and balsamic vinegar). Reserve ahead on weekends.

ℹ️ Information

Banorte (cnr Av 2a Norte & Calle Central Poniente; ☺8:30am-4:30pm Mon-Fri, 9am-2pm Sat) Changes dollars Monday through Friday and has an ATM.

Chiapas Divisas (Calle 1a Poniente 13; 8:30am-8:30pm Mon-Fri, to 6:30pm Sat, to 2:30pm Sun) Currency exchange.

Sanatorio Soconusco (☑962-626-35-66; Av 4a Norte 68, at Calle 11 Poniente) A clinic with 24-hour emergency service.

Tourist Office (www.turismochiapas.gob.mx/sectur/tapachula; Av 8a Norte; ☺8am-4pm Mon-Fri) A helpful office in the Antiguo Palacio Municipal.

ℹ️ Getting There & Away

AIR

Tapachula's modern **airport** (☑962-626-22-91; Carretera Tapachula-Puerto Madero Km 18.5; 🛜) is 20km southwest of the city. It's a drowsy place, with just three daily flights to/from Mexico City on **Aeroméxico** (☑962-626-39-21; Central Oriente 4) and Volaris (www.volaris.com).

BUS

Deluxe and 1st-class buses go from the **OCC terminal** (☑962-626-28-81; Calle 17a Oriente, btwn Avs 3a & 5a Norte), 1km northeast of Parque Hidalgo. The main 2nd-class services are by **Rápidos del Sur** (RS; ☑962-626-11-61; Calle 9a Poniente 62).

Other buses from the OCC station go to Palenque, Puerto Escondido and Villahermosa. There are also daily buses from here to Guatemala City (five to six hours), with tickets sold at the main counter: The main operator is **Tica Bus** (☑962-625-24-35; www.ticabus.com; Terminal OCC, 17 Oriente esquina) which has a 7am departure (M$407).

Trans Galgos Inter (www.transgalgosintergt.com; Terminal OCC, 17 Oriente esquina) and Tica Bus run buses to San Salvador, El Salvador (from M$800, nine hours), via Escuintla in Guatemala. Tica Bus continues all the way to Panama City (from M$2670), with several long overnight stops en route.

For destinations in western Guatemala, including Quetzaltenango, it's best to get a bus from the border.

COLECTIVO

A large **colectivo terminal** (Calle 5a Poniente) houses most of the regional taxi and combi companies. **Autotransportes Paulino Navarro** (☑962-626-11-52; Calle 7a Poniente 5) runs rather ancient combis to Ciudad Hidalgo (M$15, 50 minutes) every 10 minutes from 4:30am to 10pm.

BUSES FROM TAPACHULA

DESTINATION	FARE (M$)	DURATION (HR)	FREQUENCY (DAILY)
Comitán via Motozintla	300	6-7	5 OCC
Escuintla	68-114	1½-2	6 OCC, very frequent RS
Mexico City	792-997	17-18	frequent OCC
Oaxaca	368	13	1 OCC
San Cristóbal de las Casas via Motozintla	234-386	7½-8	7 OCC
Tonalá	198-318	3-4	very frequent OCC & RS
Tuxtla Gutiérrez	209-504	4½-6	very frequent OCC & RS

🛈 Getting Around

CAR & MOTORCYCLE

Tapachula's two rental agencies carry both automatic and manual-transmission cars.

AVC Rente un Auto (📞 962-626-23-16; www.avcrenteunauto.com; Av Tapachula 2A) In-town pickup service available.

Europcar (📞 cell 962-1208010; www.europcar.com; Airport; ⏰ 9am-11:30pm) Best rates online.

TAXI

Taxis within the central area (including the OCC terminal) cost M$30.

Sociedades Transportes 149 (📞 962-625-12-87) has a booth in the airport arrivals hall, charging M$90 per person for a *colectivo* from the airport to the center; it's M$200 for a private taxi (up to three people) in either direction.

North of Tapachula

The hills north of Tapachula are home to numerous coffee *fincas* (ranches), many of them set up by German immigrants more than a century ago and today offering tours, restaurants and overnight accommodations.

🛏 Sleeping

⭐ Finca Argovia
RESORT $$$

(📞 962-621-12-23; www.argovia.com.mx; r M$2085-3000, bungalow M$3000; ⊛🅿️📶⊠) This gorgeous boutique hotel on a working coffee farm high in the cool, misty hills north of Tapachula offers luxurious wood-panelled rooms from which you can wile away hours swinging in the hammocks on the terraces, counting orchids in the gardens, going on informative coffee farm tours and relaxing in the spa. Delicious meals are served.

Finca Hamburgo
BUNGALOW $$$

(📞 962-626-75-78; www.fincahamburgo.com; Carr a Nueva Alemania Km 54; d/ste from M$1780/2780; 🅿️⊛📶⊠) Founded by German settlers in 1888, this historic coffee farm, perched atop a hill, offers breathless views over lush, rugged countryside (best enjoyed, cup of coffee in hand, from an easy chair on your room terrace), bush-chic wooden cabins that are comfortable without being over the top, spa services, a gourmet restaurant and tours of the property and surrounds.

The road here can be very rough. Be prepared for car and body to receive a pot-hole induced battering!

Izapa

The small and peaceful pre-Hispanic **ruins** (⏰ 9am-5pm) **FREE** at Izapa contain three groups of ruins. The northern group (Grupo F) is on the left side of the road if you're arriving from Tapachula – watch for the low pyramid mounds; you'll also see a ball court and several carved stelae and altars. Grupo A has 10 very weathered stele-and-altar pairings around a field. Grupo B is a couple of grass-covered mounds and more stone sculptures, including three curious ball-on-pillar affairs.

Izapa flourished from approximately 200 BC to AD 200, and its carving style (mostly seen on tall slabs known as stelae, fronted by round altars) shows descendants of Olmec deities with their upper lips unnaturally lengthened. Some Maya monuments in Guatemala are similar, and Izapa is considered an important 'bridge' between the Olmecs and the Maya. Izapa had 91 known stele-and-altar pairings.

Group A and B are a little way from the northern group. To reach them go back 700m toward Tapachula and take a signposted road to the left. After 800m you'll reach a fork with signs to Izapa Grupo A and Izapa Grupo B, each about 250m further on and looked after by caretaker families that will request a small donation.

Izapa is around 11km east of Tapachula on the Talismán road. To get there from Tapachula, take a combi (M$16) from the *colectivo* terminal or any Talismán-bound bus.

Santo Domingo, Unión Juárez & Volcán Tacaná

 962

At 4100m, Volcán Tacaná's dormant cone towers over the countryside north of Tapachula. Even if you're not interested in climbing to its summit, two villages, Santo Domingo and Unión Juárez, on its gorgeously verdant lower slopes make an attractive day trip, their cooler climate offering welcome relief from the Tapachula steam bath. The scenic road up is winding but well paved.

◉ Sights

◉ Santo Domingo

Santo Domingo lies 34km northeast of Tapachula, amid coffee plantations. The village's gorgeous three-story wooden 1920s *casa grande* (big house) has been restored. It belonged to the German immigrants who formerly owned the coffee plantation here, but it's now the **Centro Ecoturístico Santo Domingo** (☑962-625-54-09; M$5; ⊙9am-8pm) and has a restaurant (mains M$60 to M$120), a small creaky-floored coffee museum (M$10) and a well-tended tropical garden and pool (M$10; free with a meal).

◉ Unión Juárez

About 9km beyond Santo Domingo, passing some gorgeous waterfalls tucked in around tight turns, Unión Juárez (population 2600, elevation 1300m) is the starting point for ascents of Tacaná and other, less demanding walks. Tapachula folk like to come up here on weekends and holidays to cool off and feast on *parrillada*, a cholesterol-challenging plate of grilled meat and a few vegetables.

🏃 Activities

Hiking

The best months to climb Tacaná are late November to March. There are two routes up the mountain from Unión Juárez. Neither requires any technical climbing, but you need to allow two or three days for ei-

ther, preferably plus time to acclimatize. Be prepared for extreme cold at the top. The less steep route is via Chiquihuites, 12km from Unión Juárez and reachable by vehicle. From there it's a three-hour walk to Papales, where you can sleep in huts for a small donation. The ascent from Papales to the summit takes about five hours. The other route is via Talquián (about two hours' walk from Unión Juárez) and Trigales (five hours from Talquián). It takes about six hours to climb from Trigales to the summit. The two routes meet a couple of hours below the summit, and on both you have access to camping areas.

Combis from Unión Juárez will carry you to the small town of Córdoba, about halfway to Talquián, also passing the turnoff for Chiquihuites (about 1½ hours' walk away). It's a good idea to get a guide for Tacaná in Unión Juárez or organize one to meet you. The Casa Morayma can find guides (about M$350 per day) with three days' notice.

🛏 Sleeping

Hotel Colonial Campestre HOTEL $
(☑962-647-20-15; Unión Juárez; r M$380-560; P 🗘) Rambling and Escher-esque, this hotel has spacious rooms with bathroom, TV and good views (especially from room 26). It also has a restaurant (mains M$70 to M$120, *parrillada* for two M$250). Look for the arch a couple of blocks below the plaza, and ask to see the tunnel and antique movie theater.

Casa Morayma HOTEL $$
(☑962-122-25-84; www.facebook.com/casamorayma; Unión Juárez; d M$600; ⊖🗘) Offering by far the best night's sleep in Unión Juárez, this small, arty hotel on the entrance road into town stands out for its terracotta red paintwork and vines creeping up the outside of the building. The botanical theme continues inside with a little water garden feature, bright flowery paintings and travel-inspired photo art. Staff can organise Tacaná treks (around M$350 per day).

❶ Getting There & Away

From Tapachula, first take a combi from the *colectivo* terminal to Cacahoatán (M$20, 30 minutes), 20km north. From where these terminate in Cacahoatán, other combis travel to Santo Domingo (M$18 to M$20, 30 minutes) and Unión Juárez (M$25, 45 minutes).

ℹ️ **CROSSING THE BORDER**

If you're not taking a direct bus to Guatemala from the OCC station, you can go the border for connections. It's 20km from Tapachula to the international border at Talismán, opposite El Carmen in Guatemala. The border crossing between Ciudad Hidalgo, 37km from Tapachula, opposite Ciudad Tecún Umán in Guatemala, is busier and has more onward connections. Both border points have money-changing facilities and are open 24 hours – though you should get through by early afternoon for greater security and to guarantee onward transportation. Watch out for money changers passing counterfeit bills at both crossings.

Combis for Talismán (M$18, 30 minutes) leave from the Tapachula *colectivo* terminal every 10 minutes from 5am to 9pm. The majority of bus services from El Carmen, which include around 20 a day to Guatemala City (seven hours), go via Ciudad Tecún Umán, and then head along the Pacific slope route. For Quetzaltenango, you can take one of these and change at Coatepeque or Retalhuleu, but it's easier to get a *colectivo* taxi to Malacatán, on a more direct road to Quetzaltenango via San Marcos, and then look for onward transportation from there.

From Tapachula combis head to Ciudad Hidalgo (M$29, 50 minutes) every 10 minutes from 4:30am to 10pm. Across the border in Ciudad Tecún Umán, frequent buses leave until about 6pm for Guatemala City (five hours) by the Pacific slope route, through Retalhuleu and Escuintla. Buses to Quetzaltenango (three hours) depart hourly from 5am to 6pm.

For Lake Atitlán or Chichicastenango, you need to get to Quetzaltenango first.

TABASCO

They say that the state of Tabasco has more water than land, and looking at all the lagoons, rivers and wetlands on the map you can certainly see why, especially during the rainy season. It's always hot and sweaty here, but marginally less so when you catch a breeze along the Gulf of Mexico or venture into the southern hills. Travelers to Villahermosa and coastal Tabasco should note the region is subject to seasonal floods, though few travelers linger in Tabasco longer than it takes to see the outstanding Olmec stone sculpture in Villahermosa's Parque-Museo La Venta. Located north of Chiapas and abutting the Gulf of Mexico, Tabasco is the site of extensive onshore and offshore oil exploitation by Mexico's state oil company (Pemex).

Villahermosa

📞 993 / POP 353,000

This sprawling, flat, hot and humid oil-rich city, with more than a quarter of Tabasco's population, was never the 'beautiful town' its name implies. What it lacks in the looks department, though, it makes up for with its buzzy atmosphere, welcoming inhabitants and the best range of hotels and restaurants in Tabasco. The city also makes a good base for day trips to some of the state's more alluring attractions.

👁 Sights

The central area of this expansive city is known as the Zona Luz, and extends north–south from Parque Juárez to the Plaza de Armas, and east–west from the Río Grijalva to roughly Calle 5 de Mayo. The main bus stations are between 750m and 1km north of the center.

★ **Parque-Museo La Venta**   PARK, MUSEUM
(http://iec.tabasco.gob.mx; Av Ruíz Cortines; M$50; ⊙8am-4pm; 🅿🚼) This fascinating outdoor park and museum was created in 1958, when petroleum exploration threatened the highly important ancient Olmec settlement of La Venta in western Tabasco. Archaeologists moved the site's most significant finds, including three colossal stone heads, to Villahermosa. There's also a zoo but the cages are shabby and depressing. Avoid the zoo when making your way to the sculpture trail.

Inside, you first come to the **zoo** devoted to animals from Tabasco and nearby regions: cats include jaguars, ocelots and jaguarundi, and there are white-tailed deer, spider monkeys, crocodiles, boa constrictors, peccaries and plenty of colorful birds, including scarlet macaws and keel-billed toucans. Most people prefer to rush through this part.

There's an informative display in English and Spanish on Olmec archaeology as you pass through the **sculpture trail**, the start of which is marked by a giant ceiba (the sacred tree of the Olmec and Maya). This 1km walk is lined with finds from La Venta. Among the most impressive, in the order you come to them, are **Stele 3**, which depicts a bearded man with a headdress; **Altar 5**, depicting a figure carrying a child; **Monument 77**, 'El Gobernante,' a very sour-looking seated ruler; the monkey-faced **Monument 56**; **Monument 1**, the colossal head of a helmet-wearing warrior; and **Stele 1**, showing a young goddess (a rare Olmec representation of anything female). Animals that pose no danger (such as coatis, squirrels and black agoutis) roam freely. From 8pm Tuesdays to Sundays there's a **sound and light show** (M$100).

Plan two to three hours for your visit, and take mosquito repellent (the park is set in humid tropical woodland). Parque-Museo La Venta lies 2km northwest of the Zona Luz, beside Avenida Ruíz Cortines, the main east–west highway crossing the city. It's M$30 via *colectivo*.

Museo Regional de Antropología MUSEUM
(http://iec.tabasco.gob.mx; Periférico Carlos Pellicer; M$20; ⊙9am-5pm Tue-Sun; P) Villahermosa's excellent regional anthropology museum (even the shiny modern building it's housed in is impressive) holds some stunning exhibits on Olmec, Maya, Nahua and Zoque cultures in Tabasco – including Tortuguero #6, the infamous tablet *solely* responsible for the dire 'end of world' predictions forecast for December 21, 2012, which just goes to show that you can't believe everything you read! It's in the CICOM complex, a 15-minute walk from Zona Luz and just south of the Paseo Tabasco bridge.

Museo de Historia Natural MUSEUM
(⊋933-314-21-75; Av Ruíz Cortines; M$24; ⊙8am-5pm Tue-Sun, last admission 4pm; P) Named after Tabasco's best-known naturalist, the small Museo de Historia Natural has good displays on dinosaurs, space, early humanity and Tabascan ecosystems and wildlife (all in Spanish).

🛏 Sleeping & Eating

As a major oil town, Villahermosa has scores of comfortable midrange and top-end chain hotels, most of which offer heavily discounted online and weekend rates. Inviting budget options are scarcer.

★Hotel Olmeca Plaza HOTEL $
(⊋993-358-01-02, 800-201-09-09; www.hotelolmecaplaza.com; Madero 418; d from M$500; P🅿❄@🛜❄) This good-value downtown hotel has a flash lobby, an open-air pool and a well-equipped gym. Rooms are basic, but comfortable, with ample desks and good, large bathrooms, and there's a quality on-site restaurant. The police have set up their headquarters within the hotel and you'll see heavily armed, masked police walking the corridors, which can be a bit off-putting!

Mision Express Villahermosa BUSINESS HOTEL $
(⊋993-314-46-45; www.hotelesmision.com.mx; Aldama 404; r M$330-480; ❄❄🛜) A fair option

OFF THE BEATEN TRACK

RESERVA DE LA BIOSFERA PANTANOS DE CENTLA

This 3030-sq-km **biosphere reserve** (M$31) protects a good part of the wetlands around the lower reaches of two of Mexico's biggest rivers, the Usumacinta and the Grijalva. These lakes, marshes, rivers, mangroves, savannas and forests are an irreplaceable sanctuary for countless creatures, including the West Indian manatee and Morelet's crocodile (both endangered), six kinds of tortoise, tapirs, ocelots, jaguars, howler monkeys, 60 fish species and 255 bird species.

The **Centro de Interpretación Uyotot-Ja** (⊋913-106-83-90; www.casadelagua.org.mx; Carretera Frontera-Jonuta Km 12.5; admission M$25, reserve fee M$31, boat ride M$1000; ⊙9am-5pm Tue-Sun) visitor center, or 'Casa de Agua,' is 13km along the Jonuta road from Frontera, beside the broad, winding Río Grijalva. A 20m-high observation tower overlooks the awesome confluence of the Grijalva, the Usumacinta and a third large river, the San Pedrito – a spot known as Tres Brazos (Three Arms). Boat trips are available into the mangroves, where you should see crocodiles, iguanas, birds and, with luck, howler monkeys. March to May is the best birding season.

From Villahermosa, ADO, CAT and Cardesa buses service Frontera (near the site of conquistador Hernán Cortés' 1519 first battle against native Mexicans), from where *colectivos* run the 15-minute trip to the reserve.

AIRPORT BUS TO PALENQUE

The Villahermosa airport has a handy counter for ADO (www.ado.com.mx), with almost hourly minibuses departing daily to Palenque (M$330, 2¼ hours) between 7:20am and 9:20pm. Check the website for schedules to/from 'Aeropuerto Villahermosa.'

---

located close to a number of decent, cheap taco stands. The rooms have bright Mexican art on the walls and bold red bed sashes, but they do suffer a bit from street noise, so pack some earplugs.

★ One Villahermosa Centro
BUSINESS HOTEL $$

(☑ 993-131-71-00; www.onehotels.com; Carranza 101; r incl breakfast from M$851; ✳️ 🛜) A large, business-style hotel, this one wins points for attentive staff and a super-central location. Rooms are what you'd expect for the price – big and comfortable but lacking much sense of place. Even so, if it's a good night's kip you want then you won't find a better option in the city center.

★ La Cevichería Tabasco
SEAFOOD $$

(☑ 993-345-00-35; www.facebook.com/lacevicheriatabascov; Francisco José Hernández Mandujano 114; mains M$120-200; ⊙ 11am-6pm Tue-Fri, 10am-6pm Sat & Sun; ✳️) A stellar seafood place just over the river from the city center. With bright murals inside and out and a friendly neighbourhood vibe, this busy, and slightly chaotic, place serves seafood dishes that are so arty you might prefer to just gaze in wonder at your meal rather than eat it. The tacos stuffed with marlin are espically impressive.

★ Rock & Roll Cocktelería
SEAFOOD $$

(☑ 993-334-21-90; Reforma 307; mains M$160-220; ⊙ 7am-11pm Mon & Thu, 10am-10pm Tue & Wed, 11am-9pm Sun & Fri, 10am-8pm Sat) A maelstrom of heat, swirling fans and blaring TVs. Everyone's here for the large and delicious seafood cocktails (though it also has good ceviche and seafood stew) and cheap beer. It's on a pedestrian street across from the Miraflores Hotel, and has 60 years under its belt. A Villahermosa institution if ever there were one.

La Dantesca
ITALIAN $$

(☑ 993-351-51-62; www.facebook.com/LaDantesca; Hidalgo 406, near Parque Los Pajaritos; mains M$100-150, pizzas M$180; ⊙ 1-10pm; ✳️) Locals flock to this lively trattoria for its fantastic brick-oven pizzas, house-made pastas and scrumptious desserts. Most folks come for the pizza, but the ravioli *verde* with *requesón* and *jamaica* (a ricotta-like cheese and hibiscus flowers) is superb. Give the chef the slightest hint of encouragement and he'll start spinning pizza bases around like he's mixing a cocktail.

Mar & Co
SEAFOOD $$

(☑ 993-315-05-05; http://marcompany.com.mx; Paseo Tabasco 1011; mains M$90-160; ⊙ 1-10pm Mon-Wed, 1-11:45pm Thu-Sat, noon-7pm Sun) A little out of the center, but worth the trek for its outstandingly good seafood. Culinary highlights are the octopus with garlic and the delicious shellfish. Most locals will insist it's the best seafood joint in town. The building itself, old shipping containers piled like lego atop each other, is as memorable as the food.

☆ Entertainment

La Bohemia de Manrique
LIVE MUSIC

(www.facebook.com/bohemiamanrique; Independencia 317; ⊙ 9pm-3am Thu-Sat) This cocktail bar is the place to come to catch great live music at the weekends. A lot of the performers play a distinctly Caribbean genre of music known as Trova.

ℹ️ Information

Most banks have ATMs and exchange dollars or euros.

HSBC (cnr Juárez & Lerdo de Tejada; ⊙ 9am-5pm Mon-Fri) Branch on a pedestrianized street.

Oficina de Convenciones y Visitantes de Tabasco (OCV; ☑ 993-316-35-54; www.visitetabasco.com; Paseo Tabasco 1504; ⊙ 9am-3pm Mon-Fri) Statewide information.

Tourism Information Kiosk (Mina 297, ADO bus terminal; ⊙ 9am-6pm Mon-Sat) At the ADO bus terminal; has maps and can book hotels.

ℹ️ Getting There & Away

AIR

Villahermosa's **Aeropuerto Rovirosa** (☑ 993-356-01-57; www.asur.com.mx; Carretera Villahermosa-Macuspana Km 13) is 13km east of the center, off Hwy 186. Aeroméxico is the major airline; there are daily nonstop flights to/from Villahermosa.

Aeroméxico (www.aeromexico.com) Flys daily to Mexico City; lots of international connections via Mexico City.

Interjet (www.interjet.com.mx) To Mexico City.

MAYAir (www.mayair.com.mx) To Cancún, Cozumel, Mérida and Veracruz.

BUSES FROM VILLAHERMOSA

DESTINATION	FARE (M$)	DURATION (HR)	FREQUENCY (DAILY)
Campeche	524-658	5½-7	frequent ADO
Cancún	624-1086	12½-14½	20 ADO
Comalcalco	90	2	very frequent Cardesa, 2 ADO
Mérida	698-855	8-9½	28 ADO
Mexico City (TAPO)	1022-1186	12-13	frequent ADO
Oaxaca	814	13	3 ADO
Palenque	140-190	2-2½	22 ADO, very frequent Cardesa
San Cristóbal de las Casas	466	6-6½	5 ADO
Tenosique	194-252	3-3½	11 ADO, very frequent CAT
Tuxtla Gutiérrez	384-572	4-5	16 ADO
Veracruz	610-696	6-8½	frequent ADO

TAR (www.tarmexico.com) To Mérida and Oaxaca.

United (www.united.com) To Houston.

VivaAerobus (www.vivaaerobus.com) To Cancún, Mexico City, Monterrey and Guadalajara.

Volaris (www.volaris.com) To Mexico City.

BUS & COLECTIVO

Deluxe and 1st-class buses depart from the **ADO bus station** (☎ 993-312-84-22; Mina 297), which has wi-fi and 24-hour left luggage and is located 750m north of the Zona Luz.

Transportation to most destinations within Tabasco leaves from other terminals within walking distance north of ADO, including the 2nd-class **Cardesa bus station** (cnr Hermanos Bastar Zozaya & Castillo) and the main 2nd-class bus station, the **Central de Autobuses de Tabasco** (CAT; ☎ 993-312-29-77; cnr Av Ruíz Cortines & Castillo) on the north side of Avenida Ruíz Cortines (use the pedestrian overpass).

ⓘ Getting Around

Comfortable ADO minibuses ferry passengers between the airport and the ADO bus terminal (M$225); they run hourly between 6am and 9pm. Taxis to the center cost around M$280. Alternatively, walk 500m past the airport parking lot for a *colectivo* (M$25) from the Dos Montes taxi stand. These terminate in the market on Carranza, about 1km north of the Zona Luz.

A system of *colectivo* taxis (M$25) provides the backbone of the center's public transit. Flag one down to ask if it's going your way, or join a queue at a stand outside a large store or transportation terminal, where proficient handlers ask for your destination and quickly assign you a shared taxi. There's no fee for the match-up, and no haggling necessary. Private taxis charge around M$50 within the center.

Comalcalco

☎ 933 / POP 40,000

The small town of Comalcalco, around 55km northwest of Villahermosa, is a scrappy, lowrise place of little visual appeal. However, just on the outskirts of town, is an enjoyably under-visited Maya site that is one of the big attractions of Tabasco. The town is also known for its cacao production and small chocolate factories, some of which are open to the public. Ancient monuments and divine chocolate, what better reason to make the easy day trip from Villahermosa does a person need?

⊙ Sights

Small though Comalcalco might be, there are easily enough attractions in and around the town to make for an enjoyable day trip from Villahermosa (a little over an hour away).

★ **Comalcalco** ARCHAEOLOGICAL SITE
(☎ 933-337-02-74; M$55; ⊙ 8am-4pm) Surrounded by jungle trees and little visited by tourists, the small but impressive Maya ruins of ancient Comalcalco are the most westerly known Maya ruins. Architecturally they're unique due to many of the buildings being constructed of bricks and/or mortar made from oyster shells. Comalcalco was at its peak between AD 600 and 1000, when it was ruled by the Chontals. It remained an important center of commerce for several more centuries, trading in a cornucopia of pre-Hispanic luxury goods.

At the entrance to the complex is a small **museum** with a fine array of sculptures and

DON'T MISS

MALPASITO RUINS

The Maya ceremonial site of **Malpasito** (M$40; ⊘7am-5pm) is 600m (signposted) uphill from the village of the same name. Apart from the beautiful setting, what's remarkable about this little-visited site, dating from AD 700 to 900, are its petroglyphs. More than 100 petroglyphs showing birds, deer, monkeys, people, and temples with stairways are scattered around the Malpasito area, of which about 10 are at the archaeological site. Interpretive signs are in Spanish and English.

engravings of human heads, deities, glyphs and animals, such as crocodiles and pelicans.

Beyond the museum the first building you encounter is the great brick tiered pyramid, **Templo 1**. At its base are the remains of large stucco sculptures, including the feet of a giant winged toad. Further temples line **Plaza Norte**, in front of Templo I. In the far (southeast) corner of the site rises the **Gran Acrópolis**, which has views from its summit over a canopy of palms to the Gulf of Mexico. The Acrópolis is fronted by **Templo V**, a burial pyramid that was once decorated on all sides with stucco sculptures of people, reptiles, birds and aquatic life. At Templo V's western foot is **Templo IX**, which has a tomb lined by nine stucco sculptures showing a Comalcalco lord with his priests and courtiers. Above Templo V is the crumbling profile of **El Palacio**, with its parallel 80m-long, corbel-arched galleries, probably once Comalcalco's royal residence. Information is in both Spanish and English. The site is a few minutes' walk northeast of the town center.

Hacienda La Luz   PLANTATION
(☑933-337-11-22; www.haciendalaluz.mx; Blvd Rovirosa 232; 1hr tour per person from M$100; ⊘tours 9am, 11am, 1pm & 3pm Tue-Sun) Hacienda La Luz, one of several local plantations making chocolate from home-grown cacao, offers informative guided tours (a basic tour is one hour, but longer and more detailed tours are available) round the beautiful house, gardens and cacao plantation. You

will be shown the traditional methods of turning cacao beans into chocolate, and, yep, the bit you were waiting for, the tour concludes with a chocolate drink. For a tour in English it's wise to reserve in advance.

The hacienda is just 300m from Comalcalco's central Parque Juárez: walk 250m west along Calle Bosada to its end at Blvd Rovirosa, turn right and you'll see the hacienda's white gateposts across the road.

✖ Eating

There are a number of taco stands and other cheap eats in and around the Parque Benito Juarez Garcia (a little to the west of the main road through town). There is also one exceptional place close to the archaeological site.

★Cocina Chontal   MEXICAN $
(☑933-158-56-96; www.facebook.com/nelly.cordova morillo.5; Ejido Buenavista; mains M$80-130; ⊘noon-5pm Wed-Sun) Run by the larger than life, traditionally dressed Nelly Córdova, this delightful open-air restaurant specalizes in rekindling half-forgotten traditional Tabasco dishes, including some from the Maya period. Think thick chocolate *moles,* turkey stew and bananas stuffed with beans and pork. Everything is cooked on open wood fires and served in clay bowls.

❶ Getting There & Away

There are frequent buses (M$90, two hours) to and from Villahermosa. They leave from the main road through town.

Oaxaca

Why Go?

The state of Oaxaca (wah-*hah*-kah) has a special magic felt by Mexicans and foreigners alike. A bastion of indigenous culture, it's home to the country's most vibrant crafts and art scene, some outstandingly colorful and extroverted festivities, a uniquely savory cuisine and diverse natural riches. At the center of the state in every way stands beautiful, colonial Oaxaca city, an elegant and fascinating cultural hub. Nearby, the forested Sierra Norte is home to successful community-tourism ventures enabling visitors to hike, bike and ride horses amid delicious green mountainscapes. To the south, across rugged, remote ranges, is Oaxaca's fabulous tropical coast, with its wide sandy beaches, pumping Pacific surf, seas full of dolphins and turtles, and a string of beach towns and villages that will placate even the most anxious of travelers: surfer-heaven Puerto Escondido; planned but relaxed Bahías de Huatulco; and the mellow delights of Mazunte, Zipolite and San Agustinillo.

Best Places to Eat

➡ Casa Oaxaca (p439)

➡ Almoraduz (p466)

➡ La Providencia (p473)

➡ Boulenc Pan Artesano (p437)

➡ Restaurante Los Danzantes (p439)

Best Places to Stay

➡ Heven (p473)

➡ Villas Carrizalillo (p465)

➡ La Betulia (p435)

➡ Quinta Real Oaxaca (p436)

➡ Hotel Casa de Dan (p462)

When to Go
Oaxaca City

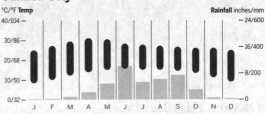

Jan–Mar Driest months: a lively winter-escapee scene; best hiking conditions in the Sierra Norte.

Jul & Aug Guelaguetza festival in Oaxaca city; summer-vacation fun time on the coast.

Late Oct & Nov Día de Muertos in Oaxaca city; Fiestas de Noviembre in Puerto Escondido.

Oaxaca Highlights

1 **Oaxaca city** (p424)
Indulging in the culture, cuisine, color, crafts – and mezcal – of this festive, colonial city.

2 **Zipolite** (p471) Chilling out at this travelers' beach hangout,

one of several laid-back villages along the coast.

3 **Puerto Escondido** (p458) Riding the surf on the gorgeous beaches of this low-key town.

4 **Pueblos Mancomunados** (p455) Hiking through otherworldly cloud forests between mountain villages.

5 **Monte Albán** (p445) Enjoying the majestic setting

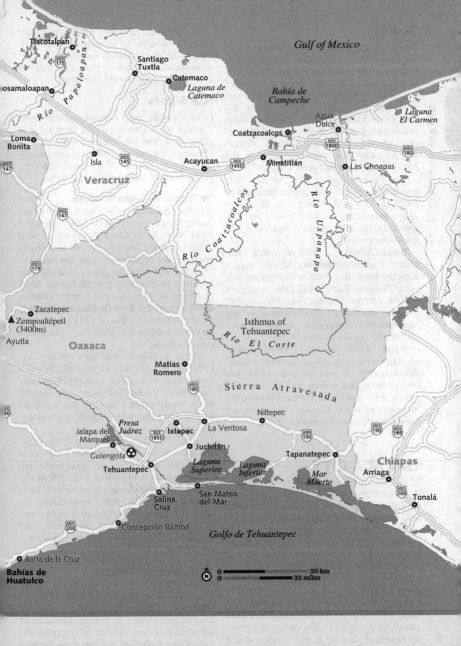

and mysterious architecture of this vista-rich archaeological site.

6 Valles Centrales (p445) Getting a feel for indigenous village life at the markets,

fiestas and artisans' workshops of this culturally laden region.

7 Chacahua (p468) Riding across bird-filled lagoons to a stunning beach at this tranquil village.

8 Playa Escobilla (p465) Seeing thousands of turtles struggling ashore to nest.

9 Bahías de Huatulco (p480) Enjoying beach life with creature comforts.

History

Pre-Hispanic cultures in Oaxaca's Valles Centrales (Central Valleys) reached heights rivaling those of central Mexico. The hilltop city of Monte Albán became the center of the Zapotec culture, which conquered much of Oaxaca and peaked between AD 350 and 700. From about 1200 the Zapotecs came under the growing dominance of Mixtecs from Oaxaca's northwest uplands. Mixtecs and Zapotecs alike were conquered by the Aztecs in the 15th and early 16th centuries.

The Spanish had to send at least four expeditions before they felt safe enough to found the city of Oaxaca in 1529. The indigenous population declined quickly and disastrously; though rebellions continued into the 20th century.

Benito Juárez, the great reforming president of mid-19th-century Mexico, was a Zapotec from the Oaxaca mountains. Another Oaxacan, Porfirio Díaz, rose to control Mexico with an iron fist from 1877 to 1910, bringing the country into the industrial age but fostering corruption, repression and, eventually, the Revolution in 1910.

Today, while tourism thrives in and around Oaxaca city and on the coast, underdevelopment still prevails in the backcountry. There is still a wide gulf between the state's rich, largely mestizo (people of mixed ancestry) elite and its poor, disempowered, heavily indigenous majority.

OAXACA CITY

📞 951 / POP 260,000 / ELEV 1550M

A cultural colossus fit to rival anywhere in Latin America for history, gastronomy and colorful manifestations of indigenous culture, Oaxaca is a complex but intensely attractive city whose majestic churches and refined plazas have deservedly earned it a Unesco World Heritage badge. Lovers of culture come here to indulge in the Mexico of Zapotec and colonial legend. Flowing through handsome yet tranquil streets, life pulsates with an unadulterated regional flavor. See it in the color palate of historic boutique hotels, a meet-the-producer artisan store or an intentionally grungy *mezcalería* (plying locally manufactured alcoholic beverages). But what makes Oaxaca especially interesting are its undercurrents. While largely safe and attractive by Mexican standards, snippets of political protest in recent years have lent the city a grittier edge. It bubbles up in satirical street art, bohemian bars and been-around-forever street markets. Trust us: there's far more to this city than just pretty churches.

👁 Sights

Oaxaca's sights start with its historic whole – listed as a Unesco World Heritage site since 1987. The city center overflows with churches, art galleries, museums and handsome green spaces. If it's your first trip, you're best off targeting the highlights.

★ Templo de Santo Domingo   CHURCH

(cnr Alcalá & Gurrión; ⊙ 7am-1pm & 4-8pm except during Mass) Gorgeous Santo Domingo is the most splendid of Oaxaca's churches, with a finely carved baroque facade and nearly every square centimeter inside decorated in 3D relief with intricate gilt designs swirling around a profusion of painted figures. Most elaborate of all is the 18th-century **Capilla de la Virgen del Rosario (Rosary Chapel)** on the south side. The whole church takes on a magically warm glow during candlelit evening Mass.

Santo Domingo was built mainly between 1570 and 1608 as part of the city's Dominican monastery, with the finest artisans from Puebla and elsewhere helping in its construction. Like other big buildings in this earthquake-prone region, it has immensely thick stone walls.

Santo Domingo de Guzmán (1172–1221), the Spanish monk who founded the Dominican order, appears as the right-hand one of the two figures holding a church in the center of the facade, and his elaborate family tree adorns the ceiling immediately inside. The Dominicans observed strict vows of poverty, chastity and obedience, and in Mexico they protected the indigenous people from other colonists' excesses.

★ Museo de las Culturas de Oaxaca   MUSEUM

(📞 951-516-29-91; Alcalá; adult/child under 13yr M$70/free; ⊙ 10am-6:15pm Tue-Sun) Got two hours? You'll need it for the Museum of Oaxacan Cultures, housed in the beautiful monastery buildings adjoining the Templo de Santo Domingo. This is one of Mexico's best regional museums. The rich displays take you right through the history and cultures of Oaxaca state up to the present day, emphasizing the continuity between pre-Hispanic and contemporary cultures in areas such as crafts, medicine and food.

A gorgeous stone cloister serves as antechamber to the museum proper. The greatest treasure is the **Mixtec hoard** from Tomb 7 at Monte Albán, in Room III (the first on the right upstairs). This dates from the 14th century, when Mixtecs reused an old Zapotec tomb at Monte Albán to bury one of their kings and his sacrificed servants, along with a stash of beautifully worked silver, turquoise, coral, jade, amber, pearls, finely carved bone, crystal goblets, a skull covered in turquoise, and a lot of gold. The treasure was discovered in 1932 by Alfonso Caso.

Halls I to IV are devoted to the pre-Hispanic period, halls V to VIII to the colonial period, halls IX to XIII to Oaxaca in the independence era and after, and the final room (XIV) to Santo Domingo Monastery itself. At the end of the long corridor past hall IX, glass doors give a view into the beautifully ornate choir of the Templo de Santo Domingo.

Surprisingly, the museum's explanatory material is in Spanish only. Also, there is a good book-and-souvenir shop.

Jardín Etnobotánico
GARDENS

(Ethnobotanical Garden; ☑951-516-79-15; cnr Constitución & Reforma; 2hr tours in English or French M$100, 1hr tours in Spanish M$50; ⊘ English tours 11am Tue, Thu & Sat, Spanish tours 10am, noon & 5pm Mon-Sat, French tours 5pm Tue) In former monastic grounds behind the Templo de Santo Domingo, this garden features plants from around Oaxaca state, including a staggering variety of cacti. Though it has been growing only since the 1990s, it's already a fascinating demonstration of Oaxaca's biodiversity. Visits are by guided tour only; be there five minutes before they start.

Zócalo
PLAZA

Traffic-free, shaded by tall trees and surrounded by elegant *portales* (arcades), the Zócalo is the perfect place to start soaking up the Oaxaca atmosphere. It bustles with life by day and night, as marimba ensembles, brass bands and roving buskers float their melodies among the crowds, hawkers try to offload pretty carpets and hideous balloons, and lovers parade in slow rounds under the trees, while anyone and everyone sits, drinks and watches from the sidewalk cafes.

Catedral
CATHEDRAL

(Av de la Independencia 700; ⊘8am-8pm) Oaxaca's cantera stone cathedral is suitably massive and old, but in a city as culturally rich as Oaxaca, it is arguably only the third most impressive church behind the Soledad (p428) and the Templo de Santo Domingo. Construction began in 1553 and finished (after several earthquakes) in the 18th century. It enjoys a grand placement just north of the Zócalo with its main facade, featuring typical if not lavish baroque carving, facing the Alameda.

Palacio de Gobierno
NOTABLE BUILDING

(Plaza de la Constitución) A 19th-century wonder of marble and murals, the State Government Palace occupies the Zócalo's southern flank. The large, very detailed stairway mural (1980), by Arturo García Bustos, depicts famous Oaxacans and Oaxacan history, including Benito Juárez, his wife Margarita Maza, José María Morelos, Porfirio Díaz, Vicente Guerrero (being shot at Cuilapan) and the 17th-century nun and love poet Juana Inés de la Cruz.

The building also houses the interactive **Museo del Palacio** (M$25, Sun free; ⊘9:30am-5pm Mon, to 6pm Tue-Sat, to 4pm Sun; ♿). Its main displays, with a primarily educational purpose and in Spanish only, range over evolution, the pre-Hispanic ball game, biodiversity and more, with a Oaxacan handle on universal themes. Also here is what is very probably the world's largest tortilla – a 300kg *tlayuda,* decorated with the history of Mexico by Enrique Ramos.

Andador Turístico
STREET

Historic, romantic, dignified and safe, the wonderful Calle Alcalá (traffic-free since the 1980s) is what Oaxaca is all about. It runs north from the Cathedral to the Templo de Santo Domingo and is lined by typical colonial-era stone buildings that are now home to artisan shops, galleries, museums, cafes and bars. Always good for a stroll, it's particularly atmospheric at night.

Museo Rufino Tamayo
MUSEUM

(☑951-516-47-50; Morelos 503; M$90; ⊘10am-2pm & 4-7pm Mon & Wed-Sat, 10am-3pm Sun) A top-class museum, even by Oaxaca's high standards, showing off a wondrous collection of pre-Hispanic art donated by the city's most famous artist, Rufino Tamayo (1899–1991). It traces artistic developments in preconquest times and includes some truly beautiful pieces laid out in color-coded back-lit cases in

Oaxaca City

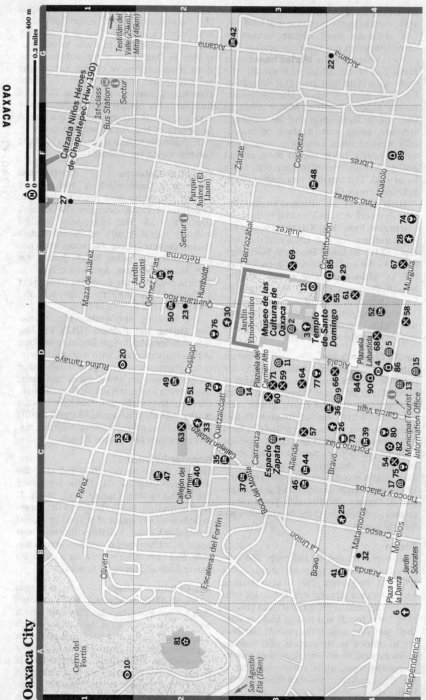

OAXACA

Santa María Atzompa (6km);
Atzompa Ruins (8km)

Huatulco 2000
Expressos Colombo Huatulco

Central de Abastos (200m);
2nd-class (500m)

Transportadora Exelencias

Transportes Villa del Pacífico

Autobuses Turísticos (to Monte Albán)

Monte Albán (6km)

Autobuses Halcón

Express Service

Zaachila Yoo

Líneas Unidas

La Cocina Oaxaqueña (450m)

(6km); Ocotlán (31km), Xochitl

Santos Degollado

González Ortega

Hidalgo

Doblado

Xicoténcatl

Ocampo

Guerrero

Colón

Rayón

Arteaga

La Noria

La Carbonera

Atlántida

Armenta y López

Bustamante

Cabrera

Zaragoza

Arista

Mina

Díaz Ordaz

Aldama

JP García

Las Casas

Trujano

Miery Terán

Hidalgo

JP García

20 de Noviembre

Flores Magón

Portal de Flores

Alameda de León

Portal Benito Juárez

Valdivieso

5 de Mayo

Reforma

Independencia

Morelos

Libres

Murguía

Galeana

Periférico

Prolongación Victoria

Victoria

Sectur
Municipal Tourist Information Kiosk

Sectur

Santos Degollado

56
38
7
45
87
83
18
72
65
16
70
24
88
62
78
19
21
34
31

Oaxaca City

a series of uncluttered rooms set around a lovely 17th-century patio.

The figurines (some as old as 1250 BC) are from sites all around Mexico and are displayed as art rather than archaeology.

★ Espacio Zapata
GALLERY

(Porfirio Díaz 509; ⊙10am-6pm) FREE In a city of provocative graphic art, this workshop and gallery is a key agitator. Founded by the art collective Asaro (Asamblea de Artistas Revolucionarios de Oaxaca) in 2006, and never satisfied to put down its paintbrush for long, it broadcasts an ever-changing menu of events, discussions, workshops and expos. Even the mural on the facade is regularly repainted.

Stick your head in for a browse, a chat, a snack (there's a courtyard cafe) or a 'Ciudad Revolucionario de México' T-shirt.

Basilica de Nuestra Señora de la Soledad
BASILICA

(Independencia 107; admission by donation; ⊙museum 9am-2pm & 3-7pm Tue-Sun) Oaxaca doesn't lack distinguished churches, but many locals rate the Soledad as their favorite. The original baroque facade dates from 1690; while the florid and gold-tinged interior, which emits an extra sparkle above the altar, is a product of the late 19th century. Among some of the finer touches are the eight sculpted angels each holding up a chandelier. Don't miss the small **museum** around the back crowded with stained glass, saintly paintings and depictions of the Virgin of Solitude.

Museo de Arte Contemporáneo de Oaxaca
MUSEUM

(MACO; ☑951-514-10-55; www.museomaco.org; Alcalá 202; M$20, Sun free; ⊙10:30am-8pm Wed-Mon) Excellent contemporary art in a beautifully revamped colonial house.

Museo Casa de Juárez
MUSEUM

(☑951-516-18-60; www.museocasajuarez.blogspot.com.es; García Vigil 609; M$50; ⊙10am-7pm Tue-Sun) The simple house of bookbinder Antonio Salanueva, who supported the great 19th-century Mexican leader Benito Juárez during his youth, is now an interesting little museum. The binding workshop is preserved, along with Benito memorabilia and period artifacts.

Museo Textil de Oaxaca　　　MUSEUM
(☎951-501-11-04; www.museotextildeoaxaca.org.
mx; Hildago 917; ☉10am-8pm Mon-Sat, to 6pm
Sun) FREE This textile museum promotes
Oaxaca's traditional textile crafts through
exhibitions, workshops, films, presentations
and a library. Themed selections from its
stock of around 5000 Oaxacan and international textile pieces, many of them a century
or more old, are always on view. There's a
top-quality crafts shop here too.

One-hour guided visits (M$10) are given
at 5pm on Wednesday, in English and/or
Spanish, if five or more people turn up.

Xochimilco Aqueduct　　　LANDMARK
Wander northwest of the historical core
and you'll ultimately encounter this arched
aqueduct rendered in typical green cantera
stone that runs the length of Calle Rufino
Tamayo. Built between 1727 and 1751, it was
designed to bring fresh drinking water from
the hillsides of Cerro de San Felipe into the
city center. It served its purpose until 1940,
where it was replaced by a more modern if
less architecturally elegant system.

Cerro del Fortín　　　HILL
Oaxaca's sentinel hill with stairs, statues, a
park and – of course – views makes a robust
early morning run, stride or walk. It starts
on Calle Crespo at the bottom of the **Escaleras del Fortín**, a wide stairway busy every
morning with exercising locals. Duck under
the muraled underpass at the top and you'll
be at the foot of the Auditorio Guelaguetza
(p432); beside which stands a noble **statue
of Benito Juárez** admiring a fine view of
the city that helped shape him.

Further up, a dirt road through trees
leads to a planetarium, a space observatory
and, beyond that, TV masts and a Christian
cross. The upper reaches of the hill are best
avoided at dusk and after dark.

🏃 **Activities**

★ **Mundo Ceiba**　　　CYCLING
(☎951-192-04-19; Berriozábal 109; ☉8am-11pm)
Oaxaca's bike hub inhabits a large garage
with an on-site cafe and is instrumental
in organizing the Paseos Nocturnos en
Bicicleta (p442), a free communal bike
ride that heads out four evenings a week

LOCAL KNOWLEDGE

CONTEMPORARY ART IN OAXACA

Of Mexico's major art hubs, Mexico City may have the most and the fanciest galleries, and Monterrey the most impressive presentations – but only in Oaxaca will you find such a dense concentration of talent, innovation and galleries within a small, accessible area.

A delight in color and light, a dreamlike feeling and references to indigenous mythology have long been trademarks of Oaxacan art. Two artists laid the basis for today's flourishing scene: the great muralist Rufino Tamayo (1899–1991) and European-influenced Francisco Gutiérrez (1906–45). The next generation was led by three artists. The colorful art of Rodolfo Morales (1925–2001) from Ocotlán, with its childlike angel figures, has deep roots in local myths. Rodolfo Nieto (1936–85) populated his work with vivid fantasy animals and dream figures. Francisco Toledo (b 1940), from Juchitán, works in many media, often focusing on grotesque beasts. He's still an active figure in Oaxacan cultural life.

Workshops for young artists organized by Tamayo in the 1970s encouraged talents such as Abelardo López, Ariel Mendoza and Alejandro Santiago. Their work is highly varied, but indigenous roots and a dreamlike quality run through a lot of it. More or less contemporary is Sergio Hernández, whose limitless imagination melds the figurative with the abstract and fantastic. Artists who appeared around the turn of the 21st century, such as Demián Flores, Soid Pastrana and Guillermo Olguín, tend to reject representation and 'folklorism' in favor of postmodernism, video and symbol-loaded graphic compositions designed to make us ponder.

Top Museums & Galleries

Museo de Arte Contemporáneo de Oaxaca (p428) Changing exhibits of first-rate contemporary Mexican and international art.

Museo de los Pintores Oaxaqueños (MUPO, Museum of Oaxacan Painters; ☑951-516-56-45; www.museodelospintores.blogspot.co.uk; Independencia 607; M$20, Sun free; ☺10am-6pm Tue-Sun) Exhibitions by artists from Oaxaca and elsewhere – often provocative contemporary work.

Arte de Oaxaca (☑951-514-09-10; www.artedeoaxaca.com; Murguía 105; ☺11am-3pm & 5-8pm Mon-Fri, 11am-6pm Sat) FREE A commercial gallery presenting a wide range of quality art, it includes a room devoted to Rodolfo Morales' work.

Centro Fotográfico Álvarez Bravo (☑951-516-98-00; www.cfmab.org; Bravo 116; ☺9:30am-8pm Wed-Mon) FREE With a taste for provocative social commentary, this photo gallery displays weird and wonderful work by international photographers.

Galería Quetzalli (☑951-514-26-06; Constitución 104; ☺10am-2pm & 5-8pm Mon-Sat) FREE A leading commercial gallery, handling big names such as Francisco Toledo and Guillermo Olguín. It has a second exhibition space, **Bodega Quetzalli** (Murguía 400; ☺hours variable), a few blocks away.

Instituto de Artes Gráficas de Oaxaca (IAGO, Oaxaca Graphic Arts Institute; ☑951-516-69-80; www.institutodeartesgraficasdeoaxaca.blogspot.com; Alcalá 507; ☺9:30am-8pm, library closed Sun) FREE Offers changing exhibitions of graphic art plus a superb arts library open to all.

La Mano Mágica (☑951-516-42-75; Alcalá 203; ☺10:30am-3pm & 4-8pm Mon-Sat) You'll find art by leading figures such as Tamayo, Morales and Hernández, plus a small but fine selection of handicrafts, at this commercial gallery founded by the master weaver Arnulfo Mendoza (1954–2014) from Teotitlán del Valle.

Espacio Zapata (p428) A bona fide art collective peddling revolutionary art, often with a political bent.

into the cobbled streets of the city center. Rental bikes for this or any other necessity go for M$70 for eight hours. Fun tandems cost M$120.

★**Tierraventura** OUTDOORS
(☑951-501-21-96; www.tierraventura.com; Porfirio Díaz 719; day trips per person M$950-1700, longer trips per day M$1500-1600; ☺10am-2pm & 4-6pm Mon-Fri) ✐ Tierraventura, set up

by a Swiss-German couple in 1999, is the antidote to the rest of the tour guide pack, offering trips to places few others think to tread. Local guides accompany travelers wherever possible.

Expediciones Sierra Norte OUTDOORS
(☑951-514-82-71; www.sierranorte.org.mx; Bravo 210A; ⊗9am-7:30pm Mon-Fri, to 2pm Sat)  Some of Oaxaca's most exhilarating outdoor experiences are to be had among the mountain villages of the Pueblos Mancomunados, where this community-run outfit maintains a network of good trails, comfortable *cabañas* (cabins), guide services, and horse and bike hire. This city office has copious information (including a useful guide map; M$50) and some English-speaking staff, and can make reservations for all services.

Horseback Mexico HORSEBACK RIDING
(☑cell 951-1997026; www.horsebackmexico.com; Murguía 403; ⊗11am-6pm Sun-Fri) This experienced, enthusiastic Canadian–American-run outfit offers equestrian adventures for all levels from beginners up. Two-hour rides on Arabian and Mexican Criollo horses in the countryside around their ranch at Rojas de Cuauhtémoc, 15km east of the city, cost US$70 per person including round-trip transportation from Oaxaca.

🍴 Courses

Language Courses
Oaxaca has numerous good, professional language schools, all offering small-group instruction at varied levels and most emphasizing spoken language. At most schools you can start any Monday (at some you can start any day). Most also offer individual tuition if wanted, plus volunteer opportunities and optional activities like dance or cooking classes, trips and *intercambios* (meetings with locals for conversation). If you're looking for some social life with other students, the bigger schools are best. Enrolment/registration fees, textbooks and materials are extra costs at some schools.

Schools can arrange accommodations with families or in hotels, apartments or their own student houses. Homestays with a private room typically cost around US$20/25/29 a day with one/two/three meals.

★Ollin Tlahtoalli LANGUAGE
(☑951-514-55-62; www.ollinoaxaca.org.mx; Ocampo 710; 15/20hr per week US$150/186)  Not just a mere language school, Ollin can teach you far more than how to conjugate Spanish verbs. It also offers courses on the Mexican revolution, Latin American economics, Mexican literature and up-to-the-minute street art. Email or call in to discuss your individual needs. They're extremely friendly and flexible.

Spanish Immersion School LANGUAGE
(☑cell 951-1964567; www.spanishschoolinmexico.com; Matamoros 502; classes per hour US$12) This school employs the novel method of giving one-on-one classes in cafes, parks, libraries, homestays or on the move while visiting markets, museums and galleries. They're very flexible: you can study from three to eight hours daily, for as long as you like, or even just take a teacher for a day's excursion.

Instituto Cultural Oaxaca LANGUAGE
(ICO; ☑951-515-34-04; www.icomexico.com; Juárez 909; 15/20/32hr per week US$140/157/178; ▣) A large, long-established school with a professional approach and ample gardens where some of the classes take place. The 32-hour-a-week main program includes eight hours of cultural workshops (dance, cooking, arts, crafts and more) and four hours' *intercambio* (meetings with locals for conversation). You can study for any period from one week up. Courses in medical and business Spanish, and for children and teachers, are also offered.

Becari Language School (Bravo) LANGUAGE
(☑951-514-60-76; www.becari.com.mx; Bravo 210; 15/20/30hr per week US$150/200/300; ▣) The Bravo branch of the highly rated, medium-sized Becari Language School. Group sizes range from one to five, and optional extras include salsa, folk dance, weaving and cooking. It also offers special courses such as Zapotec language and Spanish for children. There's another branch at **Tonatzin** (☑951-516-46-34; Quintana Roo 209).

Cooking Classes
Oaxaca has its own memorable take on Mexican cuisine, based on its famous seven *mole* sauces (p438), ancient culinary traditions and unforgettable flavor combinations. Numerous cooks regularly impart their secrets to visitors – in classes that are (or can be) held in English, and include market visits to buy ingredients and a meal to enjoy the fruits of your work!

La Casa de los Sabores

COOKING

(☎951-516-66-68; www.casadelossabores.com; La Olla, Reforma 402; per person US$75) Pilar Cabrera, owner of the excellent La Olla (p438), gives classes most Wednesday and Friday mornings. Participants prepare and eat one of 17 varied lunch menus. Make inquiries and reservations at La Olla; participants meet there at 9:30am and are delivered back there around 2:30pm after a market visit and the class and lunch at Pilar's house.

La Cocina Oaxaqueña

COOKING

(☎951-156-28-93; www.oaxacacuisine.com; Yagul 209, San José la Noria; per person US$60) A friendly mother-and-son team give well-priced, five-hour classes (morning or afternoon options) in their prettily decorated open kitchen. Normally you'll make four typical Oaxacan dishes. Try to reserve a day or two ahead; they'll pick you up and drop you back at your accommodations. Vegetarian classes available.

Alma de Mi Tierra

COOKING

(☎951-513-92-11; www.almademitierra.net; Aldama 205, Barrio Jalatlaco; per person US$75-95) Nora Valencia, from a family of celebrated Oaxacan cooks (her parents run La Casa de Mis Recuerdos; p437), conducts five-hour morning classes at her home in quaint Barrio Jalatlaco; 48 hours' notice is needed.

☞ Tours

The abundance of heavyweight sights surrounding Oaxaca make it an ideal base for guided tours. Such trips can save transportation hassles, be a lot of fun and tell you more than you might otherwise learn. A typical small-group day trip costs anywhere between M$180 and M$330 per person. Admission fees and meals are usually extra. You can book these and other tours at many accommodations, or direct with agencies such as **Turismo El Convento** (☎951-516-18-06; www.oaxacatours.mx; Quinta Real, 5 de Mayo 300; ⊙8:30am-7pm Mon-Sat, 9am-2pm Sun).

Zapotrek

HIKING, CYCLING

(☎951-502-59-57, cell 951-2577712; www.zapotrek.com) 🖋 Zapotrek specializes in hiking, biking and driving trips among indigenous Zapotec villages and their often-spectacular countryside with the help of local guides and experts, opening windows on Zapotec culture and eating local meals, often in local homes. It's run by English-fluent Eric Ramírez, a native of Tlacolula, 31km east of Oaxaca.

Fundación En Vía

CULTURAL

(☎951-515-24-24; www.envia.org; Instituto Cultural Oaxaca, Juárez 909; tour per person M$850; ⊙tours 1pm weekdays & 9am Sat) 🖋 Run out of the Instituto Cultural Oaxaca (p431) language school, nonprofit organization En Vía provides financial aid to small groups of village women to help them develop small businesses. The program's funded by En Vía's unique six-hour tours, which take you into the women's houses for lunch and explanations of local crafts and the local economy, providing a rare close-up look at village life.

Traditions Mexico

CULTURAL

(☎cell 951-2262742; www.traditionsmexico.com; day tours per person US$85-95; 🖩) These expertly guided trips yield insights into Oaxacan crafts, food, festivals and culture that few tours match, getting off the beaten track into artisans' workshops and villagers' kitchens for firsthand and hands-on encounters with indigenous Zapotec culture. Eight-hour day trips explore a different facet of Zapotec life each day (Tuesday to Sunday; minimum three people).

Bicicletas Pedro Martínez

CYCLING, HIKING

(☎951-514-59-35; www.bicicletaspedromartinez.com; Aldama 418; ⊙9am-8pm Mon-Sat) 🖋 This friendly team headed by Mexican Olympic cyclist Pedro Martínez offers mostly off-road rides (and some great day walks) amid some of Oaxaca state's best scenery. Van support cuts out the less interesting bits and hardest climbs. The most popular option is the full-day Valle de Tlacolula ride (two/four people M$1750/1500) that includes a bus transfer to Hierve El Agua.

🎎 Festivals & Events

★ Guelaguetza

DANCE

(⊙10am & 5pm, last 2 Mon of Jul) The Guelaguetza is a brilliant feast of Oaxacan folk dance staged on the first two Mondays after July 16 in the large, semi-open-air **Auditorio Guelaguetza** (Carretera Panamericano) on Cerro del Fortín. Magnificently costumed dancers from the seven regions of Oaxaca state perform a succession of dignified, lively or comical traditional dances, tossing offerings of produce to the crowd as they finish.

Excitement climaxes with the incredibly colorful pineapple dance by women of the Papaloapan region, and the stately Zapotec

Danza de las Plumas (Feather Dance), which symbolically re-enacts the Spanish conquest.

The auditorium holds about 11,000 people; tickets for the front sections of seating (A and B, together holding about 5000 people) for each show go on sale about two months ahead through the state tourism office, Sectur (p443), and www.ticketmaster.com.mx for M$850 to M$1050. The remaining 6000 or so seats (sections C and D) are free and first come, first served.

The event takes place at 10am and 5pm on each of the Mondays, lasting about three hours. The dates vary only when July 18, the anniversary of Benito Juárez' death, falls on a Monday. Guelaguetza then happens on July 25 and August 1.

The Guelaguetza period also sees many other colorful celebrations in Oaxaca, including concerts, exhibitions, a mezcal fair in Parque Juárez (El Llano) and fantastically festive Saturday-afternoon parades along Calle Alcalá. Thousands of people flock into the city for the festivities (including visiting pickpockets, so stay alert).

Smaller Guelaguetzas are held in outlying towns and villages, such as Zaachila, Tlacolula, Atzompa, Tlacochahuaya and San Agustín Etla, and even Tututepec down near the Oaxaca coast, usually on the same days, and can make a refreshing change from what might seem the overcommercialized hubbub of Oaxaca.

The Guelaguetza celebrations have their origins in a colonial-era fusion of indigenous festivities with Christian celebrations for the Virgen del Carmen. The current format dates back to 1932.

Día de Muertos TRADITIONAL

(☉ Oct 31-Nov 1) Oaxaca's Día de Muertos (Day of the Dead) celebrations are among Mexico's most vibrant, with concerts, exhibitions and other special goings-on starting days beforehand. Homes, cemeteries and some public buildings are decorated with fantastically crafted *altares de muertos* (altars of the dead); streets and plazas are decked with *tapetes de arena* (colored sand patterns and sculptures); and *comparsas* (satirical fancy-dress groups) parade the streets.

LAPIZTOLA & THE RISE OF STREET ART

Following a path first blazed by Mexican muralists, Diego Rivera and José Orozco in the 1930s and '40s, Oaxaca's modern street artists have captured a global audience in the last 10 years with provocative exhibitions in places as diverse as Brazil, Sweden, the UK and Cuba.

The street art renaissance can be traced back to a series of mass protests in 2006, when a teacher's strike in the state capital turned violent, resulting in over a dozen deaths. Against this backdrop of volatility and political turmoil, angry art collectives began to take shape using their graphic stencils as a form of political protest.

Sitting at the forefront of the movement, **Lapiztola** (http://lapiztola.tumblr.com) is an art collective, pioneered by creative luminaries Rosario Martínez and Roberto Vega, whose name is a clever juxtaposition of the words *lápiz* (pencil) and *pistola* (pistol). Never shy to comment graphically on the 2006 protests and their aftermath, the artists have been quoted as describing their vivid if often ephemeral art as 'a shout on a wall.'

While philosophically anchored in the traditions of Mexican muralism, Lapiztola's work stylistically owes more to the satirical graffiti of artists such as Banksy in the UK and Blek le Rat in France. Working under the radar, they copy their stencils guerrilla-style onto walls and buildings around the city using politically tinged graffiti to highlight the injustices in contemporary Mexico, be it drug wars, environmental degradation, migrant issues or the trials of innocent youth. Some decry it as vandalism; others see it as part of a vast public gallery that has been instrumental in shaping ideas and pushing debate.

Like it or not, Oaxaca's street art continues to highlight the dichotomies that exist in the city today: an attractive Unesco World Heritage site on one hand, yet a place where divisive political issues fester beneath the surface on the other. Not surprisingly, Lapiztola is just the point of the pencil. Other important art collectives include Asaro (Asamblea de Artistas Revolucionarios de Oaxaca; p428) and **Yescka** (http://guerilla-art.mx), while plenty more small independent galleries plying prints, pop art and T-shirts lie scattered around the city.

Oaxaca FilmFest

FILM

(www.oaxacafilmfest.com; ☉ Oct) Less than a decade old, but already being hailed as a cultural powerhouse, the Oaxaca FilmFest presents a great weeklong program of independent films from Mexico and around the world in the first half of October. All showings are free and all are in their original language with subtitles in Spanish, English or both.

🛏 Sleeping

Oaxaca is a dreamland of beautiful non-franchise accommodations loaded with authentic local charm. There's a good stash of cheap but well-kept hostels in interesting old houses, some brilliant B&Bs, an extravagant array of boutique hotels and plenty of evocative historic nooks. 'Spoiled for choice' would be a huge understatement.

Some places raise rates around four main festivals: Semana Santa, Guelaguetza, Día de Muertos and Christmas to New Year's Eve.

★ Casa Ángel

HOSTEL $

(☎ 951-514-22-24; www.casaangelhostel.com; Tinoco y Palacios 610; dm M$200-300, s/d M$700/800, without bathroom M$400/500, all incl breakfast; @ 🕾) Deservedly popular, this 'boutique' hostel is run by a friendly, helpful young team and kept scrupulously clean. Rooms are thoughtfully designed and the bright common areas include a good kitchen, a plasma screen with Netflix, and a great roof terrace with a barbecue every Sunday.

Three of the six private rooms have their own little terraces, and the dorms (two of them women only) have good solid bunks with private reading lights. The newer 'deluxe' dorms are capsule-style, with curtained, comfy, wood-paneled bunks equipped with their own electrical plugs and USB chargers. There's plenty of local info on offer too.

Azul Cielo

HOSTEL $

(☎ 951-205-35-64; www.azulcielohostel.com; Arteaga 608; dm M$150-170, d M$500 all incl breakfast; @ 🕾) This backpacker's favorite is a cross between a hostel and a B&B. A sunny, grassy garden that generates the comfy atmosphere of a private home lies at its heart. A semi-open lounge area sits at one end, along with two dorms and a clean, modern kitchen. The six brightly decorated private rooms at the other end have murals, fans and wooden furniture. Free bikes (two hours a day) and cooked breakfasts add to the appeal.

La Villada Inn

HOSTEL $

(☎ 951-518-62-17; www.facebook.com/lavillada. hostel; Felipe Ángeles 204, Ejido Guadalupe Victoria; dm/s/d/tr/q US$380/625/750/900; ℗ @ 🕾 ☒) Though it's set on the city's far northern edge, La Villada is preferred by some people for its good facilities, helpful English-speaking staff, spacious, relatively tranquil premises and rural views. The mostly adobe-built rooms have good Mexican furniture, and there's a reasonably priced cafe, plus an excellent swimming pool, bar, yoga room, tour service and hammocks. Some rooms have shared bathrooms.

If you call ahead, or from the bus station, they'll send a taxi to pick you up for M$60. It's 5.5km north of the Zócalo.

Hotel Casa Arnel

HOTEL $

(☎ 951-515-28-56; www.casaarnel.com.mx; Aldama 404, Barrio Jalatlaco; s/d M$650/700, without bathroom M$300/400; ℗ 🕾) The first joy of Casa Arnel is its location in the hushed, cobbled Jalatlaco quarter. Second joy: like most houses in the barrio, it has a lovely 'secret' garden. Rooms come third on the list but they are, nonetheless, clean, well-kept and have attractive color schemes in this traveler-friendly family-run hotel.

There are bikes or cars to rent, breakfast and helpful traveler services. The bright little Cafe El Ágora de Jalatlaco (cnr Aldama & Hidalgo; dishes M$30-85; ☉ 7:30am-10:30pm) under the same ownership, is next door.

Hostal Pochón

HOSTEL $

(☎ 951-516-13-22; www.hostalpochon.com; Callejón del Carmen 102; dm M$155, d with/without bathroom M$495/410, all incl breakfast; @ 🕾) Budget-friendly Pochón, on a quiet street, provides five dorms for four to eight people (one for women only) and four private rooms with decent beds. It's not luxe, but it's well kept and well run with a full kitchen, good common areas, included breakfast and welcome splashes of color. It also offers free drinking water and bike rentals.

Posada Don Mario

GUESTHOUSE $

(☎ 951-514-20-12; Cosijopí 219; s/d M$650/750, without bathroom M$450/650, all incl breakfast; @ 🕾) Cute, cheerful and friendly, this colorful courtyard guesthouse has an intimate feel, with neat, brightly decorated rooms – the five up on the roof terrace being particularly appealing. There's free drinking water, and helpful services include bookings for cooking classes, tours and transportation to the coast.

Hostal de las Américas HOSTEL $

(☑951-514-13-53; www.hostaldelasamericas.mx; Porfirio Díaz 300; dm/r incl breakfast M$220/600; ✳@☎) In a recently renovated city-center house, this hotel-standard hostel has seven separate-sex dorms, each with its own bathroom. Every bunk has its own reading light and electrical plug. There are three private rooms too, plus a roof terrace, filtered drinking water and a well-equipped kitchen. It's kept impeccably clean and adds up to a sound budget choice.

★ **La Betulia** B&B $$

(☑951-514-00-29; www.labetulia.com; Cabrera Carrasquedo 102; d incl breakfast M$1450; P☎) There's good service and then there's the Betulia, an eight-room B&B with a pretty walled patio where the owners sit and mingle with guests over breakfast as if they were old amigos. Nothing is too much trouble here, be it offering tips about the best local places for live music or satisfying special requests for breakfast (which is Oaxacan-themed and different every day).

The rooms are simple but highly contemporary, rendered with the kind of underlying artiness that Mexico – and, in particular, Oaxaca – seems to excel in.

Hotel La Casa de María BOUTIQUE HOTEL $$

(☑951-514-43-13; www.lacasademaria.com.mx; Juárez 103; r M$750-995; ✳☎) A subtle boutique hotel with the interior a mix of virgin white splashed with sharp color accents and the odd Frida Kahlo-esque painting or drawing. Bonuses, aside from the surgically clean rooms, are a bright patio, roof-deck, small attached restaurant (with room service available) and beyond-the-call-of-duty staff. This being Oaxaca, they also serve fabulous coffee.

Casa Adobe B&B $$

(☑951-517-72-68; www.casaadobe-bandb.com; Independencia 801, Tlalixtac de Cabrera; s/d incl breakfast US$47/57, apt US$50-55; ☎) On a quiet lane in the village of Tlalixtac de Cabrera, 8km east of the city, this is a charming retreat full of lovely art and crafts, and a good base for visits to the city and exploring outlying areas. Breakfast is served in the verdant little patio, and there's a nice roof terrace and cozy sitting room.

The amiable owners will pick you up on arrival in Oaxaca and offer free rides to town in the mornings. They'll also tell you about good restaurants locally. Minimum stay is two nights for the three rooms, and three nights for the two apartments.

Hotel Casa del Sótano HOTEL $$

(☑951-516-24-94; www.hoteldelsotano.com.mx; Tinoco y Palacios 404; s/d/tr/q M$1000/1150/1250/1400; @☎) Set off by a small but beautiful plant-filled courtyard and topped by a sunset-viewing terrace, this bargain-for-what-you-get hotel is one of the city's best deals, with attractive, spotless rooms that are pleasantly old rather than 'olde.' Enjoy the sturdy beds, traditional furniture and punctuations of antique art. There's a fine cafe on site.

Hotel Las Golondrinas HOTEL $$

(☑951-514-32-98; www.lasgolondrinasoaxaca.com; Tinoco y Palacios 411; d/tr/q M$800/900/1000; @☎) A profusion of plants of all types fills the three patios that beautify this excellent-value small hotel, which is worth the price for the gardens alone. The rooms are a little more prosaic but immaculately clean, and fruity breakfasts (dishes M$45 to M$75) served in one of the patios are well worth climbing out of your hammock for.

Hotel Casa Conzatti HOTEL $$

(☑951-513-85-00; www.casaconzatti.com.mx; Farias 218; r incl breakfast M$950-1300; P✳☎) An understated but good-value hotel named for an Italian botanist. Located opposite a quiet park about a 10-minute walk from the city-center action. Rooms are small but well equipped, with coffee machines and regularly replenished toiletries. Out front is a thoroughly decent restaurant (also understated) where you can enjoy your (included) breakfast. A rooftop terrace adds extra sparkle.

Hotel Azucenas HOTEL $$

(☑800-717-25-40, 800-882-6089; 951-514-79-18, USA & Canada; www.hotelazucenas.com; Aranda 203; s/d M$800/850; @☎) Painted in the warm colors of a Mexican sunset, the Azucenas is a small, friendly, very well-run Canadian-owned hotel in a beautifully restored century-old house. The 10 cool, tile-floored rooms have ample bathrooms, and a continental buffet breakfast (M$58) is served on the panoramic roof terrace. There's a three-night minimum stay at some peak periods. No children under eight.

Un Sueño Valle de Huajes HOTEL $$

(☑951-514-29-64; www.unsueno.com; Faustino Olivera 203; r M$1000; ☎) In the highly competitive league table of Oaxaca hotels, Un

Sueño probably wouldn't make the top 10, but there's function and tranquility in its 12 sharp minimalist rooms set on two floors around a sunny patio. Beds are comfy, and there's a pleasant roof terrace where breakfast and drinks are served with views of the hills and mountains.

Original decorative touches in the rooms include deft murals illustrating different stages in the life cycle of the locally abundant *huaje* tree.

★ Quinta Real Oaxaca   HISTORIC HOTEL $$$

(☎951-501-61-00; www.quintareal.com/oaxaca; 5 de Mayo 300; r from M$2670; ❋ 🌐 🛜 ⛲) As far as historic colonial hotels go, the Quinta is a five star among the five stars. The place is literally dripping with attention-grabbing details, from the multiple green patios to the knightly Don Quixote-esque decor. Built in the 16th century as a convent, in 1970 the Quinta was the first religious building in Mexico to become a hotel.

The old chapel is a banquet hall, one of the five palatial courtyards contains a swimming pool, and sturdy thick stone walls help to keep the place cool. The 91 rooms are sympathetically rendered in colonial styles, with high ceilings, though the ordinary (nonmaster) suites are modestly sized. If you start to feel claustrophobic, walk the colonial corridors with the ghosts of conquistadors past.

★ La Casona de Tita   HERITAGE HOTEL $$$

(☎951-516-14-00; www.hotelcasonadetita.com; García Vigil 105; r incl breakfast M$1660-1770; ❋🛜) Would you like the room with the 18th-century iron-railing bedstead, or the one with the precious 16th-century wardrobe, or perhaps the one with the beautiful Filipino chest brought over to Mexico in a Chinese boat during the colonial era? The Tita is one of Oaxaca's most exquisite and exclusive digs, with six huge rooms decorated with a seamless mix of antiques and modernity.

And if you grow attached to that fabulous modern painting hung up in your room, you can take it home with you when you leave – for a price.

★ Casa de las Bugambilias   B&B $$$

(☎866-829-6778; 951-516-11-65, USA & Canada; www.lasbugambilias.com; Reforma 402; s US$80-130, d US$90-140, all incl breakfast; ❋ @ 🛜) The nine rooms, all named after flowers, are works of art (equipped with beds embellished with

wood-carved or hand-painted headboards); breakfast in the on-site La Olla (p438) restaurant will have you thinking that Mexico is the best place in the world to wake up; and it's all stitched together by above-and-beyond service at this fabulous B&B.

Some rooms have little balconies. All are different. Gorgeous little decor details leave you in no doubt that you're in the cultural heart of Mexico.

El Diablo y la Sandía (Libres)   B&B $$$

(☑951-514-40-95; www.eldiabloylasandia.com; Libres 205; s/d incl breakfast US$80/90; 🛜) Is there a better place in the world to enjoy breakfast than Oaxaca? After a few days at the 'Devil and the Watermelon' B&B, you'll answer 'probably not.' There are six rooms painted lily white in these wonderful accommodations. All are punctuated with very Mexican color accents and sprinkled with very original Oaxacan *artesanías*.

Casa Oaxaca   BOUTIQUE HOTEL $$$

(☑951-514-41-73; www.casaoaxaca.com.mx; García Vigil 407; r US$167-220, ste US$238-362, all incl breakfast; 🅿 @ 🛜) Huge rooms, luxury pool, arty food and contemporary-meets-colonial courtyard in a converted 18th-century colonial mansion. What more could you want? Fabulous service? They have that too, along with art exhibits, an excellent little patio restaurant, mezcal tastings and cooking classes with the chefs. No kids under 12.

El Diablo y la Sandía (Boca del Monte)   B&B $$$

(☎951-514-40-95; www.eldiabloylasandia.com; Boca del Monte 121; s US$55-90, d US$65-100, all incl breakfast; 🛜) ⊘ This newer branch of the established B&B El Diablo y la Sandía has eight very white rooms set around a wide terracotta hued courtyard with colorful plants, plus two roof terraces, contemporary-styled solar-heated bathrooms (two rooms share), and slightly more understated Oaxacan *artesanías* decor than the original Libres branch. But everything is still infused with the same impeccable taste of the owner.

Ollin Bed & Breakfast   B&B $$$

(☑951-514-91-26; www.oaxacabedandbreakfast.com; Quintana Roo 213; r/ste incl breakfast US$95/130; ❋ @ 🛜) The Ollin has most of those wonderful Oaxacan calling cards: characterful rooms imbued with a tangible Mexican flavor, gourmet breakfasts, hands-on staff, and color and interest in every corner. Raising the yardstick even higher is the courtyard swimming pool, big roof terrace and lovely Oaxacan handicrafts sprinkled around. All that and they keep the room prices pretty reasonable.

La Casa de Mis Recuerdos B&B $$$
(☑951-515-56-45, USA & Canada 877-234-4706; http://lacasademisrecuerdos.com; Pino Suárez 508; s US$70-80, d US$95-110, all incl breakfast; ✳@☎) A marvelous decorative aesthetic prevails throughout this welcoming guesthouse, with old-style tiles, mirrors, masks and all sorts of other Mexican art and crafts adorning the rooms and halls. The best rooms overlook a fragrant central patio, and the Oaxacan breakfast (one of numerous highlights) is served in a beautiful dining room. There's a three-night minimum at some peak periods. Family member Nora Valencia gives cooking classes at her school Alma de Mi Tierra (p432).

✕ Eating

Surely one of the world's great food cities, Oaxaca is a gastronomic powerhouse full of creative restaurants, big-name chefs, cooking schools and curious local dishes (grasshoppers anyone?). You can eat grandly or cheaply any night of the week without complaint. The selection is quite dizzying.

★Boulenc Pan Artesano BAKERY, CAFE $
(☑951-351-3648; Porfirio Diaz 207; sandwiches M$45-55; ☉8:30am-8:30pm Mon-Wed, 8am-11pm Thu-Sat; ☎) Oaxaca's best bakery comes with an attached hipster cafe next door where the most popular dish is – guess what? – avocado on toast. Guys with beards or girls in Doc Martens serve you coffee in terracotta mugs and cakes of your choice (peruse the bakery case first) in an intentionally mildewed patio with an assortment of scuffed tables and a scribbled mural.

But, boy, are both breads and coffee good. Impossibly addictive are the almond croissants, sourdough pizzas and the *shakshouka* (poached eggs on a tangy tomato sauce).

★Jaguar Yuú CAFE $
(Murguía 202; breakfasts & light dishes M$55-95; ☉8am-10pm Mon-Sat, 10am-10pm Sun) The best coffee in Oaxaca comes from the mountains overlooking the Pacific and is served in this quietly hip but unmistakably Mexican cafe that also does a fine line in smoothies, baguettes, crepes, waffles and other appetite satisfiers.

Xuncu Choco OAXACAN $
(☑951-501-11-69; Independencia 403; mains M$60-90; ☉8am-6pm Mon-Sat, 9am-3pm Sun; ☎) A hole in the wall – there are just five tables in its little black-walled cafe plus a kitchen so small it could fit in an average-sized caravan. But, what wonderful treats emerge from it, not least a rich variety of breakfast omelettes, organic coffee and several Isthmus of Tehuantepec specials – try the *pescadillas* (fish quesadillas) or *camarones nanixhe* (spicy sautéed shrimp).

Tastavins MEDITERRANEAN $
(☑951-514-3776; Murguía 309; dishes M$50-150; ☉3pm-midnight Mon-Sat; ☎✏) The best Oaxaca tapas experience supported by some small Italy-worthy pasta, all served on typically Mexican ceramics, can be found in the pleasantly cramped confines of Tastavins (seven tables and three or four bar stools, all usually taken by around 8pm). They also ply fine Latin-world wine that tastes infinitely better with a plate of cheese and cured meat.

Cenaduría Tlayudas Libres OAXACAN $
(Libres 212; tlayudas M$30-55; ☉3pm-3am) It might smell more like a blacksmith's forge than a restaurant, but don't be put off. A dip inside the charcoal-y interior of this city institution is practically obligatory to anyone with more than a faint curiosity about Oaxacan food. The attraction is *tlayudas:* large, charcoal-grilled tortillas filled with cheese, lettuce and re-fried beans.

Don't worry, they're wonderful – just mind you don't get hit in the face by the sparks when they're smoldering on the grill.

Gourmand EUROPEAN $
(☑951-516-44-35; Porfirio Díaz 410; dishes M$55-100; ☉9am-1am Mon-Sat; ☎✏) Like a cross between a deli and a tapas bar, Gourmand does baguettes and deli sandwiches with roast beef, hummus or turkey breast, *tablas* (boards) of cold meats and cheeses, homemade sausages with mustard, assorted burgers (including veggie) and good breakfast options including eggs Benedict.

Big bonus – you can order craft beers in from the adjoining nano-brewery, La Santísima Flor de Lúpulo (p440).

Mercado 20 de Noviembre MARKET $
(cnr Flores Magón & Aldama; dishes M$25-50; ☉7am-10pm) Looking for cheap street food? Look no further. Dozens of good, clean *comedores* (food stalls) fill this large market

HOLY MOLE

Oaxaca's multicolored *moles* ('*moh*-les'; nut-, chili- and spice-based sauces) are its culinary signature. To Mexicans, the meat these sauces are served over is secondary in importance to the *mole* itself. Oaxaca's most famous variety, *mole negro* (black *mole*), is a smoky, savory delight bearing a hint of chocolate. It's the most complex and labor-intensive to create, though its popularity ensures that it's easy to find. While in Oaxaca, seek out the other colors of the *mole* family:

Mole amarillo A savory *mole* using a base of tomatillo (a small, husked tomato-like fruit), spiced with cumin, cloves, cilantro and hierba santa, and often served over beef. To the untutored eye, it's more red than *amarillo* (yellow).

Mole verde A lovely, delicate sauce thickened with corn dough and including tomatillos, pumpkin seeds, the herbs *epazote* and hierba santa, and different nuts such as walnuts and almonds. Often served with chicken.

Mole colorado A forceful *mole* based on *ancho*, *pasilla* and *cascabel* chilies, black pepper and cinnamon.

Mole coloradito (or mole rojo) This tangy, tomato-based blend might remind gringos of their neighborhood Mexican joint back home; it is exported in dumbed-down form as enchilada sauce.

Mancha manteles The brick-red 'tablecloth stainer' has a deep, woody flavor, often used to complement tropical fruit.

Chíchilo negro A rare *mole* whose defining ingredients include *chilguacle negro*, *mulato* and *pasilla* chilies, avocado leaves (which give a touch of anise flavor), tomatoes and corn dough.

where wait staff will thrust menus to within an inch of your nose as you stroll past.

The biggest treat for carnivores is the hugely popular Pasillo de Carnes Asadas (Grilled Meat Passage) on the east side, where a dozen stands specialize in grilling *tasajo* (beef) or *cecina enchilada* (slices of chili-coated pork) over hot coals.

Mercado Sánchez Pascuas   MARKET $
(cnr Porfirio Díaz & Callejón Hidalgo; dishes M$13-25; ⏱8am-4pm) The local's choice, this small indoor food market is where you'll end up shopping when you book a cooking class and go out searching for ingredients.

Its *comedores* (food stalls) provide a down-to-earth Oaxacan eating experience: head to the ones toward the west end (where you eat at counters right in front of the cooks), ask for a *tamal, memela* or empanada, and practice your Spanish in deciding what you want on or in it.

★**La Olla**   OAXACAN $$
(☎951-516-66-68; www.laolla.com.mx; Reforma 402; breakfasts M$100-125, mains M$90-210; ⏱8am-10pm Mon-Sat; ☎🖈) La Olla (the cooking pot) is very much its own invention. It's not a trying-too-hard hipster cafe, or a fancy

fusion restaurant or a purveyor of nouveau cuisine. It's just, for want of a better word, good – very good, in fact. One day, they'll be serving international dishes; another day, street food; another, whatever's on sale at the local market.

You can take stock of it all in a Scandinavian slick ground-floor restaurant, but far more attractive views await upstairs on the roof terrace where the guacamole, *moles* and tortillas seem to taste so much better.

Tobaziche   NEW MEXICAN $$
(☎951-516-81-16; www.tobaziche.mx; 5 de Mayo 311; mains M$75-155; ⏱1-11pm Mon-Thu, to midnight Fri & Sat) Named after a type of indigenous agave plant, the new and unashamedly hip Tobaziche slams down complimentary mezcals on selective nights and trumpets some skilled live bands improvising jazzy jams. They also do wonderful things with roasted squash and weave even better miracles with *chapulines* (grasshoppers), which are served unadorned with guacamole.

You should also try the prawn tacos and save at least a little space for some local cheese (*quesillo*) melted over chorizo and Oaxacan 'water chilies.' Food presentation is beautiful. So are most of the clientele.

La Popular MEXICAN **$$**
(García Vigil 519; dishes M$75-120; ☺10am-11pm Tue-Sat, 1-11pm Sun & Mon; 🛜🖉) Cheap, quick, boisterous and – as the name implies – popular, this little corner restaurant with a sideline as an art gallery does a variety of interesting *antojitos* (Mexican snacks) and other more substantial Oaxacan and Mexican dishes. Trendy it isn't, which could be something of a relief if you've been overdosing in Oaxaca's rash of hip new *mezcalerías* (mezcal bars). The soft tacos are good. The wild-mushrooms in garlic are even better. Arrive early. 'Tis busy.

Zandunga OAXACAN **$$**
(🖉951-516-2265; García Vigil 512E; mains M$85-185; ☺2-11pm Mon-Sat; 🛜) The Isthmus of Tehuantepec has its own take on Oaxacan cuisine based on ingredients like tropical fruits and seafood, with many dishes cooked in banana leaves. Festive Zandunga brings those flavors to Oaxaca, and the *botana* (a sampler of dishes which easily serves two) is perfect for whiling away a couple of hours with some of its many mezcals.

La Biznaga OAXACAN, FUSION **$$**
(🖉951-516-18-00; García Vigil 512; mains M$100-240; ☺1-10pm Mon-Thu, to 11pm Fri & Sat) Locals and visitors alike jam the large colonial courtyard for well-rendered nouveau-Oaxacan fusion dishes. The choices are chalked on blackboards: you might start with the *sopa del establo* (a creamy Roquefort and chipotle chili soup), follow up with turkey breast in a blackberry *mole negro*, and finish with the delectable chocolate mousse and guava.

★**Casa Oaxaca** FUSION **$$$**
(🖉951-516-85-31; www.casaoaxacaelrestaurante. com; Constitución 104-4; mains M$200-335; ☺1-11pm Mon-Sat, to 9pm Sun) It's not easy living up to the mantle of Oaxaca's best restaurant, but this place consistently achieves. A glamorous rooftop terrace, theatrical tableside preparation, a posh cocktail scene, and an array of ravishing dishes – seared tuna, ceviche in pimiento agua, fish stone soup, duck tacos, and octopus among them. Iron your shirt and make a reservation.

★**Restaurante Los Danzantes** FUSION **$$$**
(🖉951-501-11-84; www.losdanzantes.com; Alcalá 403; mains M$165-285; ☺1-10:30pm Sun-Tue, to 11pm Fri & Sat) Excellent Mexican fusion food in a spectacular architect-designed patio makes Los Danzantes one of Oaxaca's special dining spots. The hierba santa leaves rolled round two cheeses are a great starter, and the goat's cheese flan with figs, chocolate and honey is a perfect dessert. In between, try a fish fillet in *mole amarillo* (yellow *mole*) or a rib-eye steak with wild mushrooms.

Restaurante Catedral INTERNATIONAL **$$$**
(🖉951-516-32-85; www.restaurantecatedral.com. mx; García Vigil 105; mains M$180-320; ☺8am-11pm Wed-Mon) Perhaps Oaxaca's most refined and romantic eating choice, with sharp but non-showy service on a patio or in a variety of interior rooms. The specialty is roast pork, but there is the usual variety of moles and – highlight – the multifarious if meat-heavy *Plato Oaxaqueña*, a cocktail of the town's best food bites with *mole*, cheese, chorizo, stuffed chilies and cured meat.

Pescatarians can attempt the *pulpo a las brasas* (barbecued octopus), while vegetarians can dive figuratively into the mushroom mountain soup.

Pitiona OAXACAN **$$$**
(🖉951-514-06-90; www.pitiona.com; Allende 108; mains M$180-320, tasting menus from M$580; ☺1-11pm Mon-Sat, to 9pm Sun) Food as art. Oaxacan chef José Manuel Baños, who has worked at the renowned El Bulli in Spain, takes the ingredients and flavors of his homeland to new creative heights at Pitiona. The delicious *sopa de fideos* (noodle soup) comes with floating capsules of liquid cheese, and the beef tongue is done in a chili marinade and topped with potato foam.

Some dishes are so artistically presented it's a shame to eat them – but the restaurant's atmosphere is refreshingly relaxed. The six-course tasting menu is eternally popular.

Los Pacos OAXACAN **$$$**
(🖉951-516-17-04; www.lospacos.com.mx; Abasolo 121; mains M$175-275; ☺noon-10pm) *Moles* are the prize here and, to aid your selection, the wait staff will bring you a free selection of seven of the revered sauces along with tortillas for dipping to help you make your choice. The *mole negro* with chicken rules, OK. They also offer *tasajo* (thinly sliced grilled beef) done 15 different ways.

There's another Los Pacos – older, more local and more family-oriented – in the Colonia Reforma neighborhood in the northern suburbs.

Vieja Lira
ITALIAN $$$

(☑ 951-516-11-22; www.viejalira.com; Reforma 502; mains M$120-300; ⊙1-11pm) Every city needs an Italian restaurant and Oaxaca has several, though few are better than the authentic and casually refined Vieja Lira with its thin-crust pizzas, al dente pastas and inviting interior flecked with memories of Florence. The extensive wine list makes a welcome away day from mezcal and margaritas.

Drinking & Nightlife

Mezcal is the (sometimes slurred) word on most people's lips when ordering a drink in Oaxaca. This once poor man's alternative to tequila is now officially trendy, as exemplified by the city's large and growing cache of divey-hip *mezcalerías*. Craft beer is also making inroads. Alcalá, García Vigil and nearby streets are the main party zone on Friday and Saturday nights.

★ Los Amantes
MEZCALERÍA

(http://losamantesmezcal.blogspot.ca; Allende 107; ⊙5-11pm Tue-Sun) Squeeze into this unusual standing-room-only bar stuffed to the rafters with peculiar knickknacks for a short sharp intro to Mexico's smokiest spirit. Friendly bar staff will explain all about the three different artisanal mezcals that they give you to taste for around M$150.

Sacapalabras
BAR

(☑ 951-351-83-71; García Vigil 104; ⊙2pm-2am Mon-Sat) An agreeably moody bar back-lit by smoky blue lights where mezcal and live jazz make ideal bedfellows. One room is a de facto art gallery and they also serve a welcome medley of Mexican craft beers.

La Santísima Flor de Lúpulo
BREWERY

(☑ 951-516-44-35; Allende 215; ⊙5pm-1am Mon-Sat) Goodbye Corona, hello Lúpulo (the word means 'hop,' as in the plant). Oaxaca's cherished nano-brewery (that's a brewery even smaller than a microbrewery) offers a constantly rotating trio of made-on-site craft beers served in a space barely large enough to swing a small kitten. For full immersion, order the three glass taster board with a burger from deli/bakery Gourmand (p437), next door.

In Situ
MEZCALERÍA

(http://insitumezcaleria.com; Morelos 511; ⊙1-11pm Mon-Sat; 🛜) A don't-miss stop on any mezcal trail, In Situ stocks a vast variety of artisanal mezcals, many of them unusual, and the owner is an encyclopedia of the so-called oven-cooked agave.

Café Café
CAFE

(Bravo 219; ⊙7am-11pm) 🍃 So good they named it twice, this clean-lined corner cafe could just as well be named 'carrot cake carrot cake' or 'mango smoothie mango smoothie.' As in most Mexican cafes you can procure a sizeable snack here (the breakfasts are particularly good). It began life as a roaster supporting local bean production and several women's education projects.

Mayordomo
CAFE

(☑ 951-516-16-19; www.chocolatemayordomo.com.mx; Mina 219; ⊙7am-9pm; 🛗) A synonym for chocolate in Oaxaco, Mayordomo have several branches, but the best and biggest is just south of the Mercado 20 de Noviembre (p437). Walk in through the sweet smelling entry cum grinding room and make a beeline for the bar where you can order a cup of Oaxacan chocolate (hot or cold) and become mesmerized by the cooks making breakfast and/or lunch.

La Mezcalerita
MEZCALERÍA

(Alcalá 706C; ⊙2pm-2am) Like most of Oaxaca's *mezcalerías,* this place is small, dark and rustically trendy with an atmosphere that gets friskier as the evening wears on. The mostly 20s and 30s clientele can be seen propping up the bar downstairs or chilling on a simple roof terrace over a great selection of smoky mezcals (from M$50) and craft beers. Small snack plates also available.

Café Brújula
CAFE

(www.cafebrujula.com; Alcalá 104; cakes, cookies & sandwiches M$10-70; ⊙8am-10pm Mon-Sat, 9am-9pm Sun; 🛜) Oaxaca's most prestigious and ubiquitous local coffee roaster uses organic beans plucked from growers in the western part of the province. The company has opened four cafes since 2006, the best of them situated in a tranquil courtyard (next to several book and craft shops) in Calle Alcalá. Aside from the fruity joe, they ply fruit smoothies and handsome wedges of carrot cake.

Txalaparta
CLUB

(☑ 951-514-43-05; Matamoros 206; ⊙1pm-2am Mon-Sat, 6pm-2am Sun) Take some hipsters, a vague Wild West theme, the cool menace of

MEZCAL

....

When Oaxacans tell you mezcal is a *bebida espirituosa* (spirit), they're not just saying it's a distilled liquor; they're hinting at an almost-spiritual reverence for the king of Oaxacan drinks. When you sip mezcal, you're imbibing the essence of an agave plant that has taken at least seven, and sometimes 70, years to reach maturity. Mezcal is a drink to be respected while being enjoyed, a drink that can put people into a kind of trance – '*Para todo mal, mezcal,*' they say, '*Para todo bien, también.*' ('For everything bad, mezcal; for everything good too.)

In the past decade or so, this once little-trumpeted liquor has become positively fashionable, not just in Mexico but also in the US and beyond. *Mezcalerías* (mezcal bars), from the trendy to the seriously connoisseurish, have proliferated in Oaxaca, Mexico City and elsewhere, and a mind-boggling diversity of mezcal varieties and brands has hit the market.

It's strong stuff (usually 40% to 50% alcohol content), and best sipped slowly and savored. A glass of reasonable mezcal in a bar is unlikely to cost less than M$30 and a top-class one might cost M$300.

Mezcal-type drinks are produced in many parts of Mexico, but only those that meet established criteria from certain specific areas can legally be marketed as 'mezcal.' Otherwise they are known as *destilados de agave*. Around 60% of mezcal (and most of the best) is produced in and around Oaxaca's Valles Centrales.

Mezcal can be made from around 20 different species of agave (or *maguey* – the words are synonymous). The majority comes from the widely cultivated *espadín,* which has a high sugar content and matures relatively quickly. Mezcals from *agaves silvestres* (wild, uncultivated agaves) are specially prized for their organic nature, unique tastes and usually small-scale production methods. Best known of these is the *tobalá,* which yields distinctive herbal notes.

The mature plant's *piña* (heart), with the leaves removed, is cooked for several days over a wood fire, typically in an oven in the ground. Thus sweetened, it is crushed to fibers that are fermented with water for up to three weeks. The resulting liquid is distilled twice to produce mezcal. It can be drunk *joven* (young) or *reposado* (aged in oak for between two months and one year) or *añejo* (aged in oak for at least a year). A *pechuga* mezcal is one with flavors imparted by a chicken or turkey breast (*pechuga*) and/or fruits and spices placed in the distillation vessel.

You can observe the mezcal-making process and sample the product at dozens of mezcal factories and *palenques* (small-scale producers) in the Oaxaca area, especially around Mitla and along the road to it, and above all at the village of Santiago Matatlán, which produces about half of all Oaxaca's mezcal. If you really want to get down to grass roots and learn about the mezcal-making process firsthand and in detail, take a trip with **Mezcal Educational Tours** (☎951-132-82-03; www.mezcaleducationaltours.com) ✐.

The taste variations of different mezcals are amazingly wide, and as a general rule you get what you pay for – but the only sure way to judge a mezcal is by how much you like it!

The infamous *gusano* (worm) is actually a moth caterpillar that feeds on the agave and is found mostly in bottles of cheaper mezcal. While no harm will come from swallowing the *gusano,* there is definitely no obligation! Mezcal is, however, often served with a little plate of orangey powder, *sal de gusano,* which is a mix of salt, chili and ground-up *gusanos*. Along with slices of orange or lime, this nicely counterpoints the mezcal taste.

Reservoir Dogs and the 'everyman' appeal of The Beatles and you've got a rough feel for Txalaparta. This quietish hookah bar has plenty of dark nooks and crannies to hide away in by day, but morphs into a jiving hive at night.

Candela CLUB

(☎951-514-20-10; Murguía 413; M$50; ⊙10pm-2am Thu-Sat) Candela's writhing Latin bands and beautiful colonial-house setting have kept it high on the Oaxaca nightlife lists for years. Get there soon after opening for a good table. Latin dance classes are held here too.

DON'T MISS

NIGHTTIME BIKE RIDES

Oaxaca is a famously attractive city, but its beauty is made infinity more palatable by the lack of city center traffic. The dearth of cars is thanks, in part, to the efforts of local businesses such as Mundo Ceiba (p429), a bike-rental shop responsible for organizing regular communal bike rides designed to cut pollution and push alternative means of transportation. The so-called Paseos Nocturnos en Bicicleta began in 2008 as a once a week jaunt around Oaxaca's cobbled core, but they quickly became so popular with both locals and tourists that they now run four times a week on Wednesday, Friday, Saturday and Sunday. Cyclists meet at 9pm on Calle Alaclá outside the Templo de Santo Domingo (p424). The ride, which is leisurely and highly sociable, runs for 11/2 hours and covers 8km. A customized tricycle pedals at the front playing galvanizing music and looking out for errant drivers. On special days and festivals, riders have been known to don fancy dress. There isn't a better way to see after-dark Oaxaca while communing with the locals.

Bikes for the ride can be rented beforehand at Mundo Ceiba, a couple of blocks from the starting point.

☆ Entertainment

Teatro Macedonio Alcalá THEATER
(☑951-516-83-12; Independencia 900) The city's main theater is a riot of frescoes and gilded boxes built in Louis XV style in 1909 during a renaissance of Mexican theater known as *chico mexicano*. Performances here range from operas and plays to classical concerts. There's a ticket/info office next to the lobby.

La Nueva Babel LIVE MUSIC
(Porfirio Díaz 224; ⊘9am-2am Mon-Sat, 9pm-2am Sun) A mural of Bowie as Aladdin Sane juxtaposed with the Virgin of Guadaloupe sets the alternative tone in Babel, a kind of Mexican dive bar with regular live music from an eclectic cache of performers – it could be *son* (folk), blues, *trova* (troubadour-type folk), jazz or *cumbia* (dance music originating from Colombia). The chairs are covered in old newspaper, should you get bored.

Guelaguetza Show DANCE
(☑951-501-61-00; Quinta Real Oaxaca, 5 de Mayo 300; incl buffet dinner M$450; ⊘7pm Fri) If you're not in Oaxaca for the Guelaguetza dance festival itself (July), it's well worth attending one of the regular imitations. The highly colorful three-hour show in the beautiful Hotel Quinta Real is the best of them.

🛍 Shopping

The state of Oaxaca has the richest, most inventive folk-art scene in Mexico, and the city is its chief marketplace. You'll find the highest-quality crafts mostly in smart stores, but prices are lower in the markets. Some artisans have grouped together to market their products directly in their own stores.

Oaxaca's crowded commercial area stretches over several blocks southwest of the Zócalo. Oaxacans flock here, and to the big Central de Abastos market, for all their everyday needs.

★ Amate Books BOOKS
(Alcalá 307; ⊘10:30am-2:30pm & 3:30-7:30pm Mon-Sat, 1-7pm Sun) Probably the best English-language bookstore in the country, Arnate is a joy to browse, ponder, peruse and admire – it stocks almost every in-print English-language title related to Mexico. The ideal place to idle for a rainy hour.

Voces de Copal, Aullidos del Alma ARTS & CRAFTS
(Alcalá 303; ⊘8am-9:30pm) A classy crafts shop with superb *alebrijes* from the workshop of Jacobo and María Ángeles in San Martín Tilcajete (p452). These brightly painted wooden figurines, primarily depicting animals and birds, are one of the Valles Centrales many unique and highly sought-after crafts.

Huizache ARTS & CRAFTS
(☑951-501-12-82; Murguía 101; ⊘9am-9pm) A kind of greatest hits of Oaxacan crafts– including black pottery, rugs, clothes, shoes and painted wood carvings *(alebrijes)* – collected from around the state by a cooperative of artisans. A handy place to shop if you can't make it out to the village markets.

El Nahual ARTS & CRAFTS
(☑951-516-42-02; http://elnahualfolkart.blogspot.ca; Reforma 412A; ⊘10:30am-2pm & 4-8pm Mon-Sat) Folk art shop run by a Teotitlán

del Valle weaving family, meaning it's stuffed with quality rugs, clothes and embroidery, as well as work from other affiliated artisans.

La Casa del Rebozo
ARTS & CRAFTS

(5 de Mayo 114; ⊙9:30am-9pm Mon-Sat, 10am-6pm Sun) A cooperative of 84 artisans from around Oaxaca state, La Casa del Rebozo stocks quality pottery, textiles, *alebrijes*, tinware, bowls and baskets made from pine needles, and palm-leaf bags, baskets, mats and hats.

Unión de Palenqueros de Oaxaca
DRINKS

(☑951-513-04-85; Abasolo 510; ⊙9am-9pm) 🍶 This hole-in-the-wall place is the outlet for a group of small-scale mezcal producers from Santiago Matatlán. It has excellent and very well-priced *reposado*, *pechuga* and smoky *añejo* varieties.

Central de Abastos
MARKET

(Periférico; ⊙6am-8pm) The enormous main market, nearly 1km west of the Zócalo, is a hive of activity all week, with Saturday the biggest day. You can find almost anything here, and it's easy to get lost among the household goods, *artesanías* and overwhelming quantities of fruit, vegetables, sugarcane, maize and other produce grown from the coast to the mountaintops.

Mercado Juárez
MARKET

(cnr Flores Magón & Las Casas; ⊙6am-9pm) This daily indoor market, a block south of the Zócalo, peddles a mix of flowers, hats, shoes, cheap clothes and jewelry, baskets, leather belts and bags, fancy knives, mezcal, herbs (medicinal and culinary), spices, meat, cheese, ready-made *mole,* fruit, vegetables, grasshoppers and almost every other food a Oaxacan could need – a fascinating browse.

❶ Information

There are still a few internet cafes; most charge around M$10 per hour. There is free wi-fi in some public spaces, including Parque Juárez and in nearly all hotels.

There are plenty of ATMs around the center, and several banks and *casas de cambio* (exchange houses) will change cash US dollars.

CI Banco (Armenta y López 203; ⊙8:30am-6pm Mon-Fri, 10am-2pm Sat) Exchanges cash US and Canadian dollars, euros, pounds sterling, yen and Swiss francs, and euro traveler's checks.

Main Post Office (Alameda de León; ⊙8am-7pm Mon-Fri, to 3pm Sat)

Municipal Tourist Information Kiosk (Alameda de León; ⊙9am-6pm)

Municipal Tourist Information Office (☑951-514-28-82; Matamoros 102; ⊙9am-8pm)

Sectur (☑951-502-12-00, ext 1506; www.oaxaca.travel; Juárez 703; ⊙8am-8pm) The Oaxaca state tourism department's main information office. Also has desks at the **1st-class bus station** (5 de Mayo 900, Barrio Jalatlaco; ⊙9am-8pm), **Museo de los Pintores Oaxaqueños** (Independencia 607; ⊙10am-6pm) and **Teatro Macedonio Alcalá** (Independencia 900; ⊙9am-8pm).

❶ Getting There & Away

AIR

Oaxaca Airport (☑951-511-50-88; www.asur.com.mx) is 6km south of the city, 500m west off Hwy 175, and is served by numerous airlines.

Aeroméxico (☑951-516-10-66; www.aeromexico.com; Hidalgo 513; ⊙9am-6pm Mon-Fri, to 4pm Sat) To/from Mexico City several times daily.

Aerotucán (☑951-502-0840; www.aerotucan.com) Thirteen-seat Cessnas make half-hour hops to Puerto Escondido (M$1993) and Bahías de Huatulco (M$2042), on the Oaxaca coast, both daily – spectacular flights, but they are sometimes canceled or rescheduled at short notice.

Interjet (☑951-502-57-23; www.interjet.com.mx; Plaza Mazari, Calzada Porfirio Díaz 256, Colonia Reforma; ⊙9am-7pm Mon-Fri, to 6pm

---

❶ COLECTIVOS: A BEGINNER'S GUIDE

Colectivos are shared taxis that run along fixed routes in the localities in and around Oaxaca. However, because you are sharing the ride with other people, the cost is a lot cheaper than a regular taxi (but slightly more expensive than a bus). In Oaxaca, *colectivos* are dark red and white and display their destination on a banner at the top of the windscreen. Many congregate at the north side of Oaxaca's 2nd-class bus station, but will stop unscheduled en route to pick up passengers if they have room (stick your arm out to flag one down). *Colectivos* carry four passengers and leave when full (some try to squeeze in five people). They are generally faster than buses – some would say a little too fast!

Sat, 10am-2pm Sun) Flies to Mexico City two or three times daily.

TAR Aerolíneas (☏55-2629-5272; www.tar mexico.com) Direct flights to Guadalajara, Villahermosa, Huatulco and Tuxtla Gutiérrez.

United (☏800-900-50-00; www.united.com) Flies to Houston, Texas daily.

Vivaaerobus (☏81-8215-0150; www.viva aerobus.com) Budget airline flying to/from Monterrey two or three times weekly.

Volaris (☏55-1102-8000; www.volaris.com) Low-cost Mexican airline with flights to Mexico City (three weekly), Tijuana (five), Monterrey (two) and Los Angeles (three).

BUS & VAN

For destinations on the Oaxaca coast, buses from the 1st-class bus station take a long and expensive route via Salina Cruz. Unless you're prone to travel sickness on winding mountain roads, it's cheaper and quicker to use one of the comfortable 12- to 18-seat van services that go directly to Puerto Escondido, Pochutla, Zipolite, Mazunte or Huatulco (prices from between M$195 and M$230). Some hostels can arrange for these services to pick you up for an extra charge of around M$50.

New highways to Puerto Escondido and Tehuantepec, when they eventually open (possibly 2018, but don't bank on it), will reduce journey times to coastal destinations and are likely to affect schedules and routes of some services.

1st-class bus station (Terminal ADO; ☏951-502-05-60; 5 de Mayo 900, Barrio Jalatlaco)

Two kilometers northeast of the Zócalo; used by ADO Platino and ADO GL (deluxe service), ADO and OCC (1st class) and AU, Sur and Cuenca (2nd class). You can book online at **Mi Escape** (☏951-502-0560; www.miescape.mx; 5 de Mayo 900; ⏰7am-10pm Mon-Fri, 9am-2pm & 5-8pm Sat & Sun).

2nd-class bus station (Central de Autobuses de Segunda Clase; Las Casas) Mainly useful for some buses to villages around Oaxaca; it's 1km west of the Zócalo.

Atlántida (☏951-514-7077; La Noria 101) Direct vans to Zipolite and Mazunte.

Autobuses Halcón (☏951-516-01-83; Bustamante 606A, Oaxaca) Buses to San Bartolo Coyotepec.

Express Service (☏951-516-40-59; Arista 116) Vans to Puerto Escondido.

Expressos Colombo Huatulco (☏951-514-38-54; www.expressoscolombohuatulco.com; Trujano 600) Vans to Bahías de Huatulco.

Huatulco 2000 (☏951-516-31-54; Hidalgo 208) Vans to Bahías de Huatulco.

Líneas Unidas (☏951-187-55-11; Bustamante 601) Vans to Pochutla.

Transportadora Excelencias (Díaz Ordaz 314, Oaxaca) Vans to Yanhuitlán and Teposcolula.

Transportes Villa del Pacífico (☏951-160-51-60; Galeana 322A) Vans to Puerto Escondido.

CAR & MOTORCYCLE

Hwy 135D branches off the Mexico City–Veracruz highway (150D) to make a spectacular traverse of Oaxaca's northern mountains to Oaxaca

BUSES & VANS FROM OAXACA CITY

DESTINATION	FARE (M$)	DURATION (HR)	FREQUENCY (DAILY)
Bahías de Huatulco	230-305	7-8	13 Expressos Colombo, 9 Huatulco 2000, 5 from 1st-class terminal
Mazunte	210	7	6 daily Atlántida
Mexico City (TAPO)	310-823	6-7	27 from 1st-class terminal
Pochutla	195-446	6-10	30 Líneas Unidas, 4 from 1st-class terminal
Puebla	370-780	4½	19 from 1st-class terminal
Puerto Escondido	200-382	7-11	15 Express Service, 18 Villa del Pacífico, 4 from 1st-class terminal
San Cristóbal de las Casas	507-804	10-11	4 from 1st-class terminal
Tapachula	606	12	7pm from 1st-class terminal
Tehuantepec	154-294	4½	15 from 1st-class terminal
Veracruz	400-792	7-8	4 from 1st-class terminal
Zipolite	210	6¾	6 Atlántida

city. Automobile tolls from Mexico City to Oaxaca total M$430; the trip takes five to six hours.

The roads of Oaxaca state are mostly poorly maintained. Promised new highways to the coast have been in the works for nearly 10 years but have yet to reach fruition. The touted termination date of 2018 sounds generous. Away from Oaxaca city, traffic is light and the scenery is fantastic.

Walk-in car rental prices in Oaxaca start around M$700 a day with unlimited kilometers.

Europcar (☑951-143-83-40; www.europcar. com.mx; ☺6am-10:30pm) At the airport.

Only Rent-A-Car (☑951-514-02-55; www.only rentacar.com; 5 de Mayo 215A; ☺8am-8pm)

❶ Getting Around

TO/FROM THE AIRPORT

The Transporte Terrestre ticket-taxi desk in the airport charges M$75 per person to get anywhere downtown in a van. For the same service going to the airport, reserve a day ahead at **Transportación Terrestre Aeropuerto** (☑951-514-10-71; Alameda de León 1G; ☺9am-7pm Mon-Sat, 10am-2pm Sun). Other taxis to the airport generally cost M$300.

BUS

City buses cost M$7.50. From the main road outside the 1st-class bus station, westbound 'Juárez' buses will take you down Juárez and Ocampo, three blocks east of the Zócalo; westbound 'Tinoco y Palacios' buses go down Tinoco y Palacios, two blocks west of the Zócalo. To return to the bus station, take an 'ADO' bus north up Pino Suárez or Crespo.

TAXI

Taxis anywhere within the central area, including the bus stations, cost M$40.

VALLES CENTRALES

The historic yet sophisticated city of Oaxaca is ringed by a slightly more rustic collection of towns and villages that tout some the state's biggest calling cards: ancient Mesoamerican ruins, indigenous crafts, industrious markets, riotous festivals and fields full of mezcal-producing agave plants. There are three main geographical arteries: the Valle de Tlacolula, stretching 50km east from the city; the Valle de Zimatlán, running about 100km south; and the Valle de Etla, reaching about 40km north. All are within easy day-trip distance of Oaxaca city. The people of these Valles Centrales (Central Valleys) are mostly indigenous Zapotec.

Monte Albán

The city from which the ancient Zapotecs once ruled Oaxaca's Valles Centrales, **Monte Albán** (adult/child-under-13 M$70/free; ☺8am-5pm; ℗) towers 400m above the valley floor from a hilltop a few kilometers west of Oaxaca. This is one of Mexico's most culturally rich archaeological sites, with the remains of temples, palaces, tall stepped platforms, an observatory and a ball court all arranged in orderly fashion, with wonderful 360-degree views over the city, valleys and distant mountains.

Monte Albán traces its roots to 500 BC and its 1300-year history is usually split into five archaeological phases. The city reached its apex between AD 300 and 700, but was abandoned long before the Spanish arrived in the 1520s.

While busy compared to other Oaxaca archaeological sites, Monte Albán avoids the tour bus circus of some of the better-known ruins around Mexico City and Cancún.

History

Monte Albán was first occupied around 500 BC, probably by Zapotecs moving from the previous main settlement in the Valles Centrales, the less defensible San José El Mogote in the Valle de Etla. Monte Albán had early cultural connections with the Olmecs to the northeast.

The years up to about 200 BC (known as phase Monte Albán I) saw the leveling of the hilltop, the building of temples and probably palaces, and the growth of a town of 10,000 or more people on the hillsides. Hieroglyphs and dates in a dot-and-bar system carved during this era may mean that the elite of Monte Albán were the first people in Mexico to use a developed writing system and written calendar. Between 200 BC and AD 300 (phase Monte Albán II) the city came to dominate more and more of the Oaxaca region.

The city was at its peak from about AD 300 to 700 (Monte Albán III), when the surrounding hills were terraced for dwellings, and the population reached about 25,000. This was the center of a highly organized, priest-dominated society, controlling the extensively irrigated Valles Centrales, which held at least 200 other settlements and ceremonial centers. Many buildings here were plastered and painted red. Nearly 170 underground tombs from this period have been

Monte Albán

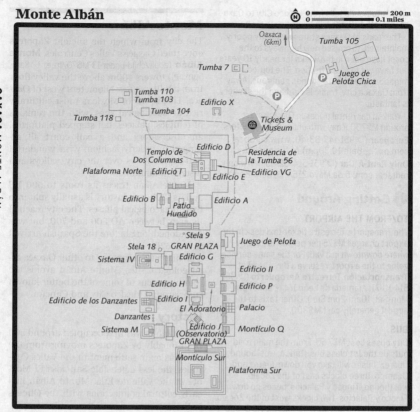

Oaxaca
(6km)

Tumba 105

Tumba 7

Juego de
Pelota Chica

Tumba 110
Tumba 103
Edificio X

Tumba 118   Tumba 104

Tickets &
Museum

Edificio D
Residencia de
la Tumba 56

Templo de
Dos Columnas
Plataforma Norte   Edificio T   Edificio VG
Edificio E

Edificio B   Edificio A
Patio
Hundido

Stela 9

Stela 18   GRAN PLAZA   Juego de Pelota

Sistema IV

Edificio G   Edificio II

Edificio H   Edificio P

Edificio de los Danzantes   Edificio I

Danzantes   El Adoratorio   Palacio

Sistema M   Edificio J   Montículo Q
(Observatorio)
GRAN PLAZA

Montículo Sur

Plataforma Sur

found, some of them elaborate and decorated with frescoes, though none of these are regularly open to visitors today.

Between about 700 and 950 (Monte Albán IV) the place was abandoned and fell into ruin. Phase Monte Albán V (950–1521) saw minimal activity, although Mixtecs arriving from northwestern Oaxaca reused some old tombs here to bury their own dignitaries – notably Tumba 7, where they placed a famous treasure hoards, now seen in the Museo de las Culturas de Oaxaca (p424).

⊙ Sights

Edificio de los Danzantes   NOTABLE BUILDING
This structure combines an early (Monte Albán I) building, which contained famous carvings known as Danzantes (Dancers), with a later structure that was built over it. There are a few original Danzantes in a short passage that you can enter, and copies of others along the wall outside. Carved between 500 and 100 BC, they depict naked

men, thought to be sacrificed leaders of conquered neighboring towns.

The Danzantes generally have thick-lipped open mouths (sometimes downturned in Olmec style) and closed eyes. Some have blood flowing where they have been disemboweled.

Plataforma Norte   VIEWPOINT
The North Platform is almost as big as the Gran Plaza, and affords the best views overall. It was rebuilt several times over the centuries. The 12 column bases at the top of the stairs were part of a roofed hall. On top of the platform is a ceremonial complex created between AD 500 and 800, which includes the **Patio Hundido** (Sunken Patio), with an altar at its center; **Edificios D**, **VG** and **E**, which were topped with adobe temples; and the **Templo de Dos Columnas**.

Edificio J   NOTABLE BUILDING
Arrowhead-shaped Building J, constructed about 100 BC and riddled with tunnels

and staircases (unfortunately you can't go inside), stands at an angle of 45 degrees to the other Gran Plaza structures and was an observatory. Astronomical observation enabled the ancients to track the seasons, calculate agricultural cycles and make prophesies. Figures and hieroglyphs carved on the building's walls record Monte Albán's military conquests.

Edificio P   NOTABLE BUILDING

Building P was topped by a small pillared temple and was probably an observatory of some sort. The sun shines directly down into a small opening near the top at the solar zenith passages (when the sun passes directly overhead at noon on May 5 and August 8).

Plataforma Sur   VIEWPOINT

The 40m-high South Platform, with its wide staircase, is the tallest in Monte Albán and is great for a panorama of the plaza and the surrounding mountains. Unlike some Mexican ruins, you are allowed to climb to the top of the structure.

Juego de Pelota   ARCHAEOLOGICAL SITE

The stone terraces of the deep Ball Court, constructed about 100 BC, were probably part of the playing area, not seats for spectators. It's thought they were covered with a thick coating of lime, meaning the ball would roll down them.

Gran Plaza   PLAZA

About 300m long and 200m wide, the Gran Plaza is the heart of Monte Albán. Some of its structures were temples; others were elite residential quarters. Many of them are now cordoned off to prevent damage by visitors' feet.

Tours

Official guides offer their services outside the ticket office (around M$250 for a small group). Alternatively, numerous companies in central Oaxaca offer Monte Albán as a half-day trip from around M$350 covering guide, transportation and entrance fees.

Getting There & Away

It's easy to get to Monte Albán from Oaxaca either independently or as part of an organized trip. **Autobuses Turísticos** (951-516-61-75; Mina 501, Oaxaca) has bus departures hourly (half-hourly on Saturday and Sunday) from 8:30am to 3:30pm, starting back from the site between noon and 5pm. The cost is M$55 round-

trip. Buses stop two blocks west of Mercado 20 de Noviembre.

Valle de Tlacolula

The Valle de Tlacolula, east of Oaxaca, has the Valles Centrales' most condensed booty of sights – it's home to two pre-Hispanic sites (Mitla and Yagul) and an even more ancient tree. Craft-wise, this is where you come for your weaving (cloths and rugs abound) and artisan mezcal (there are numerous distilleries) The cherry on the top is the glorious infinity pools and petrified waterfalls at Hierve el Agua.

Getting There & Away

El Tule, Teotitlán del Valle, Tlacolula and Yagul are all close to the Oaxaca–Mitla road, Hwy 190. Buses to Mitla (M$21, 1¼ hours) leave about every hour from Oaxaca's 2nd-class bus station and will drop you anywhere along this road.

Alternatively, you can catch taxis colectivos direct to El Tule (M$13, 15 minutes), Teotitlán (M$18, 30 minutes), Tlacolula (M$20, 40 minutes) or Mitla (M$25, one hour) from the corner of Hwy 190 and Derechos Humanos, 500m east of Oaxaca's 1st-class bus station, immediately past the baseball stadium.

Sights

El Rey del Matatlán   DISTILLERY

(951-516-23-46; Hwy 190 Km 265; 8am-8pm) FREE A popular place to taste and buy artisan mezcal right next to the fields where they grow the agave. Granted, it's a hot spot on the tour bus circuit (if you're on a tour you'll probably stop here), but the smoky-flavored mezcal is authentic and the terracotta-shaded hacienda with its bar, mill, traditional ovens and fermentation plant is more rustic than industrial. Free explanations of the mezcal-making process are given throughout the day. Afterward you can get tipsy tasting it.

Yagul Ruins   ARCHAEOLOGICAL SITE

(M$65; 8am-5pm; P) If you want photos of Zapotec ruins without tonnes of tourists milling around in the background, Yagul is your kind of place. The ruins (known as 'Pueblo Viejo' by locals) are finely sited on a cactus-covered hill, about 1.5km north of the Oaxaca–Mitla road, 34km from Oaxaca. Unless you have a vehicle, you'll have to walk the 1.5km; caution is advised on this isolated road.

Valles Centrales & Pueblos Mancomunados

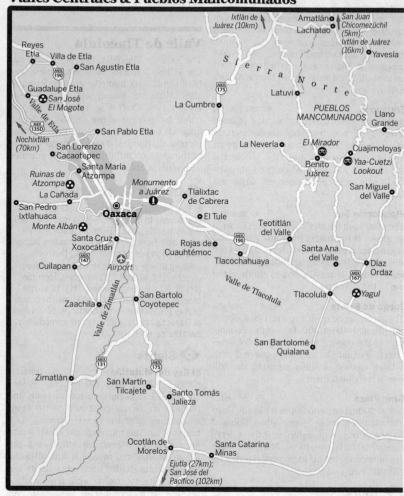

Prehistoric Caves of Yagul & Mitla   CAVE

Approaching Yagul from the main road, you can make out a large white rock painting of a person/deity/tree/sun on a cliff face on the **Caballito Blanco** rock outcrop to your right. This is the most obvious feature of the Unesco World Heritage site, the Prehistoric Caves of Yagul and Mitla, which stretches about 6km east from here. Caves here have yielded evidence of the earliest plant domestication in North America, about 10,000 years ago, and other valuable details about the transition from hunting and gathering to agriculture over a period of several thousand years.

The Unesco-protected caves are difficult to visit independently. Your best bet is to hook up with Tierraventura (p430) on a day-tour to the important Guilá Naquitz cave (M$1100). The trip includes a three-hour hike.

El Tule

🎵 951 / POP 7600 / ELEV 1550M

El Tule, 10km east of Oaxaca along Hwy 190, draws crowds of visitors for one very good reason: El Árbol del Tule, a huge tree reckoned to be as old as the Monte Albán ruins. The tree anchors a pleasant

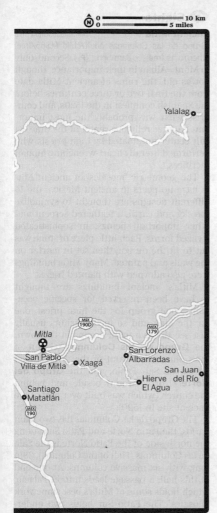

0 / 10 km
0 / 5 miles

Yalalag

MEX 190D
MEX 179

Mitla
San Pablo
Villa de Mitla · Xaagá
Santiago
Matatlán
MEX 190

San Lorenzo
Albarradas
San Juan
Hierve del Río
El Agua

cypress), 42m high, dwarfs the pretty 17th-century village church in whose churchyard it towers.

The tree is reckoned to be over 2000 years old, which means it was already growing when the ancient city of Monte Albán was in its infancy. Much revered by Oaxacans, the Árbol del Tule appears to be healthy, though there are potential threats to it from local urban growth and irrigated agriculture, which tap its water sources.

✗ Eating

Casa Embajador   OAXACAN **$$$**
(Unión 1; mains M$250; ⊘9am-6pm) A new *parador turistico* favored by passing tour groups, the Embajador is also a distillery making its own mezcal. Order lunch and you'll usually get a complimentary glass. The meat-heavy and shareable Botana Oaxaqueña is recommended (with cheese, chorizo, grilled beef and much more). The large restaurant is housed under a thatched *palapa* with an elegant fountain, gardens and even a chapel.

Teotitlán del Valle

☏ 951 / POP 4400 / ELEV 1700M

A famous weaving village, located about 25km southeast of Oaxaca, Teotitlán has been renowned for its weaving wares since pre-Hispanic times: the village had to pay tributes of cloth to the Aztecs. Quality today is high, and traditional dyes made from natural sources like indigo, cochineal and moss have been revived (though some weavers still use much cheaper synthetic dyes). The variety of designs is enormous – from Zapotec gods and Mitla-style geometric patterns to imitations of paintings by Rivera and Picasso.

Many tour groups only get as far as the larger weaving showrooms on the road approaching the village, which tend to dominate the craft here by buying up weavers' products or employing weavers directly to weave for them. For more direct interaction, head on into the village itself, where blankets and rugs wave at you from houses and workshops along the streets.

◉ Sights

**Iglesia Preciosa
Sangre de Cristo**   CHURCH
(⊘6am-6pm) From the plaza, steps rise to this handsome 17th-century church with a fine broad churchyard and colorful

little Mexican town complete with church, square and market that contrasts with the more urban scene of the big city nearby.

◉ Sights

El Árbol del Tule   LANDMARK
(Tree of El Tule; M$10; ⊘8am-8pm) Visitors flock to the village of El Tule to behold El Árbol del Tule, which is, by some counts, the fattest tree in the world. California's General Sherman sequoia is ahead in total volume, but at 14m in diameter, El Árbol del Tule certainly has the world's widest trunk. This vast *ahuehuete* (Montezuma

18th-century frescoes inside. It was built atop a Zapotec ceremonial site, many of the carved stones of which can be seen in the church walls; look especially in the inner patio.

Courses

El Sabor Zapoteco   COOKING
(☑ 951-524-46-58; www.cookingclasseselsaborzapoteco.blogspot.com; Juárez 30; per person US$75) These classes, preparing traditional village dishes by traditional methods, are given by Reyna Mendoza in her open-air kitchen. Classes are normally held on Tuesday and Friday mornings (Teotitlán's main market days; two-way transportation included). Their pickup point in Oaxaca is outside the Jardín Etnobotánico (p425).

Tlacolula

POP 14,000 / ELEV 1650M

Tlacolula, 31km from Oaxaca, holds one of the Valles Centrales' biggest markets every Sunday, with the area around the church becoming a packed throng. Crafts, foods and plenty of everyday goods are on sale. It's a treat for lovers of market atmosphere – and market food. The Templo de la Asunción with its florid side-chapel is another persuasive reason to visit.

Sights

Templo de la Asunción   CHURCH
(Av 2 de Abril; ◷ 8am-6pm) Tlacolula's main church is notable for its ornate baroque side-chapel, known colloquially as the Capilla de la Plata (Silver Chapel), a dazzling riot of indigenous-influenced decoration comparable to the Capilla del Rosario in Oaxaca's Santo Domingo (p424). Among the ceiling ornamentation, spot the plaster martyrs holding their own severed heads and the playful angels clutching various musical instruments.

San Pablo Villa de Mitla

☑ 951 / POP 8200 / ELEV 1700M

The small town of San Pablo Villa de Mitla, 46km southeast of Oaxaca, is famous for the ruins of Ancient Mitla replete with unique stone 'mosaics' that stand today in the midst of a modern Zapotec settlement.

The town is also a hive of craft shops peddling embroidery, and liquor stores selling powerful locally made mezcal.

Sights

Ancient Mitla   ARCHAEOLOGICAL SITE
(Grupo de las Columnas adult/child M$65/free, other ruins free; ◷ 8am-5pm; P) Second only to Monte Albán in their importance, though not as old, the ruins of ancient Mitla date from the final two or three centuries before the Spanish conquest in the 1520s, and comprise what was probably the most important Zapotec religious center at the time – a cult center dominated by high priests who performed literally heart-wrenching human sacrifices.

The geometric 'mosaics' of ancient Mitla have no peers in ancient Mexico: the 14 different designs are thought to symbolize the sky and earth, a feathered serpent and other important beings, in sophisticated stylized forms. Each little piece of stone was cut to fit the design, then set in mortar on the walls and painted. Many Mitla buildings were also adorned with painted friezes.

Mitla's ancient buildings are thought to have been reserved for specific occupants: one group for the high priest, one for the king and so forth. Visitors usually just see the two main groups in the town: the **Grupo de las Columnas** (Group of the Columns) in front of the three-domed Iglesia de San Pablo, and the **Grupo del Norte** (North Group) beside and behind the church (which was built over part of the ancient site in 1590).

The Grupo de las Columnas has two main patios, the Patio Norte and Patio Sur. Along the north side of the Patio Norte is the Sala de las Columnas (Hall of the Columns), 38m long with six square columns. At one end of this hall, a passage leads into El Palacio, which holds some of Mitla's best stonework 'mosaics'. The Patio Sur holds two underground tombs.

The remains of other structures are scattered around the town and for many kilometers around.

If you're coming by public transportation, ask to disembark at the fork known as La Cuchilla as you enter Mitla. From here it's 1.2km north to the Iglesia de San Pablo and the ticket office for the Grupo de las Columnas.

Sleeping & Eating

Hotel Don Cenobio   HOTEL $$
(☑ 951-568-03-30; www.hoteldoncenobio.com; Av Juárez 3; r M$830-1050; P ✿ ⛄) Set on the central plaza, this is easily Mitla's best hotel, its

23 comfortable rooms sporting multicolored carved furnishings from Guadalajara. In and around the grassy central garden are a swimming pool, bar and the hotel's restaurant (open 8am to 6:30pm), serving Oaxacan fare.

Restaurante Doña Chica OAXACAN $
(☑951-568-06-83; Av Morelos 41; mains M$75-100; ☺7am-7pm) If you're hungry after viewing the Mitla ruins, fret not. Bright Doña Chica serves delicious Oaxacan dishes like *moles*, enchiladas and *tasajo* (thin grilled slices of beef) from an open kitchen. Good soups, *antojitos* (Mexican snacks), salads and desserts round out the menu – and your stomach.

Hierve El Agua

ELEV 1800M

Hierve El Agua consists of a series of spectacularly sited mineral springs and rock formations 65km southeast of Oaxaca and 35km beyond Tlacolula. It's a popular outing for *oaxaqueños* (people from Oaxaca) on their days off and a good place to end a trip to the Valle de Tlacolula when the sun starts to dip.

◎ Sights

★ Mineral Springs POOL, LOOKOUT
(M$25; ☺7:30am-7:30pm; ℗) Natural hot tubs have never looked this good. Set in truly ethereal surroundings amid low brush-covered mountains, Hierve El Agua (meaning 'the water boils) is a set of bubbling mineral springs that run into natural infinity pools right on a cliff's edge with spectacular panoramas over the sierra. The act of the water dribbling over the cliff edge for millennia has created unique white mineral formations that resemble huge frozen waterfalls.

There are two ghostly 'waterfalls' at the site. The 'cascada chica' is the one nearer the visitor car park and supports four popular mineral pools (the one nearest to the lip of the cliff is manmade). From here you get perfect views of the more impressive 'cascada grande.' To get to the second 'waterfall' follow the trail for 1km to its end, where you can enjoy a much quieter more natural spot (with few bathers).

The mineral-laden water is actually cool to cold, though usually swimmable. Altogether it's an utterly unique bathing experience and stunningly beautiful to boot.

There are changing rooms just above the pools.

Unofficial roadblocks – the result of a local feud – sometimes spring up close to the springs and charge you an extra M$10 to enter.

❶ Getting There & Away

Hierve El Agua is on the itinerary of day tours from Oaxaca, and there's public transportation by the *camionetas* (pickup trucks) of Transportes Zapotecos del Valle Oriente (M$50 one way) from La Cuchilla in Mitla. They leave when they have enough passengers.

If you're driving, 'Hierve El Agua' signs approaching Mitla will lead you on to the new Hwy 190D toll road, which bypasses Mitla: you turn off (signposted to Hierve El Agua) after 19km then go another 7km (unpaved for the last 4km). Alternatively, drive through Mitla and follow the older Hwy 179, which more or less parallels the toll road; the signed turnoff to Hierve El Agua comes up 18km from Mitla.

Valle de Zimatlán

South from Oaxaca, Hwy 175 goes through San Bartolo Coyotepec, famed for its black pottery; Ocotlán, with one of the Valles Centrales' busiest weekly markets; and – much further on – San José del Pacífico, famed for its magic mushrooms, en route to Pochutla near the coast. The less busy Hwy 147 goes to Cuilapan just west of Oaxaca Airport.

Cuilapan

☑951 / POP 12,000 / ELEV 1560M

Cuilapan (Cuilápam), 9km southwest of Oaxaca, is one of the few Mixtec towns in the Valles Centrales. It's the site of a historic Dominican monastery, the Ex Convento Dominicano, most people's primary reason for visiting.

◎ Sights

Ex Convento Dominicano MONASTERY
(cloister M$40; ☺9am-6pm; ℗) Standing by the highway in dusty Cuilapan, the Ex Convento Dominicano (aka Santiago Apóstol) with its pale 'green' stone walls seems almost to grow out of the land. With half the building missing a roof, one's immediate conclusion is that it's just another ruin. On the contrary, the building was never actually finished. Work on the long low church in front of the monastery with its stately

arches and detailed stone carving stopped in 1560 due to financial disputes.

Behind is the church that succeeded it, which contains the tomb of Juana Donají (daughter of Cosijoeza, the last Zapotec king of Zaachila) and is normally open only for Mass (noon and 5pm Saturday and Sunday). Adjoining the church is a two-story Renaissance-style cloister. A painting of Mexican independence hero Vicente Guerrero hangs in the small room where he was held in 1831 before being executed by soldiers supporting the rebel conservative Anastasio Bustamante. Outside, a monument marks the spot where he was shot.

Aside from its roofless church and Guerrero associations, the convent is notable for its Moorish architectural influences and faded murals that incorporate some unusual indigenous themes.

ⓘ Getting There & Away

Zaachila Yoo (Bustamante 601, Oaxaca) runs buses from Oaxaca to Cuilapan (M$7, 45 minutes) about every 15 minutes.

San Bartolo Coyotepec

✎ 951 / POP 4000 / ELEV 1550M

Barro negro, the polished, surprisingly light, black pottery (candlesticks, jugs and vases, and decorative animal and bird figures) that you find in hundreds of forms around Oaxaca, comes from San Bartolo Coyotepec, 11km south of the city. For the original source, head to Alfarería Doña Rosa, a short walk east off the highway.

◉ Sights

Alfarería Doña Rosa   HANDICRAFTS
(✆ 951-551-00-11; Juárez 24; ⊙ 9am-7pm; ℗) It was doña Rosa Real Mateo (1900–80) who invented the method of burnishing the barro negro with quartz stones for the distinctive shine. Her family alfarería (potters' workshop) is now the biggest in the village, and they will demonstrate the process to anyone who asks. The pieces are hand-molded by an age-old technique that uses two saucers functioning as a rudimentary potter's wheel. They are fired in pit kilns and turn black from smoke and from the iron oxide in the clay.

The workshop doubles up as a shop and is also something of a museum. It's well worth visiting, even if you have no intention of buying.

Museo Estatal de Arte Popular de Oaxaca   MUSEUM
(✆ 951-551-00-36; Independencia; adult/child M$20/free; ⊙ 10am-6pm Tue-Sun) Recently reborn with a bright pink facade, San Bartolo's excellent, modern, folk-art museum is on the south side of the main village plaza. It's very nicely done and features a collection of fine *barro negro* plus exhibits of quality folk art from around Oaxaca state.

ⓘ Getting There & Away

Autobuses Halcón (p444) runs buses from Oaxaca city to San Bartolo (M$10, 20 minutes) about every 10 minutes.

San Martín Tilcajete

✎ 951 / POP 1600 / ELEV 1540M

San Martín Tilcajete, 1km west of Hwy 175, 24km south of Oaxaca, is the source of many of the bright copal-wood *alebrijes* – those distinctive colorful wooden animal figures – seen in Oaxaca. Dozens of villagers carve them, and you can see and buy them in makers' houses, many of which have 'Alebrijes' or 'Artesanías de Madera' (Wooden Handicrafts) signs outside.

✖ Eating

Azucena Zapoteca   OAXACAN $$
(✆ 951-524-92-27; www.restauranteazucenazapoteca.com; Hwy 175 Km 23.5; mains M$80-160; ⊙ 8am-6pm; ☏) Good *alebrijes* and other crafts are displayed and sold at this popular lunch stop, serving good Oaxacan fare, beside Hwy 175 opposite the Tilcajete turnoff. The menu even advertises an Almuerzo Jacobo (steak and onions with bacon, egg and beans) named after the skilled local wood-carver.

🛍 Shopping

★ **Jacobo & María Ángeles**   ARTS & CRAFTS
(✆ 951-524-90-47; www.jacoboymariaangeles.com; Callejón del Olvido 9; ⊙ 8am-6pm) Jacobo and María Ángeles have been making particularly wonderful *alebrijes* for over two decades and now run a workshop providing employment for 100 villagers. Visitors get a free tour and see the incredibly detailed *alebrijes* being made. It's very labor-intensive. An average-sized piece takes up to a month to make.

Many of the figures made here are based on the sacred animals of Zapotec mythology. The best pieces sell for many thousands of pesos, and some huge and very detailed pieces can take up to four years to make. The couple's work can also be found in Voces de Copal, Aullidos del Alma (p442) in central Oaxaca.

ℹ Getting There & Away

Ocotlán-bound buses from Oaxaca will drop you at the turnoff to San Martín (M$20, 35 minutes). *Taxis colectivos* run from Ocotlán itself.

Ocotlán de Morelos

✔ 951 / POP 15,000 / ELEV 1500M

Ocotlán de Morelos is a town of fine art, esoteric pottery and a dense, industrious Friday market. The art is courtesy of homegrown artist Rodolfo Morales (1925–2001), who turned his international success to the area's benefit by setting up the Fundación Cultural Rodolfo Morales (www.fcrom.org. mx), which has done marvelous renovation work on local churches and promotes the area's arts, heritage, environment and social welfare.

The pottery was put on the international map by the Aguilar family, a quartet of talented sisters who pioneered a style of sculpture captured in unusually beautiful clay figurines reflecting religion, Frida Kahlo and Day of the Dead iconography.

Most visitors come to Ocotlán on Friday, when its big spirited covered market takes over the central plaza and its surroundings.

◉ Sights

**Ex Convento
de Santo Domingo**   MUSEUM
(M$15; ⊙9:30am-5:30pm) This rehabilitated former convent, previously a dilapidated jail, is now a first-class art museum and includes a room dedicated to the work of local magic realist artist, Rodolfo Morales. Morales was responsible for driving much of the restoration of the building which began in 1995. His ashes are interred here too.

After enjoying the art-fest, it's also worth perusing the adjacent church framed by a lovely avenue of slender trees.

🛍 Shopping

Guillermina Aguilar   HANDICRAFTS
(Morelos 430; ⊙10am-6pm Mon-Sat) Ocotlán's most renowned artisans are the four Aguilar sisters and their families, who create whimsical, colorful pottery figures of women with all sorts of unusual motifs. Their houses are together on the west side of the main road entering Ocotlán from the north, almost opposite the Hotel Real de Ocotlán.

Most renowned is Guillermina Aguilar, the eldest of the sisters, who turns out, among other things, miniature 3D recreations of Frida Kahlo works. The artisan pottery work was initially inspired by Guillermina's mother and the skill has since been carried through the generations to her grandchildren.

Mercado Morelos   MARKET
(Pueblos Unidos; ⊙6:30am-8pm) This covered market, on the south side of the central plaza opens daily. Food, clothes, pottery, textiles, mezcal, chickens, art and cheap junk – it's difficult to work out what it doesn't sell. On Fridays, the stalls are integrated into Ocotlán's massive weekly market that spills over several city blocks.

ℹ Getting There & Away

Automorsa (Bustamante 601, Oaxaca) runs buses (M$20) and vans (M$25) from Oaxaca to Ocotlán (45 minutes) about every 10 minutes from 6am to 9pm.

Zaachila

✔ 951 / POP 14,000

This part-Mixtec, part-Zapotec town 6km southeast of Cuilapan is an authentic place with a big, busy Thursday market known for its food stalls – expect a noisy melange of squawking chickens, buzzing three-wheeler taxis and gossiping locals. It was a Zapotec capital from AD 1400 until the Spanish conquest. Behind the village church overlooking the main plaza, a sign indicates the entrance to Zaachila's Zona Arqueológica, a relatively unexplored site where tourism has yet to disturb the tranquility.

◉ Sights

Zona Arqueológica   ARCHAEOLOGICAL SITE
(Archaeological Zone; adult/child M$40/free; ⊙9am-5pm) Ancient Zaachila, rather like Mitla, was a post-Classic Zapotec city that took root after the demise of Monte Albán. It was later conquered by the Mixtecs. The rough date of its establishment is sketchy, but it probably reached its apogee in the 1300s. The Zona Arqueológica sits behind the village church overlooking the main plaza and consists of a small assortment of mounds where you can enter two small tombs used by the ancient Mixtecs.

ⓘ Getting There & Away

Zaachila Yoo (p452) runs buses between Oaxaca and Zaachila (M$7, 40 minutes) about every 15 minutes. *Taxis colectivos* (M$12, 20 minutes) leave from the corner of Bustamante and Zaragoza in Oaxaca.

Valle de Etla

Etla (meaning land of beans) is a sub-valley of the Valle de Oaxaca and stretches about 40km to the northeast of the state capital. It has some recently excavated ruins and an inspirational factory-turned-arts center.

Santa María Atzompa

🖉 951 / POP 22,000 / ELEV 1600M

Perched 3km above the village Santa María Atzompa (and 6km from central Oaxaca), the hilltop archaeological site of Atzompa on the Cerro El Bonete is a fascinating complement to the larger, more famous, parent city of Monte Albán. Together with Santa María Atzompa village's museum and crafts market, it provides proof of the continuity of Atzompa's pottery-making expertise from pre-Hispanic times to the present day.

◉ Sights

Atzompa Ruins ARCHAEOLOGICAL SITE
(M$25; ⊙8am-4:30pm; P) If you like your pre-Hispanic Mexican ruins suitably 'ruined' and crowd-free without compromising on authenticity or spectacular setting, opt for Atzompa. The site gets a tiny fraction of Monte Albán's visitors (it's not unusual to have the place to yourself), meaning your imagination can run wild conjuring up images of Zapotecs in feathery attire playing the Mesoamerican ball game.

Only thoroughly excavated in the early 21st century and not opened to the public until 2012 (when the access road was built), Atzompa was a residential satellite city of nearby Monte Albán. It was probably established around AD 650 and abandoned 300 years later.

Three ceremonial plazas, several ball courts (including the largest in the Oaxaca area) and the remains of two large residences have been exposed to view. A specially intriguing feature is the reconstructed pottery-firing oven on the north side – identical to ovens still used by potters in modern Atzompa. Excavation at the site is ongoing.

Museo Comunitario MUSEUM
(Calle Independencia; M$10; ⊙10am-5pm) Two kilometers down the road from the ruins toward Santa María Atzompa, the Community Museum exhibits some very fine pieces of pottery found at the archeological site, including detailed effigies of nobility or deities and huge pots used for storing water, grain or seeds.

🛍 Shopping

Mercado de Artesanías ARTS & CRAFTS
(Crafts Market; Av Libertad 303; ⊙9am-7pm) The work of over 100 contemporary Atzompa potters is on sale in the Mercado de Artesanías: items range from animal figures and lampshades to pots, plates, cups and more – some bearing Atzompa's traditional green glaze, others in more colorful, innovative styles. Prices are reasonable, but much of the best work goes to shops in Oaxaca and elsewhere.

ⓘ Getting There & Away

Access to the ruins is by paved road, either 3km up from Santa María Atzompa village, or 2.5km up from La Cañada village on the road from Oaxaca to San Pedro Ixtlahuaca. From Monte Albán, vehicles can drive direct to La Cañada and the ruins without returning to Oaxaca. There's no public transportation to the site. Taxis charge about M$180 round-trip from Oaxaca or M$60 from Santa María Atzompa, from where some elect to walk uphill (3km) to the ruins.

Taxis colectivos and buses to Santa María Atzompa leave from Trujano on the north side of Oaxaca's 2nd-class bus station and cost from M$8 to M$10 for the 20-minute journey.

San Agustín Etla

🖉 951 / POP 3700 / ELEV 1800M

Pretty San Agustín sits on the Valle de Etla's eastern slopes, 18km northwest of Oaxaca and is notable for its arts center.

◉ Sights

Centro de las Artes
de San Agustín ARTS CENTER
(CaSa; 🖉951-521-25-74; www.casa.oaxaca.gob. mx; Independencia s/n, Barrio Vistahermosa; ⊙9am-8pm) FREE Pretty San Agustín's large, early-20th-century textile mill has been superbly restored as the Centro de las Artes de San Agustín (CaSa), a spectacular arts center with two long, large halls. The lower hall is used as a gallery for often wonderful craft or art exhibitions; the upper one

is a setting for concerts, conferences and other events. The center also hosts courses and workshops in a great variety of arts and crafts. Check the website for upcoming events and expos.

ⓘ Getting There & Away

The turnoff for San Agustín is on the east side of Hwy 190, 13.5km from central Oaxaca, marked by a tiny 'San Sebastián Etla' sign beside the large-ish Instituto Euro-Americano. It's 4km up to the village. *Taxis colectivos* to San Agustín (M$15, 30 minutes), from Trujano on the north side of Oaxaca's 2nd-class bus station, will take you to CaSa .

San José del Pacífico

◢ 951 / POP 370 / ELEV 2380M

High in the misty mountains that close off the south end of the Valles Centrales, 135km from Oaxaca, San José del Pacífico is chiefly renowned for one thing – the hallucinogenic mushroom *Psilocybe mexicana*. Though their consumption is officially illegal, these *hongos mágicos* (magic mushrooms) help to make San José quite a popular travelers' stop en route between Oaxaca city and the coast. There's a significant community of alternative lifestylers here and in nearby villages. Mushrooms or no mushrooms, San José has a touch of magic anyway and is a beautiful place to break a journey. When the clouds clear, the views over pristine forested ranges and valleys are fabulous. There are good walks, a handful of surprisingly good places to stay, and several places where you can take a temascal steam bath.

🛏 Sleeping & Eating

There are several cafes and small restaurants along the main road in the village, plus a few shops selling food.

La Puesta del Sol CABAÑAS $
(◢ 951-596-73-30; www.sanjosedelpacifico.com; Hwy 175 Km 131; r incl breakfast M$350-650; 🅿🛜) Just below the highway 500m north of town, La Puesta del Sol is usually considered to be San José's posh digs. The cozy, clean *cabañas* have marvelous panoramas. All except the cheapest have fireplaces.

Refugio Terraza de la Tierra BUNGALOW $$
(www.terrazadelatierra.com; Hwy 175 Km 128; r M$500-850, breakfast/dinner M$140/180; 🅿🛜)
🍃 A beautiful mountain retreat, Terraza de

la Tierra has six lovely big rooms in adobe, wood and tile bungalows around its large organic garden, on a 1.5-sq-km hillside property with over 20 waterfalls. Excellent vegetarian meals are served, and there are cute little glass meditation pyramids and a big-windowed yoga room. They offer cooking classes and yoga retreats. It's 300m off the highway, 3.5km north of town.

ⓘ Getting There & Away

San José sits on Hwy 175, the Oaxaca–Pochutla road, 33km south of Miahuatlán. All the frequent van services running between Oaxaca (M$95, three hours) and Pochutla (M$95, 3½ hours), Mazunte (M$130 or M$140, 4¼ hours) or Bahías de Huatulco (M$140, four hours) stop here.

SIERRA NORTE

The mountains separating the Valles Centrales from low-lying far northern Oaxaca are called the Sierra Juárez, and the more southerly parts of this range, rising from the north side of the Valle de Tlacolula, are known as the Sierra Norte. These beautiful, forested highlands are home to several successful community ecotourism ventures providing a wonderful opportunity to get out on foot, mountain bike or horseback into pristine landscapes. Over 400 bird species, 350 butterflies, all six Mexican wild cats and nearly 4000 plants have been recorded in the Sierra Norte. Be prepared for cool temperatures: in the higher, southern villages it can snow in winter. The wettest season is from late May to September; there's little rain from January to April.

Pueblos Mancomunados

The Pueblos Mancomunados (Commonwealth of Villages) is eight remote villages (Amatlán, Benito Juárez, Cuajimoloyas, La Nevería, Lachatao, Latuvi, Llano Grande and Yavesía) protected under the umbrella of a unique and foresighted ecotourism project. Communally they offer great wilderness escapes and an up-close communion with Zapotec village life. More than 100km of high-country trails run between the villages and to local beauty spots and places of interest, and you can easily enjoy several days exploring them. Elevations in these hills range from 2200m to over 3200m, and the landscapes, with canyons, caves, waterfalls and panoramic lookouts, are spectacular.

For centuries these villages have pooled the natural resources of their 290-sq-km territory, sharing profits from forestry and other enterprises. In recent years they have also turned to ecotourism to stave off economic difficulties. Currently 120 local people work in a tourist industry that attracts 17,000 annual visitors. Ninety percent of the money goes directly back into the communities.

🏃 Activities

Hiking

Over 100km of trails link the eight villages. You can spend one afternoon or up to four days wandering at will. If you're short on time, the 3½-hour walk between Benito Juárez and Cuajimoloyas on the **Needa-Naa-Lagashxi trail** includes a visit to **El Mirador**, a craning lookout tower perched high above the village; the **Piedra Larga**, a giant rock you can scramble up to for views of Pico Orizaba on a clear day; and a bouncy **suspension bridge** across a ravine.

Other good day walks include the **Ruta Loma de Cucharilla** from Cuajimoloyas to Latuvi (about six hours, nearly all downhill), and two ancient tracks leading on from Latuvi: the **Camino Real** to San Juan Chicomezúchil and Amatlán, and the beautiful **Latuvi–Lachatao canyon trail** passing through cloud forests festooned with bromeliads and hanging mosses (keep your eyes peeled for trogons on this route).

Using a basic map available from Expediciones Sierra Norte (p431), it is possible to hike on your own, but beware: signposting is sometimes lacking.

Cycling

Welcome to mountain-biking paradise. Cycling routes meander between all eight villages. Of note is the **Circuito Taurino Mecinas Ceballos**, a 30km circuit linking Benito Juárez, Latuvi and La Nevería. Another possibility is the **Ruta Ka-Yezzi-Daa-Vii,** a 28km (one way) ride between Cuajimoloyas and Lachatao. Beware of rough and steep sections. Reasonable bike-handling skills are essential.

Bike rental is available in Benito Juárez and Cuajimoloyas for M$120 for three hours (M$250 with a guide).

Horseback Riding

Horseback riding is an adventurous and highly satisfying way of exploring the Sierra Norte. Costs are M$235/350/465 per three/four/five hours. Horseback Mexico (p431) offers a seven-day trek between the villages for M$2490 including transportation from Oaxaca.

Zip-Lining

A spectacular 1km-long zip-line (M$235) starts on the slopes of 3200m-high Yaa-Cuetzi and carries you over the rooftops of the village of Cuajimoloyas at speeds reaching 65km/h. There's another shorter zip-line circuit (three cables) in Benito Juárez costing M$150 per person.

ℹ️ Getting There & Away

Benito Juárez is the nearest of the villages to Oaxaca City, 60km away by road heading northeast.

Check with Expediciones Sierra Norte (p431) in Oaxaca for current public-transportation details. It can also transport up to 14 people by van to any of the villages for M$2900 round-trip; reserve at least one day before.

THE SOUTHERN VILLAGES

The Sizsa bus line runs buses from Oaxaca's 2nd-class station (p444) to Cuajimoloyas (M$50, two hours) and Llano Grande (M$45, 2½ hours) leaving daily at 7am, 2pm and 4pm. For Benito Juárez get out at the Benito Juárez turnoff ('desviación de Benito Juárez'), 3km before Cuajimoloyas, and walk 3.5km west to Benito Juárez. From Benito Juárez, La Nevería is a 9km walk west, and Latuvi 10km north.

AMATLÁN & LACHATAO

A direct bus leaves the 2nd-class bus station (p444) in Oaxaca for Amatlán via Lachatao on Saturday at 2pm and Sunday at 5pm. It takes two hours (three on Sunday) and costs M$80.

You can also head to Ixtlán de Juárez on Hwy 175 (M$50, 1½ hours, 15 daily buses from Oaxaca's 1st-class bus station; p444), then take a *camioneta* to Amatlán (M$35, 45 minutes) or Lachatao (M$35, one hour) from beside the *escuela primaria* (primary school) in central Ixtlán at 7am, 11am and 3pm, Monday to Friday, or 11am on Saturday. *Colectivos* (shared taxis) follow the same route.

WESTERN OAXACA

Western Oaxaca is dramatic and mountainous, with a fairly sparse population and some thick forests as well as overfarmed and deforested areas. Along with adjoining parts of Puebla and Guerrero states, it is known as the Mixteca, for its Mixtec indigenous inhabitants. The region offers a chance to get well off the beaten track, enjoy hiking or biking in remote areas and see some outstanding colonial architecture. Guided trips are available from Oaxaca with operators such as Tierraventura (p430) and Bicicletas Pedro Martínez (p432).

Santiago Apoala

ELEVATION 2000M / POP 190

In the heart of Oaxaca's Mixtec region, this small, remote village is nestled in a green, Shangri-la–like valley flanked by cliffs. Though still little publicized, it is a lovely spot for hiking, biking and climbing. The village, which is small and rustic, practices a form of community tourism similar to that in the Pueblos Mancomunados.

In traditional Mixtec belief, this valley was the birthplace of humanity, and the scenery around Apoala is appropriately spectacular, with the 60m waterfall **Cascada Cola de la Serpiente**, the 400m-deep **Cañón Morelos** and a number of caves, ancient rock carvings and paintings among the highlights.

The easy way to get here is with an agency from Oaxaca – Tierraventura (p430) does a good two-day tour – but it's cheaper to make your own way and arrange things directly with the village's community-tourism unit, the **Unidad Ecoturística** (Ecotourism Unit; ☑ 55-5151-9154; cnr Pino Suárez & Independencia; ⊙ 8am-5pm) ☑.

🛏 Sleeping & Eating

Unidad Ecoturística Cabañas　　CABAÑAS $
(r/cabin M$200/450, mains M$45; P) ☑ Santiago Apoala's cozy *cabañas* are run by with the village's community-tourism unit, the Unidad Ecoturística. They have hot-water bathrooms and an appealing riverside location. There are also three rooms in a small 'hotel' known as the parador.

ℹ Getting There & Away

Santiago Apoala is 40km north of the town of Nochixtlán, by a rough, unpaved road that takes about two hours to drive. Nochixtlán is served by nine daily buses from Oaxaca's 1st-class bus station (M$64 to M$148, one to 1½ hours). Between Nochixtlán and Apoala, take a taxi or the not 100% reliable *camioneta* bus, which normally leaves Apoala for Nochixtlán at 8am on Wednesday, Saturday and Sunday (M$70, two hours), and starts back from Nochixtlán to Apoala at noon or 1pm the same day. Beware: the schedule is 'flexible.'

OAXACA COAST

Oaxaca's beautiful, little-developed Pacific coast is home to several varied, relaxed beach destinations, and a near-empty shoreline strung with long golden beaches and lagoons full of wildlife. Offshore are turtles (this is a major global sea-turtle nesting area), dolphins and whales, plus diving, snorkeling, sportfishing and some of North America's best surfing swells. In this tropical climate, the pace is never too hectic, the atmosphere is relaxed and the people are welcoming. Everywhere the scenery is spectacular and you're in direct touch with the elements wherever you go, from the half-hidden sandy beaches to the crashing surf to the forest-clad, river-threaded mountains rising just inland. No need to pack too many clothes!

The area spins on three mains hubs: the restrained resort zone of Huatulco, the

Puerto Escondido

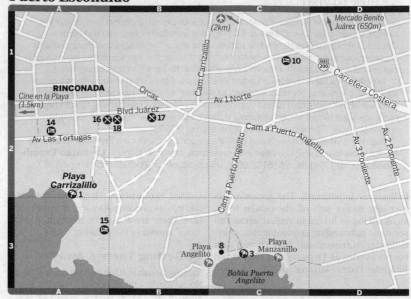

Puerto Escondido

loose federation of beach villages south of Pochutla (including nude-friendly Zipolite and yoga-practicing Mazunte) and the carefree surf town of Puerto Escondido.

Puerto Escondido

♩ 954 / POP 40,000

Is this where surfers go when they die? Many places claim to be the world's best surfing beach, but Puerto Escondido's Playa Zicatela – 3.5km of golden sand and crashing waves – would make most wave-riders' top tens. Even if you have no desire to test your balance as a 20ft wave curls over your head, Mexico's 'hidden port' is a highly desirable place, a small mellow town where Mexicans, expats and world travelers intermingle, and surfboards are as ubiquitous as cell phones.

While it's hardly undiscovered these days, PE remains pleasantly rough around the edges and, thanks to its spread-out nature, rarely feels urban. Plus there's more

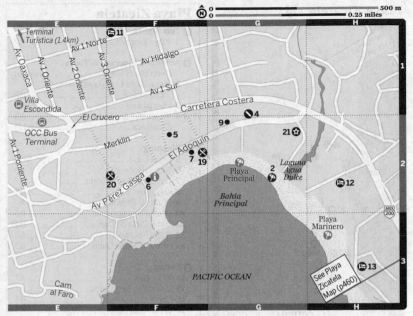

to do here than just ride white-knuckle on waves. Folks in tie-dye T-shirts stroll the sandy lanes of La Punta, master chefs have moved into residential Rinconada, while Playa Carrizalillo – the superstar of Mexico's beaches – is a gorgeous place to hang out, swim, and live vicariously as a surfer dude(ette).

◎ Sights

★ Playa Zicatela   BEACH
(Map p460; P) Legendary 3km-long Zicatela is the best-known surfing spot in Mexico courtesy the tempestuous surfing waves of the Mexican Pipeline. The heart of the action, including the Pipeline, is at Zicatela's northern end. Nonsurfers beware: the waters here have a lethal undertow and are not safe for the boardless, or beginner surfers either. Lifeguards rescue several careless people most months. Surfing aside, the beach is a beauty: wide, golden and gloriously laid-back – man!

The main beach area is backed by **Calle del Morro**, a kind of gringo-ville meets Mexican beach town where locals, along with dudes and dudettes from colder climes, mix seamlessly.

The **Punta Zicatela** area at Zicatela's far southern end has mellower surf and a mellower vibe to go with it. With its unpaved roads overlooked by vegan cafes and yoga retreats, it's favored chiefly by backpackers and beginner surfers.

★ Playa Carrizalillo   BEACH
(Map p458) Small is beautiful at Carrizalillo, set in a sheltered cove west of the center that's reached by a stairway of 157 steps. It's popular for swimming and bodyboarding, and is *the* place for beginner surfers. Book a lesson and you'll probably end up here making a splash or three 50m offshore. There's a mellow line of *palapa* (thatch-roofed) beach bars when you finish.

Bahía Puerto Angelito   BEACH
(Map p458) The sheltered bay of Puerto Angelito has two smallish beaches with shallow, usually calm waters: the western **Playa Angelito** and the eastern **Playa Manzanillo**. Both have lots of seafood *comedores* and are very popular with Mexican families at weekends and on holidays. Manzanillo has the more relaxed vibe. You can rent snorkels for around M$85 for 1½ hours.

Bahía Principal   BEACH
(Map p458) Puerto Escondido's central bay is long enough to accommodate restaurants at

its west end, a fleet of fishing boats in its center (Playa Principal), and sun worshippers and young bodyboarders at its east end (Playa Marinero), where the waters are a little cleaner. Pelicans wing in centimeters above the waves, boats bob on the swell and a few hawkers prowl up and down with a low-key sales pitch.

🏃 Activities

Diving & Snorkeling

Typical visibility is around 10m, rising to as much as 30m between May and August, when the seas are warmest. The reefs are of volcanic rock, with lots of marine life, including big schools of fish, spotted eagle rays, stingrays and turtles. Most dive sites are within a 15-minute boat ride. Both Puerto's dive outfits offer snorkeling and marine-life-spotting trips as well as dives for certified divers and a variety of courses.

Aventura Submarina
DIVING

(Map p458; ☑ cell 954-5444862; Av Pérez Gasga 609; ⊙ 9am-2pm & 6-9pm) Professional Association of Diving Instructors (PADI) instructor Jorge Pérez Bravo has three decades' experience diving local waters, and offers two-tank dives for M$1400, plus a range of diving courses and snorkeling trips.

Deep Blue Dive
DIVING, SNORKELING

(Map p460; ☑ cell 954-1003071; www.deepblue divemexico.com; Beach Hotel Inés, Calle del Morro, Zicatela; ⊙ 9am-2pm & 5:30-8pm) This professional, European-run outfit with PADI Dive Master guides does one-tank, two-tank and night dives for certified divers (US$40, US$70 and US$50 respectively), one-morning Discover Scuba sessions (US$65) and a range of PADI diving courses. One-hour snorkeling outings are US$25 per person.

Fishing

Local fishers will take two to four people fishing for marlin, sailfish, tuna or smaller inshore fish: a four-hour trip costs around M$4000 for up to four people. Contact **Omar's Sportfishing** (Map p458; ☑ cell 954-5594406; www.omarsportfishing.com; Playa Angelito). Catch-and-release is encouraged, but boat owners can also arrange for some of the catch to be cooked for you at one of the town's seafood restaurants.

Surfing

Puerto Escondido has surfable waves most days of the year. The Zicatela **Pipeline** is one of the world's heaviest and scariest beach breaks; it's normally best with the offshore winds in the morning and late afternoon, and at its biggest between about May and August. Even when the Pipeline is flat, the point break at **Punta Zicatela** works almost day in, day out. **Playa Carrizalillo** has good beginners' waves. Several professional surf contests are held annually at Zicatela: dates depend partly on swell forecasts, but there's always an event during the November fiestas. In 2015 the World Surf League's Big Wave Tour came to Zicatela for the first time.

Long- or shortboard rental is typically M$130 to M$150 per day; bodyboards are normally M$80 to M$100. You can buy secondhand boards for between M$1800 and M$5000 at several surf shops on Zicatela.

Numerous surf shops, schools and individuals at Zicatela, Punta Zicatela and Rinconada offer surfing lessons. Lessons normally last 1½ to two hours in the water, with prices including board use and transportation to wherever the waves are most suitable (often Carrizalillo).

Puerto Surf
SURFING

(Map p460; ☑ 954-122-01-72, cell 954-1096406; www.puertosurf.com.mx; Nuevo León, Punta Zicatela) Run by the amiable David Salinas, the youngest of six well-known Puerto surfer brothers, Puerto Surf offers good five-day surf courses (group/private M$2000/2800). Shorter courses or single classes (group/private M$480/650) are also available, and they have a comfortable five-room guesthouse in La Punta.

Zicazteca
SURFING

(Map p460; ☑ cell 954-1105853; www.zicazteca. com; Hotel Rockaway, Calle del Morro, Zicatela; group/private class per person M$500/700; ⊙ 7am-7pm) A relatively young surf school gaining good reports for its teaching and friendly, enthusiastic instructors. Run out of a surfing shop outside the Rockaway Hotel on Playa Zicatela.

Courses

Experiencia
LANGUAGE

(Map p458; ☑ 954-582-18-18; www.spanishpuerto. com; Andador Revolución 21; programs per week incl activities US$173-529, registration US$60, textbooks each US$20) Experiencia has a reputation for professionalism and a good atmosphere, and combines language learning with activities, excursions and volunteer projects (including turtles). Tuition is in small groups or one-to-one, and programs range from 10 to 40 classes per week, with all levels catered for. The Spanish-surfing package is popular (try conjugating the subjunctive tense while trying to stand up on a surfboard).

Instituto de Lenguajes
Puerto Escondido
LANGUAGE

(Map p460; ☑ 954-582-20-55; www.puerto-school.com; Carretera Costera, Zicatela; small-group/private classes per person per hour US$8/12) This small, student-centered school emphasizes both spoken and written Spanish and receives good reports for teaching quality. Excursions and activities including surfing, salsa and t'ai chi are available at extra cost. It's set in tropical gardens overlooking Zicatela beach, with wi-fi and student bungalows available on site. You can start any day, at any level, and study for as long as you like.

Tours

★ Gina's Tours

CULTURAL, HISTORICAL

(Map p458; ☑ 954-582-02-76, 954-582-11-86; https://ginainpuertoescondido.wordpress.com; Tourist Information Kiosk, Av Pérez Gasga) Gina Machorro, Puerto's energetic and knowledgable tourist information officer, leads a variety of personally guided tours including popular Saturday-morning visits to the Mercado Benito Juárez (p466) with an introduction to local history, food and religion (M$350 per person; two hours).

She also arranges cooking classes at a local cook's home (M$1500 and you take your lunch home to eat), and leads trips to Playa Escobilla (p465) to observe nesting turtles, and to **Tututepec** village, an ancient indigenous Mixtec capital west of Puerto Escondido, which has ruins, Mixtec *artesanías* (handicrafts) and a good little archaeological museum. Tututepec trips cost M$700 per person (minimum five), including lunch and a 20-minute local dance and music performance.

★ Lalo Ecotours

BIRDWATCHING

(Map p458; ☑ 954-582-16-11, cell 954-5889164; www.lalo-ecotours.com; Av Pérez Gasga; ☺ office 10am-6pm) 🐦 Lalo's is run by an experienced local bird guide who lives right next to the Laguna Manialtepec. *Lancha* (motorboat) trips cost M$700 per person including pickups from Puerto Escondido. A night tour to observe the bioluminescense is M$300. There are also trips to turtle-release beaches and coffee plantations.

Campamento Tortuguero Palmarito

WILDLIFE

(🐦) 🐦 A few kilometers west of Puerto Escondido, the Palmarito sea-turtle camp collects tens of thousands of new-laid turtle eggs each year, and reburies them in a fenced enclosure to protect them from human and animal predators. When the baby turtles hatch after about six weeks, visitors can help release them into the sea (donations welcome).

Lalo Ecotours and other agencies take groups from town to participate for around M$300 per person: look for 'Liberación de Tortugas' signs. The camp is down a track off Hwy 200 just after the Km 134 marker, 3km past the airport.

La Puesta del Sol

BIRDWATCHING

(☑ cell 954-1328294, cell 954-5889055; www. facebook.com/lapuestamanialtepec; Hwy 200 Km 124; ☺ restaurant 9am-6pm; 🐦) This pretty, family-run, lakeside restaurant, just off Hwy 200 about 2.5km from the eastern end of Laguna Manialtepec, is a good base if you're getting to Manialtepec under your own steam. It serves excellent food (breakfast dishes M$40 to M$65, mains M$80 to M$140), and does bird-watching boat trips for M$1200 (four to six people) or M$1000 (two or three people).

Viajes Dimar

TOURS

(Map p458; ☑ 954-582-02-59; www.viajesdimar. com; Av Pérez Gasga 905; ☺ 9am-9pm Mon-Sat, to 5pm Sun) Long-established and reliable Dimar offers a good range of day and half-day trips to Manialtepec, Chacahua, waterfalls, hot springs and other places of interest in the area, with English-speaking guides, for M$400 to M$800 per person (minimum four people). There's also a **Zicatela branch** (Map p460; ☑ 954-582-23-05; www.viajesdimar. com; Calle del Morro s/n, Zicatela; ☺ 9am-9pm Mon-Sat, to 5pm Sun).

★ Festivals & Events

Fiestas de Noviembre

CULTURAL, SPORTS

(☺ Nov) Puerto buzzes throughout November with many events and festivities, including the Festival Costeño de la Danza (folk dance), an international sportfishing tournament (www.pescapuertoescondido. com), surfing and motocross contests, and plenty more.

Sleeping

Accommodations are scattered from the Rinconada and Bacocho areas in the west of town to the central Adoquín area and out to the southeast along Playa Zicatela.

During the Christmas–New Year and Easter vacations, prices can double or even more, but in the low season many rates drop dramatically. It's worth reserving ahead in the busy seasons.

★ Hotel Casa de Dan

HOTEL $

(Map p460; ☑ 954-582-27-60; www.hotelcasa-dan.com; Jacarandas 14, Colonia Santa María; r M$400-890; 🅿 ❄ 🐦 🐦) Run by an expat Canadian, these magnificent hacienda-style accommodations just back from Zicatela beach are head and shoulders above much of the opposition. The 15 individualistic suites have all the usual bells and whistles

WORTH A TRIP

LAGUNA MANIALTEPEC

The 6km-long Manialtepec Lagoon, beginning 14km west of Puerto Escondido along Hwy 200, is an essential spot for bird enthusiasts and a fascinating place for anyone interested in nature. Ibises, roseate spoonbills, parrots, pelicans, falcons, ospreys, herons, kingfishers and several types of hawk and iguana call Manialtepec home for at least part of the year. The best bird-watching months are December to March, and the best time of day is soon after dawn.

The lagoon is mainly surrounded by mangroves, but tropical flowers and palms accent the ocean side, and the channel at the west end winds through to a pristine sandbar beach.

Several operators run three-hour bird-spotting trips in motorized *lanchas* (outboard boats), with English-speaking guides, binoculars and round-trip transportation from your accommodations in Puerto Escondido. Manialtepec is also a bioluminescent bay where phosphorescent plankton appear for a few nights several times a year. At these times nocturnal boat trips are offered, and you can swim or trail your hand in the water to activate the strange phosphorescent glow. July, August, November and December are often good months for this. Don't bother going when there's a full moon or after heavy rain.

From Puerto Escondido, take a *taxi colectivo* (shared taxi) bound for San José Manialtepec from Av 4 Poniente (M$20 to La Puesta del Sol, 15 minutes), running from about 6am to 8pm, or a Río Grande–bound minibus (M$20) from Av Hidalgo 5, leaving about every 20 minutes from 4am to 8pm.

(comfortable beds, large bathrooms and plenty of Mexican craft touches), but with a few notable extras.

Here you can enjoy a proper lap pool, a veritable library of books, a deluxe affiliated cafe and the charming presence of Dan himself (and/or his excellent staff). And it all comes at a highly reasonable price. Book ahead; it's understandably popular.

Hostal One Love
HOTEL, HOSTEL **$**

(Map p460; ☑cell 954-1298582; www.hostal puertoescondido.com; Tamaulipas s/n, Brisas de Zicatela; r from M$590; ☎) The big dilemma at One Love is whether to stay in the John Lennon room or the Jim Morrison suite or, if you're feeling a little more bluesy, the *habitación de* Janis Joplin. Classier than many of the hippie joints in La Punta, One Love is a high-walled wonderfully private domain packed with lush ferns and music legends.

The circular rooms are decorated with art and photos of the peace-loving rock heroes they are named after and are exceedingly comfortable. Bonus: there's an excellent restaurant (p466) on site that generously accepts nonguests.

Hotel Arena Surf
HOTEL **$**

(Map p458; ☑954-582-2743; 1 Norte, btwn Avs 3 & 4 Oriente; r M$300; ☎) Many of the hotels in the center of Puerto Escondido are fly-blown places and rather unappealing, but not this little hotel overseen by a friendly family who also run a shop out front. Rooms are simple but big enough to store a surfboard, plus there's a welcome water cooler, hot-ish showers and wi-fi that works.

Hostel Losodeli
HOSTEL **$**

(Map p458; ☑954-582-42-21; www.casalosodeli. com; Prolongación 2a Norte; dm M$180, r M$450-700; P🅿✳🛜🏊) Popular, well-run Losodeli, located between the bus stations and Rinconada, provides most things a budget traveler needs: clean accommodations with a choice between bunk dorms and private rooms (some very spacious), friendly staff, a well-equipped, well-organized kitchen, a good pool in the central garden, an eating area with bar service, breakfast available (M$35) and bookings for many outings and activities.

Aqua Luna
HOTEL **$**

(Map p460; ☑954-582-15-05; www.hotelaqualuna. com; Vista Hermosa s/n, Colonia Santa María; s/d/apt M$360/420/1000; ✳🛜🏊) In contrast to the beach shacks often beloved by surfers, Aqua Luna offers cool, contemporary black-and-white minimalism with a few nods to Mexican style (a poolside *palapa* and a panoramic deck with a hot tub). The brainchild of an Aussie surfer, it still attracts plenty of boarders thanks to excellent-value rooms, many with kitchens. All-day breakfasts and light dishes are served at the poolside bar.

Frutas y Verduras
CABAÑAS, ROOMS $

(Map p460; ☑cell 954-1230473; www.frutasy verdurasmexico.com; Cárdenas s/n, Punta Zicatela; s/d without bathroom M$400/600; 🔊🐾) 'Fruit & Veg' might sound like a strange name for a hotel, but this is the surfer-hippie enclave of La Punta where being weird is considered relatively normal. Gelling eloquently with the rustic jungley feel of the 'hood, this place sports tiny simple *cabañas* with mosquito nets, highly colorful screened rooms, and one apartment – all with decent shared bathrooms and kitchen.

Surprise: there's a small pool, an inviting restaurant called Café Olé, surfboards for rent and free bicycles.

Cabañas Buena Onda
HOSTEL $

(Map p460; ☑954-582-16-63; buenaondazica tela@live.com; Cárdenas 777, Punta Zicatela; camping/hammock/dm per person M$100/100/150, cabañas M$350; 🔊) Busy but relaxed Buena Onda, set in a shady palm grove with a beachfront *palapa* hangout area, can seem like surfer dude central station. It is also one of the few Zicatela joints that is actually ON the beach. The 10 rustic *cabañas* are clean and equipped with mosquito nets, fans and hammocks, and there are adequate bathrooms and kitchen.

Casamar
SUITES $$

(Map p460; ☑954-582-25-93; www.casamar suites.com; Puebla 407, Brisas de Zicatela; r US$56-147; 🅿❄🔊🐾) North American-owned Casamar is a luxurious, comfortable and health-conscious vacation retreat. The 15 spacious, air-conditioned rooms are instantly impressive and all have gorgeous kitchens and tasteful Mexican art and crafts decor, much of it locally made. At the center of things is a large, fern-draped garden with a sizable pool. From December to April there's a guests-only gourmet vegan cafe.

Fitness training services are offered, and there are free yoga and exercise-dance classes. The Monday-night cocktails also help bring guests together. Excellent discounts for stays of a week or more.

Hotel Rockaway
HOTEL $$

(Map p460; ☑954-582-32-00; www.hotelrock away.com; Calle del Morro; d/ste M$1250/2150; 🅿❄🔊🐾) This new-ish hotel is Zicatela's fledgling posh abode, advertizing itself in slick white with purple accents. Rooms are as attractive as they are spotless, the beach

is across the road and the hotel incorporates a wider complex that also includes a decent gym (guests get a free one-hour workout).

Hotel Villa Mozart y Macondo
BUNGALOW $$

(Map p458; ☑954-104-22-95; www.hotelmozart ymacondo.com; Av Las Tortugas 77, Rinconada; r incl breakfast M$800-1200; 🔊) The work of art here is not courtesy of Wolfgang Amadeus, but the verdant tropical garden (Jardín Macondo) filled with avant-garde Peruvian sculptures. Around the sides are the accommodations – three bungalows with bright, modern artistic touches and all mod cons (all have king-sized beds; two have kitchenettes).

Three obvious bonuses: there's a pleasant on-site cafe, the owners are super-welcoming, and Playa Carrizalillo (Puerto's most swimming-friendly beach) is a short walk away.

Hotelito Swiss Oasis
HOTEL $$

(Map p460; ☑954-582-14-96; www.swissoasis. com; Andador Gaviotas; r US$50-60; 🔊🐾) This good small hotel provides a guest kitchen with free coffee, tea and purified water, and a pool in the pretty garden, in addition to eight cool rooms with good beds, mosquito screens and attractive color schemes. The well-traveled Swiss owners speak four languages and are very helpful with local information. No under-15s.

Hotel Flor de María
HOTEL $$

(Map p458; ☑954-582-05-36; www.mexonline. com/flordemaria.htm; 1a Entrada a Playa Marinero; r US$50-65; 🅿🔊🐾) A popular Canadian-owned hotel with 24 ample rooms sporting good large bathrooms, folksy Mexican decor and pretty wall and door paintings. A highlight is the expansive roof terrace with its fabulous views, bar and small pool. No under-12s.

Beach Hotel Inés
HOTEL $$

(Map p460; ☑954-582-07-92; www.hotelines.com; Calle del Morro s/n; r M$1080-1350; 🅿❄🔊🐾) German-run Inés has a wide variety of bright, cheerful *cabañas*, rooms, apartments and suites, around a shaded pool area with a restaurant serving good Euro/Mexican food. Most accommodations have air-con available, and some come with kitchens or Jacuzzis. You can arrange horseback riding, surf lessons, diving and other outings – and security is particularly good here.

★ Villas Carrizalillo BOUTIQUE HOTEL $$$
(Map p458; ☎954-582-17-35; www.villascarriza
lillo.com; Av Carrizalillo 125, Rinconada; apt
US$185-215; P❋🛜🏊) There's no short-
age of inspired accommodations perched
on spectacular headlands on the Oaxacan
coast, but the Carrizalillo stands out even
on this dreamy littoral. It helps that it
overlooks one of the area's most gorgeous
beaches, has a plush restaurant, Espadin,
on a covered terrace, and spacious, stylish,
air-conditioned apartments from one to
three bedrooms.

Nearly all the grandly decorated apart-
ments have kitchens and private terraces;
some with panoramic coastal views.

A path goes directly down to the beach,
and the hotel has snorkel gear for rent, and
free surfboards and bikes. Discounts are of-
fered for cash payments.

Hotel Santa Fe HOTEL $$$
(Map p458; ☎954-582-01-70; www.hotelsantafe.
com.mx; Calle del Morro s/n; r from M$1800;
P❋@🛜🏊) Bringing some taste to the
menu of hotel architecture, the Santa Fe is
a neocolonial-style beauty filled with greenery, bird-song, terracotta pots and a subtle
folkloric theme. The 60-plus rooms with
attractive terracotta-tile floors and wood
furnishings are set around two pools shaded by palms, and the reputable restaurant
(p466) overlooking Zicatela beach is pesce-
tarian (ie it only serves fish and vegetarian
dishes).

✘ Eating

★ Lychee THAI $
(Map p460; www.facebook.com/lycheemex; cnr
Cárdenas & Héroes Oaxaqueñas, Punta Zicatela;
mains M$70-100; ⊗5pm-midnight; 🍴) La Pun-
ta resembles in some ways a sybaritic Thai
beach and Lychee doesn't have to try hard
to meld in with superb Thai dishes – tom
yum soup, red or green curries, chicken satay – and other Southeast Asian standards
cooked up in the middle of a large, rectangular wooden bar, with alfresco log tables
and benches set on the earth around it. Save
room for the dessert of caramelized banana
on filo pastry with ice cream!

Virginia's Supercafe CAFE $
(Map p458; ☎cell 954-1003453; Andador La Soledad 2; breakfast M$50-75; ⊗7am-4pm) Hidden
away behind El Adoguín, Virginia's cafe is
pretty super, particularly if you're judging it

PLAYA ESCOBILLA

This 15km-long beach, beginning about
30km east of Puerto Escondido, is one
of the world's major nesting grounds for
the olive ridley turtle (*tortuga golfina*
to Mexicans). Up to a million female
olive ridleys a year arrive at Escobilla to
lay their eggs, with numbers peaking
at night for a period of about a week
around the full moons from May to
February – a spectacular phenomenon
known as an *arribada* or *arribazón*. The
olive ridley is one of the smaller sea
turtles (around 70cm long), but still
an impressive animal, especially when
seen emerging from the surf at a rate of
several thousand per hour, as happens
during Escobilla's biggest *arribadas*.

To protect the turtles, there is no general public access to the beach, and this
is enforced by the Mexican army. Some
Puerto Escondido agencies make things
easier with organized trips; a great option is Gina's Tours (p462).

by its coffee (the best in the city and roasted
on site) and its waffles (chunky with inventive toppings). The ultimate breakfast stop.

Dan's Café Deluxe INTERNATIONAL $
(Map p460; www.facebook.com/danscafedeluxe;
Jacarandas 14, Colonia Santa María; breakfasts
M$45-65, light meals M$45-80; ⊗9am-5pm Mon-
Sat; 🛜🍴) Dan was one of the founders of
local legend El Cafecito (p466) and this
spot next to his eponymous hotel is great
for hearty, surfer-pleasing breakfasts, juices and *licuados* (smoothies), and healthy
lunch options like salads, whole-wheat
sandwiches and vegetable stir-frie. There's
table tennis and sports (and surfing) on TV.

Alaburger INTERNATIONAL $
(Map p460; Cárdenas s/n, Punta Zicatela, opposite
Cabañas Buena Onda; mains M$65-150; ⊗11am-
11pm; 🛜) Talk about simple. Alaburger inhabits a charcoal-y *palapa* under which its
congenial owners have constructed a rudimentary barbecue (ie a pile of bricks). But,
oh the food! Baked potatoes, pizzas, burgers
and a vegan menu good enough to turn you
into one. It's an ambitious undertaking, but
the best culinary alchemy often emerges
from the most modest food shacks – like
this one.

You can enjoy it all at a communal table sitting, not on a conventional seat, but a swing. This, after all, is La Punta.

El Sultán
MIDDLE EASTERN $

(Map p458; ☏ 954-582-05-12; www.el-sultan.com; Blvd Juárez, Rinconada; dishes M$20-65; ☺10am-10pm Tue-Sun; 🍴) For a puff on a hookah pipe and a dose of falafel served with strong coffee, park yourself on one of the cushions at Sultan, an unlikely oasis of cheap Middle Eastern snack food on the posh Rinconada strip (they also do shawarma and hummus). It's popular – so popular that they've opened another branch on Playa Zicatela.

Mercado Benito Juárez
MARKET $

(Av 8 Norte, btwn Avs 3 & 4 Poniente; mains M$40-60; ☺8am-7pm) For local flavors and the true PE atmosphere, head up to the main market in the upper part of town, where dozens of *comedores* serve up fresh fish and shrimp, soups and *antojitos* (Mexican snacks) at ridiculously cheap prices. Wander round the flower, food and craft stalls and try out some of the unusual offerings at the line of juice stalls. 'Mercado' buses (M$8) run up Av Oaxaca.

El Nene
MEXICAN, FUSION $$

(Map p458; Blvd Juárez, Rinconada; mains M$120-180; ☺2-10pm Mon-Sat) El Nene serves up enormous tacos (three for M$50 to M$100) and Mexican- and international-style fish, shrimp and chicken mains. Fish of the day in white wine or Cajun-style is a good choice, and you could start with a flavorsome Thai or *nopal* (prickly pear) soup. The plant-fringed patio setting adds to one of Puerto's best eating experiences.

El Cafecito
MEXICAN, INTERNATIONAL $$

(Map p460; Calle del Morro s/n; breakfast dishes M$25-80, mains M$60-250; ☺6am-11:30pm; 🛜🍴) Cafecito has cornered the market in crossover gringo-Mexican fusion food with large surfer appetites in mind. Herein are some of the best breakfasts on the coast: endless egg concoctions, huge fruit dishes, pasta and bowls of rich Oaxacan chocolate. Icing on the cake is the on-site Carmen's bakery with a walk-up window offering coffee and baked goods. You'll never forget that carrot cake. There's another equally busy branch in Rinconada.

One Love
EUROPEAN, MEXICAN $$

(Map p460; www.hostalpuertoescondido.com; Tamaulipas s/n; mains M$105-160; ☺8am-9:30pm Tue-Sun; 🛜) Excellent Euro-Mexican dishes with fresh local ingredients are served up in this restaurant run by a Mexican-French couple. You could start with the 'One Love taco' (a ceviche wrap with a mango-and-habanero-chili dressing) and follow up with 'Give Peace a Chance' (breaded catch of the day with tabbouleh and chili mayo), but there's plenty of choice, including good pasta and vegetarian dishes.

Hotel Santa Fe
VEGETARIAN, SEAFOOD $$

(Map p458; Calle del Morro s/n; mains M$90-250; ☺7:30am-10pm; 🛜🍴) The attractive colonial Hotel Santa Fe's restaurant sits on a covered terrace looking along Zicatela beach and is a pescatarian affair (no meat – just fish and veg). Options include tofu dishes, vegetarian *antojitos* (Mexican snacks) and a Mediterranean plate with hummus, tabbouleh, Greek salad and pita bread.

La Hostería Bananas
ITALIAN, MEXICAN $$

(Map p460; ☏ 954-582-00-05; Calle del Morro s/n; mains M$80-220; ☺8am-11:30pm; 🛜🍴🐾) The Hostería is an Italian labor of love, from its gleaming kitchen (with computerized wood-fired pizza oven) to the Talavera-tiled bathrooms. A broad selection of dishes, including many veggie and homemade pasta options, is paired with a great drinks list, good breakfast deals and strong coffee. The seafood skewers are epic.

Restaurante Los Tíos
SEAFOOD $$

(Map p460; ☏ 954-582-28-79; Calle del Morro; mains M$50-160; ☺8am-10pm Wed-Mon) 'The Uncles,' right on the sand's edge, serves great *licuados* (milkshakes) and fresh juices to go with its well-priced egg dishes, *antojitos* (Mexican snacks) and seafood. It's popular with locals and nicely relaxed.

★Almoraduz
MEXICAN $$$

(Map p458; ☏ 954-582-31-09; www.almoraduz.com.mx; Blvd Juárez 11-12, Rinconada; mains M$180-250; ☺2-10pm Tue-Sun; 🍴) Almoraduz' husband-and-wife culinary alliance creates memorable flavor combinations in one of the Oaxaca's coast's few true gourmet restaurants. It's not at all pretentious. The open dining space in the rising Rinconada quarter is small, tasteful and distinguished. The menu changes frequently: their most popular offerings range from fig salad or fish in green *mole* to chocolate lava cake.

For the 'full monty' opt for the eight-course tasting menu set at a very reasonable M$500. The drinks selection, including artisan mezcals, craft beers and original fruit drinks, is top-notch too.

Pascale MEXICAN, EUROPEAN **$$$**
(Map p458; ☑ cell 954-1030668; www.pascale.mx; Av Pérez Gasga 612; mains M$110-225; ☉6-11pm Tue-Sun; 🖘) An unlikely factory of gourmet food amid the grubbier fishing shacks of Playa Principal, Pascale prepares original and creative seafood, meat, homemade pasta dishes (with a choice of sauces) and French desserts with rare flair. The seafood is fresh as can be, there's a short but select wine list, and everything is served up with professional polish. The place sometimes closes in low season months.

Costeñito Cevichería SEAFOOD **$$$**
(Map p460; ☑ cell 954-1270424; Calle del Morro s/n; dishes M$130-300; ☉1-11pm) Costeñito is all about its unique *parrilla* (grill) set up in the back of an old 'hippie-mobile' camper van so that you can watch your fish (take your pick from snapper, bass, prawns and octopus) being grilled in full view. For those favoring cured seafood, this is arguably the best place in town for ceviche.

The restaurant inhabits one of the more deluxe *palapas* on Zicatela beach (look out for the camper van).

🍺 Drinking & Nightlife

★ Playa Kabbalah BAR
(Map p460; www.playakabbalah.com; Calle del Morro 312; ☉8am-midnight or later; 🖘) A hip and romantic (depending on who you're with) beach bar/restaurant good for nocturnal drinks with a Zicatela crowd either propping up the bar or relaxing post-surf on canopied loungers on the sand. It's known for its fiestas, which usually involve DJ sets playing mostly electronic dance music to flashing fluorescent lights with the odd wedding thrown in.

Tuesday, Thursday, Friday and Saturday are music nights. Advertised Ladies Nights are particularly popular. At weekends there's often live salsa and/or reggae too.

Casa Babylon BAR
(Map p460; Calle del Morro s/n; ☉9am-2am; 🖘) Psychedelic Babylon has a terrifying Mexican mask collection, a sprawling library of books to exchange and varied live music or a DJ Thursday to Saturday performing on a stage surrounded by winged angels and flying nymphs. Word on the street says the mojitos and mezcal margaritas are to die for.

☆ Entertainment

Cine en la Playa CINEMA
(Cinema on the Beach; www.facebook.com/hotelvillasol; Playa Bacocho; ☉7pm or 8pm Wed, Nov-May) A varied program of movies, from recent feature films to art house, classics and documentaries, is shown on the sands of Playa Bacocho in front of Hotel Suites Villasol's beach club. Films are generally in Spanish with English subtitles, or vice versa.

Split Coconut LIVE MUSIC
(Map p458; Playa Marinero; ☉2pm-midnight Wed-Mon) A favorite of expats, this beach bar hosts several live-music nights a week from about December to March, featuring talented local and visiting musicians playing rock, blues, jazz, world music and more. The rest of the year there's usually a gig on Saturday or Sunday. It does good gringo food (ribs, steaks, burgers...) too.

ℹ Information

Playa Zicatela has a couple of ATMs, but the ones in town work more reliably.

HSBC (Av 1 Norte, btwn Av 2 Poniente & Carretera Costera) Has a dependable ATM.

Santander (Carretera Costera; ☉9am-4pm Mon-Fri, 10am-2pm Sat) New bank with several reliable ATMs and a welcoming blast of air-con.

Tourist Information Kiosk (Map p458; ☑954-582-11-86; ginainpuerto@yahoo.com; Av Pérez Gasga; ☉10am-2pm & 4-6pm Mon-Fri, to 1pm Sat) Gina Machorro, the energetic, dedicated, multilingual information officer, knows everything that's happening in and around Puerto, happily answers your every question and conducts her own interesting tours (p462).

ℹ Getting There & Away

AIR

Airport (☑954-582-04-91) Three kilometers west of the center on Hwy 200. No international flights.

Aeromar (☑954-582-09-77; www.aeromar.com.mx; ☉9am-6pm) Up to three daily flights to/from Mexico City.

Aerotucán (☑954-582-34-61; www.aerotucan.com.mx; ☉7am-3pm Mon-Sat, noon-2pm Sun) Flies 13-seat Cessnas daily to/from Oaxaca (M$2210). Flights are sometimes rescheduled at short notice.

Interjet (☑cell 954-1079957; www.interjet.com; ☉8am-7pm) To/from Mexico City four or five times weekly.

VivaAerobus (☑81-82-150-150; www.vivaaerobus.com) Budget airline flying daily to/

BUSES FROM PUERTO ESCONDIDO

DESTINATION	FARE (M$)	DURATION (HR)	FREQUENCY (DAILY)
Acapulco	466	8	7 AltaMar
Bahías de Huatulco	81-162	2½	23 from OCC terminal
Mexico City (Sur)	703-796	12	Turistar 6pm & 6:45pm, AltaMar 5:45pm & 8:30pm
Pochutla	64-104	1¼	25 from OCC terminal
Salina Cruz	298-316	5	11 from OCC terminal
San Cristóbal de las Casas	740	13	OCC 6:30pm & 9:30pm

from Mexico City. Flights bought in advance can cost less than M$750.

BUS & VAN

OCC Bus Terminal (Map p458; ☎954-582-10-73; Carretera Costera 102) Used by OCC 1st-class and Sur and AU 2nd-class services.

Terminal Turística (Central Camionera; cnr Avs Oaxaca & 4 Poniente) In the upper part of town; used by AltaMar (1st class) and Turistar (deluxe).

Oaxaca

Travel to/from Oaxaca will become quicker and easier once a new highway, joining Hwy 200 a few kilometers east of Puerto Escondido to Hwy 175 south of Ejutla, opens (don't hold your breath, it's been 'in the works' for nearly a decade). This will reduce driving time from seven hours to about four hours and will undoubtedly alter bus and van services. Until then, the most convenient way of traveling to Oaxaca is in the comfortable van services via Hwy 131 (seven hours) offered by at least two companies. OCC's 1st-class buses (M$382, 11 hours, three daily) take a much longer route via Salina Cruz and Hwy 190.

Express Service (☎954-582-08-68; Terminal Turística, cnr Avs Oaxaca & 4 Poniente) Vans to Oaxaca (M$220) hourly from 4am to 5pm, and at 8pm, 10pm, 11pm and 11:30pm.

Villa Escondida (Map p458; Av Hidalgo s/n) Vans to Oaxaca (M$200) hourly from 3:30am to 9:30pm, and at 11pm. Has another office in Terminal Turística. Vans call at both.

Other Destinations

For Mexico City, the AltaMar and Turistar services from the Terminal Turística go via the outskirts of Acapulco and are much quicker than OCC, which takes a longer route via Salina Cruz.

CAR & MOTORCYCLE

To/from Oaxaca city, the winding Hwy 131 via Sola de Vega takes about seven hours.

Between Puerto Escondido and Acapulco, figure on about seven hours for the 400km drive along Hwy 200, which is well enough surfaced but has a lot of speed bumps.

Los Tres Reyes (☎954-582-33-35; http://lostresreyescarrent.com; cnr Carretera Costera & Belmares, Colonia Santa María; ⊗8am-7pm) Rents saloon cars from M$800 per day. They have offices on the highway above Colonia Santa María and at the airport. Cheaper is **Úcar** (☎954-149-03-04; www.u-car.mx; Calle del Morro; ⊗9am-8pm) with saloons from M$499 per day and scooters from M$150.

ℹ Getting Around

Ticket taxis from the airport will drop you in town for M$40 per person (M$70 to Punta Zicatela). You can usually find a whole cab for a similar price on the main road outside the airport. Taxi rides within town cost M$30 to M$35.

Taxis colectivos, local buses and *camionetas* marked 'Zicatela' or 'La Punta' (all M$8) run approximately every 20 minutes to Punta Zicatela from Mercado Benito Juárez up in the north of the town (near the Terminal Turística), from sunrise to about 8:30pm. They travel down 3 Poniente then east along the Carretera Costera; for El Adoquín or Playa Zicatela you can hop off and walk down in two minutes.

Parque Nacional Lagunas de Chacahua

West of Manialtepec, Hwy 200 winds its way along a coast studded with lagoons, pristine beaches and prolific bird and plant life. Settlements in this region are home to many Afro-Mexicans, descendants of slaves who escaped from the Spanish.

The area around the coastal lagoons of Chacahua and La Pastoría forms the beautiful 149-sq-km Parque Nacional Lagunas de Chacahua, which attracts many migratory birds from Alaska and Canada in winter. Mangrove-fringed islands harbor roseate spoonbills, ibises, cormorants, wood storks, herons and egrets, as well as mahogany trees, crocodiles and turtles. El Corral, a tunnel-like waterway filled with countless birds in winter, connects the two lagoons. The boat trip along the lagoons is fabulous, and at its end Chacahua village sits upon a gorgeous beach curving at least 20km eastward, inviting you to stop for a meal or a night in rustic *cabañas*.

◎ Sights

Cocodrilario de Chacahua   WILDLIFE RESERVE
(Chacahua Crocodile Sanctuary; Calle Chiapas; guided tour by donation; ⊙8am-6pm) 🌿 The Cocodrilario de Chacahua houses over 200 crocodiles, releasing some of them into the lagoons occasionally as part of a successful program to save the local wild croc population from extinction at the hands of poachers. It's not specifically set up to receive visitors, but you're welcome to drop by.

Local *lanchas* (motorboats; M$15 per person) will whiz you across the channel to the inland half of the village where the Cocodrilario is situated.

⌂ Sleeping & Eating

Many of the beach restaurants also have basic *cabañas* costing from around M$150 for two people, with shared bathrooms. You can usually sleep in a hammock or camp for free if you eat at a particular establishment.

Restaurante Siete Mares   CABAÑAS $
(☑954-114-00-62, 954-132-22-63; Playa; cabañas M$250) Siete Mares, at the beach's west end (nearest the river), has some of the better *cabañas*, each with two double beds, fans, mosquito nets, electric light and curtained-off showers in the corner. There's also a pleasant on-site restaurant.

ⓘ Getting There & Away

The starting point for boat trips along the lagoons to Chacahua village is the small fishing village of Zapotalito, at the eastern end of Laguna La Pastoría, 63km from Puerto Escondido.

From Puerto Escondido, take a minibus bound for Pinotepa Nacional from Av Hidalgo 5 (departures about every 20 minutes, 4am to 8pm) and get out at the Zapotalito turnoff (M$45, 1¼ hours), 58km from Puerto (and 8km past the town of Río Grande). From the turning, taxis will shuttle you the 5km to Zapotalito for M$70 (M$20 by colectivo).

Competing boat cooperatives offer *lancha* services from Zapotalito to Chacahua village,

charging approximately M$1500 round-trip for up to 10 people. The round-trip option lasts about four hours, including about two hours at Chacahua. When there is sufficient traffic, *colectivo* services run for M$150/200 per person one way/round-trip. All prices go up about 40% at peak holiday times such as Christmas−New Year's and Semana Santa.

For drivers, a mostly unpaved road heads 27km south to Chacahua village from San José del Progreso on Hwy 200. It's passable for normal cars except when waterlogged, which it often is between May and November.

Pochutla
📞958 / POP 14,000

Bustling, sweaty Pochutla is the market town and transportation hub for the central part of the Oaxaca coast, including the nearby beach spots of Puerto Ángel, Zipolite, San Agustinillo and Mazunte. There's no other reason to pause here.

Hwy 175 from Oaxaca runs through Pochutla as Av Lázaro Cárdenas, the narrow main street, and meets the coastal Hwy 200 about 1.5km south of town. The bus and van terminals cluster toward the southern, downhill end of Cárdenas.

⌂ Sleeping & Eating

Hotel Izala (☑958-584-01-15; Av Cárdenas 59; s/d M$250/300, with air-con M$350/500; P ❋) and **Hotel San Pedro** (☑958-584-11-23; Av Cárdenas s/n; s/d M$400/500; P ❋ 🛜), respectively 300m north and 300m south of the main bus station, are both OK for a night, but, realistically Pochutla is mainly a way station for the coastal villages nearby.

★Finca de Vaqueros   PARRILLA $$
(☑958-100-43-31; El Colorado village; mains M$145-200; ⊙10am-9pm; P ♿) This ranch-style eatery with long tables in a large, open-sided barn is worth an expedition from anywhere on the coast for its superb grilled meats. It's 2km south of Pochutla on the Puerto Ángel road (M$60 by taxi). Order some *frijoles charros* (bean soup with bacon bits) and *queso fundido* (melted cheese) to start, followed by some tender *arrachera* (skirt steak).

ⓘ Information

Banco Azteca (Av Cárdenas s/n; ⊙9am-9pm) Exchanges cash US dollars and euros; inside the Elektra store 75m south of the main bus station. Lines can be long.

BUSES FROM POCHUTLA

DESTINATION	FARE (M$)	DURATION (HR)	FREQUENCY (DAILY)
Bahías de Huatulco	39-74	1	TRP every 10-15min 5:15am-8:15pm, Sur hourly 7:20am-8:20pm, 9 OCC
Mexico City (Sur)	1089	13½	Turistar 5pm, AltaMar 4:20pm
Puerto Escondido	64-104	1¼	Sur hourly 7am-8pm, 8 OCC, 4 AltaMar
Salina Cruz	228-240	4	8 OCC
San Cristóbal de las Casas	672	11-12	OCC 8pm & 10:50pm
Tapachula	434	12	OCC 6:40pm

Scotiabank ATM (Av Cárdenas 57) About 350m up the main street from the main bus station.

ⓘ Getting There & Away

OAXACA

Oaxaca is 245km away by the curvy Hwy 175 – six hours in the convenient and fairly comfortable air-conditioned van services for around M$195 offered by several companies. The same services will drop you in San José del Pacífico (M$95, 3½ hours). Drivers will also usually stop when you need a bathroom break, or need to vomit, as a few people do on this route. OCC runs three daily 1st-class buses to Oaxaca (M$446, nine hours) from the Terminal de Autobuses San Pedro Pochutla, but they take a much longer and more expensive route via Salina Cruz.

Atlántida (☑ 958-584-92-39; Av Cárdenas 85) Eleven vans to Oaxaca daily from M$195, from their ticket office next to the Santa Cruz Hotel 50m north of the main bus station.

Líneas Unidas (☑ cell 958-5841322; Av Cárdenas 94) Across the street from the main bus terminal, with vans to Oaxaca every 30 to 60 minutes from 3:30am to midnight (from M$200).

OTHER DESTINATIONS

Terminal de Autobuses San Pedro Pochutla (cnr Av Cárdenas & Constitución) The main bus station, entered through a white-grilled doorway toward the south end of Cárdenas. It's used by Turistar (deluxe), OCC and AltaMar (1st class) and Sur and AU (2nd class) services. For distant destinations with limited service, such as San Cristóbal de las Casas and Mexico City, it's advisable to get tickets a couple of days ahead.

Taxis to the Beach Villages (TRP; cnr Jamaica & Matamoros) Follow Calle Jamaica west off Av Cárdenas just north of the main bus station. After 150m you will reach a small chapel. To the left, a car park acts as a departure point for shared *taxis colectivos* to the beach villages of Zipolite, San Agustinillo and Mazunte. Prices run from M$15 to M$20.

Puerto Ángel

☑ 958 / POP 2600

The scruffy entry point to this slice of nirvanic coast has the feel of a Mexican fishing village. Boats rather than surfboards embellish the sheltered curve of beach known as Playa Panteón and the food is more tortilla than pizza and pasta. Most travelers don't stop here at all, preferring instead to press on to the beach bliss of Zipolite or Mazunte further west without looking back. But a night or two needn't be wasted, especially if you prefer the gritty to the pretty.

⊙ Sights

Playa La Boquilla BEACH

(ℙ) The coast east of Puerto Ángel is dotted with small hidden beaches, none of them very busy. Playa La Boquilla, on a gentle bay about 7.5km from town by road, is the site of the Bahía de la Luna hotel and restaurant, and is good for snorkeling and swimming. It's fun to go by boat (M$600 each way): ask at Puerto Ángel pier or Playa del Panteón.

You can also get here by a 3.5km unpaved road from a turnoff 4km out of Puerto Ángel on the Pochutla road. A taxi from Puerto Ángel costs around M$120, or from Pochutla about M$200. Some taxis won't tackle the road in the rainy season.

🏃 Activities

Azul Profundo   WATER SPORTS
(☑cell 958-1060420; www.hotelcordelias.com;
Playa del Panteón) Well-organized Azul Profundo specializes in boat trips (with snorkeling and wildlife-watching thrown in) and
sportfishing for marlin, swordfish, sailfish,
tuna or mahimahi. Its main base is at Hotel Cordelias overlooking Puerto Ángel, but
you can also make bookings in the internet
cafe (p474) in Zipolite from where they can
arrange pickups.

Four-hour snorkeling boat trips (M$180
per person, or M$250 with Zipolite pickup)
go looking for turtles, dolphins and, with
luck (from December to April), whales
and take in four bays. You'll stop at least
once for snorkeling and get a chance to go
ashore.

A fishing boat for four people, with two
lines, costs M$600 per hour (minimum
two hours). All guides speak at least a little
English.

Kayaks are available for paddling around
in Puerto Ángel's sheltered bay for M$50
per hour.

🛏 Sleeping & Eating

Hotel Cordelias   HOTEL $$
(☑958-584-3021; www.hotelcordelias.com; Playa
Panteón; r M$500-1000; ✴🅿🗐) Not many elect
to stay in Puerto Ángel, but, if you do, head
to this bright, white hotel run by the own-
ers of boat-tour specialists Azul Profundo.
Rooms are large (most with two double
beds) and 10 overlook Puerto's merry
beach and harbor. There's a fresh-fish res-
taurant downstairs and boat trips push off
from the adjacent jetty. Just the package!

Bahía de la Luna   BUNGALOW $$$
(☑958-589-50-20;   www.bahiadelaluna.com;
Playa La Boquilla; r incl breakfast from M$1900;
🅿🗐) This rustic-chic hideaway sits in
splendid isolation at lovely Playa La Boquilla – a place for really escaping the
world. The bright adobe bungalows are
scattered over a tree-covered hillside overlooking the beach. Some have kitchens,
but there's also an informal Mexican/
international-fusion beach restaurant
(lunch dishes from M$60; two-course din-
ner from M$300), with excellent seafood
and steaks, generous margaritas and mezcal from the barrel. Snorkel gear, kayaks
and a paddleboard are free for guests.

ℹ Information

Banco Azteca (Blvd Uribe; ⊘8am-8pm)
Changes cash US dollars and euros.

ℹ Getting There & Away

A taxi colectivo costs M$10 to Zipolite and
roughly M$15 to Pochutla. A private cab to either
is M$45 to M$50 (M$60 to M$70 after about
9pm).

Zipolite

☑958 / POP 1100

There's a stark-naked dude with dreadlocks
meditating on the beach, a bobbing crowd
of surfers bravely fighting aggressive waves,
a couple of aging hippies looking (apart
from their cell phones) like they've just
arrived in a time machine from 1975, and
a local artisan shop doing a roaring trade
in Frida Kahlo bags. Welcome to Zipolite, a
chilled-out strip of palapas, beach shacks
and intentionally rustic boutique hotels
that hasn't yet been discovered by big resort developers or people who play golf.

The largest of the three beach towns that
decorate the coast west of Puerto Ángel,
Zipolite is known for its surfing, clothing-
optional beach and unashamed 'do nothing' vibe. Plenty of expats have discovered
its tranquil charms and opened small
businesses (most notably Italians), but the
place still retains a touch of erstwhile bohemian magic. Long may it continue.

👁 Sights

★Playa Zipolite   BEACH
Zipolite's beach is huge, running for a good
1.5km and dispatching massive waves. It's
famous for its nudity; you'll see people randomly swimming, sunbathing or happily
walking across the wet sand minus their
clothes at any time of day, although it is
more common in a couple of coves at the
western end of the beach and in the small
bay called Playa del Amor at the east end,
which is a favorite spot for gay men.

The eastern end of Zipolite (nearest
Puerto Ángel) is called Colonia Playa del
Amor, the middle part is Centro, and the
western end, where most of the traveler
scene is centered, is Colonia Roca Blanca, where you'll find what amounts to the
main street, Av Roca Blanca (also called El
Adoquín), a block back from the beach.

Surfing is better toward the west. For more seclusion and the best boutique hotels, retreat to the far western end of the beach behind several rocky knolls.

Activities

The essence and glory of Zipolite is that organized activity is minimal. This is a place for hanging out and doing as little as you like.

Azul Profundo (p471) provides free transportation for its fishing, diving and snorkeling trips from Puerto Ángel: you can reserve at its internet shop (p474) on Av Roca Blanca.

You can partake in daily yoga classes (M$70) at La Loma Linda at 9am and 10:30am.

🛏 Sleeping

The majority of accommodations are in and around the Roca Blanca area at the west end of Zipolite and are literally steps from the beach. A smaller, plusher cluster sits at the top of a headland to the west.

Hotel Hostal Teresa HOTEL $
(☑958-584-30-06; www.hotelhostalteresa.com; Av Roca Blanca; r M$300) A lot of what's good about a hotel is the people who run it. A case in point is Hotel Teresa managed by a lovely Mexican couple who'll cater to your every need. Sure, the rooms are modest, but this place is about fabulous service, a secure environment and highly economical prices. It's a lovely combo.

A Nice Place on the Beach ROOMS $
(☑958-584-31-95; www.aniceplaceonthebeach. weebly.com; Av Roca Blanca; d M$500, d/q without bathroom M$300/500; 🛜) Aptly named and aptly subtitled too (the second stanza reads: 'Where people come to do nothing'), Nice Place has eight basic rooms, split four upstairs with wooden walls and private bathrooms, and four downstairs with concrete walls and shared bathrooms. Step out of the door and your feet are on dry sand right beside the on-site bar and restaurant.

Lo Cósmico CABAÑAS $
(www.locosmico.com; west end Playa Zipolite; r M$400-600, without bathroom M$300; ⊘restaurant 8am-4pm Tue-Sun; 🅿🛜) Lo Cósmico is old-school Zipolite, a throwback to the days when this place really was undiscovered, except by the odd cosmically minded hippie. Despite being destroyed and rebuilt after a 1997 hurricane, it has retained its 1970s essence: simple conical-roofed *cabañas* made

out of local materials, dotted around a tall rock outcrop.

The on-site open-air restaurant (dishes M$30 to M$70) serves excellent crepes, salads and breakfasts from an impeccably clean kitchen.

Las Casitas BUNGALOW $
(☑958-100-34-55; www.las-casitas.net; cabins M$500-800; 🅿🛜) Peaceful Las Casitas sits like a lighthouse on a lane behind the west end of Playa Zipolite. Seven detached rooms done out with tasteful Mexican color schemes and cute decorative details are set in palm-thatch-and-wood bungalows scattered around a steep terraced garden. All have private bathrooms, kitchens and spacious hangout areas.

★La Loma Linda HOTEL $$
(☑958-584-31-98; www.lalomalinda.com; Carreta Puerto Ángel-Mazunte; d US$45-70, without bathroom US$28-40; 🅿🛜) Stacked on a steep hillside away from the traveler 'scene' of Colonia Roca Blanca, this handsome, reflective yoga retreat is an aesthetic joy with six exceptionally well-designed bungalows with private bathrooms and four individual rooms that share a bathroom encased in a hexagonal Mudéjar-style tower! The gardens and terraces are impeccable and there's a yoga studio offering daily classes (nonguests welcome).

Rooms have fridges, mozzie nets, hammocks and huge stone terraces with ocean or garden views. Book ahead as the German owners often host retreats.

Posada Buena Vida INN $$
(☑55-2855-2230; www.posadabuenavida.com; Andador Gaviotas, Colonia Roca Blanca; cabaña/ste from M$1250/2250; 🛜) Buena Vida takes the boutique quality up a notch with artfully designed rooms accented with striking paintings, colorful tiles and balustrades cleverly fashioned out of old driftwood. The overriding theme is Mexican arts and crafts meets Eastern mysticism. A giant Buddha statue guards a wonderful circular swimming pool and tables and sunloungers shaded by canopies line the beach. A good life indeed!

There's a mix of rooms, cabins, suites and bungalows to choose from, plus a lovely beach-facing bar/restaurant.

Hotel Nude HOTEL $$
(☑958-584-30-62; www.nudezipolite.com; Av Roca Blanca; r from M$1200; 🅿🛜🏊) Tapping into Zipolite's clothing-optional vibe, the

Nude wears its nudist reputation fairly subtly (guests usually save their nudity for the beach). Attractive two-story thatched bungalows are arranged around a kidney-shaped pool with a palm tree in the middle. Well-scrubbed interiors are simple and white, but all have large porches with hammocks. Bonuses include a spa, beachfront restaurant and eager-to-please service.

Posada México   ROOMS $$
(☑958-584-31-94; Av Roca Blanca; r M$800-1000, without bathroom M$300-600; ℗🛜) 🖋 This Italian-run beachfront joint is on a friendly, personal scale and has smallish but clean, colorful rooms with good beds, four-poster mosquito nets, ingenious water-saving showers and sandy little hammock areas. Best are the two larger, more expensive, beach-facing rooms. There's a fine **restaurant** (mains M$80-160; ◷8am-5:30pm & 6:30-11pm Thu-Tue, 8am-1:30pm Wed; 🛜☑) too.

★Heven   APARTMENT $$$
(☑cell 958-1062018; www.hevenresidence.com; Arco Iris 1; s/d incl breakfast M$1200/1600; 🛜🅿) Heven, at the risk of sounding trite, is pretty heavenly: a beautifully designed walled compound arranged around an infinity pool, lush gardens and winding stairways punctuated with balconies and a shapely tower that (intentionally) recalls the whitewashed glories of Naples and the Amalfi Coast. The rooms, which have lured musicians and writers in the past, are classy and charismatic.

Most have kitchen facilities, and all have fans and handsome hand-crafted Mexican furniture.

Casa Sol   APARTMENT $$$
(☑cell 958-1000462; www.casasolzipolite.com; Arco Iris 6; r US$110-150; ❇🛜🅿) Canadian-owned Casa Sol overlooks little Playa Camarón, a 10-minute walk west of Playa Zipolite, and its three spacious, spotless rooms make perfect vacation retreats. No meals are served, but rooms have kitchens and there's another kitchen on the large, panoramic terrace. The beach is good for snorkeling when calm (free gear is available for guests).

Vehicle access is by a signposted 400m track off the main road about 1km west of Zipolite, or it's a hot 20-minute walk.

El Alquimista   BUNGALOW $$$
(☑958-587-89-61; www.el-alquimista.com; west end Playa Zipolite; bungalow M$1100-1500, r M$1600-1800; ℗❇🛜🅿) The Alquimista has rustic-boutique thatch-roofed bungalows just off the beach (most with double bed, fan, hot-water bathroom) and big, bright rooms set back up the luxuriant hillside with ample terraces and king-sized beds. The decor is all about hammocks, lazy terraces, trance music and twinkling oil lamps at night.

One of Zipolite's best restaurants (p474) is here too, as are a good pool and a spa, **Espacio Shanti** (☑958-111-50-97; ◷10am-7:30pm), using locally made organic materials. Daily hatha yoga sessions (M$100/300 per one/four classes) take place in a bright yoga room.

✖ Eating

Sal y Pimienta   MEXICAN $
(Playa; mains M$70-130; ◷11am-10pm) So close to the ocean you barely need to get off your surfboard, the 'Salt & Pepper' serves unsophisticated but delicious *comida* from plastic tables set out on the sand. Portions are huge and prices are small, with fabulous fish and very cold beer. Enough said. It's on the beach just east of Bang Bang (p474).

Orale! Cafe   BREAKFAST $
(☑958-117-71-29; off west end Av Roca Blanca; breakfast dishes M$30-85; ◷8am-3pm Thu-Mon) This shady tropical-garden cafe feels like a rough clearing in the jungle and its food tastes pretty good too, especially if you order their branded coffee or ask for a fruit plate (with yogurt and granola) that comes full of ambrosial bites that might conceivably have fallen off a nearby tree straight onto your plate. It also serves eggs for breakfast and baguettes for lunch.

Postres del Sol   CAFE $
(☑cell 958-1070249; Carretera Puerto Ángel-Zipolite; cakes M$20-40; ◷8:30am-9pm Tue-Sun) An apparition by the dusty roadside heading west out of Zipolite, this new cafe with four alfresco tables, and usually as many dogs, lures people out of passing taxis with its strategically positioned display case full of rich cakes – carrot, nut and chocolate among them. The joe's pretty good too.

★La Providencia   MEXICAN, FUSION $$
(☑cell 958-1009234; www.laprovidenciazipolite. com; mains M$130-190; ◷6:30-10pm Wed-Sun Nov-Apr, Jul & Aug) Zipolite's outstanding dining option, on a lane behind the western end of the beach, combines exquisite flavors, artful presentation and relaxed ambience. You can sip a cocktail in the open-air lounge

while you peruse the menu. It's a contemporary Mexican treat, from amaranth-encrusted aubergine to beef medallions with red-wine reduction or coconut-crusted prawns with mango sauce. Save room for the chocolate mousse! Reservations advised during busy seasons.

El Alquimista
INTERNATIONAL $$

(☑ 954-587-89-61; west end Playa Zipolite; mains M$120-230; ⏰ 8am-11pm; 🛜☑) The Alchemist is delightfully sited alfresco in a quiet sandy cove, and atmospherically lit by oil lamps and candles at night, conjuring up an intentionally romantic air. The wide-ranging menu runs from fresh salads to good meat, seafood and pasta and hard-to-pass-up desserts. In terms of setting, it's definitely Zipolite's most refined choice.

Piedra de Fuego
SEAFOOD $$

(Mangle, Colonia Roca Blanca; mains M$70-110; ⏰ 2-10pm) If you came to Zipolite to eat Mexican rather than Italian food, this is your bag with generous servings of fresh fish fillet or shrimp, accompanied by rice, salad and potatoes. It's simple, superb and run by a local family. Good *aguas de frutas* (fruit cordials) too.

Pacha Mama
ITALIAN, MEXICAN $$

(☑ 958-106-61-64; Pelícano, Colonia Roca Blanca; mains M$90-170; ⏰ 6-11pm Fri-Wed) Named after an Inca fertility goddess, you could be forgiven for thinking that Pacha Mama is Peruvian, but no! The chefs are from Zipolite's sizable Italian community, and they turn out very professional steaks, seafood, homemade pasta with classic sauces, and wood-oven pizzas (takeout available) in a shady garden-like setting.

🍷 Drinking & Nightlife

Zipolite's beachfront restaurant-bars have perfect locations for drinks from sunset onward, and beach bonfires provide the focus for informal partying when the surfers get home.

Bang Bang
BAR

(⏰ 6pm-2am Mon-Sat) It looks more like a hobo's shack than a bar by day, but Bang Bang lights up at night with a big bonfire on the beach, winner-stays-on table-tennis tournaments, DJ sets and lots of high jinks fueled by *muchas cervezas*. It's just east from the end of the main Roca Blanca strip (a shallow wade across the town river if arriving via the beach).

☆ Entertainment

Cine Luciernaga (Firefly Cinema)
OUTDOOR CINEMA

(Pelícano) FREE A neat little makeshift cinema with indoor and outdoor seating areas and a small bar. It usually shows a matinee and evening film/TV show – everything from *Twin Peaks* to *Withnail and I*.

🛍 Shopping

Tienda de Artesanías Piña Palmera
ARTS & CRAFTS

(cnr Pelícano & Carretera, Colonia Roca Blanca; ⏰ 9am-5pm Mon-Sat) 🌿 This little shop sells wooden toys, recycled paper products, coconut oil and other stuff made at the **Piña Palmera** (☑ 958-584-31-47; www.pinapalmera. org; Colonia Roca Blanca; ⏰ 8am-3pm Mon-Sat) 🌿 rehabilitation center and in the communities where Piña Palmera works.

ℹ Information

Ostensibly Zipolite is a place for peace and tranquility and most travelers enjoy a quiet, trouble-free stay here. However, some crimes against tourists have been reported in recent years, especially on the beach after dark. Enjoy the laid-back ambience, but don't drop your guard too low. Always lock your bedroom door and think twice before spending the night on a hammock alfresco on the sand.

A more natural danger is Zipolite's surf. It's fraught with riptides, changing currents and a strong undertow. Going in deeper than your knees can be risking your life. Local voluntary lifeguards rescue many, but people still drown here every year. The shore break is one only experienced surfers should attempt. Heed the warning flags: yellow means don't go in deeper than your knees; red means don't go in period.

There are ATMs outside Hotel Playa Zipolite and inside Hotel Nude on Av Roca Blanca, but they sometimes run out of cash. The nearest other ATMs are in Pochutla and Mazunte.

Internet Cafe (☑ 958-584-34-37; Av Roca Blanca; internet per hour M$15; ⏰ 9am-10pm) Also takes bookings for Azul Profundo (p471).

ℹ Getting There & Away

After dark, taxis are your only option for getting to Puerto Ángel, San Agustinillo or Mazunte (M$50 to M$60 until around 9pm; M$70 to M$80 after that).

Atlántida (☑ 954-584-32-14; Papelería Aby, next to La Capilla, Centro) has comfortable vans that depart for San José del Pacífico (M$130, four hours) and Oaxaca (M$210, 6½ hours) almost round the clock.

San Agustinillo

958 / POP 290

True, it's a bit like comparing heaven with nirvana, but San Agustinillo might just possess the nicest slice of sand on this glorious coast. The village is smaller than Mazunte, its 'twin' to the west, with everything clinging to the main drag, Calle Principal. The waves are a little more manageable too, making this place perfect for bodyboarding and learning to surf. There's a local surf school should you need assistance.

🏃 Activities

Local fishers will take you on boat trips to observe turtles, dolphins, birds, manta rays and whales (best from November to April for these last two). The cost for three hours is normally M$250 per person (usually with a minimum of four) including a snorkeling stop. The fishers also offer sportfishing trips, usually M$450 to M$550 per hour for up to three people (minimum three or four hours). Ask at your accommodations.

🐚 Courses

Coco Loco Surf Club　　SURFING, SNORKELING

(☑cell 958-1157737; Calle Principal; ☉10am-6pm; 🖐) Coco Loco's qualified French surf instructor, David Chouard, gives excellent classes for anyone from five years old upwards (M$400). The outfit also rents out surfboards, boogie boards and snorkel gear (all per hour/day M$50/200), sells surf gear, and takes surf trips to Chacahua and Barra de la Cruz (M$600 per day per person).

🛏 Sleeping

Most places to stay and eat are right on the beach. Rooms have either mosquito-screened windows or mosquito nets.

Recinto del Viento　　GUESTHOUSE $

(☑cell 958-1135236; www.recintodelviento.com; s/d without bathroom M$380/450; 🅿) This budget option looks like some frozen relic from San Agustinillo's pre-tourist days and sits 100m up steps opposite Un Sueño (p476) with surf views from its hammock-slung terrace. The guest kitchen helps create a sociable atmosphere and there's a no-wi-fi policy to encourage guests to interact. The five rooms are simple and small. Only one has its own bathroom (single/double M$500/600).

Hotel Paraíso del Pescador　　HOTEL $$

(☑958-589-95-17; Calle Principal; r M$1000; 🅿❄🛜) Sunny rooms with adjoining kitchens (equipped with massive fridges) and broad balconies characterize this orange-hued posada above a restaurant in San Agustinillo's main drag. The rooms aren't flashy, but the view is.

Rancho Cerro Largo　　CABAÑAS $$

(www.ranchocerrolargo.wix.com/ranchocerrolargo; Playa Aragón; s M$900-1250, d M$1000-1350, all incl breakfast & dinner; 🅿) 🌿 The Rancho has all the calling cards of a quintessential Oaxacan yoga resort: quiet clifftop location; comfortable but simple ocean-view *cabañas*, most constructed of mud and wattle (and some with open walls overlooking the crashing surf below); and top-notch mainly vegan and vegetarian meals taken communally with other guests.

There probably isn't a better place to sit in the lotus position and feel at one with nature. Access is by a signed driveway from the Zipolite–San Agustinillo road.

Bambú　　CABAÑAS $$

(www.bambuecocabanas.com; Calle Principal; d/q M$1300/1500; 🅿🛜) 🌿 The half-dozen rooms here, toward the beach's east end, are large, open to as much breeze as possible, and set under high *palapa* roofs that look faintly Indonesian. All are cleverly constructed, mainly from bamboo, with pretty tilework, fans, good mozzie nets, and quirky details like seashell shower heads and trees growing inside a couple of rooms. The large guest kitchen area includes a barbecue grill and long communal table.

★ Punta Placer　　CABAÑAS $$$

(☑cell 958-1090164; www.puntaplacer.com; Calle Principal; r/apt M$1800/$2500; 🅿🛜) The eight beautiful circular rooms and one large apartment here have a fresh, open-air feel thanks to their breezy terraces and wood-slat windows. With welcome touches like good reading lights and stone-lined hot showers with excellent water pressure, they're a grade above most other San Agustinillo accommodations.

The garden of native plants opens directly on the beach, and the little restaurant here, Vidita Negra (p476), serves up well-executed Mexican and Mediterranean fare.

Hotel Casa La Ola　　BOUTIQUE HOTEL $$$

(☑55-3103-6257; www.casalaola.mx; Calle Principal; s/d/ste M$1800/2600/3100; 🅿❄🛜🏊)

San Agustinillo's newest hotel (opened December 2016) is a plush bricks-and-mortar affair set above the main road at the village's western limits. Rooms are classy and super-modern, using local wood and stone in an enviably creative way. Most are large and ocean-facing with fridges, wooden decks and relaxing deck chairs. Breakfast in the on-site cafe is an extra M$200.

Casa Aamori
BOUTIQUE HOTEL $$$

(☑55-5436-2538; www.aamoriboutiquehotel.com; Calle Principal; r M$1800-2800; ❄☎⊠) San Agustinillo's classiest accommodations, lovingly designed Casa Aamori stands toward the east end of the beach. The 12 large, attractive rooms, on themes from Copacabana to Goa to Africa, feature floor mosaics and original crafts from around the world. Four look straight out on to the ocean.

The pool-and-restaurant deck leads on to a sandy area over the beach, with hanging beds under the palms. The hotel is for adults only, with a two-night minimum stay.

Un Sueño
CABAÑAS $$$

(☑cell 958-1138749; www.unsueno.com; Calle Principal; r from M$1650; ℗☎) Un Sueño, toward the east end of the beach, has 17 lovely, good-sized rooms sporting touches of art and craft from around the world, and a semi-open-air feel from bamboo-slat windows and hammock-slung terraces. Also fronting the sands are a breeze-lapped hammock area and an excellent restaurant doing breakfasts and lunch.

✕ Eating

★ Restaurante

La Mora
MEXICAN, ITALIAN $$

(☑958-584-64-22; www.lamoraposada.com; Calle Principal; mains M$80-120, r with/without kitchenette M$600/500, apt M$1200; ⊗8am-2:30pm & 6:30-10pm Wed-Mon; ☎) Tucked onto a sheltered slice of beach, there's something of the old posada about La Mora. You can park yourself in the tavern-like interior or feel the salt spray on the narrow terrace. The food – good Italian and seafood dinners, breakfasts, massive fruit plates and organic, fair-trade coffee – will be equally memorable.

La Ola
SEAFOOD $$

(☑55-3103-6257; Playa; mains M$150-220; ⊗8am-11:30pm) A slightly more refined palapa than is standard in these parts, La Ola (the wave) is right on the beach and delivers fine fish concoctions to its wooden periwinkle tables with aplomb. Honorable mentions should go to the tuna tostadas (with raw marinated spicy tuna on a crispy base), the fish tacos and the large peel-able curried prawns.

Un Sueño Restaurant
MEXICAN $$

(Calle Principal; mains M$120-160; ⊗8am-6:30pm; ☎) The restaurant on the sands at Un Sueño serves up good breakfasts and, for lunch, sabores del Pacífico (flavors of the Pacific) with a touch of French flair. The short but sweet seafood-based menu runs from a delicious foil-wrapped fish with mint to Thai-style shrimp, and you shouldn't miss their lemon pie!

Vidita Negra
MEXICAN, MEDITERRANEAN $$

(mains M$70-190; ⊗7:30am-10:30pm; ☎) The little open-air restaurant at Punta Placer (p475) serves up a variety of well-prepared Mexican and Mediterranean dishes from beef fillet to parrillada de verduras (grilled vegetables). The fresh fish, done in three chilies or white wine, is always a good bet.

❶ Getting There & Away

San Agustinillo is linked to the other villages on the coast by regular colectivos and camionetas. Flag them down on the main road.

Mazunte

☑958 / POP 870

Mazunte is a counterpart of Zipolite, a huddle of thatch and abode buildings that hug two elemental beaches – Playas Rinconcito and Mermejita – on either side of a wave-lashed headland called La Cometa. Wellknown on the independent travelers' circuit, it's a motley melange of tattoo parlors, yoga studios, Che Guevara T-shirts and people who see their future in tarot cards. It's also very beautiful and – courtesy of a recent pueblo mágico (magical village) listing – the most visited of the beach villages hereabouts.

Mazunte is known for its sea turtles: an interesting research center just off the main drag has an aquarium open to the public. It's also a good place to learn Spanish, practice yoga or simply do nothing.

◉ Sights

★ Punta Cometa
VIEWPOINT

This rocky cape, jutting out from the west end of Mazunte beach, is the southernmost point in the state of Oaxaca and a fabulous place to hike at sunset amid crashing waves and dreamy Pacific vistas.

To walk to the cape, take the lane toward Playa Mermejita off Calle Rinconcito, and go left up the track immediately after the cemetery to reach the community nature reserve entrance after 250m. Here you have two choices. Take the path leading down to the right (Sendero Corral de Piedra Poniente) and you'll join a winding sometimes rough trail that ultimately gets you to the Punta in 20 to 30 minutes (the last part crosses a small beach). Take the central path and you'll be led more directly through trees and then across a grassy headland to the Punta. Ideally you can combine both paths for a round-trip that takes around one hour without stops.

Centro Mexicano de la Tortuga
AQUARIUM

(☏55-5449-7000, ext 19001; www.centromexi canodelatortuga.org; Paseo del Mazunte; M$32; ☉10am-4:30pm Wed-Sat, to 2:30pm Sun; 🅿🚹) 🍃 With a wonderful and very appropriate setting overlooking the ocean, this two-part turtle center ushers visitors on a walk around a collection of outdoor tanks filled with all kinds of exotic breeds of turtle before diving (metaphorically) into an indoor aquarium where you can get very close to some BIG reptiles. The research center contains specimens of all the world's eight marine-turtle species (seven of which frequent Mexico's coasts), plus some freshwater and land varieties.

🏃 Activities

Ola Verde Expediciones
RAFTING, HIKING

(☏cell 958-1096751; www.olaverdeexpediciones. com.mx; Calle Rinconcito; ☉office 10am-2pm & 4-9pm; 🚹) This professional team of adventure-sports enthusiasts leads exciting river adventures including a half-day canyon hike on the Río San Francisco inland from Mazunte (year-round; adult/child M$550/400), with swimming, floating and jumping into pools – a fun outing for families and anyone else.

🍴 Courses

Instituto Iguana
LANGUAGE

(☏cell 958-1075232; www.institutoiguana.com; Camino al Aguaje) 🍃 In keeping with the Mazunte vibe, this language school is a relaxed, friendly place where you can start classes any day and study as intensively as you like.

Run by a Mexican-German nonprofit organization, which also gives free English classes to villagers, it has a lovely breezy hilltop site centered on a beautiful big *palapa* (thatch-roofed) area.

One-on-one classes are available any time (M$2000 for a 10-hour week) and the school can help arrange accommodations in family-run guesthouses nearby (from M$100 to M$200 per night). For courses for two people using the same teacher, you'll pay M$1600 each. The school is 400m inland off the main road, signposted beside the bridge in the middle of Mazunte.

⭐ Festivals & Events

Festival Internacional de Jazz
MUSIC

(www.facebook.com/festivalinternacionaldejazz demazunte; ☉mid-Nov) This festival brings three days of top-quality international jazz and other music, plus workshops and exhibitions, to Mazunte around mid-November. All events are free!

🛏 Sleeping

Most of the accommodations are collected in two huddles – one around Playa Rinconcito at the end of the eponymous dirt street, and the other over the 'hump' overlooking Playa Mermejita. The latter area has the pick of the bunch.

Hospedaje El Rinconcito
HOTEL $

(☏984-157-30-56; Calle Rinconcito; s & d M$300-400, with air-con M$550-600; 🅿❄📶) The new kid in town inhabits a terracotta-hued building on Calle Rinconcito and is fronted by a row of crafty shops, including La Baguette (p478) bakery. Rooms are gathered on the 2nd floor around a courtyard cum car lot and are relatively simple with a few dashes of color. Most have two double beds. Some have air-conditioning.

Posada del Arquitecto
CABAÑAS $

(www.posadadelarquitecto.com; Playa Rinconcito; dm M$70-100, estrella M$100, cabins M$400-1200; 🅿📶) Arquitecto looks slightly grungy from beach level, but venture inside its rooms and the quality shines through. Its quirk is its *camas colgantes* (hanging beds) also known as *estrellas*. Some of them are set on the hillside *en plein air*, sheltered only by *palapas*; others are suspended from the ceiling on ropes inside cabins and encased in graceful white mosquito nets.

You can rock yourself to sleep to the sound of crashing waves (Playa Rinconcito is inches away). There are cheaper dorm rooms on offer too.

Cabañas Balamjuyuc
CABAÑAS $

(✆ cell 958-5837667; http://balamjuyuc.blogspot. com; Camino a Punta Cometa; camping per person M$100, tent & bedding rental M$150, dm M$150, cabañas M$500-800; P 🗢) The words *paz y amor* (love and peace) greet you at clifftop Balamjuyuc, proof of its hippie credentials. The cabins here are pretty simple, focusing instead on the real deal, the location – high up, surrounded by nature with views over the rocky coastline. There probably isn't a better place to indulge in yoga, therapeutic massage and temazcal steam-baths, all of which are on offer.

Aside from the comfortable cabins, there's a dormitory, camping and rent-a-tent deals available.

★ Hotel Arigalan
HOTEL $$

(✆ cell 958-1086987; www.arigalan.com; Cerrada del Museo de la Tortuga; cabañas M$700, without bathroom M$500-650, ste M$1800-2000; P ❄ 🗢) The best of both worlds can be found high above the lofty headland between Mazunte and San Agustinillo where you get spectacular views of two beaches. If that wasn't enough, Arigalan has trendy virgin-white rooms punctuated with some Frida Kahlo iconography, hammocks, a pool and an air of casual refinement. No under-18s accepted here. Breakfast is available on request from December to April.

Oceanomar
CABAÑAS $$

(✆ cell 958-5890376; www.oceanomar.com; Camino a Mermejita, Playa Mermejita; s/d/tr M$1600/1800/2000; P 🗢 ❄) On a lovely and cleverly landscaped hillside site with great views over Playa Mermejita, Italian-owned Oceanomar has a gorgeous pool and just five spacious, well-built rooms with nice craft details, hammock-slung terraces and good bathrooms. There's a great little on-site restaurant also called **Oceanomar** (mains M$120-200; ⊗ hotel guests 8am-10pm, public 7-10pm; 🍴), serving meals for guests all day and open to nonguests in the evening.

El Copal
CABAÑAS $$

(✆ cell 55-41942167; www.elcopal.com.mx; Playa Mermejita; cabañas M$1050-1350; P 🗢) 🍴 Hard-to-find Copal hugs a forested hill behind Playa Mermejita with steps leading up to an arty **restaurant** (mains M$95-130;

⊗ 7am-10:30pm; 🗢), along with a pool that appears as infinite as the sea beyond. It's a leafy secluded spot with *cabañas* of adobe, wood and palm-thatch, all containing a double bed on the ground floor and two or three singles above.

Recently added are some Native American tepees. The bathrooms are quaint open-air affairs with views.

Celeste del Mar
ROOMS $$

(✆ cell 958-1075296; www.celestedelmar.com; Playa Mermejita; r M$1550; 🗢) 🍴 A few steps from Playa Mermejita, this small hotel offers eight carefully designed rooms in two-story *palapa*-roofed cottages with attractive contemporary decorative details. The four airy upstairs rooms feature loft areas with big double hammocks under their high roofs; no under-18s.

Casa Pan de Miel
HOTEL $$$

(✆ cell 958-1004719; www.casapandemiel.com; r US$150-350; P ❄ 🗢 ❄) This is a place for real relaxation, equipped with a lovely infinity pool in front of an inviting large *palapa* dining/lounge area. The nine bright, elegant air-conditioned rooms are adorned with varied Mexican art, and all have sea views, kitchen or kitchenette, and terraces with hammocks. The excellent breakfasts (US$9 to US$15) include organic eggs and homemade jams, breads and yogurt.

It's up a steep track from the main road at the east end of Mazunte and enjoys wonderful views. Children are not accepted because of the clifftop position.

🍴 Eating

La Baguette
BAKERY, CAFE $

(Rinconcito; baked goods M$25-50; ⊗ 8am-9pm) On your way down Calle Rinconcito to the beach you'll surely have to stop for this little bakery well stocked with ready-made baguettes, muffins, pizza slices and coffee made in a stove-top pot.

★ Alessandro
ITALIAN $$

(✆ cell 958-1220700; El Rinconcito; mains M$95-145; ⊗ 6-10:30pm Wed-Mon; 🍴) On Oaxaca's coast you're never far from an expat Italian chef who's generously imported his/her culinary know-how and opened a restaurant. Few are as good as Alessandro. His tiny but brilliant place has just six tables in a corner of the Posada del Arquitecto (p477), but it serves up wonderful homemade pasta (eg in arugula-and-avocado pesto).

Also on offer is fresh fish (maybe served in *guajillo* chili and tomatillo sauce), *filet miñón* (beef tenderloin in white wine and olive oil, with parmesan) and desserts (don't miss the mousse of Oaxacan chocolate with orange-and-rum perfume). Good drinks include Argentine wine, Oaxacan mezcal and thirst-quenching *aguas de frutas* (fruit cordials). Go early to avoid waiting.

La Cuisine   MEDITERRANEAN, MEXICAN **$$**
(☑cell 958-1071836; Andador Barrita; 3-course comida corrida M$190; ◷6:30-11pm Tue-Sat) An immediate success when it opened in 2015, La Cuisine does a three-course *comida corrida gourmet* (gourmet set menu), with four options for each course. The menu changes daily, according to the market-fresh ingredients that the dedicated French cook acquires, and is posted each morning on the Facebook page. It's just off Calle Rinconcito in the first side lane back from the beach.

Siddhartha   INTERNATIONAL **$$**
(El Rinconcito; dishes M$70-150; ◷8am-11pm; 🛜🍴) A classic beach-bum-meets-backpacker place where you can wander in half-dressed from the beach and no one will bat an eyelid. The menu is an all-over-the-map dissertation of pesto pasta, burgers, salads, fish of the day, falafels and two-for-one cocktails. Inside young backpackers sip beer in front of giant waves and try to break their social media addiction.

🛍 Shopping

**Cosméticos
Naturales Mazunte**   ARTS & CRAFTS
(☑cell 958-5874860; www.cosmeticosmazunte.com; Paseo del Mazunte; ◷9am-4pm Mon-Sat, 10am-2pm Sun) 🌿 This very successful small cooperative, toward the village's west end, makes and sells products such as shampoo, cosmetics, mosquito repellent, soap and herbal medicines, using natural sources like maize, coconut and essential oils. You'll find its toiletries in hotel bathrooms all over Oaxaca state. It also sells organic coffee and tahini, and you can have a look at the workshop while here.

ℹ Information

Santander ATM (Paseo del Mazunte) Just west of the church on the main drag.
Tourist Information Kiosk (Paseo del Mazunte; ◷9am-5pm Sat & Sun) By the roadside at the west end of the village.

ℹ Getting There & Away

Atlántida (☑cell 958-198911) Comfortable vans depart for San José del Pacífico (M$140, 4¼ hours) and Oaxaca (M$200, 6¾ hours) 11 times daily from Paseo del Mazunte, just east of the church. Book in advance by phone or from the Pochutla office (p470).

Local transportation to the nearby villages is provided by *colectivos* and *camionetas*. Flag them down anywhere on the main street.

La Ventanilla

📞958 / POP 100

Some 2.5km along the road west from Mazunte, a sign points to the tiny beach village of La Ventanilla, 1.2km down a dirt track. La Ventanilla is home to a community-led eco-project protecting turtles, crocodiles and a long, wild beach and lagoon. You can take a boat trip on the lagoon to see crocodiles, and go bird-watching or ride a horse along the beach. Somehow this tiny village manages to have two rival cooperatives offering these services: both have some English-speaking guides and do a fine job.

🏃 Activities

Lagarto Real   WILDLIFE WATCHING
(☑cell 958-1080354; www.facebook.com/lagarto.real; 1½hr lagoon tours adult/child M$80/40; ◷tours 8am-6pm) 🌿 Lagarto Real, the members of which wear red shirts, has its office on the roadside near the beach and another in the village itself. It offers lagoon boat trips (without an island stop), early-morning bird-watching (M$150 per person per hour) and nocturnal turtle-nesting observation.

**Servicios Ecoturísticos
La Ventanilla**   WILDLIFE
(☑cell 958-1087726; www.laventanilla.com.mx; 1½hr lagoon tours adult/child M$100/50; ◷tours 8am-5pm) 🌿 With its office and restaurant by the roadside as you enter the village, this cooperative (with white-shirt wearing members) runs 12-passenger boat trips on the mangrove-fringed lagoon to spot endangered river crocodiles (there are several hundred in the local protected area), lots of water birds (most prolific from November to March) and a few deer, monkeys, eagles and coatis in enclosures on an island.

It also offers three-hour horseback rides (M$500); reserve both the day before. On certain days there's the chance to release turtle hatchlings or join night patrols to see turtles laying eggs (M$250).

❶ Getting There & Away

Camionetas and *taxis colectivos* on the Zipolite–Mazunte–Pochutla route pass the Ventanilla turnoff, leaving you with a 1.2km walk. A taxi from Mazunte should cost M$80. From Zipolite, bank on M$150.

Bahías de Huatulco

🎵 958 / POP 19,000

Huatulco is an interesting experiment in resort development. Until the mid-1980s, this thickly forested slice of Pacific coast hosted nothing more than a few hard-to-reach fishing villages. Then along came government-funded tourist agency, Fonatur, with a mandate to develop the region's nine ruggedly handsome bays for tourism. But Cancún this isn't. Huatulco's development has followed a more ecological bent. Big hotels are spread-out, low-rise and relatively low-key; tracts of virgin forest have been protected in a national park; and the area's unobtrusive infrastructure doesn't really feel like a resort at all. Indeed, the main settlement Crucecita (which houses the coast's original inhabitants) could pass off as any authentic Mexican town with its church, park and street stalls.

The softly, softly approach means that Huatulco appeals to a broad cross-section of travelers who come here to appreciate what has always been the region's raison d'être: world-class beaches nestled in sheltered coves backed by broccoli-colored forest.

◎ Sights

Huatulco's beaches are beautiful and sandy with clear turquoise waters. Some have coral offshore and excellent snorkeling. As in the rest of Mexico, all beaches are under federal control, and anyone can use them, even when hotels appear to treat them as private property.

The area is popularly described as having nine different bays protecting over a dozen named beaches.

★ Bahía San Agustín   BEACH

This long, sandy beach, 14km west of Santa Cruz Huatulco, is backed by a fishing village, and in contrast to Huatulco's other settlements, there's absolutely no resort-type development – just a line of rustic *comedores* stretching along the beach, serving seafood and fish dishes and simple *antojitos* (typical Mexican snacks). Usually the waters of the bay are calm, and there is coral with very good snorkeling around the rocks in the bay and at **Playa Riscalillo** round the corner to the east.

San Agustín is popular with Mexicans on weekends and vacations, but quiet at other times. Some *comedores* rent out snorkel gear, and most of them can arrange boats to Riscalillo or Playa La India. Many also have hammocks for rent overnight, or tent space; they may let you stay free if you eat with them. **El Tronco** (🎵 cell 958-1031808; Playa San Agustín; 2-person tents M$150, hammock per person M$50; 🅿) toward the north end is run by a friendly family and has a tent to rent as well as hammocks.

A 13km dirt road heads south to San Agustín from a crossroads on Hwy 200, 1.7km west of the airport. Buses between Huatulco and Pochutla will drop you at the crossroads, where taxis wait to carry people to San Agustín (M$115, or M$25 per person by *colectivo*).

Hagia Sofia   FARM

(www.hagiasofia.mx; Apanguito; incl round-trip transportation & breakfast M$800; 🅿 🚼) ✿ One of Huatulco's loveliest and most interesting day trips, this 'agro-ecotourism' operation includes a large organic fruit orchard and a gorgeous 500m riverside trail with 60 kinds of tropical flowering plants that attract colorful birds and butterflies. You can have a refreshing dip beneath a waterfall while you're there. It's 9km northwest of Santa María Huatulco and about 30km from La Crucecita (a 45-minute drive).

You can visit any day, but reserve the day before in person or by phoning the **office** (🎵 958-587-08-71, cell 958-5837943; Local 7, Mitla 402; ⊗ 9am-2pm & 4-7pm Mon-Fri, 11am-5pm Sat) in Santa Cruz Huatulco: tours are given in English or Spanish and most people stay about four hours.

Bahía Conejos   BEACH

The oddly named 'rabbit bay,' 3km east of Tangolunda, has a long main beach divided by a small rocky outcrop into the western **Playa Arenas** and the eastern **Playa Punta Arenas**, both reachable by short walks from the paved road. The surf can be strong here. At the east end of the bay is the more sheltered **Playa Conejos**, site of the super-plush Secrets Huatulco Resort (p484), but still accessible to Joe Public.

Bahía Cacaluta   BEACH
Cacaluta is a 1km-long slice of paradise that's protected by an island, backed by dunes and usually deliciously deserted. The Mexican road-trip movie *Y Tú Mamá También* was famously filmed there. Swimming is possible, although there can be undertow. Snorkeling is best around the island. There are no services at the beach, so bring plenty of water. *Lancha* (motorboat) is only way to currently get there. There is technically a trail to the beach, the **Sendero Zanate**, but it was closed to the public at last visit.

Bahía Maguey   BEACH
(P ♿) Three kilometers west of Santa Cruz and easily walkable along a new roadside pavement, Maguey's fine 400m beach curves around a calm bay between forested headlands. A line of a dozen or more family-friendly *palapas* serves fish and seafood dishes for M$100-plus, along with rather nice piña coladas. There's good snorkeling around the rocks on the east side of the bay; **Escualo** (snorkeling set M$100; ⊙8am-6pm) rents out gear. Plenty of taxis wait in the car park. The fare to Santa Cruz is M$70.

Bahía Chachacual   BEACH
Inaccessible by land, Chachacual has two beaches: the easterly **Playa La India** is one of Huatulco's most beautiful scimitars of sand and one of the area's best places for snorkeling. The eponymous **Playa Chachacual** is longer with strong sea currents. There are no facilities on either beach bar the odd local selling coconuts.

**Parroquia de Nuestra
Señora de Guadalupe**   CHURCH
(Plaza Principal, La Crucecita; ⊙8am-6pm) Let it not be said that the age of great church building is dead. Crucecita's pale-orange colonial-style ecclesial dame dates from – ahem – 2000, but, what it lacks in history it makes up for in neck-tilting beauty. A huge 20m-long painting of the Virgin of Guadalupe is etched on the ceiling. Complementing Mexican's patron saint are a couple of colorful side chapels filled with mosaics and other murals.

**Parque Eco-Arqueológico
Copalita**   ARCHAEOLOGICAL SITE
(☑958-587-15-91;   Blvd   Copalita-Tangolunda; Mexican/non-Mexican M$60/80;   ⊙8am-4pm Tue-Sun; P) Granted, it's no Monte Albán, but this pre-Hispanic site 600m north of La Bocana village is your only true glimpse of history in made-in-the-1980s Huatulco. Excavations are ongoing, but, to date, a ball court and two fairly modest temples have been uncovered. Adding to the appeal is a small museum, a jungle path to a spectacular clifftop lookout (site of an ancient 'guiding stone' possibly also used for sacrifices) and some new explanatory signs in Spanish and English.

The site was occupied by different groups between about 500 BC and AD 500, and again from 1000 to the 16th century. You can wander around on your own or hire a guide (M$480 for up to four people). Parking costs M$10. A taxi to Crucecita is M$1000.

Playa La Entrega   BEACH
(P ♿) La Entrega lies toward the outer edge of Bahía de Santa Cruz, a five-minute *lancha* trip or 2.5km walk/drive along a bendy road from Santa Cruz. This 300m beach, backed by a line of seafood *palapas,* can get busy, but it has decent (if sometimes crowded) snorkeling on a coral plate from which boats are cordoned off. Gear is available at **Renta de Snorkel Vicente** (☑cell 958-1168197; snokeling gear M$75, kayak per hour M$250; ⊙7:30am-dusk) at the beach's northern end.

'La Entrega' means 'The Delivery': in 1831 Mexican independence hero Vicente Guerrero was handed over here to his political enemies by a Genoese sea captain. Guerrero was then taken to Cuilapan near Oaxaca and shot.

La Bocana   BEACH
(P) About 1.5km east of Playa Conejos, just before the Parque Eco-Arqueológico Copalita, lies Hutatulco's most low-key beach. Less pretty than other spots, Bocana is the surfers' choice courtesy of a decent right-hand surf break near the mouth of the Río Copalita. There's a **surf school** (☑958-130-18-32; www.bocanasurf.com; Playa La Bocana; surf lesson US$75; ⊙hours vary) offering lessons and rentals on site (look out for the VW campervan mural) plus a couple of agreeably shabby restaurants facing the waves.

Bahía Tangolunda   BEACH
Tangolunda, 5km east of Santa Cruz Huatulco, is the site of most of the major top-end hotel developments. The long, wide, spotlessly clean beach is accessible to the public at its west end just beyond the golf

Bahías de Huatulco

5 km
2.5 miles

Río Copalita

Parque Eco-Arqueológico Copalita

Playa La Bocana

Playa Magueyito

La Bocana

Barra de la Cruz (14km)

Copalita

Playa Conejos

Playa Arenas

Bahía Conejos

Residencial Conejos

PACIFIC OCEAN

Tangolunda

Bahía Tangolunda

Playa Tangolunda

Playa Arrocito

Huatulco Expediciones

Parque Ecológico Rufino Tamayo

Playa Chahué

Bahía Chahué

Chahué

Bahía de Santa Cruz

Playa La Entrega

Las Palmas

La Crucecita

Santa Cruz Huatulco

Playa Santa Cruz

Playa El Órgano

Bahía El Órgano

Bahía Maguey

Sendero Zanate

Playa Maguey

Bahía Cacaluta

Playa Cacaluta

Parque Nacional Huatulco

Sendero Sabanal

Río Cacaluta

Parque Nacional Huatulco

Playa La India

Bahía Chachacual

Playa Chachacual

Playa Riscalillo

Bahía San Agustín

Playa San Agustín

San Agustín

MEX 200

Río San Agustín

Airport

Santa María Huatulco (9km)

Pochutla (30km)

course. A rocky headland (climbable with care) splits the beach in two.

Bahía El Órgano
BEACH

Just east of Bahía Maguey, this lush 250m beach has calm waters good for snorkeling, and no crowds because there's no vehicle access and no *comedores*. You can come by boat (most do), or walk to the beach by a 1km path through the forest. The path starts about 1.3km back toward Santa Cruz from the Maguey parking lot; the easy-to-miss entry is marked by signs telling people not to molest wildlife, light fires etc. It becomes a mini-river in the rainy season.

Corredor Turístico
STREET

One of Huatulco's more recent developments is a wide terraced walkway that leads from Crucecita to the Santa Cruz cruise terminal. The path then carries on west paralleling the road all the way out to Playa Maguey.

Bahía Chahué
BEACH

([P]) The beach here, 1km east of Santa Cruz Huatulco, is wide with soft sand, but offers little in the way of shade, plus the surf can be surprisingly strong. There's a marina at its east end. Locals use it as an impromptu football pitch.

🏃 Activities

Huatulco Expediciones
RAFTING

([☎]958-587-21-26; www.huatulcoexpediciones. com; Hwy 200 Km 256, Puente Tangolunda, Comunidad La Jabalina; [♿]) Runs rafting trips on the Río Copalita near Huatulco, from all-day outings on the Class III–IV Alemania section starting 800m above sea level (M$650 to M$700 per person; generally July to December) to a gentler 2½-hour jaunt down the Copalita's final 5km to the ocean at La Bocana (M$300 to M$350 per person; available all year and suitable for children).

Diving & Snorkeling

You can rent snorkeling gear, including life jacket and fins, at Santa Cruz harbor for M$130 a day if you're taking a boat trip from there. Renters at one or two beaches have lower rates. The best snorkeling sites include the coral plates at La Entrega, San Agustín and the inshore side of the island at Cacaluta. You can either hire a *lancha* (motorboat) from Santa Cruz to take you to snorkel sites or take a snorkeling tour with one of Huatulco's diving outfits.

The Huatulco coast has over 100 dive sites, 40 of them marked by buoys. There's a good variety of fish and corals, plus dolphins, turtles and (from about December to March) humpback whales. This is a good place to learn to dive, with warm waters, varied underwater scenery, and calm conditions almost year-round. Visibility averages 10m to 20m. There's a decompression chamber in the local navy hospital.

Huatulco Dive Center
DIVING, SNORKELING

([☎]958-583-42-95; www.huatulcodivecenter.com; Marina Chahué; [⏰]9am-6pm Mon-Fri, to 4pm Sat) A highly efficient PADI dive shop at the Marina Chahué. They offer two-tank dives (US$95), Discover Scuba courses in the open water for first-timers (US$150 – price includes two immersions) and a range of PADI courses and snorkeling trips.

Diving excursions usually set out a 9:30pm. Most dive sites are within 20 minutes of boat launch.

Hurricane Divers
DIVING, SNORKELING

([☎]958-587-11-07; www.hurricanedivers.com; Playa Santa Cruz; [⏰]9am-6pm Mon-Fri, to 4pm Sat) This very professional international crew is one of Mexico's few PADI 5-Star Dive Resorts. Options include two-tank dives (US$95) and night dives (US$70) for certified divers (plus US$5 each for buoyancy control device (BCD), regulator and wet suit if needed), and half-day PADI Discover Scuba courses (US$150) for beginners, which include two short dives.

Hiking & Mountain Biking

There are several trails within the Parque Nacional Huatulco, but travelers are strongly pushed into doing them as part of an organized excursion. Huatulco Salvaje (p484) is your best bet for interesting guided hikes and bike trips in this area.

☞ Tours

Practically every agency in town offers the 'Seven Bays Tour' that calls into seven of Huatulco's nine bays with stops for snorkeling and lunch. Prices are a fairly generic M$350.

There are also trips to local waterfalls, rafting on the Copalita River and several undemanding hiking and biking excursions. You'll see these and other trips well advertized in hotels and information kiosks all over the resort strip.

★ Huatulco Salvaje
ADVENTURE

(📱cell 958-5874028, cell 958-1193886; www.huatulcosalvaje.com; Local 2, Mitla 402, Santa Cruz Huatulco; ⏰9am-2pm & 4:30-7:30pm Mon-Sat; 🚲) 🏄 Huatulco Salvaje is a group of certified tour guides from the local community, many of them from village families displaced when the Parque Nacional Huatulco was created in the 1990s. They know their stuff when it comes to nature tours hereabouts.

Pop into their office in Santa Cruz's Ocean Park building to organize seaborne activities including five-hour snorkeling boat trips (M$2000 to M$3500 for up to 10 people), various walking trips, and whale-, dolphin- and turtle-watching (October to April, four hours, M$650 per person, minimum five).

They also rent out bikes per hour/day M$40/200.

🛏 Sleeping

You'll find all budget and many midrange options in La Crucecita. Further midrange possibilities are in Chahué and Santa Cruz. The top-end resort hotels are at Tangolunda and beyond and are typically all-inclusive.

Flight-and-lodging package deals are your best bet for a good-value vacation in a top-end Huatulco hotel.

AM Hotel y Plaza
HOTEL $

(📱958-587-14-89; www.amhotelyplaza.com; Blvd Chahué 1601, La Crucecita; r M$500-700; 🅿❄🌐🏊) An interesting new 'concept' hotel with an open reception on a roadside plaza welcoming you to slick, minimalist rooms perched in a large angular structure above the traffic. There's even a bizarre little plunge pool overlooking the otherwise dull boulevard. Everything is clean, scrubbed, and straight off the shelf, plus it's right next to the bus station and spitting distance from downtown Crucecita.

Hotel Nonni
HOTEL $

(📱958-587-03-72; Bugambilia 203, La Crucecita; r from M$500; ❄🌐) Nonni is a new hotel still in mint condition. Expect rooms with modern fittings, freshly tiled showers and an aura of underlying cleanliness. While modest in ambition, it's no ugly duckling and has some well-thought-out details, with plenty of power sockets, good lighting and large beds with mattresses comfortable enough to make getting up in the morning a chore.

Hotel María Mixteca
HOTEL $

(📱958-587-09-90; www.mariamixtecahuatulco.com; Guamuchil 204, La Crucecita; r M$550-650; 🅿❄🌐) María Mixteca offers 14 prettily decorated yellow-and-white rooms on two upper floors around an open patio, with super-comfy beds, air-conditioning, all-you-need bathrooms and room safes. It's half a block east of the Plaza Principal and shares digs with El Sabor de Oaxaca (p487) restaurant.

Hotel Jaroje Centro
HOTEL $

(📱958-583-48-01; www.hotelhuatulco.com.mx; Bugambilia 304, La Crucecita; d/q M$550/750; ❄🌐) Bright Jaroje, two blocks south of the Plaza Principal, has 13 large, clean, white rooms with mosquito screens, air-con and either one king-sized bed or two normal-sized double beds. Balconies overlook the street.

★ Misión de los Arcos
HOTEL $$

(📱958-587-01-65; http://misiondelosarcos.website; Gardenia 902, La Crucecita; r/ste M$654/892; ❄🌐) Surprise! Huatulco's best-loved hotel isn't one of the big all-inclusives but these more humble yet fiercely traditional accommodations half a block off Crucecita's Plaza Principal. While not particularly old, the Misión is nonetheless embellished by a touch of colonial style with interior greenery, bright air-conditioned rooms, very comfortable beds and homey touches, for which you would pay a lot more in other places.

There's walk-through access to the excellent Terra-Cotta (p486) restaurant, under the same ownership.

Hotel Posada Edén Costa
HOTEL $$

(📱958-587-24-80; www.edencosta.com; Zapoteco 26, Chahué; r/ste incl breakfast M$800/1200; 🅿❄🌐) Swiss- and Laotian-owned Edén Costa, 500m inland from Bahía Chahué, has attractive rooms with avian touches in the form of colorful bird murals. Most rooms have two double beds and overlook the small central pool. Suites have their own kitchens. The attached restaurant, L'Échalote (p486), is a big bonus.

Secrets Huatulco Resort & Spa
RESORT $$$

(📱USA 866-467-3273; www.secretsresorts.com.mx; Bahía de Conejos; r all-incl US$165-295; 🅿❄@🌐🏊) Opened in 2012 and still looking as plush as the day it was born, Secrets is a pretty ravishing offering. For starters, there's the location, perched above the golden ribbon of Playa Conejos between two spinach-colored headlands. Then there's the Vegas-sized super-rooms with Jacuzzi baths, Nespresso machines, dressing gowns, slippers and private pools, not to mention the more prosaic essentials.

Communal areas are equally extravagant from the exotic gardens to the polished apples on the reception desk. Indeed, the place is scrubbed so clean, you almost have to walk around in sunglasses. And did we mention the spa, gym, bird-watching trail and two kidney-shaped pools?

Las Palmas
SUITES $$$

(✆cell 958-1091448; www.laspalmashuatulco. com; Camino a Playa La Entrega; casitas/villas US$190/750; P❋🛜🏊) On a lovely site looking down on little Playa Violín, along the road between Santa Cruz and Playa La Entrega, Las Palmas is a marvelous discovery for couples, families or larger groups who have a vehicle and want to self-cater. The three bright, spacious four-bedroom villas enjoy large sitting/eating areas opening on to their own infinity pools.

The five smaller but also attractive casitas (for up to four people) share a kitchen, pool and large *palapa* (thatch-roofed) dining area. The tilework and crafts are beautiful, kayaks and mountain bikes are provided free, and the whole place has an expansive but private feel.

Camino Real Zaashila
LUXURY HOTEL $$$

(✆958-583-03-00; www.caminoreal.com; Blvd Juárez 5, Tangolunda; r from M$2410; P❋🛜🏊) The Zaashila is rendered in smooth white adobe on a lovingly manicured terraced slope above the ocean, giving it a palpable Greek Islands feel. You'll probably feel a bit like Zeus or Aphrodite when you book into your large ocean-facing room with its private pool, luxuriant sheets, Jacuzzi bathtub and king-of-the-gods-sized bed.

The other draw – if you need one – is the food. Two particularly fine restaurants slot seamlessly into the Garden of Eden grounds, including the Mexican-Thai fusion Azul Profundo (p487).

Hotel Binniguenda
RESORT $$$

(✆958-583-26-00; www.binniguendahuatulco. com.mx; Blvd Santa Cruz 201, Santa Cruz Huatulco; s/d all-inclusive M$6700/9000; P❋@🛜🏊) Not as monstrous in size as your average all-inclusive, the Binniguenda is a historical monument in Huatulco years. It was the resort's first hotel when it opened in 1987. With its refined ambience, small attractive pool and colonial-style architecture, it hasn't aged badly. Indeed, a 2012 renovation has meant it remains proudly plush.

While not on the beach, the hotel is close to Santa Cruz's sand and has a nice quiet feel. With only 80 rooms, it is just small enough to merit a more intimate personable level of service. Look out for online deals.

🍴 Eating

Around 80% of the eating options are in 'downtown' Crucecita. Several of the beaches – most notably Playas Santa Cruz, Entrega, Maquey and San Agustín – have lines of generically good *palapas* (open palm-thatch beach shacks). Being an all-inclusive area, Tangolunda is more limited, although there are a couple of lunch places.

Antojitos Los Gallos
MEXICAN $

(cnr Carrizal & Palma Real, La Crucecita; dishes M$55-70; ⊙2-10pm Tue-Sun; 🛜) The beauty of Crucecita is that is looks, feels and *is* Mexican despite its actual youth. Indeed, if you grab a cafeteria-style table in this very simple little diner, a fount of unadulterated Mexican home-cooking – it tastes authentically Mexican too.

Try tuning up with *caldo tlalpeño* (a soup of chicken, veggies, chili and herbs) before launching into a *tlayuda* (a large tortilla) with *res deshebrada* (shredded beef), or maybe some enchiladas.

It does inventive fruit drinks too, like *agua de pepino y limón* (cucumber and lemon cordial).

Xipol
CAFETERIA $

(Guanacastle 311, La Crucecita; breakfast & snacks M$45-100; ⊙7am-11:30pm; 🛜) Bivouacked beneath bohemian La Crema (p487), this new prodigy can claim to be equally arty (a mural by noted Zapotec graffiti artist Irving Cano beautifies one wall). It can deliver in the mezcal stakes and it also offers breakfast washed down with superb coffee. A couple of flat-screen TVs placate travelers missing their European soccer fix.

Casa Mayor
CAFE $

(Bugambilia 601, La Crucecita; dishes M$65-130; ⊙8am-midnight Mon-Sat, 4pm-midnight Sun) 🌿 Overlooking the Plaza Principal, Casa Mayor serves good organic Oaxacan coffee and is perfect for breakfast, baguettes, *antojitos* (Mexican snacks) and cocktails too.

OFF THE BEATEN TRACK

CONCEPCIÓN BAMBA

The coast west from Salina Cruz is spectacular, with long, sweeping sandy beaches, monster dunes and forested mountains rising just inland. It has surfers in raptures for its long-peeling, sand-bottom, right-hand point breaks and several beach and jetty breaks. Concepción Bamba, or La Bamba as it's known, 40km west of Salina Cruz, sits on a 6km beach with two point breaks in the middle, and stands out because it's home to easily the area's most appealing accommodations. The surfing season is from about March to October, but swells don't come every day so check the forecasts.

There's a community turtle camp on the beach, where turtle eggs (laid between October and March) are collected and incubated in a protected enclosure, with hatchlings being released into the ocean after about six weeks.

Cocoleoco Surf Camp (☑ cell 322-1167535; www.cabanabambasurfmx.com; camping per person US$5-7, cabañas US$15-30, bungalows US$40-50, extra person US$10; ⓟ 🛜) 🏄 is the perfect laid-back surf base, in spacious grounds with an appealing mix of bungalows, double rooms, open beds under a thatched palapa and camping space. All, except camping, are equipped with mosquito nets and fans (some with private bathroom), plus there's good French, Mexican and international meals available (lunch mains M$50 to M$80; dinner mains M$100 to M$120) and a guests' cooking area.

The signposted turnoff to Concepción Bamba is at Km 352 on Hwy 200: a 2.5km unpaved road leads to the village, with Cocoleoco Surf Camp on its far side, then it's 800m further to the beach. Buses between Huatulco and Salina Cruz will drop you at the turnoff, where three-wheeler moto-taxis (M$10 per person) run to the village from about 7am to 6pm. There are also *taxis colectivos* to the village from Salina Cruz (M$50, plus M$15 for a surfboard), leaving about hourly, 7am to 7pm, from a lot on Hwy 200 a few steps west of its intersection with Blvd Salina Cruz in the north of town.

A smaller **branch** (cnr Gardenia & Guanacastle, La Crucecita; coffees M$15-40; ⏲7am-11pm) 🏄 on the far corner of the plaza does the same excellent coffee and other drinks. There's often a live troubadour strumming plaintively in the evenings.

Restaurant La Crucecita   MEXICAN $
(☑958-587-09-06; Av Bugambilia 501; mains M$50-95; ⏲7:30am-10pm) Hometown favorite. This inexpensive plastic-bottle-on-the-table spot, a block from the Plaza Principal, proves that simple is sometimes best for fish, chicken and beef dishes when it comes to Oaxacan flavors. There's an economical M$50 *menú del día*. Early in the day, watch the chef prepare serious quantities of *salsa roja* (spicy red salsa).

★**Terra-Cotta**   MEXICAN, INTERNATIONAL $$
(☑958-587-12-28; Gardenia 902, La Crucecita; mains M$80-170; ⏲7:30am-11pm; 🛜🍴) La Crucecita's classiest restaurant is affiliated to the equally classy Misión de los Arcos (p484) and inhabits a refined small dining room air-conditioned to resemble a pleasant summer's day in Paris. The menu is international with an obvious Mexican bias, but here you get complimentary bread rather than default nachos. Choose from prawns, steaks, fish, pasta, baguettes and pizza. A strategically positioned cake cabinet makes skipping dessert tricky.

El Grillo Marinero   SEAFOOD $$
(Carrizal & Macuhitle, La Crucecita; mains M$140-160; ⏲1-8pm Tue-Sun) Huge portions of fish (try the mahimahi if it's available) served in a no-nonsense family-run restaurant that has most locals sighing with affection. Expect beer in a bottle, chipotle sauce in a plastic container, and cheap blow-away serviettes plonked down by a waiter in a Barcelona shirt. All in all, a classic.

L'Échalote   EUROPEAN, MEXICAN $$
(☑958-587-24-80; www.edencosta.com; Hotel Posada Edén Costa, Zapoteco 26, Chahué; mains M$120-230; ⏲6-11pm Tue-Fri, 2-11pm Sat & Sun) The French-Swiss kitchen prepares top-notch French, Mexican and Mediterranean dishes. Specialties include snails, osso buco and fish of the day in a creamy leek sauce. The desserts and French and Italian wines (from M$350) aren't too shabby either, and you can round things off with a super-smooth Armagnac.

El Sabor de Oaxaca OAXACAN $$
(958-587-00-60; Guamuchil 206, La Crucecita; mains M$140-180; 7:30am-11pm) Sit amid the sound of roosting birds and whirring fans and let friendly servers bring you classic Oaxacan food. Lots of local specialties are on show here, including *tlayudas* (barbecued tortillas) and *moles*. You can go the 'full monty' (Oaxacan-style) if you order your *tlayuda* with *chapulines* (grasshoppers).

Giordanas ITALIAN $$
(958-583-43-24; www.giordanas-delizie.com; cnr Gardenia & Palma Real, La Crucecita; pastas M$90-130, antipasti M$120-220; noon-10pm Tue-Sat;) The talented Italian chef here makes almost everything herself, including the pasta. Options include ravioli with a choice of five fillings and nine sauces, meat or vegetarian lasagne, and some pretty good antipasti including carpaccios and Parma ham with melon. Plus there's a choice of Italian wine. Giordanas also does a great selection of baguettes with Italian cheeses and salamis.

Azul Profundo SEAFOOD $$$
(958-583-03-00; Camino Real Zaashila, Blvd Juárez 5, Tangolunda; mains M$200-300; 7-11pm Mon, Wed, Fri & Sun) Unusually for an all-inclusive, the Camino Real Zaashila (p485) allows nonguests into its best restaurant, a romantic candlelit affair aside the ocean, to experience rich but expensive seafood. If you've ever dreamed of lobster and champagne over a tangerine sunset, polish up your credit card.

Drinking & Nightlife

Palapas (ie beach bars) are common and can usually rustle up large potent cocktails inches from the waves. All-inclusive resorts put on their own slightly canned entertainment (expect Elvis impersonators and cheesy cabaret). Downtown Crucecita has a modest bar scene embellished by mellow musicians and a bit of mezcal-fueled karaoke.

★La Crema BAR
(958-587-07-02; www.lacremahuatulco.com; Gardenia 311, La Crucecita; 7pm-2am;) Part of the success of Huatulco is that it can cough up something as cool as La Crema, a dark-lit upstairs bar where a thrown-together mesh of old sofas and retro decor attracts anyone who's into punk, piazza, mezcal and reggae. It's always an interesting

place to roll up, especially when they put on live music (weekends mainly).

El Tonel BAR
(958-587-17-90; Carrizal 504, cnr Framboyán, La Crucecita; noon-11pm) Plunge into Crucecita's newest mezcal dive, which is actually rather large compared to your average *mezcalería*, with moody lighting, lurid graffiti and plenty of stools upon which to perch. Music of the salsa-ing variety loosens the limbs on Friday and Saturday nights.

Paletería Zamora JUICE BAR
(Plaza Principal, La Crucecita; drinks M$20-65; 7:15am-11:45pm) Some get sloshed on beer, others wander into Zamora for the kind of smoothies that would make even hippies raise their eyebrows. Para la Prostrata (for the prostrate) is a combo of carrots, asparagus and lettuce; and there are other equally robust mixes for the liver, kidneys and heart.

Then there's the ice cream. If you've just OD'd on jalapeños, the rice popsicle (basically rice pudding on a stick) is a soothing joy.

Shopping

Paradise ARTS & CRAFTS
(Gardenia 803; 9:30am-9:30pm) Crucecita doesn't lack shops, but if you're looking for something a bit quirkier than underpants and socks, this local craft outlet can oblige with black clay pottery, copal-wood *alebrijes* and some psychedelic clothes.

Information

Tourist Information Kiosk (Plaza Principal, La Crucecita; 9am-9pm) This main *módulo* (kiosk) is in Crucecita's Plaza Principal, but there are several others dotted around, including in Santa Cruz.

Getting There & Away

AIR

Possibly the world's handsomest airport with white walls and a gabled thatched roof, **Huatulco Airport** (958-581-90-04) is located 400m north of Hwy 200, 15km west of La Crucecita. There are direct international flights to/from Houston, USA, with **United** (www.united.com); and from November to May (or parts of that period) to/from several Canadian airports with **Air Canada** (www.aircanada.com), **Air Transat** (www.airtransat.ca), **Sunwing Airlines** (www.flysunwing.com) and **WestJet** (www.westjet.com), and to/from Minneapolis with **Sun Country Airlines** (www.suncountry.com).

Other airlines include the following:

Aeroméxico (958-581-91-26; www.aero mexico.com; 9:30am-6:30pm) Mexico City twice daily.

Aerotucán (958-581-90-85; 8am-noon) Flies 13-seat Cessnas daily to/from Oaxaca (M$2042). Flights are sometimes canceled or rescheduled at short notice.

Interjet (958-581-91-16; 9am-5pm) Mexico City at least twice daily.

Magnicharters (800-201-14-04; www. magnicharters.com) Mexico City daily except Tuesday, plus Monterrey.

TAR Aerolíneas (www.tarmexico.com; 9am-5pm) Oaxaca four times weekly, Guadalajara twice.

Volaris (55-1102-8000; www.volaris.com) Mexico City at least twice weekly, plus flights to Chicago and Monterrey.

BUS, VAN & TAXI COLECTIVO

Some buses to Huatulco are marked 'Santa Cruz Huatulco,' but they still terminate in La Crucecita. Make sure your bus is not headed to Santa María Huatulco, which is some way inland.

Taxis colectivos to Pochutla (M$35, one hour) leave from the street corner beside Soriana hypermarket on Blvd Chahué, 200m west of the OCC Bus Station in La Crucecita.

Central Camionera (Carpinteros s/n, Sector V, La Crucecita) Located 1.2km northwest of central La Crucecita; used by Turistar (deluxe), AltaMar (1st-class), Transportes Rápidos de Pochutla (TRP; 2nd-class) and Istmeños (2nd-class) buses.

Expressos Colombo (cnr Gardenia & Sabalí, La Crucecita) Passenger vans to Oaxaca; the terminal is 400m north of the Plaza Principal.

Huatulco 2000 (Guamuchil, La Crucecita) Passenger vans to Oaxaca. Located 150m east of the Plaza Principal.

OCC Bus Station (Blvd Chahué, La Crucecita) Located 500m north of the Plaza Principal; used by ADO GL (deluxe), OCC (1st-class) and Sur and AU (2nd-class) buses.

ℹ Getting Around

TO/FROM THE AIRPORT

Taxis autorizados (authorized taxis) cost M$430 for a whole cab from the airport to La Crucecita, Santa Cruz, Chahué or Tangolunda, but you can usually get one for half this price, or less, by walking 300m down to Hwy 200, where drivers wait at the airport intersection. Or catch a bus from the same intersection to La Crucecita (M$8) or Pochutla (M$20): they pass about every 15 minutes in both directions from about 6am to 8pm. To get back to the airport from La Crucecita costs M$170 in a taxi.

BICYCLE

You can rent bikes for around M$200 per day from Huatulco Salvaje (p484). Roads are light on traffic and regular *topes* (ramps) prevent speeding.

BOAT

Some of the western bays and most of the eastern ones are accessible by road, but a boat ride is more fun, if more expensive, than a taxi. *Lanchas* (motorboats) will whisk you out to most beaches from Santa Cruz harbor any time after 8am and return to collect you by dusk. Round-trip rates for up to 10 people: Playa La Entrega M$800, Bahía Órgano M$1500, Bahía Maguey M$1500, Bahía Cacaluta M$2000, Playa La

BUS & VANS FROM BAHÍAS DE HUATULCO

DESTINATION	FARE (M$)	DURATION (HR)	FREQUENCY (DAILY)
Mexico City (Sur) via Puerto Escondido	956-1235	14-15	AltaMar 3:30pm, Turistar 4pm
Mexico City (TAPO) via Salina Cruz	765-1116	14-15	4 from OCC terminal
Oaxaca via Salina Cruz	279-305	8	4 from OCC terminal
Oaxaca via San José del Pacífico	230	7	13 Expressos Colombo, 8 Huatulco 2000
Pochutla	39-74	1	23 from OCC terminal, TRP every 10-15min 5:30am-8pm
Puerto Escondido	81-162	2½	23 from OCC terminal
Salina Cruz	164-218	2¾	Istmeños hourly 4am-6pm, 13 from OCC terminal
San Cristóbal de las Casas	630	10	OCC 9pm, 11:55pm
Tehuantepec	176-206	3½	Istmeños hourly 4am-6pm, 12 from OCC terminal

THE 2017 EARTHQUAKE

A major 8.2 magnitude earthquake (the strongest in Mexico in over a century) dealt a huge blow to the Oaxaca coast in September 2017, particularly the area around the Isthmus de Tehuantepec. Juchitán was the city that fared the worst with many of its older structures in and around central Jardín Juárez collapsing completely or suffering major damage. The most public of images was the sight of the Palacio de Ayuntamiento, a graceful 19th-century town hall with 31 arches, partially caved in. Another casualty was the 16th-century Vicente Ferrer church around the corner, which lost one tower with the other one left hanging precariously over the adjacent Lidxi Guendabiaani like a loose piece of Lego. The school in front of the church, the Centro Escolar Juchitán, had to be demolished completely due to irrevocable structural damage.

At the time of writing some business had returned to Juchitán. The outdoor market in Jardín Juárez was functioning relatively normally and so were many of the town's restaurants. However, most of Juchitán's hotels remained closed. Check ahead if you are traveling to the area as the situation is liable to change.

The town of Tehuantepec, 28km southwest of Juchitan, suffered less severe damage, although roofs on some of the older colonial structures failed to withstand the tremors. Notwithstanding, most of the town's hotels and restaurants remained operational.

Huatulco, Puerto Escondido and the coast around Zipolite were unaffected by the quake and are open for business as usual.

India M$2800 and Bahía San Agustín M$3500. For Cacaluta and Bahía Chachacual to its west, there's a M$50 fee for entering the Parque Nacional Huatulco, also collected at the harbor. Use of nonbiodegradable sunscreen is prohibited within the national park.

BUS & TAXI

Taxis are the main modus operandi around Huatulco's spread-out sights. They have set rates clearly displayed at every taxi rank. Sample rates from Crucecita are M$30 to Santa Cruz or the Central Camionera, M$43 to Tangolunda, M$60 to Playa La Entrega and M$70 to Bahía Maguey.

Blue-and-white local buses run every few minutes during daylight. To Santa Cruz Huatulco they go from Plaza El Madero mall on Guamuchil, two blocks east of the plaza in La Crucecita. Fares cost M$5.

CAR & MOTORCYCLE

Car rental is available.

Europcar (☎958-581-90-94; Huatulco Airport; ☺8:30am-6:30pm) Reasonable rates and good service.

Los Tres Reyes (☎cell 958-1051376; http://lostresreyescarrent.com; Lote 20, Blvd Chahué manzana 1, La Crucecita; ☺8am-8pm) Efficient local firm with good rates.

Zipping around on a scooter can be a fun way to get around Huatulco. **Aventura Mundo** (☎958-581-0197; www.aventuramundo.net; Blvd Benito Juárez; ☺9am-7pm) in Tangolunda rents out good Japanese bikes, with helmets and a map, from US$35 per day (discounts for more

than one day). There's generally no insurance available with scooter rental.

WALKING

The whole area from La Bocana in the east to Playa Maguey in the west has a wide, relatively smooth pavement running alongside the road making walking both safe and easy.

ISTHMUS OF TEHUANTEPEC

The southern half of the 200km-wide Isthmus of Tehuantepec (teh-wahn-teh-*pek*), Mexico's narrow waist, forms the flat, hot, humid eastern end of Oaxaca state. Indigenous Zapotec culture is strong here, with its own regional twists. In 1496 the isthmus Zapotecs repulsed the Aztecs from the fortress of Guiengola, near Tehuantepec, and the isthmus never became part of the Aztec empire. An independent spirit pervades the region to this day.

Few travelers linger here, but if you do you'll encounter a lively, friendly populace whose open and confident women take leading roles in business and government. Many fiestas feature the *tirada de frutas,* in which women climb on roofs and throw fruit on the men below!

Of the three main towns, isthmus culture is stronger in Tehuantepec and Juchitán than in Salina Cruz, which is dominated by its oil refinery. All three towns can be uncomfortable in the heat and humidity of the day, but evening breezes are deliciously refreshing.

Tehuantepec

📞 971 / POP 42,000

Tehuantepec, 245km from Oaxaca city, is a friendly but hot and sweaty town, and most travelers blow through here on their way to somewhere else. June and August are the main months for partying in the fiestas of Tehuantepec's 15 barrios (neighborhoods), each of which has its own colonial church, many of which are floodlit after dark.

👁 Sights

Ex Convento Rey Cosijopí HISTORIC BUILDING
(📞 971-715-01-14; Callejón Rey Cosijopí; ⊙ 8am-8pm Mon-Fri, 9am-2pm Sat) **FREE** This former Dominican monastery, built in the 16th century, houses Tehuantepec's Casa de la Cultura, where arts and crafts workshops and activities are held, though it was temporarily closed after the September 2017 earthquake at last visit. It bears traces of old frescoes, and some rooms hold modest exhibits of traditional dress, archaeological finds and historical photos. It's on a short lane off Guerrero, 400m northeast of the central plaza.

🛏 Sleeping & Eating

Hotel Donaji HOTEL $
(📞 971-715-00-64; www.hoteldonaji.com; Josefa O de Domínguez; s/d M$450/570; 🅿️ 🅰️) A journeyman hotel that's good enough to break a journey (which is Tehuantepec's main function). It's pretty central with a slightly dingy affiliated cafe, new air-con units and bright bedspreads.

Hostal Emilia PENSION $
(📞 971-715-00-08; Ocampo 8; r for up to 3 with/without air-con M$450/310; 🅿️ @ 🅰️) A block south of the plaza, Emilia has seven

reasonably comfy rooms, one with a bathroom outside the room. The cheaper ones only have a fan. Good meals (M$150) are cooked up in **Mariscos Silvia** (mains M$120-150; ⊙ 8am-7pm) next door.

Restaurante Scarú MEXICAN $$
(Callejón Leona Vicario 4; mains M$80-150; ⊙ 8am-9pm Mon-Sat) Scarú occupies an 18th-century house with a scruffy patio made infinitely prettier by some striking typically Mexican murals. Sit beneath a fan, quaff a *limonada* and sample one of the varied dishes on offer. Seafood is the specialty and the prawns stuffed with *acelga* (chard) are a good choice.

ℹ Information

There's an erratically staffed **Tourist Information Office** (Hwy 185; ⊙ 9am-7pm Mon-Sat) beside the highway, two blocks west from the central plaza.

ℹ Getting There & Away

Tehuantepec's main bus station (**La Terminal**; Calle de los Heroes), is by Hwy 185, 1.5km northeast of the central plaza. It's shared by deluxe, 1st-class and 2nd-class services of the ADO/OCC group. Second-class Istmeños buses to Juchitán (M$27, 30 minutes) and Salina Cruz (M$20, 30 minutes) stop on the highway outside La Terminal at least every half-hour during daylight.

Juchitán

📞 971 / POP 75,000

Isthmus culture is strong in this friendly town, where about 30 different neighborhood *velas* (festivals) fill the calendar with music, dancing, drinking, eating and fun from April to September. Juchitán is also famed for its *muxes* – openly gay, frequently cross-dressing men, who are fully accepted in local society and hold their own *vela* in November.

BUSES FROM TEHUANTEPEC

DESTINATION	FARE (M$)	DURATION (HR)	FREQUENCY (DAILY)
Bahías de Huatulco	176-206	3¼	6
Mexico City (TAPO or Sur)	624-1106	12	8
Oaxaca	154-294	5	24
Pochutla	260-286	4½	4
Puerto Escondido	316-334	5½	4

BUSES FROM JUCHITÁN

DESTINATION	FARE (M$)	DURATION (HR)	FREQUENCY (DAILY)
Bahías de Huatulco	202-288	3½-4	8
Mexico City (TAPO or Sur)	624-1064	12	7
Oaxaca	164-314	5-5½	26
Pochutla	268-294	4½-5	6
San Cristóbal de las Casas	418	5½-6	3
Tapachula	427-478	7½	3

👁 Sights

Jardín Juárez
PLAZA

Jardín Juárez is the city's always interesting central square. In the busy market on its east side you'll find locally made hammocks, isthmus women's costumes, and maybe iguana on the *comedor* menus. The splendid 19th-century **Palacio del Ayuntamiento** with its 31 arches runs down the square's east side, but it was badly damaged in the 2017 earthquake, when part of it caved in.

🛏 Sleeping & Eating

In wake of the 2017 earthquake, many of Juchitán's accommodations were closed. In normal circumstances, the town has a reasonable stash of affordable places to stay, but it may take a while for some of them to reopen.

Hotel Central
HOTEL $

(📞971-712-20-19; www.hotelcentral.com.mx; Av Efraín Gómez 30; s/d M$370/470; ✳@🛜) A good-value hotel 1½ blocks east of Jardín Juárez, offering freshly painted rooms with comfy beds, good-sized bathrooms and bottled drinking water, though some have little natural light. It was briefly closed after the earthquake (p489), but may be open by the time you read this.

La Inter
CAFETERIA $$

(📞971-711-42-08; 16 de Septiembre 25; breakfast M$120; ⏰8am-10:30pm) Suspend your judgment on this light, bright eating option. Inter might be part of a three-cafe chain and look a bit plastic on first impression, but it's rich pickings in hot, steamy post-earthquake Juchitán, with polite, fleet-footed staff, a comprehensive not unhealthy menu and life-reaffirming air-conditioning.

La Tossta
MEDITERRANEAN, MEXICAN $$

(Av 16 de Septiembre 37; mains M$160-195; ⏰7am-midnight; 🛜) With an upbeat, contemporary ambience and some creative recipe combinations (breaded shrimps with coconut; beef medallions in port sauce), this is quite a surprise in Juchitán and has continued to stay open since the 2017 earthquake.

ℹ Getting There & Away

The main **bus station** (Prolongación 16 de Septiembre), used by deluxe, 1st-class and 2nd-class services of ADO/OCC, is 100m south of Hwy 185 on the northern edge of town. Many buses depart inconveniently between 11pm and 7am. 'Terminal-Centro' buses run between the bus station and the central Jardín Juárez. A taxi costs M$30.

Second-class Istmeños buses to Tehuantepec (M$27, 30 minutes) and Salina Cruz (M$40, one hour) leave at least every 30 minutes during daylight, from the next corner south from the main terminal.

Central Pacific Coast

Includes ➡

Why Go?

Gigantic aquamarine waves provide the backdrop and pulsating rhythm to any visit to Mexico's central Pacific coast, a land of stunning beaches and giant sunsets. You can indulge in all the tropical clichés here: eating sublime seafood under simple palm-frond roofs, drinking chilled coconut water while lounging in a hammock, and enjoying poolside cocktails at an upmarket resort. The nightlife is great and there's a beach for everyone, whether you prefer yours backed by high-rise hotels or tumbledown cabins.

There's even more going on in the ocean, where you can surf world-class breaks and spot humpback whales breaching on the horizon, battalions of mother turtles arriving to lay their eggs, pelicans flying in formation or pods of dolphins rising from the waves.

Whether your thing is a cushy week of beachside pampering or a budget quest for the perfect wave, the Pacific coast has it covered.

Best Places to Eat

➡ El Presidio (p502)

➡ Paititi del Mar (p569)

➡ Café des Artistes (p531)

➡ El Manglito (p540)

➡ Pacifica del Mar (p544)

Best Places to Stay

➡ Troncones Point Hostel (p548)

➡ Aura del Mar (p556)

➡ Casa Dulce Vida (p528)

➡ Hotel Delfin (p539)

➡ Techos de México (p514)

When to Go
Puerto Vallarta

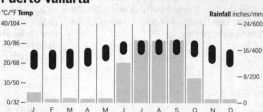

Feb Perfect beach weather. Carnaval (p498) reigns in Mazatlán.

Jun & Jul Surf's up and prices are down at Pacific Mexico's prime surfing destinations.

Nov & Dec Puerto Vallarta celebrates various festivals. December is whale-watching season.

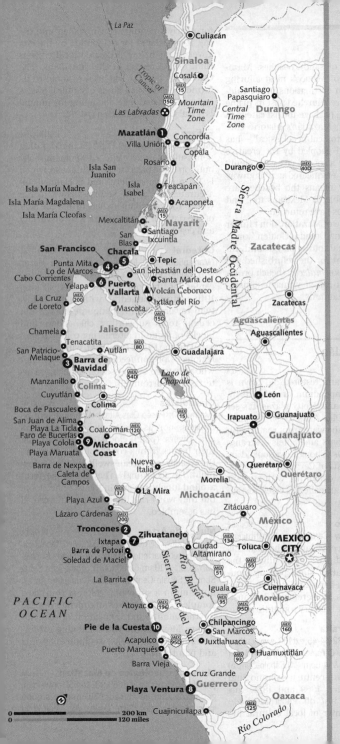

Central Pacific Coast Highlights

1 **Mazatlán** (p494) Hanging out in the beautifully restored downtown.

2 **Troncones** (p548) Dreaming of making a life in this beach town before heading out for a day of surfing.

3 **Barra de Navidad** (p539) Biking, boating and dining on fresh seafood in this laid-back mini-resort.

4 **San Francisco** (p515) Soaking up the party vibe along the sands and streets.

5 **Chacala** (p513) Whale-watching and swimming in the calm waters of this tiny fishing village.

6 **Puerto Vallarta** (p520) Cherishing the diverse flavors of the Zona Romántica and visiting remote beaches.

7 **Zihuatanejo** (p551) Savoring the culinary scene and atmospheric bars.

8 **Playa Ventura** (p575) Chilling out on the impossibly perfect beach.

9 **Michoacán Coast** (p545) Exploring surf beaches and traditional settlements.

10 **Pie de la Cuesta** (p562) Bird-watching and marveling at the bravado of cliff divers in neighboring Acapulco.

Mazatlán

📞 669 / POP 502,547

Thanks to 20km of sandy beaches, Mazatlán became one of Mexico's most alluring and inviting beach destinations in the mid-20th century, before it lurched past its prime into a mid-market, package-tourist category. Recently, however, Mazatlán's historic core – referred to as 'tropical neoclassical' – has been restored and peopled by the creative class. The result is a coastal city with plenty of allure. A boldly engineered new highway from the interior means the beaches are now more accessible to Mexicans too, and the good-time vibes have returned.

To take the pulse of Mazatlán, don't linger too long in the Zona Dorada (Golden Zone), the city's traditional tourist playground. Instead head straight for the refurbished old town and its glorious *malecón* (beach promenade), where you can view magic sunsets from bars and restaurants.

🅞 Sights

🅞 Old Mazatlán

★ Old Mazatlán
AREA

(Map p500) Mazatlán's restored old town is a picturesque compendium of noble 19th-century buildings and pretty plazas. It's set back from Playa Olas Altas (p495), a small cove beach where the waterfront road – with its old-fashioned bars and hotels – strongly evokes the 1950s. Though overlooked by the ugly radio masts of Cerro de la Nevería, this old quarter is delightful, with student life and numerous art galleries, cafes, restaurants and bars.

★ Plaza Machado
SQUARE

(Map p500; cnr Av Carnaval & Constitución; 🚊 Sábalo-Centro) Sleepy during the day, this gorgeous tree-lined plaza comes alive in the evening, when market stalls pop up, couples stroll hand-in-hand and its numerous terrace restaurants are serenaded by musicians. It's a touristy but very romantic scene.

Teatro Ángela Peralta
THEATER

(Map p500; 📞 669-982-44-46; ext 103; www.culturamazatlan.com/tap; Av Carnaval 47; self-guided visit M$20; ⊙ 9am-2pm & 4-6pm; 🚊 Sábalo-Centro) Named after a 19th-century soprano and constructed between 1869 and 1874, this 1366-seat theater just off Plaza Machado was a thriving center of local cultural life

for nearly a century. Having fallen into decay, it was slated for demolition by the city government before dedicated local citizens came to its rescue in the late 1980s. The three-level interior has been restored to its former splendor; all kinds of cultural events are again staged here, including the annual Festival Cultural Mazatlán (p498).

El Faro
LIGHTHOUSE

(Map p496; 🚊 Playa Sur) **FREE** At the Mazatlán peninsula's southern end, a prominent rocky outcrop is the base for this lighthouse, which is 135m above sea level and is claimed, inaccurately, to be the second-highest in the world. You can climb up here (avoid the heat of the day) for a spectacular view of the city and coast.

Catedral
CATHEDRAL

(Map p500; cnr Juárez & Calle 21 de Marzo; ⊙ 6:30am-7:30pm; 🚊 Sábalo-Centro) At the center of the old town is this striking 19th-century cathedral with high yellow twin towers. The dramatic interior has gilt ceiling roses supporting chandeliers and blocks of stone in alternating colors. It's located on the **Plaza Principal**, which attracts legions of pigeon feeders and local families who patronize businesses on the clogged arteries that surround it.

Clavadistas
VIEWPOINT

(Map p500; Paseo Olas Altas) Although not as famous, nor as spectacular, as Acapulco's cliff divers (p563), local *clavadistas* cast their bodies from a couple of platforms into the treacherous ocean swells for your enjoyment. Tip accordingly. They usually perform around lunchtime and in the late afternoon, but they won't risk their necks until a crowd has assembled.

Museo de Arte
MUSEUM

(Map p500; 📞 669-985-35-02; www.facebook.com/museodeartedemazatlan; cnr Sixto Osuna & Carranza; ⊙ 10am-6pm Mon-Fri, 11am-5pm Sat & Sun; 🚊 Sábalo-Centro) **FREE** This is a small museum in a sprawling colonial courtyard complex, which makes a convincing case for the vitality and innovation of contemporary Mexican art with changing exhibitions of digital works, sculptures, prints and paintings.

Museo Arqueológico de Mazatlán
MUSEUM

(INAH; Map p500; 📞 669-981-14-55; www.inah.gob.mx/es/red-de-museos/210-museo-arqueologico-de-mazatlan; Sixto Osuna 76; adult/child

CENTRAL PACIFIC COAST MAZATLÁN

under 12yr M$40/free, Sun free; ⊘ 9am-6pm Tue-Sun; 🚌 Sábalo-Centro) The small but absorbing Museo Arqueológico displays several hundred pre-Hispanic archaeological finds accompanied by fascinating wall texts in Spanish and English.

★ **Isla de la Piedra**   ISLAND
(Map p496; boat fare M$30; 🚌 Playa Sur) A popular half-day escape from the city, this island is just southeast of Old Mazatlán and boasts a beautiful, long sandy beach bordered by coconut groves. Surfers come for the waves, and its simple *palapa* (thatched-roof) restaurants draw Mexican families; outside weekends and high season, you might have it to yourself. Though there are tours, it's easy to get here by water taxi – boats depart frequently (6am to 6pm) from the Playa Sur *embarcadero* (dock).

'Playa Sur' buses leave for the *embarcadero* from the corner of Serdán and Escobedo, two blocks southeast of Plaza Principal in Old Mazatlán.

⊙ Zona Dorada

Onilikan   DISTILLERY
(Map p502; ✆ 669-668-23-70; www.onilikan.com; Av Playa Gaviotas 505; ⊘ 8:30am-5:30pm Mon-Fri, 9am-2pm Sat; 🅿; 🚌 Sábalo-Centro) FREE This tiny distillery brews up liquors from mango, agave and coffee, among other things. It's in the heart of the Zona Dorada, and you can just drop in for a friendly short explanation and free tasting.

Acuario Mazatlán   AQUARIUM
(Map p496; ✆ 669-981-78-15; www.acuariomazatlan.com; Av de los Deportes 111; adult/child 3-11yr M$115/85; ⊘ 9:30am-5pm; 🅿; 🚌 Sábalo-Centro) One of Mexico's largest aquariums has tanks with hundreds of species of fresh- and saltwater fish, a display of skeletons, and birds and frogs in the garden. Its sea lion shows and much-hyped shark-riding experience are the kinds of interaction with marine creatures that are a big concern to animal welfare groups, who say that contact of this sort is harmful to the creatures and should be avoided.

Beaches
With over 20km of beaches, it's easy to find a suitable stretch of sand. The following beaches are listed in geographic order, from south to north.

Crescent-shaped **Playa Olas Altas** (Map p500; 🚌 Sábalo-Centro) is where tourism first flourished in the 1950s. It's within walking distance if you're staying in Old Mazatlán.

Backed by a promenade popular with joggers and strollers, the golden sands of **Playa Norte** (Map p496; 🚌 Sábalo-Centro) begin just north of Old Mazatlán. The beach arcs toward **Punta Camarón**, a rocky point dominated by the conspicuous, castle-like Fiesta Land (p504) nightclub complex.

The most luxurious hotels face pretty **Playa Las Gaviotas** (Map p502; 🚌 Sábalo-Centro) and **Playa Sábalo** (Map p496; 🚌 Sábalo-Centro), the latter extending north of the Zona Dorada. Sheltered by picturesque islands, the waters here are generally calm and ideal for swimming and water sports.

Further north, past **Marina El Cid** and the ever-evolving **Marina Mazatlán**, are **Playa Bruja** (🚌 Cerritos-Juárez) – a once-serene beach that has seen a flood of high-rise development in recent years – and **Playa Cerritos** (🚌 Cerritos-Juárez). Both have a smattering of seafood restaurants and decent surf. To reach these northern beaches, catch a 'Cerritos–Juárez' bus along Avenida Camarón Sábalo in the Zona Dorada.

Islands
Resembling breaching whales, the three photogenic rocks jutting from the sea offshore from the Zona Dorada offer secluded beaches and clear waters ideal for snorkeling, plus great multitudes of seals and marine birds. On the left is **Isla de Chivos** (Goat Island); **Isla de Pájaros** (Bird Island) is on the right. Most visited is the one in the middle, **Isla de Venados** (Deer Island). The islands are part of a wildlife refuge designated to help protect the local birds and marine fauna. Any boat operator can take you out there; organized tours are also available.

🏃 Activities
Mazatlán boasts some noteworthy surfing sites, including Playa Bruja. There are several spots to rent boards and a handful of surf schools. Other water-sports equipment can be hired from the beaches of most large beachfront hotels.

Estrella del Mar Golf Club   GOLF
(✆ 800-727-46-53; www.estrelladelmar.com; Camino Isla de la Piedra 10; green fees Nov-Apr US$120, May-Oct US$75) Mazatlán's finest golf course is just south of the airport (p505) by the ocean.

Greater Mazatlán

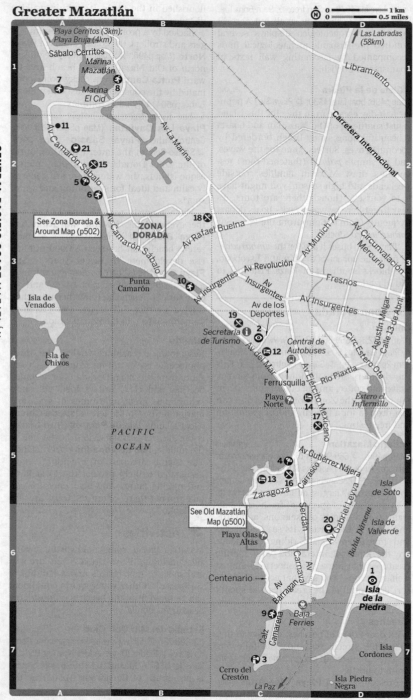

Greater Mazatlán

Jah Surf School SURFING
(📲cell 669-1494699; http://jahsurfschool.com; class US$50, board rental per hour/day US$10/25; ♿) Friendly, reader-recommended instructor who is happy to take on whole families. Also rents out boards and equipment.

Aqua Sports Center WATER SPORTS
(Map p496; 📞669-913-04-51; www.aquasports center.com; Av Camarón Sábalo s/n, Hotel El Cid Castilla; 1-tank dive US$100, snorkeling tour US$40, kayak rental US$30; ⊙9:30am-5pm; 🚌Sábalo-Centro) The place to go for all sorts of water-sports activities, including scuba diving, snorkeling rentals, jet skiing, banana-boat rides (for up to five passengers), parasailing, sailboat rentals and kayak rentals.

Sportfishing
Handily located at the confluence of the Sea of Cortez and the Pacific Ocean, Mazatlán is world famous for sportfishing – especially for marlin, swordfish, sailfish, tuna and *dorado* (mahimahi). It can be an expensive activity (US$475 to US$750 per boat per day, for boats ranging in size from 8m to 11m with four to 10 people fishing); fishing from a 7m *super panga* (fiberglass skiff) is less expensive (around US$325 per day with up to four people fishing). A fishing license costs US$10 per person, and is usually organized by the operator.

The spiffiest boats leave from the marinas north of town; for lower prices, try the operators near El Faro (p494) or negotiate directly with one of the independent fishers offering half-day *panga* trips along Paseo Claussen near Playa Norte (p495). Many operators also offer simple bottom-fishing excursions.

Flota Sábalo FISHING
(Map p496; 📞669-981-27-61; www.facebook.com/manuel.valdessalgado; Calz Camarena s/n; half-day fishing trips from M$3000; ⊙6am-6pm; 🚌Playa Sur) This friendly setup is run by two brothers, who offer two different boats – one an old faithful, the other sleeker and more modern – for very affordable fishing or other boating excursions. Lots of fun.

Bibi Fleet FISHING
(Map p496; 📞669-913-10-60; www.bibifleet.com; Marina Mazatlán, shop 8, btwn docks 7 & 8; charters per day US$300-600; ⊙9am-5pm Mon-Fri, to 1pm Sat; 🚌Sábalo-Centro) Helpful and professional setup with three different boat options. Excursions last up to eight hours and can include both fishing and snorkeling activities.

Aries Fleet FISHING
(Map p496; 📞669-916-34-68; www.elcidmarinas.com; Av Camarón Sábalo s/n, Marina el Cid; fishing tour per day from US$325, Deer Island tour adult/child US$58/38; ⊙8:30am-5pm Mon-Sat, to 2pm Sun; 🚌Sábalo-Centro) Offers fishing tours and supports some catch-and-release practices. Also runs an activities-packed excursion to Deer Island, which includes snorkeling, kayaking, open bar and lunch.

👉 Tours

★**Onca Explorations** ECOTOUR
(Map p496; 📞669-913-40-50; www.oncaexplorations.com; Av Camarón Sábalo 2100; whale-watching or wild dolphin tours adult/child US$95/65, birding US$85/65; ⊙9am-5pm; 🚌Sábalo-Centro) 🌿 Wildlife observation and conservation are the focus of these ecotours, led by marine ecologist Oscar Guzón. Most popular are his 'Humpback Whale Research

Adventure' (8am and 1pm December to April) and 'Wild Dolphin Adventure' (8am year-round) tours, which offer excellent opportunities to observe marine mammals up close.

Other options include an excursion to Las Labradas (p508) beachside petroglyph site, and custom bird-watching tours to Santa María Bay, Isla Isabel National Park and the Chara Pinta Tufted Jay Preserve.

King David
BOATING

(Map p502; ☑ 669-914-14-44; www.kingdavid. com.mx; Av Camarón Sábalo 333; tour adult/child US$45/30; ⊗ office 7:30am-5pm Mon-Fri, to 2pm Sat; ☐ Sábalo-Centro) Offers a variety of boat tours, including a 'Jungle and Beach' tour into the mangrove-fringed waterways of the Isla de la Piedra wildlife refuge. You get it cheaper by booking at its office instead of via hotels. Its 'Isla de la Piedra' tour is more cheaply (and better) done by yourself.

Vista Tours
TOURS

(Map p502; ☑ 669-986-86-10; www.vistatours. com.mx; Av Camarón Sábalo 51; tours per person M$30-129; ⊗ 9am-5pm Mon-Fri, to 3pm Sat; ☐ Sábalo-Centro) A reliable group that offers a variety of tours in and around Mazatlán, including city tours (US$30), a colonial tour (US$50) to the foothill towns of Concordia and Copala, a tequila-factory tour (US$45) and all-day jaunts to Mexcaltitán (US$129).

✷ Festivals & Events

Carnaval
CARNIVAL

(www.carnavalmazatlan.net; ⊗ Feb) Mazatlán has Mexico's most flamboyant Carnaval celebrations. For the week leading up to Ash Wednesday, the town goes on a nonstop partying spree. Reserve hotels in advance.

Festival Cultural Mazatlán
PERFORMING ARTS

(www.culturamazatlan.com; ⊗ Oct-Dec) If you love the performing arts, witness captivating theatrical and musical performances in and around the Teatro Ángela Peralta (p494).

Artwalk
ART

(www.artwalkmazatlan.com; ⊗ 4-8pm 1st Fri of the month Nov-Apr) Get a taste of Mazatlán's arts scene through this self-guided walking tour of artists' studios and galleries.

🛌 Sleeping

★ Funky Monkey Hostel
HOSTEL $

(Map p502; ☑ cell 669-4313421; www.funky monkeyhostel.net; Cerro Boludo 112; dm/d incl breakfast M$265/630; P ⊛ ❀ @ ❀ ❀; ☐ Sábalo-Centro) Genially run in a quiet residential suburb about 1.2km from the beach, this facility-packed hostel makes a fine place to hang out, with ample lounging space, a pretty pool, two kitchens and hammocks. Private rooms come with their own kitchen, bathroom and air-con, while fan-cooled dorms are spacious with colorful bed covers and decent mattresses. Surfboard rentals and free bikes.

Hotel Posada Los Tabachines
HOTEL $

(Map p496; ☑ 669-982-29-10; www.hoteltabachi nes.com; Río Elota 2; d/ste from M$400/470; P ⊛ ❀ ❀; ☐ Sábalo-Centro) Just 100m from the beach and five blocks from the bus station (p506), this convenient budget hotel has clean air-conditioned rooms with tile floors and larger suites with kitchens, making it good value if you don't mind early-morning noise from the lobby.

Hostal Mazatlán
HOSTEL $

(Map p500; ☑ 699-688-57-55; www.hostalmazat lan.com; Constitución 809; dm/d M$290/600; ❀ ❀ ❀; ☐ Sábalo-Centro) This downtown hostel has several things working in its favor: it's two blocks from the spirited Plaza Machado (p494), bike rentals are dirt-cheap and it offers a look at Mazatlán's less touristy side, with plenty of neighborhood bars and local eateries nearby. Choose between air-conditioned six-bed dorms or tidy private rooms with their own bathrooms.

Melville Suites
HOTEL $$

(Map p500; ☑ 669-982-84-74; www.themelville. com; Constitución 99; ste M$1390-2400; ❀ ❀ ❀; ☐ Sábalo-Centro) Enormous suites with high ceilings and thick walls surrounding a central courtyard give this perfectly located, relaxed option plenty of old-Mexico character. Rustic rooms also come with fans, aircon and kitchenette. The downside? There's loads of street noise in the front chambers on weekend nights. Car park opposite.

Hotel La Siesta
HOTEL $$

(Map p500; ☑ 669-981-26-40; www.lasiesta.com. mx; Paseo Olas Altas 11; r M$1178-1416; ❀ ❀ @ ❀ ❀; ☐ Sábalo-Centro) Sitting pretty above Playa Olas Altas (p495), La Siesta is a good option if you can snag one of the choice sea-view rooms. When we last visited, the spacious interior rooms were getting a makeover with new furnishings and mattresses. The pleasant central courtyard and attached restaurant are good places to meet other travelers. Books out quickly in summer.

WORTH A TRIP

SINALOA'S COLONIAL GEMS

Several small, picturesque colonial towns in the Sierra Madre foothills make pleasant day trips from Mazatlán.

Concordia, founded in 1565, has an 18th-century church with a baroque facade and elaborately decorated columns. The village is known for manufacturing high-quality pottery and hand-carved furniture. It's about a 45-minute drive east of Mazatlán; head southeast on Hwy 15 for 20km to Villa Unión, turn inland on Hwy 40 (the highway to Durango) and go another 20km.

Copala, 40km past Concordia on Hwy 40, was one of Mexico's first mining towns. It still has its colonial church (1748), period houses and cobblestone streets. It's a one-hour drive from Mazatlán.

El Rosario, 76km southeast of Mazatlán on Hwy 15, is another colonial mining town. Founded in 1655, its most famous feature is the towering gold-leaf altar in its church, the Nuestra Señora del Rosario. You can also visit the home of beloved singer Lola Beltrán, whose long recording career made *ranchera* (Mexico's urban 'country music') popular in the mid-20th century.

Cosalá, in the mountains north of Mazatlán, is a beautiful colonial mining village that dates from 1550. It has an 18th-century church, a mining museum in a colonial mansion on the plaza, and the lovely hacienda-style **Hotel Quinta Minera** (☎ 696-965-02-22; www.hotelquintaminera.com; Hidalgo 92, Cosalá; d/q M$1200/1420; P ❄ ✳ 🛜 ☀). To get here, go north on Hwy 15 for 113km to the turnoff (opposite the turnoff for La Cruz de Alota on the coast) and then climb 45km into the mountains.

Buses to Cosalá, Concordia and El Rosario depart from a small station behind Mazatlán's main bus terminal (p506).

Suitel   GUESTHOUSE $$
(Map p496; ☎ 669-985-41-40; www.facebook.com/suitel522; Río Presidio 522; r incl breakfast M$1100; ❄ ✳ 🛜; 🚌 Sábalo-Centro) 🌿 Three blocks from the beach, this is a good-value option offering spotless (but somewhat musty) rooms with kitchenettes along a pleasant plant-filled patio. It rents out bikes, bodyboards and fishing gear and has an ecologically minded policy of recycling solid waste. Turn off the coast road opposite the gold statue of a *pulmonía* taxi.

Casa Contenta   APARTMENT $$
(Map p502; ☎ 669-913-49-76; www.casacontenta.com.mx; Av Playa Gaviotas 224; apt/house M$1600/3600; P ❄ ✳ 🛜 ☀; 🚌 Sábalo-Centro) Right on the beach in the heart of Zona Dorada, these spacious apartments – each with cable TV, kitchenette, dining area, double bed and two twins – make a decent option for families. The rooms and beds could do with a bit of modernizing, but it's friendly and pretty fair value for this great location.

Motel Marley   MOTEL $$
(Map p502; ☎ 669-913-55-33; http://travelbymexico.com/sina/marley; Av Playa Gaviotas 226; 1-/2-bedroom apt M$1400/1600; P ❄ ✳ @ 🛜

☀; 🚌 Sábalo-Centro) The most atmospheric of the string of low-budget spots in Zona Dorada, this place offers dated but comfortable seafront apartments, set in four-unit blocks and staggered for airflow, with well-equipped kitchens, an oceanfront lawn, a pool and – best of all – privileged beach access.

★**Casa de Leyendas**   B&B $$$
(Map p500; ☎ 669-981-61-80; www.casadeleyendas.com; Venustiano Carranza 4; r incl breakfast M$2118-2975; ❄ ✳ @ 🛜 ☀; 🚌 Sábalo-Centro) One of Old Mazatlán's homiest B&Bs. The sprawling two-story building near Playa Olas Altas (p495) houses six comfy adults-only rooms, all with coffee makers, fridges, hairdryers, safes and other nice touches. Common areas include a library, a lively, well-stocked and reasonably priced bar, a central 'cocktail pool' with Jacuzzi jets, a fully equipped guest kitchen and two spacious upstairs patios.

Villa Serena   APARTMENT $$$
(Map p500; ☎ cell 669-1500034; www.villa-serena.blogspot.com; Heriberto Frías 1610; 1-/2-bedroom apt from US$100/120; ❄ ✳ ☀; 🚌 Sábalo-Centro) Once a cigar factory, this 19th-century

Old Mazatlán

Old Mazatlán

◉ Top Sights
| 1 Old Mazatlán | C2 |
| 2 Plaza Machado | C2 |

◉ Sights
3 Catedral	D1
4 Clavadistas	A2
5 Museo Arqueológico de Mazatlán	B3
6 Museo de Arte	B3
7 Playa Olas Altas	B3
8 Teatro Ángela Peralta	C2

🛏 Sleeping
9 Casa de Leyendas	B3
10 Hostal Mazatlán	D2
11 Hotel La Siesta	B2
12 Jonathon	C2
13 Melville Suites	C2
14 Villa Serena	C1

⊗ Eating
| 15 Angelina's Kitchen | B3 |

16 El Presidio	B2
17 Fonda de Chalio	B3
18 Gaia Bistrot	C2
19 Héctor's Bistro	C2
20 Helarte Sano	C3
21 Nieves de Garrafa de con Medrano	C2
22 Panamá	D1
23 Pedro & Lola	C2
24 Topolo	D2

🍷 Drinking & Nightlife
| 25 Looney Bean | B3 |
| 26 Vitrolas Bar | C2 |

🛍 Shopping
27 Casa Etnika	B3
28 Gandarva Bazar	D2
29 La Querencia	C2
30 Mercado Pino Suárez	D1
31 Nidart	C2

historic beauty has been converted into a 14-unit apartment complex. The best ones are the two-story digs with high wood-beamed ceilings, tiled floors, full kitchens and private patios. A small pool in the tranquil courtyard and a rooftop Jacuzzi seal the deal.

Las 7 Maravillas   B&B $$$
(Map p496; ☏ 669-136-06-46; www.las7maravillas.com; Av Las Palmas 1; r incl breakfast M$2200-3200; ⊗ ❄ 🛜; 🚌 Sábalo-Centro) A block above the waterfront but in a quiet residential area, this classy place aims at the couples market with personalized service, security

details, Jacuzzi-with-a-view and a reader-praised breakfast buffet. Each of the six rooms is lightly themed on the country after which it is named. It's an impressive over-all package that needs to be reserved in advance. No under-15s.

Jonathon BOUTIQUE HOTEL $$$
(Map p500; ☑669-915-63-60; www.jonathonhotel.com; Av Carnaval 1205; r incl breakfast M$1964-3778; ◉❄☞❄; ☐Sábalo-Centro) On a pedestrian street just off Plaza Machado (p494), set around a striking columnar courtyard with a modern spiral staircase. Rooms are a good size with floating beds, hardwood closets and shelving; the pricier setups come with Jacuzzis. It's slightly over the top, but super-comfortable with a great location and a rooftop pool with a view.

Hotel Playa Mazatlán RESORT $$$
(Map p502; ☑669-989-05-55; www.hotelplayamazatlan.com; Av Playa Gaviotas 202; r from M$2500; ℗◉❄@☞❄; ☐Sábalo-Centro) This large resort – the first built in the Zona Dorada – maintains impeccable standards. Half the rooms have ocean views, and all come equipped with cable TV, private terrace and the thoughtful touches that mark a classy operation. Manicured tropical gardens and a breezy oceanside restaurant make this Mazatlán's most stylish large hotel.

✖ Eating

Mazatlán is famous for fresh seafood. *Pescado zarandeado* is a delicious, spiced, charcoal-grilled fish; the shrimp here is as sweet as you'll ever taste.

Good locations for cheap, fresh, no-frills seafood are around the Mercado de Mariscos at the southern end of Playa Norte (p495), and the thatched kiosks on the beach opposite hotels Hacienda and Cima, a little further north.

✖ Old Mazatlán & Around

Tacos José TACOS $
(Map p496; ☑cell 669-9940467; cnr Río Presidio & Av Rotarismo; tacos M$17-35; ◷6pm-1:30am; ☐Sábalo-Centro) This wildly popular street taco stand specializes in *carne asada,* grilled beef served on a corn or flour tortilla with your choice of salsas. Regulars love a cholesterol bomb known as the *choreada* (grilled beef served on a crisp tortilla with a lard spread). Non-meat eaters can order quesadillas or hit the seafood stall across the street.

Helarte Sano ICE CREAM $
(Map p500; www.facebook.com/helartesano; Av Carnaval 1129; popsicles M$10-35, ice cream M$35-55; ◷9am-9pm Mon-Fri, 10am-10pm Sat, 11am-9pm Sun; ☐Sábalo-Centro) Makes over three dozen flavors of *paletas* (popsicles), sherbets and Mexican-inspired gelato, including unconventional fruit flavors (lemon-rosemary, kumquat, avocado), diabetic-friendly sugar-free offerings, and small popsicles for kids.

Mercado de Mariscos Playa Norte SEAFOOD $
(Map p496; Paseo Claussen s/n; fish per kg M$60-100; ◷8am-3pm; ☐Sábalo-Centro) This no-frills market sells fish and seafood straight off the boats that dock on the beach (p495) opposite. Stalls here will cook up your purchases or your own catch.

Nieves de Garrafa de con Medrano ICE CREAM $
(Map p500; www.facebook.com/nievesdegarrafaconmedrano; cnr Flores & Calle 5 de Mayo; ice cream M$20-30; ◷11am-9pm; ☐Sábalo-Centro) A local tradition since 1938, this unpretentious family-run cart near Mazatlán's Plaza Principal dishes out delicious homemade ice cream to devoted crowds. Try the vanilla, prune, coconut or guayaba flavors.

Panamá MEXICAN, BAKERY $$
(Map p500; ☑669-985-18-53; www.panama.com.mx; cnr Canizales & Juárez; mains M$68-164; ◷7am-10:30pm; ☞; ☐Sábalo-Centro) With a zillion different breakfast combos, ranging from North American standards to Mexican treats such as *chilaquiles* (tortilla strips drenched in salsa), this locally popular bakery and diner is a great place to start the day, or continue it. Has a few other locations around town.

Angelina's Kitchen MEXICAN $$
(Map p500; ☑669-910-15-96; www.facebook.com/angelinaslatinkitchen; Venustiano Carranza 18; mains M$120-200; ◷noon-11pm Tue-Fri, 8am-11pm Sat & Sun mid-Oct–Jul; ☞☑; ☐Sábalo-Centro) Behind an unobtrusive facade, this surprisingly capacious restaurant is something of a local favorite and it's easy to see why. A casual menu runs from burgers and salads to ceviches and Greek pizza, plus plenty of vegetarian options. Seafood is expertly selected and prepared, whether it's plump, sweet crustaceans or marinated fish on your plate.

Zona Dorada & Around

Fonda de Chalio MEXICAN $$
(Map p500; ☑669-910-04-80; fondadechalio33@
hotmail.com; Paseo Olas Altas 166; mains M$130-185;
⏰7am-11pm Sun-Fri, to midnight Sat; 🛜; 🚌Sábalo-
Centro) This street-front cafe across from the
malecón (beach promenade) is popular with
Mazatlán's middle-aged locals. Breakfasts
pack out for baskets of *pan dulce* (pastries),
chilaquiles with *machaca* (spiced, shredded
dried beef) and *huevos con nopales* (scram-
bled eggs with cactus paddles). Evenings get
lively with *aguachile* (a local ceviche), cold
beer and street-side music and dancing.

Pedro & Lola FUSION $$
(Map p500; ☑669-982-25-89; www.restaurant
pedroylola.com; Av Carnaval 1303; mains M$129-
238; ⏰6pm-1am; 🛜; 🚌Sábalo-Centro) This
stylish eatery on Plaza Machado (p494) does
outstanding small plates, including delectable shrimp and octopus dishes. The fresh
fish of the day comes cooked in a variety of
ways – go garlic-sautéed for the most flavor

– and there are always interesting new takes
on traditional Sinaloa dishes. Live jazz and
blues acts play Thursday to Sunday.

★Héctor's Bistro FUSION $$$
(Map p500; ☑669-981-15-77; www.facebook.com/
hectorsbistro; Escobedo 409, cnr Heriberto Frías;
mains M$165-295; ⏰8am-11pm Mon-Sat; 🛜;
🚌Sábalo-Centro) Commodious and with will-
ing service, this is the praised venture of a
popular local chef. Dishes such as seafood
carpaccios, homemade pastrami, tasty pas-
tas and salads bursting with fresh prawns
and avocado are complemented by daily
blackboard specials that might feature pork
fillet or T-bone steak. The interior combines
modern elegance with the high old beamed
ceiling to good effect.

★El Presidio MEXICAN $$$
(Map p500; ☑669-910-26-15; www.facebook.
com/elpresidiococinademexico; Blvd Niños Héroes
1511; mains M$149-329; ⏰1-11pm Sun-Thu, to

Zona Dorada & Around

midnight Fri & Sat; 🕿; 🖬 Sábalo-Centro) Dining in the courtyard of this beautifully restored 19th-century estate building takes you back to an other era. Standout menu items include *zarandeado* (grilled) shrimp with Mexican noodles and smoked pork shank, which is slow-cooked in a pit for 14 hours. Presidio's well-stocked cantina pours fine mezcal, tequila and local craft beer.

Gaia Bistrot INTERNATIONAL $$$
(Map p500; ✆ 669-112-25-25; www.gaiabistrot. com.mx; Heriberto Frías 1301; mains M$165-275; ⊘noon-11pm Tue-Sat, 1:30-10pm Sun; 🕿🍴; 🖬 Sábalo-Centro) Chef Gilberto del Toro has earned praise for a menu featuring international dishes such as braised beef in red wine sauce and *paella valenciana* (seasoned rice and seafood), which is made on Sundays only. For dessert try the vanilla panna cotta with balsamic marinated strawberries. Vegetarians can rely on a variety of salads, soups and pastas.

Topolo MEXICAN $$$
(Map p500; ✆ 669-136-06-60; www.topolomaz. com; Constitución 629; mains M$220-260; ⊘3-11pm Tue-Sun, closed Sun mid-Aug–Sep; 🕿; 🖬 Sábalo-Centro) For a romantic, mariachi-free dinner, step into this softly lit courtyard in a historic central building. Though aimed at gringos, it has plenty of

charm: waiters prepare fresh salsa at your table while chefs cook specialties such as tequila shrimp or fish in cilantro butter.

✖ Zona Dorada & Around

Pura Vida VEGETARIAN $
(Map p502; ✆ 669-916-10-10; puravidatogo@gmail. com; Bugambilias 18; mains M$85-106; ⊘8am-10:30pm; ❀🕿🍴; 🖬 Sábalo-Centro) Serves salads, sandwiches, Mexican snacks and vegetarian fare, but is most sought out for its juices and smoothies (drinks M$45–$54). Its menu is packed with creative concoctions blended from all the tropical fruit you love, as well as apples, dates, prunes, wheatgrass, spirulina and strawberries.

Tomates Verdes MEXICAN $
(Map p502; ✆ 669-913-21-36; Laguna 42; set meals M$55; ⊘8:30am-4:30pm Mon-Sat; 🕿; 🖬 Sábalo-Centro) Cozy and unpretentious, this breakfast and lunch spot serves dishes such as *pechuga rellena* (stuffed chicken breast) and flavorful soups such as *nopales con chipotle* (spicy cactus). Meals come with soup, a main dish and rice or beans. The menu changes daily.

Carlos & Lucía's CUBAN, MEXICAN $$
(Map p496; ✆ 669-913-56-77; lucialleras@yahoo. com; Av Camarón Sábalo 2000; mains M$80-220; ⊘noon-11pm Mon-Sat; 🕿; 🖬 Sábalo-Centro) What do you get when you combine the talents of a Mexican named Carlos and a Cuban-born chef named Lucía? A vibrant, colorful little restaurant serving homestyle specialties from both countries. Try the *plato Carlos y Lucía*, shrimp and fish cooked in brandy, accompanied by rice, veggies and plantains. It's opposite the Palms Resort.

Pancho's Restaurant MEXICAN $$
(Map p502; ✆ 669-914-09-11; www.lospanchosmaz-atlan.com; Av Playa Gaviotas 408, Centro Comercial Las Cabañas; mains M$165-269; ⊘7am-11pm; 🕿; 🖬 Sábalo-Centro) With two levels right on Playa Las Gaviotas (p495), this place has a spectacular outlook and the food measures up. There's a big range, whether you want tasty *aguachile* (a local ceviche) or a huge seafood platter. Or just drop by for a drink – the army of waiting staff will snappily provide a monster margarita or icy-cold beer.

Todos Santos SEAFOOD $$
(Map p496; ✆ 669-112-13-22; www.facebook.com/ todosantosmariscosoficial; cnr Av Marina & Rodolfo Gaona; dishes M$129-189; ⊘11am-11pm Sun-Thu,

CENTRAL PACIFIC COAST MAZATLÁN

to 1am Fri & Sat; P ⚡; 🖳 Sábalo-Cocos) This breezy open-air place is popular with young *mazatleco* couples for a date, offering a surf theme and a cheeky, good-time vibe, though staff show plenty of attitude. The long seafood menu has lots of innovation and quality: enjoy delicious tuna, fresh oysters, a range of ceviches and some excellent fish fillet creations. It's behind the Soriana Plus shopping center on Avenida Rafael Buelna.

Yoko   SUSHI $$
(Map p496; 📞 669-982-55-99; Av del Mar 720; mains & sushi rolls M$80-175; ⏱ 1-11pm; ⚡; 🖳 Sábalo-Centro) In a town swimming with sushi restaurants, locals consistently nominate Yoko as one of the best.

Casa Loma   INTERNATIONAL $$$
(Map p502; 📞 669-913-53-98; www.restaurant casaloma.com; Av Las Gaviotas 104; mains M$145-298; ⏱ 1:30-11pm; ⚡; 🖳 Sábalo-Centro) At this genteel eatery, enjoy chateaubriand béarnaise (steak with homemade béarnaise sauce) or poached fish *blanca rosa* (with shrimp, asparagus and mushrooms) in the swanky dining room or outdoors by the burbling fountain.

🍸 Drinking & Nightlife

Mazatlán has earned its reputation as a nightlife destination with a great selection of high-energy dance clubs frequented by visiting college students, lending a Mexican spring-break vibe. The scene starts percolating around 10pm and boils over after midnight. If you're more partial to sipping and people-watching, head to Avenida Olas Altas or deeper into Old Mazatlán (p494).

★ Cervecería Tres Islas   BREWERY
(Map p496; 📞 669-688-54-57; www.facebook.com/ cervezatresislas; Av Alemán 923; ⏱ 1pm-10:30pm Mon-Sat; ⚡; 🖳 Sábalo-Centro) Mazatlán's best craft beer is on tap in the friendly neighborhood barroom of this small brewery. The hoppy IPA and Belgian-style saison go down nicely on a warm day. On Thursday and Friday nights you're likely to catch DJ sets or live music acts. There's no kitchen, but you're allowed to order in food.

La Fiera   LOUNGE
(Map p496; 📞 669-913-16-85; www.facebook.com/ fierarest; Av Cámaron Sábalo 1968; ⏱ 6pm-1am Thu & Fri, to 3:30am Sat; ⚡; 🖳 Sábalo-Centro) The adjoining bar of restaurant La Fiera provides a much-needed escape from the Zona Dorada's raucous nightclubs. Resident and guest

DJs spin everything from house and reggae to *cumbia* (dance music originating from Colombia) and hip-hop in a low-lit cocktail lounge. The restaurant does good food, but expect small portions.

Looney Bean   CAFE
(Map p500; 📞 669-136-05-07; www.looneybean mzt.com; Paseo Olas Altas 166G; drinks M$20-50, pastries M$20-50; ⏱ 7:30am-10pm Mon-Thu, to 11pm Fri-Sun; ⚡; 🖳 Sábalo-Centro) A terrific local coffee shop on the main seaside drag with strong coffee and espresso drinks, juices and smoothies. It also has strawberry scones bigger than your face – they're almost impossible to eat in one sitting, though you may try (they are *that* good).

Vitrolas Bar   GAY
(Map p500; 📞 669-985-22-21; www.vitrolasbar. com; Heriberto Frías 1608; ⏱ 8pm-2am Thu-Sun; ⚡; 🖳 Sábalo-Centro) This gracious gay bar in a beautifully restored building is romantically lit and, overall, more button-down than mesh muscle shirt. It's also a popular spot for karaoke and it does a decent pizza. Not at all sceney.

Fiesta Land   CLUB
(Map p502; 📞 669-989-16-00; www.fiestaland. mx; Av Camarón Sábalo s/n; ⏱ 9pm-4am Thu-Sun; ⚡; 🖳 Sábalo-Centro) The ostentatious white castle on Punta Camarón at the south end of the Zona Dorada is the undisputed epicenter of Mazatlán's nightlife. Inside its walls are a half-dozen clubs, including several of the city's most popular dance spots.

Valentino's draws a mixed crowd to three dance floors throbbing with hip-hop and Latin music; **Bora Bora** is popular for its open-air dance floor and lax policy on bar-top dancing; and seasonal **Sumbawa Beach Club** is the perfect after-hours spot for dancing on the sand, lounging on an oversized mattress or cooling off in the pool.

☆ Entertainment

For entertainment listings, check Pacific Pearl (www.pacificpearl.com), available in hotel lobbies around town and online.

Cinemas Gaviotas   CINEMA
(Map p502; 📞 669-984-28-48; www.cinemas gaviotas.com.mx; Av Camarón Sábalo 218; M$30; 🖳 Sábalo-Centro) Screens recent releases, including some original version Hollywood films with subtitles.

🛍 Shopping

The Zona Dorada is replete with tourist-oriented stores that sell clothes, jewelry, pottery and crafts. Old Mazatlán has quirkier, artier offerings.

Casa Etnika ARTS & CRAFTS

(Map p500; ☑669-136-01-39; www.facebook.com/casaetnika; Sixto Osuna 50; ◷10am-7pm Mon-Sat; 🐾; 🚌 Sábalo-Centro) 🍴 Family-run Casa Etnika offers a small, tasteful inventory of unique objects, many made by local Mexican artisans. It also has a cafe that pours fair-trade coffee. Can organize shipping to the USA and Canada.

La Querencia ART

(Map p500; ☑669-981-10-36; www.facebook.com/laquerenciagaleriadearte; Heriberto Frías 1405; ◷10am-8pm Mon-Sat; 🐾; 🚌Sábalo-Centro) This sizable gallery-shop with entrances on two streets (the other one being on Belisario Dominguez) has striking ceramics, painted wood objects, sculptures and jewelry. Some of the pieces are huge – you won't be squeezing them into your carry-on luggage. La Querencia doubles as a bistro-bar.

Gandarva Bazar ARTS & CRAFTS

(Map p500; ☑669-136-06-65; www.facebook.com/gandarvabazar; Constitución 616; ◷10am-8pm Mon-Sat) This wonderfully atmospheric courtyard gallery is filled with drums, sculpture, masks, crosses, dolls made from gourds, hearts made from glass... It has a fair amount of mass-produced stuff, but there are some interesting reproduction Chinesco (an early-1st-millennium culture in Nayarit) ceramics too.

Mercado Pino Suárez MARKET

(Mercado Centro; Map p500; www.mercadopinosuarezmazatlan.com; Melchor Ocampo 7; ◷6am-6pm Mon-Sat, to 2pm Sun; 🚌 Sábalo-Centro) Old Mazatlán's central market offers a classic Mexican experience, complete with vegetable stands, spice dealers, food stalls and shops selling bargain-priced crafts.

Nidart CERAMICS, HANDICRAFTS

(Map p500; ☑669-985-59-91; www.facebook.com/nidartgallery; Libertad 45; ◷10am-2pm Mon-Sat; 🚌 Sábalo-Centro) Sells handmade leather masks, sculptures and ceramics from its in-house studio; it also represents numerous other local artisans. The leathery aromas are a real treat.

ℹ Information

Free wi-fi is available in numerous bars, restaurants and accommodations.

Go Mazatlán (www.gomazatlan.com) is a useful website proffering information about Mazatlán and around.

Hospital Sharp (☑669-986-56-78; www.hospitalsharp.com; Jesús Kumate s/n, cnr Av Rafael Buelna; 🚌 Sábalo-Centro) Competent and modern private hospital.

Secretaría de Turismo (Map p496; ☑669-915-66-00; http://turismo.sinaloa.gob.mx; Av del Mar 882; ◷9am-5pm Mon-Fri; 🚌 Sábalo-Centro) Gives out a mediocre free map and a few leaflets about the interior, but is not any help as far as practical information goes.

ℹ Getting There & Away

Most US flights to Mazatlán connect through Mexico City or Phoenix, though there are a couple that fly direct from Los Angeles and Dallas.

AIR

Rafael Buelna International Airport (Mazatlan Airport; ☑669-982-23-99; www.oma.aero/en/airports/mazatlan; Carretera Internacional al Sur s/n) is 26km southeast of the Zona Dorada. There are direct flights to several US and Canadian destinations.

The following domestic destinations are serviced by these airlines:

➔ Guadalajara – TAR

➔ Mexico City – Aeroméxico, VivaAerobús, Volaris, Interjet

➔ Monterrey – VivaAerobús

➔ Tijuana – Volaris

Aeroméxico (www.aeromexico.com) has offices in Zona Dorada (☑669-914-11-11; www.aeromexico.com; Av Camarón Sábalo 310; ◷9am-6pm Mon-Fri, to 2pm Sat; 🚌 Sábalo-Centro) and at the airport (☑669-982-34-44; www.aeromexico.com; Carretera Internacional al Sur s/n; ◷4am-11pm).

BOAT

Baja Ferries (Map p496; ☑800-337-74-37; www.bajaferries.com; Av Barragán s/n, Playa Sur; seat adult/child one way M$1240/620, car M$3200; ◷ticket office 8am-6pm Mon & Wed-Sun, to 3pm Tue; 🚌 Playa Sur) operates ferries from the terminal at the southern end of town between Mazatlán and the port town of Pichilingue (23km from La Paz in Baja California Sur). Boats depart at 6:30pm (be there at 4:30pm) on Wednesday, Friday and Sunday and take around 12 hours. They return at 8pm Tuesday, Thursday and Saturday. Winter winds may cause delays.

BUS

The full-service **Central de Autobuses** (Main Bus Station; Map p496; ☑ 669-982-02-87; Espinoza Ferrusquilla s/n; ☐ Sábalo-Cocos) is just off Avenida Ejército Mexicano, four blocks inland from the northern end of Playa Norte. All bus lines operate from separate halls in the main terminal.

Local buses to small towns nearby (such as Concordia, Cosalá and El Rosario) operate from a smaller station, behind the main terminal.

CAR & MOTORCYCLE

Local all-inclusive rental rates begin at around M$750 per day during the high season.

Alamo Airport (☑ 669-981-22-66; www.alamo.com.mx; Rafael Buelna International Airport; ☺ 6am-9pm); Zona Dorada (☑ 669-913-10-10; Av Camarón Sábalo 410; ☺ 7am-8pm Mon-Sat, 8am-7pm Sun; ☐ Sábalo-Centro)

Budget Airport (☑ 669-982-63-63; www.budget.com.mx; Rafael Buelna International Airport; ☺ 7am-10pm); Zona Dorada (☑ 669-913-20-00; Av Camarón Sábalo 413; ☺ 7am-8pm Mon-Sat, to 7pm Sun; ☐ Sábalo-Centro)

Europcar Airport (☑ 669-954-81-15; www.europcar.com.mx/en; Rafael Buelna International Airport; ☺ 7am-11pm); Zona Dorada (☑ 669-913-33-68; Av Camarón Sábalo 357; ☺ 8am-8pm Mon-Sat, to 6pm Sun; ☐ Sábalo-Centro)

Hertz Airport (☑ 669-985-37-31; https://hertzmexico.com; Rafael Buelna International Airport; ☺ 8am-8pm); Zona Dorada (☑ 669-913-49-55; Av Camarón Sábalo 314; ☺ 8am-7pm Mon-Fri, to 6pm Sat & Sun; ☐ Sábalo-Centro)

ⓘ Getting Around

TO/FROM THE AIRPORT

Taxis and *colectivos* (shuttle buses picking up and dropping off passengers along predeter-

mined routes) operate from the airport (p505) to town. Tickets for both can be purchased at a booth just outside the arrivals hall (*colectivo* M$115; taxi M$400). There is no public bus running between Mazatlán and the airport.

BICYCLE

Mazatlán is an easy town to navigate by bicycle, as the *malecón* (beach promenade) leads from the town center all the way to the Zona Dorada. There are lots of bike-rental places along the coast.

Baikas (☑ 669-910-19-99; www.baikas.mx; Paseo Olas Altas 166; city bikes per hour/day M$70/300, hybrids M$100/400; ☺ 7am-9pm; ☐ Sábalo-Centro) Professional setup with city bikes and pricier hybrids. There's another branch (☑ 669-984-01-01; www.baikas.mx; Av del Mar 1111; city bikes per hour/day M$70/300, hybrids M$100/400; ☺ 7am-9pm; ☐ Sábalo-Centro) near the Zona Dorada.

BUS

Local buses run from 6am to 10:30pm. Regular buses cost M$7; those with air-con are M$10.

From the **Central de Autobuses** bus terminal, go to Avenida Ejército Mexicano and catch any bus going south to downtown. Alternatively, walk 400m from the bus terminal to the beach and take a Sábalo–Centro bus heading south to downtown or north to the Zona Dorada.

Main routes:

Playa Sur Travels (Map p500; ☐ Playa Sur) south along Avenida Ejército Mexicano, near the bus terminal and through downtown, passing the Mercado Centro, then to the ferry terminal and El Faro.

Sábalo–Centro Travels from the Mercado Centro to Playa Norte via Juárez, then north on Avenida del Mar to the Zona Dorada and further north on Avenida Camarón Sábalo.

BUSES FROM MAZATLÁN

DESTINATION	FARE (M$)	DURATION (HR)	FREQUENCY (DAILY)
Culiacán	130-180	2¾-3	frequent
Durango	495-685	4-5½	frequent
Guadalajara	505-705	8-8½	frequent
Los Mochis	455-532	6-7	frequent
Manzanillo	909	12	2
Mexicali	1260-1470	22-25	frequent
Mexico City (Terminal Norte)	985-1275	13-16	frequent
Monterrey	1395-1580	12-14	5
Puerto Vallarta	570	9	4
Tepic	290-430	4-5	frequent
Tijuana	1370-1560	24-27	frequent

TAXI

Mazatlán is renowned for its special *pulmonía* taxis, small open-air vehicles similar to a golf cart. There are also regular taxis. Rates for rides within Mazatlán range from M$50 to M$120, depending on distance, time of day and your bargaining skills.

Mexcaltitán

📞 323 / POP 818

This shield-shaped island village is believed by some experts to be Aztlán, the ancestral homeland that the Aztecs left around AD 1091 to begin their generations-long migration to Tenochtitlán (modern Mexico City). Proponents point to the striking similarities between the cruciform design of Mexcaltitán's streets and the urban layout of early Tenochtitlán. A pre-Hispanic bas-relief in stone found in the area is also provided as evidence – it depicts a heron clutching a snake, an allusion to the sign the Aztecs hoped to find in the promised land.

These days Mexcaltitán is foremost a shrimping town. Men head out into the surrounding wetlands, which are spectacular, in the early evening in small boats, to return just before dawn with their nets bulging.

It's a very laid-back, friendly place. Tourism has scarcely made a mark here.

◉ Sights

Museo del Origen　　　　　MUSEUM
(📞 cell 323-1209323; Plaza s/n; M$5; ⊙10am-2pm & 4-7pm Tue-Sat, 10am-1pm Sun) This small but enchanting museum on the plaza offers info in Spanish on the history of museums, a small archaeological collection and pictures of ruins and petroglyphs. There's also a reproduction of a fascinating long scroll (the *Códice Boturini*), telling the story of the Aztec's travels, with their initial departure from an island looking very much like Mexcaltitán.

Activites

Arrange boat trips on the lagoon for bird-watching, fishing and sightseeing – every family has one or more boats. Trips start at M$50, which gets you a circuit of the island; otherwise expect to pay M$300 per hour.

🎊 Festivals & Events

Semana Santa　　　　　RELIGIOUS
(⊙Mar or Apr) Holy Week is celebrated in a big way here. On Good Friday a statue of Christ is put on a cross in the church, then taken down and carried through the streets.

Fiesta de San Pedro Apóstol　　RELIGIOUS
(⊙late Jun) During this raucous festival, which celebrates the patron saint of fishing, statues of SS Peter and Paul are taken out into the lagoon in decorated *lanchas* (skiffs).

🛏 Sleeping & Eating

Don't leave town without trying the local specialty *albóndigas de camarón* (shrimp meatballs), shrimp *empanadas* (turnovers) or perhaps a rich *jugo de camarón* (shrimp broth). The shrimp *tamales* sold in the morning from a wheelbarrow on the streets are another culinary highlight.

Hotel Casino Plaza　　　　HOTEL $
(📞323-235-08-50; hotelcasino.facturas@gmail. com; Ocampo s/n, cnr Rayón, Santiago Ixcuintla; s/d M$475/555; 🅿 ❄) The motel-style setup offers clean rooms, a restaurant and a location five blocks from the Mexcaltitán *colectivo* terminal (M$35). In Santiago Ixcuintla; it makes a good base for visiting the island village of Mexcaltitán.

★La Alberca　　　　　SEAFOOD $$
(📞323-235-60-27; Porfirio Diaz s/n, off Venecia; mains M$90-110; ⊙9am-6pm) On the island's east side, this has a great lagoon view. It's cheerily run, despite the fact that the staff have to spend half their days peeling crustaceans. It's all about shrimp: try shrimp *empanadas* (turnovers), shrimp ceviche and shrimp *albóndigas* (meatballs) in a delicious chili-inflected shrimp broth. The fried shrimp (called *cucarachas*) as a free appetizer are very moreish.

Mariscos Kika　　　　　SEAFOOD $$
(📞323-235-60-54; Loma China s/n; mains M$70-150; ⊙9am-6pm) For fish, shrimp and octopus cooked a dozen ways, hop on a boat to this family-run place on a small island just across from Mexcaltitán's main dock. Grassy lawns and sun loungers provide reasons to linger.

❶ Getting There & Away

Catch a bus from San Blas (M$70, one hour) or Tepic (M$71, one hour) to Santiago Ixcuintla, 7km west of Hwy 15 and 52km northwest of Tepic. Once in Santiago, take a *colectivo* (M$35, 45 minutes, four daily) or taxi (M$200) to La Batanga, a small wharf 35km away where *lanchas* (motorboats) depart for Mexcaltitán.

LOS LABRADAS

More than 600 petroglyphs, some believed to be more than 5000 years old, are depicted on volcanic rocks known as **Las Labradas** (📱 cell 696-1041144; www.facebook.com/laslabra das; via Hwy 15D Km 51, Ejido la Chicayota; M$55; ☺ 9am-5pm Mon-Thu, to 6pm Fri-Sun) along a sublime stretch of coast about 60km north of Mazatlán. Many of the carvings were made between AD 750–1250 and are tied to summer solstice, as evidenced by the solar and geometric engravings. You'll also see intriguing human and animal figures, such as a manta ray-shaped rock. Pack a swimsuit and lunch to enjoy some quality beach time.

Las Labradas is best reached by car. From Mazatlán take Hwy 15 to Hwy 15D and exit just past Km 51, then head coastward about 5.5km along a dirt road. Alternatively, Onca (p497) runs tours to the site.

The arrival and departure times of the *lanchas* are coordinated with the *colectivo* schedule. The boat journey takes 15 minutes and costs M$15 per person. If you miss the *lancha*, you can hire a private one for M$120.

From Mazatlán, catch a Tepic-bound bus, jump off at the junction for Santiago Ixcuintla and wait for further transportation.

San Blas

📞 323 / POP 10,187

The tranquil fishing village of San Blas is a peaceful, drowsy backwater, and therein lies its charm. Visitors come to enjoy isolated beaches, fine surfing, abundant birdlife and tropical jungles reached by riverboats.

San Blas was an important Spanish port from the late 16th century to the 19th century. The Spanish built a fortress here to protect their trading galleons from marauding British and French pirates. It was also the port from which St Junípero Serra, the 'Father' of the California missions, embarked on his northward peregrination. While on either side of the main drag San Blas is just another cobblestoned backwater, the uniform whitewashed facades on Avenida Juárez itself lend a dreamy revival quality that is immediately endearing.

◉ Sights

★ Playa Las Islitas   BEACH

The best beaches are southeast of town around Bahía de Matanchén, starting with Playa Las Islitas, 7km from San Blas. To get here, take the main road toward Tepic and turn right after about 4km. This paved road goes south to Matanchén, where a dirt road leads east to Playa Las Islitas and continues on to wonderfully swimmable beaches.

Playa El Borrego   BEACH

The beach closest to the town is Playa El Borrego, at the end of Azueta – look for the jet aircraft. It's a long sweep of gray sand with decent waves backed by a string of casual bar-restaurants. Swimming can be treacherous – beware of rip currents – but there are flags and a lifeguard. A handful of old gauchos offer horseback rides (M$50) on the beach, which last 15 to 30 minutes.

Cocodrilario Kiekari   ZOO

(📱 cell 311-1456231; www.facebook.com/kiekari. cocodrilario; Ejido La Palma s/n; M$30; ☺ 9am-7pm; 🅿) On the river, this crocodile nursery rears toothy reptiles that later get released into the wild as part of a repopulation program. There are also some non-release crocs, felines (jaguars and lynxes) and other captive creatures. It's usually reached by a La Tovara boat tour, but is also accessible by road (10.5km from San Blas).

La Contaduría   FORTRESS

(Del Panteón s/n; M$10; ☺ 9am-7pm; 🅿) This hill is the site of San Blas' original colonial settlement. It's worth visiting for the views and to stroll around the ruins of the 18th-century Spanish fort, where colonial riches were once amassed and counted before being shipped off to Mexico City or the Philippines. The place is still guarded by a collection of corroded cannons. On the way up are the gorgeous ruins of the settlement's church, **Templo de la Virgen del Rosario**, built in 1769.

🏃 Activities

For bird-watching, sportfishing and swimming with whale sharks, see www.sanblas-rivieranayarit.com/tours to contact local tour operators.

Surfing

Beginner and intermediate surfers choose to hone their skills at San Blas for its many beach and point breaks. The season starts in May, but the waves are fairly mellow until September and October when the south swell brings long rides. Surf spots include **El Borrego**, **La Puntilla** (by a river mouth south of Playa El Borrego), **El Mosco** (west of San Blas on Isla del Rey) and **Stoner's** (further south, between San Blas and Las Islitas), which is known for having one of the longest waves in the world.

Stoner's Surf Camp SURFING
(Playa Azul; ☎ cell 323-2322225; www.stoners surfcamp.com; Ramada 7, Playa El Borrego; classes per person M$300, board rental per hour/day from M$60/150) At Playa El Borrego, this is the nexus of the surf scene. National longboard champion 'Pompis' Cano gives lessons and holds court under the *palapa*. You can also stay (p510) at the camp.

☞ Tours

In addition to the popular La Tovara tours, more **boats** depart from landings on Estero El Pozo, running trips to **Piedra Blanca** (M$500 for up to six people, one hour) to visit a statue of the Virgin; to **Isla del Rey** (M$30 per person; five minutes) just across from San Blas; and to **Playa del Rey**, a 20km beach on the other side of the Isla del Rey peninsula.

At a **dock** north of Avenida Juárez you can hire boatmen to take you bird-watching (M$300 per hour), whale-watching (December through March M$250 per person) and fishing (M$2800 per boat). You can also make arrangements there to visit **Isla Isabel**, where the boatmen accompany you on an interesting overnight trip. It's a national park and protected ecological preserve three hours northwest of San Blas by boat. The island is a bird-watcher's paradise, but there are no facilities, so be prepared for self-sufficient camping. You can fish for your dinner, but tour operators will also help negotiate good prices with local fishers. Overnight trips generally go for M$9000 for up to six people.

★ La Tovara BOATING
(☎ cell 323-1169997; www.latovara.com; to La Tovara M$150, per person to La Tovara & cocodrilario M$200; ☺ 7am-4pm; 🚆 San Blas-Tepic) 🏄 A boat trip to the freshwater spring of La Tovara is a San Blas highlight. Small boats depart

from the *embarcadero* (dock) at the eastern edge of town or from the main dock 4.5km further east on the road to Matanchén. The three-hour trips go up the San Cristóbal *estero* (estuary) to the spring, passing thick jungle and mangroves.

La Tovara is a designated Ramsar site, and benefits from an international treaty to conserve wetlands.

There's a restaurant at La Tovara, where you can stop for lunch, or you can extend the trip to include the Cocodrilario Kiekari crocodile zoo.

Boats usually wait to head out with groups of six to eight people, so you're best off catching one at the main dock, where there are more frequent departures. From the *zócalo*, take a San Blas–Tepic combi to the main dock.

🎉 Festivals & Events

**Festival Internacional
de Aves Migratorias** BIRDWATCHING
(www.facebook.com/fiamsanblas; ☺ Jan & Feb) Bird-watchers flock to San Blas in late January and/or early February for the week-long International Migratory Bird Festival. Highlights include tours with English-speaking ornithologists and nightly entertainment in the plaza.

🛏 Sleeping

★ Casa Roxanna Bungalows BUNGALOW $
(☎ 323-285-05-73; www.casaroxanna.com; El Rey 1; d M$800-900; 🅿 ➲ ❄ 🛜 🐾 🐕) This refined haven offers eight large bungalows and two smaller rooms; angle for one of the larger upstairs units (sleeping up to five) with full kitchen and a screened porch overlooking the pool and manicured palm-treed grounds. English is spoken and discounts are offered for longer stays.

Bungalows Conny INN $
(☎ 323-285-09-86; www.bungalowsconny.com; Chiapas 26; d from M$600, bungalows M$850; 🅿 ➲ ❄ 🛜 🐕) On a quiet side of town, this place rests easy with just four modern rooms and bungalows. The largest bungalow is fresh and feels like a small apartment with a large kitchen. The sunny pool area provides plenty of relaxation. Owner Tom can offer great travel tips.

Hotelito Casa de las Cocadas HOTEL $
(☎ 323-285-09-60; www.hotellacasadelascocadas. com; Av Juárez 145; d M$800; ➲ ❄ 🛜 🐕) This pleasant hotel down by the boat docks offers

San Blas

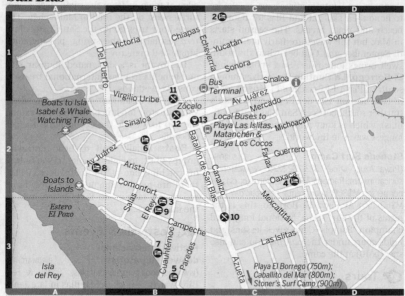

CENTRAL PACIFIC COAST SAN BLAS

clean rooms with quality beds and antique furnishings; they surround a central pool area adorned with local artwork. An appealing dining room with piano adds extra value.

Estancia Don Roberto
HOTEL $

(☎323-131-27-78; www.facebook.com/hotel estanciadonroberto; Isla María Magadalena 50; s/d M$560/795; P❀❄☎❄) The most modern of San Blas' budget offerings. Tidy rooms with air-con, sofa and satellite TV surround a colorful lobby with an enticing blue-tiled pool. Quite a deal if you're looking for affordable digs with a few creature comforts.

Stoner's Surf Camp
CABIN, CAMPGROUND $

(Playa Azul; ☎cell 323-2322225; www.stonerssurf camp.com; Playa El Borrego; campsites per person M$80, cabins without bathroom d/q M$250/500; P) The *cabañas* (cabins) at this friendly traveler hangout and surf center have electricity, mosquito nets (you'll need them), fans and suspect beds. The choicest digs are the rickety stilted cabins on the beach. There's space to camp and hammocks; the Playa Azul restaurant serves well-prepared fare. *Cabaña* guests get free use of bikes plus discounts at the surf center.

★ Hotel Hacienda Flamingos
HOTEL $$

(☎323-285-09-30; www.sanblas.com.mx/flamin go; Av Juárez 105; d from M$1200, ste M$1900; P❀❄@☎❄) This restored colonial gem provides the classiest accommodations in town. The spacious rooms and fountain-tinkling courtyard are evocative of old Mexico without even a whiff of kitsch. Some rooms have balconies and antique furniture; all have a filter coffee maker. There's a very decent pool as well as an on-site bar and small gym.

Posada del Rey
HOTEL $$

(☎323-285-01-23; www.sanblas.com.mx/posada -del-rey; Campeche 10; d M$1000; P❀❄☎❄) Neat air-conditioned rooms around an appealing pool make this a worthwhile retreat from the sometimes oppressive midday humidity of San Blas. Staff are easygoing and beds and bathrooms are more than decent, but rooms can be a bit musty.

Hotel Marina San Blas
HOTEL $$

(☎323-285-08-12; www.sanblas.com.mx/marina -san-blas; Cuauhtémoc 197; s/d M$850/990; P❀❄☎❄) Near the estuary mouth, within view of the harbor, is this meticulously maintained three-star resort. The grounds are lovely and guests get a free one-hour kayak rental. Kitschy marine-themed

San Blas

rooms have lighthouse lamps and a strange amalgamation of cinder block and tile, but they're comfy, with river views and cable TV. There's a pool and small estuary swimming beach.

🍴 Eating

San Blas is a town of casual restaurants and beachfront *palapas,* all serving fresh seafood at low prices. Cheaper sustenance, including *tortas* (sandwiches), *jugos* (juices) and *licuados* (milkshakes), can be found at the local **mercado** (cnr Sinaloa & Batallón de San Blas; mains M$45-90; ⊘7am-1pm).

★Ofro's   MEXICAN $
(☑323-285-07-50; oohlala505@outlook.es; Av Juárez 64; mains M$55-130; ⊘7am-10pm; 🛜) For honest and delicious home-cooked cuisine, head to this family-run place on the main street. It's a simply but appealingly decorated setup that does good breakfasts, great shrimp, plus chicken and potato tacos – already a substantial meal – and plates of fish and chicken with vegetables, rice and guacamole.

Juan Bananas   BAKERY, CAFE $
(La Tumba de Yako; ☑323-285-05-52; www.facebook.com/panaderiajuanbananas; Batallón de San Blas 219; loaves M$60-65, snacks M$12-55; ⊘8am-7pm) For four decades this little bakery has been cranking out some of the world's best banana bread; with any luck, you'll get a loaf hot from the oven. Juan himself is a terrific source of local information. There's also a cafe here (open November to May) doing breakfasts and tasty snacks.

★Restaurant El Delfín   FUSION $$
(☑323-285-01-12; www.garzacanela.com/en/restaurante-bar-el-delfin; Paredes 106 Sur; breakfast M$55-130, lunch & dinner M$170-189; ⊘8am-10am & 1pm-8:30pm; 🅿🛜) Under the direction of internationally renowned chef Betty Vázquez (a judge on Mexico's *MasterChef*), this restaurant at the **Hotel Garza Canela** (r M$1700, ste M$2700; ⊛❄🛜🞲) serves an impressive array of rich gourmet foods and international wines. Pick from the wonderfully cooked fish, seafood and meat dishes on offer and cap it off with homemade desserts and ice cream. Special diets are imaginatively accommodated.

Mysis III   SEAFOOD $$
(☑cell 323-1086405; horse_pedro@hotmail.com; Playa Las Islitas; mains M$90-140; ⊘9am-7pm; 🚌San Blas–Tepic combi) Sitting pretty about 2km south of the San Blas–Tepic Hwy, on Playa Las Islitas (p508), this *palapa* seafood restaurant whips up excellent shrimp dishes, *tostadas* and a flavorful *caldo de pescado* (fish soup). The calm beach and gorgeous scenery make the experience all the more memorable, and the sands south of Mysis are well worth exploring.

San Blas–Tepic combis will leave you at the Playa Las Islitas entrance, from where it's a 2km stroll.

Caballito del Mar   SEAFOOD $$

(☑ 323-216-92-04; caballitodemar10c@gmail.com; Playa El Borrego; mains M$140-160; ⊙ 11am-7pm Thu-Tue; P⛱) This is among the best of the seafood *enramadas* (thatch-covered, open-air restaurants) lined up along Playa El Borrego (p508). Popular menu items include the *cóctel de camarón* (shrimp cocktail) and *pescado zarandeado* (grilled whole fish priced by the kilo).

🍸 Drinking & Nightlife

Cafe Del Mar   BAR

(☑ 323-285-10-81; salogv76@hotmail.com; Av Juárez 5; ⊙ 6pm-2am Fri-Sun; 🐾) The coolest watering hole in town sits overlooking the plaza, with whitewashed walls hung with authentic indigenous masks. Jazz, salsa, reggae and rock pour from the sound system, mingling with the tropical breeze. The drinks don't live up to the atmosphere, but it's still a fine spot to sit.

❶ Information

Take repellent to San Blas: voracious mosquitoes and sandflies are often present in huge squadrons.

Free municipal wi-fi is available within a 150m radius of the central plaza.

Banamex ATM (Av Juárez s/n) One of a handful of ATMs in town.

Centro de Salud (☑ 323-285-12-07; cnr Azueta & Campeche; ⊙ 24hr) This central medical center is on the road that heads down to the beach.

Tourist Office (☑ cell 323-2824913; adry64 lopez@hotmail.com; Av Juárez s/n; ⊙ 2-8pm Mon-Fri) On the main road at the archway that marks your arrival at the center. Has maps and brochures about the area and the state of Nayarit, but keeps iffy office hours.

❶ Getting There & Away

The little **bus terminal** (☑ 323-285-00-43; Sinaloa s/n; ⊙ 6am-8pm) is served by Nayar and Estrella Blanca buses. From/to some destinations, including Mazatlán, you'll need to change in Tepic or at the junction (crucero de San Blas; M$40) on Hwy 15.

Daily departures include the following:

Puerto Vallarta (M$228, 3½ hours, four daily)
Santiago Ixcuintla (M$70, one hour, frequent)
Tepic (M$64, one hour, frequent 6am to 8pm)
Buses (cnr Canalizo & Mercado; M$15-20) depart from the corner of Canalizo and Mercado

several times a day, serving all the villages and beaches on Bahía de Matanchén.

Taxis and Tepic-bound combis congregate around the plaza's south side and will take you to nearby beaches or drop you off at the main dock for boat rides to national park La Tovara.

Tepic

311 / POP 332,863 / ELEV 920M

Founded by the nephew of Hernán Cortés in 1524, Tepic is the capital of Nayarit state. It's a predominantly middle-class place with a veritable hum of provincial bustle playing out on its narrow streets. Indigenous Huicholes are often seen here, wearing their colorful traditional clothing.

Across from **Plaza Principal** the ornate cathedral, dedicated in 1804, casts a regal eye over the square. Opposite is the **Palacio Municipal** (city hall), where nearby you'll often find Huicholes selling handicrafts at reasonable prices. Calle Amado Nervo, north of city hall, and nearby streets are lined with stalls where you can try local specialties such as *tejuino* (a fermented corn drink) and *guamuchil* (a small white fruit).

◉ Sights

★ Museo Regional de Nayarit   MUSEUM

(☑ 311-212-19-00; www.inah.gob.mx/es/red-de-mus eos/257-museo-regional-de-nayarit; Av México Norte 91; M$50; ⊙ 9am-6pm Mon-Fri, to 3pm Sat) Set around the courtyard of an impressive magenta *palacio* (palace), this excellent museum has a beautifully presented selection of top-quality indigenous ceramics mostly sourced from burials from around 200 BC to AD 600. Figures depicting pregnant women, houses, warriors, ball-players and musicians give a real insight into these cultures, while anthropomorphic burial urns from the local Mololoa culture (late 1st millennium AD) sport spooky faces. There's an interesting section on shells and good information in English throughout.

Museo de los Cinco Pueblos   MUSEUM

(Museum of the Five Peoples; ☑ 311-212-17-05; nay cora@hotmail.com; Av México Norte 105; ⊙ 10am-2pm & 4-7pm Tue-Sat, 10am-2pm Sun; 🅿 FREE) Displays contemporary popular arts of Nayarit's Huichol, Cora, Tepehuano, Mexicanero and mestizo peoples, including clothing, yarn art, weaving, musical instruments, ceramics and beadwork. A shop next door practicing fair trade sells a variety of items made by indigenous artisans.

BUSES FROM TEPIC

DESTINATION	FARE (M$)	DURATION (HR)	FREQUENCY (DAILY)
Guadalajara	224-375	3½-5	frequent
Mazatlán	350-360	4	hourly
Mexico City (Terminal Norte)	1190-1225	10-11	3
Puerto Vallarta	205-305	3-4	frequent
Santiago Ixcuintla	71	1	frequent

🛏 Sleeping & Eating

★ Hotel Real de Don Juan   HOTEL $$

(📞311-216-18-88;   realdedonjuan2@hotmail.com; Av México Sur 105; r/ste M$1340/1740; P👁❄ @🛜🏊) This beautifully done-up old hotel overlooking Plaza Constituyentes strikes the right balance between colonial character and urbane style. Upstairs rooms are decked out in appealing pastel colors, with luxurious king beds and marble-accented bathrooms. A good restaurant with alcove tables over the street, plus a classy bar and rooftop lounge and lap pool add points. Two imposing angel warrior statues keep watch over the tranquil lobby. Downsides? Wi-fi can be hit-and-miss, and the nearby bells can be a nuisance for late risers.

El Farallón del Pacífico   SEAFOOD $$

(📞311-213-11-24;   www.facebook.com/elfarallondel pacificotepic; Av Insurgentes 282; tostadas M$31-85, mains M$130-210; ⊙11:30am-7pm; P🛜) The standout dish here is the *pescado zarandeado* (grilled whole fish), but the menu features an ample offering of favorites from the sea, including *tostadas* piled high with ceviche and fresh shrimp.

★ Emiliano   MEXICAN $$$

(📞311-216-20-10;   www.emilianorestaurant.com; Zapata Oriente 91; breakfast M$159, lunch & dinner M$198-275; ⊙8am-midnight Mon-Sat; P🛜) One of Mexico's most acclaimed restaurants, Emiliano serves mostly regional fare in a classy courtyard setting. Breakfast is most popular: juice, coffee and fruit are included along with either one of their healthy options or a set-you-up-for-the-day meat dish. Or come in the evening and let the sommelier pick the best wines to pair with chef Marco's creative dishes.

ⓘ Information

City Tourist Office (📞311-215-30-00, ext 2000; www.facebook.com/didecotepic; 2nd flr, Amado Nervo s/n; ⊙8am-8pm) Go here for details on city tours. A nearby kiosk gives out information on Nayarit state, as does a desk at the bus terminal.

ⓘ Getting There & Away

The main **bus station** (Tepic Bus Terminal; 📞311-213-23-30; Av Insurgentes 492) is on the southeastern outskirts of town; local buses (M$6) marked 'Estación' make frequent trips between the bus station and downtown. A taxi from the terminal to the center will cost M$40.

Colectivos (Durango Norte 284; M$70; ⊙5am-9pm) to San Blas depart frequently from a small terminal on Durango Norte, between Zaragoza and Amado Nervo. For Laguna Santa María del Oro, catch a **colectivo** (Av México s/n, btwn Zaragoza Poniente y Bravo Poniente; M$30; ⊙6am-9pm) from Avenida México.

ⓘ Getting Around

Local buses (M$6) operate from around 6am to 9pm. Combis (M$6) operate along Avenida México from 6am to midnight. There are also plenty of street taxis and a taxi stand opposite the cathedral.

Chacala

📞327 / POP 319

Despite its charm and beauty, the tiny coastal fishing village of Chacala has managed to retain its status as a somewhat-secret paradise. Located 96km north of Puerto Vallarta and 10km west of Las Varas on Hwy 200, it sits pretty along a beautiful little cove backed by verdant green slopes and edged by rugged black-rock formations at either end. With just one main, sandy thoroughfare and a few cobbled side streets, it's an ideal place to unwind and contemplate the horizon.

◉ Sights

Altavista Petroglyphs   ARCHAEOLOGICAL SITE (Hwy 200–Altavista; M$20; ⊙7am-4pm) It's a drive along a rough road off Hwy 200–Altavista, then a 1.5km walk up to this site; get good directions first, as it's not signposted. The site is well stocked with petroglyphs,

LAGUNA SANTA MARÍA DEL ORO

Surrounded by forested mountains, this idyllic lake fills a volcanic crater that's over 100m deep and 2km in diameter. The clean water takes on colors ranging from turquoise to slate. It's a pleasure to walk around the lake and in the surrounding mountains, spotting birds (some 250 species) and butterflies along the way. You can also climb to an abandoned gold mine, cycle, swim, kayak or fish for black bass and perch. A number of restaurants serve fresh lake fish.

If driving, take the Santa María del Oro turnoff about 40km from Tepic along the Guadalajara road. From the turnoff it's about 9km to Santa María del Oro village, then another 8km to the lake. By bus, catch a 'Santa María del Oro' colectivo (M$30, 45 minutes) on Avenida México in Tepic, then change to a colectivo (p513) marked 'Laguna' at Santa María's town square or take a private taxi.

some geometrical, some depicting human figures. A path leads you past many carvings, with Spanish and English signs explaining them.

The visit ends in a glade with cascading water and rock pools for a dip. The site is somewhat difficult to find, but you can always hook up a tour with Xplore Chacala.

Activites

The sea provides most of the action here. Swimming in Chacala's luscious bay is safe and tranquil most of the year. You can also hike to La Caleta; it's a challenging but rewarding 3.5km walk through the jungle.

For small-boat excursions, ask at the **Chacala Fishing Cooperative** (cell 327-1020683; trinimoya2@hotmail.com; whale-watching per person M$400, fishing & surfing per boat M$800; 7:30am-5:30pm), located at a dock at the northern tip of the shoreline. They run whale-watching and fishing trips as well as surfing expeditions to La Caleta – a prime spot where a wicked left-breaking point break thrashes the rocky beach. **Xplore Chacala** (cell 327-1053504; www.xplorechacala.wixsite.com/mysite; Av Chacalilla s/n; bird-watching tour per hour M$100, petroglyphs tour per person M$350, surfboard rental per hour M$100; 9am-8pm Nov-Apr, 9am-5pm Sat & Sun May-Oct) rents out surfboards and paddleboards.

Festivals & Events

Chacala Music & Arts Festival   CULTURAL
(327-219-50-06; www.chacalamusicfestival.com; Mar) A four-day festival celebrating music, dance, local art and regional cuisine with events held in beachfront restaurants and open-air spaces.

Sleeping & Eating

Accommodations here range from the simple to the luxurious. Though there are over 50 choices, some need to be pre-booked and cater for multiday stays only.

For self-catering, **Chacala Villas** (cell 327-1030065; www.chacalavillas.com; Av Chacalilla 3; 7:30am-9:30pm) offers a variety of rental housing with full kitchens, including the recommended **Casa Mágica** (327-219-40-97; www.omcasamagica.blogspot.mx; Socorro 100; apt US$100-110).

⭐ **Techos de México**   HOMESTAY, GUESTHOUSE $
(www.techosdemexico.com; r M$400-600) Travelers interested in meeting locals should consider this organization that helps Chacala residents build good homes with adjacent guest units. Seven local families offer comfortable budget lodging through this program; check the website or look for the distinctive Techos signs as you pass through town.

Casa Norma   GUESTHOUSE $
(327-219-40-85; Golfo de México 15; r M$500-600; P) Just a minute's walk from the beach, Casa Norma offers three tidy rooms with full kitchens; two of the accommodations sport large balconies affording partial ocean views. It makes for a quiet, comfortable stay, and the family running it is *muy amable*.

Casa de Tortugas   RENTAL HOUSE $$
(cell 322-1464787; www.casadetortugas.com; Oceano Pacifico 4; d M$1300-1400, ste M$3700) This walled red house overlooking the north end of the beach enjoys privileged views over the bay and offers three excellent rooms, a large family suite, a roof terrace and an infinity pool. Rooms have a microwave and coffee maker, and there's a shared kitchen area. Must be prebooked: there's no reception.

Hotel Mar de Coral HOTEL **$$**

(☑ 327-219-41-09; www.facebook.com/mardecoral chacala; Av Chacalilla s/n; d M$1000, bungalows from M$1800; ☺❋☎☒) Set in the center of town across the road from the beach, this incongruous modern building offers spacious tiled rooms with wooden beds and furnishings. What it calls bungalows are much larger rooms with an attached kitchen. There's a pool in a shady courtyard lobby.

Around the corner, on Calle Canarias, sister property **Mar de Coral Elite** provides slightly more upscale accommodations with a sunny pool area.

Mar de Jade RESORT **$$$**

(☑ 327-219-40-00, US 800-257-0532; www. mardejade.com; Mar de Jade 1; s/d incl full board from US$321/369; ℗☺❋☎☒) This getaway at the far south end of Chacala's beachfront hosts regular yoga, meditation and wellness retreats, but welcomes independent travelers too. Crashing waves are audible everywhere on the property, from the rooms with deep, tiled bathtubs, to the sauna, Jacuzzi and spa area, to the sprawling poolside patio where vegetarian-friendly buffet meals are served. Rates include yoga classes in winter.

Mauna Kea BREAKFAST **$**

(☑ 327-219-40-67; www.casapacificachacala.com; Los Corchos 15; mains M$70-100; ☺ 8-11am Mon-Sat Nov-Apr; ☎) Watch whales over morning coffee at this seasonal rooftop eatery on the bluffs just north of town (or get your breakfast free by staying at the attached B&B!).

Quezada SEAFOOD **$$**

(☑ cell 327-1044373; Av Chacalilla s/n; grilled fish per kilo M$240; ☺ 9am-5:30pm) Beachfront *palapa* (thatched-roof) restaurant Quezada grills *pescado zarandeado* (spiced, charcoal-grilled fish) to near perfection thanks to a delightful *adobo* (seasoned tomato-chili sauce) marinade that gets brushed on the whole fish during cooking. If they happen to have corbina as the day's fresh catch, you're in luck.

Majahua INTERNATIONAL **$$**

(☑ 327-219-40-53; www.majahua.com; Sur de la Bahia de Chacala s/n; mains M$95-190; ☺ breakfast 9-11am, lunch noon-4pm, dinner 5-8pm; ☎) ✎ Perched on a jungle-covered hillside overlooking the cove, this ecolodge's terrace restaurant makes a glorious spot to greet the morning with a full breakfast, or to indulge in a romantic sunset dinner over cocktails

and fresh seafood. Reserve ahead for dinner. Majahua also runs a seasonal beachside tapas bar (November through April).

ⓘ Getting There & Away

For Chacala, get off a Puerto Vallarta–Tepic bus at Las Varas and take a *colectivo* (M$15) for 11km from there: these leave every half-hour or so from directly across the road from the bus stop (look for the chairs on a corner outside a locksmith). A taxi into Chacala runs about M$120. If you're driving, the Hwy 200 turnoff is 1km south of Las Varas.

San Francisco

☑ 311 / POP 1823

San Francisco, aka San Pancho, is another fishing pueblo turned vacation spot, with prettier beaches and a less obvious gringo footprint than you'll find in popular Sayulita, a couple of beaches south. There's less action here too, unless you count those real-life gauchos riding horses through the riverbed and along a gorgeous blond beach, long, wild and driftwood-strewn.

Avenida Tercer Mundo leads from Hwy 200 a couple of kilometers through town to the beach, where sidewalk restaurants serve the usual fish and ceviche dishes and cold beers.

🏃 Activities

Las Huertas GOLF

(☑ 311-258-45-21; www.lashuertasgolf.com; América Latina s/n; green fees 9 holes from M$420; ☺ 8am-4pm Tue-Sun) Las Huertas is a short but pretty par 32 nine-holer that will keep golfers happy for several hours.

↻ Tours

Paseos a Caballo HORSEBACK RIDING

(☑ 311-258-41-82; www.laselvasanpancho.com; Av Tercer Mundo 50; tour per hour M$350) Hostal La Selva, near the town's entrance, offers horseback tours on mountain trails and along the windswept beach.

🛏 Sleeping

★**Refugio de Sol**
& Hostal San Pancho HOSTEL, GUESTHOUSE **$**

(☑ 311-258-41-61; www.hostalsanpancho.com; Av Tercer Mundo 12; dm M$250-300, d M$1000-1500; ☺❋☎) Kitted out with travelers' needs in mind, this guesthouse-hostel is set around its surf shop near the highway. It offers super-clean, simple yet charming rooms and snazzier 'suites' (bigger rooms with an attractive design, better bathrooms and terrace). Ground-floor dorms and their outdoor bathroom are basic but comfy. Guesthouse stays include free breakfast served in an appealing common area upstairs.

There's also free bike and skateboard use – handy to zip down to the beach, 1km away. It offers surfboard rental and classes too, as well as various tours.

Bungalows Lydia
BUNGALOW $$$

(☎311-258-43-37; www.bungalowslydia.com; Clavelinas 393; bungalows US$110-150; P🚗🗐🛜🏊) Overlooking two hidden beaches and surrounded by 2000 palm trees planted by the owners themselves, this restful cliffside haven is idyllic as it gets. Of the eight fan-cooled suites on offer, the 'Sunset' and 'Panaroma' provide the most stunning ocean views (as does an infinity pool at the cliff's edge). A delightful saltwater pool awaits on the beach below.

Bungalows Lydia best suits independent-minded travelers with vehicles. There's no on-site restaurant, but the suites have full kitchens. It's 3km east of town along a dirt road.

✕ Eating & Drinking

Maria's
MEXICAN $

(☎311-258-44-39; www.facebook.com/marias.restaurant.3; Av Tercer Mundo 28A; breakfast & lunch M$50-100, dinner M$110-240; ⏰8:30am-3:30pm & 6pm-10:30pm Thu-Mon, 8:30am-3:30pm Tue; 🛜🍴) San Pancho's premier breakfast spot slings tasty Mexican faves such as *huevos divorciados* (fried eggs in red and green salsa) and it does North American dishes as well. The lunch and dinner menu offers plenty of vegetarian options and light fare including salads and fish tacos.

★Bistro Orgánico
FUSION $$$

(☎311-258-41-55; www.hotelcielorojo.com/english/bistro-organico-restaurant.html; Asia 6; mains M$215-240; ⏰breakfast 8:30am-2:30pm daily, dinner 6:30-10pm Fri-Sun Nov-Apr; 🛜🍴) Tucked into a pretty plant-filled courtyard in **Hotel Cielo Rojo** (d incl breakfast US$150; 🚗❄🛜), Bistro Orgánico is San Francisco's surprisingly sophisticated top choice for eating. Chef Calixto cooks up fish and vegetarian food as imaginative as anything in LA or New York, using mostly local, organic produce. Breakfast stretches into the afternoon, and seasonal dinner service is best finished off with chocolate tequila truffles.

★La Fresona
BAR

(☎cell 322-2315219; www.facebook.com/lafresonabeachclub; Av Tercer Mundo s/n; ⏰11am-9pm Thu-Mon; 🐾) Get your groove on at this popular on-the-beach bar where DJs spin funky electronic music or live salsa acts take the stage. Even during the quieter afternoon hours it makes quite the scenic (albeit sceney) hangout spot to chill over *micheladas* (beer cocktails) and cocktails.

❶ Getting There & Away

There are direct international flights from the US and Canada to resort towns such as Puerto Vallarta, Mazatlán, Acapulco and Zihuatanejo. For those traveling by car, the toll roads make for easy sailing, but are pricey. High-quality bus services connect the resort centers to inland Mexico.

Between towns, coastal Hwy 200 has had an up-and-down safety record, especially in the states of Michoacán and Guerrero, which still have a reputation for being unsafe at night.

Sayulita
◪329 / POP 2262

Once upon a time – well, the late 1990s – Sayulita really *was* a tranquil fishing village. Many of the town's *norteamericano* residents still describe it that way, but the truth is that in peak season the place is full of gringos, drawn here by the beautiful (if not that clean) sandy beach, rideable waves, good restaurants and tasteful B&Bs. It's a thriving hipster-surfer scene and a pleasant place to relax for a few days.

◉ Sights

Playa Los Muertos
BEACH

One popular destination near central Sayulita is Playa Los Muertos, where picnics and bodyboarding top the action. It's a 15-minute walk south along the coast road, through the Villa Amor resort and the cemetery.

🏃 Activities

Arrange bicycle hire, boat trips, horseback riding, trekking or kayaking from operators on the main street and on the beach.

Don Pedros
DANCING

(☎329-291-30-90; www.donpedros.com; Marlín 2; salsa lesson M$50; ⏰salsa class 8:30pm-11:30pm Mon, flamenco 7:30pm-9:30pm Thu Oct-Jul) Practice your salsa moves with Monday night dance classes at this oceanfront restaurant-bar. On Thursday nights, order a drink and watch flamenco dancers perform. Both dance activities run from October to July.

Stand Up Sayulita
WATER SPORTS

(☎329-291-35-75; www.standupsayulita.com; Marlín 59; board rental per hour/half-/full day US$10/30/45, lesson US$50; ⊗9am-8pm) This is the place to learn how to captain a stand-up paddleboard and ride waves too. Lessons last 90 minutes and include a free 60-minute paddle afterward.

Surfing

Sayulita is a classic 'boarder' town. Medium-sized waves pour dependably from both the left and the right – practice your moves or take up the sport for the first time. Several surf shops offer rentals and lessons.

Oceano Dive & Surf
SURFING, DIVING

(☎329-298-85-32; www.oceanoadventures.com; Av Revolución 34B; surf class US$45, Islas Marietas tour US$75; ⊗9am-5pm Mon-Sat) Friendly, recommended setup that offers really good and enthusiastic surf classes at a better price than many. A 2½-hour private lesson allows for an hour's board rental free to practice afterward. It is also a PADI-certified dive operator, and runs snorkeling excursions out to Islas Marietas.

Lunazul
SURFING

(☎329-291-20-09; www.lunazulsurfing.com; Marlín 4; SUP/surfboard/bodyboard rental per day M$300/400/200, private lessons US$60; ⊗9am-6pm) Several local surf shops offer rentals and lessons, including the well-established Lunazul.

🛏 Sleeping

A good selection of private villas can be browsed on the website Sayulita Life (www.sayulitalife.com). Low-season prices can reduce sharply.

★ Amazing Hostel Sayulita
HOSTEL $

(☎329-291-36-88; www.theamazinghostelsayulita.com; Pelícanos 102; dm/d M$350/1300; ⊖❄🛜❄) Follow the road upriver on the plaza side of the bridge to reach this modern hostel. It's run by helpful, well-traveled folk and has tip-top facilities. Dark but cool en suite dorms are downstairs; upstairs guests have use of an area with a kitchen, climbing wall and pool. Air-con private rooms are spacious, wi-fi is reliable and bike rentals are available.

WORTH A TRIP

LO DE MARCOS

There really isn't much to do in the mellow fishing town of Lo de Marcos – that's why Mexican vacationers and snowbirds like the place so much. Several seafood restaurants line the palm-fringed beach along with some decent oceanfront bungalows if you decide to spend the night. **El Caracol Bungalows** (☎33-3684-3301; www.bungalowselcaracol.com; Camino a las Minitas Km 1.5, Playa Lo de Marcos; r US$80-102; 🅿⊖❄🛜❄❄), which doubles as a trailer park, provides comfortable rooms overlooking grassy grounds, and the staff can arrange boat trips to nearby islands (OK, so there *are* a few things to do). About 2km south of Lo de Marcos, you'll find **Playa Los Venados**, a small cove accessible by a dirt road.

To reach Lo de Marcos, catch any northbound Compostela bus along Hwy 200. It's 10km north of San Francisco.

Casa Corazón
HOTEL $$

(☎cell 322-1345696; www.casacorazonsayulita.com/blog; Cocos Sur 4; d M$990-1200; 🅿⊖❄🛜) About 500m from the town square, this family-run hotel provides 10 simple yet colorful rooms varying in size from compact digs with air-con to larger units with kitchens. It's nothing extraordinary, but you get clean, cheerful accommodations that are relatively affordable for Sayulita.

Petit Hotel Hafa
HOTEL $$

(☎329-291-38-06; www.hotelhafa-sayulita.com; Av Revolución 55; r US$60-103; ⊖❄🛜) Plenty of charm is on offer at this sweet small hotel near the plaza, though the location means party noise can be an issue. Decor fuses North Africa and Mexico, with eight individually decorated rooms offering concrete floors, fans (air-con extra) and large bathrooms with brass-bowl sinks. Staff are friendly though hands-off. The downstairs boutique is a gorgeous browse.

★ Aurinko Bungalows
BUNGALOW $$$

(☎329-291-31-50; www.aurinkobungalows.com; Marlín 18; 1-/2-bedroom bungalows US$107/178; ⊖❄🛜❄❄) An exuberant thatched roof covers this enticing complex of deconstructed houses with indoor/outdoor living rooms and kitchens, and wonderful bedrooms with river-stone floors. It feels like a secluded hideaway but is actually just steps from

ℹ️ SAYULITA'S CHANGING TIME ZONE

Sayulita and Riviera Nayarit towns as far north as Lo de Marcos are on Central time, unlike most of Nayarit state, which is on Mountain time. The area made the switch in 2010 in order to synchronize its clocks with neighboring Puerto Vallarta and Jalisco. Why the shift? It turns out there was an epidemic of gringos arriving at Vallarta's airport an hour late and missing their homeward-bound flights, either ignorant of the time zone difference or too blissed out by beach life to care.

the plaza and the beach. A yoga center and small pool are the latest additions.

Siete Lunas BOUTIQUE HOTEL $$$
(📱 cell 322-1822979; www.sietelunas.mx; Camino Playa de los Muertos 714; r incl breakfast US$242-303; 🅿️❄️🐾🛜🏊) Perched above jungly slopes and boasting phenomenal coastal views, these intimate bungalows make for the perfect romantic stay. Around 2km from town, past Playa Los Muertos (p516), it's an end-of-the-road honeymoon spot where a golf cart zips you up to a lodge-style retreat of real beauty. Breakfast is included, but there's no restaurant service.

Hotel Sayulita Central HOTEL $$$
(📞 329-291-38-45; www.hotelsayulitacentral.com; Delfines 7; r US$113-169; ❄️❄️🛜) Perfectly located between the plaza and beach, this hotel has a variety of rooms named for classic rock bands. All are bright and creative, with nice touches such as water coolers, and share a sprawling lounge that is a great place to hang. Prices do reflect quality: the cheapest top-floor chambers can be furnaces in summer.

🍴 Eating

Sayulita has a beguiling selection of small bistro-style cafes, providing an agreeable contrast to the *palapas* on the beach and the lively stands (try the seafood burritos) that sprout every evening on the streets surrounding the plaza.

⭐ Naty's Kitchen TACOS $
(📱 329-291-38-18; natys.cocina@gmail.com; Marlín 13; tacos M$15-20; ⏰8:30am-4pm Mon-Sat, 9am-3pm Sun) A cute and clean taco stand where

tortillas are stuffed per your choice with sliced poblano peppers, potatoes, green beans and mushrooms, beef, smoked marlin, chicken with *mole* (chili sauce), or pork and cactus paddles. Order at the counter and sit on a bench table out front. Locals descend en masse for a reason.

Mary's MEXICAN $
(📱 cell 322-1201803; Av Revolución 36; tacos M$25-40, mains M$60-150; ⏰8:30am-11pm Mon-Sat, to 4pm Sun) Mary's keeps things simple, affordable and traditional with menu items such as fish tacos or grilled shrimp on handmade tortillas. The popular curbside eatery also has gained kudos for its poblano chili peppers stuffed with shrimp, chicken or cheese.

Yah-Yah Sayulita Cafe VEGETARIAN, BREAKFAST $
(www.facebook.com/cafeyahyah; Delfines 20; M$55-90; ⏰8am-4pm; 🛜🐾) In addition to its robust Mexican-grown coffee, this small cafe on the main square prepares full breakfasts, fruit and veggie bowls, gluten-free pastries and many vegetarian options. Makes an ideal spot to fuel up before hitting the surf.

Chilly Willy SEAFOOD $
(📱 cell 322-8897190; Av Revolución 72; dishes M$60-120; ⏰10am-7pm Wed-Mon) An unpretentious spot, this simple *taquería* (taco stall) makes a good stop for no-frills, tasty seafood. Munch *tostadas* piled with shrimp and octopus and seafood cocktails. On Saturday and Sunday it does chicken with *mole* and *chile relleno* (stuffed poblano chili pepper). Ask about its jungle-hiking, bird-watching and mountain-biking excursions.

Café El Espresso CAFE $
(www.sayulitalife.com/elespresso; Av Revolución 51; dishes M$65-130; ⏰7am-10pm; 🛜) This corner spot on the plaza – where breakfast is served until 2pm – lives up to its name. The coffee is strong and sensational, and non-dairy milk options are available. The 'Tropical Heaven' smoothie blends pineapple, yogurt, honey and papaya or strawberries with basil and coconut cream, and the Mexican breakfasts are dynamite.

Palmar Trapiche AMERICAN, SEAFOOD $$
(📱 cell 55-43607789; www.facebook.com/trapiche sayulita; Av del Palmar 10A; mains M$95-295; ⏰4-11pm Tue-Sun) Owned by the excellent Colima microbrewery, this restaurant and beer garden excels in North American fare such as

burgers and braised ribs slow-cooked in pale ale. There's also an interesting variety of fish and seafood dishes on a menu that offers beer-pairing suggestions.

Yeikame
MEXICAN **$$**

(☑ 329-291-30-22; www.facebook.com/yeikame sayulita; Mariscal 10; mains M$90-165; ☺8am-10:30pm Wed-Mon; ☎) Welcoming and reliable, this family-run place has pleasant street-side tables and produces a range of fairly traditional Mexican fare. Enchiladas, *tostadas*, tacos and more substantial plates such as chicken in *mole* or marinated pork are priced fairly and feature tasty blue-corn tortillas. There are delicious fruit drinks on offer, and breakfast fare is equally toothsome.

Drinking & Nightlife

Several bars on the plaza's west side keep fairly late hours.

Cava
BAR

(☑cell 322-1495836; berenice_praznik@hotmail.com; Av Revolución 54; ☺1pm-1am Mon-Sat, 7pm-1am Sun) Belly up to the bar at this friendly neighborhood mezcal joint where you can sip smoky *raicilla* (mezcal-like distilled agave drink), viscous *pulque* (fermented maguey beverage), local craft beer and cocktails. After a few potent *raicillas* you'll be chatting it up in no time with the stranger sitting on the barstool next to you.

Don Pato
BAR

(☑cell 322-1032006; www.facebook.com/bar donpato; Marlín 12; ☺8pm-3am Sun-Fri, to 4am Sat) At the rubber-duck sign and up a spiral staircase, this lively bar on the main plaza pumps out live music or DJ sets most nights, with an open mike on Tuesdays. Don't expect a dress code: half the folks are in bathing suits. Table football is hotly contested, and the upstairs level is often where it's all at.

Shopping

Tierra Huichol
ARTS & CRAFTS

(☑cell 322-1572725; www.huicholand.com; Av Revolución 38; ☺10am-10pm) ✍ While not the cheapest place to buy, this co-op shop gives a good introduction to the Huicholes' colorful beadwork sculptures. There are some spectacular pieces here, and you can often see an artist at work. Fair-trade crafts sold here contribute to the livelihood of artisans in Huichol communities.

Revolución del Sueno
FASHION & ACCESSORIES

(☑329-291-38-50; revoluciondelsueno.contacto@gmail.com; Navarrete 55; ☺10am-8pm) Specializes in silk-screened T-shirts and hipster beach bags – we love revolutionary Emiliano Zapata holding a bouquet of flowers. It also has throw pillows, exquisite jewelry, and quirky stickers and decorative art pieces, including outstanding papier-mâché skulls.

ⓘ Getting There & Away

Sayulita is about 40km north of Puerto Vallarta, just west of Hwy 200. Buses (M$40, 50 minutes) operate every 15 minutes or so from a stop (p535) in front of Puerto Vallarta's Walmart, just south of Marina Vallarta. Additionally, any northbound 2nd-class bus from the Puerto Vallarta bus terminal (p535) will drop you at the Sayulita turnoff, but you'll have to walk 2km into town.

Buses to San Francisco (M$20, 15 minutes), Lo de Marcos (M$30, 30 minutes) and Puerto Vallarta (M$40, 50 minutes) depart from a small **station** (Av Revolución s/n; ☺6am-10pm) on Avenida Revolución and Coral.

Punta de Mita & Riviera Nayarit

Just south of Sayulita, a stunning, jungled mountainous peninsula tumbles into the sea. Much of it has been tamed and groomed into gated resorts, and **Punta de Mita** village is now largely a service center for these resorts. Nevertheless, it has a string of beachfront restaurants popular with Vallarta families, and its little marina is a place to jump on a boat out to sea.

The beaches that grace the coast from here to Nuevo Vallarta – part of a larger 150km stretch known as **Riviera Nayarit** – are some of the best on the central Pacific coast. The water is almost always clear and aquamarine, the sand is white and the surf can get fun too. Laid-back fishing ports turned beach resorts worth exploring on this coastline include **La Cruz de Huanacaxtle** and **Bucerías**.

⚐ Activities

Punta de Mita's beachfront strip has several places offering surfing classes and rentals. After a few wipeouts, the village's several massage studios might look like a good idea. From the marina (eastern end of the strip), boats leave for the Islas Marietas; they also run whale-watching expeditions (December to March).

Punta Mita Charters — BOATING

(☑329-291-62-98; www.puntamitacharters.com; Av Anclote 17; whale-watching boat per hour US$140, fishing boat per day US$800, Islas Marietas M$500-1500; ☉office 8am-4pm) This cooperative can take you to the Islas Marietas, out fishing or – from December to March – humpback whale-watching.

⌣ Sleeping & Eating

★ Villa Bella Bed & Breakfast — B&B $$$

(☑329-295-51-61; www.villabella-lacruz.com; Monte Calvario 12, La Cruz de Huanacaxtle; ste incl breakfast from US$149; ❀❄☎❀❀) Jaw-dropping views across the Riviera Nayarit combine with contemporary/bohemian decor to make the trip up the hill to this place worth it (a car is a must). The very private Master Suite has its own outdoor kitchen and lounge, but all the suites have views and access to the lovely garden and pool area. Breakfast is served alfresco. Just down the road, the small town of La Cruz de Huanacaxtle and its marina have plenty of eating and drinking options.

La Quinta del Sol — HOTEL $$$

(☑329-291-53-15; www.laquintadelsol.com; Hidalgo 162; d from US$119; ❀❄☎) An ideal spot for surfers and beach bums alike, the seven tastefully appointed rooms here come with full kitchens, slick marble sinks, excellent beds and a sweet rooftop terrace overlooking the ocean. Right across the street awaits a quiet beach and **Stinky's**, a novice-friendly surf break. The hotel will gladly hook you up with lessons and board rentals.

★ Tuna Blanca — MEXICAN $$$

(☑329-291-54-14; www.tunablanca.com; Av Anclote 5; lunch dishes M$95-210, dinner dishes M$380-650, tasting menus M$869-950; ☉noon-10:30pm Tue-Sun; ☎❀) The exquisite surf-and-turf offerings at this gorgeously designed ocean-front restaurant feature renowned chef Thierry Blouet's tried-and-true favorites, such as prawn-and-pumpkin cream soup and *raicilla*-flambéed shrimp. If you want to splurge, go for the five-course tasting menu, which can be done up vegetarian style.

❶ Getting There & Away

From Puerto Vallarta, take Hwy 200 north through Bucerías, then veer left toward La Cruz de Huanacaxtle to follow the coast toward the Punta de Mita peninsula. Frequent buses departing from Puerto Vallarta (p535) can drop you at most Riviera Nayarit towns.

Puerto Vallarta

☑322 / POP 255,681

Stretching around the sparkling blue Bahía de Banderas and backed by lush palm-covered mountains, Puerto Vallarta (or just 'Vallarta' to many) is one of Mexico's most enticing coastal destinations. Each year millions come to laze on the dazzling sandy beaches, browse in the quirky shops, nosh in the stylish restaurants and wander the picturesque central streets and enticing *malecón* (boardwalk). There are activities aplenty, including boat trips, horseback rides, diving trips and day trips to the interior. After sunset, Vallarta takes on a new identity with pumping nightlife along the cobblestone streets and numerous LGBT-friendly options in what is the gay beach capital of Mexico.

❶ Orientation

The 'old' town center, called **Zona Centro**, is the area north of Río Cuale. Cross the river to reach the **Zona Romántica**, a characterful, spread-out tourist district with smaller hotels, restaurants and bars, the two most central beaches and the hub of LGBT life. These eminently walkable downtown neighborhoods, which remain the heart and soul of Puerto Vallarta, are where most places worth visiting, staying at or eating are located.

North of the city is a strip of giant luxury hotels, the **Zona Hotelera**, where you'll find Marina Vallarta, a large yacht marina (9km from downtown), and Nuevo Vallarta, a new area of hotel and condominium developments (18km). Just north of Marina Vallarta is the **airport** (10km; p535) and the **bus station** (12km; p535). To the south of the city is a string of winningly beautiful beaches, some backed by resort hotels.

❍ Sights

The heart of Zona Centro is the **Plaza Principal** (Plaza de Armas), where chain-store modernism blends with the old shoeshine days of pueblo yore. The wide **malecón** stretches a little south and about 10 blocks north from here, and is dotted with bars, restaurants, nightclubs and a grand collection of public sculptures.

Or you could just go to the beach. Those on the Bahía de Banderas have many personalities. Some are buzzing with cheerful activity; others are quiet and private. Two, **Playa Olas Altas** (Map p526) and **Playa de los Muertos** (Beach of the Dead; Map p522),

A DAY ON A RANCH

Hacienda El Divisadero (☑ 322-225-21-71; www.haciendaeldivisadero.com; Camino Tuito–Chacala Km 9, Las Guásimas; tour without/with hotel transportation US$50/95; ⊙ 10am-6pm Fri-Sun Nov-Mar) is a vast ranch 90 minutes south of Puerto Vallarta and offers a slew of fun activities on a one-day tour. You'll be picked up from Puerto Vallarta and shuttled to the ranch, where you'll enjoy a light breakfast before a horseback excursion to local petroglyphs, river swim and a tour of the ranch's raicilla (a knock-your-socks-off mezcal-like agave drink) distillery.

The tour includes cheese tasting and lunch at the onsite restaurant, where you may enjoy melt-in-the-mouth birria (a spicy meat stew). You'll be dropped off at your hotel at around 5pm. The price includes everything except tips for the guides. The tour is cheaper if you do not require transport from your hotel. To get here, drive south of Puerto Vallarta for 45km on Hwy 200 to the town of El Tuito, then follow the signs another 10km west to the hacienda.

CENTRAL PACIFIC COAST PUERTO VALLARTA

are handy to downtown; both are south of the Río Cuale. At the southern end of Playa de los Muertos is the stretch of sand called **Blue Chairs**, one of Mexico's most famous gay beaches.

There's a string of good hotels on the north side, in the Zona Hotelera; Nuevo Vallarta also has decent stretches of sand. But it's south of the center (p525) where the most enchanting coves are found.

★ **Jardín Botánico de Vallarta**   GARDENS
(Vallarta Botanical Garden; ☑ 322-223-61-82; www.vbgardens.org; Hwy 200 Km 24; M$150; ⊙ 9am-6pm Tue-Sun Jan-Apr, 9am-6pm Mon-Sun May-Dec) Orchids, bromeliads, agaves and wild palms line the paths of this gorgeous nature park, located 30km south of Puerto Vallarta. Follow hummingbirds through fern grottoes or head down to bask in a chair on the sand and swim amid huge boulders in the river below. Take the 'El Tuito' bus (M$30) from the corner of Carranza and Aguacate in Puerto Vallarta, or hop in a taxi (about M$350).

Isla Río Cuale   ISLAND
(Map p526) A trip to Vallarta wouldn't be complete without lingering on Isla Río Cuale, a sand island that appeared in the river mouth in the 1920s and was then consolidated. It's very pleasant for a traffic-free stroll among the trees.

Los Arcos   LANDMARK
(Map p526; Malecón s/n, Plaza Morelos) Public events such as gaucho parades and mariachi festivals bloom on the sea side of the plaza near an outdoor **amphitheater** backed by Los Arcos, a row of Romanesque arches that has become a symbol of the city.

Parroquia de Nuestra Señora de Guadalupe   CATHEDRAL
(Templo de Guadalupe; Map p526; ☑ 322-222-13-26; www.parroquiadeguadalupevallarta.com; Hidalgo 370; ⊙ 7am-10pm Mon-Sat, from 6:30am Sun) The crown-topped steeple of the Church of Our Lady of Guadalupe, the town's central cathedral, is a Vallarta icon, and the hand-ringing of the bells via a long rope is a local tradition.

🏃 Activities

Restless souls need not go far to find activities such as mountain biking and whale-watching. Snorkeling, scuba diving, deep-sea fishing, waterskiing, windsurfing, sailing and parasailing can be arranged on the beaches in front of any of the large hotels or through the tourist office (p535).

Cruises
Daytime, sunset and evening cruises are available in Vallarta. The most popular ones are the cruises to Yelapa (p525) and Las Ánimas (p525) beaches; others go to **Islas Marietas**. Prices are generally negotiable, starting at M$1200 for sunset cruises and beach trips; longer trips lasting four to six hours with meals and bottomless cocktails will set you back M$2200. Leaflets advertising cruises are available throughout town.

Diana's Gay & Lesbian Cruise   CRUISE
(Map p526; www.dianastours.com; Playa de los Muertos dock; cruise US$110; ⊙ 9am-5pm Thu or Fri Oct-May) On non-summer Thursdays or Fridays (cruise days vary by the week), Diana hosts an all-day gay and lesbian cruise, with plenty of food, an open bar and snorkeling. It leaves from the dock at Playa de los Muertos. You can book your spot via the website.

Greater Puerto Vallarta

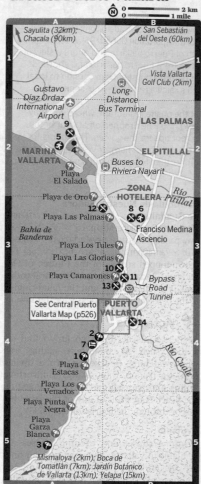

Sayulita (32km); Chacala (90km)
San Sebastián del Oeste (60km)
Vista Vallarta Golf Club (2km)
Gustavo Díaz Ordaz International Airport
Long-Distance Bus Terminal
LAS PALMAS
EL PITILLAL
MARINA VALLARTA
Buses to Riviera Nayarit
Playa El Salado
ZONA HOTELERA
Río Pitillal
Playa de Oro
Bahía de Banderas
Playa Las Palmas
Francisco Medina Ascencio
Playa Los Tules
Playa Las Glorias
Playa Camarones
Bypass Road Tunnel
See Central Puerto Vallarta Map (p526)
PUERTO VALLARTA
Río Cuale
Playa Estacas
Playa Los Venados
Playa Punta Negra
Playa Garza Blanca
Mismaloya (2km); Boca de Tomatlán (7km); Jardín Botánico de Vallarta (13km); Yelapa (15km)

cal fish and garishly colored corals. Vallarta has several diving operators. Most also offer snorkeling trips, which usually means snorkelers tag along with divers. Dives typically include transportation, gear and light meals.

Banderas Scuba Republic
DIVING
(Map p526; ☎ cell 322-1357884; www.bs-republic. com; Cárdenas 230; shore/boat dives US$95/105; ⊗ office 8am-1pm & 2-5pm Mon-Fri, 8am-1pm Sat) Maintains a high degree of professionalism with its small-group excursions to lesser-known sites.

Golf
Vallarta's golf courses are north of the city. Various golf websites, such as www.golfnow. com, often offer appealing deals.

Punta Mita Golf Club
GOLF
(☎ 329-291-55-90; www.fourseasons.com/punta mita/golf; Ramal Carretera 200 Km 19, Punta Mita; green fees 9/18 holes US$208/322) At the Four Seasons resort at Punta Mita, two Jack Nicklaus–designed golf courses enjoy some spectacular ocean vistas; the **Pacífico** has a renowned optional hole with an island green and the **Bahía** lacks little by comparison. Non-hotel guests must pay an additional US$243 (covers two people and includes daytime room) for a day pass.

Vista Vallarta Golf Club
GOLF
(☎ 322-290-00-30; www.clubcorp.com/clubs/ vista-vallarta-club-de-golf; Circuito Universidad 653, Colonia El Pitillal; green fees twilight/daylight

Deep-Sea Fishing
Deep-sea fishing is popular year-round, with a major international **fishing tournament** (☎ 322-225-54-67; www.fishvallarta.com) held mid-November every year. Prime catches are sailfish, marlin, tuna, red snapper and sea bass. Fishing trips can be arranged dockside at Marina Vallarta or through the multitude of agencies around town. Rates start at about US$250/400 for a four-/eight-hour excursion.

Diving & Snorkeling
Beneath the warm, tranquil waters of Bahía de Banderas is a world of stingrays, tropi-

US$155/209; ☉ daylight 7am-1pm, twilight 1-5pm) With Nicklaus- and Weiskopf-designed courses side by side, this is one of Mexico's premier golf resorts, and its jungle-side situation gives it a memorable appeal. It's around 9km east of the airport (p535).

Marina Vallarta Golf Club   GOLF
(Map p522; ☑ 322-221-00-73; www.clubcorp. com/clubs/marina-vallarta-club-de-golf; Paseo de la Marina 430; green fees twilight/daylight incl cart US$111/139; ☉ daylight 7am-1pm, twilight 1-4:30pm) This Joe Finger–designed 18-hole, par-72 course is just north of Marina Vallarta and features plenty of water wildlife including crocs. Could do with a little TLC though.

Horseback Riding
Vallarta's jungly mountains are wonderful to explore from a horseback perspective. Rancho El Charro runs scenic tours into the Sierra Madre.

Rancho El Charro   HORSEBACK RIDING
(Map p522; ☑ 322-224-01-14; www.ranchoelcharro. com; Pickup Av Francisco Villa 1001; horseback rides US$75-135) Rancho El Charro, 12km northeast of downtown Puerto Vallarta, is recommended for its healthy horses and scenic three- to eight-hour trots into the Sierra Madre. Some rides are suitable for kids. The pickup point in Puerto Vallarta is at the Biblioteca Los Mangos, near the corners of Avenidas Francisco Villa and De Los Tules.

🎓 Courses

Instituto Vallartense de Cultura   COURSE
(Vallarta Cultural Institute; Map p526; ☑ 322-223-00-95; www.facebook.com/ivcultura; Isla Río Cuale; enrollment fee M$100, lessons per month M$280; ☉ 8am-8pm Mon-Fri, 9am-2pm Sat) An arts complex at the easternmost plaza on Isla Río Cuale, on the more local hemisphere of the island. Theater productions and battles of the bands bloom in the modest theater, and there are regular workshops where locals and tourists can take lessons in music, printmaking and painting.

Colegio de Español y Cultura Mexicana   LANGUAGE
(CECM; Map p526; ☑ 322-223-20-82; www.cecm. udg.mx; Libertad 105-1; per course intensive/one-on-one US$500/800; ☉ office 9am-5pm Mon-Fri) Language courses at this Universidad de Guadalajara–affiliated school range from 50-hour intensive two-week courses to 30 hours of one-on-one instruction and an optional homestay program.

☞ Tours
Nature and outdoor adventure tours are one of Puerto Vallarta's strongest attributes. There's a tour agency on almost every block; some are pushier than others. **Agencia Paraíso** (Map p526; ☑ 322-222-25-49; paraiso pv1@gmail.com; Morelos 236; ☉ 9am-9:30pm) is a reliable central option. There are several zip-line courses, all regularly recommended.

★ Ecotours de México   WILDLIFE
(Map p522; ☑ 322-209-21-95; www.ecotoursvallar ta.com; Proa s/n, Marina Vallarta; whale-watching adult/child US$95/80, wild dolphin & snorkeling tour adult/child US$85/75; ☉ 9am-7pm Mon-Fri, to 5pm Sat, to 2pm Sun) 🍃 Run by enthusiastic naturalists, this outfit offers whale-watching expeditions, guided hiking and bird-watching, a wild dolphin-watching and snorkeling combo outing, tours to Islas Marietas and multiday trips further afield focusing on sea turtles and more. Operates tours that support local research projects and nature conservation efforts.

Eco Ride   CYCLING
(Map p526; ☑ 322-222-79-12; www.ecoridemex. com; Miramar 382; tours US$45-105) Surrounded by mountains, jungle and sea, Vallarta offers truly thrilling mountain biking. This welcoming outfit runs guided one-day tours suitable for beginners and bad-asses alike. The all-level 20km ride takes you upriver to a lovely waterfall. The most challenging is a 48km expedition from El Tuito (a small town at 1100m) through Chacala and down to the beach in Yelapa (p525).

Vallarta Eats   FOOD & DRINK
(Map p526; ☑ 322-178-82-88; www.vallartaeats. com; Independencia 231, 2nd fl; taco tour adult/child US$55/39; ☉ office 9am-5pm) Local bilingual guides run a variety of food-and-drink-related tours about town. The most popular one is a morning or evening taco tour, which involves sampling food at street stands, candy shops and more. They also do a boozy 3½-hour Mexican craft beer tour.

Walking Tours   WALKING
(Recorridos Turísticos; Map p526; ☑ 322-222-09-23; www.facebook.com/turismopvoficial; cnr Juárez & Independencia; ☉ 9am & noon Tue & Wed, 9am Sat) **FREE** These free walking tours of Puerto Vallarta's historic center are run from the tourist office (p535), and guides can speak Spanish, English and German. A tip is appropriate at the end.

Canopy River

TOUR

(Map p526; ☎322-223-52-57; www.canopyriver. com; Insurgentes 379; adult/child US$80/51; ☺office 8am-4pm) An exhilarating four-hour canopy tour up the Río Cuale, featuring 11 ziplines ranging in height from 4m to 216m and in length from 44m to a stunning 650m run – curl up like a cannonball to reach top speed. A tequila tour and mule riding are thrown in, and you can add ATV driving or get-wet river zip-lines. Price includes transportation.

🎊 Festivals & Events

Vallarta Pride

LGBT

(☐ cell 322-1786787; www.vallartapride.com; ☺May) A weeklong event in May celebrating the LGBT community with cultural events, concerts, parades and wild beach parties in the heart of Mexico's top gay beach destination.

Festival Gourmet International

FOOD & DRINK

(☎322-222-22-47; www.festivalgourmet.com; ☺Nov) Puerto Vallarta's culinary community has hosted this mid-November festival since 1995.

🛏 Sleeping

You're spoiled for choice here. Vallarta's cheapest lodgings lie inland, on both sides of the Río Cuale. Closer to the ocean, in the Zona Romántica, you'll find several appealing midrange options. Prices listed here are for the December to April high season; low-season rates can be 20% to 50% lower. Negotiate for discounts if you plan on staying multiple nights; monthly rates can cut your rent by half.

Hostal Suites Vallarta

HOSTEL $

(Map p526; ☎322-222-23-66; www.hostalvallarta suites.com; Corona 270; dm M$350, r incl breakfast M$650-1300; ☺❄🕯) A slightly pricier option than the other hostels in town, but the comfort level and ocean views at this hillside setup make it worthwhile. Ground-level accommodations include a mixed dorm and basic private rooms, while rooms upstairs get more natural light and catch an ocean breeze. Free vegan breakfast included. There's a rooftop terrace for watching sunsets.

Hostel Central

HOSTEL $

(Map p526; ☎cell 322-1341313; www.hostelcentral vallarta.com; Hidalgo 224; dm/d without bathroom M$250/350; ☺🕯) The little rooftop dorm here has both beds and bunks, and makes

a compact but sweet central hideaway. This is very simple hostelling, but there's something rather nice about it and the couple that runs it are helpful.

Hotel Galería Belmar

HOTEL $

(Map p526; ☎322-223-18-72; www.belmarvallarta. com; Insurgentes 161; studio/d from M$650/1200; ☺❄@🕯) Astute use of color and a plethora of original artworks enliven the tidy, comfortable rooms at this hotel in the heart of the Zona Romántica. Some have kitchenettes, others are compact studios, and many have balconies. Nicest are the top-floor chambers, which get natural light, ocean breeze and slightly less street noise.

Oasis Hostel Downtown

HOSTEL $

(Map p526; ☎322-222-92-82; jguillermov@ gmail.com; Juárez 386; dm/d without bathroom M$300/500; ☺🕯) The conveniently located Oasis Downtown (no longer affiliated with the other Oasis in town) houses three bright dorms and one simple private room with two beds and a shared bathroom. The hostel has the rather off-putting policy of not allowing walk-ins to check out the digs. There's a rooftop deck with ocean views and lockers to guard your valuables.

Hotel Azteca

HOTEL $

(Map p526; ☎322-222-27-50; www.facebook.com/ hotelaztecapvta; Madero 473; s M$350, d M$450-650; ☺❄🕯) A popular budget hotel full of brick arches. Rooms aren't huge or bright as they face an inner courtyard, but they have ceramic tile floors, satellite TV, so-so beds and enough cute hand-painted touches to make them endearing. Pricier rooms come with a kitchen and/or air-con.

Hotel Casa Anita

HOTEL $$

(Map p526; ☎322-222-00-18; www.casaanita. com; Carretera Barra de Navidad 601; d US$65-100, 1-/2-bedroom ste US$115-175; P❄❄🕯🏊) It's all about the sweet views at this jungle-backed hillside setup. Cheerful units range from studios to spacious three-bedroom apartments, all with full kitchens and balconies affording bay vistas. Guests have use of two pools (one at adjoining sister property Corona del Mar). About half of the rooms have no air-con, but the ocean breeze keeps them cool.

Hotel Catedral

HOTEL $$

(Map p526; ☎322-222-90-33; www.hotelcatedral vallarta.com; Hidalgo 166; d M$1200-1500; ☺❄❄@🕯) A charming three-star spot, steps from

THE SOUTHERN BEACHES

A string of beautiful coves and beaches graces the bay south of central Vallarta, easily accessed by bus. Further around the southern side of the bay are three more isolated beaches – from east to west, Las Ánimas, Quimixto and Yelapa – all accessible by boat but not by road, though you can walk a trail to the first two from Boca de Tomatlán.

Buses marked 'Boca' stop at both Mismaloya and Boca de Tomatlán (M$8); the 'Mismaloya' bus only goes as far as Mismaloya. Any of these buses work for Playa Conchas Chinas and Playa Palmares.

Playa Conchas Chinas (Map p522) Around 3km south of downtown is the beautiful condo enclave of Playa Conchas Chinas. It's a tiny cove favored by families for the shallow and sheltered pools created by the burly rock reef further out (that's where the snorkelers and spearfishers have fun). Although the cove is small, the beach is blond and reasonably wide, with lifeguards on duty.

Playa Palmares (Map p522) About 6km south of Zona Centro, Playa Palmares – named not for the nonexistent palms but for the condo complex of the same name – is a narrow but ample stretch of white sand. These picturesque turquoise shallows are favored by locals for swimming as the beach is far from rivers, which means clear water year-round.

Mismaloya Mismaloya, the location for the 1964 film *The Night of the Iguana*, is about 12km south of Puerto Vallarta: you can still see the dilapidated Iguana sign by the roadside. The tiny scenic cove is dominated by a gargantuan resort; villagers are up in arms about proposals to evict them so that another resort can be built.

Boca de Tomatlán Boca de Tomatlán is a seaside village that's less commercialized than Puerto Vallarta and a good place to munch ceviche *tostadas* on the beach. You can get water taxis from here to more remote beaches further along the bay. It's 16km from Puerto Vallarta, beyond Mismaloya, southwest along the coast.

Playa de las Ánimas Playa de las Ánimas is a lovely beach with a small fishing village and some *palapa* restaurants offering fresh seafood.

Playa de Quimixto This beach, just beyond Las Ánimas, has a waterfall accessible by a half-hour hike or by hiring a pony on the beach to take you up.

Yelapa Yelapa, the furthermost of the southern beaches from town, is one of Puerto Vallarta's most secluded and beloved bays, and home to a small fishing community. Lots of day-trippers turn up on organized tours, but this picturesque cove empties out when the boats leave in the late afternoon. There are several comfortable places to stay the night. Round-trip water taxis (p535) from Puerto Vallarta/Boca de Tomatlán cost M$320/180 per person; the trip takes 45 minutes from Vallarta.

the waterfront and river. The four floors of rooms surround a courtyard and have Templo de Guadalupe (p521) views from the upper reaches. Rooms are clean and cheerful with tiled floors, flat-screen TVs and a few thoughtful extras. Bathrooms are small, but soaps are great, service is helpful and prices very fair, especially in summer.

Hotel Yasmin HOTEL **$$**
(Map p526; ☏ 322-222-00-87; www.hotelyasminpv. com; Badillo 168; s/d M$800/950; ☻🛜🏊) Something of a bargain just a block from the beach, this hotel offers cordial hospitality and an attractive courtyard area with a small pool. Some of the rooms smell a little

under-ventilated, but they are enlivened by colorful artwork and rustic furnishings.

Hotel Emperador HOTEL **$$**
(Map p526; ☏ 322-222-17-67; www.hotelemper adorpv.com; Amapas 114; d/ste M$1550/2700; ☻❄@🛜) This brilliantly located beachside complex offers cheery staff and simple but homey rooms with tiled floors, comfortable beds and flat screens on the wall. The 'suites' are large rooms that have magic views over the beach and sea, and full kitchens on their spacious balconies. There are good off-season discounts. The place is gay-friendly and has a can-do attitude.

Central Puerto Vallarta

200 m
0.1 miles

ZONA CENTRO

See Inset

Bahía de Banderas

Paseo Díaz Ordaz

El Barracuda (1.2km)

Morelos

Mina

Iturbide

Galeana

Juárez

Hidalgo

Corona

Matamoros

Carranza

Miramar

Mina

Aldama

Abasolo

Iturbide

Zaragoza

Cuauhtémoc

Río Cuale

Rivera del Río

Serdán

Madero

Cárdenas

ZONA ROMÁNTICA

Insurgentes

Local Buses to North

Isla Río Cuale

Encino

Rodríguez

Libertad

Guerrero

Zaragoza

Serdán

Plaza Principal

Plaza Morelos

Plaza Serdán

62

2

5

40

30

14

64

68

21

24

51

13

44

48

3

42

20

32

17

10

19

61

8

65

1

26

12

31

22

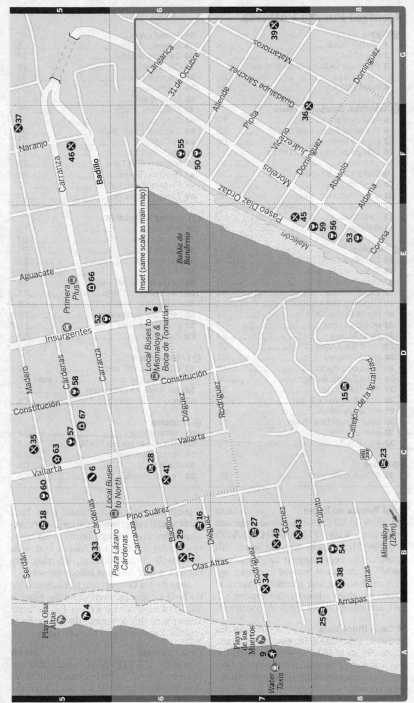

Central Puerto Vallarta

Hotel Posada de Roger   HOTEL $$
(Map p526; ☎322-222-08-36; www.hotelposada deroger.com; Badillo 237; s/d M$1300/1400; ❖❋❅❇) Three blocks from the beach, this agreeable travelers' hangout has long been one of Vallarta's most beloved midrange options and has a popular attached restaurant. Rooms are given a boost by decorative pillows, and there's a pool and leafy courtyard.

★**Casa Dulce Vida**   APARTMENT $$$
(Map p526; ☎322-222-10-08; www.dulcevida.com; Aldama 295; ste US$80-250; ❖❅❇) With the look and feel of an Italian villa, this collection of six spacious suites offers graceful accommodations and delicious privacy. Expect

a gorgeous red-bottom mosaic pool, leafy gardens and sumptuous *casas* with ceramic-tiled floors, high ceilings, sunny living areas, wrought-iron doors and windows, well-stocked kitchens, whirring ceiling fans, a roof deck and bloody sunsets.

Most rooms have private terraces and extra beds for groups. Even when the place is fully booked, it retains a quiet and intimate atmosphere. It's a setting that begs for a cocktail, then another. Then one more.

Casa Fantasía   B&B $$$
(Map p526; ☎322-223-24-44; www.casafantasia. com; Pino Suárez 203; r incl breakfast from US$135; ❖❋❅❇❇) A lovely B&B a block from the

beach with spacious, terracotta-tiled rooms sporting slanted beamed ceilings, antique furnishings and flat-screen TVs wired with satellite. A full breakfast is served every morning in the gorgeous courtyard, gushing with fountains, where a popular bar and restaurant rocks in the high season.

Rivera del Río
BOUTIQUE HOTEL **$$$**
(Map p526; ☑ cell 322-2056093; www.riveradelrio. com; Rivera del Río 104; r incl breakfast US$129-239; ☻❈🛜🌊) Along a peaceful riverside road, it's quite a surprise to come upon this place. The sumptuous interiors are eye-popping, running from Italianate frescoes and water features to 1920s plush, with not a false note. All eight rooms and suites in this vertically arranged building are strikingly different, and the overall package is very impressive. Gay-friendly.

Casa Doña Susana
HOTEL **$$$**
(Map p526; ☑ 322-226-71-01; www.casadonasu-sana.com; Diéguez 171; d from US$115; P☻❈@🛜🌊) There's old-world elegance in the lobby, plenty of stone-and-brick arches, and a pretty interior courtyard at this adults-only hotel. Rooms sport antique wood furnishings, and the rooftop pool has mountain and sea views, as well as a chapel. You get full use of the nearby sister resort-hotel's (Playa Los Arcos) facilities, including beach umbrellas and a larger pool.

Hacienda San Angel
BOUTIQUE HOTEL **$$$**
(Map p526; ☑ 322-222-26-92; www.haciendasanangel.com; Miramar 336; ste incl breakfast from US$504; ☻❈@🛜🌊) The 19 suites on this charming quiet backstreet high above the coast are set in five scattered houses, all exquisitely decorated with fine terracotta floors, antique four-poster beds, *azulejo*-tiled arches and wash basins, and knitted together by a courtyard with fountains. Two resplendent pool decks offer special city and ocean views. The rooftop restaurant earns repeat customers.

Eating

There's a thriving culinary scene in Puerto Vallarta, with choices ranging from ubiquitous street eats to gourmet restaurants.

🍴 South of the Río Cuale

Some of the tastiest and cheapest food in town comes from the taco stands that pop up in the Zona Romántica streets in the morning and early evening.

Pancho's Takos
TACOS **$**
(Map p526; ☑ 322-222-16-93; Badillo 162; tacos M$13-64; ☺6pm-2am Mon-Sat) Drawing a regular nighttime crowd, this spot near the beach serves delicious *tacos al pastor* (spit-cooked pork with diced onions, cilantro and pineapple) after many neighborhood restaurants have closed.

Tacos Revolución
TACOS **$**
(Map p526; ☑ 322-222-13-62; www.facebook. com/tacosrevolucion; Olas Altas 485; tacos M$15-85; ☺2-11pm Wed-Mon; 🛜☑) Excellent *carne asada* (grilled beef), *al pastor* (marinated pork), fish and vegetarian tacos are prepared on handmade tortillas and served with kick-ass salsas at this revolutionary-themed establishment. Unlike most *taquerías,* Revolución boasts a well-stocked bar of Mexican craft beers, tequila and wine. For a seriously decadent dessert, indulge in a *churro* (fritters) sundae with vanilla ice cream and chocolate syrup.

A Page in the Sun
CAFE **$**
(Map p526; ☑ 322-222-36-08; www.apageinthe-sun.com; Cárdenas 179; pastries & light meals M$25-100; ☺7am-11pm; 🛜) This friendly and highly recommended cafe doubles as a bookstore and social hangout, with good espresso drinks, delicious sweet treats, sandwiches, salads, beer and regular events.

Marisma Fish Taco
TACOS **$**
(Map p526; ☑ 322-222-13-95; www.marismafish taco.com; Naranjo 320; snacks M$24-30; ☺9am-5pm) Delicious tacos with shrimp, smoked marlin or fried fish are served at this genial streetside *taquería*. Pull up a stool and watch as the servers behind the counter press fresh tortillas and fry up tasty treats from a simple menu that also offers seafood quesadillas.

Coco's Kitchen
INTERNATIONAL **$$**
(Map p526; ☑ 322-223-03-73; www.cocoskitchenpv. net; Púlpito 122; mains M$78-155; ☺8am-4pm Jun-Nov, to 10pm Dec-May; 🛜) A preferred brunch choice south of the river. Tables are sprinkled on a ceramic-tiled patio beneath a stilted terracotta roof in a shady bar-side garden. Dishes range from *carnitas* (braised pulled pork) and green-chili burritos to a range of quesadillas and salads, eggs Benedict, *chilaquiles,* French toast and pecan waffles.

Joe Jack's Fish Shack
SEAFOOD **$$**
(Map p526; ☑ 322-222-20-99; www.joejacks -fishshack.com; Olas Altas 507; mains M$140-260; ☺noon-11pm; 🛜) With an extended happy

WORTH A TRIP

SAN SEBASTIÁN DEL OESTE

For a dramatic change of scenery, head for the cool climes of San Sebastián del Oeste, a former mining town (17th-century) with stunning views of the surrounding Sierra Madre mountains and beyond. A two-lane highway to the village winds past old farm houses, coconut stands, roadside *birria* (lamb) eateries and small distilleries producing *raicilla* (a mezcal-like agave drink).

With a population of about 700, San Sebastián sits pretty in a cloud forest about 1400m (4600ft) above sea level. From the highest vantage point, lookout **Cerro de la Bufa** affords a spectacular vista extending all the way to the Vallarta coast when weather permits. The easiest way to reach the lookout is by renting an ATV in town or by hooking up a three-hour tour at **Malibrí Turismo** (☑ cell 322-1400441; www.facebook.com/malibrisso; Juárez 30; tour per person M$900; ◷ office 10am-5pm), just a block north of the main square. It's best to go on a weekday when the town sees fewer visitors.

There's not a whole lot happening along the cobblestone streets of San Sebastián, but you can pleasantly while away your time over a cup of locally produced coffee, sit down to a homestyle meal on the plaza or set out for a hike in the fresh mountain air. There are several appealing hotels in town that make for a comfortable and relaxing stay, most notably the colonial-style **Mansion Real** (☑ 322-297-32-75; hotelmansionreal@yahoo.com.mx; 5 de Mayo 36A; d M$1500-2100; ❄ 🛜).

San Sebastián del Oeste lies about 70km east of Puerto Vallarta and it's best reached by car. To get there, head north along the Vallarta–Tepic Hwy 200 and veer right (about 3km past the **airport** (p535) to take Hwy 544. Follow Hwy 544 about 53km east to the town of La Estancia, where you'll find the San Sebastián del Oeste turnoff.

hour running from noon to 7pm, you can keep the mojitos coming until day blurs into night. The Shack's refreshing muddled-mint cocktail goes down nicely with the fresh ceviche, a house specialty, as well as with the Baja-style fish or shrimp tacos.

El Mole de Jovita
MEXICAN $$

(Map p526; ☑ 322-223-30-65; www.mexicanrestaurantpuertovallarta.wordpress.com; Badillo 220; mains M$130-170; ◷ noon-10:30pm; 🛜) This family-run restaurant specializes in chicken with *mole* (chili sauce), but also serves plenty of other reasonably priced Mexican standards.

Red Cabbage Café
MEXICAN $$$

(Map p522; ☑ 322-223-04-11; www.redcabbagepv.com; Rivera del Río 204A; mains M$165-375; ◷ 5-11pm Mon-Sat Oct-Jun; 🛜) Though the atmosphere is casual, with eclectic and bohemian artwork, the food is serious, featuring old recipes and uncommon indigenous sauces. It's a pleasant 10-minute walk from the Zona Romántica; from Cárdenas, turn right on Rivera del Río, just before the Río Cuale bridge. Cash only.

Chenando's
SEAFOOD $$$

(Map p526; ☑ 322-222-33-28; www.facebook.com/chenandosrestaurant; Cárdenas 520; mains M$180-298; ◷ 5:30-11pm Tue-Sun; 🛜) This delightful family-run restaurant has a simple but attractive interior with small square tables and air-con. It excels in the kitchen, producing absolutely succulent seafood burritos as well as tasty coconut shrimp and other dishes on its regularly changing menu.

Bravos
MEXICAN, ITALIAN $$$

(Map p526; ☑ 322-222-03-39; www.bravospv.com; Madero 263; mains M$195-320; ◷ 5-11pm Tue-Sun; 🛜) In the heart of the Zona Romántica, this low-lit bistro has a growing fan base for its refined and delicious preparations that draw on both Italy and Mexico for inspiration. Anything involving plump and tender shrimp is a winner, but almost everything here is tasty. Make sure you leave room for a slice of cake for dessert. Extremely welcoming service.

Archie's Wok
ASIAN $$$

(Map p526; ☑ 322-222-04-11; www.archieswok.com; Rodríguez 130; mains M$160-275; ◷ 2pm-10:30pm Mon-Sat; 🛜✏) The menu may change, but Asian fusion is always served at this elegant, urbane restaurant. Savory fish roasted in a banana leaf is a worthy option; the good selection of vegetarian options includes stir-fry vegetable dishes prepared with a Thai curry or Chinese black bean sauce. The noodle dishes are stellar, and the wines and margaritas tasty.

🍴 North of the Río Cuale

El Banquito
TACOS $

(Map p526; ☑ cell 322-1412301; Libertad 189; tacos M$12; ⊘ 9am-3pm Thu-Tue) For one of Jalisco's most emblematic snacks, head to this tiny taco joint aptly named after the sole stool (banquito) parked on the sidewalk. The specialty, taco de birria dorado, is a hard-shell taco with savory goat meat. You'll find many taquería stands in PV doing the same, but this hole-in-the-wall seems a step above the rest. Orders of three tacos include a complimentary cup of rich consommé.

El Taquito Hidalguense
TACOS $

(Map p522; ☑ cell 322-1123740; Panamá 177; tacos M$19, consommé M$25-29; ⊘ 10am-3:30pm) Hailing from Mexico's barbacoa (lamb or mutton) capital Hidalgo, this family prepares delectable tacos on handmade tortillas with tender meat that's been slow-cooked in a pit for 12 hours. The unctuous consommé adds a little oomph to the morning grease fix.

Planeta Vegetariano
VEGETARIAN $

(Map p526; ☑ 322-222-30-73; www.planetavegetariano.com; Iturbide 270; breakfast buffet M$75, lunch & dinner M$105; ⊘ 8am-10pm; 🍴) This buffet-style place with only 10 tables eschews cheese for fresh, dairy-free dishes such as soy carnitas, yam lasagna (yes, that's right) and a wide range of creatively conceived salads.

Gaby's
MEXICAN $$

(Map p526; ☑ 322-222-04-80; www.gabysrestaurant.com.mx; Mina 252; mains M$135-260, cooking class M$850; ⊘ 8am-11pm; 🛜) Since 1989, this bright and cheerful family-run place with upstairs terrace seating and a tree-shaded back patio has been serving dependably tasty Mexican classics. It's especially atmospheric in the evenings when videos are cheekily projected onto a neighboring building. Fancy a five-hour Mexican cooking class? Gaby's chef Julio Castillón teaches you how to makes salsas, mole tamales and more.

El Barracuda
SEAFOOD $$

(Map p522; ☑ 322-222-40-34; www.elbarracuda.com; Paraguay 1290; mains M$148-238; ⊘ 1-11pm Mon & Tue, noon-1am Wed-Sat, noon-11pm Sun; 🛜) This breezy open shack on the beach makes a top venue for a seafood lunch with ocean views. Grilled-shrimp tacos are famous, the tuna sashimi is more a carpaccio but still tasty, as is mariscos dinamita, a shrimp,

octopus and fish rice dish. Do-it-yourself smoked marlin tostadas are fab. Turtles still emerge here to lay eggs, and whales thrash just offshore all winter long.

Benitto's
DELI $$

(Map p522; ☑ 322-209-02-87; www.benittos.com; Paseo de la Marina 21; mains M$115-195; ⊘ 8:30am-2:30am Mon-Sat; 🛜) A gourmet deli in the marina area with big, bold modern art on the walls. It's popular among upmarket locals for creative panini, mixed carpaccios and craft beers and wines. It also does main serves of salads, soups and pastas. The kitchen is open until 1am; drinkers may linger.

La Dolce Vita
ITALIAN $$

(Map p526; ☑ 322-222-38-52; www.dolcevita.com.mx; Paseo Díaz Ordaz 674; mains M$125-242; ⊘ 11:30am-2am Mon-Sat, 5pm-midnight Sun; 🛜) A cheerful, often-crowded spot, good for wood-fired pizzas, pastas and people-watching. It's a local expat favorite. Request a table upstairs by the window for great views.

★ Barrio Bistro
FUSION $$$

(Map p522; ☑ cell 322-3060530; www.barriobistro.com; España 305, Colonia Versalles; mains M$190-320; ⊘ 6pm-10:30pm Tue-Sat; 🛜) Once you've been seated, chef Memo visits your table with a detailed explanation of each dish featured on a chalkboard menu that changes weekly. At last visit the menu featured a wonderfully cooked rack of lamb with fresh herbs plucked from the bistro's garden. Memo stocks a top-notch raicilla (mezcal-like agave beverage) and quality wines and craft beers. Cash only.

★ Café des Artistes
FUSION $$$

(Map p526; ☑ 322-226-72-00; www.cafedesartistes.com; Guadalupe Sánchez 740; mains M$260-545; ⊘ 6-11pm; 🛜) Many consider this to be Vallarta's finest restaurant. You're sure to enjoy its romantic ambience and exquisite fusion of French and Mexican influences. It has a candlelit garden, modern interior and whimsical castle-like exterior. But the food is the thing, with some memorable combinations on show. Service is formal but unobtrusive. Reservations are recommended.

El Arrayán
MEXICAN $$$

(Map p526; ☑ 322-222-71-95; www.elarrayan.com.mx; Allende 344; mains M$235-325; ⊘ 5:30-11pm Wed-Mon; 🛜) Owner Carmen Porras takes special pleasure in rescuing old family recipes

GAY & LESBIAN PUERTO VALLARTA

Come on out – the rainbow flag flies high over Puerto Vallarta. An ever-increasing stream of visitors descends on the city annually for its formidable selection of gay bars, nightclubs, restaurants and hotels, as well as its busy annual calendar of gay- and lesbian-themed events. The Gay Guide Vallarta booklet and website (www.gayguidevallarta.com) have tonnes of information and a helpful map for finding gay-friendly businesses. The nine-day Vallarta Pride (p524) event in May celebrates the LGBT community with special fervor.

Sleeping

Casa Cupula (Map p526; ✆800-223-24-84; www.casacupula.com; Callejón de la Igualdad 129; r/ste from US$343/629; ⓟ✚❄@🛜🏊) Sophisticated design and luxurious flourishes define this popular resort catering to both gays and lesbians. Each room is uniquely decorated, with amenities ranging from home-theater-sized TVs to private Jacuzzis in some suites. The beach is only a few blocks downhill, although the resort's three pools, gym, on-site restaurant and bar may give you enough incentive to linger here all day.

Hotel Mercurio (Map p526; ✆322-222-47-93; www.hotel-mercurio.com; Rodríguez 168; s/d incl breakfast M$1872/2214; ✚❄@🛜🏊) Less than two blocks from Playa de los Muertos (p520) pier, this three-story gay hotel features 28 rooms (some of which smell mustier than others) around a pleasant courtyard with a stylish pool and bar. Rooms are simple for the price, but have fridges, cable TV and double or king-sized beds. Buffet breakfasts and free international phone calls are among the other perks on offer.

Blue Chairs Beach Resort (Map p522; ✆800-561-97-17; www.bluechairsresort.com; Almendro 4; r/ste from US$85/155; ✚❄🛜🏊) Overlooking one of Mexico's most famous gay beaches, this resort is a byword for 'gay' in Vallarta. At the time of our last visit it was looking a bit down at heel, but some rooms have been renovated and the beach club scene is still worthwhile, as is the rooftop nightspot and pool. Suites are larger rooms with a kitchenette.

Villa David (Map p526; ✆322-223-03-15; www.villadavidpv.com; Galeana 348; r US$126-161; ✚❄@🛜🏊) Reservations are essential and clothing optional at this gay retreat in a beautiful hacienda-style mansion in the characterful streets high above the *malecón* (beach promenade). There are great views and sunsets from here, and the tastefully appointed rooms are all different.

Drinking & Nightlife

Gay Vallarta Bar-Hopping (Map p526; www.gaypv.mx/hop/tours; Púlpito 141; per person US$60-129; ⊙office 10am-4pm Mon-Fri) This entertaining excursion is a fun introduction to Vallarta's gay nightlife. The most expensive outing includes dinner and drinks aplenty at six different bars. Book online or visit the office.

Garbo (Map p526; ✆322-223-57-53; german_gm@yahoo.com; Púlpito 142; ⊙6pm-2am; 🛜) If you enjoy jazzy stylings and an excellent martini to go with them, make your way to this concrete-floor habitat. The jazz and torch singing are decent to good, and sing-alongs may happen.

Antropology (Map p526; ✆322-117-11-31; edward_1602@hotmail.com; Morelos 101; ⊙9pm-4am; 🛜) It's raining men at this sizzling dance mecca and male-stripper venue. Women are unapologetically disallowed. There's a two-drink minimum.

Bar Frida (Map p526; ✆322-222-36-68; www.barfrida.com; Insurgentes 301A; ⊙1pm-2am; 🛜) Named for the artist who is on a first-name basis with the world, Frida is a cozy and sociable cantina featuring enticing drink specials. It's a good spot to kick off the evening in a relaxed, non-sceney atmosphere.

La Noche (Map p526; www.lanochepv.com; Cárdenas 263; ⊙8pm-3:30am; 🛜) This pre-club venue is well loved for its convivial atmosphere, buff bartenders and go-go dancers. The soundtrack is resolutely old-school house, and there's a roof terrace.

from obscurity, with an emphasis on fresh local ingredients. Specialties include crispy duck *carnitas* (deep-fried) with orange sauce, and plantain *empanadas* (plantain dough, black beans and cheese). The restaurant, with its open kitchen and romantic courtyard, also serves as a venue for regular cooking classes.

La Leche
MEXICAN $$$

(Map p522; 322-293-09-00; www.lalecherestau rant.com; Medina Ascensio Km 2.5; mains M$230-390, tasting menu M$699, burritos M$80-100; 6pm-1am;) This milk-themed place has a dramatic entry, and the dairy gag continues in various ways throughout the meal. Service is very personal and friendly – expect pats on the back rather than kid gloves – if a bit scatty. The restaurant is strong on seafood and its duck signature dish. The eating experience is lots of fun.

There's a good wine list for west coast Mexico, plus a seven-course *degustatión* (tasting) menu. Drug lord Joaquín 'El Chapo' Guzman's son was famously kidnapped here in 2016 by armed men of a rival cartel. La Leche also runs a burrito food truck outside.

Layla's Restaurante
MEXICAN $$$

(Map p522; 322-222-24-36; www.laylasrestau rante.com; Venezuela 137; mains M$159-295; 1-11pm Tue-Sun;) Just off the strip, but unnoticed by passers-by, this place is highly recommended for quality, well-presented cooking without a hint of pretension. Sip a cucumber margarita on the upstairs terrace before a meal of fish, shrimp or beef, all exquisitely prepared and served by a friendly bevy of staff. Asparagus tempura was a standout when we visited.

La Cigale
FRENCH $$$

(Map p526; 322-222-79-38; www.lacigalebistro. com; Hidalgo 398; mains M$135-295; 5pm-11:30pm;) In the shadow of Templo de Guadalupe (p521), this casual-chic French bistro with chalkboard menus and checkerboard floors serves everything from quiche Lorraine to steak tartare, accompanied by wines from around the world.

Drinking & Nightlife

It's ridiculously easy to become inebriated in a town where two-for-one happy hours are as reliable as the sunset, margarita glasses look like oversized snifters and day drinking is almost an obligation. Admission charges are normally waived early in the week; on Friday and Saturday nights they often include one or two drinks.

A.M. Bar
BAR

(Map p526; www.facebook.com/playa.a.m.bar; Allende 116; 9pm-4am) DJs here will have you shaking your booty to *cumbia* (dance music originating from Colombia) tunes (especially after a few mezcals) in this casual bar with exposed brick walls and very affordable drinks. No uptight nightclub attitude here.

La Cervecería Unión
BAR

(Map p526; 322-223-09-29; www.lacerveceria union.com.mx; Paseo Díaz Ordaz 610; 11am-2am;) It's a real relief to come in here on a hot afternoon and leave bland beer behind. There's a fine selection of craft brews from around Mexico and imports as well. There's also an oyster bar, decent tacos, a good mezcal list and tasty *micheladas* (beer cocktails). The bay views are great.

Panchöfurter
BEER HALL

(Map p526; 322-223-13-42; www.facebook.com/ gastrocerveceria; Madero 239; 3-11pm Mon-Fri, to 1am Sat;) Mexico meets Germany at this trendy brats-and-bier haus, where you can order craft brew alongside homemade sausage, burgers or salad (dishes M$95 to M$165). Try the 'tropical' IPA produced by Vallarta microbrewery Los Cuentos – it's a hoppy delight.

Bar Morelos
BAR

(Map p526; 322-222-25-50; www.facebook.com/ barmorelospuertovallarta; Morelos 589; 8pm-3am Sun-Tue, to 5am Wed-Sat;) Stylish and with professional staff, this makes for a far classier drink than you can find a block away on the *malecón* (beach promenade). Over 50 mezcals are available, and the staff will talk you through them. Interesting midweek DJs, a decent sound system and attractive decor make this a standout. Don't miss a game of table football in the toilet area.

Los Muertos Brewing
PUB

(Map p526; 322-222-03-08; www.losmuertos brewing.com; Cárdenas 302; 11am-midnight;) An attractive brick-arched, concrete-floored pub and microbrewery. The beer comes in six varieties including an IPA called 'Revenge' and a stout called 'McSanchez.' There's good pizza and average pub grub available.

Mandala
CLUB

(Map p526; 322-224-38-27; www.facebook. com/mandala.puerto.vallarta; Paseo Díaz Ordaz 640; 6pm-6am) By far the best of three adjacent clubs here, this cinema-sized spot has privileged *malecón* frontage and keeps a youngish crowd happy until late at night under a benevolent icon's gaze. Drinks are pricey, but you can buy an open-bar wristband if you're going to hit it hard.

La Bodeguita del Medio
BAR

(Map p526; ☏ 322-223-15-85; www.labodeguita delmedio.com.mx; Paseo Díaz Ordaz 858; ⊕ 9am-3am; ☏) The walls are scrawled with handwritten poetics and inanities in several languages, the bar is blessed with fine rums and tequilas, and the staff pour a mean mojito, as well as questionable variations. Loud salsa music with nightly live acts is accompanied by plenty of dancing and good cheer. The food isn't so special.

☆ Entertainment

Vallarta's main forms of nighttime entertainment revolve around dancing, drinking and dining, much of which happens in establishments lining the busy *malecón*. There's often entertainment by the sea at Los Arcos (p521).

★ El Patio de Mi Casa
JAZZ

(Map p526; ☏ 322-222-07-43; www.facebook.com/ elpatiodemicasavallarta; Guerrero 311; ⊕ 6pm-2:30am Mon-Sat; ☏) Escape from the raucous nightclubs and take in a refreshingly calm jazz and blues scene at this open-air patio decked out with vintage furnishings. The bar pours *raicilla* (a mezcal-like agave drink) and you can order from a dinner menu featuring salads and thin-crust pizza. Live music on Friday and Saturday.

Jazz Foundation
JAZZ

(Map p526; ☏ 322-113-02-95; www.jazzpv.com; Allende 116; ⊕ 6pm-2am Tue-Sun; ☏) This appealing upstairs venue might be constructed out of breeze blocks, bricks and planks of wood, but it provides plenty of class with regular live music ranging from jazz and blues to funk and soul. The ocean views are spectacular too, making it a romantic spot for a sunset drink.

Roxy Rock House
LIVE MUSIC

(Map p526; ☏ 322-222-76-17; www.roxyrockhouse. com; Vallarta 217; ⊕ 10pm-6am; ☏) In the heart of the Zona Romántica, this place draws an enthusiastic mixed crowd with its nightly rock cover bands and no admission charge.

🛍 Shopping

Vallarta is a delight for shoppers, with many shops and boutiques selling fashionable clothing, beachwear and crafts from all over

Mexico. Tequila and Cuban cigars are also big business.

Peyote People
ARTS & CRAFTS

(Map p526; ☏ 322-222-23-02; www.peyote people.com; Juárez 222; ⊕ 10am-8pm Mon-Fri, to 6pm Sat, 11am-5pm Sun) 🍷 Sells excellent Huichol beadwork, yarn art, jewelry, Day of the Dead crafts and wood carvings from the southern state of Oaxaca. Money spent here helps support indigenous artisan communities.

Dulcería Leal
FOOD

(Map p526; ☏ 322-222-80-42; www.facebook.com/ dulcerialeal; Juárez 262; ⊕ 10am-10pm) If you have a sweet tooth, stop by this cute *tienda* (shop) packed with temptation. It sells everything from tamarind chews and exquisite caramels to any number of dried fruit and sugary nut concoctions.

Mundo de Azulejos
CERAMICS

(Map p526; ☏ 322-222-26-75; www.mundode azulejos.com; Carranza 374; ⊕ 9am-7pm Mon-Fri, to 2pm Sat) This store offers a vast array of brightly colored Talavera tiles and ceramics.

Olinalá
ARTS & CRAFTS

(Map p526; ☏ 322-222-49-95, cell 322-1213576; http://brewsterbrockmann.com; Cárdenas 274; ⊕ 11am-5pm Mon-Sat Oct-May, 11am-3pm Thu-Sat Jun-Sep) In business since 1978, this excellent little shop displays authentic Mexican dance masks, folk art and rural antiques.

Mercado Municipal Río Cuale
ARTS & CRAFTS, MARKET

(Map p526; ☏ 322-222-45-65; Rodríguez 260; ⊕ 9am-6pm) Straddling the north bank of the Río Cuale, this market sells everything from Taxco silver, *sarapes* (blankets with a head opening, worn as a cloak) and *huaraches* (woven leather sandals) to wool wall hangings and blown glass. Don't confuse it with the nearby market on Morelos, which deals in tourist tat.

ℹ Information

Although most businesses in Vallarta accept US dollars as readily as they accept pesos, rates are generally poor. Banks with ATMs and *casas de cambio* (currency exchange) are abundant.

Canadian Consulate (☏ 322-293-00-98; www. canadainternational.gc.ca/mexico-mexique; Medina Ascencio 2485, Plaza Peninsula; ⊕ 9am-1pm Mon-Fri; 🚇 Ixtapa)

Main Post Office (Map p522; ☑ 322-223-13-60; www.correosdemexico.gob.mx; Colombia 1014; ☺ 8am-5:30pm Mon-Fri, 9am-1pm Sat)

Municipal Tourist Office (Map p526; ☑ 322-222-09-23; www.visitpuertovallarta.com; Juárez s/n; ☺ 8am-8pm Mon-Fri, 9am-5pm Sat & Sun) Vallarta's busy office in the municipal building at the northeast corner of Plaza Principal has free maps, multilingual tourist literature and bilingual staff.

San Javier Marina Hospital (☑ 322-226-10-10; www.sanjavier.com.mx; Medina Ascencio 2760; ☺ 24hr) Vallarta's best-equipped hospital.

US Consular Agency (☑ 81-8047-3145; Paseo de los Cocoteros 85 Sur, Paradise Plaza, Nuevo Vallarta; ☺ 8:30am-12:30pm Mon-Thu)

❶ Getting There & Away

To reach downtown from the airport and bus station, it's a straight shoot southbound along Medina Ascencio (aka Hwy 200).

AIR

Gustavo Díaz Ordaz International Airport (Puerto Vallarta International Airport; Map p522; ☑ 322-221-12-98; www.aeropuertosgap. com.mx; Carretera Vallarta–Tepic Km 7.5; ☎; ☑ Las Juntas, Ixtapa) is located 10km north of the city. There are direct flights, some seasonal, from dozens of US and Canadian cities, as well as direct charters from the UK.

The following domestic destinations are serviced by these airlines:

➜ Acapulco – TAR

➜ Guadalajara – Aeroméxico, Interjet, TAR

➜ León – Interjet, TAR

➜ Mazatlán – TAR

➜ Mexico City – Aeroméxico, InterJet, VivaAerobús, Volaris

➜ Monterrey – Aeroméxico, TAR, VivaAerobús, Volaris

➜ Querétaro – TAR

➜ Tijuana – Volaris

➜ Toluca – Interjet

Aeroméxico (☑ 322-225-17-77; www.aeromexico.com; Medina Ascencio 1853, Plaza Santa María; ☺ 9am-7pm Mon-Fri, to 2pm Sat; ☑ Ixtapa) also has an office at the airport.

BUS

Vallarta's **long-distance bus terminal** (Central Camionera; Map p522; ☑ 322-290-10-09; Bahía Sin Nombre 363) is off Hwy 200, about 10km north of downtown and 3km northeast of the airport. Think M$180 for a cab fare to downtown.

Primera Plus (Map p526; ☑ 322-222-90-70; www.primeraplus.com.mx; Carranza 393; ☺ 7am-7pm Mon & Tue, to 10:30pm Wed-Sun) has a downtown office where you can buy tickets. If you're heading to Barra de Navidad,

Manzanillo or other points south, you can save a trip to the bus terminal by boarding here.

Northbound **buses to Riviera Nayarit** (Map p522; Blvd Medina Ascencio s/n; ☺ 5am-9pm) towns depart frequently from a bus stop in front of Walmart, just south of Marina Vallarta.

CAR & MOTOTCYCLE

Starting at about M$500 per day, on-the-spot car rentals can be pricey during high season; you'll often do better booking online, though extra insurance charges mean online rates aren't always what they appear to be. At other times, deep discounts are offered.

Numerous car rental agencies maintain adjacent counters in the **airport** arrivals hall, with offices nearby. Below is a list of agencies with Vallarta offices.

Alamo (☑ 322-221-30-30; www.alamomexico. com.mx; Medina Ascencio 4690, Coral Plaza; ☺ 8am-10pm; ☑ Ixtapa)

Avis (☑ 322-221-07-83; www.avis.mx; Medina Ascensio Km 7.5; ☺ 7am-11:30pm; ☑ Ixtapa)

Budget (☑ 322-221-17-30; www.budget.com. mx; Medina Ascencio 141, Villa Las Flores; ☺ 7am-9pm)

Europcar (☑ 322-209-09-21; www.europcar. com.mx/en; Carretera Vallarta–Tepic Km 7.5, Gustavo Díaz Ordaz International Airport; ☺ 7am-10pm)

Hertz (☑ 800-709-50-00; https://hertzmexico. com; Carretera Vallarta–Tepic Km 7.5, Gustavo Díaz Ordaz International Airport; ☺ 7am-11pm)

National (☑ 322-209-03-52; www.nationalcar. com.mx; Medina Ascencio 4172; ☺ 7am-10pm)

Sixt (☑ 322-221-14-73; www.sixt.com.mx; Medina Ascencio 7930, Villa Las Flores; ☺ 7am-10pm; ☑ Ixtapa)

Thrifty (☑ 322-221-29-84; www.thrifty.com. mx; Medina Ascencio 7926; ☺ 7am-10pm; ☑ Ixtapa)

❶ Getting Around

TO/FROM THE AIRPORT

The cheapest way to get to/from the airport is on a local bus for M$7.50. 'Centro' and 'Olas Altas' buses go into town from a stop just outside the airport. Returning from town, 'Aeropuerto,' 'Juntas' and 'Ixtapa' buses stop at a pedestrian bridge near the airport entrance.

From the airport to the city, taxis charge fixed rates ranging from M$260 to M$343, depending on which neighborhood you're traveling to. Shuttle service costs M$120 to M$139. A taxi back to the airport from downtown costs around M$150.

BOAT

Vallarta's **water taxis** (Map p526; Playa de los Muerto pier; round-trip fare M$320) serve the beautiful beaches on the southern side of the bay, some of which are accessible only by boat. Departing from the Playa de los Muertos (p520) pier, they head south around the bay, making stops at **Playa de las Ánimas** (25 minutes; p525), **Quimixto** (40 minutes; p525) and **Yelapa** (55 minutes; p525). Boats depart Puerto Vallarta every hour or two between 10am and 4:30pm, returning from Yelapa (the end of the line) with the same frequency between 7:30am and 3:45pm daily. Water taxis to the beaches also depart from Boca de Tomatlán (p525).

Private yachts and *lanchas* (motorboats) can be hired from the southern side of the Playa de los Muertos pier, starting from around M$350 per hour. They'll take you to any secluded beach around the bay; most have gear aboard for snorkeling and fishing.

BUS

Local buses operate every five minutes from 5am to 11pm on most routes, and cost M$7.50. **Plaza Lázaro Cárdenas** (Map p526; Suárez s/n) near Playa Olas Altas (p520) is a major departure hub. **Northbound** (Map p526; Insurgentes s/n) local buses also stop on Insurgentes near the corner of Madero. Southbound buses either pass through the center or loop round via a tunnel to the Zona Romántica.

Northbound buses marked 'Aeropuerto,' 'Ixtapa,' 'Mojoneras' and 'Juntas' pass through the city heading north to the airport (p535) and Marina Vallarta; the 'Mojoneras' bus also stops at Puerto Vallarta's long-distance bus terminal (p535).

White-and-orange 'Boca de Tomatlán' buses (M$8) head south along the coastal highway through **Mismaloya** (20 minutes; p525) to **Boca de Tomatlán** (30 minutes; p525). They depart from the corner of Badillo and Constitución every 15 minutes.

TAXI

Cab prices are regulated by zones; the cost for a ride is determined by how many zones you cross. A typical trip from downtown to the Zona Hotelera costs M$120; to the airport (p535) or the long-distance bus terminal (p535) it's M$160 to M$180; and to Mismaloya (p525) it's M$175.

Always determine the price of the ride before you get in. Hailing a cab is easy in the city center along Morelos. There are several taxi stands, including one on **Insurgentes and Cárdenas** (Map p526; ☏ 322-222-24-22; taxisitio9@gmail.com; cnr Insurgentes & Cárdenas), one on **Rodríguez at Matamoros** (Map p526; cnr Rodríguez & Matamoros) and one on **Olas Altas** (Map p526; ☏ 322-223-30-33; cnr Olas Altas & Carranza) at Plaza Lázaro Cárdenas.

Costalegre Beaches

South of Puerto Vallarta, the stretch of Mexico's Pacific coast from Chamela to Barra de Navidad is blessed with fine beaches and enough outdoor activities to keep nature enthusiasts thoroughly entertained; there's a sea turtle camp, uninhabited islands providing prime bird-watching and snorkeling, and mangroves that are home to large crocs. In an effort to draw more visitors to the area, tourism promoters and developers refer to this shoreline as the 'Costalegre' (Happy Coast).

◉ Sights

Playa Pérula   BEACH
(turnoff Hwy 200 Km 73) Playa Pérula, a sheltered beach at the northern end of the tranquil 11km-long Bahía de Chamela, is great for swimming and extended walks. There are cheap accommodations and a smattering of *palapa* restaurants. You can charter a *panga* (skiff) from here to the nine islands in the bay.

Campamento Majahuas   NATURE RESERVE
(☏ cell 322-2285806; www.campamentomajahuas. com; turnoff Hwy 200 Km 116; ⊙turtles nesting Jul-Nov) 🌱 This community-run project just north of Punta Pérula lets you camp and watch (with local guides) the turtles nest. It's become a destination for international students interested in turtles and their

BUSES FROM PUERTO VALLARTA

DESTINATION	FARE (M$)	DURATION (HR)	FREQUENCY (DAILY)
Barra de Navidad/ Melaque	244-332	4-5½	frequent
Guadalajara	399-635	5½-6	frequent
Manzanillo	306-421	5-5½	hourly
Mazatlán	570-695	6½-7	4
Mexico City	1019-1350	11-13¼	9 (nightly)
Tepic	205-310	3-3½	frequent

habitat, and offers volunteering programs. You'll need a vehicle to get here, or you can visit the camp on an overnight trip offered by Mex-Eco Tours. You can camp here year-round, but July through November is the best time for turtle sightings.

Playa Tenacatita   BEACH
(turnoff Hwy 200 Km 28) On the palm-fringed Bahía Tenacatita, Playa Tenacatita has clear snorkeling waters and a large mangrove lagoon with good bird-watching. There is a land title in dispute here, with a development group in the process of trying to build on and partly privatize an otherwise public and relatively undeveloped beach. You can still visit, but camping is no longer allowed.

Playa El Negrito   BEACH
(turnoff Hwy 200 Km 64) At Bahía de Chamela, Playa El Negrito is an isolated, relaxing beach with a couple of restaurants but no hotels. The nine islands in the expansive bay are beautiful to see in silhouette at sunset.

❶ Getting There & Away

You'll need a car to reach most Costalegre beaches. San Patricio-Melaque and Manzanillo buses departing from Puerto Vallarta stop at the highway crossroads to Punta Pérula, where you can hopefully catch a taxi (M$50) into town.

Bahía de Navidad

The tight arc of the Bahía de Navidad is practically ringed by deep, honey-colored sand with two resort towns waving amiably at each other from either end. Situated 5km apart by road, but only a kilometer and a bit along the beach, Barra de Navidad and San Patricio-Melaque are siblings with distinct personalities. Barra is beloved for its attractive cobbled streets and aura of good living, while Melaque, which is larger and less quaint, draws budget-minded travelers seeking that beachfront buzz.

San Patricio-Melaque

📞 315 / POP 7569
Known by most as Melaque (meh-*lah*-keh), this kick-back beach resort is a popular vacation destination for Mexican families and a low-key winter hangout for snowbirds. The main activities are swimming, lazing on the beach, watching pelicans fish at sunrise and sunset, climbing to the *mirador* (lookout) at the bay's western end, prowling the plaza and public market, and walking the beach to Barra de Navidad.

🏄 Activities

Pacific Adventures   WATER SPORTS
(📞 315-355-52-98; www.pacificadventures.mx; Gómez Farías 595; rentals per hour surfboard/ paddleboard/bike M$90/150/20; ⏰ 9am-2pm & 4-7pm Thu-Tue) An enthusiastic, youthful group that can rent you surfboards, paddleboards and more, and also teach you how to use them. They also rent out bikes if you're up for pedaling to nearby Barra de Navidad.

🧭 Tours

★ Mex-Eco Tours   ECOTOUR
(📞 315-355-70-27; www.mex-ecotours.com; Gómez Farías 59-2; coffee plantation tour M$1100, sea turtle camp M$1500-2400; ⏰ 10am-2pm & 5-7pm Mon-Fri, 10am-2pm Sat) 🌿 Competent and friendly, this knowledgable ecotourism company operates impressive day trips near Melaque and an array of multiday excursions throughout Mexico, all with a commitment to sustainable tourism. Highlights include visiting an indigenous women's cooperative coffee plantation, an overnight camping trip to a sea turtle biological station, and boat trips. It also runs tours from Bucerías, near Puerto Vallarta.

🎉 Festivals & Events

Fiesta de San Patricio   CULTURAL
(⊘ Mar) Melaque honors its patron saint with a blowout week of festivities, including all-day parties, rodeos, a carnival, music, dances and nightly fireworks, leading up to St Patrick's Day (March 17).

🛏 Sleeping

Rates rise sharply at Christmas and Semana Santa; high season is November through April. Discounts are common for longer stays.

Hotel Bahía   HOTEL $
(📞 315-355-68-94; www.melaquehotelbahia.com; Legazpi 5; d/ste M$680/890; ❄ 🌐 🛜 ♨) Aside from being one of the cleanest budget hotels in town, the Bahía lies just one block from Melaque's most swimmable beach. Rooms here feature air-con and cable TV, while suites include kitchenettes and refrigerators. The two-story property sits on Melaque's quiet north end, about 1km from downtown.

★ Villas El Rosario de San Andres
APARTMENT $$

(☑315-355-63-42; www.elrosariodesanandres.com; Hidalgo 10; d M$790-990, q M$990-1190; 🅿️🐕❄️🛜🏊) This genial, family-run central complex offers bright, ceramic-tiled studios with attractive kitchenettes, high ceilings and flat-screen TVs. Sofa beds mean that children can be easily accommodated in most rooms. The rooftop deck is a wonderful common area with special mountain and sea views. There is also a small plunge pool.

Casa Misifus
SPA HOTEL $$

(☑315-355-84-47; http://casamisifus.wixsite.com/casamisifus; Av Veracruz 27; d incl breakfast M$1250; 🅿️🐕❄️♨️🛜🏊) At the town's entrance and about five blocks from the beach, this well-run hotel exudes tranquility with its remarkably quiet pool area and rooftop terrace, full-service spa and six comfortable rooms with kitchens, balconies and snug beds.

Posada Pablo de Tarso
HOTEL $$

(☑315-355-57-07; www.posadapablodetarso.com; Gómez Farías 408; d M$1500, bungalows from M$1900; 🅿️🐕❄️🛜🏊) This leafy, brick courtyard hotel with an attractive beachside pool area offers air-conditioned rooms or bungalows (with kitchenette but no air-con) that are cool and spacious with beamed ceilings and terracotta floors. Some rooms have fridges too; those overlooking the road or the beach are largest. A couple of the bungalows are across the street.

★ La Paloma
BOUTIQUE HOTEL $$$

(☑315-355-53-45; www.lapalomamexico.com; Las Cabañas 13; r M$2050-2350, penthouse M$2450, all incl breakfast; ⊙Nov-Aug; 🅿️🐕❄️🛜🏊) Original art abounds at this oceanside boutique hotel hidden behind high walls. Singular, comfortable rooms have a kitchen/kitchenette plus terraces, and are vibrantly colorful, with quirky mirrors and bright ceramics. For the small price difference, consider the large penthouses with sea views – we loved number 14. With plush gardens and a beachside pool, it's a fabulous retreat.

✖️ Eating & Drinking

From 6pm to midnight, food stands serve inexpensive Mexican fare a block east of the plaza along Juárez. A row of pleasant *palapa* restaurants stretches along the beach at the western end of town.

La Flor del Café
CAFE $

(☑cell 314-1301222; www.facebook.com/laflordelcafemelaque07; Guzmán s/n, near Corona; mains M$60-120; ⊙7am-1pm & 6-10pm Wed-Mon; 🛜) On a friendly, brightly hued patio, this place eschews the hottest part of the day but opens mornings for tasty smoothies, juices, coffee, sandwiches and salads. In the evenings it adds a couple of heftier dishes to the menu, such as seafood fettuccine.

Quetzal de Laura
MEXICAN $$

(☑315-351-52-76; Guerrero 99; breakfast M$45-70, dinner M$120-245; ⊙8am-1pm & 5-10pm Tue-Sun; 🍴) The extensive menu at this open-air restaurant may make your head spin, but you can always go with an inexpensive Mexican breakfast, homestyle soup or the house specialty – chili pepper stuffed with shrimp or mushrooms. Vegetarians will find plenty to choose from.

Tacos Scooby
MEXICAN $$

(☑cell 315-1073499; Obregón 34; snacks M$10-50, mains M$90-270; ⊙5pm-1am; 🛜) This neighborhood eatery does the tastiest *tacos al pastor* (spit-cooked marinated pork) in town, and keeps expats coming back for the grilled ribs and seasonal prime rib steak on Sundays. Portions are generous and the owners couldn't be more welcoming. It does a fine *michelada* (beer cocktail) too.

Taza Negra
CAFE

(☑315-355-70-80; www.latazanegra.com; Guerrero 112; coffee M$25-40; ⊙8:30am-1pm Mon-Fri Oct-Apr, to noon May-Sep; 🛜) This friendly neighborhood cafe has your back if you like to kick start the day with a good strong cup of joe. Chiapas-grown beans are roasted and prepared with love here, as are pastries such as the blueberry-oatmeal-coconut muffin.

Esquina Paraíso
BAR

(☑cell 314-1624412; Obregón 13; ⊙5pm-2am Dec-Mar) This curious open-air corner bar has done its decor out of driftwood, recycled packing crates and the like; it's well worth a look. Don't expect luxury, but do enjoy the swing-seats and nightly live music.

ℹ️ Getting There & Away

Buses stop on opposite sides of Carranza at the corner of Gómez Farías. Three companies have separate ticket offices around this intersection, with similar fares.

Local orange buses to Barra de Navidad (M$7, 15 minutes) leave every 15 minutes from the corner of López Mateos and Juárez at the

BUSES FROM SAN PATRICIO-MELAQUE

DESTINATION	FARE (M$)	DURATION (HR)	FREQUENCY (DAILY)
Guadalajara	350-485	5½-6½	frequent
Manzanillo	65-90	1-1½	frequent
Mexico City (Terminal Norte)	1229	12	1 (nightly)
Puerto Vallarta	244-332	4-5½	frequent

southwest corner of the plaza, and do a slow circuit before hitting the main road. More direct green buses cost M$15.

Barra de Navidad

☑ 315 / POP 4324

Barra de Navidad greets you with a mellow happiness and easy charm that seeps into your bones. It's a pueblo on a narrow isthmus between a lagoon and the beach, boasting excellent sportfishing, bird- and crocodile-watching trips and succulent seafood. Barra first came to prominence in 1564 when its shipyards produced the galleons used by conquistador Miguel López de Legazpi and Father André de Urdaneta to deliver the Philippines to King Felipe of Spain. By 1600, however, most of the conquests were being conducted from Acapulco, and Barra slipped into sleepy obscurity.

🏃 Activities

Barra's steep and narrow beach is lovely to behold, but conditions are sometimes too rough for swimming. It's generally gentlest in the mornings.

The waters near Barra are bristling with marlin, swordfish, albacore, *dorado,* snapper and other, more rarefied catches.

Isla Navidad Golf Course   GOLF
(☑ 314-337-90-24; www.islanavidad.com.mx; Isla Navidad; 18-holes green fees incl cart US$197; ◷ 7am-7pm) Isla Navidad has 27 holes with excellent vistas and greens carved into ocean dunes against a backdrop of mountains. It's considered one of Mexico's finer courses. Given the geography of the area, it's appropriate that there are lots of water hazards.

☞ Tours

Ecojoy Adventures   ECOTOUR
(☑ cell 315-1009240; www.facebook.com/ecojoy adventures; Costa Occidental 13, cnr Av Veracruz; biking & kayaking tours M$200, horseback riding per hour M$300, bike rental per day M$150; ◷ 9am-11pm & 5-8pm Mon-Thu) This tour outfit at the

town's entrance offers biking and kayaking trips in and around the lagoon, and they can also hook you up with horseback riding along the beach. If you prefer to go it alone, Ecojoy delivers bike rentals to your hotel's doorstep.

Sociedad Cooperativa de Servicios Turísticos   BOATING
(☑ cell 315-1077909; konan_marlin@hotmail.com; cnr Veracruz & López de Legazpi; lagoon tour M$400, Tenacatita day trip per boat M$4000, fishing M$4500; ◷ 9am-5pm) Trips into the Laguna de Navidad are a Barra highlight. This boat owner's cooperative books a variety of boat tours ranging from half-hour trips around the lagoon to all-day jungle trips to Tenacatita. Fishing trips on *lanchas* (skiffs) can also be arranged; they include gear and snorkeling stops. Prices are posted at the open-air lagoonside office.

🛏 Sleeping

Barra has fewer beachfront rooms than neighboring Melaque. Book well in advance for high season (between November and May). Some of the town's options are a bit mediocre, but there are some solid choices.

Hotel Sarabi   HOTEL $
(☑ 315-355-82-23; www.hotelsarabi.com; Av Veracruz 196; d M$500-600, bungalows M$700-900; ❄ ✳ 🛜 ⛱) In the heart of things in Barra, this hotel offers three levels of excellent budget rooms with fans and air-con; the latter costs an extra M$100 if you want to turn it on. It's set around a gravel courtyard with a blue-tiled pool and everything is shipshape. Something of a bargain.

★ Hotel Delfín   HOTEL $$
(☑ 315-355-50-68; www.hoteldelfinmx.com; Morelos 23; d M$827-927, apt M$2004; 🅿 ❄ ✳ 🛜 ⛱)
🏵 The homey Delfín is one of Barra's best deals. It has large, pleasant rooms featuring shared balconies, a grassy pool area and a rooftop deck. Factor in excellent management and you have the kind of place you'd

rather not leave. Rooms with TV and air-con cost more but are otherwise identical; fans in the others usually do the trick.

Spacious apartments with full kitchens suit families well. Repeat customers fill the place in winter. The ecofriendly Delfín composts organic waste and uses a solar hot-water system.

Hotel Bogavante HOTEL $$

(☑315-355-81-09; www.bogavanteresortspa.com; López de Legazpi 259; r M$1100-1309, ste M$1750-2380; ⊛✳🛜🌊) Right on the beach in the center of town, the Bogavante boasts modern remodeled rooms, an on-site restaurant and an infinity pool with an impressive view of Melaque and beyond. The best on offer here are the oceanside rooms and pricier suites sleeping up to five people.

Hotel Barra de Navidad HOTEL $$

(☑315-355-51-22; www.hotelbarradenavidad.com. mx; López de Legazpi 250; d M$1200-1400, ste M$1400-2050; ⊛✳🛜🌊) Providing good beach access, this white beachside hotel looks somewhat tired in parts but harbors a shaded and intimate courtyard and a small but inviting pool. The open layout means you can hear the sea nearly throughout. Best are the seaside rooms, which are modern and nondescript but boast a magnificent outlook and a terrace to enjoy it from.

✗ Eating & Drinking

Bananas BREAKFAST $

(☑315-355-55-54; marydiaz805@yahoo.com.mx; López de Legazpi 250; breakfast mains M$65-88; ⏰8am-noon May-Nov, 8am-noon & 6-10pm Dec-Apr; 🛜) For breakfast with a fine ocean view, nothing beats this 2nd-floor eatery above Hotel Barra de Navidad. Angle for one of the terrace tables overlooking the beach, then sit back and enjoy the menu of Mexican and North American favorites, from the trademark banana pancakes to chilaquiles (fried tortillas with green or red salsa, eggs and/or chicken).

★ El Manglito SEAFOOD $$

(☑315-355-81-28; www.facebook.com/elmanglito restaurantbar; Av Veracruz 17; mains M$140-230; ⏰noon-11pm; 🛜) With a lovely view over the lagoon and welcome breezes, this open-air restaurant with palm-thatch roofing and sand floors produces some really excellent seafood – the shrimp is wonderful, the fresh oysters are great, and there are various standout fish dishes. Service is very cordial.

Fortino's SEAFOOD $$

(☑314-337-90-75; Isla Navidad; mains M$130-160; ⏰11am-7pm Thu-Tue; 🛜) Across the lagoon, this waterfront restaurant's family-run kitchen has been winning folks over with its superb seafood dishes for more than 50 years. The camarones costeños (coconut shrimp with a pineapple-guayaba dipping sauce) pairs oh-so nicely with refreshing coconut water served in its shell. There's a small beach here if you're up for a swim after lunch. To get here, boats just south of the malecón (beach promenade) provide free transportation to and from restaurants on the lagoon.

Jarro Beach BAR

(☑cell 315-1002020; jarrobeach@hotmail.com; López de Legazpi 154; ⏰11am-4am; 🛜) Beach bar by day, disco by night, this is one of the few spots in Barra where you'll find late-night action with danceable DJ sets usually consisting of salsa, northern banda (big-band) music and cumbia (dance music originating from Colombia) tunes. During the quiet daytime hours, it makes a mellow spot to contemplate the ocean scenery over a cold drink.

ℹ Information

Banamex (Av Veracruz s/n) One of two ATMs just south of Barra's main plaza. Bring cash in case the machines dry up.

Tourist Office (☑315-355-83-83; www. costalegre.com; Av Veracruz 98; ⏰9am-5pm Mon-Fri) This regional office has maps and information about Barra and the other towns of the Costalegre.

ℹ Getting There & Away

AIR

Barra de Navidad is served by Manzanillo's Playa de Oro International Airport (p544) – it's 30km southeast of Barra on Hwy 200. To get to town from the airport, take a taxi (M$590, 30 minutes).

BOAT

Water taxis operate on demand from a dock at the southern end of Avenida Veracruz, offering service to the marina, golf course and various restaurants. Round-trip fare to any destination is M$40.

BUS

The bus companies cluster around Avenida Veracruz just south of the marlin statue as you enter the center. There are direct **ETN** (☑315-355-84-00; www.etn.com.mx; Av Veracruz

PESCADO ZARANDEADO – A COASTAL CULINARY HIGHLIGHT

If you've never tried *pescado zarandeado* (marinated grilled fish), you're missing out on a real Pacific coast treat. Whole fish, often red snapper or corbina, is butterflied, seasoned with a marinade or rub and then barbecued in a fish cage over mesquite wood or charcoal. When cooked properly, the result is a smoky, succulent fish with an added zesty bite if the marinade includes chili pepper.

Pescado zarandeado (aka *pescado a la talla*) hails from Nayarit and Sinaloa, and to this day locals from *both* of the neighboring states adamantly claim bragging rights as the birthplace of the age-old cooking method. Nowadays you can find the signature dish up and down most of the coast and it's even featured on menus in landlocked Mexico City. But nothing beats the fresh-fish experience and know-how of the *costeños* (people from the coast). In particular, restaurants in Mazatlán, Chacala, San Blas and Barra Vieja do excellent *pescado zarandeado*. And no two versions are alike – purists, for instance, might roast the fish in old wooden ovens, while marinade ingredients and rubs can include anything from guajillo chili and crushed garlic to bottled Huichol salsa and Worcestershire sauce.

273C) and **Primera Plus** (477-710-00-60; www.primeraplus.com.mx; Av Veracruz 269; 6am-9pm) buses from Barra to Manzanillo (M$61 to M$75), Puerto Vallarta (M$259 to M$264) and Guadalajara (M$499 to M$590). Some services (called *coordinados*) stop at both Barra and Melaque, but most only visit Melaque. You can reach Melaque by local orange buses (M$7, every 15 minutes, 6am to 9pm) that do circuits of both towns; the green buses (M$15) are more direct.

TAXI

A taxi to San Patricio-Melaque costs M$70.

Manzanillo

314 / POP 161,420

Though it boasts miles of golden sands, Manzanillo puts bread on the table by being one of the Mexican Pacific's major seaports; tourism takes second place. The beaches are none too clean, and the dimensions – it's 20km from the old town to the best beach at Playa Olas Altas – make it a drag to get around without a car.

Despite that – and the fact that the beaches are backed by an ugly highway where mediocre hotels and chain restaurants jostle for space with car dealerships and filling stations – there are some super places to stay here, particularly on the picturesque Península de Santiago, which offers spectacular coastal views.

The old town is the most atmospheric area, and the huge blue sculpture on the waterside plaza is a nod to Manzanillo's self-proclaimed status as 'Sailfish Capital of the World.'

Sights

★ Playa La Boquita
BEACH

Playa La Boquita is a beach with calm waters at the mouth of a lagoon where fishermen lay out their nets to dry by day, and shove off by night. The beach is lined with seafood restaurants where you can hang out for the day. A shipwreck just offshore makes this a popular snorkeling spot.

Playa Azul
BEACH

This long, curving strip of sand can suffer from oil streaking and the water can get rough. It stretches northwest from Playa Las Brisas to the Península de Santiago.

Playa Las Brisas
BEACH

Just across the harbor from the old town, this spacious stretch of sand is backed by an appealing yet fast-growing zone of hotels, restaurants and bars.

Playa Olas Altas
BEACH

True to its name (Big Waves Beach), this attractive stretch of sand has lovely surfable breakers and is backed by a handful of simple beach restaurants.

Playa Santiago
BEACH

On the far side of the Península de Santiago from town, this is one of Manzanillo's cleaner beaches and has some good accommodations nearby.

Playa Miramar
BEACH

Boasting the best surfing and bodysurfing waves in the area, the long and beautiful Playa Miramar is an ideal place to take the plunge and rent a surfboard.

Greater Manzanillo

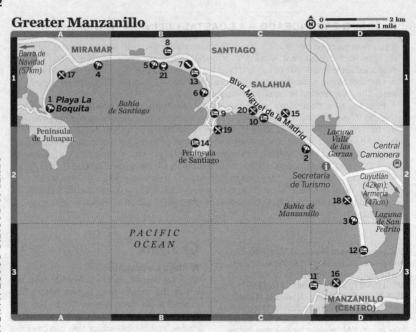

Greater Manzanillo

🏃 Activities

Diving

The scuba diving around Manzanillo can be interesting, with deep-water pinnacles luring pelagics at **Los Frailes**, and alluring swim-through arches at **Roca Elefante**.

Aquatic Sports & Adventures DIVING
(☎314-334-63-94; www.aquaticsportsadventures. com; Privada Los Naranjos 30; 2-tank dive US$110, snorkel tour per person US$55; ⊙9am-5pm Mon-Sat, to 2pm Sun; 🚌Ruta 1) In the Santiago area,

this is a PADI-accredited diving operator, catering for all levels of experience. On offer are shore and boat dives as well as a snorkeling tour visiting various sites.

🎉 Festivals & Events

Fiestas de Mayo CULTURAL
(⊙Apr & May) These fiestas celebrate the founding of Manzanillo in 1873. Festivities involve sporting competitions and other events over two weeks from late April to early May.

Sailfish Tournaments SPORTS

(📞 314-332-73-99; www.deportivodepescamanzanillo.com; ⊙ Feb & Dec) Manzanillo's famous international fishing tournament takes place in December; a smaller national tournament is held in February.

🛏 Sleeping

Manzanillo's cheapest hotels are located downtown, in the blocks surrounding the main plaza, and there are several down-on-their-luck three-star habitats on Playa Santiago (p541) disguised as proper beach hotels. Top-end places can be found on the Santiago peninsula.

Hotel Colonial HOTEL $

(📞 314-332-10-80; www.facebook.com/colonialhotelmanzanillo; Bocanegra 28; s M$640, d from $790; 🅿 ⊝ ❄ 🐾 🛜 😣) One block from Manzanillo's waterfront plaza, this atmospheric old hotel retains the character of a colonial hacienda, with tiled outdoor hallways, a spectacular exterior and a central courtyard. Big rooms are set on four floors surrounding that courtyard and have elegant drapes and wood furnishings. Downstairs rooms are darkish and suffer from a lot of noise from the **restaurant** (Av México 100; breakfast & lunch M$60-120, dinner M$140-310; ⊙ 7am-10:30pm Mon-Fri, 8am-4pm Sat & Sun; 🛜).

Hostal Tzalahua HOSTEL $

(📞 cell 311-1184546; www.facebook.com/hostaltzalahua; Pájaro de Fuego 1; dm/d M$150/400; ⊝ 🛜 😣 🐾; 🚌 Ruta 1) Guests can rest easy at this well-run hostel in a quiet residential area about a block from Playa Azul (p541). Opt to stay in a nine-bed mixed dorm or one of seven private rooms (five with bathrooms), which are all cheerful and clean. A rear garden with hammocks and a swimming pool provides a nice spot to chill.

★ Casa Artista B&B $$

(📞 314-334-47-04; www.casaartistamanzanillo.com; Calle 4 No 12, Colinas de Santiago; apt incl breakfast M$800-1200; 🅿 ⊝ ❄ 🛜 😣; 🚌 Ruta 1) A gloriously peaceful spot up a hill on the landward side of the main road, this B&B has hummingbirds thrumming in the garden. Its artistically decorated apartments have kitchenettes, and are homey, relaxing and really attractive. It's a top spot to relax with a book.

Hotel Real Posada HOTEL $$

(📞 314-334-12-12; www.realposada.com.mx; Blvd Miguel de la Madrid 13801; d M$1000; 🅿 ⊝ ❄ @ 🛜 😣; 🚌 Ruta 1) A block back from Playa Santiago (p541), this motel-style setup is on the main road and within walking distance of Playa Olas Altas (p541). Rooms are relatively modern with tiled floors, dark-wood furnishings, crisp sheets and cable TV. Staff are helpful, and there's a kiddie pool alongside the main one.

Pepe's Hideaway CABAÑAS $$$

(📞 314-334-16-90, US 213-261-6821; www.pepeshideaway.com; Camino Don Diego 67, La Punta; cabins per person incl meals US$185-225; 🅿 ⊝ 🛜 😣) Don't despair as you cruise the sanitized banality of the gated community wherein this place lies, for this spot is totally unexpected. It's set on a wild rocky point where noise means wind in the coconut palms and waves crashing below. A handful of romantic, rustic cabins with vibrant paint jobs puts you in a sort of castaway fantasy world. Rates are all-inclusive. You'll need a vehicle to get here.

Dolphin Cove Inn HOTEL $$$

(📞 314-334-15-15; www.dolphincoveinn.com; Av Vista Hermosa s/n; d incl breakfast M$2450; 🅿 ⊝ ❄ @ 🛜 😣; 🚌 Ruta 8) This cliffside hotel has awe-inspiring views and huge, spacious and bright rooms on tiered floors that cascade to a pretty bayside swimming pool. Units range from basic doubles to two-room suites sleeping four, all with marble floors, kitchens or kitchenettes, vaulted ceilings and sea-view balconies. Bathrooms and fittings are a little disappointing for this price, but the outlook is sublime.

Hotel La Posada HOTEL $$$

(📞 314-333-18-99; www.hotel-la-posada.net; Cárdenas 201; s/d incl breakfast US$69/93; 🅿 ⊝ ❄ 🛜 😣; 🚌 Ruta 8) This bright, pink beachside hotel at the end of the Playa Las Brisas (p541) peninsula lures repeat guests with cool, rustic rooms, personalized service and amenities including a library, open-air dining room and honor bar. A small pool overlooks the beach, where you can watch ships – and the occasional whale – trawling the harbor.

🍴 Eating & Drinking

Down-to-earth options are within several blocks of the main plaza, including a couple of markets, while many chain and chain-like spots line Hwy 200 around the bay.

★ Mariscos El Aliviane SEAFOOD $

(📞 cell 314-3536588; Playa Santiago; dishes M$20-120; ⊙ 11am-4:30pm Mon-Sat) A terrific little street stall across from Hotel Playa Santiago, where locals crowd wooden tables for *jaiba* (crab) *tostadas, cócteles* (seafood cocktails) and platters of shrimp, octopus, scallops and ceviche. Beers are icy and the house habanero salsa so piquant it will leave your lips burning and soul simmering. According to residents, this is the best *cevichería* in Manzanillo.

Tacos Chuy
FOOD TRUCK $

(☑ cell 314-1121010; www.tacoschuymanzanillo. blogspot.mx/p/la-carta.html; Blvd Miguel de la Madrid s/n; tacos M$13; ⊘9am-7pm; ☐Ruta 1) Dispensed from the bed of a red pickup truck, a variety of tacos – including marinated pork and *carne asada* (marinated grilled beef) – are accompanied by zesty salsas and fixings such as grilled cactus paddle and whole beans. The truck parks just south of supermarket Comercial Mexicana.

Tacos Chuy won't win any hygiene awards, but we're guessing food truck aficionados are OK with that.

Oasis Ocean Club
INTERNATIONAL $$

(☑314-334-88-22; www.oasisoceanclub.com; Delfin 15; lunch M$90-200, dinner M$150-350; ⊘11am-10pm; ☐Ruta 1) Worthwhile just to visit its very swimmable beach on Santiago Bay, this restaurant-bar also happens to prepare excellent cocktails, tasty international fare including *curricanes* (tuna rolls with crab, avocado and ponzu sauce) and a killer gelato for dessert. If you're coming by bus, it's about a 1km walk from Boulevar Miguel de la Madrid.

Mariscos El Delfín
SEAFOOD $$

(☑314-332-63-69; www.facebook.com/mariscos. e.manzanillo; Av Niños Héroes s/n, 2nd fl; dishes M$15-160; ⊘10:30am-6pm Tue-Sun; ☎) Above the fish-market building near the center of town, this place has very soothing views over foraging pelicans and bobbing boats. It does very tasty, no-frills seafood. The house specialty is swordfish in tamarind sauce, and there are also excellent marlin *tostadas*.

El Fogón
MEXICAN $$

(☑314-333-30-94; fogonypalmas@outlook.com; Blvd Miguel de la Madrid Km 9.5; mains M$140-220; ⊘1pm-midnight; ☎; ☐Ruta 1) Under a tiled roof with an open-air rustic style, this meat restaurant does excellent, tender steaks from the grill house, while fresh tortillas are busily made in the hut opposite. Portions are large – even the tortilla chips come with a whole platter of sauces – and the pork tacos and *arrachera* (hanger steak) come highly recommended.

★Pacifica del Mar
FUSION $$$

(☑314-333-63-53; www.facebook.com/pacifica delmarzlo; Del Mar 1506, Playa Las Brisas; mains M$195-265; ⊘1-11pm; [P]☎; ☐Ruta 1) Grab a cocktail and watch ginormous container ships cruise into port from this restaurant's open-air patio on Playa Las Brisas (p541). The menu, drawing from an eclectic array of cuisines, includes such items as Black Angus flank steak in beer sauce, freshly made pastas and chipotle-fried shrimp on hibiscus tortillas. The seasonal Sunday brunch buffet (November to April) is a hit.

Poco Pazzo
ITALIAN $$$

(☑314-336-85-33; pocopazzofacturacion@gmail. com; Marina Las Hadas s/n; mains M$120-280; ⊘5pm-midnight Tue-Sun; ☎; ☐Ruta 8) One of a row of restaurants on the marina within the Las Hadas resort offering a romantic waterside setting. Enjoy surprisingly authentic Italian thin-crust pizza, pastas and traditional Italian steaks and seafood dishes. Try the 'siciliano' fish fillet prepared with an olive, caper and white-wine sauce.

★Hostal Olas Altas
BAR

(☑314-333-03-90; www.hostalolasaltas.com; Blvd Miguel de la Madrid 15675; ⊘noon-2:30am; ☎; ☐Ruta1) At the center of Manzanillo's music, arts and surf scene, this hostel's beach bar hosts live bands on Saturday nights. The occasional surf tourney or art show always livens up the party atmosphere on the beach. Accommodations here are cool but noisy.

ⓘ Information

Secretaría de Turismo (☑314-333-22-77; www.visitcolima.mx; Blvd Miguel de la Madrid 875A; ⊘8:30am-4:30pm Mon-Fri) On the main waterfront boulevard, halfway between downtown and Península de Santiago. Dispenses limited information on Manzanillo and the state of Colima.

ⓘ Getting There & Away

AIR

Playa de Oro International Airport (☑314-333-11-19; www.aeropuertosgap.com.mx; Carretera Manzanillo–Barra de Navidad Km 42) lies between a long and secluded white-sand beach and tropical groves of bananas and coconuts, 35km northwest of Manzanillo's Zona Hotelera. Aeroméxico and **Aeromar** (☑314-334-05-32, 800-237-66-27; www.aeromar.com. mx; ⊘7am-8pm Mon-Fri, to 1pm Sat, noon-8pm Sun) provide direct services to Mexico City.

BUS

Manzanillo's **Central Camionera** (☑ 314-336-80-35; Obras Marítimas s/n; 🚌 Ruta 8) is 7km northeast of downtown. It's an organized place with tourist information, phones, eateries and left-luggage facilities.

CAR & MOTORCYCLE

Renting a car is not only convenient for exploring the Costalegre beaches northwest of Manzanillo's airport, but also recommended for getting the most out of Manzanillo in general. There are several firms at the airport; some also have downtown offices.

Alamo (☑ 314-333-24-30; www.alamo.com.mx; Blvd Miguel de la Madrid 1570; ☺ 8am-8pm; 🚌 Ruta 1)

Budget (☑ 314-333-14-45; www.budget.com.mx; Blvd Miguel de la Madrid Km 10; ☺ 9am-2pm & 4-7pm Mon-Fri, 9am-2pm Sat; 🚌 Ruta 1)

Sixt (☑ 314-333-31-91; www.sixt.com.mx; Playa de Oro International Airport; ☺ 7am-7pm)

Thrifty (☑ 314-334-32-82; www.thrifty.com.mx; Playa de Oro International Airport; ☺ 7am-7pm; 🚌 Ruta 1)

ℹ️ Getting Around

BUS

Local buses marked 'Santiago,' 'Las Brisas' and 'Miramar' head around the bay to the towns of San Pedrito, Salahua, Santiago and Miramar, and to beaches along the way. Route 8 runs from Playa las Brisas (p541) to the bus terminal (p545) and then does a circuit of the Península de Santiago. Take route 2 from the old town to reach the bus terminal or Playa Olas Altas (p541). Fares are M$9.

TAXI

Taxis are plentiful in Manzanillo, but always agree on a price before getting into one. From the main bus terminal (p545), a cab fare is around M$50 to the main plaza or Playa Azul (p541), and M$70 to Península de Santiago or Playa Miramar (p541).

Michoacán Coast

Highway 200 hugs the shoreline most of the way along the 250km coastline of Michoacán, one of Mexico's most beautiful states. This is one of the nation's most memorable drives: the route passes dozens of untouched beaches, and some with wide expanses of golden sand, some tucked into tiny rocky coves, some at river mouths where quiet estuaries harbor multitudes of birds. Several have gentle waves that are good for swimming; others have big breakers suitable for surfing. Many beaches are uninhabited, but some shelter communities, many of which are largely indigenous. Mango, coconut and banana plantations line the highway; the green peaks of the Sierra Madre del Sur form a lush backdrop inland. Signs along Hwy 200 mark the turnoffs for most beaches of interest, including **Ixtapilla** (Km 180), **La Manzanillera** (Km 174), **Motín de Oro** (Km 167), **Zapote de Tizupán** (Km 103), **Pichilinguillo** (Km 95) and **Huahua** (Km 84).

ℹ️ Information

DANGERS & ANNOYANCES

The 150km stretch of the Michoacán Coast between Las Brisas and Caleta de Campos has traditionally been cartel-controlled, first by the notorious La Familia, then by the Knights Templar. In the wake of cartel wars and government operations, these organizations have broken down, though their main business line certainly hasn't.

Various 'self-defense groups' operate here now, and they are difficult to classify. A range of issues including poverty, indigenous rights and lack of infrastructure and jobs are enmeshed with ongoing criminal activity, drug production and transportation, and battles of loyalties. There are no police or military bases here, though heavily armed patrols run up and down the highway.

BUSES FROM MANZANILLO

DESTINATION	FARE (M$)	DURATION (HR)	FREQUENCY (DAILY)
Barra de Navidad	61-75	1-1½	frequent
Colima	110-160	1½-2	half-hourly
Guadalajara	440-525	5-6	frequent
Lázaro Cárdenas	390-518	6-8½	8
Mexico City (Terminal Norte)	1051-1380	11½-12	4
Puerto Vallarta	360-421	5-5½	frequent
San Patricio-Melaque	66-90	1-1½	half-hourly
Zihuatanejo	616-695	8-8½	3 (nightly)

WORTH A TRIP

PLAYA MARUATA

With clear turquoise waters and golden sandy beaches, **Playa Maruata** (turnoff Hwy 200 Km 150) is the most beautiful beach in Michoacán. The Nahua fishing village has a bit of a hippie reputation, attracting beach bums from all over. It's a tranquil, friendly place to hang out with your sweetie or a large stack of paperbacks. It's also a prime nesting site for green turtles (nightly from July to December).

Maruata actually has three beaches, each with its own unique character. The left (eastern) is the longest, a 3km pristine crescent-shaped beach with creamy yellow sand and calm waves perfect for swimming and snorkeling. The small middle arc is OK for strong swimmers. It's sheltered by a climbable rocky headland riddled with caves, tunnels and blowholes, and marked by the unusual Dedo de Dios (God's Finger) formation rising from the sea. The far-right (western) beach is known as Playa de los Muertos (Beach of the Dead), and for good reason: it has dangerous currents and ferocious waves. During low tide you can scale the rocks on the far right side of Muertos to reach a secluded cove where discreet nude sunbathing is tolerated. But don't get stuck here when the tide comes in. A crucifix on the rocks serves as a stark memorial to the people who have been swallowed by the sea.

Maruata is an extremely poor pueblo (village), though a couple of recent infrastructure projects now stand in the town center. You'll find shops and simple eateries around the semi-derelict plaza. The enramadas (thatch-covered, open-air restaurants) on the left beach serve fresh seafood and are also your best bet for camping: most charge from M$50 per person to pitch a tent or rent a hammock. There are rustic cabañas for M$300 to M$400, but the best accommodations are at the **Centro Ecoturístico Ayutl Maruata** (☑ cell 555-1505110; https://nuestrodestino.jimdo.com/ecoturismo-en-michoacán/centro-ecoturístico-ayult-maruata; d/tr/q M$600/750/1000, hammock M$100; [P][❄][❁][雪]) .

Lázaro Cárdenas-bound buses from Manzanillo will leave you at the town entrance on Hwy 200, from where it's a short walk into town.

What does this mean for the visitor? Very little in practical terms. Roadblocks are sometimes enforced to protest against the government, so you might be delayed for a while, but theft or violence against tourists was never tolerated by the big cartels and the region remains comparatively safe. Locals strongly recommend not driving at night along this stretch, however, and hitchhiking should be avoided.

San Juan de Alima

☑ 313 / POP 291

Twenty kilometers into Michoacán is the cobblestoned town of San Juan de Alima (turn off Hwy 200 at Km 211). It's a pretty place with a quiet beach and is seasonally popular with surfers due to its creamy medium-sized breakers just off the coast. There are several beachfront restaurants and modern hotels.

🛏 Sleeping & Eating

Hotel Restaurant Parador　　HOTEL $
(☑ 313-327-90-38; www.facebook.com/elhotelparador; Blvd San Juan de Alima Oriente 1; s/d M$600/750; [P][❄][❁][❁][雪]) Offers a variety of rooms; the best have air-con, balconies and views. The hotel's popular restaurant perches directly above the ocean on palm-shaded terraces.

Hotel Hacienda Trinidad　　HOTEL $$$
(☑ 313-327-92-00; www.haciendatrinidad.com.mx; Blvd San Juan s/n; d M$2110; [P][❄][❁][❁][雪][雪]) The town's most upscale offering has decent rooms, a lovely pool surrounded by lush vegetation, and one of the nicest restaurants. High-season prices are ridiculously steep in July, August and December, but you can get fair deals the rest of the year.

❶ Getting There & Away

Buses (M$56, one hour) departing every two hours from the Tecomán bus terminal will leave you at the town entrance on Hwy 200.

Barra de Nexpa

☑ 753 / POP 102

At Km 55.6, just north of Puente Nexpa bridge, and 1km from Hwy 200 down a rough cobbled road, lies the small, laid-back community of Nexpa, a hamlet misty with sea spray. It's long been a haven for surfers, attracted to the salt-and-pepper sandbar and long left-hand break at the river mouth, which can rise to double overhead. Rides can go a half-kilometer or more here. There are no ATMs in town so bring cash.

🛏 Sleeping & Eating

Cabañas Alba CABAÑAS $
(📱cell 753-1185082; www.hospedajesalba.com; Barra de Nexpa; d/q M$500/700; 🅿🌀) Two-story rustic cabins, some sleeping up to six people, provide a homey feel with their full kitchens, porches and balconies with ocean views. The on-site restaurant opens during high season and there's also a temascal steam bath to sweat out those party toxins. Drawbacks? No air-con or wi-fi.

Chicho's INTERNATIONAL $
(📱cell 753-1184203; chichosnexpa@hotmail.com; Barra de Nexpa; breakfast M$60-70, lunch & dinner M$80-150; ⊙9am-9pm; 🅿) One of several *palapas* lining the beach, family-run Chicho's is a great choice for meals thanks to gargantuan breakfast smoothies, pancakes, solid plates of shrimp and burgers, and inspiring views of wave-riding surfers.

❶ Getting There & Away

Sur de Jalisco buses (M$87, 1½ hours) depart from the Galeana bus terminal in Lázaro Cárdenas five times daily.

Caleta de Campos

📞 753 / POP 2580

Set up on the bluffs, which taper toward an azure bay, Caleta (turn off Hwy 200 at Km 50) draws mostly surfers, but its small-town appeal makes it worthy of a short visit for non-boarders as well.

Also known as Bahía Bufadero, Caleta de Campos is a regional service service with most of the essentials (but no ATMs in town). There's a surf shop and a protected cove suited to novice surfers, and there are several hotels in the center.

🛏 Sleeping

Partour Caleta GUESTHOUSE $$
(📱cell 753-1141111; www.partourcaleta.com; Hwy 200 Km 51; d M$1500, ste M$2200-2500; 🅿🌀🗦) This place has a fabulous clifftop view over the wild beach and waving palms. Its comfortable ocean-view units, with terracotta floors and cable TV, surround a *palapa*-roofed bar and lounge area. The best suite has a kitchenette, dining room and private terrace with Jacuzzi. Stairs lead down to a rocky beach. It's on the highway 1km north of town.

❶ Getting There & Away

Sur de Jalisco buses (M$80, 1¼ hours) depart from the **Galeana bus terminal** in Lázaro Cárdenas five times daily. Hourly *colectivos* depart Caleta's main plaza for Lázaro Cárdenas (M$68, 1¼ hours) from 6:30am to 8pm. A taxi between Caleta de Campos and Barra de Nexpa costs M$70.

Lázaro Cárdenas

📞 753 / POP 79,200

As an industrial port city, Lázaro has nothing of real tourist interest – but because it's a hub for buses up and down the coast, travelers regularly pass through. Lázaro is also a regional service center, but with excellent beaches and waves so near, there is no reason to spend the night.

❶ Getting There & Away

Lázaro has several bus terminals, all within a few blocks of each other. From the most useful **main bus terminal** (Galeana; 📞753-532-30-06; Av Lázaro Cárdenas 1810), operators offer services to Manzanillo, Uruapan, Morelia, Colima, Caleta de Campos, Barra de Nexpa, Guadalajara and Mexico City.

Estrella Blanca (📞753-532-11-71; www. estrellablanca.com.mx; Francisco Villa 65) goes to destinations including Puerto Vallarta, Mazatlán and as far north as Tijuana. The **Estrella**

BUSES FROM LÁZARO CÁRDENAS

DESTINATION	FARE (M$)	DURATION (HR)	FREQUENCY (DAILY)
Acapulco	235-329	6-7	frequent
Guadalajara	596-650	8-10	6
Manzanillo	390-560	7	hourly
Mexico City	708-788	8-11	6
Morelia	530-563	4-5	frequent
Uruapan	330-380	3-4	frequent
Zihuatanejo	71-118	1½-2	frequent

de Oro (☑753-532-02-75; www.estrelladeoro. com.mx; Corregidora 318) terminal is one block north and two blocks west of Estrella Blanca and serves Zihuatanejo, Acapulco, Manzanillo and Mexico City.

Troncones

☑755 / POP 698

Not long ago, Troncones was a poor, sleepy fishing and farming village. These days, expat homes and B&Bs have left the long beach-front road resembling more a California sub-division than the traditional Mexican villages at either end. The attraction is obvious: fab-ulous beaches, a laid-back atmosphere and world-class surfing. Troncones is a marvelous place to kick back for several days.

The village is located about 25km north-west of Ixtapa, at the end of a 4km paved road from Hwy 200. The road ends at a T-intersection, from where the beachfront road continues 4.5km northwest to neigh-boring **Majahua** via Troncones Point and Manzanillo Bay. The majority of hotels and restaurants are along this road.

Majahua is a traditional fishing village with a few *enramadas* (thatch-covered, open-air restaurants) and a mellow beach layered with fine shells. From here, a dirt road (rough in the wet season) leads back out to Hwy 200.

🏃 Activities

The swimming in the protected cove off Pla-ya Manzanillo is glorious; on placid days the snorkeling is good too. Horseback riding is quite popular; locals stroll the beach with their steeds looking for customers. Biking, fishing and spelunking through the lime-stone cave system near Majahua can be ar-ranged through local inns.

Prime Surfboards SURFING
(☑755-103-01-80, cell 755-1143504; www.prime surfboards.com.mx; Av de la Playa s/n; surf lesson US$60, board rental per day US$25; ⊙7am-8pm) Around 500m north of the T-intersection, surfer Bruce Grimes offers two-hour lessons and board repair. He also designs custom boards and offers rentals.

Inn at Manzanillo Bay KAYAKING, BICYCLING
(☑755-553-28-84; www.manzanillobay.com; Av de la Playa s/n; surfboard & bicycle/kayak & paddleboard per day US$25/40) Near the point, this hotel rents out an excellent selection of short- and longboards, bicycles, paddleboards and kayaks.

Tours

Costa Nativa Ecotours ECOTOUR
(☑cell 755-1007499; www.tronconesecotours.com; Av de la Playa s/n; kayaking/hiking/paddleboarding US$42/45/45; ⊙office 9am-6pm Mon-Sat Oct-May) 🏄 This outfit runs low-impact ecotours such as three-hour kayaking excursions that offer excellent wildlife-watching, guided hik-ing ending at a swimming hole, and stand-up paddleboarding.

🛏 Sleeping

There are numerous places to stay; most are located along Troncones' main waterfront road. Reservations are advisable during the high season (November through April), when some places require multiple-night stays. During low season, prices can be 25% to 50% lower, but some places close during summer.

★Troncones Point Hostel HOSTEL $
(☑755-553-28-86; www.tronconespointhostel.com; Lote 49, Manzana 15, Troncones Point, off Av de la Playa; dm US$19-21, tents US$29, r US$85; P⊙🌊🐾) 🏄 Handy for the dreamy surfing at Troncones Point, this imaginatively designed place features a variety of rooms in several very easy-on-the-eye buildings. These range from slightly cramped but attractive dorms with bamboo beds to 'luxury' tents and a cu-rious duplex room with separate entrances. All are environmentally sound, and share a marvelous kitchen-lounge area with sea views. Board rental available.

★Casa Delfín Sonriente B&B $$
(☑755-553-28-03; www.casadelfinsonriente.com; Av de la Playa s/n; r/ste incl breakfast US$85/119; ⊙❄🌊🏊) With welcoming caretakers and a very laid-back atmosphere, this B&B makes a super place to stay. If available, grab one of the amazing upstairs suites, which have hanging beds, full kitchens, no doors (there's a lockable drawer for your valuables) and a shared rooftop patio with insane views of the wild Pacific. It's about a kilometer from the T-junction. There's a guest kitchen, and staff can be brought in to cook meals for you.

Hotel Playa Troncones HOTEL $$
(☑755-103-00-79; hotelplayatroncones@hotmail.com; Av de la Playa s/n; d M$1000; P❄🌊🏊) Conveniently located in the center of town and reasonably priced by Troncones stand-ards (especially during low season), rooms here are fairly straightforward with air-con,

comfortable beds, spotless bathrooms inlaid with river rock, and ocean views from the upstairs units. Kids like the small pool.

Los Raqueros
B&B $$$

([☑]755-553-28-02; www.raqueros.com; Av de la Playa s/n; d incl breakfast US$95-125; [P][◉][✴][🛜]) Offering some of the best value along the precious Playa Manzanillo beachfront, this well-run B&B provides plenty of quiet time and relaxation on its soft sands and manicured gardens. Some rooms afford sweet bay views, while family-friendly bungalows sleep four and come with open-air kitchens. It's 3km north of the T-intersection.

Inn at Manzanillo Bay
HOTEL $$$

([☑]755-553-28-84; www.manzanillobay.com; Av de la Playa s/n, Playa Manzanillo; ste US$183-204; [P][◉][✴][🛜][🏊]) In an ideal setting on Troncones' prettiest beach, this hotel has upscale thatched-roof bungalows with king-sized beds, handmade marble sinks, rain showers and hammocked terraces surrounding a pool. There's also a popular restaurant and bar, a surf shop, bike rental and easy access to the primo Troncones Point break.

✗ Eating

★ Toro del Mar
SEAFOOD $$

([☑]cell 755-1083074; Av de la Playa s/n, Playa Majahua; mains M$90-180; ⊙9am-9pm) On the southern end of Majahua beach, this rustic oceanfront restaurant in a small fishing village dishes up some mighty fine fresh fish and seafood. You might try the grilled snapper or coconut shrimp plated with fried plantain, rice and veggies.

Chenchos
MEXICAN $$

([☑]755-103-00-61; Av de la Playa s/n; M$95-175; ⊙11am-9pm; 🛜) You don't get the ocean view at this 'mini-restaurarant' one block inland, so the sand floor and sea breeze will have to do. A local favorite, this family-run place does fine homestyle Mexican cooking such as shrimp enchiladas in salsa verde and *chiles rellenos* (stuffed chilies).

Café Pacífico
CAFE $$

([☑]755-101-73-72; www.facebook.com/cafepacifico troncones; Av de la Playa s/n; mains M$70-160; ⊙8am-4pm Dec-Aug; 🛜🍴) This sweet modern place does a very decent coffee and lip-smacking juices. Service is with a smile, and there are nice shady tables outside to enjoy original breakfast omelettes, sandwiches and a range of well-prepared meals.

Roberto's Bistro
ARGENTINE $$$

([☑]755-103-00-19; www.robertosbistro.com; Av de la Playa s/n; mains M$120-270; ⊙8am-10pm; 🛜) Sizzling steaks and crashing waves create the stereophonic soundtrack at this Argentine-style beachfront grill, 1km south of the T-intersection. From chorizo starters to full-on feasts such as the *parrillada argentina* (T-bone, rib-eye and several other cuts grilled together with shrimp), this is a carnivore's paradise. It also does seafood. Saturdays in season are salsa night. Next to the restaurant, the owner's son runs a small turtle preserve that releases about 15,000 hatchlings each year.

Jardín del Edén
FUSION $$$

([☑]755-103-01-04; www.jardindeleden.com.mx; Av de la Playa s/n; mains M$140-240; ⊙8am-10pm Nov-Apr; 🛜) Just north of Troncones Point, the French chef's fusion menu ranges from Mediterranean to traditional Mexican fare. Nightly specials such as pizza, seafood ravioli and *cochinita pibil* (Yucatán-style slow-roasted pork) are cooked on the grill and in the wood-fired oven. Catch live salsa bands on Friday night.

❶ Getting There & Around

From Zihuatanejo, take a La Unión-bound bus (M$33, 30 minutes) from the Petatlán terminal (p560)– it will drop you at the turnoff. Walk down the road a little way and you'll find a stop where vans (M$15, five minutes) shuttle into Troncones every half-hour or so until 7pm; some continue to fishing village Majahua, just north of Troncones. Some 2nd-class buses heading northwest toward Morelia or Lázaro Cárdenas will also drop you at the turnoff.

Taxis ([☑]755-553-28-68; Av de la Playa s/n; ⊙8am-8pm) in Troncones offer service around the area (M$100 to Playa Majahua), to the airport (p559) (M$800) or to Zihuatanejo (M$500). A reliable air-conditioned cab is run by **Victor's Taxi Service** ([☑]755-553-28-08, cell 755-1110580; carayala2010@hotmail.com; Av de la Playa s/n).

Ixtapa

[☑]755 / POP 8698

Ixtapa was nothing more than a coconut plantation until the late 1970s when Fonatur (the Mexican government's tourism development group) decided that the Pacific coast needed a Cancún-like resort. In came the developers and up went the high-rises. The result is a long string of huge hotels backing a lovely beach, but little local community. Ixtapa's appeal is best appreciated by families

CENTRAL PACIFIC COAST IXTAPA

seeking a hassle-free, all-inclusive beach getaway, or by those who value modern chain-hotel comforts. It's close enough to Zihuatanejo – in effect, it's a suburb of it – that you can experience that town's more authentic Mexican life easily.

Sights

Playa el Palmar
BEACH

Ixtapa's longest (2.5km) and broadest stretch of blond sand is overrun by parasailing and jet-skiing concessions. The sea takes on an aquamarine sheen in the dry season, which makes it all the more inviting. Take care while swimming, as there can be a vicious shore break and a powerful undertow when the swell comes up. There aren't many public access points, thanks to the mega-resorts lined up shoulder to shoulder, but you can always cut through a hotel lobby.

Playa Escolleras
BEACH

Playa Escolleras, at the western end of Playa el Palmar near the entrance to the marina, has a decent break and attracts surfers.

Cocodrilario
WILDLIFE RESERVE

(Playa Linda; ⊙24hr) FREE Playa Linda has a small *cocodrilario* (crocodile reserve) that is also home to fat iguanas and several bird species. You can watch the hulking crocs from the safety of the well-fenced wooden viewing platform located near the bus stop and extending toward the harbor.

Isla Ixtapa
ISLAND

(round-trip boat fare M$50, snorkel rental M$150) Ixtapa's finest attraction is a beautiful oasis. The turquoise waters are crystal clear, calm and great for snorkeling (gear rentals available). **Playa Corales** on the back side of the island is the nicest and quietest beach, with soft white sand and an offshore coral reef. Thatch-covered, open-air *enramada* seafood restaurants and massage providers dot the island. Frequent boats depart from the pier at **Playa Linda**. The island gets mobbed by tourists in high season.

Activities

Cycling is a breeze along a 15km *ciclopista* (cycle path) that stretches from Playa Linda, north of Ixtapa, practically into Zihuatanejo. You can rent bikes from Adventours.

Mero Adventure
DIVING

(☑cell 755-1019672; www.meroadventure.com; Blvd Paseo Ixtapa s/n, Hotel Pacífica; 1-/2-tank dives US$65/90; ⊙9am-5pm Mon-Sat) Mero Adventure organizes diving, snorkeling, kayaking and fishing trips.

Catcha L'Ola Surf
SURFING

(☑755-553-13-84; www.ixtapasurf.com; Centro Comercial Kiosco 12, Plaza Zócalo; board rental per day/week US$20/100, 3hr lesson US$50; ⊙9am-7pm Mon-Sat, noon-5pm Sun) You'll find everything you need – rentals, repairs, classes and surfing trips – here. It's next to the well-signed **Nueva Zelanda** (☑755-553-08-38; www.restaurantsnapshot.com/nuevazelanda; Plaza Zócalo s/n; breakfast M$61-85, lunch & dinner M$125-210; ⊙8am-10pm; 🔊) restaurant.

Tours

Adventours
ADVENTURE

(☑755-553-35-84; www.ixtapa-adventours.com; Blvd Paseo Ixtapa s/n; tours M$1180-1580, bike rentals per hour/day M$60/250; ⊙8am-6pm) Opposite the Park Royal hotel, Adventours offers a variety of guided cycling, kayaking, snorkeling and bird-watching tours around Ixtapa and Zihuatanejo.

Sleeping

A couple of cheaper options are a few blocks inland from the main drag. The beachside hotels are mostly top-end and best booked through package deals or from hotel websites. Several haven't had much more than a lick of paint since they were built in the 1970s. Ixtapa hotels all have wi-fi.

Hotel Suites Ixtapa Plaza
HOTEL $$

(☑755-553-13-70; www.hotelsuitesixtapaplaza.com; Blvd Paseo Ixtapa s/n, Centro Comercial Ixtapa; r M$1200-1600, ste from M$1700; ⓟ➚@🔊🏊) This relatively small hotel is a welcome sight in the land of ginormous resorts. The rooftop pool provides a nice view of Ixtapa. Accommodations vary from basic digs and 'superior' rooms to suites with private terraces. Beware: some rooms catch noise from nearby bars and nightclubs.

★ Casa Candiles
B&B $$$

(☑cell 755-1012744; www.casacandiles.com; Paseo de las Golondrinas 65; r incl breakfast US$160-172; ➚❄🔊🏊) Far nicer than the hulking resort hotels is this intimate paradise on a quiet residential street about 500m from the beach. Three stylish but homey rooms are individually decorated – one with Balinese masks – and there's a lovely pool and garden. It backs onto jungle where you can spot birds and animals from a path. Hospitality is very genuine.

🍴 Eating & Drinking

Some of the big hotels have bars and nightclubs. In the low season most of these charge less and open fewer nights.

⭐ La Raiz de la Tierra   VEGAN $$
(☑ 755-553-15-03; www.laraizdelatierra.com; Plaza Zócalo s/n; mains M$55-145; ⊙ 8am-10pm; ☑) A vegan cafe owned by Rodrigo Sánchez of the flamenco-metal guitar duo Rodrigo Y Gabriela, this place also sells records and books and is an activities center offering salsa and guitar classes. Menu items include cold-pressed juices, vegan *tacos al pastor* (marinated mushroom on organic corn tortilla) and many other non-meat treats.

Lili Cipriani   SEAFOOD $$
(☑ cell 755-1200404; lili.cipriani@hotmail.com; Playa Coral s/n, Isla Ixtapa; mains M$150-250; ⊙ 9am-5pm) Walk to Playa Coral, on Isla Ixtapa's south side, for a mighty fine *pescado a las brasas* (grilled fish) at this beachfront *palapa* restaurant, where you can get in some snorkeling too. The whole fish comes served with handmade tortillas and a spicy habanero and *chile de arbol* (aka bird's beak chili) salsa. Boats to Isla Ixtapa depart from Playa Linda. Watch out for wild bunnies scouring the sands for table scraps.

Bistro Soleiado   INTERNATIONAL, SEAFOOD $$
(☑ 755-553-04-20; www.facebook.com/bistrosoleiadoixtapa; Blvd Paseo Ixtapa s/n; mains M$155-255; ⊙ 8am-11pm; 🔊) Opposite the Park Royal hotel, this open-fronted restaurant has an extensive international menu, but is especially recommended for its delicious seafood and tender fish bathed in delicious sauces. It's also a fine spot for breakfast.

Cuattro Café   CAFE
(☑ 755-553-01-80; www.cuattrocafe.com; Blvd Paseo Ixtapa s/n, Plaza Comercial Rafaello; ⊙ 8am-10:30pm Thu-Tue) One of the better places in town for a strong coffee. If you need something stronger, the original Zihuatanejo location (Altamirano 19) serves cocktails too.

Christine   CLUB
(☑ 755-553-04-56; Blvd Paseo Ixtapa 4, Hotel Krystal; ⊙ 11pm-4am Fri & Sat; 🔊) Christine has the sizzling sound-and-light systems you'd expect from one of the most popular discos in town. Admission varies, but is hefty in peak season and includes open bar.

ℹ️ Information

Tourist Office (☑ 755-555-07-00, ext 224; www.ixtapa-zihuatanejo.com; Blvd Paseo Ixtapa s/n; ⊙ 8am-4pm) Provides tourist info from a little kiosk directly across from the Holiday Inn.

ℹ️ Getting There & Away

Private taxis (M$460) provide transportation from the airport (p559) to Ixtapa, while shuttles making multiple stops charge M$135 per person. The return journey to the airport in private taxis costs M$280 to M$340. City cabs from Ixtapa to Zihuatanejo cost M$75 to M$105.

Rental cars can be hired at the airport or at the **Barceló Ixtapa** (☑ 755-553-71-47; www.alamo.com.mx; Blvd Paseo Ixtapa s/n; ⊙ 9am-7pm Mon-Sat) hotel.

There are bus-ticket offices, but very few long-distance buses actually stop here – for most destinations, go to Zihuatanejo.

Local buses run frequently between Ixtapa and Zihuatanejo from 5:30am to 11pm (M$12, 15 minutes). In Ixtapa, buses stop along the main street in front of all hotels. In Zihuatanejo, buses run along Morelos. Many Ixtapa-bound buses continue to Playa Linda (M$14).

Zihuatanejo

☑ 755 / POP 118,211

Zihuatanejo, or Zihua as it's affectionately called, is a Pacific paradise of beautiful beaches, friendly people and an easygoing lifestyle. Until the 1970s it was a sleepy fishing village, but with the construction of Ixtapa next door, Zihua's tourism industry boomed practically overnight.

Parts of the city have become quite touristy, especially when cruise ships are in town, and luxury hotels are slowly replacing family guesthouses. But for the most part, Zihua has retained its historic charm. The narrow cobblestone streets of downtown hide wonderful local restaurants, bars, boutiques and artisan studios. Fishers still meet every morning on the beach by Paseo del Pescador (Fishermen's Passage) to sell their catch of the day. At night, young lovers and families stroll carefree along the romantic waterfront sidewalk. Zihua is the best of both worlds. No wonder Andy and Red chose to live out their post-prison days here in *The Shawshank Redemption*.

◉ Sights

Museo Arqueológico
de la Costa Grande   MUSEUM
(Archaeological Museum of the Costa Grande; ☏755-554-75-52; museoarqueologico2@hotmail.com; cnr Plaza Olof Palme & Paseo del Pescador; M$10; ⊙10am-6pm Tue-Sun) This small museum houses six rooms with exhibits on the history, archaeology and culture of the Guerrero coast. Most displays are in Spanish, but you can get by with the free English-language handout.

Beaches
Waves are gentle at all of Bahía de Zihuatanejo's beaches: if you want big ocean waves, head west toward Ixtapa or south to Playa Larga. Water in the bay, particularly around the central beaches, isn't always the cleanest.

Playa Municipal, in the center of town, is convenient if you're staying in the neighborhood, but you can definitely find much cleaner waters elsewhere on the bay. A five-minute stroll heading east along a boardwalk leads to **Playa Madera** (▣Playa La Ropa), known for its shallow, swimmable beach.

Over a steep hill from Playa Madera is **Playa La Ropa** (Clothes Beach; ▣Playa La Ropa), about a 20-minute walk along a scenic highway with spectacular ocean views along the way. Some of the best hotels and restaurants in town are clustered in Playa La Ropa, and its sprawling beach provides fine swimming and waterskiing conditions.

Across the bay, protected beach **Playa Las Gatas** (Cat Beach; round-trip boat fare M$50) gets very crowded during the Mexican holiday season in July and August and the winter vacation period, but when the crowds thin out it makes a good snorkeling spot. Boats to Las Gatas (round-trip fare M$50) depart from Zihuatanejo's main pier.

For big-wave surfing and horseback riding, hit Playa Larga, about 12km south of the city center. Catch a 'Coacoyul' combi (p560) from the corner of Juárez and Gonzalez to the Playa Larga turnoff, then take another combi to the beach.

Near Playa Larga, **Playa Manzanillo** is considered to be one of the best snorkeling spots in the area and it draws fewer visitors than the highly popular Playa Las Gatas. The secluded beach is reachable by boat.

🏃 Activities

Sportfishing
Sportfishing is very popular in Zihuatanejo. Sailfish are caught here year-round; seasonal fish include blue or black marlin (March to May), roosterfish (September and October), wahoo (October), mahimahi (November and December) and Spanish mackerel (December). Deep-sea fishing trips start at around M$3600 for a boat holding up to four passengers. Trips run for up to seven hours and usually include equipment.

Sociedad Cooperativa
José Azueta   FISHING, BOATING
(☏755-554-20-56; https://sociedadcooperativatenientejoseazueta.com; Muelle Municipal; round-trip fare Playa Las Gatas M$50, deep-sea fishing M$3600; ⊙office 8am-6pm) Offers full-day fishing excursions and boat transportation to Playa Las Gatas from an office at the foot of the pier.

Sociedad de Servicios
Turísticos Triángulo del Sol   FISHING
(☏755-554-37-58; cooptriangulodelsol@hotmail.com; Paseo del Pescador 38B, near Muelle Municipal; fishing US$200-350, snorkeling per boat US$160; ⊙office 9am-4pm) As well as fishing in small and large boats, this place offers snorkeling at Playa Manzanillo including time at Playa Las Gatas. It also runs tours of the bay.

Water Sports
Snorkeling is good at Playa Las Gatas and even better at Playa Manzanillo. Marine life is abundant here due to a convergence of currents, and the visibility can be great – up to 35m in dry months. Migrating humpback whales pass through from December to early March.

Dive Zihua   DIVING
(☏cell 755-1023738; www.divezihuatanejo.com; Ascensio 7; 2-tank dive US$90, snorkel tour US$35; ⊙9:30am-6:30pm Mon-Sat) Offers a good variety of dives, plus snorkeling, classes in underwater photography and PADI certification. They also can arrange humpback whale tours with a biologist from December to March.

Carlo Scuba   DIVING
(☏cell 755-5546003; www.carloscuba.com; Playa Las Gatas; 1-/2-tank dives US$65/90; ⊙8am-6pm) Carlo Scuba, run by a third-generation family operation based at Playa Las Gatas, offers dives, snorkeling trips, instruction and PADI certification. Prices include pick-up and drop-off at the Muelle Municipal (pier).

Yoga

Paty's Yoga Studio   YOGA, MASSAGE

(☎ 755-554-22-13; www.zihuatanejoyoga.com; Playa La Ropa; classes US$10; ⏰ 9am-10:15am Oct-Apr) Few yogis can offer the kind of guaranteed enlightenment that comes from gazing through coconut palms into the sun-dappled Pacific from the upstairs terrace of this studio above Paty's restaurant (p558) on Playa La Ropa. Multilevel classes are offered daily in high season. Massages are also available.

🍃 Courses

⭐ **Patio Mexica Cooking School**   COOKING

(☎ cell 755-1167211; www.patiomexica.com; Adelita 32, Colonia La Madera; classes M$400-450) Mónica Durán Pérez opens her home kitchen and shares her love of Mexican culinary culture in this wonderful series of classes. Start with a trip to the market (some classes only) then return to Mónica's backyard, where you grind corn, shape tortillas, make salsa in a *molcajete* (traditional mortar and pestle), and cook up one of several different specialties.

These might be *tamales, mole poblano* (chicken or turkey in a sauce of chilies, fruits, nuts, spices and chocolate) or stuffed chilies or zucchini flowers. Check the website for details of different classes.

🧭 Tours

Picante   BOATING

(☎ 755-554-82-70; www.picantecruises.com; Muelle Puerto Mío, La Noria; sail & snorkel US$88, sunset cruise US$65) This 23m catamaran offers two enjoyable excursions. The 'Sail, Snorkel and Spinnaker Flying' trip sails south of Zihua to prime snorkeling off Playa Manzanillo . The 'Magical Sunset Cruise' heads around the bay and along the coast of Ixtapa. Prices include food and open bar. Reservations required. See website for schedule.

🛏️ Sleeping

Zihuatanejo has a huge selection for all budgets. Cheap hotels cluster around Calle Bravo in the center. High season is December through March, but even in high season, discounting of overinflated rack rates is common. Outside high season, prices drop by up to 20%. You can often negotiate lower rates, especially during slow periods or for extended stays.

Casa de la Palma   HOTEL $

(☎ 755-554-20-92; www.facebook.com/hotelcasa delapalma; Ciruelos s/n; d M$595-774; P 🅿 ❄ 🛜 🌊) In a busy market area with several boisterous dive bars nearby, this spotless and surprisingly comfy budget hotel offers a glimpse of Zihua's non-touristy side. Despite all the activity going on, you'll get a good night's rest here and the pool out back makes a decent spot for cooling off. At last visit the wi-fi was slooow.

Hotel Villas Mercedes   HOTEL $

(☎ 443-319-13-05, 755-544-67-81; www.hotelvillas mercedes.com; Adelita 59; d M$525-900; P 🅿 ❄ 🛜 🌊) Nestled in the pleasant barrio behind Playa Madera, this hotel offers remarkably good value for clean, comfortable rooms surrounding a pool area. It's a friendly place with decent security. It's popular with Mexican families.

Hotel Villas El Morro   HOTEL $

(☎ 443-319-13-05; www.zihuatanejo-villaselmorro. com; Paseo del Morro 4, Colonia El Almacén; r M$400-600, ste M$700-1300; P 🅿 ❄ 🛜 🌊) It's all about the views at El Morro, which sits high upon a hilltop on the bay's less-visited west end. Rooms are remarkably affordable here and an M$200 upgrade gets you one with a kitchen, terrace and Jacuzzi. Wi-fi is spotty and the climb up some 150 stairs to the hotel can be tiring.

Mi Casita   GUESTHOUSE $

(☎ 755-125-27-71, cell 755-1245123; micasita.alejan dra@gmail.com; Carretera Escénica s/n; r M$600-800; 🅿 ❄ 🛜; 🚌 Playa La Ropa) This humble and welcoming family-run place perches on the hillside between Playas Madera and La Ropa. The six rooms vary – some have artistic paint jobs, others a kitchen and aircon, though all open onto sweet terraces with hammocks and stirring views over the ocean far below.

Hotel Ávila   HOTEL $

(☎ 755-554-20-10; hotelavila68@yahoo.com.mx; Álvarez 8; d M$600; P 🅿 ❄ 🛜 🌊) Set just off the plaza and the main beach beyond, these older, sizable rooms have air-con and there's a small pool, but while the price is fair and the location ideal, the property could use some love. Downstairs rooms will grab the wi-fi but are dark and suffer from traffic noise.

Posada Citlali   GUESTHOUSE $

(☎ 755-554-20-43; xochramirez@live.com.mx; Guerrero 4; s/d M$400/650; 🅿 ❄ 🛜) Providing decent budget digs in the town center, this older, pleasant family-owned posada (inn) has simple, cozy and clean tiled rooms with

Zihuatanejo

Map labels:

(1.5km)

Morelos

Heroico Colegio Militar

19

Calle La Laya

21

Morelos

28

Juárez

Local Buses
to Ixtapa

Palmas

Palapas

Altamirano

La Correa Route
Bus Stop

10

Mangos

29

Cocos

Juárez

Nava

Cuauhtémoc

Colectivos
to Airport &
Playa Larga

Terminal for
Petatlán &
La Unión

González

Galeana

33

Ejido

5 de Mayo

Guerrero

Álvarez

26

Local Buses to
Playa La Ropa

Bravo

35

López Mateos

32

39

36

30

Plaza
Olof
Palme

20

Ramírez

34

16

Naval
Base

Ascencio

27

4

37

Álvarez

11

1

3

Paseo del Pescador

38

Marina

6

25

5

Bahía de Zihuatanejo

Hostel
Rincón
del Viajero
(400m)

Muelle Municipal (Pier)

Contramar Andador

Picante
(300m);
Hotel Villas
El Morro
(350m)

Playa El
Almacen

---

queen beds and rockers on a shared patio. There's a lush garden rising through the courtyard and it's steps from the sea. It can be loud on weekends with bar noise. Air-con costs an extra M$50.

Bungalows Vepao　　　　BUNGALOW $$
(☏ 755-554-36-19; www.vepao.com; Playa La Ropa; d M$1400-2000; P ⊖ ❄ 🌐 ❄; 🚌 Playa La Ropa) Quite a bargain for the super location right on Playa La Ropa (p552), these cute 'bungalows' offer plenty of space, an inviting pool and all

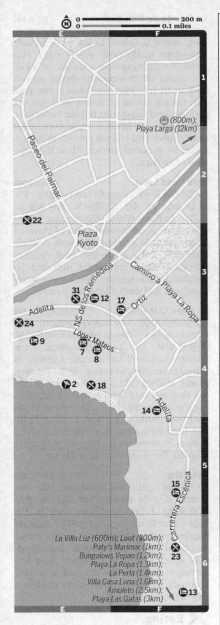

CENTRAL PACIFIC COAST ZIHUATANEJO

the beach time you can handle. There's a variety of accommodations – those with kitchen and/or sea view cost a little more.

Arena Suites APARTMENT **$$**
(☏ 755-554-40-87; www.arenasuites.com.mx; López Mateos s/n; apt US$70-95, ste US$115-180;

🅿︎⊖⊛🛜) Well kept and spacious, with unbeatable views and beach access, these bungalows are simple but likable. Most have thatched terraces with hammocks, room safes and kitchens. There's also a suite with a Jacuzzi and a terrace overlooking Playa Madera (p552). Steps descend directly to the sand, where the hotel has a bar-beach club.

Bungalows La Madera
BUNGALOW $$

(☑ 755-554-39-20; www.bungalowslamadera.com; López Mateos 25; r with kitchenette US$65-130; ⊜✸🛜❄) This sprawling place straddles the hillside between Playa Madera (p552) and downtown. The nicest ocean-facing bungalows have two rooms; many units have sea-view terraces and kitchens. In the center there's a pool and patio area. The annex across the street offers several more spacious units with spectacular balconies/living rooms with hammocks and great views over Zihua. No service at night.

★ La Villa Luz
BOUTIQUE HOTEL $$$

(☑ 755-112-18-34; www.lavillaluz.com; Carretera Escénica 97; ste incl breakfast US$170-230; P⊜✸🛜❄; 🏖 Playa La Ropa) This genuinely romantic retreat climbs the hill just above Playa La Ropa (p552; warning: plenty of stairs). The seven suites are all sweet and characterful with artful use of inlaid wood, adobe brick and pebble mosaics; we particularly loved Suite Mar, with glorious sea vistas from the comfortable bed. A couple of them are duplexes, one with a kitchen.

★ Aura del Mar
HOTEL $$$

(☑ 755-554-21-42; www.hotelauradelmar.com; López Mateos s/n; d incl breakfast from US$189; P⊜✸@🛜❄) A cliff-hugging red adobe complex perched above Playa Madera (p552), Aura del Mar is perfect for a romantic getaway. The spacious rooms and grounds are decorated with traditional Mexican furnishings, tiles and handicrafts. All have private balconies with exquisite ocean views and a hammock; some have a Jacuzzi on the balcony. Steep stairs lead to the beach and an excellent restaurant (p558).

Villas Naomi
HOTEL $$$

(La Casa del Árbol; ☑ 755-544-73-03; www.villasnaomi.com; Adelita 114; r US$85, ste with kitchenette US$90-110; ⊜✸🛜❄) Dominated by a lovely old ceiba tree, Villas Naomi is a haven near Playa Madera (p552). Run with quiet dignity, its little whitewashed abodes have built-in shelving and showers, bamboo towel racks, plush linens, a flat-screen TV and tiled floors inlaid with river rock. With only eight units, it's a peaceful spot to relax around the pool.

La Quinta de Don Andres
HOTEL $$$

(☑ 755-554-37-94; www.laquintadedonandres.com; Adelita 11, Colonia La Madera; r without/with kitchen US$130/140; P⊜✸🛜❄) This burnt-orange fauxdobe complex of modern rooms offers terracotta floors, air-con and small balconies overlooking the pool and the sea below. All rooms are large and spotless, and those with full sea views have kitchenettes. It's family friendly, with lots of public space and is small enough to feature excellent personal service. More than the sum of its parts.

Villa Casa Luna
VILLA $$$

(☑ 755-554-27-43; www.villa-casa-luna.com; Playa La Ropa s/n; d/q US$375/475; P⊜✸🛜❄; 🏖 Playa La Ropa) Within this verdant walled compound at the southern end of Playa La Ropa (p552) is a grand villa with multiple bedrooms and a gorgeously tiled designer kitchen. It sleeps up to eight, including the delightful studio cottage. There's a nice swimming pool and garden setting is tranquil.

La Casa Que Canta
BOUTIQUE HOTEL $$$

(☑ 755-555-70-30; www.lacasaquecanta.com; Carretera Escénica s/n, Playa La Ropa; ste from US$548; P⊜✸🛜❄) The 'house that sings' is the epitome of luxury and customer service in Zihuatanejo. Perched atop cliffs between Playas Madera (p552) and La Ropa (p552), the thatched-roof hotel features bold, striking use of interior space and shelters exquisitely decorated rooms and a raft of facilities. But perhaps the most valuable amenity is silence: there are no TVs and kids aren't allowed. There are separate villas too.

Amuleto
BOUTIQUE HOTEL $$$

(☑ 755-544-62-22; www.amuleto.net; Carretera Escénica 9; r incl breakfast from US$476; P✸@🛜❄) A boutique hotel high in the hills above Playa La Ropa (p552), Amuleto dazzles guests with opulent, earthy rooms decorated in stone, ceramic and wood, plus suites with private plunge pools and scrumptious views. The attached restaurant is equally fabulous. A three-night minimum stay is required. No kids.

✘ Eating

Guerrero state is famous for green *pozole*, a hearty meat-and-hominy stew that's found on most menus in town (especially on Thursdays). *Tiritas* (raw fish slivers marinated with red onion, lemon or lime and chili peppers) are Zihua's specialty.

✖ Central Zihuatanejo

Seafood here is fresh and delicious. Many popular (if touristy) fish restaurants line Paseo del Pescador, parallel to Playa Municipal (p552); however, the quality-to-price ratio tends to improve as you move inland. A hearty and inexpensive breakfast or lunch is available in the **Mercado Municipal** (☑755-544-77-82; Mangos s/n; meals M$30-60; ⊗8am-6pm), which has several eating zones.

★ Fonda Doña Licha   MEXICAN $
(☑cell 755-1153114; felisa.solis@hotmail.com; Cocos 8; mains M$59-115; ⊗8am-6pm) This place near the mercado is renowned for its downhome Mexican cooking, casual atmosphere and excellent prices. There are always several *comidas corridas* (prix-fixe menus) to choose from; all come with rice, beans and handmade tortillas. Breakfasts are huge and a special Sunday menu includes *tamales de elote* (sweet corn *tamales*).

Carmelitas   BREAKFAST $
(☑755-554-38-85; www.facebook.com/holacarmel itascafe; Av Heróico Colegio Militar s/n; mains M$65-130; ⊗8am-4:30pm Mon-Sat, to 3pm Sun; 🅿🛜) Zihua's premier breakfast spot, this open-air cafe slings a tantalizing array of Guerrero comfort food including *huevos a la pasilla* (fried eggs in tortilla bowls bathed with guajillo chili sauce and accompanied by fried plantain) with handmade tortillas on the side. Order from the menu or the daily blackboard specials, such as *pozole* (hominy stew). Cash only.

Panadería El Buen Gusto   BAKERY $
(Guerrero 11; pastries from M$5; ⊗8:30am-10pm Mon-Sat) A good traditional Mexican bakery in the heart of downtown Zihua.

★ Marisquería Yolanda   SEAFOOD $$
(☑cell 755-1282368; cnr Morelos & Cuauhtémoc; mains M$80-200; ⊗10am-8pm) Staff here open oysters with a hammer, and dice and drown ceviche on the street side, where boleros belly up to the sidewalk bar and sing about their unbridled, unrequited romance to one too many beers. And when the balladeers mosey along, the jukebox takes over. It's known as the *Catedral del Marisco* (cathedral of seafood) for a reason.

El Gabo   SEAFOOD $$
(☑755-103-41-12; mariscoselgago@hotmail.com; Morelos 55; mains M$120-195; ⊗11am-8:30pm; 🛜) A shady hideaway tucked off a major thoroughfare isn't necessarily what you'd associate with a prime seafood joint, but this open-sided place with leather saddle barstools and tables scattered beneath a vaulted, tiled roof delivers the goods. A menu of coconut shrimp, fresh fish done up 10 ways, oysters, sashimi, seafood cocktails and ceviche has a loyal following.

Chez Leo   SEAFOOD $$
(☑cell 755-1136038; www.facebook.com/chezleo restaurant; cnr Cuauhtémoc & Ascencio; mains M$120-170; ⊗2-11pm Mon-Sat; 🛜) Though it doesn't look much from outside, the chef here takes real pride in preparing delicious seafood dishes, such as great fish tartare, seared tuna and whatever's fresh that day. There are some surprising flavors and simple but handsome presentation; it's all rather good value.

La Sirena Gorda   SEAFOOD $$
(☑755-554-26-87; Paseo del Pescador 90; mains M$90-200; ⊗8:30am-10:30pm) Close to the pier, this place (The Fat Mermaid) is a casual and popular open-air restaurant that's good for garlic shrimp, curried tuna and an intriguing range of fish tacos. Fresh fish fillets are done in a variety of ways, all delicious, and this is a top spot to try spicy *tiritas* (citrus-cooked fish strips).

Restaurantes Mexicanos Any   MEXICAN $$
(☑755-554-73-73; www.restaurantesmexicanosany. com.mx; Ejido 18; mains M$60-200; ⊗8am-11pm; 🛜) This friendly place serves traditional Mexican cuisine under its big *palapa* roof. The decor is cheerfully and colorfully folkloric, while food highlights include Guerrero-style green *pozole* (hominy stew), to-die-for *tamales* and sweet, corn-based hot drinks known as *atoles*.

Mariscos Chendo's   SEAFOOD $$
(☑755-104-89-78; chendos.zihuatanejo.2017@ gmail.com; Ascencio 15; mains M$110-160; ⊗1-9pm Thu-Tue) This sweet little family-run place is all about straightforward seafood dishes and reasonably priced beer. Specialties include garlic shrimp, coconut shrimp and award-winning *tiritas* (citrus-cured fish strips).

✖ Around the Bay

Pricey restaurants with panoramic views dominate the hilltops, while casual candlelit beachside eateries are the rule on Playa La Ropa (p552). More affordable fare can be found in the 'gringo gastronomic ghetto' along Adelita, just inland from Playa Madera (p552); half of the restaurants here shut down from May to November.

Patio Mexica
BREAKFAST $

(☑ cell 755-1167211; www.patiomexica.com; Adelita 32, Colonia La Madera; mains M$40-80; ☺9am-2pm Mon-Sat Sep-Apr; ☎) Squash-blossom omelette and other Mexican delicacies get your day off to a sunny start at this informal breakfast place run by Mónica Durán Pérez of the Patio Mexica Cooking School (p553).

Restaurant El Arrayan
GRILL $$

(☑ 755-112-11-93; www.facebook.com/restaurate elarrayan; Adelita 41, Colonia La Madera; ☺8:30am-9pm Thu-Sat Jun-Oct, 8:30am-9pm Mon-Sat Nov-May; ☎) From his curbside barbecue, grill master Mauricio Cancino cooks up fresh fish (usually tuna or mahimahi with grilled veggies) to perfection, then he finishes it off with a brush of delightful guajillo chili and garlic sauce. The menu includes other items such as grilled steak, but the catch of the day is the best bet.

Las Adelitas
MEXICAN $$

(☑ cell 755-5593517; Adelita 6; breakfast M$40-60, lunch & dinner M$60-200; ☺8am-4pm Mon-Sat May-Oct, to 10pm Nov-Apr; ☎) This adorable breakfast and lunch cafe is on a little plaza with outdoor seating. It has a loyal local following thanks to its *chilaquiles* (tortilla strips in salsa) and omelettes in the morning and *tortas* (sandwiches), *chiles rellenos* (stuffed chilies) and fried and grilled fish at lunch. In gringo season it opens for great-value dinners too.

Paty's Marimar
MEXICAN $$

(☑ 755-544-22-13; www.patys-marymar.com; Playa La Ropa; mains M$100-260; ☺7am-10pm; ☎; 🚌 Playa La Ropa) On the sand at the main access to Playa La Ropa (p552), this place serves grilled octopus, snapper, and shrimp sautéed in tequila, plus an array of tasty soups, salads, omelettes and big juices. Enjoy the fare under thatched and linen umbrellas in the sand with rattan lanterns dangling from the palms.

Rufo's Grill
PARRILLA $$

(☑ 755-120-54-94; www.facebook.com/rufosgrill; Adelita 32A, Colonia La Madera; mains M$100-220; ☺5-11pm Mon-Sat Sep-May; ☎) Tucked onto a concrete patio under a bamboo roof fringed with Christmas lights, this unpretentious corner joint is popular among long-term gringos thanks to its fabulous barbecued

meat and shrimp marinated in herbs and olive oil. Tasty grilled vegetables – red peppers, carrots, zucchini, eggplant and mushrooms – accompany every main course.

Bistro del Mar
FUSION $$$

(☑ 755-554-83-33; www.bistrodelmar.com; López Mateos s/n, Playa La Madera; mains M$190-290; ☺8am-10:30pm; ☎) With its landmark sail roof over candlelit tables and its fusion of Latin, European and Asian flavors, this beachside bistro is a romantic treat. Delicious fish flavors are the mainstay, with standouts mahimahi or tuna sashimi (or whatever is the fish of the day) done in outstandingly inventive ways. The house wines are a cut above average too.

La Gula
FUSION $$$

(☑ 755-554-83-96; www.restaurantelagula.com; Adelita 8; mains M$160-260; ☺5-10pm Mon-Sat Nov-Apr; ☎) This place wins points for its beautifully presented creative cuisine. Dishes bear names such as *manjar mestizo* (eggplant raviolis filled with corn truffle and squash flower) and *negrito de zihua* (seared tuna seasoned with 10 spices). The atmosphere on a breezy upstairs terrace is most pleasant.

Il Mare
ITALIAN, SEAFOOD $$$

(☑ 755-554-90-67; www.ilmareristorante.com; Carretera Escénica 105; mains M$155-385; ☺noon-11pm Mon-Sat, 4-11pm Sun, closed Tue May-Oct; ☎) A romantic Italian restaurant with a fabulous bird's-eye view of the bay, Il Mare is well regarded for its Mediterranean pasta and seafood specialties, including linguini with fresh clams in a garlic-wine sauce. Pair your dish with wine from Spain, Italy, France or Argentina.

La Perla
SEAFOOD $$$

(☑ 755-554-27-00; www.laperlarestaurant.net; Playa La Ropa; mains M$120-240; ☺10am-10pm; ☎; 🚌 Playa La Ropa) Despite the seasonal beer-bucket NFL promos, this is a refined pavilion in dark wood right on Playa La Ropa (p552). Best dishes include grilled octopus, tuna steaks seared as rare as you like, whole grilled fish, and tacos piled with shrimp, lobster and chicken. Eat here and hang on to the beach lounges for as long as you desire.

Drinking & Nightlife

Downtown has a handful of bars offering two-for-one beers and margaritas, and you can find some live music and booty-shaking bass on weekends, but in its earthy soul, Zihuatanejo is all about the mellow.

Malagua
BAR

(☑ 755-554-42-91; www.facebook.com/malagua-1376149592406803; Paseo del Pescador 20; ⊙ 7pm-2am Wed-Sun; ⧈) A friendly neighborhood watering hole specializing in imported and Mexican craft beers. It's a nice spot to chat it up with locals and the fine music selection adds a touch of character to the fancooled bar.

Andy's Bar
BAR

(☑ cell 755-5593349; Guerrero 6; ⊙ 7pm-2am Thu-Tue) Perhaps set up by Andy Dufresne himself (of *Shawshank Redemption* fame), this two-room bar has a dance floor, screens live sporting events and does karaoke sessions. It gets packed on weekends and the lack of outdoor seating means it can get steamy in the rear room.

Temptation
CLUB

(☑ cell 755-1049998; cnr Bravo & Guerrero; ⊙ 9pm-6am Thu-Sun; ⧈) This is built like a cruise-ship disco with a raised lit dance floor, handsome center bar, the obligatory disco ball, and red vinyl booths and seats on the main floor and the mezzanine above. DJs spin *cumbia* (dance music originating from Colombia), *merengue* (a ballroom dance of Dominican origin), salsa, electronica and reggae.

☆ Entertainment

★ Loot
LIVE MUSIC

(☑ 755-544-60-38; www.loot.mx; Playa La Ropa 55; ⊙ 8am-11pm Mon-Sat; ⊟ Playa La Ropa) Hipster central Loot does a little bit of everything, including brunch in its downstairs cafe, art exhibits upstairs, and dinner and drinks on its open-air rooftop bar at night. It also happens to host some of the best fiestas in town, with live events such as dance parties, concerts and arts festivals.

🔒 Shopping

Zihua offers abundant Mexican handicrafts, including ceramics, clothing, leather work, Taxco silver, woodcarvings and masks from around the state of Guerrero. Most shops also open Sundays in high season (December to March).

Café Caracol
FOOD & DRINKS

(☑ cell 755-5574219; www.cafecaracol.com.mx; Álvarez 15; ⊙ 8am-9pm) This shop with four branches sells delicious organic coffee from Guerrero state, as well as vanilla and honey.

El Embarcadero
CLOTHING

(☑ 755-554-23-73; nataliakrebs@yahoo.com.mx; Álvarez 21A; ⊙ 10am-8pm Mon-Sat) Embroidery, textiles and handwoven clothing from Guerrero, Oaxaca, Michoacán and other neighboring states.

Alberto's
JEWELRY

(☑ 755-554-21-61; albertos@albertos.com.mx; Cuauhtémoc 15; ⊙ 9am-8pm Mon-Sat) A few shops along Cuauhtémoc sell silver from Taxco, a town famous for its quality craftwork. This jeweler has some of the finest and most original pieces.

El Jumil
ARTS & CRAFTS

(☑ 755-554-61-91; Paseo del Pescador 9; ⊙ 10am-8pm Mon-Sat, plus Sun Dec-Apr) This shop specializes in masks – a well-known traditional handicraft of Guerrero state.

Mercado de Artesanías
MARKET

(5 de Mayo s/n; ⊙ 9am-8pm) Has many stalls selling clothes, bags, crafts and knickknacks.

ℹ Information

Hospital General (☑ 755-554-36-50; cnr Morelos & Mar Egeo; ⊙ 24hr) Halfway to the bus terminal.

Post Office (☑ 755-554-21-92; www.correosdemexico.com.mx; Carteros s/n; ⊙ 8am-4:30pm Mon-Fri, 9am-1pm Sat) Beside the big blue-and-yellow Coppel department store.

Tourist Office (☑ 755-555-07-00, ext 224; www.ixtapa-zihuatanejo.com; Paseo del Pescador s/n, Muelle Municipal; ⊙ 8am-4pm) This convenient office in the Terminal Marítima at the foot of Zihua's pier stocks brochures and maps even when unstaffed.

ℹ Getting There & Away

AIR

The **Ixtapa/Zihuatanejo international airport** (ZIH; ☑ 755-554-20-70; www.oma.aero/en/airports/zihuatanejo; Hwy 200 s/n) is 12km southeast of Zihuatanejo, several kilometers off Hwy 200 heading toward Acapulco. There are direct flights from several US cities and seasonal service to Canadian destinations.

The following destinations in Mexico are serviced by these airlines:
➡ Mexico City – Aeromar, Aeroméxico, Interjet, VivaAerobús, Volaris
➡ Monterrey – Magnicharters
➡ Querétaro – TAR

BUS

Both long-distance bus terminals are on Hwy 200 (aka Paseo de Zihuatanejo) about 2km northeast of the town center (toward the airport). The main terminal, also known as Central de Autobuses or **Estrella Blanca** (Central de Autobuses; ☑ 800-507-55-00; www. estrellablanca.com.mx; Paseo de Zihuatanejo Oriente 421; ☐ La Correa), is adjacent to the smaller **Estrella de Oro** (☑ 755-554-21-75; www. estrelladeoro.com.mx; Paseo de Zihuatanejo s/n; ☐ La Correa) terminal (EDO). Buses to La Unión and Petatlán (for Troncones and Barra de Potosí respectively) leave frequently from a small **terminal** (Las Palmas s/n) one block south of the municipal market (p557).

CAR & MOTORCYCLE

There are several car rental companies at the airport. Daily rentals including liability insurance start at about M$600.

Alamo (☑ 755-553-71-47; www.alamo.com.mx/ en; ⊙ 9am-7pm Mon-Sat)

Europcar (☑ 755-553-71-58; www.europcar. com.mx; ⊙ 9am-6pm)

Hertz (☑ 755-553-73-10; https://hertzmexico. com; ⊙ 9am-6pm Mon-Thu & Sat, to 9pm Fri & Sun)

⊙ Getting Around

TO/FROM THE AIRPORT

The cheapest way to the airport (p559) is via public 'Aeropuerto' **colectivos** (Juárez s/n; M$14; ⊙ 6:30am-8pm) departing from Juárez near González between 6:30am and 8pm and making many stops before dropping you just outside the airport gate. *Colectivo* taxis are a more direct and convenient option for incoming passengers, whisking you from the arrivals area to Ixtapa or Zihua for M$135 per person. Private taxis from the airport into town cost M$400 to M$460; they're M$180 to M$250 from Zihuatanejo for the return journey.

BUS & COLECTIVO

To reach downtown Zihua or Ixtapa from Zihua's long-distance bus terminals, cross Hwy 200 using the pedestrian overpass directly opposite the main bus terminal. Buses for downtown Zihua and Ixtapa stop just west of the bridge.

From downtown Zihua to the bus terminals, catch **La Correa** (cnr Nava & Juárez; M$8; ⊙ 6am-10pm) route buses (M$8, 10 minutes), which leave regularly from the corner of Nava and Juárez between 6am and 10pm. To reach Ixtapa from Zihuatanejo Centro, take a **bus** (Morelos s/n; M$12; ⊙ 6am-10pm) (15 minutes) from the corner of Morelos and Juárez.

Playa La Ropa (Juárez s/n; M$12; ⊙ 7am-6pm) buses go south on Juárez and out to Playa La Ropa (p552) every half-hour from 7am to 6pm (M$12).

'Coacoyul' colectivos heading toward Playa Larga and to the airport (p559) depart from Juárez, near the corner of González, every 15 minutes from 6:30am to 8pm (M$14, 15 minutes).

TAXI

Cabs are plentiful in Zihuatanejo. Fares from a **taxi stand** (☑ 755-554-33-11; cnr Juárez & González; ⊙ 24hr) in central Zihua cost M$75 to Ixtapa, M$45 to M$70 to **Playa La Ropa** (p552), M$90 to **Playa Larga** (☐ Coacoyul), M$180 to M$250 to the **airport** (p559), and M$30 to the bus terminals. Rates run higher for air-conditioned cabs.

Barra de Potosí

☑ 755 / POP 396

The small fishing village of Barra de Potosí is about 26km southeast of Zihuatanejo. It's located at the far tip of Playa Larga's seemingly endless palm-fringed, sandy-white beach, and at the mouth of the brackish **Laguna de Potosí**, a saltwater lagoon about 6.5km long and home to hundreds of species of birds, including herons, kingfishers, cormorants and pelicans. The village is thankfully free of any resort hotels and makes for a marvelous wind-down stay in a friendly Mexican community.

⊙ Sights

El Refugio de Potosí   WILDLIFE RESERVE
(☑ cell 755-5572840; www.elrefugiodepotosi. org; Colonia Playa Blanca s/n) ✏ This nature center rehabilitates injured wildlife, breeds

BUSES FROM ZIHUATANEJO

DESTINATION	FARE (M$)	DURATION (HR)	FREQUENCY (DAILY)
Acapulco	195-248	4-5	9 EDO
Lázaro Cárdenas	74-118	1½-2	frequent EDO
Manzanillo	695	9	8pm main
Mexico City	723-812	8-10	4 EDO, 7 main
Morelia	570-585	5-6	4 main (nightly)
Puerto Vallarta	989-1069	14-14½	2 main (nightly)

butterflies and parrots, and contributes to environmental education in the area. The grounds are home to macaws, iguanas and an impressive 18m sperm whale skeleton exhibit. Those interested in visiting may make arrangements by contacting the center via email. It's just inland from the beachfront around 3.5km north of town.

Tours

Nearly every *enramada* (thatch-covered, open-air restaurant) in the pueblo – all of them fishing-family owned – offers 90-minute boat tours of the lagoon, where you can glimpse crocodiles for the standard M$300 price. **Paradise Bird Tours** (Eco Tours Cheli's Oregón; cell 755-1306829; www.facebook. com/araceli.oregonsalas; Barra de Potosí-Achotes s/n; birding M$350, snorkeling M$2000, fishing M$4500), based at Restaurante Rosita, is a good choice; its snorkeling trips include a buzz out to the impressive **Morros de Potosí**, a cluster of massive guano-covered rocks about 20 minutes offshore. Boats circle the Morros, affording views of the many seabirds that nest out there, before heading to nearby **Playa Manzanillo**, where the snorkeling is sublime.

Sleeping & Eating

★Casa del Encanto
B&B $$

(cell 755-1246122; www.lacasadelencanto.com; Rodríguez s/n; d incl breakfast US$70-100;) For bohemian charm and an intimate perspective on the community, nothing beats this magical space of brilliantly colored open-air rooms, hammocks, fountains and candlelit stairways. Owner Laura, a great resource for getting to know the town, has spent years organizing international volunteers to work with neighborhood children. The B&B is on a residential street about 300m inland from the beach. Rates are flexible off-season with good deals for longer stays. Adobe oven-baked pizzas with locally sourced ingredients might be on the menu in high season by the time you visit.

La Condesa
SEAFOOD $$

(cell 755-1203128; Barra de Potosí-Achotes s/n; mains M$80-140; 9am-6pm) Northernmost of the beachfront *enramadas*, this is one of the best. Try its *pescado a la talla* (grilled fish) or *tiritas* (raw fish slivers marinated with red onion, lemon or lime and chili peppers), both local specialties, or munch on some tasty *abulón* (abalone) if it's in season.

Getting There & Away

By car from Zihuatanejo, drive southeast on Hwy 200 toward Acapulco, turn off at Los Achotes and drive another 9km to Barra de Potosí.

By public transportation, catch a Petatlán-bound bus from outside Zihua's main terminals, or from the terminal near Zihua's market. Tell the driver to let you off at the Barra de Potosí *crucero* (turnoff; M$19, 30 minutes), where you can catch a *camioneta* (pickup truck; M$15, 20 minutes) the rest of the way.

Colectivos also run directly from the Ixtapa/Zihuatanejo airport (p559) to Barra de Potosí (M$14, 30 minutes).

Soledad de Maciel

758 / POP 385

Known locally as 'La Chole,' the hamlet of Soledad de Maciel sits atop the largest, most important archaeological site in Guerrero state. Since excavations began in earnest in 2007, archaeologists have discovered a plaza, a ball court and three pyramids – one crowned by five temples – all left behind by pre-Hispanic cultures including Tepoztecos, Cuitlatecos and Tomiles. A museum houses three rooms full of artifacts and Spanish-language displays.

Sights

Museo de Sitio Xihuacan
MUSEUM

(cell 758-1043188; www.inah.gob.mx/es/red-de -museos/309-museo-de-sitio-de-la-zona-arqueo logica-de-soledad-maciel-o-museo-de-sitio-xihua can; turnoff Hwy 200 Km 214; suggested donation M$10, guided tour M$100; 8am-4pm Tue-Sun) Near the archaeological site of Soledad de Maciel, a museum houses three rooms full of Spanish-language displays, which place the local archaeological finds in a broader historical context. A recent find on display is a stone carved with a glyph of the name of the town in the late pre-Hispanic era: Xihuacan. Local guide Adán Velez found many of the artifacts on display in the museum.

Getting There & Away

Soledad de Maciel is 33km southeast of Zihuatanejo off Hwy 200. From the well-marked turnoff near Km 214, a road leads 4km coastward to the **museum**, then continues another kilometer to the archaeological site and village.

Any bus heading south to Petatlán or Acapulco will get you here; ask to be dropped at the 'La Chole' intersection, where you can hop on a *camioneta* (pickup truck; M$10) into town.

Pie de la Cuesta

 744 / POP 773

Just 10km from Acapulco is the tranquil seaside suburb of Pie de la Cuesta, a rustic beach town occupied by some terrific guesthouses and seafood restaurants. But it's the odd combination of dramatic sunset views from the long beach and bloody sunrises over the lagoon that have made Pie de la Cuesta famous, for the town sits on a narrow strip of land bordered by the Pacific Ocean and the Laguna de Coyuca (where part of *Rambo: First Blood Part II* was filmed). The large freshwater lagoon contains several islands including **Isla Pájaros**, a bird sanctuary.

Pie de la Cuesta is much quieter, safer, cheaper and closer to nature than Acapulco, but still close enough for those who want to enjoy the city's attractions and nightlife.

🏃 Activities

The rugged, steep shore break is better for bodyboarders, but big December swells get over 3m and attract surfers. The riptide and strong waves make it sometimes dangerous for swimmers.

Horseback riding on the beach costs about M$200 per hour. Book through your hotel or directly from galloping gauchos.

Water Sports

Waterskiing and wakeboarding on the lagoon are both popular pastimes; there are several waterskiing clubs along the main road, all charging around M$900 to M$1000 per hour, including Club de Ski Cadena.

Several establishments offer boat trips on the lagoon and eager captains await your business along the main road and down by the boat launches at the lagoon's southeast corner.

Club de Ski Cadena   WATER SPORTS

(☎ cell 744-1598503; clubdeskicadena@gmail. com; Av Fuerza Aérea Mexicana s/n; tours per hour M$900) Does waterskiing and wakeboarding outings as well as a boat tour of the lagoon, which stops at two islands. The English-speaking owner Fernando knows a lot about the area's bird species and he also rents out decent budget rooms (M$600 to M$800) with sundecks right on the lagoon. Cadena is a much friendlier operation than the competition next door.

🛏 Sleeping

Baxar   BOUTIQUE HOTEL $$

(☎ 744-460-25-02; www.baxar.com.mx; Av Aérea Mexicana 356; r M$1533, ste M$2624-3060, all incl breakfast; P 🅿 ❄ 🛜 🌊) Trimmed in pink and exuding barefoot style, this is a popular and likable weekend getaway. Its cute rooms include sunken sitting areas, tastefully dangling rattan lampshades, mosquito nets and other sweet little details. Rates include use of kayaks, and paddleboards are available for rent.

Quinta Erika   B&B $$

(☎ 744-444-41-31; www.quintaerika.com; Carretera Barra de Coyuca Km 8.5; d/bungalows incl breakfast US$55/120; P 🅿 🛜 🌊; 🚌 Playa Luces) A hidden, jungle-like retreat located 8km west of the highway junction. Six colorful rooms and one bungalow are tastefully decorated with handmade furniture and traditional handicrafts. It sits on two hectares of lagoonside property, lovingly landscaped with palm and tropical fruit trees. Other perks include kayaks, a whimsically decorated pool, a dock boasting lagoon views, and an upstairs lounge. It's about a kilometer beyond the final bus stop in Playa Luces.

Hacienda Vayma
Beach Club   HOTEL $$

(☎ 744-460-28-82; www.vayma.com.mx; Av Fuerza Aérea Mexicana 378; r M$1102-1218, ste M$2320; P 🅿 ❄ 🛜 🌊) This relaxing ranch-style hotel is handsome in white and dark wood. It has a patch of beach with private *cabañas* (cabins) and double-width lounge chairs, a big pool with swim-up bar and a choice of room types, from rustic beach-town digs to suites with air-con and Jacuzzi. Nonguests may visit the bar here, which is open until 11pm on weekend nights.

A&V Hotel Boutique   BOUTIQUE HOTEL $$$

(☎ 744-444-43-29; www.avhotelboutique.com; Av Fuerza Aérea Mexicana Km 6.2, Colonia Luces en el Mar; r M$1600-2400; ❄ 🛜 🌊; 🚌 Playa Luces) Each of the ultra-comfortable 11 rooms in this hotel incorporates earthy design elements, such as palm-leaf wall paneling, rattan lampshades and pine-wood flooring. Most come with private balconies overlooking a free-form pool and on-site restaurant, which is worth visiting even if you're not staying at the hotel.

Eating

A long string of beachside eateries means that finding a cold beer and shrimp cocktail presents zero difficulty.

Chepina
SEAFOOD $$

(📱744-460-25-02; www.baxar.com.mx; Av Fuerza Aérea Mexicana 356; mains M$80-200; ⊙8am-10pm; 🛜) This bistro on the beach, coated in hot pink, serves standards such as ceviche, *cócteles* (cocktails) and fish tacos; it also folds shrimp with sautéed vegetables into grilled flour *taquitos* (crisp-fried, filled tortilla rolls). All of it is done with flair and flavor. It's in the Baxar hotel.

Mar de Fondo
FUSION $$$

(📱744-444-43-29; www.avhotelboutique.com; Av Fuerza Aérea Mexicana Km 6.2, Colonia Luces en el Mar; mains M$180-240; ⊙9am-8pm Tue-Sun; 🅿; 🚌Playa Luces) Tired of the fish and seafood routine? Hit this restaurant in A&V Hotel Boutique, where you can order handmade pasta and lasagna, regional Oaxacan cuisine and sweet treats including apple strudel. There's also a variety of fish dishes that you won't find elsewhere in town, and the same can be said for the restaurant-bar's cocktails.

ℹ Information

Pie de la Cuesta is strung out along the long main road (known both as Avenida Fuerza Aérea Mexicana and Calzada Pie de la Cuesta) that runs between the lagoon and beach, past an air force base and on to Playa Luces.

ℹ Getting There & Away

From Acapulco, catch a 'Pie de la Cuesta' bus (p574) on Avenida Costera across the street from the post office. Buses depart every 15 minutes from 6am until 9pm; the trip costs M$8 and takes 30 to 90 minutes, depending on traffic – on a bad day, it can be total gridlock.

Buses marked 'Pie de la Cuesta–San Isidro' or 'Pie de la Cuesta–Pedregoso' stop at the town's arched entryway on Hwy 200, leaving you with a short walk into town; more convenient 'Pie de la Cuesta–Playa Luces' buses turn off the main highway and follow Pie de la Cuesta's main street through town to Playa Luces.

A regular taxi from Acapulco costs M$200 to M$400, depending on your negotiating skills.

Acapulco

📱744 / POP 789,971

Acapulco, Mexico's original party town, has a stunning topography of soaring cliffs curling into a series of wide bays and intimate coves, fringed with sandy beaches and backed by jungle-green hills. It was dubbed the 'Pearl of the Pacific' during its heyday as a playground for the rich and famous, including Frank Sinatra, Elvis Presley and Elizabeth Taylor.

Acapulco remains gorgeous, though overdeveloped. The city's reputation has been tarnished by years of violent battles in Mexico's ongoing drug wars. Despite frightening homicide statistics, the violence is largely confined to gang disputes. International tourism has plummeted, but the city remains comparatively safe to visit. It still offers atmosphere and charm, with romantic cliffside restaurants, an impressive 17th-century fort, a world-class botanical garden, cliff divers and the old town's shady *zócalo* (main square). When you tire of the crowds, secluded beaches such as Pie de la Cuesta are a short trip away.

ℹ Orientation

Acapulco follows the 11km shore of the Bahía de Acapulco (Acapulco Bay). Old Acapulco, centered on the cathedral (p565) and adjacent *zócalo* (p565), is the western part of the city; Acapulco Dorado heads east around the bay from Playa Hornos (p567) to Playa Icacos (p567). Acapulco Diamante is a newer luxury resort area southeast of Acapulco proper, near the airport.

Acapulco's principal bayside avenue, Avenida Costera Miguel Alemán – often called 'La Costera' – hugs the shoreline all the way around the bay. Past the naval base, Avenida Costera becomes Carretera Escénica and climbs over the headland toward Diamante and the airport.

◉ Sights

Most of Acapulco's hotels, restaurants, discos and points of interest are along or near Avenida Costera, especially near its midpoint at **La Diana** (Map p570; Av Costera s/n) traffic circle. From Playa Caleta on the Península de las Playas, it curves north toward the *zócalo*, then continues east along the beachfront past Parque Papagayo (p565) – a large, shady park popular with Mexican families – all the way to Playa Icacos (p567) and the naval base at the bay's southeastern edge.

★Clavadistas de la Quebrada
VIEWPOINT

(Map p566; 📱744-483-14-00; cpqaca@prodigy.net.mx; Plazoleta La Quebrada s/n; adult/child M$40/15; ⊙shows 1pm, 7:30pm, 8:30pm, 9:30pm & 10:30pm; 🚌Caleta) Acapulco's most famous

Greater Acapulco

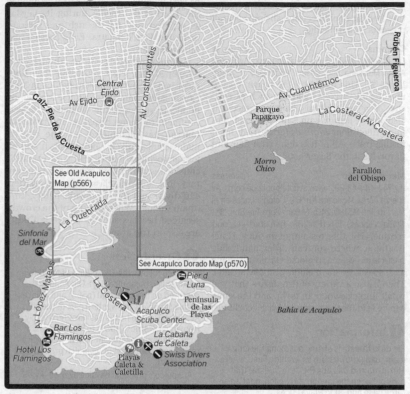

tourist attraction, the cliff divers of La Quebrada have been dazzling audiences since 1934, plunging with fearless finesse from heights of 25m to 35m into the narrow ocean cove below. Expect to see around six divers; the spectacle lasts for about 20 minutes. The last show features divers holding torches. For good road karma, tip the divers on your way out. La Perla restaurant-bar provides a great (but pricey) view of the divers from above.

★ Exekatlkalli
PUBLIC ART

(House of the Winds; Map p566; Inalámbrica 8; Caleta) While the famed Mexican art collector Dolores 'Lola' Olmedo was away on vacation in 1956, a dying Diego Rivera decided to pep up the entrance to the villa of his friend, muse and love object with spectacular serpentine mosaic murals. They are quite an unexpected sight on this quiet hillside street. Plans have long been in the works to convert the house and studio into

a cultural center/museum, but to no avail so far.

La Capilla de la Paz
CHAPEL

(Chapel of Peace; 744-446-54-58; Vientos Cardinales s/n, Alto Las Brisas; 10am-6pm) FREE Perched on a hilltop high above Acapulco is this quiet spot for reflection, an airy '70s A-frame chapel surrounded by lovely gardens and providing stunning ocean views. Despite the giant white cross that can be seen from miles away, it was built as a non-denominational chapel to welcome people of all faiths – the garden's sculpture of clasped hands perhaps better captures that spirit. Access is via a gated compound: you may have to leave ID at the gate.

Fuerte de San Diego
FORTRESS

(Map p570; 744-482-38-28; www.facebook.com/museoohistoricodeacapulcofuertedesandiego; Hornitos s/n) FREE This beautifully restored pentagonal fort was built in 1616 atop a hill east

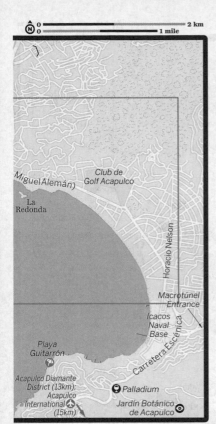

Isla de la Roqueta ISLAND

(☑ 755-410-97-07; www.yatesdeacapulco.com; round-trip boat fare M$50, glass-bottom boat M$90) This island offers a popular (crowded) beach, and snorkeling and diving possibilities. You can rent snorkeling gear, kayaks and more. From Playa Caleta, boats make the eight-minute trip regularly. Alternatively, glass-bottomed boats (by the company Yates Fondo Cristal) make a circuitous trip from here or the *zócalo*, pointing out celebrity dwellings, sea life and the **Virgen de los Mares**, a submerged bronze Virgin statue. The trip takes about 45 minutes, depending on how many times floating vendors approach your boat.

Jardín Botánico de Acapulco GARDENS

(Map p564; ☑ 744-446-52-52; www.acapulcobotanico.org; Av Heróico Colegio Militar s/n, Cumbres de Llano Largo; adult/child M$30/free, free Sun, guided visit per person M$50; ◷ 9am-6pm) Located on the campus of a Jesuit university, these botanical gardens house an impressive collection of flora and fauna. The well-marked footpath climbs from 204m to 411m above sea level through a shaded tropical forest, with plenty of benches to stop and smell the flowers at. It's 1.2km from the main road between Acapulco and Diamante; shared cabs marked 'Base–Cumbres' depart from the Icacos Naval Base and drop you right outside the gardens.

Zócalo PLAZA

(Map p566; cnr Av Costera & Madero) Every night Acapulco's leafy old town *zócalo* comes alive with street performers, mariachis and sidewalk cafes; it also hosts occasional festivals. It's especially popular with multiple generations of Mexican families on Sunday nights. The **Nuestra Señora de la Soledad Cathedral** (Map p566; ☑ 744-483-05-63; www.facebook.com/catedral.soledad; Hidalgo s/n; ◷ 7am-8pm Mon-Sat, 6:30am-9pm Sun) **FREE**, built in 1930, dominates the square and is unusual for its blue-domed, neo-Byzantine architecture.

Sinfonía del Mar VIEWPOINT

(Symphony of the Sea; Map p564; Av López Mateos s/n) The magical Sinfonía del Mar is an outdoor stepped plaza that occasionally hosts concerts, but mainly serves as an amazing place to view sunsets.

Beaches

Acapulco's beaches top the list of must-dos for most visitors. The beaches heading east around the bay from the *zócalo* – **Playa**

of the *zócalo*. Its mission was to protect the Spanish *naos* (galleons) conducting trade between the Philippines and Mexico from marauding Dutch and English buccaneers. The fort was destroyed in a 1776 earthquake and rebuilt. It remains basically unchanged today. The fort is home to the excellent **Museo Histórico de Acapulco** (Map p570; ☑ 744-482-38-28; www.facebook.com/museohistoricodeacapulcofuertedesandiego; Hornitos s/n; M$55; ◷ 9am-6pm Tue-Sun; ℗).

Parque Papagayo PARK

(Map p570; ☑ 744-486-14-14; www.facebook.com/parquepapagayoacapulcoepbs; Morín 1; ◷ 6am-8pm; ℗) **FREE** This large shaded children's park, between Morín and El Cano near Playa Hornitos, is popular with Mexican families. Attractions include a lake with paddleboats, a children's train, a bar-restaurant, an aviary, a small zoo and a petting zoo. The 1.2km circuit trail is a good place for a morning jog.

Old Acapulco

Old Acapulco

◎ Top Sights

◎ Sights

۞ Activities, Courses & Tours

🛏 Sleeping

🍴 Eating

🛍 Shopping

Hornos (Map p570), **Playa Hornitos** (Map p570), **Playa Condesa** (Map p570) and **Playa Icacos** (Map p570) – are the most popular, though the west end of Hornos sometimes smells of fish from the morning catch. The high-rise hotel district begins on Playa Hornitos, on the east side of Parque Papagayo, and sweeps east. City buses constantly ply Avenida Costera, making it easy to get up and down the long arc of beaches.

Playas Caleta and Caletilla (Map p564; 🚇 Caleta) are two small beaches on the south side of Península de las Playas. The calm waters make for safe swimming, but the immensely popular location draws throngs of family vacationers, especially in July and August and during the busy winter holiday season. From the city center along Avenida Costera, buses marked 'Caleta' arrive here. Boats to Isla de la Roqueta depart from a small dock.

Playa La Angosta (Map p566; 🚇 Caleta), a protected cove about 1.5km southwest of the *zócalo*, is reachable by walking from the main plaza; alternatively, a 'Caleta' bus will leave you one block from the beach. Locals visit La Angosta for its *palapa* seafood restaurants.

A scenic drive heading southeast of the city center along the jungle-backed Hwy 200 affords spectacular views of the Acapulco Bay before a turnoff descends to the beaches on **Bahía Puerto Marqués**, where you can get in some waterskiing and swimming on the bay's calm waters. For public transportation, take a frequent Puerto Marqués (p574) bus along Avenida Costera.

About 3km south of Puerto Marqués, rougher waters await at **Playa Revolcadero**, a popular surf spot but somewhat dangerous option for swimming. The long beach has seen a development boom in recent years, but it's still possible to find quiet stretches of sand.

The two beaches closest to Old Acapulco are **Playa Tlacopanocha** (Map p566) – not known as a swimming spot – and **Playa Manzanillo** (Map p566), a small beach where you can take a dip; note that the water quality isn't so great.

🏃 Activities

Acapulco's activities are largely beach-based.

Cruises

Various boats and yachts offer cruises around the bay. Most depart from Playa Tlacopanocha or Playa Manzanillo near the zócalo. Cruises are available day and night. Vessels range from glass-bottomed boats to multilevel craft (with blaring salsa music and open bars) to yachts offering quiet sunset cruises. Make reservations at the marina or through travel agencies, tour kiosks and most hotels. Acapulco has seen a decline in **cruise ship** (Map p570; ☎744-434-17-10; www.apiacapulcoport.com; Av Costera s/n) activity due to security concerns.

Acarey CRUISE
(Map p566; ☎744-100-36-37; www.acarey.com.mx; Av Costera s/n; adult/child under 10yr M$310/free; ⊙cruises 4:30pm & 10:30pm daily, plus 7:30pm Sat) This popular boat cruise is sold by nearly every kiosk and agency in town, plus at the booth by the dock across from the zócalo. All departures have an open bar and live music. The 4:30pm sunset outing gives a decent tour of the bay, while the night cruise is more of a fiesta. Trips last 2½ hours.

Golf

Club de Golf Acapulco GOLF
(Map p570; ☎744-484-07-81; clubgolf@prodigy.net.mx; Av Costera s/n; green fees 9/18 holes M$600/800; ⊙7am-5pm) Just back from the beach, this nine-holer is a simple but central course. Green fees include cart. You can repeat the front nine holes to play 18.

Sportfishing

Sportfishing is very popular, especially during the winter months when you can catch marlin and yellowfin tuna.

Blue Water Sportfishing FISHING
(Map p566; ☎cell 744-4282279; www.acavio.com/aventura.html; Pinzona 163; fishing charters US$250-390) Fun and friendly fishing setup that will pick you up from the pier at the zócalo. Price varies according to boat size.

Water Sports

Just about everything that can be done on or below the water is done in Acapulco. Waterskiing, boating, banana-boating and parasailing are all popular. Outfitters, based in kiosks along the Zona Dorada beaches, charge about M$500 for a five-minute parasailing flight, and M$1500 per boat for for one hour of waterskiing, jet-skiing or wakeboarding. The smaller Playas Caleta and Caletilla (p567) have sailboats, fishing boats, motorboats, pedal boats, canoes and snorkeling gear for rent.

Though Acapulco isn't really a scuba destination, there are some decent dive sites nearby.

The best snorkeling is off small Playa Las Palmitas on Isla de la Roqueta (p565). Unless you pony up for an organized snorkeling trip, you'll need to scramble over rocks to reach it. You can rent gear on the island or on Playas Caleta and Caletilla, which also have some decent spots.

Acapulco Scuba Center
DIVING

(Map p564; ☑744-482-94-74; www.acapulcoscuba. com; Av Costera 215, Club Náutico La Marina Acapulco; 2-tank dive M$1100, snorkeling M$500; ☺8am-4pm Wed-Mon) One of a few diving operators that can take you out on boat dives in the bay. Offers PADI and SSI certification. Snorkeling trips to Isla de la Roqueta (p565) are also available.

Swiss Divers Association
DIVING

(Map p564; ☑744-482-13-57; www.swissdivers. com; Cerro San Martín 325, Hotel Caleta; 2-tank boat dive US$80, snorkeling US$40; ☺9am-5pm Thu-Tue) This experienced setup offers a wide range of dives and PADI courses. Its office, tucked above wave-lashed rocks amid the semi-ruined splendor of the Hotel Caleta, is worth a look in itself. Snorkeling trips also available.

✯✯ Festivals & Events

FAcapulcoestival Francés
CULTURAL

(www.festivalfrances.com; ☺Mar or Apr) The French Festival, usually held in March or April, celebrates French food, cinema, music and literature.

🛏 Sleeping

Acapulco has tens of thousands of hotel rooms. Most of Acapulco's budget hotels are concentrated around the *zócalo* (p565). The original high-rise zone stretches from the eastern end of Parque Papagayo (p565) and curves east around the bay; other luxury strips are southeast of town near the airport.

Hotel Márquez del Sol
HOTEL $

(Map p570; ☑744-484-77-60; hotelmarquezdel sol@hotmail.com; Juan de la Cosa 22; r M$600; ☺❄🛜🏊) This budget hotel is close to the beach but just far enough away from the main road to be peaceful at night. Decor is bland, but rooms are spacious and clean enough, though bathrooms are tight; many

rooms have balconies. The hotel has little charm, but offers value for its location in the heart of the zone.

Hotel Nilo
HOTEL $$

(Map p570; ☑744-484-10-99; www.hotelnilo.mx; Calle 4 No 105; d/q M$1300/1500; 🅿❄🛜🏊) Occupying the same price band as a whole swath of Acapulco hotels, but about 40 years newer than most of them, this likable place a block back from the strip is in the pleasant eastern end of town and amiably run. Rooms are compact but comfy and modern – that includes the bathrooms. There's a pool on the top floor.

Etel Suites
HOTEL $$

(Map p566; ☑744-482-22-40; www.facebook. com/hoteletelsuites; Av Pinzona 92; r M$600-900, apt M$1500; 🅿❄🛜🏊; 🚐Caleta) High above Old Acapulco, with views of both the bay and the Pacific Ocean, this hotel has modest but well-kept rooms in a very quiet part of town. Management is benevolent, and the terraces offer outrageous city vistas. Mid-century modernists will love the apartments' dated furnishings, while families will appreciate the children's play area and accommodating rooms.

Hotel Acapulco Malibu
HOTEL $$

(Map p570; ☑744-484-10-70; www.acapulcomalibu. com; Av Costera 20; r from M$1415; 🅿❄🛜🏊) It's always nice to see a bit of originality, and the octagonal rooms here fit the bill. Compact and rather charming, they sport a small balcony, surround a creeper-draped atrium and make a fine beach base – or you could go for a dip in the pool instead, also an eight-sided job.

Bali-Hai
MOTEL $$

(Map p570; ☑744-485-66-22; www.balihai.com. mx; Av Costera 186; r from M$1071; 🅿❄🛜🏊) This Polynesian-themed motel in the heart of Bahía de Acapulco, across the street from the beach, looks a little downbeat, but has secure parking and long rows of spacious rooms flanking a pair of palm-lined pools. Upgrading to a pricier 'superior' room offers little in return.

Hotel Los Flamingos
HOTEL $$

(Map p564; ☑744-482-06-91; www.hotellosflamin gos.com.mx; Av López Mateos s/n; d/superior d/ junior ste M$714/833/952; 🅿❄🛜🏊) This affordable hotel with a million-dollar view, once owned by Johnny 'Tarzan' Weissmuller,

John Wayne and their pals, is a living, hot-pink memory of Acapulco's heyday. Perched on a cliff 135m above the ocean, this classic boasts one of the finest sunset views in town, with hammocks to enjoy them from, and a popular bar and restaurant.

Images of Hollywood's Golden Age grace the walls. The rooms are modest, if aged, but comfortable enough. It's well worth the upgrade to the 'junior suites,' which are significantly larger, air-conditioned and have a balcony.

Hotel Marzol
HOTEL **$$**

(Map p570; ✆744-484-33-96; www.hotelmarzol acapulco.com; Av Francia 1A; r M$1000; ⊝✱🛜🏊) Tucked down a narrow street leading to the beach and dwarfed by huge high-rises, this more modest construction is a polished if unremarkable three-star choice. Rooms have high-end tiled floors, dark wood furnishings and thin, hard-ish beds. It makes a clean, reliable base.

★ Pier d Luna
B&B **$$$**

(Map p564; ✆744-480-10-18, cell 744-1792072; www.pdluna.wix.com/pier-d-luna; Casa No 2, Gran Vía Tropical 34; r incl breakfast US$119-153; 🅿⊝✱🛜) This tucked-away retreat has a view so good that the enormous lounge and dining room, complete with baby grand, is wholly open-sided: what a marvelous space it is. Five sweet rooms, all with individual designs, enjoy the same outlook; some have balconies to soak it all up. Hospitable hosts make this a delightful personal experience and breakfasts are abundant.

There's a pleasant pool and Jacuzzi upstairs and a great saltwater pool on the bay, to which you can descend via private stairs. Delicious chef-cooked French-Mexican meals are available by arrangement. Pay attention to the directions you'll be sent, as there are no signs. Reserve ahead.

Hotel Elcano
HOTEL **$$$**

(Map p570; ✆744-435-15-00; www.hotelelcano. com.mx; Av Costera 75; d M$1100-1800; 🅿⊝✱ @🛜🏊) Near the center of Acapulco's crescent of beaches, the pleasantly retro Elcano has old-school grace, with art deco tiles in the breezy lobby, a sumptuous pool area and a patch of beachfront. There's a maritime theme accentuated by the white-and-blue paint job. Rooms are bright and most come with private terraces offering commanding ocean views. Low-season discounts are a steal.

Banyan Tree Cabo Marqués
RESORT **$$$**

(✆744-434-01-00; www.banyantree.com; Blvd Cabo Marqués s/n, Punta Diamante; r from US$735; 🅿⊝✱@🛜🏊) Over the ocean on a gated peninsula, 20km south of downtown, this gorgeous resort brings Asia to Acapulco. Sumptuous villas offer complete privacy to enjoy your hammock, deck and pool with vast vistas. Villas are equipped with a stylish range of robes, toiletries and thoughtful extras; in-room dining is available. Golf carts zip you around the charming facilities.

Highlights of the complex include a Thai restaurant, private massage rooms with view and a stunning infinity pool. An army of helpful staff keeps things very slick. For an utterly peaceful resort experience away from the crowds, this is hard to beat.

✖ Eating

Lots of restaurants are dotted along the coastal strip, from Playa Icacos (p567) to the old town, where you'll find many traditional eateries. On Thursdays, *pozole* (hominy stew) is typically served, and restaurants get lively with groups eating this (and other traditional food such as *tamales*) while listening to folkloric music.

El Nopalito
CAFE **$**

(Map p566; La Paz 230; mains M$50-120, set menu M$60; ⊘8am-8pm) This darkish, keep-it-real eatery attracts people for its daily menu, which includes *mole verde* (green chili sauce dish) on Thursdays and Sundays. The set menu lunch includes fruit, juice or coffee and a main such as roast chicken, beef enchilada, *carne asada* (marinated grilled beef) or fried fish, served with *nopales* (cactus paddles) and tortillas. It's one of several cafes and diners strung along the streets surrounding the *zócalo* (p565).

★ Paititi del Mar
SEAFOOD **$$**

(✆744-480-00-31; www.facebook.com/paititi delmar; Zaragoza 6, La Poza; mains M$140-220; ⊘8am-7pm Fri-Wed; 🚌Coloso) Set in a tropical garden under a *palapa,* this inland seafood restaurant prepares dishes that put most of Acapulco's beachside eateries to shame. The *ceviche paraiso* is a flavor explosion of fresh tuna, mango, ginger, strawberry

Acapulco Dorado

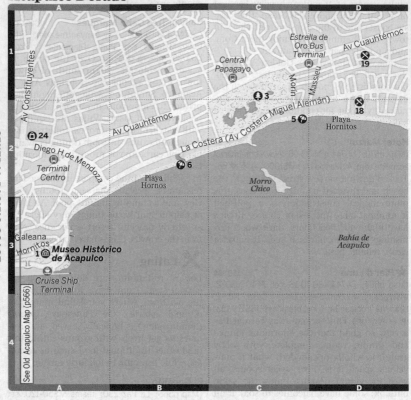

Acapulco Dorado

◉ Top Sights
1 Museo Histórico de Acapulco...............A3

◉ Sights
Fuerte de San Diego ....(see 1)
2 La Diana...E2
3 Parque Papagayo...................................C1
4 Playa Condesa.......................................F2
5 Playa Hornitos.......................................C2
6 Playa Hornos...B2
7 Playa Icacos...G3

◉ Activities, Courses & Tours
8 Club de Golf Acapulco...........................G2
9 Paradise Bungy......................................F2

◉ Sleeping
10 Bali-Hai...E1
11 Hotel Acapulco Malibu.........................G2
12 Hotel Elcano...G3

13 Hotel Márquez del Sol............................E1
14 Hotel Marzol...G3
15 Hotel Nilo..H4

◉ Eating
16 El Cabrito..H3
17 El Gaucho..F2
18 El Jacalito...D2
19 La Casa de Tere.....................................D1
Pipo's..(see 16)

◉ Drinking & Nightlife
20 Demás Factory......................................G2
21 Mezcalina...H3
22 Mojito..E2

◉ Shopping
23 La Europea..H3
24 Mercado Central....................................A2

and habanero; order it with a refreshing cucumber-lime water. For the main course, the grilled or *ajillo*-style octopus draws high praise.

'Coloso' buses, which can be picked up along Avenida Costera anywhere south of the Hwy 200 turnoff, stop about 2km north of the restaurant on Bulevar de las Naciones.

★ La Casa de Tere   MEXICAN $$

(Map p570; ☑ 744-485-77-35; www.facebook.com/lacasadetereacapulco; Martín 1721; mains M$70-225; ☺8am-6pm Tue-Sun; ☜) This homespun gem near the Estrella de Oro bus terminal (p574) is the place to go for Thursday *pozole verde* (green hominy stew). Founded on doña Tere's patio in 1990 using her mother Clarita's traditional recipes, it serves a wide-ranging menu, including the sought-after Sunday special: *barbacoa de*

carnero (slow-cooked lamb). All of it comes with house-made tortillas.

El Jacalito   MEXICAN $$

(Map p570; ☑ 744-486-65-12; Gonzalo de Sandoval 26; mains M$55-195; ☺8am-11pm; ☜) Just off the strip and a few paces from the beach, this thatched restaurant can nevertheless have a secluded vibe. It feels very authentic, with its traditional checked tablecloths and cordial staff, and the food backs it up. Great rolled chicken tacos, delicious *frijoles* (beans), affordable fish dishes and filling breakfasts make it an oasis at any time of day.

La Cabaña de Caleta   SEAFOOD $$

(Map p564; ☑ 744-482-50-07; www.lacabanadecaleta.com; Playa Caleta; mains M$80-250; ☺9am-9pm; ☜; ☐Caleta) Step back in time and into a slice of traditional Mexican beach life, c 1950, at this venerable, unpretentious seafood *palapa* straddling the sands of Playa Caleta. Bask under a blue umbrella and gaze at the bay while savoring specialties such as *cazuela de mariscos* (seafood stew) or grilled whole fish.

El Cabrito
MEXICAN **$$**

(Map p570; ☑744-484-77-11; www.elcabrito-aca pulco.com; Av Costera 1480; mains M$85-255; ⊙2-11pm Mon-Sat, 1:30-10:30pm Sun; ☏) This beloved and brightly decorated restaurant has some of the city's finest traditional Mexican food, such as Oaxaca-style black *mole* (a type of chili sauce) made from 32 ingredients. You'd also do quite well with *cabrito al pastor* (roast kid goat); eat it with your fingers, say the staff. The shrimp dishes are tasty, as are the house-made tortillas.

Pipo's
SEAFOOD **$$$**

(Map p570; ☑744-188-10-05; www.facebook. com/mariscospiposacapulco; Av Costera 105; mains M$150-270; ⊙noon-11pm) Famous for its *pescado almendrado* (mahimahi baked in a creamy Parmesan sauce with almonds), Pipo's is best after 6pm when the restaurant opens its airy terrace upstairs, offering a bird's-eye view of the carmageddon scene unfolding along the Costera. Pipo's began as a small ceviche stand seven decades ago and has become an Acapulco institution.

El Gaucho
PARRILLA **$$$**

(Map p570; ☑744-435-63-00; www.facebook. com/elgauchoacapulcomexico; Av Costera 8, Hotel Presidente; pasta M$89-120, mains M$325-545; ⊙2pm-midnight; ☏) This glass-box dining room leaves a little to be desired in terms of atmosphere, but it does do an excellent steak. Less carnivorous folk can choose from an assortment of pasta dishes or tasty grilled provolone cheese. Argentine trios play on Wednesday, Friday and Saturday nights.

🍷 Drinking & Nightlife

The strip of huge outdoor/indoor bars around the landmark **Paradise Bungy** (Map p570; ☑744-484-75-29; www.facebook.com/ paradisebungyacaoficial; Av Costera 101; M$600; ⊙5pm-12:30am Tue-Thu, 3pm-2am Fri & Sat, 3-11pm Sun) tower is lively from early evening until late, with drinks promos, go-go dancers and other revelry.

Most clubs don't get rolling until midnight or later. Admission charges vary by season and night. Dress to impress; shorts and sneakers are frowned upon.

★ Bar Los Flamingos
BAR

(Map p564; ☑744-483-98-06; www.hotelflamin gosacapulco.com; Av López Mateos s/n; ⊙10am-10pm; ☏) The clifftop bar of Hotel Los Flamingos (p568) is old-school impeccable and the best sundowner spot in Acapulco, thanks to its famed menu of signature cocktails, including *Cocos Locos* (made with rum, tequila, pineapple juice and coconut crème). The restaurant offers a traditional menu, and *pozole* (hominy stew) Thursday is a beloved local lunch tradition: reserve ahead.

Mojito
BAR, CLUB

(Map p570; ☑744-484-82-74; www.facebook.com/ mojitoaca; Av Costera s/n; ⊙10am-4pm Thu-Sat; ☏) If you prefer salsa and *cumbia* (dance music originating from Colombia) to reggaeton or techno, this should be your go-to option on the Acapulco strip. The popular club looks out over the ocean and gets lively with Latin beats and drinks until late. There's a good range of ages dancing to the live Cuban group.

Palladium
CLUB

(Map p564; ☑744-446-54-90; www.palladium. com.mx; Carretera Escénica s/n; admission varies; ⊙11pm-6am Fri & Sat; ☏) The best nightclub in town, Palladium attracts a young crowd and offers fabulous bay views from floor-to-ceiling windows. An international cast of DJs pumps out hip-hop, house, trance and techno from an ultraluxe sound system. Dress up, and expect to wait in line. Admission is pricey but usually includes unlimited drinks.

Mezcalina
BAR

(Map p570; ☑744-481-15-90; www.facebook.com/ mezcalinaacapulco; Av Costera 3007; ⊙8pm-2am Tue-Thu, to 4am Fri-Sun; ☏) This ain't your typical mezcal joint (unless dancing to loud reggaeton music is a new trend taking over *mezcalerías*), but it's easy enough to join the party while sipping on a smoky Danzantes or Bruxo.

Demás Factory
GAY

(Map p570; www.facebook.com/demasfactory; Av de los Deportes 10A; ⊙10pm-7am Wed-Sun; ☏) The city's longest-running gay club is mixed but draws a mostly male clientele. There are shows on weekend nights and M$250 gets you all you can drink on Saturdays.

☆ Entertainment

Forum Mundo Imperial CONCERT VENUE
(☑744-435-17-00; www.forumimperial.com; Blvd de las Naciones s/n, Acapulco Diamante) At the airport junction in the Diamante area, this huge, striking venue attracts big-name acts for anything from dance performances to rock. It's best reached by car or taxi.

🛍 Shopping

La Europea ALCOHOL
(Map p570; ☑744-484-80-43; www.laeuropea.com.mx; Av Costera 2908; ⊘10am-8pm Mon-Thu, to 9pm Fri & Sat, 11am-4pm Sun) Stocks a good selection of mezcals and tequilas, such as Pierde Almas and 7 Leguas.

**Mercado de Artesanías
El Parazal** MARKET
(Map p566; cnr Parana & Velázquez de Leon; ⊘many shops 10am-7pm) Bargaining is the standard at this leafy and laid-back craft market, one of several handicraft markets around town. Here you'll find better deals on everything that you see in the hotel shops, including hammocks, jewelry, ceramics, lacquer work, T-shirts and other clothing.

Mercado Central MARKET
(Map p570; Hurtado de Mendoza s/n; ⊘7am-6pm) This sprawling indoor-outdoor bazaar has everything from *atoles* (corn-based drinks) to *zapatos* (shoes), plus produce, hot food and souvenirs. Any westbound 'Pie de la Cuesta' or 'Pedregoso' bus will drop you here.

ℹ Information

DANGERS & ANNOYANCES
At the time of writing, Acapulco ranked second in the world for homicides per capita, but residents rightly claim that this doesn't reflect the reality for visitors. The vast majority of violent incidents are score-settling assassinations between members of rival drug gangs. That said, though protecting the downtown areas is an absolute priority for the city, tourists have occasionally been targeted in isolated incidents or caught in the cross fire. Acapulco isn't necessarily a dangerous place to visit, but, as with most Mexican cities, we advise caution with personal possessions, exploring unfamiliar areas and taking taxis late at night.

EMERGENCY
Tourist Police (☑744-485-04-90)

MEDICAL SERVICES
Hospital Magallanes (☑744-469-02-70; www.hospitalprivadomagallanes.com; Massieu 2) A well-established private hospital with English-speaking doctors and staff.

MONEY
Banks and *casas de cambio* (currency exchanges) cluster around the *zócalo* (p565) and line Avenida Costera. Hotels will also change money, but their rates usually stink.

POST
Main Post Office (Map p566; ☑744-483-24-05; www.correosdemexico.com.mx; Av Costera 315, Palacio Federal; ⊘8am-7pm Mon-Fri, to 2pm Sat)

TOURIST INFORMATION
CAPTA (Tourist Infomation and Assistance; Map p570; ☑744-481-18-54; www.acapulco.gob.mx/capta/; Av Costera 38A; ⊘office 9am-9pm) Office and 24-hour hotline for tourist information and assistance with problems.

The city government operates several tourist information kiosks that aren't particularly helpful. They are located on the **marina** (Map p566; ☑744-481-18-54; www.acapulco.gob.mx/capta; Av Costera s/n; ⊘9am-6pm) across from the *zócalo* (p565), at **La Diana traffic circle** (Map p570; ☑744-481-18-54; www.acapulco.gob.mx/capta; Av Costera s/n; ⊘9am-6pm), at **Playa Caleta** (Map p564; ☑744-481-18-54; www.acapulco.gob.mx/capta; ⊘9am-6pm) and by the entrance to **Walmart** (Map p570; ☑744-481-18-54; www.acapulco.gob.mx/capta; Horacio Nelson s/n; ⊘9am-6pm) near Playa Icacos (p567).

ℹ Getting There & Away

AIR
Acapulco's **airport** (Juan Álvarez International Airport; ☑744-435-20-60; www.oma.aero/es/aeropuertos/acapulco; Blvd de las Naciones s/n) has seen a marked decrease in international nonstop flights, although it's still easy to connect through Mexico City (a short hop from Acapulco). Airlines have offices at the airport; there are a couple of direct flights from the USA and Canada.

The following domestic destinations are serviced by these airlines:

➧ Guadalajara – TAR

➧ Mexico City – Aeromar, Aeroméxico, Interjet, Volaris

➧ Monterrey – VivaAerobús, Volaris

➧ Queretaro – TAR

➧ Tijuana – Interjet, Volaris

➧ Toluca – Interjet

BUS

Acapulco has four bus terminals. Fortunately, the two major ones are quite close together. There's also a bus station in the Acapulco Diamante resort area.

Central Ejido (Map p564; ☎744-469-20-30; Av Ejido 47) This bus terminal mostly serves departures to destinations in Guerrero and Oaxaca states, run by the AltaMar/Costeños group. Estrella de Oro services to Zihuatanejo also stop here on their way north.

Central Papagayo (Estrella Blanca Terminal; Map p570; ☎800-507-55-00; www. estrellablanca.com.mx; Av Cuauhtémoc 1605) Just north of Parque Papagayo (p565), this modern terminal has 1st-class and luxury services all around the country run by Estrella Blanca and its affiliates. Left luggage is available, but eating options are weak.

Estrella de Oro Bus Terminal (Central Cuauhtémoc; Map p570; ☎800-900-01-05; www. estrelladeoro.com.mx; Av Cuauhtémoc 1490) All Estrella de Oro (EDO) services leave from this modern, air-conditioned terminal, which has several ATMs and left-luggage facilities.

Terminal Centro (Map p570; ☎800-003-76-35; Av Cuauhtémoc 97) First- and 2nd-class departures to relatively nearby towns, though some services to Mexico City stop here too.

CAR & MOTORCYCLE

Several car rental companies have offices at the airport.

Alamo (☎744-466-93-30; www.alamo.com. mx/en; ⏱7am-10pm)

Europcar (☎744-466-93-14; www.europcar. com.mx/en; ⏱6am-11pm)

Hertz (☎744-466-94-24; www.hertz.com; ⏱6am-10pm)

ℹ Getting Around

Cycling in Acapulco can be a hairy ride; always wear a helmet. **Las Bicis de Aca** (www.face book.com/lasbicisdeaca.es; Av Costera s/n; rental per hour M$50; ⏱1-9pm Mon-Fri, from 9am Sat & Sun) rents out bikes.

TO/FROM THE AIRPORT

Acapulco's airport (p573) is 23km southeast of the zócalo (p565). You can buy a ticket for transportation into town from the desk at the end of the domestic terminal. The taxis for the airport run constantly, ranging in price depending on destination (think M$450 for central hotels).

Leaving Acapulco, taxis from downtown to the airport cost around M$250 to M$350, depending on the distance.

BUS

The easiest way to get around is on the 'Base–Caleta' bus route, which runs from the Icacos naval base on the southeast end of Acapulco, along La Costera, past the zócalo (p565) to Playa Caleta. Fares are M$8 and M$9.50 for buses with air-conditioning.

Another option is the Acabús system (www. acabus.gob.mx): red rapid-transit buses accessed via station platforms using rechargeable smart cards. The yellow RT4 line is a main route, plying Avenida Costera from Icacos to the zócalo. From the zócalo station, transfer to the complementary RA12 line to reach Caleta. Rides cost M$10 including free transfers to complementary routes.

Most buses operate from 5am to 11pm. A **bus stop** (Map p566; Av Costera s/n; ⏱5am-10pm) for the nearby beach towns of Pie de la Cuesta and Puerto Marqués is on Avenida Costera, about two blocks east from the zócalo.

BUSES FROM ACAPULCO

DESTINATION	FARE (M$)	DURATION (HR)	FREQUENCY (DAILY)
Chilpancingo	66-128	1½-2½	frequent Centro, EDO, Ejido & Papagayo
Cuernavaca	414-533	4-5	4 EDO, 6 Papagayo
Mazatlán	1500-1830	19-21	3 Papagayo
Mexico City (Terminal Norte)	507-667	6	frequent Centro, EDO & Papagayo
Mexico City (Terminal Sur)	525-690	5-6	frequent Centro, EDO & Papagayo
Puerto Escondido	466	8-9	7 Centro, 7 Ejido
Taxco	257-290	4-5	1 Centro, 4 EDO
Zihuatanejo	160-248	4½-5½	frequent Centro, 7 EDO, 9 Papagayo

CAR & MOTORCYCLE

Avoid driving in Acapulco if you can. The anarchic traffic is often horribly snarled. A pricey new 3.3km tunnel (M$55) called Macrotúnel runs from south of the Icacos naval base to Acapulco Diamante, but you're better off taking the pretty scenic drive along the coast.

TAXI

Legions of blue-and-white cabs scurry around Acapulco like cockroaches, maneuvering with an audacity that borders on the comical. Drivers often quote fares higher than the official ones; always agree on a price with the driver before getting in. Other blue-and-white cabs are also available. A short hop should be M$40 to M$50, while a cross-town ride will be M$100 to M$150.

Shared yellow taxis (*colectivos* or *peseros*) run along set routes and cost M$18 per journey (double if you want to sit on your own in the front and not get squashed). Their destinations are written on the windshield and they can be hailed anywhere – in fact, they'll probably hail you with their horns first.

In the hotel district, sparkling Cinderella-style horse carts are a big hit with kids at night.

Costa Chica

Guerrero's 'Small Coast,' extending southeast from Acapulco to the Oaxaca border, is much less traveled than its bigger brother (Costa Grande) to the northwest, but it has some spectacular beaches. Afro-Mestizos (people of mixed African, indigenous and European descent) make up a portion of the population. The region was a safe haven for Africans who escaped slavery, some from the interior, others (it's believed) from a slave ship that sank just off the coast.

From Acapulco, Hwy 200 traverses inland past small villages and farmlands. **San Marcos**, about 60km east of Acapulco, and **Cruz Grande**, about 40km further east, are the only two towns of significant size before Cuajinicuilapa (p576) near the Oaxaca border. Both provide basic services including banks, gas stations and simple hotels. Playa Ventura makes a great place to spend a couple days relaxing on a quiet beach with lovely rock formations.

Playa Ventura

🖉 741 / POP 555

Located 135km southeast of Acapulco, Playa Ventura (labeled Colonia Juan Álvarez on most maps) is a long, pristine beach with soft white-and-gold sands. Behind it is a simple, likable Mexican village, while uncomplicated beachfront accommodations and seafood restaurants line the beaches in both directions from the center of town.

Playa Ventura is an important turtle nesting site, and volunteers go out every night in the season (from May to January) to collect eggs and rebury them in a little beachside compound, which looks like a tiny war cemetery with its rows of information markers, but with a more hopeful purpose. Like most good places along the seldom-visited Costa Chica, including the nearby market town of **Marquelia** and its sublime beach **Playa La Bocana**, Playa Ventura leaves you no choice but to disconnect and surrender to its easy tempo and natural beauty.

🛏 Sleeping

⭐ Méson Casa de Piedra   HOTEL $

(🖉 cell 741-1013129; www.playaventura.mx; Costera Ventura s/n; d M$600-900; 🅿 ❄ 🤶) The House of Stone features beautifully designed rustic rooms fashioned from recycled objects; some include private balconies with ocean views (the 'cielo' room provides a sweet vista, and it's affordable to boot). The Mesón also boasts one of the best restaurants in town, serving excellent breakfast, pizza, vegetarian fare and fresh fish and seafood.

🍴 Eating & Drinking

⭐ Los Norteñitos   MEXICAN $

(🖉 cell 745-1163957; mains M$50-150; ⏱ 7am–10pm) Totally authentic and genuinely welcoming, this *taquería* in the center of town is run by an affable local family. Delicious *cecina* (cured beef) tacos are great with freshly made *tomatillo* (green tomato) salsa in a *molcajete* (mortar and pestle), while fish and prawns are reliably delicious – the whole snapper cooked in foil with a mellow chili sauce is a standout.

Bolumba   BAR

(🖉 741-101-30-12; felixbolumba@live.com.mx; Costera Ventura s/n; ⏱ 7am-9pm; 🤶) This *palapa* restaurant-bar occupies an excellent beach for swimming. It stays open until 9pm, which makes for a late evening by Playa Ventura standards. A refreshing *michelada* (beer cocktail) usually hits the spot here. It's about 500m south of the town center.

❶ Getting There & Away

To get here by car from Acapulco, take Hwy 200 to the signposted Playa Ventura turnoff (Km 124), just east of the village of Copala, then continue 7km to the coast. Alternatively, take a southeast-bound bus to Copala (M$110 to M$134, about 3½ hours). From the Oxxo convenience store in Copala, *camionetas* (pickup trucks) and microbuses depart for the turnoff to Playa Ventura (M$10, 10 minutes). At the turnoff, shared taxis (M$17, 10 minutes) shuttle into town. Some Cuajinicuilapa-bound buses from Acapulco will drop you directly at the turnoff.

Cuajinicuilapa

📞 741 / POP 10,282

About 200km southeast of Acapulco, Cuajinicuilapa (Cuaji for short) is the nucleus of Afro-Mestizo culture on the Costa Chica.

The main sight in town is the **Museo de las Culturas Afromestizas** (Museum

of Afro-Mestizo Cultures; 📞 cell 741-1250842; museodelasculturasafromestizas_cuaji @hotmail.com; Zárate s/n; M$10; ⏰10am-2pm & 4-7pm Mon-Fri, by appointment Sat & Sun) is a tribute to the history of African slaves in Mexico and, specifically, to local Afro-Mestizo culture. There are some interesting stories, sweet dioramas and a model slaving ship; all text is in Spanish. Behind the museum are three examples of *casas redondas,* the round houses typical of West Africa that were built around Cuaji until the 1960s. The museum is behind the basketball court on the main road in the town center.

❶ Getting There & Away

Buses to Cuajinicuilapa (M$233, 4½ hours) run by AltaMar/Costeños depart **Central Ejido bus terminal** (p574) in Acapulco nine times daily. There are also nine buses daily from Pinotepa Nacional (M$60, one hour) in Oaxaca state.

Western Central Highlands

Best Places to Eat

➡ Alcalde (p595)

➡ Chango (p621)

➡ Cox-Hanal (p637)

➡ Lu Cochina Michoacana (p621)

➡ Lulabistro (p595)

➡ Los Girasoles (p607)

Best Places to Stay

➡ Casa de las Flores (p592)

➡ Lake Chapala Inn (p605)

➡ Casa Alvarada (p613)

➡ Hotel Casa Encantada (p630)

➡ Casa Chikita Bed & Breakfast (p636)

➡ La Nueva Posada (p606)

Why Go?

Welcome to the Mexico of your imagination! Many of the elements that define the image of Mexico worldwide originated in the western central highlands amid slumbering volcanoes, sun-drenched avocado plantations and some of the country's finest 'undiscovered' pre-Hispanic ruins. Those looking for a bit of local flavor can sip the world's best tequila in a sea of blue agave, listen to mariachi music in the region of its birth or be awed by the twin-towered magnificence of Morelia's cathedral.

Less obvious (and visited) is Lago de Pátzcuaro, where the indigenous Purépecha people display their craft-making skills and observe some of the most chilling Day of the Dead rituals in the land.

Among the region's natural wonders, Volcán Paricutín is a climbable volcano that burst out of a corn field in 1943, while the Reserva Mariposa Monarca is a swath of coniferous-covered highlands visited annually by millions of monarch butterflies.

When to Go
Guadalajara

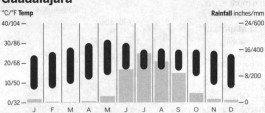

Feb Probably the best month to mingle with the monarch butter-flies in the Reserva Mariposa Monarca.

Mar–Apr Appreciate some of the finest craftwork in Mexico at the Tianguis Artesanal de Uruapan.

Nov Villages around Pátzcuaro host colorful (and spooky) Día de Muertos celebrations.

Western Central Highlands Highlights

1 **Morelia**
(p614) Getting to know Michoacán's welcoming capital, with its shimmering cathedral, animated streets and delightful architecture.

2 **Guadalajara**
(p580) Exploring the excellent art museums, ancient churches and superb restaurants of Mexico's second-largest city.

3 **Reserva Mariposa Monarca**
(p624) Absorbing the beauty of this incredible natural phenomenon: the winter retreat of millions of butterflies.

4 **Pátzcuaro**
(p626) Peering into the mystical soul of the Purépecha people in this tranquil city of art and beautiful squares.

5 **Volcán Nevado de Colima** (p612) Getting up close to this snowy and extinct volcano that shares a national park with a more active (but off-limits) one.

6 **Tzintzuntzan**
(p634) Gazing out over Lago de Pátzcuaro from the mystical and semideserted Tarascan ruins of this archaeological site.

7 **Tequila** (p603) Touring and sipping your way through the distilleries in the birthplace of Mexico's most famous beverage.

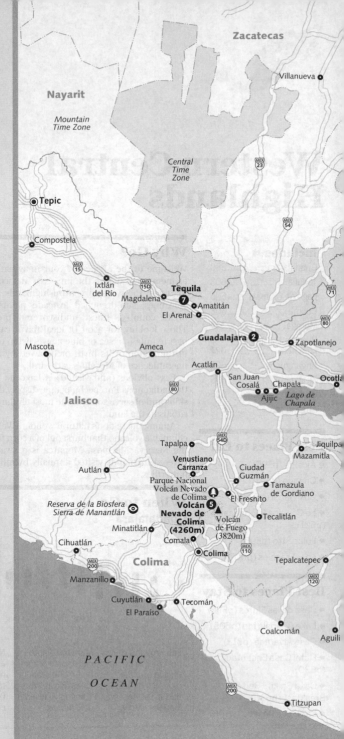

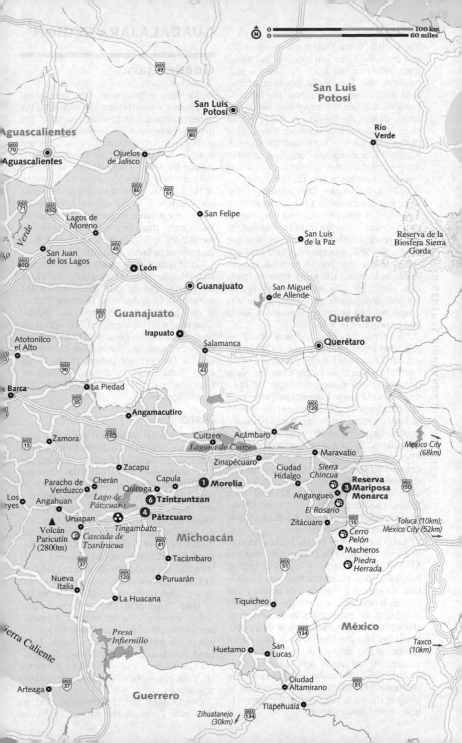

History

The western central highlands were too distant from the Maya and Aztecs to fall under their influence, but from the 14th to 16th centuries the Tarascos in northern Michoacán state developed a robust pre-Hispanic civilization. When the Aztecs took notice and attacked them, the Tarascos were able to fend them off thanks to their copper blades. West of the Tarascos was their rival, the Chimalhuacán – four indigenous kingdoms based in the present-day states of Jalisco, Colima and Nayarit. To the north were the Chichimec.

Colima, the leading Chimalhuacán kingdom, was conquered by the Spanish in 1523. The whole region, however, was not brought under Spanish control until the campaigns of the notorious Nuño de Guzmán. Between 1529 and 1536 he tortured, killed and enslaved indigenous people from Michoacán north to Sinaloa. His grisly exploits made him rich and won him governorship of his conquered lands until news of his war crimes reached home. He was sent to Spain and imprisoned in 1538.

This fertile ranching and agricultural region developed gradually and Guadalajara, established in 1542, became the 'capital of the west.' The church, with help from the Nuño de Guzmán's successor, the enlightened Bishop Vasco de Quiroga, fostered small industries and handicraft traditions around the villages of Lago de Pátzcuaro in an effort to ease the continuing poverty of the indigenous people.

In the 1920s the region's two major states, Michoacán and Jalisco, were hotbeds of the Cristero rebellion led by Catholics fighting the government's antichurch policies. As Michoacán governor (1928–32) and then federal president (1934–40), Lázaro Cárdenas instituted reforms that did much to lessen antigovernment sentiments.

Today the states of Jalisco, Michoacán and, to a lesser extent, little Colima hold many of Mexico's natural resources – especially timber, minerals, livestock and agriculture; in addition, Jalisco has a thriving tech industry and Colima boasts one of the highest standards of living in the country. But in the past these states have seen large segments of their population head for the USA for work. Michoacán reportedly lost almost half its population to emigration, and money sent home regularly exceeds US$2 billion. But with the economic slowdown and stricter immigration laws in place in the USA, the flow north appears to have slowed down somewhat.

GUADALAJARA REGION

Guadalajara

✈ 33 / POP 1.5 MILLION / ELEV 1566M

As Mexico's second-largest city, Guadalajara delivers a less frenetic alternative to the nation's capital. And, while many of the images recognized as Mexican have their roots here – mariachi music, wide-brimmed sombreros, the Mexican hat dance and *charreadas* (rodeos) – Guadalajara is as much a vanguard of the new Mexico as it is guardian of the old. An embarrassment of museums and theaters drive the cultural life forward, fusion chefs have sharpened the edges of an already legendary culinary scene and foresighted local planners are doing their damnedest to tackle the traffic.

Guadalajara can't match the architectural homogeneity of smaller colonial cities, though its historic core, anchored by the wonderful cathedral and Instituto Cultural de Cabañas, is handsome. The hipster Chapultepec neighborhood is sprinkled with fashionable restaurants, coffeehouses and nightclubs. The mellow suburbs of upscale Tlaquepaque and grassroots Tonalá are folk-art shoppers' dream destinations, while Zapopan has some interesting colonial architecture.

History

Guadalajara has weathered not a few false starts. In early 1531 Nuño de Guzmán and a few dozen Spanish families founded the first settlement near Nochixtlán, naming Guadalajara after Guzmán's hometown in Spain. Water was scarce, the land was dry and unyielding, and the indigenous people were understandably hostile. So in May 1533 the settlers moved to the village of Tonalá (today a part of Guadalajara). Guzmán disliked Tonalá, however, and several years later had the settlement moved to Tlacotán. In 1541 this site was attacked and decimated by a confederation of indigenous tribes led by chief Tenamaxtli. The survivors wearily picked a new site in the valley of Atemajac beside San Juan de Dios Creek, which ran where the boulevard called Calzada Independencia runs today. That's where the present Guadalajara was founded on February 14, 1550, near where the Teatro Degollado now stands.

Guadalajara finally prospered and in 1559 was declared the capital of Nueva

Galicia province. The city, at the heart of a rich agricultural region, quickly grew into one of colonial Mexico's most important population centers. It also became the launch pad for Spanish expeditions and missions to western and northern Nueva España (new Spain), and others as far away as the Philippines. Miguel Hidalgo, a leader in the fight for Mexican independence, set up a revolutionary government in Guadalajara in late 1810, but was defeated near the city the following year, just months before his capture and execution in Chihuahua. The city was also the object of heavy fighting during the War of the Reform (1857–61) and between Constitutionalist and Villista armies in 1915.

Despite the violence, the 19th century was a period of economic, technological and social growth for the city, and by the close of the century Guadalajara had overtaken Puebla as Mexico's second-biggest city. Its population has mushroomed since WWII, and now the city is a huge commercial, industrial and cultural center as well as the hi-tech and communications hub for the northern half of Mexico.

◎ Sights

◎ Plaza de Armas & Around

★ **Catedral de Guadalajara** CATHEDRAL
(Catedral de la Asunción de María Santísima; Map p588; ☑ 33-3613-7168; www.facebook.com/cate dralguadalajara.org; Av Alcalde 10, btwn Morelos & Av Hidalgo; ◎ 7:30am-8:30pm) FREE Guadalajara's cathedral is the city's most conspicuous landmark with distinctive neo-Gothic towers built after an earthquake toppled the originals in 1818. Begun in 1561 and consecrated in 1618, the building is almost as old as the city itself. Time your visit right and you'll see light filter through stained-glass of the Last Supper above the altar and hear a working pipe organ rumble sweetly from the rafters.

The interior includes a Gothic **crypt** (Map p588; ◎ 10:30am-2pm & 4:30-7pm Mon-Sat, 9-11am & 1:30-8:30pm Sun), where three archbishops are buried, plus massive Tuscan-style gold-leaf pillars and 11 richly decorated side altars that were bequeathed to the city by King Fernando VII of Spain (1784–1833). The 18th-century glass case nearest the west entrance is an extremely popular reliquary, containing the waxed remains of the mar-

tyred Santa Inocencia. In the sacristy, which an attendant can open for you on request, is *La Asunción de la Virgen,* painted by Spanish artist Bartolomé Murillo in 1650. Much like the city's Palacio de Gobierno, the cathedral is a bit of a stylistic hodgepodge, including baroque, Churrigueresque (late Spanish baroque) and neoclassical influences.

Palacio de Gobierno NOTABLE BUILDING
(Map p588; ☑ 33-3668-1808; Av Corona 43, btwn Morelos & Moreno; ◎ 10am-6pm Tue-Sat, to 3pm Sun) FREE The golden-hued Palacio de Gobierno, which houses the Jalisco state government offices, was finished in 1774 and is well worth visiting to see two impressive murals by local artist José Clemente Orozco (1883–1949). The real head-turner is the 400-sq-metre mural of Miguel Hidalgo painted in 1937 that dominates the main interior staircase. Hidalgo brandishes a torch in one fist while the masses at his feet struggle against the twin foes of communism and fascism.

Another Orozco mural in the Ex Congreso (former Congress Hall) upstairs to the right depicts Hidalgo, Benito Juárez and other historical luminaries. On the ground floor there's an excellent multimedia **museum** about the history of Jalisco and its capital, though labeling is largely in Spanish.

Plaza Guadalajara PLAZA
(Map p588) Plaza Guadalajara is shaded by dozens of severly cropped laurel trees and has great views of the east of the cathedral. Boasting a few fine cafes, it's a hive of activity day and night. On its north side is the **Palacio Municipal** (City Hall; Map p588; Av Hidalgo 400; ◎ 10am-7pm Mon-Fri) FREE, which was built between 1949 and 1952 but looks much older. Above the main stairway inside is a dark mural by Gabriel Flores depicting the founding of Guadalajara.

Teatro Degollado THEATER
(Map p588; ☑ 33-3614-4773; www.facebook.com/ TeatroDegollado; Degollado; ◎ viewing noon-2pm Mon-Fri) FREE Construction of this neoclassical theater, which is home to the Guadalajara Philharmonic, was begun in 1855 and completed four decades later. Above the Corinthian columns is a pediment with a mosaic depicting Apollo and the Nine Muses.

Museo Regional de Guadalajara MUSEUM
(Mapp588; ☑ 33-3613-2703; Liceo60; adult/student & child M$55/free; ◎ 9am-5:30pm Tue-Sat, to 4:30pm Sun) Guadalajara's most important

WESTERN CENTRAL HIGHLANDS GUADALAJARA

Greater Guadalajara

N
0   5 km
0   2.5 miles

Río Verde

Río Grande de Santiago

ZAPOPAN

Basílica de
Zapopan

Paseo del
Zoológico

Av de la Cruz

Calz Obrero

Calz Independencia

Circunvalación

Domínguez

Anillo Periférico

Av Alcalde

Av 16 de Septiembre

Av Federalismo

See Central Guadalajara
Map (p588)

See Chapultepec
Map (p594)

Av Camacho

Av de las Américas

Av López
Mateos

Av Acueducto

Av de la Patria

Av Vallarta

Av Otero

Av López Mateos Sur

Av Guadalupe

Av Tepeyac

Av de la Patria

CHAPALITA

Anillo Periférico

Av Vallarta

Tequila (50km);
Tepic (215km)

Av Cruz del Sur

Av Colón

Av 8 de Julio

Av de Legazpi

Calz Cárdenas

Calz Curiel

Dr Michel

Calz Gallo

Blvd Barragán

Calz Revolución

Av Javier Mina

San Jacinto Plutarco
Elías Calles

Av Osorio

Av Pesa

Av Giantes

TLAQUEPAQUE

See Tlaquepaque
Map (p592)

TONALÁ

Av Tonaltecas

Calz Río Nilo

Calz Río Nilo

Autopista Guadalajara Zapotlanejo

Av Tonalá

Aeropuerto Internacional
Miguel Hidalgo (12km)

Anillo Periférico

Greater Guadalajara

museum attempts to tell the story of the city and the surrounding region from prehistory to the revolution through chaotic monolingual displays in rooms that are often shut tight. The ground floor houses a natural history collection whose unwitting star is a mightily impressive woolly mammoth skeleton dating from 10,000 BC. Other crowd-pleasers include displays about indigenous life and a superb collection of pre-Hispanic ceramics and other artifacts taken from a shaft tomb dating from 600 BC.

The upper level of the museum is devoted to colonial paintings depicting the Spanish conquest, as well as more austere religious allegories, a revolutionary wing and exhibits devoted to the indigenous Huichol (or Wixarika) culture. The building is worth visiting for its architecture – a gorgeous, tree-studded double courtyard with a fountain acts as its centerpiece.

Plaza de la Liberación PLAZA
(Map p588) This huge plaza due east of the cathedral was a 1980s urban planner's dream project – two whole blocks of colonial buildings to be knocked down and replaced with a concrete slab.

On the north side of the plaza, next to the Museo Regional de Guadalajara, is the **Palacio Legislativo** (Map p588; República). Distinguished by thick stone columns in its interior courtyard, this is where the state congress meets. Across the Calle Belén to the east is the **Palacio de Justicia** (State Courthouse; Map p588; Belén). It was built in 1588 and began life as Guadalajara's first nunnery. Duck inside to the interior stairwell and check out the 1965 mural by Guillermo Chávez depicting legendary Mexican lawmakers, including Benito Juárez.

Rotonda de los Jaliscenses Ilustres MONUMENT
(Rotunda of Illustrious Jaliscans; Map p588; Av Hidalgo, btwn Av Alcalde & Liceo) Jalisco's hall of fame, in the plaza on the north side of the cathedral, is ringed by 30 bronze sculptures of the state's favorite writers, architects and revolutionaries, including one woman – Rita Pérez Jiménez (1779–1861), heroine of the War of Independence. Some of the greats depicted here are actually buried underneath the rotunda, the round, pillared gazebo-like monument in the center.

Museo de Arte Sacro de Guadalajara MUSEUM
(Map p588; ☎33-3613-6706; www.museodearte sacro.com.mx; Liceo 17, btwn Morelos & Av Hidalgo; adult/child M$20/10; ⊙10am-5pm Tue-Sat, to 2pm Sun) This pious collection astride the eastern flank of the cathedral is filled with dark and brooding 17th- to 18th-century religious art, as well as some spectacular ecclesiastical treasures including chalices, monstrances and vestments.

Galería Jorge Martínez GALLERY
(Map p588; ☎33-3613-2362; Belén 120; ⊙10am-7pm Mon-Fri, 11am-1pm Sat) FREE It's worth popping into this interesting modern and conceptual art gallery to see if there's an exhibition showing (there's no permanent collection on display). It's adjacent to, and benefiting, Guadalajara's top art school, Artes Plásticas, which is operated by the Universidad de Guadalajara.

WESTERN CENTRAL HIGHLANDS GUADALAJARA

DON'T MISS

AN EYE ON OROZCO

Long before Banksy and the rebirth of politically charged street art, Mexican muralists were making bold statements in giant public murals that expressed mostly revolutionary ideals in swirls of vivid color. Guadalajara's gift to the genre was substantial. The grandfather of Mexican *muralismo* is usually considered to be locally born artist Gerardo Murillo (1875–1964), who signed his work 'Dr Atl,' while one of his former pupils, José Clemente Orozco (1883–1949), came from the nearby city of Ciudad Guzmán.

Together with Diego Rivera and David Alfaro Siqueiros, Orozco is considered one of the 'Big Three' of Mexican mural art. Some argue he was the most original; his energetic brushstrokes depict fiery, sometimes pained, figures in vivid studies of polemic symbolism. Orozco's work decorates stairways, ceilings and public spaces everywhere from New York to Mexico City, but his most personal work can be found in Guadalajara. Don't miss the following.

Instituto Cultural de Cabañas Orozco painted 57 murals including the kaleidoscopic *Hombre del Fuego* in this Unesco-listed building between 1937 and 1939.

Palacio de Gobierno (p581) Astonishing 1937 painting of Miguel Hidalgo brandishing a torch, set on the government building's main staircase that will literally stop you in your tracks.

Museo de las Artes Two pieces in the auditorium – *El Hombre Creador y Rebelde* (Creator and Rebel) in the cupola and *El Pueblo y Sus Falsos Líderes* (The People and Their False Leaders) on the stage backdrop painted in 1937 – are housed in this art museum opposite the university.

Casa-Taller Orozco Contains Orozco's *La Buena Vida* (The Good Life; 1945), an uncharacteristically upbeat study of a chef holding up a fish.

⊙ East of Plaza de Armas

★ **Instituto Cultural de Cabañas**   MUSEUM
(Map p588; ☏ 33-3668-1645; http://hospicioca banas.jalisco.gob.mx; Cabañas 8; adult/student M$70/20, Tue free; ⊙ 10am-6pm Tue-Sun) Standing proudly at the eastern end of dramatic Plaza Tapatía is one of Guadalajara's architectural landmarks, and a Unesco World Heritage site since 1997. On the ceiling and inside the dome of the enchanting neoclassical **Capilla Mayor** (Main Chapel) is a most unexpected series of modernist murals by José Clemente Orozco, which rank among his best works and Guadalajara's top sights. The complex also houses a collection of 340 other pieces by Orozco, and works by leading lights of Mexico's contemporary art scene.

The beautiful building, which consists of masses of hidden arched courtyards, was founded by Bishop don Juan Cruz Ruiz de Cabañas and designed by Spanish architect Manuel Tolsá between 1805 and 1810. Its original purpose was as an orphanage and home for invalids, and it remained so for 150 years, housing 500 children at once.

From 1937 to 1939 Orozco, one of the 'Big Three' of the Mexican muralist movement, channeled the archetypal struggle for freedom into 57 magnificent murals that now decorate the domed chapel at the center of the complex. Widely regarded as Orozco's finest works, they depict pre-Hispanic Jalisco and the conquest, presented through dark, unnerving and distinctly modern images of fire, armor, broken chains, blood and prayer. Given the timeframe, the works almost certainly serve as a warning against fascism and any force that subverts humanity to cultivate power. Conveniently placed benches allow you to lie down and inspect the works more easily. Free tours of the institute in a half-dozen languages (including English) depart regularly.

Plaza Tapatía   PLAZA
(Map p588) The fabulously wide pedestrian and elevated Plaza Tapatía sprawls for more than 500m eastward from Teatro Degollado to the Instituto Cultural de Cabañas. Stroll the length of the plaza on Sunday and you'll find yourself in a sea of locals who shop at low-end crafts markets, snack (from both street vendors and cafes), watch street performers and rest on the low walls of gurgling fountains.

Plaza de los Mariachis
STREET

(Map p588) Just south of Avenida Javier Mina and the Mercado San Juan de Dios (p593), this is the very birthplace of mariachi music. By day it's just a narrow walking street, flanked by charming old buildings and dotted with a few plastic tables and chairs, with the odd mariachi musician in full regalia chatting on a cell phone and/or awaiting gainful employment. At night it can get lively, when patrons swill beer and listen to bands play requests (from M$100 per song).

⊙ West of Plaza de Armas

West of the city center, where Avenidas Juárez and Federalismo meet, is the green comma of **Parque Revolución**, a haven for skaters and the focal point of Sunday's Vía Recreativa (p601).

Museo de las Artes
MUSEUM

(MUSA; Map p588; ☑ 33-3134-1664; www.musa. udg.mx; Av Juárez 975; ⊙10am-6pm Tue-Sun) **FREE** Three blocks west of Parque Revolución is this museum of contemporary art housed in a French Renaissance building (1917) that once served as the administration building for the University of Guadalajara. The highlight is the **Paraninfo** (auditorium) on the 1st floor, whose stage backdrop and dome feature large, powerful murals by Orozco. The rest of the space – some 14 galleries, in fact – is given over to well-curated temporary exhibitions focusing on contemporary Mexican art.

Templo Expiatorio del Santísimo Sacramento
CHURCH

(Map p588; ☑ 33-3825-3410; Madero 935; ⊙7am-10pm) This fine neo-Gothic church, begun in 1897 but not completed until 1972, dominates the neighborhood thanks to its enormous stone columns, 15m-high mosaic stained-glass windows above the altar and kaleidoscopic steeple. A carillon of 25 bells plays many religious and popular tunes. When the hour strikes, a door in the clock tower opens and the 12 Apostles march out. View it best from Parque Expiatorio to the south.

Casa-Taller Orozco
GALLERY

(Orozco House & Workshop; Map p594; ☑ 33-3616-8329; https://sc.jalisco.gob.mx/patrimonio/casas -de-la-cultura/casa-taller-jose-clemente-orozco; Aceves 27; ⊙noon-6pm Tue-Sat) **FREE** Orozco's former studio, used briefly by the celebrated muralist in the early 1940s, today hosts temporary exhibitions. On permanent display in the lobby – and worth a peek if you're in the area – is *La Buena Vida* (The Good Life), an unusually joyous Orozco mural the artist was commissioned to paint for Mexico City's Turf Club in 1945. To avoid disappointment, call before you set out; the museum does not always keep to schedule.

⊙ Zapopan

The fashionable, middle-class suburb of Zapopan is just under 10km northwest of the city center. There are a few interesting sights around the main square (**Plaza de las Americas**), which is a fun place to hang out, with pilgrims and the faithful coming and going and all sorts of religious items for sale. After dark the locals get the place back to themselves and the numerous bars and restaurants turn the music up and the beer flows.

To get here from the center of Guadalajara, take any bus marked 'Zapopan' (eg bus 275 or 706 TUR) heading north on Avenida 16 de Septiembre and its continuation Avenida Alcalde and get off on Avenida Hidalgo just north of the Basílica de Zapopan. The trip takes about 40 minutes. A taxi from the city center will cost around M$120.

★ Basílica de Zapopan
CATHEDRAL

(Map p582; ☑ 33-3633-0141; Eva Briseño 152; ⊙9am-8pm) One of the city's most important churches, the Basílica de Zapopan, built in 1730, is home to Nuestra Señora de Zapopan, a petite statue of the Virgin visited by pilgrims year-round. Since 1734 on October 12, thousands of kneeling faithful crawl behind as the statue is carried here from Guadalajara cathedral. The kneeling pilgrims then make the final trek up the basilica's aisle to pray for favors at the altar.

Museo de Arte Huichol (Wixárika)
MUSEUM

(Map p582; ☑ 33-1112-8247; Eva Briseño 152; adult/child M$10/5; ⊙10am-6pm Mon-Sat, 9am-3:30pm Sun) This small but surprisingly informative museum has a worthwhile display of artifacts from the Huichol (or Wixárika) people, an indigenous group known for their bright-colored yarn art, beadwork and peyote rituals. It covers all aspects of the culture, from birth to death and everything in between through everyday items and photographs. There's an excellent shop here too. It's just to the right of the Basílica de Zapopan within the basilica grounds.

Museo de Arte de Zapopan MUSEUM

(MAZ; Map p582; ☑ 33-3818-2575; www.maz museo.com; Andador 20 de Noviembre No 166; ⊙10am-6pm Tue-Sun, to 10pm Thu) FREE One block east of the southeast corner of Plaza de las Américas in Zapopan, MAZ is dedicated to modern art. Four sleek minimalist galleries hold temporary exhibits, which have included works by Diego Rivera and Frida Kahlo as well as leading contemporary Mexican artists. Many of the exhibits are interactive, and the museum acts as a nexus for numerous cultural activities.

👁 Tlaquepaque

Though just under 8km southeast of central Guadalajara, Tlaquepaque (officially San Pedro Tlaquepaque) feels almost like a village: squint and you could well be in some small colonial town miles from anywhere. But Tlaquepaque's attractiveness is not its sole draw: artisans live behind the pastel-colored walls of the old mansions that line Tlaquepaque's narrow cobblestone streets, and their goods – such as wood carvings, sculpture, furniture, jewelry, leather items and especially ceramics – are sold on and around pedestrianized Calle Independencia. The fancy boutiques here contrast sharply with the more rough-and-ready shops and stalls of Tonalá.

The main square, **Jardín Hidalgo**, is leafy and lush with blossoms, and the benches around the fountain are always packed. The eating is very good and the strolling is even better, especially at sunset when the sky behind the gorgeous, white-domed basilica burns orange and families take to the streets, enjoying the last ticks of daylight. *Voladores* ('flying men' from Papantla) give spectacular performances from a special 30m-high pole in the plaza most afternoons between about 3pm and 4pm.

There's a handy and helpful **tourist information booth** (Map p592; ☑ 33-1057-6212; cnr Av Juárez & Calle Progresso; ⊙9am-8pm Mon-Fri, 10am-7pm Sat & Sun) close to the junction of Juárez and Progresso (opposite El Parián; p596) that gives out pictorial neighborhood maps.

To get to Tlaquepaque from central Guadalajara, take bus 275B, 330 or 647 (M$7). The turquoise 706 TUR bus marked 'Tonalá' has air-con and is more comfortable (M$12). All these buses leave central Guadalajara from Avenida 16 de Septiembre between López Cotilla and Madero; the trip takes about 20 minutes. As you near Tlaquepaque, watch for the brick arch and then a traffic circle, after which you should get off at the next stop. Up the street on the left is Independencia, which will take you to the center of Tlaquepaque.

Museo Pantaleón Panduro MUSEUM

(Museo Premio Nacional de la Cerámica; Map p592; ☑ 33-3639-5646; www.premionacionaldelaceram ica.com/museo-pantaleon-panduro; Sánchez 191; ⊙10am-5pm Tue-Sun) FREE This superb collection of over 500 pieces of national folk art is housed in a converted religious mission and includes well-displayed miniature figurines, as well as enormous, lightly fired urns and other ceramic crafts from all over the country. Its focus is on winners of the prestigious National Ceramics Prize.

Museo Regional de la Cerámica MUSEUM

(Map p592; ☑ 33-3635-5404; Independencia 237; ⊙10am-5:45pm Tue-Sat, 11am-4:45pm Sun) FREE The Museo Regional de la Cerámica is set in a great old adobe building with stone arches and mature trees in the courtyard. It's a relatively small collection that exhibits the varied styles and clays used in Jalisco and Michoacán. Don't miss the fulyl stocked traditional kitchen, the weaver at work on an old loom at 11am and the excellent shop.

👁 Tonalá

This dusty, bustling suburb is about 17km southeast of downtown Guadalajara and home to many artisans. You can feel Tonalá beginning to take Tlaquepaque's lead with a few airy, inviting showrooms and cafes opening around town, but it remains happily rough around the edges. It's fun to roam through the dark, dusty stores and workshops, browsing glassware, ceramics, furniture, masks, toys, jewelry, handmade soap and more. Anything you can buy in Tlaquepaque you can find here for much less, which is what attracts wholesale buyers from all over the world.

Ask staff at the **Tonalá tourist office** (☑ 33-3586-6062; Morelos 180; ⊙9am-3pm Mon-Fri) about two- to three-hour **walking tours** (by donation) of Tonalá's artisan workshops. They're given in English or Spanish, but need to be reserved by email (recorridos tonala@hotmail.com) a couple of days in advance.

To reach Tonalá, take bus 231, 275 Diagonal or 633V (M$7). The turquoise 707 TUR bus marked 'Tonalá' has air-con and is more comfortable (M$12). All these buses leave Guadalajara from the corner of Avenida 16 de Septiembre and Madero; the trip takes about 45 minutes. As you enter Tonalá, get off on the corner of Avenidas Tonalá and Tonaltecas. The Plaza Principal is three blocks east of Avenida Tonaltecas on Avenida Juárez. A taxi will cost about M$150.

Museo Nacional de la Cerámica MUSEUM
(Map p582; ☑ 33-3683-2519; www.facebook.com/ museonacionaldelaceramica.tonala; Constitución 104; ⊘10am-6pm Tue-Sun) FREE Our favorite of the many ceramics museums in the greater Guadalajara region, this one focuses largely on ceramics from Tonalá, arguably the finest in central Mexico, and some of the items on display reach back to 500BC. Among the most memorable styles are *barro bruñido* and *barro canela*.

Tonalá Street Market MARKET
(Map p582; ⊘8am-4pm Thu & Sun) On Thursday and Sunday, Tonalá bursts into a huge street market that sprouts on Avenida Tonaltecas and crawls through dozens of streets and alleys and takes hours to explore. With *torta* (sandwich), taco and *michelada* (beer and tomato juice) stands aplenty, the whole area takes on a carnival vibe. The best piec-

es are usually found at the workshops and warehouses, though, not on the street.

Courses

Guadalajara is a popular place to study Spanish, with classes available to students of all ages and levels. Prices and curricula can vary considerably.

**Colegio de Español y
Cultura Mexicana** LANGUAGE
(CECM; Map p594; ☑ 33-3616-6881; www.cecm. udg.mx; Gómez 125; 50hr tuition over 2 weeks US$500) Part of the University of Guadalajara, CECM offers several levels of tuition, including two-week intensive (50 hours) and four-week semi-intensive (50 hours) Spanish-language courses. Day trips, homestays (from US$240 per week) and longer excursions to other parts of Mexico are available.

IMAC LANGUAGE
(Instituto Mexico-Americano de Cultura; Map p588; ☑ 33-3614-1414; www.learnspanish.com.mx; Guerra 180; per 25hr week from US$230) Offers courses from one week upwards and private tutoring from US$21 per hour. Check its website for course fees and homestay options. Music and dance classes are also available.

COLONIAL CHURCHES

Central Guadalajara has dozens of large and small churches. The following are some of the city's most beautiful and interesting. Most are open from between 7am and 9:30am to about 1pm and then again from 4pm or 5pm to 8pm or 8:30pm.

The **Templo de Nuestra Señora del Carmen** (Map p588; cnr Avenida Juárez & Calle 8 de Julio; ⊘9:30am-12:45pm & 4:30-6:45pm), facing a small plaza, is essentially a 17th-century chapel rebuilt in the 1860s, with lots of gold leaf, old paintings and murals in the dome. Closer to the city center is the ornate **Templo de la Merced** (Map p588; cnr Calle Loza & Av Hidalgo; ⊘7am-8pm), which was built in 1650; inside are several large paintings, crystal chandeliers and lots of gold leaf. A block northeast of Plaza de la Liberación is the unremarkable **Templo de Santa María de Gracia** (Map p588; cnr Carranza & República; ⊘7am-1pm & 5-8pm), with a rather rough interior; it served as the city's first cathedral (1549–1618). South of the landmark Teatro Degollado on Plaza de la Liberación is the baroque-style **Templo de San Agustín** (Map p588; Morelos; ⊘11am-1pm & 5-8pm), all gold and white and one of the city's oldest and loveliest churches. **Templo Santa Eduviges** (Map p588; Calle Abascal y Souza; ⊘7am-1pm & 5-8pm), built in 1726, is usually packed with worshippers and, during services, perfumed with clouds of sandalwood smoke. It's just east of the Mercado San Juan de Dios.

The compact **Templo de Aranzazú** (Map p588; Av 16 de Septiembre 20; ⊘6am-1pm & 4-8:40pm) is perhaps the city's most beautiful. Built from 1749 to 1752, it has three insanely ornate Churrigueresque (Spanish baroque) golden altars and a lovely vaulted ceiling. Across the road is the larger but less impressive **Templo de San Francisco de Asís** (Map p588; cnr Sánchez & Av 16 de Septiembre; ⊘9:30am-1pm & 2-6pm), which was begun in the 1660s by the Franciscans and has lovely stained glass.

Central Guadalajara

Tours

Bike Tours   CYCLING
(Map p588; corner Av Juárez & Calle Escorzia; ⊙9:30am & 11am Sun) FREE During Guadalajara's Sunday Vía Recreativa, when the main streets are closed to traffic, an army of volunteers in Parque Revolución dispense free bikes (ID required) and offer scenic bike tours departing from the corner of Avenida Juárez and Calle Escorzia and lasting one hour. You get to use the bikes till 1pm.

Recorridos Turísticos Guadalajara   WALKING
(Map p588; ☎33-3818 3600, ext 3351; www.vivir guadalajara.com/14632-recorridos-en-guadalajara. shtml; Plaza Guadalajara) FREE The city council runs free tours (in Spanish) of central Guadalajara at 10am and 7pm. Tours, which leave from opposite the Palacio Municipal in Plaza Guadalajara, last about 1½ hours and you must register 15 minutes beforehand. Ask the tourist office (p600) for further details.

Tapatío Tour   BUS
(Map p588; ☎33-3613-0887; www.tapatiotour. com; tours weekdays/weekends adult M$130/140, senior & child M$80/90) The double-decker buses of Tapatío Tour ply the city's most popular sights on four routes: Guadalajara, Tlaquepaque, Tonalá and Zapopan. While the narration in Spanish and in English is less than riveting, the tours allow you to hop off and on wherever you wish. Buses depart hourly from the Rotonda de los Jaliscenses Ilustres 9am to 8pm daily.

✵ Festivals & Events

**Encuentro Internacional
del Mariachi y la Charrería**   MUSIC, RODEO
(www.mariachi-jalisco.com.mx; ⊙Aug-Sep) In late August and early September mariachis come to Guadalajara from everywhere in Mexico to jam, battle and enjoy. A Campeonato Nacional Charro (National Cowboy Championship) takes place at the same time.

WESTERN CENTRAL HIGHLANDS GUADALAJARA

Feria Internacional del Libro BOOK FAIR
(www.fil.com.mx; ⊙ Nov-Dec) This nine-day book fair is one of the biggest book events in Latin America. It's held during the last week of November and first week of December, headlined by major authors from around the Spanish-speaking world.

Festival Internacional del Cine FILM
(www.ficg.mx; ⊙ Mar) Mexico's most important film festival has been drawing top actors and directors to Guadalajara for a week each March for more than three decades, with screenings and parties taking place across the city.

🛏 Sleeping

During holidays (Christmas and Holy Week/Easter) and festivals such as Día de los Muertos you must reserve ahead. Ask about discounts if you arrive in the low season or will be staying more than a few days.

🛏 Centro Histórico

The Centro Histórico is full of midrange options, many of which are housed in charming colonial buildings. Southeast of Mercado San Juan de Dios, there's a cluster of budget hotels. This part of town is a bit rough and away from the action, but you can usually find a cheap room here when other places are full. Budget digs can also be found around the Antigua Central Camionera (old bus station); again, it's a bit far-flung but well served by buses.

Hospedarte Centro Histórico HOSTEL $
(Map p588; ☎ 33-3562-7520; www.hostelguadala jara.com; Maestranza 147; dm/d/ste incl breakfast M$240/550/700; @🛜) One of two Hospedarte hostels in Guadalajara, this bright-yellow downtown option is popular with a young crowd looking for a good time. The three dorms (men, women and mixed) are

Central Guadalajara

spacious and count eight metal bunk beds with lockers and fans, sharing toilets and showers around a large communal area with a huge kitchen and plenty of activities laid on.

The two private doubles share bathrooms too. There are another seven suites available in a neighboring building with a great terrace. Discounts for IH card holders.

Casa Vilasanta   HOTEL $
(Map p588; ☎33-3124-1277; www.vilasanta.com; Rayón 170; dm/s/d/tr M$250/600/700/900; ❄🛜) The bright, pastel-colored rooms of this cheery guesthouse are scattered around a cool covered interior courtyard, decorated with pottery and flowers, and there's a sunny 2nd-floor terrace. The singles can feel cramped, but the doubles (eg room 4) are large and all rooms have TV.

There's a shared kitchen with a huge communal table and plenty of chill space on both floors. But with just 17 rooms and English-speaking management, this place fills up, so book ahead. Beware: there are crosses everywhere.

Posada San Pablo   HOTEL $
(Map p588; ☎33-3614-2811; www.posadasanpablo.com; Madero 429; r with/without bathroom from M$500/370; 🛜) This cheery place comes complete with a central courtyard and sunny terrace. The 16 tiled rooms can be a little monkish, though the upstairs ones have balconies. There's a spick-and-span communal kitchen and you can even (hand) wash your clothes in the old-fashioned *lavandería* (laundry) out back. Fans help keep you cool.

**★Del Carmen
Concept Hotel**   BOUTIQUE HOTEL $$
(Map p588; ☎33-3614-2640; www.delcarmen.mx; Gálvez 45; d/ste M$1250/1450; ❄🛜) This hotel in a 19th-century mansion is a great place to stop for a spell. The concept? Nine rooms individually themed around artists from

Mexico's La Ruptura movement (an abstract reaction to the 20th-century muralists); hence the Tamayo room (with a curvaceous metallic bathtub), the Friedeberg room (a trippy patchwork of blinding surrealism) or the energetically blue Soriano room.

All mod cons (but no parking) are assured and the Chai cafe chain has an outlet with terrace on the 1st floor – handy for breakfast or a late-night beer and enchilada.

Hotel Francés   HOTEL **$$**

(Map p588; ☑33-3613-2020; www.hotelfranc es.com; Maestranza 35; r M$740-1270) Hotel Francés is one of the best midrange hotels in Guadalajara for a time-warp stay (it was founded in 1610). The 64 rooms are not as much fun as the marble courtyard bar (open noon to midnight), where waiters in bow ties treat you like a homecoming amigo, troubadours strum weepy ballads, happy hour lasts till 8pm and the bartender mixes a mean margarita.

Hotel Morales   HOTEL **$$**

(Map p588; ☑33-3658-5232; www.hotelmorales. com.mx; Av Corona 243; d/ste from M$1200/1700; ⓟ✳☎⛱) The dimly lit, four-tiered colonial lobby with the stunning ceiling mural is a suitably impressive entrance to this excellent-value, central hotel. Brighter and equally brilliant is the 2nd-floor, blue-and-white-tiled, Andalucía-style courtyard. Other nooks hide fountains, bookshelves and even a rooftop pool, spa and gym. The 98 rooms are a good size and some have Jacuzzis. Choose one (try for room 122) facing into the courtyard in the older Virreinal section of the hotel.

Casa Pedro Loza   BOUTIQUE HOTEL **$$$**

(Map p582; ☑33-1202-2423; www.casapedroloza. com.mx; Loza 360; r incl breakfast M$1200-2300; ✳☎) Housed in an impressive colonial mansion in a charming part of the Centro Histórico, this hotel is a bit away from the action and a titch attitudy. The 12 rooms are each wildly different; some are chock-full of beautiful antiques, others are like garish love nests with circular beds and bubbly furnishings. Could be fun...

The retractable roof over the courtyard and the superb roof terrace Sky Lounge are other points in the hotel's favor.

🛏 Chapultepec & Around

Top-end accommodations are generally found in Chapultepec and points west; those in the latter are generally aimed at guests with their own transportation.

Hospedarte Chapultepec   HOSTEL **$**

(Map p594; ☑33-3615-4957; www.hospedarte hostel.com; Luna 2075; dm/s/d M$200/450/600; ◉☎) On a quiet residential side street in Chapultepec, this low-key hostel has pretty much everything a backpacker requires: two spotless eight-bed dorms, 10 private rooms, a hammock-filled garden, communal kitchen, free bikes, internet and wi-fi, its own bar open Wednesday to Saturday and cheap places to eat within stumbling distance.

There are plenty of traveler-related services, and inhouse events include bar crawls and barbecues. Discounts for IH card holders.

★Villa Ganz   BOUTIQUE HOTEL **$$$**

(Map p594; ☑33-3120-1416; www.villaganz.com; López Cotilla 1739; ste incl breakfast M$2500-3500; ⓟ✳◉☎) Cross the threshold of Villa Ganz and behold a dazzling array of tiles, ferns, candelabras, original art and even a piano. Suites (rather than 'rooms') are luxury personified, with bathrobes, classic furniture, rich carpets and wonderful details. And there is a fantastic back garden with all sorts of hidden nooks and crannies.

Master suite 17 has a balcony, while bright 13 has two outlooks and a Jacuzzi. The service is equally exemplary and there's free wine from 6pm to 8pm, a real fire, evening candlelight and a fine restaurant. It's a bargain – whatever the price!

Quinta Real Guadalajara   LUXURY HOTEL **$$$**

(Map p594; ☑33-1105-1000; www.quintareal.com; Av México 2727; r M$2500-3000; ⓟ✳◉⛱) A sort of rural hacienda in a busy city, this five-star property, one of 10 in a Mexican luxury chain, is drop-dead gorgeous with its exquisite stone and ivy-covered exteriors. The lobby and bar are inviting and stylish, the grounds are impeccably manicured and the service is outstanding. Choose a suite from among the 66 rooms, like garden-facing 104.

A lovely garden pool and fully equipped gym too. It's about 2.5km northwest of Chapultepec.

🛏 Tlaquepaque

Just 20 minutes away by bus or taxi from downtown Guadalajara, Tlaquepaque is an excellent option for those who crave small-town charm but still want to visit the sights of the big city. Added bonus: the shopping here is superb.

Tlaquepaque

Map of Tlaquepaque with scale 200 m / 0.1 miles, north arrow. Streets include Blvd Barragan, Calz Niños Héroes, Cruz Verde, Medellin, Florida, Donato Guerra, Constitución, Madero, Obregón, Carillo Puerto, Allende, Zapata, Morelos, Leandro Valle, Independencia, Jardín Hidalgo, Av Juárez, Zaragoza, Reforma, Miranda, Matamoros, Progreso, Herrera y Cairo, Carranza, 16 de Setiembre, Tonalá, Porvenir, Degollado, Alfareros, Cuauhtémoc, Moctezuma, Río Tinto, Ejército. Labels include Brick Arch, Tlaquepaque State Tourist Office, Tlaquepaque Tourist Information Booth. Numbered markers 1–16.

Casa del Retoño
GUESTHOUSE $$

(Map p592; ☑ 33-3639-6510; www.lacasadelretono.com.mx; Matamoros 182; s/d incl breakfast M$825/1000; P �) The eight rooms in this very pleasant traditional house are all colorfully decorated, share an enormous garden and boast good bathrooms. It's a short walk from Tlaquepaque's main square and is run by a friendly family. It's a good idea to call ahead; reception isn't always staffed.

Casa Campos
GUESTHOUSE $$

(Map p592; ☑ 33-3838-5297; www.casacampos.mx; Miranda 30; s/d/ste incl breakfast M$1070/1310/1510; ✳ @ ☎) This pink-and-orange repurposed 19th-century mansion has a gorgeous, flower-filled courtyard, stone columns and sleek wood furnishings. The 11 rooms on two levels are spacious, tasteful and well equipped (though bathrooms are nothing special), and it's just minutes from the best shopping on Independencia.

★ Casa de las Flores
B&B $$$

(Map p592; ☑ 33-3659-3186; www.casadelasflores.com; Degollado 175; r incl breakfast M$2210-2435; @ ☎) One of our favorite places to stay in the Guadalajara region, this colorful guesthouse is positively crammed with painted ceramics (the American owner is a collector), and boasts a garden full of flowers and a decorative fireplace that defies belief. The seven rooms in an outbuilding have an engaging Mexican feel, with multicolored bedcovers, tiled sinks, haunting art and (sometimes) skylights and balconies.

You'll spend days inspecting the details in your room and the well-stocked El Nahual Gallery (p599), its inhouse shop with wonderful ceramics, figurines and masks.

Quinta Don José
BOUTIQUE HOTEL $$$

(Map p592; ☑ 33-3635-7522; www.quintadonjose.com; Reforma 139; r incl breakfast M$1675-3250; P ✳ @ ☎ ⬱) From the cozy sunken lobby

Tlaquepaque

to the sunny, flower-filled, kidney-shaped pool terrace complete with gurgling fountains, this charming hotel is a great place to escape while remaining in the heart of Tlaquepaque. The 18 rooms might not be as flamboyant as the gardens, but that's a minor niggle.

There's a good in-house Italian restaurant called **TlaquePasta** (Map p592; ☑ 33-3635-7522; www.quintadonjose.com/tlaquepasta; Reforma 139, Quinta Don José;; mains M$160-350; ◎5-10pm Tue-Thu, 2-10pm Fri-Sun) as well.

✖ Eating

Guadalajara is a foodie destination and many visitors find that meals here count among the highlights of their stay. A few local specialties to look out for include *birria* (a spicy goat or lamb stew), *carne en su jugo* ('meat in its juice,' a type of beef soup) and, above all, the ubiquitous *torta ahogada* (literally 'drowned sandwich'), a chili-sauce-soaked pork roll said to cure everything (but especially hangovers).

✖ Centro Histórico

The adventurous might head for **Mercado San Juan de Dios** (Mercado Libertad; Map p588; cnr Av Javier Mina & Calzada Independencia Sur; ◎10am-7pm Mon-Sat, to 4pm Sun), home to endless food stalls serving the cheapest and some of the tastiest eats in town. The plaza south of the Templo Expiatorio is a good place to snag late-night tacos, *tortas ahogadas* and *elote* (grilled corn on the cob with mayonnaise and cheese).

Taco La Paz   SEAFOOD $
(Map p582; ☑ 33-1200-4647; www.tacofish-lapaz.com; Av de la Paz 494; mains M$23-35; ◎9am-4:30pm Mon-Sat) Guadalajara may be a fair

distance from the ocean, but fish and seafood remain a passion. For prawn and fish tacos, this simple eatery can't be beat and you'll guess that as soon as you see the queues.

Café Madrid   CAFE $
(Map p588; ☑ 33-3614-9504; Av Juárez 264; mains M$48-145; ◎8am-10:30pm) An upgraded 1950s-style cafe that is open all day, but best for a *huevos rancheros* breakfast (fried eggs on a corn tortilla with a tomato, chili and onion sauce served with refried beans; M$60) and *chilaquiles* (fried tortilla strips cooked with chili sauce; M$77).

It lacks the historical atmosphere of similar Mexican places, although the coffee, dispensed from a vintage silver espresso machine, has plenty of zest.

★ La Fonda de la Noche   MEXICAN $$
(Map p588; ☑ 33-3827-0917; www.facebook.com/LaFondadelaNoche; Jesús 251; mains M$80-132; ◎7:30pm-midnight) Set in a rambling art nouveau house, this restaurant is a stunner in every way. The cuisine is largely from the Durango region and it would be fair to say that absolutely anything is tasty. The menu is simple and largely spoken, but the affable owner, Carlos, does speak basic English. Try the *plato combinado* – a selection of the chef's four prize dishes (M$111).

La Fonda de San Miguel Arcángel   MEXICAN $$
(Map p588; ☑ 33-3613-0793; www.fondasanmiguelarcangel.com; Guerra 25; mains M$155-240; ◎2-11pm Tue-Fri, 9am-11pm Sat, to 9pm Sun) The courtyard of this erstwhile convent is so dimly lit you can barely see what you're eating, although the semi-darkness has its

Chapultepec

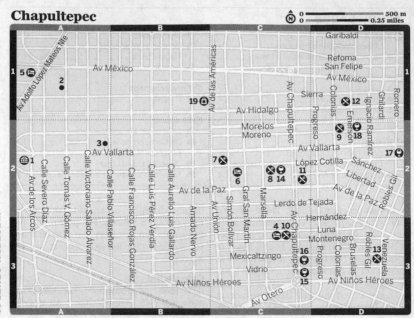

benefits, enhancing the sounds of gurgling fountains, tinkling piano keys and twittering caged birds. Sample the *filete de res oro negro* – beef with *huitlacoche* (corn fungus) sauce.

Also excellent is the *molcajete,* a spicy dish from Oaxaca served on a sizzlingly hot stone dish with fajitas.

Birriería las Nueve Esquinas   MEXICAN $$

(Map p588; 33-3613-6260; www.las9esquinas. com; Av Colón 384; mains M$74-139; 8:30am-11pm Mon-Sat, to 8:30pm Sun) Many restaurants in the village-like Nueve Esquinas (Nine Corners) neighborhood specialize in *birria,* meat stewed in its own juices until very tender. Birriería las Nueve Esquinas, a delightful semi-open-air restaurant covered in blue-and-white tiles, is renowned far and wide for being the king of *birria.*

The two main offerings here are *birria de chivo* (steamed goat) and *barbacoa de borrego* (baked lamb). Both cost M$139 and come with a stack of fresh tortillas, pickled onions, cilantro and two types of salsa. Wrap the meat in the tortilla, add various flavors and then dip the tortilla in the meat juice before putting it in your mouth.

La Chata de Guadalajara   MEXICAN $$

(Map p588; 33-3613-1315; www.lachata.com. mx; Av Corona 126; mains M$69-164; 7:30am-midnight) Quality *comida típica* (home-style food), affordable prices and ample portions mean this family diner always has a queue out front. Fortunately, hard-working staff keep the crowds moving quickly, plus you'll be happily distracted watching the energetic chefs spin tortillas as you wait in line. The specialty is the superb *platillo jaliscense* (fried chicken with five side dishes; M$108).

✕ Chapultepec & Around

★Tortas Ahogadas Migue   MEXICAN $

(Map p594; 33-3825-4520; Calle Mexicaltzingo 1727; tortas M$38-65) Take it from *tapatíos* (native Guadalajarans) in the know: this bright yellow-and-orange cafe serves the city's best *tortas ahogadas,* Guadalajara's beloved hangover cure. Baguette-like rolls called *birotes* are filled with chunks of slow-roasted pork and drenched with searing *salsa picante* – ask for yours 'media *ahogada*' (half-drowned) for less burn. Only die-hard chili-heads should request 'bien *ahogada*.'

Chapultepec

Pig's Pearls BURGERS $$
(Map p594; ☑ 33-3825-5933; www.pigspearls.com; Coronado 79; burgers M$95-112; ⊗ 1-11pm Mon-Sat) *Tapatíos* rave about the burgers here – there are a dozen to choose from – so who are we to argue? Sit in the convivial open terrace in fine weather or move behind to the small but perfectly formed bar. A small selection of salads (M$75 to M$85) and kebabs (from M$85) too.

El Cargol SPANISH $$
(Map p594; ☑ 33-3616-6035; López Cotilla 1513; mains M$115-200; ⊗ 2-11pm Mon, Tue & Thu, to 1am Fri & Sat, to 7pm Sun) You can pay homage to Catalonia (that Spanish collector of Michelin stars) in the unlikely environs of Chapultepec at the family-run 'Snail.' The Catalan menu is billed as 'slow food' – made from scratch and worth the wait. Regulars come here for a paella fix and everyone raves about the *crema catalana* dessert.

★**Alcalde** NEW MEXICAN $$$
(Map p582; ☑ 33-3615-7400; www.alcalde.com. mx; Av México 2903; mains M$295-375; ⊗ 1:30-11pm Mon-Sat, to 5:30pm Sun) One of our favorite top-end restaurants in Guadalajara, the 'Mayor' is chef Francisco Ruano's latest local venture, having cut his teeth at El Celler de Can Roca in Girona and Noma in Copenhagen. Try his green *aguachile* soup with green apples or his tomatoes in three ways to start, followed by his 'black dish' of grilled pork in rich *mole,* homemade blood sausage/pudding and blackened rice.

The decor – colorful Perspex lights setting off a black-and-white tiled floor – is stunning.

★**Lulabistro** NEW MEXICAN $$$
(Map p582; ☑ 33-3647-6432; www.lulabistro.com; San Gabriel 3030; 6-8-12-course menu M$850/ 1200/1600; ⊗ 8-11:30pm Mon, 2-5pm & 8-11:30pm Tue-Thu, 2-5:30pm & 8pm-midnight Fri & Sat) Guadalajara's most inventive restaurant is this super-chic eatery west of the center. Sleek and industrial though the setting is, it's the food people come for. The three set menus, which could best be described as a fusion of French preparation and Mexican tastes, is particularly strong on fish and seafood. Add M$600/750/1000 for wine pairings. Reservations highly recommended.

★**El Sacromonte** MEXICAN $$$
(Map p594; ☑ 33-3825-5447; www.sacromonte. com.mx; Moreno 1398; mains M$180-300; ⊗ noon-midnight Mon-Sat, to 6pm Sun) This favorite *alta cocina* (gourmet restaurant) establishment in Chapultepec has whimsical takes on classic dishes – think quesadillas sprinkled with rose petals and strawberry aioli, avocado-watermelon soup and giant prawns in lobster sauce with fried spinach. The decor pays homage to erstwhile matadors – there are cartoons of them everywhere – and moody piano music plays in the background. Reservations are recommended.

Hueso INTERNATIONAL $$$
(Map p594; ☑ 33-3615-3591; www.huesorestaurant. com; Luna 2061; mains M$295-375; ⊗ 7:30pm-midnight Mon-Sat) The preserve of acclaimed chef Alfonso Cadena (in fact, it's described as his *taller,* or 'workshop'), this restaurant gets consistently rave reviews for its innovative dishes and attention to detail. Our only problem is the Hueso (Bone) theme – some 10,000 shark, bear, deer, boar and other

animal bones adorn the place. It's like the Day of the Dead arrived and never departed.

Allium
FUSION $$$

(Map p594; 📋 33-3615-6401; www.allium.com.mx; López Cotilla 1752; mains M$230-250; ⊘1:30-5pm Tues-Sun, 7-10:30pm Tue-Fri, 7-11pm Fri & Sat) 🍴 This sleek fine-dining addition to Guadalajara's growing gourmet circuit directed by chef Sebastian Renner Hamdan puts emphasis on locally produced food: 90% of its ingredients come from the state of Jalisco. The small minimalist interior is redolent of Michelin-star restaurants in Europe, but prices and service are down-to-earth. Try the pork belly with sweet potato or the roasted octopus.

I Latina
INTERNATIONAL $$$

(Map p582; 📋 33-3647-7774; www.ilatinarest.com; Av Inglaterra 3128; mains M$150-350; ⊘7pm-1am Tue-Sat, 1:30-6pm Sun) This eccentrically decorated place requires a sharp double-take with its wall of ceramic pigs, a giant swordfish and lots of kitsch, fun touches. The Asian-leaning international menu is the reason to come, however, and the food is excellent. It's hugely popular with a smart and fashionable crowd and can get loud. But that makes it all the more fun.

🍴 Tlaquepaque

Tlaquepaque's main plaza overflows with street-food vendors – look for *jericalla* (a cross between flan and creme brûlée), coconut *empanadas* and cups of lime-drenched pomegranate seeds. Just southeast of the plaza, **El Parián** (Map p592; 📋33-3696-0488; www.facebook.com/ElParianDeTlaquepaque; Av Juárez 68; ⊘10am-midnight Sun-Thu, to 1am Fri & Sat) is a block of restaurant-bars with patio tables crowding a leafy inner courtyard. This is where you can sit, drink and listen to live mariachi music (but eat elsewhere).

Cenaduría Doña Victoria
MEXICAN $

(Map p592; 📋 33-3635-2010; Degollado 182; mains from M$80; ⊘7-11pm Fri-Wed) Victoria serves high-quality Mexican soul food from her streetside stall in Tlaquepaque. Each evening her skillet overflows with *taquitos* (small tacos), tacos, *pozole* (traditional soup or stew made with hominy, pork and chilies), quail and chicken. In fact, the *pollo dorado* (fried chicken; M$80) is the best seller. It comes with potatoes, salad, tortillas and three kinds of salsa.

Chimbombo's Grill
MEXICAN $$

(Map p592; 📋33-3954-1788; Madero 80A; tortas M$32, steaks M$75-170; ⊘8am-10pm) This streetside grill is where to come for T-bone and skirt steaks as well as deliciously spicy *tortas ahogadas* (bread rolls called *birotes* filled with chunks of slow-roasted pork and drenched with searing *salsa picante*). Steaks are rubbed with olive oil, splashed with soy sauce and served with Greek salad and garlic bread. You can eat in, or take your feast to the nearby plaza and enjoy it in the sun.

★ Casa Fuerte
MEXICAN $$$

(Map p592; 📋 33-3639-6481; www.casafuerte.com; Independencia 224; mains M$150-350; ⊘noon-9pm; 🛜) This elegant and sprawling place leans toward fine dining, with a full cocktail bar, refreshing garden patio and a rather stately feel. It's very popular with Tlaquepaque's upper crust, although you can usually get a table with no problem. Try the sizzling *queso fundido con chorizo* (melted cheese with chorizo) in a stone pot.

Casa Luna
NEW MEXICAN $$$

(Map p592; 📋33-1592-2061; www.facebook.com/CasaLunaRest; Independencia 211; mains M$245-350; ⊘noon-11pm Mon-Thu, to midnight Fri & Sat) This restaurant in the center of Tlaquepaque spreads throughout an open courtyard under the shade of a large tree and inside as well. The cuisine is Mexican, but a modern version – think cream of cilantro soup and shrimp quesadillas. The wonderful lamps and other lighting fixtures come from the attached **Origenes** (Map p592; 📋 33-3657-2405; ⊘10am-7pm Mon-Fri, 11am-7pm Sat, to 6pm Sun) shop.

Zaguan
MEXICAN $$$

(Map p592; 📋33-3614-1814; www.facebook.com/zaguan.restaurante.galeria; Juárez 5; mains M$180-250; ⊘1-9pm Tue-Sun) Touted as Tlaquepaque's best eatery, this restaurant and gallery places a lot of emphasis on colors, tastes and textures and is largely successful in its endeavors. Local favorites like *chiles en nogada* and *carne en su jugo* take on a new taste and look; go for the *degustación de moles* (M$199), a *mole*-tasting treat.

Mariscos Progreso
SEAFOOD $$$

(Map p592; 📋33-3636-6149; Progreso 80; mains M$150-300; ⊘11am-8pm) On Saturday and Sunday afternoons it feels like half of Guadalajara has packed into this Tlaquepaque patio seafood restaurant with an open fire.

Dressed-up Mexican families slurp ceviche and pass around platters of pineapple shrimp (M$162) and *huachinango al estilo Veracruz* (snapper with lime and tomatoes; M$299), while mariachis wander from table to table.

Oysters (from M$106 a dozen) are a specialty – you'll recognize the place by the oyster-shucking hut out front.

 Zapopan

Zapopan has its own multifarious food scene, although the places lining the main road to the basilica are generally best avoided. Head instead to the side streets to the southeast.

Fonda Doña
Gabina Escolatica   MEXICAN $

(Map p582; ☑ 33-3833-0883; Mina 237; mains M$16-62; ⊗2-11pm Tue-Sat, 9am-8pm Sun) This narrow, barnlike restaurant on a delightful Zapopan side-street of pastel-colored houses is bedecked with sunny colored textiles and specializes in *pozole* (traditional soup or stew made with hominy, pork and chilies) and monumental *tostada de pollo,* a huge pile of chicken and salad on a toasted tortilla.

 Drinking & Nightlife

The Centro Histórico gets fairly quiet at night, though there are several bright spots (if you know where to look) and a well-established gay scene; most gay clubs also welcome straight people. Chapultepec, however, is always hopping, with both local *antros* (literally 'dens,' but meaning dives) and international-style bars and clubs. In general, *tapatíos* (Guadalajarans) tend to dress up to go out, so when in Rome...

★**La Mutualista**   DANCING

(Map p588; ☑33-3614-2176; Madero 553; ⊗noon-2am Tue-Sat) With smoke-yellowed walls and antique chandeliers dangling from high ceilings, this vintage dance hall simmers with the decaying glamour of Old Havana. Thursdays, Fridays and Saturdays are salsa nights, the real reason to come. A Cuban band kicks off around midnight and the all-age crowd explodes with eye-popping moves on the dance floor. Prepare to perspire.

★**Café Galería André Breton**   BAR

(Café AB; Map p588; ☑33-3345-2194; Manuel 175; ⊗10am-8pm Mon, to 3am Tue-Sat) Tucked away on a side street on the eastern side of the Centro Histórico is this charming bar, cafe and live-music venue. As bohemian as its name suggests, this is one of the city's coolest hangouts. Enjoy the French menu (mains M$80) and range of craft beers from around the world, and enjoy live music (M$50 cover) most evenings from 10pm.

Bar Américas   CLUB

(Map p594; ☑cell 324-1044467; http://barameri cas.com.mx; Av Chapultepec Sur 507; ⊗9pm-5am Wed-Sat, to midnight Sun) One of the most interesting late-night clubs in town, this place caters to a slightly well-heeled, sophisticated older crowd. The all-black entrance down the steps look as though you are entering the very gates of hell.

El Grillo   CRAFT BEER

(Map p594; ☑33-3827-3090; www.facebook.com/ el.grillo.cantor; Av Chapultepec 219; ⊗noon-2:30am) This bar stocks over 50 (mainly bottled) Mexican craft beers. Of interest are the Guadalajara-brewed Diógenes IPA and the red amber Grasshoppy. The front patio is a good starting point for a Chapultepec night out – while your taste buds are still awake to the nuances of the hoppy brews.

Need to line the stomach? Order off the menu from the affiliated (and equally hip) restaurant next door, **La Nacional** (LaNaChapultepec; Map p594; ☑33-3827-3090; www. facebook.com/lanachapultepec; Av Chapultepec Sur 215; mains M$89-134; ⊗9am-2pm Sun-Thu, to 3pm Fri & Sat).

California's   GAY

(Map p588; ☑33-3614-3221; Moreno 652; ⊗6pm-4am Mon-Sat) Attracts a fairly diverse and attractive crowd usually OFB (out for business). It gets packed around 10pm, and Friday and Saturday nights are a madhouse. Great music but no dancing – this is the place to start your night before heading to a club.

La Fuente   BAR

(Map p588; Suárez 78; ⊗noon-11pm Mon-Wed, to 12:30am Thu-Sat) La Fuente, set in the old Edison boiler room, is an institution in Guadalajara and a perfect example of what a proper Mexican cantina is (ie rough around the edges). It's been here since 1921 and is mostly patronized by regulars who welcome newcomers like family. A bass, piano and violin trio sets up and jams from midafternoon until last call.

GAY & LESBIAN GUADALAJARA

Guadalajara is one of the gayest cities in Mexico – a conservative local government and fiercely Catholic population notwithstanding. In late June everyone takes to the streets when the city hosts one of Latin America's largest gay pride parades.

Guadalajara's so-called 'gay ghetto' radiates out a few blocks from the corner of Ocampo and Sánchez, in the city center, but Avenida Chapultepec, just west of the city center, is starting to see upscale establishments aimed at a gay clientele. You can read more listings at www.gaymexicomap.com.

La Taberna de Caudillos
CLUB
(Map p588; ☑ 33-3613-5445; www.facebook. com/LaTabernaDeCaudillos; Sánchez 407; M$50; ⊘ 9pm-4am) A popular multistory disco, with three dance floors and endless lounges and bars full of gorgeous young things dancing and various acts on stage (from go-go dancers to drag shows). Always fun.

Pigalle
COCKTAIL BAR
(Map p594; ☑ 33-3825-3118; Robles Gil 137; ⊘ 6pm-midnight Tue & Wed, to 2:30am Thu-Sat) Mexican baristas excel at making cocktails (from M$17), both the savory and sweet type, and Pigalle is yet another cut above. Come here to relax, sip some of the most inventive libations in Guadalajara and listen to music, both canned and live.

Romea
WINE BAR
(Map p594; ☑ 33-1817-0202; www.facebook.com/ romea.gdl; Morelos 1349; ⊘ 5:30pm-midnight Mon, 9am-midnight Tue-Sat, to 4pm Sun) This welcoming corner wine bar with large open windows stocks a wide range of Mexican vintages as well as wine from Spain, France, Portugal and even Slovenia. Blotter is available in the form of cheese (M$99) and charcuterie (M$155 to M$245) platters.

Cervecería Chapultepec
PUB
(Map p594; ☑ 33-1102-1955; www.cerveceria chapultepec.com; Mexicaltzingo 1938) This boozer is forever hopping (and jumping and somersaulting) and we think we know why. Everything but everything – from beers and mojitos to tacos and burgers – costs a uniform M$18. The front terrace is rammed from opening to closing.

Angels Club
CLUB
(Map p594; ☑ 33-4040-5030; López Cotilla 1495B; ⊘ 10pm-5am Wed-Sat, 6am-11pm Sun) Welcome to Guadalajara's mega-club. Sure, it's a gay venue, but straight guys and girls are just as welcome to join the party, which is spread across three dance floors where house, pop and techno reign supreme. Saturday nights get wild and flow freely into late Sunday morning.

☆ Entertainment

Guadalajara is a musical city, and live performers can be heard most nights of the week at any of the city's many venues (which include some restaurants). Discos and bars are plentiful, but ask around for the newest hot spots – tapatíos (Guadalajarans) love to show off their town.

Alongside the town's key cultural institutions, the Unesco World Heritage–listed Instituto Cultural de Cabañas (p584) also plays host to an array of cultural performances.

Live Music

Guadalajara is the birthplace of the mariachi tradition, and Plaza de los Mariachis (p585), east of the Centro Histórico, is a great place to sit, drink beer and soak in the serenades of passionate Mexican bands. El Parián (p596), a garden complex dating from 1878 in Tlaquepaque, is made up of almost a score of small cantinas that all share one plaza occupied by droves of mariachis. From Thursday to Monday the bands battle and jockey for your ears, applause and cash for about an hour from 3:30pm and then again from 9:30pm.

State and municipal bands present free concerts of typical música tapatía (Guadalajaran music) in the French art nouveau (1889) bandstand in the Plaza de Armas at 6:30pm Tuesday, 7:30pm Wednesday and 8pm Thursday, as well during certain holiday periods.

1er Piso Jazz Club
LIVE MUSIC
(Primer Piso Jazz Club; Map p588; ☑ 33-3825-7085; Moreno 947; ⊘ 7:30pm-3am Tue-Sat) This sophisticated jazz club on the 1er Piso (1st floor) of a city block has sets most nights from 9pm and excellent cocktails.

Sports

Fútbol (soccer) flows strongly through tapatío blood. The city has two local teams in Mexico's 18-club Liga MX (formerly called the Primera División): **Guadalajara** (www.

chivasdecorazon.com.mx), the second most popular team in the country and the only club in Mexico to exclusively field Mexican players, and Atlas (www.atlas.com.mx). The seasons last from July to December and from January to June, and teams play at stadiums around the city. You can get an up-to-date season schedule at Federación Mexicana de Fútbol (www.femexfut.org.mx).

★**Arena Coliseo**   MEXICAN WRESTLING
(Map p588; ☑ 33-3617-3401; Medrano 67; tickets M$110-350; ⊙ 8:30pm Tue, 6pm Sun) Watching masked *luchadores* (wrestlers) with names like El Terrible and Blue Panther gut-punching each other makes for a memorable night out. Expect scantily clad women, insult-hurling crowds and screaming doughnut vendors: it's all part of the fun of this classic Mexican pastime. The neighborhood surrounding the beloved coliseum can be a bit dodgy; take the usual precautions.

Campo Charro Jalisco   RODEO
(Map p582; ☑ 33-3619-0315; www.decharros.com; Av Dr Roberto Michel 577, Rincon de Agua Azul) *Charreadas* (or *charrerías*), similar to rodeos, are held at noon most Sundays in this ring just behind Parque Agua Azul south of the city center. *Charros* (cowboys) come from all over Jalisco and the rest of Mexico; *escaramuza charra* (female stunt riding) teams perform as well.

Theater

Teatro Degollado   THEATER
(Map p588; ☑ 33-3614-4773; www.facebook.com/TeatroDegollado) This historic theater is a downtown cultural center that hosts a range of drama, dance and music performances.

Teatro Diana   THEATER
(Map p582; ☑ 33-3613-8579; www.teatrodiana.com; Av 16 de Septiembre 710) The hippest venue in town hosting a wide range of range of drama, dance and music performances. It stages traveling Broadway shows, concerts with local and international artists and art installations.

🔒 **Shopping**

For most visitors, Guadalajara's most appealing shopping are the excellent handicrafts from Jalisco, Michoacán and other Mexican states available in its many markets. Tlaquepaque and Tonalá, suburbs 8km and 17km respectively from the center,

are both major producers of handicrafts and furniture – anyone with an interior-decorating habit should plan to spend some time in each. You'll find the best wholesale prices in Tonalá. There's also a craft market in Chapultepec.

Tienda de Vino Vinísfera   WINE
(Map p594; ☑ 33-1377-5647; www.tiendadevino.mx; Av Justo Sierra 2275) If you'd like to learn more about and/or taste Mexican wine, head for this combination shop and cafe-bar north of Chapultepec. Along with a large selection of red and white wines ranging in price from M$100 to M$4000, you'll also find a dozen craft beers from Jalisco state. Take away or sip same in the cafe or delightful back garden.

El Nahual Gallery   ARTS & CRAFTS
(Map p592; www.elnahualgallery.com; Degollado 175; ⊙ 10am-6pm) This well-stocked shop in the Casa de las Flores (p592) sells some of the finest ceramics pieces, figurines and masks in the region. Owner and collector Stan Singleton is ready and eager to explain the processes, organize workshop visits and advise on purchases.

Antigua de México   HOMEWARES
(Map p592; ☑ 33-3635-2402; www.antiguademexico.com; Independencia 255; ⊙ 10am-2pm & 3-6:30pm Mon-Fri, 10am-6pm Sat) A 'wow'-inducing Tlaquepaque boutique with gorgeous furniture showpieces, such as benches carved from a single tree, which are displayed in expansive, old-world courtyards. Are those ancient coaches actually for sale?

Del Corazón de la Tierra   ARTS & CRAFTS
(Map p592; ☑ 33-3657-5682; www.delcorazondelatierra.mx; Independencia 227) This lovely shop in central Tlaquepaque, whose name translates as 'From the Heart of the Country,' specialises in indigenous (mostly Maya) art. Stop by for some very affordable souvenirs and/or gifts.

Taller de Cerámica Paco Padilla   ARTS & CRAFTS
(Map p592; ☑ 33-3635-4838; www.facebook.com/tallerpacopadilla; Sánchez 142; ⊙ 10am-4pm Mon-Fri, to 2pm Sat) This is the workshop and showroom of noted Tlaquepaque ceramicist Paco Padilla. It's within easy walking distance of the famed Museo Pantaleón Panduro (p586) of award-winning ceramics pieces.

ℹ Information

EMERGENCY

If you are a victim of crime, you may first want to contact your embassy or consulate and/or the state tourist office.

Ambulance ☎ 33-3616-9616

Emergency ☎ 066, ☎ 080

Fire ☎ 33-3619-5155

Police ☎ 33-3668-0800

INTERNET ACCESS

A dwindling stash of internet cafes (M$10 to M$35 per hour) are scattered around the city, but tend to change location frequently. Nearly all hotels and hostels and the majority of restaurants, cafes and bars offer free wi-fi access.

MEDICAL SERVICES

Farmacia Guadalajara (☎ 33-3613-7509; Moreno 170; ⊗ 8am-10pm) Get your first aid, sundry items and prescribed meds here.

Hospital México Americano (☎ 33-3648-3333, free call 01-800-462-2238; www.hma.com.mx; Colomos 2110) About 3km northwest of the city center; English-speaking physicians available.

US Consulate (☎ 33-3268-2100; https://mx .usembassy.gov/embassy-consulates/guadala jara; Progreso 175, Colonia Americana) Keeps a regularly updated online list (https://mx.usem bassy.gov/embassy-consulates/guadalajara/ american-services) of local English-speaking doctors, including specialists and dentists.

MONEY

Banks are plentiful in Guadalajara and most have ATMs, known as *cajeros automáticos*.

You can change cash at competitive prices round the clock at one of the eager *casas de cambio* (money changers) on López Cotilla, between Avenida 16 de Septiembre and Maestranza. Very few change traveler's checks these days.

POST

If you go overboard stocking up on hammocks, ceramics and giant carved jaguars in one of Guadalajara's many wonderful homewares stores, **Sebastián Exportaciones** (Map p592; ☎ 33-3124-6560; sebastianexp@prodigy.net.mx; Ejército 45; ⊗ 9am-2pm & 4-6pm Mon-Fri) has you covered. This outfit ships boxes and cartons (minimum 1 cu meter) internationally.

Main Post Office (Map p588; ☎ 33-3614-2482; cnr Carranza & Av Independencia 57; ⊗ 8am-7pm Mon-Fri, to 3pm Sat)

TOURIST INFORMATION

Guadalajara Tourist Information Booth (Map p588; Plaza de la Liberación; ⊗ 8:45am-1:45pm & 2:45-7:45pm Mon-Fri, 9:45am-2:45pm Sat & Sun) One of half a dozen generic booths scattered around the city, all with the same hours. You'll find others in Jardín San Francisco, Plaza de las Américas (Zapopan) and outside the Instituto Cultural de Cabañas in Plaza de Iberoamérica.

Jalisco State Tourist Office (Map p588; ☎ 33-3668-1600/1; Morelos 102; ⊗ 9am-5pm Mon-Fri) Enter from either Morelos or Paseo Degollado. English-speaking staff offer information on Guadalajara, the state of Jalisco and the upcoming week's events.

Tlaquepaque State Tourist Office (Map p592; ☎ 33-1057-6212; www.tlaquepaque.gob.mx; Morelos 288; ⊗ 9am-3pm Mon-Fri) Upstairs in the Casa del Artesano. There is a much more helpful and conveniently located tourist information booth (p586) just next to El Parián (p596).

Tonalá Tourist Office (p586) Two blocks east of Avenida Tonaltecas and north of Avenida Constitución on Moreles.

ℹ Getting There & Away

AIR

Guadalajara's **Aeropuerto Internacional Miguel Hidalgo** (☎ 33-3688-5248; www.aeropuertosgap.com.mx) is 20km south of downtown, just off the Hwy 23 to Chapala. Inside are ATMs, money-exchange offices, cafes and car-rental companies.

A number of diiferent airlines offer direct flights to major cities in Mexico.

Aeroméxico (☎ 800-021-40-00; www.aero mexico.com; Aeropuerto Internacional Miguel Hidalgo)

Interjet (☎ 800-011-23-45; www.interjet.com. mx; Aeropuerto Internacional Miguel Hidalgo)

VivaAerobus (☎ 33-4000-0180; www.vivaaero bus.com; Aeropuerto Internacional Miguel Hidalgo)

Volaris (☎ 55-1102-8000; www.volaris.mx; Aeropuerto Internacional Miguel Hidalgo)

BUS

Guadalajara has two bus terminals. The long-distance bus terminal is the airport-like **Nueva Central Camionera** (New Bus Terminal; Map p582; ☎ 33-3600-0135), a large, modern, V-shaped terminal that is split into seven separate *módulos* (mini-terminals). Each *módulo* has ticket desks for a number of bus lines, plus restrooms, web cafes and cafeterias. The Nueva Central Camionera is 11km southeast of Guadalajara city center, past Tlaquepaque, just off the Hwy 15 to Mexico City.

Buses go to and from just about everywhere in western, central and northern Mexico. Destinations are served by multiple companies, based in the different *módulos*, making price comparisons difficult (though prices are posted) and

CAR-FREE GUADALAJARA

Every Sunday since 2004, Mexico's second largest city has celebrated the **Vía Recreativa** (www.viarecreativa.org; ⊙8am-2pm Sun), when its arterial streets are closed to cars and given over instead to bikes, skateboards, strollers, wheelchairs and any other form of nonmotorized forward propulsion.

Adding to the convenience is an army of enthusiastic volunteers in Parque Revolución dispensing free bikes (ID required) and offering scenic bike tours (p588) departing a short distance to the west at 9:30am and 11am and lasting an hour.

The aim of this car-less half-day is to reduce vehicle dependence, promote health and generate social interaction. Creative artists are encouraged to take to the streets, and Parque Revolución, the nerve center of Via Recreativa, maintains a cultural pavilion with live performances. The measure – which sees an average 200,000 *tapatíos* (Guadalajara residents) take to the streets weekly – has since been adopted by other Mexican cities, including Mexico City's DF (Distrito Federal or Federal District).

time-consuming. The good news is that if you're flexible, you won't have to wait long for a bus – there are departures at least once an hour for all major destinations. Fares given are for the best buses available. You can often find cheaper fares by going on slightly less plush buses.

ETN (☑33-3817-6618; www.etn.com.mx) and **Primera Plus** (☑800-444-16-06; www.primeraplus.com.mx) offer deluxe nonstop rides to many destinations. Buses have wi-fi, toilets, air-con, individual TV screens, mega-comfortable seats, and free food and drink. Prices are highly reasonable.

Guadalajara's other bus terminal is the scruffier **Antigua Central Camionera** (Old Bus Terminal; Map p582; ☑33-3650-0479; Dr Michel & Los Ángeles), about 2km south of the cathedral near Parque Agua Azul. From here 2nd-class buses serve destinations within 100km of Guadalajara. There are two sides to it: Sala A is for destinations to the east and northeast; Sala B is for destinations northwest, southwest and south. There's a M$0.50 charge to enter the terminal. Bus services generally run between 6am and 10pm. Buses leave multiple times an hour for nearby locations, and once an hour or so for longer trips.

CAR & MOTORCYCLE

Guadalajara is 545km northwest of Mexico City and 325km east of Puerto Vallarta. Highways 15, 15D, 23, 54, 54D, 80, 80D and 90 all converge here, combining temporarily to form the Periférico Norte and Periférico Sur, the ring roads around the city.

Guadalajara has many car-rental agencies. All the large international companies are represented, but you may get a cheaper deal from a local company, so it's worth comparing prices and availability online before you travel. Prices start at around M$350 per day for a four-door sedan; it will cost you upward of M$4000 to drop off the car in any city other than the one you rented it from.

TRAIN

The only passenger trains serving Guadalajara are the two tourist 'tequila-tasting' trains to the nearby towns of Amatitán or Tequila.

ⓘ Getting Around

TO/FROM THE AIRPORT

The airport is just under 20km south of central Guadalajara, just off the Hwy 23 to Chapala. To get into town on public transportation, exit the airport and head to the bus stop in front of the motel-like Hotel Casa Grande, about 50m to the right. Take bus 176 (M$7) or the more expensive one marked 'Atasa' (M$12) – both run every 15 minutes or so from about 5am to 10pm and take 40 minutes to the Antigua Central Camionera, where you can hop on a bus to the city center.

Taxi prices are M$330 to the city center, M$290 to the Nueva Central Camionera and M$250 to Tlaquepaque. Buy fixed-price tickets inside the airport.

To get to the airport from Guadalajara's center, take bus 604 to the Antigua Central Camionera (the stop where you get off is in front of the Gran Hotel Canada) and then get on an 'Aeropuerto' shuttle bus (every 20 minutes, 6am to 9pm) at this stop. Metered taxis cost roughly M$300.

TO/FROM THE BUS TERMINALS

To reach the city center from the Nueva Central Camionera, take any bus marked 'Centro' (M$7). You can also catch the more comfortable, turquoise-colored TUR bus (M$12). They should be marked 'Zapopan.' Don't take the ones marked 'Tonalá' or you'll be headed away from Guadalajara's center. Taxis to the city center cost M$150 unless they let the meter tick (some don't use it). A direct taxi from the airport to the Nueva Central Camionera costs M$290.

To get to the Nueva Central Camionera from the city center, take any bus marked 'Nueva Central' such as 616 or 275B. These are frequent and leave from the **corner** (Map p588) of Avenida 16 de Septiembre and Madero.

To reach the city center from the Antigua Central Camionera, take any bus going north on Calzada Independencia. To return to the Antigua Central Camionera from the city center, take bus 604 going south on **Calzada Independencia** (Map p588). Taxis cost M$50.

Bus 616 (M$7) runs between the two bus terminals.

BICYCLE

Guadalajara's large-scale bike-sharing scheme **MiBici** was introduced in 2014 and now counts some 13,000 users. Most of its users are yearly (M$365) subscribers, but you can obtain a *pase temporal* (temporary pass) for M$80/160/280 per day/3 days/week by using your credit card in a machine at any of the docking stations, such as the big one on Parque Revolución. Be advised that bikes must be returned by midnight and cannot be used before 6am.

BUS

Guadalajara has a comprehensive city bus system, but be ready for crowded, rough rides. On major routes, buses run every five minutes or so from 6am to 10pm daily and cost M$7. Many buses pass through the city center, so for a suburban destination you'll have a few stops to choose from. The routes diverge as they get further from the city center and you'll need to know the bus number for the suburb you want. Some bus-route numbers are followed by an additional letter indicating which route they take through the suburbs.

The TUR buses, painted a distinctive turquoise color, are a more comfortable alternative. They have air-con and plush seats (M$12). If they roar past without stopping, they're full; this can happen several times in a row during rush hour and may drive you mad.

BUSES FROM GUADALAJARA
From Nueva Central Camionera

DESTINATION	FARE (M$)	DURATION (HR)	FREQUENCY (DAILY)
Barra de Navidad	549	6	12
Colima	324	3	hourly
Guanajuato	482	4	13
Manzanillo	473	4½	hourly
Mexico City (Terminal Norte)	792	7	half-hourly
Morelia	495	3½	half-hourly
Pátzcuaro	438	4½	2
Puerto Vallarta	589	6	hourly
Querétaro	612	4½	half-hourly
San Miguel de Allende	648	5½	every 2hr
Tepic	351	3	5
Uruapan	459	4¾	hourly
Zacatecas	621	5	11
Zamora	274	2¼	half-hourly

From Antigua Central Camionera

DESTINATION	FARE (M$)	DURATION (HR)	FREQUENCY (DAILY)
Ajijic	55	1	hourly
Chapala	55	1	very frequent
Ciudad Guzmán	192	2	hourly
Mazamitla	170	3	hourly
Tapalpa	152	3	10
Tequila	103	1¾	half-hourly

The tourist office has a list of the complex bus routes in Guadalajara and can help you reach your destination. Following are some common destinations, the buses that go there and a central stop from where you can catch them.

Antigua Central Camionera Bus 62 going south on Calzada Independencia or bus 320, 644A or from the center.

Chapultepec Bus 707 TUR and metro line 3 bus replacement along Avenida Vallarta; buses 400 and 500 from Avenida Alcalde to **Chapultepec** (Map p588).

Nueva Central Camionera Bus 616, 275B or any bus marked Nueva Central; catch them all at the corner of Avenida 16 de Septiembre and Madero.

Tlaquepaque Bus 275B, 303, 647 or 706 TUR marked **Tlaquepaque** at Avenida 16 de Septiembre between López Cotilla and Madero.

Tonalá Bus 231, 275D, 275 Diagonal, 633V or 707b TUR marked Tonalá at Avenida 16 de Septiembre and Madero.

Zapopan Bus 275 or 706 TUR marked **Zapopan** (Map p588) going north on Avenida 16 de Septiembre or Alcalde.

METRO

At present the **SITEUR** (Sistema de Tren Eléctrico Urbano; [☎] 33-3942-5700; www.siteur. gob.mx) subway and light-rail system counts two lines that cross the city. Stops are marked with a 'T.' But the metro as it exists now isn't tourist friendly because most stops are far from the sights. Línea 1 stretches north–south for 15.5km all the way from the Periférico Norte to the Periférico Sur. It runs below Federalismo (seven blocks west of the city center) and Avenida Colón: catch it at Parque Revolución, on the corner of Avenida Juárez. Línea 2 runs east–west for 8.5km below Avenidas Juárez and Mina. Slated for December 2018, Línea 3 will extend westward from the interchange Juárez station for 19km to Zapopan. The SiTren trolleybus covers part of the route as far as Los Arcos and Centro Magno.

A single journey costs M$7 with a transfer at Juárez an additional M$3.50. A stored-value card (M$20) includes the first journey.

TAXI

Taxis are everywhere in the city center. They have meters, but drivers seldom use them. Most would rather quote a flat fee for a trip, especially at night. Generally it's cheaper to go by the meter – if you're quoted a flat fee and think it's inflated, try to bargain (and good luck). From 10pm to 6am fares rise by 25%. We've heard reports from both locals and visitors about endemic taxi rip-offs in Guadalajara; use Uber, which is reliable and invariably cheaper.

Tequila

[☎] 374 / POP 29,200 / ELEV 1180M

Surrounded by a sea of blue agave, sun-baked Tequila is a surprisingly attractive factory town that's firmly on the tour-bus circuit these days. The eponymous drink – the object of everyone's longing – is best observed and tasted in one of three big distilleries, all of which run tours.

The Tequila region's agave landscape and its ancient industrial facilities have been a Unesco World Heritage site since 2006.

⊙ Sights

Hacienda La Cofradia DISTILLERY
([☎] 374-742-6800; www.tequilacofradia.com.mx; La Cofradia 1297; tour M$195, with 3 tastings M$260; ⊙10am-6pm) Two kilometers south of Tequila sits the beautiful Hacienda La Cofradia estate where the 100% blue agave Casa Noble tequila brand is distilled. The elegant 'factory' is set amid mango trees and uses French oak barrels to age its spirits. Aside from factory tours, La Cofradia hosts the **Museo de Sitio del Tequila** and the atmospherically cavernous **La Taberna del Cofrade** restaurant.

Casa Sauza DISTILLERY
([☎] 374-742-61-00; www.casasauza.com; Luis Navarro 70; ⊙9am-6pm Mon-Fri, to 2pm Sat) The Casa Sauza estate invokes Frances Hodgson Burnett's classic fairy tale *The Secret Garden*. The colonial-style grounds are adorned with Italianate fountains, tumbling plants and even a chapel. Indeed, 'tequila factory' are the last words that spring to mind as you recline in the sun-streaked bar. Nonetheless, tequila has been made here for eons and still is. Basic tours of Casa Sauza's **Perseverancia Distillery** (Sauza 80; tour M$120, with tasting M$220) last 1½ hours.

Longer tours of the estate, lasting 2½ hours and costing M$160, take in the adjoining botanical gardens and agave fields as well as the distillery.

Mundo Cuervo DISTILLERY
([☎] 374-742-72-00; www.mundocuervo.com; José Cuervo 33; ⊙11am-5pm Sun-Fri, to 6pm Sat) Just opposite Tequila's main plaza and immediately recognisable by the enormous statue of a crow (*cuervo* in Spanish), Mundo Cuervo, which is owned by the José Cuervo distillery, is a veritable tequila theme park and the biggest game in town. Hourly tours of **La Rojeña distillery** (José Cuervo 73; tour M$240, with

Around Guadalajara

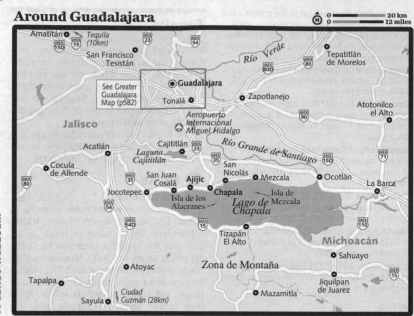

4 tastings M$385), the oldest in the Americas, can include tastings. The hour-long tour is a bit rushed so it's worth spending a little more on one of the longer tours that takes in the agave fields (M$880).

Museo Nacional del Tequila MUSEUM
(☑ 374-742-00-12; Ramón Corona 34; adult/child M$15/7; ◷ 9am-4pm) Set in an old colonial building just off the main plaza and spread over five rooms, this museum does a reasonable job of illustrating the history of tequila-making with photos and distillery apparatus. There's a decent shop here too.

☞ Tours

Tequila Tour by Mickey Marentes TOURS
(Map p594; ☑ 33-3615-6688; www.tequilatour bymm.com; Lope de Vega 25A, Guadalajara; adult US$99-195; ◷ 9am-6pm) This well-regarded agency has both private and group tours of tequila, distilleries, shops and museums. Prices depend on the number of people touring together and mode of transportation, be it van, jeep or on horseback.

Experience Tequila TOURS
(☑ 55-3060-8242; www.experiencetequila.com; 4-day package from US$1255) North American tequila aficionado Clayton Szczech offers a variety of individualized private tours

departing from Guadalajara, from basic day trips to tequila country to multiday intensive tasting seminars. Book well in advance.

José Cuervo Express TOURS
(Map p582; ☑ US 374-742-67-29; www.mundo cuervo.com/jose-cuervo-express; Washington 11, Guadalajara; adult/child from M$1900/1650; ◷ ticket office 9am-6pm Mon-Fri, to 1pm Sat & Sun) Ride in elegant carriages on this high-class train tour to the Mundo Cuervo distillery in Tequila, which departs from the Guadalajara train station (p601) at 9:30am on Saturdays and some Sundays (check website). Transportation in more exclusive coaches costs M$2100 and M$2300. Prices include transport, distillery tours, meals, a Mexican 'show' and a fair bit of tequila.

✕ Eating

La Jíma INTERNATIONAL $$
(☑ 374-742-42-42; www.losabolengos.com.mx/rest aurantelajima; México 138; mains M$135-255; ◷ 7am-11pm) This comfortable restaurant serving international favorites at the **Los Abolengos** (☑ 374-742-42-42; www.losabolen-gos.com; r M$1980-3300; ℗❄🛜) hotel has seating both inside and in the covered back garden. The lovely cellar is worth a look; it

stocks some excellent Mexican and other vintages. If you want a break from Mexican food, come here.

ⓘ Getting There & Away

Buses to Tequila leave from Guadalajara's Antigua Central Camionera roughly every 30 minutes (M$103, 1¾ hours).

Lago de Chapala

Lago de Chapala, Mexico's largest lake measuring 12.5km by 80km, lies 50km south of Guadalajara. Surrounded by dramatic mountains and enjoying a mild climate (always warm during the day and pleasantly cool at night), the lake continues to lure North American retirees and, at weekends, masses of *tapatíos* (Guadalajarans) out for some fresh air, a boat ride and a fish lunch. For foreign tourists the allure is a little less compelling, although it does make for a fun escape from Guadalajara.

Sadly, the lake is not as healthy as it is beautiful. Water levels fluctuate due to Guadalajara's and Mexico City's water needs and on-again, off-again drought conditions. Commercial fertilizers washed into the lake have polluted it and nourished water hyacinth, an invasive plant that clogs the lake's surface and kills off aquatic life. You'll see very few people swimming here.

Chapala

📞 376 / POP 21,600 / ELEV 1539M

With a commanding location from the northern shore of its namesake lake, Chapala became a well-known resort destination when President Porfirio Díaz vacationed here every year from 1904 to 1909. DH Lawrence and Tennessee Williams came later, certifying the town's literary pedigree. Today Chapala is a simple but charming working-class Mexican town with lovely lakeside walks and a buzzing weekend scene.

◉ Sights

Isla de Mezcala   ISLAND

The more interesting island to visit on Lago de Chapala is Isla de Mezcala. Here you'll find ruins of a fort where Mexican independence fighters held strong from 1812 to 1816, repulsing several Spanish attacks before finally earning the respect of, and a full pardon from, their enemies. A three-hour round-trip boat ride costs M$1800 for up to eight people.

Isla de los Alacranes   ISLAND

A ticket booth at the pier's entrance sells boat tickets to Isla de los Alacranes (Scorpion Island), 6km from Chapala, which has some restaurants and souvenir stalls but is not very captivating. A round-trip, with 30 minutes on the island, costs M$430 per boatload; for one hour on the island it's M$510.

🛏 Sleeping & Eating

⭐ **Lake Chapala Inn**   GUESTHOUSE $$$

(📞 376-765-47-86; www.chapalainn.com; Paseo Ramón Corona 23; s/d incl breakfast M$1200/1600; 🅿@🛜⌨) This very imposing white building dating from 1906 right on the lakeshore is moments from the center of town and enjoys wonderful views over the waters and off to the faraway hills. The views from two of the four rooms (Rosa and Jacaranda) and the communal terrace are unbeatable. There's a wonderful library with fireplace and a small garden with pool.

Reductions are available for stays of more than two nights, and the traditional breakfast is the real deal. Ask to borrow one of their two bikes.

Isla Cozumel   SEAFOOD $$

(📞 376-765-75-15; www.facebook.com/restaurant. isla.cozumel; Paseo Ramón Corona 22A; mains from M$160; ⊙10am-9pm Tue-Sun) Among the best of the touristy lakefront restaurants, Cozumel sits just up from the boardwalk and bills itself as a 'Caribbean Escape on the Chapala Riviera.' It is very popular with visitors who enjoy the complimentary margaritas as a prelude to the seafood-biased meals – everything from catfish to oysters.

ⓘ Getting There & Away

Buses from Guadalajara (M$55 to M$70, one hour, half-hourly) to Chapala leave from the Antigua Central Camionera. Buses connect Chapala to Ajijic (M$8 to M$10, 15 minutes) every 20 minutes.

Ajijic

📞 376 / POP 10,300 / ELEV 1577M

This town with the bizarre-sounding name of Ajijic (pronounced 'ah-hee-heek') is an outpost of North American retirees and by far the most sophisticated and energetic of the towns that line the northern shore of Lago de Chapala. While the gringos may have put Ajijic on the map by opening boutiques, galleries and restaurants galore, much of the town retains its charming, colonial-era vibe, with cobblestone lanes and quiet streets of colorfully painted houses. It makes a delightful place to sit back and relax awhile, although it's far from the typical Mexico here: English is almost as commonly heard on the streets as Spanish and prices are somewhat higher than other places on the lake.

🏃 Activities

Ajijic has a web of sinuous trails that wrap their way around the jungle-covered hills behind the town, taking in waterfalls, peek-aboo lake views and some rocky scrambles.

🛏 Sleeping

★ La Nueva Posada   GUESTHOUSE $$
(☏376-766-14-44; www.hotelnuevaposada.com; Guerra 9; r incl breakfast M$1300-1600; 🅿🛗❄) A lovely hotel with an unspoken grandeur, this lakeside retreat offers a taste of genteel, old-world Mexico. The 19 rooms are spacious, with tasteful furnishings, and almost half have expansive lake views (try room 109). The garden, with resident macaw Paco and small pool, runs right down to the lake, giving you plenty of space to feel at ease with the world.

The large and airy inhouse restaurant (mains from M$120 to M$170) is open to guests and nonguests alike daily from 8am to 8pm.

🍴 Eating & Drinking

El Chile Verde   MEXICAN $
(☏376-766-00-72; Colón 25; mains M$35-60; ☺8am-4pm Mon-Sat) A world away from all the arty expat-style restaurants and cafes, this tiny lemon-and-lime-colored eatery serves up authentic and delicious home-cooked Mexican food that pulls in both locals and resident foreigners. The lunchtime dish of the day is a bargain-priced M$50.

Ajijic Tango   ARGENTINE $$$
(☏376-766-24-58; www.ajijictango.com; Morelos 5; steaks M$117-370; ☺12:30-9pm Mon, Wed & Thu, to 10pm Fri & Sat, to 7pm Sun) Ajijic's most popular restaurant is never less than rammed with locals, resident expats and visitors, all here to enjoy the excellent steaks (it is an Argentinian restaurant after all). But there are other dishes too – Mexican, salads and pasta (M$117 to M$199).

Seating is in a colorful tented courtyard. Reservations are a must on Friday and Saturday nights.

Café Grano   CAFE
(☏376-766-51-68; www.facebook.com/Cafegrano cafeoficial; Castellanos 15D; coffee M$28-44; ☺8:30am-9pm Sun-Thu, to 9:30pm Fri & Sat) This thoroughly pleasant local cafe is everything a good coffee bar should be, with fine aromas, Mexican beans, wooden chairs tailored in coffee sacking and excellent cakes (M$22 to M$45). Bright murals tell the coffee story from plant to cup. It also sells high-quality beans from Veracruz, Oaxaca and Chiapas.

ℹ Getting There & Away

Buses from Guadalajara (M$55 to M$70, one hour, half-hourly) to Ajijic leave from the Antigua Central Camionera and drop you on the highway at Colón next to a small ticket office. Buses connect Chapala and Ajijic every 20 minutes (M$8 to M$10, 15 minutes).

Zona de Montaña

South of Lago de Chapala, Jalisco's Zona de Montaña – the 'Mountain Zone' – of seemingly endless layered peaks – is an increasingly popular weekend retreat for *tapatíos* (Guadalajarans), who come to enjoy the rangeland, pines, timeless colonial *pueblos mágicos* (magical villages), local dishes and cooler climes.

Tapalpa

☏343 / POP 15,740 / ELEV 2068M

Tapalpa, a labyrinth of whitewashed walls, red-tiled roofs and cobblestoned streets surrounding two impressive 16th-century churches, truly deserves its designation as *pueblo mágico* – it is truly one of the most beautiful mountain towns in the land. Of course, this beauty hasn't gone unnoticed – at weekends flocks of people flee Guadalajara for the hiking, trekking and generally cool and misty climate that Tapalpa offers. During the week, when visitors are few in number, Tapalpa retains a country backwater feel; horses clip-clop down the lanes and old men in cowboy hats lounge on benches in the plaza.

👁 Sights

Las Piedrotas   NATURAL FEATURE
(🏠) Las Piedrotas are a large and impressive group of rock formations set in cow pastures in what's called the Valle de las Enigmas

DON'T MISS

EL ARENAL

El Arenal is the gateway to the Tequila region, 43km northwest of Guadalajara and 22km southeast of Tequila. This small settlement is the site of one of the state's best small distilleries, **Cascahuín** (☑ 33-3614-9958, cell 374-7480010; www.facebook.com/cascahuin; Av Ferrocarril; tour M$50, with 3 tastings M$100-160; ☺ 9am-6pm Mon-Fri, to 2pm Sat). If you have time for only one distillery tour while in Tequila country, make it this one. Here you'll see the entire process, from *piña* harvesting to bottling and labeling, up close, and mostly done in the traditional manner. Some of the items used, including brick ovens, *tahona* (stone mill) and charcoal firing pits, are positive heirlooms and the product – be it *blanco* (white), *reposado* (rested) or *añejo* (aged) – is delectable.

about 6km north of town. Most people drive here, but it's an easy and rewarding 2½- to three-hour return walk along a quiet country lane through dark pine forests, past an abandoned old paper mill and up onto a flower-filled plateau.

To reach Las Piedrotas take Hidalgo westward out of town, keeping to the left and following the signs for Chiquilistlán (and some signs for Las Piedrotas). Once you've cleared the edge of town, carry on straight. A taxi costs around M$100 one way.

El Salto del Nogal   WATERFALL

El Salto del Nogal is a jaw-dropping, 105m-high waterfall about 18km south of town. A taxi costs around M$200 one way.

☞ Tours

Colores Tapalpa   TOURS

(☑ 343-432-12-70; www.colorestapalpa.mx; Matamoros 69C; ☺ 9am-8pm) This upbeat and helpful travel agency on Tapalpa's main square organizes daily excursions to Las Piedrotas at 1pm and 5pm, lasting three hours and costing M$300. A five-hour trip to El Salto del Nogal departs at 11am and costs M$400.

🛏 Sleeping & Eating

Las Margaritas
Hotel Posada   GUESTHOUSE $$

(☑ 343-432-07-99; www.tapalpahotelmargaritas. com; 16 de Septiembre 81; d/4-person villa M$800/ 1600; ☜) Sporting bright decorations and carved wardrobes, this seven-room inn uphill from the main plaza offers excellent value, comfort, and eye-pleasing rooms and villas with kitchen. There's a shop on site with a lovely range of local folk crafts.

★ Los Girasoles   MEXICAN $$

(☑ 343-432-00-86; www.facebook.com/girasole stapalpa; Obregón 110; mains M$75-165; ☺ 9am-

10pm Mon-Thu, to 11pm Fri & Sat, to 7:30pm Sun) Tapalpa's classiest restaurant is just off the main plaza and offers quality dishes such as cheese- and plantain-stuffed chilies in a cilantro sauce, *tamales de acelga* (chard-filled *tamales*) and a spicy chicken dish called *cochala de polio*. There's a starlit outdoor patio for rare warm nights or you can snuggle in front of the open log fire in the dining room.

ℹ Information

The **tourist office** (☑ 343-432-06-50, ext 125; www.tapalpaturistico.com; Portal Morelos; ☺ 8am-5pm Mon-Fri, 10am-6pm Sat, to 3pm Sun) facing the Plaza Principal has maps, info and a particularly useful website.

ℹ Getting There & Away

Some 10 buses depart daily for Tapalpa from Guadalajara's Antigua Central Camionera (M$152, three hours); three daily also leave from the Nueva Central Camionera. There are also four buses a day to/from Ciudad Guzmán (M$109, two hours). Buses in Tapalpa stop at the **Sur de Jalisco bus office** (Ignacio López 10) down the hill from the center.

Ciudad Guzmán

☑ 341 / POP 97,750 / ELEV 1535M

Large and frenetic Ciudad Guzmán is no tourist destination, but it is the closest city to Volcán Nevado de Colima, the majestic volcano about 25km to its southwest.

◉ Sights

Guzmán's crowded main plaza is surrounded by market stalls and shopping arcades set around two churches: the 17th-century **Templo del Sagrado Corazón** and the neoclassical **Catedral de San Juan**. In the center of the adjoining Jardín Municipal (City Garden) is a stone bandstand with a copy of local boy José Clemente Orozco's mural *Hombre de Fuego* (Man of Fire) painted on its ceiling. The original is in the Instituto Cultural de Cabañas (p584) in Guadalajara.

🛏 Sleeping

Gran Hotel Zapotlán   HOTEL $
(☑ 341-412-00-40; www.hotelzapotlan.com; Federico del Toro 61; d/tr from M$400/585; [P][❄][🌐]) This awesomely old-style hotel, set on the western side of the main plaza with a pretty tiled atrium full of hanging plants and enormous metal urns, has plenty of character. The 82 rooms spread over four floors and looking into the courtyard cannot be described as luxurious, but for the price they are money well spent.

ℹ Information

The **tourist office** (☑ 341-412-25-63, ext 102/110; Calz Madero y Carranza 568; ⊙ 9am-3pm Mon-Fri) is in the defunct *estación de ferrocarriles* (train station), about 2.5km due west of the center and just north of the mammoth bus station. Staff can help with planning and booking an ascent of the Volcán Nevado de Colima.

ℹ Getting There & Away

Ciudad Guzmán's modern bus terminal is about 3km west of the plaza near the entrance to (or exit from) the city from the Guadalajara–Colima highway. Hop on bus 6 (M$6) to get there and back. Destinations include Guadalajara (M$192, two hours), Colima (M$132, one to two hours), Tapalpa (M$109, two hours), Mazamitla (M$109, 2½ hours) and Zapotitlán, which passes 2km from El Fresnito (M$20, 20 minutes), the closest village to Volcán Nevado de Colima. An alternative way to reach El Fresnito is by taking the 1A, 1C or 1V *urbano* (urban bus) from the Los Mones crossroad in Ciudad Guzmán (M$6, 20 minutes).

INLAND COLIMA STATE

At just 5627 sq km and Mexico's third-smallest state, tiny but ecologically rich and diverse Colima connects lofty volcanoes in its arid northern highlands to idyllic turquoise lagoons near the hot and humid Pacific coast to the south.

Many travelers think inland Colima is poised to become Mexico's next great adventure hub. The famous volcanoes in the north – the active and constantly fuming but inaccessible Volcán de Fuego (3820m)

and the extinct, snowcapped Volcán Nevado de Colima (4260m) – remain the big draws, but the Reserva de la Biosfera Sierra de Manantlán is a jungle-and-limestone playground in waiting, with single-track mountain biking, exceptional hiking and canyons that see a few canyoneers abseiling, leaping into crystalline streams and bathing in the magical Cascada El Salto waterfall. Tourism infrastructure hasn't caught up to the area's potential yet, so those who like virgin territory should come now.

History

Pre-Hispanic Colima was removed from the major ancient cultures of Mexico. Seaborne contacts with more distant lands might have been more important: legend says one king of Colima, Ix, had regular visitors bearing treasure from China. Eventually, though, the northern tribes began moving in. The Otomí settled here from about AD 250 to 750, followed by the Toltecs, who flourished between 900 and 1154, and the Chichimecs from 1154 to 1428.

All of them left behind exceptional pottery, which has been found at more than 250 sites, mainly tombs, dating from about 200 BC to AD 800. The pottery includes a variety of comical and expressive figures. The most famous are the plump, hairless dogs known as xoloitzcuintles.

Two Spanish expeditions were defeated and repelled by the Chichimecs before Gonzalo de Sandoval, one of Cortés' lieutenants, conquered them in 1523. That year he founded the town of Colima, the third Spanish settlement in Nueva España (after Veracruz and Mexico City). In 1527 the town moved to its present site from its original lowland location near Tecomán.

Colima

☑ 312 / POP 137,500 / ELEV 498M
Colima is a laid-back city with lush subtropical gardens, fine public plazas and the warmest weather in the western central highlands. The city's university attracts students from around the world, while its burgeoning tourism potential derived from nearby canyons, forests and mountains brings in a small but growing number of visitors.

The billowing volcano you see on clear days, Volcán de Fuego – visible 30km to the north – continues to rumble and shake, and

Colima

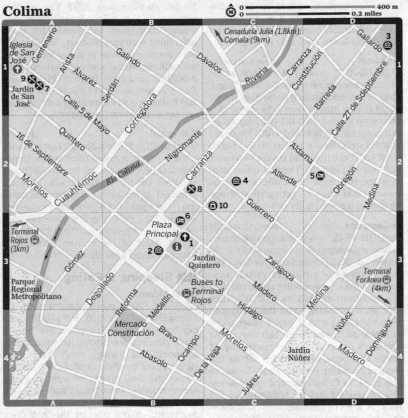

N 0 ——— 400 m
0 ——— 0.2 miles

Cenaduría Julia (1.8km);
Comala (9km)

Colima

the city has been hit by several major quakes over the centuries (the last one of 7.5 magnitude in January 2003). It's no wonder that Colima has few colonial buildings, despite having been the first city established by the Spanish in western Mexico.

Sights

Museo Universitario
de Artes Populares
MUSEUM

(📞 312-312-68-69; www.mexicoescultura.com/rec |into/66604/museo-universitario-de-artes-pop ulares-ma-teresa-pomar.html; cnr Gallardo & Barreda; adult/child & student M$20/10, Sun free; ⊙10am-2pm & 5-8pm Tue-Sat, 10am-1pm Sun) Colima's best museum, this is a showcase for folk art including a superb collection of masks, *mojigangas* (giant puppets), musical instruments, baskets and wood and ceramic sculpture from every state in Mexico. There's exhibits on farming, fishing and Colima salt-making too.

Unusual displays include an armadillo-shell guitar from Paracho, a model airplane made with animal bones and an icon of Our Lady of Guadalupe fashioned with feathers.

El Chanal
ARCHAEOLOGICAL SITE

(☑312-316-20-21; www.inah.gob.mx/es/zonas/151-zona-arqueologica-el-chanal; Camino al Chanal; M$40; ⊙9am-6pm Tue-Sun) Some 4km northeast of Colima, this extensive site was settled some time around 1300 BC, reaching its zenith between AD 1100 and 1400. There are pyramid structures, a ball court, five patios and a small catchment to collect rainwater. Just east of Plaza del Tiempo, which contains the two most impressive structures, are several blocks with petroglyphs depicting animal figures, plants and deities.

La Campana
ARCHAEOLOGICAL SITE

(☑312-313-49-45; www.zonaarqueologica.com.mx/sitio-arqueologico-de-la-campana-colima; Av Tecnológico; M$50; ⊙9am-6pm Tue-Sun) The low, pyramid-like structures at this bell-shaped (thus *campana*) archaeological site date from as early as 1500 BC. They have been excavated since the 1930s and restored, along with a small shaft tomb with objects in situ and a ball court. The structures are oriented due north toward Volcán de Fuego, which makes for an impressive backdrop on clear days. It's about 3km north of Colima city and easily accessible by buses 7 and 22; taxis cost around M$50. A word of warning: wear good shoes and socks because there are lots of fire ants.

Museo Regional de Historia de Colima
MUSEUM

(☑312-312-92-28; www.inah.gob.mx/es/red-de-museos/245-museo-regional-de-historia-de-colima; 16 de Septiembre 29, Portal Morelos 1; M$55; ⊙9am-6pm Tue-Sat, 5-8pm Sun) This excellent museum in rooms off a central patio has an extensive collection of well-labeled artifacts spanning the region's history, from ancient pottery to conquistadors' armor and a 19th-century horse-drawn carriage. Don't miss the ceramic xoloitzcuintles (Colima dogs) in room 12 or the walk-through mock tomb excavation next door. There is also an interesting collection of clay figures that may depict pelota players.

Pinacoteca Universitaria Alfonso Michel
GALLERY

(☑312-314-33-06; www.mexicoescultura.com/recinto/55240/pinacoteca-universitaria-alfonso-michel.html; Guerrero 35; ⊙10am-2pm & 5-8pm Tue-Sat, 10am-1pm Sun) FREE The modern entrance to this gallery leads into a 19th-century courtyard surrounded by seven halls filled with surrealist art. Included is a permanent collection of paintings by Colima's Alfonso Michel – whose work has been described as a cross between Picasso and Dalí – as well as works by José Luis Cuevas and Rafael Coronel. Four other *salas* are given over to temporary exhibitions.

Cathedral
CATHEDRAL

(Reforma 21; ⊙7am-8:30pm) Light floods what is officially called the Basílica Menor Catedral de Colima from its circular dome windows on the northeast side of Plaza Principal. It has been rebuilt several times since the Spanish first erected a cathedral here in 1527, most recently after the 1941 earthquake, when its northern tower collapsed. Most of the current neoclassical structure dates from 1894.

🛏 Sleeping & Eating

Hotel Aldama
HOTEL $

(☑312-330-73-07; www.hotelaldamacolima.com; Aldama 134; s/d M$550/620; ✳🛜) Four blocks northeast of the central plaza, this budget hotel punches way above its weight with 15 rooms that, though small, have some value-raising touches: think flowers strewn across the bed sheets, wrought-iron and heavy wooden furnishings, and desks to work at. The 1st-floor rooms look into the courtyard; choose one on the 2nd floor, which has a lovely roof terrace.

Hotel Ceballos
HOTEL $$

(☑312-316-01-00; www.hotelceballos.com; Constitución 11, Portal Medellín 12; r from M$1100; 🅿✳@🛜✳) A prominent Mexican plaza hotel with atmospheric portal-fronted communal areas (including a cafe and restaurant) backed by 54 not-always-inspiring rooms. The property is part of the Best Western chain; some of the better rooms have high ceilings with crown moldings and balconies that overlook the Plaza Principal. There's a pool and a small gym on the ground floor. Very welcoming staff.

Chile Amor
MEXICAN $

(☑312-160-50-96; 5 de Mayo 49; mains M$35-60; ⊙8am-3pm Mon-Sat) This very colorful corner eatery, with floor-to-ceiling painted walls and where the waitstaff wear flamboyant traditional Mexican garb, serves some of the best tacos and quesadillas in town. Specials

BUSES FROM COLIMA

DESTINATION	FARE (M$)	DURATION (HR)	FREQUENCY (DAILY)
Ciudad Guzmán	132	1-2	5
Comala	9	¼	half-hourly
Guadalajara	324	3	hourly
Manzanillo	134	1½	half-hourly
Mexico City (Terminal Norte)	1015	10	10
Morelia	579	6	3
Uruapan	425	6	1

include dishes like beef cooked in peanut sauce. Good for breakfast as well.

Cenaduría Julia
MEXICAN $

(☑ 312-312-42-44; Leandro Valle 80, Villa de Álvarez; mains M$35-75; ⊙ 6-11:30pm Mon & Wed-Fri, 2-11:30pm Sat & Sun; 🅿) This institution in the northern suburb of Villa de Álvarez is one of the area's best-loved restaurants. The dishes to try here are the *sopitos* (small circular tortillas topped with meat, spices and tomato sauce; M$40 for eight) as well as the *tacos tuxpeños* (tortillas dipped in smoky adobo sauce and fried and filled with refried beans or pork; M$35 for four).

It doesn't look like much, but at these prices for authentic *cocina colimense* (Colima-style cuisine), it's well worth the short taxi ride (M$40) from the town center.

★ El Charco de la Higuera
MEXICAN $$

(☑ 312-313-01-92; www.facebook.com/ElCharcode laHiguera; Jardín de San José, cnr Calle 5 de Mayo; mains M$90-145; ⊙ 8am-midnight) The best salt-of-the-earth restaurant in Colima doubles as a modest museum to local mask-making and offers typical *cocina colimense*. The combined *antojitos* (Mexican snacks; M$85) plate is a smorgasbord; the adventurous will want to try the *pepena* (cow's heart and intestines; M$85) with hot tortillas. Slightly less exotic are the *chilaquiles* (fried tortillas; M$70).

The excellent food is complemented by the setting in a quiet little plaza next to the San José church with live music till 8pm Thursday to Sunday.

¡Ah Qué Nanishe!
MEXICAN $$

(☑ 312-314-21-97; www.facebook.com/restaurante nanishe; Calle 5 de Mayo 267; mains M$99-120; ⊙ noon-11pm Tue-Sun) The name of this restaurant in indigenous Zapotec means 'How delicious!' and the rich, chocolatey but not overwhelming *mole* (sauce) is superb. Oth-

er unmissable Oaxacan delicacies that are available include *chiles rellenos* (stuffed chilies) or, if you're lucky, *chapulines* (crunchy fried grasshoppers). Half orders of many mains are available for 70% of the full price, making for great value.

🔒 Shopping

Huentli
ARTS & CRAFTS

(☑ 312-314-12-95; www.facebook.com/Artesanias Huentli; Andador Constitución 1, cnr Zaragoza; ⊙ 8:30am-8pm Mon-Fri, 9am-8pm Sat, to 2pm Sun) This excellent government-run *tienda de artesanías* (handicrafts shop) stocks items produced uniquely by Colima artisans such as masks, ceramics, pottery, hats and furniture.

ℹ Information

Colima State Tourist Office (☑ 312-312-83-60; www.colimatienemagia.com.mx; Reforma; ⊙ 9am-5pm Mon-Fri) Handily positioned in the Palacio de Gobierno in the main plaza.

ℹ Getting There & Away

Colima's **Licenciado Miguel de la Madrid Airport** (☑ 312-314-41-60; Av Lic Carlos de la Madrid Bejar) is near Cuauhtémoc, 12km northeast of the city center off the highway to Guadalajara (taxis M$280). **Aeromar** (☑ 312-313-13-40; www. aeromar.com.mx) flies to Mexico City three times a day. It is also serves by **Aeromexico** (☑ 312-313-80-58; https://aeromexico.com) and **Volaris** (☑ 55-1102-8000; https://flights.volaris.com).

Colima has two bus terminals. The long-distance terminal is **Terminal Foránea** (Carretera 54), 4km east of the city center at the junction of Avenida Niños Héroes and the city's eastern bypass. There's a left-luggage facility. To reach downtown, hop on bus 5. For the return trip catch the same bus on Calle 5 de Mayo or Zaragoza. There's a prepay taxi booth at the terminal and the fare to downtown is M$28.

Colima's second bus terminal (serving local towns) is **Terminal Rojos** (Bosque de Cedros), about 2km west of Plaza Principal. Ruta 4 or 6 buses run to Colima's center from this terminal. To get back here, take any bus marked 'Rojos' going north on Morelos.

Taxi fares within town cost M$15 to M$25.

Parque Nacional Volcán Nevado de Colima

This 9.5-sq-km national park, straddling over the Colima–Jalisco border, encompasses two dramatic volcanoes some 5km apart: the still-active Volcán de Fuego and the much older (and dormant) Volcán Nevado de Colima. Ciudad Guzmán is the closest city to the park, but if you have a car or hire a guide, Colima or Comala are much more pleasant bases. It can be difficult to find a guide on the fly if you only have a few days, so it's best to organize things in advance.

The national park is home to a wide range of flora and fauna, some of it endemic. Resident and/or visiting mammals include white-tailed foxes, coatimundis, coyotes, pumas and jaguars.

◉ Sights

Volcán Nevado de Colima   VOLCANO

Volcán Nevado de Colima (4260m) is accessible on foot from the last week of October till the first week of June. Patches of pine forest cover Nevado's shoulders, while alpine desert takes over at the highest altitudes. Wildlife includes deer, wild boars, coyotes and even pumas.

The best months for climbing are generally the dry months of December through May. But temperatures from December to February often dip below 0°C (32°F) and snow can fall on the upper slopes – *nevado* means 'snow-covered.' Weather changes fast here and lightning strikes the peak in stormy weather, so make sure you keep an eye on the clouds and get an early start. The park's hours November to March are from 6am to 6pm. The summer rainy season is from July to September, when park hours are longer.

To get here on your own from Ciudad Guzmán, take the bus to El Fresnito (M$20), where you must try to hire a driver (not an easy task) to take you the remaining 20km or so up a rough road to the trailhead at La Joya/Puerto Las Cruces (3500m). You'll pass the park entrance on the way, where you'll pay a M$40 entry fee. An alternative is to walk up from El Fresnito – a much

longer and tougher proposition. If you elect to walk, stay on the bus as long as you can as it covers some of the distance beyond the town.

Walkers will need camping gear and food (and some very warm clothes), because it's impossible to walk there and back in a day. Allow seven hours to get to the parking at La Joya/Puerto Las Cruces and then another three to four hours from there to the summit and about seven hours all the way back down again. You can camp at La Joya/Puerto Las Cruces a few kilometers beyond the park gates.

The hike to the summit from La Joya is around 9km and ascends 700m. Some prefer to just hike to the *micro-ondas* (radio antennae) about 90 minutes by foot from the end of the road at La Joya/Puerto Las Cruces. If you want to reach the peak, you'll need another 90 minutes, and while the peak is easy to see, you shouldn't go alone. There are many trails up and back and it's very easy to get lost or led to areas with hazardous footing. Fog can also be an impediment. You'll save a lot of time and bother going with a guide.

Driving up this volcano on the relatively good gravel road means that you'll be ascending to a high altitude very quickly. If you feel lightheaded or dizzy, you may be suffering from altitude sickness (p854). Descend as quickly as possible, as this condition can be dangerous.

Volcán de Fuego   VOLCANO

Overlooking Comala and Colima, 23km and 30km to the north respectively, is smoking Volcán de Fuego (3820m), Mexico's most active volcano. It has erupted dozens of times in the past four centuries, with a big eruption about every 70 years. In June 2005 a large explosion sent ash almost 5km into the sky, all the way to Colima; another one almost as big in July 2015 did the same thing to Ciudad Guzmán.

Fuego's peak has been off-limits to visitors since 1980 and to seismologists since 2013. To hike in the vicinity of the volcano – there is an exclusion zone within 10km of the summit – it is best to organize in advance through a reputable agency.

⊙ Tours

The guides we list are licensed to take visitors into the Parque Nacional Volcán Nevado de Colima. A 3½-hour tour to within 10km of the summit of Volcán de Fuego costs from

M$800. Trekking to the top of Volcán Nevado de Colima with a guide will cost from M$2200. Prices include transportation and entry fees.

Admire Mexico
TREKKING

(☑ 312-314-54-54; www.admiremexicotours.com; Obregón 105, Comala) The undisputed leader of hikes and tours in the national park as well as in and around Colima and Comala is this highly regarded agency led by volcano expert Júpiter Rivera. It's based out of Casa Alvarada in Comala.

Corazón de Colima Tours
TREKKING

(☑ 312-314-08-96; www.corazondecolimatours.com; Nayarit 1415, Colima) Runs tours to Comala, plus a hike in the skirts of Volcán de Fuego, and ascents of Volcán Nevado de Colima. Based in Colima.

🍸 Drinking & Nightlife

Cafe La Yerbabuena
CAFE

(☑ 312-102-17-33; La Yerbabuena; ⊙ 8am-6pm) While hiking up to as close as you are going to get to the summit of Volcán de Fuego, you might stop at 1500m at this rustic cafe in a working coffee plantation for a cup of homegrown and ground joe. It's in the original hamlet of La Yerbabuena, which disappeared under the lava flow of the 2005 eruption. Residents were moved away in good time and now live in La Yerbabuena II some 7km further down the slope.

🛈 Getting There & Away

The national park is not served by public transportation; the closest point you can reach from Ciudad Guzmán is El Fresnito (M$20). The best way to visit is under your own steam or in a guide's vehicle.

Comala

☑ 312 / POP 9500 / ELEV 600M

If you've made it as far as Colima, do not miss the gloriously idiosyncratic *pueblo mágico* (magical villages) of Comala, 10km to the north, famous for its *ponche* (alcoholic punch), *tuba* (fermented drink made from palm-tree sap), sweet bread and distinctive hand-carved wooden masks. Characterized by the kind of generic white colonial edifices that wouldn't look out of place in the so-called *pueblos blancos* (white towns) of Andalucía, Comala's centerpiece is its main plaza, one of the region's most beguiling, replete with *tuba* salespeople, shoe-

shiners, strolling mariachis and a plethora of restaurants.

Comala's red-letter event is the Feria de Ponche, Pan y Cafe (Punch, Bread and Coffee Festival) held over two weeks in April.

⊙ Sights

Ex Hacienda Nogueras
MUSEUM

(☑ 312-315-60-28; Nogueras; hacienda/museum M$10/20; ⊙ 10am-3pm Mon-Fri, to 5pm Sat & Sun) Comala's obligatory sight is this former home of Mexican artist Alejandro Rangel Hidalgo (1923–2000), which now contains a museum dedicated to the man's life and art. Here you'll see his extensive pre-Hispanic ceramics collection (including Colima dogs) and the distinctive Unicef Christmas cards for which he is largely remembered. The house also contains a chapel and the ruins of an old sugar factory. The grounds – including a botanical garden – are lush. Check out the shop in the former apothecary.

To get here on foot from the main square walk east for 450m along Calle Degollado, which runs to the left of **Templo de San Miguel Arcángel**. Turn left at Calle Saavedra then turn left at the T-intersection, go 1km, then turn right at the next T-intersection and go another 450m. You can also take a bus (M$7) from behind the church or a taxi (M$25).

Centro Estatal de los Artes
GALLERY

(☑ 312-313-99-68; Carreterra Villa de Álvarez-Comala Km 5.5; ⊙ 9am-6pm Mon-Sat, to 3pm Sun) FREE The latest addition to Comala's cultural life is the spanking new 'State Center of the Arts' gallery in an eye-catching building south of the main plaza just over the Río Suchitlán. It has temporary exhibits of modern painting and sculpture. The adjoining gardens are delightful, especially the half-dozen sculptures representing one (or the other) of the two ever-dominant volcanoes.

🛏 Sleeping & Eating

★ Casa Alvarada
B&B $$

(☑ 312-315-52-29; www.casaalvarada.com; Obregón 105; d incl breakfast M$950-1600; P ❋ 🛜) Casa Alvarada is a homey and very welcoming B&B run by English-speaking guide Júpiter Rivera and his wife Mara. The three rooms, one suite and a detached villa are themed and decorated with local folk art; the villa named after the painter Alejandro Rangel Hidalgo sleeps four and has its own kitchen.

Lavish breakfasts are served family-style, and the patio has a sumptuous hammock bed. The bathrooms have what must be the most powerful showers south of the border.

Tacos Doña Mary
MEXICAN $

(5 de Mayo 144; dishes M$45; ⊘7pm-midnight Wed-Mon) Take it from local Comalans: this simple stall with a few outside seats has the best tacos in the region. But don't start World War III by debating which of the half-dozen or so on offer is the best. (If you must know, we vote the *asado de res* – roast beef – followed by the chorizo ones.)

Don Comalón
MEXICAN $

(✆312-315-51-04; www.doncomalon.com; Progreso 5; drink & snack M$45; ⊘noon-6pm) One of many restaurants lining Comala's main plaza that serves a *botana* (free snack) with every drink you order. If you haven't got time to make your choice, opt for this place and pray the staff bring you a crispy *tostada* topped with ceviche.

❶ Getting There & Away

Buses make the 15-minute trip to/from Colima (M$9) half-hourly throughout the day and will drop you near the main square.

INLAND MICHOACÁN

Pre-Hispanic traditions and colonial-era architecture meet in Michoacán. The state is home to three of Mexico's coolest under-the-radar cities: the adobe-and-cobblestone town of Pátzcuaro, where Purépecha women sell fruit and *tamales* in the shadow of 16th-century churches; the lush agricultural city of Uruapan, gateway to the mythic Paricutín volcano; and the vibrant and cultured colonial city of Morelia, with an ancient cathedral and aqueduct built from rosy pink stone.

Michoacán is also gaining renown as a crafts capital: the Purépecha artisans of the state's Cordillera Neovolcánica highlands create wonderful masks, pottery, straw art and stringed instruments – all on display at the annual Tianguis Artesanal de Uruapan craft fair (p636). Rich in natural treasures, Michoacán has one of the world's truly unmissable sights: the annual butterfly migration to the rugged Reserva Mariposa Monarca (Monarch Butterfly Reserve), where millions of mating monarchs cover the grass and trees in a shimmering carpet.

Morelia
✦443 / POP 607,500 / ELEV 1920M

The state capital of Michoacán and its most beautiful and dynamic city, Morelia is an increasingly popular destination and rightly so: the colonial heart of the city, with its gorgeous cathedral at its center, is so well preserved that it was declared a Unesco World Heritage site in 1991.

Elegant 16th- and 17th-century stone buildings with their baroque facades and graceful archways line the downtown streets and house museums, hotels, restaurants, *chocolaterías* (chocolate shops), sidewalk cafes, a popular university and cheap-and-inviting *taquerías* (taco stalls). There are free public concerts, frequent art installations and relatively few foreign visitors. Those who do make it here often extend their stay and enrol in classes to learn how to cook or speak Spanish. Word will almost certainly get out, but for the moment unspoiled Morelia is like a Oaxaca waiting to happen.

History

Morelia, founded in 1541, was one of the first Spanish cities in the colony of Nueva España. Its first viceroy, Antonio de Mendoza, named it Valladolid after that city in Spain and encouraged Spanish nobility to move here with their families. In 1828, four years after Nueva España had become the Republic of Mexico, the city was renamed Morelia in honor of local hero José María Morelos y Pavón, a priest who led the Mexican War of Independence movement after the execution of Miguel Hidalgo y Costilla.

◉ Sights

Morelia boasts a surfeit of high-quality museums, but many of them overlap, especially on the subject of local hero José María Morelos y Pavón. Choose carefully or prepare for Morelos information overload.

★ Biblioteca Pública de la Universidad Michoacana
HISTORIC BUILDING

(✆443-312-57-25; Jardín Igangio Altamirano, cnr Av Madero Poniente & Nigromante; ⊘8am-8pm Mon-Fri) FREE Installed inside the magnificent 17th-century **Ex Templo de la Compañía de Jesús**, the shelves of the city's breathtaking university library rise up toward the domed and painted ceilings and are crammed from head to toe with tens of thousands (22,901 to be exact) of antique books and manuscripts, including seven incunabula dating from the 15th century. The murals date from the 1950s.

★ Morelia Cathedral   CATHEDRAL

(Plaza de Armas; ⊙6am-9pm) FREE Morelia's cathedral, considered by many to be the country's most beautiful, dominates the city center, where it flanks rather than faces the central plaza. It took almost a century to build (1660–1744), which explains its potpourri of styles: the twin 70m-high bell towers, for instance, have classical Herreresque bases, baroque midsections and multicolumned neoclassical tops. It is particularly impressive when lit up at night.

Much of the baroque reliefs inside were replaced in the 19th century with neoclassical work. Fortunately, one of the highlights was preserved: a sculpture of the crucified Christ called the **Señor de la Sacristía** in a chapel to the left of the main altar. It is made from *pasta de caña* (a paste made from the heart of the cornstalk) and is topped with a gold crown gifted to the church by the Spanish King Felipe II in the 16th century. The organ counts 4600 pipes; occasional organ recitals take place here – a beautiful time to be in the cathedral.

★ Centro Cultural Clavijero   MUSEUM

(☑443-312-04-12; www.ccclavijero.mx; Nigromante 79; ⊙10am-6pm Tue-Fri, to 7pm Sat & Sun) FREE From 1660 to 1767 the Palacio Clavijero, with its magnificent minimalist main patio, imposing colonnades and pink stonework, was home to the Jesuit school of St Francis Xavier. Today the enormous building houses a cultural center with exhibition spaces showing off contemporary art, photography and other creative media.

Museo de Arte Colonial   GALLERY

(☑443-313-92-60; http://morelianas.com/morelia/museos/museo-de-arte-colonial; Juárez 240; ⊙10am-8pm Mon-Fri, to 6pm Sat & Sun) FREE This ambitious museum contains five rooms chock-a-block with religious paintings and sculptures, including more than 100 depictions of the crucified Christ. Highlights include a small statue of Jesus wearing a skirt in room 3 and scale models of Columbus' three ships – the *Niña*, the *Pinta* and the *Santa Maria* – in room 4. Check out the ancient streetside windows in room 5.

Parque Zoológico Benito Juárez   ZOO

(☑443-299-36-10; www.zoomorelia.michoacan.gob.mx; Calzada Juárez; adult/child M$25/15; ⊙10am-5pm Mon-Fri, to 6pm Sat & Sun) Morelia's zoo is located 2.5km south of the Plaza de Armas and is surprisingly pleasant, with most critters in decent habitats. Animals include sea lions, giraffes, elephants and lots of winged creatures. Gravel paths make it hard for strollers, but kids will love the playground. There are additional charges for the aquarium, reptile house and little train.

Palacio de Gobierno   NOTABLE BUILDING

(http://morelianas.com/morelia/edificios/palacio-de-gobierno; Av Madero Oriente; ⊙9am-8pm Mon-Fri) FREE This 18th-century palace, originally a seminary and now housing Michoacán state government offices, has a simple baroque facade. Its soaring historical murals (1962) in the stairwell and 2nd-floor hallways are the magnum opus of Pátzcuaro-born artist Alfredo Zalce (1908–2003), and arguably the city's best. Enter from Calle Juárez.

Museo Regional Michoacano   MUSEUM

(Michoacán Regional Museum; ☑443-312-04-07; www.inah.gob.mx/es/red-de-museos/297-museo-regional-de-michoacano-dr-nicolas-leon-calderon; Allende 305; adult/child M$50/free; ⊙9am-5pm Tue-Sun) Housed in a dozen rooms of a renovated late-18th-century baroque palace, this museum contains an impressive array of pre-Hispanic artifacts, including a reconstructed open tomb from El Opeño, colonial art and relics, including a carved stone coyote from Ihuatzio and an anatomically correct Chacmool (reclining male figure with turned head). There are also several spectacular murals by Alfredo Zalce on the stairway, including *Cuauhtémoc y la Historia* (Cuauhtémoc and History) and *Los Pueblos del Mundo contra la Guerra Atómica* (Peoples of the World Against Atomic War) (both 1951).

But our favorite is the surreal mural *La Inquisición* (The Inquisition; Philip Guston and Reuben Kadish; 1935) on the wall of the back courtyard on the 1st floor. The most valuable work is *Traslado de las Monjas Dominicas a Su Nuevo Convento* (The Transfer of Dominican Nuns to their New Convent) depicting Dominican nuns moving into their new home at the **Templo de las Monjas** (Av Madero Oriente; ⊙8am-8pm) in 1738.

WESTERN CENTRAL HIGHLANDS MORELIA

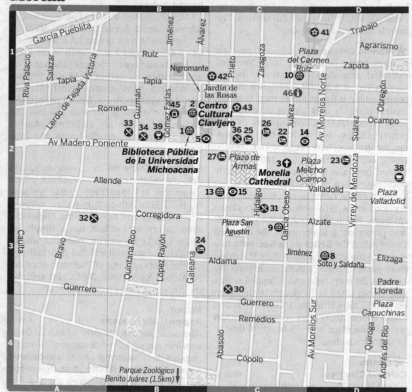

Santuario de la Virgen de Guadalupe

CHURCH

(Av Vasco 200; ⏰8am-8pm) A standard baroque structure on the outside dating from 1708 to 1716, this hushed sanctuary to Mexico's patron is a different story within. Get ready for a glistening profusion of pink, red and gold, gold, gold! The interior decorations date from 1915.

Springing out of all this elaboration is a series of large paintings depicting the conversion of the indigenous peoples to Christianity. They show scenes such as sacrificial victims about to be executed before being saved by the honest, God-fearing folk of Spain.

Beside the church, the much less splashy **Ex Convento de San Diego** (Plaza Morelos; ⏰7am-8pm) was built in 1761 as a monastery and now houses the Faculty of Law and Social Sciences of the Universidad Michoacana de San Nicolás de Hidalgo.

Colegio de San Nicolás de Hidalgo

NOTABLE BUILDING

(☎443-322-35-00; cnr Av Madero Poniente & Nigromante; ⏰8am-8pm Mon-Sat) FREE This building is now part of the Universidad Michoacana de San Nicolás de Hidalgo, which produced such scholars as Morelos, Miguel Hidalgo y Costilla and José Sixto Verduzco. Upstairs, the **Sala de Melchor Ocampo** is a memorial to another Mexican hero, a reformer-governor of Michoacán (open 8am to 2pm Monday to Friday). Preserved inside is his library and a copy of the document he signed donating it to the college, just before he was executed by a conservative firing squad in 1861.

The enormous, 72-sq-meter mural *Paisaje y economía de Michoacán* (Landscape and Economy of Michoacán) on the upper floor was painted by in 1935 by Marion Greenwood, the first foreign woman to paint a public mural in Mexico.

Museo Casa de Morelos
MUSEUM

(Morelos House Museum; ☏443-313-26-51; www.inah.gob.mx/paseos/morelos; Av Morelos Sur 323; adult/child M$40/free; ⊗9am-5pm Tue-Sun) This museum, arguably Morelia's best on the subject of José María Morelos y Pavón, resides in the former house of the independence hero, who bought the Spanish-style mansion for his sister in 1801. Well-laid-out displays have good information panels in both Spanish and English and cover Morelos' life, military campaigns and the trajectory of the independence movement thereafter. Don't miss his study, cell-like bedroom and spooky *máscara mortuoria* (death mask).

Other highlights include the wonderful old kitchen contemporary with the house and the antique coaches in the courtyard.

Acueducto
LANDMARK

Morelia's impressively preserved aqueduct north runs for just over 2km along (appropriately enough) Avenida Acueducto and then curves around Plaza Villalongín. It was built between 1785 and 1788 and supplied the city with water until 1910. Its 253 arches – some of which are now underground – are impressive when illuminated at night.

Museo del Dulce
MUSEUM

(Sweets Museum; ☏443-312-04-77; www.callereal.mx/#recorridos; Av Madero Oriente 440; adult/child M$26/21; ⊗10am-8pm Sun-Fri, to 9pm Sat) This small museum in the back of an old-fashioned sweet-shop is staffed by guides in period costume. It painlessly walks you through the history of candy-making, from the handiwork of nuns in the region's convents to mass production.

Plaza Morelos
PLAZA

This irregular, conspicuously vacant plaza southeast of the center surrounds the **Estatua Ecuestre al Patriota Morelos**, a majestic statue of Morelos on horseback, sculpted by Italian artist Giuseppe Inghilleri and unveiled in 1913.

Running from here to the **Fuente Las Tarascas** (Plaza Villalongín) is the leafy and cobbled **Calzada Fray Antonio de San Miguel**, a wide, romantic pedestrian promenade framed by exquisite old buildings. Just north of its western end, narrow **Callejón del Romance** (Romance Alley) is all pink stone, trailing vines and cavorting couples. There are a couple of bars here.

Museo Casa Natal de Morelos
MUSEUM

(Morelos Birthplace Museum; ☎443-312-27-93; http://sic.gob.mx; Corregidora 113; ☉9am-8pm Mon-Fri, to 7:30pm Sat & Sun) FREE Independence leader José María Morelos y Pavón is king in Morelia – after all, the city is named after him. He was born at the site of this house; an eternal flame in the patio marks the spot where his mother, Juana Pérez Pavón, delivered him on her way to Mass on September 30, 1765. Now housing a museum in his honor, the collection of old photos and documents in eight rooms is poignant, but not as comprehensive as the better-curated Museo Casa de Morelos (p617).

Palacio de Justicia
NOTABLE BUILDING

(http://michoacan.network/publicacion/museo-antiguo-palacio-de-justicia-morelia-michoacan; Portal Allende 267; ☉9am-6pm Mon-Fri) FREE Facing the leafy expanse of Plaza de Armas, the Palacio de Justicia is in fact two buildings rebuilt in 1884. Its flamboyant facade blends French and eclectic styles, with stairwell art in the patio. An impressive mural called *Morelos y la Justicia* (Morelos and Justice) by Agustín Cárdenas (1976) was restored to its full glory by the artist 40 years later. The on-site museum has revolving exhibitions dealing with history and government.

Courses

Relatively few foreigners and plenty of culture make Morelia an exceptional place to learn how to cook Mexican, dance salsa and speak Spanish.

Baden-Powell Institute

LANGUAGE

(☏ 443-312-20-02; www.baden-powell.com; Antonio Alzate 569; per 20hr week from US$180, private lessons per hour US$18) The small, extremely well-run and welcoming Baden-Powell Institute offers courses in the Spanish language, as well as Latin American history, Mexican art, cooking, culture, guitar, and folk and salsa dancing. It can book homestays (per day US$27) for students and has some well-appointed apartments available right around the corner from the school.

Centro Cultural de Lenguas

LANGUAGE

(☏ 443-312-05-89; www.ccl.com.mx; Av Madero Oriente 560; private lessons per hour US$17) This chaotically run outfit on the main drag concentrates mostly on teaching English to Mexicans, but does offer private (only) Spanish-language lessons. Tours and classes can also be arranged for Mexican music, dance and cooking (minimum three people).

☞ Tours

The tourist office (p623) runs daily city tours at 10am or 4pm. For tours outside the city, ask them for recommendations.

Mexico Cooks!

FOOD & DRINK

(☏ 55-1305-7194; www.mexicocooks.typepad.com; half-day market tour per person US$125) US-born Cristina Potters, a Mexican citizen and expert on Mexican cuisine, gives wonderful personalized culinary and cultural tours of Morelia and the rest of Michoacán as well as of Guadalajara, though she is based in Mexico City. Contact her in advance to arrange a tour.

✵ Festivals & Events

Festival Internacional de Guitarra

MUSIC

(http://michoacan.travel/en/events/guitar-international-festival.html; ⊙ Apr) This popular festival over four days in April features concerts by both local and internationally acclaimed guitarists, plus seminars and a large display of beautifully made guitars and other stringed instruments.

Feria de Morelia

CULTURAL

(⊙ Apr-May) Morelia's biggest fair, running for three weeks in late April through May, hosts exhibits of handicrafts, agriculture and livestock, plus regional dances, bullfights and fiestas. The city's founding date (May 18) is celebrated with a fireworks show.

Festival Internacional de Música

MUSIC

(www.festivalmorelia.mx; ⊙ Nov) The international classical-music festival unfolds over two weeks in November with orchestras, choirs and quartets giving concerts in churches, plazas and theaters around town.

Festival Internacional de Cine de Morelia

FILM

(www.moreliafilmfest.com; ⊙ Oct) This major international exhibition for Mexico's vibrant film industry brings 10 days of movies, parties and star sightings in late October.

🛏 Sleeping

There is a lot of places to stay in Morelia and not all that many tourists, so competition is fierce. Except during certain festivals, you can be sure that all accommodations, apart from the very cheapest hostels, will offer significant discounts on rack rates.

★ Baden-Powell Institute Apartments

APARTMENT $

(www.furnishedapartmentmorelia.com; Tagle 138; 2-/4-person apt per week from US$250/300; P 🛜) The fully equipped apartments in this delightful complex share a courtyard and terrace. All have complete kitchens, dining areas and one, two or three bedrooms accommodating between two and six people. They are at the eastern end of Avenida Madero Oriente, an easy walk to the sights and restaurants of Plaza de Armas and the bars at Plaza Villalongín.

Hotel Casa del Anticuario

HOTEL $

(☏ 443-333-25-21; www.hotelcasadelanticuario.com; Galeana 319; s/d from M$550/650, superior M$750/950; 🛜) This luscious yellow 16-room guesthouse has rooms with exposed stone walls and wooden roof beams, very helpful staff, a nice central courtyard bedecked with vintage radios, TVs and gramophones, and excellent wi-fi reception. In fact, it has everything required to give hotels twice its price a serious run for their money.

Hotel Real Valladolid

HOTEL $

(☏ 443-312-45-62; valladolidhotel@hotmail.com; Bartolomé de las Casas 418; d M$650; P ❄ 🛜) Putting in a solid performance in Morelia's somewhat scant budget end of the market, the Valladolid delivers the basics: 21 clean, no-frills, relatively modern rooms with flat-screen TVs and small bathrooms. It lacks the embellishments of some of Morelia's more historic establishments, but if it's just a crash pad you're after, it'll do the trick nicely.

Only Backpackers Morelia
HOSTEL $

(☑443-425-42-09; www.facebook.com/TheOnly Backpackers; Serdán 654; dm M$150, d M$ 290-400; @ 🖥) Not strictly the only backpacker hostel in Morelia, but this is probably the best of them. This one has three private rooms along with eight- to 10-bed dorms sleeping 45 and all with shared bathroom, a kitchen and two quiet courtyards in a traditional Morelian townhouse. The owners are friendly and the fruit-based breakfasts (M$35) excellent. Laundry costs M$70.

Hotel Casino
HOTEL $$

(☑443-313-13-28; www.hotelcasino.com.mx; Portal Hidalgo 229; r from M$1050; P @ 🖥) Overlooking Plaza de Armas and the cathedral, the Casino's frontage hums with the addictive energy of Mexican street life. The 42 rooms themselves, accessible by elevator, are less illuminating for a building as stately as this, but there are other bonuses: incomparable location, professional service and the excellent Lu Cochina Michoacana restaurant, which takes up the lobby and front terrace.

★Hotel Virrey de Mendoza
HISTORIC HOTEL $$$

(☑443-312-00-45; www.hotelvirrey.com; Av Madero Poniente 310; r from M$1850; P ❋ @ 🖥) The lobby of this very central, very friendly hotel, here since 1939, is drop-dead gorgeous, with a spectacular stained-glass atrium. The 55 rooms have an aging grace, with wooden floors and high ceilings. Ask for one with plenty of windows, as some rooms can be dark.

The restaurant does Morelia's swankiest Sunday brunch (mains from M$90), complete with made-to-order omelettes, platters of fresh tropical fruits and a groaning dessert table.

★Hotel de la Soledad
HISTORIC HOTEL $$$

(☑443-312-18-88; www.hsoledad.com; Zaragoza 90; r/ste incl breakfast from M$2500/3000; P ❋ @ 🖥) Wow! Bougainvillea frames the stone arches, fountains tinkle, classical music wafts on the breeze and palm trees reach for the skies – and that's all just in the central courtyard. The 41 rooms all differ, but expect showers made from ancient stone arches,

translucent stone basins, hand-carved wooden bedheads and a general sense of class.

Cantera Diez
BOUTIQUE HOTEL $$$

(☑443-312-54-19; www.canteradiezhotel.com; Juárez 63; r from M$3120; P ❋ 🖥) Facing the cathedral is Morelia's slickest boutique hotel. The 11 rooms – all suites – range from spacious to palatial, all with dark-wood floors, stylish modern furnishings in primary colors and sumptuous bathrooms you could throw a party in. There's a popular restaurant called Cantera 10 on the 1st floor.

Hosting House Congreso
BOUTIQUE HOTEL $$$

(☑443-232-02-46; www.hhcongreso.com; Av Madero Oriente 94; r/ste from M$2400/3750; P ❋ @ 🖥) Recently renamed and rebranded (they're obviously going after the conference and convention market), this hotel's 26 rooms might be small but they are crammed with pomp and a sense of royalty, including ornately carved and colorful bedheads and quality bathrooms and mattresses. There's also a lovely courtyard bar and restaurant. Front-facing rooms suffer from road noise despite the soundproofing.

✖ Eating

Morelia offers some superb eating options to suit all budgets. Street food can be harder to find; seek it out at any of the three markets.

Mercado de San Juan
MARKET

(Revolución & Plan de Ayala; ⊙8am-4pm) Also known as Mercado Revolución from its address, this is our favorite of Morelia's trinity of markets, with meat, produce, dry goods and an infinite variety of cooked foods on offer.

Cenaduría Lupita
MEXICAN $

(☑443-312-13-40; www.facebook.com/Cenaduria LupitaMR; Sanchez del Tagle 1004; mains M$67-100; ⊙6-11pm Mon-Fri, 2-10pm Sat & Sun) If you'd like to try a range of Morelian delicacies, head for this low-key eatery 2km southeast of the cathedral specializing in *antojitos regionales* (regional appetizers) like *sopa tarasca* (a rich bean soup with cream, dried chili and bits of crisp tortilla), *uchepos* (corn 'polenta' cooked in husks) and *pozole* (pork and hominy stew).

La Cocina de Licha
MEXICAN $

(☑443-312-61-65; Corregidora 669; set meals M$45; ⊙1-4pm) One of Morelia's best deals available can be found at this super-friendly hole-in-the-wall, which serves up *cocina económica* (literally 'economic cuisine') to a crowd of loyal locals to the strains of a tinkling piano. The daily changing set meal includes starter, main course, dessert and drink. Look out for a small table with a sign on the sidewalk.

Gaspachos La Cerrada
MEXICAN $

(Hidalgo 67; gaspachos M$35; ☺9am-9pm) Gaspacho – not a cold vegetable soup in Mexico but a 'salad' of diced mango, pineapple and *jicama* (Mexican 'turnip') drowned in orange and lime juice and vinegar and dashed with salt, chili sauce, onion and grated cheese – is a Morelian favorit. But word on the street says this place is the best of them all.

★Tata
MEXICAN $$

(☑443-312-95-14; www.tatamezcaleria.com; Bartolomé de las Casas 511; mains M$125-210; ☺1:30pm-12:30am Mon-Thu, to 2am Fri & Sat, 1:30-10pm Sun) It could very well be the 190 different mezcals from Michoacán, Jalisco and Oaxaca that keeps pulling us back to Tata, but we're more inclined to think it's the *cocina de autor* (signature cuisine) of chef Fermín Ambás, with such delectables as rabbit tartare with wasabi aioli and chili (M$85) and tuna in a tortilla crust (M$210) on offer. Our advice? Eat here but drink at Tata's little sister Tatita (p622) two blocks to the northeast.

★Lu Cochina Michoacana
NEW MEXICAN $$

(☑443-313-13-28; www.lucocinamichoacana.mx; Portal Hidalgo 229; mains M$120-180; ☺7:30am-10pm Sun-Thu, to 11pm Fri & Sat) This unassuming restaurant below the Hotel Casino is one of Morelia's most inventive places to dine. Talented young chef Lucero Soto Arriaga turns pre-Hispanic ingredients into exquisite gems of beautifully presented *alta cocina*. Try the *atápakua de chilacayote*, a rich seasonal vegetable soup (M$56) and the Zitácuaro trout with green *mole* (M$169). Excellent selection of Mexican wines by the glass.

Fonda Marceva
MEXICAN $$

(☑443-312-16-66; Abasolo 455; mains M$90-175; ☺9am-6pm) Specializing in the cuisine of the *Tierra Caliente* (Hot Land) region of Michoacán's southeast corner, this lovely courtyard restaurant spread over three rooms and crammed with colorful handicrafts serves a mindblowing *aporreadillo* (breakfast stew of eggs, dried beef and chili; M$90) and some of the best *frijoles de la olla* (beans slow-cooked in a pot; M$60) we've ever tasted.

★Chango
FUSION $$$

(☑443-312-62-13; www.changorestaurante.com; Sor Juana Inés de la Cruz 129; mains M$145-350; ☺1:45pm-12:30am) A lovely destination restaurant south of Plaza Villalongín, Chango offers *cocina contemporánea de autor* (contemporary signature cuisine) with maestro chef Daniel Aguilar Bernal at the helm. Seating is spread around various downstairs rooms and an upstairs terrace in a house best described as 'Mexican art meets art nouveau.' The menu is international and subtly experimental (expect sous vide cooking).

The gourmet lamb burger (M$158) deserves a mention, as does the 'orange' risotto of ginger, zucchini and prawns. But we'll go back for the fig tart with goat's cheese (M$115) and the pork confit parcel with mango glaze (M$220). Anglophiles will appreciate the banoffee pie (M$69) for dessert.

Los Mirasoles
MEXICAN $$$

(☑443-317-57-75; www.losmirasoles.com; Av Madero Poniente 549; mains M$125-295; ☺1-11pm Mon-Thu, to 11:30pm Fri & Sat) Morelian and Michoacán pride oozes from the kitchen at Los Mirasoles, where you'll dine in a fine Unesco-quality house bedecked (among other quirks) with a copy of Las Tarascas fountain. The food is doused in regional flavors. Try the *chiles capones* (seedless chilies stuffed with cheese; M$87) and *atápakua de huachinango* (fish in a *mole*-like sauce; M$210).

The latter was the dish served in Paris in 2005 during Mexico's bid to have its cuisine listed as an Intangible Cultural Heritage by Unesco (realized in 2010). The wine cellar stocks some 250 vintages.

Onix
INTERNATIONAL, MEXICAN $$$

(☑443-317-82-90; www.onix.mx; Portal Hidalgo 261; mains M$119-259; ☺1pm-1am) All the restaurants around Plaza de Armas are excellent for eavesdropping and people-watching, but some come unstuck with the food. Not Onix, locally famous for its taste-challenging menu that includes such eccentricities as crocodile in a starfruit and coconut sauce and international favorites like cheese fondue.

Less traditional than other city-center abodes, the Onix also turns heads with its seating (check out the seriously avant-garde chairs), perfectly balanced margaritas and hugely varied live music (from 9:30pm Wednesday to Saturday). Service is sharp.

THE SWEET LIFE

Dulces morelianos – delicious 'Morelian sweets' made with fruit, nuts, milk and sugar – are famous throughout the region. They're showcased both at the **Mercado de Dulces y Artesanías** and the Museo del Dulce (p617), an old-fashioned *chocolatería* stacked with truffles, preserves, candied nuts and sugary chunks of candied peaches and pumpkin and staffed by women in period costume.

There are up to 300 varieties, but these are some of our favorite sweets:

➜ *Ates de fruta* – jewel-colored squares or strips of fruit leather, commonly made from guava, mango and quince.

➜ *Cocadas* – chewy-crunchy pyramids of caramelized coconut.

➜ *Frutas cubiertas* – chunks of candied fruits such as squash, fig and pineapple.

➜ *Glorias* – cellophane-wrapped rolls of goat's milk caramel studded with pecans.

➜ *Jamoncillo de leche* – fudge-like milk sweets sold in rectangles or molded into nut shapes.

➜ *Obleas con cajeta* – gooey caramel sandwiched between two thin round wafers.

➜ *Ollitas de tamarindo* – tiny clay pots filled with a sweet-salty-tangy tamarind jam-like paste.

➜ *Rompope* – eggnog-like drink made with *aguardiente*, eggs, milk and (here) one of 16 flavorings: from pecans and walnuts to cinnamon and strawberries.

Las Mercedes
MEXICAN $$$

(☏443-312-61-13; Guzmán 47; mains M$180-295; ⊙2:30-10pm Mon-Sat, 2-7:30pm Sun) This astonishingly decorated restaurant is spread over various rooms in an erstwhile colonial mansion. The rich decor could pass for a museum with paintings and mirrors in gilded frames, religious icons, handsome columns and stone spheres. The food is equally upmarket with the kitchen serving *pechuga azteca* (Aztec chicken breast) and four cuts of steak in a number of different ways.

Drinking & Nightlife

Nightlife is more genteel than rowdy in Morelia, though a few clubs keep the music pumping into the small hours. Around the Jardín de las Rosas just north of the Centro Cultural Clavijero are several bars with terraces that start buzzing in the early evening. Another hot spot is the area around Plaza Villalongin at the eastern end of the city center.

Los 50s Bar
BAR

(Av Madero Poniente 507; ⊙5pm-midnight Sun & Mon, to 11pm Tue-Thu, to 5am Fri & Sat) Rock belts out of a handful of clubs on and around Av Madero Poniente after 10pm, but this is one of the best. Expect young, moody student bands reinterpreting Doors songs or blasting through self-penned homages to Nirva-

na. There's a cover charge (from M$30) on live-music nights.

Cafe Europa
CAFE

(www.cafeeuropa.com.mx; Bartolomé de las Casas 97; coffee from M$25; ⊙9am-9pm Mon-Sat) Part of a chain of local cafes, this tiny place would be easy to miss were it not for the aroma of roasting coffee beans, sourced from four different Mexican states, wafting from the doorway. Seating on two levels.

Tatita Mezcalería
BAR

(☏443-312-95-14; www.facebook.com/TatitaMez caleria; Jardín Villalongín 42; ⊙1pm-2:30am) A gorgeous *mezcalería* (mezcal bar) housed in a beautifully converted old villa just by the Fuente Las Tarascas, Tatita gets it all right, with cool music, superb cocktails (from M$65), great DJs and friendly, attentive staff. Mezcal flights cost M$140 (Michoacán) and M$265 (Oaxaca).

☆ Entertainment

As a university town and the capital of one of Mexico's more dynamic states, Morelia has a thriving cultural life. Stop by the tourist office or the Casa de la Cultura for a copy of *Cartelera Cultural*, a free weekly listing of films and cultural events.

For stage-acting, visit the **Teatro Ocampo** (☏443-312-37-34; www.facebook.com/TeatroOcam poMorelia; Ocampo 256) or **Teatro Morelos**

(☑ 443-314-62-02; www.ceconexpo.com; cnr Av Ventura Puente & Camelinas); the latter is part of the Centro de Convenciones complex, 3km south of the city center. The cathedral (p615) has occasional impressive organ recitals.

Conservatorio de las Rosas CLASSICAL MUSIC
(☑ 443-312-14-69; www.conservatoriodelasrosas.edu.mx; Tapia 334) Founded in 1743, this is the oldest music conservatory in the Americas and remains something of an 'old-school' music college. In its Alhambra-esque courtyard, you can sit and seek romantic inspiration as the sound of trumpet blasts and guitar riffs emanates from the surrounding classrooms. There are free concerts on at 8pm Thursdays in the Sala Niños Cantores de Morelia.

Casa de la Cultura LIVE MUSIC
(☑ 443-313-12-68; www.casaculturamorelia.gob.mx; Av Morelos Norte 485) With the Conservatorio de las Rosas (p623), this is a pillar of Morelia's cultural life. Housed in an old Carmelite monastery dating from the 17th century, it's a blissful place to hang out and soak up the musical spirit of Mexico. The cute cafe near the entrance is a good staging post, or check the website to see what performances are coming up.

Save time for other nooks and crannies too, taking in the ancient wall paintings, enormous mirrors and cell-like monks' quarters. Guitarists often sit around the cloisters quietly strumming.

🛍 Shopping

Casa de las Artesanías MARKET
(☑ 443-312-08-48; http://casart.gob.mx; Fray Juan de San Miguel 129, Plaza Valladolid; ☺ 8am-7:30pm Mon-Fri, 9am-3pm & 4-7:30pm Sat & Sun) If you don't have time to scour the Purépecha pueblos for the perfect folk-art piece, come to the House of Crafts inside a wing of the Ex Convento de San Francisco, dating from 1541. It's a cooperative marketplace launched to benefit indigenous craftspeople; arts and handicrafts from all over Michoacán are displayed and sold here. On the upper floor there's a free craft museum called the **Museo Michoacano de las Artesanías**.

**Mercado de Dulces
y Artesanías** MARKET
(Sweets & Crafts Market; Gómez Farías 55; ☺ 9am-10pm) This seductive market, on the western side of the Centro Cultural Clavijero, deals in the region's famous sweets, including

a rainbow selection of *ates de fruta* (fruit leathers) in a variety of exotic flavors.

ℹ Information

Banks and ATMs are plentiful along Avenida Madero, especially at its western end around the plazas on either side of the cathedral.

The **state tourist office** (☑ 443-312-94-14; http://michoacan.travel/en; Portal Hidalgo 245; ☺ 8am-5pm Mon-Fri) is opposite the Plaza de Armas. The helpful **city tourist office** (☑ 443-317-03-35, 443-317-80-39; www.turismo morelia.mx; Juárez 178; ☺ 9am-6pm Mon-Fri, 10am-6pm Sat & Sun) can be found along Benito Juárez north of the cathedral. In addition, there are info kiosks at the northeast corner of Plaza de Armas and in Plaza Melchor Ocampo (both open 9am to 9pm daily).

Hospital Star Médica (☑ 443-322-77-00; www.starmedica.com; Virrey de Mendoza 2000)

Main Post Office (Av Madero Oriente 369; ☺ 8am-6pm Mon-Fri, to noon Sat)

ℹ Getting There & Away

AIR

General Francisco Mujica International Airport (Aeropuerto Internacional General Francisco Mujica; ☑ 443-317-67-80; www.aeropuertosgap.com.mx/en/morelia-3.html; Carretera Morelia-Zinapécuaro Km 27) is 27km north of Morelia, on the Morelia–Zinapécuaro Hwy. There are no public buses; taxis to and from the airport cost about M$200. There are plenty of daily departures to cities in Mexico and limited flights serve destinations in North America.

Aeromar (☑ 800-237-66-27; www.aeromar.com.mx) Flies to Mexico City and Tijuana.

Volaris (☑ 55-1102-8000; www.volaris.mx) Book online or at the airport desk. Domestic flights include those to Mexico City.

BUS

Morelia's **bus station** (Terminal de Autobuses de Morelia; ☑ 443-334-10-71) is about 4km northwest of the city center. It's separated into three *módulos*, which correspond to 1st-, 2nd- and 3rd-class buses. To get into town from here take a Roja 1 combi (red) from under the pedestrian bridge, or catch a taxi (M$60). First-class buses depart hourly or more frequently for most destinations.

ℹ Getting Around

Around town, small combis and buses operate from 6am until 10pm daily (M$7). Combi routes are designated by the color of their stripe: Ruta Roja (red), Ruta Amarilla (yellow), Ruta Rosa (pink), Ruta Azul (blue), Ruta Verde (green),

BUSES FROM MORELIA

DESTINATION	FARE (M$)	DURATION (HR)	FREQUENCY (DAILY)
Colima	579	6	3 daily
Guadalajara	388	4	half-hourly
Mexico City (Terminal Norte)	414	4¾	hourly
Mexico City (Terminal Poniente)	414	4½	half-hourly
Pátzcuaro	59	1	hourly
Uruapan	175	2	hourly
Zitácuaro	187	3	half-hourly

Ruta Cafe (brown) and so on. Ask at the tourist office for help with bus and combi routes.

Reserva Mariposa Monarca

In the eastern-most corner of Michoacán, straddling the border of México state, lies the incredible 563-sq-km **Reserva de la Biósfera Santuario Mariposa Monarca** (Monarch Butterfly Biosphere Reserve; http://mariposamonarca.semarnat.gob.mx; each sanctuary adult/child M$50/40; ☉8am-dusk mid-Nov–Mar), a Unesco World Heritage site since 2008. Every autumn, in late October to early November, millions of monarch butterflies flock to these forested highlands for their winter hibernation, having flown all the way from the Great Lakes region of the US and Canada some 4500km away. It's an unforgettable sight watching clouds of the colorful insects transform the forest into a unique Technicolor world.

☉ Sights

The biosphere reserve extends over two states, with two sanctuaries in Michoacán and two in the state of México. Hotels located near the reserves can arrange guided trips starting at M$1500 including lunch.

☉ El Rosario

El Rosario is the most popular area – during the height of butterfly voyeurism (February and March) it gets as many as 8000 visitors a day. It is also the most commercial – souvenir stalls abound on the hillside and the habitat has been severely affected by illegal logging. El Rosario village and the entrance to the El Rosario reserve area are located about 12km up a good gravel road from the small village of Ocampo.

Getting to the butterflies requires a steep 2km to 4km hike (or horseback ride), a lot of it on steps, depending on the time of year. There are a couple of hotels in Ocampo, but it's a far more pleasant experience to stay in the village of Angangueo (just 45 minutes on foot from Ocampo). The entrance fee (adult/child M$50/40) includes a mandatory guide. Horses cost M$100 one way. There's a small, free **museum** (open 9am to 5pm) worth perusing at the entrance gate with exhibits and a short film about the butterflies.

☉ Sierra Chincua

Sierra Chincua is some 12km northeast of Angangueo, way up in the mountains. This area has been damaged by logging, but not as badly as El Rosario. It's a less strenuous hike, so this sanctuary is for those who want an easier walk. Price-wise it's the same deal as El Rosario (adult/child M$50/40). Horses are also available. At the attractively organized entrance are souvenir shops, places to eat and a zip-line. To get here from Angangueo, take the bus bound for Tlalpujahua or Mexico City bus (M$20) and tell the driver you're going to Sierra Chincua. Taxis from Angangueo cost M$350 and upward, depending on the wait.

☉ Cerro Pelón

Cerro Pelón, which is actually located in México state, is by far the best choice. The mountains rise high (more than 3000m) here, the forest is in great shape and there is barely a trickle of tourism compared with the Michoacán reserves. Rangers have protected the México side of the forest for the last 40 years, reducing illegal logging considerably. Expect to see huge, cathedral fir trees, moss-covered trunks, wildflowers and incredible canyon views.

Be warned that the climb here is very steep and the relentless ascent takes a good mountain walker at least 1½ hours going at a fair pace and without stopping. People not used to mountain walking are likely to struggle; we would discourage most from attempting to do so. Most people choose to ascend the mountain on horseback (M$200).

This reserve area is about a 40-minute drive southeast of Zitácuaro, Michoacán's sixth-largest city, where you can buy necessary food, water and supplies. There are a couple of access points, including Macheros and El Capulín. Both are within 1.5km of each other and can be reached by public transportation from outside Zitácuaro's bus terminal. The combis marked 'Aputzio' and waiting to the left of the Bodega Aurrera when you exit the bus terminal cost M$15. Get off in La Piedra and take a taxi from there to Macheros or El Capulín (from M$30). A taxi straight from Zitácuaro to either of the reserve areas costs M$250 to M$300.

Piedra Herrada

The sanctuary of 'Branded Rock' is 25km outside of Valle de Bravo in México state. The road to it passes through a major monarch crossing, with thousands of monarchs fluttering across to drink before returning to their roosts every day. The entrance is just past this spectacle on your left. Most of the trail up to the colony is paved. The difficulty of the hike or ride up varies by year depending on the location of the colony. Horses are available. Try to visit on a weekday to avoid the tour buses from Mexico City.

ⓘ Getting There & Away

At least one of the four reserves can be reached from Angangueo, Zitácuaro and Macheros, but it's easiest and most time-efficient to hire a guide with transportation.

Angangueo

📞 715 / POP 5030 / ELEV 2580M

This drowsy mining town is the most popular base for butterfly-watchers, because it's close to both the Sierra Chincua and El Rosario sanctuaries. The town is layered into the hills and replete with pine forest, grazing land and cornfields. Most services can be found along a single main drag with two names (Nacional and Morelos). There are two attractive churches, including the 18th-century Templo de la Immaculada Concepción, on Plaza de la Constitución, the center of town, from which Nacional runs down the hill.

🛏 Sleeping

Plaza Don Gabino GUESTHOUSE $

(📞715-156-03-22; www.facebook.com/Don.Gabino. Hotel; Morelos 147; s/d/ste M$650/850/1200; 🅿🛜) By far the best of the town's guesthouses, this family-run and exceptionally welcoming place has nine sparkling-clean rooms with fully functioning hot-water showers and a restaurant serving an excellent four-course dinner with Michoacán specialties. Some suites have fireplaces. It's around a kilometer downhill from the central plaza. Reserve ahead in butterfly season.

During the butterfly season from late October to March, Plaza Don Gabino also organizes excursions to the Sierra Chincua and El Rosario sanctuaries.

ⓘ Information

The small **tourist office** (📞715-156-06-44; Nacional 1; ⊗8am-7pm Nov-Mar, to 4pm Mon-Fri Apr-Oct) is just downhill from the main plaza.

ⓘ Getting There & Away

Frequent buses from Morelia go first to Zitácuaro (M$187, three hours), where you'll catch another bus to Angangueo (M$25, 1¼ hours). From Mexico City's Terminal Poniente you can get a Zina bus direct to Angangueo (M$226, 3½ hours, seven daily); most of the other bus lines go through Zitácuaro.

To reach the El Rosario sanctuary from Angangueo, first take a combi to Ocampo (M$12, 15 minutes, hourly), then another to El Rosario (M$20, 30 minutes, hourly), from the corner of Independencia and Ocampo. In season there are also camionetas (pickup trucks) that leave from the auditorio (auditorium) in Angangueo, or from outside hotels; these cost about M$600 for around 10 people and take 45 bumpy minutes (via a back road) to reach the sanctuary, but they go directly to the entrance.

For Sierra Chincua take the bus bound for Tlalpujahua or Mexico City bus (M$20) and tell the driver you're going to Sierra Chincua. Taxis from Angangueo cost M$350 and upward, depending on the wait.

Zitácuaro

📞 715 / POP 84,700 / ELEV 1990M

Zitácuaro is Michoacán's sixth-largest city, but it feels like a provincial working-class town. Known primarily for its specialty

MACHEROS

This quiet farming community is located close to the entrance of the Cerro Pelón sanctuary (p624). Out of season it offers excellent birding and hiking opportunities as well as year-round scenic views.

Along with a wonderful destination B&B, **JM Butterfly** (☑726-596-31-17; www.jmbutterflybnb.com; s M$850-1250, d M$950-1350, all incl breakfast), Macheros offers a campsite (from M$300) with the usual facilities, as does the village of El Capulín, a couple of kilometers to the southeast. Remember that camping is forbidden in the reserve.

breads and trout farms, it's no great looker and will confuse most visitors as they amble up and down the hilly streets. But Zitácuaro is a sensible base for visiting the butterflies at both the Cerro Pelón and the Piedra Herrada sanctuaries.

👁 Sights

Iglesia de San Pancho   CHURCH
(Morelos 74; ⏰9am-2pm & 4-6pm) This restored mid-16th-century church in the village of San Francisco Coatepec de Morelos across Hwy 51 south of Zitácuaro appeared in the great John Huston film, *The Treasure of the Sierra Madre,* starring Humphrey Bogart. Visit at sunset to see the light streaming through the stained glass. A taxi from town costs M$50.

🛏 Sleeping & Eating

Rancho San Cayetano   HOTEL $$$
(☑715-153-19-26; www.ranchosancayetano.com; Carretera a Huetamo Km 2.3; r from M$2125; P@🗑🐾) This attractive but pricey property has nine rooms, three loft apartments and three separate self-catering houses spread over 5 hectares of gardens and forest with a raging creek at the bottom. Spacious rooms are rustic chic with exposed stone walls, beamed ceilings and fireplaces. The pool and new spa are bonuses. Multi-course evening meals (M$510) available.

The *rancho* is owned and run by Pablo and Lisette, a Mexican-French couple who are passionate about butterflies. They show background videos to interested guests, have a substantial library on the subject and can arrange tours of all four sanctuaries.

La Bodega Leonesa   SPANISH $$
(☑715-153-71-55; www.facebook.com/labodegaleonesa; Revolución Sur 209; mains M$125-210; ⏰1-9:30pm Wed-Mon) This tapas bar and restaurant serves specialties from León, named the 'Spanish Capital of Gastronomy 2018,' and comes highly recommended by residents.

Try the *pulpo gallego* (Galician-style grilled octopus cooked with boiled potatoes and sweet paprika and drizzled with olive oil) or any of the salmon dishes. And no funny business; the owners are boxers.

ℹ Getting There & Away

Zitácuaro's bus terminal is on General Pueblita Norte, about a kilometer southeast of the city center. There are frequent buses to and from Morelia (M$187, three hours), Angangueo (M$25, 1¼ hours) and Mexico City's Terminal Poniente (M$194 to M$260, two hours), among other destinations.

For Cerro Pelón, take a combi marked 'Aputzio' (M$15); they wait to the left of the Bodega Aurrera when you exit the bus terminal. Get off in La Piedra and catch a taxi from there to Macheros or El Capulín (from M$30). A taxi straight from Zitácuaro costs M$250 to M$300.

Pátzcuaro Region

The area around Pátzcuaro is anchored by Lago de Pátzcuaro and a half-dozen notable lakeside villages.

Pátzcuaro

☑434 / POP 55,300 / ELEV 2140M
Terracotta-tiled roofs, warped red-and-white adobe walls and narrow cobblestone streets give the city of Pátzcuaro the air of a large village. Unlike the Spanish-founded settlements of Morelia and Guadalajara, Pátzcuaro took root in the 1320s as part of the Tarascan empire, two full centuries before the conquistadors arrived, and retains its indigenous feel.

History whispers from the cobwebbed louvers that overlook the lively but hassle-free streets fanning out from the city's attractively landscaped Plaza Vasco de Quiroga (or Plaza Grande) and Plaza Gertudis Bocanegra (AKA Plaza Chica). Adding to the atmosphere, Pátzcuaro hosts one of the most dramatic Day of the Dead celebrations in Mexico. It's also handily placed for exploring Lago de Pátzcuaro, just 3km to the north, and the craft-making Purépecha villages that cluster around its shoreline.

Make advance reservations during holidays and bring warm clothes from November to February – you're at altitude here and it gets chilly.

History

Pátzcuaro was the capital of the Tarasco (now known as the Purépecha) civilization from about AD 1325 to 1400. After the death of King Tariácuri, the Tarascan state became a three-member confederation comprising Tzintzuntzan and Ihuatzio as well. The league repulsed repeated Aztec attacks, which might explain why they welcomed the Spanish when they first arrived in 1522. Bad idea. The Spanish returned in 1529 under Nuño de Guzmán, a vicious conquistador.

Guzmán's five-year reign over the indigenous people was brutal, even for those times. The colonial government recalled Guzmán to Spain, where he was arrested and jailed, and in his place dispatched Bishop Vasco de Quiroga, a respected judge and cleric from Mexico City, to clean up the mess. Quiroga was an impressively enlightened man. When he arrived in 1536, he established village cooperatives based on the humanitarian ideals described in Sir Thomas More's *Utopia.*

To avoid dependence on Spanish mining lords and landowners, Quiroga successfully encouraged education and agricultural self-sufficiency in the Purépecha villages around Lago de Pátzcuaro, with all villagers contributing equally to the community. He also helped each village develop its own craft specialty, from masks and pottery to baskets and guitars. The utopian communities declined after his death in 1565, but the crafts traditions continue to this day. Not surprisingly, Tata Vascu (Father Vasco), as the Tarascos called Quiroga, has not been forgotten: streets, plazas, restaurants and hotels all over Michoacán are named in his honor.

⊙ Sights

★ Basílica de Nuestra
Señora de la Salud   BASILICA
(Plaza de la Basílica; ⊗8am-9pm) Built on a hill atop a pre-Hispanic ceremonial site, this cathedral-cum-pilgrimage site was intended to be the centerpiece of Vasco de Quiroga's utopia. Begun in 1540, the church was not completed until the 19th century and only the barrel-vaulted central nave is faithful to his original design. Quiroga's tomb, the **Mausoleo de Don Vasco**, is in the side-chapel to the left of the main entrance. It's a massive structure and quite austere, but always full of worshippers.

Behind the altar and up some steps at the eastern end of the basilic stands a much-revered figure of the cathedral's patron, **Nuestra Señora de la Salud** (Our Lady of Health), which 16th-century Purépechans crafted with a paste made from the heart of the cornstalk and bound with *tazingue,* a natural glue. Soon after its dedication, people began to experience miraculous healings and pilgrims still arrive from all over Mexico to pray for miracles. They crawl on their knees across the plaza, into the church and along its nave. Pinned to the image and at its feet are tiny tin *votivas* (votives) of hands, feet, legs, eyes and other body parts for which the faithful seek cures.

★ Plaza Vasco de Quiroga   PLAZA
(Plaza Grande) Pátzcuaro's leafy main square – more commonly known as 'Plaza Grande' – is Mexico's largest plaza after the Zócalo in Mexico City and the only one in the country without a church. It is framed by the 17th-century facades of old mansions that have since been converted to hotels, shops and restaurants, and is watched over by a serene **statue of Vasco de Quiroga**, which rises from the central fountain.

The plaza's colonnaded *portales* (corridors) are full of food stalls, jewelry shops and folk-art sellers, and the atmosphere, particularly on the weekend when bands play and street performers entertain, is wonderful.

Casa de los Once Patios   MARKET
(Madrigal de las Altas Torres; ⊗10am-7pm) This cool, rambling colonial edifice was built as a Dominican convent in the 1740s. (Before that, it was the site of the Hospital de Santa Martha, founded by Vasco de Quiroga and one of Mexico's first.) Today it houses small *artesanías* (handicraft shops) on two levels, each specializing in a particular regional craft. Renovations over the years mean there are now five patios rather than the previous 11 (as in the market's name – *once* is Spanish for 'eleven').

Pátzcuaro

Templo del Sagrario
CHURCH

(cnr Lerín & Portugal; ⊙8am-8pm) This creaky church is one of Pátzcuaro's oldest and built on the site of a former hospital in the 16th century. Until the early 1900s, it housed the revered statue of Nuestra Señora de la Salud, which now takes pride of place in the basilica nearby. Note the wonderful wooden tile floor and the majestic baroque altar.

Templo San Francisco
CHURCH

(Terán) This pink-stone eclectic-style church has an impressive Plateresque-style doorway, an adjoining cloister and a 16th-century figure of Christ fashioned from cornstalk paste.

Museo de Artes e Industrias Populares
MUSEUM

(☑434-342-10-29; www.inah.gob.mx/es/red-de-museos/299-museo-local-de-artes-e-industrias-populares-de-patzcuaro; cnr Enseñanza & Alcantarillas; adult/child M$50/free; ⊙9am-5pm Tue-Sun) Highlights among the dozen salas of this impressive folk-art museum include a room set up as a typical Michoacán kitchen, cases of gorgeous jewelry, copperware, ceramics and guitars from Paracho, and an entire room filled with *votivas* and *retablos* – votives and crudely rendered devotional paintings offering thanks to God for saving the creator from illness or accident.

The museum is housed in the former Colegio de San Nicolás, founded by Quiroga in 1540 as the first university in the Americas. The building was constructed on pre-Hispanic stone foundations, some of which can be seen in the patio behind the museum. Here you'll also see an all-wood decorated *troje* (traditional granary).

Biblioteca Gertrudis Bocanegra
LIBRARY

(☑434-342-54-41; http://sic.gob.mx; cnr Padre Lloreda & Títere; ⊙9am-7pm Mon-Fri, to 2pm Sat)

Pátzcuaro

◎ Top Sights
1 Basílica de Nuestra Señora de la
    Salud D2
2 Plaza Vasco de Quiroga (Plaza
    Grande) B3

◎ Sights
3 Biblioteca Gertrudis Bocanegra............ C1
4 Casa de los Once Patios C4
5 Museo de Artes e Industrias
    Populares C3
6 Plaza Gertrudis Bocanegra................... B2
7 Templo del Sagrario C3
8 Templo San Francisco............................ A3
9 Vasco de Quiroga Statue B3

⊕ Activities, Courses & Tours
10 Centro de Lenguas y Ecoturismo
    de Pátzcuaro.................................. A4

⊟ Sleeping
11 Gran Hotel Pátzcuaro B2
12 Hotel Casa del Refugio B2

13 Hotel Casa Encantada........................... B4
14 Hotel Casa Leal C3
15 Hotel Mansión de los Sueños.............. B2
16 Hotel Mansión Iturbe............................ B2
17 Hotel Misión Pátzcuaro Centro
    Histórico... B1
18 Mesón de San Antonio D2
19 Posada de la Basílica........................... C2

⊗ Eating
Doña Paca.................................... (see 16)
20 El Patio B3
21 La Surtidora B3
22 Market Food Stalls................................ B1
23 Santo Huacal B4
24 Tekare C2

⊕ Entertainment
Teatro Emperador
    Caltzontzin.................................(see 3)

⊕ Shopping
25 Market.. B1

On the northern side of Plaza Chica and oc-cupying the cavernous 16th-century Templo de San Agustín this stunning public library has a barrel-vaulted ceiling, oyster-shell sky-lights and a massive, very colorful mural (1942) by Juan O'Gorman on the rear wall that depicts the history of Michoacán from pre-Hispanic times to the 1910 Revolution. Note the remnants of original frescoes on the east and west walls.

To the west of the library, the **Teatro Emperador Caltzontzin** (☑ 434-342-14-51; www.teatroemperador.org; Plaza Chica) was a convent until it was converted into a theater in 1936; it functions today as an art-house cinema.

Plaza Gertrudis Bocanegra   PLAZA
(Plaza Chica) Pátzcuaro's second plaza, usually referred to as Plaza Chica, is officially named after a local heroine who was shot by firing squad in 1818 for her support of the inde-pendence movement. Her statue commands the center of the plaza. Hotels ring the pla-za and on the west side is the local **market** (btwn Juárez & Codallos; ☺ 7am-5pm) where you'll find everything from fruit and vege-tables to herbal medicines and traditional clothing – including the region's distinctive striped shawls and *sarapes* (blankets with an opening for the head).

Volcán del Estribo   VIEWPOINT
This hilltop lookout on an extinct volcano 3.5km west of the city center is a quintes-sential morning run for Pátzcuaro's more robust residents; but don't underestimate the altitude (2175m above sea level) or the terrain – a steep, cobbled, cypress-lined road. It's all worth it in the end when you reach the viewing pavilion with killer views of Lago de Pátzcuaro and its surroundings. For those with abnormal energy reserves, 422 steps lead up to the true summit.

To reach Volcán del Estribo, take Calle Ponce de León from the southwest corner of Plaza Grande and keep walking (or running).

⌖ Courses

**Centro de Lenguas y
Ecoturismo de Pátzcuaro**   LANGUAGE
(CELEP; ☑ 434-342-47-64; www.celep.com.mx; Navarrete 50; 2-week Spanish-language course US$350, language & cultural program US$540) Courses at this very enthusiastic center in-volve four hours of classes Monday to Fri-day. Cultural programs include seminars in Mexican literature and excursions to local villages. Homestays including meals with local families can also be arranged (from US$25 per day).

✦ Festivals & Events

Día de Muertos   RELIGIOUS
(Day of the Dead; ☺ Nov 1 & 2) The villages around Pátzcuaro, most notably Tzintzuntzan, and the Isla Janitzio stage the most popular (and crowded!) Día de Muertos celebrations in

Mexico. Parades, crafts markets, dancing, ceremonies, exhibitions and concerts are held in and around Pátzcuaro on both days, and cemeteries are packed with visitors throughout the festivities.

Pastorelas
RELIGIOUS

(☉Dec 26–Feb 2) These dramatizations of the shepherds' journey to pay homage to the infant Jesus are staged in Plaza Grande around Christmas. *Pastorelas indígenas,* on the same theme but including mask dances, enact the struggle of angels against the devils that are trying to hinder the shepherds. They're performed in eight villages around Lago de Pátzcuaro on different days between December 26 and February 2.

La Inmaculada Concepción/ Virgen de la Salud
RELIGIOUS

(☉Dec 8) A colorful procession to the basilica on the Feast of the Immaculate Conception honors 'Our Lady of Health' with traditional dance performances.

🛏 Sleeping

Pátzcuaro does 'pleasant colonial hotels' like Paris does refined streetside cafes. Nonetheless, it's usually worth reserving ahead for Friday and Saturday nights, and months ahead for Día de Muertos, when the entire town is booked well in advance. By contrast, at all other times you need normally only raise an eyebrow at the more expensive places to see prices tumble – sometimes by as much as 40%.

Gran Hotel Pátzcuaro
HOTEL $

(☎434-342-04-43; www.granhotelpatzcuaro.com; Plaza Bocanegra 6; s/d from M$650/950; P🛜) This no-frills hotel has smallish rooms but is very central, perched at the southern end of Plaza Chica. Ask for a room on the 2nd floor facing the square. The restaurant behind reception serves hearty breakfasts (M$55 to M$110).

Mesón de San Antonio
GUESTHOUSE $

(☎434-342-25-01; Serrato 33; s/d M$650/750; @🛜) Rooms at this great-value, old hacienda-style inn border a leafy, colonial-style courtyard. The beamed overhangs are held up by ancient timbers and the seven extremely large rooms are decorated with fine Purépecha pottery and have wood-burning fireplaces and cable TV. There's also a communal kitchen for guests' use.

★ Hotel Casa Encantada
B&B $$

(☎434-342-34-92; www.hotelcasaencantada.com; Dr Coss 15; r incl breakfast M$950-1750; P@🛜) Enchanting is the word for this intimate American-owned B&B offering 12 elegant rooms with local rugs and beautifully tiled bathrooms in a converted 1784 mansion. Many of the rooms like the Grand Sala at the front are enormous and some come with kitchenettes and have fireplaces. Host Virginia and her welcoming staff just can't do enough for guests.

Hotel Mansión Iturbe
BOUTIQUE HOTEL $$

(☎434-342-03-68; www.mansioniturbe.com; Morelos 59; r incl breakfast M$1265; P🛜) Right on the main square, the 14 rooms in this atmospheric hostelry are spacious, old-world in style, furnished in heavy dark woods, with beamed ceilings and crammed full of antiques. The wood- and stone-finished bathrooms are sumptuous. There's a wonderful terrace and patio out the back.

Hotel Casa del Refugio
BOUTIQUE HOTEL $$

(☎434-342-55-05; www.hotelesdelrefugio.com/casa-del-refugio; Portal Régules 9; d M$1100; P🛜) With adobe walls covered in religious motifs and portraits of saints, a palm-filled atrium with an enormous open fireplace and 23 small but immaculate rooms, this welcoming, very central hotel might just be the best deal in town if you arrive on the right day with the right bargaining skills. It's one of a group of five hotels here and in Morelia.

Hotel Misión Pátzcuaro Centro Histórico
HOTEL $$

(☎434-342-10-37; www.hotelesmision.com.mx/e_michoacan_patzcuaro.php; Obregón 10; d from M$900; P❄🛜) An impressive building once you make it past the ugly entry-level car park, the Misión, one of four dozen properties in a local chain, has a soaring central atrium, an impressive Pátzcuaro-themed painting, altarpieces and a peaceful covered courtyard. The 82 rooms are a little more institutionalized, but comfortable, with up-to-date bathrooms; nonetheless, many only have windows facing the indoor patio.

★ Hotel Casa Leal
BOUTIQUE HOTEL $$$

(☎434-342-11-06; www.hotelcasaleal.com; Portugal 1; d/ste from M$1500/3000; P❄@🛜) If there were a beauty contest among Pátzcuaro's boutique hotels, then this neoclassical plaza-facing stunner would win hands down. Examine the elegant sofas, the fabulous *Downton Abbey*–esque library, and the 14 grand but not grandiose rooms, which maintain a delicate balance between old-world exquisiteness and modern comfort. The icing on the sponge? The refined roof terrace overlooking Plaza Grande. Wow.

Posada de la Basílica   BOUTIQUE HOTEL $$$
(☑434-342-11-08; www.posadalabasilica.com.mx; Arciga 6; d/ste M$1600/2400; P @ 🛜) For rustic luxury, consider this boutique hotel with a terracotta rooftop and lake views opposite the basilica. The surprisingly bright colonial building contains 12 huge rooms with wood floors and open fireplaces; there are seven rooms more in a new wing. The master suites are truly special, and the entire place exudes elegance, charm and understatement. The in-house Tekare restaurant has panoramic views.

Hotel Mansión de los Sueños   BOUTIQUE HOTEL $$$
(☑434-342-11-03; www.mansiondelossuenos.com.mx; Ibarra 15; d/ste incl breakfast from M$1950/2950; P 🛜) This restored mansion built around three adjacent courtyards offers some of the most luxurious accommodations in town. There is art on every wall, coffee machines and minibars in each of the 13 rooms, and fireplaces and lofts in a few. The decor in some rooms is a bit over the top, though, so ask to see a few before deciding.

✖️ Eating

Pátzcuaro has some atmospheric eating options. Some of the town's best street food can be found at the **food stalls** (Juárez; ⊘8am-11pm) fronting the market on the northwest corner of Plaza Chica.

★Santo Huacal   MEXICAN $
(☑434-117-63-87, cell 434-1096942; www.facebook.com/santohuacal; Navarrete 32; mains M$60-120; ⊘10am-6pm Wed-Fri, 11am-7pm Sat & Sun) This tiny garden restaurant run by a young couple from Oaxaca is a wonderful find. From the weekly-changing blackboard menu, choose such delectables as root vegetable salad in a honey-mustard dressing, stuffed dates wrapped in bacon, and quiche made with poblano chilies and *huitlacoche* (mushroom-like corn mold). Desserts are to die for here.

Doña Paca   MEXICAN $
(☑434-342-03-68; Morelos 59; mains M$59-109; ⊘8am-8pm) This restaurant below the Hotel Mansión Iturbe is surprisingly stylish and the food – revamped Mexican favorites – is in fact something to write home about. The only down side is the bankers' hours, shutting shop when the rest of the world is reaching for the menu.

★La Surtidora   MEXICAN $$
(☑434-342-28-35; Hidalgo 71; mains M$89-160; ⊘8am-10pm) This downright heavenly place to flop down for refueling is living proof that no other country does atmospheric colonial cafes quite as well as Mexico. La Surtidora's cafe-cum-deli has been knocking out breakfasts (M$35 to M$89), *comidas* (lunch) and *cenas* (suppers) on Plaza Grande since 1916. The enchiladas, cakes, balletic waitstaff and home-roasted coffee can all be recommended.

Tekare   NEW MEXICAN $$
(☑434-342-11-08; Arciga 6; mains M$120-190; ⊘9am-9pm) This posh place on two levels above the Posada de la Basilica serves wonderful modern Mexican meat and fish dishes – though not all of the latter originate in the nearby lake. Perhaps the main reason for coming to Tekare ('lookout' in Purépecha) are the fabulous views of the town and the Lago de Pátzcuaro.

El Patio   MEXICAN $$
(☑434-342-04-84; www.facebook.com/elpatiorest; Aldama 19; mains M$60-160; ⊘8am-10pm) With much coveted seating on the portales of the Plaza Grande, this restaurant attracts as many locals as tourists and is unquestionably a pleasant place for a meal, with decent Mexican staples and some well-prepared

BUSES FROM PATZCUARO

DESTINATION	FARE (M$)	DURATION (HR)	FREQUENCY (DAILY)
Guadalajara	438	4½	2
Ihuatzio	20	15min	very frequent
Mexico City (Terminal Norte)	553	5½	6
Mexico City (Terminal Poniente)	553	5½	9
Morelia	68	1	hourly
Tzintzuntzan	20	20min	very frequent
Uruapan	79	1	very frequent

local dishes like *corundas* (triangular *tamales*; M$60). *Fiesta méxicana* decor.

ℹ Information

Several banks in the city center with ATMs will also change currency.

Municipal Tourist Office (☏434-344-34-86; Portal Hidalgo 1; ⊗9am-9pm)

Post Office (Obregón 13; ⊗8am-4:30pm Mon-Fri, to noon Sat)

ℹ Getting There & Away

Pátzcuaro's bus terminal is a walkable 1.5km southwest of the city center. It has a cafeteria and left-luggage facilities (M$20 per item; open 7am to 7pm).

To catch a bus heading to the city center, walk outside the terminal, turn right and at the corner take any bus marked 'Centro' (M$8). Taxis cost M$35.

Buses back to the terminal (marked 'Central') leave from the northeast corner of Plaza Chica. Buses to the **boat pier** (marked 'Lago'; M$8, five minutes) leave from the eastern side of the square and run from about 6am to 10pm daily.

Lago de Pátzcuaro

About 3km north of central Pátzcuaro, you will come over a rise to find a lake so blue that its edges blend seamlessly with the sky. Within it are a few populated islands. It is stream-fed and natural, and though pollution is a concern, it's still beautiful.

ISLA JANITZIO

Isla Janitzio is a popular weekend and holiday destination. It's heavily devoted to tourism, with lots of low-end souvenir stalls, fish restaurants and drunk college kids on holiday. But it is car-free and threaded with stepped footpaths (275 at last count) that eventually wend their way to the top

of the island, where you'll find a 40m-high statue of independence leader José María Morelos, erected in 1934. You can climb up inside the **Morelos Monument** (M$10) where an ascending 56 panels painted by Ramón Alva de la Canal (between 1936 and 1940) tell Morelos' story. The last part ingeniously climbs the statue's raised arm to a lookout with panoramic lake views in the see-through wrist.

A new 1200m-long zip-line links Isla Janitzio with Isla Tecuéna and costs M$250 one way. A boat will return you to Janitzio.

Round-trip boat trips to Janitzio depart from the Muelle General on the lake's southeastern edge and cost M$60 (free for children under seven years old) and take 25 minutes each way; they leave when full (about every 30 minutes; more often on Saturday and Sunday). The last one back is around 8pm.

Lakeside Villages

The villages surrounding Lago de Pátzcuaro make perfect day trips from Pátzcuaro, and most can be reached by public transportation. The villages differ quite a bit one from the other and some specialise in one particular type of craft.

ERONGARÍCUARO
☏434 / POP 2575 / ELEV 2084M

A pretty town 20km northwest from Pátzcuaro, Erongarícuaro (or 'Eronga') is one of the oldest settlements on the lake. French poet André Breton (1896–1966), who found Mexico to be 'the most surrealist country in the world', lived here for a time in the late 1930s, where he met Leon Trotsky and was visited occasionally by Diego Rivera and Frida Kahlo. Breton designed the unusual wrought-iron cross in the forecourt of the **Templo de Nuestra Señora de la Asunción**, 50m east of Avenida Morelos. There are gorgeous gardens behind the old Franciscan monastery attached to the church. You may find the gate to them open.

ℹ Getting There & Away

Combis run to Erongarícuaro from Pátzcuaro (M$20) frequently.

IHUATZIO
☑ 434 / POP 3575 / ELEV 2057M

Ihuatzio, 15km north of Pátzcuaro, was capital of the Tarascan kingdom after Pátzcuaro (but before Tzintzuntzan). Today it's just a slow, dusty village renowned for its weavers of animal figures – elephants, pigs, bulls etc – from *tule,* a reed that grows on the edge of the lake.

◉ Sights

**Ihuatzio
Archaeological Site**   RUINS
(☑ 443-312-88-38; http://inah.gob.mx/es/zonas/155-zona-arqueologica-ihuatzio; adult/child M$40/free; ⊙ 9am-6pm) The Ihuatzio site contains a partially restored set of pre-Tarascan ruins, some of which date back as far as AD 900. The site lies about 1.5km up a cobbled road from the village's small plaza. The ruins' best attraction is the **Plaza de Armas**, an open ceremonial space some 200m long, which doubled as a ball court and features two 15m-high squared-off pyramids at its west end. The piled stones enclosing the site are *muro-calzadas* (wall-causeways) used for transportation.

ℹ Getting There & Away

Buses to Ihuatzio (M$20) run directly from Pátzcuaro's Plaza Chica.

QUIROGA
☑ 435 / POP 14,700 / ELEV 2080M

The bustling market town of Quiroga, 25km northeast of Pátzcuaro and 8km beyond Tzintzuntzan, is named for Vasco de Quiroga, the man responsible for many of its buildings and handicrafts. Every day there's a busy **mercado de artesanías** (crafts market) on Avenida Vasco de Quiroga and the Plaza Principal, with hundreds of stalls and shops selling brightly painted wooden, ceramic and leather goods, as well as colorful woolen sweaters and *sarapes,* the long, blanket-like shawls worn here. The town is set at the crossroads of Hwys

15 and 120, so there is seldom a dearth of shoppers.

On the first Sunday in July the **Fiesta de la Preciosa Sangre de Cristo** (Feast of the Most Precious Blood of Christ) is celebrated with a long torchlight procession led by a group carrying an image of Christ crafted from a paste made of corncobs and honey.

ℹ Getting There & Away

Transportation between Quiroga and Erongarícuaro is infrequent, so travel between those two may be quicker via Pátzcuaro.

TZINTZUNTZAN
☑ 434 / POP 3500 / ELEV 2050M

The tiny town of Tzintzuntzan (tseen-TSOON-tsahn), some 17km northeast of Pátzcuaro, was once the Tarascan capital and served as Vasco de Quiroga's first base in the region. It has a beautiful sprawling cemetery that blooms with flowers and crepe paper during heady Día de Muertos celebrations, crumbling Tarascan ruins and some relics from the early Spanish missionary period. The town's pulse comes from its thriving Saturday and Sunday **mercado de artesanías** (crafts market) at the entrance to saintly Quiroga's beloved *atrio de los olivos* (olive grove) and two old churches and a former monastery now converted into a fascinating museum.

◉ Sights

★**Antiguo Convento
Franciscano de Santa Ana**   MONASTERY
South of the lake and just west of Hwy 120 lies this enormous religious compound built partly with stones from the Tarascan *yácatas* (temples) taken from the site up the hill. This is where Franciscan monks began the Spanish missionary effort in Michoacán in the 16th century. The complex is composed of two churches fronted by shady olive trees in the churchyard planted by Vasco de Quiroga. Most of the monastery now houses a fascinating new **museum** (☑ cell 434-3443005; www.inah.gob.mx/es/red-de-museos/317-antiguo-convento-franciscano-de-santa-ana-tzintzuntzan-michoacan; M$15; ⊙ 10am-5pm).

The museum showcases Purépecha culture and history and documents the arrival of the Spanish and the people's conversion to Christianity via excellent multimedia displays set up in the cloisters, refectory and

Lago de Pátzcuaro

0 ____ 5 km
0 ____ 2.5 miles

Chupícuaro

San Jerónimo
Purenchécuaro

Santa Fe
de la Laguna

San Andrés
Tziróndaro

Morelia
(40km)

Quiroga

Oponguo

Lago de Pátzcuaro

Tzintzuntzan • Tzintzuntzan

Puacuaro

Isla
Pacanda

Napizaro

Isla
Yunuén

Erongarícuaro • Janitzio-Tecuéna
Zipline

Isla
Tecuéna

Cucuchucho

San Francisco
Uricho

Isla
Janitzio

Statue of
José María
Morelos

Ihuatzio

Sanabría

Jarácuaro

Ihuatzio

Arocutín

Isla
Uranden
Morelos

Muelle General
(boat dock)

Tzurumútaro

Tócuaro • San Pedro
Pareo

Tzentzénguaro

Huecorio

Morelia
(50km)

Nocutzepo

San
Bartolo
Pareo

Santa Ana
Chapitiro

See Pátzcuaro
Map (p628)

Pátzcuaro

Tingambato (40km);
Uruapan (65km)

Santa Clara
del Cobre
(15km)

Uruapan
(Toll; 60km)

two open chapels. The galleries include a number of faded murals and Mudéjar-patterned wooden ceiling ornamentation, as well as a carved portal at the main entrance. Attached is the crumbling but still-functioning **Templo de San Francisco**.

★ Tzintzuntzan
Archaeological Site
RUINS

(☑cell 443-3128838; http://inah.gob.mx/es/zonas/179-zona-arqueologica-de-tzintzuntzan; adult/child M$55/free; ⊙9am-6pm) This site comprises an impressive group of five semicircular reconstructed temples known as *yácatas*, which are all that remain of the mighty Tarascan empire. The hillside location offers wonderful views of the town, lake and surrounding mountains and is rarely crowded. A small but well-curated **museum** showcases finds from the site. Don't miss the replica of the Ihuatzio coyote.

Down the hill to the east there are boulders with carved petroglyphs of barely recognisable deities. A small info point and some flowering bushes highlight a project that's trying to entice the once-abundant hummingbird back to the area; 'Tzintzuntzan' means 'place of the hummingbird' in Purépecha.

Cerámica
Tzintzuntzan
WORKSHOP

(☑cell 443-3948167; moralestz@yahoo.com; del Hospital & Tariacuri; ⊙10am-8pm Mon-Sat, to 1pm Sun) A converted missionary hospital now houses the rustic ceramics studio of Manuel Morales, a fifth-generation local potter. His colorful, intricate work is sold in galleries throughout Mexico and the USA. Inside you'll see ceramics in all stages of production and a cool, underground showroom in the back. Morales gives classes and accepts apprentices as well.

ℹ️ Getting There & Away

There are direct buses to Tzintzuntzan from Pátzcuaro's bus terminal (M$20).

Uruapan

📞452 / POP 279,000 / ELEV 2140M

All praise the thundering Río Cupatitzio, which brings lifeblood to Uruapan. This impressive river begins life underground, then rises to the surface, feeding a subtropical garden of palms, orchids and massive shade trees in the city's Parque Nacional Barranca del Cupatitzio. Without the river, Uruapan would not exist.

When Spanish monk Fray Juan de San Miguel arrived here in 1533, he was so taken with his surroundings that he gave the area the Purépecha name, Uruapan (oo-roo-AH-pahn), or 'Eternal Spring.' Fray Juan designed a large market square, built a hospital and chapel, and arranged streets into a grid that survives today.

Uruapan quickly grew into a productive agricultural center renowned for its macadamia nuts and high-quality aguacates (avocados); it still holds the title 'Capital Mundial del Aguacate.' Uruapan is 500m lower than Pátzcuaro and a bit warmer. It's not as enchanting a place as the latter, but is worth a stopover for a day or so.

◉ Sights

★ Parque Nacional Barranca del Cupatitzio   PARK

(Parque Nacional Eduardo Ruíz; 📞452-523-23-09; www.uruapanvirtual.com/acerca.php?item=parque-nacional; Independencia & Culver City; adult/child M$25/10; ⊙7:30am-6pm) This incomparable urban park is just 15 minutes west of the main plaza, but it's another world. Tropical and subtropical foliage is thick and aflutter with birds and butterflies. The Río Cupatitzio bubbles over boulders, cascades down waterfalls and spreads into wide, crystalline pools. Cobbled paths (labeled 'Recorrido Principal') follow the riverbanks to the river's source at the icy and gin-clear Rodilla del Diablo pool.

The main entrance to the 458-hectare gardens is where Calles Independencia and Culver City meet (though you can also enter at the western end of Calzada Rodilla del Diablo). There are a few fruit stands and *taquerías* inside, and there's even a trout farm where you can net your own catch.

Fábrica San Pedro   FACTORY

(📞452-524-14-63; www.facebook.com/FabricadeSanPedro; Treviño; ⊙9am-6pm Mon-Sat) FREE This old textile factory from the 19th century is essentially a living museum. Hand-loomed and hand-dyed bedspreads, tablecloths and curtains are still made here from pure cotton and wool, and are available for sale at the in-house shop (p638). The original machines are more than 150 years old and many are still used.

Museo Indígena Huatápera   MUSEUM

(📞452-524-34-34; www.gob.mx/cdi/galerias/museo-indigena-huatapera-uruapan-michoacan; Portal Mercado; ⊙9:30am-1:30pm & 3:30-6pm Tue-Sun) FREE Embedded in the Huatápera, an old colonial courtyard building on the northeast corner of the main plaza, this small museum showcases handsome *artesanías* (handicrafts) from Michoacán's four main indigenous groups: Purépecha, Nahua, Mazahua and Otomí. Built in the 1530s by Fray Juan de San Miguel, the Huatápera once housed the first hospital in the Americas. The decorations around the doors and windows were carved by Purépecha artisans in a Mudéjar style.

Cascada de Tzaráracua   WATERFALL

(📞452-106-04-41; www.tzararacua.com; adult/child M$15/5; ⊙8:30am-6pm) Some 12km south of central Uruapan, the wild Río Cupatitzio makes its last act count. It pumps hard over the vine-covered, 30m-high red-rock cliffs and crashes into a misty pool forming Tzaráracua waterfall. A meandering hike down the 557 slippery steps leads to the falls framed in foliage, or you can mount a horse (M$150 round-trip with a 30-minute wait at the falls).

There are a couple of zip-lines. One shoots you over the forest canopy, while a separate operator offers short 'flights' over the pool in front of the falls (M$50 to M$150). An arched stone bridge leads to the best viewing point, or ride in the little airborne cart (M$10) suspended about it.

Hourly buses to Tzaráracua (M$8) depart from in front of the Hotel Regis on the south side of Uruapan's main plaza. A round-trip with a taxi will cost from M$120 with a wait.

WORTH A TRIP

TINGAMBATO RUINS

Stroll through luscious avocado groves to the beautiful ruins of this ceremonial site called **Tinganio** (☎443-312-88-38; http://inah.gob.mx/es/zonas/177-zona-arqueologica-tingambato; M$50; ◷9am-6pm) in Purépecha, which predates the Tarascan empire and thrived from about AD 450 to 900. Rarely visited and beautifully atmospheric as a result, the site is located outside the town of Tingambato, 33km northeast of Uruapan on the old road to Pátzcuaro. The ruins, which include two plazas, three altars and a ball court, have a Teotihuacán influence.

There's also an 8m-high stepped pyramid to the east and an underground tomb where 15 skeletons and 32 scattered skulls were found – hinting at beheading or trophy-skull rituals. The wooded knoll behind the fence to the west of the ball court contains an unexcavated pyramid.

Buses to Morelia and Pátzcuaro leave from Uruapan's terminal every half-hour and stop in Tingambato (M$44, 30 minutes) on the way. The ruins are 1.5km downhill on Terán, the continuation of Juárez, the sixth street on the right as you enter Tingambato.

🎎 Festivals & Events

Semana Santa (Tianguis Artesanal de Uruapan)
FAIR

(◷Mar or Apr) Palm Sunday is marked by a procession through the city streets and the **Tianguis Artesanal de Uruapan**, which starts with a major crafts competition and for the next two weeks fills the main square with exhibitions and sales of Michoacán handicrafts.

Día de Muertos
CULTURAL

(◷Nov 1 & 2) Celebrated across Mexico but with extra enthusiasm here, the famous 'Day of the Dead' festival brings many visitors to Uruapan for the colorful local celebrations.

Feria del Aguacate
FOOD & DRINK

(◷Nov-Dec) The Avocado Fair erupts for 2½ weeks from late November into December and is celebrated with agricultural, industrial and handicraft exhibitions.

🛏 Sleeping

Uruapan offers a relatively wide range of accommodations, but reserve a room well in advance for the Día de Muertos (November 1 and 2) and Semana Santa (March/April) festivities.

Hotel Regis
HOTEL $

(☎452-523-58-44; www.hotelregis.com.mx; Portal Carrillo 12; s/d/tr M$500/600/700; ⓅⓈ) This is probably the best value among the budget plaza hotels. The public areas and central patio are charming in a borderline eccentric manner and, while the 43 rooms are small and have poky bathrooms, the hand-painted bedheads add a splash of exotic color. Some rooms (such as rooms 35 and 36) have little balconies overlooking the main square.

★Hotel Mi Solar Centro
BOUTIQUE HOTEL $$

(☎452-524-09-12; www.hotelmisolar.com; Delgado 10; r from M$1150; Ⓟ❄@Ⓢ) Uruapan's oldest hotel opened in the 1940s to accommodate tourists flooding in to see the newborn Volcán Paricutín. Today it's a wholly remodeled boutique place, with 17 spacious rooms on three floors surrounding an atrium bar. Rooms have luscious king beds, high ceilings and hand-carved wooden furniture.

Over the road is a newer annex with larger rooms that are very comfortable but lack the character of those in the main building. The rack rates shown here only apply in busy periods; count on discounts of up to 40% at other times.

★Casa Chikita Bed & Breakfast
B&B $$

(☎452-524-41-74; www.casachikita.com; Carranza 32; r incl breakfast M$850-1200; ⓅⓈ) This 19th-century house has four lovely rooms set around a garden decorated with local pottery. The rooms vary quite a bit, but the best are extremely comfortable and decorated with lovely touches, such as granite or wooden counters in the bathroom, tiled floors and local art on the walls.

Hotel Mansión del Cupatitzio
HOTEL $$$

(☎452-523-20-60; www.mansiondelcupatitzio.com; Calz Rodilla del Diablo 20; s/d standard from M$1620/1970, executive from M$2235/2735; Ⓟ@Ⓢ⅏) Enter this beautiful 57-room hacienda-style property and you come face to face with mounds of flower arrangements and over-the-top religious art. This is further enhanced by the carefully tended gardens and beautiful pool. The standard rooms, while perfectly pleasant and comfy, are a bit dowdy in comparison. Upgrading to an excutive room will make all the difference.

✕ Eating & Drinking

★ Cox-Hanal
MEXICAN $

(☑ 452-524-61-52; Carranza 31A; mains M$40-110; ☉ 4-11pm Tue-Fri, noon-11pm Sat & Sun) The chairs are plastic, there's not much to look at decor-wise and service can be a bit slow, but so what? This place is about mix-and-match *antojitos yucatecos* (small dishes from the Yucatán; M$12 to M$18) and they are well worth the wait. Try the hard *tacos de cochinita* (pulled pork) and the exquisite *sopa de lima* (lime soup with chicken).

Cocina Económica Mary
MEXICAN $

(☑ 452-519-48-69; Independencia 59; set menu M$60; ☉ 8:30am-5pm Mon-Sat) This busy family eatery always smells delicious. The cafeteria-style open kitchen serves filling meals with your choice of main – eg, chicken *mole*, pulled pork with squash or *chiles rellenos* (stuffed chilies with cheese or meat) – along with soup, rice, beans and freshly made tortillas. Breakfast costs M$30 to M$50.

La Lucha
CAFE $

(☑ 452-524-03-75; Ortiz 20; coffee M$30; ☉ 8am-9pm) The vaulted interior of this charming cafe makes for a very pleasant place for a coffee and a piece of cake. There are black-and-white photos on the wall and a great courtyard out the back. It does a brisk trade in selling its own beans. There's another smaller **branch** (☑ 452-523-32-69; Portal Matamoros 16A; coffee from M$30; ☉ 8am-9pm) with takeout in the main plaza.

Gratíssima
MEXICAN $$

(☑ 452-148-87-82; www.gratissima.mx; Calz Rodilla del Diablo 13A; mains M$70-135; ☉ 10:30am-6:30pm Thu-Tue) This delightful restaurant perched above the Río Cupatitzio near the northern entrance to the Parque Nacional Barranca del Cupatitzio has wonderful modern Mexican dishes, every one of which contains avocado in some form. The *enchiladas suizas de aguacate* are stuffed with chicken and avocado.

La Cantinita Cafe
BAR

(☑ 452-519-37-45; Ocampo; ☉ 3pm-midnight Tue-Sun) Going strong since 1907, this little cantina just up from the main square has turned its attention to cocktails, and the one made with mezcal and avocado is to die for. Perch on stools and high tables almost on the pavement below, or settle in to more comfortable seating on the loft-like 2nd floor.

Salt
COCKTAIL BAR

(☑ 452-116-68-30; Carranza 37; cocktails M$17; ☉ 3:30-11pm Sun-Thu, to 2am Fri & Sat) This trendy new place, all black and white at the front and green and intimate in the tiny back garden, serves food, especially seafood (mains from M$160) – note the fish-trap lamps – but we come here to sip one of their fabulous cocktails, like the unnamed concoction made with mezcal, strawberry juice, pepper and lime.

🛍 Shopping

Mercado de Antojitos
MARKET

(Quiroga; ☉ 8am-11pm) The Mercado de Antojitos, north of the main plaza, sells local snacks and small dishes and is the perfect place to try Michoacán specialties.

BUSES FROM URUAPAN

DESTINATION	FARE (M$)	DURATION (HR)	FREQUENCY (DAILY)
Angahuan	25	1	half-hourly
Colima	539	6	1
Guadalajara	425	4½	half-hourly
Mexico City (Terminal Norte)	626	6	hourly
Morelia	180	2	half-hourly
Paracho	52	1	every 15min
Pátzcuaro	74	1	every 15min
Tingambato	44	30min	half-hourly

Fábrica
San Pedro Shop   CLOTHING, HOMEWARES
(☑ 452-524-14-63; Treviño; ☺ 9am-6pm Mon-Sat)
This shop sells exquisite (mostly) hand-made textiles produced at the Fábrica San Pedro (p635).

❶ Information

Several banks with ATMs can be found on or near the central plaza.

Main Post Office (Jalisco 81; ☺ 8am-5pm Mon-Fri, 9am-noon Sat) East of the center.

❶ Getting There & Away

Uruapan's bus terminal is 2km northeast of central Uruapan on the highway to Pátzcuaro and Morelia. For Tingambato (M$44, 30 minutes) take the same bus as those heading for Pátzcuaro or Morelia.

Local buses marked 'Centro' run from just outside the bus terminal to the plaza (M$8). For taxis, prepay inside the bus terminal (M$30). For the return trip catch a 'Central Camionera' bus from the south side of the plaza.

Angahuan

📱 452 / POP 5775 / ELEV 2380M

Angahuan, 40km northwest of Uruapan and the nearest town to the incredible Volcán Paricutín, is a typical Purépecha town: there are wooden houses, dusty streets, as many horses as cars, women in ankle-length skirts and colorful shawls, and loudspeakers booming announcements in the Purépecha tongue. *Jaru je sesi* (Welcome)!

◉ Sights

★ **Volcán Paricutín**   VOLCANO
The upstart Volcán Paricutín (2800m) might be less than 80 years old, but clambering up the volcanic scree slopes to its summit and looking out across blackened, village-engulfing lava fields will be a highlight of your travels in this part of Mexico. You can trek to it on horseback or on foot, though the final ascent is always by foot. Whatever you choose, prepare for a long but rewarding day.

The story behind this volcano is as extraordinary as the views from its summit. On February 20, 1943, Dionisio Pulido, a Purépecha farmer, was ploughing his corn-field some 40km west of Uruapan when the ground began to quake and spurt steam, sparks and hot ash. The farmer struggled to cover the blast holes, but he quickly realized his futility and ran for safety. It was a good thing, because like some Hollywood B-grade movie, a growling volcano began to rise from the bowels of the earth. Within a year it had reached an elevation of 410m above the rolling farmland and its lava had flooded the Purépecha villages of San Salvador Paricutín and San Juan Parangaricutiro. Thankfully, the lava flowed slowly, giving the villagers plenty of time to escape.

The volcano continued to grow until 1952. Today its large black cone spits warm steam in a few places, but otherwise it appears dormant. Near the edge of the 20-sq-km lava field, the belfry of the swamped Templo de San Juan Parangaricutiro protrudes eerily from a sea of black lava; it and the altar awash in colorful offerings of candles and flowers are the only visible traces of the two buried villages. It's a one-hour (3km) walk to the church from Angahuan.

You should be striding out of Angahuan before 9am if you want to climb Volcán Paricutín comfortably. There's no shortage of guides with horses at the tourist center offering their services to the volcano and back via the ruined church, and they will meet you at the bus from Uruapan. Horses and a guide should cost around M$800 in total per person per day. There are two standard routes up the volcano: a 14km round-trip short route and a 24km round-trip long route. Horses always go via the long route as the short route crosses a lava field. If you're going by horse allow five to six hours (including at least four in an unforgiving, wooden saddle).

Whichever route you take, the final scramble up the volcano – a half-hour steep grunt through gravel and unstable rock – is on foot. Coming down is a different matter altogether; sliding down smooth black sand you'll be on terra firma in two minutes. The standard route visits the San Juan church on the way back. The altar is almost always blessed with colorful offerings of candles and flowers. Close to the church are a number of food stalls serving fabulously tasty blue-corn quesadillas cooked on old, wood-burning, oil-can skillets. Bring enough water and wear decent shoes.

If wooden saddles intimidate you and/or you have energy to burn, you can walk to the volcano, but you'll still need a guide (M$400) as the trail through the pine forest can be hard to follow. The long route follows a sandy track for around 12km through avocado groves, agave fields and wildflowers. The short route (7km one way) starts in pine forest but then switches to difficult rock-hopping across an expansive lava field. If you're fit and want variety, ask your guide to hike out on the short route and back on the longer trek.

Iglesia de Santiago Apóstol
CHURCH

This sensational 16th-century church on the main square has a beautifully carved portal at the entrance carved in the Moorish Mudéjar style by an Andalusian stonemason who accompanied the early Spanish missionaries here.

ℹ️ Information

Centro Turístico de Angahuan (☏ 452-443-03-85; www.staspe.org/centro-turistico-de-angahuan; M$10; ⏱24hr) This tourist center with a dusty little museum, accommodations and a restaurant is effectively the entrance to Volcán Paricutín. It's located around 2km southwest of the main square.

ℹ️ Getting There & Away

Angahuan is 40km northwest of Uruapan. Buses leave the Uruapan bus terminal for Angahuan every 30 minutes or so from 5am to 7pm (M$25, one hour).

Buses return to Uruapan every 30 minutes until about 8pm (double-check on arrival) and very few cabs are available in town, so make sure you don't miss that last bus.

Northern Central Highlands

Best Places to Eat

➡ Áperi (p673)

➡ El Jardín de los Milagros (p659)

➡ Las Mercedes (p659)

➡ Nomada (p673)

➡ La Parada (p672)

Best Places to Stay

➡ Mesón de Abundancia (p689)

➡ Rosewood San Miguel de Allende (p671)

➡ Hotel Museo Palacio de San Agustín (p685)

➡ Villa María Cristina (p657)

➡ La Casa del Atrio (p645)

Why Go?

From cobbled lanes and shaded plazas to vast deserts and cloud forest, Mexico's northern central highlands is a region as varied as its history, cuisine and cultures. It was here that enormous mineral wealth created rich colonial cities before revolutionary activity left ghost towns in its wake. Known as the Cuna de la Independencia (Cradle of Independence), the territory is renowned for its part in the country's fight for autonomy, spurred on by the famous *Grito de Dolores,* which called the Mexican people to arms against the Spanish.

Unmissable highlights of the region include arty and achingly gorgeous San Miguel de Allende, the waterfalls and the turquoise-colored water of the Huasteca Potosina and the grand colonial silver cities of Guanajuato and Zacatecas. Elsewhere you'll find pre-Hispanic sites, art museums, nightlife, crowded festivals and *artesanías* shopping to rival anywhere else in the country. Get ready to join the (exceptionally loud) party.

When to Go
Guanajuato

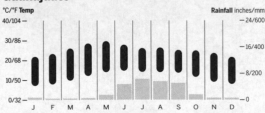

Jul & Aug Days are mild and wildflowers bloom; it's the perfect time for do-it-yourself explorations.

Oct–Apr It's dry season in the Huasteca Potosina; great for visiting waterfalls and turquoise rivers.

Late Mar or Apr Traditional religious festivities abound during Semana Santa (Holy Week).

Northern Central Highlands Highlights

❶ San Miguel de Allende (p664) Wandering with awe through this gorgeous colonial city, which specializes in art, food, hot springs and fiestas.

❷ Guanajuato (p650) Meandering through winding cobbled alleys and discovering marvelous museums.

❸ Huasteca Potosina (p690) Plunging into the remarkable turquoise rivers and surveying extraordinary waterfalls.

❹ Real de Catorce (p687) Sensing the glorious past in this very picturesque highland ghost town that is gradually coming back to life.

❺ Reserva de la Biosfera Sierra Gorda (p651) Marveling at the mission churches and visiting communities within this wilderness jewel.

❻ Zacatecas (p694) Discovering the fascinating museums that crowd this charming old silver city.

History

Until the Spanish conquest, the northern central highlands were inhabited by fierce seminomadic tribes known to the Aztecs as Chichimecs. They resisted Spanish expansion longer than other Mexican peoples, but were ultimately conquered in the late 16th century. The wealth subsequently amassed by the Spanish was at the cost of many Chichimecs, who were used as slave labor in the mines.

This historically volatile region sparked the criollo fight for independence from Spain, which was plotted in Querétaro and San Miguel de Allende and launched from

Dolores Hidalgo in 1810. A century later Francisco Madero released his revolutionary Plan de San Luis Potosí and the 1917 signing of Mexico's constitution in Querétaro cemented the region's leading role in Mexican political affairs.

In more recent times the region has flourished economically, due in part to the boom in the motor, aerospace, manufacturing and agricultural industries, particularly around Querétaro, while San Miguel attracts many weekenders from Mexico City and a constant stream of well-heeled creatives from the USA.

QUERÉTARO STATE

POP 1.9 MILLION

Querétaro state is full of surprises. Billed primarily as an agricultural and ranching region – with handsome and fast-developing Querétaro city as its capital – it is actually packed with diverse geography, quirky sights and historical gems. Natural phenomena, such as the world's third-largest monolith, La Peña de Bernal, pre-Hispanic ruins and the stunning Sierra Gorda Biosphere Reserve are located within its borders. The reserve protects several mission towns, from where local people run some excellent, community-owned tourism ventures – a must for the more intrepid traveler.

Querétaro

442 / POP 879,000 / ELEV 1800M

Wandering through the delightful colonial heart of Querétaro with its shady squares, grand fountains and historic mansions, you'd never guess that this is one of the fastest-growing cities in the northern hemisphere thanks to a booming aerospace and technologies industry. Except perhaps you can, as in order to reach the colonial heart of Querétaro, you'll have to first pass through some fairly striking examples of urban sprawl and contend with the powerhouse city's legendary bad traffic. However, it's well worth the effort to do that, as Querétaro's star is clearly in the ascendent, with an optimistic and mercantile population rising to the challenges of life in modern Mexico. The town's historic heart is characterized by charming *andadores* (pedestrian streets), gorgeous plazas and historic churches. The sophisticated restaurants serve up quality cuisine and the many museums reflect Querétaro's important role in Mexican history.

History

The Otomí founded a settlement here in the 15th century that was soon absorbed by the Aztecs, then by the Spaniards in 1531. Franciscan monks used it as a missionary base not only to Mexico but also to what is now southwestern USA. In the early 19th century, Querétaro became a center of intrigue among disaffected criollos plotting to free Mexico from Spanish rule. Conspirators, including Miguel Hidalgo, met secretly at the house of doña Josefa Ortiz (La Corregidora), who was the wife of Querétaro's former *corregidor* (district administrator). When the conspiracy was uncovered, the story goes, doña Josefa was locked in her house (now the Palacio de Gobierno), but managed to whisper through a keyhole to a coconspirator, Ignacio Pérez, that their colleagues were in jeopardy, leading to Padre Hidalgo's call to arms. This key event is still celebrated today as part of Mexico's independence celebrations every September.

In 1917 the Mexican constitution was drawn up by the Constitutionalist faction in Querétaro. The PNR (which later became the PRI, the Institutional Revolutionary Party) was organized in Querétaro in 1929, and dominated Mexican politics for the rest of the 20th century.

⊙ Sights

★ MUCAL   MUSEUM
(Museo del Calendario; www.mucal.mx; Madero 91; M$25; ⊙10am-6pm Tue-Sun) The first of its kind in the world, this extraordinary museum is the labor of love of its owner Señor Landin, whose family has been producing calendars in Mexico for decades. There are two parts to the museum: 19 exhibition rooms that house the original artworks (including reproductions) that featured in decades of Mexico's calendars, along with over 400 original retro-style calendars themselves. The second is the building itself, a stunningly renovated mansion, complete with beautiful gardens and courtyards.

The outdoor areas and the excellent cafe set on its lawns provide a perfect oasis from the heat, and a place to reflect on the sometimes amusing (and often titillating and politically incorrect) retro calendar depictions.

Mirador   VIEWPOINT

From this viewpoint there's a fine view of 'Los Arcos,' Querétaro's emblematic 1.28km-long aqueduct, with 74 towering sandstone arches built between 1726 and 1738. The aqueduct runs along the center of Avenida Zaragoza.

Templo y Convento
de la Santa Cruz   CHURCH

(Independencia 148 at Felipe Luna; M$10; ⊘9am-2pm & 4-6pm Tue-Sat, to 5:15pm Sun) One of the city's most interesting sights, this convent was built between 1654 and about 1815 on the site of a battle in which a miraculous appearance of Santiago (St James) apparently led to the Otomí surrender to the conquistadors and Christianity. Emperor Maximilian had his headquarters here while under siege in Querétaro from March to May 1867. After his surrender and subsequent death sentence, he was jailed here while awaiting the firing squad.

Today it's used as a religious school. You must visit with a guide – you wait at the entrance until a group has formed – although tours are in Spanish. The site's main legend is the growth of the Árbol de la Cruz, an ancient tree in the convent's garden, whose thorns are in the shape of crosses. This miracle was the result of a walking stick stuck in the earth by a pious friar in 1697.

Museo de Arte de Querétaro   MUSEUM

(www.museodeartequeretaro.com; Allende Sur 14; M$30, Tue free, photos M$15; ⊘10am-6pm Tue-Sun) Querétaro's art museum, adjacent to the Templo de San Agustín, occupies a splendid baroque monastery built between 1731 and 1748. It's worth visiting to see the building alone: angels, gargoyles, statues and other ornamental details abound, particularly around the stunning courtyard. The ground-floor display of 16th- and 17th-century European paintings traces influences from Flemish to Spanish to Mexican art. Here, too, you'll find 19th- and 20th-century Mexican paintings. The top floor has works from 16th-century Mannerism to 18th-century baroque.

Templo de Santa Rosa de Viterbo   CHURCH

(cnr Arteaga & Montes) FREE The 18th-century Templo de Santa Rosa de Viterbo is Querétaro's most splendid baroque church, with its pagoda-like bell tower, unusual exterior paintwork, curling buttresses and lavishly gilded and marbled interior. The church also boasts what some say is the earliest four-sided clock in the New World.

Templo de San Francisco   CHURCH

(cnr Av Corregidora & Andador 5 de Mayo; ⊘8am-9pm) This impressive church fronts Jardín Zenea. Pretty colored tiles on the dome were brought from Spain in 1540, around the time construction of the church began. Inside are some fine religious paintings from the 17th, 18th and 19th centuries.

Museo Regional de Querétaro   MUSEUM

(cnr Av Corregidora 3 & Jardín Zenea; M$55; ⊘9am-6pm Tue-Sun) The ground floor of this museum holds interesting exhibits on pre-Hispanic Mexico, archaeological sites, the Spanish occupation and the state's various indigenous groups. The upstairs exhibits reveal Querétaro's role in the independence movement and post-independence history. The table at which the Treaty of Guadalupe Hidalgo was signed in 1848, ending the Mexican-American War, is on display, as is the desk of the tribunal that sentenced Emperor Maximilian to death.

The museum is housed in part of what was once a huge monastery and seminary. Begun in 1540, the seminary became the seat of the Franciscan province of San Pedro y San Pablo de Michoacán by 1567. Building continued until at least 1727. Thanks to its high tower, in the 1860s the monastery was used as a fort both by forces supporting Maximilian and by those who defeated him in 1867.

Teatro de la República   THEATER

(⊘442-212-03-39; cnr Juárez & Peralta; ⊘10am-3pm & 5-8pm) FREE This lovely old functioning theater, complete with impressive chandeliers, was where a tribunal met in 1867 to decide the fate of Emperor Maximilian. Mexico's constitution was also signed here on January 31, 1917. The stage backdrop lists the names of its signatories and the states they represented. In 1929 politicians met in the theater to organize Mexico's political party, the PNR (now called PRI).

Casa de la Zacatecana   HOUSE

(⊘442-224-07-58; www.museolazacatecana.com; Independencia 59; M$45; ⊘10am-6pm) This is a finely restored 17th-century home with an impressive collection of 18th- and 19th-century furniture and decorations, which veer between the chintzy and the austere (check out the wall of gruesome crucifixes). It's a good place to get a sense of life in colonial-era Querétaro.

Querétaro

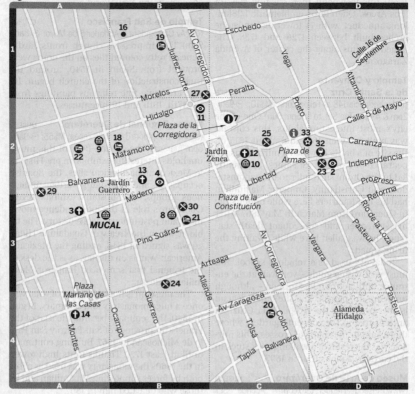

Monumento a la Corregidora
MONUMENT

(cnr Corregidora & Andador 16 de Sepiembre) FREE
Plaza de la Corregidora is dominated by the
Monumento a la Corregidora, a 1910 statue
of doña Josefa Ortiz bearing the flame of
freedom. It's a rather impressive and inspiring sight and there's a busy book market
that gathers here most days.

Cathedral
CATHEDRAL

(cnr Madero & Ocampo) FREE The 18th-century
cathedral features both baroque and neoclassical styles, with an emphasis on straight
lines and few curves; it's said that the first
Mass in the cathedral (then known as San
Felipe Neri) was led by Padre Hidalgo, of Independence fame.

Templo de Santa Clara
CHURCH

(cnr Madero & Allende) The 17th-century Templo de Santa Clara has an extraordinarily
ornate baroque interior. Masses are held

frequently so you'll have to inquire as to the
best time to enter.

Mausoleo de la Corregidora
MAUSOLEUM

(Ejército Republicano s/n; ⏰9am-6pm) The
Mausoleo de la Corregidora, opposite the
mirador (p643), is the final resting place of
local independence heroes doña Josefa Ortiz and her husband, Miguel Domínguez de
Alemán.

Museo de la Ciudad
MUSEUM

(www.museodelaciudadqro.org; Guerrero Norte 27;
M$5; ⏰11am-7pm Tue-Sun) Inside the ex-con-
vent and old prison that held the deposed
Emperor Maximilian, the 11-room Museo de
la Ciudad has some good alternating contemporary art exhibits.

Fuente de Neptuno
FOUNTAIN

(Neptune's Fountain; cnr Madero & Allende) A
block west of Jardín Zenea is the Fuente
de Neptuno, designed by noted Mexican

neoclassical architect Eduardo Tresguerras in 1797.

🎓 Courses

Olé Spanish Language School
LANGUAGE

(📞 442-214-40-23; www.ole.edu.mx; Escobedo 32) Offers a range of courses with homestay options and extracurricular programs. Week-long courses range from moderate group classes (15 hours; US$185) to 35-hour intensive courses (US$470).

🛏️ Sleeping

Santa Lucha Hostel
HOSTEL **$**

(📞 442-214-36-45; www.santalucha.com; Hidalgo 47; dm/d from M$285/850; 🛜) This brightly painted Mexican wrestling-themed hostel has an enviable old-town location and is housed in a pleasantly converted building. All dorms and rooms – save one private – share bathrooms, but there are plenty of

them and they're clean. There's a big kitchen and common area perfect for hanging out.

El Petate Hostel
HOSTEL **$**

(📞 442-212-79-87; www.elpetatehostel.com; Matamoros 20; dm/d from M$200/500; 🛜📶) This hostel in a gorgeous little side street has been very attractively designed with clean and bright dorms and rooms, some of which have their own bathroom.

Blue Bicycle House
HOSTEL **$**

(📞 442-455-48-13; www.bluebicyclehouse. com; Ejercito Republicano 15; dm M$230-250, d M$590-750; 🛜) Located just on the edge of the center, with a view of the aqueduct, the Blue Bicycle House (look for the bicycle hanging outside) is a highlight of Querétaro's budget sleeping scene. It's small and simple and offers dorms, including one for women only. Beds are long by Mexican standards and one-hour bike use is included in the price.

Hotel Quinta Lucca
HOTEL **$$**

(📞 442-340-44-44; www.hotelquintalucca.com; Juárez Norte 119A; r M$990-1100, ste M$1200-1400; 🅿️🛜) The spacious and good-value rooms here have Mexican-modern interiors and are sparkling clean. Those in the rear are more pleasant, and surround a luscious green courtyard, where a continental breakfast is served.

⭐ La Casa del Atrio
B&B **$$$**

(📞 442-212-63-14; www.lacasadelatrio.com; Allende Sur 15; r M$1850-2750; 🛜📶) This gorgeous spot has morphed from its original three-rooms-in-an-antique-store to a stunning boutique hotel, with 12 rooms, several glorious courtyard spaces and an on-site spa. The bilingual host, Antonio, will go out of his way to run a professional ship and ensure everything – from each artistic, art-filled room to the delicious breakfasts – are to your liking.

Rooms and bathrooms are spacious, though if you insist on open windows at night (all rooms feature massive doors, but not windows, that open on to courtyards), then communicate this on reservation. Otherwise it's a win-win choice.

La Casa de los Dos Leones
BOUTIQUE HOTEL **$$$**

(📞 442-212-45-85; www.lacasadelosdosleones. com; Colón 4; r incl breakfast from M$2690; ❄️🛜📶) If you want a very comfortable experience with spacious modern rooms and

Querétaro

superfriendly staff, this place may be for you. While it's a block outside the old town, it's an easy wander away, and its location means that there's far more space to be had. There's a gym and rooftop pool.

✖ Eating

★ Breton
FRENCH $

(Andador Libertad 82B; mains M$115-190; ⊙8am-5pm Tue-Sat; 🛜🌱) A delightful French bakery that has a lovely semi-open-air upstairs terrace. As well as doing excellent coffee and pastries to go, it serves up delicious breakfasts and lunches, including dishes such as beef bourguignon, steak frites and mussel marinara. Vegetarians and vegans are also lovingly catered for.

★ La Mariposa
CAFE $

(Peralta 7; snacks M$25-120; ⊙8am-9:30pm) Unchanged since 1940, as the photos and coffee machine testify, this Querétaro institution is more about the quaint atmosphere than the food. Don't leave without trying the mouthwatering *volteado de piña* (a version of a pineapple cake) or the *mantecado* (egg-based ice cream).

La Vieja Varsovia
BAKERY $

(www.laviejavarsovia.com.mx; Plaza de los Fundadores; snacks M$50-150; ⊙10am-11pm Tue-

Sun) This sweet cafe and bakery has tables scattered over the Plaza de los Fundadores and is a great place for breakfast before a day exploring the old city. Later on you can sample the scrumptious wood-fired pizzas with gourmet toppings.

La Biznarga Arte-Cafe
CAFE $

(Gutiérrez Najera 17; mains M$38-62; ⊙9am-2pm & 6-11pm Mon-Sat) Their friends liked their cooking so much the owners of Biznarga opened their kitchen to the public. It's a rather chaotic and dark place, but it's also hugely popular and a fun experience, complete with graffiti, artworks and other paraphernalia on the walls. Salads, homemade pizzas, juices and more are all on the menu.

La Antojería
MEXICAN $

(Calle 5 de Mayo; mains M$60-110; ⊙10am-11pm; 🛗) This family-friendly, fun Mexican-themed place serves up every style of *antojito* (typical Mexican snacks) known in Mexico.

Restaurante Las Monjas
MEXICAN $$

(Ezequiel Montes 22; mains M$170-285; ⊙7:30am-11pm Mon-Sat, to 6pm Sun) You can almost feel the history in this deeply traditional Querétaro establishment, where charming and smartly dressed waiters attend the tables with relish and great expertise, which you'll see on display when they prepare your salad right in front of you. The menu contains lots of local dishes, including a wonderful *cazuela de quesillo fundido* (melted-cheese stew with chorizo).

Tikua
MEXICAN $$

(📞442-455-33-33; www.tikua.mx; Allende Sur 13; mains M$110-230; ⊙9am-midnight Mon-Sat, to 9pm Sun; 🐱) This gorgeously set restaurant specializes in Southeastern Mexican cuisine and the dishes – from the *xi'i*, a mushroom salad, to the Oaxacan chorizo recipes – are true to their roots. The rice with *chapulines* (grasshoppers), *tasajo* (salted beef) and chocolate *mole* (a traditional sauce) are especially good. Serves up a mezcal menu and cocktails too.

Brewer Gastro Pub
INTERNATIONAL $$

(www.erlum.com.mx; Arteaga 55; mains M$130-235; ⊙1pm-1am Wed-Sat, to 8pm Sun; 🐱) 🥢 This is what happens when a local artisanal brewer joins forces with a good eatery: a casual drinking spot that serves up fabulous brews, from honey IPAs *(miel de abeja)* to a mezcal beer mix (Agave Ale), to excellent dishes. The chef uses all local products of which the provenance is known. Excellent charcuterie, pizzas and salads.

🍷 Drinking & Nightlife

There's a thriving bar scene in Querétaro. Bars and clubs pack the historic center and beyond. Calle 5 de Mayo is the fashionable drinking strip in the center; barflies hit these places after 10pm.

★ El Faro
BAR

(Calle 16 de Sepiembre 128) A shining light on the local drinking scene, the Lighthouse exudes elements of old with a recent polish (it originally opened in 1927 and is believed to be the city's oldest bar). The current owners took over in early 2015 so the interior is a little hipper for it. But the swinging cantina doors and friendly vibe are standing legacies. Guests are addressed by their first names, free bar snacks keep you standing and happy hour runs all afternoon.

Gracias a Dios
BAR

(Calle 5 de Mayo; snacks M$60-120; ⊙2pm-1:30am Tue-Sat) One of the many bars near Calle 5 de Mayo, this place revives traditions of old: a *cantina-botanero* (bar with snacks) complete with barrels and stools and just a touch of grimy-bar-syndrome. However, it also has a touch of feminine funk and attracts a young crowd out for whiskey, tequila and brandy-fueled fun.

☆ Entertainment

Querétaro is action-packed with cultural activities. For the latest on what's happening around town, look out for posters on bulletin boards, or pick up a copy of freebie listing mag *Asomarte* from the tourist office. On Sunday, free concerts usually take place in Plaza de Armas at 1pm and in the evenings in Jardín Zenea.

Teatro de la República
THEATER

(cnr Juárez & Peralta; tickets M$80-200) Has regular symphony concerts most Fridays.

Casa de la Cultura
CONCERT VENUE

(📞442-212-56-14; Calle 5 de Mayo 40; ⊙9am-2pm & 4-8pm Mon-Fri) Sponsors concerts, dance, theater and art events; stop by to view the bulletin board.

ⓘ Information

H+ Querétaro (📞442-477-22-22; www. hmasqueretaro.mx; Zaragoza 16B) This private hospital comes recommended by expats.

Hospital Angeles (📞442-192-30-00; www. hospitalangelesqueretaro.com; Bernardo Del Razo 21, El Ensueño) Southwest of Querétaro's city center, this hospital has English-speaking doctors.

Tourist Office (📞800-715-17-42, 442-238-50-67; www.queretaro.travel; Pasteur Norte 4; ⊙9am-7pm) This helpful office has English-speaking staff and gives out free city maps and brochures, plus a useful publication *Asomarte* with listings of what's on.

ⓘ Getting There & Away

AIR

The **Aeropuerto Intercontinental de Querétaro** (📞442-192-55-00; www.aiq.com. mx), 8km northeast of the downtown area, is around a M$300 taxi ride from the center. Primera Plus also runs from the bus terminal to Mexico City airport (M$365, three hours). As well as flights to Mexico City, there are direct services to various US cities from Querétaro.

BUS

Querétaro is a hub for buses in all directions; the modern **Central Camionera** (Parque del Cimatario) is 5km southeast of the center. There's one building for deluxe and 1st class (labeled A), one for 2nd class (B) and another for local buses (C). Facilities include luggage storage.

BUSES FROM QUERÉTARO

DESTINATION	FARE (M$)	DURATION (HR)	FREQUENCY (DAILY)
Ciudad Valles	735	7½	3
Guadalajara	410-620	4½-5½	frequent
Guanajuato	239	2½-3	7
Mexico City (Terminal Norte)	280-395	3-4½	every 20min 4am-11:30pm
Mexico City Airport	393	3½	every 30min
Morelia	219-305	3-4	frequent
San Luis Potosí	228-280	2½-2¾	frequent
San Miguel de Allende	74-130	1-1½	every 40min 6am-11pm
Tequisquiapan	50	1	every 30min 6:30am-9pm
Xilitla	355-400	5-8	4

❶ Getting Around

Once you have reached downtown, you can easily visit most sights on foot. City buses (M$9) run from 6am until 9pm or 10pm. They gather in an area at the end of the bus terminal; turn right from the 2nd-class terminal, or left from the 1st-class side. Several routes go to the center (the numbers change, so check.) For a taxi, get a ticket first from the bus station booth (M$50 for up to four people.)

To get to the bus station from the center, take city bus marked 'Central' (ie Central Camionera) from Calle Zaragoza, or any bus labeled 'TAQ' (ie Terminal de Autobuses de Querétaro) or 'Central' heading south on the east side of the Alameda Hidalgo.

Tequisquiapan

📞 414 / POP 30,000 / ELEV 1870M

This small town (teh-kees-kee-ap-an), 70km southeast of Querétaro, is a quaint weekend retreat from Mexico City or Querétaro. Once known for its thermal springs – Mexican presidents came here to ease their aches and stresses – the town's natural pools may have long since dried up, but its pretty, bougainvillea-lined streets, colorful colonial buildings and excellent markets make for an enjoyable browse and the town comes alive on the weekend with couples and families wandering the streets and browsing the many artesanías stalls.

◉ Sights

Plaza Miguel Hidalgo   PLAZA
The wide and attractive Plaza Miguel Hidalgo is surrounded by portales (arcades) filled with bustling cafes and handicrafts stores, and overlooked by the 19th-century neoclassical **La Parroquia de Santa María de la Asunción** (🕐7:30am-8:30pm) with its pink facade and decorated tower.

Quinta Fernando Schmoll   GARDENS
(📞441-276-10-71; Pilancon 1, Cadereyta de Montes; M$25; 🕐9am-5pm Tue-Sun) If you have your own wheels, this impressive botanical garden, with over 4400 varieties of cactus, is on the east edge of the village of Cadereyta de Montes. It's 38km from Tequisquiapan.

🏃 Activities

Horseback Riding   HORSEBACK RIDING
(Fray Junípero; rides per hour M$80-100; 🕐10am-6pm Sat & Sun) Guided trail rides around the surrounding countryside are offered at weekends. Guides and their hacks congregate on Fray Junípero, just north of Parque La Pila.

🎊 Festivals & Events

Feria Nacional del Queso y del Vino   FOOD & DRINK
(www.feriadelquesoyvino.com.mx; Parque La Pila; 🕐mid-May–early Jun) The National Wine & Cheese Fair, run by Tequisquiapan's tourist office, has been running for over four decades and includes tastings, dinners and concerts over two weeks. Most events are ticketed; buy tickets on the website.

🛏 Sleeping & Eating

The best budget accommodations are the posadas along Moctezuma. Demand is low Monday to Thursday, when you may be able to negotiate a discount.

Posada Tequisquiapan
GUESTHOUSE $

(☑414-273-00-10; Moctezuma 6; s/d M$350/500; ℗) With simple but spacious rooms set around a leafy courtyard complete with its own well, this is a great-value option. Breakfast is not included and you'll need to find it elsewhere in town, as there's no restaurant here.

La Granja
BOUTIQUE HOTEL $$$

(☑414-273-20-04; www.hotelboutiquelagranja.com; Morelos 12; r from M$1925; ℗✳🛜❄) Located in a pretty part of town, this colonial building has been renovated into an impressive hotel, though the rooms don't quite live up to the promise of the very attractive public areas. There's a large back garden with a pool and a big on-site restaurant, though breakfast is not included.

Madre Selva
PIZZA $$

(Niños Heroes 54; pizza M$110-170; ☉2-10pm Wed-Sun) This rather charming pizzeria has a wood-fired oven and a big list of toppings to choose from to create your ideal pizza.

🛍 Shopping

Mercado de Artesanías
MARKET

(Carrizal; ☉8am-7pm) This crafts market can be found a block north of Tequisquiapan's main plaza.

ℹ Information

Tourist office (☑414-273-08-41; Plaza Miguel Hidalgo; ☉9am-7pm) Has town maps and information on Querétaro state.

ℹ Getting There & Away

Tequisquiapan's **Terminal de Autobuses** (Carretera San Juan del Río-Tequisquiapan 546) is around 2km north of the center in the new part of town. Local buses (M$8) from outside the bus station run to the markets on Carrizal, one block northeast of the Plaza Principal.

Flecha Azul runs half-hourly to/from Querétaro between 6:30am and 8pm (M$50, one hour). Buses also run regularly throughout the day to Ezequiel Montes (change here for Bernal; M$14, 20 minutes), and there's also a direct bus to Bernal (M$35, one hour) at 5:40pm daily. ETN has deluxe buses to/from Mexico City's Terminal Norte (M$280, three hours, eight daily). Coordinados (Flecha Amarilla) and Flecha Roja has 2nd-class services to the same destination (M$205, 3½ hours, regular departures). There are also three buses a day to Xilitla (M$322, five hours).

Jalpan
☑441 / POP 11,000 / ELEV 760M

The attractive town of Jalpan centers on its famous mission church; the town is the gateway to the other four famous mission churches sprinkled liberally around the region. Jalpan itself is quite a charmer, with a lovely central square and an attractive hillside location. Not surprisingly, given its tropical climate, Jalpan specializes in artisanal – and very delicious – ice creams served in the many *heladerías* (ice-cream shops) around town.

◉ Sights

Mission Church
CHURCH

Constructed by Franciscan monks and their indigenous converts in the 1750s, the original of the five missions in the Sierra Gorda is in the middle of the town of Jalpan. It has an elaborate exterior and is devoted to the first evangelist, James the Greater.

🛏 Sleeping & Eating

Cabañas Centro Tierra
BUNGALOW $

(☑441-296-07-00; www.sierragordaecotours.com; Centro Tierra Sierra Gorda, Av La Presa s/n, Barrio El Panteon; d M$600-750; 🛜) 🅿 The best budget choice in Jalpan, these simple but charming and comfortable rooms can be found in a pleasant garden site a 15-minute walk from the center of Jalpan, near the *presa* (reservoir). Ecologically sound construction has been carried out, all rooms have fans, and the bigger ones even have mezzanines and sleep up to five people in them.

★Hotel Misión Jalpan
HOTEL $$

(☑441-296-02-55; www.hotelesmision.com.mx; Fray Junípero Serra s/n; r from M$870; ✳🛜❄) On the west side of the Jardín Principal and right in the heart of the town, Hotel Misión Jalpan has attractive gardens and a good restaurant, plus well-cared for rooms that enjoy comfy mattresses and high-pressure showers. Prices are high on the weekend, but during the week it's a great deal.

El Aguaje del Moro
MEXICAN $$

(Vicente Guerrero 8; mains M$100-200; ☉7am-10:30pm Mon-Sat) Famous for its exceptionally spicy enchiladas (though you'll have to request spice – gringos automatically seem to get a fairly tame order unless they insist), this pleasant place has a breezy balcony with views toward the mountains, as well as over the main road. It's a good-value and cozy place for a meal.

ℹ️ Getting There & Away

Jalpan's **Terminal de Autobuses** (Heroico Colegio Militar) has hourly services to Ciudad Valles (M$246, three hours) and Xilitla (M$92, 1¾ hours), as well as four services a day to San Luis Potosí (M$342, four hours).

There are also services to Mexico City's Terminal Norte (M$415 to M$509, five hours, five daily), to Querétaro (M$343, 3½ hours, three daily) and to Tequisquiapan (M$235, 3¼ hours, four daily).

Bernal

📍 441 / POP 4000

Dominated by the impressive Peña de Bernal, a giant rock that is the third-largest monolith in the world, pretty and quaint Bernal is a likable but otherwise fairly unremarkable town known locally for its cheese, candies and street food. The town comes to life during the weekends when it's bursting with Mexican visitors; however, if you come during the week you'll avoid the crowds and find a provincial town quietly going about its business.

Bernal has several lovely churches scattered around its old town and El Castillo, a 16th-century viceregal building. For a more in-depth explanation of the area, friendly La Peña Tours offers an array of tours (M$150 to M$700) plus climbing sessions on the Peña.

◉ Sights

Peña de Bernal MOUNTAIN
This 350m-high rock spire is the third-largest monolith in the world and is considered mystical by many Mexicans. During the vernal equinox thousands of pilgrims converge on the rock to take in its positive energy. Visitors can climb to the rock's halfway point (allow one hour both ways); only professional rock climbers can climb to its peak.

☞ Tours

La Peña Tours TOURS
(📞 441-296-73-98, 441-101-48-21; www.lapenia tours.com; cnr Independencia & Colon) The friendly Peña Tours offers an array of tours (M$170 to M$900), including a wine and

cheese tour. They also offer climbing sessions on the Peña (half-day M$1500).

🛍️ Shopping

La Aurora ARTS & CRAFTS
(Jardín Principal 1; ⊙ 10am-8pm) This interesting *artesanías* shop sells an array of rugs made on the premises; request permission to see the weavers at work at their looms in the workshop behind the shop.

ℹ️ Getting There & Away

There are regular buses to/from Querétaro (around M$70, 45 minutes). The last return bus to Querétaro departs from the main road around 5:30pm. For connections to/from Tequisquiapan, change buses at Ezequiel Montes (M$15, 30 minutes).

GUANAJUATO STATE

POP 5.5 MILLION

The rocky highland state of Guanajuato is full of riches of every kind. In colonial times, mineral resources attracted Spanish prospectors to mine for silver, gold, iron, lead, zinc and tin. For two centuries the state produced enormous wealth, extracting up to 40% of the world's silver. Silver barons in Guanajuato city enjoyed opulent lives at the expense of indigenous people who worked the mines, first as slaves and then later as wage slaves. Eventually, resenting the dominance of Spanish-born colonists, the well-heeled criollo class of Guanajuato and Querétaro states contributed to plans for rebellion.

These days, the state's treasures are the quaint colonial towns of Guanajuato and San Miguel de Allende. Visitors to this region can enjoy its precious legacies: stunning colonial architecture, established cultural scenes and a stream of never-ending festivals...not to mention friendly, proud locals and a lively university atmosphere.

Guanajuato

📍 473 / POP 155,000 / ELEV 2045M

The extraordinary Unesco World Heritage city of Guanajuato was founded in 1559 due to the region's rich silver and gold deposits. Opulent colonial buildings, stunning tree-filled plazas and brightly colored houses are crammed together on to the steep slopes of a narrow ravine where excellent museums,

RESERVA DE LA BIOSFERA SIERRA GORDA

The Reserva de la Biosfera Sierra Gorda, in the rugged Sierra Madre Oriental mountain range, covers a huge swath of the northeastern third of Querétaro state. Known as the 'green jewel' of central Mexico, the reserve boasts 15 vegetation types, making it the most ecosystem-diverse protected area in the country. Its stunning wilderness areas encompass old-growth cloud forests, semideserts and tropical forests; jaguars, rare orchids and endemic cacti are just some of the fauna and flora on offer here.

Over the past few years, sustainable ecotourism projects have been established, with varying success. Travelers can head into villages with local guides, stay in basic cabins and camping areas, and partake in a range of activities. These include hikes to waterfalls, rafting, rappeling and kayaking. Many communities here have functioning workshops that produce pottery, natural remedies, dried foodstuffs, honey products and embroidery.

Several companies offer trips in the reserve:

Aventúrate (441-296-07-14, cell 441-1033129; www.aventurate.mx; Benito Juárez 29) This professional outfit has young, enthusiastic and experienced guides who will take you to any number of local sights: the missions (M$1800 for two people including transportation and guide), Río Escanela (to Puente de Dios), El Chuveje waterfall, Sotano de Barro, Las Pozas and more. It is also the only operator that takes trips to Gruta Jalpan, the local cave.

Sierra Gorda Eco Tours (441-296-02-42, 441-296-07-00; www.sierragordaecotours.com; Av La Presa s/n, Barrio El Panteón) Promotes programs within local communities. Prices start at M$1700 per person (based on two people) including transportation, accommodations, meals and activities, entrance fee, plus community guide (where necessary). At least a day's notice is required, a week in high season. Guides speak English.

Arnoldo Montes Rodríguez (441-108-88-24, 441-101-81-31; www.sierragordaguides. com) One of Jalpan's original independent guides who can show you the missions. Located in what's billed as a tourist office inside the Hotel Misión Jalpan (p649), it's actually a shop from where excursions are sold.

handsome theaters and a fine marketplace punctuate cobblestone streets. The city's main roads twist around the hillsides and plunge into long dank subterranean tunnels, formerly rivers.

The city is best known internationally for its acclaimed annual arts event, the Festival Cervantino. Yet this colorful and lively place holds center stage all year; much of the youthful vibrancy and prolific cultural activities – *callejoneadas,* films, theater and orchestras – can be attributed to the 20,000 students of the city's own University of Guanajuato. In short, Guanajuato is the state's slightly gritty but fascinating capital city and should not be missed by anyone traveling in the region.

History

One of the hemisphere's richest silver veins was uncovered in 1558 at La Valenciana mine; for 250 years the mine produced 20% of the world's silver. Colonial barons benefiting from this mineral treasure were infuriated when King Carlos III of Spain slashed their share of the wealth in 1765. The King's 1767 decree banishing the Jesuits from Spanish dominions further alienated both the wealthy barons and the poor miners, who held allegiance to the Jesuits.

This anger was focused in the War of Independence. In 1810 rebel leader Miguel Hidalgo set off the independence movement with his Grito de Independencia (Cry for Independence) in nearby Dolores. Guanajuato citizens joined the independence fighters and defeated the Spanish and loyalists, seizing the city in the rebellion's first military victory. When the Spaniards eventually retook the city they retaliated by conducting the infamous 'lottery of death,' in which names of Guanajuato citizens were drawn at random and the 'winners' were tortured and hanged. Independence was eventually won, freeing the silver barons to amass further wealth. From this wealth arose many of the mansions, churches and theaters.

Guanajuato

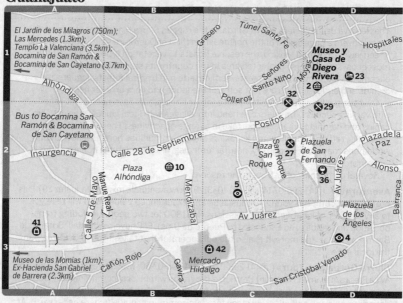

Guanajuato

◎ Top Sights

◎ Sights

◎ Activities, Courses & Tours

◎ Sleeping

◎ Eating

◎ Drinking & Nightlife

◎ Entertainment

◎ Shopping

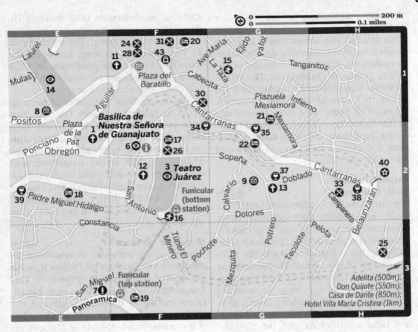

◉ Sights

★ Museo y Casa de Diego Rivera
MUSEUM

(Positos 47; M$20; ⊙10am-6:30pm Tue-Sat, to 2:30pm Sun) Diego Rivera's birthplace is now an excellent museum honoring the famous artist, who was *persona non grata* here for years. It's worth spending an hour here – longer if you're a Rivera fan. Rivera and his twin brother were born in the house in 1886 (Carlos died at the age of two) and lived here until the family moved to Mexico City six years later. The museum's ground floor is a recreation of the Rivera family home, furnished with 19th-century antiques.

The labyrinth of upper floors exhibit a permanent collection of his original works and preliminary sketches (completed for some of his famous murals in Mexico City), plus there's a nude of Frida Kahlo. Several *salas* also host temporary exhibitions of work by Mexican and international artists. An intimate theater upstairs features black-and-white photographs of Kahlo and Rivera.

★ Templo La Valenciana
CHURCH

(Iglesia de San Cayetano) On a hill overlooking Guanajuato, 5km north of the center, is the magnificent Templo La Valenciana. Its facade is spectacular and its interior dazzles with ornate golden altars, filigree carvings and giant paintings. Ground was broken here in 1765 and the church was completed in 1788.

One legend says that the Spaniard who started the nearby San Ramón mine promised San Cayetano that if it made him rich, he would build a church to honor the saint. Another says that the silver baron of La Valenciana, Conde de Rul, tried to atone for exploiting the miners by building the ultimate in Churrigueresque churches.

★ Teatro Juárez
THEATER

(Sopeña s/n; M$35; ⊙9am-1pm & 4-6pm Tue-Sun) Don't leave Guanajuato without visiting the magnificent Teatro Juárez. It was built between 1873 and 1903 and inaugurated by the dictator Porfirio Díaz, whose lavish tastes are reflected in the plush red-and-gold interior. The outside features 12 columns with brass capitals, lamp posts and eight of the nine muses; inside the impression is Moorish, with the bar and lobby gleaming with carved wood, stained glass and precious metals. It's only open when no performances are scheduled.

★ **Basílica de Nuestra Señora de Guanajuato**   CHURCH

(Plaza de la Paz) The attractive and arresting Basílica de Nuestra Señora de Guanajuato contains a jewel-covered image of the Virgin, patron of Guanajuato. The wooden statue was supposedly hidden from the Moors in a cave in Spain for 800 years. Felipe II of Spain gave it to Guanajuato in thanks for the wealth it provided to the crown. Next door, the small **Galería Mariana** is dedicated to images of Mary and other Catholic relics.

Parador Turístico Sangre de Cristo   MUSEUM

(Carretera Silao Km 8; adult/student M$50/30; ☺11am-6pm Wed-Sat, 10am-6pm Sun) Three museums are sited in one impressively designed complex in the hills above Guanajuato. One collection explores the mining history of the region. The second has 36 mummies discovered in local churches (they look pretty gruesome so consider missing this one if you have young children with you). The last looks at Day of the Dead celebrations and the *Catrina* dolls (an image/figurine of a skeleton in female clothing) that are a key part of the tradition. Shops and a cafe are on site. To get here, take a 'Cristo Rey' bus, which depart every hour or so from near Alhóndiga (M$40 return).

Casa de Arte Olga Costa & José Chávez Morado   MUSEUM

(Pastita 158, Torre del Arco; adult/student M$20/5; ☺10am-4pm Tue-Sat, to 3pm Sun) In 1966 artists José Chávez Morado and Olga Costa converted a massive old well into their home and studio; before their deaths, they donated their home and its contents for public use. On display is a small, but fascinating, collection of items from the 16th to 18th centuries, including pre-Hispanic and modern ceramics, embroidery, furniture, masks and their own artworks. It's worth heading to the 'suburb' of Pastita to experience a side of Guanajuato you might otherwise miss.

The pretty approach follows the former aqueduct that ends at their house. Take any bus marked 'Pastita' from the eastern end of town.

Monumento a El Pípila   MONUMENT

(Panoramica) The monument to El Pípila honors the hero who torched the Alhóndiga gates on September 28, 1810, enabling Hidalgo's forces to win the first victory of the independence movement. The statue shows El Pípila holding his torch high over the city. On the base is the inscription *Aún hay otras Alhóndigas por incendiar* (There are still other Alhóndigas to burn).

Two routes from the center of town go up steep, picturesque lanes. One goes east on Sopeña from Jardín de la Unión, then turns right on Callejón del Calvario (this becomes Pochote; turn right at Subida San Miguel). Another ascent, unmarked, goes uphill from the small plaza on Alonso. Alternatively, the 'Pípila-ISSSTE' bus heading west on Avenida Juárez will let you off right by the statue, or you can ride up in the funicular.

Museo de las Momias   MUSEUM

(Museum of the Mummies; www.momiasdeguanajuato.gob.mx; Explanada del Panteón Municipal s/n; adult/student M$55/36; ☺9am-6pm) This famous museum is one of the most bizarre (some might say distasteful) sights at the *panteón* (cemetery). The popular attraction is a quintessential example of Mexico's acceptance of, celebration of and obsession with death; visitors come from all over to see more than 100 disinterred corpses.

While technically these are mummified remains – due to the dry atmosphere in their former crypts – the bodies are not thousands of years old. The first remains were unearthed in 1865 to make room for more bodies in the cemeteries. What the authorities uncovered were not skeletons but mummified flesh (many feature grotesque forms and facial expressions).

The complex is on the western edge of town, a 10-minute ride from Avenida Juárez on any 'Momias' bus (M$6).

Bocamina de San Ramón & Bocamina de San Cayetano   MINE

(www.bocaminasanramon.com; M$35; ☺10am-6pm) These neighboring mines are part of the famous Valenciana mining district. Silver was discovered here in 1548. At **San Ramón** you can descend via steps into a mine shaft to a depth of 60m (note: not for claustrophobes). **San Cayetano** has an interesting museum and former miners take you on a brief tour – including a shaft visit.

To reach the mines, take a 'Cristo Rey' or 'Valenciana' bus from the bus stop on the corner of Alhóndiga and Calle 28 de

Septiembre. Get off at Templo La Valenciana and follow the signs behind the church.

Cristo Rey
MONUMENT

Cristo Rey (Christ the King) is a 20m bronze statue of Jesus erected in 1950 on the summit of the Cerro de Cubilete, 15km west of Guanajuato. The location of the statue at the supposed geographical center of the country holds particular significance for Mexican tourists, with impressive views an added draw. Tour agencies offer trips here, but you can also simply take a bus marked 'Cubilete' or 'Cristo Rey,' departing every hour or so from near Alhóndiga (M$40 return).

Museo del Pueblo de Guanajuato
MUSEUM

(Positos 7; adult M$20; ⊙10am-6:30pm Tue-Sat, to 2:30pm Sun) Located beside the university, this fascinating art museum displays an exquisite collection of Mexican miniatures, and 18th- and 19th-century artworks by Guanajuatan painters Hermenegildo Bustos and José Chávez Morado, plus temporary exhibitions. It occupies the former mansion of the Marqueses de San Juan de Rayas, who owned the San Juan de Rayas mine. The private baroque chapel (built 1696) upstairs in the courtyard contains an interesting three-paneled mural by José Chávez Morado depicting the Spanish colonization.

Jardín de la Reforma
SQUARE

This attractive cafe-lined and shady square is Guanajuato's social hub and is packed full of locals, mariachis and tourists throughout the day.

Jardín de la Unión
PLAZA

This triangular plaza is lined by cafes, bars and restaurants and full of shade-giving trees in a neatly maintained garden.

Museo Regional de Guanajuato Alhóndiga de Granaditas
MUSEUM

(☑473-732-11-12; Calle 28 de Sepiembre; M$52, camera/video M$30/60; ⊙10am-5:30pm Tue-Sat, to 2:30pm Sun) Built between 1798 and 1808 as a grain storehouse, the Alhóndiga became a fortress in 1810 when 300 Spanish troops and loyalist leaders barricaded themselves inside after 20,000 rebels led by Miguel Hidalgo attempted to take Guanajuato. On September 28, 1810, a young miner nicknamed El Pípila tied a stone slab to his back and, thus protected from Spanish bullets, set the entrance ablaze.

COLONIAL CHURCHES

Aside from the **Basílica de Nuestra Señora de Guanajuato**, other fine colonial churches include **Templo de San Diego** (Jardín de la Union s/n), opposite the Jardín de la Unión; **Templo de San Francisco** (Doblado s/n); and large **Templo de la Compañía de Jesús** (Lascuraín de Retana s/n), which was completed in 1747 for the Jesuit seminary whose buildings are now occupied by the University of Guanajuato.

The rebels moved in and killed everyone inside.

The Alhóndiga was later used as an armory, then a school, before it was a prison for 80 years (1864–1948). It became a museum in 1958, though it's arguably more interesting for its history than its display today. Don't miss José Chávez Morado's dramatic murals of Guanajuato's history on the staircases.

Ex-Hacienda San Gabriel de Barrera
MUSEUM, GARDEN

(Camino Antiguo a Marfil Km 2.5; adult M$30; ⊙9am-6pm) To escape Guanajuato's narrow streets, head to this magnificent colonial home that is now a museum with tranquil and attractive gardens. Built at the end of the 17th century, this was the grand hacienda of Captain Gabriel de Barrera, whose family was descended from the first Conde de Rul of the famous La Valenciana mine. Opened as a museum in 1979, the hacienda, with its opulent period European furnishings, provides an insight into noble lifestyles of the viceregal period.

The hacienda is 2.5km west of the city center. Take one of the frequent 'Marfil' buses heading west in the subterranean tunnel under Avenida Juárez and ask the driver to drop you at Hotel Misión Guanajuato.

Callejón del Beso
STREET

(Alley of the Kiss) Narrowest of the many alleyways in Guanajuato's streets is this *callejón*, where the balconies of two houses practically touch. In a local legend, a fine family once lived on this street and their daughter fell in love with a common miner. They were forbidden to see each other, but the miner rented a room opposite and the lovers exchanged furtive *besos* (kisses) from these balconies. Inevitably, the romance was discovered and the couple met a tragic end.

From the Plazuela de los Ángeles on Avenida Juárez, walk about 40m up Callejón del Patrocinio to see the tiny alley on your left.

Universidad de Guanajuato
NOTABLE BUILDING

(UGTO; www.ugto.mx; Lascuraín de Retana 5) The main building of this university, whose ramparts are visible above much of the city, is one block up the hill from the basilica. The distinctive multistory white-and-blue building with the crenelated pediment dates from the 1950s. The design was (and some might say continues to be) controversial, as this dominating structure disrupts the characteristic, historic cityscape, but it's unusual enough to be worth searching out.

Museo Iconográfico del Quijote
MUSEUM

(☑473-732-67-21; www.museoiconografico.guana juato.gob.mx; Manuel Doblado 1; adult/student M$30/10; ☉9:30am-7pm Tue-Sat, noon-7pm Sun) This surprisingly interesting museum is worth half-hour of your time. Every exhibit relates to Don Quixote de la Mancha, Cervantes' classic literary hero, depicted in numerous different media by different artists in different styles. Paintings, statues, tapestries, even chess sets, clocks and postage stamps and all feature the quixotic icon and his bumbling companion Sancho Panza.

🏃 Activities

★ Funicular
FUNICULAR

(Plaza Constancia s/n; one-way/round-trip M$25/50; ☉8am-9:45pm Mon-Fri, 9am-9:45pm Sat, 10am-8:45pm Sun) This incline railway inches up (and down) the slope behind the Teatro Juárez to a terminal near the El Pípila monument, from where there are stunning views of Guanajuato and the surrounding valley. Heading up is fun, but to descend, you can save your pennies by walking down one of the two obvious, well-paved routes.

🐾 Courses

Guanajuato is a university town and has an excellent atmosphere for studying Spanish. Group classes range from around US$160 to US$220 for 20 lessons (one week's worth) and private lessons average US$20 an hour.

Schools can arrange homestays with meals for around US$200 per week. Language schools to consider include **Adelita** (☑473-732-64-55; www.learnspanishadelita.com; Agua Fuerte 56), **Don Quijote** (☑cell 923-268860; www.donquijote.org; Calle Pastita 76, Barrio Pastita) and **Escuela Falcon** (☑473-732-65-31; www.escuelafalcon.com; Callejón de Gallitos).

Mika Matsuishi & Felipe Olmos Workshops
COURSE

(☑cell 473-1204299; www.felipeymika.wix.com/mojigangas) Hands-on, fun art workshops for creative souls (mask-making, clay classes etc) are run by talented artists and *mojiganga* (farce) specialists. Materials are included; prices vary according to activity.

🎭 Festivals & Events

★ Festival Internacional Cervantino
ART

(www.festivalcervantino.gob.mx; ☉Oct) Beginning in the 1950s as merely *entremeses* (interludes) from Miguel Cervantes' work performed by students, the Festival Internacional Cervantino has grown to become one of Latin America's foremost arts extravaganzas. Music, dance and theater groups from around the world perform diverse works (mostly non-Cervantes related) for two weeks in October.

Tickets for single events range from M$30 to M$650 and should be booked in advance (www.ticketmaster.com.mx) along with hotels. In Guanajuato, tickets are available from a booth by Teatro Juarez two months before the festival.

Baile de las Flores
RELIGIOUS

(☉Mar or Apr) The Flower Dance takes place on the Thursday before Semana Santa. The next day, mines are open to the public for sightseeing and celebrations. Miners decorate altars to La Virgen de los Dolores, a manifestation of the Virgin Mary who looks after miners.

Fiestas de San Juan y Presa de la Olla
RELIGIOUS

(☉late Jun-early Jul) The festivals of San Juan are celebrated at the Presa de la Olla park in late June. The 24th is the big bash for the saint's day itself, with dances, music, fireworks and picnics. Then on the first Monday in July, everyone comes back to the park for another big party celebrating the opening of the dam's floodgates.

🛌 Sleeping

Guanajuato has some excellent accommodations for all budgets. Particularly atmospheric are a number of midrange and top-end hotels and guesthouses in the old town. During the Festival Internacional Cervantino in October, and at Christmas, Semana Santa and, in some cases, summer vacation, prices may be hiked well above regular rates.

Corral d Comedias   HOSTEL $
(📞 473-732-40-54; Av María 17; dm/d M$200/650; 📶) This hostel joined the scene in 2016 and is run by volunteers whose presence makes it feel like more of a hangout than traditional hostel setup. There's lots of communal space and lounging room, and breakfast is great. Some of the three dorms and one private room are a little on the simple side, but the location is excellent.

Hostel La Casa del Tío   HOSTEL $
(📞 473-733-97-28; www.hostellacasadeltio. mx; Cantarranas 47; dm/r M$190/560; 📶) The sweet and simple rooms here are clean, even if many lack natural light. Fear not though: there's a brightly painted roof terrace and it's centrally located in the heart of Guanajuato. The upstairs dorms get more light and a good breakfast is included.

El Zopilote Mojado   HOTEL $$
(📞 473-732-53-11; www.elzopilotemojado.com; De Mexiamora 51; r M$1400; 📶) This welcoming place has traditional fan-cooled rooms in a converted old colonial home, many of which feature lovely colorful tiling, wooden furniture and (from some) views on to a delightful square. There's a cafe downstairs where breakfast can be had, though it's not included in the room rate.

Casa Zuniga   B&B $$
(📞 473-732-85-46; www.casazunigagto.com; Callejón del Pachote 38; r incl breakfast from M$1250; 🅿️📶🏊) This charming B&B is run by the charismatic duo Carmen and Rick, who are famous for their warm welcome and generous breakfasts. It's located on the hill near El Pípila, to the left of the funicular (heading uphill), or by car and bus along Panoramica. Rates include a funicular pass throughout your stay. The lap pool is a plus.

Mesón de los Poetas   HOTEL $$
(📞 473-732-07-05; www.mesondelospoetas.com; Positos 35; r M$1200-3500; 🚭📶) Built against the hillside, this hotel's labyrinth of rooms – each named after a poet – offers spacious, comfortable and very clean lodgings. While natural light is limited, it's good value and service is friendly. We particularly like rooms 401, 402 and 403, which share a sunny terrace.

★ Hotel Villa
María Cristina   LUXURY HOTEL $$$
(📞 473-731-21-82; www.villamariacristina.net; Paseo de la Presa de la Olla 76; ste M$5300-12,100; 📶🏊) This series of stunning converted colonial mansions, joined by a maze of patios and gardens, is one of Guanajuato's most exclusive addresses. The decor in the spacious rooms features neoclassical French designer furniture, original paintings by local artist Jesús Gallardo, and beds and bathrooms with all the fluffy trimmings. There are fountains, two swimming pools and wonderful views. It's in La Presa, a 15-minute walk from the center of Guanajuato.

1850 Hotel   BOUTIQUE HOTEL $$$
(📞 473-732-27-95; www.hotel1850.com/index. php/en; Jardín de la Unión 7; r M$2950-4550; ❄️📶) In a marvelous location right on El Jardín and equipped with double-glazed windows to ensure the sound of the mariachis doesn't reach your bedroom, this is one of the smartest addresses in town. The decor is sleek and smart in a converted mansion with lots of silver and contemporary sculptures. Each room is individually designed and the rooftop bar is unbeatable.

Alonso10 Hotel
Boutique & Arte   BOUTIQUE HOTEL $$$
(📞 473-732-76-57; www.hotelalonso10.com.mx; Alonso 10; ste M$2950-3500; ❄️📶) A stylish boutique hotel located a street away from the centralized chaos. White and taupe hues rule, as do smart rooms with all the trimmings. The front two suites have great balconies with quirky views of the basílica and the back of Teatro Juárez. Downstairs is an elegant restaurant and bar with a fabulous wine cellar.

🍴 Eating

Eating in Guanajuato won't blow your culinary world apart; options are limited. Having said that, there are a few superb exceptions. For fresh produce and cheap lunches, head to Mercado Hidalgo (p660), a five-minute walk west of Jardín de la Unión on Avenida Juárez. Another two blocks further down

CALLEJONEADOS – THE TRADITIONAL WAY TO PARTY

The *callejoneada* tradition is said to have come from Spain. A group of professional singers and musicians, dressed in traditional costumes, starts up in a central location such as a plaza, a crowd gathers, then the whole mob winds through the alleyways, streets and plazas playing, dancing and singing heartily. In Guanajuato they are also called *estudiantinas*. Stories and jokes (in Spanish) are told in between songs, often relating to the legends of the alleys. In Zacatecas there are no stories, but hired bands called *tamboras* (dressed in uniform, not traditional attire) lead dancing revelers. On special occasions a burro laden with wine is brought along. Often, strangers are just expected to join the party and the crowd swells. Occasionally, the organizers foot the bill; sometimes you pay a small amount for the wine you drink (or you bring your own). In Guanajuato the groups themselves or tour companies sell tickets (around M$100 for 1¼ hours; Tuesday through Sunday) for the *callejoneadas* and juice (not alcohol) is provided. It's great fun.

on the right is **Central Comercio** (Av Juárez; ⊙8am-8pm), with a large supermarket.

★ La Vie en Rose
FRENCH $

(Cantarranas 18; pastries & snacks M$30-80; ⊙10am-10pm Tue-Sun; 🎅) At this old-town institution you'll find some of the most genuine, mouthwatering, flavorsome French pastries and desserts around. All made by a French pastry chef.

★ Delica Mitsu
JAPANESE $

(Cantaritos 37; sushi M$43-93; ⊙noon-6pm Mon-Sat) This tiny Japanese-run deli may not look like much (and is all but hidden in a side street off a pretty plaza), but it serves up some of the biggest, freshest and best Japanese flavors around.

Escarola
INTERNATIONAL $

(Positos 38; mains M$40-70; ⊙11am-8pm Tue-Sat, to 6pm Sun; 🎅📶) 🌿 This excellent little place in the middle of the old town makes for a superb lunch stop. Food is prepared from scratch, however, so don't come here if you're in a hurry, but rather enjoy the pleasant sun-dappled terrace and the delicious offerings of burgers, sandwiches, salads and soups.

Café Tal
CAFE $

(Temezcuitate 4; snacks M$30-50; ⊙7am-midnight Mon-Fri, 8am-midnight Sat & Sun; 🎅) Spread over two buildings on either side of a steep, narrow side street, this student favorite is always busy with modish young things who love the owners' passion for roasting coffee right here on the premises. Don't miss the *beso negro* ('black kiss'), ultra-concentrated hot chocolate (M$20). If you're lucky, Tal the cat might sit on your lap.

Santo Café
CAFE $

(www.facebook.com/santocafe; Puente de Campanero; mains M$50-150; ⊙10am-11pm Mon-Sat, noon-8pm Sun; 🎅📶) Stop by this casual but cozy spot on the quaint Venetian-style bridge and check the latest university vibe. It serves good salads and snacks; try the *queso fundido* (melted cheese) or the soy burger, both great for vegetarians. Some tables overlook the alley below.

★ Los Campos
TAPAS $$

(www.loscampos.mx; 4A de la Alameda, off Plaza Baratillo; mains M$75-185; ⊙2-10pm Tue-Sun) A Canadian-Mexican husband-and-wife team runs this small cozy, candlelit restaurant. The innovative menu, which runs from tapas plates to full dishes such as stuffed ancho chili on a bed of pearl barley with *huitlacoche* (corn mushrooms), *nopal* and corn, is a cut above other Guanajuato eateries in terms of variety and ingredients. Reserve ahead for evenings.

A Punto
INTERNATIONAL $$

(📞473-732-61-32; Casa Cuatro, San José 4; M$180-310; ⊙2-10pm Tue & Wed, to 11pm Thu-Sun) Located in the restored Casa Cuatro mansion complex, this is among Guanajuato's most cosmopolitan spots and serves up good international dishes. It's a great choice for a long lunch or dinner, and you can also come just for drinks.

Mestizo
INTERNATIONAL $$

(📞473-732-06-12; Positos 69; mains M$120-280; ⊙1-10pm Tue-Sat, to 5pm Sun; 🎅) There's interesting art on the walls, a great menu and three breezy dining rooms, not to mention changing daily specials, so why is the lighting so poor and the carpeting so ugly? Yes,

Guanajuato's eating scene has a long way to go to catch up with other cities in Mexico, but this place does at least do some tasty cuisine.

Casa Valadez
MEXICAN $$

(☑ 473-732-03-11; Jardín de la Unión 3; mains M$150-800; ⊙ 8:30am-11pm; 🐾) This classic place enjoys an impressive perch on Jardín de la Unión and is a smart choice in every respect. As you'd expect, it attracts a loyal crowd of well-dressed locals who like to see and be seen. Servings are generous. Dishes are mainly international with a few Mexican favorites such as *pollo con enchiladas mineras* (chicken enchiladas).

★ El Jardín de los Milagros
MEXICAN $$$

(☑ 473-732-93-66; www.eljardindelosmilagros. com.mx; Calzada Alhondiga 80; mains M$230-350; ⊙ 1:30-10pm Wed-Mon; 🐾) This superb place is hidden away from the busy road outside by thick walls that encircle an ancient hacienda and well-tended garden. It's a stunning setting, whether you eat outside or in one of the charming hacienda dining rooms. Staff are incredibly solicitous and the food is an epic tour de force of creatively presented high-style Mexican cookery with international elements.

★ Las Mercedes
MEXICAN $$$

(☑ 473-733-90-59; www.casamercedes.com.mx; Arriba 6, San Javier; mains M$200-350; ⊙ 2-10pm Tue-Sat, to 6pm Sun; 🐾) In a residential area overlooking the city is Guanajuato's best restaurant, where Mexican cuisine *como la abuela* – grandmother's cooking that takes hours to prepare – is served. Dishes include *moles* hand-ground in a *molcajete* (traditional mortar and pestle) with a contemporary twist and stylish presentation. Reservations recommended. Take a taxi to get here.

El Midi Bistró
FRENCH $$$

(Casa Cuatro, San José 4; mains M$230-300; ⊙ 9am-10pm Mon, Wed & Thu, to 11pm Fri & Sat, to 9pm Sun; 🐾) This tastefully decorated part-bistro, part-bar on the top floor of a gorgeously restored mansion serves up a delectable array of à la carte French classic dishes including beef bourguignon, duck confit and bouillabaisse. There's live music on Thursday evenings and brunch served daily (9am to 2pm). All in all one of the town's most pleasant places to kick back.

🍷 Drinking & Nightlife

Every evening, the Jardín de la Unión comes alive with people crowding the outdoor tables, strolling and listening to the street musicians and mariachi bands. The city's immense student population means that there is a very busy and accessible bar scene in town. Thursday is generally their big night out, though drinking and dancing establishments in Guanajuato generally start late.

Los Lobos
BAR

(Doblado 2; ⊙ 6pm-3am Mon-Sat, to 1am Sun) This cool, gay-friendly place is decked out with images of devils and *Catrinas* (skeleton dolls) plastered on every available surface. The crowd is far less ghoulish, however, and there's a great soundtrack and a pool table in the back room.

Golem
BAR

(Cantarranas 38; ⊙ 6:30pm-3am Mon-Sat, 2pm-midnight Sun) This punk bar is a veritable maze of rooms with foosball, repurposed airplane seats and Anglo-indie music on the speakers. Margaritas are served in champagne glasses, and upstairs there's more of the same plus a roof terrace. It's definitely one of Guanajuato's liveliest spots.

Why Not?
CLUB

(Alfonso 34; ⊙ 9:30pm-3am Mon-Sat) You may not be asking yourself 'why not?' after you wake up with a throbbing headache from drinking all night with the hordes of local students who head to this Guanajuato institution (especially Thursday to Saturday, when it's packed). The fun starts after midnight.

La Inundación de 1905
BAR

(San Fernando Plaza; ⊙ 10am-midnight Tue-Sun) Students love this relaxed spot, named after the city's 1905 flood, for its flowing beer and the beer-garden atmosphere.

El Midi Bistró
BAR

(Casa Cuatro, San José 4; ⊙ 9am-10pm Mon, Wed & Thu, to 11pm Fri & Sat, to 9pm Sun) This pleasant place, which is also an upmarket restaurant, is housed in a refurbished mansion. It offers a touch of class and culture with frequent live-music performances and exhibitions in its next-door gallery space, as well as a fabulous old-fashioned bar. It's is a relaxing spot to head to for a pre- or post-dinner drink.

El Incendio BAR

(Cantarranas 39; ⊘11am-11pm) A former old-school cantina – whose legacy is swinging doors, an open urinal (as per the old cantinas, but no longer used) and mural-covered walls – that caters to a fun and rowdy student crowd.

Whoopees BAR

(Manuel Doblado 39; ⊘9pm-4am Tue-Sat) This friendly bar is the center of Guanajuato's gay scene.

☆ Entertainment

Teatro Cervantes THEATER

(☎473-732-11-69; Plaza Allende s/n) Has a full schedule of performances during the Cervantino festival and less regular shows at other times. Statues of Don Quixote and Sancho Panza grace the small Plaza Allende, in front of the theater.

🛍 Shopping

Xocola-T FOOD

(Plazuela del Baratillo 15; ⊘noon-8pm Mon, 9am-8pm Tue-Sat, 10am-6pm Sun) This chocoholic's nirvana sells delectable handmade chocolates of pure cocoa with natural flavors and not a trans fat in sight. Quirkier fillings include *chapulines* (grasshoppers), *gusanos* (caterpillars) and *nopal* (cactus).

Mercado Hidalgo MARKET

(Av Juárez; ⊘8am–9pm) Guanajuato's atmospheric and bustling market is chockablock with tourist paraphernalia, artisan's products and food stalls. It's well worth a visit.

ℹ Information

Incredibly, the only formal information points in Guanajuato are two small tourist kiosks, located at **Jardín de la Unión** (⊘9am-6pm) and an extension of this, in Calle Allende. Note: do not confuse these with official-looking booths marked 'Información Turística' that are dotted around town. The latter are private companies touting specific hotels and other services.

Banks along Avenida Juárez change cash, offer advances on credit cards and have ATMs.

Centro Médico la Presa (☎473-102-31-00; www.centromedicolapresa.mx; Paseo de la Presa 85; ⊘24hr)

Hospital General (☎473-733-15-73, 473-733-15-76; Carretera a Silao, Km 6.5)

Post Office (Ayuntamiento 25; ⊘8am-4:30pm Mon-Fri, to noon Sat)

ℹ Getting There & Away

AIR

Guanajuato is served by the **Aeropuerto Internacional de Guanajuato** (Aeropuerto Internacional del Bajío; ☎472-748-21-20; www.aeropuertosgap.com.mx; Silao), which is about 30km west of the city, near the town of Silao.

BUS

Guanajuato's **Central de Autobuses** (☎473-733-13-44; Silao 450) is around 5km southwest of town (confusingly, to get there you go northwest out of town along Tepetapa). Deluxe and 1st-class bus tickets (ETN and Primera Plus) can be bought in town at **Viajes Frausto** (☎473-732-35-80; www.frausto.agenciasviajes.mx; Obregón 10; ⊘9am-2pm & 4:30-7:30pm Mon-Fri, 9am-1:30pm Sat).

Primera Plus and ETN are the main 1st-class operators, while Flecha Amarilla has cheaper services to Dolores Hidalgo, León and San Miguel de Allende.

ℹ Getting Around

A taxi to Aeropuerto Internacional de Guanajuato will cost about M$400 (there's a set rate of M$450 from the airport; you buy your ticket at a taxi counter inside the airport). A cheaper option from Guanajuato is one of the frequent buses to

BUSES FROM GUANAJUATO

DESTINATION	FARE (M$)	DURATION (HR)	FREQUENCY (DAILY)
Dolores Hidalgo	60	1½	every 30min 5:30am-10:30pm
Guadalajara	420-515	4	frequent
León	75-98	1-1¼	very frequent
Mexico City (Terminal Norte)	540-680	4½	very frequent
Querétaro	200-230	2½	frequent
San Miguel de Allende	130-170	1½-2	very frequent
Zacatecas	465	4	daily at 12:15pm

MIGUEL HIDALGO: ¡VIVA MEXICO!

The balding head of the visionary priest Father Miguel Hidalgo y Costilla is familiar to anyone who has ogled Mexican statues or murals. A genuine rebel idealist, Hidalgo sacrificed his career and risked his life on September 16, 1810, when he launched the independence movement.

Born on May 8, 1753, son of a criollo (Mexican-born person of Spanish parentage) hacienda manager in Guanajuato, he earned a bachelor's degree and, in 1778, was ordained a priest. He returned to teach at his alma mater in Morelia and eventually became rector. But he was no orthodox cleric: Hidalgo questioned many Catholic traditions, read banned books, gambled, danced and had a mistress.

In 1800 he was brought before the Inquisition. Nothing was proven, but a few years later, in 1804, he found himself transferred as priest to the hick town of Dolores.

Hidalgo's years in Dolores show his growing interest in the economic and cultural welfare of the people. He started several new industries: silk was cultivated, olive groves were planted and vineyards established, all in defiance of the Spanish colonial authorities. Earthenware building products were the foundation of the ceramics industry that today produces fine glazed pots and tiles.

When Hidalgo met Ignacio Allende from San Miguel, they shared a criollo discontent with the Spanish stranglehold on Mexico. Hidalgo's standing among the mestizos (people of mixed European and indigenous ancestry) and indigenous people of his parish was vital in broadening the base of the rebellion that followed.

Shortly after his Grito de Independencia, Hidalgo was formally excommunicated for 'heresy, apostasy and sedition.' He defended his call for Mexican independence and stated furthermore that the Spanish were not truly Catholic in any religious sense of the word but only for political purposes, specifically to rape, pillage and exploit Mexico. A few days later, on October 19, Hidalgo dictated his first edict calling for the abolition of slavery in Mexico.

Hidalgo led his growing forces from Dolores to San Miguel, Celaya and Guanajuato, north to Zacatecas, south almost to Mexico City and west to Guadalajara. But then, pushed northward, their numbers dwindled and on July 30, 1811, having been captured by the Spanish, Hidalgo was shot by a firing squad in Chihuahua. His head was returned to the city of Guanajuato, where it hung in a cage for 10 years on an outer corner of the Alhóndiga de Granaditas, along with the heads of fellow independence leaders Allende, Aldama and Jiménez. Rather than intimidating the people, this lurid display kept the memory, the goal and the example of the heroic martyrs fresh in everyone's mind. After independence the cages were removed, and the skulls (and bodies) of the heroes are now in the Monumento a la Independencia in Mexico City.

Silao (M$30, every 20 minutes) and a taxi from there (around M$120). Note: in reverse – from the airport to Silao – the taxi rates are set at M$250.

Between the bus station and downtown, 'Central de Autobuses' buses (M$6) run round the clock. From the center, you can catch them heading west on Avenida Juárez. From the bus terminal, you will enter a tunnel running east under the *centro histórico*. Alight at one of several entry/exit points: Mercado Hidalgo, Plaza de los Ángeles, Jardín de la Unión, Plaza Baratillo/Teatro Principal, Teatro Cervantes or Embajadoras. A taxi to/from the bus station costs around M$50.

To get around town keep a look out – local buses display their destination. For the *centro histórico* the rule of thumb is as follows: all buses heading east go via the tunnels below

Avenida Juárez (eg if you want to go from the market to the Teatro Principal). Those heading west go along Avenida Juárez.

City buses (M$6) run from 7am to 10pm. Taxis are plentiful in the center and charge about M$40 for short trips around town (slightly more if heading uphill to El Pípila and the like).

Buses to Bocamina San Ramón and Bocamina de San Cayetano (Insurgencia) leave from Calle Insurgencia near Plaza Alhóndiga.

León

📍 477 / POP 1.5 MILLION / ELEV 1815M

There's no real reason to visit industrial León, 56km west of Guanajuato, but due to its importance as a main bus hub within the

BUSES FROM LEÓN

DESTINATION	FARE (M$)	DURATION (HR)	FREQUENCY (DAILY)
Aguascalientes	195	2-2½	frequent
Guadalajara	320-370	3	10
Guanajuato	80-112	¾	hourly
Mexico City (Terminal Norte)	450-600	5	very frequent (24 hr)
San Miguel de Allende	185-250	2¼	6
Zacatecas	430	4	8

state of Guanajuato you may well have to change buses here. Also, it's only 20km from Aeropuerto Internacional de Guanajuato (p660). It's unlikely you'll need to stay here; bus connections are plentiful.

If you want to fill an hour or two before a bus connection, it's worth wandering the streets surrounding the bus terminal, known as Zona Piel (Leather District). León has a long history of supplying goods: in the 16th century it was the center of Mexico's ranching district, providing meat for the mining towns and processing hides.

❶ Getting There & Away

Aeropuerto Internacional de Guanajuato (p660) is 20km southeast of León on the Mexico City road. Many US airlines offer flights between US cities and here. Unfortunately, no bus service operates between Aeropuerto Internacional de Guanajuato and central León. A taxi between León and the airport costs around M$300 (M$380 from the airport using the official airport taxis).

The **Central de Autobuses** (Blvd Hilario Medina s/n), just north of Blvd López Mateos and 2.5km east of downtown, has a cafeteria, left luggage and a money exchange. There are regular 1st- and 2nd-class services to most cities in northern and central Mexico.

Dolores Hidalgo

📞 418 / POP 61,000 / ELEV 1920M

Dolores Hidalgo is a compact town with a pretty, tree-filled plaza, a relaxed ambience and an important history. Amazingly enough, the Mexican independence movement began in earnest in this small place when at 5am on September 16, 1810, Miguel Hidalgo, the parish priest, rang the bells to summon people to church earlier than usual and issued the Grito de Dolores (Cry of Dolores), also known as the Grito de Independencia (Cry of Independence).

Today Hidalgo is one of Mexico's most revered heroes. Dolores was renamed in his honor in 1824. Mexicans swarm here for Independence Day (September 16), during which time the price of accommodations can more than double. The town's *centro histórico* is worth a half-day visit for history buffs, not only for its interesting independence-themed museums but also for its colored Talavera ceramics workshops and famous ice cream.

◉ Sights

Parroquia de Nuestra Señora de Dolores   CHURCH
(Plaza Principal) The Parroquia de Nuestra Señora de Dolores is the church where Hidalgo issued the now world famous Grito (a call to arms for the country's independence) and is the focal point for the town's independence day celebrations each year. It has a fine 18th-century Churrigueresque facade. Legends surround his 'cry'; some say that Hidalgo uttered his famous words from the pulpit, others claim that he spoke at the church door to the people gathered outside.

Cuna De Tierra   WINERY
(📞 418-690-22-09; www.cunadetierra.com; Carretera Dolores Hidalgo–San Luis de la Paz Km 11; ⊘ Wed-Sun by appointment) The first and biggest winery in Guanajuato opened in 2005, heralding the reintroduction of wine production in the area 200 years after the Spanish banned it, insisting instead on Mexicans drinking only Spanish wine. Tastings, for which you should book in advance, take place in the award-winning buildings. The white uses Sémillon grapes; reds are a mixture. Around 80,000 bottles are produced each year.

Hidalgo Statue MONUMENT

(Plaza Principal) The town's main square naturally boasts a statue of the man himself, Hidalgo (in Roman garb, on top of a tall column). Here too is a tree that, according to the plaque beneath it, was a sapling of the tree of the Noche Triste (Sad Night), under which Cortés is said to have wept when his men were driven out of Tenochtitlán in 1520.

Museo Bicentenario 1810–2010 MUSEUM

(Casa del Capitán Mariano Abasolo; adult/student M$20/10, Sun free; ⊙10am-5pm Mon-Sat, to 3pm Sun) Previously the Presidencia Municipal, this museum was inaugurated in 2010 for Mexico's bicentennial celebrations. Despite its name, the majority of its seven rooms provide a cultural and historical context of the first hundred years of independence, including mementos produced for the centenary of 1910. Quirkier items include a stunning silk scarf embroidered with hair (depicting the image of Alejandro Zavala Mangas, an architect from Guanajuato city) and the original painted poster promoting the first century of independence.

Museo de la Independencia Nacional MUSEUM

(Zacatecas 6; adult/student M$15/10, Sun free; ⊙9am-5pm Mon-Sat, to 3pm Sun) Although this museum has few relics, it has plenty of information on the independence movement. The exhibition spans seven rooms and charts the appalling decline in Nueva España's indigenous population between 1519 (an estimated 25 million) and 1605 (one million), and identifies 23 indigenous rebellions before 1800 as well as several criollo conspiracies in the years leading up to 1810. There are vivid paintings, quotations and details on the heroic last 10 months of Hidalgo's life.

Museo Casa de Hidalgo MUSEUM

(cnr Hidalgo & Morelos; adult/student M$40/20, free Sun; ⊙9am-5:45pm Tue-Sat, to 4:45pm Sun) Miguel Hidalgo lived in this house when he was Dolores' parish priest. It was from here, in the early hours of September 16, 1810, that Hidalgo, Ignacio Allende and Juan de Aldama set off to launch the uprising against colonial rule. The house is now something of a national shrine – think memorials, replicas of Hidalgo's furniture and independence-movement documents, including the order for Hidalgo's excommunication.

★☆ Festivals & Events

Día de la Independencia HISTORICAL

(⊙Sep 16) As the scene of the Grito de Independencia, Dolores is the scene of major Día de la Independencia celebrations on September 16, which the Mexican president may officiate – according to tradition – in his fifth year of office.

🛏 Sleeping & Eating

Don't leave without sampling a hand-turned ice cream (around M$20) from an ice-cream vendor on the plaza or around town. You can test your taste buds on the flavors: *mole* (chili sauce), *chicharrón* (fried pork skin), avocado, corn, cheese, honey, shrimp, beer, tequila and tropical fruits.

Posada Cocomacán HOTEL $

(📱418-182-60-86; www.posadacocomacan.com.mx; Plaza Principal 4; s/d M$420/600; 🕸) The centrally located and absolutely apricot Cocomacán is an aged but reliable option and has lots of Mexican ambience. Of the 37 rooms, those on the upper levels, with windows on to the street, are the best. There's also a restaurant (open 8am to 10:30pm).

BUSES FROM DOLORES HIDALGO

DESTINATION	FARE (M$)	DURATION (HR)	FREQUENCY (DAILY)
Guanajuato	85	1¼	frequent
León	160	2¼	3
Mexico City (Terminal Norte) via Querétaro	375	5-6	frequent
Querétaro	150	2	hourly
San Luis Potosí	170	2¼	hourly
San Miguel de Allende	50	¾	frequent

Hotel Hidalgo
HOTEL $

(☏ 418-182-04-77; www.hotelposadahidalgo.com; Hidalgo 15; s/d M$550/650; 🕸) The reception feels a bit like a doctor's surgery, but this super-clean and well-managed place offers comfortable if rather dated rooms. It's conveniently located between the bus stations and the Plaza Principal.

★ DaMónica
ITALIAN $$

(Nayarit 67; mains M$80-200; ⊙10:30am-10:30pm Tue-Sun) This cozy and inviting culinary marvel is hosted by Mónica, the Italian owner, who will whip up very genuine Italian delights such as lasagna, pizza and gourmet seafood treats.

🛍 Shopping

Talavera ceramics have been the signature handicraft of Dolores ever since Padre Hidalgo founded the town's first ceramics workshop in the early 19th century. Head to the Zona Artesanal; the workshops along Avenida Jiménez, five blocks west of the plaza; or (by car) to Calzada de los Héroes, the exit road to San Miguel de Allende.

ℹ Information

Tourist office (☏ 418-182-11-64; www.do-lores-hidalgo.com; Plaza Principal; ⊙9am-5pm Mon-Fri, 10am-2pm Sat) On Plaza Principal's southeastern side. The helpful staff provide maps and information.

ℹ Getting There & Away

The **Primera Plus/Coordinados (Flecha Amarilla) bus station** (Hidalgo) is 2½ blocks south of the plaza, near the **Herradura de Plata/ Autovías bus station** (☏ 418-182-29-37; cnr Chiapas & Yucatán).

San Miguel de Allende

☏ 415 / POP 73,000 / ELEV 1900M

With its gorgeous colonial architecture, enchanting cobblestone streets and striking light, San Miguel de Allende is rightly one of Mexico's biggest draws and has been popular with aesthetes and romantics for much of the past century. This includes a large population of Americans who either live full time in the town or maintain winter homes here, bringing with them a cosmopolitan atmosphere you'll find in few other Mexican towns.

With superb restaurants and high-class accommodations, numerous galleries stocked with quality Mexican *artesanías* (handicrafts), a fantastic spring-like climate and a surfeit of cultural activities including regular festivals, fireworks and parades, San Miguel is an unmissable highlight for anyone visiting the northern central highlands. The entire ensemble was declared a Unesco World Heritage site in 2008, and despite receiving huge numbers of visitors, San Miguel absorbs them well and locals mix warmly with their foreign guests and residents.

History

The town, so the story goes, owes its founding to a few overheated dogs. These hounds were loved by a Franciscan friar, Juan de San Miguel, who started a mission in 1542 near an often-dry river 5km from the present town. One day the dogs wandered off from the mission; they were found reclining at the spring called **El Chorro**. The mission was moved to this superior site.

San Miguel was then central Mexico's most northern Spanish settlement. Tarascan and Tlaxcalan allies of the Spanish were brought to help pacify the local Otomí and Chichimecs. San Miguel was barely surviving the fierce Chichimec resistance, until in 1555 a Spanish garrison was established to protect the new road from Mexico City to the silver center of Zacatecas. Spanish ranchers settled in the area and it grew into a thriving commercial center and home to some of Guanajuato's wealthy silver barons.

San Miguel's favorite son, Ignacio Allende, was born here in 1779. He became a fervent believer in the need for Mexican independence and was a leader of a Querétaro-based conspiracy that set December 8, 1810, as the date for an armed uprising. When the plan was discovered by the authorities in Querétaro on September 13, a messenger rushed to San Miguel and gave the news to Juan de Aldama, another conspirator. Aldama sped north to Dolores where, in the early hours of September 16, he found Allende at the house of the priest Miguel Hidalgo, also one of the coterie. A few hours later Hidalgo proclaimed rebellion from his church. After initial successes Allende, Hidalgo and other rebel leaders were captured in 1811 in Chihuahua. Allende was executed, but on independence in 1821 he was recognized as a martyr and in 1826 the town was renamed San Miguel de Allende.

The Escuela de Bellas Artes was founded in 1938 and the town started to take on its current character when David Alfaro Siqueiros began mural-painting courses that attracted artists of every persuasion. The Instituto Allende opened in 1951, also attracting foreign students. Many were US war veterans (who could settle here under the GI Bill); an influx of artists has continued ever since.

◉ Sights

Parque Benito Juárez
PARK

(🐾) The shady Parque Benito Juárez is a lovely place to relax and meander through, with benches, well-maintained pathways and a popular play area for children.

La Esquina: Museo del Juguete Popular Mexicano
MUSEUM

(www.museolaesquina.org.mx; Núñez 40; adult/child M$50/20; ⊙10am-6pm Tue-Sat, to 4pm Sun; 🐾) This bright, modern museum is a must-visit for all kids, big or small. The toy collection of museum owner Angélica Tijerina has taken over half a century to amass and aims to preserve and continue various traditions by showcasing pieces from different regions of Mexico. The exhibits – divided into four main themed areas – are made of a range of materials, from wheat to plastic, and wood to fabric.

Oratorio de San Felipe Neri
CHURCH

(Plaza Cívica) Located near the east end of Insurgentes, this multitowered and domed church dates from the 18th century. The pale-pink main facade is baroque with an indigenous influence. A passage to the right of this facade leads to the east wall, where a doorway holds the image of Nuestra Señora de la Soledad (Our Lady of Solitude). You can see into the cloister from this side of the church.

Inside the church are 33 oil paintings showing scenes from the life of San Felipe Neri, the 16th-century Florentine who founded the Oratorio Catholic order. In the east transept is a painting of the Virgin of Guadalupe by leading colonial painter Miguel Cabrera. In the west transept is a lavishly decorated 1735 chapel, the **Santa Casa de Loreto**, a replica of a chapel in Loreto, Italy, legendary home of the Virgin Mary. Although rarely open, the *camarín* (chapel behind the main church) has six elaborately gilded baroque altars. In one is a reclining

wax figure of San Columbano; it supposedly contains the saint's bones.

Jardín Botánico El Charco del Ingenio
GARDENS

(📞415-154-47-15; www.elcharco.org.mx; off Antiguo Camino Real a Querétaro; M$40; ⊙9am-6pm) San Miguel's excellent 88-hectare botanical garden is also a wildlife and bird sanctuary. Pathways head through wetlands and magnificent areas of cacti and native plants. The deep canyon at the bottom boasts the eponymous freshwater spring, El Charco del Ingenio. Don't miss the Conservatory of Mexican Plants, which houses a wonderful array of cacti and succulent species. Two-hour tours (in English) depart every Tuesday and Thursday at 10am (M$80).

The garden is 1.5km northeast of town and each Tuesday, Thursday, Saturday and Sunday a complimentary bus service leaves Calles Mesones in front of Plaza Cívica at 9:30am, returning at 1pm. Alternatively, a 2km vehicle track leads north from the Soriana shopping center, 2.5km southeast of the center on the Querétaro road. This can be reached on 'Soriana' buses from the bus stop from Mesones, near Plaza Cívica (10 minutes, M$5). A taxi to the gardens from the center costs from around M$50 to M$60.

Parroquia de San Miguel Arcángel
CHURCH

San Miguel's most famous sight is its parish church, characterized by its pink 'wedding cake' towers that soar above the town. These strange pinnacles were designed by indigenous stonemason Zeferino Gutiérrez in the late 19th century. He reputedly based the design on a postcard of a Belgian church and instructed builders by scratching plans in the sand with a stick. The rest of the church dates from the late 17th century.

Biblioteca Pública
NOTABLE BUILDING

(📞415-152-02-93; Insurgentes 25; ⊙10am-7pm Mon-Fri, to 2pm Sat) As well as housing one of the largest collections of books and magazines in English in Latin America, this excellent public library functions as a cultural center. It's also the editorial offices of the weekly English-Spanish *Atención San Miguel* newspaper and has an on-site cafe that provides a pleasant spot from which to view the cultural action. The tiny **Teatro Santa Ana** (📞415-152-02-93; Reloj 50A; tickets M$40-250) also hosts talks and performances.

San Miguel de Allende

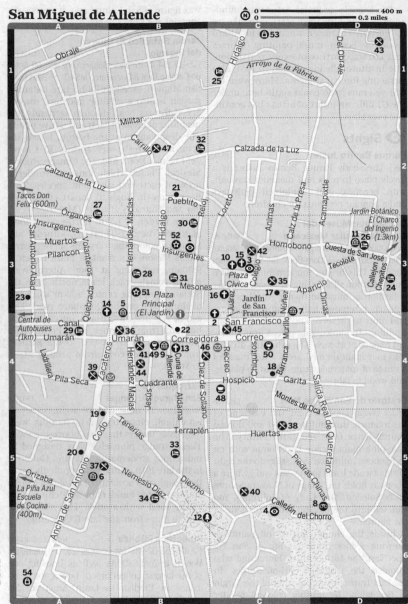

Escuela de Bellas Artes

GALLERY

(School of Fine Arts, Centro Cultural Nigromante; 415-152-02-89; Hernández Macías 75; 10am-6pm Mon-Sat, to 2pm Sun) This former monastery was converted into a fine-arts school in 1938. Don't miss the murals of Pedro Martínez, plus the Siqueiros Room, which features the extraordinary unfinished mural by David Alfaro Siqueiros in the far corner of the complex. The rest of the gallery holds temporary exhibitions from local artists, many of whom graduated from the school.

San Miguel de Allende

⊙ Sights

⊙ Activities, Courses & Tours

⊙ Sleeping

⊙ Eating

⊙ Drinking & Nightlife

⊙ Entertainment

⊙ Shopping

Mirador   VIEWPOINT
One of the best views over the town and surrounding country is from the *mirador* southeast of town.

**Museo Histórico de
San Miguel de Allende**   MUSEUM
(Museo Casa de Allende; Cuna de Allende 1; M$50, free Sun; ⊙9am-5pm Tue-Sun) This is the house where Mexican independence hero Ignacio Allende was born in 1769, a fact that draws a steady stream of Mexican pilgrims year-round. The building is also home to the town's history museum, which relates the interesting history of the San Miguel area alongside reproductions of the Allende family's furnishings and possessions, though all signage is in Spanish only.

Other Face of Mexico Gallery   MUSEUM
(☏415-154-43-24; www.casadelacuesta.com; Casa de la Cuesta, Cuesta de San José 32; M$50) This fascinating private collection of more than 500 masks provides an excellent context to the Mexican mask tradition. It is open by appointment only. The admission fee goes to charity.

Instituto Allende   HISTORIC BUILDING
(Ancha de San Antonio 20) This large 1736 complex, originally the home of the aristocratic De La Canal family, was later used as a Carmelite convent, eventually becoming an art and language school in 1951. These days it's split into two – one area of gardens and an old chapel is used for functions, the other for courses. Above the main entrance is a carving of the Virgin of Loreto, patroness of the De La Canal family, while inside an impressive mural depicts the history of Mexico.

NORTHERN CENTRAL HIGHLANDS SAN MIGUEL DE ALLENDE

Templo de la Salud
CHURCH

(Plaza Cívica) With its blue and yellow tiled dome and a big shell carved above its entrance, this church is just east of San Felipe Neri. The facade is early Churrigueresque. The church's paintings include one of San Javier by Miguel Cabrera. San Javier (St Francis Xavier; 1506–52) was a founding member of the Jesuits. It was once part of the Colegio de Sales.

Templo de la Concepción
CHURCH

(Church of the Conception; cnr Zacateros & Canal) A splendid church with a fine altar and several magnificent old oil paintings. Painted on the interior doorway are a number of wise sayings to give pause to those entering. The church was begun in the mid-18th century; its dome, added in the late 19th century by the versatile Zeferino Gutiérrez, was possibly inspired by pictures of Les Invalides in Paris.

Capilla de la Tercera Orden
CHAPEL

(Chapel of the Third Order; cnr San Francisco & Juárez) Built in the early 18th century, this chapel, like the **Templo de San Francisco** (cnr San Francisco & Juárez), was part of a Franciscan monastery complex. The main facade shows St Francis and symbols of the Franciscan order.

Colegio de Sales
NOTABLE BUILDING

(Plaza Cívica; ⊘8am-2pm & 5-8pm) Once a college founded in the mid-18th century by the San Felipe Neri order, the Colegio de Sales has regained its educational status; it currently houses part of the University of León. Many of the 1810 revolutionaries were educated here, while later Spanish nobles were locked up here when the rebels took San Miguel.

Activities

Balnearios

Balneario Santa Veronica
SWIMMING

(☑415-109-63-73; Carretera San Miguel de Allende –Dolores Hidalgo Km 5.5; M$30; ⊘10am-6pm Fri-Sun) This is one of the easiest of the hot springs to reach as it's right on the main road. A lovely old hacienda with an enormous swimming pool and two hot-spring-fed baths, Santa Veronica has definitely seen better days, but it's wonderfully relaxed, you're welcome to bring your own food and drinks and, yes, swig beer in the pool.

Balneario Xote
SWIMMING

(☑415-155-83-30; www.xoteparqueacuatico.com. mx; adult/child M$100/50; ⊘9am-6pm; ⓐ) The family-oriented Balneario Xote water park is 3.5km off the highway down a cobblestone road. It's a great place to go with kids, as it has multiple areas for children and several waterslides and pools.

La Gruta
SWIMMING

(☑415-185-21-62; www.lagruta-spa.com; Carretera Dolores Hidalogo–San Miguel de Allende Km 10; M$150; ⊘7am-5pm) Upmarket La Gruta is justifiably a local and tourist favorite; it has three small pools where a thermal spring is channeled. The hottest is in a cave entered through a 27m tunnel, with water gushing from the roof, lit by a single shaft of sunlight. It also offers quality spa treatments and has a good restaurant.

Escondido Place
SWIMMING

(☑415-185-20-22; www.escondidoplace.com; Carretera San Miguel de Allende–Dolores Hidalgo Km 10; M$150; ⊘8am-5:30pm) Escondido Place has seven small outdoor pools and three connected indoor pools, each progressively hotter. The picturesque grounds have plenty of picnicking space and there's a kiosk for drinks and snacks.

Courses

Several institutions offer Spanish courses, with group or private lessons and optional classes in Mexican culture and history. Most private lessons cost around US$20 an hour; group and long-term rates are much lower. Homestays with Mexican families, including a private room and three daily meals, cost around US$35 per day. Cooking courses are also very popular here.

La Piña Azul
Escuela de Cocina
COOKING

(www.kirstenwest.blogspot.de; Orizaba 39A; class per person US$75) Kirsten West, former private chef to Mick Jagger and a world expert on Mexican cuisine, opened her own Mexican cookery school in 2016. The lessons – where you won't actually be cooking yourself – focus on indigenous and traditional Mexican dishes. Classes require a minimum of four participants and are taught in English.

SANCTUARIO DE ATOTONILCO

Known as Mexico's Sistine Chapel, this vitally important **church** (Calle Principal, Atotonilco) in the hamlet of Atotonilco, 11km north of San Miguel, is defined by its connection to the independence struggle, which has made it an important icon for Mexicans. Nationalist hero Ignacio Allende married here in 1802, and eight years later he returned with Miguel Hidalgo and a band of independence rebels en route from Dolores to San Miguel to take the shrine's banner of the Virgin of Guadalupe as their flag.

A journey to Atotonilco is the goal of pilgrims and penitents from all over Mexico, and the starting point of an important and solemn procession two weekends before Easter. Participants carry the image of the Señor de la Columna to the church of San Juan de Dios in San Miguel. Inside, the sanctuary has six chapels and is vibrant with statues, folk murals and paintings. Traditional dances are held here on the third Sunday in July. The church was named a Unesco World Heritage site in 2008.

From San Miguel, taxis charge around M$120 to M$150 for a one-way trip. Local buses signed 'Atotonilco' or 'Cruz del Palmar' depart from Calzada de La Luz every hour on the half hour (M$10, 45 minutes).

El Liceo de la Lengua Española
LANGUAGE

(☑415-121-25-35; www.liceodelalengua.com; Callejón del Pueblito 5) A small, centrally located and extremely professional Spanish school, where classes never exceed five pupils.

Academia Hispano Americana
LANGUAGE

(☑415-152-03-49; www.academiahispanoamericana.com; Mesones 4) Housed in a beautiful colonial building, this place runs quality immersion courses in the Spanish language and incorporates history classes.

Warren Hardy Spanish
LANGUAGE

(☑415-154-40-17; www.warrenhardy.com; San Rafael 6) An American-run school offering Spanish instruction including its own range of printed learning materials, Warren Hardy Spanish is a favorite among local expats of a mature age.

⟳ Tours

★ Bookatour
TOURS

(☑415-152-01-98; www.bookatour.mx; Codo 1; ⏱9am-6:30pm Mon-Fri, to 3pm Sun) Offers a range of walking tours with bilingual guides, including illuminating three-hour strolls around San Miguel (US$40), arts and crafts tours (US$120), cantina 'crawls' (US$35 per person) and hot-air-balloon rides (US$175 per person). Prices are the same for up to three people and include transportation. Also offers rental cars, the only place in San Miguel to do so.

★ Bici-Burro
CYCLING

(☑415-152-15-26; www.bici-burro.com; Hospicio 1; trips US$70-120) Friendly and professional, English-speaking owner Alberto conducts 11 different guided mountain-bike tours for groups of two or more. Popular trips include six- or seven-hour excursions to Atotonilco or Mineral de Pozos and a wonderful 'mezcal tour' that takes in a number of haciendas. Bike rental is also available (US$45 per day), as are hiking tours.

Historical Walking Tour of San Miguel de Allende
WALKING

(☑415-152-77-96; www.historicalwalkingtour.org; Jardín Allende; M$300) This excellent tour takes place every Monday, Wednesday and Friday at 10am, departing from El Jardín. Tickets go on sale at 9:45am; be sure to allow good time as tours leave promptly. The English-speaking volunteer guides provide a fascinating historical, architectural and cultural commentary on the town's sights. Specialized architecture and private tours are also available.

Xotolar Ranch Adventures
HORSEBACK RIDING

(☑415-154-62-75; www.xotolarranch.com; rides from US$95) Xotolar Ranch Adventures, based on a working ranch, specializes in canyon trail rides, which can be booked as half- or full-day excursions. One tour involves riding to the pyramid of Cañada de la Virgen (US$145 per person; p676).

⚔️ Festivals & Events

San Miguel boasts a surfeit of churches (over 40) and patron saints (it has six) and enjoys a multitude of festivals, many imbued with strong spiritual themes. You'll probably be alerted to a festival event by firework bursts, while parades seem to be an almost weekly occurrence. For a full list, check with the tourist office (p674) or its website: www.visit sanmiguel.travel.

Semana Santa   RELIGIOUS

(⊙ Mar/Apr) A week of religious activities. Two Sundays before Easter, pilgrims carry an image of the Señor de la Columna from Atotonilco, 11km north, to San Miguel's church of San Juan de Dios, departing at midnight on Saturday. During Semana Santa, activities include the solemn Procesión del Santo Entierro on Good Friday and the burning or exploding of Judas effigies on Easter Day.

Fiesta de la Santa Cruz   FIESTA

(⊙ late May) This deeply spiritual spring festival has its roots in the 16th century. It happens at Valle del Maíz, 2km from the town center. Oxen are dressed in lime necklaces and painted tortillas and their yokes are festooned with flowers and fruit. A mock battle between 'Indians' and 'Federales' follows. There are *mojigangas* (giant puppets), dancing and musicians, plus 96 hours of fireworks.

Fiesta de los Locos   RELIGIOUS

(⊙ mid-Jun) Part of the Festividad de San Antonio de Padua in mid-June, the 'festival of the crazies' is a colorful Carnavalesque parade through town with floats, blaring music and costumed dancers throwing out candy to – sometimes at! – the crowd. It takes place on the first Sunday after June 13.

San Miguel Arcángel   RELIGIOUS

(Jardín Allende; ⊙ Sep) Celebrations honoring the town's chief patron saint are held around the weekend following September 29. The party is celebrated with an *alborada,* an artificial dawn created by thousands of fireworks around the cathedral, and turns into an all-night festivity with extraordinary pre-Hispanic dances.

Guanajuato International Film Festival   FILM

(GIFF; www.giff.mx; ⊙ Jul) Shared with the city of Guanajuato, this short-film festival in July was founded with the intention of promoting homegrown cinema production, something it's done to great acclaim. Events include Cine entre Muertos, where horror films are screened in graveyards.

🛏️ Sleeping

Accommodations are often full during festivals and high season, so make reservations well in advance. Thanks to a couple of recent hostel additions, the city now boasts accommodations for all budgets. In the higher budget ranges, San Miguel has some of Mexico's best luxury B&Bs, boutique hotels and guesthouses.

Hostal Punto 79   HOSTEL $

(☎ 415-121-10-34; www.punto79.com; Mesones 79; dm M$180-210, r from M$780; 🛜) This centrally located sprawling spot touts itself as a hotel-hostel, but the hostel rooms are far better value. The dorm rooms are segregated for male and female guests and are a decent place to bed down, especially if you're on a budget. There are few facilities (and no breakfast), but you're bang in the middle of town.

Hostal Alcatraz   HOSTEL $

(☎ 415-152-85-43; www.facebook.com/alcatrazhostal; Reloj 54; dm incl breakfast from M$235; 🛜) This centrally located hostel has simple but perfectly serviceable dorms and a shared kitchen, even if it is a bit short on bathrooms. The included breakfast is excellent.

Hostel Inn   HOSTEL $

(☎ 415-154-67-27; www.hostelinnmx.com; Calzada de La Luz 31A; dm M$180-250, s M$580, r without bathroom M$550-750, all incl breakfast; 🛜) This functional converted house offers dorms and simple fan-cooled private rooms, a kitchen for guests to use, cheap laundry services and a small back garden with grassy lawns and a pleasant common area. It's on a busy main road, but most of the rooms don't look over the street.

Casa Carly   APARTMENT $$

(☎ 415-152-89-00; www.casacarly.com; Calzada de la Aurora 48; s/d/q incl breakfast M$1200 /1600/1800; ⊙ Jul-May; ❄️🛜) Part of a former hacienda, the seven delightful rooms surrounding this wonderfully secluded garden are all individually decorated in tasteful, brightly colored Mexican designs. Those with kitchenettes provide great alternatives for longer-term stays, while the charming garden, complete with pond and fountains, is a welcome oasis from the town outside.

★ Rosewood
San Miguel de Allende   HERITAGE HOTEL **$$$**
(☑ 415-152-97-00; www.rosewoodhotels.com/
en/san-miguel-de-allende; Nemesio Diez 11; r/ste
incl breakfast from M$11,750/17,300; ☯ ✳ 🛜 🏊)
San Miguel's most exclusive and impres-
sive address, the Rosewood is a magnifi-
cent palace of a place, where seamless ser-
vice, gorgeous classically decorated rooms
and fairly staggering levels of opulence
combine to create the ultimate weekend
address. There's a great pool, beautiful
manicured gardens and a rooftop bar with
dizzying views over the domes and hills of
San Miguel.

★ Casa de la Noche   GUESTHOUSE **$$$**
(☑ 415-152-07-32; www.casadelanoche.com; Orga-
nos 19; r incl breakfast US$100-160; ✳ 🛜) This
fascinating former brothel wears its history proudly and owner Barbara will tell you
interesting stories about past employees,
whose photographs adorn the walls and
some of whose descendants work as staff at
the hotel to this day. Despite its racy origins,
the hotel today is a model of respectability,
popular with artists and writers.

Rooms vary enormously in layout and
size, but are all comfortable and cozy with
underfloor heating. Guests can use the
shared kitchen and the generous communal
areas. A restaurant is planned.

★ Antigua Capilla   BOUTIQUE HOTEL **$$$**
(☑ 415-152-40-48; www.antiguacapilla.com; Callejon
Chepitos 16; r incl breakfast US$175-200; 🅿 ☯ 🛜)
Constructed around a tiny 17th-century chapel, this utterly stylish, spick-and-span place is
hard to fault; it boasts every mod con and service imaginable plus extraordinary breakfasts
and a gorgeous plant-lined courtyard. The
English- and Spanish-speaking owners are
delightful. Access is up a hill, but the rooftop
terrace affords one of the best views in San
Miguel. Excellent price-to-quality ratio.

Hotel Matilda   BOUTIQUE HOTEL **$$$**
(☑ 415-152-10-15; www.hotelmatilda.com; Aldama 53; r incl breakfast from US$410; ✳ 🛜 🏊) A
slice of thoroughly modern luxury makes a
striking contrast to the rest of San Miguel's
staunchly colonial accommodations, but it
works well here. Almost everything is white,
including the sleek and understatedly fabulous rooms. There's an infinity pool, spa and
popular bar-restaurant too, where a great
continental breakfast is served.

Art, including a copy of Diego Rivera's
1940s portrait of Matilda Stream (the American hotel owner's mother), is displayed
throughout the property.

Casa Florida   BOUTIQUE HOTEL **$$$**
(☑ 415-154-81-95; www.casafloridasma.com; Macias 60; r incl breakfast US$130-170; ✳ 🛜) Muted
tones and subtle design choices define this
ultra-attractive, intimate boutique hotel in
the heart of San Miguel. The four rooms
vary in size, but all are delightful and feature plush pillows and locally made throws.
There's a shared roof terrace, and the pent-
house even has its own private one. Uncom-
monly for such a place, guests can use the
kitchen. Prices increase by about 30% on
weekends.

Dos Casas   BOUTIQUE HOTEL **$$$**
(☑ 415-154-40-73; www.doscasas.com.mx; Quebrada 101; d incl breakfast from US$210; ☯ ✳ 🛜)
This sleek sleep oozes contemporary style
with its cream and black hues, fireplaces and private terraces. Twelve stunning
rooms across two adjoining properties provide a touch of avant-garde luxury overseen
by its architect owner. There's a spa, plus
the restaurant Áperi (p673) in the courtyard, which is easily a culinary highlight of
the region.

Casa de la Cuesta   B&B **$$$**
(☑ 415-154-43-24; www.casadelacuesta.com;
Cuesta de San José 32; r incl breakfast US$180;
☯ 🛜) Perched on a hill behind the Mercado
El Nigromante, this ornate and deeply Mexican place has spacious rooms in a decorative colonial mansion, lavish breakfasts and
friendly, knowledgable owners. Minimum
stay of two nights.

🍴 Eating
San Miguel has a superb eating scene showcasing a startling variety of quality Mexican
and international cuisine, and has repeatedly
proven its reputation as one of Mexico's leading culinary capitals. A thriving cafe society
prevails and gorgeous bakeries proliferate.
For budget bites, several reliable food stands
are on the corner of Ancha de San Antonio
and tree-shaded Calle Nemesio Diez.

Tacos Don Felix   TACOS **$**
(www.tacosdonfelix.com; Fray Juan de San Miguel 15;
tacos M$25-40, mains M$70-200; ☺ 6pm-midnight
Fri & Sat, 2-9:30pm Sun) An opportunity to get
off the tourist trail presents itself at this

pleasantly local establishment in the Colonia of San Rafael, a short way outside the center. Delicious tacos and friendly service await you either in the shady courtyard or the surprisingly large main restaurant. Take a taxi after dark.

Baja Fish Taquito   TACOS $
(☑ 415-121-09-50; Mesones 11B; tacos M$25-40, set meals M$80-120; ☺ 11:30am-8pm; ☎) You'll find extraordinarily solicitous staff here at this fabulous little joint specializing in mind-blowingly good Baja-style fish tacos and *tostadas*. While it may not look like much downstairs where you can sit at the counter and watch the tacos being made, there's also a lovely upstairs terrace with good views of San Miguel's rooftops.

La Mesa Grande   BAKERY $
(☑ 415-154-08-38; www.lamesagrande.com; Zacateros 149; breakfasts M$50-100, pizzas M$90-130; ☺ 8am-5pm Mon-Thu, to 10pm Fri, 9am-5pm Sat; ☎) An American-run contemporary *panadería*-cafe with excellent pastries, great breakfasts, tasty salads, and wood-fired oven pizzas that you can design yourself. The large communal table of the name is a great place for neighborly chats, and the entire place is something of a meeting point for locals.

El Manantial   BAR, CANTINA $
(Barranca 78; tacos M$85-95 tostadas M$40-60; ☺ 1pm-1am Tue-Sun) Behind the swinging doors of a former saloon, 'The Spring' serves fabulously fresh ceviche in a dark and rather loud space with a cantina feel. It has a real buzz compounded by habanero salsa, the spiciest of chili sauces, and even though the staff can be somewhat surly, it's nearly always packed full. Try their ginger margaritas (M$65).

San Agustín   CAFE $
(☑ 415-154-91-02; San Francisco 21; snacks M$30-80, mains M$70-180; ☺ 8am-11pm Mon-Thu, 9am-midnight Fri-Sun) This is a 'don't leave San Miguel without...' experience. This sweet-tooth's paradise is the best place in Mexico for chocolate and *churros* (doughnut-like fritters), though you'll often have to wait in line just to get inside. Most people seem to think that it's well worth it, however.

★ Vía Orgánica   MEXICAN $$
(www.viaorganica.org; Ledesma 2; mains M$120-200; ☺ 8am-9pm; ☎🅟) 🌿 This fantastic and pioneering spot has won the hearts of well-to-

do San Miguelense expats thanks to its wonderful menu of Mexican food with an international twist (try a sage-seasoned turkey burger or the vegetarian lasagna). The shop sells locally sourced organic food and also offers free workshops every Thursday on subjects including agriculture and healthy eating.

★ Lavanda   CAFE $$
(Macías 87; ☺ 8:30am-4pm Mon-Sat, to 2pm Sun; ☎🅟) 🌿 A guitarist strums away during super-popular breakfasts – get there at opening time or be prepared to queue – at this lovely place where killer coffee, superb egg dishes and delicious *cazuelas* are served. The charming premises are divided into two: one high-ceilinged dining room and one garden courtyard.

★ La Parada   PERUVIAN $$
(☑ 415-152-04-73; www.laparadasma.com; Recreo 94; mains M$105-250; ☺ noon-10pm, Wed-Sat, to 9pm Sun & Mon; ☎) This hot spot showcases Peruvian cuisine at its best. Dish presentation is as exquisite as the names ('El Quiquiriquí,' aka chicken breast and 'Chino Cochino' pork, but much fancier). The ubiquitous (and delicious) ceviche is superb. The owners are young, hip and, most importantly, passionate chefs. Vegetarians can enjoy the 'veggie muncher' (M$105) – an elaborate grilled zucchini sandwich. Reservations essential.

Muro   MEXICAN $$
(☑ 415-152-63-41; www.cafemuro.com; Cerrada de San Gabriel 1; M$130-195; ☺ 9am-4pm Thu-Tue; ☎) Now in its fabulous new premises a short walk from Centro, Muro serves up everything from *chilaquiles con arrachera* to french toast and pastries, plus fabulous freshly made juices, which combine to make it an awesome breakfast spot. Local ingredients are used where possible and the ultra-professional and friendly owners ensure you'll receive a warm welcome.

Café Rama   BAR, RESTAURANT $$
(☑ 415-154-96-55; www.cafe-rama.com; Nemesio Diez 7; mains M$165-290; ☺ 8am-midnight Tue-Sun; ☎🅟) This cool cafe-bar-gallery comprises two separate rooms that are lovingly furnished with quirky antiques and eclectic curios, plus cozy couches near the open fireplace. It's changing menu proffers excellent international dishes and is fearsomely popular, especially for breakfast, which is served daily until noon, and 1pm on the weekend. Try the curried mussels or the divine shrimp tacos.

Berlin
INTERNATIONAL **$$**

(📞415-152-94-32;   www.berlinmexico.com;
Umarán 19; mains M$130-385; ⏰5pm-late; 🛜)
This cool, artsy spot serves up some good
international feeds, including several hearty
German classics such as spätzle. There's
also an impressive range of steaks. The at-
mospheric and highly social bar is great for
a glamorous tipple.

★Nomada
MEXICAN **$$$**

(📞415-121-91-63;   http://nomada-cocina.mx;
Macias 88; mains M$70-180; ⏰1-10pm Mon-Sat;
🛜📶) This gorgeous place with friendly
English-speaking staff serves up some of
San Miguel's best contemporary Mexican cuisine. Try its sublime pork-belly
tacos, cactus salad with charred avocado
or octopus tortilla with salsa verde, locally sourced cheese and cilantro. There's a
highly recommended four-course tasting
menu (M$350) served on Monday and
Wednesday only.

★Áperi
INTERNATIONAL **$$$**

(📞415-152-09-41; www.aperi.mx; Dos Casas,
Quebrada 101; 5-course tasting menu with/without
wine pairing M$1200/900, mains M$360-480;
⏰2-4pm & 6:30-10:30pm Wed-Mon; 📶) This
courtyard restaurant inside a boutique
hotel is perhaps the best spot in town for
fine dining. The chef here has been given
the freedom to do whatever he wants and a
regularly changing menu featuring the likes
of duck, pork and seafood dishes, prepared
with San Miguelense ingredients, is the re-
sult. Farm-to-table cuisine has never looked
so glamorous.

The Chef's Table – a multicourse tast-
ing menu for two to five people – starts
at 6:30pm (by reservation). If you want to
loosen the purse strings, this is the place
to do it.

The Restaurant
INTERNATIONAL **$$$**

(📞415-154-78-77;   www.therestaurantsanmiguel.
com; Diez de Sollano 16; mains M$245-480;
⏰noon-10pm Sun, Tue & Wed, to 11pm Thu-Sat)
This fine-dining establishment set within a
patio of a colonial building boasts a thoroughly international menu with occasional
Mexican influences, and features seasonal,
organic produce inventively combined to
sublime effect. Try the duck tacos or the
sweet-corn risotto with *huitlacoche* (corn
fungus) for a memorable meal.

🍷 Drinking & Nightlife

In San Miguel, drinking and entertainment
are often synonymous. Many bars (and restaurants) host live music. Most of the action
is on Thursday to Saturday nights, but some
places have live music nightly. Calle Umarán
has plenty of bars.

La Mezcalería
BAR

(Correo 47; ⏰5-11pm) It's mezcal-mania time
in San Miguel and this cool bar, where you
can get your tongue around a mighty mix
of mezcals from Oaxaca, plus good tapas
plates, is a local favorite. Don't miss the superb mezcal margarita.

Mama Mía
CLUB

(www.mamamia.com.mx; Umarán 8; ⏰8am-
midnight Sun-Thu, to late Fri & Sat) This perenni-
ally popular place has separate areas for differing entertainment purposes; hit Mama's
Bar for live rock/funk on Fridays and Saturdays (or karaoke on weeknights), or join a
more sophisticated crowd in the restaurant
patio for live folk music. Up front, Bar Leonardo's shows big-screen sports and La Ter-
razza, the terrace bar, offers a fine view of
the town. The joint gets going by 11pm.

La Azotea
BAR

(Umarán 6) This roof-terrace cocktail lounge
is a gay-friendly, laid-back place with a
young and smart crowd; it's a top spot for
sundowners.

El Café de la Mancha
CAFE

(www.facebook.com/elcafedelamancha; Recreo
21A; ⏰9am-6pm Mon-Fri, 10am-6pm Sat; 🛜)
Just larger than a hole-in-the-wall, this
is the place for coffee snobs. Need we say
more. The trained owner-barista does magic with his Mexican beans and adopts every
extraction method known to coffee culture
(French press, chemex, aeropress, espresso).

☆ Entertainment

It's one big cultural party in San Miguel;
check out what's on in *Atención San Miguel.*
The Escuela de Bellas Artes (p666) and the
Biblioteca (in the Sala Quetzal) host a variety of cultural events, many in English; check
their noticeboards for schedules.

Teatro Ángela Peralta
THEATER

(📞415-152-22-00; http://teatro.sanmigueldeal
lende.gob.mx; cnr Calles Mesones & Hernández
Macías) Built in 1873, this elegant venue
is the most impressive in town and hosts

local productions, classical-music concerts and other cultural events. The ticket office is around the corner. Tickets cost between M$50 and M$500 depending on the production.

Shopping

San Miguel has a mind-boggling number of craft shops, selling folk art and handicrafts from all over the country. Anyone serious about buying should book an appointment at the excellent **Galeria Atotonilco** (☑ 415-185-22-25; www.folkartsanmiguel.com; Camino Antiguo Ferrocarril 14, El Cortijo; ☺ by appointment only). Local crafts include tinware, wrought iron, silver, brass, leather, glassware, pottery and textiles. Many shops are along Canal, San Francisco, Zacateros and Pila Seca. Price and quality varies widely.

Arts & Crafts

Part of the joy of wandering around San Miguel is to stumble upon the many galleries tucked away in streets around town; there are more commercial galleries than cafes (and perhaps even real-estate agents) in San Miguel. The largest concentration of contemporary art galleries and design studios (mainly expatriates' work) is housed in the trendy **Fábrica La Aurora** (☑ 415-152-13-12; www.fabricalaaurora.com; Aurora s/n; ☺ 10am-6pm), a remodeled raw-cotton factory on the north end of town.

Markets

An interesting excursion is the famous **Tianguis** (☺ 7am–6pm Tue), a huge outdoor affair beside the Soriana shopping center, 2.5km southeast of the center on the Querétaro road. Here you'll find a fantastic choice of fresh produce as well as lots of lurid plastic goods, though some may find the scale and crowds overwhelming. More centrally, **Mercado El Nigromante** (Colegio s/n; ☺ 8am-8pm) sells fruit, vegetables and other foodstuffs. A rather upmarket alternative to both is **TOSMA** (www.tosma.net; Ancha de San Antonio 32; ☺ 9am-4pm Sat), which runs all day Saturday in a lot off the Ancha de San Antonio and where you can find artisanal products, souvenirs and food stands.

Information

Don't even contemplate spending time in town without buying the weekly English- and Spanish-language newspaper *Atención San Miguel* (M$15). Published every Friday, it's chockablock with what's on for the coming week, including tours, concerts and gallery openings. It also lists yoga, Spanish, art and dance class schedules. You can buy it at the public library and many cafes or from roaming vendors.

Most banks have their own ATMs and are located on, or within two blocks of, El Jardín. There are also *casas de cambio* (money changers) on Correo.

The main **post office** (cnr Correo & Corregidora; ☺ 8am-6pm Mon-Sat) can be found just off the Jardín, although for sending handicrafts or art home, it's better to use a delivery service such as **La Unión** (☑ 415-185-92-00; www.launionsanmiguel.com; Pila Seca 13; ☺ 9am-6pm Mon-Sat).

H+ San Miguel de Allende (☑ 415-152-59-00; www.hmas.mx/sanmiguel; Libramiento Jose Manuel Zavala 12) is your best bet for modern medical care and English-speaking doctors should you have a medical emergency.

Tourist Office (☑ 415-152-09-00; www.visitsanmiguel.travel; Plaza Principal 8; ☺ 9am-8pm Mon-Fri, 10am-8pm Sat, to 6pm Sun) is on the northern side of El Jardín. Good for maps of the town, promotional pamphlets and information on events.

Getting There & Away

AIR

Local debate rages about the small local airport planned by San Miguel's authorities, many fearing that its construction will change the city forever. In the meantime, the nearest airport is the Aeropuerto Internacional de Guanajuato (p660), between León and Silao, around 1½ hours away by car. The obvious alternatives are Querétaro or Mexico City's airports.

BUS

The Central de Autobuses is on Canal (Calzada de la Estación), 3km west of the center. Second-class services (Coordinados/Flecha Amarilla and Herradura de Plata) also leave from this station. Other 1st-class buses serve Aguascalientes, Monterrey and San Luis Potosí.

CAR & MOTORCYCLE

The only San Miguel–based car-hire agency is Bookatour (p669). Prices start at about M$750 per day including insurance. Most of the bigger agencies are in Guanajuato or Bajío Airport.

Getting Around

TO/FROM THE AIRPORT

Many agencies provide shuttle transportation to/from Guanajuato airport. These include **Viajes Vertiz** (☑ 415-152-18-56; www.facebook.com/viajesvertiz; Hidalgo 1; ☺ 9am-6:30pm

BUSES FROM SAN MIGUEL DE ALLENDE

DESTINATION	FARE (M$)	DURATION (HR)	FREQUENCY (DAILY)
Celaya	60	1¾	every 15min
Dolores Hidalgo	53	1	every 40min 7am-7pm
Guadalajara	590-680	5¼-5½	4 daily
Guanajuato	113-175	1-1½	hourly
León	224	2¼-2½	12 daily
Mexico City (Terminal Norte)	328	3½-4¼	8 daily
Querétaro	74	1-1½	every 40min 7am-8:30pm

Mon-Fri, 10am-2pm Sat), **Viajes San Miguel** (☑ 415-152-25-37; www.viajessanmiguel.com; Mesones 38, Interior 7; ⊗ 9am-7pm Mon-Fri, 10am-2pm Sat), **Bajío Go** (☑ 415-152-19-99; www.bajiogo.com; Jésus 11; ⊗ 8am-8pm Mon-Sat, 10am-3pm Sun) and **Bookatour** (p669). Alternatively, take a bus to Silao and get a taxi from there to the airport (around M$60). For Mexico City airport, get a bus to Querétaro and a bus direct to the airport from there.

If heading from the airport to San Miguel by bus, it's easiest to go to León by taxi and take a bus from there. No bus service operates between Guanajuato airport and central León. A taxi to León costs M$380 and to San Miguel M$1200 (for up to four people).

TO/FROM THE BUS STATION

Local buses (M$6) run from 7am to 9pm daily. 'Central' buses run regularly between the bus station and the town center. Coming into town these terminate at the eastern end of Insurgentes after winding through the streets. Heading out of the center, you can pick one up on Canal. A taxi between the center and the bus station costs around M$40; trips around town cost around M$35.

Mineral de Pozos

☑ 442 / POP 3500

Less than a century ago, Mineral de Pozos was a flourishing silver-mining center of 70,000 people, but with the 1910 Revolution and the flooding of the mines, the population dwindled. Empty houses, a large and unfinished church and discarded mine shafts were the legacy of abandonment. Today this tiny place is gradually winning back its place on the map. Visitors can explore the crumbling buildings and tour the fascinating surrounds – including several mine ruins – by mountain bike, horse or guided tour. As well as galleries, many craft shops are dotted around town, where community members sell their work.

🏃 Activities

Be sure to explore beyond the Jardin Juarez and head up the hill to Plaza Zaragoza and down the hill to Plaza Mineros. The mines are all located outside the town itself and are best visited on a guided tour, which can be arranged through Cinco Señores.

Cinco Señores TOURS
(☑ 468-106-06-35, 468-103-06-50; mineral-de-pozos@outlook.com; Juárez; M$150 per tour; ⊗ 11am-6pm Sat & Sun) This certified tour agency is the best in town. It offers guided tours of one (M$150) or two (M$220) mining haciendas, including transportation, entrances fees and a guided tour through the mineshaft. It also provides helmets for all participants. Find them on Mineral de Pozos' main square.

🛏 Sleeping & Eating

★**Posada de las Minas** BOUTIQUE HOTEL $$
(☑ 442-293-02-13; www.posadadelasminas.com; Doblado 1; r incl breakfast M$1000-1800; 🅿) This beautifully restored 19th-century hacienda offers ornate rooms and apartments complete with Mexican ceramics and antique furnishings. The 'Santa Brigida' room has corner windows with views over town, and many others have balconies. It has a bar and restaurant, an impressive cactus garden and charming staff.

El Secreto B&B $$
(☑ 442-293-02-00; www.elsecretomexico.com; Jardín Principal 4; r incl breakfast from M$1500; 🅿🐾) On the plaza, this small B&B nestled in a lovely garden featuring cacti, flowers and birds aplenty has three elegant rooms. Pets are welcome.

NORTHERN CENTRAL HIGHLANDS MINERAL DE POZOS

WORTH A TRIP

CAÑADA DE LA VIRGEN

Cañada de la Virgen is an intriguing pre-Hispanic pyramid complex and former ritual and ceremonial location, dating from around AD 300 and in use until around 1050. Bones, believed to be from sacrificial ceremonies, and remnants were discovered here. The most interesting aspects include the alignment of the main temple to the planets, and the design of the site, which reflects the surrounding landscape.

The **site** (M$50; ☉10am-4pm Tue-Sun) is around 25km southeast of San Miguel: possibly the easiest and most rewarding visit for non-Spanish speakers is to take a tour with **Coyote Canyon Adventures** (☑415-154-41-93; www.coyotecanyonadventures.com; rides per person half-/full-day from M$1550/2450, 4-person minimum). The guides include archaeologists and anthropologists who discuss the site's fascinating cultural and historical context. A shuttle bus is the compulsory transportation for visitors at the site. It runs between the office and the ruins (several kilometers away); these depart on the hour between 10am and 4pm and cost M$30. The tours are in Spanish. Wear sensible shoes as you'll be walking on cobbled surfaces and steep steps.

★**La Cantina Mina**   MEXICAN $$
(www.posadadelasminas.com; Doblado 1; mains M$100-175; ☉8:30am-9pm Sun-Thu, to 11pm Fri & Sat; 🛜) This wonderful patio restaurant around a small fountain inside the Posada de las Minas is the best place for a leisurely meal in Mineral de Pozos. The menu is sophisticated and delicious and includes dishes such as coconut shrimp with pineapple sauce and a salmon burger, as well as Mexican classics, such as a show-stopping *queso fundido* (melted cheese).

Shopping

Casa del Venado Azul   MUSIC
(☑468-117-03-87; azulvenado@hotmail.com; Calle Centenario 34; ☉10am-6pm) Among Mexico's folk instrument makers, shop owner Luis Cruz stands out. The accomplished musician heads his own musical ensemble, which tours internationally. The location doubles as a budget **hotel** (r M$500-600).

❶ Getting There & Away

If you have your own wheels, Mineral de Pozos is a one-hour trip from San Miguel de Allende. Alternatively, the easiest way to get to Pozos is with Bookatour (p669). Its five-hour trips cost US$45 per person (minimum three). Alternatively, Bici-Burro (p669) offers day-long bike tours to the town and mines.

Unfortunately, by bus (from San Miguel de Allende or Querétaro) it will take the best part of a day to get to this backwater: you must go first to Dolores Hidalgo, then to San Luis de la Paz (14km north of Pozos, a detour east of Hwy 57) and then take a third bus to Pozos, making it a real slog.

AGUASCALIENTES STATE

POP 1.2 MILLION

The state of Aguascalientes is one of Mexico's smallest and its focus is squarely on the city of the same name. According to local legend, a kiss planted on the lips of dictator Antonio López de Santa Anna by the wife of a prominent local politician brought about the creation of a separate Aguascalientes state from neighboring Zacatecas.

Beyond the museum-rich capital city formal tourist sites are few, but it's a pleasant-enough drive en route to or from Zacatecas, through fertile lands of corn, beans, chilies, fruit and grain. The state's ranches produce beef cattle as well as bulls that are sacrificed at bullfights countrywide.

Aguascalientes

☑449 / POP 935,000 / ELEV 1880M

This prosperous industrial city is home to more than half the state's population. Despite its messy outskirts, which are defined by ring roads and the kind of urban sprawl you'll find on the outskirts of almost all cities in Mexico, at its heart is a fine plaza and several blocks of handsome colonial buildings. Museums are its strong point: the Museo Nacional de la Muerte justifies a visit in itself, as do those devoted to José Guadalupe Posada and Saturnino Herrán. If you're passing through the state, its pleasant capital is worth stopping in for lunch or even overnight if you're not in a hurry.

History

Before the Spanish arrived, a labyrinth of catacombs was built here; the first Spaniards called it La Ciudad Perforada (The Perforated City). Archaeologists understand little of the tunnels and unfortunately they are off-limits to visitors.

Conquistador Pedro de Alvarado arrived in 1522, but was driven back by the Chichimecs. A small garrison was founded here in 1575 to protect Zacatecas–Mexico City silver convoys. Eventually, as the Chichimecs were pacified, the region's hot springs sparked the growth of a town; a large tank beside the Ojo Caliente springs helped irrigate local farms that fed hungry mining districts nearby.

Today the city's industries include textiles, wine, brandy, leather, preserved fruits and car manufacturing.

◉ Sights

★ Museo Nacional de la Muerte   MUSEUM

(www.museonacionaldelamuerte.uaa.mx; Jardín del Estudiante s/n; adult/student M$20/10, Tue free; ⊙10am-6pm Tue-Sun) The excellent Museo Nacional de la Muerte exhibits all things relating to Mexico's favorite subject – death – from the skeleton La Catrina to historic artifacts and modern depictions. The contents – over 2500 items, drawings, literature, textiles, toys and miniatures – were donated to the Universidad Autónoma de Aguascalientes by collector and engraver, Octavio Bajonero Gil. Over 1200 are on display. They span several centuries, from Mesoamerican to contemporary artistic interpretations.

While a section on the funeral rites of children is a little harrowing – not to mention pictures of a dead Frida Kahlo elsewhere – otherwise the tone is kept surprisingly light. In the second to last room, look out for the (very) miniature crystal skull. It's believed to be from Aztec times and there are only two like it in the world. The upstairs gallery includes an interesting section on the different representations of death from countries around the world, and it becomes apparent that an obsession with the macabre is far from unique to Mexico. This wonderful place provides a colorful, humorous and insightful encounter and is easily a highlight of Aguascalientes.

Palacio de Gobierno   HISTORIC BUILDING

(Plaza de la Patria; ⊙8am-8:30pm Mon-Fri, to 2pm Sat & Sun) FREE On the south side of Plaza de la Patria, the red-and-pink stone Palacio de Gobierno is Aguascalientes' most noteworthy colonial building. Once the mansion of colonial baron Marqués de Guadalupe, it dates from 1665 and has a striking courtyard with two levels of murals. Noteworthy is the mural depicting the 1914 convention by the Chilean artist Osvaldo Barra. Barra, whose mentor was Diego Rivera, also painted the mural on the south wall, a compendium of the forces that forged Aguascalientes.

Museo José Guadalupe Posada   MUSEUM

(☑449-915-45-56; Jardín El Encino s/n; adult/student M$10/5, Sun free; ⊙11am-6pm Tue-Sun) Aguascalientes native José Guadalupe Posada (1852–1913) was in many ways the founder of modern Mexican art. His engravings and satirical cartoons broadened the audience for art in Mexico, highlighted social problems and were a catalyst in the later mural phase, influencing artists including Diego Rivera, José Clemente Orozco and Alfaro David Siqueiros. Posada's hallmark is the *calavera* (skull or skeleton) and many of his *calavera* engravings have been widely reproduced.

Museo de Aguascalientes   MUSEUM

(Zaragoza 505; adult/student M$10/5, free Sun; ⊙11am-6pm Tue-Sun) Housed in a handsome neoclassical building, this museum houses a permanent collection of work by the brilliant Aguascalientes artist Saturnino Herrán (1887–1918), and there are also temporary exhibitions. His works are some of the first to honestly depict the Mexican people. The sensual sculpture *Malgretout* on the patio is a fiberglass copy of the marble original by Jesús Fructuoso Contreras.

Catedral   CATHEDRAL

(Plaza de la Patria) The well-restored 18th-century baroque cathedral, on the plaza's west side, is more magnificent inside than out. Over the altar at the east end of the south aisle is a painting of the Virgin of Guadalupe by Miguel Cabrera. There are more works by Cabrera, colonial Mexico's finest artist, in the cathedral's *pinacoteca* (picture gallery), which is open at Easter only, though if you ask a priest, he might let you in.

Aguascalientes

Aguascalientes

Museo Regional de Historia MUSEUM
(☑449-916-52-28; Av Carranza 118; adult M$50;
⊗9am-6pm Tue-Sun) This history museum
was designed by Refugio Reyes as a family
home and features a small chapel. Its exhibits run all the way from the big bang to
the colonial conquest. It also has a beautiful chapel with *ex voto* paintings and works

attributed to Correa. Anyone interested in Mexican history will appreciate these displays. There are also temporary exhibitions.

Templo del Encino CHURCH
(Jardín El Encino; ⊙7am-1pm & 6-9pm) This church contains a black statue of Jesus that some believe is growing. When it reaches an adjacent column, a worldwide calamity is anticipated. The huge *Way of the Cross* murals are also noteworthy.

Activities

★Baños Termales de Ojocaliente THERMAL BATHS
(☑449-970-07-21; Av Tecnológico 102; private baths per hour from M$420; ⊙8am-8pm) Despite the city's name, these beautifully restored and colorful thermal baths are the only ones near the center. The brightly tiled 1808 complex truly turns back the clock; the waters are said to help all sorts of ailments. The easiest way to get there is by taxi (around M$50).

Festivals & Events

Feria de San Marcos FAIR
(www.feriadesanmarcos.gob.mx; Expoplaza; ⊙mid-Apr) This is Mexico's biggest annual three- to four-week fair. It centers on Expoplaza and attracts thousands of visitors with exhibitions, bullfights, cockfights, rodeos, concerts and cultural events. The big parade takes place on the saint's day, April 25. The Feria is Aguascalientes' biggest event and at this time all accommodations are at a premium.

Festival de las Calaveras CULTURAL
(⊙Nov) During the 10-day Festival de las Calaveras (the dates vary but always encompass November 1 and 2), Aguascalientes celebrates Día de Muertos (Day of the Dead) with an emphasis on the symbolism of *calavera* – the edible or decorative skull so beloved by Mexicans at this time of year.

Sleeping

Aguascalientes has a decent range of accommodations suited to most budgets, and a couple of recently opened hostels have made it cheap for backpackers to stay here too. Note that prices skyrocket during the Feria de San Marcos in April and accommodations are always completely booked for the fair's final weekend; residents run a lucrative homestay service at this time.

Hostal La Vie en Rose HOSTEL $
(☑449-688-71-69, 437-479-24-00; lavieenrosehostal@gmail.com; Nieto 457; dm/d M$200/400; ☏) This friendly and good-value hostel has rather simple decor, but enjoys the odd pleasing vintage touch. Dorms are clean and share bathrooms, while double rooms have their own facilities. There's a foosball table, a good kitchen, a lounge area and a roof terrace with a bar, all of which combine to give the place a social vibe.

El Giro Hostel HOSTEL $
(☑449-917-93-93; www.elgirohostal.com; Ignacio Allende Oriente 341; dm from M$180) This colorful spot is the best hostel in town. It has rather tightly packed bunk rooms, but each has its own bathroom except one. There's also a kitchen, friendly staff and its location is excellent. Take bus 31 from the bus station and disembark at the corner of Calles Elizondo and Rayon.

Art Hotel BOUTIQUE HOTEL $$
(☑449-269-69-95, 449-917-95-95; Nieto 502; r weekdays/weekends M$650/1050; ✴☏) Housed in a brutalist concrete building and displaying plenty of its namesake art (including a rather striking bull in reception), this place is striking out to be memorable and rather neatly succeeds. Its comfortable and stylish rooms may rather lack natural light, but they are excellent value during the week, with prices spiking at the weekend. There is no breakfast.

Eating & Drinking

There are some decent and fairly varied eating options in Aguascalientes. Fresh produce and cheap eats are available in three markets: **Mercado Juárez** (Plazuela Juárez), **Mercado Jesús Terán** (Arteaga) and **Mercado Morelos** (Morelos), each of which is open daily from 7am to 7pm. Carranza is lined with eateries. Callejón del Codo is the place to go for small cafes and coffee.

★Mesa Verde CAFE $
(Elizondo 113; ⊙9:30am-5pm Mon, Wed-Fri, 10:30am-6pm Sat & Sun; ☏📶) This delightful find is a fabulous spot for a relaxed lunch, with its vegetarian-friendly *comida saludable* – health food – that is freshly made right in front of you. Artisanal beers are on the menu, as well as great coffee. There's also a roof terrace with wooden tables and a lovely vibe.

Rincón Maya
YUCATECAN $$

(Abasolo 113; mains M$100-200; ⊙ 2pm-midnight Mon-Sat, to 10:30pm Sun) Until lunchtime, this place has service at La Mestiza Yucateca (open 8am to 2pm), its alter ego next door. Both are located in a former hacienda and both serve delectable Yucatecan specialties.

Restaurant Mitla
MEXICAN $$

(Madero 220; mains M$75-230; ⊙ 7am-10pm, to 9pm Sun; 🛜) This large, pleasant and popular restaurant is caught in a time warp; specifically 1938, the year it opened. There are white-shirted waiters carrying silver trays, plus a grand menu with a choice of Mexican specialties, set breakfasts (from M$90) and buffet lunches (M$140).

Pulquería Posada
BAR

(La Pulque; Nieto 445; ⊙ 10am-2:30pm, 5:30-11pm Tue-Sun) Aguascalientes used to be renowned for its *pulque,* and this popular student hangout has reintroduced the tradition. It's fun and cheap, with a half-liter *jarra* (jug) of *pulque* (a traditional Aztec tipple made from fermented agave sap) costing M$20. There's also a good range of mezcals, flavored with everything from lime to guava.

☆ Entertainment

Aguascalientes has two theaters, **Teatro de Aguascalientes** (☑449-978-54-14; cnr Calles Chávez & Aguascalientes) and **Teatro Morelos** (☑449-915-19-41; Nieto 113, Plaza de la Patria), which stage a variety of cultural events.

Casa de la Cultura
ARTS CENTER

(☑449-910-20-10; Av Carranza 101) In a fine 17th-century building, the Casa de la Cultura hosts art exhibitions, concerts, theater and dance events.

🛍 Shopping

Casa de las Artesanías
ARTS & CRAFTS

(Nieto 210) This lovely Casa de las Artesanías showcases a range of stunning handicrafts made in the region, from local sweets to leather products (using the intricate *piteado* technique).

ℹ Information

Banks with ATMs are common around Plaza de la Patria and Expoplaza. *Casas de cambio* (money changers) cluster on Hospitalidad, opposite the post office.

Star Médica (☑449-910-99-00; www.star medica.com; Universidad 101)

State Tourist Office (☑449-910-20-88, ext 4300; www.aguascalientes.gob.mx; Palacio de Gobierno, Plaza de la Patria; ⊙ 9am-8pm Mon-Sat, 10am-5pm Sun)

ℹ Getting There & Away

AIR

Aéropuerto Internacional Jesús Terán (☑449-918-28-06) is 26km south of Aguascalientes off the highway to Mexico City. There are domestic flights from here to Mexico City and Monterrey, as well as direct services to Los Angeles, Houston and Dallas/Fort Worth.

BUS

The **bus station** (Central de Autobuses Aguascalientes; Av Convención) is 2km south of the center. It has several food outlets and luggage storage. Deluxe and 1st- and 2nd-class buses operate to/from Aguascalientes. Deluxe and 1st-class companies include ETN, Primera Plus, Futura and Ómnibus de México. The main 2nd-class line is Coordinados (Flecha Amarilla).

ℹ Getting Around

Most places of interest are within easy walking distance of each other. Regular city buses (M$6) run from 6am to 10pm. From the city center,

BUSES FROM AGUASCALIENTES

DESTINATION	FARE (M$)	DURATION (HR)	FREQUENCY (DAILY)
Guadalajara	255-310	2¾-3	frequent
Guanajuato	240	3	2 daily
León	180-240	2-3½	frequent
Mexico City (Terminal Norte)	470-680	6	frequent
Queretaro	395-550	5	frequent
San Luis Potosí	175-245	3-3½	hourly
Zacatecas	165-230	2	hourly

several buses head to the bus station from the corner **Galeana** (Galeana & Insurgentes; near Insurgentes).

Taxis charge as per metered fares. Between the bus station and the center the taxi fare is from around M$25 to M$30.

SAN LUIS POTOSÍ STATE

One of Mexico's most scenic and varied states, San Luis Potosí manages to charm all those who visit, whether it be with the enchanting green valleys, steep mountainsides and towering waterfalls of the Huasteca Potosina, or with its eponymous historic capital, the genteel colonial center of which looks more like a film set than the workaday medium-sized Mexican city it is. Elsewhere there's the fascinating 'ghost town' of Real de Catorce, the epic journey to which culminates in a long drive down a mildly terrifying tunnel through the mountainside: quite an unforgettable experience that is instantly rewarded by arrival in one of the most striking *pueblos mágicos* (magical villages) in Mexico. Finally, do not miss a trip to charming Xilitla, the nearest town to Edward James' epic sculpture garden of Las Pozas, a delightful dadaist treat complete with waterfalls and rushing streams flowing down the thickly forested hillside.

San Luis Potosí

🏅 444 / POP 762,000 / ELEV 1860M

A grand old dame of a colonial city, San Luis Potosí was once a revolutionary hotbed, an important mining town and a seat of government to boot. Today the city has maintained its poise as the prosperous state capital, orderly industrial center and university seat, though it sees relatively few visitors.

A great place to wander through, the city's historic core is made up of numerous plazas and manicured parks that are linked by attractive pedestrian streets. Although not as striking as Zacatecas or Guanajuato, and definitely lacking the magic of San Miguel de Allende, this lively city's cultural elegance is reflected in its delightful colonial architecture, impressive theater and numerous excellent museums.

History

Founded in 1592, San Luis is 20km west of the silver deposits in Cerro de San Pedro, and was named Potosí after the immensely rich Bolivian silver town, which the Spanish hoped it would rival. The mines began to decline in the 1620s, but the city was established enough as a ranching center to remain the major city of northeastern Mexico until overtaken by Monterrey at the start of the 20th century.

Known in the 19th century for its lavish houses and imported luxury goods, San Luis was twice the seat of President Benito Juárez's government during the 1860s French intervention. In 1910 in San Luis, the dictatorial president Porfirio Díaz jailed Francisco Madero, his liberal opponent, during the presidential campaign. Freed after the election, Madero hatched his Plan de San Luis Potosí (a strategy to depose Díaz), announcing it in San Antonio, Texas, in October 1910; he declared the election illegal, named himself provisional president and designated November 20 as the day for Mexico to rise in revolt – the start of the Mexican Revolution.

◎ Sights

★ Museo Federico Silva   MUSEUM
(www.museofedericosilva.org; Obregón 80; adult/student M$30/15, free Sun; ⊙10am-6pm Wed-Mon, to 2pm Sun) This excellent museum devoted to the work of Mexican artist Federico Silva (b 1923) should not be missed. The 17th-century building was once a hospital and later a school, but has been exquisitely transformed into a museum of sculpture, ingeniously integrating the building's previous neoclassical finish with the haunting monolithic sculptures of Silva.

As well as the permanent exhibition on the ground floor, the museum hosts high-quality temporary exhibitions of international sculptors upstairs.

Jardín de San Francisco (Jardín Guerrero)   PLAZA
Dominated by the bulk of the Templo de San Francisco (p683) and convent, and with a lovely fountain gracing its interior, this square is one of the city's most fetching.

Museo del Ferrocarril   MUSEUM
(Av Othón; M$25; ⊙9am-6pm Tue-Fri, 1-5pm Sat & Sun; 🚋) Once an important stop on two of Mexico's main train lines, San Luis Potosí

San Luis Potosí

San Luis Potosí

has cleverly brought the past to life in this excellent museum housed inside its glorious former train station, which dates from 1936. Don't miss the two murals by Fernando Leal (completed in 1943) that grace the station interior, or a wander through the old train carriages waiting by the platforms. Kids will love the miniature train ride that rings the museum (M$25).

Centro de las Artes Centenario
ARTS CENTER

(Antigua Penitenciaria; Calz de Guadalupe; M$20; ◷10am-2pm & 5-8pm Mon-Fri, 11am-5pm Sat & Sun) Up until 1999, this striking building was a prison believed to have briefly held Francisco Madero. Ten years later, it was transformed – without losing its fundamental design – into an arts and cultural center. Some of the former cells have been maintained; others have been converted into offices. It's a must visit for architects. At 5pm, 6pm and 7pm there are guided tours (in Spanish; tip the guides).

Museo Regional Potosino
MUSEUM

(Plaza de Aranzazú s/n; M$50, Sun free; ◷9am-6pm Tue-Sun) This fetching museum was originally part of a Franciscan monastery founded in 1590. The ground floor – part of which is housed in the small Capilla de San Antonio de Padua – has exhibits (predominantly pottery) of pre-Hispanic Mexico, especially the indigenous people of the Huasteca. Upstairs is the lavish, gold and aqua **Capilla de Aranzazú**, an elaborate private chapel constructed in the mid-18th century in Churrigueresque style. New monks were ordained here.

Templo del Carmen
CHURCH

(◷8am-1pm & 5-8pm) The Churrigueresque Templo del Carmen (1749–64) is San Luis's most spectacular structure. On the vividly carved stone facade, hovering angels show the touch of indigenous artisans. The Camarín de la Virgen, with a splendid golden altar, is to the left of the main altar inside. The entrance and roof of this chapel are a riot of small plaster figures.

Catedral
CATHEDRAL

(Plaza de Armas) FREE This impressive three-nave baroque cathedral was built between 1660 and 1730. Originally it had just one tower; the northern tower was added in the 20th century. The marble apostles on the facade are replicas of statues in Rome's St

Peter's Basilica. On the hour, the electronic bells, a more recent addition, ring out.

Museo Nacional de la Máscara
MUSEUM

(National Mask Museum; www.museonacionalde lamascara.com; Villerías 2; adult/student M$20/10, camera M$10; ◷10am-6pm Tue-Fri, to 5pm Sat, to 3pm Sun & Mon) This excellent museum displays a fascinating collection of ceremonial masks from across Mexico and around the world, and does a good job at explaining the evolution of pre-Columbian masks in Mexico. There are good descriptions in English and interesting videos of dances performed during community festivals.

Templo de San José
CHURCH

(Av Othón) Inside the Templo de San José, facing the Alameda's south side, lies the image of El Señor de los Trabajos, a Christ-like figure attracting pilgrims from near and far. Numerous *retablos* (altarpieces) around the statue testify to prayers answered in finding jobs and other miracles.

Plaza de los Fundadores
PLAZA

The least pretty of the plazas, Plaza de los Fundadores (Founders' Plaza) is where the city was born. On the north side is a large building constructed in 1653 as a Jesuit college. Today it houses offices of the Universidad Autónoma de San Luis Potosí.

Alameda
PARK

(Av Othón) The Alameda Juan Sarabia marks the eastern boundary of the downtown area. It used to be the vegetable garden of the monastery attached to the Templo del Carmen. Today it's a large, attractive park with shady paths.

Museo de Arte Contemporáneo
MUSEUM

(MAC; ☎444-814-43-63; www.macsanluispotosi. com; Morelos 235; adult/student M$20/10; ◷10am-6pm Tue-Sat, to 2pm Sun) This museum is housed in the city's former post office. These days the brilliantly transformed space houses temporary art exhibitions that change every three months.

Templo de San Francisco
CHURCH

(Jardín de San Francisco) The altar of the 17th- and 18th-century Templo de San Francisco was remodeled in the 20th century, but the sacristy (the priest's dressing room), reached by a door to the right of the altar, is original and has a fine dome and carved pink stone. The Sala De Profundis, through the arch at the south end of the sacristy, has more paintings and a carved stone fountain. A beautiful crystal ship hangs from the main dome.

Templo de la Tercera Orden & Templo del Sagrado Corazón   CHURCH

(Jardín de San Francisco) The small Templo de la Tercera Orden, built in 1694 and restored in 1960, and Templo del Sagrado Corazón (1728–31), both formerly part of the Franciscan monastery, stand together at the south end of Jardín de San Francisco.

Museo del Virreinato   MUSEUM

(www.museodelvirreinato.mx; Villerías 155; adult/student M$15/10, camera M$20; ⊙10am-7pm Tue-Sat, to 5pm Sun) Beside the Templo del Carmen (p683), this museum has a large collection of paintings and artifacts from the Spanish vice-regency. More of interest might be its temporary exhibitions – check what's on.

🗘 Tours

Operatour Potosina   TOURS

(☏444-151-22-01; www.operatourpotosina.com. mx; Hotel Napoles, Sarabia 120) This is the SLP-based tour operator most used to working with foreign tourists. It's run by friendly and knowledgable English-speaking Lori, who offers tours around the city, as well as to *haciendas,* Real de Catorce, Zacatecas and the Huasteca Potosina (minimum two people). Custom tours also available.

🎎 Festivals & Events

Semana Santa   RELIGIOUS

(⊙Mar/Apr) Holy Week is celebrated with concerts, exhibitions and other activities; on Good Friday at 3pm, Christ's passion is reenacted in the barrio of San Juan de Guadalupe, followed at 8pm by the Silent Procession through the city center (one of the city's most important events).

Feria Nacional Potosina   FAIR

(FENAPO; www.fenapo.mx; ⊙Aug) San Luis' National Fair, normally in the last three weeks of August, includes concerts, bullfights, rodeos, cockfights and agricultural shows.

Festival Internacional de Danza Contemporánea Lila López   DANCE

(www.facebook.com/festivalinternacionaldedanzacontemporanealilalopez; ⊙Jul) This wonderful annual national festival of contemporary dance is usually held on changing dates during July.

Día de San Luis Rey de Francia   RELIGIOUS

(⊙Aug 25) On August 25 the city's patron saint, St Louis IX, is honored as the highlight of the Feria Nacional. Events include a parade, concerts and plays.

🛏 Sleeping

Corazón de Xoconostle   HOSTEL $

(☏444-243-98-98; www.corazondexoconostle. com; 5 de May 1040; dm with shared bathroom M$190, r M$425-500; ☏) The best hostel in San Luis is this delightfully renovated house named after the flowering fruit of the *nopal* cactus. The hostel has good dorms with lockers, including one female-only dorm. There's also a kitchen where guests can prepare food, free use of laundry facilities, a roof terrace and a friendly atmosphere.

The downside is the bathroom shortage – it might keep you hopping on your feet at peak bathroom hours.

Hikuri Eco Hostal   HOSTEL $

(☏444-814-76-01; hikuriecohostal@gmail.com; Iturbide 980; dm M$175, r from M$500; ☏) A pleasantly converted house on the edge of the colonial old town, this fun place sets the tone by placing one end of a combi van in reception. Elsewhere there's a funky assortment of recycled furniture and simple but comfortable dorms and private rooms. The well-traveled Italian owner speaks several languages and ensures a social environment.

Hotel San Francisco   HOTEL $$

(www.sanfranciscohotel.mx; Universidad 375; r M$1030; P⊙❄☏) This converted historic building offers modern, business-style rooms that won't thrill anyone with their office-style furniture, but are perfectly clean and comfortable. Rooms at the front with external windows are susceptible to traffic noise, while interior rooms don't get the fresh air. But it's a good choice either way.

Hotel Panorama   BUSINESS HOTEL $$

(☏444-812-17-77, 800-480-01-00; www.hotel panorama.com.mx; Av Carranza 315; r/ste M$1050/1400; P❄❄☏⛱) It's the best of San Luis' rather average lot of midrange accommodations and has its position going for it – opposite Plaza de los Fundadores. Beyond that, it's smart(ish) and all 126 rooms have floor-to-ceiling windows; those on the south side overlook the pool and lovely garden. It's understandably popular with business travelers, though the welcome could be warmer.

HUICHOL VISIONS

The remote Sierra Madre Occidental, in and around the far north of Jalisco, is the home of the Huicholes, one of Mexico's most distinctive and enduring indigenous groups. A fiercely independent people, they were one of the few indigenous groups not subjugated by the Aztecs.

The arrival of the Spanish had little immediate effect on the Huicholes and it wasn't until the 17th century that the first Catholic missionaries reached the Huichol homelands. Rather than convert to Christianity, the Huicholes incorporated various elements of Christian teachings into their traditional animist belief systems. In Huichol mythology, gods become personalized as plants, totem animal species and natural objects, while their supernatural form is explored in religious rituals.

Every year the Huicholes leave their isolated homeland and make a pilgrimage to the Sierra de Catorce, in northern San Luis Potosí state. In this harsh desert region, they seek out the mezcal cactus (*Lophophora williamsii*), known as peyote cactus. The rounded peyote 'buttons' contain a powerful hallucinogenic drug (whose chief element is mescaline) that is central to the Huicholes' rituals and complex spiritual life.

The fact is that peyote is illegal in Mexico though many travelers seem intent on ignoring this. Under Mexican law, the Huicholes are permitted to use it for their spiritual purposes. For the Huicholes, indiscriminate use is regarded as offensive, even sacrilegious.

Traditionally the main Huichol art forms were telling stories and making masks and detailed geometric embroidery, or 'yarn pictures.' In the last few decades, brightly colored beads have replaced the yarn. This is painstaking work, where the beads are pressed into a beeswax-covered substrate. This exquisite artwork is sold in craft markets, shops and galleries. Prices are usually fixed and the Huicholes don't like to haggle. To see the best work, visit one of the specialist museums or shops in Zapopan (Guadalajara), Tepic, Puerto Vallarta or Zacatecas.

★ Hotel Museo Palacio de San Agustín

HISTORIC HOTEL **$$$**

(☏ 444-144-19-00; www.hotelmuseopalaciode sanagustin.com; Galeana 240; r from M$4000; P ☯ ❋ ☎) Formerly a house for retired monks of the nearby San Agustín monastery, this extraordinary property has been restored to its original condition, including hand-painted gold-leaf finishes, crystal chandeliers and 700 certified European antiques. Rooms are elaborately decorated in the style of the Mexican 19th-century upper classes, and feature gorgeous marble bathrooms complete with L'Occitane toiletries. One to splurge on.

✕ Eating & Drinking

There's a fairly ho-hum dining scene in San Luis, though don't miss the delightful Cafe Cortáo, perhaps the city's most enjoyable eatery. One local specialty to look out for is *tacos potosinos* – red, chili-impregnated tacos stuffed with cheese or chicken and topped with chopped potato, carrot, lettuce and loads of *queso blanco* (white cheese).

★ Cafe Cortáo

MEXICAN **$**

(Independencia 1150; mains M$45-85; ☯ 8:30am-1:30pm & 6:20-9:30pm Mon-Fri, 9:30am-1:30pm & 6:20-9:30pm Sat) This simple spot is our top pick as it's the perfect example of a fuss-free local that serves up lashings of quality Mexican meals to an appreciative crowd. All done with efficient service and a warm welcome from a charismatic owner. Don't miss the heavenly *huevo abolengo* (eggs on bread with a mushroom and manchego-cheese sauce).

Antojitos El Pozole

MEXICAN **$**

(cnr Calles Carmona & Arista; mains M$50-100; ☯ noon-11:30pm Tue-Sun) The is the place for the local *enchiladas potosinas* – the tortilla dough is red from chili. This place was started by a woman selling *antojitos* (Mexican snacks) in her home in the 1980s. Demand for her goods was so high she opened several restaurants specializing in what she knows best – *tacos rojos,* delicious *pozole* (hominy stew) and *quesadillas de papa* (potato quesadillas).

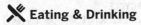

NORTHERN CENTRAL HIGHLANDS SAN LUIS POTOSÍ

La Oruga y La Cebada
INTERNATIONAL $$

(Callejón de Lozada 1; mains M$115-200; ⊙ noon-1am Tue-Sat, to 11pm Sun, to 10pm Mon; 🕾) 'The caterpillar and the barley' is a large and hugely popular restaurant divided between the downstairs dining room, dominated by a normally busy bar, and the upstairs roof terrace complete with retractable roof. There's a big menu that includes Mexican favorites as well as international dishes. The pizza is excellent, as is the craft beer.

Cielo Tinto
INTERNATIONAL $$

(✆ 444-814-00-40; www.cielotinto.com.mx; Carranza 700; mains M$140-295; ⊙ 8am-11:30pm) Generally held to be San Luis Potosí's best restaurant, the 'red sky' is an attractive upscale place housed in a renovated hacienda with a beautiful courtyard. The menu is international and runs from skilfully presented grilled dishes to Mexican standards. Good set breakfasts (M$90 to M$130).

La Gran Vía
SPANISH $$$

(✆ 444-812-28-99; www.lagranviaslp.com; Carranza 560; mains M$230-380; ⊙ 1pm-midnight Mon-Sat, 1-7pm Sun) Notes of expensive perfume mingle with the aromas of paella, *lechón asado* (roasted piglet) and cod fish – just a few of the dishes on this culinary institution's extensive menu. Great for a special meal out.

Callejon 7B
CRAFT BEER

(www.7barrios.com.mx; Universidad 153; ⊙ 6pm-1am Mon-Fri, 2pm-1am Sat & Sun) A hip bar named after the very beer it produces, Siete barrios, which is in turn named after the seven main regions of the city. After you've tried one of its artisanal brews, from blonde ales to robust porters, you can bar hop your way down the laneway to surrounding drinking dens.

☆ Entertainment

San Luis has an active cultural scene. Ask in the tourist office about what's on and keep your eye out for posters and the free monthly *Guiarte* booklet.

Teatro de la Paz
CONCERT VENUE

(✆ 444-812-52-09; Villerias 2) This exceptionally handsome neoclassical theater completed in 1894 contains a concert hall with 1500 seats where San Luis Potosí's Orquesta Sinfónica performs. There is also an exhibition gallery and a theater here. Posters announce upcoming dance, theater and music events.

Shopping

Casa Grande

Esencia Artesanal
ARTS & CRAFTS

(Universidad 220; ⊙ 10am-8pm Mon-Sat, 11am-6pm Sun) This cooperative of small stalls sells a great range of *artesanías potosinas* that are 100% locally made. There's also clothing and more standard souvenirs.

La Casa del Artesano
ARTS & CRAFTS

(www.elrebozo.gob.mx; Jardín Colón 23; ⊙ 8am-3pm & 5-7pm Mon-Fri, 10am-5pm Sat) For local products, try this shop full of *potosino* pottery, masks, woodwork and canework.

ⓘ Information

Hospital Lomas de SLP (✆ 444-102-59-00; www.hls.com.mx; Av Palmira 600, Villas del Pedregal)

Post Office (Av Universidad 526; ⊙ 8am-3pm Mon-Fri)

Sectur (State Tourist Office; ✆ 444-812-99-39; www.visitasanluispotosi.com; Av Manuel José Othón 130; ⊙ 8am-9pm Mon-Fri, 9am-3pm Sat & Sun) Has maps and good information on off-the-beaten-track attractions in San Luis Potosí state.

Tourist Office (✆ 444-812-57-19; Palacio Municipal; ⊙ 8am-8pm Mon-Sat, 10am-5pm Sun) On the east side of Plaza de Armas.

ⓘ Getting There & Away

AIR

Aeropuerto Internacional Ponciano Arriaga (✆ 444-822-00-95; www.oma.aero/en) is 10km north of the city off Hwy 57. A new terminal was under construction at the time of writing. There are several daily flights to Mexico City and a once- or twice-daily flight to Monterrey.

BUS

The **Terminal Terrestre Potosina** (TTP; ✆ 444-816-46-02; Carretera 57), 2.5km east of the center, is a busy transportation hub that has deluxe, 1st-class and 2nd-class bus services. Its facilities include 24-hour luggage storage and fast-food outlets.

CAR & MOTORCYCLE

Car-rental prices are around US$25 per day (excluding some insurances); week-long packages also available. All car-hire outlets can be found at the airport.

ⓘ Getting Around

Taxis charge around M$200 to M$250 for the half-hour trip to/from the airport. Coming into the city there's a fixed rate of M$260 (you'll need to line up and buy a voucher inside the terminal building).

BUSES FROM SAN LUIS POTOSÍ

DESTINATION	FARE (M$)	DURATION (HR)	FREQUENCY (DAILY)
Aguascalientes	196-245	2½-3	hourly
Ciudad Valles	690	4½	hourly
Guadalajara	485-660	5-6	hourly
Guanajuato	275	3	1
Matehuala	265	2½	4
Mexico City (Terminal Norte)	550-710	5-6½	hourly
Monterrey	690-785	6	5
Querétaro	286-340	2½-4	frequent
San Miguel de Allende	245	4	3
Xilitla	451	6	3
Zacatecas	290	3	frequent

To reach the center from the bus station, take any 'Centro' or bus 46. A convenient place to get off is on the Alameda, outside the former train station. A booth in the bus station sells taxi tickets (M$35 to M$70) to the center.

From the center to the bus station, take any 'Central TTP' or bus southbound on Avenida Constitución from the Alameda's west side.

City buses run from 6:30am to 10:30pm (M$8). For places along Avenida Carranza, catch a 'Morales' (bus 9) or 'Carranza' (bus 23) at the bus depot behind Museo de Ferrocaril.

Real de Catorce

📍 488 / POP 1300 / ELEV 2730M

A wealthy silver-mining town until early last century, Real de Catorce's fortunes changed overnight when the price of silver plummeted, its mine closed and much of the population left, leaving it a 'ghost town' located an inconveniently long distance from anywhere, deep in the giant hills of the Sierra Madre Oriental. Not long ago Real was nearly deserted, its streets lined with crumbling buildings and just a few hundred unfortunates eking out an existence.

But then somebody invented the weekend break and the boutique hotel and Real de Catorce slipped into a new element, attracting outsiders who have helped with the slow (and very much ongoing) transformation of the town into a getaway destination. Although Real is no longer a ghost town, doors still creak in the breeze, cobblestone streets end abruptly and many buildings are ruins, but the fabulous scenery and charming architecture make it a delight to visit.

History

The 14 in the town's name may have been derived from the 14 Spanish soldiers killed here by indigenous resistance fighters around 1700. The town was founded in the mid-18th century and the church built between 1790 and 1817. The town reached its peak in the late 19th century, vying to surpass the famed Valenciana mine of Guanajuato. It had opulent houses, a bullring and shops selling European luxury goods.

⊙ Sights

Templo de la Purísima Concepción
CHURCH

(Lanzagorta; ⊙7am-7pm) FREE This charming church is an impressive neoclassical building where thousands of Mexican pilgrims descend annually in a pilgrimage to the supposedly miraculous image of St Francis of Assisi, displayed at the front of the church. A cult has grown up around the statue, whose help is sought in solving problems and cleansing sins. Walk through the door to the left of the altar to find a roomful of *retablos*, small pictures depicting threatening situations in which St Francis interceded.

Retablos have become much sought after by collectors and are very occasionally seen in antique shops. Sadly, most of those on sale have been stolen from churches such as this one.

Centro Cultural de Real de Catorce
MUSEUM

(Casa de la Moneda; M$10; ⊙10am-6pm Wed-Sun) Opposite the Templo de la Purísima Concepción's facade, the Centro Cultural

Real de Catorce

Real de Catorce

de Real de Catorce, the old mint, made coins for 14 months (1,489,405 pesos to be exact) in the mid-1860s. This classic monument has been exquisitely restored over the last few years and now houses a cultural-center-cum-gallery with several levels of temporary exhibitions. The bottom floor has a permanent exhibition depicting photos and machinery from the original mint.

Capilla de Guadalupe
CHURCH, CEMETERY

(Zaragoza; ⊙ 8am-5pm) This fine old 19th-century church has an interesting interior of once-glorious but now very faded and decaying frescoes.

🏃 Activities

Hiking

The hilly and stark desert setting makes up for the lack of major sights around town. If you're into walking, there's plenty to keep you occupied for a couple of days. Don't miss the Pueblo Fantasmo or Socavón de Purísima hikes.

Pueblo Fantasmo
HIKING

Allow at least one hour to get to this hillside ghost town, which is visible from the town. There is also a second set of ruins, not visible from Real, 100m further on. Beware that there are also two large shafts in the ruins, so take care while wandering about. From Real, head along Lanzagorta and stay left.

To extend this hike, head northwest along the ridge to the antennas and the cross over the town (make sure you note this from the town before you leave, as it becomes obscured when on the ridge). Follow the path behind the cross before you weave your way down to the cemetery. Allow three to four hours in total for the longer hike.

Socavón de Purísima
HIKING

Socavón de Purísima is the large chimney of a former mine. To get here from Real, head off down Allende and veer right at its end. Follow this road until you reach the chimney (about 45 minutes one way). The road passes through a cut or split rock, the Cerro

Trocado. If open, you can enter the mouth of the mine.

To return, it's a longer and harder slog back up the hill. Be sure to take water, a hat and strong footwear; it's dry and unforgiving country out here.

Horseback Riding

Numerous trails lead out into the dry, stark and fascinating desertscapes around Real. The most popular guided trail ride is the three-hour trip to El Quemado, the sacred mountain of the Huicholes. Here you'll find expansive views of the high-desert plateau and a small shrine to the sun god. The horses and guides congregate every morning around Plaza Hidalgo.

Horse guides now belong to an association, approved by the municipality, and you'll find **Caballerangos del Real** (Plaza Hidalgo; 2hr trip M$150-200) around Real's main square offering rides. Note that no protective hats are provided; you clomp off at your own risk.

Jeep Rides

Trips in 'Jeep Willys' can also be arranged to many of the same locations, mainly on weekends. Ask any of the drivers along Lanzagorta or Allende, or at the tourist office. Rates vary according to the trip and numbers; they work out cheaper if you share the cost with other visitors.

Cycling

Cyclists of all levels can head out around Real de Catorce on some great-value rides with **Lalo Bike** (cell 488-1051981; www.facebook.com/mtb-bicitours-expeditions; Lanzagorta 5; 1½hr ride per person M$150; Fri-Sun Nov-Sep). Lalo speaks Spanish only, but can arrange an English-speaking guide) Prices include mountain bike, helmet and guide. Spanish speakers can email or ring ahead or, if you are in Real, inquire at Mesón de la Abundancia

★ Festivals & Events

Fiesta de San Francisco   RELIGIOUS

(end Sep-Oct) From the end of September to the end of October, 150,000 pilgrims pay homage to the figure of St Francis of Assisi in the town's church. Many of them just come for the day, while thousands stay in the town, filling every rentable room and sleeping rough in the plazas.

The streets are lined with stalls selling religious souvenirs and food, while many of the town's more upmarket restaurants close for a month. Note: travelers who desire the tranquil 'ghost-town experience' of Real de Catorce are best staying away during this festival period to avoid disappointment.

Festival del Desierto   CULTURAL

(www.festivaldeldesierto.com.mx; Jun) This cultural festival features folkloric music and dance performances in towns all around the region. Dates vary annually; check before you come with the tourist office.

🛏 Sleeping

There's a good number of hotels for such a remote place, and it's a good idea to reserve on the weekend. Also note that it can be very cold here in winter in the cheapest digs; bring a sleeping bag or extra layers of clothing, or request extra blankets.

★ Mesón de Abundancia   HOTEL $$

(488-887-50-44; www.mesonabundancia.com; Lanzagorta 11; d M$850-1500;) Easily one of Mexico's most atmospheric hotels, this 19th-century former treasury building has been wonderfully renovated and is Real's best option by far. A massive old-fashioned key lets you into one of 11 rooms; these are grandly appointed and tastefully decorated with local crafts and make a cozy retreat on chilly nights. Rates are significantly lower outside high season.

Hotel Mina Real   HOTEL $$

(488-887-51-62; www.hotelminareal.com; Corona 5B; r from M$1250;) This stylish place is no museum of Real's past but a thoughtfully and boldly renovated stone building whose tone is set by the modern wooden staircase leading up through its center to the 11 tastefully modern rooms and the gorgeous roof terrace. It's a good choice for those seeking contemporary comforts. There's no breakfast.

Hotel Amor y Paz   HOTEL $$

(488-887-50-59; hotelayp@gmail.com; Juárez 10; d M$1100;) How you feel about this hotel's spiritual pretensions (its business cards come with Buddha quotations) might affect your overall opinion, but what cannot be denied is its historic charm, built around a lovely courtyard and stuffed with period furniture. The rooms are a little dark, but have gorgeous wooden ceilings and colorfully tiled bathrooms.

✕ Eating & Drinking

Café Azul
CAFE $

(Lanzagorta 27; breakfasts M$50-90; ☺ 8:30am-5pm Thu-Tue, to 10pm Fri & Sat) Open all day, this airy, Swiss-run spot is perfect for breakfast, freshly baked cakes and light meals, including excellent crepes. The delightful owners are very helpful with local info.

Mesón de Abundancia
MEXICAN, ITALIAN $$

(www.mesonabundancia.com; Lanzagorta 11; mains M$100-200; ☺ 7am-10pm; 🛜🖉) There are several cozy eating areas at the restaurant in this hugely atmospheric hotel, one with a bar and fireplace. The hearty servings of Italian and Mexican dishes are delicious and its wood-fired oven pizza is a delicious evening treat. It's open all day, every day, including for breakfast.

Amor y Paz
BAR

(Juaréz 10; ☺ 6pm-late Fri & Sat) Real's reputation as a ghost town may in part be due to the fact that its residents and visitors are often all hiding out at this funky bar, hidden behind the walls of **Hotel El Real** (www.hotelreal.com.mx; Morelos 20). It's decked out in antiques (note the amazing wooden bar), retro seating and quirky chandeliers, and serves a range of mezcals.

❶ Information

There's one ATM in Real de Catorce, located in the tourist office, but on busy weekends it occasionally runs out of money and is often out of order thanks to electricity cuts and the like, so it's wise to bring cash.

There's a small but helpful **tourist office** (Palacio Municipal, Constitución s/n; ☺ 9am-4pm) by the church.

❶ Getting There & Away

BUS

To get to Real de Catorce, you need to catch a bus from the town of Matehuala (M$95, 1½ hours). These leave Matehuala's bus station at 8am, midday, 2pm and 6pm. Matehuala is easy to reach from elsewhere in the region, with multiple daily connections from San Luis Potosí (M$247, three hours) and Querétaro (M$515, 5½ hours).

On arrival in Real, buses stop on the outskirts of town before the Ogarrio tunnel. There, in order to pass through the tunnel to the town proper, you change to a smaller bus that takes you the final part of the journey, dropping you on the market square.

Returning from Real to Matehuala, the small buses leave the market square in Real at 7:40am, 11:40am, 3:40pm and 5:40pm (M$88, 1½ to two hours), and once again passengers pick up the bigger bus on the other side for the rest of the journey. Buy tickets on board the bus.

CAR & MOTORCYCLE

If driving from Hwy 57 north of Matehuala, turn off toward Cedral, 20km west. After Cedral, you turn south to reach Catorce on what must be one of the world's longest cobblestone roads. It's a slow but spectacular zigzag drive up a steep mountainside. The 2.3km-long Ogarrio tunnel (M$30 per vehicle) is only wide enough for one vehicle; workers stationed at each end with telephones control traffic flow between 7am and 11pm. If it's really busy, you'll have to leave your car at the eastern tunnel entrance and continue by pickup or cart. If you drive through, as a nonresident you are supposed to leave your car in the parking area where you exit the tunnel, rather than park in the narrow streets of the town.

La Huasteca Potosina

The stunning, tropical Huasteca Potosina is a lush, remote subregion of San Luis Potosí but worlds away from it in both geography and climate. Filled will incredible waterfalls and swimming holes, the result of the rivers that flow eastward from the slopes of the Sierra Madre Oriental, this alluring region offers some of central Mexico's most breathtaking scenery. The waterfalls here look as though they've been photoshopped, so rich is their aquamarine hue due to the high calcium content in the surrounding rocks. The rich culture of the local Huastec people (Tének), plus extraordinary sinkholes, caves and bird-watching, make a visit here extremely rewarding. The best time to visit is in dry season, between November and March. Wet season brings heavy rains and high, less-clear waters.

⊙ Sights

Sótano de las Golondrinas
CAVE

(Aquismón; M$35; ☺ dawn-dusk) The extraordinary limestone sinkhole, known as Swallows' Cave, is located near Aquismón. One of the world's deepest pits at over 500m (over 370m freefall), it's known for the thousands of *vencejos* (white-collared swifts) that nest in the caves. At dawn, flocks of swifts leave the cave, spiraling their way up to the opening. At dusk, on return to the cave, they circle above the cave

LAS POZAS

Take a wealthy English eccentric, an idyllic tract of Mexican jungle and an extremely hyperactive imagination, and you'd still struggle to come up with the audacious, bizarre and – frankly – madcap experiment that is **Las Pozas** (The Pools; www.xilitla.org; M$70; ☺9am-6pm).

Situated on the sweeping slopes of the Sierra Madre Oriental, Las Pozas is a monumental sculpture garden built in thick jungle that links a series of concrete temples, pagodas, bridges, pavilions and spiral stairways with a necklace of natural waterfalls. The surreal creation stands as a memorial to the imagination and excessive wealth of Edward James (1907–84). A drop-out English aristocrat and poet, he became a patron of Salvador Dalí in the late 1930s and subsequently went on to amass the largest private collection of surrealist art in the world. In 1945 James' adventures took him to Xilitla where he met Plutarco Gastelum, who helped build Las Pozas. It began with 40 local workers crafting giant, colored concrete flowers beside an idyllic jungle stream. Then, for 17 years, James and Gastelum created ever larger and stranger structures – many of which were never finished – at an estimated cost of US$5 million.

James died in 1984, leaving no provision to maintain his creation, which, since 2008, has been in the hands of a Mexican-run nonprofit foundation. The extravagant labyrinth of surreal sculptures and edifices with stairways leading nowhere covers 36 hectares and is worth a significant diversion for anyone with the vaguest creative inclinations. If you're in fairly good shape, you could spend the whole day contemplating the lovely swimming holes and mazelike trails.

Las Pozas has a good on-site restaurant (open 10am to 6pm) and there are several small campsites and posadas nearby. For the true Las Pozas experience, you should stay at **Posada El Castillo** (p694), the surrealist-inspired former Gastelum home where James himself also lived, now transformed into a verdant Pozas-esque guesthouse run by the Gastelum family.

mouth before they break off in groups and dive-bomb into the abyss.

It's popular with rappelers and base jumpers who drop from the cave's mouth. To get there, you must walk from the car park, down hundreds of steps (and back again), which is about a 20-minute walk.

Sótano de las Huahuas   CAVE
(San Isidro Tampaxal; M$35; ☺dawn-dusk) This impressive sinkhole is one of two in the Huasteca Potosina where you can view swift flocks exiting and entering their cavern. A favorite for rappeling enthusiasts, the chasm itself is around 478m deep. Accessing the cave is a little tricky – from the car park you must walk 1km through remarkable jungle – but it's worth it for its beautiful cedar and local tree and bird species.

Laguna de la Media Luna   HOT SPRINGS
(El Jabalí; adult/child M$40/20; ☺9am-6pm) This extraordinary prehistoric lagoon is fed by six thermal springs with temperatures ranging between an appealing 27°C and 30°C (80.6°F and 86°F). Its crystal-clear waters mean snorkelers and divers can view beds of water lilies, an ancient pet-

rified forest and several fish species. Hundreds of families flock here on weekends, when it can get very busy. You can hire snorkeling gear from one of the many stalls inside the area (M$20).

Diving courses are available. The most highly recommended is **Escuela de Buceo Media Luna** (☎487-872-81-89; www.buceomedialuna.com; diving courses from M$950), run by master scuba diver and oceanographer Ossiel Martinez.

Waterfalls
The region's main draw is its incredible waterfalls, which in most cases you can swim near or take boat trips to. A self-guided tour with your own wheels or an agency-run day trip is the perfect way to discover them all.

Los Micos   WATERFALL
(M$30; ☺8am-5pm) One of the most visited of Huasteca Potosina's falls it may be, but there's a reason for that: here seven waterfalls of different heights cascade down a river bed, which makes for an incredible sight. You can do a quick boat tour (M$90 for 10 minutes; minimum four people) or

jumping expeditions down the seven waterfalls (M$175 per person for two hours; helmet and life jacket supplied). Many operators located in the car park offer the same activity.

★ Cascadas de Minas Viejas   WATERFALL

(El Platanito; M$30; ⊘ 7am-8pm) The stunning cascades of Minas Viejas are well worth the 78km trip northwest from Ciudad Valles, if only to see the gorgeous turquoise waters here. The site comprises a principal waterfall with a drop of 55m plus a stunning water pool. From here, a series of smaller cascades and pools drop over terraces. It's a popular destination for adventure groups who jump over the terraces.

Puente de Dios   WATERFALL

(M$30) Around 5km northeast of Tamasopo along a rough road, Puente de Dios features a 600m-long wooden walkway with stunning rain-forest views and fabulous swimming opportunities. The main feature, 'God's Bridge' is a turquoise-colored water hole with an adjoining cave entrance, though this is not accessible or recommended in high waters.

★ Cascada de Tamul   WATERFALL

(M$20; ⊘ 8am-6pm) Tamul is the Huasteca Potosina's most spectacular waterfall. Water plunges 105m into the pristine Río Santa Maria (which becomes the Tampaón). Its setting, in a canyon surrounded on all sides with thick forest, is quite simply breathtaking. Best of all, you'll often have this amazing place to yourself, due to its remote location.

To see the falls, you can drive almost all the way to the top entrance (you'll need to pay M$20 to drive along this private dirt track). When you reach the river, you'll need to park, wade across to the campsite on other side (if the river is flowing heavily, it's best to be helped across by one of the campsite employees), from where it's an easy 1km hike to the waterfall itself. You'll emerge at its top, where there is a lovely pool to swim in, but be sure to take the rickety wooden ladder down to the bottom of the valley and see the falls from there, where they are truly a spectacular sight with thousands of butterflies flapping about in the spray.

Another way to reach the waterfall is to paddle up river in a wooden *lancha* (boat), a return journey of around 3½ hours (M$800 to M$1000 per boat depending on your hag-

gling skills). You can arrange trips on arrival into Tanchachín or La Morena.

If you don't have your own transportation, MS Xpediciones arranges excellent day trips from Ciudad Valles, complete with lunch at the home of a hospitable local (M$800 per person including transportation; minimum two people). It also arranges rafting trips in the area.

🏃 Activities

La Huasteca Potosina is a dream for activities enthusiasts, with swimming, hiking, rappeling, rafting and kayaking all possible on and around its rushing rivers and soaring peaks. Agencies in Xilitla, Ciudad Valles and San Luis Potosí can arrange day trips and multiday tours, though it's best to make arrangements at least several days in advance.

🛏 Sleeping

El Molino   GUESTHOUSE $$

(www.hotelelmolino.webs.com; Porfirio Díaz 1417, Rio Verde; r from M$950; P 🛜) Based in the rather scrappy agricultural town of Rio Verde, on the edge of the Huasteca Potosina, 'The Mill' has 15 neat and tasteful rooms (some of which are around the central living room) and a pretty garden. Built on the ruins of an 18th-century sugarcane factory, El Molino provides sweet respite from the heat. The owners also offer meals.

It's a lovely place to stay if you plan to visit the nearby Laguna de la Media Luna (p691). Breakfast costs M$70.

ℹ Getting There & Away

You can get to the towns of Xilitla and Ciudad Valles easily by public transportation, but the nature of the region beyond these population centers means you really need your own transportation to reach the best places. Of course, you can also hire taxis or arrange trips with a local tour operator, which you'll find in both Xilitla and Ciudad Valles.

Ciudad Valles

📶 481 / POP 177,000

Ciudad Valles, while not a very attractive city, is the chief town of La Huasteca Potosina and is useful for its adventure organizations and potentially as a transportation hub and a place to spend the night. The town itself is fairly unattractive, but it does boast two interesting museums that focus on the history of the region's Huastec and Nahuatl peoples.

⊙ Sights

Museo Regional Huasteco Joaquín Meade　　　MUSEUM
(Rotarios 623; ⊘9am-4pm Mon-Fri) FREE Showcases over 10,000 archaeological and ethnological pieces from the region, from around 600 BC until the Spanish conquest.

Museo de Cultura de la Huasteca Tamuantzán　　　MUSEUM
(☑481-381-26-75; Carretera México-Laredo y Libramiento Sur; ⊘9am-6pm Mon-Fri) FREE An excellent starting point to learn more about the Huasteca region and local cultures.

🏃 Activities

★MS Xpediciones　　　ADVENTURE
(☑481-381-18-88; www.msxpediciones.com; Blvd México Laredo, Escontría 15B, Interior Hotel Misión; ⊘9am-8pm Mon-Sat, plus 9am-noon Sun Jul & Aug) 🌊 The pick of the region's operators for its community-aware, friendly and professional approach. Its range of activities and adventures includes trips to Xilitla and Las Pozas, to the bird caves, and to many of the region's waterfalls. It also arranges excellent canoeing adventures, including to Tamul (M$800 minimum two people; including transportation and a meal with a local family) plus rafting expeditions.

🛏 Sleeping & Eating

Hotel Misión Ciudad Valles　　　HOTEL $$
(☑481-382-00-66; www.hotelesmision.com.mx; Blvd México-Laredo 15; r M$1438; ❀🛜🏊) This attractive 1930s hacienda-style building may be in need of a little love and a fresh lick of paint, but it has good bones. There's a big pool (a plus in this climate) and spacious and clean rooms with coffee facilities. Breakfast is not included in the price, but is available.

La Leyenda　　　MEXICAN $$
(Morelos 323; M$115-225; ⊘8am-11pm Mon-Sat, to 5pm Sun; P❀) This rather dark but mercifully air-conditioned restaurant is housed in a ranch-like building where smart and attentive staff work hard for their tips. The meaty menu is pure Mexican, with tasty tacos, enchiladas and steaks.

ⓘ Getting There & Away

Ciudad Valles is well connected throughout the region, and the busy **Terminal Ciudad Valles** (Contreras s/n) can be found 3km southeast of the downtown area. To get to Real de Ca-

torce from here, you'll need to change buses twice; first in the town of Río Verde and then in Matehuala.

Xilitla

📷 489 / POP 6500 / ELEV 489M

Surrounded by the jaw-dropping tropical scenery of the Huasteca Potosina, the remote hillside town of Xilitla (hee-leet-la) is an agreeable spot notable for its precariously steep streets and proximity to Las Pozas, the British eccentric Edward James' fantastical jungle sculpture garden. Built just outside the town in the 1950s and constantly embellished and expanded over the following decades, Las Pozas is still the main reason for most people to come here.

As the Huasteca Potosina continues to grow in popularity as a travel destination, however, Xilitla has found itself at the center of a small but quickly growing tourism bubble, and now has dozens of hotels and guesthouses as well as numerous tour operators offering rafting, rappeling, hiking and mountain-bike excursions in the surrounding countryside. There's definitely a bit of magic in the air here, as all who make it this far quickly discover.

ⓖ Tours

Mundo Extreme Tours　　　OUTDOORS
(☑489-105-30-00; www.mundoextreme.com.mx; Hidalgo 104) A highly recommended outfit specializing in extreme sports and all sorts of outdoor activity, Mundo Extreme offers a number of 'rutas' through the Huasteca Potosina, combining elements of hiking, climbing, kayaking, rafting and rappeling.

Ruta Xilitla　　　OUTDOORS
(☑489-109-65-40; www.rutaxilitla.com) A good Xilitla-based agency that offers a wide range of activities throughout the Huasteca Potosina, including visits to the waterfalls and caves, plus rafting and rappeling.

🛏 Sleeping & Eating

While things have improved noticeably in the past few years, there's still not much culinary choice. What there is can be found on and around the Jardín Principal, Xilitla's main square.

★Hotel Camino Surreal　　　HOTEL $$
(☑489-365-03-67; www.caminosurreal.com; Ocampo 311; r M$1500; ❀🛜🏊) This is the friendliest and most comfortable place in town and

BUSES FROM XILITLA

DESTINATION	FARE (M$)	DURATION (HR)	FREQUENCY (DAILY)
Ciudad Valles	132	2	hourly
Jalpan	94-128	2	hourly
Mexico City (Norte)	440-561	8	5
Querétaro	440	5½	1
San Luis Potosí	451	5½	2
Tampico	413	5	5
Tequisquiapan	322	5	3

makes for a very pleasant oasis of cool after a day tramping around the jungle. There are just six rooms, but they're all spacious, spotlessly clean and most enjoy balconies overlooking the pool and garden out back.

Posada El Castillo GUESTHOUSE $$
(☑489-365-00-38; www.junglegossip.com; Ocampo 105; d incl breakfast M$1570; 🕸🏊) The former Gastelum home where Edward James stayed in Xilitla is now a verdant, Pozas-esque guesthouse run by his niece and her family. Its unique rooms are decorated with antiques and art, and some claim fantastic views. Based only on room quality, it's quite overpriced, and while the welcome is warm, they do not accept walk-ins, so reserve ahead.

Querreque MEXICAN $$
(Hidalgo 201; mains M$115-220; ⊙9am-10pm; 🕸🅿) There are wonderful views over the town and distant hills from this place's large terrace. Inside you'll find two brightly colored dining rooms and friendly staff working hard serving up Mexican dishes of all types, including *mole de mariscos* (traditional *mole* served with a range of seafood), spicy enchiladas and *chile hojaldrado relleno* (a stuffed chili wrapped in puff pastry).

ⓘ Getting There & Away

Xilitla's makeshift **bus station** (Independencia s/n) is a small lot surrounded by several ticket offices in the middle of the town. From here you can find buses to the following destinations.

ZACATECAS STATE

The state of Zacatecas (za-ka-*te*-kas) is a dry, rugged, cactus-strewn expanse on the fringe of Mexico's northern semideserts. The state is best known for the wealthy silver city of the same name, an elegant and enjoy-able place full of colonial architecture and boasting an impressive cathedral. Visitors can enjoy the region's historical and natural monuments, including the mysterious ruins of La Quemada, a testament to centuries of cultures. The state is one of Mexico's largest in area (73,252 sq km) but smallest in population (1.5 million); it is believed that as many people again, who come from the state, currently live in the USA.

Zacatecas

🅹492 / POP 147,000 / ELEV 2430M

The most northern of Mexico's silver cities, fascinating Zacatecas – a Unesco World Heritage site – runs along a narrow valley overlooked by a steep and imposing hillside. The large historic center is jampacked with opulent colonial buildings, a stupendous cathedral, magnificent museums and steep, winding streets and alleys that simply ooze charm.

Zacatecas was where thousands of indigenous slaves were forced by the Spanish to toil in the mines under terrible conditions. Pancho Villa enjoyed a historic victory in 1914, and he is still feted by locals today. Today travelers can have their own lofty experiences in a *teleférico* (cable car) to the Cerro de la Bufa, the impressive rock outcrop that soars above the town and affords great views of the church domes and tiled rooftops below. Alternatively, visitors can drop below the surface to tour the infamous Edén mine, a sobering reminder of the city's brutal colonial past.

History

Indigenous Zacatecos – one of the Chichimec tribes – mined local mineral deposits for centuries before the Spanish arrived; it's said that the silver rush here was started when a Chichimec gave a piece

LA QUEMADA RUINS

The remote and scenic ruins of **La Quemada** (M$55; ⏰9am-5pm) stand on a hill 45km south of Zacatecas. The exact history and purpose of the site are extremely vague and many suppositions surround the area – one theory is that it was where the Aztecs halted during their legendary wanderings toward the Valle de México. What is known for sure is that the constructions were destroyed by fire – and thus they came to be called La Quemada (meaning 'burned city').

La Quemada was inhabited between about AD 300 and 1200, and it is estimated to have peaked between 500 and 900 with as many as 3000 inhabitants. From around 400 it was part of a regional trade network linked to Teotihuacán, but fortifications suggest that La Quemada later tried to dominate trade in this region. A recent study suggests that during the settlement's peak its inhabitants engaged in cannibalism of their enemies, the remains of whom they hung up ceremonially.

Of the main structures, the nearest to the site entrance is the **Salón de las Columnas** (Hall of the Columns), probably a ceremonial hall. Slightly further up the hill are a ball court, a steep offerings pyramid and an equally steep staircase leading toward the site's upper levels. From the upper levels of the main hill, a path leads westward for about 800m to a spur hilltop (the highest point) with the remains of a cluster of buildings called **La Ciudadela** (the Citadel). To return, follow the defensive wall and path back around to the small **museum**, which has an interesting collection of artifacts recovered from the site and a good video summary of what is known. Take water and a hat and be on the look out for rattlesnakes, which have been seen at the site.

From Zacatecas's Plaza del Bicentenario, board a combi bus for Villanueva (M$40) and ask beforehand to be let off at *las ruinas;* you'll be deposited at the turnoff, from where it's a 2.5km walk to the site entrance. Returning to Zacatecas, you may have to wait a while for a bus – don't leave the ruins too late. Alternatively, hire a taxi to take you here, which will cost around M$800 including waiting time.

of the fabled metal to a conquistador. The Spaniards founded a settlement in 1548 and started mining operations that sent caravan after caravan of silver off to Mexico City, creating fabulously wealthy silver barons in Zacatecas.

By the early 18th century, the mines of Zacatecas were producing 20% of Nueva España's silver and the city became an important base for Catholic missionaries.

In the 19th century political instability diminished the flow of silver. Although silver production later improved under Porfirio Díaz, the Revolution disrupted it. In 1914 in Zacatecas, Pancho Villa defeated a stronghold of 12,000 soldiers loyal to President Victoriano Huerta. After the Revolution, Zacatecas continued to thrive on silver until the final closure of the last mines.

◉ Sights

★ Museo Rafael Coronel   MUSEUM

(cnr Abasolo & Matamoros;   adult/student M$30/15; ⏰10am-5pm Thu-Tue) The excellent Museo Rafael Coronel is not to be missed. Imaginatively housed in the ruins of the lovely 16th-century Ex-Convento de San Francisco, it houses Mexican folk art collected by Zacatecan artist Rafael Coronel, brother of Pedro Coronel and son-in-law of Diego Rivera. Take your time to wander through the various spaces by following the arrows. The collection of masks is truly incredible, as are collections of totems, pottery, puppets and other fascinating objects. All labeling is in Spanish only.

★ Museo del Arte Abstracto Manuel Felguérez   MUSEUM

(www.museodearteabstracto.com;   Ex-Seminario de la Purísima Concepción, Colón s/n; adult/student M$30/20; ⏰10am-5pm Wed-Mon) This superb abstract-art museum is worth visiting for the building alone; originally a seminary, it was later used as a prison and has been renovated to create some remarkable exhibition spaces, transforming the former dark, depressing cells and steel walkways into a beautiful site. It has a stunning and varied collection of abstract painting and sculpture, particularly the work of Zacatecan artist Manuel Felguérez. You can easily while away an hour or two in contemplation of extraordinary forms here.

Zacatecas

N
0 —————— 200 m
0 —————— 0.1 miles

Los Dorados de Villa (200m);
Museo Rafael
Coronel (200m)

**Museo del
Arte Abstracto
Manuel Felguérez** 1

Duranzo
Fortin
Bosque
la del Seminario
Abasolo
Moral
Juan de Tolosa

Tirolesa 840
(650m);
Museo Toma de
Zacatecas (1km)

Triste
Unizar

Cerro del Grillo
Teleférico Station

19

Cerro de la
Bufa (250m);
Capilla de la Virgen
del Patrocinio (400m);
Cerro de la Bufa (400m)

Paseo Díaz Ordaz

5

Bosque

Mante
Mante
Del Salto
Rojas

Av Hidalgo

Mercedita
Lopez
De Los Bolos

Pankhurst

Grillo

Del Auxilio

Mina Club
(250m)

Gomez
Serdán
Lancaster

**Museo Pedro 2
Coronel** 11

Genaro Codina

13
9 10
8

Plazuela
de Santo
Domingo

3

24 17
7 Dr Hierro 18
21 Plazuela
Francisco
Goitia 12

De la Loma
Del Cobre
Villalpando

4
Plaza
Miguel Auza 22
15 Callejón del Lazo 25

Parque
Alameda

Del Estudiante

Cadena

Aguascalientes
Medina

Tenorio

14 23
20 Jardín
Morelos Jardín
Juárez

Amador

Av Juárez

Plazuela
Genaro
Codina

Av González Ortega

Trabajo

Jardín
Independencia

Arroyo de la Plata
Av Guerrero
Aurora
Correa

Ponce

6

Estrada

Parque
Enrique
Estrada

García de la Cadena

Salinas
Estrada

Independencia
Salazar

Plaza del
Bicentenario Calz de la Paz

16

Rayón
Calderón
Morelos

Blvd López Mateos

Local Buses
to Guadalupe

Zacatecas

★**Museo Pedro Coronel** MUSEUM
(Plaza de Santo Domingo s/n; adult/student M$30/15; ⊙10am-5pm Tue-Sun) The extraordinary Museo Pedro Coronel is housed in a 17th-century former Jesuit college and, given that it was recently remodeled, is one of provincial Mexico's best art museums. Pedro Coronel (1923–85) was an affluent Zacatecan artist who bequeathed his collection of art and artifacts from all over the world, as well as his own works. The collection includes 20th-century works by Picasso, Rouault, Dalí, Goya and Miró; and pre-Hispanic Mexican artifacts, masks and other ancient pieces.

Cerro de la Bufa LANDMARK
The most appealing of the many explanations for the name of the hill that dominates Zacatecas is that *bufa* is an old Basque word for wineskin, which is apparently what the rocky formation looks like. The views from the top are superb and there's an interesting group of monuments, a chapel and a museum. It is also the site of a zip-line, **Tirolesa 840** (☑cell 492-9463157; rides M$250; ⊙10am-6pm), a 1km ride cross a former open-pit mine.

Once up the hill you can also visit **Capilla de la Virgen del Patrocinio**, as well as three imposing equestrian statues of the victors of the battle of Zacatecas – Villa, Ángeles and Pánfilo Natera, which stand opposite the chapel. To the right of the statues, a paved path along the foot of the rocky hilltop leads to the **Mausoleo de los**

Hombres Ilustres de Zacatecas, with the tombs of Zacatecan heroes from 1841 to the present.

A convenient way to ascend La Bufa (to the church and museum) is by **teleférico** (☑492-922-01-70; one-way ticket M$50; ⊙10am-6pm). Alternatively, you can walk up, starting at Calle del Ángel from the cathedral's east end. To reach it by car, take Carretera a la Bufa, which begins at Avenida López Velarde, a couple of kilometers east of the center. A taxi costs around M$60. You can return to town by the *teleférico* or by a footpath leading downhill from the statues.

Plaza de Armas PLAZA
This recently renovated plaza is north of the cathedral. The **Palacio de Gobierno** (⊙8am-8pm Mon-Fri) `FREE` on the plaza's east side was built in the 18th century for a colonial family. In the turret of its main staircase is a mural of the history of Zacatecas state, painted in 1970 by Antonio Rodríguez. Across the road, and directly opposite the Palacio, the **Palacio de la Mala Noche** was built in the late 18th century for a mine owner and now houses state government offices.

Mina El Edén MINE
(☑492-922-30-02; www.minaeleden.com.mx/english; Mante s/n; tours adult/child M$100/50; ⊙tours every hour 10am-6pm) Visiting one of Mexico's richest mines (1586–1960s) provides an insight into a source of wealth

NORTHERN CENTRAL HIGHLANDS ZACATECAS

and the terrible price paid for it. Digging for hoards of silver, gold, iron, copper and zinc, enslaved indigenous people worked in horrific conditions. Up to five people a day died from accidents or tuberculosis and silicosis. These days, it's rather different: a miniature train takes you inside Cerro del Grillo, while guides lead you along floodlit walkways past shafts and over subterranean pools.

The mine has two entrances. To reach the higher one (the east entrance), walk 100m southwest from Cerro del Grillo teleférico (p697) station; from this entrance, tours start with an elevator descent. To reach the west entrance from the town center, walk west along Avenida Juárez and stay on it after its name changes to Avenida Torreón at the Alameda. Turn right immediately after the IMSS hospital (bus 7 from the corner of Avenida Hidalgo goes up Avenida Juárez and past the hospital) and a short walk will bring you to the mine entrance. Tours begin here with a trip on the narrow-gauge railway (540m), after which you walk another 350m or so.

Catedral
CATHEDRAL

(Plaza de Armas) Built between 1729 and 1752, the pink-stone cathedral is an ultimate expression of Mexican baroque. The stupendous main facade is a wall of detailed carvings; this has been interpreted as a giant symbol of the tabernacle. Indeed, a tiny figure of an angel holding a tabernacle is in the middle of the design, the keystone atop the round central window. Above this, in the third tier, is Christ and above Christ is God.

The southern facade's central sculpture is of La Virgen de los Zacatecanos, the city's patroness. The north facade shows Christ crucified, attended by the Virgin Mary and St John. Unveiled in 2010, the grand altar is the work of Javier Marín, a famous Mexican artist. It features 10 large bronze figures and the figure of Christ, arranged on a backdrop of golden blocks.

Museo Toma de Zacatecas
MUSEUM

(☑492-922-80-66; Cerro de la Bufa; adult/student M$20/10; ⊙10am-4:30pm; ☖) This museum memorializes the 1914 battle fought on the slopes of the Cerro de la Bufa in which the revolutionary División del Norte, led by Pancho Villa and Felipe Ángeles, defeated President Victoriano Huerta's forces. This gave the revolutionaries control of Zacatecas, which was the gateway to Mexico City. The child-friendly museum, which reopened in 2014 after a full renovation, is a technological delight, with talking ghosts, actual footage of the battle and all kinds of other interactive displays.

Museo Zacatecano
MUSEUM

(Dr Hierro 301; adult/student M$30/15; ⊙10am-5pm Wed-Mon) Zacatecas' former mint (Mexico's second-biggest in the 19th century) now houses the wonderful Museo Zacatecano. Spread over a number of rooms, this contemporary museum exhibits a weird mix of all things *zacatecano*. Unfortunately, the first few *salas* are text-heavy information boards (in Spanish). The highlight – in the last halls – is the superb collection of Huichol art. Videos (all in Spanish) provide each hall's context.

Templo de Santo Domingo
CHURCH

(Plazuela de Santo Domingo) The Templo de Santo Domingo, in a *plazuela* of the same name, is in a baroque style, with fine gilded altars and a graceful horseshoe staircase. Built by the Jesuits in the 1740s, the church was taken over by Dominican monks when the Jesuits were expelled in 1767.

Ex-Templo de San Agustín
CHURCH

(⊙10am-4:30pm Tue-Sun) FREE The Ex-Templo de San Agustín was built for Augustinian monks in the 17th century. During the 19th-century anticlerical movement, the church became a cantina and Masonic lodge. In 1882 it was purchased by American Presbyterian missionaries who destroyed its 'too Catholic' main facade, replacing it with a blank white wall. One surviving feature is the church's plateresque carving of the conversion of St Augustine over the north doorway. It's now used as a venue for temporary exhibitions.

Museo Francisco Goitia
MUSEUM

(☑492-922-02-11; Estrada 101; M$30; ⊙10am-4:45pm Tue-Sun) The Museo Francisco Goitia displays work by several 20th-century Zacatecan artists, including some evocative paintings of indigenous people by Goitia (1882–1960) himself. Other artists represented include Pedro Coronel, Rafael Coronel and Manuel Felguérez. The museum is in a former governor's mansion, above Parque Enrique Estrada, and is worth it for the building and manicured gardens, overlooking the aqueduct.

🎊 Festivals & Events

La Morisma
RELIGIOUS

(⊙Aug) Usually held the last weekend in August, La Morisma features a spectacular mock battle commemorating the triumph of the Christians over the Muslims in old Spain. Two rival 'armies' – around 10,000 participants from the *barrio* of Bracho – parade through the streets in the morning, then, accompanied by bands of musicians, enact two battle sequences between Lomas de Bracho and Cerro de la Bufa.

Feria de Zacatecas
CULTURAL

(FENAZA; www.fenaza.com.mx; ⊙Sep) An annual fair with a folkloric focus, held during the first three weeks of September, featuring renowned matadors fighting famous local bulls. There are also *charreadas* (rodeos), concerts, plays, agricultural and craft shows. On September 8 the image of La Virgen del Patrocinio is carried to the cathedral from its chapel on Cerro de la Bufa (p697).

🛏 Sleeping

Disappointingly, there are limited budget options in Zacatecas, though there is one very pleasant hostel. Midrange and top-end accommodations tend to double their rates during Zacatecas' high seasons – September's festivals, Christmas and Semana Santa (March/April).

★ Cielito Lindo Hostal
HOSTEL $

(☑492-921-11-32; www.cielitolindohostal.com; Aguascalientes 213; dm M$220, d from M$500; 🛜) This delightful and stylish hostel right in the center of the city is the former home of a religious *padre* that has been lovingly converted into a charming – and much-needed – space for budget travelers. There's a big choice of rooms including dorms that come with lockers and recharging stations, as well as a (rather basic) kitchen. Welcome is warm.

La Terrasse
BOUTIQUE HOTEL $$

(☑492-925-53-15; www.terrassehotel.com.mx; Villalpando 209; d M$700-880, tr M$1000, all incl breakfast; ⊜❄🛜) This small, friendly and centrally located boutique option is run by a proud owner. It has 14 contemporary and slightly sparse rooms, but is by far the best midrange option. Back rooms have internal-facing windows: claustrophobic for some, quiet for others.

GUADALUPE

About 10km east of Zacatecas, Guadalupe boasts a fascinating historic former monastery, the Convento de Guadalupe. The Convento was established by Franciscan monks in the early 18th century as an apostolic college. It developed a strong academic tradition and was a base for missionary work in northern Nueva España until the 1850s. It is now the excellent **Museo Virreinal de Guadalupe** (Jardín Juárez Oriente; M$52, Sun free; ⊙9am-6pm Tue-Sun), the reason for travelers to come here.

Visitors can enter two parts of the convento: the impressive **church**, which attracts pilgrims to honor the country's beloved Virgin, and museum itself, which features one of Mexico's best colonial-art collections.

Hotel Mesón de Jobito
HOTEL $$

(☑492-922-70-95; www.mesondejobito.com; Jardín Juárez 143; r from M$1270; 🅿⊜❄🛜) Guests come here to soak up the old-fashioned charm and sense of history that permeates pretty much every corner of this atmospheric hotel. Its 53 rooms are comfortable and spacious, if a little faded; there's a good restaurant and bar (plus slanting balcony, a legacy of its construction 200 years ago). Its Sunday breakfast buffet (M$160) is a local institution.

Quinta Real Zacatecas
LUXURY HOTEL $$$

(☑492-922-91-04, 800-500-40-00; www.quintareal.com; Rayón 434; ste from M$2700; 🅿⊜❄🛜) This luxury treat is hands down the best hotel in Zacatecas. Spectacularly situated around the country's oldest – and now retired – bullring and near El Cubo aqueduct, the 49-room hotel is one of Mexico's most contemporary and fetching. Even the least expensive rooms are spacious, comfortable master suites. The elegant Restaurant La Plaza (p700), overlooks the ring.

Hotel Emporio Zacatecas
LUXURY HOTEL $$$

(☑492-925-65-00; www.hotelesemporio.com; Av Hidalgo 703; r from M$3195; 🅿⊜🛜) Zacatecas' most upmarket hotel boasts a superb location, large and luxurious if somewhat bland rooms and pleasant public areas.

Service is professional, and the rooms provide a quiet oasis from external noise. The downer is there's no air-conditioning. The rack rates are high, though you can sometimes find big discounts online. Breakfast is not included.

Santa Rita Hotel
BOUTIQUE HOTEL $$$

(☑492-925-11-94; www.hotelsantarita.com; Av Hidalgo 507A; ste M$2300-3500; P✴☎) A stylish and contemporary choice, this boutique hotel has delightful, attentive staff and some unusual decorative choices. Be aware that some of the 41 suites have internal-facing windows, an inevitability in colonial buildings but one that might surprise you at these prices.

✗ Eating

Zacatecas has a rather disappointing dining scene in general, though there are some notable exceptions. Local specialties feature ingredients such as *nopal* (cactus) and pumpkin seeds. In the morning, look around Avenida Tacuba for the *burro* (donkey) carrying pottery jugs of *aguamiel* (honey water), a nutritional drink derived from the *maguey* cactus.

Acrópolis Café
MEXICAN $

(www.acropoliszacatecas.wixsite.com/restaurante; cnr Av Hidalgo & Plazuela Candelario Huizar; mains M$110-200; �8am-10pm; ☎) Near the cathedral, this Greek-owned cafe has a quirky '50s-style diner feel, and is *the* breakfast place for locals and visitors alike – perhaps more for its location than its food. It offers light meals, set breakfasts and good coffee.

El Pueblito
MEXICAN $

(Hidalgo 802; mains M$60-180; �lpm-10pm Wed-Mon) Furnished in the hues of Mexico – bright purples, yellows, pinks and oranges – this casual spot is the place for Mexican cuisine. Come when the locals do for late afternoon lunches, as it can feel a bit barn-like when no one else is here.

El Recoveco
MEXICAN $

(Torreón 513; buffet breakfast/lunch M$89/99; �8:30am-7pm Mon-Sat, 9am-7pm Sun) 'Cheap and good' is how the locals describe this long-standing, cafeteria-style eatery. This means buffet style (as much as you can eat and as many plates as you like) and tasty enough Mexican fare that holds no surprises but is outstanding value. Come hungry.

Los Dorados de Villa
MEXICAN $$

(☑492-922-57-22; Plazuela de García 1314; mains M$80-240; �80pm-12:30am; ☎) You may have to reserve to get into this popular revolutionary-themed restaurant: knock at the door – it's always locked. Inside it's a blast of warmth and color chockablock with atmosphere and relics. Its menu offers a delicious array of everything, including an amazing selection of different enchiladas and a fabulous *caldillo durangueño* (Durango beef stew), a northern Mexican delicacy.

Restaurant La Plaza
INTERNATIONAL $$$

(Quinta Real Zacatecas, Rayón 434; mains M$200-390; ☎) The elegant dining room at the Quinta Real Zacatecas is especially memorable for its outlook to the aqueduct and bullring, as well as for its refined ambience and good international cuisine with a few Mexican standards. Head here for Sunday brunch (M$250), a local institution. Reservations are advisable for the evening.

🍷 Drinking & Nightlife

Mina Club
BAR

(www.minaeleden.com.mx; Dovali s/n; cover M$70-150; �10pm-late Sat) For a different experience do not miss your chance to descend into the earth and party in the tunnel of the Mina El Edén (p697). On Saturday the popular attraction morphs into a club; check opening hours as these change seasonally.

Cantina 15 Letras
BAR

(☑492-922-01-78; Mártires de Chicago 309; �1pm-3am Mon-Sat) Stop for a drink at this oft-crowded classic, filled with bohemians, drunks and poets. The art showcases some well-known local and international artists, including Pedro Coronel.

La Famosa Cantina Típica
BAR

(Callejón Cuevas 110; �7pm-2am Tue-Sun) This popular and atmospheric bar is patronized by a well-dressed crowd of students and arty types. Like most bars in Zacatecas, it gets going late.

Dalí Café & Bar
BAR

(Plaza Miguel Auza 322; �noon-1am Mon-Sat, 5pm-1am Sun; ☎) This sprawling cafe-bar in front of Ex-Templo de San Agustín (p698) offers a surreal mix of furniture, cocktails and post-drink munchies (plus good hot-chocolate drinks).

BUSES FROM ZACATECAS

DESTINATION	FARE (M$)	DURATION (HR)	FREQUENCY (DAILY)
Aguascalientes	165-196	2-3	hourly
Durango	460-520	4½-7	hourly
Guadalajara	545-580	4-7	hourly
León	365	3-4	4
Mexico City (Terminal Norte)	810-975	6-8	frequent
Monterrey	556-601	7-8	frequent
Querétaro	560-640	5-6¼	frequent
San Luis Potosí	305	3-3½	hourly

 Entertainment

Teatro Calderón THEATER
(☑492-922-81-20; http://teatrocalderon.uaz.edu.mx; Av Hidalgo s/n) This top venue hosts a variety of cultural events including theater, dance and music performances. Check the posters or with the tourist office for current events.

 Shopping

Zacatecas is known for silver and leather products and the colorful *sarape* (a blanket with an opening for a head). Try along Arroyo de la Plata (and its indoor market) and at **Casa de las Artesanías** (Plazuela Miguel Auza 312; ⊙9am-6pm).

Centro Platero JEWELRY
(☑492-899-45-03; www.centroplaterodezacatecas.com; Ex-Hacienda de Bernardez; ⊙10am-5pm Mon-Fri, to 2pm Sat) The Zacatecas silversmith industry sells Its work at this workshop a few kilometers east of town on the road to Guadalupe. Here, young artisans produce various designs, from the traditional to the contemporary. To get here, take a taxi (around M$60).

ℹ Information

Hospital Santa Elena (☑492-924-29-28; Av Guerrero 143)

Post Office (Allende 111; ⊙8am-4pm Mon-Fri, to 2pm Sat)

Tourist Office (☑492-924-40-47; www.zacatecastravel.com; Av Hidalgo s/n; ⊙9am-8pm Mon-Sat, to 6pm Sun) This information kiosk is run by Securz, the municipal tourist organization, and offers maps and information. Ask for a copy of *Agenda Cultural*, an excellent month-by-month listing.

Tourist Office (☑492-925-12-77, ext 625; www.zacatecastravel.com; Av González Ortega s/n; ⊙9am-4pm Mon-Fri) The formal headquarters of Securz.

ℹ Getting There & Away

AIR
Zacatecas International Airport is 20km northwest of the city. There are two daily flights to Mexico City as well as direct services to Los Angeles, Dallas/Fort Worth and Chicago.

BUS
Central de Autobuses Zacatecas (Carretera 45) is on the southwest edge of town, around 3km from the center. Deluxe, 1st- and 2nd-class buses operate to/from here. Some buses to nearby destinations including Villanueva (for La Quemada) leave from **Plaza del Bicentenario** (Blvd López Mateos). **Local buses to Guadalupe** (Blvd López Mateos) leave from the other side of the road here. There is no direct service to Guanajuato from Zacatecas, so take a León bus and change there. For San Miguel de Allende, change buses in San Luis Potosí or Querétaro.

ℹ Getting Around

The easiest way to get to/from the airport is by taxi (M$350 to M$400).

Taxis from the bus station to the center of Zacatecas cost around M$50. Bus 8 from the bus station (M$6) runs directly to the cathedral. Heading out of the center, catch a 'route 8' bus heading south on Villalpando.

Jerez

☑494 / POP 58,000 / ELEV 2000M
The delightful country town of Jerez, 30km southwest of Zacatecas, is as Mexican as can be: full of cowboys, churches and marching bands. As such, it's a great place to head for a day to soak up the traditional atmosphere. Sunday – market day – is especially fun as you'll see saddle-bound *rancheros* drinking outside the saloons, while on Saturdays you'll see wedding processions and

mariachis playing around the main plaza, Jardín Páez, with its old-fashioned gazebo, trees and benches. Jerez is also known for its lively one-week-long Easter fair, featuring, among other activities, *charreadas* (Mexican rodeos) and cockfights.

◉ Sights

Teatro Hinojosa
HISTORIC BUILDING

(Reloj Esq Salvador Varela; ⊙10am-5pm Tue-Sun) Construction of this remarkable and very beautiful building is said to have taken place over two decades, thanks to the organization of a local Don Higinio Escobedo Zauza who got things rolling in 1867. Then Don José María Hinojos organized generous locals who volunteered their time and donations of materials until the project was completed. It is renowned for its extraordinary shape, said to create among the best acoustics in the world. Ask the caretaker if you can look inside.

Casa Museo Interactivo Ramón Lopez Velarde
HISTORIC BUILDING

(Calle de la Parroquia 33; M$20; ⊙10am-5pm Tue-Fri, 11am-5pm Sat & Sun) One of Mexico's favorite poets, Ramón Lopez Velarde, was born in this house on June 15, 1888 and lived here first eight years or so of his life. The museum is well curated and full of interactive displays, which can be interesting even if you're unfamiliar with Lopez Velarde's work.

✖ Eating

★ Botica del Cafe
CAFE $

(Calle del Espejo 3; sandwiches M$60-80; ⊙5:30-10:30pm Tue-Fri, 10am-10:30pm Sat & Sun; 🛜🖉)
🍽 This utterly delightful cafe is quite the find in a small town like Jerez. Housed in an old pharmacy, Botica del Cafe serves up delicious *chapatas* (ciabatta sandwiches), salads and cakes, and does an array of coffee likely to satisfy even the most demanding customer, including chemex and aeropress.

❶ Getting There & Away

There are regular services from Zacatecas' bus station to Jerez (M$50 to M$60, one hour). Jerez' **bus station** is on the east side of town, 1km from the center along Calzada La Suave Patria. From here, 'Centro' buses (M$6) run to/from the center.

Baja California

Best Places to Eat

➡ Sur Beach House (p741)

➡ Tras/Horizonte (p707)

➡ Deckman's (p715)

➡ Heirbabuena (p745)

➡ Taco Fish La Paz (p731)

Best Places to Stay

➡ Posada la Poza (p744)

➡ Bungalows Breakfast Inn (p741)

➡ Casa Natalia (p737)

➡ El Ángel Azul (p731)

➡ Pension Baja Paradise (p731)

Why Go?

Baja, the earth's second-longest peninsula, offers over 1200km of the mystical, ethereal, majestic and untamed. Those lucky enough to make the full Tijuana to Los Cabos trip will find that the Carretera Transpeninsular (Hwy 1) offers stunning vistas at every turn. The middle of nowhere is more beautiful than you ever imagined, and people are friendly, relaxed and helpful – even in the border towns. Side roads pass through tiny villages and wind drunkenly along the sides of mountains. Condors carve circles into an unblemished blue sky. Some people simply sip drinks, eat fish tacos and watch the sun disappear into the Pacific. Some choose to feel the rush of adrenaline as they surf that perfect wave. Others walk through sherbet-colored canyons or stare up at the night's canopy of scattered-diamond stars. Whichever way you choose to take it, you'll discover some of Baja's many joys.

When to Go
Cabo San Lucas

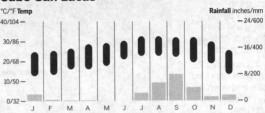

Jan–Mar Flowers bloom, things get green; whales and whale sharks play; and big waves delight surfers.

Aug–Sep Beaches all but empty. You'll have Baja all to yourself, but it's *hot*.

Oct–Nov The seas are crystal clear for un-crowded diving and snorkeling.

Baja California Highlights

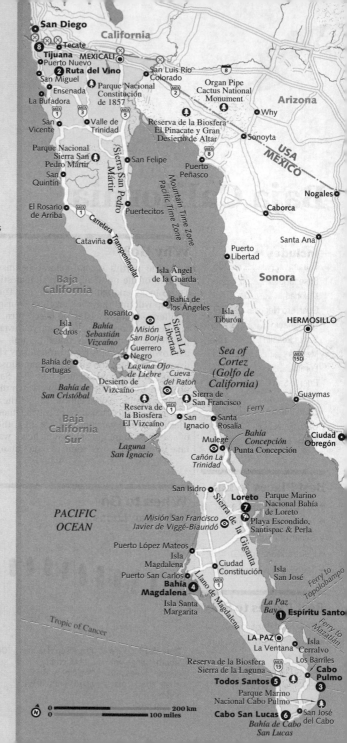

1 **Espíritu Santo** (p730) Kayaking the blue bays and picnicking on empty white beaches.

2 **Ruta del Vino** (p713) Sipping and savoring the bucolic delights of northern Baja's unspoiled Valle de Guadalupe.

3 **El Bajo** (p736) Diving with a giant ball of schooling jacks in Cabo Pulmo, home to the Sea of Cortez' only living coral reef.

4 **Bahía Magdalena** (p729) Boating from Puerto San Carlos into clear waters where whales come to calve.

5 **Todos Santos** (p743) Wandering cobblestone streets, dining farm-to-table at Heirbabuena and surfing till the sun goes down.

6 **Land's End** (p740) Paddling through clear waters to romantic Lovers Beach before crossing to wild Divorce Beach.

7 **Loreto** (p727) Boating and snorkeling by day; drinking and dining on the historic town square by night.

8 **Tijuana** (p705) Gorging on 'Baja Med' cuisine and downing tasty craft beers at Plaza Fiesta.

History

Before Europeans arrived, an estimated 48,000 mobile hunter-gatherers were living in today's Baja; their mysterious murals still grace caves and canyon walls. European settlement failed to reach Baja until the Jesuit missions of the 17th and 18th centuries, and the missions soon collapsed as European-introduced diseases ravaged the indigenous people. Ranchers, miners and fishers were the next to arrive. During the US Prohibition era of the 1920s, Baja became a popular south-of-the-border destination for gamblers, drinkers and other 'sinners.' Today the region is growing in economic power, population and popularity, albeit with problematic ecological and environmental consequences.

❶ Getting There & Away

There are six official border crossings from the US state of California to Baja.

Mexican mainland, US and international flights leave from and arrive at La Paz, Loreto, San José del Cabo and Tijuana. Ferries from Santa Rosalía and Pichilingue (near La Paz), connect Baja California to the mainland by sea.

❶ Getting Around

Air-conditioned, nonsmoking but relatively expensive buses operate daily between towns all along the peninsula; however, car travel is often the only way to reach isolated villages, mountains and beaches. You can rent cars in larger cities and major tourist destinations.

Highways are good and there are few toll roads. Drivers using the scenic (*cuota*; toll highway) route to Ensenada will need M$32; the Tijuana–Mexicali route costs M$170. Denominations larger than US$20 or M$200 are not accepted. You'll also encounter a number of military checkpoints.

NORTHERN BAJA

Tijuana, Tecate and Mexicali form the northern border of an area known as La Frontera, which extends as far south as San Quintín on the west and San Felipe on the east. Increasingly, the Ruta del Vino (between Ensenada and Tecate) is gaining Napa Valley–like fame for its boutique, award-winning wines. Though northern Baja's border cities and beaches are undeniably hedonistic, Tijuana and Mexicali are also major manufacturing centers and retain a workaday feel.

Parque Nacional
Constitución de 1857   NATIONAL PARK

At the end of a challenging 43km road out of Ojos Negros (east of Ensenada), Parque Nacional Constitución de 1857 has beautiful conifers, fields of wildflowers and a sometimes-dry lake, Laguna Hanson, at an altitude of 1200m. **Cabañas** (cabins; US$30) or **campsites** (☑686-554-44-04; included with US$4 park fee; ☉8am to 3pm) are available; the water may be contaminated so bring your own.

It's a sublime spot for mountain biking, hiking or just getting away from it all, as long as everyone else isn't getting away at the same time – in peak holiday times it can be busy, but it's a beautiful spot any time of year. The park is also accessible by a steeper road east of Km 55.2, 16km southeast of the Ojos Negros junction.

La Bufadora   LANDMARK

La Bufadora is a popular 'blowhole' (really a notch in the rock that sprays waves upwards) 40km south of Ensenada. If conditions are right it sends a jet of water up to 30m into the sky, drenching cheering onlookers.

Conditions aren't always ideal, but if you're up for a gamble you can drive south on the Transpeninsular to the 'Bufadora' sign, then follow the road all the way around to the Pacific side. Parking costs M$20 and the approach is flanked by souvenir stalls (and touts).

Tijuana

☑ 664 / POP 1.4 MILLION

Tijuana boasts the 'most crossed border in the world,' and in many ways offers the full border-town experience with its vibrant cocktail of cultures, vigorous nightlife, great range of restaurants and bars, and sleazy red-light district. Yes it's gritty and yes, there's plenty of violent crime, but in reality tourists are rarely a target. What's changed about Tijuana over the years is the emergence of a dynamic craft beer, dining and urban art scene. Several *pasajes* (passages) off main thoroughfare La Revolución (or La Revo, as it is commonly known) are now home to contemporary galleries and arty cafes. Many hip, lauded restaurants have opened in Zona Río, the upscale commercial center that runs alongside the river. Here you'll also find Plaza Fiesta, the rough-around-the-edges center of the craft beer and bar scene that perhaps more than anywhere embodies the ever-evolving, hedonistic yet distinctly Mexican soul of Tijuana.

History

At the beginning of the 20th century, TJ was literally just a mud hole. Prohibition drove US tourists here for booze, gambling, brothels, boxing and cockfights, causing Tijuana's population to balloon to 180,000 by 1960. With continued growth have come the inevitable social and environmental problems. Today the drug and illegal-immigrants trade into the US are the city's biggest concerns.

◉ Sights

★ Museo de las Californias   MUSEUM
(Museum of the Californias; ☑664-687-96-00; www.cecut.gob.mx; Centro Cultural Tijuana, cnr Paseo de los Héroes & Av Independencia; adult/child under 12yr M$27/free; ☺10am-6pm Tue-Sun; P♿) The Museo de las Californias chronicles the history of Baja California from prehistoric times to the present. The exhibit kicks off with replica cave paintings, then covers important historical milestones, illustrated in many cases by realistic dioramas and scale models, including replicas of a 16th-century ship, several missions and even a freestone chapel.

★ Pasaje Rodríguez   ARTS CENTER
(Av Revolución, btwn Calles 3a & 4a; ☺noon-10pm) This atmospheric arty alley reflects TJ's growing urban art scene. The walls are painted with vibrant graffiti-style murals – the perfect backdrop to the boho-style cafes, Oaxacan food stalls, locally made fashion, music bars, bookstores and craft shops.

Frontón Palacio Jai Alai   PALACE
(Av Revolución, btwn Calles 7a & 8a) Oddly baroque in style, the striking Frontón Palacio Jai Alai dates from 1926 and for decades hosted the fast-moving ball game of jai alai – a sort of hybrid between squash and tennis, originating in Spain's Basque country. A strike by players combined with lack of attendance led to its closure. Today it's a massive music venue.

⚡ Activities

Vinícola L.A. Cetto   WINE
(L.A. Cetto Winery; ☑664-685-30-31; www.lacetto.mx; Cañón Johnson 2108; ☺10am-5pm Mon-Sat) Still operated by descendants of Italian immigrants who arrived in Baja in 1926, L.A.

Cetto produces a range of tasty varietals, as well as sparkling wines and a decent brandy. If you can't make it to its Valle de Guadalupe **vineyards** (☑646-175-23-63; www.lacetto.com; Carretera Tecate–El Sauzal Km 73.5; tour & tastings M$50; ☺9am-5pm), stop at this shop for a tasting.

⚐ Tours

Turista Libre   TOURS
(www.turistalibre.com; day tours from US$70) Tours to Tijuana and beyond, focusing on harder-to-find stuff like cultural events, quirky markets, craft breweries, amazing street tacos and more.

✨ Festivals & Events

Expo Artesanal   ART
(Centro Cultural; cnr Paseo de los Héroes & Av Independencia; ☺early May) A superb arts and crafts festival held at the Cultural Center with handicrafts for sale from all over Mexico.

Tijuana Craft Beer Expo   BEER
(www.facebook.com/TjBeerFest; Mercado Hidalgo; ☺early Jun) This boozy festival serves some of the best beers, both new and old. Mix with Clamato for the true Mexican experience.

Expo Tequila   TEQUILA
(Tequila Festival; cnr Ave Revolucion & Calle 8a; ☺mid-Oct) Your chance to become a tequila pro with a vast variety available for tasting and purchase.

🛏 Sleeping

Hotel Baja   HOTEL $
(☑664-688-22-88; Calle 5a 8163; r from M$660; P♿❄☎) This small, modern, relatively new hotel, just off La Revo, has motel-style rooms set around a small astroturf garden. The decor is a dazzle of green-and-white paintwork and, while the rooms are tiny, the bathrooms are spacious with walk-in showers. It's secure, friendly and a very good deal.

Hotel Nelson   HISTORIC HOTEL $
(☑664-685-43-02; Av Revolución 721; r from M$650; P♿❄☎) The friendly Nelson is a longtime favorite, with high ceilings and 1950s-era touches, such as a real live barbershop of old. The carpeted rooms are scuffed and some are maybe a little too authentically old (check out a few), but they come with color TV, and some have a view of the (less-than-soothing!) Avenida Revolución.

★ Hotel Caesar's
HISTORIC HOTEL **$$**

(☎ 664-685-16-06; www.hotelcaesars.com.mx; Av Revolución 1079; r M$1360-1530; P⊝✳🖥🖧) If walls could talk! Tijuana's most famous historic hotel dates from the 1920s Prohibition era when it was popular with movie stars from over the border. Today only the facade reflects this belle epoque; the rooms are large, exceptionally clean, carpeted and blandly comfortable. But it's great value, central and the adjacent restaurant holds the historic charm the hotel lacks. Rates are cheaper online.

Hotel La Villa de Zaragoza
MOTEL **$$**

(☑ 664-685-18-32; www.hotellavilla.biz; Av Madero 1120; r from M$900; P⊝✳@🖧) Rooms here are set around a central courtyard and car park, and are typical, faded motel-style, sporting a decor predictably business-style bland with a predominantly cream-and-brown color scheme. However, the location is central yet quiet, rooms are immaculate and clean, and there's a good on-site restaurant, plus room service.

Hotel Real del Río
HOTEL **$$$**

(☑ 664-634-31-00; www.realdelrio.com; Av Velasco 1409; r incl breakfast M$1650; P⊝✳🖧) The contemporary building-block-style exterior here sets the tone for a slick, modern hotel with comfortable carpeted rooms, a gym, a rooftop sundeck for catching the rays and an excellent restaurant and bar, well known among locals for its Sunday brunch. It's located in the less-gritty-than-central-Tijuana Zona Río area, near many hip restaurants and brew pubs.

✗ Eating

★ Tras/Horizonte
MEXICAN **$**

(Río Colorado 9680; dishes M$28-119; ⊙1-10pm Tue-Sat, 1-7pm Sun; 🖧) With sunsets and sea creatures painted on the walls, and ferns, cacti, driftwood and fairy lights throughout, this indoor warehouse restaurant feels like a magical outdoor space. The food is even better, with generous, creative starters and tacos, from shrimp-stuffed *chili relleno* in adobe chili to portobello mushroom in cilantro mesquite pesto. Pair them with a house specialty mezcal cocktail.

Colectivo 9
INTERNATIONAL **$**

(Av Revolución 1265; mains M$70-95; ⊙1-8pm Tue-Thu & Sun, to midnight Fri & Sat; ♿) The narrow-lane approach provides a taster of what's to come with its hip small boutiques

---

BAJA SAFETY

The US State Department has issued travel warnings as gang violence, particularly in San José del Cabo and La Paz, skyrockets; the two cities have become two of the top cities for murders per capita in Mexico. These murders have been almost entirely within the drug cartels, and in the main tourist areas you'd hardly realize that violence is going on in the fringes. Border towns such as Tijuana have also received awful press due to drug-trade-related killings. It's important to know that, so far, tourists have not been targeted. Basic caution, common sense and awareness, such as staying clear of dodgy areas and not driving at night, is imperative. Keeping valuables (including surfboards) out of sight and doors locked will minimize risk of theft, which, at present, is still your greatest worry.

Sanitation standards in Baja are higher than in other states, and water – even tap water – is usually safe to drink.

---

and cafes; the Colectivo comprises nine small restaurants set around a central courtyard and fountain. What do you fancy? A burger, handmade sausage, pizza, Japanese food? Take your pick; the standard is superb, while the setting has a contemporary feel that's lacking in downtown TJ.

Tacos El Gordo
TACOS **$**

(Av Constitución 1342; tacos M$24; ⊙10am-5pm Mon-Sat) Locals in the know flock to this clean-cut, semi-outdoor joint decked out in white and red. Tacos include the normal suspects like *asada* and *pastor* (marinated roast pork), but also include delicacies like tender *lengua* (tongue) and fatty and tasty *ojo* (cow eye). *Sopas* (soups), *tortas* (sandwiches) and *tostadas* (deep-fried tortillas) are also on the menu.

Praga
CAFE **$**

(Av Revolución, btwn Calles 4a & 5a; breakfasts M$75-98; ⊙8am-11pm; 🖧) Good coffee (including espresso drinks) and yummy breakfasts from Benedicts and pancakes to particularly good *chilaquiles* make this an early morning no-brainer. The Parisian-style marble tables and European vibe make it an escape from the dusty streets outside.

Tijuana

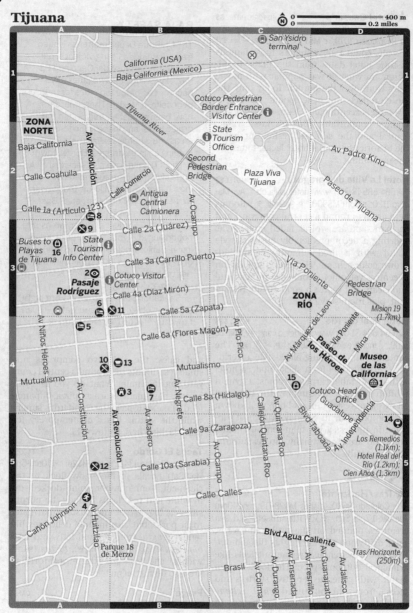

BAJA CALIFORNIA TIJUANA

Cine Tonala   MEXICAN **$$**
(http://tj.cinetonala.mx; Av Revolución 1317; dishes M$45-160; ⊙1pm-2am Tue-Sun) Taking Av Revolución to chic new standards, this cosmopolitan rooftop bar and restaurant serves insanely good and unusual tacos like sea urchin with avocado and guajilio chilies or smoked tuna with prawns, garlic lime and nine chilies. Or, just go with a rib eye steak or veggie burger with a cocktail. Don't miss checking out the art-house cinema downstairs.

Tijuana

Caesar's   ITALIAN $$

(📞 664-685-19-27; www.caesarstijuana.com; Av Revolución 1927; small Caesar salad M$90, mains M$110-120; ⊙noon-10:30pm Mon-Wed, to midnight Thu-Sat, to 9pm Sun; 🅿) Step inside and you are transported to the 1950s. Sepia pics of Hollywood movie stars line the walls, while the dark-wood decor oozes elegance. The exceptional Caesar salad, prepared with panache at your table, was apparently invented here by the restaurant's founder Caesar Cardini, an Italian immigrant from the 1920s.

Casa Cacao   MEXICAN $$

(Calle 2 No 8172; mains M$60-190; ⊙8:30am-8pm Mon-Sat, 10:30am-3pm Sun) Like stepping into a Mexican grandmother's home, this warm cafe is our favorite breakfast stop with chicken *emolades* (layered meat and tortillas) smothered with one of the best *moles* (chili sauce) in Baja and paired with an off-the-charts delicious *cafe olla* (Mexican cinnamon coffee) or hot chocolate. Lunch and dinner are great too.

Mision 19   INTERNATIONAL $$$

(📞664-634-24-93; www.mision19.com; Misión de San Javier 10643, Zona Río; mains M$150-395; ⊙1-10pm Mon-Sat) Star Mexican chef Javier Plascencia's ode to revitalizing his hometown, Mision 19 is the city's chic-est address with sparse black-and-white decor and formal service. Ingredients aim to come from a 120-mile radius to create true 'Baja cuisine.' Try the roast duck with mezcal, guava and chili or the tuna parfait with avocado meringue, Meyer lemon caramel and pork crackling.

Cien Años   MODERN MEXICAN $$$

(📞664-634-30-39; Av Velasco 2331, Zona Río; mains M$169-399; ⊙7:30am-11pm Mon-Sat, to 5pm Sun; 🅿🛜) Delicious, innovative contemporary Mexican cuisine plus traditional dishes such as *sopa Azteca* with avocado and tortilla strips, *crepes de huitlacoche* (corn fungus) with a creamy pistachio-flavored sauce and *chiles rellenos* (chilies stuffed with meat or cheese) with shrimps and lobster bisque. Ask the waiter to prepare the classic *salsa de molcajete* (roasted salsa made with a mortar and pestle) at your table.

🍸 **Drinking & Nightlife**

Drinkers in TJ may feel like hounds let loose in a fire-hydrant factory. Go wild in bars or attempt refinement with craft beers, fine tequilas and local wines.

⭐ **Plaza Fiesta**   CRAFT BEER

(Erasmo Castellanos Q. 9440; ⊙4pm-2am) Step into what seems like an aging shopping mall, to some gritty alleyways that, behold, house the heart of Tijuana's craft-beer scene as well as a slew of mezcal and sports bars and hopping clubs. Our favorite beers come from tiny yet lauded Insurgente Tap Room, but edgy Border Psycho and fun Mamut are also worth a stop.

Evenings are mellow at the craft-beer shops, but get much, much crazier as the night rolls on at the clubs that line the back of the complex. There's no for-tourist stuff here, just full-on Mexican partying.

BAJA CALIFORNIA TIJUANA

Norte Brewing Co. BREWERY

(Diaz Miron y o cuarta 8160; beer flights M$80; ⊘2-10pm Mon-Wed, to midnight Thu-Sat) Feel cool just finding this gray and black-themed brewery with windows overlooking the US–Mexico border. Try the hoppy yet easy-drinking 4 Play Session IPA or the Foreign Club Porter to go as dark as the music playing on the stereo. To find it, go through an unmarked entrance next to the casino and take the elevator to the 5th floor.

Container Coffee COFFEE

(Av Revolución 1348; espresso drinks from M$35; ⊘8am-9pm Mon-Sat) If you seriously need a coffee and are serious about the coffee you need, make a beeline to this hip roastery, with seats made from coffee sacks and model airplanes on the ceiling, in the heart of downtown. Choose from espresso or coffee brewed as you like from drip to French press.

Los Remedios CANTINA

(Av Rivera 2479, Zona Río; meals M$100-300; ⊘1pm-12:30am) Enjoy fabulous festive decor at this cavernous cantina/restaurant with its bullfighting posters, classic '50s movie posters, colorful paper flags and ceiling papered with lotto tickets. You can't miss the canary-yellow facade right on the roundabout in Zona Río. Live music at weekends. Choose from a veritable encyclopedia of tequilas.

☆ Entertainment

Domo Imax CINEMA

(www.cecut.gob.mex; Centro Cultural Tijuana; cnr Paseo de los Héroes & Av Independencia; tickets from M$52; ⊘1-11pm Tue-Sun) Located in the Centro Cultural Tijuana and showing predominantly art-house films.

Centro Cultural Tijuana ARTS CENTER

(CECUT; ☑664-687-96-00; www.cecut.gob.mx; cnr Paseo de los Héroes & Av Independencia; ⊘9am-7pm Mon-Fri, 10am-7pm Sat & Sun; ☑) Tijuana's sophisticated arts and cultural center would make any comparably sized city north of the border proud. It houses an art gallery, the superb Museo de las Californias (p706), a theater, and the globular cinema Domo Imax.

🛍 Shopping

Tijuana is great for souvenirs, but be cautious when buying gold and silver as much of it is fake (at those prices it would have to be, right?). You'll note the many drugstores here; they specialize in selling discounted generic pharmaceuticals to US citizens. Be sure to check out some of the local markets for another side of TJ.

Mecado Hidalgo MARKET

(Guadalupe Victoria 2; ⊘6am-6pm) Tijuana's most well-known market is also one of the biggest and most visited by tourists. It's still a great place to peruse everything from exotic fruits to fresh pastries and colorful piñatas.

Mercado El Popo MARKET

(cnr Calle 2a & Av Constitución; ⊘8am-8:30pm) El Popo is the most colorful downtown market, with stacks of fresh cheeses, sweets, wooden spoons, piles of dried chilies, kitchenware, herbs, incense, santeria, candles, love soaps, stacks of bundled cinnamon sticks, bee pollen and fruit. It's like a condensed version of the bigger, better-known markets.

ⓘ Information

DANGERS & ANNOYANCES

If you're street smart and not after trouble, then it is unlikely you'll have problems. Touts are sometimes irksome but they deserve a respectful 'no' – they are trying to make a living.

Don't drink on the streets. As in any big city, being plastered late at night can invite trouble.

Coyotes and *polleros* (both mean 'people smugglers') congregate along the river west of the San Ysidro crossing. After dark, avoid this area and Colonia Libertad, east of the crossing.

EMERGENCY

Tourist Assistance Hotline (☑078)

MEDICAL SERVICES

Hospital General (☑664-684-00-78; Centenario 10851) Hospital with a good reputation northwest of the junction with Avenida Rodríguez.

MONEY

Use caution when changing money, especially at night. Everyone accepts US dollars and most banks have ATMs.

TOURIST INFORMATION

Cotuco Visitor Center (☑664-685-31-17; www.descubretijuana.com; Av Revolución, btwn Calle 3a & Calle 4a; ⊘9am-6pm Mon-Sat) There is also a visitor center at the **border** (☑664-607-30-97; www.descubretijuana.com; pedestrian border entrance visitor center; ⊘9am-6pm Mon-Sat, 9am-3pm Sun) and a **head office** (☑664-684-05-37; www.descubretijuana.com; ste 201, Paseo de los Héroes 9365; ⊘9am-6pm Mon-Fri) on Paseo de los Héroes.

State Tourism Info Center (☑664-973-04-24; Av Revolución 842; ⊘8am-8pm Mon-Fri, 9am-1pm Sat) This small information kiosk

WORTH A TRIP

RUTA DEL VINO – SELF-GUIDED WINERIES TOUR

Here are a few of Valle de Guadalupe's many excellent, scenic and quirky wineries that are worth adding to your itinerary (in order heading from Ensenada toward Tecate):

Clos de Tres Cantos (☑558-568-92-40; Carretera Ensenada-Tecate Km 81; tastings US$8 incl bread & cheese; ☉10am-5pm Wed-Sun) ✿ From the old-seeming stone buildings and modern murals to the views, friendly staff and our favorite rosé in the valley, this is a near perfect place to sip vino with a plate of locally made bread and cheese.

El Pinar de 3 Mujeres (vinicola3mujeres@gmail.com; Carretera Tecate-Ensenada Km 87; set menu M$450; ☉1-6pm Thu-Mon, Apr-Oct) Named after the three women owners and winemakers, it combines a winery, restaurant and craft shop; meals are served under the trees with scenic vineyard views.

Castillo Ferrer (☑646-132-03-56; www.castilloferrer.com; Carretera Ensenada-Tecate Km 86.3; tastings from M$200; ☉11am-5pm) Taste wines (their Aurum is particularly noteworthy) on the Mediterranean-inspired terrace accompanied by mouthwatering rosemary-infused focaccia. It sits in an orange grove.

Bibayoff (☑646-176-10-08; http://bibayoff.mx; Carretera Franciso Zarco-El Tigre Km 9.5; tastings US$7; ☉10am-4pm Tue-Sun) A winery set off the beaten path with a small museum recounting the fascinating history of the Russians who immigrated here in the early 1900s (the current owner is a descendant). Be sure to ask for a taste of the fruity muscatel.

Adobe Guadalupe (☑646-155-20-94; www.adobeguadalupe.com; Parcela A-1 s/n, Rusa de Guadalupe; tastings from M$200; ☉10am-6pm) The most Mexican-feeling winery in the valley serves its vintages in a replica of a Spanish mission and surrounded by grapevines and a horse ranch. Its Jardin Secreto blend of grenache and tempranillo is the favorite.

L.A. Cetto (p706) Mexico's largest producer, and often filled with the tour-bus crowd, L.A. Cetto is worth checking out to see how it contrasts with the smaller, boutique places. It's highlight is its cabernet sauvignon.

can provide a handy map of town and that's about it.

State Tourism Office (Secretaría de Turismo del Estado; ☑664-682-33-67; www.descubre bajacalifornia.com; Alarcón 1572; ☉8am-8pm Mon-Fri, 9am-1pm Sat) This is the main state tourism office in town.

❶ Getting There & Away

Mexican tourist permits are available 24 hours a day at the San Ysidro–Tijuana border's *Instituto Nacional de Migración* (INM) office at a cost of M$500, or free if you're visiting Mexico for under one week. They can be issued for up to 180 days.

AIR

Several airlines service Tijuana, predominantly **Aeroméxico** (☑664-683-84-44, 664-684-92-68; www.aeromexico.com; Plaza Rio) and **Volaris** (☑55-1102-8000; www.volaris.com; Aeropuerto Internacional de Tijuana), which serve many mainland Mexican and US destinations. International destinations include Shanghai, Guatamala City, Managua and San Salvador.

Aeropuerto Internacional General Abelardo L Rodríguez (☑664-607-82-00; www. tijuana-airport.com; Carretera Aeropuerto-Otay Mesa) is in Mesa de Otay, east of downtown.

BUS

The main bus terminal, about 5km southeast of downtown, is the **Central Camionera** (☑664-621-29-82; Chapultepec Alamar), where Elite (www.autobuseselite.com.mx) and Estrella Blanca (www.estrellablanca.com.mx) offer 1st-class buses with air-con and toilets. Destinations in mainland Mexico include Guadalajara (from M$1900, 36 hours) and Mexico City (from M$2015, 44 hours, 12 daily, hourly). ABC (www. abc.com.mx) and Auto Transporte Águila (www. autobusesaguila.com) operate mostly 2nd-class buses to mainland Mexico's Pacific coast and around Baja California.

Suburbaja (☑664-688-00-45) local buses use the handy downtown **Antigua Central Camionera** (cnr Av Madero & Calle 1a), with buses leaving for Tecate (M$85), one hour, every 15 minutes).

Between 3am and 10pm, buses leave from the **San Diego Greyhound terminal** (☑800-231-22-22, US 619-515-1100; www.greyhound.com; 120 West Broadway, San Diego) and stop at the **San Ysidro terminal** (☑619-428-62-00; 4570 Camino de la Plaza) en route to Tijuana's Central Camionera bus terminal or the airport. Fares from San Diego/San Ysidro to the Central Camionera or airport are M$150 each way.

CAR & MOTORCYCLE

The **San Ysidro** (📞 US 619-428-1194; 799 East San Ysidro Blvd) border crossing, a 10-minute walk from downtown Tijuana, is open 24 hours, but motorists may find the Mesa de Otay crossing (also open 24 hours) less congested – it's 15km to the east of San Ysidro.

Rental agencies in San Diego are the cheapest option, but most of them only allow journeys as far as Ensenada. Renting a car in Tijuana or taking the bus may be your best option for heading further south, although few offer one-way rentals and those that do add a US$600 or more surcharge.

TROLLEY

San Diego's popular and easy trolley (www.sdmts.com) runs from downtown San Diego through to the border at San Ysidro (US$2.50) every 15 minutes from about 5am to midnight. From San Diego's Lindbergh Field airport, city bus 992 (US$2.50) goes to the Plaza America trolley stop in downtown San Diego, across from the Amtrak depot.

ⓘ Getting Around

For about M$12, local buses go everywhere, but the slightly pricier route taxis are much quicker. To get to the Central Camionera take any 'Buena Vista,' 'Centro' or 'Central Camionera' bus from Calle 2a, east of Avenida Constitución. Alternatively, take a gold-and-white 'Mesa de Otay' route taxi from Avenida Madero between Calles 2a and 3a (M$15). Regular taxis will charge about M$100 for rides in and around Avenida Revolucíon or the Zona Río. The airport is about M$250.

Buses to Playas de Tijuana leave from Calle 3a near Ave Martinez in Zona Central. Grab route taxis for Blvd Agua Caliente and to Central Camionera.

Uber rideshare is popular in Tijuana and rides around town cost around M$35 – you'll need to have the app or download it on your phone. You can request an English-speaking driver on the app at no extra cost.

Playas de Rosarito

📞 661 / POP 78,247

Once a deserted, sandy beach and then a Hollywood film location (Fox Studios Baja, built in 1996 for the filming of *Titanic*), Playas de Rosarito is finally coming into its own. Developments and condos are everywhere, but despite the construction clamor, Rosarito is a quieter place to party or just chill out, and is an easy day trip (or overnight trip) from Tijuana or San Diego. There are also several excellent surf breaks nearby including the famous K28 around 15km south of town.

🛏 Sleeping & Eating

Robert's K38 Surf Motel   MOTEL $$

(📞 661-613-20-83; www.robertsk38.com; Carretera 1D Km 38; r US$40-75; 🅿 ❄ 🖥) Eleven kilometers south of Rosarito and walking distance from the famous K28 surf break, this super-fun, comfortable bargain of a place is, as you'd guess, popular with surfers. You can rent gear or rack up your gear then just chill out on the beach, walk to cheap places to eat and become a beach bum. No reservations.

Hotel del Sol Inn   HOTEL $$

(📞 661-612-25-52; www.del-sol-inn.com; Blvd Juárez 32; d M$1500; 🅿 🐾 ❄) The Sol is a motel-style lodging right on the main drag with clean, carpeted rooms with TV, bottled water and simple furniture. Note that prices triple during the short spring-break holiday.

★ Tacos El Yaqui   TACOS $

(cnr Palma & Mar del Norte; tacos M$20-45; ⊙ 8am-5pm Mon, Wed & Thu, 9am-9:30pm Fri-Sun) This delicious taco stand with an outdoor grill is so popular that it often closes early when the ingredients run out. Get in line before 4pm if you don't want to risk missing out.

BUSES FROM TIJUANA

DESTINATION	FARE (M$)	DURATION (HR)	FREQUENCY (DAILY)
Ensenada	205	1½	frequent
Guerrero Negro	1300	11	3
La Paz	2505	24	3
Loreto	1945	18	2
Mexicali	325	2¾	frequent
Santa Rosalía	1616	14	3

PARQUE NACIONAL SIERRA SAN PEDRO MÁRTIR

Bobcats, deer and bighorn sheep await visitors to San Pedro Mártir national park, but its real claim to fame isn't what's on the ground but what's in the air: this park is one of only six places in the world where the almost-extinct California condor has been successfully reintroduced into the wild.

Even if one of the world's largest birds doesn't soar over your head, there are lots of other reasons to make the detour. Conifers scrape the sky, the air is pine scented and clean, and the (tortuously winding) drive passes through boulder-studded, ethereal landscapes that seem more Martian than something here on earth.

To reach the park, turn left at the sign at approximately Km 140 on the Transpeninsular, south of Colonet. A 100km paved road climbs to the east through an ever-changing desert landscape, affording satisfying vistas all along the way. Camping is possible (no toilets; bring water) in designated areas, but there are no other facilities.

Susanna's MODERN AMERICAN $$
(www.susannasinrosarito.com; Blvd Juárez 4356; mains US$15-30; ⏰1-9:30pm Wed-Mon; 🛜) Owner Susanna dishes up delightful plates of tasty fare based on fresh seasonal produce spiked with Californian pizzazz. Light salads with innovative dressings, and pasta, meat and fish dishes can be enjoyed in a court-yard setting or homey dining room with chintzy furniture and olive-green walls. The wines are from Valle de Guadalupe.

El Nido STEAK $$$
(Blvd Juárez 67; mains M$225-510; ⏰8am-9:30pm; 🅿🛜♿) You can't miss the vine-covered, wagon-wheel-decorated frontage of this steakhouse in the center of town. And the atmosphere continues with exposed brick and beams, strings of garlic and a foliage-filled back terrace, complete with aviary. Tortillas are made fresh to order and the menu includes venison, rabbit and chicken, plus the star billing: steak.

ℹ Getting There & Away

From downtown Tijuana, *colectivos* (shared cars) for Playas de Rosarito (M$18) leave from Avenida Madero between Calles 3a and 4a.

Ruta del Vino & Valle de Guadalupe

📞646 / POP 2664

Beloved by residents of Mexico and Southern California, but a surprise to just about everyone else, Baja's wine country is an intoxicating blend of luxury lodging, wine tasting and fine dining with dirt roads, cacti amid the grapevines and a very laid-back attitude. It's actually one of the oldest wine-producing regions in the Americas,

now with over 60 wineries, and it attracts a very hip crowd of 20- to 40-somethings looking to relax and indulge in the finer things on a relatively low budget. Once people began whispering that this is the next Napa, the word spread further afield and the wines are gaining attention internationally.

⊙ Sights

Museo de la Vid y El Vino MUSEUM
(www.museodelvinobc.com; Carretera Federal Tecate–Ensenada Km 81.3; M$50; ⏰9am-5pm Tue-Sun) Who knew that the first wines in the Americas were produced in Baja? Follow the fascinating history of wine in the region via diaromas (in Spanish, but English speakers are given a binder with English translations) and a few artifacts. The bright, modern building makes this even more of a worthwhile stop.

🎊 Festivals & Events

Fiesta de la Vendimia WINE
(Grape Harvest Festival; ⏰early Aug) Midsummer wine harvest with galas, special tastings, elite parties around Valle de Guadalupe. Reserve far in advance with wineries for events. Cheers!

🛏 Sleeping

Glamping Ruta de Arte y Vino CARAVAN PARK $
(📞646-185-33-52; www.rutadearteyvino.wixsite.com/rutadearteyvino; Carretera Ensenada–Tecate Km 13, San Marcos; s/d campervans US$50/96) A quirky place in a field with 12 vintage 1960s Airstream campervans. Lodging is rustic and gets hot when the weather is sweltering, but otherwise expect to barbecue with your neighbors, get tips from the friendly hosts,

TOP SPOTS FOR FANTASTIC FISH TACOS

Simple and versatile, the humble fish taco is Baja's comfort food. Done right they're magical. These spots are all worth seeking out for a taste of this sublimely delicious snack:

Taco Fish La Paz (p731), La Paz. Superb, crispy seafood tacos at one of the longest-standing places in town.

La Guerrerense (p718), Ensenada. Good enough to win an international street food competition and Anthony Bourdain's pork-loving heart. Enough said.

La Lupita (p738), San José del Cabo. Creative new twists on the classic plus 15 mezcals to choose from as a chaser.

Tacos del Rey (p728), Loreto. Clean, simple, perfect. Pick your toppings then stuff your face on a park bench.

enjoy the stars through a telescope and have a grand 'ole time communing with nature. It's overpriced but fun.

Hotel Meson del Vino   HOTEL $$

(646-151-21-37; www.mesondelvino.net; Carretera Federal 3 Ensenada–Tecate Km 88.4; d US$55; P ❋ ❈ ☎) A mustard-yellow exterior with vines up the walls gives this place a hacienda vibe, but the comfortable rooms feel more like grandma's house. There's a small pool and a rather bizarre semi-outdoor weights room, but service is nonexistent (we were handed the room key and never saw the owner again). Overall though it's clean, central and a great deal.

Encuentro   DESIGN HOTEL $$$

(646-155-27-75; www.grupoencuentro.com.mx; Carretera Tecate-Ensenada Km 75; r US$320-390; ☎❈) Architecturally beautiful Encuentro features 22 minimalist, glass, steel and wood 'loft' bungalows perched on a dry grassy hill overlooking the valley. This is the type of place where people dress stylishly and take selfies. There's a photo-worthy infinity pool as well as a restaurant with not only one of the greatest views around but also some of the best food we sampled in the wine country.

La Villa del Valle   B&B $$$

(646-156-80-07; www.lavilladelvalle.com; Carretera Tecate–San Antonio de las Minas Km 88; d US$275-295; P ❋ ❈ ☎) A beautiful B&B overlooking the rolling vineyards and fields in the Ruta del Vino. The owners grow their own lavender, make their own personal-care products and have fantastic meals. It feels like a modern, ultra-luxe place in Tuscany. No pets or children.

✖ Eating

La Cocina de Doña Estela   MEXICAN $

(646-156-84-53; Ranchos San Marcos; mains M$60-115; ☺8am-6pm Tue-Sun) Everyone's favorite breakfast in the valley. Doña Estella's is a welcome slice of traditional Mexico with huge egg dishes including the house specialty *machaca con huevos* (scrambled eggs with dried Sinola-style beef). Lunch moves on into *birria de res* (beef stew) territory. Don't miss the addictive *cafe olla* (Mexican coffee) – the best we've had.

Taquería Los Amigos   MEXICAN $

(cnr Av Hidalgo & Ortiz Rubio, Tecate; tacos from M$22; ☺Fri-Wed) Join the locals for absolutely superb (and massive) flour quesadillas filled with beans, cheese, excellent guacamole and *carne asada* (marinated grilled beef). The tacos are tasty too. Don't leave Tecate without trying this place.

Lupe   FOOD TRUCK $$

(Carretera Tecate–Ensenada Km 83; tortas M$60-130; ☺1pm-9pm Tue-Fri, noon-10pm Sat & Sun) Just want a quick bite between wineries or maybe want a budget meal in the land of upscale dining? Fortunately celebrity chef Javier Placensia offers this humble yet delicious food cart. Fillings range from simple yet gourmet-like ham and cheese to creative wonders like crispy suckling pig with refried beans and avocado, or Mexican stewed beef and onion.

Troica   FOOD TRUCK $$

(646-156-80-30; Rancho San Marcos Toros Pintos; dishes M$45-160; ☺1-7pm Tue-Sun) Right in the middle of the vineyards and set on a little hill, this is a fabulous place to enjoy fish, *asada* (grilled beef) or *lechon* (roasted suckling pig) tacos or perhaps a salad or octopus *tostada* (deep-fried tortillas) to break up a day of wine tasting.

★ Deckman's
CALIFORNIAN $$$

(☑646-188-39-60; www.deckmans.com; Carretera Ensenada–Tecate Km 85.5; mains M$190-400; ☺1-8pm Wed-Mon; ℗) ✐ Good luck not having fun at this warm-hued, adobe-walled, gravel-floored restaurant with the grill as aflame as the wine-drinking diners' spirits. Run by Michelin-starred chef Drew Deckman, it has hearty dishes like roast quail or rack of lamb, with ingredients nearly entirely sourced from sustainable, local supplies. The five-course tasting menu for M$500 is a steal.

Finca Altozano
CALIFORNIAN $$$

(☑646-156-80-45; www.fincaltozano.com; Carretera Tecate–Ensenada Km 83; mains M$95-380; ☺1-9pm Tue-Sun) Our favorite of celebrity Mexican chef Javier Placensia's restaurants, this laid-back-feeling place looking out over the vineyards has a cracking oyster bar and not-to-miss starters like chocolate clams with tuna, scallop and oak-smoked bacon. Mains include everything from risotto and confit duck in *mole* (chili sauce) to locally sourced beef brisket or wood-fired tacos.

ℹ Getting There & Away

You can skip Tijuana's long lines and treat yourself to some beautiful scenery by entering Mexico via Tecate. The border crossing (open 6am to 10pm) is far less congested, and south of Tecate lies the Ruta del Vino in the intoxicatingly beautiful Valle de Guadalupe (Hwy 3).

Ruta del Vino and Valle de Guadalupe are not reliably accessed by public transportation; you'll need your own car.

ℹ Getting Around

If you're taking your own vehicle and will be wine tasting, obviously designate a nondrinking driver first. Maps of the wine route (available at local hotels, tourist offices and wineries) will help you locate the vineyards.

If you don't want to drive but don't fancy a group tour either, you can hire a driver for the day via Uber with **UberVALLE** (www.uber.com; day trips for up to four people around US$150) within the Uber app, although there have been clashes between Uber and locals supporting taxi drivers in the area. For this reason, some people prefer a private taxi for the day, found through hotels and word of mouth – these should cost around US$160 for a day trip for up to four people.

Ensenada

⏹ 646 / POP 519,813

Ensenada, 108km south of the border, is hedonistic Tijuana's cosmopolitan sister. The city has a quirky mix of just-off-the-boat cruise shippers, drive-by tourists from California, visitors from mainland Mexico and seen-it-all locals. In case you've forgotten you're in Mexico (what with all those US dollars and English menus), just look up: a Mexican flag, so large it's probably visible from space, flutters proudly over the *malecón* (waterfront promenade). Wander Avenida López Mateos (Calle 1a) and you'll find almost anything ranging from delicious French food to tasteless T-shirts. Don't miss the dancing musical fountain on the waterfront if you've got kids.

Ensenada was the capital of Baja territory from 1882 to 1915, but the capital shifted to Mexicali during the revolution. The city subsequently catered to 'sin' industries until the federal government outlawed gambling in the 1930s. Today the town is a tourist resort for more than four million visitors annually.

◉ Sights

★ Riviera del Pacífico
HISTORIC BUILDING

(☑646-177-05-94; Blvd Costero; ℗) FREE Opened in the 1930s as Hotel Playa Ensenada, the extravagant Riviera del Pacífico, a Spanish-style former casino, is rumored to have been a haunt of Al Capone. It now houses the **Museo de Historia de Ensenada** (M$25; ☺10am-5pm Mon-Sat, noon-5pm Sun) and **Bar Andaluz** (☑646-176-43-10; ☺10am-midnight Mon-Fri, 9am-1am Sat; ☎); while the Casa de Cultura offers classes, film screenings and exhibitions. Just strolling around the building and grounds is a delight.

Museo Historico Regional de Ensenada
MUSEUM

(Museo del INAH; ☑646-178-25-31; www.lugares.inah.gob.mx; Av Gastelum; ☺9am-5pm Mon-Sat) FREE Built in 1886 and once the Aduana Marítima de Ensenada, the city's oldest public building now houses this historical and cultural museum. It has a relatively small but comprehensive collection of artifacts, and discusses (mainly in Spanish) the area's history. The most interesting part is the old prison cells where paintings by ex-inmates are preserved on the walls.

Ensenada

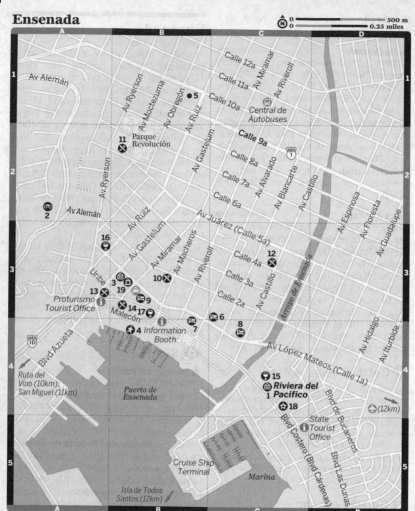

El Mirador

VIEWPOINT

Atop the Colinas de Chapultepec, El Mirador offers panoramic views of the city and Bahía de Todos Santos. Climb or drive (note: there's no off-street parking) to this highest point in town, up Avenida Alemán from the western end of Calle 2a in central Ensenada.

🏃 Activities

Surfing

Isla de Todos Santos

SURFING

This island off Ensenada's coast (not to be confused with the town near Los Ca-

bos) hosts one of the world's top big-wave surfing contests each year. **El Martillo** (The Hammer) is legendary, with swells often triple overhead or even bigger when conditions are right. Boats can be chartered out from the harbor. Prices start at about M$900 per person (four people minimum).

San Miguel

SURFING

(parking M$75) There's not much here but a few campers, a parking lot, and a wonderful point break just offshore. When the waves are big it's an awesome ride.

Ensenada

Fishing & Whale-Watching

Ensenada is known the world over for its excellent sportfishing, though you must have a valid Mexican fishing license (available at state tourism offices) if you want to reel in a live one. Most charter companies also offer whale-watching tours from mid-December to mid-April.

Sergio's Sportfishing Center   FISHING
(☏646-178-21-85; www.sergiosfishing.com; day trips from US$70; ◷8am-6pm) Well-regarded Sergio's can be found on the sportfishing pier off Ensenada's *malecón*. Fishing trips include the necessary gear. Day trips are available as well as private charter trips.

🎓 Courses

Spanish School Baja   LANGUAGE
(☏646-190-60-49; www.spanishschoolbaja.com; Calle 10a, btwn Avs Ruiz & Obregón; courses per week US$270) Small classes with 25 hours of instruction per week run throughout the year.

🎊 Festivals & Events

Baja 1000   RACING
(◷mid-Nov; 🏴) Baja's biggest off-road race. See 'truggies' (truck-buggies) tear up the desert to the cheers of just about everyone. The Baja 500 is in June.

Carnaval   CARNIVAL
(◷Feb; 🏴) A Mardi Gras–type celebration 40 days before Ash Wednesday when the streets flood with floats and dancers.

Baja Seafood Expo   FOOD & DRINK
(Calle 9a 340; ◷Sep) Sample scrumptious seafood with industry folks.

🛏 Sleeping

Hotel demand can exceed supply at times, particularly at weekends and in summer. Many places raise their rates significantly at these times, but don't expect a lot of bang for your pesos at any time.

Hotel Santo Tomás   HOTEL $
(☏646-178-33-11; hst@bajainn.com; Blvd Costero 609; d from M$590; 🅿❄🌐🛜) Although the furnishing and carpets are a little tired, this vast hotel with its pea-green-and-purple exterior is still a great choice. The quirky lobby has a grand sweeping staircase, an elevator with disco mirrors and a cage of cuddly-looking chinchillas. Rates nearly double on Friday and Saturday (along with the noise levels outside).

Hotel Cortez   HOTEL $$
(☏646-178-23-07; www.bajainn.com; Av López Mateos 1089; r from M$1470; 🅿❄🌐🛜🏊) This is one of the best choices right in the heart of things, with facilities that include a small gym. The (heated) pool is surrounded by lofty trees. Some of the rooms are a tad dark. If you can, go for the premium rooms, with their chic and contemporary look: all earth colors and plush fabrics. It books out fast.

Hotel Bahía   HOTEL $$
(☏646-178-21-01; www.hotelbahia.com.mx; Av López Mateos 980; r M$1062; 🅿❄🛜🏊) Despite

the unintentionally retro, 1960s-ish exterior, this hotel offers pleasant and spacious carpeted rooms. An attractive pool area with adjacent bar and service direct to your sunbed is another perk. It's as central as central gets.

Best Western Hotel El Cid
HOTEL **$$$**

(☑646-178-24-01; www.hotelelcid.com.mx; Av López Mateos 993; d from M$1495; P🅿🚭 ❄@🛜🐾❄🐾) This four-star hotel has comfortable rooms with firm beds, a respected restaurant and a lively bar. The bilingual staff are particularly gracious and friendly and the situation is central, in the more upmarket part of town.

🍴 Eating

Ensenada's dining options range from outrageously delicious corner taco stands to places serving excellent Mexican and international cuisine.

★ La Guerrerense
TACOS **$**

(www.laguerrerense.com; cnr Avs Alvarado & López Mateos; tacos from M$25; ⊙10:30am-5pm Wed-Mon) Sabina Bandera's award-winning seafood stand dates from the 1960s and attracts long lines with its outstanding seafood tacos, juicy ceviche (seafood marinated in lime juice) and *tostadas* (deep-fried tortillas). There's usually some streetside guitar strumming to add to the atmosphere. Try the sea snail or sea urchin on a *tostada* (M$25) for a real treat.

Birreria La Guadalajara
MEXICAN **$**

(Av Macheros 154; tacos M$25-39; ⊙7am-8pm; 🎵) A great barn of a place, rightfully famous for its *birria de chivo* (goat stew), but also serving excellent tacos and charcoal grilled meats. Popular with families, the atmosphere is boisterous and noisy with a large open-plan kitchen, a few TVs, strolling mariachis and decor that has changed little since its opening in 1972.

Mariscos El Norteño
SEAFOOD **$**

(Local 4, mercado de mariscos; tacos M$30; ⊙8am-9pm Mon-Sat, from 7am Sun) You can't go wrong at any of the seafood stalls across from the *mercado de mariscos* (fish market), but this popular one has plenty of seating and a superb range of salsas; including roasted jalapeños and red chili. Try an original Baja-style taco, which is a deep-fried fish or shrimp taco with shredded cabbage in a creamy white sauce.

El Parián
MEXICAN **$**

(☑646-128-82-32; cnr Calle 4a & Av Castillo; mains M$80-95; ⊙7:30am-11:30pm; 🎵) Streamers, murals, painted tables and sherbert-colored furniture give a festive atmosphere to enjoying great enchiladas, quesadillas, burritos, *agua de jamaica* (hibiscus water) and friendly service. Flat-screen TVs in every corner mean you (or the waitstaff) never have to miss a moment of that cheesy Mexican soap.

Muelle 3
SEAFOOD **$$**

(☑646-17-40-318; Teniete Azueta 187a; dishes M$60-150; ⊙noon-6:30pm Wed-Sun) Right on the marina, this place looks like a hole in the wall but on closer inspection you'll see a sophisticated crowd savoring artistically presented ceviches and other Mexican classics. The flavors are balanced and subtle and everything is fresh and prepared to perfection. It gets crowded, especially at lunchtime.

Boules
INTERNATIONAL **$$$**

(☑646-175-87-69; Av Moctezuma 623; mains around M$250; ⊙2pm-midnight Wed-Sun) Creamy risottos, pasta and fresh seafood are a draw here, but it's the setting under the trees on a deck with lights strung up above that make it taste even better. Owner Javier greets and mingles with all guests like they're regulars. Choose from a huge selection of wines at the on-site shop then bring them to your table.

Drinking & Nightlife

On weekends most bars and cantinas along Avenida Ruiz are packed from noon to early morning. If that's not your scene, head for one of the many quality hotels and fine restaurants where you're likely to find a laid-back spot to sip a margarita (said to have been invented here) or sample a top-shelf tequila.

★ Hussong's Cantina
CANTINA

(http://cantinahussongs.com/home.html; Av Ruiz 113; ⊙11am-2am Tue-Sun) The oldest and perhaps liveliest cantina in the Californias has been serving tequila since 1892. A Friday or Saturday night will be packed with locals, a sprinkling of tourists and touting mariachis. The history is fascinating, so request the leaflet (in English and Spanish).

Wendlandt
BEER HALL

(www.wendlandt.com.mx; Blvd Costero; ⊙6pm-midnight Tue-Sat) Enjoy craft beers made by the owners, as well as from national and international small breweries; five samplers will cost you just 60 pesos. The surroundings have an

BUSES FROM ENSENADA

DESTINATION	FARE (M$)	DURATION (HR)	FREQUENCY (DAILY)
Guerrero Negro	1705	10	3
La Paz	2140	22	3
Mexicali	300-380	4	12
Playas de Rosarito	135	1	frequent
Tecate	200-300	2	frequent
Tijuana	145-250	1½	frequent
Tijuana Airport	300	1¾	frequent

urban-chic vibe with chunky wood furniture, exposed brick walls and clever quirky lighting incorporating beer bottles.

Ojos Negros WINE BAR
(Av Ruiz 105; ⊘11am-midnight Tue-Sat, 2-10pm Sun; 🖝) Suffering from margarita melt-down? Then head to this relaxed wine bar for a glass of fruity Passion Meritage, an award-winning red from the owners' vineyards: Bodegas San Rafael. Lounge-like seating, chill-out music and burgundy-washed walls set the scene nicely. Nibbles include gourmet flatbread pizzas.

☆ Entertainment

Centro Estatal de las Artes ARTS CENTER
(☑646-173-43-07; www.cenart.gob.mx/2015/07/ensenada/; cnr Av Riviera & Blvd Costero; ⊘8am-8pm Mon-Sat, noon-7pm Sun, plus evening events) The Centro Estatal de las Artes has shows and exhibits throughout the year.

🔒 Shopping

Tequila Room DRINKS
(Av López Mateos; ⊘10am-6pm Tue-Thu, to midnight Fri & Sat) The Irish-Mexican owner is passionate about tequila, but you won't find any of the more commercial brands here; these are sourced from all over Mexico. Even if you don't fancy a tipple (tastings are free), you can admire the bottles, many of which are art-works in themselves.

ℹ️ Information

EMERGENCY

Municipal Police ☑646-165-20-34, ☑911
State Police ☑646-176-13-11, ☑911
Tourist Assistance ☑078

MEDICAL SERVICES

Sanatorio del Carmen (☑646-178-34-77; cnr Av Obregón & Calle 11a) A small, clean, well-respected private hospital.

TOURIST INFORMATION

Proturismo Tourist Office (☑646-178-24-11; www.proturismoensenada.org.mx; Blvd Costero 540; ⊘8am-8pm Mon-Fri, 9am-5pm Sat & Sun) Dispenses maps, brochures and current hotel information. There's an **information booth** (☑646-178-30-70; ⊘Tue-Sun) in the Plaza Cívica.

State Tourist Office (☑646-172-54-44; www.descubrebajacalifornia.com; Blvd Costero 1477; ⊘8am-6pm Mon-Fri, 9am-1pm Sat & Sun) Carries similar information to the Proturismo office.

ℹ️ Getting There & Away

Immigration Office (☑646-174-01-64; Blvd Azueta 101; ⊘document delivery 8am-6pm Mon-Fri, document pickup 1-3pm Mon-Fri) Sells tourist permits for those arriving into the country by boat.

BUS

Central de Autobuses (Av Riveroll 1075) Ten blocks north of Avenida López Mateos, serving far-flung destinations like Guadalajara (M$1680, 36 hours) and Mexico City (M$1800, 48 hours) as well as local Baja destinations.

CAR & MOTORCYCLE

The drive from Tijuana to Ensenada on the scenic (cuota) route has three tolls (total M$99).

ℹ️ Getting Around

The main taxi stand is at the corner of Avenidas López Mateos and Miramar; taxis also congregate along Avenida Juárez. Most fares within the city cost from M$50 to M$120. Uber ride-share is also available in Ensenada, with trips in town averaging M$30.

Mexicali

☑686 / POP 763,162
Mexicali is what Tijuana must have been before the tourist boom – gritty, even scary – and most tourists just head southward. The city has the largest concentration of ethnic

Chinese in Mexico and offers some decent Chinese as well as Mexican restaurants plus some fun nightlife, if you can handle a rougher scene. In summer, Mexicali is one of the hottest places on earth – stay away, if possible.

◉ Sights

Catedral de la Virgen
de Guadalupe
CATHEDRAL
(cnr Morelos & Av Reforma) This cathedral is the city's major religious landmark.

🛏 Sleeping & Eating

Araiza
LUXURY HOTEL $$$
(☑686-564-11-00; www.araizahoteles.com; Calz Juárez 2220, Zona Hotelera; d incl breakfast from US$100; P❄✳@☎🏊) This family-friendly hotel has well-appointed spacious rooms, two excellent restaurants, a bar, tennis courts, a gym and a convention center. For a quieter stay, request a room in the executive wing away from the road and pool area.

Los Arcos
SEAFOOD $$
(☑686-556-09-03; Av Calafia 454; mains M$126-300; ☉11am-10pm) Dating from 1977, this is Mexicali's most popular seafood restaurant. The *shrimp culichi* (shrimp in a creamy green chili sauce) is spectacular. Live music brightens the night on Thursday and Friday. Reservations recommended.

❶ Getting There & Away

AIR
Aeropuerto Internacional General Rodolfo Sánchez Taboada (☑686-552-23-17; www.aeropuertosgap.com.mx/es/mexicali; Carretera Mesa de Andrade Km 23.5) is 18km east of town. **Aeroméxico** (☑686-555-70-47; www.aeromexico.com) flies many destinations via Mexico City, while **Calafia Airlines** (www.calafiaairlines.com) flies from Mexicali to La Paz and San José del Cabo.

BUS
Long-distance and mainland bus companies leave from the **Central de Autobuses** (☑686-556-19-03; Calz Independencia 1244; ☉24hr), near Calzada López Mateos. Autotransportes del Pacífico (www.tap.com.mx) and Elite (www.autobuseselite.com.mx) serve mainland Mexican destinations, while ABC (www.abc.com.mx) serves the Baja peninsula.

Greyhound (☑760-357-18-95, 800-231-22-22; www.greyhound.com; Calz Independencia 1244; ☉5:30am-11:30pm) has offices in Mexicali and directly across the border in Calexico. There are several departures daily from Mexicali to Los Angeles (one way from US$25) and 12 to San Diego (one way from US$22), as well as other destinations in the USA.

CAR & MOTORCYCLE
Vehicle permits are available at the border. The main Calexico–Mexicali border crossing is open 24 hours, while the newer crossing east of downtown (built to ease congestion) is open from 6am to 10pm.

SOUTHERN BAJA

Cardón cacti, boojum trees, ocotillo, cholla and other desert marvels thrive in this beautiful desert area that sometimes doesn't receive any rain for a decade. Look out for crumbling missions, date palms, coconuts and mangrove swamps as you meander southward.

The 25,000-sq-km **Reserva de la Biosfera El Vizcaíno** is one of Latin America's largest protected areas. It sprawls from the Península Vizcaíno across to the Sea of Cortez and includes the major gray-whale calving areas of Laguna San Ignacio and Laguna Ojo de Liebre, and the Sierra de San Francisco with its stunning pre-Hispanic rock art.

The southernmost part of the peninsula contains the cosmopolitan city of La Paz, small seaside towns and villages, and the popular resorts of San José del Cabo and Cabo San Lucas, aka 'Los Cabos.' After the quiet isolation of the state's north, Los Cabos will either be a jarring shock or a welcome relief.

BUSES FROM MEXICALI

DESTINATION	FARE (M$)	DURATION (HR)	FREQUENCY (DAILY)
Ensenada	498	4	12
La Paz	2931	25	2
Mexico City	1797	37	5
Tijuana	235	2½	frequent

Guerrero Negro

🗹 615 / POP 13,054

Guerrero Negro is an unassuming, ramshackle kind of town that sprang up to service the lone salt factory. Though the main tourist draw is the proximity to the seasonal migrations of gray whales, there's also excellent bird-watching in the shallow marshes, and the salt factory's odd white crystalline plains are quite beautiful.

◉ Sights

Misión San Borja   CHURCH
(btwn Rosarito & Bahía de los Ángeles; ⊙ 8am-6pm)
This well-restored mission is set a in pristine, spectacular boojum tree-and-cardón desert. The (bumpy) drive alone makes it worth the trip. A family descended from the original preconquest inhabitants is restoring it by hand and will proudly show you the mission, a freshwater spring, a secret nowwalled-up tunnel and the old Jesuit ruins. Heading east from Hwy 1, turn right about 45km after leaving the highway.

🏃 Activities

Guerrero Negro can surprise you. If whales aren't around, try bird-watching or touring the **salt factory**. On the east side of the inlet is a mini Sahara of 3m-to-6m sand dunes made of powdery white sand.

Bird-Watching
Head to the **Old Pier** and *faro* (lighthouse) if you're a bird-watcher, as there is a pleasant 11km drive through salt flats and marshland: prime territory for ducks, coots, eagles, curlews, terns, herons and other birds.

Whale-Watching
During whale-watching season agencies arrange trips on the waters of **Laguna Ojo de Liebre**, where visitors are virtually guaranteed a view of whales in their natural habitat.

Malarrimo Eco Tours   WILDLIFE
(🗹 615-157-01-00; www.malarrimo.com; Blvd Zapata 42; whale-watching US$50; 🚸) Located beside the hotel of the same name, Malarrimo is one of the most respected and longstanding operators in town and offers fourhour whale-watching tours.

Other Activities
Salt Factory   TOURS
(🗹 615-157-50-00; 1-2hr tour per person M$200) Tours of the salt factory can be arranged via

TIPS FOR DRIVING THE TRANSPENINSULAR
••••••••••••••••••••••••••••••••••••
If time permits, driving the length of the Carretera Transpeninsular (1625km) is an experience not to be missed. Most importantly, it is overall very safe; although driving at night is not recommended due to the possibility of cows wandering onto the road. The road surface is good and, in general, traffic is surprisingly light. There are several military checkpoints along the way, although tourists are rarely pulled over. Keep an eye on your gas gauge, fill up regularly, and be aware that from El Rosario to Guerrero Negro, a distance of some 350km, there is no gas station.

any hotel or tour agency in Guerrero Negro. If your Spanish is good you can also try calling the salt factory itself for a free tour, although you'll miss getting all the information you'd get from a guide.

🛏 Sleeping & Eating

The whale-watching season can strain local accommodations; reservations are advisable from January through March.

Aside from the restaurants, a few cheap and tasty taco trucks set up along the main drag from around 10am to 5pm.

Terra Sal   MOTEL $
(🗹 615-157-01-33; Emiliano Zapata s/n; s/d incl breakfast M$550/620; 🅿 ✳ 🛜) Located on the approach to town, this big, new, charmless motel has rooms in a much classier category than elsewhere in town, with earthy colors, chunky wood furniture, mosaic tiling and a choice of either Jacuzzi tubs or walk-in showers. There's a decent restaurant as well.

Hotel Malarrimo   HOTEL $
(🗹 615-157-01-00; www.malarrimo.com; Blvd Zapata 42; s/d M$490/590; 🅿 ⊖ ✳ @ 🛜) Hot, strong showers and a lot more ambience than the other options in town. Whale headboards and a general whale theme make it impossible to forget why you've come here. There is also a small gift shop and an excellent restaurant, plus whale-watching tours can be arranged. Campsites and RV hookups available.

Los Caracoles
HOTEL $$

(📞 615-157-10-88; www.hotelloscaracoles.com. mx; Calz de la República s/n; r M$850; P🗑️❄️ @🛜) This attractive, sand-colored hotel blends well with its desert surroundings, as do the modern rooms and, come to that, the bathrooms – all are decorated in tones of yellow and gold. There's a souvenir shop and several computer terminals for the use of guests.

Malarrimo
MEXICAN $$

(www.malarrimo.com; Blvd Zapata 42; mains M$145-275; ⏱️7:30am-10:30pm; P🛜) A solid dining choice at this long-standing hotel, serving primarily seafood dishes; the fish soup comes highly recommended. Vegetarian meals are available on request and the adjacent bar and pool table could equal an evening's entertainment in this somewhat sleepy town.

Santo Remedio
MEXICAN $$

(📞615-157-29-09; Carballo Félix; mains M$120-260; ⏱️8am-10pm; P) One of the fancier Guerrero Negro options, with exceptional service, soft lighting, ocher-washed walls, a pretty patio and a variety of meat and seafood dishes, ranging from T-bone steak to Galician-style octopus.

ⓘ Information

There's an ATM at Banamex.

Clínica Hospital IMSS (📞 615-157-03-33; Blvd Zapata) is Guerrero Negro's main medical facility.

ⓘ Getting There & Away

Guerrero Negro's tiny airport is 2km north of the state border, west of the Transpeninsular.

Aéreo Calafia (📞 615-157-29-99; www.aereo calafia.com.mx; Blvd Zapata; ⏱️8am-7pm Mon-Fri, to 4pm Sat) Runs flights to Hermosillo and Guyamas and offers charters.

Bus Station (Blvd Marcello Rubio; ⏱️24hr) Offers wide range of bus services throughout Baja.

San Ignacio
📍 615 / POP 667

With its lush, leafy date palms and pretty, tranquil river, sleepy San Ignacio is a welcome oasis after the seemingly endless Desierto de Vizcaíno. Jesuits located the Misión San Ignacio de Kadakaamán here, but Dominicans supervised construction of the striking church (finished in 1786) that dominates the picturesque, laurel-shaded plaza.

👁️ Sights

Misión San Ignacio de Kadakaamán
CHURCH

With lava-block walls nearly 1.2m (4ft) thick, the former Jesuit Misión San Ignacio de Kadakaamán stands directly across from San Ignacio's small plaza and is flanked by a grove of citrus trees. Occupying the site of a former Cochimí *ranchería* (indigenous settlement), the mission has been in continuous use since its founding in 1728. It's possibly the prettiest mission in Baja.

One of the three 18th-century altarpieces inside is dedicated to the San Ignacio de Loyola, the town's patron saint. The mission was initiated by the famous Jesuit Fernando Consag, and was completed in 1786 under the direction of Dominican Juan Crisóstomo Gómez. Epidemics reduced the Cochimí population from about 5000 to only 120 by the late 18th century, but the mission lasted until 1840.

Museum
MUSEUM

(Misión San Ignacio de Kadakaamán; ⏱️8am-5pm Mon-Fri) **FREE** This small museum offers a glimpse of the area's natural history and also recreates the famous cave drawings found in the Sierra de San Francisco.

Casa Lereé
MUSEUM

(📞615-154-01-58; www.casaleree.com; Morelos 20; ⏱️10am-1pm & 4-5pm Mon-Sat) **FREE** Part museum and part bookstore, this beautiful old building sits around a verdant garden

BUSES FROM GUERRERO NEGRO

DESTINATION	FARE (M$)	DURATION (HR)	FREQUENCY (DAILY)
Ensenada	1705	10	3
La Paz	1730	11	4
Loreto	825	5-6	2
Santa Rosalia	396	3	1
Tijuana	1300	11	3

with magnificent trees, including a soaring (and shady) *ficus indiga*. The US owner is a wealth of information about the area and has one of the best collections of books on Baja anywhere.

👉 Tours

Ecoturismo Kuyima ADVENTURE
(☑ 615-154-00-70; www.kuyima.com; Plaza Benito Juaréz 9; cave painting day tours per person US$60-95; ☺ 8am-8pm) This very friendly and helpful local cooperative on the plaza arranges whale-watching trips to the beautiful **Laguna San Ignacio**, and can help arrange visits to the otherwise difficult-to-reach rock-art sites in the Sierra de San Francisco.

🛏 Sleeping & Eating

★ Ignacio Springs B&B $$
(☑ 615-154-03-33; www.ignaciosprings.com; San Ignacio; d US$68-130; 🅿🌐🛜🐕) This Canadian-owned B&B comprises yurts and *cabañas* (cabins). Idyllically situated fronting the lagoon, the decor ranges from conventional US-style to Aztec ethnic, with brightly colored rugs and ceramics. Breakfast includes homemade breads, preserves and (even) sausages. Kayaks available.

Hotel Desert Inn HOTEL $$
(☑ 615-154-03-00; mmabarca@fonatur.gob.mx; Camino a San Ignacio Km 72; d M$1200; 🅿🛜🐕) It looks like a prison from the outside, but past the bleak facade is a modern mission-style hotel with spacious, airy rooms decorated in a soothing palette of creams, browns and ocher, plus plenty of wardrobe

space and large walk-in showers. Rooms are set around a central pool area landscaped with lofty palms and dazzling bougainvillea bushes.

Rice & Beans CAFE $
(www.riceandbeansoasis.com; meals M$80-250; ☺ 8am-9pm) For something different, stop at this clean, American-diner-style biker joint serving cheap breakfasts, *comidas corridas* (set lunches), stuffed potatoes and excellent *tortas* (sandwiches). The road-weary can also stay in one of the large but dingy and old rooms for US$40.

ℹ Getting There & Away

The **bus station** (☑ 615-154-04-68) is near the San Lino junction outside of town. Buses pick up passengers here, arriving about every four hours from 5am to 11pm, both north- and southbound to locations such as Tijuana (M$1855), La Paz (M$1480) and Cabo San Lucas (M$1844).

Sierra de San Francisco

The sheer quantity of beautiful petroglyphs in this region is impressive, and the ocher, red, black and white paintings remain shrouded in mystery. In recognition of its cultural importance, the Sierra de San Francisco has been declared a Unesco World Heritage site. It is also part of the **Reserva de la Biosfera El Vizcaíno**. Although day trips are possible, to see the region's highlights you'll need to trek for a few days with local rancher guides and donkeys to carry gear.

CALIFORNIA GRAY WHALES

The migration of gray whales from Siberian and Alaskan waters to the lagoons of Baja is an amazing animal event. In the calving grounds of Laguna Ojo de Liebre and Laguna San Ignacio, 700kg calves will draw their first breaths and begin learning the lessons of the sea from their ever-watchful mothers. The season is long but varies due to the fact that some whales arrive early in the Pacific lagoons, while others take weeks or months to round Land's End and find their favorite bays in the Sea of Cortez.

Peak months to see mothers and calves in the lagoons are February to early April, but the official whale-watching season begins December 15 and lasts until April 15.

If you've got *ballena* (whale) fever, one of these destinations will provide a cure:

➡ Laguna Ojo de Liebre (Scammon's Lagoon)

➡ Laguna San Ignacio

➡ Puerto López Mateos

➡ Puerto San Carlos (p729)

ON A MISSION FROM GOD

Baja's missions have a dubious history – built by Jesuits and Dominicans intent on bringing salvation, they instead brought death through introduced European diseases. Many missions were abandoned as populations dropped below sustainable levels. Today, however, these beautiful buildings, whether in use or out in the middle of nowhere, make for great photos and fun day trips, and they're an undeniable part of Baja's checkered past. You should not need a 4WD to visit any of those listed here, though the roads can be impressively bad (or impassable) at times.

Misión Nuestra Señora de Loreto (p727) The oldest mission and an impressive monument still in use today.

Misión San Borja (p721) Out in the middle of nowhere but well worth the drive. Its treasures include a hot spring and a secret tunnel (now walled up). José Gerardo, a descendant of the original preconquest inhabitants, will show you around.

Misión San Francisco Javier de Viggé-Biaundó (p727) Remote and beautifully preserved, it feels like stepping back in time. The drive here offers awesome vistas and even some cave paintings along the way.

Misión Santa Rosalía de Mulegé (p726) Extremely photogenic. Don't miss the view from behind looking out over the palm-edged river.

Resources for further reading include *Las Misiones Antiguas*, by Edward W Vernon, and www.vivabaja.com/bajamissions; both feature beautiful photos.

◉ Sights

Cueva del Ratón ARCHAEOLOGICAL SITE

Named for an image of what inhabitants once thought was a rat (or mouse) but is more likely a deer, this is the most easily accessible cave in the Sierra de San Francisco.

Drivers can get here on their own after registering and paying the park entry (M$65) and guide fee (M$150 for two people) at the office of the **Instituto Nacional de Antropología e Historia** (INAH; ☑615-154-02-22; Misión San Ignacio de Kadakaamán museum; ☺8am-5pm Mon-Sat Apr-Oct, daily Nov-Mar), inside the Misión San Ignacio de Kadakaamán museum (p722) in San Ignacio, then picking up their guide in the pueblo closest to the paintings. Bringing a camera costs M$45 per day. INAH fees for guides for other trips start at M$150 per day, and each pack animal adds M$250. These are INAH fees only, and guides themselves charge additional (varying) fees.

ℹ Getting There & Away

The beautiful mule-back descent of Cañón San Pablo requires at least two days, and preferably three, and is best done through a tour operator like Ecoturismo Kuyimá (p723), which can arrange three-day trips for around US$240 per person (four-person minimum; supplies not included). Longer tours are also available.

Self drivers should head to the Instituto Nacional de Antropología e Historia for advice and directions before heading off.

Santa Rosalía

☑615 / POP 12,000

Southbound travelers will welcome their first sight of the Sea of Cortez after crossing the Desierto de Vizcaíno. Santa Rosalía's brightly painted and strangely Wild West–feeling clapboard-sided houses, Eifel Tower–design-cousin Iglesia Santa Bábara, French cowboy bakery, *malecón* (seaside promenade) and mining museum are prime attractions, although they're rivaled by the black-sand beaches, lazy pelicans and great views from the surrounding hills. This is no holiday-haven to be sure, but it is a unique stop worth a look.

The town has become a prosperous mining center once again, with the reopening of the historic El Boleo copper and cobalt opencast mine in 2013 adding around 3800 jobs to the local economy. As such there's a real industrial, hard-working vibe to the town.

◉ Sights

★ Iglesia Santa Bárbara CHURCH

(Av Obregón 20) Designed and erected for Paris' 1889 World's Fair, then disassembled and stored in Brussels for shipping to West Africa, Gustave Eiffel's (yes, of Eiffel Tower fame) prefabricated Iglesia Santa Bárbara was, instead, shipped here when a Boleo Company director signed for its delivery to the town in 1895.

🛏 Sleeping & Eating

Hotel Las Casitas
de Santa Rosalia
BOUTIQUE HOTEL **$$**

(📞615-152-30-23; www.facebook.com/Las-Casitas-Santa-Rosalia-164100420829302; Carretera Sur Km 195; s/d M$850/1150; P 🛜) US-owned Las Casitas has a real five-star holiday-in-the-sun look with large rooms that have balconies, seamless Sea of Cortez views, exquisite tilework and tasteful artwork. The less expensive doubles share the views, but are considerably smaller; there is a small communal space with some cooking facilities plus a state-of-the art exercise bike for the use of guests.

Hotel Francés
HISTORIC HOTEL **$$**

(📞615-152-20-52; www.hotelfrances.com; Av Cousteau 15; r incl breakfast M$920; P 🛜❄) Overlooking the Sea of Cortez and rusting hulks of mine machinery, historic Hotel Francés is a colonial gem. Built in 1886 and originally the dormitory for the 'working girls' of a brothel near the mine, the hotel features beautiful rooms with high ceilings, cool cloth-covered walls and charming stained-wood details.

★ Panadería El Boleo
BAKERY **$**

(📞615-152-03-10; Av Obregón 30; baked goods M$8-12; ⊗8am-9pm Mon-Sat, 9am-2pm Sun) Since 1901 this has been an obligatory stop for those in search of Mexican pastries and, more unusually, French baguettes in a weirdly Wild West ramshackle building. While the pastries may not be world class, the setting is so unusual you have to cowboy up to the counter and order at least one. No seating.

❶ Getting There & Away

The passenger/auto ferry *Santa Rosalía* sails to Guaymas at 8:30am on Wednesday and Friday and 8pm on Saturday, arriving 10 hours later. It returns from Guaymas at 8pm Tuesday, Thursday and Saturday. Double-check in advance as timings may change.

The ticket office is at the **ferry terminal** (📞615-152-12-46; www.ferrysantarosalia.com; ⊗9am-1pm & 3-6pm Mon-Sat, 9am-1pm & 3-8pm Sun) on the highway. Passenger fares are around M$930 (children's tickets are half price). Vehicle rates vary with vehicle length.

The **bus terminal** (📞615-152-14-08; ⊗24hr) is found just south of the entrance to town, in the same building as the ferry terminal.

Mulegé
📞615 / POP 3821

The palm- and mangrove-lined Río Mulegé, with its delta, birds, wildlife and nearby snorkeling and diving opportunities, makes Mulegé a great stop for the outdoorsy or those with kids. Set down in a narrow *arroyo* (stream), Mulegé is prone to flooding when it gets pummeled by hurricanes and major storms (which tends to happen every two to three years). The river setting plus the 18th-century mission and town square give the town a remote, old-town feeling unique in Baja.

As you wind your way south from Mulegé, you'll pass some of the peninsula's most beautiful, turquoise-lapped *playas* (beaches) along Bahía Concepción, The pelican colonies, funky rock formations and milky, blue-green water make it a top stop for kayakers, even though several of the beaches are becoming more built up.

◉ Sights

★ Bahía Concepción
BEACH

One of the most stunningly beautiful stretches of coast in Baja with blue-green waters, white sandy coves and comparably less construction. Great for kayaking.

BUSES FROM SANTA ROSALÍA

DESTINATION	FARE (M$)	DURATION (HR)	FREQUENCY (DAILY)
Ensenada	1652	13	2
Guerrero Negro	396	3	1
La Paz	1021	8	5
Loreto	461	3½	6
Mulegé	120	1	5
San Ignacio	145	1	4
San José del Cabo	1402	13	1
Tijuana	1616	14	3

CAÑON LA TRINIDAD

Trinity Canyon is great for bird-watchers, with the chance to see vermilion flycatchers, gila woodpeckers and a host of raptors and buteos. The narrow, sherbet-colored canyon walls and shimmering pools of water are stunning, as are the pre-Hispanic cave paintings.

Rendered in shades of ocher and rust, the paintings feature shamans, manta rays, whales and the famous Trinity Deer, leaping gracefully from the walls of the cave as arrows pass harmlessly over its head. You're not allowed to enter by yourself, but Mulegé native Salvador Castro Drew of **Mulegé Tours** (☑ 615-161-49-85; mulegetours@hotmail. com; day excursions per person M$600-700) knows just about everything about the site you'd want to know, including how to avoid the two nasty beehives that 'guard' the paintings. He also does taxi runs to other area sites.

Museo Mulegé
MUSEUM

(Barrio Canenea; ⊘9am-2pm Mon-Sat; ⍩) `FREE`
This former territorial prison was famed for allowing prisoners to roam free in town during the day, although the women inmates stayed to cook and clean. Now it holds a small collection of fairly mundane prison artifacts plus a mummified cat. Note the blackened cell where a prisoner apparently set fire to himself after hearing his wife was having an affair.

Misión Santa Rosalía de Mulegé
CHURCH

Come to the imposing, stone hilltop Misión Santa Rosalía de Mulegé (founded in 1705, completed in 1766 and abandoned in 1828) for great photos of the site and river valley.

🕴 Activities

Mulegé's best diving spots can be found around the Santa Inés Islands (north of town) and just north of Punta Concepción (south of town). Diving tour operators come and go, so ask around. The beautiful river, the estuary delta and the southern beaches make Mulegé a prime spot for kayaking.

NOLS Mexico
KAYAKING

(☑ US 800-710-6657, US 307-332-5300; www.nols. edu/courses/locations/mexico/; ⊘1-week sailing courses US$1900) 🕊 Runs sea-kayaking, sailing and wilderness courses and trips out of its sustainable, ecofriendly facility on Coyote Bay, south of Mulegé.

🛏 Sleeping & Eating

Mulegé is a very popular expat and snowbird haunt where people own their property, and short-term lodging options are pretty sparse.

Hotel Las Casitas
HOTEL $

(☑ 615-153-00-19; javieraguiarz51@hotmail.com; Madero 50; s/d M$550/650; P⊖❄🛜) Perhaps inspired by its very pretty courtyard, fountains, statues and shady garden of tropical plants, beloved Mexican poet Alán Gorosave once inhabited this hotel. The restaurant serves decent food and has an open-fire grill. The rooms are simple and somewhat threadbare, but smell like cinnamon and oranges and are decorated with traditional fabrics and artwork.

Hotel Mulegé
HOTEL $

(☑ 615-153-00-90; Moctezuma s/n; d M$550; P❄@🛜) Located just beyond the arch at the entrance to town, this place is an unmemorable motel on the outside, but the spotless, modern, brightly painted rooms make it the best deal in town. The staff are extra-friendly and helpful as well.

Hotel Serenidad
HOTEL $$

(☑ 615-153-05-30; www.serenidad.com.mx; Mulegé; d/tr M$1200/1400, cabañas M$2100; P⊖❄🛜🏊) Dating back to the 1960s, this hotel is a local institution. Plenty of famous folk have flown into the bumpy private airstrip here, including John Wayne. The rambling, dusty property has loads of backcountry character, with a vast restaurant, rustic and authentic-to-the-era double rooms and small *cabañas*. There's a pig roast every Saturday with live music. It's 3.8km from town, off the highway to the south.

Ana's
SEAFOOD $$

(Playa Santispac; mains M$140-240; ⊘8am-9pm; P) In the mood for seafood? Then it is well worth the 10km drive southwest of town to this lovely beachside restaurant where you can dine on a succulent seafood platter comprising shrimp, clams and whatever has been caught that day. If you're here earlier in the day, grab a fresh cinnamon bun. Popular with families at weekends.

Doney Mely's MEXICAN $$
(☎615-153-00-95; Moctezuma s/n; mains M$90-180; ⊙7:30am-10pm Wed-Mon; 🛜🅿) A colorfully decorated restaurant and bar with a special weekend menu for two that includes a gut-busting choice of local favorites like *chiles rellenos* (chilies stuffed with meat or cheese) and enchiladas *verdes*. Breakfasts complete with espresso beverages come recommended as well.

Los Equipales INTERNATIONAL $$$
(☎615-153-03-30; Moctezuma s/n; mains M$100-375; ⊙8am-10pm; 🛜) Just west of Zaragoza, this restaurant and bar has gargantuan meals and bright, enclosed balcony seating that's perfect for an evening margarita with friends. Lobster salad, T-bone steak and fried chicken are a sampling of the surf and turf fare.

❶ Getting There & Away

Bus Terminal (Transpeninsular Km 132; ⊙8am-11pm) Located near the large entry arch, northbound destinations include Santa Rosalía (M$120, one hour) and Tijuana (M$2030, 16 hours) and stop three times daily. Southbound buses pass to destinations including Loreto (M$225, two hours) and La Paz (M$1170, six hours) five times daily.

Loreto

☎613 / POP 17,000
Loreto feels like somewhere between an old and new world. Linger along cobblestone streets, past shops selling pottery and a centuries-old mission to find local teenagers practicing a hip-hop act in the square. Perhaps sit at an outdoor cafe to try some local craft beer or stroll along the *malécon* (beach promenade) where an old man hobbles along with a cane and young women jog by in the latest workout gear. Out in that blue water is a water-sports paradise and the magnificent Parque Nacional Bahía de Loreto, where the shoreline, ocean and stunning offshore islands are protected from pollution and uncontrolled fishing.

Anthropologists believe the Loreto area to be the oldest human settlement on the Baja Peninsula. Indigenous cultures thrived here due to plentiful water and food. In 1697 Jesuit Juan María Salvatierra established the peninsula's first permanent mission at this modest port backed by soaring mountains.

◎ Sights

★**Parque Marine Nacional Bahía de Loreto** PARK
(entry fee M$33) This park makes Loreto a world-class destination for all types of outdoor activities; a number of outfitters offer everything from kayaking and diving to stand-up paddleboarding and snorkeling along the reefs around Islas del Carmen and dormant-volcano-dominated Coronado Islands. Aside from gray whales that frequent the Sea of Cortez, this is the best place to see blue whales. Pay the entrance fee at the park's office in the marina. Staff can advise on water activities.

Sierra de la Giganta OUTDOORS
The trails in the rugged, striated mountains that rise up behind Loreto are seldom marked, but there's great hiking for the fit and adventurous. Guides can be found at the Municipal Department of Tourism (p729) or via www.hikingloreto.com (you can also order a hiking guidebook here). Take lots of precautions out here as there's no cell-phone service.

Misión San Francisco Javier de Viggé-Biaundó CHURCH
(San Javier) FREE This wonderful mission is well worth a daytime detour. The windy road passes some beautiful *arroyos* (streams) before arriving at the mission. Be sure to wander to the back garden to see the 300-year-old olive tree with rope-like bark that looks like something out of a Tolkien fantasy. The mission itself is almost unchanged from its look of three centuries ago.

Head south on the Transpeninsular for around 35km and look for the sign to the right shortly after you leave Loreto. Guides at the mission may offer to take you to see cave paintings (guide fee M$300; entry to the caves M$100). Note that this involves driving 15km on a very rough road and climbing a steep rocky hill to see a very small wall with several red paintings.

Misión Nuestra Señora de Loreto CHURCH
Dating from 1697, this was the first permanent mission in the Californias and was the base for the expansion of Jesuit missions up and down the Baja peninsula. Alongside the church, the **Museo de las Misiones** (☎613-135-04-41; Salvatierra 16; M$50; ⊙9am-1pm & 1:45-6pm Tue-Sun) chronicles the settlement of Baja California.

⚡ Activities

Home to the beautiful waters and islands in Parque Marine Nacional Bahía de Loreto (p727), Loreto is a world-class destination for all types of ocean activities from kayaking and fishing to diving and snorkeling. The gorgeous coast is backed by the equally stunning Sierra de la Giganta (p727), perfect for off-the-beaten-path horseback riding, hiking and mountain biking.

Loreto is awash with companies offering outdoor sports.

Loreto Sea and Land Tours　　WATER SPORTS
(☑613-135-06-80; www.toursloreto.com; Madero; diving/snorkeling/whale-watching from US$110/65/130; 🖐) 🎣 This recommended ecofriendly place covers a wide range of activities, including diving, kayaking and snorkeling.

🛏 Sleeping

★Hostal Casas Loreto　　HOTEL $
(☑613-116-70-14; Misioneros 14; s/d M$600/800; 🖐🛜) Rooms here are set around a long covered courtyard, are spotless and charmingly decorated with rustic furniture and stone walls. There's a well-equipped kitchen for guests and the owner, Abel, likes to bring everyone together to hang out in the common areas.

La Damiana Inn　　HISTORIC HOTEL $$
(☑613-135-03-56; www.ladamianainn.com; Madero 8; r US$75, casitas US$90; 🖐🛜) This historical posada has spacious, individually furnished rooms with decor ranging from brightly colored Baja fabrics, ceramics and artwork to mellow earth tones and native American pieces. There's a communal kitchen and a gorgeous mature garden with fruit trees and hammocks.

There is also a charming casita (small house) that sleeps up to four people, with its own kitchen and secluded terrace. It's well worth the extra pesos.

Posada de las Flores　　LUXURY HOTEL $$
(☑613-135-11-62; www.posadadelasflores.com; Plaza Cívica; r incl breakfast from US$100; 🖐🛜) Sitting majestically on the main plaza in town, the interior has a palatial feel due to its stone columns and arches, trickling fountains and an earthy color palette. Rooms are surprisingly small, dark and characterless. Not to worry: the stunning public spaces extend to a rooftop pool, bar and terrace that have views stretching to the mission.

Posada del Cortes　　BOUTIQUE HOTEL $$
(☑613-135-02-58; www.posadadelcortes.com; El Pipila 4; r M$1500; 🖐🛜) This elegant small hotel exudes a chic atmosphere with ocher-and-cream paintwork, forest-green tilework, dark-wood furniture and lashings of white linen. There's a small terrace with wrought-iron furniture and a trickling fountain. Rooms include coffee makers.

🍴 Eating

Enjoy the regional standards: excellent seafood with plenty of tasty lime and cilantro, potent margaritas and fruity *aguas frescas* (ice drinks).

★Asadero Super Burro　　MEXICAN $
(Fernández; tacos M$25-40, burritos M$95-120; ⊙6pm-midnight Thu-Tue) At this locals' favorite, watch this team of women press fresh tortillas, and stew and grill the beef and chicken at the open kitchen. Super Burro is known for it's flavorful *arrachera* (grilled skirt steak), gigantic burritos and equally huge stuffed potatoes. If you're not sharing, famished or used to eating things the size of your head, stick with the tacos.

Tacos del Rey　　MEXICAN $
(cnr Juárez & Misioneros; tacos M$30; ⊙9am-2pm) The best fish tacos in town are sold at this simple kiosk-cum-restaurant, which is clinical in its cleanliness. The *carne asado* (roasted meat) is another standout and there is plenty of topping choice to custom-design your taco.

Pan Que Pan　　MEXICAN, ITALIAN $
(Hidalgo s/n; breakfasts M$25-95; ⊙8am-4pm Tue-Sun) 🎣 Serving simply awesome breakfasts, this friendly, funky alfresco cafe and bakery offers big omelettes served with beans, avocado, local cheese and fresh bread, continental-style lighter breakfasts of granola or pastries and a decadent French toast with caramelized bananas. Stay for lunch for salads, pizzas, baguette sandwiches and homemade pasta.

El Zopilote
Brewery & Cocina　　MEXICAN, ITALIAN $$
(Davis 18; mains M$99-160; ⊙noon-10pm Tue-Sun) Owned by a Mexican-Irish couple (ask how they met; now there's a story!), this restaurant and microbrewery has cuisine that is fittingly diverse, ranging from creamy pastas to fillet steak and chicken fajitas. Its decor and airy terrace make it a good choice for a romantic dinner. Don't miss trying one of its locally brewed beers.

BUSES FROM LORETO

DESTINATION	FARE (M$)	DURATION (HR)	FREQUENCY (DAILY)
Guerrero Negro	825	5-6	2
La Paz	800	5	6
San José del Cabo	1382	8	6
Santa Rosalía	461	3½	6
Tijuana	1945	18	2

🛍 Shopping

Baja Books   BOOKS
(Hidalgo 19; ⊙10am-5pm Mon-Sat) The most comprehensive collection of books on Baja in the region, plus maps, art materials, pottery and a bottomless coffee pot for browsers.

Silver Desert   SILVER
(📞613-135-06-84; Salvatierra 36; ⊙9am-2pm & 3-8pm Mon-Sat, 9am-2pm Sun) Sells good-quality Taxco sterling-silver jewelry. There's a second outlet at **Magdalena de Kino 4** (📞613-135-06-84; ⊙9am-2pm & 3-8pm Mon-Sat, 9am-2pm Sun).

ℹ️ Information

Municipal Department of Tourism (📞613-135-04-11; Plaza Cívica; ⊙8am-3pm Mon-Fri) has a few brochures and list of guides, but not much else.

ℹ️ Getting There & Away

Aeropuerto Internacional de Loreto (📞613-135-04-99; Carretera Transpeninsular Km 7) Served by several airlines, including Calafia Airlines (www.calafiaairlines.com) and Alaska Airlines (www.alaskaair.com), which run direct flights to Los Angeles. Taxis from the airport, 4km south of Loreto, cost M$250.

Bus Station (⊙24hr) Near the convergence of Salvatierra, Paseo de Ugarte and Paseo Tamaral, a 15-minute walk from the town center.

Puerto San Carlos

📞613 / POP 5538

Puerto San Carlos is a deep-water port and bustling little fishing town located 57km west of Ciudad Constitución on Bahía Magdalena. The town turns its attention to whales and travelers when the *ballenas* arrive in January through March to calve in the warm lagoon.

🏃 Activities

Pangueros (boatmen) take passengers for whale-watching excursions (about M$850 per hour for six people) or you can sign up with a more organized outfit like **Ecotours Villas Mar y Arena** (📞613-136-00-76; www.villasmaryarena.com; Carretera Federal Km 57; 3hr private whale-watching tours US$210; ⊙Oct-Jun; 🚹) 🌿 or **Magdalena Bay Whales** (📞US 855-594-2537; www.magdalenabaywhales.com; Puerto La Paz; 6hr tours US$90-100; ⊙4am-noon; 🚹).

🛌 Sleeping & Eating

Hotel Mar y Arena   CABAÑAS $$
(📞613-136-00-76; www.villasmaryarena.com; Carretera Federal Km 57; r US$70-100; 🅿️🐕❄️📶) 🌿 These *palapa*-style *cabañas* have chic earth-toned interiors and luxurious bathrooms. Solar power, desalinated water and a sensitivity to feng shui principles are all part of the local owner's eco-vision.

Hotel Alcatraz   HOTEL $$
(📞613-136-00-17; www.hotelalcatraz.mx; Calle San Jose del Cabo s/n; r incl breakfast M$820-990; 🅿️❄️📶) Nothing like its namesake prison, this pretty, rambling hotel has rooms set around a mature leafy courtyard, complete with sunbeds under the trees. Attractive pale-blue tilework gives the decor a sunny seaside feel. There is also a bar and restaurant (mains M$100 to M$250).

Los Arcos   SEAFOOD $$
(Puerto La Paz 170; mains M$90-280; ⊙10am-9pm) A simple place with tables set under the palm fronds, but the seafood dishes are the town's best. Go for one of the nine shrimp dishes or a simple *pescado de la plancha* (grilled fish). Note that the taco stand across the road from here is great too.

ℹ️ Getting There & Away

Autotransportes Águila (📞613-136-04-53; Calle Puerto Morelos; ⊙7-7:30am, 11:30am-1:45pm & 6:30-7:30pm) Runs buses daily to/from Ciudad Constitución (M$110) and La Paz (M$665), where you can connect to other destinations.

La Paz

📞 612 / POP 258,000

At first glance La Paz is a sprawling, slightly dingy city, but after an hour or so you'll discover there's a lot more to it. Laid-back, old-world beauty can be found on a stroll along the waterfront *malecón* or in the older architecture around the Plaza Constitución; chichi restaurants, cafes and bars cunningly hide in between the cracks. It's a surprisingly international town – you're as likely to hear French, Portuguese or Italian here as English or Spanish, and yet paradoxically it's the most 'Mexican' city in all of Baja. Its quirky history includes American occupation and even being temporarily declared its own republic.

All in all, it's a great place to meander, and you can shop uninterrupted by touts' invitations as you blend in to the urban vibe. The city makes a good base for day trips to Espíritu Santo, Cabo Pulmo and Todos Santos.

◉ Sights

★ Espíritu Santo
ISLAND

A treasure trove of shallow azure inlets and sorbet-pink cliffs, Espíritu Santo is one of La Paz's gems. It's part of a Unesco World Heritage site comprising 244 Sea of Cortez islands and coastal areas, and is a worthy day trip. A number of operators run activities here, including kayaking and snorkeling.

★ Museo de la Ballena
MUSEUM

(www.museodelaballena.org; Paseo Obregón; adult/child M$160/120; ⊙9am-6pm Tue-Sun) This recently remodeled museum comprises five exhibition spaces with models, audiovisual displays and multilingual explanations concerning the gray whales that live and breed in the local waters. A soundtrack of whales in the wild adds to the atmosphere, as does the well-lit and airy gallery spaces. The museum's foundation promotes the study and conservation of whales.

There is also a section dedicated to local turtles covering the seven different species native to Mexico, plus a cafeteria and a gift shop.

Malecón
WATERFRONT

La Paz's waterfront, with its wide sidewalk, tiny beaches, tourist pier, benches, sculptures by local artists and unimpeded sunset views, is the city's highlight. It stretches 5.5km, from the Marina de la Paz in the south to Playa Coromuel in the north. It started getting a face-lift in 2017 that may continue in stages over a few years.

Museo Regional de Antropología e Historia
MUSEUM

(cnr Calles 5 de Mayo & Altamirano; adult/child under 12yr M$40/free; ⊙9am-6pm Mon-Sat; ♿) This is a large, well-organized museum chronicling the peninsula's history (in Spanish) from prehistory to the Revolution of 1910 and its aftermath.

🕴 Activities

★ Baja Outdoor Activities
KAYAKING

(BOA; 📞612-125-56-36; www.kayactivities.com; Pichilingue Km 1; multiday kayak trips from US$585; ⊙8am-1pm & 3-6pm Mon-Fri, 9am-5pm Sat, 9am-3:30pm Sun) Kayak and camp around Espíritu Santo or take the ultimate eight-day circumnavigation tour. This is the very best way to experience the beautiful island.

Red Travel Mexico
ECOTOUR

(📞612-122-60-57; www.redtravelmexico.com; Salvatierra 740, Colina de la Cruz; walking tours US$25; ⊙9am-6pm; ♿) Finances major conservation projects throughout Baja like endangered sea-turtle monitoring. Other activities include walking tours, educational activities for children and deep-sea diving in Cabo Pulmo.

Mar y Aventuras
KAYAKING

(📞612-122-70-39; www.kayakbaja.com; Topete 564; day trips US$40-115; ♿) A well-respected company offering sea-kayaking, whale-watching, diving and fishing trips. Also has kayak rentals for self-guided tours.

Carey Dive Center
DIVING, SNORKELING

(📞612-128-40-48; www.buceocarey.com; Topete 3040; snorkeling US$85, two-tank dives US$150; ♿) A family-run establishment that offers snorkeling, diving, whale-watching, trips to see a sea-lion colony and other tours.

🕞 Tours

Espíritu & Baja
OUTDOORS

(📞612-122-44-27; www.espiritubaja.com; Paseo Obregón 2130-D; full-day trips US$85) This company has knowledgable, fun guides that are passionate about the science and history of the area. Choose from Espíritu Santo day trips, shorter whale-shark tours (three-hour tour US$70) and gray-whale-watching from Bahia Magdalena on the Pacific Coast.

Whale Shark Mexico
WILDLIFE

(📞612-154-98-59; www.whalesharkmexico.com; Paseo Obregón 2140; day trips US$85, two-month internships US$3000; ⊙9am-5pm Mon-Fri) 🌿 From October to March you can help researchers study juvenile whale sharks, which congregate in the placid waters of La Paz bay. Duties vary each trip: you can assist with tagging and even get a chance to name one. These researchers do not rent or provide any gear, and trips must be arranged in advance and only when the weather conditions are right.

⚜ Festivals & Events

Carnaval
CARNIVAL
(⊙ Feb) The annual carnival here is considered to be one of the country's best, with parades, concerts and plenty of partying in the streets.

⌷ Sleeping

★ Pension Baja Paradise
PENSION $
(Madero 2166; s without bathroom M$300, d/t with bathroom from M$400/580) Spotless, with comfy modern beds, reliably hot showers and cold air-conditioning plus touches of art and driftwood all around, this Mexican-Japanese-run place is a lovely place to stay. There's a kitchen and a coin laundry for guest use and it's near lots of great places to eat. The only downfall is the loud music from a local bar some nights, so bring earplugs!

Posada de la Mision
HOTEL $
(☑ 612-128-77-67; www.posadadelamision.com; Paseo Obregón 220; studio M$595, ste M$1100-1400; ⊝❋✿) With a fantastic location right on the central waterfront, this classic hacienda-style hotel offers great value, especially for families. The large studio double rooms are often full, but for those with kids in tow, it's the multistory suites with kitchenettes and two or more bedrooms that are a real boon. Decor is simple and floral, and service is lovely.

Baja Bed & Breakfast
B&B $$
(☑ 612-156-07-93, 612-158-21-65,; Madero 354; s/d incl breakfast US$66/72; ✿❋) Located in the trendiest part of town with organic stores and cafes, this homey, aging B&B has rooms and a leafy patio set around a small pool and outdoor kitchen for the use of guests. Terracotta tiles, pastel paintwork and tasteful art on the walls contribute to the very welcoming feel. Book by phone or third-party website.

★ El Ángel Azul
BOUTIQUE HOTEL $$$
(☑ 612-125-51-30; www.elangelazul.com; Av Independencia 518; r US$100-110; ℗⊝❋✿) Possibly the loveliest of La Paz' lodging options, the Blue Angel offers simply furnished, pastel-washed rooms, which surround a beautiful courtyard that is filled with palms, cacti, birdsong and bougainvillea. There is a color-

fully cluttered bar and sitting room, plus a kitchen for the use of guests.

Casa Tuscany
B&B $$$
(☑ 612-128-81-03; www.tuscanybaja.com; Av Bravo 110; d incl breakfast US$79-118; ⊝❋✿) Situated a seagull's swoop from the *malecón,* this picturesque B&B has homey rooms decorated with brightly colored paintwork, local rugs and traditional ceramics. Set around a tranquil central courtyard, the rooms vary in size; the most expansive, 'Romeo & Juliet,' has three terraces on several levels with sea views. Breakfast includes *aebleskiver* (Danish pancakes).

✕ Eating

La Paz' restaurant scene has become increasingly sophisticated – you'll find most of the top culinary choices on Calles Domínguez and Madero, north of Calle 5 de Mayo.

Organic Market
MARKET
(Madero s/n; ⊙ 9am-2:30pm Sat) This small organic market is fun for a browse around and sells all kinds of locally produced gourmet goodies, as well as local cheeses, homemade cakes and bread.

★ Taco Fish La Paz
SEAFOOD $
(cnr Avs Márques de León & Héroes de la Independencia; tacos M$24-30; ⊙ 8am-4pm Tue-Sun) Largely undiscovered by tourists, locals have been coming here in droves since 1992. Expect pristine stainless-steel surfaces and the best fish tacos in town. The extra battered, crispy fish style is reminiscent of an outstanding British fish and chips. The ceviche is off the charts as well.

Dulce Romero Panaderia Gourmet
BAKERY $
(Allende 167; breakfasts M$58-98; ⊙ 8am-10pm, closed Sun; ❋) Come to this clean, modern, white-brick space for delicious all-organic breakfasts of perfectly poached eggs, local cheeses, veggies, salsas and more on straight-from-the-oven breads and croissants. Sandwiches and salads are served at lunch, and pizza, pasta and burgers for dinner. Then the scrumptious cakes, pastries and myriad baked goods will have you drooling for dessert.

Bagel Shop
BAGELS $
(Domínguez 291; bagels from M$45; ⊙ 8am-3pm Tue-Sun) Owner Fabrizio learned the art of bagel making in the USA, and he makes a steaming batch daily. Fillings range from classic lox and cream cheese to smoked marlin with German sausage.

La Paz

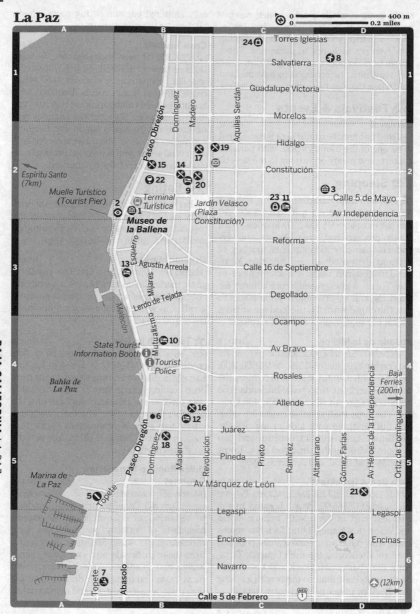

★ **Maria California** MEXICAN **$$**
(Juárez 105; breakfast mains M$69-116; ⏰ 7:30am-
2pm Mon-Sat) Great for breakfast with live
music and a fabulous atmosphere through-
out the cozy cluttered dining rooms and
terraces. Local artwork, photos and bril-
liant colored paintwork adorn the walls.
Order Mexican classics, pancakes and fresh
smoothies and juices.

La Paz

Bismarkcito   MEXICAN, SEAFOOD $$
(cnr Obregón & Constitución; mains from M$150; ⊙9am-10pm) This seafront restaurant, fronted by its own taco stand, is always packed with locals here for the superb seafood. Consider ordering the lobster chowder. TVs, exposed brick walls and jaunty blue-and-white table linen decorate the huge dining room. Service can be slow, but who's in a hurry?

Nim   INTERNATIONAL $$$
(www.nimrestaurante.com; Revolución 1110; mains M$190-360; ⊙1-10:30pm; 🐾) In a sumptuous historic house with art deco floor tiles and a chic pale-gray painted interior, organic produce is used in dishes that span the continents, like Moroccan tagines, Italian pastas, clam chowder and locally sourced sautéed oysters. Hugely popular with the resident expat population, it's La Paz at its most cosmopolitan.

Las Tres Virgenes   INTERNATIONAL $$$
(☑612-165-62-65; Madero 1130; mains M$120-500; ⊙1-11pm) An elegant oasis of a restaurant where you can dine in an atmospheric courtyard surrounded by leafy trees and statues. The menu includes both traditional and innovative dishes like grilled baby octopus, lots of export-quality Mexican beef cuts, spicy sea snails and a classic Caesar salad. Reservations recommended.

🍷 Drinking & Entertainment

The highest concentration of bars is between Calles 16 de Septiembre and Agustín Arreola, across from the *malecón* .

Harker Board   BAR
(cnr Constutución & Paseo Obregón; ⊙2pm-2am Wed-Mon; 🐾) Head upstairs to the terrace for sweeping views over the bay and a *cerveza* (beer). The local Baja Brewery beer is on tap, and there are 17 more bottled varieties. Pizza is also available. This great place doubles as a rental place for stand-up paddleboards (M$200 per hour) and kayaks (M$150 per hour) with rentals available 11am to 6pm.

Club Marlin   BAR
(El Centenario; ⊙noon-10pm Tue-Sat, 10am-8pm Sun; 🐾) Located in El Centenario, around 5km north of the center, this hotel, bar and restaurant dates from the 1980s and has long served as the resident expat haunt. The views of the bay are sublime and the place (and patrons) have plenty of sun-kissed warmth and character. Regular live music.

Teatro de la Ciudad   LIVE PERFORMANCE
(☑612-125-00-04; Altamirano; ⊙hours vary) Features performances by musical and theatrical groups, often by performers from mainland Mexico, as well as occasional film series. The giant theater is within the **Unidad Cultural Profesor Jesús Castro Agúndez** (☑612-125-02-07; ⊙Cultural Center 8am-2pm & 4-6pm Mon-Fri).

🛍 Shopping

Local stores that cater to tourists have plenty of junk but a smattering of good stuff.

Ibarra's Pottery
CERAMICS

(Prieto 625; ⊘9am-3pm Mon-Fri, to 2pm Sat) See potters at work at this ceramics workshop and store that dates back to 1958 – it is famed throughout Baja.

Allende Books
BOOKS

(☑612-125-91-14; www.allendebooks.com; Av Independencia 518; ⊘10am-6pm Mon-Sat) English-language bookstore with a good selection of books on Baja California and mainland Mexico.

ℹ Information

The majority of banks (most with ATMs) and *casas de cambio* (exchange houses) are on or around Calle 16 de Septiembre.

There's an **immigration office** (☑612-122-04-29; Paseo Obregón; ⊘8am-8pm Mon-Fri, 9am-3pm Sat) near the center of town.

Hospital Salvatierra (☑612-175-05-00; Av Paseo de los Deportistas 86; ⊘24hr) The largest hospital in southern Baja, located 4.6km southwest of the center, via calles 5 de Febrero and Forjadores de Sudcalifornia.

Main post office (cnr Constitución & Revolución; ⊘8am-3pm Mon-Fri, 9am-1pm Sat)

State Tourist Information Booth (☑612-122-59-39; cnr Paseo Obregón & Av Bravo; ⊘8am-10pm) Brochures and pamphlets in English, plus some maps; very helpful.

Tourist Police (☑078, 612-122-59-39; ⊘8am-10pm) Small booth on Paseo Obregón; hours may vary.

Viva La Paz (www.vivalapaz.com) La Paz' official tourism site.

ℹ Getting There & Away

AIR

Aeropuerto General Manuel Márquez de León (☑612-124-63-36; www.aeropuertosgap.com.mx; Transpeninsular Km 9) is about 9km southwest of the city. It has an immigration office.

Aeroméxico (☑612-122-00-91; www.aeromexico.com; Paseo Obregón) flies to many cities via Mexico City while **Calafia Airlines** (www.calafiaairlines.com; cnr Santiago & Mulege) offers the most direct flights to La Paz, including to/from Guadalajara and Tijuana.

BOAT

Ferries to Mazatlán and Topolobampo leave the ferry terminal at Pichilingue, 23km north of La Paz. Baja Ferries has a **small office** (☑612-125-63-24) at the port and a **larger office** (☑612-123-66-00; www.bajaferries.com; Allende 1025; ⊘8am-5pm Mon-Fri, to 2pm Sat) in town.

Ferries to Mazatlán depart at 8pm Tuesday, Thursday and Saturday and arrive 16 to 18 hours later; return ferries leave Mazatlán at 6:30pm Wednesday, Friday and Sunday. Passenger fares in *salón* (numbered seats) are M$1240.

Topolobampo services depart at 2:30pm Monday to Friday and 11pm on Saturday. The return ferry from Topolobampo to La Paz leaves at 11pm Sunday to Friday, arriving in Pichilingue six to seven hours later. Passenger fares in *salón* are M$1000. Ensure that you arrive at the pier two hours before departure. Vehicle rates vary with vehicle length and destination.

Before shipping any vehicle to the mainland, officials require a vehicle permit. You can obtain one at **Banjército** (www.banjercito.com.mx; ⊘7am-3pm Mon, Wed & Fri-Sun, to 7pm Tue & Thu) at the ferry terminal, or from its vehicle permit modules in Mexicali or Tijuana.

BUS

The **Terminal Turística** (☑612-122-78-98; cnr malecón & Av Independencia) is centrally located on the *malecón*. Convenient local services include five daily buses to Playa Tecolote (M$100, 30 minutes) and six to Playa Pichilingue (M$100, 20 minutes) between 10am and 5pm.

CAR & MOTORCYCLE

Car-rental rates start around M$400 per day, not including insurance.

Budget (☑612-122-60-40; www.budget.com; cnr Paseo Obregón & Allende) has several agencies with locations both on the *malecón* and at the airport.

ℹ Getting Around

Uber has started in La Paz and rides cost about M$40 around town or around M$120 from the airport to the *malecón* area.

CAR FERRIES FROM LA PAZ

DESTINATION	VEHICLE	FARE (M$)
Mazatlán	car 5.4m or less/motorcycle/motorhome	6380/3200/22,550
Topolobampo	car 5.4m or less/motorcycle/motorhome	4600/3730/17,500

BUSES FROM LA PAZ

DESTINATION	FARE (M$)	DURATION (HR)	FREQUENCY (DAILY)
Cabo San Lucas	370	3	frequent
Ciudad Constitución	450	3	12
Ensenada	2140	22	3
Guerrero Negro	1730	11	4
Loreto	800	5	6
Mulegé	1170	6	5
San Ignacio	1480	9	4
San José del Cabo	340-370	3½	frequent
SJD Airport	545	3½	frequent
Tijuana	2505	24	3
Todos Santos	160	1½	frequent

La Ventana

📞 612 / POP 183

Attracting kitesurfers from around the world with its consistent wind, this strip of seaside is also a great place to watch whale sharks, sea lions, whales, sea turtles and a myriad of fish – without the crowds. Diving is best in the summer when the water visibility reaches 25m or 30m (80ft or 100ft).

🛏 Sleeping & Eating

Baja Joe's
HOTEL $$

(📞 612-114-00-01; www.bajajoe.com; s US$40, d US$50-115; P ❄ 🛜 🏊) This place is good value with tidy small rooms fronting a communal terrace and sharing a kitchen and common room. The property encompasses a kitesurfing school, two kitchens and **Joe's Garage**, a popular bar with 10 frothy ales on tap.

⭐ Palapas Ventana
CABAÑAS $$$

(📞 612-114-01-98; www.palapasventana.com; cabañas incl breakfast M$2260-3350; P ⊖ ❄ 🅰 🛜 🏊) Stay in a delightful *palapa*-style *cabaña* (cabin) on a hillside just over the main beach. Palapas Ventana outfits for diving, snorkeling, windsurfing, kitesurfing, sportfishing, petroglyph hikes and more. It also organizes adventure tours to the Reserva de la Biosfera Sierra de la Laguna (and elsewhere). The restaurant is perfect for chilling out with an ocean view post-activities.

Playa Central
PIZZA $$

(www.facebook.com/playa.central.kiteboarding/; La Ventana; pizza M$125-250; ⊙ 9am-10pm; P 🛜) Located beachside in the center of town, this cavernous former shrimp factory with a rooftop patio not only serves terrific thin-crust pizza but also has regular live music, a popular bar, and kitesurfing rental and instruction. Don't miss its margaritas.

Las Palmas
MEXICAN $$

(El Sargento; mains M$90-230; ⊙ 8am-10pm) Find this great big orange restaurant in El Sargento, a couple of kilometers north of La Ventana, in a sublime spot overlooking the water and Isla Cerralvo. The Mexican dishes are definitely a notch above the norm; try the *chiles rellenos* (chilies stuffed with meat or cheese).

ℹ Getting There & Away

A bus leaves La Paz at 2pm daily for La Ventana (one way M$100) and makes the return trip to La Paz at around 7am daily. Most people, however, rent a car to get here.

Los Barriles

📞 624 / POP 1200

South of La Paz, the Transpeninsular brushes the gulf at this attractive small town. It is a spectacular spot for wind- and kitesurfing thanks to brisk winter westerlies that average 20 to 25 knots. During whale season you can see spouts close to shore and hundreds of leaping mobula rays in the waves.

🏃 Activities

Vela Windsurf
WINDSURFING

(www.velawindsurf.com; Hotel Playa del Sol; kitesurfing lessons from US$90; ⊙ 9am-5pm Dec-Apr) One of the longer-established water-sports companies with centers worldwide, it caters to windsurfers, kitesurfers and stand-up paddleboarders. The winds die down considerably between April and August, so that is not a good time to take out a board.

Sleeping & Eating

Hotel Los Barriles
HOTEL $$

(624-141-00-24; www.losbarrileshotel.com; 20 de Noviembre s/n; s/d US$65/80;) This hotel has a comfortable laid-back feel. Rooms are set around a pretty lagoon-style pool area, complete with outside bar and hot tub. The owner prides himself on his superior German mattresses and regularly updates the rooms; all have fridges.

Caleb's Cafe
CAFE $$

(20 de Noviembre s/n; mains M$65-160; 7:30am-3pm Tue-Sat;) This delightful, American-run cafe is famed for its gooey, buttery, sticky buns. Other favorites include zucchini bread and carrot cake, while breakfasts are healthy and hearty (think broccoli scrambled eggs and feta-cheese omelette).

Shopping

Plum Loco
ARTS & CRAFTS

(20 de Noviembre s/n; 9am-5pm) The US owner, Paul, imports crafts from all over Mexico, as well as further afield. He also has free books and coffee for browsers and, as an amiable long-term resident, is a great source of information.

Getting There & Away

Several daily buses run to Los Barriles from San José del Cabo (M$98, 1½ hours), en route to La Paz.

Cabo Pulmo

624 / POP 58

Cabo Pulmo, a tiny village and a 17,571-acre Marine Protected Area (MPA), is one of the most successful national marine parks in the world and arguably offers the best diving and snorkeling in Baja. It's also home to the only Pacific coral reef in the Sea of Cortez. You don't need a 4WD to enjoy the drive out here along the spectacular Eastern Cape (from the south) coastal road or through the Sierra de la Laguna (to the west), although the road can get rough at times. You will escape the crowds and find a very mellow scene that can be hard to leave.

Activities

People come from all around southern Baja to dive or snorkel at Cabo Pulmo. Highlights include the coral reef and sandy-bottom **El Bajo**, where a large school of bigeye jacks regularly school into a giant, astonishing ball.

Snorkelers should head for the beach at **Los Arbolitos** (entry fee M$40 per person) 5km south of Cabo Pulmo, then follow the shoreline hiking trail to **Las Sirenitas**, where wind and wave erosion has made the rocks look like melting wax sculptures. Eerie and beautiful, they're accessible by boat as well.

Offshore snorkeling and diving trips can be booked via several companies that operate out of kiosks down by the water. Our favorite is **Cabo Pulmo Divers** (624-184-81-42; 2-tank dives US$125; 2½ hour snorkeling tours US$45), run by the Castro family who were key in creating the national park and continue to be the biggest champions in protecting it.

Sleeping & Eating

Cabo Pulmo Casas
BUNGALOW $$

(www.cabopulmocasas.com; casitas US$80-150;) Marly Rickers rents out these five well-maintained and comfy little bungalows

---

SURF'S UP

Baja is a prime surfer's paradise with swells coming in off the Pacific that, even on bad days, are challenging and fun. Boards can be rented from surf shops (rental costs around M$250), but use extreme care at all times, as rips, undertow and behemoth waves are dangerous even for experienced surfers. If you're looking for good breaks, check out the following:

Costa Azul Needs southerly swell, but this intermediate break is a whole lot of fun and it's close to either of the Cabos.

Los Cerritos (p744) Beautiful sand, good waves, and a mellow vibe – this is a great beginner beach with a powerful Pacific swell...and eagle rays below.

San Miguel (p716) Rocky point break that offers awesome rides when the waves are big. Isla de Todos Santos is another option for the serious.

For more info on surfing, check out the no-nonsense *Surfer's Guide to Baja* by Mike Parise. For surf lessons, contact **Mario Surf School** (p744).

right in the village. All run on solar power, are equipped with full kitchens and have outdoor gardens with space to hang out. Definitely the best option in Cabo Pulmo.

Eco Adventure Bungalows CABAÑAS $$
(☑ 624-158-97-31; www.tourscabopulmo.com; cabañas US$60; 🅿) 🔊 These two solar-powered *palapa*-style *cabañas* (cabins) near the water are plain but pleasantly furnished. The owners organize water sports and whale-watching tours from their Eco Adventures kiosk on the waterfront.

Palapa Cabo Pulmo SEAFOOD $$
(mains M$105-300; ⊗noon-9pm) With its unbeatable position right on the beach, this friendly place with its terrace seating serves superb seafood dishes like coconut shrimp, fried calamari and fresh fish, shrimp or chicken done to your liking with a choice of delicious Mexican sauces. Wash it down with a killer mango margarita.

El Caballero MEXICAN $$
(mains M$90-190; ⊗7am-9:30pm Fri-Wed) This place serves huge dishes of traditional Mexican cuisine, including superb fish tacos. Breakfast are great too. There's a small shop here as well for snacks and supplies.

❶ Getting There & Away

Many people go to Cabo Pulmo to dive on day trips from all around Baja Sur. Otherwise you'll need your own vehicle.

San José del Cabo
☑ 624 / POP 70,000
San José del Cabo is like the 'mild' sister of 'wild' Cabo San Lucas, offering quiet shopping, an attractive plaza, a beautiful church and excellent dining opportunities in its inland, historic center. It's Zona Hotelera beach area a couple of kilometers away has miles of white sand lining a mostly riptide laden ocean and is backed by large hotels, condos and eyesores, er, timeshares.

⊙ Sights

The best beaches for swimming are along the road to Cabo San Lucas and include **Playa Santa María** at Km 13.

Iglesia San José CHURCH
(Plaza Mijares; ⊗sporadic) The colonial-style Iglesia San José, built in 1730 to replace the Misión San José del Cabo, faces the spacious Plaza Mijares.

WORTH A TRIP

RESERVA DE LA BIOSFERA SIERRA DE LA LAGUNA

Hard-core backpackers can strap on hiking boots, fill water bottles and head into the uninterrupted wilds of this lush and rugged biosphere reserve, south of the intersection of the Transpeninsular and Hwy 19. It's not a place for inexperienced hikers, or anyone unfamiliar with the unique challenges presented by desert trails, but the rewards are great: stunning vistas, close encounters with wildlife, and a meadow that was once a lake bed (the feature from which the area gets its name).

Baja Sierra Adventures (☑ 624-166-87-06; www.bajasierradventures.com; day trips from US$60), in a tiny ranch called El Chorro, offers a variety of day and overnight trips, biking and trekking through this unique region. **Palapas Ventana** is another option for tours to this region.

🛏 Sleeping

Reserve ahead during the peak winter months.

Hotel Colli HOTEL $$
(☑ 624-142-07-25; www.hotelcolli.com; Hidalgo s/n; r M$850; 🅿😊❄🖤) Friendly and family-owned for three generations, the Colli has sunny yellow paintwork in the rooms and is in a great position, only steps away from the plaza and next to the best bakery (p739) in town. Great value.

★ Casa Natalia BOUTIQUE HOTEL $$$
(☑ 624-146-71-00; www.casanatalia.com; Blvd Mijares 4; r US$190-300; 😊❄🖤🏊) The fabulous Natalia opens onto San José's plaza and has rooms overlooking a descending series of luxurious swimming pools with hammocks and lounges all around. Arty and grand paintings on the walls, contemporary furnishings and giant bathrooms make each unique room a delight. The restaurant is superb. Standards share terraces (with woven dividers) but are the most updated.

Drift BOUTIQUE HOTEL $$$
(☑ 624-130-72-03; www.driftsanjose.com; Hidalgo; r US$99-145; 😊❄🖤🏊) Polished concrete, white walls with brick detail and exposed copper piping bring an austere luxuriousness to the bright, airy rooms here. Head

San José del Cabo

San José del Cabo

| | 0 | | | 400 m |
| N | 0 | | | 0.2 miles |

downstairs to hang out by the pool under tall palms or upstairs to a hammock-strewn rooftop patio, with one of the hotel's 15 artisenal mezcals to sip. Thursdays a food truck comes to the grounds and the mezcal bar opens to the public for a night of beer, burritos and song. Adults only.

Tropicana Inn HOTEL $$$
(☎624-142-15-80; www.tropicanainn.com.mx; Blvd Mijares 30; s/d incl breakfast US$104/113; ❈ 🕏 🛇) The spacious rooms are attractively decked out with terracotta tiles and pretty floral-tiled bathrooms. The classically Mexican, hacienda-style courtyard has a huge, partially *palapa*-shaded pool, a jungle of flowers and tropical plants, and a squawking parrot named Paco. Excellent, central location.

✗ Eating & Drinking

There are some fabulous places to eat here, from cheap taco joints to upscale international cuisine.

★ La Lupita TACOS $$
(☎624-688-39-26; Morelos s/n; tacos M$25-55; ⓢ2pm-2am Tue-Sun) Pair flavorful, unique tacos – including Mediterranean octopus, duck *mole* or miso fish – with mezcal cocktails, amazing margaritas, live music and an all-around fun scene. Bright colors, rustic wood tables and ethnic patterns make it as hip as it is delicious. Just go.

La Osteria MEDITERRANEAN $$
(Obregón 1907; tapas M$90-150; mains from M$150; ⓢ11am-9pm) The old-world, leafy courtyard setting combined with live music make this an atmospheric venue in which to eat, drink

and be merry. Share a tapas plate with 14 choices or go for a grilling with steak, chicken or fish. While the food won't knock your socks off, the drinks and ambience might.

French Riviera

BAKERY, CAFE $$

(www.facebook.com/FrenchRivieraBistro/; cnr Hidalgo & Doblado; pastries around M$40, mains M$150; ⊘7am-11pm) A French-inspired spot with tasty breads, delicious croissants and pastries, gelati that hits the spot on a hot day, and excellent dinners. The Med-inspired decor is tasteful and contemporary.

★ Flora's Field Kitchen

INTERNATIONAL $$$

(☑624-142-10-00; www.flora-farms.com; mains M$200-520; ⊘11am-2:30pm & 6-9:30pm Tue-Sat, 10am-2:30pm Sun) Head to this farm oasis to splurge on meals finely crafted from ingredients harvested from the surrounding gardens, crusty fresh breads, locally made cheeses and refreshing cocktails, all in a rustic-chic setting right off the pages of a classy lifestyle magazine. You can also buy produce, chichi soaps and explore the relaxing, bucolic grounds. It's about 5km northeast of the colonial town center.

Baja Brewing Co

BREWERY

(www.bajabrewingcompany.com; Morelos 1227; ⊘noon-1am) A pub-style environment offering local microbrews. Sample 4oz measures of eight different beers in a flight to find your favorite. Popular choices include the Raspberry Lager and the put-hairs-on-your-chest Peyote Pale Ale.

Los Barriles de Don Malaquias

BAR

(☑624-142-53-22; cnr Blvd Mijares & Juárez; ⊘10am-8pm Mon-Sat) Los Barriles stocks over 300 varieties of tequila and keeps at least two dozen bottles open for tasting. Prices are a bit steep, but the selection is great.

🛍 Shopping

Blvd Mijares is the self-proclaimed art district and boasts numerous galleries, studios and stores. The district has an Art Walk on Thursdays from 5pm to 9pm, with open studios, wine tasting and more. For info on art galleries in the area, check out www.artcabo.com.

La Sacristia

ARTS & CRAFTS

(Hidalgo 9; ⊘10am-8pm) This multigallery space showcases art and crafts from throughout Mexico. Don't miss the rainbow-colored beaded animal sculptures made by the mainland Mexican Huichol people.

Old Town Gallery

ART

(www.theoldtowngallery.com; Obregón 1505; ⊘10am-6pm Mon-Sat) Duck into this gallery to view the distinct different styles of seven Canadian artists, most of whom are local residents.

Necri

CERAMICS

(www.necri.com.mx; Obregón 17; ⊘10:30am-8pm) One of the longest-established ceramic stores in town, Necri also sells pewter pieces, original Talavera jewelry and mainland crafts.

ⓘ Information

Several *casas de cambio* (exchange houses) here keep long hours.

IMSS Hospital (☑emergency 624-142-01-80, nonemergency 624-142-00-76; www.imss.gob. mx; cnr Hidalgo & Coronado) is where to go should you need to.

Secretaria Municipal de Turismo (☑624-142-29-60, ext 150; Plaza San José, Transpeninsular; ⊘8am-5pm Mon-Sat) Stocks brochures and maps.

ⓘ Getting There & Away

AIR

Aeropuerto Internacional de Los Cabos (SJD; ☑624-146-51-11; www.aeropuertosgap. com.mx; Carretera Transpeninsular Km 43.5), north of San José del Cabo, also serves Cabo San Lucas. All airline offices are found here.

Calafia Airlines (☑624-143-43-02; www. calafiaairlines.com) flies direct to some mainland Mexico destinations like Los Mochis, Guadalajara and Mazatlán, while **Aeroméxico**

BAJA CALIFORNIA SAN JOSÉ DEL CABO

BUSES FROM SAN JOSÉ DEL CABO

DESTINATION	FARE (M$)	DURATION (HR)	FREQUENCY (DAILY)
Cabo San Lucas	65	1	frequent
Ensenada	2348	24	1
La Paz	340-370	3½	frequent
Los Barriles	98	1½	6
Tijuana	2281	27	2

(☎ 624-146-50-98; www.aeromexico.com) has domestic and international connections via Mexico City, and daily flights to Los Angeles. **Alaska Airlines** (☎ 624-146-55-02; www.alaskaair.com) has the most flights to the US.

BUS

Buses depart from the **main bus terminal** (☎ 624-130-73-39; González Conseco s/n), east of the Transpeninsular.

CAR & MOTORCYCLE

The usual agencies rent from the airport. Rates start at about M$600 per day.

ⓘ Getting Around

The official government-run company runs bright-yellow taxis and minibuses to the airport for about M$280. The toll road from the Transpeninsular to the airport costs M$32.

Cabo San Lucas

☎ 624 / POP 88,539

Cabo San Lucas's white beaches, fecund waters and spectacular arching stone cliffs at Land's End have become the backdrop for Baja's most raucous tourism. Where else do clubs round up conga lines so that waiters can pour tequila down dancers' throats? The next morning you can be boating next to dolphins and spouting whales for a hangover cure. The activities are endless: jetskiing, banana-boating, parasailing, snorkeling, kitesurfing, diving and horseback-riding can all be found just by walking down to the beach. Outside city limits, you'll be surrounded by majestic cardón cacti, caracara birds and mystical *arroyos* (streams) that will impress you just as much as that crazy club you partied at the night before.

Unfortunately the desert is disappearing fast. The 'Corridor,' the once-spectacular coastline between San José del Cabo and Cabo San Lucas, is being built up with cookie-cutter resorts, American chain stores, aquifer-depleting golf courses and all-inclusive hotels.

◉ Sights

★ Land's End   LANDMARK

Land's End is the most impressive attraction in Cabo. Hop on a *panga* (skiff), kayak or stand-up paddleboard SUP) and head to **El Arco** (the Arch), a jagged natural feature that partially fills with the tide. Pelicans, sea lions, sea, sky – this is what brought people

to Cabo in the first place, and it's still magical, despite the backdrop of cruise ships.

Beaches

For sunbathing and calm waters **Playa Médano**, on the Bahía de Cabo San Lucas, is ideal. **Playa Solmar**, on the Pacific, is pretty but has a reputation for dangerous breakers and riptides. Nearly unspoiled **Playa del Amor** (Lover's Beach) shouldn't be missed; near Land's End, it is accessible by water taxi from Playa Médano or Plaza Las Glorias docks or you can paddle out on a SUP or kayak. Appropriately, **Playa del Divorcio** (Divorce Beach) is nearby, across the point on the Pacific side. **Playa Santa María**, at Km 13 toward San José del Cabo, is one of the best for swimming.

🏃 Activities

The best diving areas are **Roca Pelícano**, the sea-lion colony off Land's End, and the reef off **Playa Chileno**, at Bahía Chileno east of town. **Tio Sports** (☎ 624-143-33-99; www.tiosports.com; Playa Médano; 2-tank dives from US$120) at Playa Médano is one of the largest water-sports outfitters, but there are numerous alternatives.

Surprisingly good snorkeling can be done right from Playa del Amor, swimming left, toward the marina. A mask, a snorkel and fins should run about M$200 per day. *Panga* rides cost about M$200 for a round-trip if you bargain directly with a captain. Tipping is expected.

🛥 Tours

★ Cabo Expeditions   OUTDOORS

(☎ 624-143-27-00; www.caboexpeditions.com.mx; Bvd Marina s/n, Plaza de la Danza Local 6; whale-watching tours US$89; ⊙ 8am-5pm Mon-Sat) This well-run, eco-minded company specializes in small-group tours and is constantly seeking out new twists like trips on camel back or boat trips to 'whale concerts' where whale song is piped up through tubes. Of course there is also whale-watching, kayaking, diving and trips as far as Espiritu Santo Island. All are led by experienced guides alongside fantastic commentary.

Ecocat   BOATING

(☎ 624-157-46-85; www.caboecotours.com; dock N-12; tours per person from US$60; 🚼) Offers two-hour sunset sailing tours, snorkeling and whale-watching trips, and also plays host to a variety of other options off its giant catamaran.

✦ Festivals & Events

Fishing Tournaments   FISHING
(☺May-Nov) Cabo San Lucas is a popular staging ground for fishing tournaments in the autumn. The main events are the **Gold Cup**, **Bisbee's Black & Blue Marlin Jackpot** and the **Cabo Tuna Jackpot**.

Sammy Hagar's Birthday Party   DANCE
(Cabo Wabo; ☺early Oct) This is a major Cabo event with lots of drinking and dancing. Invitations (free) are required – try concierges at the larger hotels or look out for giveaways.

Día de San Lucas   RELIGIOUS
(☺18 Oct) A local celebration honoring the town's patron saint, with fireworks, food stalls and a fiesta spirit.

🛏 Sleeping

Cabo Inn Hotel   INN $
(☎624-143-0819; www.caboinnhotel.com; 20 de Noviembre; s/d/r from US$40/54/62; 🛜❄) This place is in town, but the *palapa* roof, colorful decor and plant-filled courtyard make you feel like you're in nature. It's close to tonnes of restaurants and shops, but about 15 minutes' walk to the beach. Add a communal kitchen, rooftop hangout area and pool and you have one of the best deals in Cabo San Lucas.

Hotel Los Milagros   HOTEL $$
(☎624-143-45-66, USA 718-928-6647; www.losmilagros.com.mx; Matamoros 116; d US$85-85; 🅿❄🛜❄) The tranquil courtyard and 12 unique rooms provide a perfect escape from Cabo's excesses. A desert garden (complete with resident iguanas), beautiful deep-blue pool, and friendly, courteous service make a stay here unforgettable.

★ Bungalows Breakfast Inn   B&B $$$
(☎624-143-05-85; www.thebungalowshotel.com; cnr Libertad & Herrera; bungalows incl breakfast from US$165; 🅿❄❄🛜❄) Extremely attentive service, delicious breakfasts, tastefully furnished rooms, fragrant palm-thatched *palapas*, hammocks and an expansive swimming pool set this B&B apart. Fresh-fruit smoothies, fruit juices, excellent coffee and warm, welcoming bilingual staff make the bungalows feel like home. Beautiful handmade soaps are one of the many tiny details that makes this *the* place to splurge.

Bahia Hotel & Beach Club   HOTEL $$$
(www.bahiacabo.com; Av El Pescador; r US$150-350; 🅿❄🛜❄) This whitewashed grande dame is a classy choice only a few minutes' walk from the heart of Médano beach. High-ceilinged rooms with tile floors, comfy beds and all the mod-cons surround a lounge-inducing pool. The on-site **Bar Esquina** means you won't have to go far for the classiest nightlife around.

🍴 Eating
Cabo's culinary scene ranges from humble taco stands to gourmet restaurants.

Tacos Gardenias   TACOS $
(www.tacosgardenias.com; Paseo de la Marina 3; tacos from M$35; ☺8am-10pm) Arrive off-hours if you want a table at this cafeteria-like, cavernous joint. This is *the* place for outrageously fresh fish or shrimp (breaded or grilled) tacos, although there are meat and vegetarian options too. Tacos arrive with homemade tortillas and all the fixings so you can build your own masterpiece. The seafood cocktails, salads and more are great too.

Taqueria Las Guacamayas   TACOS $
(Morelos; meals M$70-110; ☺5:30pm-midnight) The perfect mix of outrageously delicious tacos to devour at chunky wood Mexican tables in a just-fancy-enough-to-feel-special atmosphere with stellar service. Pair with fresh juices, a beer or a margarita. All three branches of Las Guacamayas are great for families and couples alike, but our favorite is this quieter, backstreet location. For a treat order the *molcajete mixto*!

Mariscos Las Tres Islas   SEAFOOD $$
(cnr Revolución & Mendoza; mains M$50-195; ☺8am-10pm) A lively thatched restaurant in the middle of town, swarming with locals who come for the best, classic Mexican seafood in the area. Prices are reasonable, the beers are cold and the marisco band has talent. Try the shrimp scampi or the garlic octopus.

★ Sur Beach House   INTERNATIONAL $$$
(☎624-143-18-90; www.bahiacabo.com; Playa Médano; mains M$170-395; ☺7:30am-midnight) With an exceptional location on the beach looking toward El Arco, this elegant yet laid-back place serves up ceviche and tacos using the freshest ingredients and beautifully balanced flavors. The fancier grilled fish and meat meals are just as spectacular and service is the best in town. Get lunch and drinks right on the beach or dine by candle-light for dinner.

During high season sit around the small nighttime bonfire and watch the boat lights sparkle off sea.

Cabo San Lucas

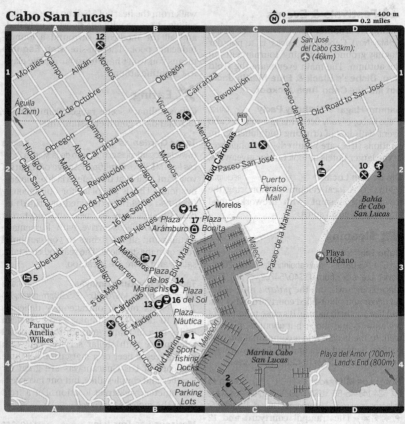

Cabo San Lucas

Mi Casa　　　　　　　　　MEXICAN $$$
(www.micasarestaurant.com.mx; cnr Cárdenas & Cabo San Lucas; mains US$13-27; ⏰10am-11pm) This place has real wow factor. The courtyard-style interior has rooms on several levels and feels like something out of a 1950s Mexican musical – plants, statues, folksy murals, wicker lights, painted furniture, Día de Muertos figurines and wandering mariachis all set the stage. Stick with the more simple dishes. The food is good, but come here more for the atmosphere.

🍷 Drinking & Nightlife

Cabo is a proud party town, and alcoholic revelry is encouraged all day long. You have been warned.

Canela
BAR

(Plaza del Sol; ⊙8am-11pm) A classier option than most for a Corona or cocktail. Moody lighting, rustic furniture and a curious (and entertaining) Día de Muertos theme.

Slim's Elbow Room
BAR

(Blvd Marina s/n; ⊙10am-midnight) In the shadow of Cabo Wabo, this teeny, easy-to-miss watering hole, wallpapered in dollar bills and clients' signatures, claims to be the world's smallest bar. With four seats inside and two standing spaces, it's a contender for sure.

Cabo Wabo
CLUB

(📞624-143-11-88; www.cabowabo.com; cnr Guerrero & Madero; ⊙9am-2am; 📶) The most famous bar and club in town, established by legendary rocker Sammy Hagar of solo career and Van Halen fame. Come here for live music and the legendary margaritas made with Hagar's own-label tequila.

El Squid Roe
CLUB

(📞624-143-12-69; cnr Blvd Cárdenas & Zaragoza; ⊙10am-5am) Crazy. Just crazy. Jello shooters, tequila congo lines. Waiters (and drunk clientele) dance on tabletops to cheering crowds. The everyday epicenter of Cabo's drunken nightlife scene.

🛍️ Shopping

Dos Lunas
FASHION & ACCESSORIES

(📞624-143-19-69; Blvd Marina, Plaza Bonita; ⊙9am-6pm) This bright, colorful shop will get you in the holiday mood. Stocking reasonably priced resort wear made of natural fibers, as well as great handbags, hats, jewelry and kiddies' clothing, it's well worth a pre-beach visit. It also has a branch in Puerto Paraíso.

Mercado Mexicano
MARKET

(cnr Hidalgo & Zapata) This sprawling market, which contains dozens of stalls with crafts from around the country, is Cabo's most comprehensive shopping area, but there's a lot of junk too. Touts beckon you in.

ℹ️ Information

It's an indication of who calls the shots here that Cabo has no government-sanctioned tourist offices. The 'info' booths you'll see are owned by timeshares, condos and hotels. The staff are friendly and can offer maps and info, but their only pay comes from commissions from selling timeshare visits: expect a firm, sometimes desperate, pitch for you to visit model homes. Be warned – the promised freebies are rarely worth wasting precious vacation time on.

Call 078 for tourist assistance.

There's an **immigration office** (📞624-143-01-35; cnr Blvd Cárdenas & Farías; ⊙9am-1pm Mon-Sat) near the center.

All About Cabo (www.allaboutcabo.com) is a useful site for visitors.

Amerimed American Hospital (📞624-143-96-70; www.amerimed.com.mx; Blvd Cárdenas) Near Paseo de la Marina.

ℹ️ Getting There & Away

AIR

The closest **airport** (p739) is at San José del Cabo. The **Cabo Airport Shuttle** (📞USA 1-877-737-9680; www.caboairportshuttle.net; per person around US$19) is one of the cheapest and best services to/from the airport and will take you directly to your hotel.

BUS

Buses depart from either the **Águila** (www.autotransportesaguila.net; Hwy 19; ⊙24hr) company, located at the Todos Santos crossroad, north of downtown, or the bus station, a 40-minute walk northwest from the tourist zone and waterfront.

CAR & MOTORCYCLE

Numerous car-rental agencies have booths along Paseo de la Marina and elsewhere in town,

BUSES FROM CABO SAN LUCAS

DESTINATION	FARE (M$)	DURATION (HR)	FREQUENCY (DAILY)
La Paz	370	3	frequent
Loreto	995	8¾	3
San José del Cabo	65	1	frequent
Tijuana	2630	27	2
Todos Santos	151	1	frequent

although booking in advance with a pickup at the airport can be cheaper.

ℹ️ Getting Around

Cab van fares within town are around US$10, and a taxi to the airport is around US$80. Avoid rides offered by the timeshare touts.

Todos Santos

📞 612 / POP 5200

With a quirky mix of locals, fishers, surfers and New Age spiritualists, the town of 'All Saints' has thus far escaped the rampant tourism of the other cape towns. With it's charming cobblestone streets lined with art galleries, romantic restaurants and a cactus or three, it's also, by far, the prettiest town in the far south of Baja. Long beaches and wild surf breaks mean there's a lot to do for those who want to get out of town as well. Think Taos, New Mexico, before Ansel Adams and Georgia O'Keefe brought the world there. Be prepared for high prices, however.

Like many other parts of Baja, Todos Santos is changing and local development is rampant. So come here now before it changes forever.

👁️ Sights

Scattered around town are several former *trapiches* (mills), many of which have been repurposed over the years. The restored **Teatro Cine General Manuel Márquez de León** is one – it's on Legaspi, facing the plaza. **Molino El Progreso**, the ruin of what was formerly El Molino restaurant, is another. On Juárez, opposite the hospital, is **Molino de los Santana**.

Centro Cultural MUSEUM
(📞 612-145-00-41; Juárez; ⏰ 8am-8pm Mon-Fri, 9am-4pm Sat & Sun; 👶) FREE Housed in a former schoolhouse with a lovely central courtyard, the Centro Cultural is home to some interesting nationalist and revolutionary murals dating from 1933. Also on display is a dusty collection of regional artifacts, fascinating old photos and a replica ranch house. Take note of the cradle 'cage' hanging from the ceiling.

🏃 Activities

Surfers come here for some of the nicest swells in all of Baja. **San Pedrito** offers Hawaii-like tubes (and Hawaii-like sea urchins if you wipe out). Catch that perfect wave as eagle rays glide below you, or just hang out with the mellow crowd on **Los Cerritos** and watch the coral sun plunge into the Pacific. Boards can be rented for M$250 to M$350 per day at Pescadero Surf Camp, or from vendors on the beaches.

Mario Surf School SURFING
(📞 612-142-61-56; www.mariosurfschool.com; Hwy 19 Km 64; 1hr surf lesson from US$60; 👶) Offers excellent lessons for all levels in the Todos Santos and Pescadero area.

🛏️ Sleeping

Most places fall in the midrange to high-end category and many of these can be rated as some of the most lovely places to stay in Baja.

Pescadero Surf Camp CABAÑAS $
(📞 612-130-30-32; www.pescaderosurf.com; Hwy 19 Km 64; casita M$800-900, penthouse M$1200, campsites per person M$200; P@🏊) Located on a side of the highway 13km south of Todos Santos near the Pescadero surf break, this clean and surprisingly stylish place caters to wave riders with rentals, lessons and advice. Some of the thatched casitas have enough open space between the walls and ceiling that they almost feel outdoors. There's a pool and community kitchen, but all accommodations share bathrooms.

⭐ **Posada La Poza** SUITES $$$
(📞 612-145-04-00; www.lapoza.com; Camino a la Poza 282; ste incl breakfast US$150-325; P➖❄️🛜🏊) Boasting 'Mexican hospitality combined with Swiss quality,' (meaning, we found, colorful surrounds and meticulous, incongruously formal service), this very private retreat is in a drop-dead gorgeous palm oasis right on the Pacific. A saltwater swimming pool, freshwater lagoon, lush garden and superb restaurant with excellent Mexican wines set it apart. Suites are large and bright but the furnishings could use updating. No kids under 13 allowed.

Hotel San Cristóbal BOUTIQUE HOTEL $$$
(📞 800-990-02-72; www.sancristobalbaja.com; Carretera Federal 19 Km 54; r from US$350; P❄️🛜🏊) Style is paramount at this sleek boho resort of white walls, wood-bead chandeliers, bright throw pillows and decorative cacti. With a killer location on a long expanse of pristine beach, with crashing surf and fishing boats pulled ashore, it's too dangerous to swim in the sea but the pool is an inviting hangout with cocktails and basket-like lounge chairs. It's about 4km south of Todos Santos.

Todos Santos Inn
BOUTIQUE HOTEL $$$

(612-145-00-40; www.todossantosinn.com; Legaspi 33; d US$125-325;) Fashioned from an exquisitely restored 19th-century brick hacienda, Todos Santos Inn has only eight intimate rooms, each with a four-poster bed and a luxurious, bygone-era atmosphere. Murals, palm-beam ceilings and painted ceramic sinks are just some of the touches. A tiny swimming pool sits within a verdant tropical courtyard and the on-site bar and restaurant are truly romantic.

Guaycura
BOUTIQUE HOTEL $$$

(612-175-08-00; www.guaycura.com; cnr Legaspi & Topete; r from US$218;) All soothing colors, restful lighting and tasteful traditional furniture and artwork, the Guaycura also offers guests the free use of its beach club with its celebrated restaurant, plus a skydeck bar and small book-lined library, complete with sink-into sofas for kickback reading time, old-fashioned style.

Hotel California
HOTEL $$$

(612-145-05-25; www.hotelcaliforniabaja.com; Juárez s/n; r US$125-175;) You can check out but you may never want to leave the arty-yet-homey, lively-yet-serene Hotel California. The public spaces, in particular, are lovely, especially around the pool, which is surrounded by lush foliage, blood-red hibiscus and lofty palms. There's plenty of space plus bright and tasteful artwork throughout the rooms and they're furnished with classy, traditional Mexican pieces. It's open year-round.

Eating & Drinking

★ Loncheria La Garita
MEXICAN $

(612-176-5792; Hwy 19; dishes from M$40; 6am-6pm) A great stop 19Km on the way to La Paz or a trip on it's own, this family-run, always-busy, ranch-style-meal-slinging restaurant is as authentic as you'll find in this area. Try the *asada rancheros* (roast beef with beans, eggs and salsa), empanadas and local-style *talega* brewed coffee. It's great for kids since there are some farm animals out back amid the dust and towering cacti.

★ Heirbabuena
MEXICAN $$

(612-149-25-68; www.hierbabuenarestaurante.com; Hwy 29 Km 62, Pescadero; meals M$170-250; 1-9pm Wed-Mon, closed Sep) Walk past growing fruit and vegetables to this farm-to-table restaurant and be greeted by a vivacious crew who will serve you one of the

PUNTA LOBOS

This point in Todos Santos, named for its sea-lion colony, is where the fishers launch *pangas* (skiffs). It's just a sandy beach and a bit out of the way, but anytime from 1pm to about 3pm you can come and bargain for just-off-the-boat fish to cook at home. Pelicans joust for scraps, and a hiking trail winds up the point to an unparalleled lookout spot.

best meals in the area. The menu changes depending on what's fresh in the organic garden, sea and surrounds; the chef cooks it all up simply, to perfection. It's around 11km south of Todos Santos.

Chicken is roasted to crispy deliciousness, salads are dressed just enough and the wood-fired pizzas are flavorful and divine.

Ristorante Tre Galline
ITALIAN $$

(612-145-02-74; cnr Topete & Juárez; dinner mains from M$140; noon-10pm Tue-Sun Nov-Apr) This stone and timber, plant-laden Italian restaurant has tables arranged on descending terraces, which gives everyone a little more privacy (candlelight adds to the atmosphere). The seafood platters are particularly scrumptious and the pasta is made fresh daily.

Jazamango
NEW MEXICAN $$$

(612-688-15-01; www.facebook.com/jazamango; Naranjos s/n; dishes M$95-350; 1-9pm Tue-Sun) Star Mexican chef Javier Placensia brings his signature Baja Med cuisine to Baja Sur via this warm, open-concept place just out of town and up a tiny hill for terrestrial views. Nearly every ingredient is sustainably and locally produced, meaning plenty of seafood, meat and vegetable dishes on a menu that changes with what's available.

Los Adobes de Todos Santos
MODERN MEXICAN $$$

(www.losadobesdetodossantos.com; Av Hidalgo; mains M$200-365; 11am-9pm;) Check out the stunning desert garden at the back of this popular restaurant with its *alta cocina* menu of creatively prepared traditional dishes like *caldo pepita:* a homespun chicken broth with dumplings and cilantro spiked with guajillo chili peppers and sprinkled with pumpkin seeds. Excellent, sweet service.

El Gusto! FUSION, MEXICAN $$$

(612-145-04-00; www.lapoza.com; Posada La Poza, Camino a la Poza 282; mains M$180-450; noon-3pm & 7-10pm Fri-Wed; P) Reservations are recommended in high season at this beautiful restaurant, which was recently voted a top place to watch a Pacific sunset – sip a margarita on the terrace or in the beautifully decorated dining area. In season, whales head by as you eat. The extensive wine list is made up of Mexico's finest vintages.

Café Santa Fe ITALIAN $$$

(612-145-03-40; Centenario 4; dinner mains M$310-550; noon-9pm Wed-Mon Nov-Aug) The *insalata Mediterranea* (steamed seafood drizzled in lemon juice and oil) will make even seafood haters change their ways. The open-air kitchen, designed by the owner himself, allows you to see the food as it's being prepped. Anything on the menu will delight, surprise and tantalize.

If you need suggestions, however, go for the mussels in wine or any one of the various handmade raviolis: lobster, meat, or spinach and ricotta.

Cafelix CAFE

(Juárez; frappé M$65; 8am-9pm Wed-Mon;) This arty cafe is always packed with the local expats here for great coffee and gut-busting breakfasts. On hot days, go for one of its dozen-plus frappés or a creamy mango smoothie.

Shopping

There are numerous galleries to wander through, especially around the plaza.

Faces of Mexico ARTS & CRAFTS

(Morelos; 11am-6pm Wed-Mon) Duck into the warren of dark rooms here to discover an extraordinary collection of masks, sculpture, ethnic art, antique baubles and plenty of somber Día de Muertos beaded and painted decorative skulls. This is not your usual souvenir shop – check it out.

Agua y Sol Joyería JEWELRY

(cnr Centenario & Analia Gutiérrez; 10am-5pm) The silver jewelry here is made by local artisans and well priced with some stunning, unusual designs.

Information

El Tecolote (612-145-02-95; cnr Juárez & Av Hidalgo) The town lacks an official tourist office, but this English-language bookstore has magazines with town maps and a sketch map of nearby beach areas. Jan, the owner, is super-helpful.

Getting There & Away

Hourly between 6:30am and 10:30pm, buses head to La Paz (M$122, one hour) and to Cabo San Lucas (M$135, one hour) from the **bus stop** (612-148-02-89; Heróico Colegio Militar; 7am-10pm) between Zaragoza and Morelos.

Copper Canyon & Northern Mexico

Best Places to Eat

➡ Teresitas (p777)

➡ Madre Oaxaca (p804)

➡ Plaza del Mariachi (p785)

➡ Restaurante Barranco (p760)

➡ Cremería Wallander (p792)

Best Places to Stay

➡ Hacienda de los Santos (p777)

➡ Dream Weaver Inn (p770)

➡ La Troje de Adobe (p763)

➡ Hotel San Felipe El Real (p785)

➡ Foggara Hotel (p796)

Why Go?

Northern Mexico is the ultimate frontier land: vast cactus-strewn deserts, craggy mountains and breathtaking canyons define this most iconic of regions, which is familiar to almost anyone from its role in countless Wild West movies. If the landscape is diverse, then the people of the north are equally so: cowboys, revolutionaries and bandits have, over the centuries, left their mark on the region, while the varied and still deeply traditional indigenous peoples remain some of Mexico's least Westernized.

Though the narco wars have impacted the north terribly in recent years, it remains a safe place to visit for anyone taking a few sensible precautions, and these days you'll find you have it pretty much to yourself. The Ferrocarril Chihuahua Pacífico (Copper Canyon Railway), Mexico's only remaining long-distance passenger train ride, is the region's most outstanding sight, but its colonial towns, superb beaches and diverse wildlife are other strong lures.

When to Go
Chihuahua

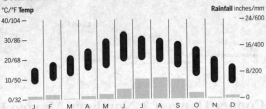

Jun & Jul Heavy rainfall. Key festivals like Las Jornadas Villistas in Parral.

Late Sep–Oct Pleasantly hot during the day. Good time to visit the coming-into-bloom Copper Canyon.

Dec & Jan Balmy, dry weather makes for a popular beach escape though Festival Tirado lures many inland.

Copper Canyon & Northern Mexico Highlights

1 **Ferrocarril Chihuahua Pacífico** (p751) Riding Mexico's last passenger train through canyon scenery.

2 **El Pinacate Biosphere Reserve** (p771) Experiencing the lunar landscapes of this spectacular desert reserve.

3 **Cuatro Ciénegas** (p797) Exploring this oasis reserve, one of the most biodiverse places in the world.

4 **Álamos** (p775) Checking into a colonial hotel and taking in the beauty of this old silver town.

5 **Horno3** (p800) Being awed by Monterrey's heavy metal heritage.

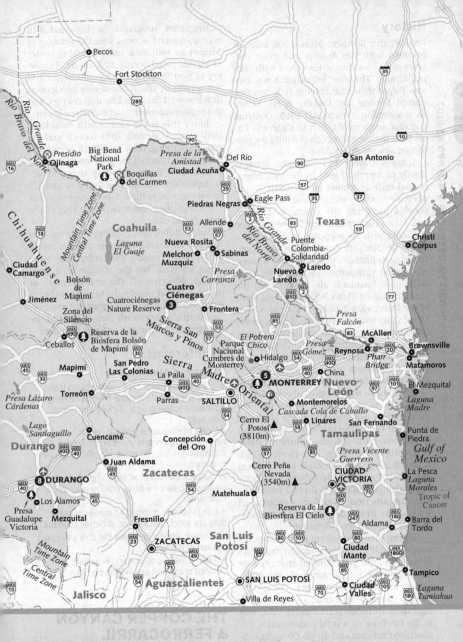

6 Playa los Algodones
(p773) Relaxing in San Carlos's finest beach: white sand and turquoise waters.

7 Cascada de Basaseachi
(p764) Floating in the plunge pool of Mexico's highest full-time waterfall.

8 Durango (p789) Soaking up history and culture in this charming colonial town.

9 Parque de Aventura Barrancas del Cobre (p761) Zip-lining over the incredible Copper Canyon at adrenaline-pumping speed.

History

Pre-Hispanic northern Mexico had more in common with the Anasazi and other cultures of the southwest USA than with central Mexico. The most important town here was Paquimé, a vital trading link between central Mexico and the dry north before its destruction around AD 1340. Outlying Paquimé settlements such as Cuarenta Casas built their dwellings on cliffsides for protection against attack.

Spanish slavers and explorers, arriving chiefly in search of gold in the 16th century, had mixed fortunes in the north. In the northwest they encountered indigenous peoples including the Opata, Seri, Yaqui and Mayo. Rather than the fabled province of Cíbola with its supposed seven cities of gold, the Spanish found silver and, conscripting indigenous people as slave miners, established prosperous mining cities such as Álamos. Spaniards also soon forged the Camino Real de Tierra Adentro (Royal Road of the Interior), a 2560km trade route from Mexico City to Santa Fe, New Mexico, which helped make towns en route such as Durango extremely wealthy. In the northeast, however, harsh conditions and attacks by indigenous Chichimecs and Apaches meant settlement and development came more slowly.

The Spanish never tightened control here sufficiently to quell revolts. In the fight for Mexican Independence (1810), the Mexican–American War of the 1840s and the Mexican Revolution (1910–20) the northern states necessarily played a key role. Frontiers radically changed with Mexico's loss of Texas and New Mexico (1830s–1850s); the Treaty of Guadalupe Hidalgo (1848) that ended the Mexican–American War finally established today's Río Bravo del Norte (Rio Grande) frontier between the two nations.

Glaring inequities of land ownership between the elite – grown wealthy from the mines – and the impoverished majority contributed to the unrest that made the north a Mexican Revolution hot spot. The revolutionary División del Norte, an army led by legendary Durango-born Pancho Villa, was in the forefront of several major battles. Venustiano Carranza and Álvaro Obregón, other main revolutionary figures, were, respectively, from the northern states of Coahuila and Sonora. All three were initially allies and subsequently enemies in the Revolution, which meant the split of allegiances in the north was acute.

Irrigation programs in the mid-20th century turned Sonora into the granary of Mexico as well as a cattle-ranching center alongside neighboring Chihuahua. Discovery of petroleum, coal and natural gas and the arrival of the railroad also accelerated development from the late 19th century, and the region emerged as an industrial leader.

Today this is the most North Americanized part of Mexico, with money and resources surging back and forth across the border and baseball the main sport in many towns. The Texan economy is particularly dependent on Mexican workers and US investment is behind most *maquiladoras* (assembly-plant operations) that ring all the region's big cities.

Since 2006, drug cartel violence has plagued northern Mexico as gangs compete for territory. Initially the border cities were worst affected, but the violence has since spread, affecting all the main centers of population. Yet despite the headlines, the region's economy remains relatively prosperous, with steady growth rates (except in the tourism sector, which continues to suffer).

ℹ Information

DANGERS & ANNOYANCES

While the vast majority of visitors to northern Mexico enjoy a safe, trouble-free trip, the region does have active drug trafficking and related violence.

➔ Use a trusted local guide for any off-the-beaten-path excursions to avoid encountering drug cultivation fields and areas plagued by cartels or gangs.

➔ Violence can occur at bars, nightclubs and casinos – take care when visiting such establishments.

➔ Use toll roads (*cuotas*) whenever possible; they are safer, quicker and in better condition.

➔ In cities, always lock your car doors to guard against carjackings.

➔ Avoid traveling after dark, especially in isolated areas and around the border.

THE COPPER CANYON & FERROCARRIL CHIHUAHUA PACÍFICO

The highland scenery of this region is nothing short of spectacular. Northern Mexico does not lack for amazing attractions, but none compares to the Copper Canyon for sheer wow-factor, with its astonishing cliff-top vistas, towering pine-clad mountains and the fascinating culture of the native Tarahumara people.

A labyrinth of six main canyons covers an area four times larger than Arizona's Grand Canyon system, and is deeper, narrower and more verdant than its American counterpart. Tropical fruit trees grow in the canyon bottoms while the high ground is covered in alpine vegetation and, often, winter snows.

A handful of towns make convenient base camps for exploring the region. Creel is the largest and home to several recommended hotels. Further into the canyon system are Divisadero, Arepo and Cerocahui, all along or near the famous Chepe train route, and the more remote (yet readily accessible) canyon-bottom villages of Batopilas and Urique.

🏃 Activities

All manner of natural wonders are accessible by foot, horse, bike or motor vehicle – cliffs, towering rock massifs, rivers, waterfalls, lakes and forests. For the ultimate buzz, head to the Parque de Aventura Barrancas del Cobre, where you can soar over death-defying drops on a series of Mexico's most hair-raising zip-lines.

★ Ferrocarril
Chihuahua Pacífico   RAIL

(El Chepe; ☑614-439-72-12, 800-122-43-73; www.chepe.com.mx; full journey 1st/2nd class M$3276/1891; 🚹) The stats say everything: 656km of track, 37 bridges, 86 tunnels and more than 60 years in the making. The Copper Canyon Railway is one of the world's most incredible rail journeys, and northern Mexico's biggest single attraction. Nicknamed 'El Chepe' (using the Spanish initials of 'Chihuahua' and 'Pacífico'), the railway operates one daily train in each direction, taking a full day.

Completed in 1961, the railway is as phenomenal in its engineering prowess as in the canyon views it yields.

The line is the major link between Chihuahua and the coast, heavily used for freight as well as passengers. It connects the Pacific coast with the mountainous, arid interior of northern Mexico via tricky canyon gradients that force it to rise up over 2400m.

Between Los Mochis and El Fuerte, the train trundles through flat farmland, then begins to climb through hills speckled with dark pillars of cacti. It passes over the long Río Fuerte bridge and through the first of the 86 tunnels about four hours after leaving Los Mochis. The train hugs the sides of deepening canyons and makes a spectacular zigzag ascent into a tunnel above Témoris, after which pine trees appear on the hillsides. By the next station, Bahuichivo, you are in the Sierra Madre uplands, with flower-dotted meadows punctuating an entrancing alpine landscape. The biggest highlight of the train ride is stopping at Divisadero, where you get your only glimpse of the actual Copper Canyon. The train circles back over itself in a complete loop to gain height at the suitably named El Lazo (the Lasso), before chugging on to Creel and Chihuahua.

There's not that much difference between *primera* and *económica* carriages – the former has a dining room, the latter a canteen. Snacks cost M$20 and meals around M$100. Coffee is instant in both classes. Neither has wi-fi. All carriages are rather showing their age (dating from the 1980s), and tickets are overpriced given the moderate comfort levels. Both classes have air-conditioning, heating and reclining seats with ample leg room. The *clase económica* is certainly nice enough for most travelers, although often you'll have no choice but *primera*.

Note that you're not allowed to consume alcohol on any of the trains, but that smoking is tolerated in the open-air gap between carriages. All trains are staffed with machine-gun-toting plainclothes police.

ℹ Information

TICKETS

You can board the train at any station without a ticket if there are free seats, and pay the conductor. Outside the peak seasons (Semana Santa, July, August, Christmas and New Year), you will almost always be able to do this. However, it's advisable to reserve tickets a month or more ahead for peak-season travel, and a day ahead at other times, although in practice most of the time you'll have no problem buying tickets on the day of travel.

Tickets are sold at Los Mochis station and Chihuahua station for trips starting at any station. *Primera express* tickets are sold up to a month in advance, and *clase económica* tickets a day in advance. Tickets can be made up to a year in advance by telephone (English speakers available) and email. On the *primera express*, you can make stopovers (usually up to three) at

Copper Canyon

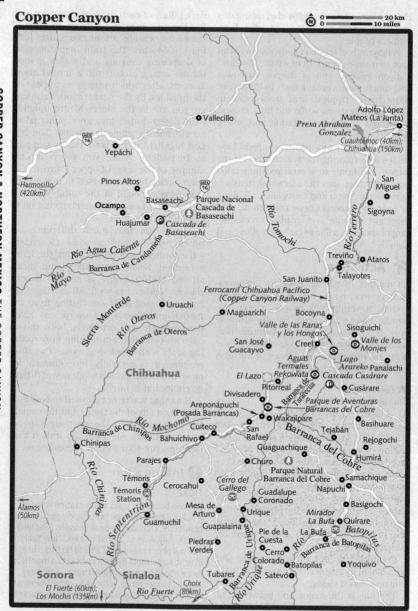

no Copper Canyon (m)extra cost, if you specify places and dates when you make the booking.

For same-day tickets, you should be at Los Mochis or Chihuahua station an hour ahead of departure. Only Los Mochis, Creel, Cuauhtémoc and Chihuahua stations have ticket offices.

When purchasing your tickets, request a seat on the south side of the railcar (from Los Mochis to Chihuahua, that's the right side of the train; from Chihuahua to Los Mochis, the left side) – you'll enjoy the best views.

See p754 for the Ferrocarril Chihuahua Pacífico schedule and ticket prices.

El Fuerte

☑ 698 / POP 11,900 / ELEV 90M

Clustered around a striking plaza and with a center packed full of brightly painted colonial houses, El Fuerte oozes historic character. For many centuries the most important commercial center in northwestern Mexico due to its proximity to the silver mines in the canyons, this is now a picturesque little town surrounded by one of Latin America's last-standing dry tropical forests. Far preferable to Los Mochis as a place to start or end a trip on the Ferrocarril Chihuahua Pacífico, it's worth a stay of more than just a night to take a trip on the Río Fuerte and explore the unique subtropical countryside.

El Fuerte was founded in 1564, and is named for a 17th-century fort built on its distinctive high point of Cerro de las Pilas to protect settlers from indigenous attacks.

◉ Sights

Bosque Secreto
FOREST

(Secret Forest) ☑ Five hundred years ago, over 550,000 sq km of dry tropical forest stretched down the coast from northern Mexico to Panama. Much of the remaining 10% is around El Fuerte, an area known as Bosque Secreto. The delightful Río Fuerte, which is incredibly rich in birdlife (including herons, osprey, kingfishers and flycatchers), winds through much of the forest.

Hotel Río Vista leads recommended boat trips (M$300 per person) along the river, taking in some 2000-year-old petroglyphs.

🛏 Sleeping

Hotel La Choza
HOTEL $

(☑ 698-893-12-74; www.hotellachoza.com; 5 de Mayo 101; r M$700; ⓟ⊝❄🛜♨) This deceptively large hotel has a colonial facade, but becomes rather more modern as you enter its enormous courtyard. It boasts inviting rooms, all with quaint touches such as hand-painted sinks, enormous crucifixes over the beds and high, brick-vaulted ceilings. It's excellent value, and the in-house **Diligencias** (mains M$70-220; ⊙7am-10pm; 🛜) restaurant is a good bet too.

Hotel Guerrero
HOTEL $

(☑ 698-893-05-24; www.hotelyhostelguerrero.jimdo.com; Juárez 106; r M$400; ⊝❄🛜) This budget hotel in the center of El Fuerte has charming staff who go the extra mile to look after their guests. The rooms, set around a shady pillared patio, are colorful and comfortable, if a bit shabby. Avoid the cell-like rooms on the left, and try for one of the older but roomier ones on the right.

Hotel Río Vista
HOTEL $$

(☑ 698-893-04-13, cell 698-1042647; hotelrio vista@hotmail.com; Progreso s/n; r M$670; ⓟ❄🛜♨) This quirky place tucked behind the town's hilltop museum has been hosting travelers for years. Stylistically it's a bit of a shock to the senses with murals, garish colors and an excess of Mexicana and other bizarre curios. But hey, the superb river views compensate. Plus there's a pool. The hotel also organizes recommended boat trips along the Bosque Secreto.

★ Posada del Hidalgo
HERITAGE HOTEL $$$

(☑ 800-552-56-45, 698-893-02-42; www.hotel posadadelhidalgo.com; Hidalgo 101; s/d/tr M$1525/1625/1950; ⓟ❄@🛜♨) This highly atmospheric hotel inside a rusty red colonial hacienda offers bundles of classic charm with spacious, elegant rooms grouped around shady garden courtyards and jaw-dropping public areas. There's a beautiful open-air restaurant, a pool, a massage room and a popular bar for socializing. Hummingbirds join guests for breakfast.

Torres del Fuerte
BOUTIQUE HOTEL $$$

(☑ 698-893-19-74; www.facebook.com/Torresdel Fuerte; Robles 102; s/d/tr US$100/110/130; ⓟ⊝❄🛜) A 400-year-old hacienda that fuses colonial class and contemporary art, set around gorgeous gardens. All rooms are individually themed – China, India, Morocco – many with slate bathrooms and exposed adobe walls. Giant cacti frame the rooms, while high ceilings with wooden beams soar overhead. There's also a gourmet restaurant, **Bonifacio's** (mains M$70-250; ⊙7am-noon & 6:30-9:30pm; ☑).

🍴 Eating

The wealth of fresh water around El Fuerte produces must-have local specialties such as *cauques* or *langostinos* (freshwater crayfish) and *lobina* (black bass). That said, restaurant choices are very limited in town.

★ SU-FÓ Sushi & Cocina Bistro
BISTRO $

(☑ 698-893-50-17; www.facebook.com/pg/Sufo Sushi.Bistro; Constitucion 112; dishes M$60-90; ⊙6pm-midnight Tue-Sun; 🛜) SU-FÓ serves

RAILWAY SCHEDULE – FERROCARRIL CHIHUAHUA PACÍFICO

There's one daily train in each direction. *Primera express* (1st-class only, and with fewer stops) trains run on Monday, Wednesday, Thursday and Saturday from Los Mochis. From Chihuahua they run on Sunday, Tuesday, Wednesday and Friday. On other days, the train has both *primera* and *clase económica* carriages, meaning it travels rather slower and makes more stops, which impacts the timetable and means that the entire journey takes around an hour longer (13½ hours in total).

Schedules change and both trains tend to run a little late (by an hour or two), so timetables comprise just a rough guideline. If you are heading to Los Mochis with hopes of catching the Baja ferry from Topolobampo the same day, don't count on it; you'll find it far easier to schedule an overnight stop in Los Mochis. There is no time change between Los Mochis and Chihuahua.

Eastbound – Los Mochis to Chihauhau

	PRIMERA EXPRESS		CLASE ECONÓMICA	
Station	Arrives	Fare from Los Mochis (M$)	Arrives (Tue, Fri, Sun)	Fare from Los Mochis (M$)
Los Mochis	6am (departs Los Mochis)	–	6am (departs Los Mochis)	–
El Fuerte	8:16am	602	8:19am	348
Témoris	11:20am	1074	11:24am	620
Bahuichivo	12:20pm	1269	12:35pm	733
San Rafael	1:25pm	1430	1:28pm	825
Posada Barrancas (Arepo)	1:43pm	1480	1:46pm	854
Divisadero	2:22pm	1500	2:25pm	866
Creel	3:44pm	1791	3:42pm	1034
Cuauhtémoc	6:37pm	2609	7:07pm	1506
Chihuahua	8:54pm	3276	9:34pm	1891

Westbound – Chihuahua to Los Mochis

	PRIMERA EXPRESS		CLASE ECONÓMICA	
Station	Arrives	Fare from Chihuahua (M$)	Arrives (Mon, Thu, Sat)	Fare from Chihuahua (M$)
Chihuahua	6am (departs Chihuahua)	–	6am (departs Chihuahua)	–
Cuauhtémoc	8:25am	667	8:25am	385
Creel	11:20am	1490	11:47am	860
Divisadero	1:04pm	1781	1:41pm	1028
Posada Barrancas (Arepo)	1:11pm	1801	1:52pm	1040
San Rafael	1:37pm	1851	2:16pm	1069
Bahuichivo	2:28pm	2012	3:12pm	1161
Témoris	3:25pm	2208	4:12pm	1274
El Fuerte	6:23pm	2870	7:19pm	1657
Los Mochis	8:22pm	3276	9:28pm	1891

up an eclectic menu of sushi rolls (all with signature cream cheese), rice bowls, hamburgers with hand-cut fries and even fancy chicken nuggets. Somehow it works – the place is hopping most nights. Seating is in an open-air lot with murals, urban-chic decor and twinkling lights. A staff member plays DJ most nights.

Taco Stands
TACOS $

(Juárez s/n; meal M$30-50; ⊙7am-3pm) A row of taco stands, set up in stand-alone concrete huts, do brisk business in all manner of grilled meats, from *al pastor* (seasoned pork) to *cabeza* (cow head; typically cheeks). Join the locals at a counter and order tacos 'til you're full. BYO drinks. Located next to the bus stop for Los Mochis.

El Mesón del General
SEAFOOD $$

(☑698-893-02-60; Juárez 202; mains M$110-270; ⊙11am-9:30pm) A traditional, formal restaurant that specializes in fish and seafood, with several styles of *pulpo* (octopus) and combo plates of various river delicacies. You'll find it on El Fuerte's main drag, an oasis from the bustle of the nearby market.

❶ Information

Tourist Information Kiosk (5 de Mayo s/n; ⊙8am-3pm Mon-Fri) On the central plaza, this tourist kiosk offers brochures and maps of town. Guides linger nearby to offer tips and tours.

❶ Getting There & Away

Buses to Los Mochis (M$70, two hours) depart about every half-hour, 5am to 7:30pm, from Juárez near Calle 16 de Septiembre, right in the center of town. From Los Mochis it's easy to connect to elsewhere in northern Mexico.

The train station is 6km south of town (M$150 by taxi). Many hotels offer station pickup and drop-off for clients, for which they may or may not charge (up to the taxi rate). If you arrive by train in the evening, waiting shared taxis charge M$50 a person for a run into the town center.

The dirt road to Álamos from here requires 4WD and takes five hours: it's actually quicker heading to Los Mochis and taking the highway.

Cerocahui

☑635 / POP 1300 / ELEV 1600M

The tiny, attractive village of Cerocahui, dedicated mainly to forestry, sits in the middle of a verdant, vista-laden valley, and is easily reached from El Chepe (p751) stop Bahuichivo, 16km away. The canyon country around here sees far fewer tourists than the region near Creel, and the enticing canyon-bottom village of Urique is within striking range.

On the Central Plaza, Cerocahui's pretty yellow-domed church, **San Francisco Javier de Cerocahui**, was founded in 1680.

There's good hiking around Cerocahui, and the excursions (offered by all accommodations) to **Cerro del Gallego**, a spectacular lookout over the Barranca de Urique, 25km along the Urique road, are well worth it.

🍴 Sleeping & Eating

Hotel Jade
HOTEL $$

(☑635-456-52-75; www.hoteljade.com.mx; Plaza del Poblado; s/d M$450/900, apt from $500; ⊙❋) This simple place has 10 clean and comfortable rooms, each with full beds and big windows. The warm welcome from hosts Alberto and Francia and the outstanding cooking (including homemade bread, fish dishes and veggie options; meals M$100) really make this place stand out. Area tours are also offered (M$100 to M$600 per person; minimum two people). English spoken.

Cabañas San Isidro
CABAÑAS $$

(☑635-293-75-02; www.coppercanyonamigos. com; Carretera a Urique Km 24; s/d/tr incl full board & transfers US$85/115/140; ℗) ⬤ High in the hills above Cerocahui, 8km along the road to Urique, this working farm makes a perfect (if isolated) rural base for all kinds of hikes, horseback riding and trips in canyon country. Brothers and co-owners Mario and Tito have excellent connections to the Tarahumara community's runner-guides. The cozy and artful adobe-and-wood cabins have wood-burning stoves. Meals are tasty and plentiful.

★Hotel Paraíso del Oso
HOTEL $$$

(☑635-109-01-88, Chihuahua 614-421-3372; www. mexicohorse.com; Carretera Bahuichivo-Cerocahui s/n; dm US$15, s/d incl full board US$120/185; ℗⊙☎) This excellent family-owned rural lodge is a great base for bird-watching, hikes (from M$50), horseback rides (M$150 per hour) and community tourism (the owners have good Tarahumara contacts). The setup includes spacious, ranch-style rooms overlooking a lush garden courtyard and a fascinating book collection to browse. There's also a dorm, with several beds that sleep two (meals not included). Located 4km from the center of Cerocahui, on the road to Bahuichivo.

Hotel Misión
HOTEL $$$

(☑ 635-456-52-94; www.hotelmision.com; Plaza del Poblado; s/d incl full board from M$3054/3997; P⊕@🐾) This delightful former hacienda on the town's central plaza offers rustic chic accommodations with *chimeneas* (fireplaces), an evocative bar-restaurant, a games room with a pool table and lovely gardens planted with vines. It's popular with tour groups 'doing' the canyon, but discounts are often available to independent travelers.

ⓘ Getting There & Away

Cerocahui hotels will pick you up at El Chepe's (p751) Bahuichivo train stop if you have reserved a room. If you haven't, you can often catch a ride with one of their vans anyway, though they'll be expecting you to check in on arrival.

Alternatively, a local bus leaves Abarrotes El Teto, a small grocery store at the entrance to town that doubles as a bus stop, and is a M$50 taxi ride from the train station. The bus leaves for Cerocahui (M$50, 40 minutes) and Urique (M$230, 3½ hours or more) daily at around

1:30pm; it waits for the train from Chihuahua but does not always wait for the one from Los Mochis. Returning, it leaves Urique at 7am and passes through Cerocahui at around 10am and Bahuichivo at 11am. From Bahuichivo, buses depart every two hours from 6am to 2pm to San Rafael (M$50, 45 minutes), Areponápuchi (M$60, one hour), Divisadero (M$10, 70 minutes), Creel (M$100, two hours) and Chihuahua (M$350, seven to eight hours).

There are several intriguing back roads from Cerocahui that look temptingly direct on maps but should not be attempted without expert local advice. These roads have tough 4WD-only stretches, traverse isolated lands harboring drug plantations and parts can be washed out after heavy rains. A track connects Cerocahui to Choix (from where there's a paved road to El Fuerte), and another links Bahuichivo with Álamos via Témoris. Consult the owners of Hotel Paraíso del Oso (p755) or Cabañas San Isidro (p755) about security and road conditions.

Urique

☑ 635 / POP 1000 / ELEV 550M

This starry-skied ex-mining village lies at the bottom of the deepest of all the canyons, the spectacular Barranca de Urique, measuring 1870m from rim to river. The trip there is nothing short of spectacular. The mostly unpaved road weaves through

---

ULTRAMARATHONS IN URIQUE

Normally held in Urique in early March, the **Ultra Caballo Blanco** (www.facebook.com/caballoblancoultramarathon) is an 82km ultramarathon on tough canyon trails and at altitude. It was established by Micah True, a legendary American runner known locally as Caballo Blanco (The White Horse) who lived for years in the Copper Canyon region, and gained international attention when featured in Christopher McDougall's book *Born to Run*.

The ultramarathon pays homage to the native Tarahumara (or Rarámuri) people, who have a centuries-old tradition of long-distance running and whose very name is thought to mean 'the running people' or 'having light feet.' Tarahumara *huaraches* (sandals made from a thin strip of recycled tires) are said to have inspired the barefoot running method (which tests have shown also reduces energy use and running-related injuries) that has now gone global.

Another event, **Carrera de los Pies Ligeros** (Race of the Light Feet), held each December, is a *rarajipari*, a long-distance Tarahumara relay-style running race with two teams kicking a ball along a course. Rarajipari are actually much truer to Tarahumara traditions than pure running races. There are two races, one for each sex, each involving two teams (who run with torches at night) over a distance of more than 100km. This race lasts between 12 and 24 hours, and is only open to Tarahumara people.

The races were canceled in years past due to drug cartel flare-ups, but security and stability have returned to the region, and so the races have returned too.

rolling pine forest before diving suddenly into the canyon proper. Just past the rim is **Mirador Cerro del Gallego**, one of the most spectacular viewpoints in the Copper Canyon, with Urique town and river visible far below. From there, the narrow road winds down the nearly sheer canyon wall, a stomach-lurching 15km descent with more hairpin bends than straight sections.

While Urique is a charming and safe place, it is nevertheless known for significant marijuana and poppy cultivation. (That unusually wide street at the edge of town doubles as an airstrip, ostensibly for medical evacuations but handy for transportation of all kinds.) Most visitors won't notice or experience anything unusual, though, especially if you stick to main routes and tours.

🏃 Activities

For day hikes you can go up the Río Urique to **Guadalupe Coronado** village (7km) or downriver to **Guapalaina** (6km), both wonderful walks along the riverside dirt roads. The two- to three-day trek to Batopilas is a bigger challenge. Local guides charge around M$4000 to M$5000 for this trip. As ever in northern Mexico, check the safety situation carefully on the ground before setting out.

🛏 Sleeping & Eating

Hotel El Paraíso Escondido　　HOTEL **$**
(☑635-592-74-04; escondidodeurique@hotmail.com; Principal s/n; s/d M$300/400; P❄) Squeaky clean, sponge-painted and centrally located, rooms at this friendly and cheap motel are great value. All have flat-screen TVs, hot water and air-con. Units on the first floor have heating too. To get here, turn right when you get to the main drag as you enter the town; the hotel will be on your right-hand side.

Entre Amigos　　CABAÑAS, CAMPGROUND **$**
(☑635-110-62-60, USA 503-434-6488; www.amongamigos.com; Principal s/n; campsites per person US$10, dm/r US$15/50; P😊🐾) 🍃 This artful place has been hosting travelers since 1975. Homey stone cabins, aging dorms and decent campsites (BYO gear) are dotted around grounds that are dominated by fruit trees and an unbelievably gigantic cactus. No meals are offered, but there's a good guests' kitchen. Staff can hook you up with dependable local guides for hiking,

camping or fishing and there's an impressive library.

It's located near the riverbank, a 10-minute walk beyond the town center. If arriving by bus, the driver will normally be happy to drop you off.

Restaurant Plaza　　MEXICAN **$$**
(☑635-456-60-03; Principal s/n; meals M$100-120; ⊙6am-9pm) This excellent family-run restaurant offers fine food with real home-cooked flavor. The specialty is *aguachile* – a soupy, spicy shrimp cocktail full of onions and tomatoes served in a *molcajete* (traditional mortar and pestle). Don't be fooled by the tiny front dining room – there's a large shady courtyard in back and a sunny rooftop patio with views of the towering canyon walls.

Restaurante del Centro　　MEXICAN **$$**
(mains M$70-180; ⊙7:30am-9pm) The entrance of this sleepy restaurant is through a knick-knack shop, but the spacious dining room is bright and pleasant, with long family-style tables. There's a breakfast menu, a buffet lunch once a week and plenty of choices for dinner, including several well-prepared steaks. You'll find it just off the central plaza, set back from the main drag.

ℹ Information

The town hall on the main street has a small, efficient **tourist office** (☑635-456-60-42; turismo.urique@gmail.com; Palacio Municipal, Principal s/n; ⊙8am-3pm Mon-Fri).

ℹ Getting There & Away

El Chepe (p751) stops twice daily in Bahuichivo, the closest train station to Urique. A daily bus leaves the station for Urique (M$230, 3½ hours or more) after the last train of the day arrives. Otherwise, Abarrotes El Teto, a small grocery store located at the entrance to town, doubles as a local bus stop, and is a M$50 taxi ride from the train station. The bus travels to Cerocahui (M$50, 40 minutes) and Urique (M$230, 3½ hours or more) daily at around 1:30pm; it waits for the first train from Chihuahua but does not always wait for the later one from Los Mochis.

Returning, the bus circles town and leaves Urique at 7am, stopping in Cerocahui and Bahuichivo. Hotels in Urique can arrange transfers from Bahuichivo for about M$1500. Cerocahui hotels also offer transportation: Cabañas San Isidro and Hotel Jade both charge M$1800 for a return day trip to Urique with a guide.

ℹ BORDER CROSSINGS

There are more than 40 official US–Mexico border crossing points, many open 24 hours daily. US Customs & Border Protection (www.cbp.gov) provides opening hours and estimated waiting times for drivers.

Tourists visiting Mexico must carry a passport or (for Americans entering and leaving by land or sea) a US passport card. All tourists must also obtain a Mexican tourist permit (*forma migratoria para turista*, FMT; or *forma migratoria múltiple*, FMM) on arrival, unless they are staying within the border zone and not staying over 72 hours. The border zone generally extends 20km to 30km south from the border, but also stretches as far as Puerto Peñasco in Sonora and Ensenada and San Felipe in Baja California.

Travelers taking a vehicle must purchase Mexican insurance (available at borders). If you're heading beyond the border zone deeper into Mexico (except in Baja California), you must obtain a temporary vehicle importation permit or a Sólo Sonora permit. Each costs M$1014 and can be obtained for less if ordered way in advance and either delivered by mail or picked up at Banjército outlets around the border.

To organize the vehicle permit in advance use the Banjército website (www.banjercito.com.mx) or simply apply at one of Mexico's 38 IITV (Importación e Internación de Vehículos) offices at northern borders and some locations past the border, including in Sonora at Agua Zarca (21km south of Nogales), in Chihuahua state 30km south of Ciudad Juárez, and in Baja California at Pichilingue (near La Paz) and Ensenada. All IITV locations are given at www.banjercito.com.mx (click on 'Red de Módulos IITV').

If you're only traveling in Sonora, the Sólo Sonora program is worth considering. This allows North Americans to bring a vehicle into northwest Sonora with less hassle (reduced paperwork and no bond to deposit) and is also available from Banjército or at IITV offices. Sólo Sonora is limited to Hwy 2 between Agua Prieta and Imuris and Hwy 15D between Imuris and the checkpoint at Km 98 east of Empalme near Guaymas. To travel beyond these points, you must get a full vehicle permit; staff at the Km 98 checkpoint can authorize one pretty rapidly if you have the paperwork, and are friendly, efficient and speak English.

If you take a vehicle into Baja California, and then ship it to mainland Mexico by ferry from Pichilingue, you must get a vehicle permit before embarking your vehicle.

The main border crossings (ordered west to east) are as follows:

San Diego (California)–Tijuana (Baja California) The three border crossings here include San Ysidro–El Chaparral (24 hours), the world's busiest border crossing. Others include the cross-border terminal at Tijuana's international airport (24 hours, for ticketed passengers only) and the Otay Mesa crossing (24 hours).

Calexico (California)–Mexicali (Baja California) The two border crossings here are Calexico West (24 hours) and Calexico East (3am to midnight).

Lukeville (Arizona)–Sonoyta (Sonora) Best for Puerto Peñasco (6am to midnight).

Nogales (Arizona)–Nogales (Sonora) Hwy 15/15D is the main highway south to the Deconcini crossing (24 hours).

Areponápuchi

📞 635 / POP 210 / ELEV 2220M

Stretched along a 2km road near the lip of the canyon, the tiny settlement of Areponápuchi or 'Arepo' is just a couple of dozen houses, a church and a few hotels, the pricier of which are right on the canyon edge with mind-blowing views. This is the most touristy bit of the Copper Canyon, with its superb adventure park (p761) that allows you to take a series of seven zip-lines almost to the canyon bottom before soaring back up to the rim by cable car – a must-do half-day out.

The village itself is unremarkable, with most people just spending a night or two to visit the adventure park before continuing on El Chepe (p751). An easy path with several good viewpoints runs along the canyon edge to the left (north) of Hotel Mirador, and several lookouts (as well as the adventure park) lie short distances off the road between here and Divisadero.

Santa Teresa crossing Some 20km west of Juárez in Chihuahua state; good for avoiding security risks near Juárez (6am to midnight).

El Paso (Texas)–Ciudad Juárez (Chihuahua) Bridge of the Americas (24 hours); Paso del Norte (24 hours); Stanton St–Avenida Lerdo (6am-midnight); and Ysleta (24 hours). Pedestrian crossings are via the bridges of Bridge of the Americas, Paso del Norte or Ysleta. To return on foot you must use Paso del Norte. Access for vehicles is via the Bridge of the Americas (Puente Córdova). Tourist permits are available at the end of the Stanton St–Avenida Lerdo bridge and Bridge of the Americas. Hwy 45D from Juárez is the principal southbound route.

Presidio (Texas)–Ojinaga (Chihuahua) From Ojinaga, it's 225km along Hwy 16 direct to Chihuahua (24 hours).

Del Rio (Texas)–Ciudad Acuña (Coahuila) Open 24 hours.

Eagle Pass (Texas)–Piedras Negras (Coahuila) Two crossings: Bridge 1 (7am to 11pm) and Bridge 2 (24 hours).

Laredo (Texas)–Nuevo Laredo (Tamaulipas) Four crossings: Puente Internacional 1 (24 hours); Puente Internacional 2 (24 hours); Colombia Solidarity (8am to midnight); World Trade Bridge (8am to midnight). Puente Internacional 2 bypasses the city and is the safest option, connecting with Hwy 85D from Nuevo Laredo to Monterrey, from where there are good connections to elsewhere in Mexico (24 hours).

McAllen/Hidalgo/Pharr (Texas)–Reynosa (Tamaulipas) Three US towns, sitting side-by-side, serve Reynosa: Anzalduas International Bridge (6am to 10pm), Hidalgo (24 hours) and Pharr (6am to midnight).

Brownsville (Texas)–Matamoros (Tamaulipas) B&M (24 hours), Gateway (24 hours), Los Indios (6am to midnight) and Veterans International (6am-midnight).

There are plenty of cross-border bus services into the region from US cities, most involving a change of buses in a city on the US or Mexican side of the border. Given the time it can take to get through the border, it is often quicker to disembark before the border, make the crossing on foot, and pick up further transportation on the other side.

If you want to avoid staying long in Mexico's border towns, some services will take you directly deeper into Mexico, including Phoenix–Puerto Peñasco via Sonoyta with **Transportes Express** (p772); Chihuahua via Juárez from Dallas, Denver, Los Angeles and Las Vegas (among others) with **Los Paisanos Autobuses** (p787); and Tufesa (www.tufesa.com.mx), which operates many cross-border buses to California and Arizona.

Many border towns rank among Mexico's most dangerous places. The security situation can change quickly. Ciudad Juárez and Nuevo Laredo have been notorious for years and are best avoided, or at least transited during daylight hours, but you should be careful anywhere. The Sonoran border crossings were deemed pretty *tranquilo* at the time of research.

🛏 Sleeping & Eating

Cabañas Díaz Family CABAÑAS $
(☑ 635-578-30-08; off Principal; cabin per person M$300; ℗) This friendly family-run lodge has several comfortable cabins overlooking a peach orchard, many with lofts, and all with fireplaces and fully equipped kitchenettes. Basic but clean hotel-type rooms (M$500) are also offered. Affordable home-style meals are served in a huge dining room in the main building. Excellent guided hikes and horseback rides (four-hour outing for two by foot/horse M$350/650) are offered too.

Hotel Mansión Tarahumara HOTEL $$
(El Castillo; ☑ 635-578-30-30, Chihuahua 614-415-47-21; www.hotelmansiontarahumara.com.mx; off Principal; s/d incl breakfast from M$1026/1445, incl full board from M$1386/1938; ℗ 🛜 🖭) This castle-like hotel (complete with turrets and battlements) offers a comfortable accommodations just a few minutes up the hill from

the station. Rooms on the canyon rim (commanding the highest prices) are the showstoppers, with plush beds and balconies. There's a huge restaurant (meals M$220) plus a pool and Jacuzzi.

Hotel Mirador HOTEL $$$
(☑ 800-552-56-45, 635-578-30-20; www.mexicos coppercanyon.com; off Principal; s/d/ste incl full board M$3045/3997/4845; P🐶🐕📶) Suspended over the canyon, this hotel's 75 rooms (each with private balcony, beamed ceilings and somewhat dated furnishings) enjoy unbeatable views, as does the restaurant where buffet meals are served at communal tables. It's popular with tour groups and is a bit overpriced, but it's just about worth it for the extraordinary canyon panorama. Located on the east end of town.

Cabañas Díaz Eatery MEXICAN $
(☑ 635-578-30-08; off Principal; meals M$80-90; ☺7am-8pm; 🐾) Tasty home-cooked meals are served at long communal tables at this family-run establishment. There's no menu, just a daily special, freshly made. Service is friendly and attentive. The most reliable place in the village to eat if you're not staying at one of the big hotels.

★Restaurante Barranco INTERNATIONAL $$
(☑ 664-143-23-05; www.parquebarrancas.com; Parque de Aventura Barrancas del Cobre; mains M$90-250; ☺9am-4pm; 🐾) Built over a gobsmacking fissure in the canyon walls – and with floor-to-ceiling windows and plexiglass flooring to prove it – the views from this restaurant are jaw-droppingly gorgeous. Meals are generous with a good variety of steaks, salads and breakfast classics. Located in the main building of the adventure park.

❶ Getting There & Away

Most visitors arrive on El Chepe (p751) at the Posada Barrancas train station, which is within easy walking distance of the Arepo hotels and the must-see adventure park. If heading straight to the park, cross the train line and head up the hill around to the left.

Five daily buses operated by Autotransportes Noroeste (p765) connect Creel with Arepo (M$90, one hour) and San Rafael (M$10, 15 minutes) every two hours between 11:30am and 7:30pm. Buses drop off passengers either at the entrance to the adventure park or on the main highway entrance to Arepo.

Divisadero
ELEV 2240M

Divisadero, a train stop without a village, is your only chance to see into the miraculous canyon if you're just doing the train ride. All trains halt here for 20 minutes, giving you enough time to jump out, gawk, snap some pics at the viewpoint and hop back on. You can just discern a tiny fragment of the Río Urique at the bottom of the actual Copper Canyon. Ration your time carefully, as the station is also a souvenir market and spectacular food court. *Gorditas* (masa cakes, some made with blue corn), burritos and *chiles rellenos* (chilies stuffed with meat or cheese), cooked up in makeshift oil-drum stoves, are worth the stop alone. Gobble your food up quickly – the conductors aren't supposed to allow food back onto the train. All this, together with the nearby adventure park 1.5km south, means a stay of longer than 20 minutes is a great idea.

🛏 Sleeping & Eating

Hotel Divisadero Barrancas HOTEL $$$
(☑ 614-415-11-99, US 888-232-4219; www.hotel divisadero.com; Av Mirador 4516; s/d incl full board from M$2629/3135; P🐶🐕📶) Right by the canyon viewpoint, rooms are modern with a log-cabin feel, though are a bit pricey for the digs. The original units lack views (what were they thinking?), but the newer rooms (Nos 35 to 52) have astonishing vistas. At the very least, all guests can enjoy the views from the picture windows in the restaurant and lounge.

★Mercado Divisidero MARKET $
(Av Mirador; dishes M$15-40; ☺noon-3pm; 🍴🐾) At the foot of the train station sits the Divisidero market with stall-upon-stall of eateries selling mostly tacos, burritos and *gorditas* (stuffed thick tortillas) filled with a huge variety of homemade goodness like grilled steak, seasoned chicken, *nopales* (cactus) and even *chiles rellenos* (chilies stuffed with meat or cheese).

❶ Getting There & Away

El Chepe (p751) stops at the Divisidero station twice daily as it chugs toward Los Mochis or Chihuahua. Tickets can be purchased on board as long as there are open seats, which is the case most of the year. If traveling during the peak seasons (Semana Santa, July, August,

WORTH A TRIP

PARQUE DE AVENTURA BARRANCAS DEL COBRE

This astonishing **adventure park** (Copper Canyon Adventure Park; ☑ 664-143-23-05, US 800-887-4766; www.parquebarrancas.com; M$20, zip-lining M$600-1000; ⊘9am-5pm; ⓐ) on the canyon rim between Arepo and Divisadero includes Mexico's longest series of *tirolesas* (zip-lines), suspended over some of the world's most profound canyon scenery. The park's seven lines take you from a height of 2400m to over halfway to the canyon floor and they include one single line that is an extraordinary 2.5km in length, the world's longest.

A couple of heart-in-mouth wobbly bridges help you to complete the cross-canyon odyssey. Safety standards are excellent: you're always accompanied by a team of experienced zip-liners and all participants are decked out in full safety gear. Allow at least two hours to descend to the spectacular viewpoint of Mesón de Bacajípare, as you have to travel in a group, meaning that there's some waiting time as each person takes each line. If zip-lining isn't your thing, you also can experience the park through a combo rappelling–rock climbing excursion (MS450) to the same viewpoint; allow at least 1½ hours to complete the journey.

The Mesón de Bacajípare viewpoint doubles as the lower station for the *teleférico* (cable car), which you will have to take back up; it's included in the zip-lining and rappelling–rock-climbing prices. If you aren't up for adventure sports but still want to see the spectacular views, you can head straight down from the canyon edge on the cable car (adult/child M$250/130;10 minutes each way, plus a 20-minute stop). Hiking (M$50 to M$200) and downhill mountain biking (M$400) also can be arranged with Tarahumara guides.

The main building houses the ticket office, a **restaurant** with amazing views plus a souvenir shop.

The nearest public transportation is at Arepo, an easy 1.5km walk away via a great canyon-lip-hugging trail. Divisidero is about 3km away, with equally impressive views along the way.

Christmas and New Year), reserve tickets a month or more in advance.

Buses serving Areponápuchi, San Rafael and ultimately Bahuichivo also run through Divisadero, stopping below the train station – which is quicker and cheaper than continuing by train.

Creel

☑ 635 / POP 5300 / ELEV 2345M

The Copper Canyon's main tourism center, Creel is actually no more than a low-key highland town strung out along the railway line. It's a very likable place, surrounded by pine forests and interesting rock formations and it boasts several good hotels and restaurants. The Tarahumara, in their multihued dress, are commonly seen about town, and there's a consistent tourist presence here, mainly in the form of tour groups.

The area around Creel is rich in natural wonders, from waterfalls and hot springs to surreal rock formations and expansive parklands, all perfect for a day's hike, ride

or drive. Local guides offer various tours, or you can go solo on a rented bicycle, scooter or 4WD.

Creel can be very cold in winter, even snowy, and it's none too warm at night in autumn either. In summer, the alpine air is a welcome relief from Mexico's coastal lowland and desert heat.

⊙ Sights

Museo de Arte Popular
de Chihuahua
MUSEUM

(☑635-456-00-80; casaartesanias@prodigy.net. mx; Av Vías del Ferrocarril 178; adult/child M$10/5; ⊘9am-6pm; ⓟⓐ) Offers excellent exhibits with text in English on local history and Tarahumara culture and crafts. Here you'll see gorgeous woven baskets, traditional clothing, photos and more. The gift shop also sells high-quality Tarahumara folk art.

⌁ Activities

Seriously consider exploring the region yourself. This is prime riding country, and many attractions near Creel can be enjoyed

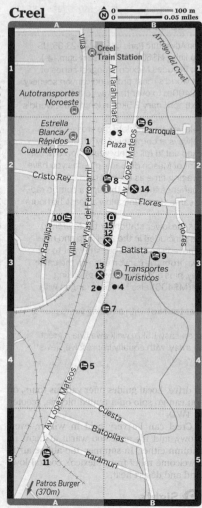

Creel

Km 133 and Km 150 winds around the great ocher walls of the Copper Canyon itself then descends to the Humira Bridge beside the foaming waters of the Urique River. It's the same route back, via Cusárare and Lago Arareko.

☞ Tours

As soon as you check into a hotel (or even before that), you'll be approached to sign up for a tour. Standard minivan tours tend to be rushed, ticking off a roster of nearby sights in a short time frame (most are half-day trips), such as canyons, waterfalls, Tarahumara settlements, hot springs and other places. Themed excursions tend to be more rewarding. Most tours require a minimum number of people, typically four. One popular trip of around five hours covers Cusárare village and waterfall, Lago Arareko and the Valley of the Frogs and Mushrooms. Typical prices are M$300 per person for half-day trips and up to M$600 for full-day trips. Other good half- or full-day destinations include the adventure park (p761) near Areponápuchi, Cascada de Basaseachi (p764) and Rekowata (p768) hot springs.

on horseback, bicycle or scooter. This is particularly attractive as you can cover terrain the minivans can't manage, and with significantly more peace and quiet. The whole area is a mountain-bike playground: you could just rent a bike and take in all the area's attractions independently.

With a scooter or car, you've the chance to reach the bottom of the Copper Canyon with your own wheels. Grab a packed lunch in Creel first. The route is very simple: you follow the excellent paved highway southeast of town toward Guachochi. The scenery is staggering; the best section between

★ 3 Amigos
TOURS

(☎635-456-00-36; www.amigos3.com; Av López Mateos 46; ⏰9am-6pm; 🚲) A passionate and well-run English-speaking agency, 3 Amigos has built its reputation on helping you 'be your own guide in the Copper Canyon'; to do this it provides trail maps (M$20), rents out Rockhopper mountain bikes (M$350 per day) and scooters (M$1000 per day), and offers personalized multiple-day guided trips with drivers (US$160 per day).

The full-day self-guided mountain bike route to the Rekowata hot springs and full-day scooter ride to the canyon bottom by the Humira Bridge pass through simply mind-blowing scenery and are highly recommended. The agency is also the best source of information in town, and its website is a great place to start planning your Copper Canyon adventure. Pickup in Chihuahua and Los Mochis also available.

Tarahumara Tours
TOURS

(☎635-199-61-64; creeltour@hotmail.com; Callejón Parroquial s/n; ⏰9am-7pm) Local driver-guides offering escorted trips, from two hours to two days, at competitive rates. Prices range from M$200 per person for a two-hour tour taking in five local beauty spots to M$1000 for a two-day trip to Batopilas, not including food or accommodations. Look for the agency on the central plaza.

Umarike Expediciones
ADVENTURE

(☎635-456-06-32, cell 614-4065464; www.umarike.com.mx; Av López Mateos s/n) Mountain-biking specialist offering guided bike and hiking adventure trips from one to eight days. Rental bikes (M$500 per day), maps and information are also available.

🛏 Sleeping

★ La Troje de Adobe
INN $

(☎635-102-10-11; www.lodgeatcreel.com; Chapultepec s/n; r M$595-795; 🛜) Reminiscent of a Swiss ski lodge, this three-story inn has just seven rooms. All have a upscale boho feel, with Tarahumara designs woven throughout, handcrafted furnishings and slate tile bathrooms. Several of the rooms have mountain views too. The affable owners – one a retired anthropologist – have excellent recommendations on area sights and guides.

★ Hotel La Estación
INN $$

(☎635-456-04-72; www.facebook.com/hotellaestacioncreel; Av López Mateos s/n; r incl breakfast M$1050; 🛜) An homage to El Chepe (p751), every room in this movie-house-turned-inn is dedicated to a different stop along the Copper Canyon Railway. Think murals and photos, even original train doors. Each unit has an urban-chic feel, with clean lines and creature comforts like rain shower heads, fine linens and flat-screen TVs. Breakfast includes organic and homemade regional goodies.

Hotel Plaza Mexicana
HOTEL $$

(☎635-456-02-45; hotelesmargaritas@hotmail.com; Batista s/n; r incl half board M$850; P🐶🛜) This second hotel from the family that runs the **Casa Margarita** (☎635-456-00-45; Av López Mateos 11; r incl half board from M$850; P🐶🛜) is a step up from the bustling original; friendly staff welcome guests and comfortable rooms are grouped around a pretty yellow painted courtyard. Rates include good breakfasts (with eggs cooked to order) and evening meals that focus on Mexican classics.

Hotel Cascada Inn
HOTEL $$

(☎635-456-01-51; www.hotelcascadainn.com; Av López Mateos 49; r incl breakfast M$950-1495; P🐶🛜) This long-standing family-run spot has updated rooms that are simple and modern in style, with marble bathrooms and vast flat-screen TVs. The grounds could use some attention, but beyond the overgrown greenery this is a solid choice. Best of all, it's located in the middle of Creel's main drag.

Quinta Mision
HOTEL $$$

(☎635-456-00-21; www.quintamision.com; Av López Mateos s/n; r from M$1730; P🐶❄🛜) 🌿 Perhaps Creel's most ecologically sensitive hotel, this swanky place recycles water and uses wind and solar power. Twenty suite-sized rooms have been created from the shell of an old furniture factory, all with fridge and enough space for a small family. Check the website for regular specials.

Best Western The Lodge at Creel
LODGE $$$

(☎635-456-07-07; www.thelodgeatcreel.com; Av López Mateos 61; r from M$1928; P🐶@🛜) Utterly fascinating in its determination to be a Wild West hotel catering to traveler fantasies, this Best Western boasts antler chandeliers and cow skins on the wall. Its 41 rooms are spacious and smart, with fireplaces, exposed stone, sitting nooks and swing seats on their verandas. There's a small fitness

DON'T MISS

MEXICO'S HIGHEST FULL-TIME WATERFALL

Cascada de Basaseachi (☑642-135-28-74) Few natural sites in Mexico boast the exquisitely pristine beauty of the country's highest full-time waterfall, Cascada de Basaseachi, where a plume of water tumbles 246m to swimmable pools below. Basaseachi is 140km northwest of Creel, so allow a full day to visit (including three hours to walk to the falls and back). The waterfall is part of the national park of the same name, south of which is the old mining town of **Maguarachi**, where there are delightful hot springs.

Both sites are accessible via San Juanito, 35km north of Creel. To visit you'll really need your own wheels or a tour with a Creel agency.

center and spa, plus numerous eating and drinking options.

✗ Eating

Creel has a limited choice of restaurants, though by the standards of smaller villages on the canyon floor, quality is high. For a packed lunch, grocery stores on the main drag sell tasty *queso menonita* (Menonite cheese) and bread.

Simple BISTRO $
(☑635-456-08-44; www.facebook.com/simple bistrocreel; Av López Mateos 17A; mains M$45-75; ⊗8am-10pm; 🛜) Big sandwiches, made-to-order burgers and a huge variety of crepes are offered at this little bistro, just steps from the central plaza. Service can be somewhat abrupt, but the food more than makes up for it. Boxed lunches offered early for those hitting the sights. On warm days, sidewalk seating is a plus.

Patros Burger TACOS $
(☑635-102-10-05; Av López Mateos; mains M$45-75; ⊗noon-8pm) Despite the name, the showstoppers at this colorful place are the *tortas* (Mexican-style sandwiches) and tacos. Offering entirely meat-based meals, the grill sizzles all day, while rolls and tortillas wait in the kitchen, lined up to be stuffed with steak, pork and toppings. A steady flow of customers keeps the restaurant busy most of the day.

La Lupita MEXICAN $
(☑635-456-10-01; Av López Mateos 44; mains M$60-110; ⊗7am-9pm; 🛜) This brightly decorated thee-room space with plastic coverings on the tablecloths is run by a team of friendly locals who are well used to travelers killing time between bus and train rides. The menu includes a range of breakfasts, the full spectrum of Mexican dishes and several seafood options as well.

La Cabaña INTERNATIONAL $$
(☑635-456-06-64; Av López Mateos 36; mains M$60-180; ⊗7:30am-10:30pm; 🛜) This Catalan-owned restaurant is one of the fancier places in town. As well as good breakfasts (M$60 to M$100), La Cabaña does a mean *tampiqueña* (steak accompanied by several side orders), not to mention tasty salads, grills and changing daily specials such as local trout stuffed with shrimp. Service can be painfully slow.

🍷 Drinking & Nightlife

La Troje de Adobe Cafe COFFEE
(☑635-102-10-11; Chapultepec s/n; ⊗4:30-9:30pm Mon-Sat; 🛜) This homey cafe serves up all manner of coffee drinks, Italian sodas and milkshakes to local intellectuals and visiting hipsters. Desserts and savory snacks, made with organic and local ingredients, also offered. Stays open late if there's a crowd.

🛍 Shopping

Shops in Creel sell Tarahumara handicrafts as well as distinctive Mata Ortiz pottery.

★ No Name Gift Shop ARTS & CRAFTS
(Av López Mateos s/n; ⊗noon-8pm) A group of Tarahumaras from nearby San Ignacio sell their folk art, clothing and musical instruments at this small shop. The quality is excellent and the prices more than fair. There's no sign. Look for it next to the Telcel office on the north end of town.

ℹ Information

Santander (☑800-501-00-00; www.santander.com.mx; Av López Mateos 3; ⊗9am-4pm Mon-Fri, 10am-2pm Sat) Has the only two ATMs in town.

Tourist Information Office (☑635-456-05-06; Av López Mateos s/n; ⊗9am-1pm & 3-6pm Mon-Fri)This office – more a desk in a public space – has brochures and maps. Staff are marginally helpful. Located on a small park, just south of the central plaza.

Unidad Medica Santa Teresita (☑635-456-01-05; Parroquia s/n; ⊘24hr) This clinic offers basic health-care services.

ⓘ Getting There & Away

BUS

If speed and convenience is the name of the game, then bus is actually the most efficient way to travel between Creel and Chihuahua, not to mention between Creel, Divisadero and Areponápuchi: trips are shorter, far cheaper and more frequent than the train.

Autotransportes Noroeste (☑635-456-09-45; www.turisticosnoroeste.com; Francisco Villa s/n) Runs buses to Cuauhtémoc (M$125, 2½ hours) and Chihuahua (M$240, 4½ hours) eight times daily at 1½-hourly intervals from 6:30am until 5pm. Noroeste also offers buses to Divisadero (M$60, one hour), Areponápuchi (M$60, one hour) and San Rafael (M$90, 1¼ hours) every two hours between 10:30am and 6:30pm. The first bus to San Rafael connects with the 1pm departure from there to Bahuichivo.

Estrella Blanca/Rápidos Cuauhtémoc (☑635-456-07-04; www.estrellablanca.com.mx; Francisco Villa s/n) Has nine daily buses to Chihuahua (M$240, 4½ hours) via Cuauhtémoc (M$120, three hours); these leave at roughly hourly intervals between 6:30am and 4:45pm. Also has four daily departures to Bahuichivo (M$120, 2½ hours) every two hours from 10:15am to 6:15pm; they stop along the way in Divisidero (M$55, one hour), Areponápuchi (M$55, one hour) and San Rafael (M$55, 1½ hours).

Transportes Turisticos (☑635-106-43-09; Av López Mateos) Runs a minibus to Batopilas (M$300, four hours) that leaves daily except Sunday from outside Hotel Los Pinos on Avenida López Mateos. The bus departs at 9am on Monday, Wednesday and Friday, while on Tuesday, Thursday and Saturday it departs at 7:30am. The return bus leaves Batopilas at 5am Monday to Saturday.

CAR & MOTORCYCLE

There are paved roads all the way from Chihuahua to Creel and on to Divisadero, Batopilas and Bahuichivo. Motorbikes and 4WDs (with drivers only) can be rented from **3 Amigos** (p763). If you want to self-drive in the region, bring a rental car from Los Mochis or Chihuahua, but proceed with caution: some areas are controlled by drug cartels, so always check your planned route with someone who has plenty of up-to-date local knowledge before setting off.

TRAIN

El Chepe (p751) stops in Creel twice daily as it's headed either toward Los Mochis or Chihuahua.

Primera express, or first-class, train tickets are sold at **Creel station** (☑635-456-00-15; www.chepe.com.mx; Av Tarahumara s/n) from one hour before trains depart; second-class tickets can only be purchased aboard the train.

Batopilas

☑649 / POP 1220 / ELEV 580M

A charming town at the bottom of the Copper Canyon, the former silver-mining village of Batopilas is a sleepy place where everybody knows everyone and whose laid-back air works a gentle magic on all who visit. The town itself sits along 2km of its winding namesake river. A paved road into the jaw-dropping Barranca de Batopilas brings you there with relative ease and it has more twists, turns and heart-in-mouth vertical drops than any amusement-park ride.

Batopilas was founded in 1708, and peaked in prominence in the late 19th century when silver mining boomed. The climate is subtropical here year-round, which means scorching in the summer months and pleasantly warm the rest of the year.

Batopilas can be slightly rough around the edges, with marijuana fueling the local economy, but while the odd robbery has occurred, foreign tourists aren't usually targeted, though it's important to take local advice about out-of-town excursions.

⊙ Sights

Museo de Batopilas
MUSEUM

(Donato Guerra s/n; ⊘9am-5pm Mon-Sat) FREE Offers a good overview of the town's history with a mock-up of a silver mine and some interesting photos and artifacts. English-speaking director Rafael Ruelas guides visitors through the exhibits, embellishing proceedings with his own anecdotes. Located on the central plaza, tourist information is available here too.

⚒ Activities

Ruta de Plata
HORSEBACK RIDING

(Silver Trail; ☑649-123-07-77; per day M$250; ⊘mid-Oct) One of northern Mexico's best horseback rides, the Ruta de Plata is an annual event that follows the ancient mule route between Batopilas and Chihuahua. The event celebrates this historic trail and its place in mining history, with the convoy passing through some of the most beautiful, if arduous, landscapes in the country.

It takes about 2½ weeks to complete, camping along the way. The cost includes the horse and its care; BYO camping gear. Food can be purchased along the way.

Urique Trek
HIKING

(with/without mule M$5000/4000) This challenging, spectacular two- to three-day trek is one of the very best in the Copper Canyon region, taking trekkers along little-traveled trails over two canyons to the village of Urique. BYO camping gear and food. Be sure to ask about the local safety situation before setting out. For recommended guides, contact the tourist information center or ask at your hotel.

Misión Satevó Hike
HIKING

(🖼) One of the most popular hikes from Batopilas is to the 18th-century Misión Satevó church, in a remote spot 8km down Copper Canyon. Simply follow the Batopilas River downstream (the mission suddenly appears, framed in a forested river gorge); it's also possible to drive there. The mission itself is only occasionally open.

🛏 Sleeping & Eating

Hotel Juanita's
HOTEL $

(☑649-488-00-43; Degollado s/n; s/d M$300/400; ☺❋) Basic, well-kept rooms each get their own crucifix plus a shared river-facing courtyard with a gurgling fountain. Some rooms have air-con, but all have a fan. Ask for a room off the main street, facing the river. There's no food on offer, so you'll have to eat out.

Riverside Lodge
HOTEL $$$

(☑649-427-30-97; www.coppercanyonlodges.com; Juárez s/n; ☺r incl breakfast US$190; P😊❋) For sensory overload hacienda-style, check into this labyrinthine colonial mansion, expertly and sympathetically renovated and decorated with lavish murals, oil paintings, rugs and oak furniture. All 14 rooms are individually furnished and boast vast bathrooms with claw-foot tubs. Look out for its blue domes across from the church: there's no sign otherwise. Enter through the gate under an anchor.

Doña Mica
MEXICAN $

(Plaza de la Constitución; meals M$70-100; ☺7am-7pm; ☑) Run by Velia and her husband, this place hits the spot for hearty home-cooked meals. Served in the front room of their house, there's usually no menu, just a few choices daily delivered in rapid-fire Spanish.

Restaurant Carolina
MEXICAN $$

(☑649-456-90-96; Plaza de la Constitución; dishes M$50-145; ☺8am-8:30pm) Rifles on the walls, pickles in jars and local scenes captured in paintings sum up this family-run restaurant a block beyond Batopilas' main plaza. Choose between filling breakfasts (M$50 to M$90), delicious tacos (ask for the mango salsa) or more elaborate dishes such as freshwater trout. The whole place is inside Carolina's home, and there are always several generations at work in the kitchen.

❶ Information

Tourist Information Center (☑649-123-07-77; www.visitbatopilas.com; Donato Guerra s/n; ☺9am-5pm Mon-Sat) This small tourist information center in the town museum – a table with brochures and maps, more than anything – is a good place to start your visit. Rafael Ruelas, the director of the museum, doubles as the director of tourism. Friendly and helpful, he often is on hand to give recommendations and tips.

❶ Getting There & Away

The paved road to Batopilas from Creel is one of Mexico's most scenic drives, and most drivers will stop at the incredible Mirador La Bufa (p768) for some mind-blowing views.

Minibuses (M$300, four hours) run by Transportes Turisticos (p765) leave from Creel every morning except Sunday outside Hotel Los Pinos on Avenida López Mateos. They depart at 9am on Monday, Wednesday and Friday, while on Tuesday, Thursday and Saturday they depart at 7:30am. Buses back to Creel leave from outside the church in Batopilas every morning except Sunday at 5am sharp.

Two-day van tours from Creel (normally a four-person minimum) cost from US$1330 per person. If you have your own wheels, it's simple to visit Batopilas independently – now that the new road is complete you don't even need a 4WD.

A back road (high-clearance 4WD needed), affording canyon-lip views, runs from Batopilas to Urique, fording the Río Urique (passable November to April). Check the security situation before heading out on this route, which is also perfect for mountain biking.

Cusárare

☑635 / POP 200

About 25km from Creel is the quiet Tarahumara village of Cusárare. Spread out along 2km of dirt road, it features an 18th-century

THE TARAHUMARA

A fascinating part of canyon life is the presence of one of Mexico's most distinctive indigenous groups, the Tarahumara, who live in caves and small houses across the countryside here. Most easily identifiable are the women, dressed in colorful skirts and blouses and often carrying infants on their backs. They sell beautiful hand-woven baskets and carved wooden dolls and animals at ridiculously low prices at tourist sites around the sierra. Most men now wear modern clothes like jeans instead of the traditional loincloth, but both sexes still often walk in *huaraches* – sandals made from tire tread and strips of leather.

The Tarahumara remain largely an enigma. Even their name is debated. Many believe it was originally 'ralamuli,' which was Hispanicized to 'Rarámuri' and evolved to 'Tarahumara,' the term by which they usually refer to themselves. Contrary to popular belief, the Spanish incursion did not force the Tarahumara into the canyons: they were here when the first Jesuits arrived in 1608.

There are two main Tarahumara groups: the Alta (high) and the Baja (low), with whom outside contact was made by Jesuit priests from higher-altitude Parral and lower-altitude El Fuerte respectively. Culture and language are radically different between the Altas and Bajas, and because of long-term isolation, every community has a slightly different culture and language. No one even knows how many Tarahumara exist. Estimates vary between 50,000 and 120,000.

Rarámuri means 'those who run fast' – and these people are most famous for running long distances swiftly, sometimes up to 20 hours without stopping. They used their aptitude for running to hunt deer by bow and arrow as little as a generation ago. The Copper Canyon area even has its own annual **ultramarathon** (p756) at Urique.

But a better cultural insight into the Tarahumara is their sense of fairness. 'Korima' is a custom where someone who has a good crop is 'blessed' and obliged to share his good fortune with others. Another tradition is the *tesgüinada*, a raucous social gathering at which Tarahumara relax their natural reserve and celebrate communal work and festivals with plenty of *tesgüino*, a potent corn beer.

Even these traditionally isolated people have been influenced by incomers, and many have adopted a type of Catholicism. However, their take on Christianity and Christian festivals is often idiosyncratic – regularly accompanied by drumming and lots of *tesgüino*.

But the Tarahumara have maintained their lifestyle despite incursions of conquistadors, missionaries, railways, drug gangs and tourism. They have one word to refer to all non-Tarahumara people: *chabochi*, which means 'with spider-webbing on the face,' a reference to bearded Spanish colonists. The majority continue to live a subsistence life in the remote Sierra Madre Occidental countryside.

The Tarahumara are also generally materially poor, and their communities have some serious health problems: there are high rates of infant mortality, malnutrition and teenage pregnancy, with some of the little relief coming from Catholic missions.

mission church with impressive Tarahumara murals and a museum with an exceptional collection of colonial religious paintings. Nearby is a set of like-named falls, perfect for a hike, swim and several selfies.

◉ Sights & Activities

Misión Cusárare
CHURCH

(Cusárare s/n) This mission was built by Jesuits in 1741 as a religious meeting place as well as a school to teach the locals Spanish and different trades. In 1826 Franciscan friars added side altars, a choir loft and an adobe bell tower; the last collapsed in 1969, taking down a corner of the church with it. The church was repaired and restored in the early 1970s, adding striking Tarahumara patterned murals. A new stone bell tower was built too.

Museo Loyola
MUSEUM

(Cusárare s/n; M$20) Sitting alongside the Cusárare Mission church, this museum holds an exceptional collection of colonial religious paintings, representing 13 scenes from the Virgin Mary's life. The paintings,

LA BUFA CANYON VIEW

Along the scenic drive to Batopilas, about 100km south of Creel, is one of the region's most spectacular views: **La Bufa canyon** (Carretera Samachíque-Batopilas; P). Dropping 1800m, it's deep and verdant, with the Batopilas river rushing through its middle, a stunning set of roadway switchbacks leading to the bottom, and a spectacular rock formation that, squinting, looks like a massive seven-layer cake. Look for the parking area, teetering on the canyon rim, with a handful of stands with Tarahumara crafts for sale.

created by Miguel Correa in 1713, were brought to the Mission by Franciscan Friars in the early 1800s. The museum is only open occasionally. However, the caretaker – Doña Rosa – will gladly open shop. She lives in the blue house just downhill from the Diconsa community store.

Cascada Cusárare   HIKING

(Hwy 25 Km 112; M$25; ⊗8am-5pm; 🖭) This lovely 30m waterfall is perfect if you're looking to take a short hike. A 3km walk from the road, the trail is shady and very beautiful, offering the chance of a dip along the way. To get here, head south on the highway 400m past the Cusárare turnoff; at Km 112, turn right at the 'Cascada de Cusárare' sign, which leads to a trail that follows a bubbling stream, then passes through a sweeping highland valley to the falls.

There are two road signs to the trailhead. If you're driving, go past the first one at Km 108 – the road is too rough unless you have a 4WD vehicle.

❶ Getting There & Away

Creel is the closest train stop if traveling on **El Chepe** (p751). Just north of Creel's train station, travelers can catch buses, which will drop you at Cusarare's highway entrance – take any bus with signage for 'Guacochi.' From the highway, it's a 1km walk into town. Many tours include a stop here too. Otherwise arrange for a cab driver to take you there and back, with an hour or so to visit the church and museum.

San Ignacio de Arareko

📞 635 / POP 4000

Four kilometers southeast of Creel is the Tarahumara *ejido* (communal farming district) of San Ignacio, which spreads over some 200 sq km and is home to about 4000 people living in caves and small houses among farmlands, small canyons and pine forests. Here you'll find the photogenic 18th-century San Ignacio Mission Church, several spectacular rock formations and the scenic Lake Arareko. A bit further, but still within the *ejido* reach, are the popular Rekowata hot springs. Visitors to San Ignacio are charged admission (M$25). The cost includes access to most of the *ejido's* sights – be sure to keep your ticket handy!

◉ Sights

★ Valle de los Monjes   NATURAL FEATURE

(Valley of the Monks; San Ignacio s/n; ⊗24hr; 🖭) Around 7km east of San Ignacio's town center, through verdant farmland, is the Valle de los Monjes. A spectacular outcrop of vertical red rock formations that inspire its Tarahumara name Bisabírachi, meaning 'Valley of the Erect Penises,' it is well worth exploring and less visited than the **Valle de las Ranas y los Hongos** (Valley of Frogs and Mushrooms; San Ignacio s/n; 🖭). Admission (M$15) is occasionally charged.

Lago Arareko   LAKE

(Hwy 25 Km 8) Meaning 'Horseshoe' in Rarámuri, the peaceful waters of this U-shaped lake reflect the surrounding pines and rock formations. Paddleboats can be rented along the lakeshore (M$50) for exploring and finding good swimming spots. Access to the lake is included in the San Ignacio admission cost (M$25); there also are viewpoints of the lake along the Creel–Cusárare highway. Located about 8km south of Creel.

A visit to this Lago Arareko can be easily combined with stops at Valle de las Ranas y Los Hongos as well as Valle de los Monjes – a perfect day trip.

🏃 Activities

Aguas Termales Rekowata   THERMAL BATHS

(Rekowata Hot Springs; Hwy 77 Km 7; M$25; ⊗9am-5pm; 🖭) These hot springs, averaging about 37°C (98.6°F), are channeled into modern-day pools near the bottom of the Barranca de Tarárecua. To get here, follow a signposted dirt road for 11km from the Creel–Divisidero Hwy to the parking lot. From there, it's a 3km hike down a rough cobblestone track to the blissfully warm bathing pools. Vans (M$70 return) shuttle visitors from the parking lot; otherwise it's a beautiful walk down and a sweaty one back up. Weekends get busy.

There's also a superb mountain bike trail to Rekowata. This route initially takes the Cusárare road, but then heads off road down tracks to the right (south) near San Ignacio. You pass through a scenic river valley then an utterly astonishing canyon viewpoint before beginning a steep descent to Rekowata. It's a full-day return-trip ride; 3 Amigos (p763) can provide a map.

Admission to the hot springs is included in the entrance fee to San Ignacio *ejido* – be sure to save your ticket!

❶ Getting There & Away

Most people visit here on a tour, but it's fairly easy to walk, cycle or taxi from Creel to San Ignacio's northern entrance (just outside town, past the cemetery); from there it's 1.6km to the Misión San Ignacio and Valle de las Ranas y los Hongos on a good dirt road. Buses headed to Guacochi can drop you at San Ignacio's highway entrance, but you're still 1.6km away from its main attractions.

NORTHWEST MEXICO

The dramatic beaches of the Sea of Cortez and the abundant marine life, including some 40 sea lion colonies and 27 species of whale and dolphin, are magnets for visitors: Puerto Peñasco, Bahía de Kino and San Carlos all beckon travelers. The region, encompassing Sonora and northern Sinaloa, still bursts with homespun character. The strains of *norteña* (country) music and the inviting smell of *carne asada* (grilled beef) waft past cowboy-hatted locals on the streets.

The perfunctory towns and cities won't detain you long: Los Mochis harbors little of interest except as a jumping-off point for the spectacular train ride through Copper Canyon or the ferry to Baja. The state capital, Hermosillo, is a vast and faceless place with little cultural interest. The glorious exception is Álamos, a colonial jewel surrounded by peaks of the Sierra Madre Occidental, which is replete with atmospheric hotels and restaurants and well worth a side trip.

Sonora

Mexico's second-largest state (neighboring Chihuahua is first) has remarkable cultural and ecological diversity within its 180,000 sq km. It boasts miles and miles of gorgeous beaches, desert moonscapes in El Pinacate Reserve, near Puerto Peñasco, and everything in between. It's still undiscovered by mass tourism, but the word is definitely getting out for Mexican travelers – beach towns like San Carlos and Bahía de Kino get packed with weekend warriors from Hermosillo and beyond – and those near the US border get a steady stream of American 'snowbirds' (retired North American citizens who head south for winter). Even so, Sonora sees far fewer travelers, especially foreigners, than its myriad attractions and drop-dead beauty would suggest. But hey, who's complaining?

Puerto Peñasco

☑ 638 / POP 65,200

Until the 1920s, 'Rocky Point,' as Americans affectionately call this Sea of Cortez coastal town, was just that: a landmark on military maps and no more. Its location alongside one of the driest parts of the Sonoran Desert deterred all would-be settlers bar intrepid fishers until Prohibition gave the fledgling community an unexpected boost. When the global economy nosedived in the 1930s, Peñasco enjoyed a (very) lengthy siesta, until state investment and a desalination plant kick-started the local economy in the early 1990s. The result has been a boom in both development and population, and now this beach town has become the seaside destination Arizona never had.

The historic core – El Malecón (Old Port) – hugs the rocky point itself, while just north sits the pleasant beach, Playa Bonita. Heading west is Sandy Beach, home to a sprawling stretch of condo-hotel resorts, expensive restaurants and golf courses carved out of the desert.

⊙ Sights

★ **Isla San Jorge**   ISLAND

(🐦) Also known as Bird Island, Isla San Jorge is one of the best boat excursions in northern Mexico. This rocky island 40km southeast of Peñasco is home to nesting seabirds and also a large community of sea lions (which are curious by nature and will swim alongside boats). Dolphins are often spotted en route, while whales (fin, gray, killer and pilot) are sometimes encountered between October and April. Full-day cruises are offered by **Del Mar Charters** (☑ 638-383-28-02, US 520-407-6054; www.delmarcharters.com; Calle Pelícano s/n; ⊙ 7am-6pm; ⊕).

Playa Bonita   BEACH
(Calle 13; P ⊕) Puerto Peñasco's main town beach, Playa Bonita is a gorgeous swath of tawny sand with small waves and views of the rocky landscape in the distance. Vendors hawk everything from mangos to jewelry, and beach shade, including chairs, can be had for $20 per day. For action beyond sand castle making, banana boat rides (US$6 per 12 minutes) and jet-ski rentals (US$35 per 30 minutes) are available too.

CEDO   VISITOR CENTER
(Intercultural Center for the Study of Desert & Oceans; ☑ 638-382-01-13, US 520-320-5473; www.cedo.org; Blvd Las Conchas s/n; ⊙ 9am-5pm Mon-Sat, 10am-2pm Sun; ⊕) 🆓 CEDO is a wonderful place to learn about Rocky Point's fascinating desert-meets-sea ecosystem. Dedicated to the conservation of the upper Gulf of California and surrounding Desierto Sonorense, CEDO has a visitor center where it hosts free natural-history talks in English at 2pm Tuesdays and 4pm Saturdays. CEDO also runs a fascinating program of nature tours, some in collaboration with local cooperatives.

Tours include tidepool walks (US$15), kayaking on Morúa estuary (US$50), snorkeling trips to Isla San Jorge (US$115) and excursions to El Pinacate Biosphere Reserve with an English-speaking naturalist (US$60).

Cholla Bay   BEACH
(La Choya; ⊕) Located about 12km west of Puerto Peñasco, Cholla Bay is a fishing village turned expat enclave with sand roads and quiet, calm beaches. At low tide, the water recedes dramatically, revealing oysters and other shellfish. Come with a shovel and bucket to collect dinner.

🏃 Activities
Fishing, snorkeling, diving, kayaking and sunset cruises are all popular. There are extensive rock pools to explore at low tide, and trips around the estuary and beyond to the remarkable Reserva El Pinacate y Gran Desierto de Altar can be set up by the likes of the CEDO.

🛏 Sleeping
El Malecón (Old Port) has agreeable down-to-earth options – though it's slim pickings for tight budgets, unless you're up for camping. All the mega-hotel complexes are at Sandy Beach, to the northwest. Note that Spring Break in Peñasco is popular with US college students, so book early if coming then.

Concha Del Mar   CAMPGROUND $
(☑ 638-113-04-67; Calle 19 No 680; campsite M$200; P 🛜) Sitting on a huge empty lot right on Playa Bonita, this campground offers clean bathrooms, wi-fi, laundry facilities and even 24-hour security. BYO tent or buy the basics at SAMS Club or Bodega Aurrera on your way into town. During high season, arrive mid-week for an oceanfront site. Reservations not accepted.

★ Dream Weaver Inn   APARTMENT $$
(☑ 638-125-60-79; www.facebook.com/dreamweaverinn; Calle Pescadores 3, El Malecón; apt US$65-95; ❇ 🛜 ❄) This welcoming and well-cared-for inn has excellent apartment-style units, each lovingly decorated with local handicrafts in true Mexican style. Each unit has cooking facilities and some have sea views. It feels like a home away from home. Located near the Old Port's main plaza, with restaurants, shops and traveling oompah bands just steps away. Kid and pet friendly.

Hospedaje Mulege   GUESTHOUSE $$
(☑ 638-383-29-85, US 760-235-4870; www.hospedajemulege.com; cnr Av Circunvalación & Calle 16 de Sepiembre, El Malecón; r incl breakfast US$75; P ⊖ ❇ 🛜) It's all about hospitality and the personal touch here at one of Puerto Peñasco's most popular guesthouses. Lupita and Israel preside over guests with real pride to show them the flip side to the town's mega-resorts in this friendly and unpretentious Old Port villa. The seven rooms are comfortable and homey, some with spectacular ocean views.

🍴 Eating
Max's Cafe   CAFE $
(☑ 638-383-10-11; www.maxsmx.com; Centro Comercial La Marina, Calle 13 s/n; dishes US$5-15; ⊙ 8am-10pm; 🛜 ⊕) Max's serves up solid

OFF THE BEATEN TRACK

GRAN DESIERTO DE ALTAR

About 30km from Puerto Peñasco are the lunar landscapes of El Pinacate, one of the driest places on earth. This remote, spectacular 7145-sq-km **reserve** (El Pinacate; ☎638-383-14-33, 638-108-00-11; http://elpinacate.conanp.gob.mx; Carretera Sonoyta–Peñasco Km 72; M$60; ☉8am-5pm) is a Unesco World Heritage site and contains ancient eroded volcanoes, giant craters, petrified lava flows, 400-plus ash cones and the continent's largest concentration of active sand dunes. Wildlife includes pronghorn antelope (the fastest land mammal in the Americas), bighorn sheep, pumas, reptiles and bountiful birdlife. There's an excellent, highly informative solar-powered visitor center, interpretive hiking trails and two campgrounds.

The extraordinary landscapes here are so unusual that Neil Armstrong and Buzz Aldrin used this region in the 1960s to prepare themselves for their Apollo 11 moon landing.

Today over 70km of dirt roads (4WD only in parts) penetrate the reserve. Visitors must register to climb the 1190m Cerro del Pinacate volcano.

The visitor center is about 8km west of Km 72 on Hwy 8 (27km from Puerto Peñasco). The craters are accessed by a separate turnoff further north at Km 52 on Hwy 8.

CEDO in Puerto Peñasco organizes excellent tours to the reserve: good walking shoes are recommended, and note that there's no water or electricity available anywhere in the reserve, except at the visitor center.

Mexican eats, hamburgers and sandwiches in a setting reminiscent of a cozy railcar. Located steps from Playa Bonita, it's a convenient place to take a break from the sun, or do like local expats do and stop here for a huge American-style breakfast. Cash only.

The Blue Marlin
SEAFOOD $$

(El Marlin Azul; ☎638-383-65-64; www.facebook.com/pg/thebluemarlinrestaurant; Ignacio Zaragoza s/n, El Malecón; dishes M$50-250; ☉11am-10pm Thu-Tue) At the swankier end of the dining spectrum, the Blue Marlin specializes in seafood, serving everything from simple fish tacos to hearty coconut shrimp meals. Service can be painfully slow, but the wait is worth it. Seating is indoors in a small nautical-themed dining room or outside on a pleasant street-front patio.

La Curva
MEXICAN $$

(☎638-383-34-70; www.facebook.com/pg/RestaurantLaCurva.puertopenasco; Blvd Kino 100; mains M$150-280; ☉8am-9:30pm Sun-Thu, to 10pm Fri & Sat; ⊛) Set in the middle of town, this restaurant is the opposite of a glitzy beach restaurant (and you'll barely see a wristband in the whole place). Huge plates of traditional Mexican cooking are served up in a simple and unfussy environment; try the amazing *mariscada* (seafood platter) or the *carne asada* (grilled steak).

Kaffee Haus
CAFE $$

(☎638-388-10-65; Blvr Benito Juarez 216B; breakfasts M$80-110, lunches M$80-140; ☉7am-3:30pm Mon-Sat, 7am-2pm Sun; ⊛⊛) A long-standing favorite, this local institution remains an excellent choice, with its enormous breakfast served daily until 2pm, great house burger and superb apple strudel, to name just a few menu highlights. It's fearsomely popular, however, and you may have to line up to get a table at peak times. Portions are huge, so consider sharing a plate. Cash only.

★Chef Mickey's Place
INTERNATIONAL $$$

(☎638-388-95-00; Plaza del Sol 4, Blvd Freemont; mains M$180-350; ☉1-10pm) Eponymous chef Mickey has been cooking up a storm here for years, and you'll be hard pressed to find better quality and innovation elsewhere in town. Steak, seafood and fresh fish dominate the eclectic menu in a sleek upscale setting. Mickey's is beloved by the local expat community, so reservations are a good idea.

Shopping

Tequila Factory
FOOD & DRINKS

(☎638-388-06-06; www.tequilafactory.mx; cnr Blvd Benito Juárez & Calle 12; ☉10am-6pm Wed-Sun) FREE Despite it's name, this family-owned shop doesn't produce any tequila on site, but it does offer informative and fun presentations on tequila production. Tastings of its artisanal tequilas are part of the experience (and you can always try before you buy in the shop). The flavored tequilas and oak-aged Añejo are favorites.

ℹ Information

Convention & Visitors Bureau (☑ 800-552-28-20, 638-388-04-44; www.cometorocky point.com; Av Coahuila 444; ⊙ 9am-2pm & 4-7pm Mon-Fri, 9am-1pm Sat) is a helpful tourist office located on the 2nd floor of Plaza Pelícanos. Its English-speaking staff can assist with booking accommodations and tours and its website has lots of useful information about the town and surrounding areas.

Rocky Point 360 (www.rockypoint360.com) is another useful online resource.

ℹ Getting There & Away

Puerto Peñasco International Airport (Aeropuerto Mar de Cortés; ☑ 638-383-60-97; www. aeropuertomardecortes.com; Libramiento Caborca-Sonoita 71) is 35km east of town. At the time of writing there were only infrequent chartered flights.

A handful of shuttle-van services operate between Puerto Peñasco and Arizona, including **Transportes Express** (☑ 638-383-36-40, US 602-442-6670; www.transportes-express.com; cnr Lázaro Cárdenas & Sinaloa), which runs to/from Phoenix four times daily (US$50, four hours).

Albatros (☑ 638-388-08-88, 800-624-66-18; www.albatrosautobuses.com; Blvd Juárez, btwn Calles 29 & 30) runs six daily buses to Hermosillo (M$370, 5½ hours), six to Nogales (M$320, six hours), three to Guaymas (M$440, eight hours), five to Navojoa ($625, 12 hours) and two to Álamos ($665, 13 hours). **Autobuses de la Baja California** (ABC; ☑ 800-025-02-22, 664-104-74-00; www.abc.com.mx; cnr Constitución & Bravo), one block north of Blvd Juárez, heads to Tijuana (M$555, eight hours) four times daily.

ℹ Getting Around

Travelers without a car, beware: there is no reliable local public transportation around town. **Bufalo** (☑ 638-388-99-99; ventas_rentacars@ hotmail.com; cnr Freemont & Chiapas; ⊙ 8am-8pm) rents out new-ish well-maintained cars, starting at M$1000 per day.

Taxis cost around M$30 for short rides around town. Beyond Puerto Peñasco, cabs cost M$60 from the Old Port to the Sandy Beach resorts and M$150 to Cholla Bay – and can be double that or more coming back.

Bahía de Kino

☑ 662 / POP 6050

Laid-back Bahía de Kino is a gorgeous stretch of beach paradise named after Padre Eusebio Kino, who established a small mission here for the indigenous Seri people

in the 17th century. The old part, Kino Viejo, is a rough-and-ready Mexican fishing village that fans out along the lengthy main beach. By contrast Kino Nuevo, a couple of kilometers to the north, is a far smarter place with nice homes and beachfront restaurants; it is the destination of choice for many 'snowbirds'. Kino Nuevo also boasts the best strip of beach, a seemingly endless swath of pristine golden sand. High season is from November to March; at other times, you may find yourself blissfully alone by the water.

◉ Sights

Isla del Tiburón   ISLAND
This mountainous island, Mexico's largest, lies 3km off the coast from Punta Chueca. It was once a Seri homeland, but was depopulated when the island was declared a nature reserve in 1963. Today it's administered by the Seri tribal authorities. An intact desert ecosystem, it's home to bighorn sheep and large colonies of seabirds. There's good snorkeling around its coast. For a permit and guide to the island, ask at the Consejo de Ancianos at the entrance to Punta Chueca.

Museo de los Seris   MUSEUM
(Museo Comca'ac; ☑ 662-212-64-19; cnr Av Mar de Cortez & Progreso, Kino Nuevo; M$10; ⊙ 9am-6pm Wed-Sun; 🅿 🖼) This small but well-curated museum displays an interesting collection of artifacts, handicrafts and panels about Seri culture and history, including videos on the tradition of basket weaving. Signage is in Spanish only. On weekends, Seri women sell their *artesania* (arts and crafts) and traditional food items at the museum entrance, sometimes accompanied by music and dance performances too.

Punta Chueca   AREA
This village is home to the Seri people, one of Mexico's smallest indigenous groups (fewer than 1000 people). The Seri are known for their handicrafts, including their highly regarded baskets and carvings from ironwood. Look for **Soccaaix**, a small shop near the entrance to town, for high-quality items; ask for Doña Guillermina if it's closed. A paved road leads to the settlement, 34km north of Bahía de Kino.

La Casa del Mar   VISITOR CENTER
(☑ 662-366-04-65; cnr Bilbao & Esqueda, Kino Nuevo; ⊙ 9am-4pm Tue-Sun) 𝗙𝗥𝗘𝗘 This visitor

center services the 900-island **Área de Protección de Flora y Fauna Islas del Golfo de California**, a biodiverse protected area of islands in the Sea of Cortez. It has very informative displays in Spanish and English, and offers assistance in obtaining permits for visiting the islands (M$50 per person, per island, per day).

🛌 Sleeping

Eco Bay Hotel   HOTEL **$$**
(☑ 662-242-04-91; www.ecobayhotel.com; cnr Guaymas & Tampico, Kino Viejo; r/ste incl breakfast from M$900/1500; ☑ 🎜 🅰 🛜 ⚄) Spacious rooms surround a small pool and parking lot at this good-value and friendly option a few blocks from the beach in Kino Viejo. There are spotless bathrooms, a social atmosphere in the bar area (though music can be loud if your room is nearby) and a decent cooked breakfast is included.

Casa Tortuga   APARTMENT **$$$**
(☑ 662-173-03-01; www.facebook.com/RentCasa TortugaBahiaKino; Av Mar de Cortez 2645, Kino Nuevo; apt US$95-115; ☑ 🎜 🅰 🛜) Beachfront Casa Tortuga has three atmospheric, very comfortable apartments: Pelican, with its stunning ocean-facing, *palapa*-roofed terrace (complete with sunbeds, barbecue and table for outdoor dining) is particularly recommended. There are complimentary kayaks, and the owners sometimes take guests out in a boat to Isla Pelícano for birdwatching. Prices increase slightly in the summer months.

Casablanca Inn   HOTEL **$$$**
(☑ 662-242-07-77; www.facebook.com/Casablanca kinobay; cnr Av Mar de Cortez & Santander, Kino Nuevo; r incl breakfast M$1500-1800; ☑ 🎜 🅰 🛜) This beautifully cared-for hotel is a real find. With rain showers, tiled floors, white painted walls and attractive wooden furniture, the rooms are both stylishly minimalist and high quality. Don't miss breakfast at the on-site restaurant; tasty dishes and good service makes it a popular spot for expats.

🍴 Eating

Seafood rules this little town. You'll find most restaurants along the main drag in Kino Nuevo.

Restaurant Dorita   CAFE **$**
(☑ 662-252-03-49; cnr Blvr Kino & Salina Cruz, Kino Viejo; breakfast M$55, mains M$60-95; ⊙ 8am-8pm Tue-Sun; 🎜) Dorita and her daughter

turned their front room into a restaurant more than 20 years ago and have been kicking out the best breakfast around since. *Omelette rancheros* (a twist on *huevos rancheros*, replacing fried eggs with an omelette) is the specialty.

★ El Pargo Rojo   SEAFOOD **$$**
(☑ 662-242-02-05; Av Mar de Cortez 1426, Kino Nuevo; mains M$120-250; ⊙ noon-8pm Mon-Fri, 10am-10pm Sat, to 9pm Sun; 🎜) This thatch-roofed shack is the most popular place in Kino Nuevo and is often full of regulars enjoying delicious fish dishes and hearty Mexican breakfasts. The *camarones rellenos* (stuffed shrimp) are a real treat.

ℹ Getting There & Around

Buses to Hermosillo (M$150, two hours) run roughly hourly from the bus station about halfway along the strip – the white lumbering buses with 'Costa de Hermosillo' signage are impossible to miss. You can use these services to get around (local rides cost M$10) as there's no other public transportation. Taxis cost M$50 for a ride of up to 5km, and more after dark.

San Carlos

☑ 622 / POP 7000

With its striking desert-and-bay landscape, the low-key beach retreat of San Carlos feels a universe apart from its gritty port neighbors. It's presided over by some dramatic hills – notably the majestic twin peaks of Cerro Tetakawi – that glow an impressive red-earthed hue as the sun descends.

San Carlos' beaches are a mix of dark sand and pebbles. Head beyond the busy and built-up central strip to remoter and quieter Playa Algodones (famed for its role in the movie *Catch-22*) and you'll find white sands and turquoise water on one of the best beaches in northern Mexico.

ℹ Orientation

San Carlos, spread-eagled over some 8km, is not pedestrian friendly. Most amenities are on the 2.5km stretch of Blvd Beltrones. Head right at the intersection by the Oxxo store on the north end of the Beltrones strip to get out to Playa Algodones (6km northwest), or straight on for Marina San Carlos (500m west).

◉ Sights

★ Playa Los Algodones   BEACH
(Hwy 124 Km 19; parking M$30) Named for the cotton-ball-like dunes on the south end of

the beach, Playa Los Algodones is arguably the most beautiful beach in northern Mexico. The sand is fine and white, the water blue and calm, and the view is of dramatic mountains. High season can bring crowds and traveling oompah bands – join the party or head north along the sand for a patch of peace.

Isla San Pedro Nolasco
DIVE SITE

(Seal Island) A popular spot for snorkeling and dive excursions 28km west of San Carlos, Isla San Pedro Nolasco is a rocky island nature reserve that's home to a large population of sea lions. These playful creatures are active year-round. To see pups exploring their underwater surroundings, book a trip during the summer months with **Ocean Sports** (622-226-06-96; www.deportesoceano. com; Edificio Marina San Carlos; 8am-4pm Mon-Fri, 7am-5pm Sat & Sun) or **Gary's Dive Shop** (622-226-00-49; www.garysdiveshop.com; Blvd Beltrones Km 10; 7am-5pm).

Activities

Gorgeous coves, as well as a nearby sea lion colony on Isla San Pedro Nolasco, make snorkeling and kayaking top activities. Sportfishing also is popular: April to September are best for big fish and there are several annual tournaments.

Enrike's Adventures
OUTDOORS

(622-130-73-38; http://sancarlosadventures. com; Blvd Beltrones s/n; tours US$35-45; 9am-5pm;) Personalized and bilingual service is offered on a variety of excursions, including hiking Cerro Tetakawi and paddleboarding or kayaking in the area's bays. Tours vary from two to five hours, depending on the destination. Gear rental – bikes, paddleboards, kayaks and snorkel gear – is also available.

Sleeping

San Carlos is geared toward visitors from north of the border – especially 'snowbirds' – making budget places tough to find and condos a popular option.

Playa Blanca Condo-Hotel
CONDO $$$

(622-227-01-00; www.playablancasancarlosren tals.com.mx; Paseo Mar Bermejo s/n; apts from US$155;) The biggest building on the best beach around, this 14-story complex houses updated one- to three-bedroom condos with spectacular views of Playa Los Algodones and the surrounding bays. Units

are spacious and individually decorated, each with a private balcony. There's a well-kept pool, beachfront *palapas* and a restaurant too. It's located outside of town, so consider renting a car to explore beyond the beach.

La Posada Condominiums
APARTMENT $$$

(622-226-10-31; www.posadacondominiums. com; Blvd Beltrones Km 11.5; apts from M$2000;) Right on the beach (you can hear the waves lapping on the shore at night), these attractive studio, one- and two-bed condos all enjoy fine sea vistas from their generous balconies. All boast fully equipped kitchens, attractive living rooms and all mod cons. They're also a short walk from the Marina San Carlos. Rates drop significantly at quiet times of year.

Eating & Drinking

★ Boye's Burger Joint
BURGERS $

(622-226-03-69; www.facebook.com/boye burgers; Blvd Beltrones s/n; burgers M$100-125; noon-10pm Fri & Sat, to 9pm Sun & Thu;) Huge juicy burgers, fresh and made to order, are served at this hopping restaurant. You'll find 14 varieties – everything from classic to pineapple – and even 'light' burgers served with iceberg lettuce and no bread. Wash it all down with a thick Oreo shake. Popular with hungry locals and expats missing the States.

Soggy Peso Bar & Grill
SEAFOOD $$

(622-125-72-38; Playa Algodones; mains M$85-240; 11am-sunset;) With sand floors and families dining in their swimsuits, this lively and popular seafood restaurant where fresh fish and seafood are king makes for a fun and informal lunch. It's on the north end of San Carlos' best beach and also functions as a popular bar, serving up strong batches of margaritas. Live music starts around 5pm every day but Monday.

La Palapa Griega
MEXICAN, GREEK $$

(622-226-18-88; Blvd Beltrones Km 11.5; mains M$95-200; 11am-9pm;) Right on the beach, this long-standing Greek-owned restaurant offers a memorable setting for a meal. Try a sampler (hummus, taramasalata, baba ghanoush), a Greek salad or freshly caught local seafood. At night, eat under neon blue lights.

4ever Happy Hour
CLUB

(622-165-61-22; www.facebook.com/4everhappy hour; Blvd Beltrones s/n; cover M$50; 9pm-3am

Fri-Sun) A pumping dance club with an often packed rooftop bar, this is the place to get your groove (and drink) on. Especially popular with the 20-something crowd from Guaymas.

ℹ️ Getting There & Around

Buses from Guaymas run as far as Marina San Carlos; local rides within San Carlos cost M$9. Taxis charge M$50 to M$200 in the San Carlos area.

Long-distance buses will drop you at either the **Grupo Estrella Blanca** (☑ 800-507-55-00, 622-222-12-71; www.estrellablanca.com.mx; Calle 14 No 96) or **Tufesa** (☑ 622-222-54-53; www.tufesa.com.mx; Blvd García López 927) terminals in Guaymas. From Grupo Estrella Blanca, walk north on Calle 14 to Blvd García López and catch the white San Carlos bus (M$14, every 30 minutes). From Tufesa, cross the road to catch the same bus. A taxi from either terminal to San Carlos is M$200.

The nearest **airport** (☑ 622-221-05-11; Carr a San Jose de Guaymas Km 4.5) is 8km north of Guaymas. At the time of research, there were no commercial flights from the US or Canada; only commuter flights to Hermosillo, Los Mochis and Loreto were offered.

Ferry service (p780) to and from Santa Rosalía in Baja California leave Guaymas three times a week, taking passengers and vehicles across in a 10-hour overnight trip.

Álamos

☑ 647 / POP 9400 / ELEV 432M

One of the most architecturally rich towns in northwest Mexico, Álamos is a cultural oasis. Sheltered in the forested foothills of the Sierra Madre Occidental, its hushed cobblestone streets and imposing colonial buildings hint at a fascinating history, much of it to do with Álamos' role as Mexico's northernmost silver mining town. The town is both a national historical monument and one of Mexico's *pueblos mágicos* (magical villages).

Álamos' charms have proven irresistible to many US retirees and creative types who, since the '50s, have snapped up decaying colonial buildings to renovate into second homes and hotels. These well-heeled expats comprise a small but influential segment of Álamos' population, and their establishments dominate the colonial center of town.

More bizarrely, Álamos and vicinity is where most of the world's jumping beans – beans that 'jump' due to the presence of a larva inside – originate. Look for them sold around town.

History

The area's silver mines were discovered around La Aduana (10km west of Álamos) in the 16th century. Álamos itself was founded in the 1680s, probably as a dormitory suburb for La Aduana's wealthy colonists. Despite hostilities from the indigenous Yaqui and Mayo, Álamos boomed into one of Mexico's principal 18th-century mining centers.

During Mexico's 19th-century turmoils, Álamos was attacked repeatedly: by French invaders, by factions seeking its silver wealth and by the fiercely independent Yaqui. The Mexican Revolution took a further toll, and by the 1920s most mines were abandoned and Álamos was practically a ghost town.

In 1948 Álamos was reawakened by William Levant Alcorn, a Pennsylvania dairy farmer who bought the Almada mansion on Plaza de Armas and converted it into Hotel Los Portales. Other *norteamericanos* followed, restoring crumbling mansions to their former glory. Recently they've been joined by wealthy Mexicans, seduced by the relaxed ambience and benign winter climate, creating something of a real estate boom, which is still visible in the multiple realtor signs you see around town today.

👁️ Sights

Álamos is ideal for sauntering around and soaking up one of Mexico's most idyllic colonial centers, with perhaps a break at one of its atmospheric restaurants.

El Mirador   VIEWPOINT
(Camino al Mirador s/n; 🅿️ 🚻) This magnificent lookout tops a hill on Álamos' southeastern edge, affording sweeping views of the town and its mountainous surroundings. It's accessible by steps (370 of them) from the Arroyo Agua Escondida, two blocks down Obregón from Victoria, and is best climbed first thing in the morning or late in the afternoon, when the light is better and the heat not so fierce.

**Parroquia de la Purísima
Concepción**   CHURCH
(Plaza de Armas; ⊙8am-7pm; 🚻) **FREE** Álamos' parish church is the tallest building in town. It was built between 1786 and 1804 and its altar rail, lamps, censers and candelabra were all originally fashioned from silver, but were melted down in 1866 on the orders of General Ángel Martínez after he

booted French troops out of Álamos. Seven or so subterranean passageways between the church and Álamos mansions – probably escape routes for rich families in times of attack – were blocked off in the 1950s.

Museo Costumbrista de Sonora
MUSEUM

(☑647-428-00-53; Plaza de Armas; M$10; ⊙9am-6pm Wed-Sun) This well-done museum of Sonoran customs has extensive exhibits (all in Spanish) on the history and traditions of the state. Special attention is paid to the influence of mining on Álamos and the fleeting prosperity it created for the town's well-off, including rooms filled with antiques, period furniture and even a few vintage carriages.

🗘 Tours

Emiliano Graseda
TOURS

(☑647-101-48-75; Madero s/n; tours M$300; 🖈) English-speaking Emiliano Graseda, who can be found at the state tourist office, offers local tours that take in Álamos' landmarks and private homes and continue in the nearby village of La Aduana to visit a brickworks, artesanías (arts and crafts) workshops and a mission.

Solipaso
ADVENTURE

(☑647-428-15-09, US 888-383-0062; www.solipaso.com; Privada s/n, Barrio el Chalatón; half-/full-day tours US$80/150) Runs expert bird-watching trips to spot some of the 300 tropical bird species living around Álamos. Groups are small – one to four people – and guides are highly knowledgable. There are no regular office hours; call directly to book. Located at El Pedregal lodge.

Homes & Gardens Tour
WALKING

(☑647-428-02-67; tours M$100; ⊙10am Sat) Meet outside Museo Costumbrista de Sonora for a two-hour tour of three lovingly restored colonial homes, all owned by expats. Volunteer guides lead the tours. Proceeds go to Amigos de Educación de Álamos, a local charity providing educational scholarships for school-age children. Late October to May only.

✹✹ Festivals & Events

★ Festival Alfonso Ortíz Tirado
MUSIC

(☑662-213-44-11; www.festivalortiztirado.gob.mx; ⊙late Jan) One of northern Mexico's premier cultural events, Álamos' nine-day late-January festival features top-class classical and chamber music, blues, bossa nova and trova (troubadour-type folk music) performed by artists from across the globe. The festival's namesake, an Álamos native, was a revered opera singer and well-respected physician (Frida Kahlo was among his patients).

Tens of thousands of people descend upon the city during this festival – be sure to book your hotel well in advance.

🛏 Sleeping

Álamos has atmospheric and attractive accommodations, many in converted colonial mansions featuring gorgeous interior design. However, peso-watchers should be aware that budget options are limited.

Such is the summer heat, the cooler months (October to April) are high season in Álamos, although year-round it's largely a weekend town, with Mexicans coming from nearby cities to get away from it all. Midweek discounts are often available year-round.

Hotel Dolisa
HOTEL $

(☑647-428-01-31; www.dolisa.com; Madero 72; s/d M$700/800; P🅿❄🖈) Spacious, modern rooms with a colonial-era touch – think high ceilings, stenciled walls and even adobe chimeneas (fireplaces) – make this a comfortable place to stay. Some have kitchenettes. All open onto breezy arched walkways. A huge parking lot (once used for RVs) makes it a good spot for those traveling with wheels. Located two long blocks from Plaza Alameda.

Hotel Luz del Sol
BOUTIQUE HOTEL $$

(☑647-428-04-66; www.luzdelsolalamos.com; Obregón 3; r incl breakfast M$1300-1500; ❄❄🖈🖈) Set in a updated colonial home, this small hotel has a warm ambience thanks to welcoming staff and the presence of one of the town's best cafes. The three rooms open onto a central courtyard, each simply decorated but very spacious with sultan-sized beds, high ceilings and vast bathrooms with vintage tiling. A plunge pool and rooftop terrace are pluses.

Casa de las Siete Columnas
B&B $$

(☑647-428-01-64; www.lassietecolumnas.com; Juárez 36; r incl breakfast M$900-1000; ⊙mid-Oct–mid-Apr; ❄❄🖈🖈) An inviting Canandian-owned hotel in an imposing centuries-old building – look for the stunning seven-columned front portico. Rooms surround a pretty, plant-filled courtyard and small heated pool, and feature beamed ceilings, fireplaces and tasteful decor. There's a guests' lounge with a TV and pool table.

★ Casa Serena Vista
B&B $$$

(☑647-428-01-49; www.facebook.com/casaserenavista; Loma de Guadalupe 9; r incl breakfast US$85; ✳☎❄✉) Perched above the central plaza, this homey 18th-century *casona* (mansion) has just three rooms. Each is decorated with touches that make you feel at home – a set of art books, a Persian rug, a flower-printed chair. There's an airy living room where guests gather, a well-tended pool, and a sweeping patio with a koi pond and enviable views of downtown Álamos.

Two of the rooms have kitchenettes; the third has a microwave and small refrigerator. Casa Serena is owned and operated by longtime expat Diane Carpenter – an affable host with loads of tips about the town and stories about her native Alaska.

★ Hacienda de los Santos
LUXURY HOTEL $$$

(☑647-428-02-22; www.haciendadelossantos.com; Molina 8; r/ste incl breakfast from US$189/290; ℙ❄✳@❄✉) By far Álamos' most exclusive place to stay, this hacienda encompasses three restored colonial houses and a sugar mill, three pools, three restaurants, a movie theater, spa, gym and bar (with a 520-strong tequila collection). Accommodations are luxurious and highly atmospheric, while the sheer size of the place and its lush gardens is simply remarkable. Children 12 and over only. Rates plummet in the hot months; M$50 tours of the property are given most days at 2pm.

Hotel Colonial
HOTEL $$$

(☑647-428-13-71; www.alamoshotelcolonial.com; Obregón 4; r/ste incl breakfast from M$2080/4050; ℙ❄✳❄) The attention to detail at this historic mansion is highly impressive: it feels more like you are stepping into an Edwardian period drama than a Mexican hotel. The nine units mirror the sumptuous public areas, featuring tapestries, oil paintings, antiques and stately fireplaces. Also has an elegant restaurant as well as a spectacular rooftop bar/lounge.

El Pedregal
LODGE $$$

(☑647-428-15-09, US 888-383-0062; www.elpedregalmexico.com; Privada s/n, Barrio el Chalatón; d/q incl breakfast US$110/140; ℙ❄✳@❄✉) 🍃 There are just eight lovely adobe and straw-bale cabins here, all with stylish artistic furnishings and luxury bedding scattered around 8 hectares of tropical deciduous forest on the edge of Álamos, 2km from the plaza. The welcoming owners are expert birders and lead tours. A good-sized pool, 3km of trails, a yoga studio and a massage parlor complete the scene.

✗ Eating & Drinking

Mexicanadas
MEXICAN $

(☑647-482-76-54; Rosales s/n; mains M$40-80; ☺7am-9:30pm; ☑🖐) You'll be greeted by high ceilings, whirring fans and watercolor paintings of the local-turned-icon Maria Felix at this locals' favorite. The menu is mostly Mexican classics – quesadillas, enchiladas, *tostadas, chilaquiles* – with a few hamburger and sandwich options thrown in. Meals are big and cheap so expect a full house most days.

Koky's
MEXICAN $

(Restaurant Dōna Lola; ☑647-428-11-09; Volantín s/n, off Juárez; mains M$50-110; ☺7am-10pm; 🖐) This fan-cooled, family-run place is both simple and welcoming, with a covered terrace at the rear. The soups are crammed with ingredients and there's a huge menu of delicious *antojitos* (typical Mexican snacks – enchiladas, tacos, *chilaquiles* etc) and breakfasts as well. It can be found on a small side street south of the Plaza de Armas.

★ Teresita's
BISTRO, BAKERY $$

(☑647-428-01-42; www.teresitasalamos.com; Allende 46B; mains M$110-300; ☺8am-9pm Mon-Sat, 9am-6pm Sun; ☎☑) It's quite amazing that somewhere as small and remote as Álamos boasts this simply outstanding bakery-cum-bistro. There's an open kitchen and a changing menu that features mouthwatering salads, pastas, steaks and paninis, as well as offerings less usual in rural Mexico: spicy chicken wings, gazpacho and Middle Eastern veggie bowls. Desserts are fully catered for with sublime cakes and pastries. Either eat in the fountain-flanked garden or enjoy the comfort of a royal-blue banquette inside.

Charisma Restaurant
INTERNATIONAL $$

(☑647-428-09-68; www.facebook.com/pg/CharismaRestaurant; Obregón 2; mains M$160-250; ☺5:30-10pm Wed-Sat; ☑) The menu changes often at this artful restaurant, but typically delivers big with traditional dishes like boeuf bourguignon, paella and chicken piccata, all served with flair. The setting is a colonial dining room with original art and twinkling lights. The bar is a popular hangout for expats. Located inside La Mansion hotel.

Café Luz del Sol
CAFE $$

(Café Luchy; ☑ 647-428-04-66; Obregón 3; mains M$90-190; ⊙ 7:30am-6:30pm; ☎) In a region cruelly deprived of decent coffee shops, this colonial cafe is a better find for caffeine-starved travelers than any silver mine. Devour beautifully prepared breakfasts, Mexican and North American lunches, homemade cakes and good coffee. There's a cozy interior dining room hung with locally produced art, and a small patio replete with tropical flowers.

Patagonia
COFFEE

(☑ 647-428-17-65; Plaza de Armas, Guadalupe Victoria 5; ⊙ 9am-1pm & 5-9pm Mon & Tue, 9am-9pm Wed-Sun; ☺) This sleek coffee shop offers a full range of coffee drinks, smoothies and healthy shakes. Grab a seat in its colonial courtyard or bring a sweater and enjoy the Arctic temperatures inside.

ℹ Information

There are two tourism information offices in town – one run by the **state** (☑ 647-428-04-50; Madero s/n; ⊙ 8am-3pm Mon-Fri), the other by the **city** (☑ 647-428-04-40; Palacio Municipal, cnr Juárez & Sinaloa; ⊙ 8am-3pm Mon-Fri). While both are helpful, the state office is better run and is often staffed by a bilingual rep; it is located near the entrance to town.

Banorte (☑ 800-226-67-83; www.banorte. com; Madero 37; ⊙ 9am-4pm Mon-Fri) ATM; money exchange.

Hospital General de Álamos (☑ 647-428-02-25; Madero s/n; ⊙ 8am-8pm) Basic local hospital with no emergency services.

ℹ Getting There & Away

Álamos is 53km east of Navojoa and 156km north of Los Mochis. Álamos' **Transportes Baldomero Corral** (☑ 647-428-00-96; Morelos 7) bus terminal is serviced by **Albatros** (☑ 647-428-00-96; www.albatrosautobuses.com; cnr Guerrero & No Reelección, Navojoa) 2nd-class buses from Navojoa (M$40, one hour) between 6:30am to 8:30pm (late bus at 10pm).

From Álamos, Albatros provides service to Navojoa from 5:30am to 7:30pm (late bus at 9pm); Hermosillo (M$290, six hours) four times daily; and Puerto Peñasco (M$650, 12 hours) at 3am.

In Navojoa, both Albatros and **Tufesa** (☑ 642-421-32-10; www.tufesa.com.mx; cnr Hidalgo &

No Reelección, Navojoa) have onward services to Hermosillo, Puerto Peñasco, Los Mochis, Mazatlán and Guaymas.

If you're coming by car from Los Mochis, stick to the longer paved road via Navojoa, as the shorter back road is unpaved and rather wild for much of the journey.

Los Mochis

☑ 668 / POP 256,600

There is nothing much to detain you in Los Mochis, a giant urban sprawl mainly notable for being the first or last stop on El Chepe (Ferrocarril Chihuahua Pacífico; p751), and within an easy hop of ferries that link the mainland to Baja California. The climate here is perpetually humid and there are no real sights worth stopping for. However, if you're venturing to Baja by boat or to the Copper Canyon by train, you may well find yourself staying overnight, and in that case you'll actually find decent eating and sleeping options available, including what is said to be northern Mexico's best seafood.

◉ Sights

Jardín Botánico
Benjamin Francis Johnston
GARDENS

(Parque Sinaloa; ☑ 668-818-18-14; www.jbbfj.org; Blvd Rosales 750; ⊙ 5am-8pm Mon-Fri, to 7pm Sat & Sun; ☺☺☺) **FREE** This verdant park occupies part of the former estate of Benjamin Johnston, the American who founded the sugar mill around which Los Mochis grew up in the early 20th century. Beyond an array of international trees and plants, there are running trails, water features, picnic areas and even a huge greenhouse (M$20) and butterfly pavilion with live specimens flitting about (M$20). Workshops and events are hosted year-round. Guided tours also available.

Museo Regional
del Valle del Fuerte
MUSEUM

(☑ 668-812-46-92; Obregón s/n; adult/child M$15/10; ⊙ 9:30am-6pm Tue-Sat, 10am-1pm Sun) Set in a small two-story building, this museum covers the history of Sinaloa state from precolonial times to the present. One section highlights Los Mochis – it's growth and economic importance as a top sugar producer. Exhibits incorporate video, artifacts and well-presented signage (in Spanish only).

Los Mochis

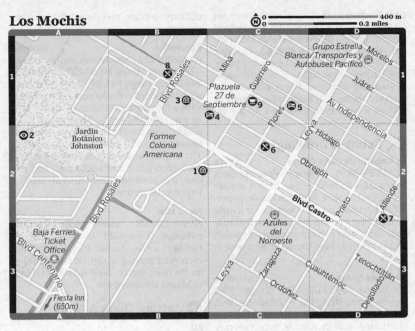

Los Mochis

⊙ Sights
1 Casa del Centenario B2
2 Jardín Botánico Benjamin Francis
   Johnston..A2
3 Museo Regional del Valle del Fuerte.......B1

🛏 Sleeping
4 Best Western Plus....................................C1
5 Hotel Fénix C1

✖ Eating
6 El Farallón...C2
7 La Cabaña de Doña Chayo...................D2
8 The Tuna Shop..B1

🍸 Drinking & Nightlife
9 Alma Mía C1

Casa del Centenario　　　MUSEUM
(📞668-817-25-52; Blvd Castro 667 Poniente; ⊙8am-4pm Mon-Fri, to 1pm Sat) This one-time family home was built in 1945 by Conrado Ochoa Beltrán, then superintendent of the *Ferrocarril Mexicano del Pacífico* and second in command of the United Sugar Company. Today it houses government offices as well as a one-room museum on the economic development of Los Mochis from 1903 to 2003. Signage in Spanish only.

🛏 Sleeping

Hotel Fénix　　　HOTEL $
(📞668-812-26-23; hotelfenix@email.com; Flores 365 Sur; r M$545; 🅿✳🛜) This is the best moderately priced hotel in town, with welcoming staff, a sparkling lobby, an excellent

restaurant and renovated rooms that represent good value. Accommodations can be on the small side, and some lack natural light, but as an overnight stop it's a great choice.

★**Fiesta Inn**　　　HOTEL $$
(📞800-343-78-21, 668-500-02-00; www.fiestainn. com; Blvd Rosales 1435 Sur; r incl breakfast M$1286; 🅿➖✳@🛜✳) Fiesta Inn is a spanking new hotel with an urban hipster vibe. Rooms are mid-century modern in design with simple lines and comfort in mind: thick mattresses, high thread count linens, rain-shower baths and lots of natural light. There's a cozy lounge, gym and pool. And the breakfast buffet? Made-to-order omelettes and fresh squeezed juices – need we say more?

Best Western Plus
HOTEL $$$

(☑ 668-816-30-00, 800-700-42-43; www.bestwest ern.com; Obregón 691 Poniente; r/ste incl breakfast M$1665/2713; P⊖✳@🛜🐕) Enjoying a prime spot overlooking the central plaza, this business-class hotel offers professional staff and service and very comfortable, carpeted rooms with modern bathrooms. It may be a big leap in price, but it's a solid option.

✗ Eating & Drinking

La Cabaña de Doña Chayo
TACOS $

(☑ 668-818-54-98; Obregón 99 Poniente; tacos & quesadillas M$35-50; ⊘8am-1am) A simple yet enjoyable place with delectable quesadillas, burritos and tacos with *carne asada* (grilled beef) or *machaca* (spiced, shredded, dried beef). It's fearsomely popular, and yet even at busy times the welcome is warm.

The Tuna Shop
SEAFOOD $$

(La Medusa; ☑ 668-176-61-64; Obregón 878A Poniente; mains M$100-180; ⊘7:30pm-1am Wed, 1pm-midnight Thu-Sat, 1-8pm Sun; 🛜) This sophisticated and thoroughly contemporary self-described 'fish kitchen' is a real find. The menu includes an excellent tuna burger, salmon teriyaki and *dorado* (dolphin fish) tacos, and you'll even find a selection of excellent local-brewed artisanal beers. There's an attached deli selling all manner of local culinary goodies that make for excellent souvenirs.

El Farallón
SEAFOOD $$

(☑ 668-812-12-73; www.farallon.com.mx; Obregón 499 Poniente; mains M$150-230; ⊘7am-11pm Sun-Thu, to midnight Fri & Sat; ✳🛜) A furiously air-conditioned, swanky seafood restaurant with a far-ranging selection of dishes: stick to the tried-and-tested Mexican and Sinaloan dishes (rather than fusion-style sushi rolls and the like) and you won't go wrong. The ceviche (seafood marinated in lemon or lime juice, garlic and seasonings) and *pescado a la plancha* (grilled fish) are particularly recommended.

Alma Mía
CAFE

(☑ 668-812-7576; www.facebook.com/almamia. coffeeshop; Guerrero 401 Sur; ⊘7am-11pm; 🛜) Excellent coffee drinks, friendly staff and even valet parking at this perky coffee shop on the main square. Good breakfasts (M$50 to M$80) are served too.

❶ Getting There & Away

AIR

Los Mochis Airport (Aeropuerto Federal del Valle del Fuerte; ☑ 668-818-68-70; www.aero puertosgap.com.mx; Carretera Los Mochis–Topolobampo Km 12.5) is located 18km south of town. It has regular flights to Mexico City, Chihuahua, Tijuana, Cabo San Lucas, Loreto, La Paz and Guadalajara with airlines including

---

FERRIES TO BAJA

Two ferry services link mainland northwest Mexico with Baja California:

From Topolobampo near Los Mochis, **Baja Ferries** (☑ 668-818-68-93, 800-012-87-70; www.bajaferries.com; Local 5, cnr Blvds Rosales & Centenario; ⊘10am-6pm Mon-Fri, 9am-3pm Sat) leaves at 11:59pm Monday to Friday and 11pm on Sunday to Pichilingue near La Paz in Baja; the trip takes around seven hours. On the return, the ferry leaves Pichilingue at 2:30pm Monday to Friday and 11pm on Saturday. If traveling around Semana Santa and Christmas–New Year and in June and July, reserve a month ahead. You can buy tickets in Los Mochis or, on departure day, at the Topolobampo terminal. Vehicles can also be transported on this route.

The **Ferry Santa Rosalía** (☑ 622-222-02-04, 800-505-50-18; www.ferrysantarosalia. com/tarifas.php; Calz García López 1598 Bis, Guaymas; ⊘8am-2pm & 3:30-8pm Mon-Sat) sails from Guaymas for Santa Rosalía, Baja California, at 8pm Tuesday, Thursday and Saturday, arriving the next morning around 6am. From mid-November to mid-March, strong winds may cause delays, and Tuesday and Wednesday sailings are occasionally canceled in low season. The ferry returns from Santa Rosalía on Wednesday and Friday at 8:30am (arriving the same day around 6:30pm) and on Sunday at 8pm (arriving the following day at 6am). The ticket office is 2km east of Guaymas city center, though reservations are only necessary if you want a cabin or are taking a vehicle (three days in advance is sufficient). All passengers and vehicles should be at the terminal by 6:30pm.

BUSES FROM LOS MOCHIS

DESTINATION	FARE (M$)	DURATION (HR)	FREQUENCY (DAILY)
Guadalajara	945-1155	13-15	half-hourly TAP, 13 Tufesa
Guaymas	345-421	5-6	25 Tufesa
Hermosillo	469-576	6-7	half-hourly 1st-class GEB, half-hourly Tufesa
Mazatlán	469-662	6-7	frequent GEB/TAP, 11 Tufesa
Mexico City	1310-1600	23	11 GEB/TAP
Navojoa	223-291	2	frequent 1st-class GEB, 32 Tufesa
Phoenix	1316-1709	14-16	10 Tufesa

Aeroméxico Connect (☑ 668-812-02-16; www.aeromexico.com.mx; Obregón 1104 Poniente; ☺ 8:30am-7pm Mon-Fri, to 4pm Sat), Aéreo Calafia (www.aereocalafia.com.mx) and Volaris (www.volaris.com).

BUS

Despite being a big transportation hub, Los Mochis lacks a central bus station, meaning that each bus company operates from its own depot in the city. Particularly useful lines are Grupo Estrella Blanca (GEB), Transportes y Autobuses Pacífico (TAP) and Tufesa. The main intercity bus stations all have round-the-clock departures.

Azules del Noroeste (☑ 668-812-34-91; Tenochtitlán 399 Poniente) Has 2nd-class buses to El Fuerte (M$70, one hour, 5am to 8:15pm). Tickets sold on the bus.

Grupo Estrella Blanca/Transportes y Autobuses Pacífico (GEB/TAP; ☑ 800-507-55-00; www.estrellablanca.com.mx; Pino Suárez 325) Deluxe and 1st-class buses to Mexico City, Guadalajara, Hermosillo and more.

Tufesa (☑ 668-818-22-22, 644-410-24-44; www.tufesa.com.mx; Blvd Antonio Rosales 2465) Offers 1st-class buses to Phoenix, Navojoa (for Álamos), Mazatlán and Guadalajara. The terminal is 3km northeast of the center of Los Mochis (M$50 in a taxi).

TRAIN

Los Mochis train station (☑ 668-824-11-51, 800-122-43-73, Chihuahua 614-439-72-11; www.chepe.com.mx; Bienestar s/n; ☺ 5am-5:30pm Mon-Fri, 5-9am & 10:30am-1pm Sat & Sun) is a hub of activity during arrival and departure times of the train. There's an ATM and plenty of cabs.

The ticket office sells railway tickets up to a month ahead of travel; opening hours are notoriously unreliable, however. Alternatively, purchase your ticket by phone (recommended in the high season) or arrive an hour before departure to buy a ticket.

The station is located 4km southeast of the town center at the end of Bienestar; a taxi from downtown is around M$50.

ⓘ Getting Around

TO/FROM THE AIRPORT

A cab to the airport costs around M$180.

CHIHUAHUA & CENTRAL NORTH MEXICO

Off the tourist radar, and with an affable frontier feel, this region offers some of Mexico's most important historic sights across a triptych of colonial cities (Chihuahua, Parral and Durango). The landscape itself is typified by the starkly beautiful Desierto Chihuahuense (Chihuahuan Desert), which covers most of Chihuahua, Mexico's largest state – and while it rises in the west into the fertile folds of the Sierra Madre Occidental, you'll be forgiven for thinking you've wandered into a B-grade western (Durango, incidentally, is where many famous westerns *were* filmed).

Tourism, unfortunately, has been ravaged by drug-gang violence, so don't venture off the beaten track without a guide. The 'Golden Triangle' – where Chihuahua, Durango and Sinaloa converge – is noted for its opium production and particularly high levels of violence. While there is some danger of being caught in the wrong place at the wrong time, tourists are not generally targeted.

Chihuahua

614 / POP 867,700 / ELEV 1440M

Chihuahua, capital of Mexico's biggest state, is a quirky but pleasant combination of *norteño* character, revolutionary history and bohemian hangouts. Many travelers use it only as an overnight stop before or after riding the Ferrocarril Chihuahua Pacífico, but Chihuahua is worth more of your time. The city center combines grand colonial buildings, several beautiful plazas, pedestrianized lanes and a healthy crop of restaurants, cafes and bars. Its museums bear witness to the key episodes of Mexican history that unfolded here. In short, it's an intriguing city with a strong sense of identity.

History

Founded in 1709, Chihuahua soon became the key city of the Nueva España's Provincias Internas (stretching from California to Texas and Sinaloa to Coahuila). The Spanish brought pro-independence rebels, including Miguel Hidalgo, to be condemned and shot here in 1811. The Porfirio Díaz regime brought railways and helped consolidate the wealth of the area's huge cattle fiefdoms. Luis Terrazas, one-time Chihuahua state governor, held lands nearly the size of Belgium: 'I am not *from* Chihuahua, Chihuahua is mine,' he once said.

After Pancho Villa's forces took Chihuahua in 1913 during the Mexican Revolution, Villa established his headquarters here, arranged various civic projects and soon acquired the status of local hero. Today the city has one of Mexico's highest living standards, with *maquiladora* (parts factory) jobs contributing significantly to this.

Sights

★ Casa Chihuahua   MUSEUM

(614-429-33-00; www.casachihuahua.org.mx; Libertad 901; M$75; 10am-6pm Wed-Mon;) Chihuahua's former Palacio Federal (built 1908–10) has been used as a mint, a monastery, a military hospital and a post office, but is now a beautifully restored cultural center full of excellent exhibits, with most explanations in English and Spanish. Modern displays concentrate on the culture and history of Chihuahua state with features on Mormons, Mennonites and the Tarahumara people. The most famous gallery is the Calabozo de Hidalgo, the subterranean dungeon where Miguel Hidalgo was held prior to his execution.

The historic dungeon and the church towering above it were preserved within the later buildings erected on the site. A short audiovisual heightens the mournful atmosphere of the dungeon, which contains Hidalgo's bible and crucifix. A plaque outside recalls the verses the revolutionary priest wrote in charcoal on his cell wall in his final hours thanking his captors for their kindness.

Casa Chihuahua also hosts live music performances every Thursday afternoon – from classical to experimental. Entrance is free.

Museo Casa Redonda   MUSEUM

(Museo Chihuahuense de Arte Contemporáneo; 614-414-90-61; www.facebook.com/museocasa redonda; Colón s/n; adult/child M$22/10; 10am-7pm Tue-Sun) Once a locomotive maintenance and repair shop, this renovated warehouse is home to the city's small but excellent modern art museum, with one room dedicated to the fascinating history of the building, including railroad gear and antiquities. The building itself was built curved to accommodate a huge turntable that allowed one mechanic to turn an entire railcar.

Museo Casa de Villa   MUSEUM

(Museo Historico de la Revolucion; 614-416-29-58; mus_histrevol@mail.sedena.gob.mx; Calle 10 No 3010; adult/student M$10/5; 9am-7pm Tue-Sat, 10am-4pm Sun;) Housed in Quinta Luz, Pancho Villa's 48-room former mansion, this museum is a must-see for anyone who appreciates a made-for-Hollywood story of crime, stakeouts and riches. The interior is loaded with Villa's personal effects and photographs, and in the back courtyard you'll find the bullet-riddled black Dodge that Villa was driving when he was murdered. Information is in Spanish and English.

After his assassination in 1923, 25 of Villa's 'wives' filed claims for his estate. Government investigations determined that Luz Corral de Villa was the *generalísimo*'s legal spouse; the mansion was awarded to her and became known as Quinta Luz. She opened the museum and the army acquired it after her death in 1981.

The rear of the museum concentrates on Mexican revolutionary history with detailed signage, newspaper articles, weapons and other artifacts.

Plaza de Armas · PLAZA

(Independencia 209;) Chihuahua's historic heart, with its mass of pigeons, shoe-shiners and cowboy-hatted characters, is a simple but pretty place. A bronze sculpture of the city's founder, Don Antonio de Deza y Ulloa, presides over the daily hubbub. The plaza also is home to the majestic baroque **cathedral** (614-416-84-10; Libertad 814; 7am-8pm;), built between 1725 and 1826 and still containing the original organ installed in 1796.

Poliforum de UACH · GALLERY

(ext 2026 614-439-15-00; www.uach.mx; Escorza 900; 9am-6pm Mon-Fri) **FREE** Located just east of **Templo San Francisco** (Libertad s/n; 8am-1pm & 3-7pm), this University of Chihuahua gallery has two permanent exhibits that showcase the work of two prominent Chihuahuense artists: Águeda Lozano and Sebastián. Temporary exhibits of up-and-coming Mexican artists are also displayed. Free guided tours are available until 3pm.

Grutas de Nombre de Dios · CAVE

(614-432-05-18; Vialidad Sacramento s/n; adult/child M$50/25; 9am-3pm Tue-Fri, from 10am Sat & Sun;) These caves on Chihuahua's northeast edge boast impressive stalagmites, stalactites and rock formations, making the one-hour, 17-chamber underground journey fun, especially for kids. Visitors enter with guides and typically in groups of 15 to 20 people. To get here take either a taxi (M$90) or a 'Nombre de Dios Ojo' bus (M$7) from outside Posada Tierra Blanca on Niños Héroes. Ask the driver where to get off.

Palacio de Gobierno · HISTORIC BUILDING

(614-429-35-96; Aldama 901; 8am-8pm) **FREE** The courtyard of this handsome, 19th-century, state-government building features striking 1960s murals by Aarón Piña Mora showing Chihuahua's highly eventful history. You can get a free e-guide to the murals through the tourist office (p786), which is located here. Hidalgo and the Mexican independence are the subjects of a small museum: **Museo de Hidalgo** (614-429-36-95; Aldama 901; 9am-5pm Tue-Sun) **FREE**.

Casa Sebastián · GALLERY

(614-200-48-00; Av Juárez 601; 8am-7pm) **FREE** The main draws of this restored 1880s gallery are the small-scale models of the massive metal sculptures by renowned Chihuahuan artist Sebastián, whose work

HIGHEST BRIDGE IN THE AMERICAS

Soaring an incredible 402m above the Río Baluarte, this incredible feat of engineering, **Puente Baluarte** (Autopista Durango-Mazatlán) is the highest bridge in the Americas. It's one of many incredible bridges on the Durango–Mazatlán Hwy, a magnificent toll road that boasts some of Mexico's most incredible scenery, with epic tunnels through mountains, hairpin bends and jaw-dropping views all the way. If you only drive one road in Mexico, make it this one.

is recognized in cities worldwide. There are five real Sebastianes around Chihuahua, including one just above Parque El Palomar.

Quinta Gameros · HISTORIC BUILDING

(614-238-20-05; www.uach.mx; Paseo Bolívar 401; adult/child M$30/10; 11am-7pm) Built in an incredibly elaborate belle epoque architectural style by a wealthy mine owner, this museum is filled with a mix of period furnishings and art. Every room is unique, with quality stained glass and ornate carved wood and moldings. Upstairs, several rooms have temporary art exhibits. Definitely worth a look around, as it is one of Chihuahua's most unforgettable buildings.

Museo Casa de Juárez · MUSEUM

(Museo de la Lealtad Republicana; 614-410-42-58; Av Juárez 321; adult/child M$11/5; 9am-6pm Tue-Sun;) President Benito Juárez' residence in this house during the French occupation made Chihuahua the capital of the Mexican republic from 1864 to 1866. Now a museum with the 1860s feel still intact, it includes documents signed by the great reformer, as well as period exhibits, including weapons, uniforms and replicas of Juárez' furniture.

Tours

Chihuahua Bárbaro · TOURS

(614-425-00-06; www.chihuahuabarbaro.com;) This trolleybus offers tours of Chihuahua's main historic sights (narrated in Spanish) and beyond. Its three-hour city tour (M$100) departs from the Plaza de Armas (where there's a ticket booth) four times daily, and includes the Pancho Villa museum and Quinta Gameros. Entrance fees not included.

Chihuahua

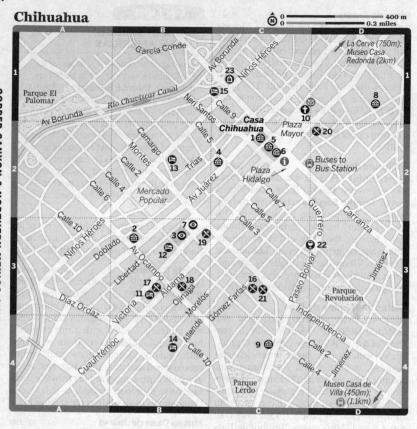

🛏 Sleeping

Hotel Jardín del Centro   HOTEL $

(☎614-415-18-32; www.hoteljardindelcentro.com; Victoria 818; s/d M$480/590; P🐶❄🛜) Offering fine value, this pleasant, inviting little hotel has cozy, attractive rooms around a pretty plant-filled courtyard, plus a good little restaurant. Twins in the back are not as atmospheric as the doubles with high ceilings at the front. Staff are sweet and its location is conveniently close to the center.

Motel María Dolores   MOTEL $

(☎614-416-74-20; motelmadol@hotmail.com; Calle 9A No 304; s/d M$380/450; P❄🐶🛜) Just down from Plaza Mayor, this impeccably run motel's basic rooms aren't much to look at, but they are clean and a very good deal given the excellent location. It's particularly handy for drivers, with its secure parking lot.

★Hotel San Felipe El Real   BOUTIQUE HOTEL $$

(☎614-437-20-37; www.hotelsanfelipeelreal.com; Allende 1005; r/ste incl breakfast M$1130/1428; P🐶❄@🛜) Unassuming it may be from the outside, but inside this gorgeous 1880s house you'll find a courtyard with a bubbling fountain and six individually furnished rooms, all replete with antiques and period furniture. The owners spoil guests, and serve breakfast on one long table in the homey kitchen. Airport and train station pickups are offered.

Hotel Posada Tierra Blanca   HOTEL $$

(☎614-415-00-00; www.posadatierrablanca.com.mx; Niños Héroes 102; s/d M$799/849; P🐶❄🛜🐶) An old-school motel that recently got a face-lift, most rooms here are spacious and clean with hardwood floors and sleek furnishings (a few had yet to be updated). There's a well-tended pool plus a dated diner serving up Mexican classics. Best of all is the cavernous lounge, with a psychedelic three-story mural.

Hotel Plaza   HOTEL $$$

(☎614-415-12-12, 800-752-92-01; www.hotelplazachihuahua.com; Cuarta 204; r incl breakfast M$1684; P🐶❄🛜) Clean, modern and spacious rooms with wood floors, modish furniture and quality bed linen await you here, just a stone's throw from the cathedral. The roof terrace, where the buffet breakfast is served, boasts fine city views. Service is friendly and attentive.

🍴 Eating & Drinking

Chihuahuenses love a good steak. You'll find most places oblige with a variety of cuts.

Café Cortez   CAFE $

(☎614-415-38-07; www.facebook.com/CafeCortezCuu; Gómez Farías 8; mains M$45-90; ⊗9am-11pm Mon-Fri, 10am-11pm Sat, 4-11pm Sun; 🛜) Chihuahua hardly does hipster, but this hangar-like place painted black outside and a riot of colors inside is probably the most likely environment to find the nearest local equivalent. The real reason to come here though is the excellent coffee, as well as the tasty and enormous paninis, salads and sandwiches, which make it a great lunch stop.

La Casa de los Milagros   MEXICAN $

(☎614-261-55-04; www.facebook.com/pg/CasaDeLosMilagrosCuu; Victoria 812; mains M$75-110; ⊗7:30am-midnight Sun-Thu, to 1:30am Fri & Sat; 🛜) Legend has it that Pancho Villa and his pals hung out in this atmospheric 110-year-old mansion featuring tiled floors, lots of snug little rooms and an airy covered courtyard. The menu is enormous and features typical Mexican dishes, all humorously renamed. There's live music Thursday through Saturday evenings starting at 8pm.

★Plaza del Mariachi   FOOD HALL $$

(www.plazadelmariachi.com.mx; Aldama 256; mains M$100-280; ⊗8am-1:30am; 🛜🍴) An upscale food court set in a colonial-style building with exposed brick, a central courtyard and a gentle mist to keep patrons cool. There are eight restaurants – with more to come – featuring mostly Mexican menus with a couple focused on steak and seafood. Mariachis stroll through the complex on Friday and Saturday nights as well as Sunday afternoons. In the evenings, many restaurants double as bars. Come here for a taste of the local nightlife too.

Taller del Chef   BISTRO $$

(☎614-410-20-84; www.facebook.com/pg/tallerdelchefcuu; Independencia 1414; mains M$90-140; ⊗1-10pm Mon-Sat, 2-10pm Sun) A stylish Asian-fusion bistro restaurant, this downtown eatery serves up delicious ramen bowls overflowing with noodles, veggies and proteins. A good selection of local craft beers is also offered. If soup isn't your thing, there is a variety of (dry) noodle dishes plus salads too.

Mesón de Catedral INTERNATIONAL $$
(☑ 614-410-15-50; www.facebook.com/MesonDe Catedral; Plaza de Armas; mains M$120-220; ☺ 8am-midnight Mon-Wed, to 2am Thu-Sat, to 10pm Sun; ☎) Go to the 2nd floor of this modern building to find the best vista in Chihuahua. With a terrace overlooking the city's cathedral, this upmarket place is worth spending a little extra on: try the fish fillet stuffed with peppers or the beefsteak with giant shrimp in a red wine dressing. There's live music on Thursday, Friday and Saturday evenings.

La Casona STEAK $$$
(☑ 614-410-00-43; www.casona.com.mx; cnr Aldama & Av Ocampo; mains M$190-450; ☺ 8am-midnight Mon-Sat, 2-6pm Sun; ☎) An elaborate 19th-century mansion where polished waiters serve up steaks, seafood and pasta alongside an ample wine list. The menu itself changes every two to three months. There's a bar and a smoking room too. Booking is recommended.

Momposina BAR
(☑ 614-410-09-75; Coronado 508; ☺ 4pm-1am Mon-Sat; ☎) A brilliant bohemian bar where creative types gather during the day to lounge on mismatched seats, snack on paninis and sip espressos. Later on it morphs into a bar, and on Thursday to Saturday evenings there's live music. Beers are inexpensive and the vibe is chilled.

La Cerve BEER GARDEN
(☑ 614-413-08-60; www.facebook.com/pg/ cervechihuahua; Av Pacheco Villa 3331; ☺ noon-11pm Wed-Sat, to 10pm Tue & Sun) A massive parking lot surrounded by beer stands and picnic tables make this a popular place for drinks. The beer isn't fancy – Tecate, Miller, Amstel Lite – but it's more about the laid-back crowd and vibe. Live music on weekends too. When you get hungry, the on-site taco stands hit the spot.

🛍 Shopping

Chihuahua is a big city with little to recommend it for shoppers. However, the strong cowboy culture here means there are plenty of cowboy-related items to be found for those on the prowl. Cowboy-boot shoppers should make a beeline to Libertad between Independencia and Avenida Ocampo, where lots of boot shops line the street.

Casa de las Artesanías
del Estado de Chihuahua ARTS & CRAFTS
(☑ 614-437-12-92; Niños Héroes 1101; ☺ 9am-5pm Mon-Fri, 10am-5pm Sat) Has a good selection of *chihuahuense* crafts (including Mata Ortiz pottery) and Mexican foodstuffs such as pecans, oregano oil and *sotol*, a local spirit made from desert spoon plants.

❶ Information

Clínica del Centro (☑ 614-439-81-00; www. clinicadelcentro.com.mx; Ojinaga 816) Has a 24-hour emergency department.

Post Office (☑ 800-701-70-00; Libertad 1700; ☺ 8am-5pm Mon-Fri, 10am-2pm Sat)

State Tourist Office (☑ 614-429-35-96, 800-508-01-11; www.chihuahuamexico. com; Aldama 901, Palacio de Gobierno; ☺ 9am-8pm Mon-Sat) Delivers hit-or-miss service though there are plenty of maps and brochures. **Tourist information kiosks** (Blvd Juan Pablo II No 4107; ☺ 9am-5pm Tue-Sun) just outside and at the bus station are more helpful.

❶ Getting There & Away

AIR
Located 15km northeast of town, **Chihuahua's airport** (☑ 614-478-70-00; www.oma.aero; Blvd Juan Pablo II Km 14) has regular flights to San Francisco, Miami, Mexico City, Guadalajara and Monterrey. It's serviced by **Aeroméxico** (☑ 800-262-40-12, 614-201-96-96; www.aeromexico.com;

BUSES FROM CHIHUAHUA

DESTINATION	FARE (M$)	DURATION (HR)	FREQUENCY (DAILY)
Ciudad Juárez	670	5-6	hourly
Durango	985	10-13	10
Guadalajara	1505	13	2
Monterrey	805-865	11-12	8
Nuevo Casas Grandes	505	4½	hourly
Parral	340	3-5	hourly
Saltillo	775	10	7
Zacatecas	950	8	6

Ortiz Mena 2807; ⊘ 9am-7pm Mon-Fri), **Interjet** (☑ 614-430-25-46; www.interjet.com.mx; Av de la Juventud 3501; ⊘ 11am-9pm Mon-Fri, to 8pm Sat & Sun), Viva Aerobus (www.vivaaerobus.com) and Volaris (www.volaris.com).

BUS

Chihuahua's busy main **bus station** (☑ 614-420-53-98; Blvd Juan Pablo II No 4107) is 7km east of the center.

Los Paisanos (☑ 614-418-73-68, US 866-771-7575; www.lospaisanosautobuses.com; cnr Calle 78 & Degollado) offers first-class bus service to the US from its stand-alone depot. Destinations include Dallas (US$65, 17 to 19 hours) and Los Angeles (US$69, 22 hours).

For Cuauhtémoc (M$110, 1½ hours) and Creel (M$420, 4½ hours) there are regular departures from both **Rápidos Cuauhtémoc** (☑ 614-416-48-40; Blvd Juan Pablo II No 4107) and **Autotransportes Noroeste** (☑ 614-411-57-83; www.turisticosnoroeste.com; Blvd Juan Pablo II No 4107). The latter also has five daily departures (6am to 4pm) to the Copper Canyon hot spots of Divisadero (M$510, 5½ hours) and San Rafael (M$540, six hours) via Parque de Aventura Barrancas del Cobre.

TRAIN

Chihuahua is the northeastern terminus for the **Ferrocarril Chihuahua Pacífico** (p751), with departures at 6am daily. All trains have 1st-class carriages, while on Monday, Thursday and Saturday, *clase económica* carriages are coupled on the back. The **station** (☑ 614-439-72-12, 800-122-43-47; www.chepe.com.mx; Méndez 2205; ⊘ 5am-5:30pm Mon-Fri, 9am-12:30pm Sat) is 1.5km south of Plaza de Armas; there are no amenities – just a ticket office. You can nearly always buy tickets on the day of travel, just be sure to arrive at least one hour before departure.

ℹ️ Getting Around

To get to the main bus station, catch a **'Circunvalación Sur' bus** (Av Carranza s/n; M$7, 30 to 50 minutes) heading northwest on Carranza, almost opposite Plaza Hidalgo.

From the center, there are taxis to the train station (M$50), bus station (M$80) and airport (M$200). Airport taxis back to town are pricey (around M$350).

Nuevo Casas Grandes & Casas Grandes

☑ 636 / POP 60,800 / ELEV 1457M

Nuevo Casas Grandes, 345km northwest of Chihuahua, is a prosperous but unremarkable country town, with small communi-

ties of Mormon and Mennonite settlers. Tourism-wise it's a transportation hub for those heading to the prettier village of Casas Grandes by the pre-Hispanic ruins of Paquimé (7km south) and the pottery center of Mata Ortiz (27km south).

◉ Sights

★**Paquimé**   ARCHAEOLOGICAL SITE

(☑ 636-692-41-40; zapaquime.museo@gmail.com; Allende s/n, Casas Grandes; adult/child under 13yr M$70/free; ⊘ 9am-5pm Tue-Sun) These ruins, in a broad valley with panoramas to distant mountains, contain the maze-like adobe remnants of northern Mexico's most important trading settlement. Paquimé was the center of the Mogollón or Casas Grandes culture, which extended north into New Mexico and Arizona and over most of Chihuahua. The site's impressive, meticulously detailed **Museo de las Culturas del Nort**e has displays about Paquimé and the linked indigenous cultures of northern Mexico and the southwest USA.

The site was sacked, perhaps by Apaches, around 1340. Excavation and restoration began in the 1950s; Unesco declared it a World Heritage site in 1998. Plaques, in Spanish and English, discuss Paquimé culture: don't miss the clay macaw cages and the distinctive T-shaped door openings. The Paquimé people revered the scarlet macaw and some structures here represent this beautiful bird, which has never been native to northern Mexico and is evidence of Paquimé's far-reaching trade network.

The Paquimé people were great potters and produced striking cream-colored earthenware with red, brown or black geometric designs; some amazing original examples are on display in the museum, and modern reproductions are for sale.

🛏️ Sleeping & Eating

★**Las Guacamayas B&B**   B&B $$

(☑ 692-699-09-97; www.mataortizollas.com; Av 20 de Noviembre, Casas Grandes; s/d incl breakfast US$50/70; P☉❀🛜) ❂ This adobe-walled place has charming rooms with beamed roofs, all built using recycled materials, and a lovely garden area. Owner Mayte Lujan has a world-class collection of Mata Ortiz pottery and is extremely knowledgable about the region. It is located just a stone's throw from the entrance to the ruins of Paquimé.

PANCHO VILLA: BANDIT TURNED REVOLUTIONARY

Macho womanizer, revolutionary, cattle rustler, lover of education, a man of impulsive violence who detested alcohol – no hero in Mexico's history is as colorful or contradictory as Francisco 'Pancho' Villa.

Villa is best known as a leader of the Mexican Revolution, but as much of his adulthood was given over to theft and chasing women as to any noble cause. Born Doroteo Arango to hacienda workers in northern Durango state in 1878, he turned to banditry by the age of 16, taking the name Francisco Villa, possibly in honor of his grandfather. The story goes that Villa became an outlaw after shooting one of the hacienda-owning family who tried to rape his sister. Between 1894 and 1910, Villa's life veered between spells of banditry and attempts to lead a legitimate existence.

In 1910, amid intensifying opposition to the dictatorial regime of President Porfirio Díaz, Villa was lobbied for support by Abraham González, leader in Chihuahua state of the revolutionary movement headed by Francisco Madero. González knew he needed natural fighting leaders and encouraged Villa to return to marauding. Villa soon raised a fighting force to join the Revolution, which began on November 20, 1910.

When Villa's rebels took Ciudad Juárez in May 1911, Díaz resigned. Madero was elected president, but in 1913 he was toppled from power by one of his own commanders, General Victoriano Huerta, and executed. Villa fled across the US border to El Paso, but within a couple of months he was back as one of four revolutionary leaders opposed to Huerta. He quickly raised an army of thousands, the famed División del Norte, and by the end of 1913, with the help of US-supplied guns, he had taken Ciudad Juárez (again) and Chihuahua, installing himself as state governor for the next two years. He expropriated property and money from rich *hacendados* (landowners), lowered prices of basic necessities and established schools, but favored his troops over noncombatants and tolerated no dissent. His victory over a pro-Huerta army at Zacatecas in June 1914 signaled the end for Huerta. But the four revolutionary forces soon split into two camps, with liberal leaders Venustiano Carranza and Álvaro Obregón on one side, and the more radical Villa and Emiliano Zapata on the other. Villa was routed by Obregón in the Battle of Celaya (1915) and never recovered his influence.

After the USA recognized Carranza's government in October 1915, Villa decided to simultaneously discredit Carranza and seek revenge on US president Wilson. On March 9, 1916, Villa's men sacked the US town of Columbus, New Mexico, which was home to both a US cavalry garrison and Sam Ravel, who had once cheated Villa on an arms deal. Though as many as half of Villa's 500 militiamen may have died that day (there were 18 US deaths) and Ravel wasn't found (he was at the dentist in El Paso), the attack ended up a success for Villa because it drew a punitive US Army expedition into Mexico in pursuit of him, and boosted his legend. Villa carried on fighting the Carranza regime, raiding cities and haciendas, but now had to maintain his fighting force by conscription, and sometimes allowed his men to pillage and slaughter.

In 1920 Carranza was deposed by his former ally Obregón, and Villa signed a peace treaty with provisional president Adolfo de la Huerta. Villa pledged to lay down his arms and retire to a hacienda in Canutillo, for which the Huerta government paid M$636,000. Villa was given money to cover wages owed to his troops and help the widows and orphans of the División del Norte. He settled 759 of his former troops at Canutillo, setting up a school for them and their children.

For the next three years, Villa led a relatively quiet life. He bought a hotel in Hidalgo del Parral and regularly attended cockfights. He installed one of his many 'wives,' Soledad Seañez, in a Parral apartment, and kept another at Canutillo. Then, one day while he was leaving Parral in his Dodge touring car, a volley of shots rang out and the legendary revolutionary was killed. The light prison sentences the eight-man assassin team received led many to conclude that the order for the killing came from President Obregón, though with all the enemies Villa made over the years, there are many suspects.

El Mesón del Kiote
STEAK **$$**

(📞 636-690-06-98; Av Juárez 1201, Casas Grandes; mains M$145-230; ⏰8am-10pm) For a fine steak, there's no better spot than this two-story restaurant with an alpine feel. There's a great variety of cuts, but go all out with the rib eye, a tender, flavorful – and substantial – plate of meat. Most orders come with a baked potato and sides.

Pompeii
MEXICAN **$$**

(📞 636-661-46-03; www.pompeii-restaurant.com.mx; Av Juárez 2601, Nuevo Casas Grandes; mains M$140-200; ⏰11am-midnight) Don't be turned off by its bright-red neon facade, reminiscent of a sleazy nightclub. This friendly and smart spot is actually quiet mellow – no thumping music here – and favored by groups visiting Mata Ortiz. It serves up scrumptious modern Mexican dishes with an emphasis on the area's specialty, *pavo* (turkey).

ℹ️ Information

Tourist Information Office (📞 ext 110 636-692-43-13; Palacio Municipal, Constitución s/n, Casas Grandes; ⏰9am-3pm) Staff in this small office are friendly and quick to hand out brochures and maps.

ℹ️ Getting There & Away

In Nuevo Casas Grandes, **Ómnibus de México** (📞 636-694-05-02; www.odm.com.mx; Obregón 312) and **Estrella Blanca/Chihuahuenses** (📞 636-694-07-80, 800-507-5500; www.estrellablanca.com.mx; Obregón 308) offer 1st-class buses to Chihuahua (M$505 to M$550, 4½ hours, eight daily), the border at Nogales (M$545 to M$710, seven hours, six daily) and Ciudad Juárez (M$400, four hours, six daily).

To get to Paquimé from Nuevo Casas Grandes, 'Casas Grandes' buses (M$9, 20 minutes, 8:30am to 7:30pm Monday to Saturday, to 4:30pm Sunday) depart every hour, northbound from Constitución, just north of Calle 16 de Septiembre. Get off in Casas Grandes' plaza and walk 800m south on Constitución to the ruins. A taxi from Nuevo Casas Grandes to Paquimé is around M$120.

Durango

📞 618 / POP 519,000 / ELEV 1880M

Durango, capital of the eponymous desert state, is an immensely likable place, with an attractive, beautifully kept and laid-back city center and a friendly local populace. It is also one of Mexico's most isolated cities: you have to travel hours through the desert or the Sierra Madre mountains from here before you hit another significant settlement. Yet isolation has fostered unique regional traits, such as the distinctive local cuisine and wry humor.

Founded in 1563, Durango's early importance was due to nearby iron-ore deposits, along with gold and silver from the Sierra Madre. Today hundreds of *maquiladoras* (assembly plants) dominate the economy. For visitors, the city's striking colonial center commands attention with over 70 historic buildings and several fascinating museums, while good accommodations and restaurants are plentiful.

Note: Durango state's time zone is one hour ahead of Chihuahua and Sinaloa.

👁️ Sights

Constitución, pedestrianized between Jardín Hidalgo past the Plaza de Armas to Plazuela Baca Ortiz, is among Mexico's most appealing traffic-free streets, lined with restaurants and cafes and lively day and night.

⭐ Museo Francisco Villa
MUSEUM

(📞 618-811-47-93; 5 de Febrero s/n; adult/child M$20/10; ⏰10am-6pm Tue-Fri, 11am-6pm Sat & Sun; 🚻) Housed in a spectacular colonial mansion, this well-conceived museum pays deep homage to the Mexican revolutionary hero Pancho Villa. Sixteen rooms worth of multimedia displays, films and personal effects tell the story of Durango's most famous native son. Be sure to leave some time to check out the gorgeous murals, which depict the history of the country and state. Signage is in English, Spanish and even braille.

⭐ Museo de la Ciudad 450
MUSEUM

(📞 618-137-84-90; cnr Av 20 de Noviembre & Victoria; adult/child M$22/5; ⏰9am-8pm Mon-Fri, 11am-6pm Sat, to 5pm Sun; 🚻) This impressive city museum features an interesting collection of interactive exhibits, from pre-Hispanic times through colonization to the present day, and deal with Durango's economy, mining, traditions and culture. The museum has an entire section dedicated to the film industry, highlighting the more than 130 films that have been made in and near the city, including *The Wild Bunch* (1968), *Zorro* (1997) and *Texas Rising* (2014). Don't miss the *alacraneo*, a black-light-lit tank with over 5000 scorpions.

Durango

◎ Top Sights
1 Museo de la Ciudad 450 .... C3
2 Museo Francisco Villa B3

◎ Sights
3 Catedral del Basílica Menor C3
4 Museo de Arqueología de Durango
   Ganot-Peschard B3
5 Museo Palacio de los Gurza B3
6 Museo Regional de Durango C2
7 Plaza de Armas C3
8 Túnel de Minería C3

◎ Activities, Courses & Tours
9 Paseo Teleférico A3

◎ Sleeping
10 Hostal de la Monja C3
11 La Casa de Bruno B4
12 Posada de María B3

◎ Eating
13 Birriería Mendoza B3
14 Cremería Wallander A2
15 Fonda de la Tía Chona A3
16 Gorditas Durango B4
17 La Tetera Bistro Cafe A3
18 Restaurant Playa Azul B1

◎ Drinking & Nightlife
19 Wirikuta Cafe A3

Paseo del Viejo Oeste   FILM LOCATION
(☑ 618-113-12-92; Hwy 45 Km 12; adult/child
M$35/25; ☺ 11am-7pm; ⓐ) Many of the big-
screen cowboys have swaggered through this
film set. Today the set is a souvenir-drenched

theme park with regular mock film productions (2pm and 4pm Monday to Friday; 1pm,
3pm and 5pm Saturday and Sunday). It's located 12km north of town; a free shuttle bus
leaves for here from the Plaza de Armas 30

minutes before each show and returns two hours later (though visitors are welcome to stay longer). Great fun for families. Horseback riding and wagon rides available too.

Plaza de Armas
PLAZA

Flower- and fountain-filled Plaza de Armas is graced by the handsome baroque **Catedral del Basílica Menor** (⏏618-811-42-42; ⊗8am-9pm). A popular meeting spot, there's a bandstand, shade trees and loads of benches. In the late afternoon and evening, vendors do brisk business in everything from corn on the cob to crepes.

The entrance to the **Túnel de Minería** (Tunnel of Mining; ⏏618-137-53-61; Juárez 313; M$20; ⊗10am-9:30pm Tue-Sun), a museum devoted to the history of mining in Durango, is located on the east side of the plaza.

Museo de Arqueología de Durango Ganot-Peschard
MUSEUM

(⏏618-813-10-47; Zaragoza 315 Sur; adult/child M$10/5; ⊗10am-6pm Tue-Fri, 11am-6pm Sat & Sun) This small, somewhat dated museum has fascinating displays and collection of artifacts from the different indigenous peoples who've lived in the region since the Paleolithic era. Particularly impressive (and a little eerie) is an exhibit of deformed skulls and funerary items of the Aztlan tribe. Kids may enjoy the recreation of an archaeological dig, complete with dim lighting, skeletons and pottery.

Museo Palacio de los Gurza
MUSEUM

(⏏618-811-17-20; Negrete 901 Poniente; adult/child M$10/5; ⊗10am-6pm Tue-Sun) This small museum, housed in a gorgeous 18th-century home, has rotating exhibits of modern art by up-and-coming Mexican artists; pieces often have politicized messages about Mexico or its neighbor to the north. Oddly, there's also a permanent exhibit showcasing a collection of old Mexican coins and antique money-making machines.

Museo Regional de Durango
MUSEUM

(El Aguacate; ⏏618-813-10-94; www.museo.ujed.mx; Victoria 100 Sur; adult/child M$10/5; ⊗8am-3pm Mon, 8am-6pm Tue-Fri, 11am-6pm Sat & Sun; ⏳) In a palatial French-style, 19th-century mansion, this museum has thorough displays on Durango state's geology, history and culture. Durango's main indigenous population, the Tepehuan people, and the area's impressive array of minerals get special attention; there also are paintings by Miguel Cabrera. Most explanations are in English and Spanish.

🏃 Activities

Paseo Teleférico
CABLE CAR

(Av Florida 1145; adult/child M$20/10; ⊗10am-9pm Tue-Sun; ⏳) This gondola takes visitors from a small hill in the center of Durango, Cerro del Calvario, to a viewpoint just 680m away, Cerro de los Remedios. A simple ride, it's all about the journey as the views from the air far outshine those at the destination. An easy, cheap outing.

🎊 Festivals & Events

Feria Nacional
FAIR

(⏏618-161-00-70; www.ferianacionaldurango.gob.mx; Hwy 23 Km 3.5; M$15; ⊗late June–mid-July; ⏳) For three weeks between late June and mid-July, Durango's big annual party remembers its agricultural roots with *charreadas* (Mexican rodeos) plus a *duranguense* music and culture fest. Amusement-park rides and food vendors round out the festivities. Free transportation is typically offered to the fairgrounds, which are 9km from the center; check the website for pick-up/drop-off spots.

🛏 Sleeping

★La Casa de Bruno
HOSTEL $

(⏏618-811-55-55; www.lacasadebrunohostal.com; Bruno Martínez 508 Sur; dm/r M$230/350; ⊜🛜) An artsy, welcoming place, this downtown hostel has three dorms, all with tall bunks that have thick mattresses, cozy bedding and privacy curtains. Two tiny private rooms are set apart from the dorms, but follow suit in comfort. There's a small common kitchen and coffee and pastries are offered each morning. A great place to meet other travelers.

Posada de María
BOUTIQUE HOTEL $$$

(⏏618-158-12-17; www.posadademaria.mx; 5 de Febrero 922; r/ste incl breakfast from M$2500/3100; 🅿✳❄⊛) Located in the heart of downtown Durango, each room in this renovated colonial *casona* (mansion) is modern and plush with Victorian-era-meets-Mexico flair (think Tiffany lamps and Oaxacan fabrics). There are loads of inviting lounge areas, including a lap pool and rooftop with enviable views. A restaurant and massage room (even a hair salon) are pluses.

Hostal de la Monja

HOTEL $$$

(☎618-837-17-19; www.hostaldelamonja.com.mx; Constitución 214 Sur; r/ste incl breakfast from M$1693/1994; P ⊕ ❄ 🛜) This 19th-century mansion facing the cathedral has been tastefully converted into an atmospheric 20-room hotel and is one of the best addresses in central Durango. The comfortable rooms manage to combine tradition and modern amenities well and there's a good restaurant too. Request a room at the back if you're noise sensitive, however, as sound from the restaurant carries. Wi-fi is hit and miss in the lobby and almost nonexistent in the rooms.

✗ Eating & Drinking

Specialties in Durango include *caldillo duranguense* (Durango stew), made with *machaca* (dried shredded meat) and *ate* (pronounced 'ah-tay' – a quince paste enjoyed with cheese).

★ Cremería Wallander

DELI $

(☎618-811-77-05; www.wallander.com.mx; Independencia 128 Norte; meals M$60-140; ⊙8:30am-9pm Mon-Sat, 9am-4pm Sun; ❄ 🛜 🖉 🖶) This delightful deli sells the artisanal products of the Wallander family farm as well as regional delicacies, fresh bread, preserves and pastries. Outside in the back courtyard you can enjoy healthy breakfasts, mega *tortas* (sandwiches) and sublime pizzas. Foodies will love the selection here, while for everyone else it'll be a welcome break from standard Mexican dishes.

La Tetera Bistro Cafe

BISTRO $

(☎618-195-53-78; Callejon Florida 1135; meals M$65-95; ⊙8am-10pm Sun-Thu, to 11pm Fri-Sat; 🛜) This cool-cat cafe specializes in light meals – crepes, sandwiches, salads – made with fresh, locally sourced ingredients. Seating is open-air, at wood tables or any number of cozy couches; plants and boho art fill the space. Not hungry? There's a huge array of teas, coffee drinks and smoothies too. Friday and Saturday evenings bring twinkling lights and live music. Located on a pedestrian side street, just up an outdoor set of stairs.

Gorditas Durango

MEXICAN $

(☎618-164-44-98; Plaza Centenario, cnr Pino Suárez & Zaragoza; meal M$30-50; ⊙8am-5pm; ⓘ) For good cheap eats, pop into this locals' eatery. Specializing in *gorditas* (a small, thick tortilla stuffed with your choice of fillings) – two or three are enough to make a hefty meal. Fillings range from *bistek* (steak) and *chicharrón* (fried pork belly) to *nopales* (cactus) and *mole* (chicken in a spicy chocolate sauce). Burritos also offered.

Fonda de la Tía Chona

MEXICAN $$

(☎618-812-77-48; www.facebook.com/FondaTia Chona; Negral 110; mains M$80-180; ⊙5-11:30pm Mon-Sat, 1-5:30pm Sun) A Durango institution, this richly atmospheric, venerable place is dedicated to local cuisine such as *caldillos* (beef stews) and delicious *chiles en nogadas* (peppers in walnut sauce).

Birriería Mendoza

MEXICAN $$

(☎618-811-56-43; www.facebook.com/Birrieria MendozaDurango; Hidalgo 317; mains M$70-150; ⊙8am-5pm Sun-Thu, to 11pm Fri & Sat) *Antiques Roadshow* meets colonial Mexico in this quirky restaurant. Here, *birria* (goat stew, typical of Jalisco) gets Duranguense twists by incorporating guajillo and pasilla chilies or substituting lamb chops and ribs. Tables themselves are set in a colonial building decorated with loads of antiques like old radios, milk jugs and grandfather clocks. A memorable stop for your belly and eyes.

BUSES FROM DURANGO

DESTINATION	FARE (M$)	DURATION (HR)	FREQUENCY (DAILY)
Chihuahua	840	8½-11	12
Los Mochis	1090	6	3
Mazatlán	600	3	11
Mexico City (Terminal Norte)	1270	11-13	14
Monterrey (via Saltillo)	835	7	8
Parral	595	6	10
Zacatecas	415	4-5	hourly

Restaurant Playa Azul
SEAFOOD $$

(☑ 618-811-93-73; www.facebook.com/playaazul durango; Constitución 241 Norte; dishes M$90-200; ⊙ 10am-10pm; ⏺) Fish and shrimp don't immediately leap to mind in an inland city such as Durango, but this seafood specialist is one of the best restaurants in town. Service in the colorfully decorated 18th-century patio is professional, and you can choose from 20 ways of preparing grouper fillets or a range of seafood cocktails, including the six-ingredient Molotov.

★Wirikuta Cafe
CAFE

(☑ 618-812-69-52; www.facebook.com/pg/wiri kutacafe; Florida 1201; ⊙ 8am-11pm; 🛜) Mindblowingly good coffee is dispensed at this sleek cafe, where coffee culture is taken seriously. The friendly and passionate baristas also sell excellent pastries and artisanal breads. For something more substantial, there's also a menu featuring crepes, sandwiches and fresh salads.

❶ Information

Durango State Tourist Office (☑ 618-811-11-07; www.durango.gob.mx; Florida 1106; ⊙ 8am-8pm Mon-Fri, 10am-6pm Sat & Sun) has friendly and enthusiastic English-speaking staff and lots of brochures; it has a satellite **information kiosk** (Blvd Villa 101; ⊙ 9am-9pm Mon, Tue, Thu, Fri & Sat, 9am-3pm Sun & Wed) at the bus station. The city also has a **kiosk** (☑ 618-137-84-31; www.durangotravel. mx; ⊙ 9am-8pm Tue-Sun) on the Plaza de Armas, inside the bandstand.

Hospital General (☑ 618-813-00-11; cnr Av 5 de Febrero & Fuentes; ⊙ 24hr) For emergencies or walk-in medical care.

Post Office (Av 20 de Noviembre 1016 Oriente; ⊙ 8am-4pm Mon-Fri, 9am-1pm Sat) Durango's main post office.

❶ Getting There & Away

Aeropuerto Guadalupe Victoria (☑ 618-118-70-12; www.oma.aero; Autopista Durango-Gómez Palacios Km 15.5), 20km northeast of town on Hwy 40D, is a relatively quiet regional airport. It is serviced by Aeromexico (www.aeromexico.com) and TAR Aerolíneas (www.tarmexico.com). A taxi here from central Durango costs about M$250.

The **Central Camionera de Durango** (☑ 618-818-36-63; Blvd Villa 101), 5km east of the center, has frequent bus departures, including several 1st-class options.

❶ Getting Around

'ISSSTE' or 'Centro' buses (M$9) from the Central de Autobuses parking lot get you to the Plaza de Armas. Metered taxis cost about M$40 to the center.

To reach the Central de Autobuses from downtown, catch **'Camionera' buses** (Negrete s/n) on Calle Negrete, one block south of the Museo Regional. Get off before the major intersection with the Pancho Villa equestrian monument and a McDonald's, and walk a short way northeast.

NORTHEAST MEXICO

The northeast has never been Mexico's main tourism draw, and news of cartel-related violence has turned off travelers even more. But the northeast's history, sights and people are remarkable, and all the more rewarding for being unexpected. Monterrey is a lively modern city, while nearby Saltillo oozes colonial charm. You can check out the idyllic wine country of Parras and the unique desert ecosystem at Cuatro Ciénegas, one of Mexico's most biologically diverse regions.

The security situation is serious but not paralyzing. Although news of the drug wars have faded considerably, border towns like Nuevo Laredo and Matamoros, and the surrounding areas can be tense. Monterrey also has neighborhoods that are best avoided. That said, virtually all the violence pits one cartel against the other, and tourists are rarely affected. Keep your wits about you and discover the myriad treasures the northeast has to offer.

Saltillo

🗐 844 / POP 762,000 / ELEV 1600M

Set high in the arid Sierra Madre Oriental, Saltillo is a large and fast-growing place with the normal endless sprawl of any big Mexican city, but with a center that maintains a relaxed small-town feel. Founded in 1577, it's the northeast's oldest town, boasting fine colonial buildings and cracking cultural surprises (some leading art galleries and museums). Most attractions are conveniently central, and a burgeoning student population adds energy. It's also on the main routes between the northeast border and central Mexico, making it a decent spot to break a journey.

◉ Sights

Saltillo's cultural core around the expansive Plaza de Armas is replete with historic buildings and ideal for exploring on foot. Alameda Zaragoza, Saltillo's green lung, is six blocks northwest of the plaza.

★ Museo del Desierto   MUSEUM

(☑ 844-986-90-00; www.museodeldesierto.org; Parque Maravillas, Blvd Davila 3745; adult/child M$110/60; ☉ 10am-5pm Tue-Sun; 🖼) Saltillo's top attraction, this no-expense-spared natural history museum is highly enjoyable and informative (even if you don't speak Spanish). Exhibits explore the Chihuahuense Desert (the largest desert is North America), reveal why sea currents can create deserts and how sand dunes are formed. Children will love the dinosaurs, particularly the *Tyrannosaurus rex*. There's also a reptile house, prairie dogs, gray wolves and a botanical garden with more than 400 cactus species.

Centro Cultural Vito Alessio Robles   HISTORIC BUILDING

(☑ 844-412-86-45; cnr Hidalgo & Aldama; ☉ 10am-6pm Tue-Sat, 11am-6pm Sun; 🖼) FREE Once Saltillo's city hall, this cultural center houses the most extensive mural painted by a woman in Mexico. At 500 sq m, it is remarkable and inspiring work of art that tells the history of Saltillo; it took almost three years for Helena Huerta Muzquiz to complete. Beyond the murals, there are several rooms exhibiting Huerta Muzquiz' range of works, including drawings in charcoal and wood engravings.

Museo del Sarape y Trajes Mexicanos   MUSEUM

(☑ 844-481-69-00; Allende 160 Sur; ☉ 10am-6pm Tue-Sun; 🖼) FREE An excellent museum devoted to the Mexican *sarapes* (blankets with an opening for the head) that Saltillo is famous for. There's a priceless collection to admire, and lots of fascinating background information about weaving techniques, looms, natural dyes and regional variations. There's also a small section of regional dresses from around the country. You'll find very detailed English information in each room and there's a store next door for purchases.

Museo de las Aves de México   MUSEUM

(Museum of Mexican Birds; ☑ 844-414-01-68; www.museodelasaves.org; Hidalgo 151; adult/child M$40/20; ☉ 10am-6pm Tue-Sat, 11am-6pm Sun; 🖼) Mexico ranks 10th in the world in terms of avian diversity, and this fascinating museum displays more than 800 stuffed and mounted species, many in convincing dioramas of their natural habitat. Exhibits are divided by ecosystem: desert, ocean, rain forest, mangrove etc. There are special sections featuring multimedia exhibits on feathers, beaks, migration and similar subjects too. Signage in Spanish and English. Guided tours available.

Catedral de Saltillo   CHURCH

(☑ 844-414-02-30; www.facebook.com/santocristo saltillo; Plaza de Armas; ☉ 9am-1pm & 4-7:30pm; 🖼) Built between 1745 and 1800, Saltillo's cathedral has one of Mexico's finest Churrigueresque facades, with columns of elaborately carved pale-gray stone. In an unusual touch, given the Catholic church's traditionally dim view of indigenous religions, the central dome features carvings of Quetzalcóatl, the Aztec rain god.

🛏 Sleeping

Hotel Colonial San Miguel   HOTEL $$

(☑ 844-410-30-44; www.hotelcolonialsaltillo.com; General Cepeda Sur 410; r M$850; 🅿❄✱🛜🏊) This fine little hotel pays kitschy homage to the Italian Renaissance: ornamental columns next to the pool, statues and stone angels everywhere, even a Sistine Chapel replica on the restaurant ceiling. Rooms themselves are spared the theme; instead, they are modern, sleek and squeaky clean with good beds and linens. Some have Juliette balconies with nice city views. Service is excellent.

Hotel Rancho el Morillo   HISTORIC HOTEL $$

(☑ 844-417-40-78; www.ranchoelmorillo.com; Coahuila 6; r US$60-75; 🅿❄🛜🏊) Founded in 1934, this highly atmospheric hacienda on the edge of Saltillo is set in extensive grounds with trails that take in a pine forest, orchard and semi-desert. The family owners are very welcoming and good meals are prepared – after which the homemade *licor de membrillo* (quince liquor) is the perfect digestif.

✗ Eating & Drinking

The foodie scene ranges from superb *fondas* (family-run eateries) to smart restaurants near the Plaza de Armas.

Flor y Canela CAFE $

(📞 844-414-31-43; www.facebook.com/florycanela centro; Juárez 257; meals M$70-120; ⏱8:30am-9:30pm Mon-Fri, 4:30-9:30pm Sat & Sun; 🛜🅿) A welcoming cafe with a boho ambience, Flor y Canela specializes in homey breakfasts, daily set-lunch specials (three courses for M$110), paninis and salads. There's an espresso machine for organic coffee drinks, and lots of *postre* (dessert) action on the menu. Wine and cocktails are available.

El Tapanco Restaurante INTERNATIONAL $$$

(📞 844-414-00-43; www.facebook.com/ElTa pancoSaltillo; Allende 225; mains M$180-350; ⏱noon-11pm Mon-Sat, to 5pm Sun; 🅿) One of the most elegant restaurants in town, this family-run place has an atmospheric interior and courtyard seating accented by a gurgling fountain. The menu includes seafood and fish dishes, as well as a long list of meat grills. Try the *cabrería azteca* (beef with black mushrooms), the duck tacos or the house specialty, *perejil frito* (fried parsley).

Taberna El Cerdo de Babel BAR

(📞 844-135-53-60; www.facebook.com/ElCer dito; Ocampo 324; ⏱4pm-1am Mon, 3pm-2am Tue-Sat) Once a 16th-century Franciscan convent, this boho-hipster tavern has live music, regular art exhibits and film showings. Seating is spread over two floors, including a leafy front patio, along a pedestrian walkway. A popular spot, this place is a go-to for university students, professors and professionals.

La Puerta al Cielo COCKTAIL BAR

(📞 844-139-97-51; Allende 148; ⏱5pm-1am Tue-Sat) Mixologists serve up beautiful and delicious concoctions and craft beers at this open-air bar in the heart of town. The patio setting features graffiti art, twinkling lights, and live music on weekends. A menu of innovative burgers, salads and pastas is offered too.

🛍 Shopping

El Sarape de Saltillo ARTS & CRAFTS

(📞 844-414-96-34; elsarapedesaltillo@gmail.com; Hidalgo 305; ⏱9:30am-1:30pm & 3:30-7:30pm Mon-Sat) With rooms upon rooms, this seemingly endless shop sells fine quality, colorful *sarapes* (blankets with an opening for the head) and other Mexican arts and crafts; see wool being dyed and woven on looms inside.

ℹ Information

Municipal Tourist Office (📞 844-439-71-95; Allende 124; ⏱8am-3pm Mon-Fri) This small office is staffed by knowledgable and friendly folks. English spoken.

ℹ Getting There & Away

AIR

Saltillo's **Plan de Guadalupe Airport** (📞 844-488-00-40; Carretera Saltillo–Monterrey Km 13.5, Ramos Arizpe) is 16km northeast of town and has regular flights to Mexico City. There are buses between Saltillo's bus terminal and Monterrey's airport (M$200), which has many more flights.

BUS

The **bus station** (📞 844-417-01-84; Periférico Echeverría s/n; 🛜) is on the south side of town, 2.5km from the center. Direct departures to many destinations leave at least hourly, with the exceptions of Durango (it's often quicker to change in Torreón) and Cuatro Ciénegas. Bus

BUSES FROM SALTILLO

DESTINATION	FARE (M$)	DURATION (HR)	FREQUENCY (DAILY)
Cuatro Ciénegas	300	5	1
Durango	535-660	6½	5
Mexico City (Terminal Norte)	955-1230	10	12
Monterrey	120-140	1¾	every 45min
Nuevo Laredo	340-463	4-5	every 45min
Parras	140	2½	7
San Luis Potosí	540	5	hourly
Torreón	355-385	3	hourly
Zacatecas	455	4½-5½	hourly

lines include Transportes Chihuahuenses, Futura, ETN and Omnibus de México.

To reach the city center from the bus station, take bus 9 (M$9) from in front of the station; on the return, catch bus 9 on Aldama, between Zaragoza and Hidalgo.

❶ Getting Around

TO/FROM THE AIRPORT
There are car rental agencies at the airport. A taxi to/from the center costs around M$150.

Parras

☑ 842 / POP 44,900 / ELEV 1520M

A graceful and historic oasis town in the heart of the Coahuilan desert some 160km west of Saltillo, Parras has a beautifully cared-for center of real colonial character and a delightfully temperate climate, both of which have contributed to its reputation for being one of northern Mexico's next big things.

However, Parras is most famous for its wine: the *parras* (grapevines) that give the town its name have grown here since the late 16th century, and its most famous vineyard, Casa Madero, is the oldest winery in the Americas.

With great places to stay, gorgeous surroundings and all that vino, this is a place where you can easily linger for days.

❍ Sights

The biggest attractions in Parras are the town's wineries, located on the outskirts.

Casa Madero   WINERY
(☑ 842-422-01-11; www.madero.com.mx; Carretera 102 Pila-Parras Km 18.2; tour adult/child under 12yr M$20/free; ☺ 9am-5pm; ☖) This, the first winery in the Americas, was established at Parras in 1597, a year before the town itself sprang up. It's now an industrial-sized operation exporting wine all over the world, although it's still housed on pleasingly old-fashioned premises. Casa Madero offers 45-minute tours through the history of winemaking, featuring equipment old and new.

You can buy quality wine and brandy on site though there are no tastings, unfortunately. From near the main plaza in Parras, catch one of the regular buses (M$20) that pass the winery; just tell your driver where you want to get off. Or take a taxi (M$80); the winery is 7km north of Parras.

Vinos El Vesubio   WINERY
(☑ 842-422-38-88; andres.rdemingo@gmail.com; Madero 36; ☺ 10am-7pm) FREE Founded in 1891, this quaint winery is known for its artisanal sweet red wines. Tours take visitors through its homegrown production process, a few barrel rooms and the bottling area. Tastings are in its small shop, in front of the family home. It's well worth a visit to soak up the wonderful atmosphere, as much to purchase wine.

Iglesia del Santo Madero   CHURCH
(Morales Padilla s/n; ☺ 10am-5pm) This deeply striking and rather iconic church perched precariously on the rocky outcrop on the south edge of town has – once you've undergone the steep-but-rewarding 293-step climb up – some wonderful, expansive views over the town and its vineyards. It's a 30-minute walk from the center, east along Madero then up Aguirre Benavides.

✦✦ Festivals & Events

★ Feria de la Uva   FERIA
(☺ early–mid-Aug; ♠) Every August thousands of people descend upon Parras to celebrate wine, the lifeblood of the region. For two weeks there are parades featuring *vendimiadoras* (barefoot grape crushers), live dance and music performances, sporting events, religious ceremonies, a crowning of the queen of the fair, and wine, wine, wine. The entire event comes to cacophonous climax – a dance party at Casa Madero.

⌶ Sleeping

★ Foggara Hotel   BOUTIQUE HOTEL $$
(☑ 842-422-04-59; www.foggara.com.mx; Cazadores 111; r M$1000-1200; ☖☎) At this gorgeous hotel set in a historic home, rooms combine colonial structure with high-end mid-century moden decor. Bathrooms are spacious with colorful tile work. Outdoor common areas include a pleasant courtyard and leafy terrace with loungers and hanging wicker chairs. The common thread: a sense of pampering and ease. A perfect getaway.

Casona del Banco   BOUTIQUE HOTEL $$$
(☑ 842-422-19-54; www.lacasonadelbanco.com; Ramos Arizpe 285; r/ste incl breakfast from M$3273/3808; ᴘ☖☀☎) For a proper splurge, opt for shabby-chic luxury on a grand and impressive scale at this wonderful – if definitely overpriced – conversion of a bank. The 24 plush rooms surround two

grassy courtyards, and the public areas, including a lounge and stylish bar, are breathtaking. Children 10 and over only. Located toward the northern entrance to town.

✕ Eating

Parras is packed with *dulcerías* (candy stores) selling the region's famous *queso de higo* (fudgy candy with figs), but sadly its eating options still have a way to go to catch up.

Tortas y Tacos Cri Cri MEXICAN $
(Plaza del Reloj, Colegio Militar s/n; meals M$40-60; ⊙ 11am-8pm; 🖘) As the name suggests, this hole-in-the-wall serves up mouthwatering *tortas* (Mexican sandwiches), tacos and – surprise! – hamburgers too. Sitting on Plaza del Reloj, it's a bustling place so its two tables are almost always full. Do like locals do and order your meal to go and enjoy it on a bench, just a few meters away.

★ Las Parras
de Santa Maria INTERNATIONAL $$
(☎ 842-422-00-60; www.lasparrasdesantamaria.com; Cayuso 12; mains M$55-195; ⊙ 9am-10pm Mon-Sat, to 6pm Sun; 🖘) With massive wood doors, 18-foot ceilings, arches upon arches and whitewashed walls, there's no doubt you're in a colonial-era building. Meals are more international – from Mexican classics to pasta dishes, all carefully prepared. The highlight, though, is the paella. Award-winning, it comes with loads of shrimp, clams and fish plus a glass of sangria and even tapas. Come hungry!

El Méson de Don Evaristo MEXICAN $$
(☎ 842-422-64-53; www.facebook.com/Mesonde DonEvaristo; cnr Madero & Cayuso; mains M$80-210; ⊙ 8am-10pm; 🖘) In the middle of town, this friendly courtyard restaurant serves up meals on tables surrounding a small fountain. The mood is colonial splendor, but the food is pretty standard Mexican fare, including a good selection of breakfasts (M$50 to M$80) and even espresso when the machine is working.

ⓘ Information

The **main tourist office** (☎ 842-422-31-84; Ramos Arizpe 122; ⊙ 10:30am-3:30pm Mon-Sat) has helpful staff who give out free town maps. Some English is spoken. There's a small **information kiosk** (cnr Ramos Arizpe & Colegio Milltar; ⊙ 10am-3pm) on the Plaza del Reloj as well.

ⓘ Getting There & Away

There are two bus stations in town, both with only 2nd-class service, though buses are perfectly comfortable and air-conditioned.

The **Parras-Saltillo bus station** (☎ 842-422-08-70; García 2B) is a small but modern station with seven daily buses to/from Saltillo (M$140, 2½ hours) and four daily to/from Monterrey (M$220, 3½ hours).

The **Parras-Torreón station** (Ramos Arizpe 179) is near the Plaza de Armas but is very run down. From here, you can make your way to Cuatro Ciénegas without backtracking to Saltillo. To do so, catch a bus to San Pedro Las Colonias (M$100, 1½ hours, five daily) and then a bus from there to Cuatro Ciénegas (M$150, two hours, nine daily).

Cuatro Ciénegas

☎ 869 / POP 13,000 / ELEV 747M

The serene and remote frontier town of Cuatro Ciénegas is bespeckled with adobe and colonial buildings and a handful of hotels and restaurants. It's a pleasantly out-of-the-way spot to enjoy the natural world of northern Mexico, and the perfect base for exploring the remarkable Área de Protección de Flora y Fauna Cuatrociénegas – a 843-sq-km nature reserve in the Chihuahuense desert with turquoise rivers, strikingly white sand dunes, and breathtaking mountain views – considered one of the most biologically diverse places in the world.

⊙ Sights

★ Área de Protección
de Flora y Fauna
Cuatrociénegas NATURE RESERVE
(Cuatrociénegas Nature Reserve; ☎ 869-696-02-99; http://cuatrocienegas.conanp.gob.mx; Hwy 30; M$30; ⊙ 10am-5pm; 🅿 🖘 🐾) With hundreds of shimmering cerulean *pozas* (pools) and streams in the middle of the Desierto Chihuahuense (Chihuahuan Desert), this 843-sq-km nature reserve is a surreal sight. Fed by more than 500 underground springs, it's a desert habitat of extraordinary biological diversity, often compared to the Galapagos Islands. It's home to over 70 endemic species, including three kinds of turtles and 11 kinds of fish, as well as primitive organisms called *estromatolitos* (stromatolites), which are linked to the creation of Earth's oxygen-rich atmosphere.

Some pools and the nearby river have been set aside for recreational activities, including swimming. Much of the area is off-limits to the public, as it's being studied by researchers from organizations as diverse as NASA and UNAM.

Even if you don't have your own transportation, exploring the area alone is tricky, as the desert tracks are not always signposted. Using the services of a guide is wise. Certified guides can be hired at the **Poza Azul Visitors Center** (☑ 869-107-72-50; www.cuatrocienegas.conanp.gob.mx; Hwy 30; ⊙10am-5pm; P ♿ 🐾); in town, both tourist information offices have lists of recommended guides.

Though it is theoretically possible to visit the park without a car (buses to Torreón will drop you at the entrances to sites around the park, but usually won't stop to pick people up), it's not advisable: distances are long, tracks are poorly marked and there is little shade.

★ Dunas de Yeso   DUNES
(Los Arenales; Hwy 30; 🐾) Located within the Cuatrociénegas Reserve, these blinding-white gypsum sand dunes – the second largest in North America – contrast superbly with the six rocky mountain ranges that ring the valley. To visit you'll need your own transportation and a guide. (The gate to the dunes is locked and only they have access to the key.) A licensed guide can be hired at the Poza Azul Visitors Center. The dunes are located 18km southwest of town, at the end of a sand road.

Mina de Mármol   VIEWPOINT
(Hwy 30; M$30; ⊙9:30am-5:30pm Mon-Fri; P ♿) Massive slabs of marble, much of it encrusted with fossils of fish and other marine life that swam in this valley when it was an ocean, greet you at this one-time mine. Beyond the spectacular rocks, this site has impressive vistas of the Cuatrociénegas Reserve with views of the cerulean pools and rivers, starkly white dunes, and mountain ranges all around.

Museo Casa
Venustiano Carranza   MUSEUM
(☑ 869-696-13-75; Carranza 109; ⊙10am-6pm Tue-Sun; ♿) **FREE** Housed in Venustiano Carranza's childhood home, this well-conceived museum relates the life story of Cuatro Ciénegas' most famous son. From mayor to senator to governor to revolutionary leader to Mexican president, Carranza was a lifelong politician who was known as

savvy but stubborn. (He was assassinated in 1920.) Multimedia exhibits, personal effects and photos are displayed throughout the gorgeously restored home. Knowledgable guides walk visitors through the exhibits, highlighting special pieces. Signage in Spanish only. Donations requested.

🏃 Activities

★ Río Los Mezquites   SWIMMING
(☑ 869-696-04-08; Hwy 30; adult/child M$85/65; ⊙10am-6:30pm Mon-Fri, to 7pm Sat & Sun) Swimming with the fish and turtles in this sublime stretch of slow-flowing blue water amid the desert landscape of the Cuatrociénegas nature reserve is a surreal, revitalizing experience. There are *palapas* (thatched shelters), picnic tables and even grills. Several sets of ladders and steps lead visitors into the water (or do as the kids do and cannonball in). Last visitors admitted at 5pm. From town, look for the turnoff just before the Poza Azul Visitor Center.

🍃 Tours

One- to three-day excursions of the spectacular Cuatrociénegas Reserve (p797) can be organized with certified guides for about M$700 per person per day. Contact them through either of the tourist information offices. Rates include car transportation.

If you have your own wheels, guides also can be hired directly at the Poza Azul Visitors Center. Tours organized by the Hotel Misión Marielena also are recommended.

🛏 Sleeping & Eating

Hotel Misión Marielena   HOTEL $$
(☑ 869-696-11-51; www.hotelmisionmarielena.com.mx; Hidalgo 200; r M$650-940; P ♿ ❄ 🛜 ♿) Excellent value, this historic hotel on the central plaza has large, well-maintained rooms with modern furnishings reminiscent of a Motel 8: clean, comfortable and totally unremarkable. Rooms are set around two leafy courtyards with a pool and mountain views. The on-site restaurant is one of the best in town. Information about area sites is freely given and tours easily arranged too.

Gorditas   MEXICAN $
(Hidalgo s/n; meal M$25-50; ⊙5am-1pm; 🖊 ♿) A mom-and-pop eatery with plastic tables and chairs, Gorditas specializes in just that – *gorditas*, small thick tortillas stuffed to the brim with all manner of taste treats for meat- and veggie-lovers alike. On Sundays,

locals fill the place for the big steaming bowls of *menudo* (a spicy tripe-based soup) on offer. Look for the bright yellow building abuzz with diners.

La Misión
MEXICAN $

(☑ 869-696-11-51; Hidalgo 200; dishes $50-110; ⊙ 7:39am-10:30pm; ☑) La Misión serves up some of the best meals in town with quality ingredients and made-to-order care. The menu is mostly traditional Mexican, but there are pasta, sandwich and salad options too. Servings are huge, so come hungry. Local wines offered too. Located inside the Hotel Misión Marielena.

Cantina El 40
MEXICAN $$

(☑ 869-696-00-40; www.facebook.com/el40cuatrocienegas; Zaragoza 204; dishes M$90-130; ⊙ noon-2am Wed-Mon; ☑) A swanky restaurant-bar with a colonial-meets-cowboy theme, Cantina El 40 serves up solid Mexican eats with flair. Think gourmet street tacos and sizzling *molcajete* dishes (meals served in a stone mortar and pestle) paired with top-shelf cocktails and local wines. Seating is either indoors at thick wood tables with cow-patterned chairs or outdoors in a breezy courtyard.

ℹ Information

There are two tourist information offices: the tiny but helpful **municipal tourist office** (☑ 869-696-06-50; Carranza 100; ⊙ 9am-3pm Mon-Fri) on Plaza Central and the **state tourist office** (☑ 869-696-05-74; Zaragoza 206; ⊙ 9am-4pm Mon-Fri), which is only occasionally open.

ℹ Getting There & Away

The **bus terminal** (Blvd Juárez s/n) is in front of a paint shop, near the eastern entrance to town. First-class buses run to Torreón (M$367, 3½ hours, seven daily), Saltillo (M$300, five hours, one daily) and Monterrey (M$344, 5½ hours, one daily); a 2nd-class bus heads to the border at Piedras Negras (M$411, six hours, six daily).

Monterrey

☑ 81 / POP 1.1 MILLION / ELEV 540M

Cosmopolitan Monterrey is Mexico's third-largest city, second-largest industrial center and *número uno* in per-capita income. This economic powerhouse has a strong entrepreneurial ethos, humming cultural scene, vibrant universities and an urban hipster nightlife scene.

With sprawling suburbs of gargantuan air-conditioned malls and manicured housing estates, this is also one of Mexico's most Americanized cities. Boasting world-class museums and a jagged mountain backdrop that offers terrific outdoor adventure sports, the city's attractions are diverse and myriad.

All of this makes Monterrey fiercely independent and very different from any other Mexican metropolis. Notably, the city experienced the drug wars up close and personal, but by 2017 cultural life was back with aplomb, especially around the Macroplaza, with thriving restaurants and bars in the newly safe Barrio Antiguo. Nevertheless, narco gangs still affect some neighborhoods, including Colonia Independencia just across the Río Santa Catarina – avoid it day or night.

History

Dating from 1596, the city did not begin to prosper until after Mexican independence – thanks to its proximity to the US, which gave it advantages in trade and smuggling.

In 1900 the first heavy industry in Latin America, a vast iron and steel works (now the site of the Parque Fundidora), rose to dominate the cityscape. Monterrey was soon dubbed the 'Pittsburgh of Mexico,' and still produces about 25% of Mexico's raw steel. The city also churns out around 60% of the nation's cement and half of its beer.

◉ Sights

Most major sights are concentrated around the extraordinary Macroplaza in the center and the atmospheric Barrio Antiguo quarter. Further east, at the far end of a beautiful river walk, is the city's other main cultural hub: the Parque Fundidora. Also adding to Monterrey's charm is the awe-inspiring nearby scenery. Just be sure to check the local security situation before embarking on a trip outside the city.

★ Paseo Santa Lucía
PARK

(Plaza 400 Años; ⊙ 24hr; ☑ ☑) The stunning 2.4km promenade of Paseo Santa Lucía is a world-class example of urban regeneration. This (artificial) river forms a turquoise ribbon through the heart of industrial Monterrey. Take a stroll down this delightful leafy pathway, or hop in one of the regular river boats (10:30am to 9pm; adult/child return

Monterrey

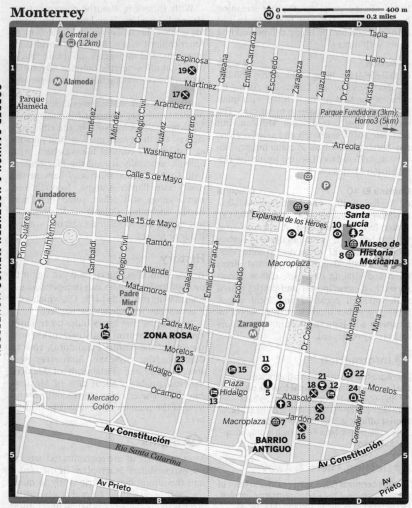

M$60/40). The landscaping is amazing, with lighting illuminating the water at night plus the 27 striking bridges and 13 fountains spanning the river.

There's 24-hour security, a few bars and restaurants at its western end and the whole promenade has free public wi-fi. Boats leave from a dock on Plaza 400 Años (p802).

★ Horno3

MUSEUM

(Museum of Steel; ☑ 81-8126-1100; www.horno3. org; Parque Fundidora; adult/child M$100/60; ⏱10am-6pm Tue-Thu, 11am-7pm Fri-Sun; Ⓜ Parque Fundidora) Blast Furnace No 3 in the for-

mer industrial site of the Parque Fundidora (p802) has been converted into Horno3, an exceptionally impressive high-tech, hands-on museum devoted to Mexico's steel industry. No expense has been spared here, from the steaming rocks at the entrance to the metal open-air elevator that climbs to the summit for dramatic bird's-eye views of Monterrey (included in admission). The entire process of steel-making is explained (with some English translations) along with its vital relevance to Monterrey and Mexico.

Monterrey

Don't miss the dramatic furnace show, beamed from the bulk of Horno3 itself, and ask about combo zip-lining-rappelling tour (adult/child M$440/270) from the top of the metal tower. Last tickets are sold one hour before closing. There's a good cafe-restaurant, **El Lingote** (🗹 ext 3003 81-8126-1100; www.ellingoterestaurante.com; mains M$90-460; ⊘1pm-midnight Tue-Sat, to 11pm Sun; P🖥; 🚇Parque Fundidora), here too. Had enough of museums but are hankering to see the views from the top? Tickets on the open-air elevator to the summit can be purchased separately (M$45), with rides continuing until 10pm.

★Museo de
Historia Mexicana   MUSEUM
(🗹 81-2033-9898; www.museohistoriamexicana.org.mx; Doctor Coss 445 Sur; adult/child M$40/free; ⊘10am-8pm Tue & Sun, 10am-6pm Wed-Sat; 🚻; 🚇Zaragoza) This sleek modernist museum on the Plaza 400 Años presents an extensive but easily manageable chronological history of Mexico. In the heart of the museum, there's also an Earth section, full of mounted animals and realistic-looking landscapes, representing Mexico's remarkable biodiversity. Signage is mostly in Spanish, though there are strategically placed screens with overviews in English. Free tours –in either language – can be arranged by phoning in advance. Entry is free on Tuesdays and Sundays.

Admission also covers the Museo del Noreste (p802), to which it's attached via a glass-enclosed bridge.

Macroplaza   PLAZA
(Gran Plaza; 🚇Zaragoza) A monument to Monterrey's late-20th-century ambition, this city-block-wide series of interconnected squares, also known as the Gran Plaza, was created in the 1980s by the demolition of a prime chunk of city-center real estate. A controversial but ultimately successful piece of redevelopment, its charm has increased over the years as the once-naked urban space – said to form the largest public square in the world – has been softened by parks, trees and fountains.

Vistas of the surrounding mountains open up between the roster of iconic edifices – classically designed municipal buildings and incongruously modern structures housing some of Mexico's finest museums – that line the Macroplaza. For visitors, it's a delight to explore on foot, as most traffic is directed away from the area by underpasses.

At the southern end of the Macroplaza, the 70m concrete tower **Faro del Comercio** (Lighthouse of Commerce; Zuazua s/n) soars above the city, its green lasers piercing the night sky. The Faro abuts the baroque form of the **Catedral Metropolitano de Monterrey** (🗹81-8342-7831; Zuazua Sur 1100; ⊘7:30am-8pm Mon-Fri, 9am-8pm Sat, 8am-8pm Sun; 🚻), capped by a neon cross. North of here is a shady park, **Plaza Zaragoza**

WORTH A TRIP

PARQUE ECOLÓGICO CHIPINQUE

This stunning **mountainside section** (☎ 818-303-21-90; www.chipinque.org.mx; Carretera a Chipinque Km. 2.5, San Pedro Garza García; pedestrian/cyclist/vehicle M$20/45/60; ☺ 6am-7:30pm) of the Parque Nacional Cumbres de Monterrey is just 12km from downtown. There's great hiking and mountain-biking on almost 80km of trails through dense forest and up rocky peaks, including highest point Copete de Águilas (2200m). A park museum with interactive exhibits, a butterfly atrium and an insect house are especially fun for kids. The visitor center has maps, snacks, trail advice and permits for those heading to the summits. Entry is free at weekends.

Mountain bike rentals (M$200 per hour) and three-hour bike excursions (M$650 per person, including bike) also can be arranged at the visitor center.

Buses to Chipinque leave from the southwest corner of Parque Alameda at 8am, 10am and noon; be sure to ask when the last bus returns. Alternatively, a taxi from downtown costs M$120; ask the driver to return at an agreed-upon time to be sure you have a ride back to town.

(Zuazua s/n; 🚇🚲), popular with snacking families and smooching lovers, and also the venue for open-air concerts and old-school Latin dancing every Sunday.

Continuing north, the rest of the Macroplaza is lined with a succession of concrete municipal structures. If you're a fan of brutalism, you'll love the **Teatro de la Ciudad** and its architectural cousin, the lofty **Congreso del Estado**. Then down some steps is the **Explanada de los Héroes** (Esplanade of the Heroes; cnr Zaragoza & Zuazua; 🚇🚲) lined with statues, and finally the 1908 neoclassical **Palacio de Gobierno** (☎ 81-2020-1021; 5 de Mayo s/n).

Parque Fundidora   PARK
(☎ 81-8126-8500; www.parquefundidora.org; cnr Fundidora & Adolfo Prieto; ☺ 6am-10pm; 🅿🚲; Ⓜ Parque Fundidora) FREE Formerly a vast steel-factory complex, this once-blighted industrial zone has been transformed into a huge urban park. Designers cleverly retained the iconic smoke stacks and industrial relics to give a surreal and at times apocalyptic feel, but also a vibe very much in keeping with Monterrey's heritage. You can jog the trails, rent bikes (from M$40 per hour), ice skate (M$100 per hour), and visit the cultural sights, of which the Horno3 (p800) museum is the undoubted star of the show.

Four other disemboweled redbrick factories comprise the **Centro de las Artes** (www.parquefundidora.org; ☺ 11am-9pm Tue-Sun) FREE, two galleries with high-class rotating exhibitions, a theater and a movie house that screens independent and foreign films.

The metro stops within a 10-minute walk of the park, but the most enjoyable way to get here is to walk or take a boat along Paseo Santa Lucía (p799).

Plaza 400 Años   PLAZA
(Ⓜ Zaragoza) This plaza, graced with fountains and pools, forms an impressive approach to the sleek, modernist Museo de Historia Mexicana (p801) and the **Museo del Noreste** (☎ 81-2033-9898; www.3museos.com; Doctor Coss 445; adult/child M$40/free; ☺ 10am-8pm Tue & Sun, 10am-6pm Wed-Sat; 🚲). It is the terminus of the lovely Paseo Santa Lucía (p799) promenade.

Museo de Arte Contemporáneo   MUSEUM
(MARCO; ☎ 81-8262-4500; www.marco.org.mx; cnr Zuazua & Jardón; adult/child M$90/60; ☺ 10am-6pm Tue & Thu-Sun, 10am-8pm Wed; 🅿; Ⓜ Zaragoza) Don't miss the terrific Museo de Arte Contemporáneo, its entrance marked by Juan Soriano's gigantic black dove sculpture. Inside, its idiosyncratic spaces are filled with water and light, and major exhibitions (almost all temporary; the permanent collection is quite modest) of work by contemporary Mexican and Latin American artists. There's also a small sculpture garden. Call in advance for a tour in English. MARCO also has fine gift shop (p804) and a gourmet restaurant. Admission is free on Wednesdays.

🎊 Festivals & Events

Aniversario de Independencia   CULTURAL
(Explanada de los Héroes, cnr Zaragoza & Zuazua; ☺ Sep 15-16; 🚲; Ⓜ Zaragoza) Monterrey's

biggest celebrations are held on Mexico's Independence Day, September 16, with fireworks, *musica norteña* (country ballads) and a parade. The festivities typically kick-off the evening prior at the Explanada de los Héroes with the traditional cry of independence from city leaders: 'Viva México! Viva la independencia!'

Festival Internacional de Cine en Monterrey   FILM

(www.monterreyfilmfestival.com; per film M$30-40; ☺ late Aug) This impressive festival held in late August showcases Mexican and international art-house films. It's held in different venues around town, including Parque Fundidora's Centro de las Artes.

🛏 Sleeping

Monterrey has few standout accommodations in the center of the city, though most of the main cultural attractions are clustered close by and you'll have the Barrio Antiguo on your doorstep.

Amatle Café Orgánico y Hostal   HOSTAL $

(📱 81-8342-3291; www.amatle.com.mx; Abasolo 881; dm/r incl breakfast from M$240/750; 🛜; Ⓜ Zaragoza) Set behind a boho cafe in Barrio Antiguo, this welcoming hostel has sparse but comfortable dorms, all with wall art, decent beds and air-conditioning. Private rooms are similar in style, only more spacious. Homemade breakfast breads and fresh coffee are served every morning. This place sells out fast, even in the low season – call in advance to secure a bed.

iStay   HOTEL $$

(📱 81-8228-6000; www.istaymty.istay.com.mx; Morelos 191 Poniente; r M$1028-1622; 🅿 ❄ ✳ 🛜 ☒; Ⓜ Padre Mier) A huge concrete hotel that enjoys a great location, facing pedestrianized Morelos and close to Monterrey's Macroplaza. The branding screams 'hip hotel' but iStay's carpeted rooms are actually very standard fare, though comfortable enough and fair value. Rates vary enormously: try booking online to access the best offers.

Krystal Monterrey Hotel   HOTEL $$$

(📱 81-8319-0900; www.krystal-hotels.com; Corregidora 519; r US$77-98, ste US$108; 🅿 ❄ ✳ @ 🛜 ☒; Ⓜ Zaragoza) A 10-story building with spectacular views of the Macroplaza, rooms here are plush and modern, all a study in gray-meets-purple. A business hotel at heart, there are still several lounging areas, a tony restaurant and a pool. The location – just steps from several museums and the Barrio Antiguo – is tough to beat.

Gran Hotel Ancira   HOTEL $$$

(📱 81-8150-7000; www.gammahoteles.com; Ocampo 443 Oriente; r/ste incl breakfast from M$1862/2503; 🅿 ❄ ✳ @ 🛜 ☒; Ⓜ Zaragoza, Padre Mier) One of Monterrey's smartest and most atmospheric hotels is this grand dame, which dates from 1912 and was built in a French art nouveau style. The mirror-ceilinged, gingham-tiled reception and restaurant area is quite something, and how many hotels have a live classical pianist at breakfast? Rooms are spacious and sleek with comfortable, modern amenities. Check the website for deals.

🍴 Eating

Monterrey's signature dish is *cabrito al pastor* (roast kid goat). Barrio Antiguo has a good selection of places to eat (and drink). Nearby **Mercado Juárez** (Av Juárez s/n; mains M$30-50; ☺ 8am-7pm Mon-Sat, to 3pm Sun; Ⓜ Alameda) has family-run eateries selling tasty, cheap grub – though be sure to keep a close eye on your belongings as the market is known as a hot spot for pickpockets.

Taqueria y Carniceria La Mexicana   TACOS $

(📱 81-8340-7175; www.taquerialamexicana.mx; Guerrero 244; meals M$45-60; ☺ 6am-7:45pm Mon-Sat, to 3pm Sun; 🚼; Ⓜ Alameda) Done up like a Mexican party dress, this eatery/butcher shop is an explosion of colors – think talavera tiles and piñatas. *Tacos de Canasta* (steamed tacos) are the specialty and come filled with everything from beans or spicy potatoes to ground beef or *chicharrón* (fried pork belly). Order at the counter and eat at one of the bustling communal tables.

Taller Veganico   VEGETARIAN $

(📱 81-8336-7809; Abasolo 859; dishes M$60-120; ☺ 9am-10pm Mon-Sat, 1-5pm Sun; 🍴🚼; Ⓜ Zaragoza) A variety of healthy plant-based meals – Mexican dishes, sandwiches and Mediterranean delights – are offered at this 2nd-story restaurant in the Barrio Antiguo. Dining is in a sunlight room with concrete floors and handcrafted tables or under umbrellas on an outdoor patio. There's a fresh salsa bar and free refills on the daily *agua* (fruit drink) too.

RECLAIMING THE STREETS

Monterrey has long been known as one of Mexico's most prosperous and business-friendly cities, and it largely avoided the worst narco-troubles during the early part of the country's drug wars. But Mexico's woes caught up with Monterrey in 2011 and 2012, when several high-profile battles between members of the Gulf Cartel and the Zetas killed dozens (mostly gang members) and left locals shocked and terrified.

Governor Rodrigo Medina responded by purging local police forces, which were deemed to be deeply infiltrated by the cartels; over 4000 officers were fired or even jailed. A new state police force, the Fuerza Civil (civil force), was formed, with officers being paid relatively high salaries and given secure compounds to live in. Around the same time, Mexico's newly elected president dialed back federal interventions, and violence subsided in the northeast and throughout Mexico beginning in 2013.

There was an uptick in overall violence in the country during 2016 and 2017, though less noticeably in the northeast, and the streets of Monterrey and elsewhere are returning to normal. (Extortion and kidnapping remain an issue, mostly targeting wealthy business people, both Mexican and foreign.) Tourists were rarely caught in the middle, even in the bad years, and the core areas, like the Macroplaza and the Barrio Antiguo, are safe and pleasant, and well worth visiting.

★ **Madre Oaxaca** MEXICAN $$$
(☎81-8345-1459; www.facebook.com/MadreOax aca.Mty; Jardón 814; mains M$140-260; ☺1-11pm Mon-Sat, to 8pm Sun; ☑; M̄Zaragoza) One of Monterrey's best restaurants, this charmer is set in a historic building and decked out with an extraordinary collection of handicrafts and folk art over its several intimate dining rooms. The menu is loaded with authentic Oaxacan dishes using rich *moles* (chili sauces) – try a mixed *tlayuda oaxaqueña* (huge flat bread with toppings), and save room for the sublime desserts.

Trece Lunas INTERNATIONAL $$
(☎81-1352-1127; http://cafe13lunas.50webs.com; Abasolo 870; mains M$80-180; ☺8am-10pm Sun-Thu, to 12:30am Fri & Sat; ☑; M̄Zaragoza) If you like your decor eclectic, your spaces multicultural and your food purposefully slow, this innovative Barrio Antiguo place may just be right for you. There's a huge menu that is focused on shared plates called *botanas*, which are piled high with food. Throw in vegetarian options, salads, sandwiches and good coffee, and you have a winner.

🍷 Drinking & Nightlife

The heart of Monterrey's nightlife is the Barrio Antiguo, where bars, beer gardens and clubs sit side by side.

Almacén 42 CRAFT BEER
(☎81-8343-2817; www.almacen42.com; Morelos 852 Oriente; ☺5pm-midnight Wed & Thu,

2pm-2am Fri & Sat, 2-10pm Sun; M̄Zaragoza) Shipping containers and guys with bushy beards and tats greet you as you enter this urban hipster bar. Over 42 craft beers are on tap at any given time – all domestic and ranging from sours to stouts. There's a breezy stone patio in back and, when you get the munchies, a solid menu of shared plates and tacos too.

☆ Entertainment

Café Iguana LIVE MUSIC
(☎81-8343-0822; www.cafeiguana.com.mx; Montemayor 927 Sur; ☺7pm-1am Thu, 8pm-2am Fri & Sat; M̄Zaragoza) The epicenter of alternative Monterrey, where the pierced, multi-tattooed, punk-loving tribe gathers en masse, both inside and on the street out front. Cover charge only for live bands.

🛍 Shopping

★**Corredor del Arte** ARTS & CRAFTS, MARKET
(Art Corridor; ☎81-1243-8848; www.facebook. com/CorredorDelArte; cnr Mina & Abasolo; ☺noon-7pm Sun; ⊕; M̄Zaragoza) On Sundays, Calle Mina in the Barrio Antiguo becomes the Corredor del Arte, a wonderful combination of antiques, arts and crafts, and flea market. The whole area comes out to play and you can find one-off items amid the piles of junk. Bands play too.

MARCO Gift Shop ARTS & CRAFTS
(☎81-8262-4500; www.marco.org.mx; cnr Zuazua & Jardón; ☺10am-6pm Tue & Thu-Sun, 10am-8pm

Wed) For high-end gifts and souvenirs, the gift shop at the Museo de Arte Contemporáneo (p802) is a good option. An extensive shop, it features everything from handcrafted jewelry and quirky T-shirts to fine pottery and artsy coffee table books.

Carápan ARTS & CRAFTS
(☎ 81-1911-9911; www.mexicanfolkartdealers.com; Hidalgo 305 Oriente; ⊙10am-7pm Mon-Sat; Ⓜ Padre Mier) This shop is in a whole other class, and is Monterrey's best outlet for *artesanías* (crafts). The genial owner, who is full of advice about what to see and do in Monterrey, stocks museum-quality work from across Mexico. English, Spanish and French spoken.

ⓘ Information

DANGER & ANNOYANCES
The Zona Rosa area on the west side of the Macroplaza, and Barrio Antiguo on the east, are both largely considered safe by day and night, but as in many big cities, it's advisable to avoid walking alone after dark and to stick to the main roads. Across the Río Santa Catarina, the crime-plagued barrio of Colonia Independencia is still affected by narco gangs and should not be entered day or night.

TOURIST INFORMATION
The **Tourist Information Center** (☎ 81-2033-8414; www.nuevoleon.travel; Palacio de Gobierno, 5 de Mayo s/n; ⊙9am-5pm Mon-Fri, 10am-6pm Sat & Sun; Ⓜ Zaragoza) has friendly, English-speaking staff offering plentiful information about sights and events across Nuevo León.

There are kiosks at the **bus station** (Av Colón 855; Ⓜ Cuauhtémoc) and **Parque Fundidora** (cnr Fundidora & Aramberri; ⊙9am-3pm Mon-Sat; Ⓜ Parque Fundidora) too.
Hospital Christus Muguerza (☎ 81-8399-3400; www.christusmuguerza.com.mx; Hidalgo 2525 Poniente; ⊙24hr) Monterrey's main hospital.
Post Office (☎ 80-0701-7000; Washington 648 Oriente; ⊙8am-5pm Mon-Fri, 10am-2pm Sat; Ⓜ Zaragoza)

ⓘ Getting There & Away

AIR
Monterrey's busy **airport** (☎ 81-8288-7700; www.oma.aero; Carretera Miguel Alemán Km 24, Apodaca) has direct flights to all of Mexico's major cities, plus direct international flights to Atlanta, Chicago, Dallas, Houston, Los Angeles, Miami and New York. The airport is located 27km from the city center, in the suburb of Apodaca.

BUS
Monterrey's colossal bus station, **Central de Autobuses** (Av Colón 855; Ⓜ Cuauhtémoc), is busy day and night with departures and arrivals from across Mexico. Use the official taxi desk inside the station; the fare is M$60 to most central locations.

ⓘ Getting Around

TO/FROM THE AIRPORT
Noreste (☎ 80-0765-6636; www.noreste.com.mx; Central de Autobuses, Av Colón 855; Ⓜ Cuauhtémoc) runs hourly buses from 5am to 8pm (M$85, 60 minutes) between the airport and the main bus terminal. A taxi to/from the center is around M$260.

BUSES FROM MONTERREY
Prices are for 1st-class buses.

DESTINATION	FARE (M$)	DURATION (HR)	FREQUENCY (DAILY)
Chihuahua	892	9-11	12
Dallas, US	935-1377	12	8
Durango	745-819	8-9	14
Houston, US	748-1309	11	5
Mazatlán	1255	16	1
Mexico City (Terminal Norte)	1065-1215	11	half-hourly
Nuevo Laredo	340	3	every 20min
Piedras Negras	665	5-7	9
Reynosa	340	3	half-hourly
Saltillo	100-106	1¾	every 45min
San Luis Potosí	620-745	6½	every 45min
Zacatecas	449-635	7	every 45min

BUS

Frequent city buses (M$12 to M$15) get you most places you can't reach by metro.

METRO

Monterrey's modern, efficient metro system **Metrorrey** (☑ 81-2033-5000; www.facebook.com/MetrorreyOficia; single trip M$4.50; ☺ 5am-midnight) currently consists of two lines. Elevated Línea 1 runs from the northwest of the city to the eastern suburbs, passing the Parque Fundidora. Línea 2 begins underground at the Gran Plaza and runs north past Parque Niños Héroes up into the northern suburbs. The two lines cross right by the bus station at Cuauhtémoc station.

Several metro stations are connected with metrobuses (specialized buses with set stops) to outlying areas. Construction has also started on Línea 3, which will connect Zaragoza station by the Macroplaza to the northeastern suburbs. Work is expected to be completed in 2018.

TAXI

Taxis (☑ 81-1709-7753, 81-8310-5051; ☺ 24hr) are ubiquitous in Monterrey and reasonably priced; all have meters. From the Zona Rosa to the bus terminal or Parque Fundidora is usually about M$60.

Understand Mexico

Mexico Today

As President Enrique Peña Nieto, of Mexico's longtime ruling party Partido Revolucionario Institucional (PRI), approaches the end of his six-year term in 2018, a number of problems remain unsolved. While his economic reforms have given the economy a boost, crime has been on the rise, and government investigations into the 2014 case of the 43 murdered students have been discredited, with the case still unsolved. On top of that, Mexico's relations with its neighbor to the north have rarely been frostier.

Best on Film

Amores Perros (Love's a Bitch; 2000) Gritty groundbreaker that set director Alejandro González Iñárritu and actor Gael García Bernal on the path to stardom.

Y Tu Mamá También (And Your Mother Too; 2001) Classic coming-of-age road trip movie about two privileged Mexico City teenagers.

Heli (2013) Amat Escalante won Cannes' best-director garland for this tale of a young couple caught up in the drugs war.

600 Miles (2015) Tim Roth plays a kidnapped US law-enforcement agent in Gabriel Ripstein's thriller.

Best in Print

Pedro Páramo (Juan Rulfo; 1955) Compelling tale of a hallucinatory ghost town; considered the world's first published work of magical realism.

El Narco (Ioan Grillo; 2011) An exposé on Mexico's drugs war, researched in dangerous territories.

Quesadillas (Juan Pablo Villalobos; 2013) Hard-hitting, almost surreal satire on poverty and corruption in a small Jalisco town in the 1980s.

God's Middle Finger (Richard Grant; 2008) Perilous journey into the narco-riddled Sierra Madre Occidental.

Sliced Iguana (Isabella Tree; 2008) Warm, perceptive account of Mexico and its indigenous cultures.

Crime & the 43

Mexico has been struggling with over three decades of increasingly violent activity involving drug gangs, who have corrupted many government officials, politicians and members of the security forces along the way. President Peña Nieto came to power with the stated intention of trying to tackle the root causes of cartel violence at a local level. But according to Mexico's Citizens' Council for Public Security, organized-crime-related killings were happening at a rate of about 23,000 per year in late 2016. The government scored a much-needed triumph when Mexico's most wanted man, Joaquín 'El Chapo' Guzmán, leader of the powerful Sinaloa cartel, was captured in 2014 – and suffered a desperate disaster when he escaped the following year. The government regained some credibility when he was recaptured in early 2016.

The drug gangs don't just ship drugs to the USA. They traffic people too, and kidnap people for ransom, and practice extortion. Mexico has one of the world's highest kidnapping rates, estimated by the country's Human Rights Commission at a staggering 274 per day. The common perception that the authorities are often in league with the cartels is what unleashed the wave of disgust after the Iguala incident.

On September 26, 2014, three trainee teachers from Ayotzinapa in Guerrero state were killed by municipal police in the city of Iguala, and another 43 students disappeared. The event sparked months of protests around the country in an outpouring of Mexicans' anger and grief about the insecurity of their country and the perceived corruption, criminality and impunity of so many in authority. It has now been officially established that the 43 were kidnapped by police, though the government's version that the students were then handed over to cartel members who massacred them after mistaking them for a rival gang has been discredited.

Independent investigations conducted by the Inter-American Commission on Human Rights and a group of Argentine forensic experts, in conjunction with a data platform provided by the British research group Forensic Architecture, have established that the attacks that night involved highly coordinated local and federal police forces. The level of government involvement is yet to be determined. With the remains of only two students identified to date, the families of the disappeared continue to seek answers.

The Economy

Mexico's crime problem and international relations aside, the economy has been growing at a fairly steady rate of around 2.5% per year ever since Peña Nieto's technocrat government embraced market- and investor-friendly reforms in order to boost both production and competition. Opening the oil industry to private investment and competition was a bold move, since the hugely inefficient Pemex, or Petroleos Mexicanos, was state-owned and responsible for around a fifth of the government's budget. The reform paid off, increasing foreign investment and making Mexico's economy less vulnerable to fluctuating oil prices. Laws passed in 2014 finally allowed more competition into telecoms, and other Peña Nieto reforms have involved overhauling the financial system in order to lower borrowing costs and to strengthen competition. However, a growing economy alone has been insufficient in tackling Mexico's endemic corruption problem or the vast wealth inequality, and the wealthiest 10% of the population still earns around 30 times as much as the poorest 10%.

While organized crime has been encroaching on previously untouched parts of Mexico, particularly those popular with tourists, the latter don't seem to be put off. International tourist arrivals in Mexico reached a record 29.3 million in 2014, and the numbers in 2015 and 2016 eclipsed that record.

US-Mexico Relations

There is a stark contrast between the warm relations between President Peña Nieto and former US president Barack Obama, and Nieto's relationship with Donald Trump. During Obama's presidency, Mexico was lauded as one of the USA's closest trading partners, with the two governments working together to promote clean energy and protect the environment, with bolstered security cooperation regarding the US–Mexico border. With the advent of Trump, much has changed. During the campaign trail and into his presidency, Trump repeatedly cast aspersions on the character of Mexican immigrants. While the Trump-promised wall between the US and Mexico was nowhere near being constructed during research time, Trump's repeated claims that Mexico would pay for the wall was ridiculed both in the Mexican press and by former president Vicente Fox in a viral video recording. Claiming that Mexico is a threat to the US economy, Trump has also threatened to pull the US out of the NAFTA agreement, which is an additional headache for Mexico's government.

POPULATION: **127.5 MILLION**

AREA: **1,972,550 SQ KM**

GDP PER CAPITA: **US$9707**

POPULATION BELOW POVERTY LINE: **47%**

RECOGNIZED NATIONAL LANGUAGES: **69**

if Mexico were 100 people

30 would have predominantly indigenous ancestry
9 would have predominantly European ancestry
61 would have mixed ancestry

belief systems
(% of population)

83 — Roman Catholic

10 — Protestant & Evangelical

5 — No Religion

2 — Other Religions

population per sq km

MEXICO   USA   UK

🚶 ≈ 30 people

History

Mexico's story is always extraordinary and at times barely credible. How could a 2700-year tradition of sophisticated indigenous civilization crumble in two short years at the hands of some adventurers from Spain? How could Mexico's 11-year war for independence from Spain lead to three decades of dictatorship by Porfirio Díaz? How could the people's revolution that ended that dictatorship yield 80 years of one-party rule? Mexico's past is present everywhere you go, and is key to understanding Mexico today.

The Ancient Civilizations

The political map of ancient Mexico shifted constantly as cities, towns or states sought domination over one another, and a sequence of powerful states rose and fell through invasion, internal conflict or environmental disaster. These diverse cultures had much in common. Human sacrifice, to appease ferocious gods, was practiced by many of them; they observed the heavens to predict the future and determine propitious times for important events like harvests; society was heavily stratified and dominated by priestly male ruling classes. Versions of a ritual ball game were played almost everywhere and seem to have always involved two teams trying to keep a rubber ball off the ground by flicking it with various parts of the body. The game sometimes served as an oracle, and could also involve the sacrifice of some players.

A common framework divides the pre-Hispanic era into three main periods: pre-Classic (before AD 250); Classic (AD 250–900); and post-Classic (AD 900–1521). The most advanced cultures in Mexico emerged chiefly in the center, south and east of the country. Together with Maya lands in what are now Guatemala, Belize and a small part of Honduras, this zone is collectively known to historians and archaeologists as Mesoamerica.

Early Arrivals

The pre-Hispanic inhabitants of the Americas arrived from Siberia in several migrations during the last Ice Age, between perhaps 60,000 and 8000 BC, crossing land now submerged beneath the Bering Strait. Early Mexicans hunted big animal herds in the grasslands of the highland val-

Books on Ancient Cultures

Mexico: From the Olmecs to the Aztecs by Michael Coe

The Aztecs by Richard Townsend

The Maya by Michael Coe

Chronicle of the Maya Kings & Queens by Simon Martin and Nikolai Grube

TIMELINE	8000–3000 BC	1200–400 BC	AD 0–150
	Agriculture develops in places such as the Tehuacán valley and Yagul. Chili seeds and squashes are planted, then corn and beans are cultivated, enabling people to live semipermanently in villages.	Mexico's 'mother culture', the Olmecs, flourishes on the Gulf coast at San Lorenzo and La Venta. Jade, a favorite pre-Hispanic material, appears in a tomb at La Venta.	A huge planned city, including the 70m-high Pyramid of the Sun, is laid out in a grid arrangement at Teotihuacán in central Mexico.

leys. When temperatures rose at the end of the last Ice Age, the valleys became drier, ceasing to support such animal life and forcing the people to derive more food from plants. In central Mexico's Tehuacán Valley and at Yagul near Oaxaca, archaeologists have traced the slow beginnings of agriculture between about 8000 and 3000 BC.

The Olmecs

Mexico's 'mother culture' was the mysterious Olmec civilization, which appeared in the humid lowlands of Veracruz and Tabasco. The evidence of the masterly stone sculptures they left behind indicates that Olmec civilization was well organized and able to support talented artisans, but lived in thrall to fearsome deities. Its best-known artifacts are the awe-inspiring 'Olmec heads,' stone sculptures up to 3m high with grim, pug-nosed faces and wearing curious helmets. Far-flung Olmec sites in central and western Mexico may have been trading posts or garrisons to ensure the supply of jade, obsidian and other luxuries for the Olmec elite.

Olmec art, religion and society had a profound influence on later Mexican civilizations. Olmec gods, such as the feathered serpent, persisted right through the pre-Hispanic era.

Teotihuacán

The first great civilization in central Mexico arose in a valley about 50km northeast of the middle of modern Mexico City. The grid plan of the magnificent city of Teotihuacán was laid out in the 1st century AD. It was the basis for the famous Pyramids of the Sun and Moon as well as avenues, palaces and temples that were added during the next 600 years. The city grew to a population of about 125,000 and became the center of the biggest pre-Hispanic Mexican empire, stretching as far south as modern El Salvador. It may have had some hegemony over the Zapotecs of Oaxaca, whose capital, Monte Albán, grew into a magnificent city in its own right between AD 300 and 600, with architecture displaying clear Teotihuacán influence. Teotihuacán's advanced civilization – including writing, and a calendar system with a 260-day 'sacred year' composed of 13 periods of 20 days – spread far from its original heartland.

Teotihuacán was eventually burned, plundered and abandoned in the 8th century. But many Teotihuacán gods, such as the serpent Quetzalcóatl (an all-important symbol of fertility and life) and Tláloc (the rain and water deity), were still being worshipped by the Aztecs a millennium later.

The Classic Maya

Maya civilization during the Classic period (AD 250–900) was the most brilliant civilization of pre-Hispanic America in the view of many experts, and flowered over a large area stretching from the Yucatán Peninsula

Virtual Visits

Colecciones Especiales Street View (street view for 27 archaeological sites; www.inah.gob.mx/es/inah/322-colecciones-especiales-street-view)

Museo Nacional de Antropología (Mexico City; www.inah.gob.mx/paseos/mna)

Teotihuacán (http://www.inah.gob.mx/paseos/sitioteotihuacan)

Templo Mayor (Mexico City; www.inah.gob.mx/paseos/templo-mayor)

HISTORY THE ANCIENT CIVILIZATIONS

Books on Modern Maya

The Caste War of Yucatán by Nelson Reed

Time Among the Maya by Ronald Wright

The Modern Maya: A Culture in Transition by Macduff Everton

250–600	250–900	695	750–900
Teotihuacán's Pyramid of the Moon is built; the city grows to an estimated 125,000 people and comes to control the biggest of Mexico's pre-Hispanic empires.	The brilliant Classic Maya civilization flowers in southeast Mexico, Guatemala, Belize and parts of Honduras and El Salvador.	The great Maya city of Tikal (in modern-day Guatemala) conquers Maya rival Calakmul (in Mexico), but is unable to exert unified control over Calakmul's subjects.	Maya civilization in the central Maya heartland – Chiapas (southeast Mexico), El Petén (northern Guatemala) and Belize – collapses, probably because of prolonged severe droughts.

ANCIENT RELIGION & BELIEF

The Maya developed a complex writing system, partly pictorial, partly phonetic, with 300 to 500 symbols. They also refined a calendar used by other pre-Hispanic peoples into a tool for the exact recording and forecasting of earthly and heavenly events. Temples were aligned to enhance observation of the heavens, helping the Maya predict solar eclipses and movements of the moon and Venus. The Maya measured time in various interlocking cycles, ranging from 13-day 'weeks' to the 1,872,000-day 'Great Cycle.' They believed the current world to be just one of a succession of worlds, and this cyclical nature of things enabled the future to be predicted by looking at the past.

To win the gods' favors they carried out elaborate rituals involving dances, feasts, sacrifices, consumption of the alcoholic drink *balche,* and bloodletting from ears, tongues or penises. The Classic Maya seem to have practiced human sacrifice on a small scale, the post-Classic Maya on a larger scale.

The Maya universe had a center and four directions, each with a color: the center was green; east was red; north, white; west, black; and south, yellow. The heavens had 13 layers, and Xibalbá, the underworld to which the dead descended, had nine. The earth was the back of a giant reptile floating on a pond.

The later Aztecs similarly observed the heavens for astrological purposes and also saw the world as having four directions, 13 heavens and nine hells. Those who died by drowning, leprosy, lightning, gout, dropsy or lung disease went to the paradisaical gardens of Tláloc, the rain god, who had killed them. Warriors who were sacrificed or died in battle, merchants killed while traveling far away, and women who died giving birth to their first child all went to heaven as companions of the sun. Everyone else traveled for four years under the northern deserts in the abode of the death god Mictlantecuhtli, before reaching the ninth hell, where – perhaps a blessed relief – they vanished altogether.

The Aztecs believed they lived in the 'fifth world,' whose four predecessors had each been destroyed by the death of the sun and of humanity. Aztec human sacrifices were designed to keep the sun, and themselves, alive.

into Belize, Guatemala, Honduras and the lowlands of Chiapas (Mexico). The Maya attained heights of artistic and architectural expression, and of learning in fields like astronomy, mathematics and astrology, that were not surpassed by any other pre-Hispanic civilization.

Politically, the Classic Maya were divided among many independent city-states, often at war with each other. A typical Maya city functioned as the religious, political and market hub for surrounding farming hamlets. Its ceremonial center focused on plazas surrounded by tall temple pyramids (usually the tombs of rulers, who were believed to be gods). Stone causeways called *sacbeob*, probably for ceremonial use, led out from the plazas, sometimes for many kilometers. In the first part of the

Maya Websites

Mesoweb (www. mesoweb.com)

Maya Exploration Center (www.maya exploration.org)

c 1000	1325	1487	1519–20
Chichén Itzá, an abandoned Maya city on the Yucatán Peninsula, is reoccupied, developing into one of Mexico's most magnificent ancient cities, in a fusion of Maya and central Mexican styles.	The Aztecs settle at Tenochtitlán, on the site of present-day Mexico City. Over the next two centuries they come to rule an empire extending over nearly all of central Mexico.	Twenty thousand human captives are sacrificed in four days for the rededication of Tenochtitlán's Great Temple after a major reconstruction.	A Spanish expedition from Cuba, under Hernán Cortés, reaches Tenochtitlán. Initially well received, the Spaniards are attacked and driven out on the Noche Triste (Sad Night), June 30, 1520.

Classic period most of these appear to have been grouped into two loose military alliances, centered on Tikal (Guatemala) and Calakmul (in the south of the Yucatán Peninsula).

Classic Maya Zones

Within Mexico, there were four main zones of Classic Maya concentration. Calakmul lies in a now-remote area known as the Río Bec zone, where Maya remains are typically long, low buildings decorated with serpent or monster masks and with towers at their corners. A second zone was the Chenes area in northeastern Campeche state, with similar architecture except for the towers. A third area was the Puuc zone, south of Mérida, characterized by buildings with intricate stone mosaics, often incorporating faces of the hook-nosed rain god Chaac. The most important Puuc city was Uxmal. The fourth zone was lowland Chiapas, with the cities of Palenque (for many people the most beautiful of all Maya sites), Yaxchilán and Toniná.

The Classic Maya Collapse

In the second half of the 8th century, conflict between Maya city-states started to increase, and by the early 10th century, the several million inhabitants of the flourishing central Maya heartland (Chiapas, Guatemala's Petén region and Belize) had virtually disappeared. The Classic era was at an end. A series of droughts combined with population pressure is thought to have brought about this cataclysm. Many Maya probably migrated to the Yucatán Peninsula or the highlands of Chiapas, where their descendants live on today. The jungle grew back up around the ancient lowland cities.

The Toltecs

In central Mexico, for centuries after the fall of Teotihuacán, power was divided between various locally important cities, including Xochicalco, south of Mexico City; Cacaxtla and Cantona to the east; and Tula to the north. The cult of Quetzalcóatl remained widespread, society in at least some places became more militarized, and mass human sacrifice may have started here in this period. The Quetzalcóatl cult and large-scale human sacrifice were both exported to the Yucatán Peninsula, where they're most evident at the city of Chichén Itzá.

Central Mexican culture in the early post-Classic period is often given the name Toltec (Artificers), a name coined by the later Aztecs, who looked back to the Toltec rulers with awe.

The Mel Gibson–directed *Apocalypto* (2006), a violent tale of a young man trying to escape becoming a human sacrifice, gives some idea of what ancient Maya life might sometimes have been like.

The Mesoamerican Ballgame (http://interactiveknowledge.com/ballgame) is an interesting website, with video, explaining the indigenous ball game, believed to have been the first team sport in human history.

HISTORY THE ANCIENT CIVILIZATIONS

1521	1524	1534–92	1540s
The Spanish, with 100,000 native Mexican allies, capture Tenochtitlán, razing it building by building. They rename it 'México' and go on to rebuild it as the capital of Nueva España (New Spain).	Virtually all the Aztec empire, plus other Mexican regions such as Colima, the Huasteca and the Isthmus of Tehuantepec, have been brought under Spanish control.	The Spanish find huge lodes of silver at Pachuca, Zacatecas, Guanajuato and San Luis Potosí, north of Mexico City.	The Yucatán Peninsula is brought under Spanish control by three (related) conquistadors all named Francisco de Montejo. Nueva España's northern border runs roughly from modern Tampico to Guadalajara.

The Aztecs

Legend tells that the Aztecs built their capital at Tenochtitlán because there they witnessed an eagle on a cactus, devouring a snake – a sign, their prophecies told, that they should stop their wanderings. The temple they built on the spot (the Templo Mayor) was considered the center of the universe.

The Aztecs' legends related that they were the chosen people of the hummingbird deity Huizilopochtli. Originally nomads from somewhere in western or northern Mexico, they were led by their priests to the Valle de México, the site of modern Mexico City, where they settled on islands in the valley's lakes. By the 15th century the Aztecs (also known as the Mexica) had fought their way up to become the most powerful group in the valley, with their capital at Tenochtitlán, where downtown Mexico City stands today.

The Aztecs formed the Triple Alliance with two other valley states, Texcoco and Tlacopan, to wage war against Tlaxcala and Huejotzingo, east of the valley. The prisoners they took became the diet of sacrificed warriors that voracious Huizilopochtli (no sweet hummingbird himself) demanded to keep the sun rising every day.

The Triple Alliance brought most of central Mexico, from the Gulf coast to the Pacific, under its control. This was an empire of 38 provinces and about five million people, geared to extracting tribute (tax in kind) of resources absent from the heartland – items like jade, turquoise, cotton, tobacco, rubber, fruits, vegetables, cacao and precious feathers, all needed for the glorification of the Aztec elite and to support their war-oriented state.

Aztec Society

Tenochtitlán and the adjoining Aztec city of Tlatelolco grew to house more than 200,000 people. The Valle de México as a whole had more than a million people. They were supported by intensive farming based on irrigation, terracing and swamp reclamation.

The Aztec emperor held absolute power. Celibate priests performed cycles of great ceremonies, typically including sacrifices and masked dances or processions enacting myths. Military leaders were usually elite professional soldiers known as *tecuhtli*. Another special group was the *pochteca* – militarized merchants who helped extend the empire, brought goods to the capital and organized large daily markets in big towns. At the bottom of society were pawns (paupers who could sell themselves for a specified period), serfs and slaves.

Other Post-Classic Civilizations

On the eve of the Spanish conquest, most Mexican civilizations shared deep similarities. Each was politically centralized and divided into classes, with many people occupied in specialist tasks, including professional priests. Agriculture was productive, despite the lack of draft animals, metal tools and the wheel. Corn tortillas, *pozol* (corn gruel) and beans were staple foods, and many other crops, such as squash, tomatoes,

1605	1767	1810	1811
Mexico's indigenous population has declined from an estimated 25 million at the time of the Spanish conquest to a little over a million, mainly because of new diseases from Europe.	The Jesuits, important missionaries and educators in Nueva España and many of them criollos (Mexican-born people of Spanish ancestry), are expelled from all Spanish dominions, unsettling criollos in the colony.	On September 16 priest Miguel Hidalgo launches Mexico's War of Independence with his Grito de Dolores (Cry of Dolores), a call to rebellion in the town of Dolores.	After initial victories, the rebels' numbers shrink and their leaders, including Hidalgo, are captured and executed in Chihuahua. José María Morelos y Pavón, another priest, assumes the rebel leadership.

chilies, avocados, peanuts, papayas and pineapples, were grown in various regions. Luxury foods for the elite included turkey, domesticated hairless dog, game and chocolate drinks. War was widespread, and often connected with the need for prisoners to sacrifice to a variety of gods.

Several important regional cultures arose in the post-Classic period:

Michoacán

The Tarascos, who were skilled artisans and jewelers, ruled Michoacán from their base around the Lago de Pátzcuaro. They were one group that managed to avoid conquest by the Aztecs.

Oaxaca

After 1200 the Zapotecs were dominated by the Mixtecs, skilled metalsmiths and potters from the uplands around the Oaxaca–Puebla border. Much of Oaxaca fell to the Aztecs in the 15th and 16th centuries.

Yucatán Peninsula

The abandoned Maya city of Chichén Itzá was reoccupied around AD 1000 and developed into one of ancient Mexico's most magnificent cities, in a fusion of Maya and central Mexican (Toltec) styles. The city of Mayapán dominated most of the Yucatán after Chichén Itzá declined around 1200. Mayapán's hold dissolved from about 1440, and the Yucatán became a quarreling ground for many city-states.

Enter The Spanish

Ancient Mexican civilization, nearly 3000 years old, was shattered in two short years by a tiny group of invaders who destroyed the Aztec empire, brought a new religion, and reduced the native people to second-class citizens and slaves. Rarely in history has a thriving society undergone such a transformation so fast. So alien to each other were the newcomers and the indigenous Mexicans that each doubted whether the other was human (Pope Paul III declared indigenous Mexicans to be human in 1537). From this traumatic encounter arose modern Mexico. Most Mexicans today are mestizo, of mixed indigenous and European blood, and thus descendants of both cultures.

The Spanish Background

In 1492, the year Christopher Columbus arrived in the Caribbean, Spain was an aggressively expanding state, fresh from completing the 700-year Reconquista (Reconquest), in which Christian armies had gradually recovered the Spanish mainland from Islamic rule. With their mix of brutality and bravery, gold lust and piety, the Spanish conquistadors of the Americas were the natural successors to the crusading knights of the Reconquista.

1813	1821	1821–22	1824
Morelos' forces blockade Mexico City for several months. A congress at Chilpancingo adopts principles for the independence movement, but Morelos is captured and executed two years later.	Rebel leaders Vicente Guerrero and Agustín de Iturbide devise the Plan de Iguala, for an independent Mexico with constitutional monarchy and Catholic religious supremacy.	The Plan de Iguala wins over all influential sections of society, and the Spanish viceroy agrees to Mexican independence. Iturbide takes the new Mexican throne as Emperor Agustín I.	A new constitution establishes a federal Mexican republic of 19 states and four territories. Guadalupe Victoria, a former independence fighter, becomes its first president.

Seeking new westward trade routes to the spice-rich Orient, Spanish explorers and soldiers landed first in the Caribbean, establishing colonies on the islands of Hispaniola and Cuba. They then began seeking a passage through the land mass to the west, and soon became distracted by tales of gold, silver and a rich empire there. Spain's governor on Cuba, Diego Velázquez, asked a colonist named Hernán Cortés to lead one such expedition westward. As Cortés gathered ships and men, Velázquez became uneasy about the costs and Cortés' loyalty, and tried to cancel the expedition. But Cortés, perhaps sensing a once-in-history opportunity, ignored him and set sail on February 15, 1519, with 11 ships, 550 men and 16 horses.

The Conquest

The Cortés expedition landed first at Cozumel island, then sailed around the coast to Tabasco, defeating inhospitable locals in the Battle of Centla near modern-day Frontera, where the enemy fled in terror from Spanish horsemen, thinking horse and rider to be a single fearsome beast. Afterward the locals gave Cortés 20 young women, among them Doña Marina (La Malinche), who became his indispensable interpreter, aide and lover.

Unhappy Aztec subject towns on the Gulf coast, such as Zempoala, welcomed the Spaniards. And as the Spaniards moved inland toward Tenochtitlán, they made allies of the Aztecs' longtime enemies, the Tlaxcalans.

Aztec legends and superstitions and the indecision of Emperor Moctezuma II Xocoyotzin also worked to the Spaniards' advantage. According to the Aztec calendar, 1519 would see the legendary Toltec god-king Quetzalcóatl return from banishment in the east. Was Cortés actually Quetzalcóatl? Omens proliferated: lightning struck a temple, a comet sailed through the night skies and a bird 'with a mirror in its head' was brought to Moctezuma, who saw warriors in it.

Anna Lanyon's *The New World of Martin Cortes* tells the fascinating and poignant story of the first mestizo, the son of Hernán Cortés and La Malinche, from his birth in 1522 in Tenochtitlán to his death, forty-something years later, near Granada.

The Taking of Tenochtitlán

The Spaniards, with 6000 indigenous allies, were invited to enter Tenochtitlán, a city bigger than any in Spain, on November 8, 1519. Aztec nobles carried Moctezuma out to meet Cortés on a litter with a canopy of feathers and gold, and the Spaniards were lodged, as befitted gods, in the palace of Moctezuma's father, Axayácatl.

Though entertained in luxury, the Spaniards were trapped. Unsure of Moctezuma's intentions, they took him hostage. Believing Cortés a god, Moctezuma told his people he went willingly, but tensions rose in the city. Eventually, after six or seven months, some of the Spaniards killed about 200 Aztec nobles in an intended pre-emptive strike. Cortés persuaded Moctezuma to try to pacify his people. According to one version

1836 〉	1845–48 〉	1858–61 〉	1861–63 〉
US settlers in the Mexican territory of Texas declare independence. Mexican forces under President Santa Anna wipe out the defenders of the Alamo mission, but are then routed on the San Jacinto River.	US Congress votes to annex Texas, sparking the Mexican–American War (1846–48). US troops occupy Mexico City. Mexico cedes Texas, California, Utah, Colorado and most of New Mexico and Arizona.	Liberal government laws requiring the church to sell property spark the War of the Reform: Mexico's liberals (with their 'capital' at Veracruz) defeat the conservatives (based in Mexico City).	Liberal Benito Juárez becomes Mexico's first indigenous president, but Mexico suffers the French Intervention: France invades Mexico, taking Mexico City in 1863 despite a defeat at Puebla on May 5, 1862.

of events, the emperor tried to address the crowds from the roof of Ax-ayácatl's palace, but was killed by missiles; other versions say it was the Spaniards who killed him.

The Spaniards fled, losing several hundred of their own and thousands of indigenous allies, on what's known as the Noche Triste (Sad Night). They retreated to Tlaxcala, where they built boats in sections, then carried them across the mountains to attack Tenochtitlán from its surrounding lakes. When the 900 Spaniards re-entered the Valle de México in May 1521, they were accompanied by some 100,000 native allies. The defenders resisted fiercely, but after three months the city had been razed to the ground and the new emperor, Cuauhtémoc, was captured. Cuauhtémoc asked Cortés to kill him, but he was kept alive until 1525 as a hostage, undergoing occasional foot-burning as the Spanish tried to make him reveal the whereabouts of Aztec treasure.

Mexico as a Colony

The Spanish crown saw Mexico and its other American conquests as a silver cow to be milked to finance its endless wars in Europe, a life of luxury for its nobility, and a deluge of new churches, palaces and monasteries that were erected around Spain. The crown was entitled to one-fifth of

SOME WE LOVE, SOME WE LOVE TO HATE

Mexicans have strong opinions about some of their historical characters. Some are immortalized by statues and street names all over the country. Others, just as influential, are considered objects of shame and ridicule.

Heroes

Cuauhtémoc Aztec leader who resisted the Spanish invaders.

Benito Juárez Reforming indigenous president who fought off French occupiers.

Miguel Hidalgo Priest who launched the War for Independence.

Pancho Villa Larger-than-life revolutionary.

Villains

Hernán Cortés The original evil Spanish conqueror.

Carlos Salinas de Gortari President from 1988 to 1994, blamed for the drugs trade, corruption, peso crisis, the North American Free Trade Agreement (Nafta), you name it...

Santa Anna Winner at the Alamo, but loser of Texas, California, Arizona, Utah, Colorado and New Mexico.

La Malinche Doña Marina, Hernán Cortés' indigenous translator and lover.

1864–67	1876–1911	1910–11	1913–14
Napoleon III sends Maximilian of Hapsburg over as emperor in 1864, but starts to withdraw his troops in 1866. Maximilian is executed by Juárez' forces in 1867.	The Porfiriato: Mexico is ruled by conservative Porfirio Díaz, who brings stability but curbs civil liberties and democratic rights, and concentrates wealth in the hands of a small minority.	The Mexican Revolution starts when the country rises against the Díaz regime on November 20, 1910. Díaz resigns in May 1911; reformist Francisco Madero is elected president in November.	Madero is deposed and executed by conservative Victoriano Huerta. Northern revolutionary leaders unite against Huerta. Huerta's troops terrorize the countryside, but he is forced to resign in July 1914.

all bullion sent back from the New World (the *quinto real,* or royal fifth). Conquistadors and colonists, too, saw the American empire as a chance to get rich. Cortés granted his soldiers *encomiendas,* which were rights to the labor or tribute of groups of indigenous people. Spain asserted its authority through viceroys, the crown's personal representatives in Mexico.

The populations of the conquered peoples of Nueva España (New Spain), as the Spanish named their Mexican colony, declined disastrously, mainly from new diseases introduced by the invaders. The indigenous peoples' only real allies were some of the monks who started arriving in 1523. The monks' missionary work helped extend Spanish control over Mexico – by 1560 they had converted millions of people and built more than 100 monasteries – but many of them also protected local people from the colonists' worst excesses.

Northern Mexico remained beyond Spanish control until big finds of silver at Zacatecas, Guanajuato and elsewhere spurred efforts to subdue it. The northern borders were slowly extended by missionaries and a few settlers, and by the early 19th century Nueva España included (albeit loosely) most of the modern US states of Texas, New Mexico, Arizona, California, Utah and Colorado.

Colonial Society

A person's place in colonial Mexican society was determined by skin color, parentage and birthplace. At the top of the tree, however humble their origins in Spain, were Spanish-born colonists. Known as *peninsulares,* they were a minuscule part of the population, but were considered nobility in Nueva España.

Next on the ladder were the criollos, people of Spanish ancestry born in the colony. As the decades passed, the criollos began to develop a distinct identity, and some of them came to possess enormous estates (haciendas) and amass huge fortunes from mining, commerce or agriculture. Not surprisingly, criollos sought political power commensurate with their wealth and grew to resent Spanish authority.

Below the criollos were the mestizos, and at the bottom of the pile were the indigenous people and African slaves. Though the poor were paid for their labor by the 18th century, they were paid very little. Many were *peones* (bonded laborers tied by debt to their employers), and indigenous people still had to pay tribute to the crown.

Social stratification follows similar patterns in Mexico today with, broadly speaking, the 'pure-blood' descendants of Spaniards at the top of the tree, the mestizos in the middle and the indigenous people at the bottom.

1917	1920–24	1926	1929
Reformists emerge victorious over radicals in the revolutionary conflict, and a new reformist constitution, still largely in force today, is enacted at Querétaro.	President Álvaro Obregón turns to post-Revolution reconstruction. More than a thousand rural schools are built; some land is redistributed from big landowners to peasants.	President Plutarco Elías Calles closes monasteries, outlaws religious orders and bans religious processions, precipitating the Cristero Rebellion by Catholics (until 1929).	Elías Calles founds the Partido Nacional Revolucionario: it and its later mutations, the Partido de la Revolución Mexicana and the Partido Revolucionario Institucional (PRI), will rule Mexico until 2000.

Mexico as a Republic

Criollo discontent with Spanish rule really began to stir following the expulsion of the Jesuits (many of whom were criollos) from the Spanish empire in 1767. The catalyst for rebellion came in 1808 when Napoleon Bonaparte occupied Spain, and direct Spanish control over Nueva España evaporated. The city of Querétaro became a hotbed of intrigue among criollos plotting rebellion against Spanish rule. The rebellion was launched on September 16, 1810 by Padre Miguel Hidalgo in his parish of Dolores (now Dolores Hidalgo). The path to independence was a hard one, involving almost 11 years of fighting between rebels and loyalist forces, and the deaths of Hidalgo and several other rebel leaders. But eventually rebel general Agustín de Iturbide sat down with Spanish viceroy Juan O'Donojú in Córdoba in 1821 and agreed on terms for Mexico's independence.

Mexico's first century as a free nation started with a period of chronic political instability and wound up with a period of stability so repressive that it triggered a revolution. A consistent thread throughout was the opposition between liberals, who favored a measure of social reform, and conservatives, who didn't. Between 1821 and the mid-1860s, the young Mexican nation was invaded by three different countries (Spain, the USA and France), lost large chunks of its territory to the US and underwent nearly 50 changes of head of state.

Santa Anna had a leg amputated after being wounded by French forces in 1838. He later had the leg buried with military honors in Mexico City. Its whereabouts are now unknown but its prosthetic replacement was captured by Americans in 1847 and now resides in the Illinois State Military Museum.

Juárez & Díaz

It was an indigenous Zapotec from Oaxaca who played the lead role in Mexican affairs for two tumultuous decades after the midpoint of the century. Lawyer Benito Juárez was a key member of the new liberal government in 1855, which ushered in the era known as the Reform, in which the liberals set about dismantling the conservative state that had developed in Mexico. Juárez became president in 1861. With the French Intervention soon afterward, his government was forced into exile in

THE TRAGICOMEDY OF SANTA ANNA

Intervention in politics by ambitious soldiers plagued Mexico throughout the 19th century. Antonio López de Santa Anna first hit the limelight by deposing Emperor Agustín I in 1823. He also overthrew President Anastasio Bustamante in 1831, then was himself elected president in 1833, the first of 11 terms in 22 chaotic years. Above all, Mexicans remember Santa Anna for losing large chunks of Mexican territory to the US. After his 1836 post-Alamo defeat in Texas and his disastrous territorial losses in the Mexican–American War of 1846–48, a Santa Anna government sold Mexico's last remaining areas of New Mexico and Arizona to the US for US$10 million in 1853.

1934–40	1940s & '50s	1964–70	1970s
President Lázaro Cárdenas redistributes 200,000 sq km of land and expropriates foreign oil operations, forming the state oil company Petróleos Mexicanos (Pemex). Foreign investors avoid Mexico.	The Mexican economy expands, helped by growth during WWII, major infrastructure projects and tourism development. The population almost doubles in two decades, and millions migrate to urban areas.	President Gustavo Díaz Ordaz resists democratizing the PRI. During demonstrations against one-party rule before the 1968 Olympics, an estimated 400 protestors are massacred at Tlatelolco, Mexico City.	Mexico enjoys an economic boom thanks to a jump in world oil prices. On the strength of the country's vast oil reserves, international institutions begin lending Mexico billions of dollars.

provincial Mexico, eventually to regain control in 1866. Juárez set an agenda of economic and social reform. Schooling was made mandatory, a railway was built between Mexico City and Veracruz, and a rural police force, the *rurales*, was organized to secure the transportation of cargo through Mexico. Juárez died in 1872 and remains one of the few Mexican historical figures with a completely unsullied reputation.

A rather different Oaxacan, Porfirio Díaz, ruled as president for 31 of the following 39 years, a period known as the Porfiriato. Díaz brought Mexico into the industrial age, stringing telephone, telegraph and railway lines and launching public works projects. He kept Mexico free of civil wars – but political opposition, free elections and a free press were banned. Peasants were cheated out of their land by new laws, workers suffered appalling conditions, and land and wealth became concentrated in the hands of a small minority. All this led, in 1910, to the Mexican Revolution.

The Mexican Revolution

The Revolution was a tortured 10-year period of shifting conflicts and allegiances between forces and leaders of all political stripes. The conservatives were pushed aside fairly early on, but the reformers and revolutionaries who had lined up against them could not agree among themselves. Successive attempts to create stable governments were wrecked by new outbreaks of devastating fighting. All told, one in eight Mexicans lost their lives.

Francisco Madero, a wealthy liberal from Coahuila, would probably have won the presidential election in 1910 if Porfirio Díaz hadn't jailed him. On his release, Madero called successfully on the nation to revolt, which spread quickly across the country. Díaz resigned in May 1911, and Madero was elected president six months later. But Madero could not contain the diverse factions now struggling for power throughout the country. The basic divide was between liberal reformers like Madero and more radical leaders such as Emiliano Zapata, who was fighting for the transfer of hacienda land to the peasants, with the cry *'¡Tierra y libertad!'* (Land and freedom!).

In 1913 Madero was deposed and executed by one of his own generals, Victoriano Huerta, who had defected to conservative rebels. The liberals and radicals united (temporarily) to defeat Huerta. Three main leaders in the north banded together under the Plan de Guadalupe: Venustiano Carranza, a Madero supporter, in Coahuila; Francisco 'Pancho' Villa in Chihuahua; and Álvaro Obregón in Sonora. Zapata also fought against Huerta.

But fighting then broke out again between the victorious factions, with Carranza and Obregón (the 'Constitutionalists', with their capital at Veracruz) pitted against the radical Zapata and the populist Villa.

Freedom from Spain: Key Sites

Alhóndiga de Granaditas (Guanajuato)

Dolores Hidalgo

Calabozo de Hidalgo, Casa Chihuahua (Chihuahua)

Ex-Hotel Zevallos (Córdoba)

Museo Casa de Morelos (Morelia)

1980s	1985	1988–94	1994
Oil prices plunge and Mexico suffers its worst recession in decades. Amid economic helplessness and rampant corruption, dissent and protests increase, even inside the PRI.	On September 19 a massive earthquake, with a magnitude of 8.1 on the Richter scale, strikes Mexico City. At least 10,000 people are killed.	The PRI's Carlos Salinas de Gortari narrowly defeats left-of-center Cuauhtémoc Cárdenas in a disputed presidential election. Salinas reforms Mexico's economy toward private enterprise and free trade.	The North American Free Trade Agreement (NAFTA) takes effect. The Zapatista uprising in Chiapas begins. Luis Donaldo Colosio, Salinas' chosen successor as PRI presidential candidate, is assassinated.

Zapata and Villa never formed a serious alliance, and it was Carranza who emerged the victor. He had Zapata assassinated in 1919, only to be liquidated himself the following year on the orders of his former ally Obregón. Pancho Villa was killed in 1923.

Mexico as a One-Party Democracy

From 1920 to 2000, Mexico was ruled by the reformists who emerged victorious from the Revolution and their successors in the political party they set up, which since the 1940s has borne the name Partido Revolucionario Institucional (Institutional Revolutionary Party), or PRI as it's universally known. Starting out with some genuinely radical social policies, these governments became steadily more conservative, corrupt, repressive and self-interested as the 20th century wore on. Mexico ended the century with a bigger middle class but still with a yawning wealth gap between the prosperous few and the many poor.

Between the 1920s and '60s more than 400,000 sq km of land was redistributed from large estates to peasants and small farmers. Nearly half the population received land, mainly in the form of *ejidos* (communal landholdings). Meanwhile, Mexico developed a worrying economic dependence on its large oil reserves in the Gulf of Mexico. The 1970s and '80s saw the country veer from oil-engendered boom to oil-engendered slump as world oil prices swung rapidly up, then just as suddenly down. The huge government-owned oil company Pemex was just one face of a massive state-controlled economic behemoth that developed as the PRI sought control over all important facets of Mexican life.

Decline of the PRI

The PRI was discredited forever in the minds of many Mexicans by the Tlatelolco Massacre of 1968, in which an estimated 400 civil-liberties protesters were shot dead. The PRI came to depend increasingly on strong-arm tactics and fraud to win elections.

Mexicans' cynicism about their leaders reached a crescendo with the 1988–94 presidency of Carlos Salinas de Gortari, who won the presidential election only after a mysterious computer failure had halted vote-tallying at a crucial stage. During Salinas' term, drug trafficking through Mexico – on the rise since the early '80s when traffickers from Colombia began shifting their routes from the Caribbean to Mexico – grew into a huge business, and mysterious high-profile murders proliferated. Salinas did take steps to liberalize the monolithic state-dominated economy. The apex of his program, the North American Free Trade Agreement (Nafta), boosted exports and industry, but was unpopular with food growers and small businesses threatened by imports from the US. The last year of his presidency, 1994, began with the left-wing Zapatista uprising in Mexico's

In the 1920s outstanding Mexican artists such as Diego Rivera were commissioned to decorate important public buildings with large, vivid murals on historical and social themes. Many of these can be seen in Mexico City.

HISTORY MEXICO AS A ONE-PARTY DEMOCRACY

1994–2000	2000	2006	2006–12
Under President Ernesto Zedillo, Mexico emerges from a recession triggered by a currency collapse days after he took office. Crime and migration to the US increase.	Vicente Fox, of the right-of-center Partido Acción Nacional (PAN), wins the presidential election under a new, transparent electoral system, ending eight decades of rule by the PRI and its predecessors.	The PAN's Felipe Calderón narrowly defeats Andrés Manuel López Obrador of the left-of-center Party of the Democratic Revolution (PRD) in the presidential election, and declares war on Mexico's drug mobs.	In the six years of Calderón's war on drugs, 50,000 troops are deployed around the country and some 60,000 people are killed, most of them in intergang turf wars.

southernmost state, Chiapas, and shortly before Salinas left office he spent nearly all of Mexico's foreign-exchange reserves in a futile attempt to support the peso, engendering a slump that he left his successor, Ernesto Zedillo, to deal with.

It was also left to Zedillo to respond to the rising clamor for democratic change in Mexico. He established a new, independently supervised electoral system that opened the way for his own party to lose power when Vicente Fox of the business-oriented Partido Acción Nacional (PAN) won the presidential election in 2000.

PAN Rule

Vicente Fox's election itself – a non-PRI president after 80 years of rule by that party and its predecessors – was really the biggest news about his six-year term. He entered office backed by much goodwill. In the end, his presidency was considered a disappointment by most. Lacking a majority in Mexico's Congress, Fox was unable to push through reforms that he believed were key to stirring Mexico's slumbering economy.

Fox was succeeded in 2006 by another PAN president, Felipe Calderón. During Calderón's term Mexico's economy sprang back surprisingly fast after the recession of 2009, and Mexico became something of a global environmental champion when it enshrined its carbon-emissions targets in law in 2012. But his presidency will be remembered far more for its war on drugs.

The Drugs War

Presidents Zedillo and Fox had already deployed the armed forces against the violent mobs running the multi-billion-dollar business of shipping illegal drugs into the USA, but had failed to rein in their violence or their power to corrupt. By 2006 over 2000 people a year were already dying in violence engendered chiefly by brutal turf wars between rival gangs.

Calderón declared war on the drug mobs and mobilized 50,000 troops plus naval and police forces against them, predominantly in cities along the US border. Some top gang leaders were killed or arrested, and drug seizures reached record levels, but so did the killings – an estimated 60,000 in the six years of Calderón's presidency. The gangs' methods grew ever more shocking, with street gun-battles, gruesome beheadings and torture. Cities such as Monterrey, Nuevo Laredo, Acapulco and Veracruz saw violence spike when local turf wars erupted; as of 2016, Acapulco had the highest murder rate in Mexico. When the numbers of killings finally started to fall at the end of Calderón's presidency, many people believed this was simply because the two strongest mobs – the Sinaloa cartel in the northwest of Mexico and Los Zetas in the northeast – had effectively wiped out their weaker rivals.

2012	26 Sep 2014	11 Jul 2015	Sep 2017
The PRI returns to power as Enrique Peña Nieto wins the presidential election, promising reforms to propel the economy forward. López Obrador of the PRD again comes a close second.	Forty-three students from Ayotzinapa, Guerrero state, disappear after clashing with police in Iguala, sparking national outrage at perceived corruption and criminality in Mexico's governing and security apparatus.	Drug kingpin Joaquín 'El Chapo' Guzmán escapes from Mexico's top maximum security prison, causing major embarrassment to Peña Nieto's government. He is recaptured in Los Mochis six months later.	Mexico is struck by two powerful earthquakes (8.1 and 7.1 on the Richter scale, respectively) in quick succession. The second earthquake takes place near Puebla and is more destructive, with over 230 dead.

The Mexican Way of Life

Travels in Mexico quickly reveal that Mexicans are a vastly diverse bunch, from the industrial workers of Monterrey to the rich sophisticates and bohemian counterculture of Mexico City, and indigenous villagers eking out subsistence in the southern mountains. But certain common threads run through almost everyone here – among them a deep vein of spirituality, the importance of family, and a simultaneous pride and frustration about Mexico itself.

Life, Death & Family

One thing you can never do with Mexicans is encapsulate them in simple formulas. They're hospitable, warm and courteous to guests, yet are most truly themselves within their family group. They will laugh at death, but have a profound spiritual awareness. They embrace modernity while remaining traditional in essence.

Many Mexicans, however contemporary and globalized they may appear, still inhabit a world in which omens, coincidences and curious resemblances take on great importance. When sick, some people still prefer to visit a traditional *curandero* – a kind of cross between a naturopath and a witch doctor – rather than resort to a modern *médico*.

While most Mexicans are chiefly concerned with earning a living for themselves and their strongly knit families, they also take their leisure time very seriously, be it partying at clubs or fiestas, or relaxing over an extended-family Sunday lunch at a restaurant. Holidays for religious festivals and patriotic anniversaries are essential to the rhythm of life, ensuring that people get a break every few weeks.

Mexicans may despair of their country ever being governed well, but at the same time they are fiercely proud of it. They naturally absorb a certain amount of US culture and consciousness, but they also strongly value what's different about Mexican life – its more humane pace, its strong sense of community and family, its unique food and drinks, and the thriving, multifaceted national culture.

Nobel Prize–winning Mexican writer Octavio Paz argues in *The Labyrinth of Solitude* that Mexicans' love of noise, music and crowds is just a temporary escape from personal isolation and gloom. Make your own judgment,

The Great Divides

Fly into Mexico City and you'll get a bird's-eye view of just how little space is not occupied by buildings or roads. Around the edges of the city, streets climb the steep slopes of extinct volcanoes, while the city's fringes are ringed with shacks made from a few concrete blocks or sheets of tin that 'house' the poorest. In the most affluent neighborhoods, imposing detached houses with well-tended gardens sit behind high walls with strong security gates.

One in every two Mexicans now lives in a city or conurbation of more than a million people. A quarter of them live in smaller cities and towns, and another quarter in villages. The number of urban dwellers continues to rise as rural folk are sucked into cities.

The secrets of physical and spiritual health of a Nahua *curandera* (literally 'curer') are revealed in *Woman Who Glows in the Dark* by Elena Ávila.

Out in the villages and small towns, people still work the land, and members of an extended family typically live in yards with separate small buildings of adobe, wood or concrete, often with earth floors. Inside these homes are few possessions – beds, a cooking area, a table with a few chairs and a few family photos. Few villagers own cars.

Mexico's eternal wealth gap yawns as wide as ever. The world's second-richest man, entrepreneur Carlos Slim Helú, is a Mexican. His net worth was estimated at US$77 billion by *Forbes* magazine in 2015. At the other extreme, the poorest city dwellers barely scrape an existence as street hawkers, buskers or home workers in the 'informal economy', rarely earning more than M$90 (US$5) a day.

While rich kids zoom about in flashy cars and attend private schools (often in the US), and the bohemian urban counterculture enjoys its mezcal bars, state-funded universities and underground dance clubs, economically disadvantaged rural laborers may dance only at local fiestas and often leave school well before they reach 15.

Land of Many Peoples

Mexico's ethnic diversity is one of its most fascinating aspects. The major distinction is between mestizos – people of mixed ancestry (mostly Spanish and indigenous) – and the *indígenas*, the indigenous descendants of Mexico's pre-Hispanic inhabitants. Mestizos are the majority that holds most positions of power and influence, but the *indígenas*, while mostly materially poor, are often culturally rich. Approximately 60 Mexican indigenous peoples survive, each with their own language and, often, unique costumes. Their way of life is still imbued with communal customs, beliefs and rituals bound up with nature. According to the National Comission for the Development of Indigenous Peoples, 25.5 million people in Mexico (21.5% of the population) are indigenous. The biggest group is the Nahua, descendants of the ancient Aztecs, over three million of whom are spread around central Mexico. The approximately two million Maya on the Yucatán Peninsula are direct descendants of the ancient Maya, as (probably) are the Tzotziles and Tzeltales of Chiapas (totaling just over one million). Also directly descended from well-known pre-Hispanic peoples are the estimated one million Zapotecs and over 800,000 Mixtecs, mainly in Oaxaca; over 400,000 Totonacs in Veracruz; and over 200,000 Purépecha (Tarascos) in Michoacán.

The Spiritual Dimension

Yoga, the *temascal* (pre-Hispanic steam bath) and New Age cosmic energies may mean more to some Mexicans today than traditional Roman Catholicism, but a spiritual dimension of some kind or other remains important in most Mexicans' lives.

Roman Catholicism

Around 10% of Mexicans adhere to non-Catholic varieties of Christianity. Some are members of Protestant churches set up by US missionaries in the 19th century. Millions of indigenous rural poor from southeast Mexico have been converted in recent years by a wave of American Pentecostal, Evangelical, Mormon, Seventh-Day Adventist and Jehovah's Witness missionaries.

About 83% of Mexicans profess Roman Catholicism, making this the world's second-biggest Catholic country after Brazil. Almost half of Mexican Catholics attend church weekly and Catholicism remains very much part of the nation's established fabric. Most Mexican fiestas are built around local saints' days, and pilgrimages to important shrines are a big feature of the calendar.

The church's most binding symbol is Nuestra Señora de Guadalupe, the dark-skinned manifestation of the Virgin Mary. She appeared to an Aztec potter, Juan Diego, in 1531 on Cerro del Tepeyac hill; in what's now northern Mexico City. A crucial link between Catholic and indigenous spirituality, the Virgin of Guadalupe is now the country's religious patron, an archetypal mother whose blue-cloaked image is ubiquitous and whose name is invoked in political speeches and literature as well as

COMMUNING WITH DEPARTED SOULS

Few festivals reveal more about Mexican spirituality than Día de Muertos (Day of the Dead), the remembrance of departed loved ones at the beginning of November. Muertos originated in colonial times, when the Catholic Church fused indigenous rites honoring and communing with the dead with its own celebrations of All Saints' Day (November 1) and All Souls' Day (November 2).

Today Muertos is a national phenomenon, with people everywhere cleaning graves and decorating them with flowers, holding graveyard vigils, sprinkling the graves with liquor (the dead also like to party!) and building elaborate altars to welcome back their loved ones with their favorite dishes. For the mestizo (mixed ancestry) majority, it's a popular folk festival and family occasion. The Catholics believe that departed souls are in heaven or in purgatory, not actually back on a visit to earth. Nevertheless, many find comfort in a sense that lost loved ones are somehow more present at this time. Among many indigenous communities, Muertos is still very much a religious and spiritual event. For them, the observance might more appropriately be called Noche de Muertos (Night of the Dead), because families actually spend whole nights at the graveyard communing with the dear departed.

Sugar skulls, chocolate coffins and toy skeletons are sold in markets everywhere, both as Muertos gifts for children and graveyard decorations; this tradition derives in great measure from the work of artist José Guadalupe Posada (1852–1913), renowned for his satirical figures of a skeletal Death cheerfully engaging in everyday life, working, dancing, courting, drinking and riding horses into battle.

religious ceremonies. December 12, her feast day, sees large-scale celebrations and pilgrimages all over the country, biggest of all in Mexico City.

Though some church figures have supported causes such as indigenous rights, the Mexican Catholic Church is a socially conservative body. It has alienated some sectors of the population by its strong opposition to the legalization of abortion and to gay marriages and civil unions.

Indigenous Religion

The Spanish missionaries of the 16th and 17th centuries won indigenous Mexicans over to Catholicism by grafting it onto pre-Hispanic religions. Old gods were renamed as Christian saints, old festivals were melded with Christian feast days. Indigenous Christianity is still fused with ancient beliefs today. Jalisco's Huichol people have two Christs, but Nakawé, the fertility goddess, is a more important deity. In the church at the Tzotzil Maya village of San Juan Chamula, you may see chanting *curanderos* (healers) carrying out shamanistic rites. In the traditional indigenous world almost everything has a spiritual dimension – trees, rivers, hills, wind, rain and sun have their own gods or spirits, and illness may be seen as a 'loss of soul' resulting from wrongdoing or from the malign influence of someone with magical powers.

Letting Off Steam

Mexicans have many ways of releasing their emotional and physical energy. Religion, artistic expression and the countless fiestas are among them. So are sports.

Fútbol

No sport ignites Mexicans' passions more than *fútbol* (soccer). Games in the 18-team Liga MX, the national First Division, are played at weekends almost year-round before crowds averaging 25,000 and followed by millions on TV. Attending a game is fun, and rivalry between opposing fans is generally good-humored.

The 2008 film *Rudo y Cursi* tells the (fictional) tale of two brothers from a poor Mexican village rising to professional playing success in a corrupt Mexican *fútbol* (soccer) world. It's a comical and lovable movie that stars two of the country's top actors, Gael García Bernal and Diego Luna.

SANTA MUERTE

A challenge to mainstream religion comes from the cult of Santa Muerte (Saint Death) – condemned as blasphemous by the Vatican in 2013 it has, by some estimates, over ten million followers in Mexico. Mexicans disillusioned with the traditional Catholic Trinity and saints now pray and make offerings to a cloaked, scythe-wielding female skeleton, the goddess of death whose origins date to pre-Hispanic Mexico. Criminal gangs are notoriously among the cult's most loyal followers, and there have even been reports of alleged human sacrifices to Santa Muerte, though she is also seen as a protector of LGBT communities and other outcasts from society. The best known Santa Muerte Altar (p81) is in Mexico City's crime-ridden Tepito neighborhood.

The two most popular teams with large followings everywhere are América, of Mexico City, known as the Águilas (Eagles), and Guadalajara, called Chivas (Goats). Matches between the two, known as Los Clásicos, are the biggest games of the year. Other leading clubs include Cruz Azul and UNAM (Pumas) of Mexico City, Monterrey and UANL (Los Tigres) from Monterrey, Santos Laguna from Torreón, and Toluca.

Bullfights

Bullfighting arouses strong passions in many Mexicans. While it has many fans, there is also a strong antibullfighting movement spearheaded by groups such as Mexican Animal Rights Association (AMEDEA) and AnimaNaturalis. Bullfights are now banned in the states of Sonora, Guerrero and Coahuila.

Bullfights usually take place on Sunday afternoons or during local festivals, chiefly in the larger cities. In northern Mexico the season generally runs from March or April to August or September. In central and southern Mexico, including Mexico City's Monumental Plaza México, one of the world's biggest bullrings, the main season is from October to February.

Other Sports

The highly popular *lucha libre* (wrestling) is more showbiz than sport. Participants give themselves names like Último Guerrero (Last Warrior), Rey Escorpión (Scorpion King) and Blue Panther, then clown around in Day-Glo tights and lurid masks. Mexico City's 17,000-seat Arena México (p129) is the big temple of this activity.

Charreadas (rodeos) are popular events, particularly in the northern half of Mexico, during fiestas and at regular venues often called *lienzos charros* – www.decharros.com has plenty of information.

Mexico has produced many world champions in boxing. The legendary Julio César Chávez won five world titles at three different weights, and achieved an amazing 87 consecutive wins (or 90 unbeaten) after turning pro in 1980.

The Arts

Mexicans are an obsessively creative people. Wherever you go in their country, you'll be impressed by the marvelous artistic expression on display. Colorful painting, stunning architecture and beautiful crafts are everywhere; Aztec dancers vibrate in the very heart of Mexico City and musicians strike up on the streets and in bars and buses. This is a country that has given the world some of its finest painting, music, movies and writing.

Architecture

Mexico's priceless architectural heritage from pre-Hispanic and colonial times is one of its greatest treasures.

Pre-Hispanic

At places like Teotihuacán, Monte Albán, Chichén Itzá, Uxmal and Palenque you can still see fairly intact, spectacular pre-Hispanic cities. Their grand ceremonial centers were designed to impress, with great stone pyramids (topped by shrines), palaces and ritual ball courts – all built without metal tools, pack animals or wheels. While the architecture of Teotihuacán, Monte Albán and the Aztecs was intended to awe with its grand scale, the Maya of Chichén Itzá, Uxmal, Palenque and countless other sites paid more attention to aesthetics, with intricately patterned facades, delicate stone 'combs' on temple roofs, and sinuous carvings, producing some of the most beautiful human creations in the Americas.

The technical hallmark of Maya buildings is the corbeled vault, a version of the arch: two stone walls leaning toward one another, nearly meeting at the top and surmounted by a capstone. Teotihuacán architecture is characterized by the *talud-tablero* style of stepped buildings, in which height is achieved by alternating upright (*tablero*) sections with sloping (*talud*) ones.

Colonial Period

The Spaniards destroyed indigenous temples and built churches and monasteries in their place, and laid out new towns with handsome plazas and grids of streets lined by fine stone edifices – contributing much to Mexico's beauty today. Building was in Spanish style, with some unique local variations. Renaissance style, based on ancient Greek and Roman ideals of harmony and proportion, with shapes such as the square and the circle, dominated in the 16th and early 17th centuries. Mérida's cathedral and Casa de Montejo are outstanding Renaissance buildings, while Mexico City and Puebla cathedrals mingle Renaissance and baroque styles.

Baroque, which reached Mexico in the early 17th century, layered new dramatic effects – curves, color and increasingly elaborate decoration – onto a Renaissance base. Painting and sculpture were integrated with architecture, notably in ornate, enormous *retablos* (altarpieces) in churches. Mexico's finest baroque buildings include Zacatecas cathedral and the churches of Santo Domingo in Mexico City and Oaxaca. Between 1730 and 1780 Mexican baroque reached its final, spectacularly out-of-control form known as Churrigueresque, with riotous ornamentation.

Mexico's Biggest Pyramids

Pirámide Tepanapa (Cholula)

Pirámide del Sol (Pyramid of the Sun; Teotihuacán)

Pirámide de la Luna (Pyramid of the Moon; Teotihuacán)

Check out the latest (and the future) in Mexico City architecture and planning – from Design Week Mexico installations to plans for a Hyperloop corridor between Mexico City and Guadalajara – at www.dezeen.com/tag/mexico-city.

Indigenous artisans added profuse sculpture in stone and colored stucco to many baroque buildings, such as the Rosary Chapels in the Templos de Santo Domingo at Puebla and Oaxaca. Spanish Islamic influence showed in the popularity of *azulejos* (colored tiles) on the outside of buildings, notably on Mexico City's Casa de Azulejos and many buildings in Puebla.

Neoclassical style, another return to sober Greek and Roman ideals, dominated from about 1780 to 1830. Outstanding buildings include the Palacio de Minería in Mexico City, designed by Mexico's leading architect of the time, Manuel Tolsá.

19th to 21st Centuries

Independent Mexico in the 19th and early 20th centuries saw revivals of colonial styles and imitations of contemporary French or Italian styles. Mexico City's semi–art nouveau Palacio de Bellas Artes is one of the most spectacular buildings from this era.

After the 1910–20 Revolution came 'Toltecism,' an effort to return to pre-Hispanic roots in the search for a national identity. This culminated in the 1950s with the Ciudad Universitaria campus in Mexico City, where many buildings are covered with colorful murals.

The great icon of more recent architecture is Luis Barragán (1902–88), who exhibited a strong Mexican strain in bringing vivid colors and plays of space and light to the typical geometric concrete shapes of the International Modern Movement. His strong influence on Mexican architecture and design is ongoing today. His oeuvre includes a set of wacky colored skyscraper sculptures in Ciudad Satélite, a Mexico City suburb, and his own house in Mexico City, which is on the Unesco World Heritage list. Another modernist, Pedro Ramírez Vázquez (1919–2013), designed three vast public buildings in Mexico City: the Estadio Azteca and Museo Nacional de Antropología in the 1960s and the Basílica de Guadalupe in the '70s. The capital has seen its share of eye-catching, prestigious structures popping up in the last decade or so: undoubtedly the top conversation piece is the Museo Soumaya Plaza Carso which opened in 2011 to house part of the art collection of multi-multi-billionaire Carlos Slim. Designed by Slim's son-in-law Fernando Romero, it's a love-it-or-hate-it six-story construction that resembles a giant, twisted blacksmith's anvil covered in 16,000 honeycomb-shaped aluminium plates.

Painting & Sculpture

Since the earliest times Mexicans have exhibited a love of color and form, and an exciting talent for painting and sculpture. The wealth of art in mural form and in Mexico's many galleries is a highlight of the country.

Pre-Hispanic

Mexico's first civilization, the Olmecs of the Gulf coast, produced remarkable stone sculptures depicting deities, animals and wonderfully lifelike human forms. Most awesome are the huge Olmec heads, which combine the features of human babies and jaguars.

The Classic Maya of southeast Mexico between about AD 250 and 800 were perhaps ancient Mexico's most artistically gifted people. They left countless beautiful stone sculptures, complicated in design but possessing great delicacy of touch.

Colonial & Independence Eras

Mexican art during Spanish rule was heavily Spanish-influenced and chiefly religious in subject, though portraiture advanced under wealthy patrons. Miguel Cabrera (1695–1768), from Oaxaca, is widely considered the most talented painter of the era.

Art Books

The Art of Mesoamerica by Mary Ellen Miller

Mexican Muralists by Desmond Rochfort

Mexicolor by Tony Cohan & Masako Takahashi

Top Art Museums

Museo Frida Kahlo (Mexico City)

Museo Jumex (Mexico City)

Museo Nacional de Arte (Mexico City)

Museo de Arte de Tlaxcala (Tlaxcala)

Museo Pedro Coronel (Zacatecas)

The years before the 1910 Revolution finally saw a break from European traditions. Mexican slums, brothels and indigenous poverty began to appear on canvases. José Guadalupe Posada (1852–1913), with his characteristic *calavera* (skull) motif, satirized the injustices of the Porfiriato period, launching a tradition of political and social subversion in Mexican art.

The Muralists
In the 1920s, immediately following the Mexican Revolution, education minister José Vasconcelos commissioned young artists to paint a series of public murals to spread a sense of Mexican history and culture and of the need for social and technological change. The trio of great muralists – all great painters in smaller scales, too – were Diego Rivera (1886–1957), José Clemente Orozco (1883–1949) and David Alfaro Siqueiros (1896–1974).

Rivera's work carried a left-wing message, emphasizing past oppression of indigenous people and peasants. His art, found in many locations in and around Mexico City, pulled Mexico's indigenous and Spanish roots together in colorful, crowded tableaux depicting historical people and events, with a simple moral message.

Siqueiros, who fought in the Revolution on the Constitutionalist (liberal) side, remained a political activist afterward and his murals convey a clear Marxist message through dramatic, symbolic depictions of the oppressed and grotesque caricatures of the oppressors. Some of his best works are at the Palacio de Bellas Artes, Castillo de Chapultepec and Ciudad Universitaria, all in Mexico City.

Orozco, from Jalisco, focused more on the universal human condition than on historical specifics. He conveyed emotion, character and atmosphere. His work was at its peak in Guadalajara between 1936 and 1939, particularly in the 50-odd frescoes in the Instituto Cultural de Cabañas.

Other 20th-Century Artists
Frida Kahlo (1907–54), physically crippled by a road accident and mentally tormented in her tempestuous marriage to Diego Rivera, painted anguished self-portraits and grotesque, surreal images that expressed her left-wing views and externalized her inner tumult. Kahlo's work

For shots of street art in 41 cities all around the country, from San Miguel de Allende and Tijuana to Puebla and León, check out Fatcap's Mexico pages: www.fatcap.com/country/mexico.html.

THE ARTS PAINTING & SCULPTURE

Diego & Frida Books

Frida Kahlo and Diego Rivera by Isabel Alcántara and Sandra Egnolff

The Diary of Frida Kahlo with an introduction by Carlos Fuentes

Frida by Hayden Herrera

Rivera by Andrea Kettenmann

STREET ART – THE NEW MURALISTS
The contemporary art having the most public impact in Mexico – and which you are most likely to set eyes on – is street art, whose direct popular appeal provides a powerful channel for Mexicans to express themselves and reach an audience. Mexico City, Oaxaca and Guadalajara lead the way in truly accomplished street art, often with a powerful political-protest message. Check out Street Art Chilango (www.streetartchilango.com), the psychedelic images with pre-Hispanic motifs created by the Axolotl Collective (www.facebook.com/axolotlcollective); the striking, often monochrome works by internationally renowned Paola Delfin (www.urban-nation.com/artist/paola-delfin); and the kaleidoscopic portrayals of animal by Farid Rueda (www.widewalls.ch/artist/farid-rueda) in Mexico City. Find works by Lapiztola (www.facebook.com/lapiztola.stencil) and Guerillaart.mx (www.guerilla-art.mx) in Oaxaca.

Today's street artists follow in the footsteps of the 20th-century muralists, with the difference that they tend to be independent and rebellious and do not serve governments. Some do, however, use their art for specific positive social projects – none more so than the Mexico City-based Germen Crew (www.facebook.com/muralismogermen), who in 2015 turned the entire Las Palmitas neighborhood in the city of Pachuca into one big rainbow-colored mural. It's a remarkable work, sponsored by the local city hall, which by all accounts has restored pride and smiles to a formerly sketchy area.

suddenly seemed to strike an international chord in the 1980s and '90s. She's now better known worldwide than any other Mexican artist, and her Mexico City home, the Museo Frida Kahlo (p96), is a don't-miss for any art lover.

Rufino Tamayo (1899–1991) from Oaxaca is sometimes thought of as the fourth major muralist, but he was a great artist at other scales too, absorbed by abstract and mythological images and effects of color. After WWII, the young artists of La Ruptura (the Rupture), led by José Luis Cuevas (b 1934), reacted against the muralist movement, which they saw as too obsessed with *mexicanidad* (Mexicanness). They opened Mexico up to world trends such as abstract expressionism and pop art. Sculptor Sebastián (b 1947), from Chihuahua, is famed for his large, mathematics-inspired sculptures that adorn cities around the world.

Contemporary Art

Today, thanks to dynamic artists, galleries and patrons and the globalization of the world art scene, contemporary Mexican art is reaching galleries the world over. Mexico City has become an international art hot spot, while other cities such as Monterrey, Oaxaca, Mazatlán and Guadalajara also have thriving art scenes. Mexican artists attempt to interpret the uncertainties of the 21st century in diverse ways. The pendulum has swung away from abstraction to hyper-representation, photorealism, installations, video and street art. Rocío Maldonado (b 1951), Rafael Cauduro (b 1950) and Roberto Cortázar (b 1962) all paint classically depicted figures against amorphous, bleak backgrounds. Check out Cauduro's murals on state-sponsored crime in Mexico City's Suprema Corte de Justicia. Leading contemporary lights such as Minerva Cuevas (b 1975), Miguel Calderón (b 1971), Betsabeé Romero (b 1963) and Gabriel Orozco (b 1962) spread their talents across many media, always challenging the spectator's preconceptions.

Music

Music is everywhere in Mexico. Live performers range from marimba (wooden xylophone) teams and mariachi bands (trumpeters, violinists, guitarists and a singer, all dressed in smart Wild West–style costumes) to ragged lone buskers with out-of-tune guitars. Mariachi music, perhaps the most 'typical' Mexican music, originated in the Guadalajara area but is played nationwide. Marimbas are particularly popular in the southeast and on the Gulf coast.

Rock & Hip-Hop

Mexico can claim to be the most important hub of *rock en español*. Talented Mexico City bands such as Café Tacuba and Maldita Vecindad emerged in the 1990s and took the genre to new heights and new audiences, mixing influences from rock, hip-hop and ska to traditional Mexican folk music. They're still popular and active today, as is the Monterrey rap-metal band Molotov, who upsets just about everyone with their expletive-laced lyrics, and El Tri, a legendary rock band active since the 1960s. Mexico's 21st-century indie rock wave threw up successful bands such as Zoé from Mexico City, which is popular throughout the Spanish-speaking world, and Monterrey's Kinky. The Mexico City five-piece Little Jesus has been winning fans with its catchy, dancey brand of pop-rock; the band's most recent album was *Río Salvaje* (2016).

Mexican rap is the true sound of the streets, and top homegrown talents include Eptos One (or Eptos Uno), from Ciudad Obregón (Sonora), Bocafloja (Mexico City), C Kan from Guadalajara, and Monterrey's Cartel de Santa.

MÚSICA TROPICAL

Although their origins lie in the Caribbean and South America, several brands of percussion-heavy, infectiously rhythmic *música tropical* are highly popular throughout the country. Mexico City, in particular, has clubs and large dance halls devoted to this scene, often hosting international bands.

Two kinds of dance music – *danzón*, originally from Cuba, and *cumbia*, from Colombia – both took deeper root in Mexico than in their original homelands. The elegant, old-fashioned *danzón* is strongly associated with the port city of Veracruz but is currently enjoying quite a revival in Mexico City and elsewhere too. The livelier, more flirtatious *cumbia* has its adopted home in Mexico City. It rests on thumping bass lines with brass, guitars, mandolins and sometimes marimbas. *Cumbia* has spawned its own subvarieties: *cumbia sonidera* is basically electronic *cumbia* played by DJs, while 'psychedelic *cumbia*' harks back to Peruvian *cumbia* of the 1970s.

Almost every town in Mexico has some place where you can dance (and often learn) salsa, which originated in New York when jazz met son (folk music), cha-cha and rumba from Cuba and Puerto Rico. Musically, salsa boils down to brass (with trumpet solos), piano, percussion, singer and chorus – the dance is a hot one with a lot of exciting turns. *Merengue*, mainly from the Dominican Republic, is a blend of *cumbia* and salsa.

Powerful, colorful Alejandra Guzmán is known as La Reina del Rock (Queen of Rock) and has sold 10 million albums during a two-decade career. The Mexican rock band most famous outside Mexico is undoubtedly Guadalajara's unashamedly commercial Maná.

Pop

Paulina Rubio is Mexico's answer to Shakira, who has also starred in several Mexican films and TV series. Hot on her heels is 'Queen of Latin Pop', Thalía from Mexico City, who has sold 25 million records worldwide. Natalia Lafourcade, a talented singer-songwriter who mixes pop and bossa nova rhythms, won Record of the Year and several other 2015 Latin Grammys with her album *Hasta La Raíz*. Another versatile singer-songwriter and diva of the pop world is Julieta Venegas from Tijuana, best known for her 2007 album, *Limón y Sal*.

Balladeer Luis Miguel is Mexico's Julio Iglesias and incredibly popular, as was Juan Gabriel, who had sold millions of his own albums and written dozens of hit songs for others before his death in 2016.

Ranchera & Norteño: Mexico's 'Country Music'

Ranchera is Mexico's urban 'country music' – mostly melodramatic stuff with a nostalgia for rural roots, sometimes with a mariachi backing. The hugely popular Vicente Fernández, Juan Gabriel and Alejandro Fernández (Vicente's son) are leading artists.

Norteño or *norteña* is country ballad and dance music, originating in northern Mexico over a century ago and now nationwide in popularity. Its roots are in *corridos*, heroic ballads with the rhythms of European dances such as waltz or polka. Originally the songs were tales of Latino-Anglo strife in the borderlands or themes from the Mexican Revolution. Modern *narcocorridos* tell of the adventures and exploits of people involved in the drugs trade. Some gangs even commission *narcocorridos* about themselves.

Norteño groups *(conjuntos)* go for 10-gallon hats, with instruments centered on the accordion and the *bajo sexto* (a 12-string guitar), along with bass and drums. *Norteño's* superstars are Los Tigres del Norte, originally from Sinaloa but now based in California. They play to huge audiences on both sides of the frontier, with some *narcocorridos* in their

Vive Latino (www.vivelatino.com.mx), a festival held over a weekend in March or April at Mexico City's Foro Sol, is one of the world's major annual *rock en español* events. Big electronica events with top Mexican or international DJs are frequent in and around the big cities: www.facebook.com/kinetik.tv and www.trance-it.net/proximos-eventos have details.

repertoire. Other top stars include Los Huracanes del Norte, Los Tucanes de Tijuana and accordionist/vocalist Ramón Ayala.

Also very popular, especially in the northwest and along the Pacific coast, is *banda* – Mexican big-band music, with large brass sections replacing *norteño* guitars and accordion, and playing a range of styles from *ranchera* and *corridos* to tropical *cumbia* and Mexican pop. Sinaloa's Banda El Recodo have been at the top of the *banda* tree for decades.

Son – Mexico's Folk Roots

Son (literally 'sound') is a broad term covering Mexican country styles that grew out of the fusion of Spanish, indigenous and African music. Guitars or similar instruments (such as the small *jarana*) lay down a strong rhythm, with harp or violin providing the melody. *Son* is often played for a foot-stomping dance audience, with witty, sometimes improvised, lyrics. There are several regional variants. The exciting *son jarocho*, from the Veracruz area, is particularly African-influenced: Grupo Mono Blanco have led a revival of the genre with contemporary lyrics. The famous 'La Bamba' is a *son jarocho*. *Son huasteco* (or *huapango*), from the Huasteca area in northeastern Mexico, features falsetto vocals between soaring violin passages. Listen out for top group Los Camperos de Valles.

Trova

This popular genre of troubadour-type folk music, typically performed by solo singer-songwriters *(cantautores)* with a guitar, has roots in 1960s and '70s folk and protest songs. Many *trova* singers are strongly inspired by Cuban political musician Silvio Rodríguez.

Cinema

The historical golden age of Mexican movie-making was the 1940s, when the country was creating up to 200 – typically epic, melodramatic – films a year. Then Hollywood reasserted itself, and Mexican cinema struggled for decades, though it has made quite a comeback in the 21st century. Fine, gritty movies by young Mexican directors have won commercial success as well as critical acclaim, and Morelia, Guadalajara, Oaxaca, Monterrey, Los Cabos and the Riviera Maya now stage successful annual film festivals.

21st-Century Film

Nuevo Cine Mexicano (New Mexican Cinema) confronts the ugly, tragic and absurd in Mexican life, as well as the beautiful and the comical. The first to really catch the world's eye was *Amores perros* (Love's a Bitch; 2000), directed by Alejandro González Iñárritu and starring Gael García Bernal, who have since both become international celebrities. Set in contemporary Mexico City, with three plots connected by one traffic accident, it's a raw, honest movie with its quota of blood, violence and sex as well as ironic humor.

Y tu mamá también (And Your Mother Too), Alfonso Cuarón's 2001 coming-of-age road trip movie about two privileged Mexico City teenagers (Gael García Bernal and Diego Luna), was at the time the biggest grossing Mexican film ever, netting more than US$25 million. Carlos Carrera's *El crimen del Padre Amaro* (The Crime of Father Amaro; 2003), again starring Gael García Bernal, painted an ugly picture of church corruption in a small town.

Success has spirited some of these talents away from Mexico. González Iñárritu moved to Hollywood to direct two more great movies with interconnected multiple plots and a theme of death – *21 Grams* (2003) and *Babel* (2006). He followed up with *Biutiful* (2010), a stunning Mexican-Spanish production starring Javier Bardem in a harrowing 'down and out in Barcelona' tale. He then scooped four Oscars, including Best Picture and Best Director, with *Birdman* (2014), the brilliantly crafted story of an aging Hollywood superhero (Michael Keaton) trying to revive his career on Broadway. Alfonso Cuarón moved on to *Harry Potter and the Prisoner of Azkaban* (2004) and the multi-Oscar-winning (including Best Director) science-fiction epic *Gravity* (2013), while Guillermo del Toro has scored success with the triple-Oscar *Pan's Labyrinth* (2006).

Meanwhile, homegrown Mexican films have been raking in awards at Cannes and other festivals. Pedro González-Rubio's *Alamar* (To the Sea) in 2010 is a gentle, thoughtful exploration of father-son bonding between a Mexican with Mayan roots and his half-Italian son, while Michel Franco's *Después de Lucía* (After Lucia) is a grim, uncomfortable look at the high school bullying at its worst. Carlos Reygadas took Cannes' 2012 Best Director award for *Post tenebras lux*, a confusing mix of fantasy and reality about a middle-class family living in the countryside. Amat Escalante was Cannes' 2013 best director with *Heli*, the story of a young couple caught in Mexico's violent drug wars. Another acclaimed 2013 movie was Diego Quemada-Diez's *La jaula de oro* (The Golden Cage), about young Central American migrants trying to get to the USA through Mexico. Migrants, this time Mexican, also take center stage in the 2015 thriller *Desierto*, starring Gael García Bernal and directed by Alfonso Cuarón's son Jonás Cuarón.

Also in the 2015 crop, Gabriel Ripstein's arms-smuggling thriller *600 Miles*, starring Tim Roth as a kidnapped US law-enforcement agent, was garlanded at the Berlin and Guadalajara festivals, and became Mexico's candidate for the 2016 Best Foreign Language Film Oscar. Tim Roth featured again, this time as a male nurse for terminally ill patients, in the moving *Chronic*, directed and written by Mexican Michel Franco and named best screenplay at Cannes in 2015. Another 2015 release, *Los jefes*, digs into the brutal reality of the narco world in Monterrey, an added curiosity being that its lead roles are played by rap musicians Cartel de Santa. In 2017, Ernesto Contreras' *Sueño en otro idioma* (I Dream in Another Language) is a meditation on the demise of indigenous languages.

On a more commercial note, Gary Alazraki's comical 2013 film addressing Mexican class divisions, *Nosotros los nobles* (We the Nobles), became the all-time biggest-grossing Mexican film in Mexican cinemas, with 3.3 million viewers. The first Mexican 3D horror movie, *Más negro que la noche* (Darker than the Night; 2014) directed by Henry Bedwell, also did well, both at the box office and with critics.

Literature

Mexicans such as Carlos Fuentes, Juan Rulfo and Octavio Paz have written some of the great Spanish-language literature.

Fuentes (1928–2012), a prolific novelist and commentator, is probably Mexico's best-known writer internationally. His most famous novel, *The Death of Artemio Cruz* (1962), takes a critical look at Mexico's postrevolutionary era through the eyes of a dying, corrupted press baron and landowner. Less known is the magical-realist *Aura* (1962), with a truly stunning ending.

In Mexico, Juan Rulfo (1918–86) is widely regarded as the supreme novelist, even though he only ever published one full-length novel: *Pedro Páramo* (1955), about a young man's search for his lost father among ghostlike villages in western Mexico. It's a scary, desolate work with confusing shifts of time – a kind of Mexican *Wuthering Heights* with a spooky, magical-realist twist.

Octavio Paz (1914–98), poet, essayist and winner of the 1990 Nobel Prize for Literature, wrote a probing, intellectually acrobatic analysis of Mexico's myths and the national character in *The Labyrinth of Solitude* (1950).

Novels Set in Mexico

The Power and the Glory by Graham Greene

Under the Volcano by Malcolm Lowry

Treasure of the Sierra Madre by B Traven

All the Pretty Horses by Cormac McCarthy

The 1960s-born novelists of the *movimiento crack* take their name from the sound of a limb falling off a tree, representing their desire to break with the past and move on from magical realism. Their work tends to adopt global themes and international settings. Best known is Jorge Volpi, whose *In Search of Klingsor* (1999) and *Season of Ash* (2009) weave complicated but exciting plots involving science, love, murder, mysteries and more, with a strong relevance to the state of the world today.

The *crack* seemed to open the way for a new generation of novelists who are right now putting Mexico back in the vanguard of world literature. These are typically superimaginative, impossible-to-classify writers whose multilayered works leap around between different times, places, voices and perspectives. Valeria Luiselli's *Faces in the Crowd* (2012) and *The Story of My Teeth* (2015) are, on the surface, respectively about a woman writing a novel and a man who replaces his own teeth with (supposedly) Marilyn Monroe's. Then there's Álvaro Enrigue with *Sudden Death* (2013), a novel of vast scope set among the many world-changing events of the 16th century in Europe and the Americas, and Yuri Herrera, whose *Signs Preceding the End of the World* (2009) illuminates small-town and big-city Mexico, the Mexico–US border and the US itself through a young woman sent to retrieve her brother from across the border. Carmen Boullosa's 17 novels range from *They're Cows, We're Pigs* (1991), examining the world of 17th-century Caribbean pirates, to *Texas, the Great Theft* (2014), a reimagining of the Tex-Mex borderlands in the 19th century. In *Quesadillas* (2014), Juan Pablo Villalobos takes a satirical look at poverty and corruption in Mexico.

Folk Art

Mexicans' skill with their hands and their love of color, fun and tradition find expression everywhere in their wonderful *artesanías* (handicrafts). Crafts such as weaving, pottery, leatherwork, copperwork, hat-making and basketry still fulfill key functions in daily life as well as yielding souvenirs and collectibles. Many craft techniques and designs in use today have pre-Hispanic origins, and it's Mexico's indigenous peoples, the direct inheritors of pre-Hispanic culture, who lead the way in *artesanías* production.

Traditional Textiles

In some of Mexico's indigenous villages you'll be stunned by the variety of colorful, intricately decorated attire, differing from area to area and often from village to village. Traditional costume – more widely worn by women than men – serves as a mark of the community to which a person belongs. The woven or embroidered patterns of some garments can take months to complete.

The 'yarn paintings' of the indigenous Huichol people – created by pressing strands of yarn onto a wax-covered board – depict scenes resembling visions experienced under the influence of the drug *peyote*, which is central to Huichol culture.

Three main types of women's garments have been in use since long before the Spanish conquest:

Huipil A long, sleeveless tunic, found mainly in the southern half of the country.
Quechquémitl A shoulder cape with an opening for the head, found mainly in central and northern Mexico.
Enredo A wraparound skirt.

Spanish missionaries introduced blouses, which are now often also embroidered with great care and detail.

The primary materials of indigenous weaving are cotton and wool, though synthetic fibers are also common. Natural dyes have been revived – deep blues from the indigo plant, reds and browns from various woods, and reds and purples from the cochineal insect.

The basic indigenous weavers' tool, used only by women, is the backstrap loom *(telar de cintura)* on which the warp (long) threads are stretched between two horizontal bars, one of which is fixed to a post or tree, while the other is attached to a strap around the weaver's lower back; the weft (cross) threads are then intricately woven in, producing some amazing patterns. Backstrap-loom *huipiles* from the southern states of Oaxaca and Chiapas are among Mexico's most eye-catching garments.

Treadle looms, operated by foot pedals (usually by men) can weave wider cloth than the backstrap loom and tend to be used for rugs, *rebozos* (shawls), *sarapes* (blankets with an opening for the head) and skirt material. Mexico's most famous rug-weaving village is Teotitlán del Valle, Oaxaca.

Ceramics

Many small-scale potters' workshops turn out everything from plain cooking pots to elaborate works of art. One highly attractive pottery variety is Talavera, made chiefly in Puebla and Dolores Hidalgo and characterized by bright colors (blue and yellow are prominent) and floral designs. The Guadalajara suburbs of Tonalá and Tlaquepaque produce a wide variety of ceramics. In northern Mexico, the villagers of Mata Ortiz make a range of beautiful earthenware, drawing on the techniques and designs of pre-Hispanic Paquimé, similar to some native American pottery in the US southwest. Another distinctive Mexican ceramic form is the *árbol de la vida* (tree of life). These elaborate, candelabra-like objects are molded by hand and decorated with numerous tiny figures of people, animals, plants and so on. Some of the best are made in Metepec in the state of México, which is also the source of colorful clay suns.

Masks & Beadwork

For millennia Mexicans have worn masks in dances, ceremonies and shamanistic rites: the wearer temporarily becomes the creature, person or deity represented by the mask. You can admire mask artistry at museums in cities such as San Luis Potosí, Zacatecas and Colima, and at shops and markets around the country. The southern state of Guerrero makes probably the broadest range of fine masks.

Wood is the basic material of most masks, but papier-mâché, clay, wax and leather are also used. Mask-makers often paint or embellish their masks with real teeth, hair, feathers or other adornments. Common masks include animals, birds, Christ, devils, and Europeans with comically pale, wide-eyed features.

The Huichol people of Jalisco, Durango, Zacatecas and Nayarit use centuries-old symbols and designs when covering masks and wooden sculptures with psychedelic patterns consisting of colourful beads, attached with wax and resin.

Lacquerware & Woodwork

Gourds, the hard shells of certain squash-type fruits, have been used in Mexico since antiquity as bowls, cups and small storage vessels. The most eye-catching decoration technique is lacquering, in which the gourd is coated with paste or paint and then varnished, producing a nonporous and, to some extent, heat-resistant vessel. Lacquering is also used to decorate wooden boxes, trays and furniture, with a lot of the most appealing ware coming from remote Olinalá in Guerrero, where artisans create patterns using the *rayado* method of scraping off part of the top coat of paint to expose a different-colored layer below.

The Seri people of Sonora work hard ironwood into dramatic human, animal and sea-creature shapes. Villagers around Oaxaca city produce brightly painted imaginary beasts carved from copal wood, known as *alebrijes*.

Craft Books

The Crafts of Mexico by Margarita de Orellana and Alberto Ruy Sánchez

Arts and Crafts of Mexico by Chloë Sayer

Mexican Textiles by Masako Takahashi

Directed by Duncan Bridgeman, the 2012 documentary *Hecho en México* is a fascinating, colorful look at contemporary Mexican life and arts, with participation from many of the country's top musicians, actors and writers.

Mexican Kitchen

In Mexico, we love food, especially our own. Ask a group of Mexicans where to find, say, the best *carnitas* (braised pork) in Mexico City, and you're launching a passionate, well-informed, lengthy debate. Visiting Mexico, you'll find out why. The food will be fresh, often locally grown, and enormously varied from one place to another, a far cry from most 'Mexican' fare served in restaurants outside the country. If you want to know Mexico and its people, you must try our food.

What's on the Menu?

This chapter was written by Mauricio Velázquez de León, a food writer born in Mexico City; his food writing has been published in Mexico and the US. He is the author (under the name Puck) of *My Foodie ABC: A Little Gourmet's Guide* (duopress, 2010). Additional research by Kate Armstrong and Anna Kaminski.

A Mexican menu will vary with the region you are visiting, but in most cases you can find food that is made with a few staples: corn, dry and fresh chilies, and beans. Contrary to popular belief, not all food in Mexico is spicy. Chilies are used as a flavoring for ingredients and to provide intensity in sauces, *moles* and *pipiáns*, and many appreciate their depth over their piquancy. But beware, some dishes do indeed have a kick, sometimes reaching daredevil levels. The *habanero* chili in the Yucatán is one of the world's spiciest peppers, and the *chile de árbol* can be fierce. A good rule of thumb is that when chilies are cooked and incorporated into the dishes as sauces they tend to be on the mild side, but when they are prepared for salsas (relishes or sauces) they can be really hot.

There are other staples that give Mexican food its classic flavoring. Among them are spices such as cinnamon, clove and cumin, and herbs such as thyme, oregano and, most importantly, cilantro (coriander), *epazote* and *hoja santa*. A pungent-smelling herb (called pigweed or Jerusalem oak in the US), *epazote* may be the unsung hero of Mexican cooking and is used for flavoring beans, soups, stews and certain *moles*. *Hoja santa* is an aromatic herb that has heart-shaped leaves; it is used as an essential ingredient in *mole verde* and is often used to make tamales.

Whimsical Eating

Antojitos are at the center of Mexican cooking. The word *antojo* translates into English as 'a whim, a sudden craving,' so an *antojito* is a little whim but, as any Mexican will quickly point out, it is not just a snack. An *antojito* can be an entire meal, an appetizer, or a *tentempié* (quick bite).

Markets are perfect places to munch on some really good *antojitos*. In the gargantuan Mercado de la Merced (p129) in Mexico City, the best *antojito* may be the *huarache*, a 30cm-long tortilla shaped like the shoe for which it is named, grilled and topped with salsa, onions, cheese and a choice of *chorizo* sausage, steak, squash blossoms and more. The *huarache* competitor can be found in the markets of Oaxaca city, where large flat tortillas called *tlayudas* are spread with refried beans and topped with Oaxacan string cheese, salsa and pork strips.

American award-winning chef and Mexican food expert Rick Bayless has a great way to define *antojitos* by grouping them according to the one component present in all: corn *masa* (dough). There are eight types of *antojitos*:

Tacos The quintessential culinary fare in Mexico can be made of any cooked meat, fish or vegetable wrapped in a tortilla, with a dash of salsa and garnished with onion and cilantro. Soft corn tortillas are used to wrap grilled meats in *tacos al carbón,* a range of stews in *tacos de guisado,* or with griddle-cooked meats and vegetables in *tacos a la plancha.* When tacos are lightly fried they are called *tacos dorados.* If you are in northern Mexico, chances are you will find tacos with flour tortillas *(tortillas de harina)* and the fillings will be more meat-based than vegetarian.

Quesadillas Fold a tortilla with cheese, heat it on a griddle and you have a quesadilla. (*Queso* means cheese, hence the name.) But real quesadillas are much more than that. In restaurants and street stalls quesadillas are stuffed pockets made with raw corn *masa* that is lightly fried or griddled until crisp. They can be stuffed with *chorizo* and cheese, squash blossoms, mushrooms with garlic, *chicharrón* (fried pork fat), beans, stewed chicken or meat.

Enchiladas In Spanish *'enchilar'* means to put chili over something, so enchiladas are a group of three or four lightly fried tortillas filled with chicken, cheese or eggs and covered with a cooked salsa. Enchiladas are usually served as a main dish, and can also be baked, like the famous *enchiladas suizas* (Swiss-style enchiladas).

Tostadas Tortillas that have been baked or fried until they get crisp and are then cooled. In this state they can hold a variety of toppings. *Tostadas de pollo* are a beautiful layering of beans, chicken, cream, shredded lettuce, onion, avocado and *queso fresco* (a fresh cheese).

Sopes Small *masa* shells, 5cm to 7.5cm in diameter, that are shaped by hand and cooked on a griddle with a thin layer of beans, salsa and cheese. *Chorizo* is also a common topping for *sopes.*

Gorditas Round *masa* cakes that are baked until they puff. Sometimes *gorditas* are filled with a thin layer of fried black or pinto beans, or even fava beans.

Chilaquiles Typically served as breakfast. Corn tortillas are cut in triangles and fried until crispy. At this point they are indeed tortilla chips *(totopos).* When cooked in a tomatillo sauce (for *chilaquiles verdes*) or tomato sauce *(chilaquiles rojos)* they become soft and then are topped with shredded cheese, sliced onions and Mexican crema.

Tamales Made with *masa* mixed with lard, stuffed with stewed meat, fish or vegetables, wrapped and steamed. Every Mexican region has its own, the most famous being the Oaxacan-style *tamales* with *mole* and wrapped in banana leaves, the Mexico City *tamales* with chicken and green tomatillo sauce wrapped in corn husks, and the Yucatecan style, made with chicken marinated in *achiote* (annatto paste) and wrapped in banana leaves.

Top Mexican Cookbooks

Authentic Mexican, 20th Anniversary Edition: Regional Cooking from the Heart of Mexico by Rick Bayless

The Essential Cuisines of Mexico by Diana Kennedy

Nopalito: A Mexican Kitchen by Stacy Adimando, Gonzalo Guzmán

The Food and Life of Oaxaca: Traditional Recipes from Mexico's Heart by Zarela Martínez

MULLI (MOLE)

Mexican chef and author Zarela Martínez once told me that in *mole* the sauce is the dish. What she meant was that when we eat *mole* we eat it because we want the sauce. The meat – whether it be chicken, turkey or pork – plays a secondary role. A complex sauce made with nuts, chilies and spices, *mole* defines Mexican cuisine. Although *mole* is often called chocolate sauce, only a very small percentage of *moles* include this ingredient. The confusion is understandable since the recipe for *mole poblano* (*mole* from the state of Puebla), the most widely known *mole* in the country, includes a small amount of chocolate. But most Mexicans would agree that when it comes to *mole*, Oaxaca is the place to go. It's known as 'The Land of Seven Moles (p438)'.

A Day of Eating: From Sunrise to Sunset & Beyond

It's easy to find a place to eat in Mexico. From an early *antojito* at a small *puesto* (street or market stall) to a lavish late dinner at a fine restaurant, food is always available.

Desayuno (breakfast) Usually served in restaurants and *cafeterías* from 8:30am to 11am; it tends to be on the heavy side. Egg dishes are popular morning fare. *Huevos rancheros*, two fried eggs atop lightly fried tortillas with a layer of black beans and topped with a tomato, onion and chili salsa, are widely served. In the Yucatán region, you will find *huevos motuleños*, a similar preparation that also includes diced ham, peas and plantains. Many *cafeterías* offer an array of *pan de dulce* (sweet breads) with amusing names such as *bigotes* (mustaches), *conchas* (shells), *besos* (kisses) and *orejas* (ears).

Almuerzo Those who have a light breakfast or skip it altogether can have an *almuerzo* (a mid-morning snack) or an *antojito* or other quick bite. *Taquerías* (places specializing in tacos), *torterías* (small establishments selling *tortas*) and *loncherías* (places that serve light meals) are good options for *almuerzo*.

Comida This is the main meal in Mexico. It is usually served from 2pm to 4:30pm in homes, restaurants and cafes. Places called *fondas* are small, family-run eateries that serve *comida corrida*, an inexpensive fixed-price menu that includes soup, rice, a main dish, beverage and dessert. In many big cities it's common to see people enjoying long business lunches or gatherings with friends where food, conversation and drinks mingle for a couple of hours. Popular *comida* fares are soups, such as *sopa de fideo* (vermicelli noodles in a soupy tomato broth), or *sopa de frijol* (bean soup), while main dishes include *guisados* (stews), such as slowed-braised meats and vegetables in cooked chipotle, tomatillo or tomato salsas.

Cena Frequently dinner is not served until 9pm and it is usually light when eaten at home. In restaurants, however, dinner is often a social gathering where eaters share a complete meal that can last until midnight.

And... When people go to a bar, a club or a late movie, they often stop off for a quick taco before returning home. Many famous *taquerías* cater to hungry insomniacs and don't close until the wee hours. On Fridays and Saturdays so many customers visit these places that sometimes you have to wait for a table at 3am!

Have You Heard the Word Fiesta?

Food and fiestas go hand-in-hand in Mexico. They can be national holidays, religious festivals, local fiestas or personal celebrations, but chances are you will get caught in one of them during your visit. During national

Under the Jaguar Sun by Italian writer Italo Calvino is a compelling account of a husband and wife discovering Mexico and its cuisine. The couple in the story becomes so enamored of the cuisine that their passion is transferred from the bedroom to the dining table.

THE NEW BREED OF CHEFS

The typical Mexican kitchen is very much a matriarchal place, where the country's culinary traditions are preserved and practiced year in, year out. But it's mostly men who are garnering celebrity status from the new wave of creative contemporary restaurants that meld the traditional and the innovative in ingredients and recipes with a flair for presentation. Mexico City is the epicenter of this movement and Enrique Olvera of the famed **Pujol** (p118) is often considered the father of New Mexican cuisine. He has been mentor to other leading lights in the capital like Eduardo García of **Maximo Bistrot Local** (p117). Ricardo Muñoz is famed for his reinventions of traditional recipes at **Azul y Oro** (p119), while Monica Patiño of **Taberna del León** (p118) and Elena Reygadas of Rosetta (Mexico City) keep the flag flying for women. Benito Molina of Manzanilla in Baja California and Pablo Salas of Amaranta (Toluca) are known for their progressive cuisine. Chefs such as Alejandro Ruiz at **Casa Oaxaca** (p439) and Diego Hernández Baquedano at **Corazón de Tierra** (www.corazondetierra.com), in Baja California's Valle de Guadalupe wine region, are spreading the word to the regions.

VEGETARIANS & VEGANS

In many parts of Mexico, 'vegetarian' is not a word in the local lexicon. Many Mexicans still think of a vegetarian as a person who doesn't eat red meat. Many more have never even heard the word *veganista* (vegan), though this is changing, particularly in Mexico City, where 'vegan food' is now a byword for hipness. The good news is that almost every city, large or small, has real vegetarian restaurants (some even have vegan ones) and their popularity is increasing. Also, many traditional Mexican dishes are vegetarian: *ensalada de nopales* (cactus-leaf salad); quesadillas made with *huitlacoche* (corn fungus), cheeses and even flowers such as zucchini flowers; *chiles rellenos de queso* (cheese-stuffed poblano chilies); and *arroz a la mexicana* (Mexican-style rice). Be warned, however, that many dishes are prepared using chicken or beef broth, or some kind of animal fat, such as *manteca* (lard).

holidays, food's always present, but toasting with tequila is a prerequisite, especially during Día de la Independencia (September 16), which celebrates independence from Spain. The largest religious festivity is the Día de Nuestra Señora de Guadalupe (December 12), where *tamales, mole* and an array of *antojitos* are traditional fare. During Lent, meatless dishes such as *romeritos* (a wild plant that resembles rosemary served with dried shrimp, potatoes and *mole*) show up on most menus. On the Día de los Santos Reyes (Three Kings Day; January 6) Mexicans celebrate by eating *rosca de reyes,* a large oval sweetbread decorated with candied fruit. The *rosca* is served with corn *tamales* and hot chocolate. During Christmas, a traditional Mexican menu includes turkey, *bacalao* (dried codfish cooked with olives, capers, onions and tomatoes) and *romeritos*.

There is no celebration in Mexico with more mystique than Día de Muertos (Day of the Dead; November 2). Its origins date to pre-Hispanic times and it commemorates lost relatives and loved ones. By celebrating death, Mexicans salute life and they do it the way they celebrate everything else, with food, drinks and music. An altar to death is set up in a house or, as some families prefer, in the graveyard. It is decorated with bright *cempasuchil* (marigold) flowers, plates of *tamales,* sugar-shaped skulls and *pan de muerto* (bread of the dead: a loaf made with egg yolks, mezcal and dried fruits). The favorite foods of the deceased are laid out so that they feel welcomed upon their return.

Josefina Velázquez de León (1899–1968) is considered the mother of Mexican cuisine. She ran a successful culinary school and wrote more than 140 cookbooks, the most ambitious being *Platillos regionales de la República Mexicana,* considered the first book to collect Mexico's regional cuisine in one volume.

¡Salud!
Tequila

Mexicans love tequila. They drink it on large and small national holidays, at funerals and anniversaries, at casual lunches, and at dinner and in bars with friends. Legally, tequila is Mexico's Champagne. All tequila has to come either from the state of Jalisco, or specifically designated areas in the states of Guanajuato, Michoacán, Nayarit and Tamaulipas, and is protected with a Designation of Origin (DO) by the Consejo Regulador del Tequila (Tequila Regulatory Council). This organization ensures that all tequila sold throughout the world comes from these parts of western Mexico. This arid area with highland soil creates the perfect conditions for the blue agave, the plant from which tequila is distilled, to grow. No tequila made in China (or elsewhere), *por favor*.

Taste is a key word when it comes to tequila. Tequila has become more and more sophisticated and today is considered a refined drink that rivals an imported single-malt whiskey or a quality cognac, and not only in price but in its smooth, warm taste. Today's finest tequilas are meant to be enjoyed in a small glass, with pleasure, in tiny sips.

The process of making tequila starts by removing the *piña* (heart) of the blue agave plant. This *piña* is then steamed for up to 36 hours, a process

CANTINAS

Cantinas are the traditional Mexican watering holes. Until not long ago, women, military personnel and children were not allowed in cantinas, and some cantinas still have a rusted sign stating this rule. Today, everybody is allowed, although the more traditional establishments retain a macho edge. Beer, tequila and *cubas* (rum and coke) are served at square tables where patrons play dominos and watch *fútbol* (soccer) games on large TV screens. Cantinas are famous for serving *botanas* (appetizers) such as *quesadillas de papa con guacamole* (potato quesadillas with guacamole) or snails in chipotle sauce.

that softens the fibers and releases the *aguamiel* (honey water). This liquid is funneled into large tanks where it is fermented. Fermentation determines whether the final product will be 100% agave or *mixto* (mixed). The highest-quality tequila is made from fermenting and then distilling only *aguamiel* mixed with some water. In tequilas *mixtos*, the *aguamiel* is mixed with other sugars, usually cane sugar with water. When tequila is 100% agave it will say so on the label. If it doesn't say 100%, it is a *mixto*.

The next step in the tequila-making process is to distill the *aguamiel* and store it in barrels for aging. The aging is important, especially for today's fancier tequilas, because it determines the color, taste, quality and price. Silver or *blanco* (white) is clear and is aged for no more than 60 days. Tequila *blanco* is used primarily for mixing and blends particularly well into fruit-based drinks. Tequila *reposado* (rested) is aged from two to nine months. It has a smooth taste and light gold color. Tequila *añejo* (old) is aged in wooden barrels for a minimum of 12 months. The best-quality *añejos* are aged up to four years. Tequila *añejo* has a velvety flavor and a deep, dark color. These three kinds of tequilas are equally popular in Mexico, and it is entirely a matter of personal taste that determines which one to drink.

Mezcal

Mezcal is tequila's brother and it is currently experiencing a boom with people who believe tequila has gone too mainstream (and expensive!). *Mezcalerías* (bars specializing in mezcal) are a recent trend, especially in cities. Like tequila, mezcal is distilled from agave plants, but mezcal doesn't have to come from blue agave, or from the tequila-producing areas of Jalisco. In other words, all tequila is mezcal, but not all mezcal is tequila. Since mezcal can be made with any type of agave plant, it is produced throughout the country; methods of production and quantities of agave involved vary widely from place to place.

In February 2017, the controversial NOM 70 legislation passed into law, stipulating that, according to the CRM (Consejo Regulador Mezcal), all mezcal that's not produced within the newly designated area consisting of the states of Durango, Guerrero, Guanajuato, Michoacán, Oaxaca, Puebla, San Luís Potosí, Tamaulipas and Zacatecas may not use the name 'mezcal' but must instead be called 'aguardiente de agave'. Since 'aguardiente' carries negative connotations and since it is felt by many that the law is less about proper regulation of mezcal and more about forcing out smaller producers, this is set to impact negatively on independent distilleries.

Pulque

If tequila and mezcal are brothers, then *pulque* would be the father of Mexican spirits. Two thousand years ago ancient Mexicans started to extract the juice of agave plants to produce a milky, slightly alcoholic drink that the Aztecs called *octli poliqhui*. When the Spanish arrived in Mexico they started to call the drink *pulque*. Even though *pulque* has a lower alcohol content than tequila or mezcal, it is much harder on the palate. Because it is not distilled, it retains an earthy, vegetal taste and has

Micheladas are prepared chilled beers ranging from simple drinks to complex cocktails. The basic *michelada* is a mix of the juice of one or two key limes in a chilled mug, a few ice cubes, a dash of salt and a Mexican cold beer. They are often served with a few drops of hot sauce, Worcestershire sauce and Maggi seasoning.

a thick, foamy consistency that some people find unpleasant. In some places it is mixed with fruit juices, such as mango or strawberry, to make it more palatable. When *pulque* is mixed with juices it is called *curado*.

Beer

For some visitors, *'Una cerveza, por favor'* is their most commonly used Spanish phrase while in Mexico. This makes sense. Mexican *cerveza* is big, and it's a great match with, well, Mexican food! Most Mexican brands are light and quench beautifully the spiciness of a plate of enchiladas. Beers are also a great companion for the thousands of *fútbol* matches that we follow in this country with religious zeal.

Two major breweries dominate the Mexican market. Grupo Modelo, now owned by Belgium-based AB InBev, makes around 18 brands, among them Corona, Victoria, Modelo Especial, Pacífico, Montejo and Negra Modelo. Although Corona is one of the world's best-selling beers, beer aficionados regard Negra Modelo, a darker beer, as the brewery's jewel. In the industrial city of Monterrey, Cervecería Cuauhtémoc Moctezuma (now a subsidiary of Heineken International) produces Sol, Carta Blanca, Dos Equis, Superior, Tecate and Bohemia, among others. The original early-20th-century version of Dos Equis, the darker and fuller-bodied Dos Equis Ámbar, is enjoying a resurgence in popularity today. In the last few years, however, microbrews *(cervezas artesanales)*, have exploded onto the beer scene and a mind-boggling choice of local brews is increasingly offered in the better restaurants and bars. The variety of Mexican beers allows for drinking them in many different environments. A day on the beach calls for a Corona, a Superior or a Pacífico. Victoria and Montejo are good matches for seafood; Modelo Especial and Carta Blanca go really well with meat; and a Bohemia or Negra Modelo would pair perfectly with a very good, decadent dinner.

Wine

Now may be the right time to expand your Spanish vocabulary to include *'Una copa de vino, por favor.'* Although the wine industry is still much smaller than that of tequila or beer, Mexican wines are leaping forward at a great rate. Since the 1990s, challenged in part by the success of Californian, Chilean and Argentinean wines, Mexican producers began yielding good wines in nine regions, from Querétaro to Sonora, with the best coming from Valle de Guadalupe, in the north of Baja California (the area even boasts a wine route). The two larger wineries in Mexico, Pedro Domecq and LA Cetto, offer solid table wines and some premium labels such as Chateau Domecq and Private Reserve Nebbiolo. 'Boutique wineries' with names such as Monte Xanic, Casa de Piedra and Casa Valmar are also producing great wine in smaller quantities.

Nonalcoholic Drinks

The great variety of fruits, plants and herbs that grow in this country are a perfect fit for the kind of nonalcoholic drinks Mexicans love. All over the country you will find classic *juguerías*, street stalls or small establishments selling fresh-squeezed orange, tangerine, strawberry, papaya or carrot juices. These places also sell *licuados*, a Mexican version of a milkshake that normally includes banana, milk, honey and fruit. There are some creative combinations too, with ingredients such as *nopal* (cactus leaves), pineapple, lemon and orange, or vanilla, banana and avocado.

In *taquerías* and most restaurants you will find *aguas frescas*, juices diluted with water and sugar. Some of them resemble iced teas. In *agua de tamarindo*, the tamarind pods are boiled and then mixed with sugar before being chilled, while *agua de jamaica* is made with dried hibiscus leaves. Others such as *horchata* are made with melon seeds and/or rice.

English sailors coined the term 'cocktail' upon discovering that their drinks in the Yucatán port of Campeche were stirred with the thin, dried roots of a plant called *cola de gallo*, which translates as 'cock's tail.' Cocktail bars are a fixture in large cities with a diverse nightlife, such as Mexico City and Guadalajara.

MEXICAN KITCHEN ¡SALUD!

In Tenochtitlán (present-day Mexico City), chocolate was considered the 'drink of the gods' and it was called *tlaquetzalli* (precious thing) in the Náhuatl language. Chocolate was so valued by the Aztecs that the cacao bean, from which chocolate is derived, was also used as a form of currency.

Landscapes & Wildlife

One of the thrills of travel in Mexico is the incredible, ever-changing scenery. From the cactus-strewn northern deserts and the snowcapped volcanoes of central Mexico to the tropical forests and wildlife-rich lagoons of the south, there's rarely a dull moment for the eye. Nature lovers will revel in this country which, thanks to its location straddling temperate and tropical regions, is one of the most biologically diverse on earth.

The Land

Nearly two million sq km in area, Mexico is the world's 14th-biggest country. With 10,000km of coastline and half its land above 1000m in elevation, the country has a spectacularly diverse and rugged topography. Almost anywhere you go, except the Yucatán Peninsula, there'll be a range of mountains in sight, close or distant.

Central Volcanic Belt

The Cordillera Neovolcánica, the spectacular volcanic belt running east–west across the middle of Mexico, includes the classic active cones of Popocatépetl (5452m), 70km southeast of Mexico City, and Volcán de Fuego de Colima (3820m), 30km north of Colima. Popocatépetl's eruptions (at low to intermediate intensity) have been ongoing from 2006; over 30 million people live within the area that could be directly affected should smoking 'Popo' erupt in a big way. Both Popocatépetl and Colima have spewed forth clouds of ash in 2017. Also in the volcanic belt, but dormant, are Mexico's highest peak, Pico de Orizaba (5611m), and the third-highest peak, Popo's 'sister' Iztaccíhuatl (5220m). Mexico's youngest volcano, and the easiest to get to the top of, is Paricutín (2800m), which popped up in 1943 near the Michoacán village of Angahuan.

The upland valleys between the volcanoes have always been among the most habitable areas of Mexico. It's in one of these – the Valle de México (a 60km-wide basin at 2200m elevation) – that Mexico City, with its 20 million people, sits ringed by volcanic ranges.

Northern Plains & Sierras

Along its 1400km length, the Sierra Madre Occidental is crossed by only one railway and three paved roads: the Ferrocarril Chihuahua Pacífico (Copper Canyon Railway) from Los Mochis to Chihuahua, Hwy 16 (Hermosillo to Chihuahua), and Hwys 40 and 40D (Mazatlán to Durango).

A string of broad plateaus, the Altiplano Central, runs down the middle of the northern half of Mexico, fringed by two long mountain chains – the Sierra Madre Occidental in the west and Sierra Madre Oriental in the east. The *altiplano* and the two *sierras madre* end where they run into the Cordillera Neovolcánica.

The *altiplano* is criss-crossed by minor mountain ranges, and rises from an average elevation of about 1000m in the north to more than 2000m toward the center of the country. The sparsely vegetated Desierto Chihuahuense (Chihuahuan Desert) covers most of the northern *altiplano* and extends north into the US states of Texas and New Mexico. The landscape here is one of long-distance vistas across dusty brown plains to distant mountains, with eagles and vultures circling the skies. The southern *altiplano* is mostly rolling hills and broad valleys, and includes some of the best Mexican farming and ranching land in the area known as El Bajío, between the cities of Querétaro, Guanajuato and Morelia. The extremely rugged Sierra Madre Occidental is fissured by many spectacularly deep canyons, including the famous Barranca del Cobre (Copper Canyon) and its 1870m-deep continuation, the Barranca de Urique. The Sierra Madre Oriental includes peaks as high as 3700m, but has semitropical zones on its lower, eastern slopes.

Baja California

Baja California, one of the world's longest peninsulas, runs down Mexico's northwest coast. It is believed to have been separated from the 'mainland' about five million years ago by tectonic forces, with the Sea of Cortez (Golfo de California) filling the gap. Baja is 1300km of starkly beautiful deserts, plains and beaches, with a mountainous spine that reaches up to 3100m in the Sierra San Pedro Mártir.

Coastal Plains

Coastal plains stretch all along Mexico's Pacific coast and as far south as the Tabasco lowlands on the Gulf coast. Both coasts are strung with hundreds of lagoons, estuaries and wetlands, making them important wildlife habitats.

On the Pacific side, a dry, wide plain stretches south from the US border almost to Tepic, in Nayarit state. As they continue south to the Guatemalan border, the lowlands narrow to a thin strip and become increasingly tropical.

The Gulf coast plain, an extension of a similar plain in Texas, is crossed by many rivers flowing down from the Sierra Madre Oriental. In the northeast, the plain is wide, with good ranchland, but is semimarsh near the coast. It narrows as it nears Veracruz.

The South

Yet another rugged, complicated mountain chain, the Sierra Madre del Sur stretches across the states of Guerrero and Oaxaca, roughly paralleling the Cordillera Neovolcánica, from which it's divided by the broiling hot Río Balsas basin. The Sierra Madre del Sur ends at the low-lying, hot and humid Isthmus of Tehuantepec, Mexico's narrow 'waist', which is just 220km wide.

In the southernmost state of Chiapas, the Pacific lowlands are backed by the Sierra Madre de Chiapas. Dormant Volcán Tacaná, whose 4110m cone rises on the Mexico–Guatemala border, is the westernmost of a string of volcanoes that stretch across Guatemala. Behind the Chiapas highlands, the land sinks to the lowlands of the Lacandón Jungle and the flat expanses of the huge limestone shelf that is the Yucatán Peninsula. The Yucatán's soft, easily eroded limestone has led to the formation of many underground rivers and more than 6000 sinkholes, known as cenotes, many of which make fantastic swimming holes. Off the Yucatán's Caribbean coast is the world's second-largest barrier reef, known variously as the Great Maya, Mesoamerican or Belize Barrier Reef. It's home to a fantastic variety of colorful marine life that makes it one of the world's top diving and snorkeling destinations.

Wildlife

From the whales, sea lions and giant cacti of Baja California to the big cats, howler monkeys and cloud forests of the southeast, Mexico's fauna and flora are exotic and fascinating. Getting out among it all is becoming steadily easier as growing numbers of local outfits offer trips to see birds, butterflies, whales, dolphins, sea turtles and more.

LANDSCAPES & WILDLIFE WILDLIFE

Volcano Watch

Monitoreo Volcánico Popocatépetl (www.cenapred.unam.mx:8080/monitoreoPopocatepetl)

Volcán Colima y Más Volcanes (www.facebook.com/volcancolima)

Webcams de México (www.webcamsdemexico.com) streams video of Volcán de Colima and Popocatepetl

Those that Walk

The surviving tropical forests of the southeast are still home to five species of large cat (jaguar, puma, ocelot, jaguarundi and margay) in isolated pockets, plus spider and howler monkeys, tapirs, anteaters and some mean reptiles, including a few boa constrictors. Small jaguar populations are scattered as far north as the northern Sierra Madre Occidental, just 200km from the US border, and the Sierra Gorda in the Sierra Madre Oriental. You may well see howler monkeys – or at least hear their eerie growls – near the Maya ruins at Palenque and Yaxchilán.

In the north, urban growth, ranching and agriculture have pushed the larger wild beasts – such as the puma (mountain lion), wolf, bobcat, bighorn sheep, pronghorn and coyote – into isolated, often mountainous pockets. Raccoons, armadillos and skunks are still fairly common – the last two in much of the rest of Mexico too.

In all warm parts of Mexico you'll encounter two harmless, though sometimes surprising, reptiles: the iguana, a lizard that can grow a meter or so long and comes in many different colors; and the gecko, a tiny, usually green lizard that may shoot out from behind a curtain or cupboard when disturbed. Geckos might make you jump, but they're good news – they eat mosquitoes.

Those that Swim

Baja California is famous for whale-watching in the early months of the year. Gray whales swim 10,000km from the Arctic to calve in its coastal waters. Between Baja and the mainland, the Sea of Cortez hosts more than a third of all the world's marine mammal species, including sea lions, fur and elephant seals, and four types of whale. Humpback whales follow plankton-bearing currents all the way down Mexico's Pacific coast between December and March, and, like dolphins and sea turtles, are commonly seen on boat trips from coastal towns.

Mexico's coasts, from Baja to Chiapas and from the northeast to the Yucatán Peninsula, are among the world's chief nesting grounds for sea turtles. Seven of the world's eight species frequent Mexican waters. Some female turtles swim unbelievable distances (right across the Pacific Ocean in the case of some loggerhead turtles) to lay eggs on the beaches where they were born. Killing sea turtles or taking their eggs is illegal in Mexico, and there are more than 100 protected nesting beaches – at many of which it's possible to observe the phenomenon known as an *arribada*, when turtles come ashore in large numbers to nest, and to assist in the release of hatchlings.

Dolphins play along the Pacific and Gulf coasts, while many coastal wetlands, especially in the south of the country, harbor crocodiles. Underwater life is richest of all on the coral reefs off the Yucatán Peninsula's Caribbean coast, where there's world-class diving and snorkeling. Near Isla Contoy, off the Yucatán's northeast tip, you can snorkel with whale sharks, the world's biggest fish.

Those that Fly

All of coastal Mexico is a fantastic bird habitat, especially its estuaries, lagoons and islands. An estimated three billion migrating birds pass by or over the Yucatán Peninsula each year, and Veracruz state is a route of passage for a 'river of raptors' over 4 million strong every fall. Inland Mexico abounds with eagles, hawks and buzzards, and innumerable ducks and geese winter in the northern Sierra Madre Occidental. Tropical species such as trogons, hummingbirds, parrots and tanagers start to appear south of Tampico in the east of the country and from around Mazatlán in the west. The southeastern jungles and cloud forests are home to colorful macaws, toucans, guans and even a few quetzals. Yucatán has spectacular flamingo colonies at Celestún and Río Lagartos. Dozens of local operators around the country, especially along the coasts, offer bird-watching trips.

Mexico's most unforgettable insect marvel is Michoacán's Reserva Mariposa Monarca (p624), where the trees and earth turn orange when millions of monarch butterflies arrive every winter.

Endangered Species

By most counts, 101 animal species are in danger of disappearing from Mexico. Eighty-one of these are endemic to Mexico. The endangered list includes such wonderful creatures as the jaguar, ocelot, northern tamandua (an anteater), pronghorn, Central American (Baird's) tapir, harpy eagle, resplendent quetzal, scarlet macaw, Cozumel curassow, loggerhead turtle, sea otter, Guadalupe fur seal, four types of parrot, and both spider and howler monkeys. The beautiful little vaquita (harbor porpoise), found only in the northern Sea of Cortez, was down to less than 30 individuals by 2017, prompting a controversial last-ditch campaign by the government and consevartionsts to save them by banning all nets from the coast and compensating fishermen for loss of work. The Margarita Island kangaroo rat and Hubbs freshwater snail may be less glamorous, but their disappearance too will forever affect the other plants and animals around them. Additionally, they're endemic to Mexico, so once gone from here, they're gone from the universe. A host of factors contribute to these creatures' endangered status, including deforestation, the spread of agriculture and urban areas, species trafficking and poaching.

Mexico's main tools for saving endangered species are its network of protected areas such as national parks and biosphere reserves, which covers 13% of the national territory, and a range of specific schemes aimed at conserving certain habitats or species. Government programs are supplemented by the work of local and international conservation groups, but progress is slowed by large gaps in the protected areas network, patchy enforcement and limited funding.

WWF's Wildfinder (worldwildlife. org/science/ wildfinder) is a database of over 26,000 animal species, searchable by species or place. For each of 23 Mexican eco-regions, it will give a list of hundreds of species with their names in English and Latin, their threatened status, and often pictures.

Plants

Northern Mexico's deserts, though sparsely vegetated with cacti, agaves, yucca, scrub and short grasses, are the world's most biodiverse deserts. Most of the planet's 2000 or so cactus species are found in Mexico, including more than 400 in the Desierto Chihuahuense alone, and many of them unique to Mexico. Isolated Baja California has a rather specialized and diverse flora, from the 20m-high cardón (the world's tallest cactus) to the bizarre boojum tree, which looks like an inverted carrot with fluff at the top.

Mexico's great mountain chains have big expanses of pine (with half the world's pine species) and, at lower elevations, oak (135 types). In the southern half of the country, mountain pine forests are often covered in clouds, turning them into cloud forests with lush, damp vegetation, many colorful wildflowers, and epiphytes growing on tree branches.

The natural vegetation of the low-lying southeast is predominantly evergreen tropical forest (rainforest in parts). This is dense and diverse, with ferns, epiphytes, palms, tropical hardwoods such as mahogany, and fruit trees such as the mamey and the chicozapote (sapodilla), which yields chicle (natural chewing gum). Despite ongoing destruction, the Selva Lacandona (Lacandón Jungle) in Chiapas is Mexico's largest remaining tropical forest, containing a significant number of Chiapas' 10,000 plant species.

The Yucatán Peninsula changes from rainforest in the south to tropical dry forest and savanna in the north, with thorny bushes and small trees (including many acacias).

Parks & Reserves

Mexico has spectacular national parks, biosphere reserves and other protected areas – over 910,000 sq km of its terrestrial and marine territory is under some kind of federal environmental protection. Governments have never had enough money for fully effective protection of these areas, but gradually, with some help from conservation organizations, more 'paper parks' are becoming real ones.

TOP PARKS & RESERVES

PARK/RESERVE	FEATURES	ACTIVITIES	WHEN TO VISIT
Área de Protección de Flora y Fauna Cuatro-ciénegas (p846)	Desert; underground streams; *pozas* (swimming holes); extraordinary biodiversity	Swimming; wildlife-watching; hiking	year-round
Parque Nacional Archip-iélago Espíritu Santo (p846)	Waters around Espíritu Santo & neighboring islands in Sea of Cortez	Kayaking with whale sharks; snorkeling with sea lions; sailing	year-round
Parque Nacional Bahía de Loreto (p846)	Islands, shores & waters of the Sea of Cortez	Snorkeling; kayaking; diving	year-round
Parque Nacional Iztaccíhuatl-Popocatépetl (p846)	Active & dormant volcanic giants on rim of Valle de México	Hiking; climbing	Nov-Feb
Parque Nacional Lagunas de Chacahua (p846)	Oaxacan coastal lagoons; beach	Boat trips; bird-watching; surfing	year-round
Parque Nacional Volcán Nevado de Colima (p846)	Active & dormant volcanoes; pumas; coyotes; pine forests	Volcano hiking	late Oct-early Jun
Reserva de la Biosfera Banco Chinchorro (p846)	Largest coral atoll in northern hemisphere	Diving; snorkeling	Dec-May
Reserva de la Biosfera Calakmul (p846)	Rainforest with major Maya ruins including Calakmul, Hormiguero and Chicanná	Visiting ruins; wild-life-spotting	year-round
Reserva de la Biosfera El Pinacate y Gran Desierto de Altar (p771)	Petrified lava flows, sand dunes, giant craters; one of the driest places on earth	Hiking; wildlife-spotting	year-round
Reserva de la Biosfera El Vizcaíno (p846)	Coastal lagoons where gray whales calve; deserts	Whale-watching; hikes to ancient rock art	Dec-Apr
Reserva de la Biosfera Mariposa Monarca (p624)	Forests festooned with millions of monarch butterflies	Butterfly observation; hiking	late Oct-Mar
Reserva de la Biosfera Montes Azules (p846)	Tropical jungle; lakes; rivers	Jungle hikes; canoeing; rafting; bird-watching; wildlife-watching	Dec-Aug
Reserva de la Biosfera Ría Celestún (p846)	Estuary & mangroves with plentiful bird life, incl flamingos	Bird-watching; boat trips	Nov-Mar
Reserva de la Biosfera Ría Lagartos (p846)	Mangrove-lined estuary full of bird-life, incl flamingos	Bird-, crocodile- and turtle-watching	Apr-Sep
Reserva de la Biosfera Sian Ka'an (p846)	Caribbean coastal jungle, wetlands & islands with incredibly diverse wildlife	Bird-watching; snorkeling & nature tours, mostly by boat	year-round
Reserva de la Biosfera Sierra Gorda (p651)	Transition zone from semidesert to cloud forest	Hiking; bird-watching; colonial missions	year-round

National Parks

Mexico's 67 terrestrial *parques nacionales* (national parks) cover 14,320 sq km of territory. Many are tiny (smaller than 10 sq km), and around half of them were created in the 1930s, often for their archaeological, historical or recreational value rather than for ecological reasons. Several recently created parks protect coastal areas, offshore islands or coral reefs. In November 2017, Mexico announced the creation of the biggest marine reserve in North America, Parque Nacional Revillagigedo (150,000 sq km), that will protect the eponymous islands, the 'Galapagos of North America', and the marine species that inhabit the surrounding waters. Despite illegal logging, hunting and grazing, terrestrial national parks have succeeded in protecting big tracts of forest, especially the high, coniferous forests of central Mexico.

Biosphere Reserves

Reservas de la biosfera (biosphere reserves) are based on the recognition that it is impracticable to put a complete stop to human exploitation of many ecologically important areas. Instead, these reserves encourage sustainable local economic activities within their territory. Today Mexico has over 50 Unesco-protected and/or national biosphere reserves, covering over 210,000 sq km. The most recent are the largest, with the Mexican Caribbean Biosphere Reserve (57,000 sq km) covering virtually the entire coastline of Quintano Roo, and Baja's Pacific Islands Biosphere Reserve (10,926 sq km) encompassing the Coronado Islands near the US border. Biosphere reserves protect some of the country's most beautiful and biologically fascinating areas, focusing on whole ecosystems with genuine biodiversity. Sustainable, community-based tourism is an important source of support for several of them, and successful visitor programs are in place in reserves like Calakmul, Sierra Gorda, Montes Azules, Mariposa Monarca, La Encrucijada and Sian Ka'an.

Ramsar Sites

Nearly 90,000 sq km of Mexican landmass and coastal waters are protected as Wetlands of International Importance, known as Ramsar sites (www.ramsar.org). They are named for the Iranian town where the 1971 Convention on Wetlands of International Importance was signed. Mexico's 142 separate sites include whale calving grounds, turtle nesting beaches, coral reefs, and coastal lagoons and mangrove forests that are of crucial importance for birds and many marine creatures.

Environmental Issues

Mexico achieved the status of a global standard-bearer on climate change in 2012 when it became only the second country (after the UK) to enshrine carbon-emission commitments into law. The climate-change law committed Mexico, currently the world's 13th biggest carbon emitter, to be producing 35% of its electricity from renewable and nuclear energy by 2024, and to cut its carbon emissions by 50% from previously expected levels by 2050.

In 2015 it became the first non-European country to formally submit its climate-change commitments to the United Nations, with a minimum 25% cut in greenhouse-gas emissions from previously expected levels by 2030. Mexico also set a target of zero deforestation by 2030.

Air pollution and deforestation are among Mexico's own biggest environmental problems, and while the country is one of the world's major exporters of crude oil, it has had to import half of its gasoline because it is short on refineries. Replacing costly imports with home-grown renewable energy makes much sense. Sunny Mexico has plenty of potential for

Parks & Reserves Websites

Comisión Nacional de Áreas Naturales Protegidas (www.conanp.gob.mx)

Unesco biosphere reserves (www.unesco.org/new/en/natural-sciences/environment/ecological-sciences/biosphere-reserves/)

LANDSCAPES & WILDLIFE ENVIRONMENTAL ISSUES

The Nature Conservancy (www.nature.org), Conservation International (www.conservation.org) and WWF (wwf.panda.org; www.wwf.org.mx; www.worldwildlife.org) all provide lots of information on the Mexican environment, including on their programs in the country.

solar power, and already at least 15% of its electricity comes from hydro sources and 5% from wind and geothermal.

How the country can meet its targets is another matter. Enormous offshore discoveries in July 2017 will boost Mexico's oil output significantly starting from 2019, with critics arguing that prospects of reducing the country's oil dependency are slim. Wind power is the only renewable energy source that has generated significantly increased amounts of electricity in recent years.

Water & Forests

President Peña Nieto's six-year national development plan, announced in 2013, prioritized the crucial issue of water sustainability – a key question in a nation where the south has 70% of the water, but the north and center have 75% of the people, and around 9% of the population still lacks access to clean drinking water. The country's water supplies are often badly polluted (which is why Mexicans are the world's leading consumers of bottled water), and sewage is seriously inadequate in many areas. In 2015, the government moved to privatize the water system, or parts of it, on the theory that private companies could provide water cheaper, cleaner and more efficiently than the state. This decision was met with protests across the country, yet partial privatization went ahead regardless.

On another key issue – forest conservation – Mexico has achieved some success. The country has lost about three-quarters of the forests it had in pre-Hispanic times, as all types of forest from cool pine-clad highlands to tropical jungles have been cleared for grazing, logging and farming. Today only about 17% of the land is covered in primary forest, though a further 16% has regenerated or replanted forest. The good news is that, on government figures at least, deforestation rates declined from about 3500 sq km a year in the 1990s to under 1600 sq km a year today. Part of the success story is that around 70% of forests are controlled by local communities, who tend to manage them in a sustainable way.

Urban Problems

Mexico's largest and probably most influential environmental group is Pronatura (www.pronatura.org.mx), which has numerous programs around the country working to protect species, combat climate change, preserve ecosystems, and promote ecotourism, environmental education and sustainable development.

Mexico City is a high-altitude megalopolis surrounded by a ring of mountains that traps polluted air in the city. The capital consumes over half of Mexico's electricity and has to pump up about a quarter of its water needs from lowlands far below, then evacuate its waste water back to the lowlands via 11,000km of sewers. Efforts to improve air quality are intensifying. For years, most vehicles have been banned from the roads one day every week. The city's climate action plan for 2014–2020 aims to cut CO_2 emissions by 30% through such means as energy-efficient buses, electric-powered taxis, more bicycle use, and a switch to energy-saving light bulbs.

The capital's problems of water supply, sewage treatment, overcrowding and air pollution are mirrored on a smaller scale in most of Mexico's faster-growing cities.

Tourism, a key sector of Mexico's economy, can bring its own environmental problems with large-scale development. In 2012, then-President Felipe Calderón canceled plans for the large-scale Cabo Cortés tourism development in Baja California, because its developers had failed to show that it would be environmentally sustainable. This delighted campaigners who had argued for years that the project would seriously damage the Cabo Pulmo Marine National Park.

On the Caribbean coast's Riviera Maya, organizations such as Centro Ecológico Akumal and Mexiconservación (www.mexiconservacion.org) work to limit damage from reckless tourism development to coral reefs, turtle-nesting beaches, mangrove systems and even the water in the area's famed cenotes (limestone sinkholes). A slowly growing number of hotels and resorts in the region are adopting green policies.

Survival Guide

Directory A–Z

Accommodations

Price Categories

Many midrange and top-end establishments in tourist destinations raise their rates during the Semana Santa (Easter) and Christmas–New Year holiday periods and local festival times. Budget accommodations are more likely to keep the same rates all year.

Budget ($) Most cities popular with international budget travelers have hostels, as well as cheap hotels. Budget accommodations also include campgrounds, hammocks, *cabañas* (cabins) and guesthouses. Airbnb (www.airbnb.com) and other room-sharing websites are also gaining popularity in Mexico.

Midrange ($$) Many midrange places have a restaurant and a bar, almost all have wi-fi and many have swimming pools. Many are atmospheric old mansions and inns turned into hotels. You'll also find some B&Bs, apartments, bungalows and more comfortable *cabañas* that are midrange.

Top end ($$$) Accommodations in this category offer the expected levels of luxury – pools, gyms, bars, restaurants, design, professional service – at prices that are sometimes agreeably modest. They range in style from converted haciendas or small, chic boutique hotels to expansive modern resorts and spas. To save money, look for deals on hotel websites. Triple or family rooms tend to be a bargain for groups.

Taxes

The price of accommodations in Mexico is subject to two taxes:

IVA (value-added tax; 16%)

ISH (lodging tax; 2% or 3% depending on the state)

Many of the less-expensive establishments only charge you these taxes if you require a receipt, and they quote room rates accordingly (ie not including taxes).

Types of Accommodations

Apartments In some resort towns you can find tourist apartments with fully equipped kitchens. They're good value for three or four people, especially if you're staying more than a few days.

B&Bs Mexican B&Bs are usually small, comfortable, midrange or top-end guesthouses, often beautifully designed and offering friendly, personal attention. Many of them are effectively boutique hotels.

Cabañas Cabins or huts (of wood, brick, adobe or stone): they often have a palm-thatched roof, and are most often found at beach destinations. The most basic have dirt floors and a bed, and you provide the padlock for the door. Other *cabañas* are positively deluxe, with electric lights, mosquito nets, large comfy beds, bathrooms, hammock-strung decks and even air-con and a kitchen. The most expensive *cabañas* are on the Caribbean, where some luxury units can cost over M$2000.

Campgrounds & Trailer Parks Most organized campgrounds are actually trailer parks set up for RVs (recreational vehicles, campers) and trailers (caravans) that are also open to tent campers at lower rates. Some restaurants and guesthouses in beach spots or country areas will let you pitch a tent on their patch for around M$60 per person.

Hammocks Hammock space is available in many of the more low-key beach spots. A hammock can be a very comfortable and cheap place to sleep in hot areas (keep mosquito repellent handy). Some places have hammocks to rent for anywhere between M$60 and M$110. It's easy to buy hammocks in Mexico, especially in Oaxaca and Chiapas states and on the Yucatán Peninsula.

BOOK YOUR STAY ONLINE

For more accommodations reviews by Lonely Planet authors, check out http://lonelyplanet.com/hotels. You'll find independent reviews, as well as recommendations on the best places to stay. Best of all, you can book online.

SLEEPING PRICE RANGES

The following price ranges refer to accommodations for two people in high season, including any taxes charged.

$ less than M$800

$$ M$800–1600

$$$ more than M$1600

Hostels Hostels provide dormitory accommodations typically from M$170 to M$250 per person, plus communal kitchens, bathrooms, living space, and nearly always wi-fi. Often private double rooms are available for a bit more than the price of two dorm beds. The best hostels have pools, bars, gardens and sundecks. Cleanliness and security vary, but popular hostels are great places for meeting fellow travelers. International hostel websites such as Hostelworld (www.hostelworld.com) provide plentiful listings and online reservations.

Posadas & Casas de Huéspedes Posadas are inns, meaning anything from basic budget hotels to tastefully designed, small, midrange places. A *casa de huéspedes* is a guesthouse, a home converted into simple, inexpensive guest lodgings, usually family run.

Activities

Some outdoor activities, such as bird-watching and trekking, are great year-round. The best seasons for other adventures are as follows:

➧ Diving & Snorkeling: Humpback whales and whale sharks are seen off Pacific coast and Baja in the winter months, while September and October are best for spotting hammerheads in the Sea of Cortez. Visibility is best off the Caribbean coast in August and September.

➧ Whitewater Rafting: October is considered the best month, though rafting is possible year-round.

➧ Surfing & Kitesurfing: April to October is the surfing and kitesurfing season in Baja and the Pacific Coast. The following websites help you figure out ahead of time the best places and times to go surfing and to find providers for your outdoor activity of choice.

Magic Seaweed (www.magic seaweed.com) Webcams, surfing forecasts, surf-spot info and more.

Planeta.com (www.planeta.com) Good resource on active and responsible tourism.

Mexiconline.com (www.mex online.com) Includes listings of activity providers.

SAFETY GUIDELINES FOR DIVING

Before embarking on a scuba-diving, free-diving or snorkeling trip, consider the following to ensure a safe and enjoyable experience:

➧ Possess a current diving-certification card from a recognized scuba-diving instruction agency.

➧ Be sure you are healthy and feel comfortable diving.

➧ If you don't have your own equipment, ask to see the dive shop's before you commit. Make sure you feel comfortable with your dive master: after all, it's your life.

➧ Obtain reliable information about physical and environmental conditions at the dive site from a reputable local dive operation, and ask how local trained divers deal with these considerations.

➧ Be aware of local laws, regulations and etiquette about marine life and the environment.

➧ Dive only at sites within your level of experience. Engage the services of a competent, professionally trained dive instructor or dive master.

➧ Find out if your dive shop has up-to-date certification from **PADI** (www.padi.com), **NAUI** (ww.naui.org) or the internationally recognized Mexican diving organization **FMAS** (www.fmas.com.mx).

➧ Know the locations of the nearest decompression chambers and the emergency telephone numbers.

➧ Avoid diving less than 18 hours before a high-altitude flight.

Customs Regulations

You may bring the following into Mexico duty-free:

➡ two cameras

➡ two cell phones or other portable wireless devices

➡ one laptop or notebook

➡ three surfboards

➡ two musical instruments

➡ medicine for personal use, with prescription in the case of psychotropic drugs

See www.aduanas.gob.mx for further details.

Discount Cards

For reduced-price air tickets at student- and youth-oriented travel agencies, use:

➡ ISIC student card

➡ IYTC (under 26 years) card

➡ ITIC card for teachers

Reduced prices on Mexican buses and at museums and archaeological sites are usually only for those with Mexican residence, but the IYTC, ITIC and the ISIC may get you a reduction.

Electricity

127V/60Hz

127V/60Hz

Embassies & Consulates

The website of Mexico's foreign ministry, the **Secretaría de Relaciones Exteriores** (www.gob.mx/sre), has links to the websites of all Mexican diplomatic missions worldwide. If you will be travelling in Mexico for a long period of time, and particularly if you're heading to remote locations, it's wise to register with your embassy. This can be done over the phone or by email.

Australian Embassy (☑55-1101-2200; www.mexico. embassy.gov.au; Rubén Darío 55, Mexico City)

Belizean Embassy (☑55-5520-1274; www.belizeembassy.bz/mx; Bernardo de Gálvez 215, Lomas de Chapultepec, Mexico City; ☐76-A-X)

Canadian Embassy (☑55-5724-7900; www.mexico.gc.ca; Schiller 529, Polanco, Mexico City; Ⓜ Polanco)

French Embassy (☑55-9171-9700; https://mx.ambafrance. org; Campos Elíseos 339, Polanco, Mexico City; ☺9am-1pm Mon-Fri; Ⓜ Auditorio)

German Embassy (☑55-5283-2200; www.mexiko.diplo.de; Horacio 1506, Los Morales, Mexico City; ☺8:30am-4pm Mon-Fri; Ⓜ Polanco)

Guatemalan Embassy (☑55-5520-9249; www.mexico.minex. gob.gt; Av Explanada 1025, Lomas de Chapultepec, Mexico City; ☺9am-1pm; ☐76-A-X)

Irish Embassy (☑55-5520-5803; www.irishembassy. com.mx; Cerrada Blvd Ávila Camacho 76-3, Lomas de Chapultepec, Mexico City; ☺9:30am-1:30pm Mon-Fri; ☐76-A-X)

Netherlands Embassy (☑55-5258-9921; http://mexico. nlambassade.org; 7th fl, Edificio Calakmul, Av Vasco de Quiroga 3000, Mexico City; ☺8:30am-12:30pm Mon-Fri; ☐76-A-X)

New Zealand Embassy (☑55-5283-9460; www. nzembassy.com/mexico; 4th floor, Jaime Balmes 8, Mexico City; ☺9:30am-5pm Mon-Fri; ☐57-X)

UK Embassy (Embajada Británica; ☑55-1670-3200; http://ukinmexico.fco.gov.uk; Río Lerma 71, Colonia Cuauhtémoc, Mexico City; ☺8am-4:30pm Mon-Thu, to 2pm Fri; Ⓜ Insurgentes)

US Embassy (☑55-5080-2000; https://mx.usembassy. gov; Paseo de la Reforma 305, Mexico City; ☺8:30am-5:30pm Mon-Fri; Ⓜ Insurgentes)

Food

There is a 16% value-added tax (IVA) on restaurant prices, nearly always included in the menu prices.

Gay & Lesbian Travelers

Mexico is increasingly broad-minded about sexuality, although the conservative influence of the Catholic Church remains strong. The LGBT community don't generally adopt a high profile, but rarely attract open discrimination or violence. The legalization of gay marriages in Mexico City has energized gay life in the capital, which has a hip, international bar and club scene. Puerto Vallarta is the gay beach capital of Mexico. There are also lively scenes in places such as Guadalajara, Veracruz, Cancún, Mérida and Acapulco. In June 2016, amidst erupting protests and demonstrations against same-sex marriage, the Supreme Court in Mexico legalised same-sex marriage in a landmark legal ruling that concluded it was unconstitutional for Mexican states to bar gay marriages.

The website www.gaymexico.com.mx has a clickable map linking to gay guides for many cities, while www.gaymexicomap.com also has listings of accommodations, bars and clubs in many cities, and www.gaycities.com is good for Mexico City, Guadalajara, Puerto Vallarta and Cancún. Also well worth checking out is the **International Gay & Lesbian Travel Association** website (www.iglta.org), with worldwide information on travel providers in the gay sector, and www.outtraveller.com.

The **Clínica Condesa** (☑55-5515-8311; www.condesadf.mx; Gral Benjamín Hill 24; ☺7am-7pm Mon-Fri; ☐De La Salle) is the first of its kind in the country. A flagship health center specializing in sexual health, especially (but not only) LGBT issues, with treatment at no charge, even for foreigners.

Free, confidential HIV rapid testing (*prueba rápida de VIH*) is available in Mexico City's Zona Rosa gay enclave by AHF Mexico (www.pruebadevih.com.mx).

Health

Travelers to Mexico need to guard chiefly against food- and mosquito-borne diseases. Besides getting the proper vaccinations, carry a good insect repellent and exercise care in what

you eat and drink. Medical care in Mexico is generally of a high standard, particularly in private hospitals in big cities.

Availability & Cost of Healthcare

Private hospitals in urban areas generally provide better care than public ones and have the latest medical equipment. The best are in Mexico City and Guadalajara and many doctors speak English. Note that some private hospitals do not accept international travel insurance and you have to pay for your treatment upon being discharged. Your country's embassy or consulates in Mexico and the national tourism secretariat, **Sectur** (☑55-5250-0151, 800-903-92-00, in the US 800-482-9832; www.visitmexico.com), can usually provide information on local hospitals.

Recommended Vaccinations

Make sure all routine vaccinations are up to date and check whether all vaccines are suitable for children and pregnant women. See the Centers for Disease Control & Prevention website (www.nc.cdc.gov/travel) for more details. There are no required vaccinations for entering Mexico, but the following are recommended:

Diphtheria Travelers visiting rural areas

Hepatitis A All travelers (except children less than one year of age)

Hepatitis B Long-term travelers and trekkers

Rabies Trekkers and travelers who may come in contact with animals

Tetanus All travelers

Tuberculosis Travelers visiting rural areas

Typhoid All travelers

Mexico requires proof of a **yellow fever vaccination** if you're arriving from a country with risk of yellow fever.

Infectious Diseases & Parasitic Infections

Chikungunya Viral disease transmitted by infected aedes mosquitoes, causing fever and severe joint pain. Growing number of cases reported, mostly in Guerrero, Oaxaca, Chiapas and Michoacán, with isolated cases in 12 other states. There is no vaccine or treatment, but it's very rarely fatal and you may only contract it once.

Cutaneous leishmaniasis Lesions caused by sandfly bites in coastal and southern Mexico.

Dengue Fever Viral infection transmitted by aedes mosquitoes, which usually bite during the day. Usually causes flu-like symptoms. No vaccine or treatment except analgesics.

Malaria Transmitted by mosquito bites, usually between dusk and dawn. The main symptom is high spiking fevers. Present in Campeche, Chiapas, Chihuahua, Nayarit, and Sinaloa. Rare cases in Durango, Jalisco, Oaxaca, Sonora, Tabasco and Quintana Roo. Consult your doctor about the best antimalarial treatment. Protecting yourself against mosquito bites is just as important as taking malaria pills.

Rickettsial Disease Tick-borne diseases include Rocky Mountain spotted fever (potentially fatal unless treated promptly with

EATING PRICE RANGES

The following price ranges refer to prices of typical main dishes, including value-added tax (IVA).

$ less than M$100

$$ M$100–200

$$$ more than M$200

antibiotics), common in Northern Mexico, and flea-borne typhus (similar symptoms to dengue fever). Take precautions against flea and tick bites.

Zika Viral disease transmitted by infected aedes mosquitoes. It has spread across the entire country since 2015 and the majority of cases are reported in southern Mexico. Symptoms such as rash, fever and joint pain can be treated, but there's no vaccine. Infections in adults have been linked to Guillain–Barré syndrome. Pregnant women are advised against travel to Mexico as zika increases the risk of brain malformations in babies.

Environmental Hazards

Altitude Sickness May develop in travelers who ascend rapidly to altitudes greater than 2500m. Symptoms may include headache, nausea, vomiting, dizziness, malaise, insomnia and loss of appetite. Severe cases can lead to death. To lessen the chance of altitude sickness, ascend gradually to higher altitudes, avoid overexertion, eat light meals and avoid alcohol. People showing any symptoms of altitude sickness should not ascend higher until the symptoms have cleared. If the symptoms become worse, or if someone shows signs of fluid in the lungs (high-altitude pulmonary edema) or swelling of the brain (high-altitude cerebral edema), descend immediately to a lower altitude. Descent of 500m to 1000m is generally adequate except in cases of cerebral edema.

Mosquito Bites Wear long sleeves, long pants, hats and shoes. Use a good insect repellent, preferably one containing at least 50% DEET, but don't use DEET-containing compounds on children under the age of two. If sleeping outdoors or in accommodations without bug netting, use a bed net, ideally treated with permethrin.

Snake & Scorpion Bites In the event of a venomous snake bite or scorpion bite, keep the bitten area immobilized and move the victim immediately to the nearest medical facility. For scorpion stings, immediately apply ice or cold packs.

Sun Stay out of the midday sun, wear sunglasses and a wide-brimmed hat and apply sunscreen with SPF 30 or higher. Drink plenty of fluids and avoid strenuous exercise when the temperature is high.

Insurance

A travel-insurance policy to cover theft, loss, adventure sports and medical problems is a very good idea. Some policies specifically exclude dangerous activities such as scuba diving, motorcycling and even trekking, so check carefully to make sure you're covered for all your activities of choice.

Worldwide travel insurance is available at www.lonelyplanet.com/travel-insurance. You can buy, extend and claim online anytime – even if you're already on the road.

Internet Access

Wi-fi is common in Mexican accommodations, is mostly free, and is also available in a growing number of restaurants, cafes, bars, airports and city plazas. Our wi-fi icon means that wi-fi is available on the premises. Internet cafes in Mexican cities are going the way of the dinosaurs, since it's easy and cheap to purchase a local SIM card with mobile data for your smartphone or device.

Language Courses

Mexico has many professional, experienced Spanish schools, offering everything from short courses for beginners, with emphasis on the spoken language, to longer courses for serious students. Many schools are located in Mexico's most attractive and interesting cities, such as Oaxaca, Guanajuato, San Cristóbal de las Casas, Mérida, Cuernavaca, Morelia and Guadalajara, as well as Puerto Morelos and Playa del Carmen. They present a great opportunity to get an inside experience of Mexican life, with plenty of extracurricular activities such as dance, cooking, music, excursions and volunteering usually available.

Some courses are geared mainly to college students wanting credits for courses back home, while other schools focus on travelers or independent language students. Some Mexican universities have special departments with tailor-made courses for foreigners (usually lasting between one month and one semester). Private schools typically offer shorter courses, from a few days to three months, with more flexible schedules and, often, smaller classes.

The website **123 Teach Me** (www.123teachme.com) offers listings of over 70 language schools in Mexico.

The **National Registration Center for Study Abroad** (www.nrcsa.com), **CIEE** (www.ciee.org), **AmeriSpan** (www.amerispan.com) and **Spanish Abroad** (spanishabroad.com) are among US-based organizations offering a range of study programs in Mexico.

Costs

➡ A typical rate for group classes in private schools is around US$14 to US$20 per hour.

➡ Most schools offer a choice of living options, including homestays, apartments and their own student accommodations. Homestays are often the cheapest option (typically around US$150 to US$170 per week for your own room in a family's home and two meals a day).

➡ All up, 25 hours of classes per week, plus homestay accommodation and meals, averages around US$370 to US$470.

➜ Some schools charge extra for enrollment and registration and/or materials.

Legal Matters

Mexican law is based on the Roman and Napoleonic codes, presuming an accused person guilty until proven innocent.

A law passed in 2009 determined that possession of small amounts of certain drugs for personal use – including cannabis (5g), cocaine (500mg), heroin (50mg) and methamphetamine (40mg) – would not incur legal proceedings against first-time offenders. But those found in possession of small amounts may still have to appear before a prosecutor to determine whether it is for personal use. The easiest way to avoid any drug-related problems is not to use them. As of June 2017, the medicinal use of marijuana is legal.

It's against Mexican law to take any firearm or ammunition into the country (even unintentionally).

Police corruption is a big problem in Mexico. If confronted by police soliciting bribes for bogus driving offences, you can either pretend to speak no Spanish, or else hand over photocopies of your legal documents (not the documents themselves), ask for their names and badge numbers and call their bluff by offering to accompany them to the police station.

Useful warnings on Mexican law are found on the website of the **US State Department** (http://travel.state.gov).

Getting Legal Help

If a foreigner is arrested in Mexico, the Mexican authorities, according to international law, are supposed to promptly contact the person's consulate or embassy if asked to do so. They may not. If they do, consular officials can tell you your rights, provide lists of lawyers, monitor your case, try to make sure you are treated humanely and notify your relatives or friends – but they can't get you out of jail. By Mexican law, the longest a person can be detained without a specific accusation after arrest is 48 hours (though official arrest may not take place until after a period of initial questioning).

Tourist offices in Mexico, especially those run by state governments, can often help you with legal problems such as complaints and reporting crimes or lost articles. The national tourism ministry, **Sectur** (☏55-5250-0151, US 800-482-9832), has a toll-free number offering 24-hour telephone advice.

If you are the victim of a crime, your embassy or consulate, or Sectur or state tourist offices, can give advice. In some cases, there may be little to gain by going to the police, unless you need a statement to present to your insurance company. If you go to the police, take your passport and tourist permit, if you still have them. If you just want to report a theft for insurance purposes, say you want to 'poner una acta de un robo' (make a record of a robbery). This should make it clear that you merely want a piece of paper, and you should get it without too much trouble.

Maps

Nelles, ITM and Michelin all produce good country maps of Mexico that are suitable for travel planning. ITM also publishes good larger-scale maps of many Mexican regions.

Tourist offices in Mexico provide free city, town and regional maps of varying quality. Bookstores and newsstands sell commercially published ones, including Guía Roji's recommended all-Mexico road atlas, *Por Las Carreteras de México*.

Inegi (www.inegi.org.mx) sells large-scale 1:50,000 and 1:250,000 topographical maps at its Centros de Información in every Mexican state capital (detailed on the website), subject to availability.

Maps.me is a very useful iPhone/Android app that allows you to download different regional/city maps of Mexico. The GPS function works offline.

Money
ATMS

ATMs (*cajero automático*) are plentiful. You can use major credit cards and Maestro, Cirrus and Plus bank cards to withdraw pesos. The exchange rate you'll get is normally better than the 'tourist rate' for currency exchange at banks and *casas de cambio* (exchange offices), though that advantage may be negated by the M$30 to M$70 fee the ATM company charges and any foreign-transaction fees levied by your card company.

For maximum security, use ATMs during daylight hours and in secure indoor locations.

Banks & Casas de Cambio

US dollars are the best currency to bring with you; Canadian dollars and euros are also widely accepted. You can exchange cash at *casas de cambio* and some banks. *Casas de cambio* exist in just about every large town and many smaller ones. They are often open evenings or weekends and usually offer similar exchange rates to banks. Banks go through more time-consuming procedures, and usually have shorter exchange hours (typically 9am to 4pm Monday to Friday and 9am to 1pm Saturday).

Cash

It's a good idea to carry cash. In tourist resorts and many Mexican cities along the US border, you can make some purchases in US dollars, though the exchange rate won't be great.

Credit Cards

Visa, MasterCard and American Express are accepted by most airlines and car-rental companies, plus many upper midrange and top-end hotels, and some restaurants and stores. Occasionally there's a surcharge for paying by card. Paying by credit card normally gives you a similar exchange rate to ATM withdrawals. In both cases you'll normally have to pay your card issuer a foreign-exchange transaction fee of around 2.5%.

Opening Hours

Where there are significant seasonal variations in opening hours, we provide hours for high season. Some hours may be shorter in shoulder and low seasons. Hours vary widely but the following are fairly typical.

Banks 9am to 4pm Monday to Friday, 9am to 1pm Saturday

Bars and clubs 1pm to midnight

Cafes 8am to 10pm

Restaurants 9am to 11pm

Shops 9am to 8pm Monday to Saturday (supermarkets and department stores 9am to 10pm daily)

Photography

It's polite to ask before taking photos of people. Some indigenous people can be especially sensitive about this.

Lonely Planet's *Travel Photography* is a comprehensive, jargon-free guide to getting the best shots from your travels.

Special permits are required for any photography or filming with 'special or professional equipment' (which includes all tripods but not amateur video cameras) at any of the 187 archaeological sites or 129 museums administered by INAH, the National Archaeology and History Institute. Permits cost M$5113 per day for still photography and M$10,227 per day for movie or video filming, and must be applied for at least two weeks in advance. You can apply by email; details are given in Spanish at www.tramites.inah.gob.mx.

Post

The Mexican postal service (www.correosdemexico.gob.mx) is slow, inexpensive and fairly reliable. Mail to the US or Canada typically takes a week to 10 days to arrive. Mail to Europe averages one to two weeks.

If you're sending a package internationally from Mexico, be prepared to open it for customs inspection at the post office; it's better to take packing materials with you, or not seal it until you get there. For assured and speedy delivery, you can use one of the more expensive international courier services, such as **UPS** (www.ups.com), **FedEx** (www.fedex.com) or Mexico's **Estafeta** (www.estafeta.com). A 1kg package typically costs around US$37 to the US or Canada, or from US$56 to Europe.

Public Holidays

On official national holidays, banks, post offices, government offices and many other offices and shops close throughout Mexico.

Año Nuevo (New Year's Day) January 1

Día de la Constitución (Constitution Day) Observed on the first Monday of February.

Día de Nacimiento de Benito Juárez (anniversary of Benito Juárez's birth) Observed on the third Monday of March.

Día del Trabajo (Labor Day) May 1

Día de la Independencia (Independence Day) September 16

Día de la Revolución (Revolution Day) Observed on the third Monday of November.

Día de Navidad (Christmas Day) December 25

National holidays that fall on Saturday or Sunday are often switched to the nearest Friday or Monday.

In addition, many offices and businesses close on the following optional holidays:

Día de los Santos Reyes (Three Kings' Day, Epiphany) January 6

Día de la Bandera (Day of the National Flag) February 24

Viernes Santo (Good Friday) Two days before Easter Sunday; March or April

Cinco de Mayo (anniversary of Mexico's victory over the French at Puebla) May 5

Día de la Madre (Mother's Day) May 10

Día de la Raza (commemoration of Columbus' arrival in the New World) October 12

Día de Muertos (Day of the Dead) November 2

Día de Nuestra Señora de Guadalupe (Day of Our Lady of Guadalupe) December 12

Safe Travel

Mexico's drug war is undeniably horrific and frightening, but the violence is almost exclusively an internal matter between the drug gangs; tourists have rarely been victims. Top safety precautions throughout Mexico include the following:

➡ Travel by day and on toll highways where possible, and don't wander into neighborhoods unfrequented by tourists after dark.

➡ Beware of undertows and rips at ocean beaches, and don't leave your belongings unattended while you swim.

➡ Watch out for tainted (badly produced) alcohol that has been linked to a couple of deaths in Quintana Roo resorts.

Theft & Robbery

Pickpocketing and bag snatching are risks on crowded buses and subway trains, at bus stops, bus terminals, airports, markets and in packed streets and plazas, especially in large cities. Pickpockets often work in teams, crowding their victims and trying to distract them.

Mugging is less common but more serious. These robbers may force you to remove your money belt, watch, rings etc. Do not resist, as resistance may be met with violence, and assailants may be armed.

There are occasional victims of 'express kidnappings', with people forced to go to an ATM and withdraw money, but this rarely happens to foreign visitors.

The following precautions will minimize risks:

➡ Avoid semideserted places, such as empty streets and empty metro cars at night, little-used pedestrian underpasses and isolated beaches.

➡ Use taxis instead of walking in potentially dodgy areas. In Mexico City, make sure you take the right kind of cab.

➡ Be alert to the people around you.

➡ Leave valuables in a safe at your accommodations unless you have immediate need of them. If no safe is available, divide valuables into different stashes secreted in your room or a locker.

➡ Carry just enough cash for your immediate needs in a pocket. If you have to carry valuables, use a money belt, shoulder wallet or pouch underneath your clothing.

➡ Don't keep cash, credit cards, purses, cameras and electronic gadgets in open view any longer than necessary. At ticket counters in bus terminals and airports, keep your bag between your feet.

If you are a victim of crime, report the incident to a tourist office, the police or your country's nearest embassy or consulate.

Telephone
Cell (Mobile) Phones

Mexico's main cell-phone (*teléfono celular*) companies are **Telcel** (www.telcel.com), **Movistar** (www.movistar.com.mx) and **AT&T Mexico** (www.att.com.mx). Telcel has the most widespread coverage, and both Telcel and AT&T Mexico offer both roaming and calling in both Canada and the United States without extra charges.

➡ Roaming in Mexico with your own phone from home is possible if you have a GSM, 3G or 4G phone, but can be expensive. **Roaming Zone** (www.roamingzone.com) is a useful source on roaming arrangements. A number of cell-phone service providers in the USA now offer packages that allow customers to roam in Mexico at no (or a small) extra charge.

➡ Much cheaper is to put a Mexican SIM card ('chip') into your phone, but your phone needs to be unlocked for international use. Many Mexican cell-phone stores can unlock it for around M$400.

GOVERNMENT TRAVEL ADVICE

These government websites have information on potentially dangerous areas and general safety tips:

Australia (www.smartraveller.gov.au)

Canada (http://travel.gc.ca)

Germany (www.auswaertiges-amt.de)

Netherlands (www.rijksoverheid.nl)

New Zealand (www.safetravel.govt.nz)

UK (www.fco.gov.uk)

USA (http://travel.state.gov)

➡ SIMs are available from countless phone stores, often for around M$50.

➡ For around M$350 you can buy a new, no-frills Mexican cell phone with a chip and some call credit included. New smartphones start around M$1700, plus M$300 to M$500 a month for calling and data credit. Take your passport for ID when you go to buy a chip or phone; you may also have to provide a local address and postcode.

➡ You can buy new credit at convenience stores, newsstands, pharmacies and department stores.

PHONE CODES

Like Mexican landlines, every Mexican SIM card has an area code. The area code and the phone's number total 10 digits.

Cell phone to cell phone	10-digit number
Cell phone to landline	Area code + number
Landline to cell phone	☎044 + 10-digit number (same area code); ☎045 + 10-digit number (different area code)
Abroad to Mexican cell phone	International access code + 52 + 1 + 10-digit number

Collect Calls

A *llamada por cobrar* (collect call) can cost the receiving party much more than if they call you, so you may prefer to arrange for the other party to call you. If you don't have access to a smartphone/wi-fi/Skype you can make collect calls from public card phones without a card. Call an operator on ☎020 for domestic calls, or ☎090 for international calls.

Landlines

Mexican landlines (*teléfonos fijos*) have two- or three-digit area codes.

Landline to landline (same town)	7- or 8-digit number
Landline to landline (different town)	☎01 + area code + local number
International call from Mexico	☎00 + country code + area code + local number
Mexican landline from abroad	International access code + ☎52 + area code + local number

Operator & Toll-Free Numbers

Directory assistance	☎040
Domestic operator	☎020
Emergency	☎911
International operator	☎090
Mexican toll-free numbers	☎1 + 800 + 7-digit number

Public Card Phones

You'll usually find some at airports and bus terminals and around town. Most are run by **Telmex** (www.telmex.com). To use a Telmex card phone you need a *tarjeta Ladatel* (phone card), sold at kiosks and shops everywhere, usually in denominations of M$50, M$100 and M$200. Insert the card into the phone to make the call.

Time
Time Zones

Hora del Centro The same as CST (US Central Time; GMT minus six hours in winter, and GMT minus five hours during daylight saving), this time zone applies to most of Mexico,

including Campeche, Chiapas, Tabasco and Yucatán.

Hora de las Montañas The same as MST (US Mountain Time; GMT minus seven hours in winter, GMT minus six hours during daylight saving), this time zone applies to five northern and western states in Mexico – Chihuahua, Nayarit, Sinaloa, Sonora and Baja California Sur.

Hora del Pacífico The same as PST (US Pacific Time; GMT minus eight hours in winter, GMT minus seven hours during daylight saving), this time zone applies to Baja California Norte.

The state of Quintana Roo observes US Eastern Standard Time (GMT minus five hours year-round).

Daylight Saving

Daylight saving time (*horario de verano;* summer time) in nearly all of Mexico runs from the first Sunday in April to the last Sunday in October. Clocks go forward one hour in April and back one hour in October. Exceptions to the general rule:

➡ The northwestern state of Sonora ignores daylight saving (like its US neighbor Arizona), as does Quintana Roo, so they remain on MST all year.

➡ Ten cities on or near the US border – Ciudad Acuña, Ciudad Anahuac, Ciudad Juárez, Matamoros, Mexicali, Nuevo Laredo, Ojinaga, Piedras Negras, Reynosa and Tijuana – change their clocks on the second Sunday in March and the first Sunday in November to synchronize with US daylight-saving periods.

Tourist Information

Most towns of interest to tourists in Mexico have a state or municipal tourist office. These are generally helpful with maps and brochures, and some staff members usually speak English.

You can call the Mexico City office of the national tourism secretariat, **Sectur** (☎55-5250-0151, 800-903-92-00, in the US 800-482-9832; www.visitmexico.com), 24 hours a day, seven days a week, for information or help in English or Spanish. You'll find links to tourism websites of each Mexican state at www.sectur.gob.mx.

Travelers with Disabilities

A gradually growing number of hotels, restaurants, public buildings and archaeological sites provide wheelchair access, but sidewalks with wheelchair ramps are still uncommon. Mobility is easiest in major tourist resorts and more expensive hotels. Bus transportation can be difficult; flying or taking a taxi is easier. The absence of formal facilities is partly compensated by Mexicans' helpful attitudes, and special arrangements are gladly improvised. Companies such as **Mind's Eye Travel** (www. mindseyetravel.com) organise cruises to Mexico for the visually impaired. However, in general, few provisions are made for travellers with hearing or sight loss. **Mobility International USA** (www. miusa.org) offers useful info. You can also download Lonely Planet's free Accessible Travel guides from http:// lptravel.to/accessibletravel.

Visas & Tourist Permits

Every tourist must have a Mexican-government tourist permit, easily obtained on arrival. Citizens of the US, Canada, EU countries, Argentina, Australia, Brazil, Israel, Japan, New Zealand, Norway and Switzerland are among those who do not need visas to enter Mexico as tourists. Chinese, Indians, Russians and South Africans are among those who do need a

visa. But Mexican visas are not required for people of any nationality who hold a valid US, Canadian or Schengen visa.

If the purpose of your visit is to work (even as a volunteer), report, study or participate in humanitarian aid or human-rights observation, you may well need a visa whatever your nationality. Visa procedures might take a few weeks and you may be required to apply in your country of residence or citizenship.

The websites of some Mexican consulates, including the **London consulate** (http://consulmex.sre.gob. mx/reinounido) and **Washington consulate** (http:// consulmex.sre.gob.mx/ washington), give useful information on visa regulations and similar matters. The rules are also summarized on the website of Mexico's **Instituto Nacional de Migración** (www.inm.gob.mx).

Non-US citizens passing (even in transit) through the USA on the way to or from Mexico should check well in advance on the US's complicated visa rules. Consult a US consulate or the **US State Department** (http:// travel.state.gov) or **Customs and Border Protection** (www.cbp.gov) websites.

Tourist Permits & Fees

You must fill out the Mexican *Forma migratoria múltiple* (FMM; tourist permit) and get it stamped by Mexican immigration when you enter Mexico, and keep it till you leave. It's available at official border crossings, international airports and ports. At land borders you have to ask for the tourist permit.

The length of your permitted stay in Mexico is written on the card by the immigration officer. The maximum is 180 days, but they may sometimes put a lower number unless you tell them specifically what you need.

The fee for the tourist permit is around M$500, but it's free for people entering by land who stay less than seven days. If you enter Mexico by air, the fee is included in your airfare. If you enter Mexico by land, you must pay the fee once you arrive or at a bank in Mexico at any time before you re-enter the border zone to leave Mexico (or before you check-in at an airport to fly out of Mexico). The border zone is the territory between the border itself and the INM's control points on highways leading into the Mexican interior (usually 20km to 30km from the border).

Most Mexican border posts have on-the-spot bank offices where you can pay the DNR fee immediately on arrival in Mexico. Your tourist permit will be stamped to prove that you have paid.

Look after your tourist permit because you need to hand it in when leaving the country. Tourist permits (and fees) are not necessary for visits shorter than 72 hours within the border zones.

EXTENSIONS & LOST PERMITS

If the number of days given on your tourist permit is fewer than 180, its validity may be extended up to this maximum. To get a permit extended, apply to the INM, which has offices in many towns and cities: they're listed on the **INM website** (http://www.inm.gob.mx/ gobmx/word/index.php/ horarios-y-oficinas/). The procedure costs the same as the tourist permit and should only take half an hour or so. You'll need your passport, tourist permit, photocopies of them and, at some offices, evidence of 'sufficient funds' (a major credit card is usually OK). Most INM offices will not extend a permit until a few days before it is due to expire.

If you lose your permit, contact your nearest tourist office, which should be able to give you an official note to take to your local INM office, which will issue a replacement for about M$500.

Volunteering

A good way to engage with and contribute to Mexican communities is to do some volunteer work. Many organizations can use your services for periods from a few hours to a year or more. Work ranges from protecting sea turtles to WWOOFing. Some organizations are looking for people with relevant experience and/or Spanish-language skills, while others can use almost any willing hand.

Many language schools offer part-time local volunteering opportunities to complement the classes you take.

Volunteer Directories

Go Abroad (www.goabroad.com)

Go Overseas (www.gooverseas.com)

Idealist.org (www.idealist.org)

The Mexico Report (http://themexicoreport.com/non-profits-in-mexico)

Volunteer Oaxaca (http://volunteer-oaxaca.com)

Mexico-Based Programs
SOCIAL PROGRAMS

Casa de los Amigos (www.casadelosamigos.org) Mexico City-based, with volunteer programs to assist refugees and migrants.

Centro de Esperanza Infantil (www.oaxacastreetchildrengrassroots.org) Center for street kids in Oaxaca.

Entre Amigos (www.entreamigos.org.mx) Nayarit-based project that arranges educational projects and workshops for the children of San Pancho.

Feed the Hungry (www.feedthehungrysma.org) Offers nutricious meals to several thousand disadvantaged children in San Miguel de Allende.

Fundación En Vía (Map p426; ☏951-515-24-24; www.envia.

org; Instituto Cultural Oaxaca, Juárez 909; tour per person M$850; ⊘tours 1pm weekdays & 9am Sat) ✈ Oaxaca-based nonprofit organization providing micro-finance loans to help village women develop small businesses.

Junax (www.junax.org.mx) Offers information and lodging in San Cristóbal de las Casas for people wanting to volunteer with indigenous communities in Chiapas; Spanish-language skills needed.

Misión México (www.lovelifehope.com) A children's refuge and surf school in Tapachula.

Piña Palmera (www.pinapalmera.org) Work with physically and intellectually disabled people at Zipolite on the Oaxaca coast.

ENVIRONMENTAL PROGRAMS

Campamento Majahuas (☏cell 322-2285806; www.campamentomajahuas.com; turnoff Hwy 200 Km 116; ⊘turtles nesting at night Jul-Nov) ✈ Excellent turtle conservation project in Costalegre (with short-term volunteering options).

Centro Ecológico Akumal (www.ceakumal.org) Environmental work, including coastal management and turtle protection.

Flora, Fauna y Cultura de México (☏984-188-06-26; www.florafaunaycultura.org; ⊘9am-5pm Mon-Fri) Conservation volunteering with turtles on the Caribbean coast.

Grupo Ecologista Vida Milenaria (www.vidamilenaria.org.mx) Excellent turtle project at Tecolutla.

Nataté (www.natate.org.mx) Turtle conservation and other projects in Chiapas and elsewhere.

Nomad Republic (www.nomadrepublic.net) Assisting with local cooperatives throughout Mexico in agriculture, education, tourism, health, water, energy and other fields.

Pronatura (www.pronatura-ppy.org.mx) Marine conservation and other projects in the Yucatán.

Tortugueros Las Playitas (www.todostortugueros.org) Sea-turtle hatchery in Todos Santos, Baja.

WWOOF Mexico (www.wwoofmexico.org) Volunteering on organic farms around Mexico. Suitable for families.

Organizations Based Outside Mexico

Global Vision International (www.gviusa.com) Anything from marine conservation to teaching projects.

Los Médicos Voladores (www.flyingdocs.org) Lend your medical skills to communities throughout Mexico and Central America.

Projects Abroad (www.projects-abroad.org) Volunteer projects involving teaching, conservation, agriculture and more.

Women Travelers

Gender equality has come a fair way, and Mexicans are generally a very polite people, but machismo is still a fact of life and solo women travelers may still be subject to wolf whistles, cat-calls and attempts to chat them up.

Avoiding drinking alone in cantinas and hitchhiking can help to minimise the risk of hassle, or worse. On the streets of cities and towns and on local transportation, following the lead of local women, who don't typically display too much skin, may also help women travelers avoid unwanted attention.

Work

Mexico's economy is the 15th largest in the world and there are work opportunities for foreigners, particularly in the service industry. A helpful website detailing how to get a work visa in Mexico is https://transferwise.com/gb/blog/mexico-work-visa, while www.mexperience.com/lifestyle/working-in-mexico/ and www.internations.org/mexico-expats/guide provide useful insights into working in Mexico.

Transportation

GETTING THERE & AWAY

As well as flying in, you can enter Mexico by car or bus from the US, Guatemala or Belize and take a boat from the Belizian coast to Quintana Roo. Flights, tours and rail tickets can be booked online at www.lonelyplanet.com/bookings.

Entering the Country

US citizens traveling by land or sea can enter Mexico and return to the US with a passport card, but if traveling by air will need a passport. Citizens of other countries need their passport to enter Mexico. Some nationalities also need a visa.

Air

More than 30 Mexican airports receive direct flights from the US (some from several US cities, some from just a couple), and some of them also receive direct flights from Canada. Mexico City (www.aicm.com.mx), Cancún (www.cancun-airport.com), Guadalajara, Monterrey (http://www.oma.aero/en/airports/monterrey/) and Puerto Vallarta are Mexico's busiest international airports. Only Mexico City and Cancún receive direct scheduled flights from European, Caribbean and Central and South American countries, with Cancún offering the most options from Europe.

Mexico's flagship airline is **Aeroméxico** (www.aeromexico.com); its safety record is comparable to major US and European airlines. Mexico's **Interjet** (www.interjet.com.mx) and **Volaris** (www.volaris.com) fly to several US cities. Interjet also flies to Havana and Varadero in Cuba, Guatemala City, San Jose, Costa Rica and Lima, Peru.

Land

Border Crossings

BELIZE

Frequent buses run from Chetumal's Nuevo Mercado Lázaro Cárdenas to the Belizean towns of Corozal (M$50, one hour) and Orange Walk (M$100, two hours). Some continue on to Belize City (M$300, four hours).

Each person leaving Belize for Mexico needs to pay a US$15 exit fee for visits of less than 24 hours and US$20 for longer stays. All fees must be paid in cash, in Belizean or US currency; officials usually won't have change for US currency. Exit fees are likely to increase in 2018.

GUATEMALA

The road borders at Ciudad Cuauhtémoc–La Mesilla, Ciudad Hidalgo–Ciudad Tecún Umán and Talismán–El Carmen are all linked to

---

CLIMATE CHANGE & TRAVEL

Every form of transport that relies on carbon-based fuel generates CO_2, the main cause of human-induced climate change. Modern travel is dependent on airplanes, which might use less fuel per kilometer per person than most cars but travel much greater distances. The altitude at which aircraft emit gases (including CO_2) and particles also contributes to their climate change impact. Many websites offer 'carbon calculators' that allow people to estimate the carbon emissions generated by their journey and, for those who wish to do so, to offset the impact of the greenhouse gases emitted with contributions to portfolios of climate-friendly initiatives throughout the world. Lonely Planet offsets the carbon footprint of all staff and author travel.

DEPARTURE TAX

The airport departure tax Tarifa de Uso de Aeropuerto (TUA) is almost always included in your airline ticket cost, but if it isn't, you must pay in cash during airport check-in. It varies from airport to airport and costs approximately M$900 for international flights and a little less for domestic flights. This tax is separate from the fee for your tourist permit, which is always included in airfares.

Guatemala City and nearby cities within Guatemala and Mexico by plentiful buses and/or combis. The Ciudad Hidalgo–Ciudad Tecún Umán border is the busiest, and famous for shakedowns on the Guatemalan side; Talismán–El Carmen is definitely the border crossing to go for.

The following companies run daily buses between Tapachula, Chiapas and Guatemala City (five to six hours):

Tica Bus (www.ticabus.com) M$407; 7am.

Trans Galgos Inter (www.facebook.com/TransGalgos Internacional) M$330-445; 6am, noon and 11.45pm.

Between Chetumal and Flores, Línea Dorada runs one daily bus each way (M$700, 7½-8 hours) via Belize City.

For the Río Usumacinta route between Palenque, Mexico, and Flores, there are vans between Palenque and Frontera Corozal (M$130, 2½ to three hours), from where it's a 40-minute boat trip to Bethel, Guatemala (M$80 to M$450 per person, depending on numbers). From Bethel hourly 2nd-class buses run to Flores (four hours) until 4pm.

Travel agencies in Palenque and Flores offer bus-boat-bus packages between the two places for around M$610 (nine hours), typically departing at 6am, but if you're traveling this route it's well worth taking the time to visit the outstanding Maya ruins at Yaxchilán, near Frontera Corozal.

Another possible route between Mexico and Flores is via the border at El Ceibo, near Tenosique, Tabasco. Vans, buses and taxis run between Tenosique and El Ceibo, and there are vans between the border and Flores.

USA

There are more than 40 official crossing points on the US–Mexico border. Some Mexican cities on the border and elsewhere in northern Mexico are affected by drug-gang violence, so check travel warnings before you go. Ciudad Juárez and Nuevo Laredo are best avoided altogether, or at least passed through as quickly as possible. Hwys 101 and 180 between Matamoros and Tampico were ones to avoid at the time of research due to frequent armed robberies and carjackings.

In Baja, the Santa Inés border crossing is the busiest, so it's best for travelers to use another, such as Tecate, for visiting the Valle de Guadalupe.

A pedestrian-only crossing has been operating between the US and Mexico at Boquillas del Carmen–Big Bend National Park since 2014.

Cross-border bus services link many US and Mexican cities. On most trips you will transfer between a US and a Mexican bus on the US or Mexican side of the border, although you can usually buy a ticket right through to your final destination thanks to affiliations between different bus lines.

Greyhound (www.greyhound.com.mx) From California, Arizona and Texas to border cities, with onward transfers into northwest Mexico.

Ómnibus Mexicanos (www.omnibusmexicanos.com.mx) From Texas to northeast, central north and central Mexico.

Transportes Supremo (www.facebook.com/Transportes-Su premo-1614999715450044/) Shuttle-van service between Phoenix, Sonoyta, Nogales, Yuma, Agua Prieta and Puerto Peñasco.

Tufesa (www.tufesa.com.mx) From many cities in the US southwest and California to northwest Mexico, Mazatlán and Guadalajara.

Turimex Internacional (www.turimex.com) From Chicago, Texas and southeastern US to northeast, central north and central Mexico.

Most routes are covered by several buses daily. You can (often as quickly) go to the border on one bus (or train – see www.amtrak.com), cross it on foot or by local bus then catch an onward bus when you get to the other side.

Car & Motorcycle

The rules for taking a vehicle into Mexico change from time to time. Check with a Mexican consulate, **Sanborn's** (www.sanborns insurance.com) or, in the US, the free Mexican tourist information number (800-482-9832).

Driving into Mexico is most useful for travelers who have plenty of time, like independence, have surfboards, diving equipment or other cumbersome luggage and/or will be traveling with at least one companion. Drivers should know at least a little Spanish and have basic mechanical knowledge. A sedan with a trunk (boot) provides safer storage than a station wagon or hatchback.

Mexican mechanics are resourceful, but take as many spare parts as you can manage (spare fuel filters are very useful). Tires (including spare), shock absorbers and suspension should be in good condition. For security, have something to immobilize the steering wheel and consider getting a kill switch installed.

Motorcycling in Mexico is not for the fainthearted. Roads and traffic can be rough, and parts and mechanics hard to come by. The parts you'll most easily find will be for Kawasaki, Honda and Suzuki bikes.

Finding a gas station at or near the border crossings is not a problem.

VEHICLE PERMIT

You will need a *permiso de importación temporal de vehículo* (temporary vehicle import permit), costing US$45 (not including IVA tax), if you want to take a vehicle into Mexico beyond the border zone that extends 20km to 30km into Mexico along the US frontier and up to 70km from the Guatemalan and Belizean frontiers. The only exceptions to this are the Baja California peninsula, where the permit is not needed, and Sonora state as far south as Guaymas, which offers a cheaper, simplified procedure – but you will need a permit if you embark a vehicle at Pichilingue (La Paz) in Baja California, on a ferry to 'mainland' Mexico.

The vehicle permits are issued by offices at border crossings, or at posts a few kilometers into Mexico, and also at Ensenada port and Pichilingue ferry terminal in Baja California. Details of all these locations, including their opening hours, are given on the website of Banjército (www.banjercito.com.mx), the bank that deals with vehicle-import procedures. US and Canadian residents can also apply for the permit (at least a couple of weeks before your trip) on Banjército's website ('Application for Temporary Import Permit for Vehicles'), in which case it will be delivered to you by courier. The online procedure also involves obtaining electronic pre-authorization for your Mexican tourist permit.

The person importing the vehicle will need to carry the original and one or two photocopies of each of the following documents, which must all be in their own name (except that you can bring in your spouse's, parent's or child's vehicle if you can show a marriage or birth certificate proving your relationship):

➡ tourist permit (FMM); at the border go to *migración* before you process your vehicle permit

➡ certificate of title, or registration certificate, for the vehicle (you should have both of these if you plan to drive through Mexico into either Guatemala or Belize)

➡ a Visa or MasterCard credit or debit card issued outside Mexico, or a cash deposit of between US$200 and US$400 (depending on how old the car is). Your card details or deposit serve as a guarantee that you'll take the car out of Mexico before your FMM expires

➡ passport or US passport card

➡ if the vehicle is not fully paid for, a credit contract, or invoice letter not more than three months old, from the financing institution

➡ for a leased or rented vehicle, the contract, in the name of the person importing the vehicle and notarised letter of permission

➡ for a company car, proof of employment by the company as well as proof of the company's ownership of the vehicle

When you leave Mexico, you must have the import permit canceled at the border to insure that your deposit is returned to you. A permit is valid for six months, during which you may enter Mexico multiple times. You have to exit Mexico before the expiration date or else the authorities may deny you permission to bring a vehicle into the country next time.

Sea

Belize Water Taxi (www.belizewatertaxi.com) sails daily between Chetumal, Mexico and San Pedro (US$50) and Caye Caulker (US$55) in Belize.

GETTING AROUND

Air

More than 60 Mexican cities have airports with scheduled passenger services. Flying can be good value on longer journeys.

Aeroméxico (including its subsidiary, Aeroméxico Connect) has the biggest network, but Interjet, TAR Aerolíneas, Volaris and VivaAerobus also serve many cities, often with lower fares. VivaAerobus offers some particularly low fares, but its website may not accept all foreign credit or bank cards.

Volaris and Interjet serve some international destinations. Mexico's regional airlines tend to have a decent safety record.

Boat

Vehicle and passenger ferries connecting Baja California with the Mexican mainland sail between Santa Rosalía and Guaymas (one-way seat/cabin M$930/1030, car M$3200); La Paz and Mazatlán

AIRLINES IN MEXICO

AIRLINE	WEBSITE	AREAS SERVED
Aéreo Calafia	www.aereocalafia.com.mx	Baja California, Pacific Coast, Guadalajara, Monterrey, León, Chihuahua, Puerto Vallarta
Aéreo Servicios Guerrero	www.asg.com.mx	9 cities in Baja and the Pacific Coast
Aeromar	www.aeromar.com.mx	25 cities nationwide, excluding Baja
Aeroméxico	www.aeromexico.com	44 cities nationwide; most flights from Mexico City and Monterrey
Interjet	www.interjet.com.mx	34 cities nationwide
Magnicharters	www.magnicharters.com	16 destinations nationwide, including Riviera Maya coastal resorts
Mayair	www.mayair.com.mx	Yucatán Peninsula, Veracruz
TAR Aerolíneas	www.tarmexico.com	25 cities nationwide, excluding Baja
VivaAerobus	www.vivaaerobus.com	32 cities nationwide
Volaris	www.volaris.com	41 cities nationwide

(one-way seat M$1240, three services weekly); and La Paz and Topolobampo (one-way seat ticket M$1100, car M$2200).

Bus

Mexico has a good road network and comfortable, frequent, reasonably priced bus services connect all cities. Most cities and towns have one main bus terminal from which all long-distance buses operate. It may be called the Terminal de Autobuses, Central de Autobuses, Central Camionera or La Central (not to be confused with *el centro*, the city center!).

Bus stations in major cities tend to be generally clean, safe and highly functional.

Classes

Mexico's buses (called *camiones*, unlike in other Spanish-speaking countries) have three classes.

DELUXE & EXECUTIVE

De lujo services, *primera plus* and the even more comfortable *ejecutivo* (executive) buses run mainly on the busier intercity routes. They are swift and comfortable, with reclining seats, plenty of legroom, air-conditioning, movies on (individual) video screens, few or no stops, toilets on board (sometimes separate ones for men and women) and often drinks, snacks and even wi-fi. They use toll roads wherever available.

FIRST CLASS

Primera (1a) clase buses have a comfortable numbered seat for each passenger. All sizable towns are served by 1st-class buses. Standards of comfort are adequate at the very least. The buses have air-conditioning and a toilet, and they stop infrequently. They show movies on TV screens. They also use toll roads where possible.

SECOND CLASS

Segunda (2a) clase or '*económico*' buses serve small towns and villages and provide cheaper, slower travel on some intercity routes. A few are almost as quick, comfortable and direct as 1st-class buses. Others are old, slow and shabby. Few have toilets. These buses tend to take non-toll roads and will stop anywhere to pick up passengers, so if you board midroute you might make some of the trip standing. In remoter areas, they are often the only buses available.

BUSES – PRACTICAL TIPS

➡ Buses do occasionally get held up and robbed. Traveling by day and on deluxe or 1st-class buses, which use toll highways where possible, minimizes this risk.

➡ Baggage is safe if stowed in the baggage hold – get a receipt for it when you hand it over. Keep your most valuable possessions in the cabin with you.

➡ Air-conditioned buses can get cold, so wear long pants or a skirt and take a sweater or jacket and maybe a blanket on board. Eye-masks and earplugs can be handy if you don't want to watch videos the entire trip!

Reservations

For 1st-class, deluxe and executive buses, buy your ticket in the bus terminal before the trip; it may also be possible to purchase tickets online, depending on the bus company, and have the ticket emailed to you. For trips of up to four or five hours on routes with frequent service, you can usually just go to the bus terminal, buy a ticket and head out without much delay. For longer trips, or routes with infrequent service, or for any trip at busy holiday times, it's best to buy a ticket a day or more in advance. You can usually select your seat when you buy your ticket. Try to avoid the back of the bus, which is where the toilets are located and also tends to give a bumpier ride.

Many 2nd-class services have no ticket office; you just pay your fare to the conductor.

In some cities you can buy bus tickets from downtown bus service agencies to avoid an extra trip to the bus terminal.

Car & Motorcycle

Having a vehicle in Mexico gives you a whole lot of flexibility and freedom, and with a little adaptation to local road conditions is no more difficult than in most other countries.

Driver's License

To drive a motor vehicle in Mexico, you need a valid driver's license from your home country.

Fuel

All *gasolina* (gasoline) and diesel fuel in Mexico is sold by the government's monopoly, Pemex (Petróleos Mexicanos). Most towns, even small ones, have a Pemex station, and stations are pretty common on most major roads. In remote areas, fill up whenever you can. Gasoline is all *sin plomo* (unleaded). There are two varieties:

Magna (87 octane) Roughly equivalent to US regular unleaded, costing about M$15.99 per liter (US$3.40 per US gallon).

Premium (91 octane and lower in sulfur content) Roughly equivalent to US super unleaded, costing about M$17.79.

Diesel fuel is widely available at around M$20.59 per liter. Regular Mexican diesel has a higher sulfur content than US diesel, but a *bajo azufre* (low sulfur) variety has started to become available in Mexico City and some nearby areas. Gas stations have pump attendants (who appreciate a tip of around M$5).

Insurance

It is essential to have Mexican liability insurance. If you are involved in an accident in Mexico, you can be jailed and have your vehicle impounded while responsibility is assessed. If you are to blame

BUS COMPANIES

Mexico has hundreds of bus companies. Many of the major ones belong to the four large groups that dominate bus transportation in different parts of the country. Their websites have schedule information.

BUS COMPANY	WEBSITE	DESTINATIONS SERVED
ETN Turistar	www.etn.com.mx	All major cities along the Pacific coast, central, northern and eastern Mexico and destinations as far south as Oaxaca. Also Tuscon, El Paso and San Diego.
Grupo ADO	www.ado.com.mx	Connects Mexico City with numerous cities in the Yucatán, Campeche, Quintana Roo, Tabasco, Chiapas, Oaxaca, Puebla, Guerrero and Veracruz.
Grupo Estrella Blanca	www.estrellablanca.com.mx	Mexico City and the center, north and west of Mexico. Major cities such as Guadalajara, Tijuana, Puebla, Monterrey, Puerto Vallarta, Ciudad Juárez.
Primera Plus	www.primeraplus.com.mx	Destinations around the center of the country include Mexico City, Guadalajara, Mazatlan, Puerto Vallarta, San Luis Potosí and San Miguel de Allende.

THE GREEN ANGELS

The Mexican tourism secretariat, Sectur, maintains a network of Ángeles Verdes (Green Angels) – bilingual mechanics in green uniforms and green trucks who patrol 60,000km of major highways and toll roads throughout the country daily from 8am to 6pm looking for tourists in trouble. They can give you directions, make minor repairs, change tires, provide fuel and oil and arrange towing and other assistance if necessary. Service is free, and parts, gasoline and oil are provided at cost. If you have access to a telephone, you can call the hotline by dialling ☏078.

for an accident causing injury or death, you may be detained until you guarantee restitution to the victims and payment of any fines. Adequate Mexican insurance coverage is the only real protection: it is regarded as a guarantee that restitution will be paid.

Mexican law recognizes only Mexican motor insurance (*seguro*), so a US or Canadian policy, even if it provides coverage, is not acceptable to Mexican officialdom. You can buy Mexican motor insurance online through the long-established **Sanborn's** (www.sanborns insurance.com) and other companies. Mexican insurance is also sold in border towns in the US and at some border points. At the busiest border crossings there are insurance offices open 24 hours a day.

Short-term insurance is about US$18 a day for full coverage on a car worth under US$10,000. For periods longer than two weeks, it's often cheaper to get a semi-annual or annual policy. Liability-only insurance costs around half the full coverage cost.

Rental

Auto rental in Mexico can be expensive by US or European standards, but is not difficult to organize. Many major international rental firms have offices throughout the country.

Renters must provide a valid driver's license (your home license is OK), passport and major credit card, and are usually required to be at least 21 years of age (sometimes 25, or if you're aged 21 to 24 you may have to pay a surcharge). Read the small print of the rental agreement. In addition to the basic rental rate, there will be tax and insurance costs. Comprehensive insurance can more than double the basic cost quoted in some online bookings – you'll usually have the option of liability-only insurance at a lower rate. Ask exactly what the insurance options cover: theft and damage insurance may only cover a percentage of costs, or the insurance might not be valid for travel on rough country tracks. It's best to have plenty of liability coverage.

Rental rates typically start around M$600 to M$700 per day, including unlimited kilometers, basic insurance and tax. In some beach resorts you may pay as little as M$500. If you rent by the week or month, per-day costs come down. The extra charge for drop-off in another city, when available, is usually about M$10 per kilometer.

Motorbikes or scooters can be rented in a few tourist centers. You're usually required to have a driver's license and a credit card. Many renters do not offer any insurance, however.

Road Hazards & Conditions

➡ Mexico's highways are serviceable and fairly fast when traffic is not heavy. There are more than 6000km of toll highways (autopistas), which are generally good, four-lane roads. Tolls cost around M$2.50 per kilometer.

➡ Driving at night is best avoided, since unlit vehicles, hard-to-see speed bumps, rocks, pedestrians and animals on the roads are common, and drunk drivers are more numerous – and general highway security is better by day.

➡ Some hijackings, holdups and illegal roadblocks connected with drug-gang activities occur, mainly in the north. The northeastern states of Tamaulipas and Nuevo León are especially notorious – particularly the Tampico–Matamoros road and Hwys 101 and 180 in Tamaulipas, which are particularly renowned for armed robberies and carjackings. In this part of the country especially, it is best to stick to toll highways, avoid driving after dark, and keep doors locked and windows closed when driving through cities. Check travel warnings and seek local advice. If you do become a victim, do not try to resist.

➡ There are also some perfectly genuine military and police roadblocks, which are generally looking for illegal weapons, drugs, migrants or contraband. They are unlikely to give tourists a hard time and are no cause for alarm.

➡ It's best to leave vehicles in secure lock-up parking lots overnight. These are fairly common in cities, and hotels can tell you where they are if they don't have their own secure parking.

➡ About 13 out of every 100,000 Mexicans die in

road accidents each year – more than double the rate of most Western countries. Driving under the influence of alcohol and non-use of seat belts are more prevalent here, but otherwise Mexicans seem to drive as cautiously and sensibly as people anywhere. Traffic density, poor surfaces, speed bumps, animals, bicycles and pedestrians all help to keep speeds down.

➡ Be wary of Alto (Stop) signs, *topes* (speed bumps) and potholes in the road (quite often on motorways, too). They are often not where you'd expect them and missing one can cost you in traffic fines or car damage. 'Tope' or 'Vibradores' signs warn you of many speed bumps – the deadly ones are the unmarked ones with no warning signs!

➡ There is always the chance that you will be pulled over by traffic police. If this happens, stay calm and polite. If you don't think you have committed an infraction, you don't have to pay a bribe, and acting dumb may eventually make the cop give up. You can also ask to see the officer's identification, the documentation about the law you have supposedly broken, ask to speak to a superior, and note the officer's name, badge number, vehicle number and department (federal, state or municipal). If you're told that it's cheaper to pay a ticket on the spot, make it clear that you want to pay any fines at a police station and get a receipt; bribe-seekers are likely to let you go at this point. If you then wish to make a complaint, head for a state tourist office.

Road Rules

➡ Drive on the right-hand side of the road.

➡ Speed limits range between 80km/h and 120km/h on open highways (less when the highways pass through areas that are built-up), and between 30km/h and 50km/h in towns and cities.

➡ One-way streets are the rule in cities.

➡ Legal blood-alcohol limits for drivers range from 0.5g/L to 0.8g/L – roughly two or three beers or tequilas.

➡ Antipollution rules in Mexico City ban most vehicles from the city's roads on one day each week.

Local Transportation

Bicycle

Cycling is not a common way to tour Mexico. The size of the country, poor road surfaces, careless motorists and other road hazards are deterrents. If you're up for the challenge, take the mountainous topography and hot climate into account when planning your route. All cities have bicycle stores: a decent mountain bike suitable for a few weeks' touring costs around M$5000.

Consider the bring-your-own-bike tours of southern Mexico and the central volcano country offered by the fun and friendly ¡El Tour (www.bikemexico.com) or else join an Exodus Travels (www.exodus.co.uk) tour of the Yucatán Peninsula.

Bicycle culture is on the up in Mexican cities, however. Most of them are flat enough to make cycling an option and there is a growing number of designated bicycle lanes in Mexico City, Guadalajara, Puebla, Monterrey and some other large cities. Mexico City offers free bike rental. There are bicycle-sharing schemes in Guadalajara (www.mibici.net), Mexico City (www.ecobici.cdmx.gob.mx) and Puebla (www.bicipuebla.com). They work in the same way as other global bike-shares. You can hire decent road and mountain bikes

in several other towns for M$300 to M$700 per day. Seek out routes that are less traffic-infested and you should enjoy it. Mass rides on Sundays are a growing phenomenon, particularly in Mexico City.

Colectivo, Combi, Minibus & Pesero

These are all names for vehicles that function as something between a taxi and a bus, running along fixed urban routes usually displayed on the windshield. They're cheaper than taxis and quicker than buses. They will pick you up or drop you off on any corner along their route – to stop one, go to the curb and wave your hand. Tell the driver where you want to go. Usually you pay at the end of the trip and the fare (a little higher than a bus fare) depends on how far you go.

Local Bus

Generally known as *camiones*, local buses are usually the cheapest way to get around cities and out to nearby towns and villages. They run frequently, and fares in cities are just a few pesos. In many cities, fleets of small, modern *microbuses* have replaced the noisy, dirty older buses.

Buses usually halt only at fixed *paradas* (bus stops), though in some places you can hold your hand out to stop one at any street corner.

Taxi

Taxis are common in towns and cities, and surprisingly economical. City rides cost around M$20 to M$25 per kilometer. If a taxi has a meter, you can ask the driver if it's working ('¿Funciona el taxímetro?'). If the taxi doesn't have a functioning meter, establish the price of the ride before getting in (this may involve a bit of haggling).

Many airports and some big bus terminals have

a system of authorized ticket-taxis – you buy a fixed-price ticket to your destination from a special *taquilla* (ticket window) and then hand it to the driver instead of paying cash. This saves haggling and major rip-offs, but fares are usually higher than you could get on the street.

Renting a taxi for a day-long out-of-town jaunt generally costs something similar to a cheap rental car – around M$600 to M$700.

Uber has become increasingly popular, as well as a similar app-based taxi service called Cabify.

Train

The spectacular **Ferrocarril Chihuahua Pacífico** (El Chepe; ☎614-439-72-12, from Mexico 800-122-43-73; www.chepe.com.mx; full journey 1st/2nd class M$3276/1891; 🚻), running through the Sierra Madre Occidental between Los Mochis and Chihuahua,

is one of the highlights of travel in Mexico and the country's only remaining passenger train (p751).

Mexico City, Guadalajara and Monterrey all have metro (subway, underground railway) systems. Mexico City's, in particular, is a quick, cheap and useful way of getting around. With 195 stations and over four million passengers every weekday, it's the world's third-busiest subway, so avoid using it in rush hour.

Language

Mexican Spanish pronunciation is easy, as most sounds have equivalents in English. Also, Spanish spelling is phonetically consistent, meaning that there's a clear and consistent relationship between what you see in writing and how it's pronounced. Note that kh is a throaty sound (like the 'ch' in the Scottish *loch*), v and b are like a soft English 'v' (between a 'v' and a 'b'), and r is strongly rolled. There are also some variations in spoken Spanish across Latin America, the most notable being the pronunciation of the letters *ll* and *y*. In some parts of Mexico they are pronounced like the 'll' in 'million', but in most areas they are pronounced like the 'y' in 'yes', and this is how they are represented in our pronunciation guides. In other Latin American countries you might also hear them pronounced like the 's' in 'measure', the 'sh' in 'shut' or the 'dg' in 'judge'. The stressed syllables are indicated with italics in our pronunciation guides. Bearing these few things in mind and reading our colored pronunciation guides as if they were English, you should be understood just fine.

The polite form is used in this chapter; where both polite and informal options are given, they are indicated by the abbreviations 'pol' and 'inf'. Where necessary, both masculine and feminine forms of words are included, separated by a slash and with the masculine form first, eg *perdido/a* (m/f).

BASICS

| Hello. | *Hola.* | o·la |
| Goodbye. | *Adiós.* | a·dyos |

WANT MORE?

For in-depth language information and handy phrases, check out Lonely Planet's *Mexican Spanish Phrasebook*. You'll find it at **shop.lonelyplanet.com**, or you can buy Lonely Planet's iPhone phrasebooks at the Apple App Store.

How are you?	*¿Qué tal?*	ke tal
Fine, thanks.	*Bien, gracias.*	byen *gra*·syas
Excuse me.	*Perdón.*	per·*don*
Sorry.	*Lo siento.*	lo *syen*·to
Please.	*Por favor.*	por fa·*vor*
Thank you.	*Gracias.*	*gra*·syas
You're welcome.	*De nada.*	de *na*·da
Yes.	*Sí.*	see
No.	*No.*	no

My name is ...
Me llamo ... — me *ya*·mo ...

What's your name?
¿Cómo se llama Usted? ko·mo se *ya*·ma oo·*ste* (pol)
¿Cómo te llamas? ko·mo te *ya*·mas (inf)

Do you speak English?
¿Habla inglés? a·bla een·*gles* (pol)
¿Hablas inglés? a·blas een·*gles* (inf)

I don't understand.
Yo no entiendo. yo no en·*tyen*·do

ACCOMMODATIONS

I'd like a ... room.	*Quisiera una habitación ...*	kee·*sye*·ra oo·na a·bee·ta·*syon* ...
single	*individual*	een·dee·vee·*dwal*
double	*doble*	*do*·ble

How much is it per night/person?
¿Cuánto cuesta por kwan·to *kwes*·ta por
noche/persona? no·che/per·so·na

Does it include breakfast?
¿Incluye el een·*kloo*·ye el
desayuno? de·sa·*yoo*·no

campsite	*terreno de cámping*	te·*re*·no de *kam*·peeng
hotel	*hotel*	o·*tel*
guesthouse	*pensión*	pen·*syon*

KEY PATTERNS

To get by in Spanish, mix and match these simple patterns with words of your choice:

When's (the next flight)?
¿Cuándo sale   kwan·do sa·le
(el próximo vuelo)?   (el prok·see·mo vwe·lo)

Where's (the station)?
¿Dónde está   don·de es·ta
(la estación)?   (la es·ta·syon)

Where can I (buy a ticket)?
¿Dónde puedo   don·de pwe·do
(comprar un billete)?   (kom·prar oon bee·ye·te)

Do you have (a map)?
¿Tiene (un mapa)?   tye·ne (oon ma·pa)

Is there (a toilet)?
¿Hay (servicios)?   ai (ser·vee·syos)

I'd like (a coffee).
Quisiera (un café).   kee·sye·ra (oon ka·fe)

I'd like (to hire a car).
Quisiera (alquilar   kee·sye·ra (al·kee·lar
un coche).   oon ko·che)

Can I (enter)?
¿Se puede (entrar)?   se pwe·de (en·trar)

Could you please (help me)?
¿Puede (ayudarme),   pwe·de (a·yoo·dar·me)
por favor?   por fa·vor

Do I have to (get a visa)?
¿Necesito   ne·se·see·to
(obtener   (ob·te·ner
un visado)?   oon vee·sa·do)

youth hostel	albergue juvenil	al·ber·ge khoo·ve·neel
air-con	aire acondicionado	ai·re a·kon·dee·syo·na·do
bathroom	baño	ba·nyo
bed	cama	ka·ma
window	ventana	ven·ta·na

DIRECTIONS

Where's ...?
¿Dónde está ...?   don·de es·ta ...

What's the address?
¿Cuál es la dirección? kwal es la dee·rek·syon

Could you please write it down?
¿Puede escribirlo,   pwe·de es·kree·beer·lo
por favor?   por fa·vor

Can you show me (on the map)?
¿Me lo puede indicar   me lo pwe·de een·dee·kar
(en el mapa)?   (en el ma·pa)

at the corner	en la esquina	en la es·kee·na

at the traffic lights	en el semáforo	en el se·ma·fo·ro
behind ...	detrás de ...	de·tras de ...
far	lejos	le·khos
in front of ...	enfrente de ...	en·fren·te de ...
left	izquierda	ees·kyer·da
near	cerca	ser·ka
next to ...	al lado de ...	al la·do de ...
opposite ...	frente a ...	fren·te a ...
right	derecha	de·re·cha
straight ahead	todo recto	to·do rek·to

EATING & DRINKING

Can I see the menu, please?
¿Puedo ver el menú,   pwe·do ver el me·noo
por favor?   por fa·vor

What would you recommend?
¿Qué recomienda?   ke re·ko·myen·da

Do you have vegetarian food?
¿Tienen comida   tye·nen ko·mee·da
vegetariana?   ve·khe·ta·rya·na

I don't eat (meat).
No como (carne).   no ko·mo (kar·ne)

That was delicious!
¡Estaba buenísimo!   es·ta·ba bwe·nee·see·mo

Cheers!
¡Salud!   sa·loo

The bill, please.
La cuenta, por favor.   la kwen·ta por fa·vor

I'd like a table for ...	Quisiera una mesa para ...	kee·sye·ra oo·na me·sa pa·ra ...
(eight) o'clock	las (ocho)	las (o·cho)
(two) people	(dos) personas	(dos) per·so·nas

Key Words

bottle	botella	bo·te·ya
breakfast	desayuno	de·sa·yoo·no
cold	frío	free·o
dessert	postre	pos·tre
dinner	cena	se·na
fork	tenedor	te·ne·dor
glass	vaso	va·so
hot (warm)	caliente	kal·yen·te
knife	cuchillo	koo·chee·yo
lunch	comida	ko·mee·da
plate	plato	pla·to
restaurant	restaurante	res·tow·ran·te
spoon	cuchara	koo·cha·ra

Meat & Fish

bacon	tocino	to·see·no
beef	carne de vaca	kar·ne de va·ka
chicken	pollo	po·yo
crab	cangrejo	kan·gre·kho
duck	pato	pa·to
goat	cabra	ka·bra
ham	jamón	kha·mon
lamb	cordero	kor·de·ro
lobster	langosta	lan·gos·ta
mutton	carnero	kar·ne·ro
octopus	pulpo	pool·po
oysters	ostras	os·tras
pork	cerdo	ser·do
shrimp	camarones	ka·ma·ro·nes
squid	calamar	ka·la·mar
turkey	pavo	pa·vo
veal	ternera	ter·ne·ra
venison	venado	ve·na·do

Fruit & Vegetables

apple	manzana	man·sa·na
apricot	albaricoque	al·ba·ree·ko·ke
banana	plátano	pla·ta·no
beans	frijoles	free·kho·les
cabbage	col	kol
cactus fruit	tuna	too·na
carrot	zanahoria	sa·na·o·rya
cherry	cereza	se·re·sa
corn	maíz	ma·ees
corn (fresh)	elote	e·lo·te
cucumber	pepino	pe·pee·no
grape	uvas	oo·vas
grapefruit	toronja	to·ron·kha
lentils	lentejas	len·te·khas
lettuce	lechuga	le·choo·ga
mushroom	champiñón	cham·pee·nyon
nuts	nueces	nwe·ses
onion	cebolla	se·bo·ya
orange	naranja	na·ran·kha
peach	melocotón	me·lo·ko·ton
peas	guisantes	gee·san·tes
pepper	pimiento	pee·myen·to
pineapple	piña	pee·nya
plantain	plátano macho	pla·ta·no ma·cho

plum	ciruela	seer·we·la
potato	patata	pa·ta·ta
pumpkin	calabaza	ka·la·ba·sa
spinach	espinacas	es·pee·na·kas
strawberry	fresa	fre·sa
(red) tomato	(ji)tomate	(khee·)to·ma·te
watermelon	sandía	san·dee·a

Other

bread	pan	pan
butter	mantequilla	man·te·kee·ya
cake	pastel	pas·tel
cheese	queso	ke·so
cookie	galleta	ga·ye·ta
(fried) eggs	huevos (fritos)	we·vos (free·tos)
French fries	papas fritas	pa·pas free·tas
honey	miel	myel
ice cream	helado	e·la·do
jam	mermelada	mer·me·la·da
pepper	pimienta	pee·myen·ta
rice	arroz	a·ros
salad	ensalada	en·sa·la·da
salt	sal	sal
soup	caldo/sopa	kal·do/so·pa
sugar	azúcar	a·soo·kar

Drinks

beer	cerveza	ser·ve·sa
coffee	café	ka·fe
juice	zumo	soo·mo
milk	leche	le·che
smoothie	licuado	lee·kwa·do
sorbet	nieve	nye·ve
(black) tea	té (negro)	te (ne·gro)
(mineral) water	agua (mineral)	a·gwa (mee·ne·ral)
(red/white) wine	vino (tinto/blanco)	vee·no (teen·to/blan·ko)

QUESTION WORDS

How?	¿Cómo?	ko·mo
What?	¿Qué?	ke
When?	¿Cuándo?	kwan·do
Where?	¿Dónde?	don·de
Who?	¿Quién?	kyen
Why?	¿Por qué?	por ke

EMERGENCIES

Help!	¡Socorro!	so·ko·ro
Go away!	¡Vete!	ve·te
Call ...!	¡Llame a ...!	ya·me a ...
a doctor	un médico	oon me·dee·ko
the police	la policía	la po·lee·see·a

I'm lost.
Estoy perdido/a.	es·toy per·dee·do/a (m/f)

I'm ill.
Estoy enfermo/a.	es·toy en·fer·mo/a (m/f)

It hurts here.
Me duele aquí.	me dwe·le a·kee

I'm allergic to (antibiotics).
Soy alérgico/a a (los antibióticos).	soy a·ler·khee·ko/a a (los an·tee·byo·tee·kos) (m/f)

Where are the toilets?
¿Dónde están los baños?	don·de es·tan los ba·nyos

SHOPPING & SERVICES

I'd like to buy ...
Quisiera comprar ...	kee·sye·ra kom·prar ...

I'm just looking.
Sólo estoy mirando.	so·lo es·toy mee·ran·do

Can I look at it?
¿Puedo verlo?	pwe·do ver·lo

NUMBERS

1	uno	oo·no
2	dos	dos
3	tres	tres
4	cuatro	kwa·tro
5	cinco	seen·ko
6	seis	seys
7	siete	sye·te
8	ocho	o·cho
9	nueve	nwe·ve
10	diez	dyes
20	veinte	veyn·te
30	treinta	treyn·ta
40	cuarenta	kwa·ren·ta
50	cincuenta	seen·kwen·ta
60	sesenta	se·sen·ta
70	setenta	se·ten·ta
80	ochenta	o·chen·ta
90	noventa	no·ven·ta
100	cien	syen
1000	mil	meel

I don't like it.
No me gusta.	no me goos·ta

How much is it?
¿Cuánto cuesta?	kwan·to kwes·ta

That's too expensive.
Es muy caro.	es mooy ka·ro

Can you lower the price?
¿Podría bajar un poco el precio?	po·dree·a ba·khar oon po·ko el pre·syo

There's a mistake in the bill.
Hay un error en la cuenta.	ai oon e·ror en la kwen·ta

ATM	cajero automático	ka·khe·ro ow·to·ma·tee·ko
credit card	tarjeta de crédito	tar·khe·ta de kre·dee·to
internet cafe	cibercafé	see·ber·ka·fe
market	mercado	mer·ka·do
post office	correos	ko·re·os
tourist office	oficina de turismo	o·fee·see·na de too·rees·mo

TIME & DATES

What time is it?	¿Qué hora es?	ke o·ra es
It's (10) o'clock.	Son (las diez).	son (las dyes)
It's half past (one).	Es (la una) y media.	es (la oo·na) ee me·dya

morning	mañana	ma·nya·na
afternoon	tarde	tar·de
evening	noche	no·che
yesterday	ayer	a·yer
today	hoy	oy
tomorrow	mañana	ma·nya·na

Monday	lunes	loo·nes
Tuesday	martes	mar·tes
Wednesday	miércoles	myer·ko·les
Thursday	jueves	khwe·ves
Friday	viernes	vyer·nes
Saturday	sábado	sa·ba·do
Sunday	domingo	do·meen·go

January	enero	e·ne·ro
February	febrero	fe·bre·ro
March	marzo	mar·so
April	abril	a·breel
May	mayo	ma·yo
June	junio	khoon·yo
July	julio	khool·yo
August	agosto	a·gos·to

September	*septiembre*	sep·*tyem*·bre
October	*octubre*	ok·*too*·bre
November	*noviembre*	no·*vyem*·bre
December	*diciembre*	dee·*syem*·bre

TRANSPORTATION

boat	*barco*	*bar*·ko
bus	*autobús*	ow·to·*boos*
plane	*avión*	a·*vyon*
train	*tren*	tren
first	*primero*	pree·*me*·ro
last	*último*	*ool*·tee·mo
next	*próximo*	*prok*·see·mo
A ... ticket, please.	*Un billete de ..., por favor.*	oon bee·*ye*·te de ... por fa·*vor*
1st-class	*primera clase*	pree·*me*·ra *kla*·se
2nd-class	*segunda clase*	se·*goon*·da *kla*·se
one-way	*ida*	*ee*·da
return	*ida y vuelta*	*ee*·da ee *vwel*·ta

I want to go to ...
Quisiera ir a ...   kee·*sye*·ra eer a ...

Does it stop at ...?
¿Para en ...?   *pa*·ra en ...

What stop is this?
¿Cuál es esta parada?   kwal es es·ta pa·*ra*·da

What time does it arrive/leave?
¿A qué hora llega/ sale?   a ke o·ra ye·ga/ *sa*·le

Please tell me when we get to ...
¿Puede avisarme cuando lleguemos a ...?   pwe·de a·vee·*sar*·me *kwan*·do ye·*ge*·mos a ...

I want to get off here.
Quiero bajarme aquí.   *kye*·ro ba·*khar*·me a·*kee*

airport	*aeropuerto*	a·e·ro·*pwer*·to
aisle seat	*asiento de pasillo*	a·*syen*·to de pa·*see*·yo
bus stop	*parada de autobuses*	pa·*ra*·da de ow·to·*boo*·ses
cancelled	*cancelado*	kan·se·*la*·do
delayed	*retrasado*	re·tra·*sa*·do
platform	*plataforma*	pla·ta·*for*·ma
ticket office	*taquilla*	ta·*kee*·ya
timetable	*horario*	o·*ra*·ryo
train station	*estación de trenes*	es·ta·*syon* de *tre*·nes

window seat	*asiento junto a la ventana*	a·*syen*·to *khoon*·to a la ven·*ta*·na
I'd like to hire a ...	*Quisiera alquilar ...*	kee·*sye*·ra al·kee·*lar* ...
4WD	*un todo-terreno*	oon to·do·te·*re*·no
bicycle	*una bicicleta*	*oo*·na bee·see·*kle*·ta
car	*un coche*	oon *ko*·che
motorcycle	*una moto*	*oo*·na *mo*·to
child seat	*asiento de seguridad para niños*	a·*syen*·to de se·goo·ree·*da* pa·ra nee·nyos
diesel	*petróleo*	pet·*ro*·le·o
helmet	*casco*	*kas*·ko
hitchhike	*hacer botella*	a·*ser* bo·te·ya
mechanic	*mecánico*	me·*ka*·nee·ko
petrol/gas	*gasolina*	ga·so·*lee*·na
service station	*gasolinera*	ga·so·lee·*ne*·ra
truck	*camión*	ka·*myon*

Is this the road to ...?
¿Se va a ... por esta carretera?   se va a ... por es·ta ka·re·*te*·ra

(How long) Can I park here?
¿(Cuánto tiempo) Puedo aparcar aquí?   (*kwan*·to *tyem*·po) pwe·do a·*par*·kar a·*kee*

The car has broken down (at ...).
El coche se ha averiado (en ...).   el *ko*·che se a a·ve·*rya*·do (en ...)

I had an accident.
He tenido un accidente.   e te·*nee*·do oon ak·see·*den*·te

I've run out of petrol.
Me he quedado sin gasolina.   me e ke·*da*·do seen ga·so·*lee*·na

I have a flat tyre.
Tengo un pinchazo.   *ten*·go oon peen·*cha*·so

MEXICAN SLANG

Pepper your conversations with a few slang expressions! You'll hear many of the following expressions all around Mexico, but some are particular to Mexico City.

¿Qué onda?
What's up?/What's happening?

¿Qué pasión? (Mexico City)
What's up?/What's going on?

¡Qué padre!
How cool!

fregón
really good at something/way cool/awesome

Este club está fregón.
This club is way cool.

El cantante es un fregón.
The singer is really awesome.

ser muy buena onda
to be really cool/nice

Mi novio es muy buena onda.
My boyfriend is really cool.

Eres muy buena onda.
You're really cool.

pisto (in the north)
booze

alipús
booze

echarse un alipús/trago
to go get a drink

Echamos un alipús/trago.
Let's go have a drink.

tirar la onda
try to pick someone up/flirt

ligar
to flirt

irse de reventón
go partying

¡Vámonos de reventón!
Let's go party!

reven
a 'rave' (huge party with loud music and a wild atmosphere)

un desmadre
a mess

Simón.
Yes.

Nel.
No.

No hay tos.
No problem. (literally: 'there's no cough')

¡Órale! (positive)
Sounds great! (when responding to an invitation)

¡Órale! (negative)
What the ...? (taunting exclamation)

¡Caray!
Shit!

¿Te cae?
Are you serious?

Me late.
Sounds really good to me.

Me vale.
I don't care./Whatever.

Sale y vale.
I agree./Sounds good.

¡Paso sin ver!
I can't stand it!/No, thank you!

¡Guácatelas!/¡Guácala!
How gross!/That's disgusting!

¡Bájale!
Don't exaggerate!/Come on!

¡¿Chale?! (Mexico City)
No way!?

¡Te pasas!
That's it! You've gone too far!

¡No manches!
Get outta here!/You must be kidding!

un resto
a lot

lana
money/dough

carnal
brother

cuate/cuaderno
buddy

chavo
guy/dude

chava
girl/gal

jefe
father

jefa
mother

la tira/julia
the police

la chota (Mexico City)
the police

GLOSSARY

(m) indicates masculine gender, (f) feminine gender, (sg) singular and (pl) plural

adobe – sun-dried mud brick used for building

agave – family of plants with thick, fleshy, usually pointed leaves, from which tequila, mezcal and *pulque* are produced (see also *maguey*)

Alameda – name of formal parks in some Mexican cities

alebrije – colorful wooden animal figure

Ángeles Verdes – Green Angels; government-funded mechanics who patrol Mexico's major highways in green vehicles; they help stranded motorists with fuel and spare parts

arroyo – brook, stream

artesanías – handicrafts, folk arts

atlas (sg), atlantes (pl) – sculpted male figure(s) used instead of a pillar to support a roof or frieze; a telamon

autopista – expressway, dual carriageway

azulejo – painted ceramic tile

bahía – bay

balneario – bathing place; often a natural hot spring

baluarte – bulwark, defensive wall

barrio – neighborhood of a town or city

boleto – ticket

brujo/a (m/f) – witch doctor, shaman; similar to *curandero/a*

burro – donkey

cabaña – cabin, simple shelter

cabina – Baja Californian term for a public telephone call station

cacique – regional warlord; political strongman

calle – street

callejón – alley

calzada – grand boulevard or avenue

camioneta – pickup truck

campesino/a (m/f) – country person, peasant

capilla abierta – open chapel; used in early Mexican monaster-ies for preaching to large crowds of indigenous people

casa de cambio – exchange house, place where currency is exchanged; faster to use than a bank

casa de huéspedes – cheap and congenial accommodations; often a home converted into simple guest lodgings

caseta de teléfono, caseta telefónica – public telephone call station

cenote – a limestone sinkhole filled with rainwater; often used in Yucatán as a reservoir

central camionera – bus terminal

cerro – hill

Chaac – Maya rain god

chac-mool – pre-Hispanic stone sculpture of a hunched-up figure; the stomach may have been used as a sacrificial altar

charreada – Mexican rodeo

charro – Mexican cowboy

chilango/a (m/f) – person from Mexico City

chinampa – Aztec garden built from lake mud and vegetation; versions still exist at Xochimilco, Mexico City

chultún – cistern found in the Chenes region, in the Puuc hills south of Mérida

Churrigueresque – Spanish late-baroque architectural style; found on many Mexican churches

clavadistas – cliff divers of Acapulco and Mazatlán

colectivo – minibus or car that picks up and drops off passengers along a predetermined route; can also refer to other types of trans-portation, such as boats, where passengers share the total fare

colonia – neighborhood of a city, often a wealthy residential area

combi – minibus

comedor – food stall

comida corrida – set lunch

completo – no vacancy (literally 'full up'); a sign you may see at hotel desks

conde – count (nobleman)

conquistador – early Spanish explorer-conqueror

cordillera – mountain range

criollo – Mexican-born person of Spanish parentage; in colonial times considered inferior by *peninsulares*

cuota – toll; a *vía cuota* is a toll road

curandero/a (m/f) – literally 'curer'; a medicine man or woman who uses herbal and/ or magical methods and often emphasizes spiritual aspects of disease

de paso – a bus that began its route somewhere else, but stops to let passengers on or off at various points

DF – Distrito Federal (Federal District); about half of Mexico City lies in DF

edificio – building

ejido – communal landholding

embarcadero – jetty, boat landing

entremeses – hors d'oeuvres; also theatrical sketches such as those performed during the Cervantino festival in Guanajuato

escuela – school

esq – abbreviation of *esquina* (corner) in addresses

ex-convento – former convent or monastery

feria – fair or carnival, typically occurring during a religious holiday

ferrocarril – railway

fonda – inn; small, family-run eatery

fraccionamiento – subdivision, housing development; similar to a *colonia*, often modern

gringo/a (m/f) – US or Cana-dian (or other Western) visitor to Latin America; can be used derogatorily

grito – literally 'shout'; the Grito de Dolores was the 1810 call to independence by priest Miguel Hidalgo, sparking the struggle for independence from Spain

gruta – cave, grotto

guayabera – man's shirt with pockets and appliquéd designs up the front, over the shoulders and down the back; worn in hot regions in place of a jacket and tie

hacha – ax; in archaeological contexts, a flat, carved-stone object connected with the ritual ball game

hacienda – estate; Hacienda (capitalized) is the Treasury Department

henequén – *agave* fiber used to make sisal rope; grown particularly around Mérida

hostal – small hotel or budget hostel

huarache – woven leather sandal, often with tire tread as the sole

huevos – eggs; also slang for testicles

huipil (sg), huipiles (pl) – indigenous woman's sleeveless tunic(s), usually highly decorated; can be thigh-length or reach the ankles

Huizilopochtli – Aztec tribal god

iglesia – church

INAH – Instituto Nacional de Antropología e Historia; the body in charge of most ancient sites and some museums

indígena – indigenous, pertaining to the original inhabitants of Latin America; can also refer to the people themselves

isla – island

IVA – *impuesto de valor agregado*, or 'ee-vah'; a sales tax added to the price of many items (16% on hotel rooms)

jai alai – the Basque game *pelota*, brought to Mexico by the Spanish; a bit like squash, played on a long court with curved baskets attached to the arm

jardín – garden

Kukulcán – Maya name for the plumed serpent god *Quetzalcóatl*

lancha – fast, open, outboard boat

larga distancia – long-distance; usually refers to telephone calls

local – refers to premises, such as a numbered shop or office; a *local* bus is one whose route starts from the bus station you are in

maguey – *agave;* sometimes refers specifically to *Agave americana,* from which *pulque* is made

malecón – waterfront boulevard or promenade

maquiladora – assembly-plant operation importing equipment, raw materials and parts for assembly or processing in Mexico, then exporting the products

mariachi – small ensemble of street musicians playing traditional ballads on guitars and trumpets

marimba – wooden xylophone-like instrument popular in southeastern Mexico

mercado – market; often a building near the center of a town, with shops and open-air stalls in the surrounding streets

Mesoamerica – historical and archaeological name for central, southern, eastern and southeastern Mexico, Guatemala, Belize and the small ancient Maya area in Honduras

mestizo – person of mixed (usually indigenous and Spanish) ancestry

Mexican Revolution – 1910 revolution that ended the *Porfiriato*

milpa – peasant's small cornfield, often cultivated using the slash-and-burn method

mirador (sg), miradores (pl) – lookout point(s)

Mudejar – Moorish architectural style imported to Mexico by the Spanish

municipio – small local government area; Mexico is divided into 2394 of them

Nafta – North American Free Trade Agreement

Náhuatl – language of the Nahua people, descendants of the Aztecs

nao – Spanish trading galleon

norteamericano – North American; someone from north of the US–Mexican border

Nte – abbreviation for *norte* (north); used in street names

Ote – abbreviation for *oriente* (east); used in street names

palacio de gobierno – state capitol, state government headquarters

palacio municipal – town or city hall, headquarters of the municipal corporation

palapa – thatched-roof shelter, usually on a beach

PAN – Partido Acción Nacional (National Action Party); the political party of Felipe Calderón and his predecessor Vicente Fox

panga – fiberglass skiff for fishing or whale-watching in Baja California

parada – bus stop, usually for city buses

parque nacional – national park; an environmentally protected area in which human exploitation is banned or restricted

parroquia – parish church

paseo – boulevard, walkway or pedestrian street; the tradition of strolling around the plaza in the evening, men and women moving in opposite directions

Pemex – government-owned petroleum extraction, refining and retailing monopoly

peninsulares – those born in Spain and sent by the Spanish government to rule the colony in Mexico

periférico – ring road

pesero – Mexico City's word for *colectivo;* can mean 'bus' in the northeast

peyote – a hallucinogenic cactus

pinacoteca – art gallery

piñata – clay pot or papier-mâché mold decorated to resemble an animal, pineapple, star, etc and filled with sweets and gifts, then smashed open at fiestas

pirata – literally 'pirate'; used to describe passenger-carrying pickup trucks in some parts of Mexico

playa – beach

plaza de toros – bullring

plazuela – small plaza

poblano/a (m/f) – person from Puebla; something in the style of Puebla

Porfiriato – reign of Porfirio Díaz as president-dictator of Mexico for 30 years until the 1910 *Mexican Revolution*

portales – arcades

posada – inn

PRI – Partido Revolucionario Institucional (Institutional Revolutionary Party); the political party that ruled Mexico for most of the 20th century

Pte – abbreviation for *poniente* (west), used in street names

puerto – port

pulque – milky, low-alcohol brew made from the *maguey* plant

quetzal – crested bird with brilliant green, red and white plumage native to southern Mexico, Central America and northern South America; quetzal feathers were highly prized in pre-Hispanic Mexico

Quetzalcóatl – plumed serpent god of pre-Hispanic Mexico

rebozo – long woolen or linen shawl covering women's head or shoulders

refugio – a very basic cabin for shelter in the mountains

reserva de la biosfera – biosphere reserve; an environmentally protected area where human exploitation is steered toward sustainable activities

retablo – altarpiece, or small painting placed in a church as

thanks for miracles, answered prayers etc

río – river

s/n – *sin número* (without number); used in addresses

sacbé (sg), sacbeob (pl) – ceremonial avenue(s) between great Maya cities

sanatorio – hospital, particularly a small private one

sarape – blanket with opening for the head; worn as a cloak

Semana Santa – Holy Week – the week from Palm Sunday to Easter Sunday; Mexico's major holiday period when accommodations and transportation get very busy

sierra – mountain range

sitio – taxi service

stela/stele (sg), stelae/steles (pl) – standing stone monument, usually carved

sur – south; often seen in street names

taller – shop or workshop; a *taller mecánico* is a mechanic's shop, usually for cars; a *taller de llantas* is a tire-repair shop

talud-tablero – stepped building style typical of Teotihuacán, with alternating vertical (*tablero*) and sloping (*talud*) sections

taquilla – ticket window

telamon – statue of a male figure, used instead of a pillar to hold up the roof of a temple; an *atlas*

teleférico – cable car

teléfono (celular) – (cell/mobile) telephone

temascal – pre-Hispanic–style steam bath, often used for curative purposes; sometimes spelt *temazcal*

templo – church; anything from a chapel to a cathedral

teocalli – Aztec sacred precinct

Tezcatlipoca – multifaceted pre-Hispanic god; lord of life and death and protector of warriors; as a smoking mirror he could see into hearts; as the sun god he needed the blood of sacrificed warriors to ensure he would rise again

tezontle – light red, porous volcanic rock used for buildings by the Aztecs and *conquistadores*

tianguis – indigenous people's market

tienda – store

típico/a (m/f) – characteristic of a region; used to describe food in particular

Tláloc – pre-Hispanic rain and water god

tope – speed bump; found on the outskirts of towns and villages; they are only sometimes marked by signs

trapiche – mill; in Baja California usually a sugar mill

UNAM – Universidad Nacional Autónoma de México (National Autonomous University of Mexico)

universidad – university

voladores – literally 'fliers'; Totonac ritual in which men, suspended by their ankles, whirl around a tall pole

War of Independence – war for Mexican independence from Spain (from 1810 to 1821), ending three centuries of Spanish rule

War of the Castes – 19th-century Maya uprising in the Yucatán Peninsula

zócalo – literally 'plinth'; used in some Mexican towns for the main plaza or square

FOOD GLOSSARY

For basic food terms, see p837
For basic menu terms, see p47

adobada – marinated with adobo (chili sauce)

al albañil – 'bricklayer style' ie served with a hot chili sauce

al mojo de ajo – with garlic sauce

al pastor – cooked on a pit, shepherd's style

albóndigas – meatballs

antojitos – 'little whims': tortilla-based snacks like tacos and enchiladas

arroz mexicana – pilaf-style rice with a tomato base

atole – gruel made with ground corn

avena – oatmeal

barbacoa – pit-smoked barbecue

bolillo – French-style roll

brocheta – shishkabob

burrito – filling in a large flour tortilla

cajeta – goat's milk and sugar boiled to a paste

calabacita – squash

carnitas – pork simmered in lard

cecina – thin cut of meat, flavored with chili and sautéed or grilled

chicharrones – fried pork skins

chile relleno – chili stuffed with meat or cheese, usually fried with egg batter

chiles en nogada – mild green chilies stuffed with meat and fruit, fried in batter and served with a sauce of cream, ground walnuts and cheese

chorizo – Mexican-style bulk sausage made with chili and vinegar

chuleta de puerco – pork chop

churros – doughnut-like fritters

cochinita pibil – pork, marinated in chilies, wrapped in banana leaves, and pit-cooked or baked

coctel de frutas – fruit cocktail

costillas de res – beef ribs

crepas – crepes or thin pancakes

empanada – pastry turnover filled with meat, cheese or fruits

filete a la tampiqueña – Tampico-style steak: a thin tenderloin, grilled and served with chili strips and onion, a quesadilla and enchilada

flor de calabaza – squash blossom

frijoles a la charra – beans cooked with tomatoes, chilies and onions (also called *frijoles rancheros*)

guacamole – mashed avocado, often with lime juice, onion, tomato and chili

horchata – soft drink made with melon seeds

huachinango veracruzana – Veracruz-style red snapper with a sauce of tomatoes, olives, vinegar and capers

huevos motuleños – fried eggs sandwiched between corn tortillas, and topped with peas, tomato, ham and cheese

huevos rancheros – fried eggs served on a corn tortilla, topped with a sauce of tomato, chilies, and onions, and served with refried beans

huevos revueltos – scrambled eggs

huitlacoche – a much esteemed fungus that grows on corn

lomo de cerdo – pork loin

machacado – pulverized jerky, often scrambled with eggs

menudo – tripe stew

milanesa – thin slices of beef or pork, breaded and fried

mixiote – chili-seasoned lamb steamed in agave membranes or parchment

mole negro – chicken or pork in a very dark sauce of chilies, fruits, nuts, spices and chocolate

mole poblano – chicken or turkey in a sauce of chilies, fruits, nuts, spices and chocolate

nopalitos – sliced cactus paddles, sautéed or grilled

picadillo – ground beef filling that often includes fruit and nuts

pipián verde – stew of chicken, with ground squash seeds, chilies and tomatillos

pozole – soup or thin stew of hominy, meat, vegetables and chilies

queso fundido – cheese melted, often with chorizo or mushrooms, and served as an appetizer with tortillas

rajas – strips of mild green chili, often fried with onions

tinga poblana – stew of pork, vegetables and chilies

Behind the Scenes

SEND US YOUR FEEDBACK

We love to hear from travelers – your comments keep us on our toes and help make our books better. Our well-traveled team reads every word on what you loved or loathed about this book. Although we cannot reply individually to your submissions, we always guarantee that your feedback goes straight to the appropriate authors, in time for the next edition. Each person who sends us information is thanked in the next edition – the most useful submissions are rewarded with a selection of digital PDF chapters.

Visit **lonelyplanet.com/contact** to submit your updates and suggestions or to ask for help. Our award-winning website also features inspirational travel stories, news and discussions.

Note: We may edit, reproduce and incorporate your comments in Lonely Planet products such as guidebooks, websites and digital products, so let us know if you don't want your comments reproduced or your name acknowledged. For a copy of our privacy policy visit lonelyplanet.com/privacy.

OUR READERS

Many thanks to the travelers who used the last edition and wrote to us with helpful hints, useful advice and interesting anecdotes:

Alejandra Robertson, Daniel de Vries, Fleur Broers, Irving W Levinson, Jessica Groenestijn, Joseph T Stanik, Michael Dahlquist, Michael Weber

WRITER THANKS

Brendan Sainsbury

Muchas gracias to all the bus drivers, tourist information staff, hoteliers, chefs, hiking guides and innocent passers-by who helped me, unwittingly or otherwise, on my research trip. Special thanks to my wife, Liz and my son, Kieran for their special company (and patience) on the road in Oaxaca.

Kate Armstrong

Muchísimas gracias first and foremost to Tom Williams, advisor and chatter extraordinaire of Luz en Yucatan for his ongoing enthusiasm and love for the region, and Donard O'Neill. For the extra research thank you to Raul LiCausi Salerno of Hostel Nómadas, Silvia Carrillo Jiménez of Tourism Valladolid and Director Jorge Romero Herrera of SEFOTUR in Mérida. Thanks to Destination Editor Sarah Stocking for her help and a big shout-out to fellow 'Yucatecano', Ray Bartlett, plus Alex Egerton and Lucas Vigden.

Ray Bartlett

Huge shout out to my family, such fun having you along some of the time. Thanks too to the amazing people who helped along the way: Rob and Joanne, Mauricio, Bailey, Corina, Tanya, Ivonne, Rudolf and many more. Huge thanks to my editors, especially Sarah Stocking, who put so much effort in behind the scenes, and to my coauthors. Thanks to all the amazing locals and travelers I met. You are what makes Mexico so magical. Don't ever change!

Celeste Brash

Thanks to Cesar and Oscar in Cabo; the Castro family in Cabo Pulmo plus Mary for support; the whole boat crew in La Paz; Carillo, Abel and the two Juans in Loreto; tow truck driver in Mulege; Kuyima in San Ignacio; Chrissie for Ensenada and beyond; and my esteemed colleague Anna Kaminski for joining me for tacos, beer and wine. As always, thanks to my husband Josh and kids Jasmine and Tevai for support and home.

Stuart Butler

Once again I would like to thank my wife, Heather, and young children, Jake and Grace, for their patience while I worked on this project. Next time I promise you'll come too! A huge thank you to all the many people inside and outside of Mexico who helped out with my research and enjoyment on this project.

Steve Fallon

Muchísimas gracias to the lovely folk who offered assistance, ideas and/or hospitality along the way, including Michael Eager in Ajijic; Alicia McNiff in Chapala; Júpiter Rivera in Comala; Luis Enrique Ruiz,

Katy Thorncroft and Carlos Ibarra in Guadalajara; Ellen Sharp in Macheros near Zitácuaro; Victoria Ryan in Pátzcuaro; Clayton J Szczech and David Arce Uribe in Tequila; Irene Pulos in Tlaquepaque; and Aline Avakian and Salvador Luna in Uruapan. *Y a mi querido México, país de amistad, buen humor y coraje.* (And to my beloved Mexico, land of friendship, good humor and courage.) As always, my share is dedicated to my now spouse, Michael Rothschild.

John Hecht

Special thanks to Julio Morales in Mazatlán; Roberto Langarica in Majahuas, Myles Estey and Gus Condado in Mexico City; Memo Wulff in Vallarta and to all the generous *costeños* for their support; and good times along the way. Above all, my heartfelt gratitude to Lau (aka *la milanesas*) for always being there for me.

Anna Kaminski

I'd like to thank Cliff and Sarah for entrusting me with the Veracruz chapter and the Mexico front and back matter and everyone who helped me along the way. In particular: Juana and David in Veracruz, the helpful site custodians at El Cuajilote and Quiahuiztlán, my rafting guide in Jalcomulco, the helpful tourist office staff in San Andres Tuxtla, my wonderful hostess in Catemaco, Diego in Xalapa, Rafael in Tlacotalpan and Toni in Orizaba.

Tom Masters

Huge thanks to Anna, Josh, Tenzin and Catherine in San Miguel de Allende. You all made my time there an absolute pleasure. Gratitude also to Joe Kellner for companionship on the road, to staff at Mesón de los Dos Leones in Querétaro and Camino Surreal in Xilitla for their help on the ground. Thanks also to staff and cowriters at LP for their patience with me after a life-changing health event during write up.

Liza Prado

Mil gracias to Alejandra Reina and Luz Vasquez for sharing your knowledge about El Norte. *Abrazos para toda la familia*, especially Abuelita Trini, Tío Enrique, Tía Lupita, Tato, Tío Miguel, Tía Ana Lilia and Tío Jaime for the warm welcome. Huge shout outs to Mom for being game for backroad travel with the kids, to Dad for cheering us on and to Susan for holding down the fort once school started. *Gracias*, Eva and Leo, for being such sweet travel companions. And to Gary, always, thank you for being my best friend, for having my back and for seeing beauty everywhere.

Phillip Tang

Thank you Stephen Hu (Ren Jie) for Puebla, Cholula, Tlaxcala and Taxco photo moments and food taste-testing. Thanks Anna Glayzer and your face for Valle de Bravo, Cuernavaca and Tepoztlán colorful times. *Mil gracias de nuevo a Armando Palma, Jocsan L Alfaro and Fiona Ross por tus sugerencias en CDMX.* Thank you Sarah Stocking and Clifton Wilkinson for having me on board again. And thanks for guidance from afar to Vek Lewis, Lisa N'paisan and Géraldine Galvaing.

ACKNOWLEDGEMENTS

Climate map data adapted from Peel MC, Finlayson BL & McMahon TA (2007) 'Updated World Map of the Köppen-Geiger Climate Classification', Hydrology and Earth System Sciences, 11, 1633-44.

Cover photograph: Parroquia de San Miguel Arcángel, San Miguel de Allende, Danita Delimont Stock/AWL ©

Chichén Itzá illustration pp328-9 by Michael Weldon.

THIS BOOK

This 16th edition of Lonely Planet's *Mexico* guidebook was researched and written by Brendan Sainsbury, Kate Armstrong, Ray Bartlett, Celeste Brash, Stuart Butler, Steve Fallon, John Hecht, Anna Kaminski, Tom Masters, Liza Prado and Phillip Tang. The Mexican Kitchen chapter was written by Mauricio Velázquez de León. This guidebook was produced by the following:

Destination Editors Sarah Stocking, Clifton Wilkinson

Product Editors Rachel Rawling, Alison Ridgway, Kate Mathews, Vicky Smith

Senior Cartographer Corey Hutchison

Book Designer Meri Blazevski

Assisting Editors Judith Bamber, Carolyn Boicos, Peter Cruttenden, Melanie Dankel, Paul Harding, Gabrielle Innes, Kellie Langdon, Rosie Nicholson, Lauren O'Connell, Susan Paterson, Monique Perrin, Sarah Reid, Tamara Sheward, Sarah Stewart, Fionnuala Twomey, Simon Williamson

Assisting Cartographer Michael Garrett

Cover Researcher Naomi Parker

Thanks to Hannah Cartmel, Kate Chapman, Andi Jones, Virginia Moreno, Kathryn Rowan, Wibowo Rusli, Tony Wheeler, Amanda Williamson

Index

Map Legend

Sights
- Beach
- Bird Sanctuary
- Buddhist
- Castle/Palace
- Christian
- Confucian
- Hindu
- Islamic
- Jain
- Jewish
- Monument
- Museum/Gallery/Historic Building
- Ruin
- Shinto
- Sikh
- Taoist
- Winery/Vineyard
- Zoo/Wildlife Sanctuary
- Other Sight

Activities, Courses & Tours
- Bodysurfing
- Diving
- Canoeing/Kayaking
- Course/Tour
- Sento Hot Baths/Onsen
- Skiing
- Snorkeling
- Surfing
- Swimming/Pool
- Walking
- Windsurfing
- Other Activity

Sleeping
- Sleeping
- Camping
- Hut/Shelter

Eating
- Eating

Drinking & Nightlife
- Drinking & Nightlife
- Cafe

Entertainment
- Entertainment

Shopping
- Shopping

Information
- Bank
- Embassy/Consulate
- Hospital/Medical
- Internet
- Police
- Post Office
- Telephone
- Toilet
- Tourist Information
- Other Information

Geographic
- Beach
- Gate
- Hut/Shelter
- Lighthouse
- Lookout
- Mountain/Volcano
- Oasis
- Park
- Pass
- Picnic Area
- Waterfall

Population
- Capital (National)
- Capital (State/Province)
- City/Large Town
- Town/Village

Transport
- Airport
- Border crossing
- Bus
- Cable car/Funicular
- Cycling
- Ferry
- Metro station
- Monorail
- Parking
- Petrol station
- Subway/Subte station
- Taxi
- Train station/Railway
- Tram
- Underground station
- Other Transport

Routes
- Tollway
- Freeway
- Primary
- Secondary
- Tertiary
- Lane
- Unsealed road
- Road under construction
- Plaza/Mall
- Steps
- Tunnel
- Pedestrian overpass
- Walking Tour
- Walking Tour detour
- Path/Walking Trail

Boundaries
- International
- State/Province
- Disputed
- Regional/Suburb
- Marine Park
- Cliff
- Wall

Hydrography
- River, Creek
- Intermittent River
- Canal
- Water
- Dry/Salt/Intermittent Lake
- Reef

Areas
- Airport/Runway
- Beach/Desert
- Cemetery (Christian)
- Cemetery (Other)
- Glacier
- Mudflat
- Park/Forest
- Sight (Building)
- Sportsground
- Swamp/Mangrove

Note: Not all symbols displayed above appear on the maps in this book

Stuart Butler
Chiapas & Tabasco Stuart has been writing for Lonely Planet for a decade and during this time he's come eye to eye with gorillas in the Congolese jungles, huffed and puffed over snowbound Himalayan mountain passes, interviewed a king who could turn into a tree, and had his fortune told by a parrot. Oh, and he's met more than his fair share of self-proclaimed Gods. When not on the road for Lonely Planet he lives on the beautiful beaches of Southwest France with his wife and two young children.

Steve Fallon
Western Central Highlands A native of Boston, Massachusetts, Steve graduated from Georgetown University with a Bachelor of Science in modern languages. After working for several years for an American daily newspaper and earning a master's degree in journalism, his fascination with the 'new' Asia and led him to Hong Kong, where he lived for over a dozen years, working for a variety of media and running his own travel bookshop. Steve lived in Budapest for three years before moving to London in 1994. He has written or contributed to more than 100 Lonely Planet titles.

John Hecht
Central Pacific Coast Los Angeles native John Hecht has contributed to more than a dozen Lonely Planet guidebooks and trade publications, mostly focused on Mexico and Central America. He is also a published food and entertainment writer and wrote a screenplay for a short film shot in Mexico City, his adopted home where he enjoys merrymaking in cantinas and chowing down greasy-good street eats.

Anna Kaminski
Veracruz Originally from the Soviet Union, Anna grew up in Cambridge, UK. She graduated from the University of Warwick with a degree in Comparative American Studies, a background in the history, culture and literature of the Americas and the Caribbean, and an enduring love of Latin America. Her restless wanderings led her to settle briefly in Oaxaca and Bangkok and her flirtation with criminal law saw her volunteering as a lawyer's assistant in the courts, ghettos and prisons of Kingston, Jamaica. Anna has contributed to almost 30 Lonely Planet titles. When not on the road, Anna calls London home.

Tom Masters
Northern Central Highlands Dreaming since he could walk of going to the most obscure places on earth, Tom has always had a taste for the unknown. This has led to a writing career that has taken him all over the world, including North Korea, the Arctic, Congo and Siberia. Despite a childhood spent in the English countryside, as an adult Tom has always called London, Paris and Berlin home.

Liza Prado
Copper Canyon & Northern Mexico Liza Prado has been a travel writer since 2003, when she made a move from corporate lawyering to travel writing (and never looked back). She's written dozens of guidebooks and articles as well as apps and blogs to destinations throughout the Americas. She takes decent photos too. Liza is a graduate of Brown University and Stanford Law School. She lives very happily in Denver, Colorado, with her husband and fellow LP writer, Gary Chandler, and their two kids.

Phillip Tang
Mexico City; Around Mexico City Phillip Tang grew up on a typically Australian diet of pho and fish'n'chips before moving to Mexico City. A degree in Chinese- and Latin-American cultures launched him into travel and then writing about it for Lonely Planet's *Canada*, *China*, *Japan*, *Korea*, *Mexico*, *Peru* and *Vietnam* guides.

OUR STORY

A beat-up old car, a few dollars in the pocket and a sense of adventure. In 1972 that's all Tony and Maureen Wheeler needed for the trip of a lifetime – across Europe and Asia overland to Australia. It took several months, and at the end – broke but inspired – they sat at their kitchen table writing and stapling together their first travel guide, *Across Asia on the Cheap*. Within a week they'd sold 1500 copies. Lonely Planet was born.

Today, Lonely Planet has offices in Franklin, London, Melbourne, Oakland, Dublin, Beijing and Delhi, with more than 600 staff and writers. We share Tony's belief that 'a great guidebook should do three things: inform, educate and amuse'.

OUR WRITERS

Brendan Sainsbury

Oaxaca Born and raised in the UK in a town that never merits a mention in any guidebook (Andover, Hampshire), Brendan spent the holidays of his youth caravanning in the English Lake District and didn't leave Blighty until he was 19. He's since squeezed 70 countries into a sometimes precarious existence as a writer and professional vagabond. In the last 11 years, he has written more 40 books for Lonely Planet from Castro's Cuba to the canyons of Peru.

Kate Armstrong

Yucatán Peninsula Kate Armstrong has spent much of her adult life traveling and living around the world. A full-time freelance travel journalist, she has contributed to more than 50 Lonely Planet guides and trade publications and is regularly published in Australian and worldwide publications. She is the author of several books and children's educational titles.

Ray Bartlett

Yucatán Peninsula Ray has been travel writing for nearly two decades, bringing Japan, Korea, Mexico, and many parts of the United States to life in rich detail for top-industry publishers, newspapers, and magazines. His acclaimed debut novel, *Sunsets of Tulum*, is set in Yucatán and was a Midwest Book Review 2016 Fiction pick. Among other pursuits, Ray surfs regularly and is an accomplished Argentine tango dancer. Follow him on Facebook, Twitter, Instagram, or contact him via his website www.kaisora.com.

Celeste Brash

Baja California Like many California natives, Celeste now lives in Portland, Oregon. She arrived, however, after 15 years in French Polynesia, a year and a half in Southeast Asia and a stint teaching English as a second language in Brighton, England – among other things. She's been writing guidebooks for Lonely Planet since 2005 and her travel articles have appeared in publications from *BBC Travel* to *National Geographic*. She's currently writing a book about her five years on a remote pearl farm in the Tuamotu Atolls and is represented by the Donald Maass Agency, New York.

OVER PAGE | MORE WRITERS

Published by Lonely Planet Global Limited
CRN 554153
16th edition – September 2018
ISBN 978 1 78657 080 2
© Lonely Planet 2018   Photographs © as indicated 2018
10 9 8 7 6 5 4 3 2 1
Printed in Singapore

Although the authors and Lonely Planet have taken all reasonable care in preparing this book, we make no warranty about the accuracy or completeness of its content and, to the maximum extent permitted, disclaim all liability arising from its use.